AN EXPLORER'S GUIDE

C0-AUV-850

Georgia

Georgia

Carol Thalimer and Dan Thalimer

Interior photographs by the authors

The Countryman Press ✳ Woodstock, Vermont

We welcome your comments and suggestions. Please contact Explorer's Guide Editor, The Countryman Press, P.O. Box 748, Woodstock, VT 05091, or e-mail countrymanpress@wwnorton.com.

First Edition

No entries or reviews in this book have been solicited or paid for.

ISBN-13: 978-0-88150-639-6

Cover and text design by Bodenweber Design
Cover photograph © Bob Krist
Interior photographs by the author unless otherwise specified
Maps by Mapping Specialists Ltd., Madison, WI
Text composition by PerfectType, Nashville, TN

Published by The Countryman Press, P.O. Box 748, Woodstock, Vermont 05091

Distributed by W. W. Norton & Company, Inc., 500 Fifth Avenue, New York, NY 10110

Printed in Canada

10 9 8 7 6 5 4 3 2 1

DEDICATION
To Elaine, our own intrepid explorer.

EXPLORE WITH US!

We've lived in Georgia for 27 years and have been writing about it for newspapers, magazines, and guidebooks for 19 years. In the course of living here, enjoying our state for our own pleasure, and researching Georgia for our readers, we've traveled the state countless times—constantly seeking out the new and checking up on the tried and true. More and more communities are recognizing the value of tourism, so the number of attractions, lodging, dining opportunities, and fairs and festivals continues to grow. We make our recommendations selectively based on years of research and personal experience.

WHAT'S WHERE

This section is an alphabetical listing of special highlights and other important information. Here you'll find recommendations on everything from where to buy fresh seafood to where to write, call, or go online to find information about parks and camping.

LODGING

We selected hotels, bed & breakfasts, resorts, and other lodgings based on their merit. Although we may not have stayed in every accommodation, we've tried to visit each or, in some rare cases, have relied on the advice of locals in the know. Accommodations cannot pay to be included in this guide.

RESTAURANTS

We've made a distinction between *Dining Out* and *Eating Out.* In the *Dining Out* category, we've generally listed more formal restaurants with entrée prices higher than $20. The *Eating Out* restaurants are generally more casual and more inexpensive. Note that we list entrée prices—you can easily double a meal price by adding appetizers, soups and salads, desserts, and alcoholic beverages.

PRICES

Changes are inevitable—especially with information in a book, which is hopefully in use for many years. We give prices only to give you a ballpark figure for whether a lodging is inexpensive, moderate, or expensive. In almost all cases, there will be some kind of local tax added to the basic rate. When you make your reservation, you might want to check about taxes or gratuities that are added on to the basic rate.

SMOKING

Georgia recently passed a law banning smoking in buildings open to the public. There's still a lot of leeway, however. Large hotels, for example, may still have smoking and nonsmoking rooms available. B&Bs, which are often in someone's home, are usually smoke-free for various reasons, including insurance requirements. Restaurants are generally smoke-free unless they do not admit anyone younger than 18. If smoking is an issue because of allergies or personal preference, be sure to ask.

KEY TO SYMBOLS

🎗 **Special Value.** This symbol appears next to lodgings, restaurants, and attractions that are inexpensive.

✐ **Family-friendly.** This symbol appears next to attractions, eateries, and lodgings that are of particular value or appeal for families.

♿ **Handicapped access.** This symbol appears next to attractions, lodgings, and restaurants that are partially or completely handicapped accessible. Note that in the case of lodgings such as bed & breakfasts, in particular, there may be a ramp to get into the building, but bathrooms may not be completely outfitted for the handicapped.

🐾 **Pets.** This symbol appears next to lodgings, campgrounds, and attractions that accept pets. Please note that many of these have restrictions, may require advance notice, and may have additional fees associated with your pet.

We would appreciate any comments (good or bad) or corrections so that our next edition will be as complete as possible. Please write to Explorer's Guide Editor, The Countryman Press, P.O. Box 748, Woodstock, VT 05091, or e-mail countrymanpress@wwnorton.com.

ACKNOWLEDGMENTS

Although we've written 15 other books about Georgia and the South, the gargantuan size and complexities of this book resulted in a process we'd liken to birthing an elephant: it was quite often painful, but we're proud of the result. We'd especially like to thank our editors at The Countryman Press—Kermit Hummel, Jennifer Thompson, and Kathryn Flynn—for their guidance, suggestions, and infinite patience.

Our daughter, Elaine Pyle, was an invaluable researcher and fact checker, and we also thank her husband, Eric, for lending her to us for prolonged periods.

No matter how much traveling we do throughout the state, we could never keep up to date with the latest activities, attractions, lodgings, restaurants, shopping, and events in Georgia without the assistance of the state regional representatives at the Georgia Department of Economic Development, Tourism Division: Becky Bassett, director; Atlanta Metro, Brittney Warnock; Colonial Coast, Carey Ferrara; Classic South, Jeannie Buttrum; Historic Heartland, Fay Tripp; Magnolia Midlands, Lindsey Hammock; Northwest Georgia Historic High Country, Alice Carson; Northeast Georgia Mountains, Cheryl Smith; Plantation Trace, Jeff Stubbs; and Presidential Pathways, Maggie Potter. We've worked with most of these representatives for almost 20 years, and they are amazing founts of information.

We've also had assistance from the staffs at almost every convention and visitors bureau, chamber of commerce, welcome center, and travel association in the state. Just a few of them include these: Alpharetta CVB, Candice Cocco and Brooke Atha; Athens CVB, Hannah Smith; Atlanta CVB, Amanda Dyson and Lauren Jarrell; Brunswick and the Golden Isles CVB, Patrick Saylor; Cartersville/Bartow County CVB, Regina Wheeler; Cobb County CVB, Judy Renfroe; Columbus CVB, Shelby Guest; Dahlonega CVB, Hal Williams; Dawson County Chamber of Commerce and CVB, Marty Williams and Linda Williams; DeKalb CVB, Jeff Mills; Georgia Coast Travel Association, Melissa Chatterton and Katerina Murray; Gwinnett CVB, Cricket Elliott and Gay VanOrt; Henry County Chamber of Commerce/CVB, Sarah Robbins and Michelle Lassiter; Historic Roswell CVB, Marsha Saum; Macon CVB, Lisa Love; Marietta Welcome Center and Visitors Bureau, Christy Duffner and Theresa Jenkins; Northeast Georgia Travel Association, Joan Zitzelman; Rome CVB, Jennifer Collins, and Erika Backus of the Savannah Area Convention and Visitors Bureau and Chamber of Commerce. These and many others too numerous to list can be found at the offices listed in the Guidance section of each chapter. We're sure these professionals will be as helpful to you as they have been to us.

To the countless others at specific activities, attractions, lodgings, restaurants, shopping, and events—thank you.

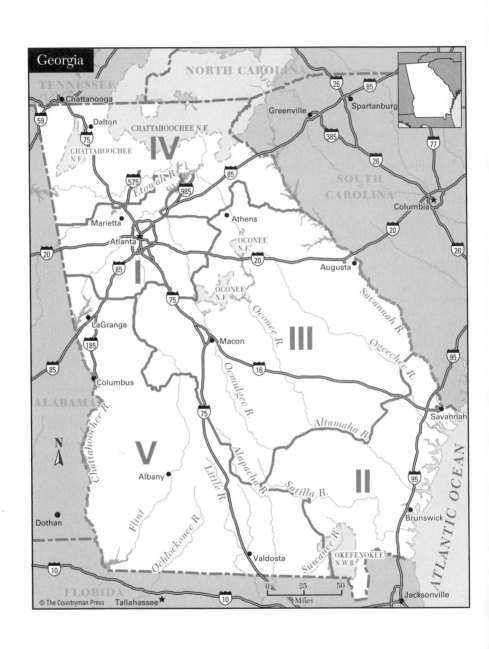

CONTENTS

6   Appendix / 703

WHAT'S WHERE IN GEORGIA

This section offers some general information that is helpful to travelers but would be too repetitive to include in each individual chapter—information about airports and airlines, car rentals, mass transit, bus and train travel, and the like. In addition, in this section we offer information about some of the state's most outstanding attractions, fairs and festivals, activities, and lodgings to spur your curiosity. These brief mentions are more fully described in the pertinent chapters. In this chapter, we merely reference these without contact information; in the separate chapters, for each entry we give you the telephone number(s), web site if there is one, address, hours of operation, and admission, lodging, or meal price. We also give you some information about associations and councils that might be helpful, references to other books or web sites, and regulations such as those regarding fishing, hunting, smoking, building fires, and littering.

AFRICAN AMERICAN SITES In a state where a major part of the economy was once based on slave labor, where the Civil War often intruded, and where there were numerous events connected with the Civil Rights Movement of the 1960s, it's not surprising that there are many significant historical sites related to the lives and history of African Americans. The most significant of these sites and one of the most-visited attractions in the state is the **Martin Luther King Jr. National Historic Site** on Auburn Avenue in Atlanta. The site contains Dr. King's birthplace and Ebenezer Baptist Church. Adjacent to the historic site is the **King Center for Nonviolent Social Change.** Also in Atlanta is a collection of six prestigious black colleges, known collectively as **Atlanta University.**

Throughout the state some other significant African American sites or tours include the **Black Heritage Trail Tour** in Columbus, the **Coweta County African American Heritage Museum and Research Center** in Newnan, **Hog Hammock** community on Sapelo Island, the **King-Tisdell Cottage** in Savannah, **Lucy Craft Laney Museum of Black History** in Augusta, **Morgan County African American Museum** in Madison, the **Mount Zion Albany Civil Rights Movement Museum** in Albany, **Ralph Mark**

Gilbert Civil Rights Museum in Savannah, **Seabrook Village** in Midway, and the **Tubman African American Museum** in Macon. Numerous festivals celebrate African American heritage.

AGRICULTURAL FAIRS Outside of Atlanta and a few other large municipalities, Georgia is largely rural with an economy based on agriculture and forestry. These industries are often celebrated at annual agricultural fairs, the largest of which is the **Georgia National Fair** in Perry. Some other agricultural fairs include the **Georgia State Fair** in Macon, **Georgia Mountain Fair** in Hiawassee, **North Georgia State Fair** in Marietta, **Sunbelt Agricultural Exposition** in Moultrie, and the **South Georgia Jaycee Fair** in Swainsboro. Some of these are described in the pertinent chapter. For more information about fairs, contact the **Georgia Association of Agricultural Fairs** (478-477-2334).

AIRPORTS AND AIRLINES Many travelers to Georgia will fly into Atlanta. Others may fly into Athens, Augusta, Brunswick, Columbus, Macon, or Savannah, although they may have to connect in Atlanta. In fact, there used to be a T-shirt on sale at the airport that read "I died and went to heaven, but I had to change planes in Atlanta." No matter which airport travelers choose, they will then often need to rent a car to complete their journey, and the major airports have car rental firms on-site. Because travelers to the destinations described in so many additional chapters will fly into one of those airports, we do not give specific contact information about these airports, the airlines that fly into them, and on-site car rental

firms in each individual chapter but simply reference What's Where in Georgia. In some parts of Georgia, the most convenient airport may actually be in another state: Dothan, Alabama; Chattanooga, Tennessee; Greeneville/ Spartanburg, South Carolina; or Jacksonville or Tallahassee, Florida. The specifics about those airports are given in the appropriate chapter.

The following are the major airlines that serve Georgia (there are dozens of others): **Aeromexico** (1-800-237-6639; www.aeromexico .com), **Air Canada** (1-888-247-2262; www.aircanada.com), **Air France** (1-800-237-2747; www.airfrance.com), **Air Jamaica** (1-800-523-5585; airjamaica.com), **AirTran** (1-800-247-8726; www.airtran.com), **American** (1-800-433-7300; www.aa.com), **America West** (1-800-327-7810; www.americawest.com), **Atlantic Southeast Airlines** (1-800-325-1999; www.flyasa.com), **British Airways** (1-800-247-9297; www.britishairways .com), **Comair** (1-800-325-1999; www.comair.com), **Continental** (1-800-231-0856; www.continental .com), **Continental Express** (1-800-525-0280; www.continental.com), **Delta** (1-800-221-1212; www.delta .com), **Frontier** (1-800-432-1359; www.frontierairlines.com), **Independence Air** (1-800-359-3594; www.flyi.com), **Korean Air** (1-800-438-5000; www.koreanair.com), **Lufthansa** (1-800-645-3880; www.lufthansa.com), **Midwest** (1-800-452-2022; www.midwestairlines .com), **Northwest** (1-800-225-2525; www.nwa.com), **South African Airways** (1-800-722-9675; www.flyssa .com), **United** (1-800-241-6522; www .united.com), and **US Airways** (1-800-428-4322; www.usair.com).

The primary airport, which serves

much of Georgia, is **Hartsfield-Jackson Atlanta International Airport** (1-800-897-1910; www.atlanta-airport.com). One of the busiest airports in the world, the airport is served by 23 airlines. The primary airlines are Delta and Air Tran, but the entire list includes **Aeromexico, Air Canada, Air France, Air Jamaica, Air Tran, American, America West, Atlantic Southeast Airlines, British Airways, Comair, Continental, Corporate, Delta, Frontier, Independence Air, Korean Air, Lufthansa, Midwest, Northwest, South African Airways, United,** and **US Airways.** Transportation into the city is available from the airport by taxi (see Taxis), MARTA rail (see Bus/Rail Service), limousine, and rental car (see Car Rentals).

Travelers to Athens and surrounding destinations will use the **Athens–Ben Epps Airport** (706-613-3420; www.athensairport.net), which is served by **US Airways Express.**

Visitors to Augusta and nearby destinations arrive at **Augusta Regional Airport** (706-798-3236; 1-866-860-9809; www.AugustaRegionalAirport.com), which is served by **Atlantic Southeast Airlines** and **US Airways Express.**

Travelers to Columbus and nearby destinations will use the **Columbus Metropolitan Airport** (706-324-2449; www.flycolumbusga.com), which is served by **ASA/Delta Connection, Northwest,** and **US Airways Express.** Car rentals are available.

Visitors to the southern Georgia coast and resort islands may fly into the **Brunswick–Golden Isles Airport** (912-265-2070), which is served by **Delta.** Car rentals are available.

The most convenient airport for some destinations is **Middle Georgia Regional Airport Macon** (478-788-3760), which is serviced by Delta's affiliate, **Atlantic Southeast Airlines.** Car rentals are available.

Travelers to several destinations on or near the Georgia coast will fly into **Savannah/Hilton Head International Airport** (912-964-0514; www.savannahairport.com), which is served by **Air Tran, Continental Express, Delta** and **Delta Connection, Independence Air, Northwest Airlink, United Express,** and **US Airways.** Numerous car rental companies, public transportation, hotel shuttles, and taxis offer transportation from the airport to Savannah and Tybee Island (see Car Rentals).

AMTRAK Amtrak (1-800-USA-RAIL; www.amtrak.com) makes only five stops in Georgia. The Crescent route, which runs from New York to New Orleans, stops in Toccoa and Gainesville in northeast Georgia and Atlanta in northwest Georgia. The Silver Service/Palmetto route, which runs along the Atlantic seacoast from the Northeast to Florida, stops in Savannah and Jesup. Because the **Atlanta station** (404-881-3067; 1-800-USA-RAIL; www.amtrak.com), 1688 Peachtree Street NW, is the closest station to so many towns described in this book, we give that information only here and do not list it in each chapter—simply referencing What's Where in Georgia. There is bus service between the Atlanta station and Hartsfield-Jackson Atlanta International Airport. We give the Toccoa, Gainesville, Savannah, and Jesup information in the appropriate chapters and simply reference those in chapters about towns close to them. Several extreme-south Georgia towns are closer to Amtrak stops in Florida; the specifics are noted in those chapters. On the whole, arrival in Georgia by train and sight-seeing throughout the state is not very practical unless your sole destination is one of the towns in which the trains stop (or very nearby) or you plan on renting a car.

AMUSEMENT PARKS No matter what your age, you can indulge the kid in you at Georgia's amusement parks, which can be found all over the state—some large, others small. All have rides; some have entertainment and even small zoos. The granddaddy of theme parks is **Six Flags over Georgia** in Austell just outside Atlanta. Six Flags also operates two sibling parks in Georgia: **Six Flags American Adventures** (geared toward young children) and **Six Flags White Water** water park, both in Marietta just outside Atlanta. Hot on their heels in size and number and variety of rides, entertainment, and other attractions is **Wild Adventures Theme Park** in Valdosta. Other amusement parks include the **All-American Fun Park** in Albany, **Alpine Amusement Park** in Helen, **Dixieland Fun Park** in Fayetteville, **Funsville** in Martinez, **Fun Town of Henry County** in McDonough, **Lake Lanier Islands Beach and Water Park** in Buford, **Lake Win-nepesaukah** in Rossville, **Splash in the Boro** in Statesboro, **Starcadia Entertainment Park** in Macon, **Summer Waves Water Park** on Jekyll Island, and **WaterWiz** in LaGrange.

ANTIQUARIAN BOOKS C. Dickens in the Buckhead section of Atlanta sells fine, rare, and collectible books, as well as maps, historical documents, autographs, and manuscripts. **E. Shaver, Bookseller** in Savannah specializes in architecture, decorative arts, regional history, and antique maps.

ANTIQUES For information about antiques shops in Georgia, consult the web site www.antiqueshopsa2z.com/ga-city.htm. In the Atlanta metro area, contact the **Antique Dealers Association of Marietta** (www.antiques ofmarietta.com) and the **Chamblee Antiques Dealers Association** (www.antiquesrow.com). **Georgia's Antiques Trail** (www.historicgeorgia .org/trails) stretches 200 miles, from Conyers to McDonough, and lists 200 shops and dealers.

APPALACHIAN TRAIL The beginning and first 80 miles of the 2,144-mile Georgia-to-Maine trail is at Springer Mountain in north Georgia. The **Georgia Appalachian Trail Club** (404-634-6495; www.georgia-atclub .org) was founded in 1930 in Dahlonega. In cooperation with the Appalachian Trail Conservancy and the U.S. Forest Service, the club maintains and manages the Georgia portion of the trail, much of which passes through the Chattahoochee National Forest. For information about the entire trail, contact the **Appalachian Trail Conference,** P.O. Box 807, Harpers Ferry, WV 25425-0807.

APPENDICES The limitations of space in even so gargantuan a guide book prohibited us from including many of Georgia attractions and activities. At the end of the book, you will find a set of appendices covering everything from Activities to Parks. Under each category you'll find the names, contact information, and a brief description for even more things to see and do in Georgia.

APPLES A combination of favorable climate and soil conditions makes north Georgia ideal for apple production. The apple is so important to the economy of north Georgia that the fruit is honored with the **Apple Monument** in Cornelia. A particularly good place to find apples is **Apple Orchard Alley** along GA 52 in Gilmer County. In the autumn some farms offer visitors the opportunity to pick their own. Others offer apples and innumerable apple products for sale. Some of these farms include **Appletree Farms** and **Jaemor Farm Market,** both in Alto, **Hillcrest Orchards** in Ellijay, and **Mercier Orchards** in Blue Ridge. A popular annual fair is the **Georgia Apple Festival** (www.n-georgia.com/travel/apple.html). To learn more about apple-related activities or to find apple orchards, consult the web site at www.allaboutapples.com/orchard/ga01.htm.

AQUARIUMS The **Georgia Aquarium,** opened in November 2005, is the largest aquarium in the world. Expectations were that the aquarium would attract 2 million visitors in its first year, but with an average daily attendance of 10,000, the 2 million mark was passed in only six months. Visitors are particularly entranced with the beluga whales and the whale sharks. Tickets are for specified days and times, so be sure to make your reservations well in advance to avoid disappointment. In southwest Georgia, the new **Flint RiverQuarium** in

Albany is on a much smaller scale but is educational and enjoyable nonetheless and is not to be missed if you're in the area. The **University of Georgia Marine Science Complex and Aquarium** on Skidaway Island near Savannah is the state's only public saltwater marine aquarium.

AREA CODES Georgia has several area codes. The Atlanta metropolitan area alone has three (soon to be four), making it necessary to dial all 10 digits whenever you make a call. It is not unheard of for a business with more than one phone line to have two different area codes. In general, the area of the metropolitan region inside the I-285 perimeter highway that circles Atlanta uses the 404 area code, while the areas outside the perimeter highway use 678 and 770. There are exceptions, however, so be sure to check the number. Other area codes include 706 and 762 in the northern areas of the state outside the Atlanta metro area; 478 in the central part of the state; 912 along the coast and in southeastern Georgia, and 229 in southwestern Georgia. With the proliferation of cell phones, all bets are off when it comes to how many area codes will be in use when you travel

FLINT RIVERQUARIUM IN ALBANY

to Georgia and whether you may have to dial all 10 digits in areas other than metro Atlanta.

ART ASSOCIATIONS AND COUNCILS
Georgia has 200 arts associations and 30 local arts groups as well as 11 symphony orchestras, eight major art museums, and 30 community theaters. For the most complete information about arts in the state, contact the **Georgia Council for the Arts** (404-685-2787; www.gaarts.org). Another major arts group is the **Middle Georgia Art Association** (404-744-9557; www.mgaa-art.com) in Macon. Some of the other groups in the state include the **Albany Area Arts Council, Albany Concert Association, Atlanta Art Association, Blue Ridge Mountain Arts Association, Macon Concert Association, Ohoopee Regional Council for the Arts** in Vidalia, **Rome Area Council for the Arts,** and the **Thomasville Entertainment Foundation,** all of which are described in the pertinent chapters.

ART MUSEUMS The **High Museum of Art** in Atlanta is the state's premier art museum. Not only are the collections impressive, but the structure is an outstanding work of art itself. The striking primary building was designed by Richard Meier, and a recently opened addition was designed by Renzo Piano. The second-biggest art museum in the state is the **Columbus Museum** in Columbus. The official Georgia art museum is the **Georgia Museum of Art** in Athens. Other significant art museums, which are described in separate chapters, include the **Albany Museum of Art** in Albany, **Madison Museum of Art** in Madison, **Mariet-**ta/**Cobb Museum of Art** in Marietta, **Michael C. Carlos Museum of Emory University** in Decatur, **Morris Museum of Art** in Augusta, and the **Telfair Museum of Arts and Science/Jepson Center for the Arts** in Savannah. There are also entries in several chapters describing smaller and university art museums. For more information, consult the **Georgia Association of Museums and Galleries** (www.gamg.org) or these web sites: www.georgia.worldweb.com/SightsAttractions/Museums, www.artcyclopedia.com/museums/art-museums-in-usa-georgia.html, or www.masmacon.com/links.htm.

ATTRACTION/RESTAURANT/SHOP HOURS We list the days of the week and the hours that attractions, restaurants, and shops are open as of publication time. Obviously many of these will change in the future. In general, museums, some other attractions, and many restaurants are closed on Monday, and almost all attractions and many restaurants are closed on Christmas and some other holidays. It would make the individual entries about these sites too unwieldy to list all the days they are closed. To avoid disappointment, please check ahead if you're traveling on major holidays such as New Year's Day, Martin Luther King Day, St. Patrick's Day (in Savannah), Easter, Memorial Day, Labor Day, and Thanksgiving. Many of Georgia's state parks and historic sites are also closed on Monday, except when a major holiday falls on a Monday. Always check the appropriate web sites or call before you travel to get the most up-to-date times of operation for attractions, restaurants, and shops.

AUTO RACING Auto racing in the state was supposedly spawned in mountainous north Georgia in the days of fast cars and moonshine—a combination that resulted in whirl-wind races between whiskey runners and revenuers. Georgia is dotted with racetracks—everything from the **Atlanta Motor Speedway** and **Road Atlanta,** which rival the tracks in Daytona, Indianapolis, and Talladega, to quarter-mile dirt tracks in small towns. Space prohibits us from describing more than a few of these tracks. For the locations of many more tracks, see the Other Activities Appendix.

BALLOONING There's an exciting and romantic way to get a bird's-eye view of parts of Georgia: a ride in a hot-air balloon. In the mountains of north Georgia, rides are available from **David Bristol Hot-Air Balloon Rides** in Helen. Near the coast, rides are available from **Feather Air Hot-Air Balloons** in Ellabelle. In general, rides are offered in the early morning or just before dusk and are highly dependent on the weather, so check ahead.

BEACHES Georgia may have a small coastline compared to states such as Florida, but the state offers many wonderful, wide, hard-packed beach-es perfect for sunning, swimming, bike riding, fishing, and other activi-ties. The most pristine beaches are found at the **Cumberland Island National Seashore** on Cumberland Island and the beaches of privately owned **Little St. Simons Island,** both of which accept a limited num-ber of overnight guests and daytrip-pers. Some of Georgia's barrier islands are national wildlife refuges and are also in a pristine state. **Tybee Island** and the Golden Isles of **Jekyll Island, St. Simons Island,** and **Sea Island** are developed resort areas with hotels, condominiums, rental cottages, restaurants, and shops. Parks at many of Georgia's lakes have man-made beaches, as do several state parks. Other beaches include the **Beach at Clayton County Interna-tional Park** in Jonesboro, **Lake Lanier Islands Beach and Water Park** in Buford, **Lake Tobesofkee Recreation Area** in Macon, and **Robin Lake Beach** at Callaway Gar-dens in Pine Mountain.

BED & BREAKFASTS Many travelers prefer accommodations in small his-toric properties with breakfast includ-ed. Georgia has many such properties in cities and rural areas. These range from grand plantation homes in the deep southern part of the state to Painted Ladies in Atlanta to rustic homes in the mountains. A smaller portion of B&Bs are contemporary, and some were built specifically to be bed & breakfasts. Savannah has the largest concentration of B&Bs in the state. Prices vary from $50 to 650, but average $150–200 per night.

Not all that long ago Carol was the only person who had ever seen every single B&B in Georgia. With new ones opening all the time, however, it's hard to keep up, and there are a few listed here that we haven't visited but depended on the recommenda-tion of tourism officials in the area.

The upside of a stay in a bed & breakfast is personal attention, recom-mendations about attractions and restaurants from your host, and the greater likelihood that guests will interact with each other than if you stayed in impersonal hotels. If you think you'd like to try a B&B, keep in mind that bed & breakfasts are usually in someone's home and that there are often strict rules about pets, children, and smoking, as well as deposit and cancellation policies that are more stringent than at other types of accommodations. B&Bs may not be wheelchair accessible and certainly don't have all the amenities of a large hotel. A stay in a B&B is usually by reservation only with no walk-ins.

The prices we quote are for one night for one or two people; there is almost always an additional charge for more than two guests. In addition to the B&Bs we describe, some other places to get recommendations include www.abaa.org, www.georgia bedandbreakfasts.com, www.usinns .com/html/regions/GA, and www .bblist.com/ga/ga.htm. Savannah has so many bed & breakfasts, some are represented by **Sonja's R.S.V.P. Savannah** (1-877-728-2662; www .iloveinns.com/bed.and.breakfasts/ georgia/rsvpsavannahreservation service.htm). See also Farm Bed & Breakfasts.

BICYCLING Every biker, from the occasional weekend recreational rider to the serious mountain biker, can find what he or she is looking for in Georgia. The entire southern part of the state is relatively flat, making recreational biking easy even for young family members. Biking is particularly popular at and around the beaches, which are usually hard-packed and easy to ride on, and rentals are plentiful. The mountains in north Georgia offer enough challenges for mountain bikers. For information on biking in Georgia, consult the state's travel web site, www.georgia.org, and choose the "Adventure" link. Also consult the **Dirt World** web site (www.dirtworld.com).

Readers might like to contact the following organizations about bicycling in the state: **Atlanta Bicycle Campaign** (404-881-1112; www .atlanta.bike.org), a bicycle advocacy group in the Atlanta metro area; **Georgia Bicycle Federation** (www .bicyclegeorgia.com), which is dedicated to making Georgia a friendlier place to ride; and **Georgia Bikes** (404-634-6745; www.georgiabikes .org), a nonprofit organization dedicated to improving bicycling conditions and promote bicycling.

Several excellent books describe bicycling in Georgia: *Cycling through Georgia* by Susan Hunter and *Road Bike North Georgia* by Jim Parham. See also Mountain Biking.

BIRDING The **Audubon Society** (www.audubon.org/states) has several chapters in Georgia. The society has designated 29 regions of Georgia as important bird areas, including Jekyll Island and the entire mountainous area of north Georgia. Several birding trails attract casual and serious birdwatchers. The **Colonial Coast Birding Trail** stretches 112 miles from St. Marys to Savannah along Georgia's coast and has 18 stops. More than 300 species of birds have been spotted along the trail that includes shoreline, salt marshes, old rice fields, woodlands, tidal rivers, and freshwater wetlands. Part of the Colonial Coast Birding Trail is the **Devendorf Forested Flyways Birding Trail at Melon Bluff** (1-888-246-8188; www .melonbluff.com). These are trails described in the Savannah, Brunswick, and Darien chapters. Another important birding trail is the Georgia Department of Natural Resources' **Southern Rivers Birding Trail,** which stretches from the piedmont area through the coastal plain, ending at the Okefenokee Swamp. It is described in the Bainbridge chapter.

Avid birders would probably like to consult "Birds of Georgia," the **Georgia Wildlife Federation**'s species list (www.gwf.org/commonbirds.htm). Another source of information is the web site www.georgianature.org/member.spotlight/index.html. Some excellent book resources include *Birding Georgia* by Giff Beaton, *Birds of Georgia Field Guide* by Stan Tekiela, *Georgia Birds* by James Cavanaugh, and *Georgia Bird Watching: A Year-Round Guide* by Bill Thompson III.

BOAT EXCURSIONS See Canoeing, Cruises, Kayaking, Tubing, and White-Water Rafting.

BOOKS Georgians traveling within their own state and visitors from elsewhere can get the flavor of different eras in the state's past by reading fictional and nonfictional accounts set in Georgia—most written by Georgians. Still the second-best-selling book in the world after the Bible, *Gone with the Wind* by Margaret Mitchell paints the stereotypical portrait of the Old South. *Tobacco Road* by Erskine Caldwell is a searing portrayal of the life of a tenant farmer during the Great Depression. Lillian Smith's 1944 novel *Strange Fruit* is a gripping story of miscegenation and murder. In more recent years, *Peachtree Road* by Anne Rivers Siddons and *A Man in Full* by Tom Wolfe put the old and new moneyed classes of Atlanta at the end of the 20th century under the microscope.

Some other books set in the state or by Georgia authors include *Ugly Ways* by Tina McElroy Ansa; *Cold Sassy Tree* by Olive Ann Burns; *The Lonely Hunter* by Virginia Spencer Carr; *The Gospel Singer* and *Feast of Snakes* by Harry Crews; *Deliverance* by James Dickey; *A Circuit Rider's Wife* by Corra Harris; *Told by Uncle Remus: New Stories of the Old Plantation* by Joel Chandler Harris; *Lamb in His Bosom* by Caroline Miller; *Wise Blood* and short stories by Flannery O'Connor; *The Beloved Invader* and *New Moon Rising,* books set on St. Simons by Eugenia Price; *Run with the Horsemen* by Ferrol Sams Jr.; *The Color Purple* by Alice Walker; and *The Foxes of Harrow* by Frank Yerby.

In the humor genre, two authors immediately come to mind: Lewis Grizzard and Bailey White. Some of Grizzard's books include *If I Ever Get Back to Georgia, I'm Gonna Nail My Feet to the Ground; Chili Dawgs Always Bark at Night;* and *When My Love Returns from the Ladies Room, Will I Be Too Old to Care?* Some of White's books include *Mama Makes Up Her Mind and Other Dangers of Southern Living, Sleeping at the Starlite Motel,* and *Quite a Year for Plums.*

In the nonfiction category, *Midnight in the Garden of Good and Evil* by John Berendt examines a real-life murder mystery at the same time it skewers Savannah's eccentricities. "The Book," as it is known in Savannah and elsewhere, has earned a worldwide cultlike following that brings scores of visitors to Savannah. Going back to the early 19th century, the recounting of the horrifying conditions endured by slaves in *Journal of a Residence on a Georgia Plantation in 1838–1839* by English actress Frances Anne "Fanny" Kemble was instrumental in keeping England out of the Civil War. In the mid-20th century, *The Year the Lights Came On* by Terry Kay recounts the electrification of rural Georgia. Some other factual accounts about Georgia include *A Childhood: The Biography of a Place* by Harry Crews; *The Souls of Black Folk* by W.E.B. Du Bois; *Praying for Sheetrock* by Melissa Fay Greene, a sociological study of coastal Georgia; *In My Place* by Charlayne Hunter-Gault, who broke the color barrier at the University of Georgia; and *And the Dead Shall Rise: The Murder of Mary Phagan and the Lynching of Leo Frank* by Steve Oney, a shocking case of anti-Semitism in Atlanta at the turn of the 20th century. As a matter of fact, Georgia seems to have spawned a large number of books about infamous murders—not only *And the Dead Shall Rise* and *Murder in the Garden of Good and Evil,* but others such as *Murder in Coweta County* by Margaret Ann Barnes. Several of these have been made into movies.

In the children's book category, Joel Chandler Harris is, of course, famous for the tales he incorporated into the Uncle Remus stories in the late 19th century. He also wrote *Little Mr. Thimblefinger and His Queer Country: What the Children Saw and Heard There,* a collection of Negro tales outside the Uncle Remus genre, as well as middle Georgia folklore tales and pure inventions. *Turn Homeward, Hannalee* by Patricia Beatty is a fictionalized version—told from a child's point of view—of the true story of the women and children taken from Roswell during the Civil War, charged with treason, and sent north to be imprisoned or placed in servitude. Youngsters will enjoy *A Tree That Owns Itself and Other Adventure Tales from Georgia's Past*

by Gail Langer Karwoski. Some of these oddities, such as the tree in question, are described in our various chapters.

Some other travel guides you might want to consult include two of our other guides: *Fun with the Family: Georgia,* a collection of activities, attractions, festivals, lodgings, and restaurants specifically of interest to families with young children; and *Romantic Days and Nights in Atlanta,* themed long weekend getaways for couples. Both *Georgia Off the Beaten Track* and *Georgia Curiosities* by William Schemmel examine some of Georgia's most eccentric or hard-to-find attractions.

Within the various categories of this What's Where in Georgia section of the book, you'll find numerous suggestions for books under the categories Bicycling, Birding, Camping, Hiking, and Mountain Biking.

BUS/RAIL SERVICE The **Greyhound Lines** (404-584-1738; www.greyhound.com) station at 232 Forsyth Street in Atlanta is open 24 hours a day and is the eighth-busiest station in the country. Because the Atlanta station is the closest one to towns described in many other chapters, we simply reference What's Where in Georgia rather than repeat the information. In addition, Greyhound stops at 32 other locations throughout Georgia. Those stops are noted in the appropriate chapters with the address of the station. In our opinion, bus travel is not a viable way to see the state. Although it is possible to map out a route that includes only towns with Greyhound service, once in each town, a traveler would have to use a taxi service if one was available or get a rental car. To see any of the state outside the towns where Greyhound stops, a visitor would need a rental car.

Only the largest cities such as Atlanta, Macon, Savannah, and a few others have mass transit, so a visit to any town other than these would require using a taxi or a rental car. Because the areas described in several chapters include the Atlanta metro area, to avoid repetitive material, we describe the various mass transit systems that serve the metro area here and simply reference What's Where in Georgia in the individual chapters. We describe mass transit systems in Macon, Savannah, and a few other cities within the pertinent chapters.

The Atlanta metro area is served by the **Metropolitan Atlanta Rapid Transit Authority,** known locally as **MARTA; BUC (Buckhead's Uptown Connection); Georgia Tech Technology Square Trolley; Cobb Community Transit; Gwinnett County Transit;** and **Xpress,** which serves several outlying counties.

MARTA (404-848-4711; www .itsmarta.com), the city's bus/rail system, is the most cost-effective and convenient way to get around the metro Atlanta area (specifically Fulton County), with a variety of routes and pass options available. A station at the airport makes access to the city and suburbs easy. The regular fare is $1.75 one way, and transfers are available between buses or buses and trains. Exact change, tokens, or fare cards (available at all station entrances) can be used. Visitor passes are available beginning at $7 for one-day unlimited use up to $13 for a seven-day pass. Buses generally run between 5 AM and 1 AM weekdays and between 6 AM and 1 AM on weekends and holidays. Trains run 5 AM to 1 AM daily. MARTA allows bicycles on all

its trains, and there are bike racks on the front of most buses (the racks handle only two bikes at a time). Many MARTA stations have bike racks for commuters who wish to bike to the train. Transfers are free between MARTA and Cobb Community Transit (CCT) Gwinnett County Transit (GCT), and Xpress.

While in the Buckhead area of Atlanta, take advantage of the free **BUC** shuttle, which connects the Lenox Square and Buckhead MARTA rail stations with major hotels, dining locations, retail centers (including Lenox Square and Phipps Plaza), and key office buildings. The BUC operates 7 AM to 10 PM weekdays. For information, contact the **Buckhead Area Transportation Management Association** (404-842-2682; www .batma.org; www.bucride.com).

Another option for getting around a limited area of the city is the free **Georgia Tech Technology Square Trolley** (404-894-9645). These rubber-tired, alternative-fuel vehicles, designed to look like old-fashioned trolleys, provide free service throughout the campus to the Midtown MARTA station. This means out-of-town visitors can take MARTA rail from the airport to the Midtown station, then transfer to the trolley to reach the campus and the Georgia Tech Hotel and Conference Center. The Tech Trolley runs every four minutes and is available to students, faculty, staff, and visitors.

In Marietta and Cobb County, mass transit is provided by **Cobb Community Transit** (770-427-4444; www.cobbdot.org/cct.htm). The transit authority provides bus service throughout the county and connecting service to MARTA at the Arts Center Station. Fare is $1.25 one way.

For mass transit transportation in Gwinnett County, **Gwinnett County Transit** (770-822-5010) provides express, local, and paratransit services. Express buses to and from Atlanta operate weekdays and include six routes using the HOV lanes on I-85. Free park-and-ride lots are located at I-985, Discover Mills shopping mall, and Indian Trail. Local bus service within Gwinnett County operates five routes Monday through Saturday, connecting neighborhoods and businesses to cultural, shopping, and educational opportunities.

Xpress (404-463-4782; www .xpressga.com) is metro Atlanta's newest public transit service. Fares are $3 one-way, $5 round-trip. Routes operate 5:30 AM TO 9:30 PM weekdays. Operated in partnership with the Georgia Regional Transportation Authority and 11 counties, the service provides an easy-to-use connection to downtown Atlanta from Cumming, Fairburn, Jonesboro, and Morrow, where passengers can transfer to the MARTA bus/rail system.

CAMPING Georgia is dotted with campgrounds on the shores of lakes and rivers, in forests or near the beach, in developed tourist areas or in the wilderness. Some of them are in state or national parks, while others are privately operated. Because of the mild climate, most of these campgrounds are open year-round, but it's always wise to check ahead. An excellent resource is *Camping Georgia* by Alex Nutt. There are also dozens of camping web sites, of which avid campers are probably already aware.

Most state parks have a campground, and we note that in each state park description along with the nightly camping fee. A two-night minimum stay is required for most reservations, except a three-night minimum is required for Memorial Day, Labor Day, and Independence Day weekends. RV and most other campsites offer electric and water hookups, grills or fire rings, and picnic tables. Comfort stations with hot showers, flush toilets, and electrical hookups are conveniently located. All campgrounds have a dump station, and some offer cable TV hookups. Campers younger than 18 must be accompanied by an adult, and pets are welcome if kept on a 6-foot leash and attended at all times. Separate group camps and pioneer camps are available. A deposit is required, and there are cancellation penalties. To find out about camping at specific state parks, consult the web site at www.gastateparks.org.

CANOEING, KAYAKING, TUBING, AND WHITE-WATER RAFTING
Because Georgia is crisscrossed with rivers, dotted with lakes, and edged by the Atlantic Ocean, the state offers all kinds of water conditions for any paddler's experience and interest level: smooth-as-glass lakes, slow-moving rivers, tumultuous white-water rivers, calm estuaries, and the ocean, which may be calm or rough depending on the weather. Canoeing, kayaking, and tubing can be good ways to see Georgia's wildlife. Families with small children might enjoy floating down a placid river in an inner tube or gliding across a tranquil lake in a canoe or kayak. Tubing is popular in the Helen area of the northeast Georgia mountains as well as in the Chattahoochee River National Recreation Area, which runs from Lake Lanier through the metro Atlanta area. Those who want

a little more adventure might like hurtling down a white-water river in a raft or challenging themselves to an ocean tour in a sea kayak. Two rivers in north Georgia—the Chattooga and the Toccoa/Ocoee, site of the 1996 Centennial Summer Olympic Games white-water events—provide plenty of thrills for white-water rafters. Some sections of the Flint River in western Georgia have rapids as well.

Sea kayaking is very popular around Tybee Island and the Golden Isles, while canoeing is a popular way to see the Okefenokee Swamp. Except for white-water rafting, which is usually offered only spring through fall, most of these paddling sports are available year-round. There is no shortage of outfitters who provide rentals, lessons, and guided tours, some of which may include overnight trips. Just a few outfitters include the **Chattahoochee River Outfitters** in Roswell, **Flint River Outdoor Center** near Thomaston, **Nantahala Outdoor Center** near Clayton, **Sea Kayak Georgia** on Tybee Island, and **Up the Creek Xpeditions and Outfitters** near St. Marys. Some guided excursions are led by **Altamaha Coastal Tours** near Darien, **Appalachian Outfitters River Trips** in Helen, and **Three Rivers Expeditions** in Hazelhurst. In most chapters we describe various outfitters in the area and describe canoe trails such as the **Altamaha Canoe Trail** near Baxley.

CAR RENTALS All the major car rental companies have numerous locations throughout Georgia, although all of them are not found everywhere. Rather than give car rental contact information in every chapter, we list that information here and simply reference What's Where in

Georgia in most cases. These car rental firms include **Alamo** (1-800-462-5266; www.alamo.com), **Avis** (1-800-331-1212; www.avis.com), **Budget** (1-800-527-0700; www.budget.com), **Dollar** (1-866-434-2226; www.dollar.com), **Enterprise** (1-800-261-7331; www.enterprise.com), **Hertz** (1-800-654-3131; www.hertz.com), **National** (1-800-CAR-RENT; www.national.com), and **Thrifty** (1-800-847-4389; www.thrifty.com).

Car rentals are available on-site at Hartsfield-Jackson Atlanta International Airport from **Avis, Budget, Dollar, Enterprise, Hertz, National/Alamo,** and **Thrifty**. Off-site car rentals include **Airport Rent A Car of Atlanta** (1-800-905-4997), **EZ Rent A Car** (404-761-4999), and **Payless Car Rental** (404-766-5034).

Car rentals are available at Athens–Ben Epps Airport in Athens from **Hertz.**

Passengers arriving at Columbus Metropolitan Airport can rent cars from **Avis, Budget, Enterprise, Hertz,** and **National.**

Car rentals are available from **Avis** and **Hertz** at the Brunswick–Golden Isles Airport in Brunswick.

At Middle Georgia Regional Airport, rentals are available from **Alamo/National, Avis, Budget, Enterprise,** and **Hertz.**

At Savannah's airport, car rentals are available from **Alamo, Avis, Budget, Economy Rent-A-Car** (912-352-7042), **Enterprise, Hertz, National,** and **Thrifty.**

CHAPTER HEADINGS Chapters are divided among the five principal regions of the state: Atlanta Metro, a vast area including the city as well its suburbs and some towns that have been swallowed up by urbanization;

the Coast, which includes many of Georgia's barrier islands as well as towns that line the mainland; Historic South, the central heartland of Georgia; the Mountains, which covers the northern part of the state; and Southern Rivers, towns and areas in the southern part of the state. Whether the chapter title lists only one city or several, the text of the chapter will cover a broader area then just those identified in the title. Descriptions will also be included for attractions, activities, special events, restaurants, and/or lodgings in small towns in the immediate vicinity of the featured town(s).

CHILDREN, ESPECIALLY FOR
Throughout this book, attractions, restaurants, and lodgings that are of special interest to families with children or that are particularly child-friendly are indicated with the 𝄞 icon.

CHILDREN'S MUSEUMS Youngsters aren't neglected when it comes to Georgia's museums. There are several museums geared specifically to the small-fry, including the **Georgia Children's Museum** in Macon, **Imagine It! The Children's Museum of Atlanta,** the **Interactive Neighborhood for Kids** in Gainesville, and the **Museum of Arts and Sciences** in Macon. Several important museums aren't just for adults but offer interactive children's rooms in their facilities, including the **Columbus Museum** in Columbus, the **High Museum of Art** in Atlanta, and the **Jepson Center for the Arts** in Savannah. The **Center for Puppetry Arts** in Atlanta is of special interest to both adults and children.

CHILDREN'S PROGRAMS A real vacation for parents often includes special activities and programs geared to children so that the youngsters are occupied while the parents are enjoying other pursuits. One program that has been attracting families for several generations is **Camp Cloister** at the Cloister at Sea Island. Some other programs include the **Brasstown Valley Family Summer Adventure Program** in Young Harris, the **Callaway Summer Family Adventure Program** in Pine Mountain, and **Club Juniors** at the Jekyll Island Club on Jekyll Island.

CHRISTMAS TREES AND WREATHS
Many folks prefer to choose and cut their own Christmas tree both for the fun of doing so and to ensure freshness. A couple places where you can cut your own Christmas tree are **Bradley's Pumpkin Patch and Christmas Trees** near Dawsonville and **Southern Tree Plantation** near Blairsville. To find more about Christmas tree farms and to find other locations, consult the **Georgia Christmas Tree Association** web site (www.ga christmas.com) and click on the "Find a Farm" link. Or call the organization, which is located in Concord (770-884-0022 or 1-800-383-6585).

CIVIL WAR SITES Georgia has significant Civil War history. As Union troops pushed into the state from Chattanooga, the Confederacy had an important victory at Chickamauga (now a national battlefield park), but later couldn't stop the relentless advance toward Atlanta, which was targeted by the Union because it was the Confederacy's primary rail center and supply distribution point. After taking Atlanta, Union General William Tecumseh Sherman's March to the Sea headed across central

MARIETTA'S CONFEDERATE CEMETERY

Chickamauga, and the **Tunnel Hill Heritage Center/Western and Atlantic Railroad Tunnel** in Tunnel Hill. All these sites and many more are described more fully in the appropriate chapters. Numerous battle reenactments, living-history camps, and other Civil War–related activities occur throughout the year and are described in the Special Events section of individual chapters. See also Reenactments.

Georgia to Savannah, destroying just about everything in his path. One of the most infamous Civil War prisons was Camp Sumter in Andersonville (now the **Andersonville National Historic Site**).

When in Georgia, don't be surprised to hear the Civil War described as The War, as if there were no other. You'll also hear it referred to as the War of Northern Aggression and, our personal favorite, the Recent Unpleasantness. General Sherman is snidely referred to as That Pyromaniac from the North. Hardly a chapter in this book doesn't feature something about the Civil War and William Tecumseh Sherman.

Just a few of the Civil War sites in Georgia are **Allatoona Pass Battlefield Trail** in Cartersville, **Andersonville Civil War Village** and **Andersonville National Historic Site,** both in Andersonville, **Chickamauga and Chattanooga National Military Park** at Fort Oglethorpe, **Gordon-Lee Mansion** in Chickamauga, **Kennesaw Mountain National Battlefield Park** in Kennesaw, **Lee and Gordon's Mill** in

COTTAGE RENTALS Cottage rentals are a popular and usually reasonably priced lodging alternative for stays of a week or more at the beach, a lake, the mountains, or a state park. We list rentals of individual cottages as well as rental agencies in many chapters. Another source of information about cottage rentals is a local chamber of commerce; many of these are listed in the Guidance section of each chapter.

Most of Georgia's state parks offer cottages, and we note those that do in state park descriptions with the nightly rental rate. In general, state parks require a two-night minimum stay (three nights on Memorial Day, Independence Day, and Labor Day weekends), although some require a five- or seven-night minimum in the summer. Shorter stays may be available at the last minute. There is a maximum 14-night stay, although if you have vacated the cottage for four nights, you may return. Young people under the age of 18 must be accompanied by an adult. After a successful experiment with allowing pets in selected cottages at three state parks in 2005, all state parks with cottages now welcome pets in selected cottages. Prior arrangements are required, so don't just show up with your pet. Deposits are required, and there are cancellation penalties. To learn more about state parks with cottages, consult the web site www.gastateparks.org.

COUNTIES Georgia has 159 counties; most of them are very small, and many have only one municipality. Years ago the thinking was that a county shouldn't be any larger than the distance a person could travel by horseback from his farm to the county seat, transact his business, and return home in the same day. Today the small sizes mean individual boards of education and other county services that might be better consolidated, but most visitors are totally unaware of crossing many counties as they travel. The only impact on a traveler would be if a medical emergency arose in one of the nine counties that do not yet have 911 service. These are noted under Emergencies/Medical in this chapter and in the pertinent chapters. Fortunately the small size of these counties means that medical attention can be found in a surrounding county. The large number of counties has created a collection of Georgia treasures: impressive county courthouses. Most of these were constructed after the Civil War but before the turn of the 20th century and are magnificent examples of a variety of styles of architecture. Most are still in use and may contain small museums; others have been converted to other uses, including museums. Unfortunately a few have burned and been replaced by much more forgettable structures. Some folks have made it their mission to see and photograph every historic courthouse in Georgia.

COVERED BRIDGES Georgia once had more than 200 covered bridges. Today there are only 16 and not all of them

are historic. The following historic covered bridges are described in separate chapters: **Auchumpkee Creek** near Thomaston, **Coheelee Creek** near Blakely, **Concord** near Smyrna, **Cromer's Mill** near Carnesville, **Elders Mill** near Watkinsville, **Euharlee Covered Bridge and Historic Museum** near Cartersville, **Parrish Mill** in George L. Smith State Park near Twin City, **Red Oak** near Woodbury, **Stovall Mill** near Sautee, and **Watson Mill Bridge** in Watson Mill Bridge State Park near Comer. For more information about these and other Georgia covered bridges, consult the **Georgia Department of Transportation**'s web site (www.dot.state.ga.us/special subjects/specialinterest/covered).

CRAFTS Locally made crafts can be found all over Georgia. Appalachian crafts are most often found in the mountainous areas of north Georgia. Pennsylvania Dutch crafts are created and sold by the Mennonite community in Montezuma in southwest Georgia. Amish furniture, artwork, quilts, and crafts from Pennsylvania and Ohio can be purchased from the **Amish Red Barn** in Clarkesville. Many crafts created along the coast reflect the African American Gullah culture.

Just a few excellent places to find a variety of quality crafts created by numerous Georgia artisans and craftspeople include **Genuine Georgia, an Artist Marketplace** in Greensboro and **Mark of the Potter** near Clarksville. In the individual chapters, we often describe shops that sell Georgia arts and crafts. See also Georgia Made.

If you have an interest in a particular craft and want to find the best locations to purchase examples, there are dozens of craft guilds such as the **Chattahoochee Handweavers Guild** (www.chgweb.com), the **Georgia Basketry Association** (www.geocities.com/ga_basketry_assoc), and the **Peachtree Arts and Crafts Association** (770-457-5510). To find contact information for other guilds, check out the *Crafts Report Online* (www.craftsreport.com/resources/south/georgia.html).

CRUISES The term "cruise" can cover a lot of territory, but in the context of this guide it generally means a boat ride or excursion of fairly short duration and might be focused on sightseeing, wildlife observation, fishing, or even gambling. These cruises may be on the ocean or an inland lake or river. **Emerald Princess II Casino Cruises** out of Brunswick offers gambling cruises in international waters. **River Street Riverboat Company** offers sight-seeing cruises on the Savannah River aboard nostalgic paddlewheelers. **Romantic Lake Cruises** offer sight-seeing cruises on Lake Chatuge near Hiawassee. **Weadore Sailing,** operating out of Jekyll Island, offers sunset, dolphin, and moonlight cruises aboard the 31-foot *Bombay Clipper*. Check various chapters for dolphin watching and nature cruises (see also Dolphin Watching).

CULTURAL ORGANIZATIONS The world-renowned **Atlanta Symphony Orchestra** offers classical and pops series. There are also symphonies based in Albany, Athens, Augusta, Buford, Columbus, Decatur, LaGrange, Rome, Savannah, Statesboro, Stockbridge, Toccoa, and Valdosta. Atlanta also offers the **Atlanta Ballet,** the **Atlanta Opera,** and the **Capitol City Opera. Company.** (See Theaters/Summer and Theaters/Year-Round).

CURIOSITIES Part of the fun of traveling around any state is finding the offbeat attraction. Georgia is no exception. The state's oddities include the **Big Chicken** in Marietta, an unusual Kentucky Fried Chicken restaurant; the **Double-Barreled Cannon** in Athens, an innovative but unsuccessful weapon developed during the Civil War; the **Georgia Guidestones** in Elberton, a gargantuan Stonehenge-like structure erected in a field by an anonymous group; **Pasaquan** in Buena Vista, the flamboyantly decorated home and compound of the late visionary artist Eddie Owens Martin; **Rock Eagle Effigy** in Eatonton, a gigantic figure of a bird created thousands of years ago by Native Americans; the **Smallest Church in America** in Eulonia, which seats only 12; and the **Tree That Owns Itself** in Athens. You'll find many more in the individual chapters and may discover some we haven't listed on your travels.

DINING AND EATING OUT The prices we list for your guidance are for entrées only, unless otherwise noted. You could easily more than double the price of a meal by adding appetizers, soup, salad, side dishes, dessert, and cold beverages, tea, or coffee. Certainly the meal price would be greatly increased by adding alcoholic beverages. The **Dining Out** category is considered to be fine dining in a more formal setting. This category is usually more expensive, too; in general, we list restaurants here when entrées are $20 or higher. The **Eating Out** category is much more casual and also more affordable, with entrées less than $20. Some restaurants are hard to categorize. Perhaps a restaurant's entrées are less than $20, but the ambience is formal with linen tablecloths and napkins, mood lighting, candlelight, soft music, and flowers. In that case, we've listed it with fine dining. Although we try to put each restaurant in the category in which we think it fits best, it might also fit into the other category, so we hope our description makes it possible for you to make a decision about whether this is what you're looking for or not. Also be aware that prices will almost inevitably have changed by the time you travel.

DOLPHIN WATCHING Although whales may occasionally pass by the Georgia coast on their way somewhere else, it's not common to see them. Visitors are entranced, however, with cavorting dolphins, which are often seen. Just a few companies that offer dolphin-watching tours are **Dolphin Magic** out of Savannah, **Capt. Mike's Dolphin Tours** out of Tybee Island, **Weadore Sailing** out of Jekyll Island, and **St. Simons Transit Company** out of St. Simons Island. Anglers on deep-sea fishing charters often sight dolphins. Better yet, do as our multigenerational extended family does and stay several weeks each year in a cottage on the Back River on

Tybee Island, where schools of dolphins cruising up and down the river keep us entertained all day long. Sometimes they come in almost to the shore. When various family members have been sailing or kayaking in the calm waters of the Back River, they've actually been sprayed by dolphins that were that close to them.

DRIVING TOURS Throughout the book we describe many state-designated trails, just a few of which include the **Andersonville Trail** from Perry to Cordele, the **Blue and Gray Trail** from Chattanooga to Dallas, **Chattahoochee–Flint River Heritage Highway** from Roscoe to St. Marks, **Chieftains Trail** from Carrollton to Dalton, **Colonial Coast Birding Trail** from St. Marys to Savannah, **Georgia's Antebellum Trail** from Athens to Macon, **Heartland of the Confederacy Civil War Trail** from Athens to Madison, the **Liberty Trail** from Hinesville to Riceboro, and the **Russell-Brasstown Scenic Byway** from Helen to Blairsville.

Many cities and towns have devised driving tours of historic neighborhoods. Just a few of these include the **Azalea Trail, Camellia Trail,** and **Valdosta Historic Driving Tour** in Valdosta; *Gone with the Wind* **Driving Tour of Homes** in Jonesboro; the **Thomasville Black History Heritage Trail Tour;** and driving tours in Historic Grantville, Moreland, and Senoia.

EMERGENCIES/MEDICAL Georgia's 159 counties are almost universally covered by 911 service. The following counties/towns are the only exceptions: Baker County/Newton, Berrien County/Nashville, Crawford

County/Knoxville and Roberta, Johnson County/Wrightsville, Pulaski County/Hawkinsville, Randolph County/Cuthbert, Stewart County/Lumpkin and Richland, Talbot County/Talbotton, and Treutlen County/Soperton.

EVENTS We list outstanding and often highly unusual annual events within each chapter. In addition to large festivals such as the **Atlanta Dogwood Festival,** the **Renaissance Festival** in Fairburn, and the **Savannah Irish Festival** and **St. Patrick's Day Parade** in Savannah, there are dozens of festivals dedicated to buggies, fire ants, honeybees, mayhaws (a type of berry), mules, peanuts, rattlesnakes, swine, Vidalia onions, watermelon, wild chickens, and wild hogs. We give a brief description, contact information, and an admission price if there is one. More events can be found by checking the web sites of convention and visitors bureaus and chambers of commerce, which are listed in the Guidance section of each chapter. Other listings can be found at the state's travel web site (www.georgia.org). Even more information can be obtained from the **Georgia Festivals and Events Association** (www.gfea.com); **Georgia Mountain Festivals, Fairs, Music, Competition** (www.jwww.com/fairs); and the **International Association of Fairs and Expositions** (www.fairsandexpos.com).

FACTORY OUTLETS Georgia has clusters of outlet stores scattered throughout the state, primarily along I-75, I-85, and I-95, but other places as well. These are described in the pertinent chapters. If you're in the market for carpet, Dalton, which is located 90 miles north of Atlanta and 25 miles south of Chattanooga on I-75, boasts more than 100 carpet outlets. Other outlet centers include **Commerce Factory Stores** in Commerce, **Georgia Islands Factory Shoppes** in Darien, **King Frog Factory Outlet** in Adel, **Lake Park Outlets** in Lake Park, **North Georgia Premium Outlets** in Dawsonville, **Peach Festival Outlet Shops** in Byron, **Prime Outlets of Calhoun, Tanger Outlet Center** in Locust Grove, and **Tanger Outlets of Commerce**. Many individual off-price shops can be found throughout the state. Atlantans were particularly happy when the famous **Filene's Basement** opened in Buckhead.

FALL FOLIAGE Autumn colors are usually at their most flamboyant in north Georgia the last week in October through the first week in November. The air is usually clear and crisp, making travel especially appealing. The downside is that the winding, two-lane, mountainous country roads are clogged with sight-seers. Restaurants and shops are crowded, and it's essential to have made overnight reservations far in advance. Unlike some other states where leaf season is considered off-season with reduced prices, in Georgia fall is still high season. In fact, hostelries may require three-night minimum stays and full nonrefundable payment in advance. Some web sites to consult about fall foliage include www.forestry.about.com, www.atlanta.citysearch.com, www.tripspot.com/foliagefeature.htm, www.fs.fed.us/conf/fall/falcolor.htm, www.11alive.com, www.ajc.com, www.appalachiantrail.com, and www.trails.com.

FARM BED & BREAKFASTS Farm B&Bs offer a complete change of pace for city dwellers: lots of wide-open spaces, farm animals, hearty breakfasts, and a casual atmosphere. Some are on working farms, some are not. One of the most outstanding is **Serenbe Bed and Breakfast Farm** located in Palmetto just south of Atlanta. Accommodations exude casual elegance; meals are gourmet delights. In addition to farm animals to feed or pet, guests enjoy a collection of folk art, the swimming pool, hiking trails, and a waterfall. Some others include **Come Home to the Country B&B** in Dublin, the **Farmhouse Inn** in Madison, **Second Time Around Mini Farm** in Washington, and **Sugar Creek Farm and Inn,** an alpaca farm in Blue Ridge. See Bed & Breakfasts for a list of B&B resources.

FARMER'S MARKETS The state's numerous farmer's markets are the best source of fresh fruit, produce, and many other food and plant items. The largest is the **Atlanta State Farmer's Market** in Forest Park just south of the city, which even offers a trolley tour of the huge site. State farmer's markets also can be found in Brunswick, Cordele, Fitzgerald, Moultrie, and Thomasville. Other popular farmer's markets include **Buford Highway Farmer's Market** in Atlanta, **Harry's Farmer's Market** in Roswell, **International Farmer's Market** in Chamblee, **Your DeKalb Farmer's Market** in Doraville, and the **Sweet Auburn Curb Market** in downtown Atlanta. For more information about farmer's markets, consult the web site at www.n-georgia.com and click on "Farmers Markets."

FARM TOURS Agriculture is an important part of Georgia's economy. Many farms throughout the state have branched out from merely growing crops to also offering tours, fruit and berry picking, shopping for food and other items, and recreational activities such as hayrides, petting zoos, and Halloween activities. Some of these farms include **Bradley's Pumpkin Patch and Christmas Trees** near Dawsonville, **Burt's Farm** near Dawsonville, **Cagle's Dairy** near Canton, **Paradise Pastures Farm and Petting Zoo** near Taylorsville, **Pecan Orchard Plantation** near Vidalia, **Pettit Creek Farms** near Cartersville, **Pumpkin Patch Farm** near Adairsville, **Southern Tree Plantation** near Blairsville, **Sugar Creek Alpaca Farm** near Blue Ridge, and **Sweet Grass Dairy** near Thomasville. The number of pick-your-own farms is so large that we could not include very many of them. Many are listed in the Other Activities Appendix.

FERRIES Georgia does not need regular ferry service for use as public transportation as some other states do. There are, however, several places that you can get to only by ferry: **Cumberland Island National Seashore, Little St. Simons Island,** and **Sapelo Island.** Details about ferries to these locations are found in the appropriate chapters. **Belles Ferry** (912-447-4000; www.savtcc.com) provides water taxi service from the City Hall dock in Savannah's historic district to the hotel and attractions across the Savannah River on Hutchinson Island. The cost is $3 per person round trip, and the taxis operate every 10 to 15 minutes between 7 AM and 11 PM daily.

FILM Since the inception of the **Georgia, Film, Video, and Music Office** (404-962-4052; www.film georgia.org) in 1973, 500 major motion pictures and television programs have been filmed in Georgia, including *Midnight in the Garden of Good and Evil, Forrest Gump, The Legend of Bagger Vance, Driving Miss Daisy, Glory, Sweet Home Alabama, Fried Green Tomatoes, The Fighting Temptations, In the Heat of the Night,* and the Emmy-winning HBO film *Warm Springs.* Savannah also has a film commission, which can be contacted at 912-651-3696 or through its web site, www.savannahfilm.org. Several film festivals occur annually, chief among them **Robert Osborne's Classic Film Festival** in Athens, which includes not only films but workshops, speakers, and other activities. The **Summer Film Festival** at the Fox Theatre in Atlanta is a series of films shown in the magnificent theater.

FIRE PERMITS Permits are not required for campfires, but campers are responsible for any damage caused by their fire, which may include the cost of fighting the fire and the cost of timber destroyed, so exercise extreme caution. Only dead or downed wood can be used. Better yet, use a portable stove fueled by propane gas or Sterno. Permits are required for all other outdoor burning. You must contact the local **Georgia Forestry Commission** office (1-800-GA-TREES; www.gfc.state.ga .us) to obtain a permit before you proceed with any other outdoor burning.

FISH HATCHERIES Many lakes and streams are stocked with fish raised in several fish hatcheries found around the state. These hatcheries are open to the public for tours and some even offer fishing. Space limitations prohibited us from describing them within the various chapters, but they are listed in the Other Attractions Appendix.

FISHING Licenses are required for both fresh- and saltwater fishing. Call

1-800-ASK-FISH for detailed information about fishing in Georgia. In addition to fishing regulations and license information, the recording gives a weekly update on fishing conditions, as well as locations of boat ramps and the answers to commonly asked questions. Alabama, Florida, and South Carolina have reciprocal freshwater fishing agreements with Georgia, so residents of those states don't have to get a Georgia license if they already have a valid one. There may be differences between the states, however, in the number or size of fish caught, so be sure to check local regulations. Licenses can be purchased at most sporting goods stores, bait and tackle stores, and large stores such as Wal-Mart that have a sporting goods department. You also can get a license by going to www.permit.com. A complete list of fishing regulations is available in the Georgia Department of Natural Resources, Wildlife Resources Division, brochure "Georgia Sport Fishing Regulations." A downloadable version of the brochure can be found on the web site at www.gofishgeorgia.com.

FOLK PLAYS To keep Georgia's unique rural heritage alive, several communities produce folk plays, including a *Cotton Hall Christmas* and *Swamp Gravy*, both in Colquitt, and *Tales from the Altamaha* in Lyons.

FORTS Georgia boasts forts that span the history of the area from the time of early settlers through the Revolutionary and Civil wars to World War II and the present. Currently active bases that have one or more attractions interesting to travelers include **Fort Benning** near Columbus, home

of the National Infantry Museum; **Fort Gordon** near Augusta, which has a museum and recreational opportunities for visitors; and **Fort Stewart** near Hinesville, which has an interesting museum. Historical forts open to the public include **Fort Frederica National Monument,** St. Simons; **Fort Jackson,** Savannah; **Fort King George Historic Site,** Darien; **Fort McAllister Historic Park,** Richmond Hill; **Fort Morris Historic Site,** Midway; **Fort Oglethorpe,** home of the **Chickamauga and Chattanooga National Military Battlefield; Fort Pulaski National Monument,** Tybee Island; and **Fort Yargo,** which is located in a state park near Winder. These forts offer living history programs and numerous annual special events.

FRUIT AND BERRY PICKING If you want the freshest and most succulent fruits and berries, you might like to pick your own. The activity also can provide a pleasant couple of hours' entertainment for the whole family. Georgia has a seemingly endless supply of opportunities to pick your own farms throughout the state. We describe a few of them in various chapters and list many more in the Other Activities Appendix. For more information about pick-your-own facilities, consult the web site at www .pickyourown.org/GA/htm.

GARDENS Georgia's ideal climate makes gardens possible year-round in all but the most mountainous areas of north Georgia. The largest and most famous garden in Georgia and the Southeast is **Callaway Gardens** in Pine Mountain, which features numerous types of gardens but is most famous for its azaleas. Some other outstanding gardens include **American Camellia Society/ Massee Lane Gardens** in Fort Valley, the **Atlanta Botanical Garden**, gardens at the **Atlanta History Center, Bamboo Farm and Coastal Gardens** near Savannah, **Dunaway Gardens** near Newnan, **Ferrell Gardens at Hills and Dales** in LaGrange, **Founders Memorial Garden** in Athens, **Fred Hamilton Rhododendron Gardens** near Hiawassee, **Georgia Golf Hall of Fame's Botanical Garden** in Augusta, **Georgia Southern University Botanical Gardens** in Statesboro, **Japanese Garden** at the **Jimmy Carter Presidential Library and Museum in Atlanta**, **Robert L. Stanton Rose Garden** in Atlanta, **Rock City Gardens** in Lookout Mountain, the **State Botanical Garden of Georgia** near Athens, and the **Thomasville Rose Garden** in Thomasville. Some of these gardens offer classes, talks, and demonstrations as well as special events and festivals.

GEORGIA FACTS Georgia is the largest state east of the Mississippi River, stretching 322 miles from Dalton near the Tennessee border in northwest Georgia to Valdosta near Florida in the southern part of the state, and 255 miles from Savannah on the coast to Columbus on the Alabama border. Its geographic regions are the Coastal Plain, the Piedmont Plateau in the center of the state, the Ridge and Valley area in the northwest, and the Appalachian Mountains in the northeast.

GEORGIA GROWN Georgia boasts 11.1 million acres devoted to farms. The state leads all others in the production of poultry, pecans, peanuts, eggs, and rye and is in second place in cotton production. Georgia, which is known as the Peach State, is actually behind California and South Carolina in peach production, although production is still significant. Other important food crops include tomatoes, watermelon, and Vidalia onions. While you're traveling through the state you might want to sample the Georgia-grown products of **Ellis Bros. Pecans** in Vienna, **Farm Fresh Tattnall** in Reidsville, **Gooseneck Farms** in Hawkinsville, **Jolly Nut Company** in Fort Valley, **Lane Packing Company** in Fort Valley, and **Merritt Pecan Company** in Weston. Be on the lookout for farms and orchards that offer pick-your-own fruits, nuts, or vegetables. See also Apples.

GEORGIA MADE Although Georgia is not known as a manufacturing state (it has lost almost all its textile and car manufactories), some products such as carpets are made here (see Factory Outlets). On a smaller scale, Georgia craftspeople and companies create some other famous products, including rocking chairs produced by the **Brumby Chair Company** in Marietta, **Claxton Old-Fashioned Fruitcake,** knitted items created by **Georgia Mountain Fibers** in Blue Ridge, and clothing produced by the **Tog Shop** in Americus.

GEORGIA PUBLIC BROADCASTING There's almost nowhere you can go in Georgia that you'd be out of range of a Georgia Public Broadcasting radio or television station. GPB television stations are found in Albany (WABW, channel 14), Atlanta (WGTV, channel 8), Augusta (WCES, channel 20),

Chatsworth (WCLP, channel 18), Columbus (WJSP, channel 28), Dawson (WACS, channel 25), Macon (WDCO, channel 29), Savannah (WVAN, channel 9), and Waycross, (WXGA, channel 8). Keep in mind that depending on the cable company that represents the area, these channel numbers may be different. Radio stations are found in Albany (WUNV, 91.7 FM), Athens (WUGA, 91.7/97.9), Augusta (WACG, 90.7), Brunswick (WWIO, 88.9), Carrollton (WUWG, 90.7), Columbus (WJSP, 88.1), Dahlonega (WNGU, 89.5), Demorest (WPPR, 88.3), Fort Gaines (WJWV, 90.9), Macon (WDCO, 89.7), Savannah (WSVH, 91.1), St. Marys (WWIO, 1190 AM), Tifton (WABR, 91.1), Valdosta (WWET, 91.7), and Waycross (WXVS, 90.1). For information in Atlanta, call 404-685-4788; outside Atlanta call 1-800-222-4788; or consult the web site at www.gpb.org. Atlanta also has public television (WABE, channel 30) and radio (WPBA, 90.1) stations operated by the Atlanta Board of Education. Call 678-363-7425 for the television station or 404-892-2962 for the radio station.

GHOST TOURS A state with so much history is bound to have more than a few ghosts. Savannah is called the "Most-Haunted City in America" by many. When visiting Savannah, be sure to take one of the spine-tingling walking or driving ghost tours—always scheduled after dark for the best effect (see Savannah chapter for details). Several other options for ghost tours include **City Segway Tours Ghost Glide** in Atlanta, **Dalton Ghost Tours, Roswell Ghost Tours, Spirits of Barnsley Ghost Tours** at Barnsley Gardens near Adairsville, and **St. Simons Ghost Tours.**

GOLD MINING Most travelers don't know that the first gold rush in the country was not in California, but in Dahlonega in the north Georgia mountains. In fact, the phrase "There's gold in them thar hills" was coined in Georgia. It was the discovery of gold in Georgia that precipitated the removal of Native Americans along the Trail of Tears. The dome of Georgia's capitol in Atlanta is covered with gold mined in Dahlonega. Enough remnants of gold remain in the mountains to provide entertainment for tourists. Several locations around Dahlonega offer gold panning and/or mine tours: **Consolidated Gold Mine, Crisson Gold Mine, Dukes Creek Mine,** and **Gold 'n Gem Grubbin' Mine.**

GOLF Although Augusta is famous for the Masters golf tournament, very few members of the general public are ever lucky enough to attend and certainly can't play at Augusta National, but there are 468 golf courses across Georgia where they *can* play. We describe the state park golf courses and some resort courses in the appropriate chapters and list many of the other courses in the Golf Appendix.

Eight state parks offer golf courses. Three are in north Georgia: the **Creek** at Hard Labor Creek State Park near Rutledge, **Highland Walk** at Victoria Bryant near Royston, and **Arrowhead Pointe** at Lake Richard B. Russell near Elberton. Five are in the southern part of the state: **Meadow Links** at George T. Bagby near Fort Gaines, **Georgia Vets** at Georgia Veterans near Cordele, **Wallace Adams** at Little Ocmulgee near McRae, **Brazell's Creek** at Gordonia-Alatamaha near Reidsville, and **The Lakes** at Laura S. Walker near Waycross. For more information about the state park golf courses, consult the web site at www.georgiagolf.com.

The major resorts that cater to golfers are: **Lake Blackshear Resort and Golf Club** in Cordele; **The Cloister at Sea Island** (restricted to guests only); **King and Prince Beach and Golf Resort** on St. Simons Island; **Sea Palms Golf and Tennis Resort** on St. Simons; **Kingwood Golf Club and Resort** in Clayton; **Innsbruck Resort and Golf Club** in Helen; **Chateau Elan Winery and Resort** in Braselton; **Emerald Pointe Resort** at Lake Lanier Islands; **Brasstown Valley Resort** in Young Harris; **Westin Savannah Harbor Golf Resort and Spa;** and **Cuscowilla Resort** on Lake Oconee and **The Ritz-Carlton Lodge at Reynolds Plantation,** both near Greensboro.

For information about all the golf courses in Georgia, consult the web site www.golflink.com/golf-courses/state.asp?state=GA. More information can be obtained from the **Georgia State Golf Association** (770-955-4272; 1-800-949-4742; www.gsga.org).

GORGES North Georgia is the mountainous area of the state, but travelers won't find spectacular gorges such as those in the western part of America. These ancient mountains have been worn down for millions of years. There are a few gorges, however. **Cloudland Canyon** is found in Cloudland Canyon State Park in Rising Fawn near the Tennessee border, and **Tallulah Gorge,** one of the deepest in the East, is found in Tallulah Falls in northeast Georgia. The canyon that comes as a complete surprise is **Providence Canyon** near Lumpkin. Located in a relatively flat area near the Alabama state line, the canyon is the result not of millions of years of upheaval, but of erosion caused by a mere 100 years of poor agricultural practices. The gorge, contained in the Providence Canyon State Conservation Area, is the home of the biggest concentration of wildflowers in the state.

GUIDE SERVICES See Canoeing, Kayaking, Tubing, and White-Water Rafting; Fishing; and Hunting/Shooting Sports. Numerous guide services also are described in individual chapters.

GUIDED TOURS When we travel to a new place, we like to take a guided tour first to get the flavor of the area so we'll know which attractions we'd like to see in more detail. Many companies in the larger cities and towns offer guided tours—some walking, some by bus, trolley, or horse-drawn carriage. In Atlanta tours are offered by **American Sightseeing Atlanta, Atlanta Preservation Center Tours, City Segway Tours,** and **Gray Line Tours**. In Athens tours are provided by **Classic City Tours** and **UGA Visitor Center Tours.** Savannah has dozens of tour companies. Some other guided tours throughout the state include **Around Town Tours of Historic Macon, Milledgeville Historic Trolley Tour, Rome Visitors Center Tours, St. Simons Trolley Tours, Saturday Guided History Tours** in Augusta, and **Spirit of Sapelo Tours** on Sapelo Island.

HANDICAPPED ACCESS Attractions, lodgings, and restaurants that are at least partially handicapped accessible are identified with the ♿ icon. Keep in mind, however, that just because an entry is listed as wheelchair accessible doesn't mean it is fully wheelchair-friendly. A multistory attraction such as a historic home may have a ramp to allow access to the first floor, but others floors may not be accessible at all. A hotel or other lodging may have wheelchair access to guest rooms on the first floor or access to rooms on other floors via an elevator, but bathrooms don't necessarily have full accessibility with roll-in showers, handrails, or other modifications. Likewise, restaurants may have access to rooms on the first floor only, and rest rooms may have limited wheelchair accessibility. New or remodeled structures must conform to federal regulations; older sites may still have accessibility problems. We try to indicate the true conditions in each entry if we think the distinction needs to be made, but it's probably best to call ahead.

HIKING Georgia's vast areas of undeveloped land are conducive to both easy and challenging hiking. The most famous trails in the state are the 80-mile section of the **Appalachian Trail** in north Georgia and the 75-mile portion of the **Bartram Trail** from Augusta to Crawfordville, as well as the Georgia portion of the 300-mile **Benton MacKaye Trail** (www.bmta.org) and the **Pine Mountain Trail** between Warm Springs and Pine Mountain. The Bartram Trail actually runs from the North Carolina border in northeast Georgia 220 miles to Augusta, the Savannah River, and Savannah. The 55-mile Georgia Loop of the Benton MacKaye Trail is called "the toughest hike in Georgia." There are hundreds of miles of trails in the **Chattahoochee-Oconee National Forests**. State parks (www.gastate parks.org) and other nature preserves

are good places to hike. Some other trails include the **Aska Trails** in Blue Ridge and the **Disney Trail** on Rocky Face Mountain and the **Pinhoti** Trail, both in northwest Georgia.

Even the big-city areas have parks and other areas that provide hiking opportunities. The **PATH Foundation** (404-875-7284; www.path foundation.org) is a nonprofit organization working to build and maintain greenway trails throughout metro Atlanta and Georgia.

Some books particularly helpful to hikers are *Atlanta Walks* by Ren and Helen Davis, 45 self-guided tours in the metro area, including walking, running, and bicycling information; *Georgia Walks* by Ren and Helen Davis; *60 Hikes Within 60 Miles of Atlanta* by Randy and Pam Golden; *The Hiking Trails of North Georgia* by Tim Homan; *A Walk in the Woods* by Bill Bryson; *Hiking Georgia* by Donald Pfitzer; *Touring the Backroads of North and South Georgia* by Frank and Victoria Logue; and *Touring the Coastal Georgia Backroads* by Nancy Rhyne.

HISTORIC HOMES AND SITES It's no surprise that, as one of America's original 13 colonies and a player in the Civil War, the state has many historic treasures—some of them open for public tours. **Pebble Hill Plantation** in Thomasville is an example of a grand sporting plantation retreat of the early 20th century. **Callaway Plantation** in Washington, **Jarrell Plantation Historic Site** in Juliette, and **Hofwyl-Broadfield Plantation State Historic Site** are examples of working farms.

Three presidents called Georgia home, either full- or part-time: Jimmy Carter, Franklin D. Roosevelt, and

Woodrow Wilson. The **Jimmy Carter National Historic Site** in Plains, the **Boyhood Home of President Woodrow Wilson** in Augusta, and the **Little White House State Historic Site** in Warm Springs give glimpses into their lives.

Savannah has one of the largest historic districts in the country, and many entire small Georgia towns are on the National Register of Historic Places. The **Jekyll Island National Historic Landmark District** is a large and impressive restoration area.

In every chapter you'll find historic homes that are open for tours either because of the importance of the people who lived there or because of the architectural significance of the structure itself, or both. See also African American Sites, Bed & Breakfasts, Civil War Sites, Covered Bridges, Forts, Lighthouses, Maritime Museums, Museum Villages, Native American Sites, Railroad Excursions and Museums, and Theaters.

HISTORY The history of Georgia can be traced through visits to the state's many historical sites. Thousands of years ago Native Americans inhabited the area. A strange remnant of their occupation is the **Rock Eagle Effigy,** a stone tumulus near Eatonton in central Georgia that represents a bird with outstretched wings. Mound Builders left evidence of their occupation along the western part of Georgia at what are now **Kolomoki Mounds State Historic Park** near Baxley and **Etowah Indian Mounds Historic Site** near Cartersville, as well as in central Georgia at what is now the **Ocmulgee National Monument** near Macon. Some shell middens offer evidence that Native Americans of the Guale (pronounced

WAHL-ee) Mocama tribe inhabited the coast and barrier islands. Numerous other sites depict the lives of Native American until they were driven out of the state in 1838 after the first gold rush in the country. This forced migration was known as the Trail of Tears. The Cherokee capital at New Echota, now the **New Echota Cherokee Capital Historic Site** near Calhoun, is a must-see stop in northwest Georgia, as are the homes of three Cherokee chiefs. See also Native American Sites.

Explorer Hernando de Soto and his men passed through Georgia in 1540. The Spanish later made more permanent incursions into what would become Georgia to build a chain of missions and establish a large Jesuit mission-presidio that later became a Franciscan mission on St. Catherine's Island. Although there is enough evidence of this occupation to interest archaeologists, little evidence remains that would attract tourists.

Fort King George, built in 1721 near present-day Darien, was the first English settlement in the area that would become Georgia. It was garrisoned by British soldiers for seven years. Now the **Fort King George State Historic Site,** the site contains a replica of the blockhouse and a museum that interprets the Native American, colonial, Scottish, and sawmilling periods of the immediate area.

Contrary to popular myth, Georgia was not founded as a penal colony nor settled by convicts but by yeoman farmers and small businessmen. Because the area lies roughly at the same latitude as China, Persia, and the Madeira Islands, Georgia's founders envisioned a robust economy based on silk and wine production. The state's charter banned slavery, Catholics, hard liquor, and lawyers.

Georgia was chartered and became the 13th colony in 1732. Savannah was settled in 1733 under the leadership of General James Oglethorpe and was the first planned city in North America. Most of the city's original squares survive, although much of the historic architecture is from the postbellum years at the end of the 19th century. Oglethorpe and his Scottish Highlanders also moved down the coast to protect the colony from the Spanish in northern Florida. Sunbury became an important port, and Fort Morris, now the **Fort Morris Historic Site,** was built to protect it. The fort fell to the British in 1779, but it was used in the War of 1812. The town of Sunbury completely disappeared with the exception of its cemetery.

Fort Frederica on St. Simons Island was established in 1736 and, at its peak in the early 1740s, was the most elaborate British fortification in North America. After the British victory over the Spanish in the Battle of Bloody Marsh in 1742, the regiment disbanded and the fort was abandoned. The significance of this battle was that it cemented Britain's control of the southernmost colony and ended the threat of incursions by the Spanish. The site, now the **Fort Frederica National Monument,** has an interpretive center and ruins.

Because the initial crops and industries the founders envisioned never flourished, farmers turned to the planting of rice, indigo, and cotton, all of which were labor intensive. The ban against slavery was overturned in 1750. By 1760 one-third of the population was slaves, and by the Revolutionary War that figure had increased to almost half. A small affluent planter class developed.

Georgia played a relatively minor role in the American Revolution. It was the only colony to comply with the Stamp Act, and although there were three Georgia signers of the Declaration of Independence, Georgia didn't send a representative to the First Continental Congress. An important Revolutionary War battle was fought in Savannah in 1779 when occupying British forces repulsed an American and French assault. Confiscation of Tory property after the Revolution resulted in a vast reapportionment of land, which was particularly helpful to the average man away from the large plantations of the low country. Heads of household could claim 200 acres of land, and few white men failed to qualify. More than 100,000 families claimed three-fourths of Georgia. Stripping the Native Americans of their lands in 1838 put even more property in the hands of individuals.

The invention of the cotton gin at the end of the 18th century made it possible for cotton production to increase 20-fold, which also increased the number of slaves. On the eve of the Civil War, Georgia had more slaves and slave owners than any other state.

Savannah's strategic importance continued after the Revolutionary War. It became a primary port, shipping cotton and other commodities from all over the state. Two brick forts were constructed near the city: **Fort Jackson** in 1808 and **Fort Pulaski** in 1829. Fort Jackson was manned during the War of 1812 and enlarged in 1845 and 1860. It didn't, however, prevent the Union from taking Savannah in 1864. The construction of Fort

Pulaski, now **Fort Pulaski National Monument,** was overseen by Robert E. Lee. It was thought to be impregnable, but 30 hours of bombardment with rifled cannon by Federal troops resulted in its fall.

Georgia's dependency on slavery and its belief in the primacy of states' rights drove the state to secede from the Union on January 2, 1861, although only 51 percent of the legislature meeting at the capital in Milledgeville favored secession.

Fort McAllister, now **Fort McAllister State Historic Site,** was built by the Confederacy in 1862 to defend the Ogeechee River, the river plantations in the area, and Savannah's southern flank. It withstood Federal assaults in 1862 and 1863, but fell to Union troops in December 1864.

The war touched every area of the state—from Chickamauga in the northwest corner of the state to Atlanta and across the heartland to Savannah—whether any battles were fought in a particular area or not (see Civil War Sites). Margaret Mitchell's opus *Gone with the Wind* memorialized the war and its aftermath for people all over the world.

During the war and afterward under Reconstruction, the citizens of Georgia suffered terrible deprivation. The cotton economy never recovered after the war, which resulted in the tenant farmer system that continued to plague both blacks and whites until World War II. It was during this period that the Jim Crow and "separate but equal" laws were passed. Segregation became an urban way of life because so many African Americans were moving to the cities. Poll taxes, white-only primaries, literacy tests, and the county-unit systems disenfranchised blacks.

Georgia was in desperate straits in 1935 because of the Great Depression, the devastation wrought by the boll weevil, and a governor who fought all the New Deal programs designed to help the citizenry. The author of the New Deal, Franklin D. Roosevelt, got many of his ideas while visiting his home in Warm Springs, now the **Little White House State Historic Site.**

At the same time that much of the state was suffering, wealthy Northerners were enjoying an idyllic lifestyle in Georgia. From the late 1800s through the beginning of World War II, 100 northern millionaires and their families spent winters at their exclusive retreat on Jekyll Island. Much of the area is preserved as the **Jekyll Island National Historic Landmark District.** Meanwhile, northern industrialists maintained opulent plantations in the area of south Georgia between Thomasville and Tallahassee. Travelers can visit **Pebble Hill Plantation,** one of those retreats.

World War II was the pivotal event in turning around Georgia's economy because massive federal spending was infused into the state. Georgia was second only to Texas in military training facilities. Airplanes were built at Bell Aircraft (now Lockheed) in Marietta, and Liberty Ships were constructed in Savannah and Brunswick. After the war, automobile manufacturing came to Atlanta, and for the first time income earned by Atlanta workers surpassed the national average.

In the early 1960s, the Civil Rights Movement was in full force in the South. The first sit-in in Atlanta was in 1960. The Albany Civil Rights Movement, although not terribly successful, served as a training ground for Martin Luther King Jr., John

Lewis, Julian Bond, and many other familiar names. Atlanta, the "city too busy to hate," peacefully integrated its schools, and when King was assassinated, his funeral and mourning were also peaceful. Today one of the most visited sites in the state is the **Martin Luther King Jr. National Historic Site.**

Over the past 50 years Georgia has lost its textile manufacturing plants and is now losing its automobile manufacturing plants as well as several of its military bases. But the state's economy is still vibrant, and the population is multihued and multiethnic. CNN, the Cable News Network, makes its home in Atlanta, as does Coca-Cola. Tourists can take the **Inside CNN Tour** and visit the **World of Coca-Cola**. The 1996 Centennial Olympic Summer Games were a coup for Atlanta and the entire state. A lasting legacy in downtown Atlanta is **Centennial Olympic Park.**

Indigenous folk arts, from the African American Gullah-Geechee culture on the coast to the Appalachian culture of the mountains, persist in pottery, folk plays, festivals, and the like. Travelers can visit **Hog Hammock** on Sapelo Island, the **Foxfire Museum** in Mountain City, and dozens of places in between. In addition to culture from the past, there have been striking changes in the fine arts, particularly the establishment of symphonies, operas, art museums, and ballets—not just in Atlanta but throughout the state.

Rapacious urbanization and suburbanization in the metro Atlanta area and some of the state's other cities have resulted in what we call "Anywhere USA," which can even be found in smaller towns. This is the strip or area of fast-food joints,

big-box stores, shopping and strip malls, and gas station/convenience stores so familiar you could be anywhere in the country. Despite this intrusion of modern life, the state's natural beauty endures in many, many places. Georgia has well-maintained state highways and secondary roads, so get off the interstates and enjoy the nonhomogenized character of the state.

See also African American Sites, Forts, Historic Homes and Sites, and Native American Sites.

HORSEBACK RIDING Horseback riding is a popular activity here, whether along the beaches of southeastern Georgia, in the pastures of the heartland, or in the northern forests or mountains. For several years, companies offering horseback riding declined precipitously because of liability issues. The Georgia Legislature, however, passed a law that requires participants to sign a waiver releasing the company from liability. Since then, many companies are offering horseback riding once again. Several even offer overnight rides with meals, camping, and entertainment. Options for horseback riding can be found in almost every chapter. Some of the most outstanding are **Barnsley Gardens Resort** in Adairsville, **Fort Mountain Stables** at Fort Mountain State Park near Chatsworth, **Lake Lanier Islands Equestrian Center** near Buford, **Roosevelt Riding Stables** at F. D. Roosevelt State Park near Pine Mountain, **Victoria's Carriages and Beach Trail Rides** on Jekyll Island, and **Zion Farms** near Rome. These and many other options are described in the appropriate chapters.

HORSE RACING Horse racing is not a widely available activity in Georgia, which makes the racing here that much more special. Two highly anticipated and well-attended annual events are the **Atlanta Steeplechase** in Kingston and the **Steeplechase at Callaway** in Pine Mountain. These events include the races themselves along with tailgating, special food tents, terrier races, other events, and, of course, fancy hats for the ladies.

Many Northern harness-racing horses winter and train in Hawkinsville at the **Lawrence Bennett Harness Training Facility.** Visitors can watch them daily during the season. Before the horses depart for the North at the beginning of April, the **Hawkinsville Harness Horse Festival and Spring Celebration** fills two days with racing and other festivities.

There are a few other horse races and events. Contact the **Georgia Thoroughbred Owners and Breeders Association** (1-866-66-GTOBA; www.gtoba.com) for information about races. Contact the

National Barrel Horse Association (706-823-3728; www.nbha.com) for information about shows and events.

HOURS OF OPERATION The hours listed here for attractions, restaurants, shops, and so on are the most up to date we could get at publication time. Hours will undoubtedly change, however, so call ahead or consult an attraction or restaurant's web site before traveling to avoid disappointment. Although we don't mention it when listing the hours for each entry, it should be understood that most attractions and many restaurants are closed on major holidays such as Thanksgiving, Christmas, and New Year's Day and some other holidays. Assume attractions are closed on holidays or check ahead when in doubt.

HUNTING/SHOOTING SPORTS Georgia is famed for its game bird hunting—particularly in the plantation country of southern Georgia. Other types of hunting—including deer, wild boar, and turkey—are permitted in

the national forests and most wildlife management areas throughout the state. Space prevents us from describing the many hunting plantations that offer guided hunts, but we list many hunting opportunities in the Other Activities Appendix. Hunting regulations for all types of birds and animals can be found on the web site for the **Georgia Department of Natural Resources** (www.georgiawildlife.dnr.state.ga.us). State laws concerning raptors and migratory birds can be found at the **Georgia Wildlife Federation's** web site (www.gwf.org/birdlaw.htm). Some sources for more hunting information, including guide services, are www.gunnersden.com, www.huntfind.com, and www.huntingsociety.org/Georgia.html.

Georgia is also filled with facilities that offer trap, skeet, and sporting clays, including the facility that was used for the 1996 Centennial Summer Olympic Games. Space limitations dictate that we can describe only a few of them. For a comprehensive list of shooting sports facilities, see the Other Activities Appendix.

(OFFICIAL) INFORMATION ABOUT GEORGIA After reading this book, the place to go for more information about traveling in Georgia is the **Georgia Department of Economic Development, Tourism Division** (1-800-847-4842; www.georgia.org/Travel). You can request a free Georgia road map and a free "Georgia Travel Guide." The state also publishes a guide to African American–related attractions, a calendar of events, and a golf guide. You also can request or download brochures via the web site at www.georgia.org/Travel/InfoDownloads/Brochures.htm.

The state operates 11 welcome centers, most of which are at primary interstate highway access points into Georgia from other states: on I-20 westbound in Augusta, US 185 in Columbus, I-95 northbound in Kingsland, I-85 southbound in Lavonia, US 280 in Plains, I-75 southbound in Ringgold, I-95 southbound in Savannah, US 301 in Sylvania, I-20 eastbound in Tallapoosa, I-75 northbound in Valdosta, and I-85 northbound in West Point. These staffed centers can provide you with maps, the state travel guide, brochures on attractions and lodgings, and advice. Other sources of information include the **Georgia Department of Transportation** (404-656-5269) and the **Georgia Department of Natural Resources, Environmental Protection Division** (404-656-0099; 404-656-0069).

INNS Over almost 30 years, we have personally stayed in and inspected hundreds of accommodations throughout the state. It's hard to keep up, however, so we've also relied on recommendations from travel professionals and others. No lodging has paid to be in this book.

ISLANDS Georgia is blessed with a small coastline and a series of coastal and barrier islands, most of which are accessible to travelers by road, ferry, or private boat. From north to south these are Tybee, Little Tybee, Skidaway, Wilmington, Wassaw, St. Catherine's, Blackbeard, Sapelo, Wolf, Little St. Simons, Sea, St. Simons, Jekyll, and Cumberland. Georgia's islands provide opportunities for numerous water sports, hiking, biking, and other outdoor pursuits. Lodging (when available) may be in hotels, cottages, and campgrounds.

KAYAKING See Canoeing, Kayaking, Tubing, and White-Water Rafting.

LAKES When you look at a map and see how many significant lakes Georgia has, it's amazing to learn that the state has no large natural lakes. The major lakes were created for power generation and flood control, with recreation as a pleasant by-product. Some of the lakes are so large they are featured in several chapters. In addition, the state is filled with many small natural lakes, so access to a lake is available almost everywhere. Some lakes boast state parks, resorts, golf, and rental cottages.

Some of the most significant lakes in Georgia are **Clarks Hill Lake, Lake Hartwell,** and **Lake Richard B. Russell** in northeast Georgia; **Lake Allatoona** and **Lake Lanier** in north Georgia; **Lake Oconee** and **Lake Sinclair** in central Georgia; and **Lake Seminole, Lake Walter F. George,** and **West Point Lake** and in western and southwestern Georgia. These lakes and the lands surrounding them provide innumerable opportunities for water sports, hiking, camping, and other outdoor pursuits. These lakes and dozens of lesser lakes are described more fully in the appropriate chapters.

LIGHTHOUSES They once used their lights and day marks to warn sailors of danger or to guide them safely to harbor. Today several of these sentinels are open for visitors, and a climb to the top is rewarded with a spectacular view of the ocean and surrounding mainland: **Sapelo Island Lighthouse, St. Simons Lighthouse and Museum of Coastal History,** and **Tybee Island Lightstation and Tybee Museum. Cockspur Light-** house and **Little Cumberland Island Lighthouse** can be viewed only from afar.

LITTER There are 11 litter control laws in Georgia. Fines for littering may range from $200 to $1,200. Contact local law enforcement agencies to report violations. For more information, contact **Keep Georgia Beautiful** (404-679-4910; www.keepgeorgia beautiful.org).

LLAMA TREKKING Llama trekking offers the height of luxury in hiking— you simply walk, while the llamas carry the picnic and any other equipment you'd otherwise have to carry. Try **Crystal River Llama Treks** near Hiawassee.

LODGES AT STATE PARKS Several state parks boast lodges with handicapped-accessible rooms, restaurants, and meeting facilities. Occupancy is limited to four in regular hotel rooms and six in loft rooms. A deposit is required, and cancellation penalties are imposed within 72 hours of the anticipated arrival date. Visitors younger than 18 must be accompanied by an adult. Pets are not allowed in or around the lodges. Smoking is prohibited. For more information, consult the web site at www.gastateparks.org.

MARITIME MUSEUMS Several museums along the coast are dedicated to Georgia's longtime relationship with the sea: **Maritime Center at the Historic Coast Guard Station** and **St. Simons Lighthouse and Museum of Coastal History** on St. Simons, **Ships of the Sea Museum** in Savannah, and **Tybee Island Lightstation and Tybee Museum** on Tybee Island.

MARITIME CENTER ON ST. SIMONS ISLAND

MAPS Sources for Georgia maps include the **Georgia Atlas and Gazetteer**—available from Amazon, REI, and other sources—which provides DeLorme topographic maps that show highways and back roads as well as information on campgrounds, scenic routes, and natural features. The **Georgia Department of Economic Development, Tourism Division** (www.georgia.org) can provide a state road map. **Georgia Department of Transportation** (www.dot.state.ga.us) maps include the Georgia Bicycle Map, State Highway Transportation Map, city and county maps, and online maps. The **Chattahoochee-Oconee National Forests** (www.fs.fed.us/conf) can provide maps of the forests.

MOUNTAIN BIKING The best source of information about mountain biking in north Georgia is the **U.S. Forest Service** (770-297-3000), which maintains many of the trails and can give you maps and advice. Places to ride are described in many chapters.

A good place to rent bikes is **Woody's Mountain Bikes** in Helen. Woody's also sponsors some guided rides. Some books that are helpful to mountain bikers include *Backroad Bicycling in the Blue Ridge and Smoky Mountains: 27 Rides for Touring and Mountain Bikes from North Georgia to Southwest Virginia* by Hiram Rogers, *Mountain Biking Georgia: A Guide to Atlanta and Northern Georgia's Greatest Off-Road Bicycle Rides* by Alex Nutt, and *Off the Beaten Track: Guide to Mountain Biking in Georgia* by Jim Parham. See also Bicycling for information about bicycling organizations and other references.

MOUNTAINS Georgia's Appalachian and Blue Ridge mountains are ancient and worn down—and sometimes ridiculed by travelers from the western United States to whom Georgia's "mountains" are little more than bumps or hills. Not to be laughed at, however, is **Brasstown Bald**—one of the tallest mountains in the East. At almost 5,000 feet in elevation, it has weather comparable to that in Vermont. Visitors can drive almost to the top, and then a short hike offers them breathtaking views of four states. **Kennesaw Mountain** north of Atlanta was the scene of fierce fighting during the Civil War. A climb to the top rewards hikers with an excellent view of Atlanta on a clear day. **Stone Mountain** is the world's largest exposed granite monadnock and the centerpiece of a recreational park. A carving of Confederate generals on its side was begun by the same sculptor who created Mount Rushmore. Visitors can hike to the top or take a cable car. Once at the top, they have excellent views of Atlanta. The entire northern part of Georgia is mountainous.

MUSEUMS We mention many different types of museums under the headings Art Museums, Children's Museums, Maritime Museums, Museum Villages, and Railroad Excursions and Museums. Some of Georgia's museums are special and difficult to categorize. Some unusual museums include **Booth Western Art Museum** in Cartersville, **Georgia Music Hall of Fame** in Macon, **Georgia Rural Telephone Museum** in Leslie, **Georgia Sports Hall of Fame** in Macon, and, perhaps the most unusual of all, the **Loudermilk Boarding House Museum** in Cornelia, which houses the "Everything Elvis" exhibit. For an extensive list of museums, consult the web site at www.answers.com/museumsingeorgia.

MUSEUM VILLAGES Museum villages provide a window into the past, and several of these villages exist in Georgia. Some were actual villages or townships; others have been created by moving historic buildings from around the state. The **Jekyll Island National Historic Landmark District** was the home of 100 millionaire families from the late 1800s to World War II. **Seabrook Village** near Midway was home to poor African Americans. These museum villages were created: **Frontier Village** in Fort Gaines, **Georgia Agrirama Living History Museum** in Tifton, and **Westville** in Lumpkin. Both the Georgia Agrirama and Westville are staffed by costumed interpreters.

MUSIC CONCERT SERIES Georgia boasts not only the acclaimed **Atlanta Symphony Orchestra,** but a dozen other symphonies, not counting several college and university symphonies. The ASO offers a classical series, a pops series, family concerts, and free summer concerts in metro area parks. All the other symphonies have some kind of concert series, which are described in the appropriate chapters. Just a few of the state's concert series include **Arts and Entertainment Series/First Tuesday Series/ Stafford Steinway Series** in Tifton; **Chateau Elan Summer Concert Series** in Braselton; **Fine Arts on the River** concerts in Savannah; **Live at Five Happy Hour Concerts** and **Georgia Music Week,** both at the Georgia Music Hall of Fame in Macon; **River Music Concert Series** in Bainbridge; and **SunTrust Lunch on Broad Concert Series** in Atlanta.

A pleasant spring-through-fall diversion in Atlanta is to attend an outdoor concert. One of the most famous venues is **Chastain Park Amphitheater** in Atlanta, which hosts two different series of musical acts, including one series with the Atlanta Symphony Orchestra. Other towns and cities that offer concert series, which may occur on the town square or in a park, include Blue Ridge, Dahlonega, Decatur, Kennesaw, Marietta, McDonough, Roswell, and Stockbridge (see Outdoor Venues below and Entertainment and Special Events in the appropriate chapters). Numerous music festivals may vary in length from a day to a week or more. Some of the best-known festivals include the **Atlanta Jazz Festival** and the **Midtown Music Festival,** both in Atlanta, and the **Savannah Jazz Festival,** but there are many more described in individual chapters.

NATIVE AMERICAN SITES Before European explorers and settlers came to Georgia, Native Americans inhab-

INDIAN STATUE IN FORT GAINES

ited the region—primarily Cherokees in the north and Creeks and Seminoles in the south, but also Guale Indians on the coast. Even before these tribes, however, the state was inhabited by Mound Builders. Close to a dozen significant Native American sites, including a national monument and several state historic sites, are open to the public: **Chieftains Museum/Major Ridge Home** in Rome, **Chief Vann House Historic Site** in Chatsworth, **Etowah Indian Mounds Historic Site** in Cartersville, **Funk Heritage Center** in Waleska, **John Ross House** in Rossville, **Kolomoki Mounds State Historic Park** in Blakely, **New Echota Cherokee Capital Historic Site** in Calhoun, and **Ocmulgee National Monument** in Macon. **Fort Mountain State Park** surrounds an ancient wall built by Native Americans. Many of these sites are on the 150-mile **Chieftains Trail** from Carrollton to Dalton.

NATURE PRESERVES/COASTAL Most of Cumberland Island—Georgia's largest barrier island, accessed by ferry from St. Marys—has been preserved as the **Cumberland Island National Seashore.** The national seashore offers 17 miles of pristine beaches, maritime forest, wild horses, and other wildlife as well as campgrounds, mansion ruins, and a small museum. Some of the other coastal preserves include **Blackbeard Island National Wildlife Refuge,** which is accessed through several outfitters based in Brunswick, Darien, Savannah, St. Simons, and Tybee Island; **Melon Bluff Nature and Heritage Reserve** near Midway; and the **Sapelo Island National Estuarine Research Reserve** accessed from Meridian. More nature preserves are listed in the Parks Appendix.

NATURE PRESERVES/INLAND The **Chattahoochee-Oconee National Forests** cover a vast area of north and central Georgia, providing endless opportunities for hiking, bird-watching, camping, and other outdoor pursuits. Some other important nature preserves in the state include the **Bartram Forest** near Milledgeville; **Chattahoochee River National Recreation Area** in metro Atlanta; **Marshall Forest** in Rome; **Moody Forest Natural Area** near Baxley; **Okefenokee National Wildlife Refuge,** which can be accessed from Fargo, Folkston, and Waycross; **Panola Mountain State Conservation Park** near Stockbridge; **Phinizy Swamp National Park** near Augusta; **Piedmont National Wildlife Refuge** near Juliette; **Providence Canyon State Conservation Park** near Lumpkin; and **Scull Shoals Archaeological Site** near Greensboro. More nature preserves are listed in the Parks Appendix.

OUTDOOR VENUES Chastain Park Amphitheater, a horseshoe-shaped venue developed as a government works project in the 1930s, remains beloved by Atlantans, who bring gourmet dinners, fancy table settings, candles, and floral arrangements to enhance their concert experience. More casual are the **Frederick Brown Jr. Amphitheater** in Peachtree City, **HIFI Buys Amphitheater** south of Atlanta, and the **Villages Amphitheater** in Fayetteville. Many individual chapters list outdoor concerts or series that may take place in small towns across the state in a park or on the courthouse square (see Entertainment or Special Events). See also Music Concert Series.

PARKING Nearly all the small towns and villages in Georgia have plentiful free on-street parking. Unless otherwise noted, assume that such parking is available. The larger cities, on the other hand, rarely have free on-street parking. In those cases, we give details about the parking situation, including metered parking, parking lots and garages, and special event parking. In Atlanta, for example, you may pay up to $15 for special event parking.

PARKING/STATE PARKS With one exception, the day-use parking fee (called the Daily ParkPass) in state parks is $3, except Wednesdays, which are free. The Daily ParkPass is valid for all state parks visited on the same day. Overnight guests in lodges, cabins, or campgrounds pay only one fee for the duration of their stay. Diners in lodge restaurants and conference attendees are exempt. Parking for golfers is included in the greens fee. Frequent visitors can purchase an Annual ParkPass for $25 (call 770-389-7401). There are discounted Annual ParkPass fees for seniors and disabled

veterans. For more information, see the web site at www.gastateparks.org.

PARKS AND FORESTS See Nature Preserves.

PARKS/NATIONAL Georgia boasts the following national parks: **Andersonville National Historic Site** in Andersonville, the **Appalachian Trail** in north Georgia, **Chattahoochee River National Recreation Area** in the metro Atlanta area, **Chickamauga and Chattanooga National Military Park** in Fort Oglethorpe, **Cumberland Island National Seashore** off the south Georgia coast near St. Marys, **Fort Frederica National Monument** on St. Simons Island, **Fort Pulaski National Monument** on Tybee Island, **Jimmy Carter National Historic Site** in Plains, **Kennesaw Mountain National Battlefield Park** in Kennesaw, **Martin Luther King Jr. National Historic Site** in Atlanta, and **Ocmulgee National Monument** in Macon. Each is described with its contact information in the appropriate chapter. For more information, consult the web site at www.nps.gov.

PARKS/STATE Georgia State Parks celebrated its 75th anniversary in 2006. The system includes 48 state parks and 18 historic sites. Although every park doesn't have every feature, combined the state parks offer accommodations in cabins, campgrounds, lodges, and even yurts; beaches; covered bridges; golf; hiking; historic homes and other structures; horseback riding; flying model airplanes; forts; miniature golf; museums; Native American sites; waterfalls; water sports; and wildlife observation. Consult the web site at www.gastateparks.org, then click on the link "75 Things to Do at Georgia's State Parks and Historic Sites" for more ideas. See also Camping, Golf, Lodges at State Parks, and Parking/State Parks.

PEACHES Peaches were introduced into what is now St. Simons Island and Cumberland Island in the 1570s by Franciscan monks who had come from St. Augustine, Florida. The Cherokees were growing them by the mid-1700s, and the first commercial production began in the mid-1800s. The first peaches were shipped to the New York market between 1858 and 1860. Georgia rapidly became associated with peach production and earned the nickname the Peach State. Today, however, the state is third in peach production behind California and South Carolina. The primary peach-growing area is in Crawford, Macon, Peach, and Taylor counties in middle Georgia along the fall line between the Piedmont and the Coastal Plain. The area is far enough north for the necessary winter chilling but far enough south to avoid late frosts. At **Lane Packing Company** in Fort Valley you can watch peaches being sorted and packed. You can buy peaches and peach products at **Dickey Farms** in Musella, the oldest packing house in Georgia. Consult the web site at www.pickyourown.org to find other places to get fresh peaches. A much-anticipated annual event to celebrate the peach is the **Georgia Peach Festival,** held in June in Fort Valley and Byron.

PETS Unless you're traveling in the winter; visiting the relatively cooler mountains, lakes, or forested areas; or driving directly to and from your des-tination, traveling with your dog can be problematic. We tried touring the state with one of our five dogs in an RV and ran into problems we didn't anticipate. Although Nero was perfectly comfortable while on the road with the air conditioning running (in fact he was often sitting regally in the passenger seat while one of us was working at the computer at the kitchen table), what to do when we stopped at a restaurant or attraction? We couldn't leave him in the RV unless we left the air conditioner running, and with today's gasoline prices that wasn't a very attractive option. We couldn't leave him tied outside the RV because it was too hot and we were concerned about his safety or the risk of him being stolen. We ended up running the RV so the air conditioner would be on. Although pets are welcome in state park camp-grounds and selected cottages, they must be leashed at all times. And uncivilized though it may be, dogs are not welcome on Georgia's beaches. Knowing that many of our readers won't be happy leaving their best friend at home, however, we've indicated with the 🐾 icon those lodgings, parks, and the like that are pet-friendly. For more information about travel with pets, consult the **Pet Friendly Travel** web site (www.petfriendly travel.com/locations/US/Georgia/GA), which primarily lists cabins and cottages.

POPULATION The 2000 census reports Georgia's population as 8,186,453 and the Atlanta metro area's population as 4,708,000. Projections for 2010 are more than 9 million for Georgia and more than 6 million for the metro Atlanta area.

PUBLIC REST ROOMS In general, visitors can find public rest rooms at welcome/visitor centers, government buildings such as city halls and courthouses, office buildings, public buildings such as libraries, restaurants, rest stops along major highways, large shopping centers, major attractions, city and state parks, and convenience stores/gasoline stations.

RAILROAD EXCURSIONS AND MUSEUMS Atlanta's existence was based on it being a railroad terminus and later a major rail hub, and rail traffic continues to play a significant role in the city's economy. Savannah was also a major rail center. Many, many small towns in Georgia were created as stops along the state's many railroad routes, and their fortunes waned as the railroads declined. Fortunately, many quaint, once-abandoned railroad depots enjoy new lives as museums, offices, restaurants, art galleries, and other uses. Several railbeds have been converted to Rails-to-Trails paths used by walkers, joggers, cyclists, and skaters. A few nostalgic rail excursions bring back pleasant memories to adults and create new ones for youngsters.

Among the excursions are the **Blue Ridge Scenic Railway,** which runs from Blue Ridge to McCaysville; the **Okefenokee Railroad Tour** in Waycross; the **Roosevelt Railroad Museum** in Griffin; and the **SAM Shortline/Southwest Georgia Excursion Train,** which runs from Cordele to Archery.

Museums range from large facilities with rolling stock such as the **Roundhouse Railroad Museum** in Savannah and the **Southeastern Railway Museum** in Duluth to smaller facilities with model trains such as **Charlemagne's Kingdom** in Helen, the **Misty Mountain Train Museum** in Blairsville, and the **Walker County Regional Heritage Train Museum** in Chickamauga. The **Southern Museum of Civil War and Locomotive History** in Kennesaw contains *The General*, the famous locomotive that was stolen during the Civil War and resulted in the Great Locomotive Chase.

RAIL SERVICE See Amtrak for interstate rail transportation and see MARTA under Bus/Rail Service for a description of Atlanta's rapid rail service.

RATES The prices listed in all categories were the most up to date we could find at press time, but undoubtedly rates will change, so check ahead before you travel. The prices listed are merely a guideline so you can tell whether something is economical, moderate, or expensive. We've marked some entries with a 🏵 icon to indicate that it's an especially good value. In order to categorize an attraction, restaurant, or lodging as economical, we've decided that an attraction should have an admission fee of $10 or less, a restaurant should offer entrées at $20 or less, and lodgings should have room rates of $100 or less. This system isn't foolproof, however. An attraction such as a theme park, for example, may have an admission fee of considerably more than $10 but have so much to offer that it's actually economical.

REENACTMENTS Many Georgians have not forgotten the Civil War. The Sons of the Confederacy and other organizations reenact some of the battles that occurred in the state, including the **Battle of Jonesboro** which occurred south of Atlanta, and the **Battle of Resaca** and the **Battle of Tunnel Hill,** both of which occurred north of Atlanta. Reenactments consist of costumed soldiers, horses, the firing of weapons, and camps set up to reflect the life of a soldier. Sutlers often sell replica period clothing, weapons, and other wares. More detailed descriptions are given in the Special Events section of the pertinent chapters. See also Civil War Sites.

RESORTS We define resorts as properties with lodging, restaurants, and activities such as boating, children's programs, golf, horseback riding, tennis, spas, and the like. From the beaches to the mountains, Georgia boasts numerous properties that fit this definition. Among them are **Barnsley Gardens Resort** in Adairsville, **Brasstown Valley Resort** in Young Harris, **Callaway Gardens** in Pine Mountain, **Chateau Elan Winery and Resort** in Braselton, the **Cloister at Sea Island, Cuscowilla Resort** on Lake Oconee near Eatonton, **Emerald Pointe Resort** at Lake Lanier Islands near Buford, **Fieldstone Resort** in Hiawassee, **Forrest Hills Mountain Hideaway Resort** near Dahlonega, **Innsbruck Resort and Golf Club** in Helen, **King and Prince Beach and Golf Resort** on St. Simons Island, **Kingwood Golf and Tennis Resort** near Clayton, **Lake Blackshear Resort and Golf Club** in Cordele, **Lodge on Little St. Simons** Island; the **Ritz-Carlton Lodge at Reynolds Plantation** on Lake Oconee near Greensboro, **Sea Palms Golf and Tennis Resort** on St. Simons Island, and the **Westin**

Savannah Harbor Golf Resort and Spa in Savannah.

RESTAURANTS A few restaurants enjoy a multidecade life, while unfortunately most others turn over quickly. Even though they may not be the trendiest restaurants in town, we've tried to suggest eateries that have shown some staying power, but of course even some of those may be closed when you visit a particular locale, so it's best to call ahead to avoid disappointment. In the event that a restaurant you particularly want to visit has closed, consult our other suggestions, ask your concierge for help, or check with the welcome/visitor center.

Cuisine ranges from the sublime to the ridiculous, from gourmet to takeout. As you read the individual chapters, you'll find that BBQ and down-home-cookin' restaurants are prominently featured throughout the state—partly because these two cuisines are so popular and partly because in many small towns those are the only choices other than fast food. Fresh seafood is the top choice on the coast and islands, but good seafood can be found almost anywhere.

Some casual eateries that have enjoyed longtime renown in Georgia include the **H&H Restaurant** in Macon, where the Allman Brothers band members used to eat; **Nu Way Weiners** in Macon; the **Varsity**, a hot doggery in Atlanta and Athens; **Mrs. Wilkes Dining Room** in Savannah; and the **Whistle Stop Café** in Juliette, which achieved fame in the movie *Fried Green Tomatoes*. A not-to-be-missed all-you-can-eat restaurant is the **Blue Willow Inn** in Social Circle.

RIVERS Georgia is laced with rivers and streams—some of them dammed into lakes. You'll notice that practically all of them still bear their Indian names. The major rivers in the state include the **Chattahoochee,** which flows all the way from Lake Lanier north of Atlanta to the Florida border and creates the border between Georgia and Alabama, and the **Flint,** which flows from the Atlanta metro area along the western border of the state and provides some white-water rapids. The best white-water river is the **Chattooga Wild and Scenic River** in northeast Georgia near Clayton. White-water conditions are also found on the **Ocoee River** in northwest Georgia, where the 1996 Centennial Olympic Games white-water events were held. Other rivers provide excellent conditions for canoeing: **Alapaha** (Lakeland), **Altamaha** (ends near Darien), **Ochlocknee** (Cairo), **Ocmulgee** (Macon), **Ogeechee** (Piedmont region to the sea at Ossabaw Island), and **Toccoa.** The **Conasauga, Coosawattee,** and **Oostanaula rivers** meet in Rome.

ROCKHOUNDING See Gold Mining. Those particularly interested in rocks and minerals will want to be sure to include a visit to the **William Weinman Mineral Museum** in White in northwest Georgia.

SAILING The waters off Georgia's coast, which were the site of the 1996 Centennial Olympic Games sailing competitions, provide exhilarating sailing adventures for those who have their own boats as well as those who rent a boat or take a guided cruise. Georgia's many lakes are also meccas for sailors, although some lakes reputedly have "dead air" zones. **Lanier Sailing**

Academy on Lake Lanier north of Atlanta offers sailing classes and rentals. **Weadore Sailing** on Jekyll Island offers guided tours. Numerous sailing companies, marinas, and boat ramps are either described in the individual chapters or listed in the Other Activities Appendix.

SHOPS Shops have the same problem as eateries in regard to staying power or lack thereof (see Restaurants). We tried to pick not the hottest flash-in-the-pan shops but those that have been around for a while. As with restaurants, in the event that a store you want to visit has closed, consider

SAILING AT LAKE LANIER

our other suggestions, ask your concierge, or check with the welcome/visitor center. These travel professionals also will be the best source of advice about the newest up-and-coming shops.

SKIING For those readers who were aware that Georgia actually had a ski resort (one of the southernmost in the United States) for more than 30 years, we're sad to report that it has closed. Several years of mild winters when it was impossible to make snow and/or maintain a snow base spelled the doom of the resort. In Georgia, if someone is talking about skiing, he or she is undoubtedly talking about waterskiing.

SKYDIVING Few are brave enough to jump out of an airplane or soar off a cliff in a hang glider, but if you're among those who thrive on an adrenaline rush, there are several adventures awaiting you in Georgia. Among these are **Adventure Skydiving Center** in Cedartown, **Georgia Skydiving Center** in Rome, **Skydive Atlanta** in Thomaston, and the **Lookout Mountain Flight Park and Training Center** in Rising Fawn.

SMOKING Beginning July 1, 2005, Georgia enacted a ban on smoking in any buildings open to the public, much to the joy of nonsmokers. That should have meant that we could simply list all hotels, lodgings, and so forth as nonsmoking. Nothing's ever that simple, though. As with most laws, there are still many loopholes and exceptions. Establishments such as bars and nightclubs that don't admit anyone younger than 18 can still allow smoking. Many restaurants

still permit smoking in their bars and on patios and decks, so these areas may be even more packed with smokers than before. Few bed & breakfasts, which are often housed in historic homes, allow smoking indoors but may allow it on porches or decks. Insurance companies, however, may decree that bed & breakfasts not allow smoking even on the porches because of the possibility of fire. We have, therefore, still tried to indicate whether an establishment allows smoking or not, and if they do, where.

SPECIAL LODGINGS Several historic homes and hotels offer exquisite accommodations. Among these are the **Greyfield Inn** on Cumberland Island, which was once a Carnegie family mansion; **Henderson Village** in Perry, which offers accommodations in historic homes and updated sharecroppers cottages; the **Jekyll Island Club Hotel** on Jekyll Island, which was once the private playground of 100 millionaires and their families; the **Mansion at Forsyth Park** in Savannah, a newly opened small luxury hostelry; **Melhana,** a plantation in Thomasville; the **Partridge Inn** in Augusta, a historic hotel dating from Augusta's grand hotel days in the late 1800s; and the **Windsor Hotel** in Americus, a fanciful concoction of styles. The Greyfield Inn, Jekyll Island Club Hotel, Partridge Inn, and Windsor Hotel, as well as the **King and Prince** on St. Simons Island and the **Mulberry Inn** and **River Street Inn** in Savannah, are Georgia's only seven members of the National Trust for Historic Preservation's prestigious Historic Hotels of America. At the other end of the spectrum is the **Len Foote Hike Inn** in Dawsonville, which actually requires overnight guests to make a 5-mile hike to the inn. See also Resorts.

SPORTS TEAMS This is the South, and college sports are still king, but there are numerous professional major- and minor-league teams. Atlanta has "America's Team"—the last-to-first **Braves** baseball team—as well as the **Falcons** football team, **Hawks** basketball team, **Thrashers** hockey team, and **Georgia Force** arena football team.

Not to be outdone, several other small cities have sports teams as well. Augusta has the **Greenjackets** minor-league baseball team and the **Lynx** hockey team. Macon has the **Blaze** basketball team and the **Trax** hockey team. Columbus has the **Cottonmouths** hockey team. Rome has the **Braves** minor-league baseball team, the **Gladiators** basketball team, and

TAXIS

Sometimes getting around Atlanta is best via taxi. Atlanta's professional taxi-cab drivers know the city's streets like the back of their hands and are used to the massive traffic jams. What's more, Atlanta has more than 1,500 taxis available to take you between accommodations and attractions. With preset rates for trips to and from the airport, downtown, and Buckhead, taxis provide an economical mode of transportation in Atlanta. Ask the concierge at your hotel for a list of taxi services in the area or simply flag down an on-duty cab. All cab companies are regulated under the same rate schedule, so it seldom makes any difference which taxi you take. From the airport the following flat rates apply:

Flat Rate Zone from Hartsfield	One Person	Two People	Three People	Four or More People
To Downtown	$25	$26 ($13 each)	$30 ($10 each)	$40 ($10 each)*
To Midtown	$28	$30 ($15 each)	$35 ($11.66 each)	$40 ($10 each)*
To Buckhead	$35	$36 ($18 each)	$39 ($13 each)	$45 ($11.25 each)*

*There is an additional $2 charge for each person beyond the fourth.

Rates to areas outside the central business district are computed by a meter. These are the standard charges:
$2 for the first $\frac{1}{7}$ mile
25¢ for each additional $\frac{1}{7}$ mile
$18 per hour wait time

the **Renegades** arena football team. Savannah has the **Sand Gnats** baseball team. Other teams include the **Atlanta Silverbacks** soccer team and the Gwinnett **Gladiators** hockey team.

THEATERS/SUMMER Most theater in Georgia is offered during a September-to-May season, but theater lovers don't have to be bereft during the summer season. Six Broadway musicals are brought to Atlanta each summer by **Theater of the Stars** and performed at the Fox Theatre. The **Atlanta Shakespeare Festival** performs the Bard's plays and those of other playwrights on the campus of Oglethorpe University in the Buckhead section of Atlanta. In the southern part of the state, the **Peach State Summer Theater** performs three musicals in the Sawyer Theater in the Valdosta State University Fine Arts Building in Valdosta.

THEATERS/YEAR-ROUND Professional and amateur theater is alive and well in Georgia. The Atlanta metro area alone has dozens of theater groups ranging from the renowned **Alliance Theater** at the Woodruff Arts Center to the **Theatre in the Square** in Marietta. Large-cast traveling Broadway shows often perform at Atlanta's **Fox Theatre** or the **Boisfeuillet Jones Atlanta Civic Center.** Towns from Albany to Warner Robins have active community theater groups, and towns with colleges or universities offer theater as well. We try to include some choices for theatrical entertainment in every chapter.

Some historic theater structures, worth seeing in their own right in addition to attending a performance there, include the **Fox Theatre** in

Atlanta, **Cotton Hall Theater** in Colquitt, **Rylander Theater** in Americus, **Madison-Morgan Cultural Arts Center** in Madison, and **Springer Opera House** (the official state theater) in Columbus.

TRAFFIC AND HIGHWAY TIPS One of the things the Atlanta metro area is most infamously known for is horrendous traffic. With I-75, I-85, and I-20 meeting in downtown Atlanta (one of only five American cities where that happens), it's no wonder that traffic is a problem—especially in the morning and evening. The I-285 perimeter freeway around Atlanta does little to speed you on your way. GA 400, a toll road that stretches north from Atlanta to near Dahlonega, is one of the most congested roads in the state. In the Atlanta metro area, getting off the major highways and using surface roads and streets gains you little except perhaps being easier on the nerves. And to make matters worse, the Atlanta metro area now stretches practically from Macon to the Tennessee border and from the Alabama line past Covington. Friday nights and Sunday nights are particularly heavily traveled as folks try to get away for the weekend.

Not that any of our readers would ever run a red light, but be forewarned that some municipalities are using photo enforcement at traffic lights. And be aware in driving around the Savannah Historic District that, as you approach a square, cars already in a square have the right of way over cars entering from a side street.

Happily, traffic is rarely a problem throughout the rest of the state. I-16 from Macon to Savannah, for example, is lightly traveled. I-95, which skirts the coast, is heavily traveled but not often snarled. There are hundreds of two-lane country roads where you'll rarely see another car.

TRAILS See Driving Tours, Hiking, and Walking Trails.

TROLLEYS Seeing the sights via a nostalgic trolley is a popular choice for travelers. Savannah has a plethora of choices, including **Gray Line Trolley Tours** (912-234-8687; www.grayline .com), **Old Savannah Tours** (912-234-8128; 1-800-517-9007; oldsavannah tours.com), and **Old Town Trolley** (912-233-0083; www.oldtowntrolley .com). The **Express Trolley Tour** at the Atlanta State Farmer's Market in Forest Park is an interesting way to see the giant fresh market. See Guided Tours for a list of trolley tours in Macon, Milledgeville, and St. Simons. More details are given in the appropriate chapters.

VACATION RENTALS In addition to campgrounds and cottages, condominiums are another lodging option for stays of a week or more (shorter stays may be available at the last minute) and are most often found at the beach resorts. On St. Simons Island condominium accommodations are offered by the **Beach Club, North Breakers Condominiums, Shipwatch Condominiums,** and **St. Simons Grand Oceanfront Villas.** On Jekyll Island, various types of rentals are represented by **Jekyll Realty Vacation Rentals** and **Parker-Kaufman Realtors.** On Tybee Island, accommodations including condominiums are available through **Tybee Cottages.** In the north Georgia mountains, condo accommodations are offered by **Fieldstone Resort Condominiums** on Lake Chatuge in Hiawassee. See also Cottage Rentals.

WALKING TOURS Both guided (see Guided Tours) and self-guided walking tours are available throughout Georgia. One interesting tour is **Lights on Macon.** Various homes in one of Macon's historic districts participate in a special lighting project so that visitors can walk by and enjoy their outstanding architecture at night.

Athens is well known as the cradle of many rock bands such as REM and the B52s. The **Athens Music History Walking Tour** points out many clubs and other sites where these bands got their start. While in Athens, a totally whimsical tour is **Who Let the Dawgs Out,** a tour of amusing public art represented by bulldogs (that's Dawgs to the uninitiated), the mascot of the University of Georgia.

At the other end of the spectrum are nature walks such as **Sea Turtle Walks** on Jekyll Island. Many small towns and historic neighborhoods with structures from the turn of the 20th century are particularly conducive to walking tours. Some of these are **City of Decatur Walking Tours, Fort Gaines Walking Tour, Historic Darien Walking Tours, Historic Downtown LaGrange Walking Tours, Historic Walking and Driving Tours of Thomasville, Walking Tour of Madison,** and **Walking Tour of Moultrie**.

WALKING TRAILS While hiking trails in the mountains and national forests can be strenuous, many other trails are more conducive to walking, jogging, bicycling, and in-line skating. Some of them are also stroller and wheelchair accessible. Some of these include the **Augusta Canal Trail** in Augusta; **Earth Day Nature Trail** in Brunswick; **Ocmulgee Heritage**

Trail in Macon; **Savannah-Tybee Railroad Historic and Scenic Trail** on Tybee Island; the **Silver Comet Trail,** which stretches from northwest Georgia to the Alabama line; and the **Wild Horse Creek Trail** in Powder Springs, which connects with the Silver Comet Trail.

WATERFALLS North Georgia's mountains are conducive to sudden changes in elevation, creating many waterfalls along rivers and streams. The most accessible is **Amicalola Falls** in Amicalola Falls State Park near Dawsonville and Dahlonega. You can drive almost to the base of the falls or to an overlook near the top. Some other easily accessible waterfalls are **Anna Ruby Falls,** which is actually two falls near Helen, and **Toccoa Falls** on the campus of Toccoa Falls College in Toccoa.

From north to south in Georgia, the topography changes from mountains to the rolling Piedmont region and then to the flat Coastal Plain. The fall line where the Piedmont changes to the Coastal Plain is the site of **High Falls,** one of the farthest south waterfalls.

Many other waterfalls are listed and described in individual chapters. For information on other waterfalls in Georgia, a good web site to consult is www.waterfalls-guide.com/ga_waterfalls-guide.htm. Some other waterfalls-related web sites are www.n-georgia.com/naturally/waterfalls.htm, www.yahoovista.com/waterfalls, and www.georgiatrails.com/waterfalls.html.

WEB SITES The intent of our descriptions of individual attractions, activities, lodgings, restaurants, special events, and the like is simply to whet your appetite. With the entries that particularly strike your fancy, we assume you'll want to know much more. Whenever they are available, therefore, we include web sites with the contact information for each entry. Accessing the web site enables you to learn more about an entry we describe, see numerous color pictures—perhaps even a live web cam—and check for the latest hours and prices before you travel. Be aware, however, that a web site is only as good as the last time it was updated; we've found many that haven't been updated for years. We've listed many web sites under specific entries and appropriate categories, but in order to reduce repetition, we list a few here that would be found under several categories.

You can access lists of Georgia's ATV trails, bike trails, hiking clubs, hiking trails, horse trails, and waterfalls at the web site at www.mountaintravelguide.com/georgia/georgia.htm. The e-library of the **Georgia Wildlife Federation** (www.gwf.org/wildlife.htm) includes lists of amphibians (www.gwf.org/commonamphibians.htm), birds (www.gwf.org/commonbirds.htm), mammals (www.gwf.org/commonmammals.htm; www.gwf.org/protectedanimals.htm), reptiles (www.gwf.org/commonreptiles.htm), and other categories. The web site of the **Georgia Nature-Based Tourism Association** is www.georgianature.org.

WHEN TO GO Georgia is blessed with a moderate climate year-round and doesn't really have a high season and low season as some states do. Spring and fall are long, pleasant, and colorful with flamboyant flowers or leaves. Winters are mild except in the mountainous areas in the northern part of the state, where freezing temperatures and snow and ice are rare but not unheard of. In the northern part of the state, some bed & breakfasts, campgrounds, and attractions close for the winter months, so it's best to call ahead if you're traveling there during this period to avoid disappointment. Occasional cold snaps, snowstorms, or ice storms in the rest of the state are rare and short-lived. In the majority of the state, winter daytime temperatures average 55 degrees, so a blazer or lightweight coat is usually sufficient for being outdoors. Nights can drop down to the 40s or even 30s, so a warmer coat, gloves, and hat may be necessary then.

Summers, on the other hand, can be quite hot, with daytime temperatures around 95 degrees for prolonged periods and sometimes even breaking 100 degrees for several days. Humidity can be high all over the state, but more so in south Georgia and the coastal areas. Temperatures and humidity on the barrier islands and in the immediate coastal areas are usually ameliorated by sea breezes, but as soon as you get inland, temperatures and humidity can be unpleasant. It is more comfortable, therefore, to travel to those areas in the fall through spring. Autumn is a good time to visit the coastal and barrier islands region, for example, because air temperatures have abated while the water temperature remains at its highest and the area is less crowded once children go back to school. (In Georgia, most schools start very early in August, so you don't even have to wait for Labor Day to reap the benefits of fewer crowds, although it is still quite hot.) Very warm temperatures can extend well into October.

Because weather in most parts of the state is so similar, we do not describe it in each separate chapter unless the weather in the area being described is unusual. We also give some information in the When to Go section about times when it might be better not to visit an area because of special events or other reasons that make the area crowded and lodging hard to get. The very things that make folks want to visit an area—fall foliage, for example—also make it the most crowded.

WHITE-WATER RAFTING See Canoeing, Kayaking, Tubing, and White-Water Rafting.

WINERIES Climate, topography, elevation, and soil conditions make wine production in Georgia viable, although the industry is still in its infancy. Most of the wineries and the widest variety of grapes are found in the northern part of the state. The **Georgia Wine Highway** stretches from Clayton to Braselton and includes eight wineries. Wineries in the southern part of the state primarily grow muscadine grapes, which are sweet and often used in dessert wines.

The primary wineries in the state include **Chateau Elan Winery and Resort** in Braselton, **Crane Creek Vineyards** in Young Harris, **1810 Country Inn and Winery** in Thomson, **Fox Vineyards and Winery** in Social Circle, **Frogtown Cellars** in Dahlonega, **Habersham Winery** in Helen, **Meinhardt Vineyards and Winery** in Statesboro, **Persimmon Creek Vineyards** in Clayton, **Still Pond Vineyard and Winery** in Arlington, **Three Sisters Vineyards and Winery** in Dahlonega, **Tiger Mountain Vineyards** in Tiger, and **Wolf Mountain Vineyards and Winery** in Dahlonega. Some of the wineries have free tours and tastings; others charge a small fee. Several also offer a restaurant and/or shop.

There are also several tasting rooms around the state where you can sample a variety of Georgia wines rather than just those produced by an individual winery: **Dahlonega Tasting Room** in Sautee and **Georgia Winery Taste Centers** in Pine Mountain and in Ringgold.

For more information, contact the **Wine Growers Association of Georgia** (706-878-9463; www.georgia wine.com). Other sources of information are **Georgia Wine Country** (www.georgiawinecountry.com) and the **Georgia Wine Council** (www .georgiawinecouncil.org).

ZOOS/ANIMAL PRESERVES You don't have to travel to exotic foreign countries to see wild animals that aren't native to America or Georgia. Several zoos throughout the state showcase a variety of these wild animals. Other zoos may have more docile farm animals just right for petting.

Zoo Atlanta is the most prestigious of Georgia's zoos. It is one of only a few zoos in America to have an adorable pair of pandas on loan from China. It also boasts an exceptional primate collection as well as other wild and tame animals. Most travelers will be surprised to find that the largest collection of kangaroos outside Australia is in north Georgia at the **Kangaroo Conservation Center** in Dawsonville. Some other organizations with wild and tame animals are the **Center for Wildlife Education and Lamar Q. Ball Jr. Raptor Center** at Georgia Southern University in Statesboro, **Chestatee Wildlife Preserve** in Dahlonega, **Noah's Ark Animal Rehabilitation Center** in Locust Grove, the **Parks at Chehaw** in Albany, **Wild Adventures Theme Park** in Valdosta, **Wild Animal Safari** in Pine Mountain, and the **Yellow River Game Ranch** in Lilburn. Look for other small zoos and preserves listed in individual chapters.

Atlanta Metro

1

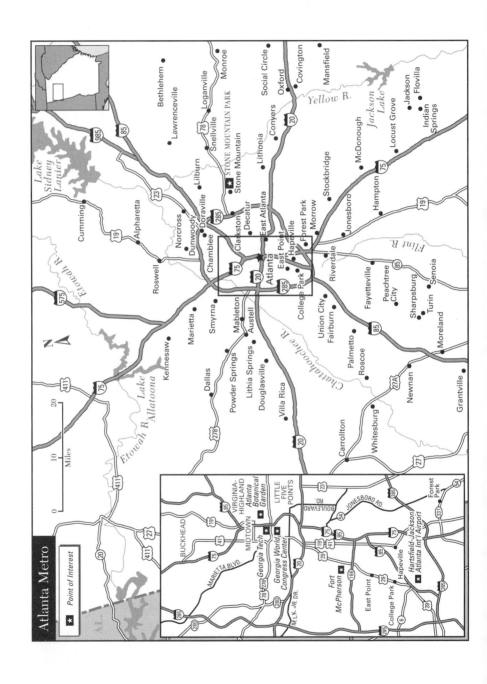

Atlanta Metro

★ *Point of Interest*

ATLANTA

In 1782 a thriving Creek Indian village and trading post called Standing Peach Tree (some say it was actually Pitch Tree) existed along what is now called Peachtree Creek where it empties into the Chattahoochee River. Historians theorize that there was either a single peach tree or a pine (pitch) tree on the spot. From these humble beginnings grew what is now the capital of the South and a plethora of things named Peachtree.

Atlanta began taking shape in 1837, when the Western and Atlantic Railroad decided to make the area the southern end of its operations. (The honor had been offered to nearby Decatur, which turned it down; otherwise there might never have been an Atlanta at all.) The town was originally called Terminus since that's what it was—the end of the line. In 1843, it was renamed Marthasville for the daughter of Governor Wilson Lumpkin. In 1847, the town was renamed once again; this time it was called Atlanta—probably a feminine form of Atlantic (as in Western and Atlantic), and the name finally stuck.

By the beginning of the Civil War in 1861, Atlanta was a major rail hub, a manufacturing center, and a supply depot, so it's no wonder that the city was a target of destruction by Union forces under General William Tecumseh Sherman. When the Union forces finally took Atlanta in 1864, all the railroad facilities, almost every business, and more than two-thirds of the city's homes were destroyed—making Atlanta the only major American city ever destroyed by war.

But the city wasn't held down for long—giving rise to the city's association with the Egyptian legend of the phoenix rising from the ashes. In 1868, the Georgia capital was moved from Milledgeville to Atlanta—making the city the fifth and last state capital. Newspaperman Henry Grady almost single-handedly created the image of the reconciled "New South," where business opportunities were rife. Colleges and universities opened, telephones and trolleys were introduced, and the 1895 Cotton States Exposition introduced 800,000 visitors to the vibrant city, all of which began a long upward economic surge that lasts to this day.

"The city too busy to hate" took the lead in peacefully strengthening minority rights in the Southeast during the 1950s and 1960s. In 1963, Mayor Ivan Allen Jr. was the only white Southern mayor to testify before Congress in support of the pending Civil Rights Bill. When native son Martin Luther King Jr. was assassinated in 1968, Mayor Allen pleaded for calm and was rewarded with peaceful mourning.

Ever optimistic, the city decided to build a stadium when it didn't even have a professional team to play there. That optimism paid off when major-league baseball's Braves moved from Milwaukee to Atlanta and the city was awarded the Falcons expansion football team. Today the city boasts not only baseball and football franchises but also basketball, hockey, and arena football teams.

Now a world-class city, Atlanta has one of the nation's busiest airport, an efficient public transportation system, convention facilities that have made it second in the nation in convention business, the Underground Atlanta shopping and entertainment complex, a new stadium, a sports dome, and a sports and entertainment arena. The city has hosted the 1988 Democratic National Convention, Super Bowls in 1994 and 2000, the NCAA Men's and Women's Basketball Final Four, and the NBA All-Star Game.

Another jewel in the city's crown was added when the 1996 Centennial Olympic Summer Games were awarded to Atlanta and 2 million people visited the city during the two-week event. The Olympics served as an impetus for a resurgence of downtown, with more than $2 billion in construction projects and other changes, the major legacy of which is Centennial Olympic Park.

Depending on whose statistics you're using, the metropolitan Atlanta area consists of nine to 16 counties, up to 100 municipalities, and a population of more than 4 million people, but this chapter focuses on the area inside the city limits, which is generally also the area inside the I-285 perimeter highway.

GUIDANCE To plan a trip to Atlanta, contact the **Atlanta Convention and Visitors Bureau** (404-521-6688; 1-800-ATLANTA; www.acvb.com), 233 Peachtree Street NE, Suite 100, Atlanta 30303. Open 8:30–5:30 weekdays. Also consult the web site at www.atlanta.net for up-to-date information on hotel and restaurant reservations, directions, guidebooks, maps, and help in creating an itinerary. There are several Atlanta CVB Visitor Centers at various locations around the city to aid visitors. The **Visitor Center at Hartsfield-Jackson Atlanta International Airport,** 6000 North Terminal Parkway, Suite 435, is open 9–9 weekdays, 9–6 Saturday, and 12:30–6 Sunday. Downtown, the **Visitor Center at the Georgia World Congress Center,** 285 International Boulevard, is open only during Georgia World Congress Center events, but the **Visitor Center at**

ATLANTA AMBASSADOR FORCE

Begun during the 1996 Centennial Olympic Summer Games to aid the vast number of visitors from around the world, the 60-person Atlanta Ambassador Force was such a success it's still around to help present-day visitors. The AAF keeps an eye out for anyone who looks lost and can give directions, suggest attractions and restaurants, and relate history. For other information about the ambassadors, contact the Atlanta Downtown Improvement District (404-215-9600). Look for their pith helmets.

Underground Atlanta, 65 Upper Alabama Street, is open 10–6 Monday through Saturday, noon–6 Sunday. In Buckhead there is also a **Visitor Center at Lenox Square Mall,** 3393 Peachtree Road, which is open 11–5 Tuesday through Saturday, noon–6 Sunday. To plan a trip specifically to Buckhead, contact the **Buckhead Coalition** (404-233-2228; www.buckhead.org/buckheadcoalition) or the **Buckhead Business Association** (404-467-7607; www.buckheadbusiness.org).

Also check out **AtlanTIX** (678-318-1400) at the Atlanta Convention and Visitors Bureau Underground Atlanta Visitor Center or the Visitor Center at Lenox Square Mall. Atlanta's same-day, half-price outlet offers tickets to a wide variety of theater, dance, and musical performances as well as half-price tickets to Zoo Atlanta, the Atlanta History Center, the High Museum of Art, the Margaret Mitchell House and Museum, and other attractions. AtlanTIX is open 11–6 Tuesday through Saturday, noon–4 Sunday.

GETTING THERE *By air:* Visitors to Atlanta fly into **Hartsfield-Jackson Atlanta International Airport.** Car rentals are available both on- and off-site. There are also numerous shuttle companies (some to distant cities), and several hotels have free shuttles to their properties (check ahead when you make your hotel reservation). See What's Where in Georgia for airline, car rental, and shuttle details.

By bus: **Greyhound Lines** (404-584-1738; www.greyhound.com), 232 Forsyth Street, is open 24 hours a day.

By car: Access to Atlanta is easy with I-75 and I-85 running north-south and I-20 running east-west. All of them meet in downtown Atlanta.

By train: **Amtrak** (404-881-3067; 1-800-USA-RAIL; www.amtrak.com), 1688 Peachtree Street NW. The station is not located downtown but in Buckhead. Transportation from the station to downtown is available by taxi or MARTA bus (see *Getting Around*).

GETTING AROUND For car rental agencies, see What's Where in Georgia.

Mass transit is another easy and economical alternative. The city's bus/rail system, &. **Metropolitan Atlanta Rapid Transit Authority,** known locally as **MARTA** (404-848-4711; www.itsmarta.com), is the most cost-effective and convenient way to get around Atlanta, with a variety of routes and pass options available (see What's Where in Georgia). MARTA also operates the **Braves Stadium Shuttle.** On days when the Atlanta Braves are playing at Turner Field (known locally as "the Ted"), MARTA offers easy service to the stadium from the Five Points rail station. Proceed from the station through Underground Atlanta to the shuttle buses waiting at the plaza. (Golf cart transportation from the rail station to the bus is available for elderly or disabled game-goers.) The shuttle begins service 90 minutes before game time and continues until the stadium is empty. Each passenger needs a rail-to-bus or bus-to-bus transfer or a regular fare to ride the shuttle.

While in Buckhead, take advantage of the free **BUC** ❧ **(Buckhead's Uptown Connection)** shuttle, which connects the Lenox Square and Buckhead MARTA

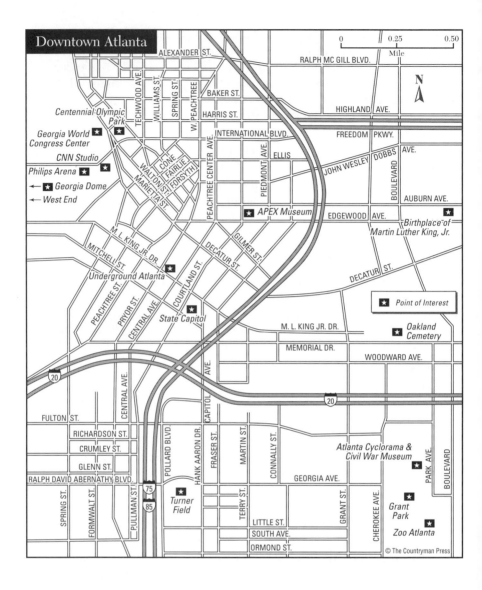

Centennial Olympic Park

Georgia World Congress Center

CNN Studio

Philips Arena

← Georgia Dome

← West End

Underground Atlanta

State Capitol

APEX Museum

Birthplace of Martin Luther King, Jr.

Oakland Cemetery

★ Point of Interest

Turner Field

Atlanta Cyclorama & Civil War Museum

Grant Park

Zoo Atlanta

© The Countryman Press

rail stations with major hotels, dining locations, retail centers, and key office buildings. The BUC operates 7 AM–10 PM daily. For information, contact the **Buckhead Area Transportation Management Association** (404-842-2682; www.batma.org; www.bucride.com).

In Midtown, another option for getting around town is the free **Georgia Tech Technology Square Trolley** (404-894-9645). These rubber-tired, alternative-fuel vehicles, designed to look like old-fashioned trolleys, provide service from the center of the campus to Technology Square to the Midtown MARTA station. This means out-of-town visitors can take MARTA rail from the airport to the Midtown station, then transfer to the trolley to reach the campus and the Georgia Tech Hotel and Conference Center. The Tech Trolley runs every four minutes and is available to students, faculty, staff, and visitors.

PARKING There is little free parking downtown, in Buckhead, or in Midtown. What little on-street parking exists is metered, but free after 6 PM and on Sunday. There are, however, plentiful for-fee parking lots and parking decks. In the Buckhead entertainment district, some streets are closed off in the evening (especially on weekends) because of traffic congestion, which means visitors have to park farther away and walk to the restaurants and nightclubs. There is plentiful free on-street parking in the residential neighborhoods, which may be within walking distance of your destination.

WHEN TO GO Some times to avoid might include the Chick-fil-A Bowl, Big Peach Drop on New Year's Eve, or other major events that draw big crowds. It might be best to call the CVB before planning a trip to find out which events might be happening during your visit.

MEDICAL EMERGENCY For life-threatening situations, call 911. In less urgent cases, immediate care is available downtown at **Grady Memorial Hospital** (404-616-6200; www.gradyhealthsystem.org), 80 Jesse Hill Jr. Drive SE, and its associated **Hughes Spalding Children's Hospital** (404-616-6600; www .gradyhealthsytem.org), 35 Jesse Hill Jr. Drive SE. Immediate care is also available at **Emory Crawford Long Hospital** (404-686-4411; www.emory healthcare.org), 550 Peachtree Street NE. If you are out and about in Buckhead and need immediate assistance, there are 20 bright-yellow emergency 911 telephone boxes with fluorescent blue signs placed throughout the business district. These give direct links to police, fire, and medical assistance 24/7 and automatically register the caller's location. The nearest immediate care to Buckhead and Midtown is **Piedmont Hospital** (404-605-5000), 1968 Peachtree Road.

NEIGHBORHOODS Atlanta was almost completely destroyed during the Civil War and also has been accused of tearing down everything more than a few decades old to build something new, so there are not as many historic buildings as might be found in a city of comparable age or size. There are, however, several historic neighborhoods dating from the late 1800s and early 1900s.

Ansley Park was built more than a century ago to attract Atlanta's wealthiest and most prestigious families. While downtown's Inman Park was the city's first trolley suburb, Midtown's Ansley Park was its first driving suburb. Today Ansley Park contains gracious residences and grand estates, tree-lined streets, broad lawns, and bucolic parks. The entire neighborhood is a National Register Historic District. Ansley Park is convenient to the arts district in Midtown.

Atlantic Station, Midtown Atlanta's newest, from-the-ground-up neighborhood, is being built on the site of the old Atlantic Steel Mill manufacturing complex, a long-abandoned eyesore along the I-75/I-85 corridor. The site is rapidly becoming an upscale mixed-use neighborhood.

Glitzy **Buckhead,** Atlanta's Beverly Hills, is a 28-square-mile district 4 miles north of downtown and immediately north of Midtown. Buckhead has been called "Where old money lives and new money parties" by the *Atlanta Journal-Constitution.* The area has the most beautiful and expensive neighborhoods, the finest restaurants, the most luxurious hotels, the best shopping, and the most nightlife. It's *the* place to see and be seen.

The historic neighborhood of **Candler Park**, which is listed on the National Register of Historic Places, was a large residential neighborhood near Chamblee dating from the late 19th and early 20th centuries. Candler Park is characterized by late-Victorian and bungalow/Craftsman architecture.

Downtown is primarily commercial, but in recent years many buildings have been converted to residential use and new neighborhoods have been built, resulting in a resurgence of in-town living. Downtown offers hotels, restaurants, and a wide range of attractions for visitors.

The vibrant **Fairlie-Poplar Historic District,** a short walk from major downtown attractions and hotels, is a National Register Historic District characterized by classic examples of commercial architecture largely developed in the early 20th century. Restaurants and boutiques occupy the street level of many of these buildings, and the district is the site of several popular events.

Grant Park Historic District, bounded by Glenwood and Atlanta avenues and Kelly and Eloise streets, is one of Atlanta's oldest neighborhoods. Centered around **Grant Park** (see *Green Space—Nature Preserves and Parks*), the majority of the district's structures are residences built between the late 1800s and early 1900s. Grant Park is also home to the **Atlanta Cyclorama and Civil War Museum** (see *Historic Homes and Sites*) and **Zoo Atlanta** (see *To Do—For Families*).

Once trolley transportation was available, Atlanta's well-to-do moved away from downtown. Begun in 1889, **Inman Park** was Atlanta's first suburb. Elegant Victorian-era homes were built northeast of downtown by wealthy magnates such as Coca-Cola's Asa Candler and Ernest Woodruff. The neighborhood is nationally renowned for its preservation efforts.

Little Five Points, located northeast of the residential Inman Park neighborhood, is a dining, entertainment, and shopping mecca for Atlanta's youthful consumers. Little Five Points (affectionately known as L5P) is the "in" place to go, with numerous offbeat restaurants, clubs, shops, and theaters—each with its own peculiar twist.

Midtown is the 9-square-mile district situated between downtown and Buckhead. Once known as Uptown, Midtown was developed in the 1870s as a streetcar suburb. It grew and prospered until the 1960s, when suburban growth moved even farther from the city. During the next decades, Midtown became much more commercial and much less residential. In the 1980s, however, the Midtown Alliance and renewed interest in in-town living sparked a renaissance in Midtown that continues to this day. The area's principal claim to fame is that it is Atlanta's arts district and the home of the city's most revered cultural institutions—the **Atlanta Symphony Orchestra,** the **Alliance Theater,** the **High**

Museum of Art, and the **Atlanta Botanical Garden**—as well as several other museums, swanky hotels, trendy restaurants, and the city's largest park. Midtown is known for its residential diversity and its energetic business district where bungalows coexist with skyscrapers, restaurants, and churches.

Poncey-Highland centers around the intersection of Ponce de Leon and Highland avenues and blends almost imperceptibly into Virginia-Highland. Businesses, shops, restaurants, and music venues make this a great place to walk and hang out.

Sweet Auburn is centered around Auburn Avenue, which was the epicenter of African American enterprise from the 1890s to the 1940s, when it was hailed as the richest black street in America. But once civil rights laws were passed and blacks were free to shop anywhere, Auburn Avenue began to decline and, in fact, became quite seedy. Today, with sites to see including the **Martin Luther King Jr. National Historic Site** and the **African American Panoramic Experience Museum** (APEX), the district is undergoing a renaissance.

The trendy **Virginia-Highland** neighborhood is one of Atlanta's most popular for shopping, dining, and nightlife. The name derives from the intersection of Virginia and Highland avenues, and its history is traced to its initial settlement by farmers in the early 1800s. When the Atlanta Street Railway Company opened the area to development in the 1890s, the farms were subdivided into building lots for residential and commercial use. One of the earliest neighborhoods was Atkins Park at Highland and Ponce de Leon avenues, and the bungalow was the predominant style of architecture here through the 1920s. **Atkins Park** restaurant opened in 1927 and is said to have the oldest liquor license in the city of Atlanta. Virginia-Highland thrived into the 1960s but, like many other in-town neighborhoods, suffered deterioration and a loss of population soon thereafter. In the '70s, however, a few families moved into the neighborhood and the rehabilitation of homes and businesses began. Today, Virginia-Highland is one of Atlanta's most desirable neighborhoods.

Around the turn of the 20th century, Atlanta's most affluent African Americans began to build or buy impressive homes in **West End.** But by the 1960s, West End's star had waned and it was threatened with the loss of most of its historic architectural treasures to commercial development. In the 1970s, however, preservationists began restoring the remaining homes, and today the neighborhood is socially diverse and culturally rich. Sights to see in West End include the **Wren's Nest,** home of Joel Chandler Harris, creator of the Uncle Remus tales; the opulent Victorian-era **Westview Cemetery; the Herndon Home; Hammonds House Galleries and Resource Center;** and the **Atlanta University Center** complex of six historic black colleges and universities.

✳ To See

CULTURAL SITES & **Robert W. Woodruff Arts Center** (404-733-5000; www.woodruffcenter.org), 1280 Peachtree Street. Open daily. The Woodruff, the fourth-largest arts center in the country, offers the finest in visual and performing arts in the Southeast. The center encompasses the **Alliance Theatre,** and the **Atlanta Symphony Orchestra** under one roof, the **High Museum of Art** on the same campus (see separate entries under *Museums* and *Entertainment*), and the **14th Street Playhouse** nearby. Free access to the center, gift shop, and galleries; admission fee for plays, concerts, and events.

See also Attractions Appendix.

FOR FAMILIES ✇ ⅙ **Georgia Aquarium** (678-581-4000; www.georgiaaquarium .org), 225 Baker Street. Open 8–6 daily; check web site for days with extended hours. Tickets are by reservation for a specific day and time, so make reservations before you travel to avoid disappointment. The aquarium, which resembles a huge ship (some have called it a modern-day Noah's Ark), is the largest aquarium in the world, with 5 million gallons of water containing more than 55,000 animals from 500 species. Conveniently located near Centennial Olympic Park and the Georgia World Congress Center, the aquarium uses innovative technologies and interactive and interdisciplinary techniques to entertain visitors. Reptiles, amphibians, and invertebrates are also represented. But the sea life exhibited here isn't just to look at; it's meant to educate the public and impress upon them the need for protection and preservation. Guided tours are available. Adults $22.75, seniors $19.50, children $17.

✇ ❀ ⅙ **Imagine It! The Children's Museum of Atlanta** (404-659-KIDS; www.imagineit-cma.org), 275 Centennial Olympic Park Drive NW. Open 10–5 daily. This is one place youngsters will never hear "Don't touch!" Instead, everything is designed to be touched. Geared for ages three to eight, the museum's high-energy, hands-on, larger-than-life, out-of-the-ordinary interactive displays encourage the smallfry to explore and discover. Anyone age three or older $11.

GUIDED TOURS ❀ **Atlanta Preservation Center Tours** (404-688-3353; www .preserveatlanta.com), 327 St. Paul Avenue. Office open 9–5 weekdays. The organization offers separate guided walking tours showcasing the Fox Theatre, historic downtown, Sweet Auburn/MLK Jr. Historic District, Inman Park, Druid Hills, Grant Park, and Ansley Park. Call or consult the web site for tour schedules, which, with the exception of the Fox Theatre, are offered April through November. Fox Theatre tours are offered year-round. Reservations are not required. Tours last one to two hours and are canceled in the event of rain, except for the Fox Theatre tour. Adults $10, seniors and students $5.

City Segway Tours-Atlanta (1-877-734-8687; www.citysegwaytours.com/ atlanta), 50 Upper Alabama Street, Suite 256 (on the upper level of Underground Atlanta). Tours at 9 and 2:30 daily, February 15 through December 15; reservations required. The two-wheeled Segway Human Transporter, a self-balancing personal transportation device, is perfect for a guided tour of downtown Atlanta because you can cover more territory than you could on foot. After a brief training session, the 3- to 3½-hour tour includes Atlanta's highlights: the World of Coca-Cola, State Capitol, the Olympic torch and Turner Field, the Sweet Auburn neighborhood and Martin Luther King Jr. National Historic Site, the CNN Center, Centennial Olympic Park, and more. Imagine the looks you'll get from passersby as you cruise past. An evening Ghost Glide is also offered.

Tours depart rain or shine (ponchos are provided for inclement weather). City tour, $65, ghost tour, $55. Everyone must sign a liability waiver, and each party must sign a damage waiver that includes a deposit of $450 on a credit card. All riders must be at least 12 years old.

✔ ⚑ ♿ **Georgia Dome** (404-223-TOUR; www.gadome.com), One Georgia Dome Drive NW. Tours are offered on the hour 10–3 Tuesday through Saturday during football season. Tours of the world's largest cable-supported dome are truly awe-inspiring. The 70,000-seat facility is not only the home of the Atlanta Falcons football team and the Chick-fil-A Bowl, but the complex also hosts many national and international championships and other events. Guests visit the observation level, press box, exclusive Dome suites, and the locker room before ending on the field, where they can toss a football. To commemorate annual college rivalries, a section of the Georgia Dome's floor level is dedicated to mini museums highlighting Southeastern Conference football and basketball championships, the Chick-fil-A Bowl, and the Bank of America Atlanta Football Classic. Adults $6, seniors and students $4 ($1 discount with a Falcons ticket stub, CNN tour stub, or Turner Field tour stub).

✔ **Gray Line of Atlanta** (404-767-0594; 1-800-965-6665; www.grayline.com). The tour company offers three options: two different half-day tours and a full-day tour that combines both the half-day tours. Each tour includes admission to several attractions, and each leaves from the Visitor Center at Underground Atlanta, 65 Upper Alabama Street. Half-day tour: adults $40–45, children $32–35; full-day tour: adults $68, children $60.

⚑ ♿ **Inside CNN Studio Tour** (404-827-2300; 1-800-426-6868; www.cnn .com/studiotour), One CNN Center (Marietta Street at Centennial Olympic Park Drive). Open 9–5 daily; tours begin every 20 minutes. Reservations for a specific time are required a day in advance, but visitors can take a chance to purchase same-day tickets. Tours of the high-tech, fast-paced, 24/7 news network show visitors behind-the-scenes action of the actual on-the-air newsrooms via glass-enclosed overhead walkways. A special, longer VIP tour is also available for an additional fee. Adults $10, seniors $8, children $7 (children younger than 6 are not admitted).

✔ ⚑ ♿ **Turner Field Tours** (404-614-2311; www.bravesmuseum.com), 755 Hank Aaron Drive. Tours leave on the hour 10–2 Monday through Saturday, October through March. During the April-through-September baseball season, the museum and tours are available 9–3 Monday through Saturday, 1–3 Sunday. On game days, the last tour leaves at noon. No tours are offered on the day of any Sunday or afternoon home game. Tours begin at the Braves Museum and include Coca-Cola Sky Field, a luxury suite, the press box, broadcast booth, locker room, dugout, Scouts Alley, and the Braves Clubhouse Store. Eating out at the stadium is easy thanks to several fast-food outlets. Adults $10, children $5; admission to museum only during games is $2. Free parking in the North Lot.

HISTORIC HOMES AND SITES ✔ ⚑ ♿ **Atlanta Cyclorama and Civil War Museum** (404-624-1071; 404-658-7625; www.bcaatlanta.com/index.php?pid=81), Grant Park, 800-C Cherokee Avenue SE. Open 9:30–4:30 daily, until 5:30 in summer. Before there were movies and television, there were cycloramas—

huge, larger-than-life-sized, wraparound paintings that could keep viewers occupied for hours. A major attraction since 1887, this cyclorama is the longest running show in the country. Depicting the July 22, 1864, Battle of Atlanta, it measures 358 feet long (that's longer than a football field) by 42 feet high, covering 15,000 square feet. Revolving stadium seating has been introduced into the circle created by the painting, and the addition of narration, dramatic lighting, and sound effects puts viewers right into the action. Before viewing the painting, watch the introductory film, *The Atlanta Campaign*. Also displayed at the museum are period photos, weapons, and uniforms, but another star shares the spotlight with the cyclorama painting: the locomotive *Texas*, which figured prominently in the Civil War episode known as the Great Locomotive Chase (see the Northern Suburbs chapter). Adults $6, seniors $5, children 6–12 $4.

✒ ✆ ⚬ **Georgia State Capitol** (404-656-2844; www.sos.state.ga.us), Capitol Avenue and Martin Luther King Jr. Drive. Open 8–5:30 weekdays. Tours available. The imposing Atlanta capitol was completed in 1889 in the Renaissance Revival style with strong Victorian influences. Its gleaming dome rising 37 feet from the floor is plated in 23-karat gold mined in the north Georgia mountains and brought to the city by wagon train. The capitol has recently undergone extensive renovations. The tour includes a short film and showcases paintings and sculptures of prominent Georgians. Stop to visit the **Georgia Capitol Museum** (see *Museums*). Outside, stroll the grounds and admire the statues and monuments dedicated to well-known Georgians. Free.

✒ ✆ ⚬ **Governor's Mansion** (404-261-1776; www.gov.state.ga.us/about_mansion .shtml), 391 West Paces Ferry Road NW. Open 10–11:30 Tuesday through Thursday; additional hours at Christmastime. Tour and learn about the traditionally Southern, 30-columned Greek Revival mansion, which was built in 1967. The three-story, 24,000-square-foot home boasts 30 rooms; the ceremonial rooms on the first floor are those open for tours. Set among 18 acres of sweeping wooded lawns, the mansion contains what is considered to be one of the country's finest collections of 19th-century neoclassical furnishings from the Federal period as well as fine paintings and porcelain. Free.

THE GEORGIA CAPITOL STANDS BEHIND A STATUE OF GOVERNOR AND MRS. JOE BROWN.

✆ ⚬ **Herndon Home** (404-581-9813; www.herndonhome.org), 587 University Place Northwest. Open 10–4 Tuesday through Saturday with tours on the hour. Designed and built in 1910 by Alonzo and Adrienne Herndon using African American craftsmen, this 15-room, 6,000-square-foot Beaux-Arts National Register of Historic Places home tells the couple's story. Mr. Herndon was born into slavery in Social Circle, Georgia, in 1858 and when freed after the Civil War became a successful barber. Later he became wealthy after acquiring the Atlanta Life Insurance Company, which became the largest African American insurance company in the nation (it is still in business today). Mrs. Herndon was a Shakespearean actress who had traveled the world and also taught drama at Atlanta University. Together they determined to fill their new home with magnificent furnishings and art purchased on their world travels. On display are original Herndon family belongings such as period furnishings, elaborate Persian carpets, Venetian and Roman glass dating to 200 B.C., and artwork. Wheelchair accessible only on first floor. Adults $5, students $3.

&. **Margaret Mitchell House and Museum** (404-249-7015; www.gwtw.org), 990 Peachtree Street NE. Open 9:30–5 daily; museum shop open 10–6. Within this turn-of-the-20th-century Tudor Revival residence called the Crescent Apartments was the small, cramped flat of Margaret Mitchell. She lived there from 1925 to 1932, and it's where she wrote most of *Gone with the Wind,* which still sells a copy every 2½ minutes. Mitchell and her husband, John Marsh, lived in No. 1, which she dubbed "the Dump." The tour of the Midtown site starts in the visitor center with an exhibit titled "Before Scarlett: The Writings of Margaret Mitchell," an introductory movie called *It May Not Be Tara,* and changing exhibits. In the apartment, visitors can see original Mitchell pieces such as her typewriter and her 1937 Pulitzer Prize, appropriate period furnishings, and other treasures such as the famous leaded-glass window out of which Mitchell looked while writing the book. After touring the apartment, guests proceed to the *Gone with the Wind* Movie Museum. Adults $12, seniors and students $9, youth 6–17 $5. Free parking is available adjacent to the property, and the Midtown MARTA station is only one block away.

THE STORY BEHIND GONE WITH THE WIND

Although Margaret Mitchell was somewhat of a tomboy, she was unfortunately also fragile. A series of accidents and arthritis caused high-spirited "Miss Peggy" to resign her job as a reporter at *The Atlanta Journal* in 1926 to convalesce at "the Dump." At first she devoured every book her husband could bring her from the library, and when she exhausted that resource he suggested that she write a book herself. He counseled her to write about what she knew, so she began her opus by fictionalizing the stories told by her family and Civil War veterans. Mitchell took the manuscript (all 60 manila envelopes of it packed into a suitcase) to Harold Latham of Macmillan Publishing at the Georgian Terrace Hotel, where she told him, "Take it before I change my mind." The book won a Pulitzer Prize, has been translated into many languages, and is the second-best-selling book of all time, surpassed only by the Bible.

✎ ✦ & **Martin Luther King Jr. National Historic Site** (404-331-5190 for the visitor center; 404-331-6922 for recorded information; www.nps.gov/malu), 450 Auburn Avenue NE. Open 9–5 daily; hours extended to 6 between June 15 and August 15. A memorial to the revered civil rights leader, the site consists of King's birthplace and home, historic Ebenezer Baptist Church, his gravesite in the midst of a reflecting pool, an interpretive center, and the crypt of Coretta Scott King. The Gothic-Revival-style Ebenezer Baptist Church is now used as a museum and a place for special services. Free, but tickets for the birthplace tour are required for scheduling purposes. They can be picked up at the visitor center. Adjacent to the historic site is the **King Center for Nonviolent Social Change** (404-526-8900; www.thekingcenter.org), 449 Auburn Avenue NE. Also open 9–5 daily, until 6 in the summer. The center serves as the international clearinghouse of official King programs, public information, and educational materials. Free.

✦ **Rhodes Hall** (404-885-7800; www.rhodeshall.org), 1516 Peachtree Street NW. Open 11–4 weekdays, noon–3 Sunday (closed Saturday). Along with the Margaret Mitchell House, this is one of the few grand homes left along what was once a fashionable residential street in Midtown. In 1904 furniture magnate Amos Rhodes had the Romanesque-Revival, castlelike house built of Stone Mountain granite to resemble several Rhine Valley castles he'd seen in Europe. $5.

✎ ✦ & **Underground Atlanta** (404-523-2311; 1-866-494-6187, ext. 1494; www .underground-atlanta.com), 50 Upper Alabama Street SW. Shops are generally open 10–9 Monday through Saturday, noon–6 Sunday; restaurants and nightspots are open later. When Atlanta was a youngster in the mid-1880s, trains and horse-drawn buggies created the first traffic jams where streets crossed railroad tracks. At that time, the solution was to build viaducts over the tracks, but that left adjacent business owners with their entrances below street level. They responded by opening new entrances on the second floor at the new street level. Long forgotten, the lower level got a new lease on life as a shopping and entertainment mecca. Six blocks encompassing 12 acres are crammed with 100 shops, 12 restaurants, nightspots, street vendors' carts, and sculptures that line both levels and create an urban playground for all ages. Street performers often keep visitors entertained. Free.

✎ ✦ & **Wren's Nest House Museum** (404-753-7735), 1050 Ralph David Abernathy Boulevard SW. Open 10–2:30 Tuesday through Saturday. This turn-of-the-20th-century building, Atlanta's oldest house museum, was the home of Joel Chandler Harris, a newspaperman, folklorist, novelist, and poet who preserved in print the folksy Uncle Remus tales he had heard as a child from slaves. (For more information about him and the Uncle Remus yarns, see the Madison chapter in Part 3, Historic South.) The "briar patch" is furnished with original family pieces and Uncle Remus memorabilia such as a diorama built by the Disney Studios when it produced the movie *Song of the South*, which is based on the Uncle Remus tales. The museum hosts quarterly storytelling events. Adults $3, seniors and teens $2, children 4–12 $1.

MUSEUMS ✎ ✦ & **African American Panoramic Experience Museum** (404-523-2739; www.apexmuseum.org), 135 Auburn Avenue. Open 10–5 Tuesday through Saturday; also open 1–5 Sunday in February and June through August.

Known as APEX for short, the museum is dedicated to presenting and preserving the culture, history, and traditions of people of African descent by tracing the details of that history and documenting the stories of Atlanta's African American pioneers, inventors, and storekeepers. The museum presents a visual journey through the historic Sweet Auburn district. Adults $4, seniors and children $3.

✐ ✆ ♿ **Atlanta History Center** (404-814-4000; www.atlantahistorycenter.com), 130 West Paces Ferry Road NW. Open 10–5:30 Monday through Saturday, noon–5:30 Sunday; last ticket sold at 4:30. Four permanent and two changing exhibits in the architecturally striking main museum give historical perspectives about Atlanta and regional history, black history, the Civil War, and folk art, among other subjects. The DuBose Civil War Collection is the largest collection of Civil War artifacts in America, with 5,000 Confederate and Union pieces. In addition to the main museum, the complex includes two historic homes. The elegant **Swan House,** built for the wealthy Inman family in 1928, takes its name from the swan motif found discreetly throughout the mansion. In complete contrast to the Swan House, the house and outbuildings of the 1840s **Tullie Smith Farm,** which was moved to the site, show life on a simple farm. The modest Plantation Plain–style house is furnished with simple antiques. The grounds surrounding all three of the main buildings comprise 33 acres of formal and natural gardens with nature trails (see *Green Space—Gardens*). The **Coca-Cola Café** serves lunch and snacks daily, while the elegant **Swan Coach House Restaurant,** located in the estate's former carriage house–garage, serves lunch Monday through Saturday (see *Eating Out—In Buckhead*). Some attractions have limited wheelchair access. Adults $12, seniors and students older than 13 $10, children 4–12 $7.

✐ ✆ ♿ **Center for Puppetry Arts** (404-873-3391; www.puppet.org), 1404 Spring Street NW. Museum open 9–5 Tuesday through Saturday, 11–5 Sunday. Call for a schedule of performances. The center, dedicated to exploring the dazzling art of puppetry as an ancient, international, and popular art form, was opened in 1978 by Kermit the Frog and his creator, Jim Henson. The first puppetry center in the country and still the largest American organization solely dedicated to the art of puppet theater, the center boasts an astounding collection of 350 one-of-a-kind puppets from different time periods and different countries—the largest permanent collection in the country. The center also produces daytime shows for children and families as well as cutting-edge evening shows for adults (see *Entertainment—Theater*). Museum admission: adults $8, seniors and students $7, children $6; shows $12; behind-the-scenes tours $5 with a single show ticket, $4 for members and Flex Pass holders.

✐ ♿ **Fernbank Museum of Natural History** (404-929-6300; tickets 404-929-6400; www.fernbank.edu/museum/visitordining.html), 767 Clifton Road NE, Atlanta. Open 10–5 Monday through Saturday, noon–5 Sunday. "Martinis and IMAX" 5:30–10:30 Friday evenings except December. Visitors can introduce themselves to some of the earth's earliest inhabitants at the largest museum of its type in the Southeast. The Giants of the Mesozoic gallery features the largest dinosaurs ever discovered, including *Argentinosaurus*; at 123 feet long and weighing 100 tons, it was not only the most massive plant eater but also the largest known dinosaur ever to walk the earth. The much smaller, 47-foot long, 8-ton *Gigantosaurus* was the largest meat eater. Visitors also see a flock of 21 *Pterodaustro*, small pterosaurs, and three *Anhanguera*, larger pterosaurs. In complete contrast, when looking down at the limestone floors, visitors see fossil remains of tiny sea creatures that lived during the Jurassic Period more than 150 million years ago. There's so much to see at this exemplary museum near Decatur, it's almost impossible to describe here. Other galleries include the Star Gallery; the World of Shells, with its 900-gallon living-reef aquarium; A Walk Through Time in Georgia; the Martha Hodgson Ellis Discovery Rooms for ages 3–5 and 6–10; First Georgians; Sensing Nature; Cultures of the World; and Wings Over Water. The **Rankin M. Smith Sr. IMAX Theatre** offers spectacular movies on its five-story-high, 72-foot-wide screen with surround sound. Fernbank also offers special programs such as "Super Saturday," "In My World," and family days. Children's crafts are offered on weekends outside the Discovery Rooms. Plan to make a day out of a visit here; there is even a café for meals or snacks (see *Where to Eat—Eating Out*). Adults can enjoy a touch of class on Friday nights at "Martinis and IMAX," which includes a movie on the giant screen, live music, specialty martinis, a wine bar, and dinner. Also on the grounds is the **Robert L. Stanton Rose Garden** (see *Green Space—Gardens*). Adults $12, seniors and students $11, children 3–12 $10; IMAX $8–10; museum and movie $13–17.

✸ ❀ ♿ **Fernbank Science Center** (678-874-7102; fsc.fernbank.edu), 156 Heaton Park Drive NE, Atlanta. Open 8:30–5 Monday, 8:30–10 Tuesday through Friday, 10–5 Saturday, 1–5 Sunday. At this, one of the country's largest planetariums, visitors can explore the vastness of the universe with one of the center's specially choreographed shows. The center boasts an observatory, two electron microscopes, a NASA aeronautics education lab, a greenhouse, a botanical garden, and a 65-acre old-growth forest with paved walking trails, some adapted for heart patients and the visually impaired. The forest is the largest urban woodland forest in the Piedmont region. Seasonal guide sheets identify the flora and fauna. Free except for planetarium; admission to planetarium: adults $4, seniors and students $3.

✸ ❀ ♿ **Georgia Capitol Museum** (404-651-6996; www.sos.state.ga.us/museum), 206 Washington Street. Open 8–5 weekdays. Located inside the state capitol, this modest museum preserves and interprets the history of the building and the state through memorabilia, artwork, Native American artifacts, fossils and minerals, scenes from Georgia's five diverse geographic regions, and 1939 World's Fair dioramas depicting Georgia industry, state symbols, and a replica of *Miss Freedom*, the statue that adorns the top of the Georgia Capitol. Free.

❀ ♿ **Hammonds House Galleries and Resource Center for African American Art** (404-752-8730; www.hammondshouse.org), 503 Peeples Street. Open 10–6 Tuesday through Friday, 1–5 Saturday and Sunday. The 1857 Eastlake-style residence in the West End, the home of African American physician and art patron Otis Thrash Hammonds until his death in 1988, houses Georgia's only exclusively African American fine art museum. Adults $2, seniors and students $1.

❀ ♿ **High Museum of Art** (404-733-HIGH; 404-733-4400; www.high.org), 1280 Peachtree Street NE. Open 10–5 Tuesday through Saturday, noon–5 Sunday; extended hours until 9 on first Thursday of each month, until 10 on third Friday. Guided tours at 1 Sunday and Wednesday. Located in the heart of Midtown as an integral part of the Woodruff Arts Center complex, the Richard Meier–designed High Museum of Art was already Atlanta's largest museum but has just added another 177,000 square feet designed by Renzo Piano. The makeover includes new gallery space, special exhibition halls, a coffee bar, and a pedestrian-friendly "village of the arts." Among the museum's collections are 19th- and 20th-century European and American paintings, art, and furniture; English ceramics; prints by French and German Impressionists; sub-Saharan African pieces; decorative and folk art; modern and contemporary works; and photography. Linger for a snack at the **High Café.** Adults $10, seniors and students with ID $8, children 6–17 $6; free to Fulton County residents on first Saturday of each month.

🎨 ♿ **High Museum of Art Folk Art and Photography Galleries** (404-577-6940; www.high.org/visitor_information/folkart_photography/folkart.html), 133 Peachtree Street NE. Open 10–5 Monday through Saturday, 10–8 every first Thursday. Located in the lower level of the **Georgia-Pacific Center**, this intimate satellite facility to the High Museum of Art showcases revolving and traveling exhibits concentrating on photography and folk art. Free.

✏ 🎨 ♿ **Jimmy Carter Presidential Library and Museum** (404-865-7100; www.cartercenter.org), 441 Freedom Parkway. Open 9–4:45 Monday through Saturday, noon–4:45 Sunday. See a life-sized re-creation of part of the Oval Office as it looked during the Carter administration and view state gifts from heads of foreign governments received during Carter's tenure, reproductions of first lady Rosalynn Carter's inaugural gowns, a formal White House dinner setting, and memorabilia from the 1976 campaign. Take time to stroll the rose garden and the beautiful and serene Japanese garden, where visitors can admire an unobstructed view of the Atlanta skyline (see *Green Spaces—Gardens*). Adults $7, seniors $5, children younger than 16 free.

✏ 🎨 ♿ **The National Museum of Patriotism** (404-875-0691; 1-877-276-1692; www.museumofpatriotism.org), 1405 Spring Street NW. Open 10–4 Tuesday through Thursday, Saturday, and Sunday. The Midtown museum is 2½ blocks from the Arts Center MARTA station. A five-minute film in the America Room Theater sets the stage for exploring the meaning of patriotism before viewing the exhibits. Adults $6, seniors $4, children younger than 6 and active military free.

✏ 🎨 ♿ **The William Breman Jewish Heritage Museum** (404-873-1661; www.thebreman.org), 1440 Spring Street. Open 10–5 Monday through Thursday, 10–3 Friday, 1–5 Sunday; closed Saturdays and most Jewish and many secular holidays. The largest museum of its kind in the Southeast, this repository explores Atlanta's Jewish history from 1845 to the present through exhibits of everyday items. There is also an exhibit on the Holocaust and survivors who live in Georgia, a hands-on Discovery Center for children, educational programs, and genealogical archives. Adults $10, seniors $6, children 3–6 $2.

✏ 🎨 ♿ **World of Coca-Cola Museum** (404-676-5151; 1-800-676-COKE; www.woccatlanta.com), 55 Martin Luther King Jr. Drive. Open 9–5 Monday

WORLD OF COCA-COLA MUSEUM

through Saturday (until 6 June through August), 11–5 Sunday. Last admission one hour prior to closing. Reservations strongly recommended. The story of Coca-Cola— from its development as an 1886 drugstore drink to its current position as a worldwide phenomenon—is told through exhibits of 1,000 items of memorabilia, classic ads, and a representation of the bottling process. Adults $7, seniors $5, children 6–11 $4.

NATURAL BEAUTY SPOTS The **Chattahoochee River** skirts the western side of Buckhead in the metro region as it stretches from Lake Lanier north of Atlanta, through the city and its suburbs on its 542-mile course to Apalachicola Bay, Florida. The river corridor is one of America's premier urban greenways—a wild oasis within the metropolis. Because the river is not navigable and doesn't flow through downtown, the waterway and the land surrounding it create one of metro Atlanta's best-kept secrets. It was due to former President Jimmy Carter, a Democrat, and former Speaker of the House Newt Gingrich, a Republican—two Georgians whose outlook about many issues could hardly be more dissimilar— that this section of the river was designated the **Chattahoochee River National Recreation Area** (see *Green Space—Recreation Areas*). The 6,500-acre, 14-unit recreation area is the most popular of Georgia's 10 National Park Service units, welcoming more than 3 million visitors annually. Its parks contain more than 900 species of plants, old- and new-growth hardwood forests, 20 species of fish, and numerous other animal species. The park is a popular escape from the city for those who enjoy hiking, fishing, boating, and other outdoor pursuits. One of the most popular activities is "shooting the 'Hooch"—floating down the river on a raft on a hot summer day.

❋ To Do

BICYCLING You can rent bikes from Skate Escape in Midtown (see entry), but there are no rentals downtown or in Buckhead. **MARTA** (see *Getting Around*) allows bicycles on all its trains, and there are bike racks on the front of some buses (the racks handle only two bikes at a time). Many MARTA stations have bike racks for commuters who wish to cycle to the bus or train.

PATH Foundation (404-875-7284; www.pathfoundation.org), mailing address: P.O. Box 14327, Atlanta 30324. The foundation has been instrumental in developing bike paths throughout the metro area. The Atlanta–DeKalb

Greenway Trail System includes the **Freedom Parkway Trail.** The east-west section, with its switchbacks and straightaways, was an immediate hit with cyclists, joggers, in-line skaters, and strollers. The 3.3-mile **Chastain Park Trail** is one of PATH's most popular trails.

SKATE ESCAPE (404-892-1292 www.skatescape.com), 1086 Piedmont Ave., NE at 12th Street, Atlanta 30309. Open daily 11–7. Located across the street from Piedmont Park, the company rents bikes, in-line skates, or roller skates that can be enjoyed in the park. Conventional or in-line skates can be rented for $5 per hour or $15 per day. Single-speed and children's bikes can be rented for $6 per hour, $25 per day.

BIRDING See the Chattahoochee River National Recreation Area under *Green Space—Recreation Areas.*

BOATING The **Chattahoochee River** provides numerous opportunities year-round for canoeing and kayaking, as well as motorboating and other small-boat use. Boating is allowed from sunrise to sunset; night boating is not permitted, nor are Jet Skis. No boat rentals are available in the park. Consult the web site at www.nps.gov/chat for information about nearby outfitters who rent equipment.

CANOEING AND TUBING An approximate float-time chart for seven possible canoe trips can be found in the **Chattahoochee River National Recreation Area** brochure (see *Green Space—Recreation Areas*).

CARRIAGE RIDES ✎ **Amen Carriage Company** (404-653-0202), office at 290 Martin Luther King Jr. Drive, Unit 7A; carriage stands at Peachtree Street and International Boulevard and at Centennial Olympic Park and International Boulevard. Available 6 PM –1 AM weekday evenings, noon–1 AM weekends, except during exceptionally hot weather when it is dangerous for the horses to be out. These romantic carriage rides cover most of historical downtown and Centennial Olympic Park. Adults $25, children $10.

FISHING The **Chattahoochee River** is the southernmost habitat in the United States for trout. The state stocks the river with rainbow, brook, and brown trout, so fishing along the river's banks or from small boats is a popular activity. Several fishing outfitters, instructors, and guides are available for hire. A Georgia fishing license and trout stamp are required. There are special regulations along three sections of the river, so it's best to check ahead before planning to fish (consult the web site at www.nps.gov/chat). Night fishing is not allowed.

FOR FAMILIES ✎ ⚿ ♿ **Turner Field–Ivan Allen Jr. Braves Museum and Hall of Fame** (404-614-2311; www.bravesmuseum.com), 755 Hank Aaron Drive. Open 9–3 Monday through Saturday, 1–3 Sunday; open 9–noon on game days. No tours on the afternoons of home games. Located at Turner Field and named for a former mayor rather than a baseball player, the museum contains 500 Braves artifacts, which trace the team's 130-plus-year history, from its begin-

LUN LUN AND YANG YANG, GIANT PANDAS ON LOAN FROM CHINA, FROLIC AT ZOO ATLANTA.

ning in Boston (1871–1952) to Milwaukee (1953–1965) to Atlanta (1966–present). The Hall of Fame honors the careers of 15 Braves legends. Included in the tour of the stadium are stops at a luxury suite, the terrace and service levels, and the press box and broadcast booth (see **Turner Field Tours** under *To See—Guided Tours*). Tour price: adults $10, children $5.

✦ ♿ **Zoo Atlanta** (404-624-5600; 1-888-945-5432; www.zooatlanta.org), 800 Cherokee Avenue SE. Open 9:30–4:30 daily, until 5:30 on weekends during daylight-saving time. Gates close one hour prior to closing. Zoo Atlanta, one of the 10 oldest, continuously operating zoos in the nation, is located in the historic Grant Park neighborhood. More than 700 animals representing 200 species from all over the world roam freely in habitats such as an Asian rain forest and an African savanna. The most popular stars right now are Lun Lun and Yang Yang, adorable giant pandas on loan from China. Not to be upstaged, however, is the outstanding primate collection, the largest in the country, which includes gorillas and orangutans. Keeper talks, training demonstrations, wildlife shows, and animal feedings are other popular activities. Adults $16.50, seniors $12.50, children $11.50.

GOLF ✦ ♞ **Bobby Jones Golf Course at Atlanta Memorial Park** (404-355-1009), 384 Woodward Way. Open sunrise to sunset daily. The 18-hole, par-71 course is well suited to any level of play. The course meanders through beautiful neighborhoods and along Peachtree Creek and boasts two clubhouses. $35 Monday through Thursday, $42.50 Friday through Sunday; seniors $20 Monday through Thursday, $25 Friday through Sunday.

✦ ♞ **Candler Park Golf Course** (404-371-1260), 585 Candler Park Drive. Open 8–6:30 daily. The nine-hole, 2,064-yard, par-31 course provides a rare opportunity for in-town golfing. Built in 1928, it was once the private course of Coca-Cola founder Asa Candler. A forest of pines and oaks bisects the course, and the terrain varies from flat to hilly, which creates challenges for all levels of players. $10.

🎾 **North Fulton Golf Course at Chastain Memorial Park** (404-255-0723), 216 West Wieuca Road. Open sunrise to sunset daily. Opened in 1939, the 18-hole, par-71 course features 6,570 yards of challenging play. The facility features a putting green, chipping area, pro shop, snack bar, club and cart rentals, and pro instruction. Residents, $32 Monday through Thursday, $37 Friday through Sunday; nonresidents, $37 Monday through Thursday, $40 Friday through Sunday. Discounts available for seniors.

TENNIS 🎾 🎾 **Bitsy Grant Tennis Center at Atlanta Memorial Park** (404-609-7193), 2125 Northside Drive. Open 9–9 weekdays, 9–6 Saturday and Sunday. Named for tennis star Bryan M. "Bitsy" Grant, who was a dynamo on the court despite his 5-foot-4-inch frame, the complex offers 13 clay courts (open 9–8 daily) and 10 hard courts (open 9–9 daily). The center is also home to the **Georgia Tennis Hall of Fame.** $2.50–3.25 an hour for hard courts; $4–5 an hour for clay courts; seniors $3.25 for either; 50¢ extra for lighted night play.

🎾 🎾 **Chastain Memorial Park Tennis Center** (404-255-1993), 110 West Wieuca Road. Open 9–9 weekdays, 9–6 Saturday, 10–6 Sunday. The park features nine tennis courts. $2.50 before 5, $3 after 5 and on weekends, free for those younger than 18. (For more information about the park, see *Green Space—Nature Preserves and Parks.*)

❋ Green Space

GARDENS 🎾 🎾 ⟨ **Atlanta Botanical Garden** (404-876-5859; www.atlanta botanicalgarden.org), 1345 Piedmont Avenue NE. Open 9–7 Tuesday through Sunday, April through September; 9–6 Tuesday through Sunday, October through March. This tranquil 30-acre oasis bordering Piedmont Park (see *Nature Preserves and Parks)* has something blooming year-round in annual, dwarf conifer, fragrance, herb, ornamental grass, perennial, rose, spring and summer bulb, vegetable, and vine arbor gardens. The **Dorothy Chapman Fuqua Conservatory and Fuqua Orchid Center** overflows with exotic tropical plants, including lowland orchids, while Desert House showcases endangered succulents. Throughout the year, the garden sponsors festivals, flower and plant shows, demonstrations, plant sales, and social events such as "Cocktails in the Garden" and concerts on the lawn. Adults $12, seniors $9, children $7.

🎾 🎾 ⟨ **Atlanta History Center** (404-814-4000; www.atlantahistorycenter.com), 130 West Paces Ferry Road NW. Open 10–5:30 Monday through Saturday, noon–5:30 Sunday; last ticket sold at 4:30. See the Japanese maples and U.S. and Asian species in the Cherry-Sims Asian-American Garden; azaleas and rhododendrons in the Frank A. Smith Rhododendron Garden; native plants and wildflowers in the Mary Howard Gilbert Memorial Quarry Garden; formal boxwoods, fountains, and statuary in the Swan House Gardens; the sculpture *The Peach Tree* in the Garden of Peace on the Swan Woods Trail; and the gardens and cotton patch at the **Tullie Smith Farm**. For the serious gardener, the center's Cherokee Garden Library houses more than 3,000 books and periodicals about gardening. Adults $12, seniors and students older than 13 $10, children 4–12 $7.

✏ 🏛 ♿ **Jimmy Carter Presidential Library and Museum** (404-865-7100; www.cartercenter.org), 441 Freedom Parkway. Open 9–4:45 Monday through Saturday, noon–4:45 Sunday. Outside the facility (see *To See—Museums*) there is a 2,500-square-foot rose garden with 80 varieties, a wildflower meadow, and a tranquil Japanese garden with two waterfalls. Cherry trees blossom in the spring. Adults $7, seniors $5, children younger than 16 free.

✏ 🏛 ♿ **Robert L. Stanton Rose Garden** (404-378-4311; www.fernbank.edu), 767 Clifton Road NE, Atlanta. Open daylight hours Tuesday through Sunday. This beautiful garden is located on the grounds of the Fernbank Museum of Natural History but maintained by the Fernbank Science Center (see *To See— Museums*). The garden is named in honor of Robert L. Stanton, who first established a rose garden at the museum in 1983. A trained horticulturist and employee of the science center, Stanton had a lifelong interest in roses and was a consulting rosarian. His interest in educating the public about roses and his realization that there was no test site in Atlanta led to the establishment of this garden. Today the garden contains more than 1,000 rosebushes (the rose garden in Thomasville, "the Rose City," has only 500). The Stanton garden tests regular roses and devotes another garden to testing miniature roses. Free.

NATURE PRESERVES AND PARKS ✏ 🏛 ♿ **Centennial Olympic Park** (404-223-4412; 404-222-PARK for recorded message; www.centennialpark.com), 265 Park Avenue NW. Open 7 AM–11 PM daily. This 21-acre park is the living legacy of the 1996 Centennial Olympic Summer Games. Features of the park include gigantic lighted columns, Quilt Plaza, Centennial Plaza, the visitor center, water

A CHILD COOLS OFF IN THE FOUNTAIN OF RINGS IN ATLANTA'S CENTENNIAL OLYMPIC PARK.

CENTENNIAL OLYMPIC PARK TRIVIA
• Some 800,000 bricks were used in the park. Laid end to end, they would stretch 100 miles, from Turner Field to Columbus, Georgia.
• The person-hours required to complete the park are equivalent to one person working full time for 100 years.
• Granite from each of the five continents represented by the Olympic Games was used in the park.
• Each of the five Olympic rings in the fountain is 25 feet in diameter—large enough to park two cars side by side.

gardens, sculptures, lawns, and playgrounds, but few trees—all connected by walkways laid with bricks donated by local citizens to help pay for the park. The highlight of the park is the gigantic Fountain of Rings, the largest interactive depiction of the Olympic logo in the world. During the warm-weather months, different heights of water spurt out of 250 jets in the ground and invite the young and young-at-heart to jump in and get wet. An hourly dancing water show is set to music. Even in balmy Atlanta, modern technology makes it possible to have an outdoor ice-skating rink at Christmastime, when the park is aglitter with a holiday lights display. Free.

✨ 🐾 ♿ **Chastain Memorial Park** (404-255-0863), 135 West Wieuca Road. Open daily. The Buckhead park boasts nine tennis courts, seven ball fields, a swimming pool, 18-hole golf course, gymnasium with basketball court, weight facility, the Chastain Arts and Crafts Center, stables, a new state-of-the-art children's playground, an amphitheater (see *Entertainment—Music*), and a 3.3-mile circuit for jogging, bicycling, and walking (see *To Do—Bicycling*). Access to the 158-acre city park is free; some activities have a fee.

✨ 🐾 ♿ **Grant Park.** The 131-acre green space and recreational area in the center of the Grant Park Historic District was a gift to the city from Colonel Lemuel P. Grant, the district's earliest settler. Today the park boasts a beautiful lake, numerous springs, playgrounds and picnicking facilities, the **Atlanta Cyclorama and Civil War Museum** (see *To See—Museums*), and **Zoo Atlanta** (see *To Do—For Families*). Park and its attractions are free.

✨ 🐾 ♿ **Piedmont Park** (404-875-7275; www.piedmontpark.org), 14th Street and Piedmont Road. Open 6 AM–11 PM daily. Entrances at Park Drive Bridge, Charles Allen Drive Gate, 12th Street Gate, and 14th Street Gate in Midtown. Known and utilized as Atlanta's backyard for more than 100 years, Piedmont Park was created for the 1895 Cotton States and International Exposition. Today the 180-acre park with tiny Lake Clara Meer attracts cyclists, joggers, picnickers, rollerskaters, and walkers. In addition, the park features tennis courts, softball fields, a swim center, playgrounds, 0.7- to 1.7-mile walking loops, and a community garden. The city's most popular park also hosts festivals and special events. During the year the park is the scene of the **Atlanta Dogwood Festival** (see *Special Events*), **Screen on the Green** film festival, **Atlanta Jazz Festival** (see

Special Events), **Atlanta Pride Festival,** and **Peachtree Road Race.** The **Park Tavern Restaurant** and **Willy's Mexicana Grill** anchor the two ends of the park. Adjacent to the park is the **Atlanta Botanical Garden** (see *Gardens*). All entrances and most areas are wheelchair accessible. With all these attractions, there is one drawback: The park has very little parking. Free admission to Atlanta Botanical Garden.

RECREATION AREAS ✅ ❀ **Chattahoochee River National Recreation Area, East and West Palisades Unit.** The headquarters for the park is in Dunwoody at the **Island Ford Unit** (678-538-1200; www.nps .gov/chat), 1978 Island Ford Parkway. The Palisades Unit, accessible from Northside Parkway at the Chattahoochee River, is the only unit physically within Buckhead. Open daily. The 50-acre unit features hiking, fishing, boating, tubing, picnicking, bird-watching, wildlife observation, and swimming. $3 parking fee.

❋ Lodging
BED & BREAKFASTS

In Ansley Park
⅙ **Ansley Inn Bed and Breakfast** (404-872-9000; 1-800-446-5416; www .ansleyinn.com), 253 15th Street NE. This boutique hostelry is an elegant and beautifully restored 1907 English Tudor mansion with exquisite furnishings and decorative accents. The inn has taken this wonderful home and created a residential flavor with the luxury and service of top-class hotels. Each sumptuous guest room in the main house features a whirlpool tub, and some boast a gas-log fireplace. A real plus in Midtown is free off-street parking, so you can leave your car here and walk to many attractions. Smoking outdoors only. Wheelchair accessible in one room on the first floor. $160–250 in the main house; $120–175 in the annex. Ask about the $99 weekday special offered Sunday through Thursday night.

Shellmont Inn (404-872-9290; www .shellmont.com), 821 Piedmont Avenue NE. The Shellmont is an exquisitely restored 1891 National Register mansion. Outstanding architectural features include stained, beveled, and leaded glass; curved and bow windows; intricately carved woodwork; coved ceilings; and hand-painted stenciling. Public areas and guest rooms are furnished with antiques, Oriental carpets, and period wall treatments. Wicker-filled verandas overlook lawns, gardens, and a Victorian fish pond. Smoking outdoors only. Not wheelchair accessible. $125–250.

In Buckhead
⅙ **Beverly Hills Inn** (404-233-8520; 1-800-331-8520; www.beverlyhills inn.com), 65 Sheridan Drive. This simple, unassuming but cozy European-style inn attracts a clientele that's 35 percent international. Each guest chamber features antique furnishings, a balcony, hardwood floors, and a kitchen, which makes the inn particularly appealing for a long-term stay. Two nonsmoking rooms. $99–165.

In Inman Park
1890 King-Keith House Bed and Breakfast (404-688-7330; 1-800-728-3879; www.kingkeith.com), 889 Edgewood Avenue NE. The opulent

Queen Anne–style King-Keith House, one of the most photographed houses in Atlanta, is characterized by 12-foot ceilings, carved fireplaces, spacious rooms, stained-glass windows, and period antiques. Accommodations include rooms, suites, and a private cottage with a Jacuzzi tub for two. Guests enjoy elegant public spaces, private gardens, complimentary snacks and beverages, and a full gourmet breakfast. $95–180.

🌸 **Heartfield Manor** (404-523-8633; www.inmanpark.org/heart.html), 1882 Elizabeth Street NE. This 1903 Craftsman cottage features a two-story entrance with a grand balcony, stained-glass windows, and wainscoting. All rooms and suites are furnished with period pieces. Some guest accommodations offer a full kitchen; some have a small refrigerator and microwave. No smoking. Not wheelchair accessible. $55–85.

Sugar Magnolia Bed and Breakfast (404-222-0226; www.sugar magnoliabb.com), 804 Edgewood Avenue NE. Accommodations are offered in a magnificent, well-preserved Queen Anne–Victorian mansion. Built in 1892, the house is embellished with gables, ornate chimneys, whimsical turrets, and an inviting wraparound porch. The inside is characterized by 12-foot ceilings, a grand staircase, six fireplaces, beveled glass, and hand-painted plasterwork. Smoking outdoors only. Not wheelchair accessible. $95–135.

In Virginia-Highland
Gaslight Inn Bed & Breakfast (404-875-1001; www.gaslightinn.com), 1001 St. Charles Avenue NE. Built in 1913, this Craftsman home actually has some flickering gaslight fixtures. A variety of accommodations—located in the Primary Residence, the Carriage House, and the Victorian Cottage—range from affordable guest rooms to luxurious suites. Some rooms and suites feature a fireplace, double whirlpool tub, private garden, or kitchen. Another plus to staying at this B&B is that it's within easy walking distance of the shops and restaurants of Virginia-Highland. Smoking is permitted only outdoors. Not wheelchair accessible. $115–215; ask about numerous packages. Two-night minimum required on weekends.

Virginia-Highland Bed and Breakfast (404-892-2735; 1-877-870-4485; www.virginiahighlandbb.com), 630 Orme Circle NE. This restored 1920s Craftsman bungalow is nestled within a cottage garden, creating a true urban retreat. Guest rooms feature a queen- or king-sized bed, and some boast a whirlpool tub or a private entrance. The B&B is within walking distance of Highland Avenue shopping, dining, and entertainment. No smoking on the property. Not wheelchair accessible. $125 and up.

INNS AND HOTELS

In Buckhead
🌿 ♿ **Grand Hyatt Atlanta** (404-237-1234; www.grandatlanta.hyatt.com), 3300 Peachtree Road NE. Recognized by AAA as a four-star hostelry, the Grand Hyatt is known for sumptuous accommodations, superior restaurants, exciting nightlife, and a solicitous staff. Other amenities include a heated outdoor pool, **Cassis** restaurant, and the **Onyx** lobby lounge. Smoking and nonsmoking rooms available. $189–275.

🌿 🍽 ♿ **InterContinental Buckhead** (404-946-9000; www.ichotels group.com), 3315 Peachtree Road

NE. This newly opened, swanky, five-star hotel features such amenities as in-room libraries, BOSE wave sound systems, marble baths, a pool, and a whirlpool. Its restaurant, **Au Pied de Cochon** (see *Where to Eat—Dining Out*) is the Les Frères Blanc food group's first U.S. venture. The hotel is adjacent to the Atlanta Financial Center and within easy walking distance of two upscale shopping malls, numerous restaurants, and the Buckhead MARTA station. Pets allowed. Most rooms nonsmoking. $149–379.

✍ ♿ **JW Marriott Buckhead Atlanta** (404-262-3344; 1-800-228-9290; www.marriotthotels.com/atljw), 3300 Lenox Road. This AAA four-diamond hotel is physically connected to Lenox Square mall, which certainly makes it a favorite with shoppers. It's also within easy walking distance of the Lenox MARTA station. The sophisticated hotel features 377 elegantly appointed rooms and four luxury suites. Smoking is permitted on the seventh floor, otherwise nonsmoking. $169–189 weekends, $299 weekdays; ask about special packages.

✍ ♿ **The Ritz-Carlton Buckhead** (404-237-2700; 1-800-241-3333; www.ritzcarlton.com), 3434 Peachtree Road. Ritz-Carlton is synonymous with unparalleled luxury and service, and this AAA five-diamond hotel, one of only three in Georgia, is always voted Atlanta's best. Accommodations are enhanced with ultraluxurious linens, rich upholstery, and marble baths. The swanky hotel features a swim and fitness center with an indoor heated lap pool, whirlpool, sauna, steam room, and weight machines. The hotel's five-star **Dining Room** (see *Where to Eat—Dining Out*) is the uncontested finest dining

experience in Atlanta, and the **Lobby Lounge** is the "in" place in Atlanta to spy visiting celebrities. The Ritz's afternoon tea, light tea, or royal tea are high-class affairs, and the hotel is known for imaginative room packages and fabulous holiday feasts. A jazz band plays in the Lobby Lounge Friday and Saturday nights. Smoking and nonsmoking rooms. $249 and up.

✍ ♿ **The Westin Buckhead Atlanta** (404-365-0065; 1-800-253-1397; www.westinbuckhead.com), 3391 Peachtree Road NE. Those who have been to Atlanta before will recognize this outstanding hotel as the former Swissotel. The AAA four-diamond property features breathtaking architecture and an outstanding expressionist art collection. The hotel is also the home of the famed the **Palm Restaurant** (see *Where to Eat—Dining Out*). The Westin is adjacent to Lenox Square mall and within easy walking distance of Phipps Plaza mall, two MARTA stations, and many highly rated restaurants. Smoking and nonsmoking rooms. Reserve in advance one of 17 rooms with adapted bathrooms. $250–375.

Downtown

✍ ♿ **Howard Johnson Plaza Hotel at Underground** (404-223-5555; www.suitehotel.com), 54 Upper Alabama Street. This intimate boutique hotel is adjacent to Underground Atlanta and the World of Coca-Cola, across the street from the MARTA Five Points rail station, and within walking distance of the Georgia Capitol and downtown shopping. The hotel occupies a converted turn-of-the-20th-century office building that has been transformed to offer one-bedroom suites with all the modern conveniences and luxuries. Smok-

ing and nonsmoking rooms available.
$89–159.

☞ ♿ **Omni Hotel at CNN Center**
(404-659-0000; 1-800-843-6664; www
.omnicnn.com), 100 CNN Center.
The AAA four-diamond hotel's downtown location and easy accessibility to
the MARTA rail system make it a
popular base of operations when visiting the city. Attached to the CNN
Center, the hotel has the advantage of
its restaurants, bars, shops, and movie
theaters. The hotel is adjacent to
Philips Arena, where scores of sporting events and concerts occur, and
across from the Georgia World Congress Center, Georgia Dome, and
Centennial Olympic Park. Smoking
and nonsmoking rooms available.
$289 and up.

☞ ♿ **The Ritz-Carlton Atlanta**
(404-659-0400; 1-888-241-3333; www
.ritz-carlton.com), 181 Peachtree
Street NE. Ritz-Carltons are world-
renowned for their not-to-be-topped
personal service, flawless facilities,
and superior dining. This AAA five-
diamond downtown Atlanta property
is no exception. The 25-story, 444-
room hotel is situated in the heart of
Downtown's business, finance, and
government district within walking
distance of many attractions, bars,
restaurants, shops, and a MARTA station. Gracious guest rooms and suites
have bay-window views of the downtown skyline. Exquisite dining is available at the **Atlanta Grill** (see *Where
to Eat—Dining Out*). Smoking and
nonsmoking rooms available. $400
and up.

☞ ♿ **Westin Peachtree Plaza** (404-
589-7424; 1-888-447-8159; www
.westin.com), 210 Peachtree Street
NW. The cylindrical-shaped hotel still
reigns as the best publicly accessible

place to get a view of Atlanta, not only
from guest rooms but also from its
revolving 73rd-floor **Sun Dial
Restaurant, Bar, and View** (see
Where to Eat—Dining Out). The
hotel's 1,000 rooms are furnished with
Westin's signature Heavenly Beds and
Heavenly Baths. Amenities include a
swimming pool, shops, a fitness center, 24-hour room service, and high-
speed Internet access in all rooms.
Smoking and nonsmoking rooms
available. $295–500.

In Midtown
♿ **Best Western Granada Suites**
(404-876-6100), 1302 West Peachtree
Street. This boutique hotel with a
Spanish hacienda feel occupies a historic property that began life in 1922
as an apartment building. Today it
offers guest rooms, suites, and a penthouse suite. In keeping with the
Spanish architecture, the intimate inn
wraps around a courtyard with a bubbling fountain. The lobby is decorated
with Spanish art and opulent Victorian-
era antiques. Smoking and nonsmoking rooms available. $89–259.

☞ ♿ **Four Seasons Hotel Atlanta**
(404-881-9898; www.fourseasons.com/
atlanta), 75 14th Street NE. All Four
Seasons Hotels are renowned for
incomparable personal service, outstanding amenities, elegant rooms and
suites, and wonderful restaurants. The
swanky AAA five-diamond Four Seasons Hotel Atlanta meets each of
these standards. For a room with a
view of both Downtown and Midtown, ask for an upper-level corner
Premier Room. The hotel's palatial
Romanesque indoor pool is Atlanta's
only saltwater pool, and its **Park 75
Restaurant** (see *Dining Out*) offers
gourmet meals. The hotel is located
in the heart of Midtown's arts district

and offers special packages in conjunction with the High Museum of Art, the Atlanta Symphony Orchestra, and other cultural institutions. Smoking and nonsmoking rooms available. Weekend packages start at $210.

♂ ♿ **Georgian Terrace Hotel** (404-897-1991; 1-800-651-2316; www .thegeorgianterrace.com), 659 Peachtree Street. Known as the Grande Dame of Peachtree Street, this stately 1911 hotel has numerous connections with *Gone with the Wind.* Margaret Mitchell met Harold Latham of Macmillan Publishing in the dining room to deliver her manuscript. In 1939, when the movie premiered in Atlanta, the stars of the film stayed here and attended gala parties. Today the hotel consists of the original 10-story building with marble floors, Palladian and French windows, spiral staircases, stained-glass skylights, intricate plaster moldings, crystal chandeliers, elegant latticework, and large murals. A stunning atrium connects a modern 19-story wing to the original building. Accommodations, which are offered in standard rooms and junior to three-bedroom suites, feature antique-style furnishings, "dream" beds, and large bathrooms. Suites boast a living-dining area, a fully appointed kitchen, and even a washer and dryer. Other amenities include the elegant **Savoy Bar & Grill** and a fitness center. On the roof is a junior Olympic-sized pool with a sweeping view of downtown Atlanta. The hotel is located directly across the street from the Fox Theatre and a block from the North Avenue MARTA rail station. Smoking and nonsmoking rooms available. Getaway packages start at $154.

♿ **Georgia Tech Hotel and Conference Center** (404-347-9440; www .gatechhotel.com), 800 Spring Street. Located in the university's new Technology Square complex, this high-tech, upscale hotel offers 252 comfortable guest rooms, each with a flat-screen television, marble bath with upgraded amenities, and cutting-edge technology. The hotel also offers a full-service club lounge with limited menu service from 3 PM to midnight, a lobby bar, advanced fitness center, indoor swimming pool, and concierge service. Technology Square features retail stores, restaurants, a day spa, and restaurants. Smoking and nonsmoking rooms available. $159–209.

♂ ♿ 🐾 **Hotel Indigo-Atlanta Midtown** (404-874-9200; www.ichotels group.com), 683 Peachtree Street NE. This trendy boutique hotel is located in a historic building across the street from the Fox Theatre. Plush bedding, area rugs on hardwood floors, spa-inspired baths, and a seashore theme make it a standout. The hotel also features the **Golden Bean** bar and restaurant, self-service laundry facilities, and a health and fitness center. Pets are allowed. In fact, from 5 to 8 on Tuesdays, guests and locals can have cocktails with their dogs (Poochy gets a bowl of ice water). A dollar from each cocktail goes to the **Piedmont Park** dog park (see *Green Space—Nature Preserves and Parks*). Smoking and nonsmoking rooms available. $119–200.

♂ ♿ 🐾 **Sheraton Colony Square Hotel** (404-892-6000; 1-800-422-7895; www.sheratoncolonysquare .com), 188 14th Street NE. Location, location, location—this hotel is across from the High Museum of Art and the Woodruff Arts Center. It's also within very easy walking distance of

Piedmont Park, the Atlanta Botanical Garden, and the Arts Center MARTA rail station. Guest rooms feature the plush Sheraton Sweet Sleeper Bed (the hotel even has comparable cribs for babies and beds for dogs), rainforest showerheads, and high-speed Internet access. Hotel amenities include the **14th Street Bar and Grill,** the **Lobby Lounge,** a Starbucks coffee kiosk, an outdoor pool (open seasonally), and a fitness center. Smoking and nonsmoking rooms available. $139 Sunday through Thursday, $119 Friday and Saturday.

In Poncey-Highland
✏ ♿ **Emory Conference Center Hotel** (404-712-6000; 1-800-933-6629; www.emoryconferencecenter .com), 1615 Clifton Road NE. The hotel, inspired by the architectural designs of Frank Lloyd Wright, provides a tranquil setting, contemporary elegance, spectacular landscapes, and exceptional service. Nestled on 28 acres of forest preserve on the university campus, it offers 197 beautifully appointed rooms, a full-service restaurant serving three meals daily, a lounge, an indoor pool, whirlpool, fitness center, putting green, and spa. No smoking. Many rooms wheelchair accessible. $160.

✏ ♿ **Emory Inn Atlanta Bed and Breakfast** (404-712-6000; 1-800-933-6629), 1641 Clifton Road. Located adjacent to the Emory Conference Center Hotel and connected to it by a covered walkway, this more intimate inn offers 107 guest rooms, complimentary continental breakfast, a restaurant open for lunch and dinner, and an outdoor pool and hydrotherapy pool available seasonally. Some smoking rooms. Many rooms wheelchair accessible. $110.

✏ ☛ ⛪ **The Highland Inn** (404-874-5756; www.thehighlandinn.com), 644 North Highland Avenue. This quaint hotel was built in the 1920s as the Wynne Hotel and Tea Room. Today it offers simple, affordable rooms and suites with Old World charm. In addition to being pet-friendly, the hotel has laundry facilities and offers continental breakfast. More than 60 restaurants are within walking distance. No smoking. Not wheelchair accessible. $69.95–105.95.

✽ **Where to Eat**
DINING OUT

In Buckhead
♿ **Anthony's Plantation Restaurant** (404-262-7379; www.anthonysfine dining.com), 3109 Piedmont Road. Open 5:30–9 Monday through Saturday. Located in an authentic 1797 Pope-Walton plantation house, Anthony's exudes Old South elegance. Twelve dining rooms, many with working fireplaces, are sumptuously furnished with 18th-century pieces. Anthony's serves a variety of beef, buffalo, duck, game, pork, and seafood accompanied by excellent wines and to-die-for desserts. No smoking. Wheelchair accessible on the ground level. $18.95–35.95.

♿ **Aria** (404-233-7673; www.aria-atl .com), 490 East Paces Ferry Road. Open 6–10 Monday through Saturday. This upscale gourmet bistro, located in a historic house, specializes in slow-cooked food and organic produce. The sophisticated decor features unusual lighting and other flashy details. The lounge is sexy and the wine cellar table is one of the most romantic in town. Smoking in the bar only. $19–32.

♿ **Atlanta Fish Market** (404-262-3165; www.buckheadrestaurants.com), 265 Pharr Road NE. Open 11:30–11:30 Monday through Thursday, 11–midnight Friday and Saturday, 4–10 Sunday. Look for the gigantic 65-foot steel and copper spawning salmon outside this seafood restaurant. So fresh are the fish and seafood here that the menu is updated twice a day. In terms of sheer variety of seafood, including everything from oysters to stone crab to halibut, no other Atlanta restaurant can compare. No smoking. $19.50–38.

♿ **Au Pied de Cochon** (404-946-9070), 3315 Peachtree Road. Open 24/7. Located in the new InterContinental Hotel, the fancifully decorated restaurant is based on a Parisian brasserie open since 1946. The restaurant's menu ranges from signature pig's feet to foie gras to raw seafood trays to steaks. For a perfectly romantic tête-à-tête, try one of the private rooms curtained in red velvet. The restaurant's **XO** bar has an extensive selection of cognacs. No smoking. $9–26.

Bluepointe (404-237-9070; www.buckheadrestaurnts.com), 3455 Pharr Road. Open 11:30–2 weekdays; 5:30–10:30 Monday through Thursday, 5:30–11:30 Friday and Saturday, 5:30–10 Sunday. This restaurant features Pacific Rim cuisine. The scene is dramatic and glamorous, and there is an oyster and seafood bar as well as a sushi table. No smoking. Not wheelchair accessible. Lunch $9–14, dinner $17–39.

♿ **Bone's** (404-237-2663; www.bonesrestaurant.com), 3130 Piedmont Road. Open 11:30–2:30 Monday through Thursday; 5:30–10:30 Sunday through Thursday, 5:30–11:30 Friday and Saturday. This private-club-like steakhouse has been a meeting place for the powerful for many years. The old-boys-network ambience is characterized by huge steaks, stiff drinks, and big cigars. The wine list is extensive. No smoking. Limited wheelchair access from a side entrance. Lunch $9.95–16.95, dinner $24.95–39.95.

♿ **Buckhead Diner** (404-262-3336; www.buckheadrestaurants.com), 3073 Piedmont Road NE. Open 11:30–midnight Monday through Saturday, 10–10 Sunday. Pairing nostalgia and retro style, the glitzy, chrome, 1950s-style diner is no fast-food joint. Rather, it is a high-energy, upscale eatery where celebrities and other notables go to see and be seen. The American menu features chic comfort food such as sweet and sour calamari or veal meatloaf with wild mushrooms. No smoking. Lunch $8–15, dinner $12–25.

♿ **The Café at the Ritz-Carlton Buckhead** (404-237-2700; www.ritzcarlton.com), 3434 Peachtree Road. Open 6:30–11, 11:30–2:30, and 6–9 Monday through Saturday; 11–2:30 Sunday for brunch; afternoon tea at 2:30 and 3:30 Monday through Saturday. Of course, the fine dining outlet at the hotel is the Dining Room (see below), but the Café is almost as fine, earning four stars. No smoking. Fixed price $23 for breakfast and lunch; $25 and up for dinner; $30–40 for afternoon tea; Sunday brunch $58 for adults, $34 for children 6–12.

♿ **Canoe** (770-432-2663; www.canoeatl.com), 4199 Paces Ferry Road. Open 11:30–2 Monday through Saturday; 5:30–10 daily; 10:30–2:30 Sunday for brunch. Reservations required for dinner. This is one of the prettiest places in the metro area to dine. The Chattahoochee River just barely skirts the metro area, and this is one of the only restaurants located along its banks. In good weather the posh patio is the place to dine. Large windows overlooking the river and lush gardens are an acceptable substitute when the weather's less than ideal. The eclectic American menu features regional cuisine such as Vidalia spring onion soup, slow-roasted Carolina rabbit, and other delicacies. Try to visit Canoe for Sunday brunch, too. No smoking. Lunch $12.50–19.50, dinner $18–28.

& **Chops** (404-262-2675; www.buck headrestaurants.com), 70 West Paces Ferry Road. Open 11:30–2:30 weekdays; 5:30–11 Monday through Thursday, 5:30–midnight Friday and Saturday, 5:30–10 Sunday. This opulent surf-and-turf steakhouse is a longtime favorite with both locals and visitors. Not surprisingly, beef is heavily featured on the menu, but seafood is flown in fresh daily. At the lobster bar, you can feast on Savannah lump-crab cocktail or Chops's famous batter-fried lobster tail. Smoking in the bar only. $15–40.

& **The Dining Room at the Ritz-Carlton Buckhead** (404-237-2700; www.ritzcarlton.com), 3434 Peachtree Road. Open 6–9 Tuesday through Friday, 6–9:30 Saturday. Reservations required. Dine like royalty at one of Atlanta's finest restaurants, one of the very few in the city to earn five stars and diamonds. Located in the poshest hotel in the city, the restaurant's traditional decor sets an elegant backdrop for innovative gourmet cuisine created by French chef Bruno Menard. For a special occasion, splurge on the five-course menu with pairing wines. In this rarefied atmosphere, coats and ties for gentlemen and appropriate attire for ladies required. No smoking. $79–118.

& **Joël** (404-233-3500; www.joel restaurant.com), 3290 Northside Parkway. Open 11:30–2 Tuesday through Friday; 5:30–10 Monday through Thursday, 5:30–10:30 Friday and Saturday. This upscale brasserie is the brainchild of Joël Antunes, who once presided over the Dining Room at the Ritz-Carlton Buckhead. The cuisine blends rustic French flavors and highly sophisticated contemporary flavors. Smoking in the bar only. Lunch $6–8, dinner $19–38; fixed-price three-course dinner $39 (available weekdays only).

& **NAVA** (404-240-1984; www.buck headrestaurants.com), 3060 Peachtree Road. Open 11:30–2:30 and 5:30–11 weekdays, 5–11 Saturday, 5:30–10 Sunday. The cuisine is Southwestern with Native American and Latin influences. In addition to such dishes as enchiladas and tacos, the restaurant specializes in entrées such as sun corn-crusted snapper and cowboy-cut beef tenderloin. Unusual desserts include banana enchilada, Southwest *tres leches* slice, or apple-piñon empanada. Smoking in the bar only. $14.95–24.95.

& **New York Prime** (404-846-0644; www.newyorkprime.com), Monarch Tower, 3424 Peachtree Road NE, Suite 100. Open 5–11 Monday through Saturday, 5–10 Sunday. Jerry Greenbaum and his crew serve classic New York strip, bone-in rib steak, barrel-cut filet, and other favorites such as lamb, veal, and lobster with delicious sides and salads. Diners also enjoy the martini bar and live entertainment. No smoking. $19.50–58.50.

& **The Palm Restaurant** (404-814-1955; www.thepalm.com), Westin Hotel, 3391 Peachtree Road NE. Open 6:30–11 daily. The famous full-service restaurant specializes in beef, lobster, and surf-and-turf combinations as well as chops, veal, and other seafood. No smoking. $35–50.

&. **Pano's & Paul's** (404-261-3662; www.buckheadrestaurants.com), 1232 West Paces Ferry Road. Open 5:30–10:30 weekdays, 5–10 Saturday. For more than 20 years, this opulent restaurant has been attracting diners with an ever-evolving menu that is mostly American contemporary. Favorites such as Dover sole and fried lobster tails are always on the menu. Smoking in the lounge only. $24–44.

&. **Pricci** (404-237-2941; www.buck headrestaurants.com), 500 Pharr Road. Open 11:30–2:30 weekdays; 5–11 Monday through Saturday, 5–10 Sunday. A dramatic interior and a creative menu of classic Italian cuisine with a modern flair guarantee an unforgettable dining experience. Selections include sliced Italian meats and cheeses, antipasti, salads, pizza, pasta, risotto, fish, and meat. No smoking. $15–27.

&. **Prime** (404-812-0555; www.hereto serverestaurants.com), 3393 Peachtree Road, Lenox Square. Open 11–2:30 Monday through Saturday; 5–11 Monday through Saturday, 5–10 Sunday. Many celebrities frequent this upscale surf-and-turf steakhouse, which offers steaks, seafood (including sushi), and even vegetarian options. Smoking in the bar only. $17–35.

&. **Twist** (404-869-1191; www.hereto serverestaurants.com), Phipps Plaza, 3500 Peachtree Road. Open 4–10 Sunday and Monday, 4–11 Tuesday through Thursday, 4–midnight Friday and Saturday. Tom Catherall is a legendary chef in Atlanta. His hand-picked team of professionals creates innovative tapas, wraps, snacks, sushi,

and other finger food, as well as a few entrées and delicious desserts. Smoking allowed. $4–29.

Downtown

&. **Atlanta Grill** (404-659-0400), 181 Peachtree Street NE. Open 6:30–2:30 and 5:30–10 daily; Sunday brunch 11–2:30. Located in the Ritz-Carlton, this upscale AAA four-diamond restaurant offers Southern-inspired cuisine in a clublike atmosphere. Smoking in the lounge only. $15–35.

&. **City Grill** (404-524-2489; www .citygrillatlanta.com), 50 Hurt Plaza at Edgewood Avenue. Open 11:30–2 weekdays; 5–10 Monday through Saturday; pre-show menu 5–6:30 Monday through Saturday. This beautiful classical building was once a bank, and diners may feel as though they need to take out a loan to pay for the $60–90 prix fixe dinner, so save this swanky, sophisticated restaurant for a special occasion. The imaginative Southern cuisine might feature sweetbreads, escargot, quail, seafood, lamb, veal, duck, beef, or pork with suitable accompaniments. Nonsmoking. Reservations strongly suggested. Gentlemen should wear a coat and ladies should dress appropriately. Lunch $9–19, dinner $14–32; pre-show menu $25 for two courses, $30 for three courses.

&. **Nikolai's Roof** (404-221-6362; www.nikolaisroof.com), 255 Courtland Street NE. Open 6–11 Monday through Saturday. Located atop the Atlanta Hilton, this restaurant is the Fabergé jewel among the city's restaurants, being the first eatery downtown to earn a four-star rating. Russian influences are seen in the depictions of Fabergé eggs that adorn the gold-rimmed service plates, the waiters dressed in red Imperial Russian uniforms, the ambience, and twists to the French-continental menu. Entrées include beef, seafood, duck, and even wild boar. The extensive wine list features more than 400 wine labels. Service is especially attentive. Smoking is permitted in the adjacent Point of View Lounge, but not in the restaurant. Restaurant is wheelchair accessible; rest rooms are not. Reservations are required, as are a jacket and tie for gentlemen. Average entrée $60; fixed price for two-course meal $95, three-course meal $99 (neither includes wine).

&. **Prime Meridian** (404-818-4450), 100 CNN Center. Open 6:30–11, 11:30–2:30, and 5:30–11:30 daily. The restaurant's location in the Omni Hotel at CNN Center provides views of Centennial Olympic Park and the downtown skyline. Fine continental cuisine is blended with local and regional specialties. Smoking in the bar only. $4–6.50 for breakfast, $6–13 for lunch, $20–34 for dinner.

&. **Ruth's Chris Steak House** (404-223-6500; 1-800-544-0808; www .ruthschris.com/locations/atlanta steakhouse.html), 267 Marietta Street, Centennial Park. Open 11–11. Located in the Embassy Suites Hotel overlooking Centennial Olympic Park, the Atlanta incarnation of the world-famous restaurant chain serves aged USDA prime steaks as well as seafood and other favorites accompanied by an exceptional wine list and classic desserts. Smoking in the bar only. $41–80.

&. **Sun Dial Restaurant, Bar, and View** (404-589-7506; www.sundial restaurant.com), 210 Peachtree Street NW. Open 11:30–2:30 daily; 6–11 Sunday through Thursday, 6–11:30 Friday, 5:30–11:30 Saturday. This trilevel revolving complex atop the Westin Peachtree Plaza hotel offers superb views of downtown as well as exquisite cuisine in the restaurant and wonderful jazz by the Mose Davis Trio in the bar. Visitors who are not customers of the restaurant or lounge may ride the glass elevators to the View level for $5. No smoking. Lunch $10–17, dinner $26–36.

In Midtown

&. **Bacchanalia** (404-365-0410; www .starprovisions.com/bacc), 1198 Howell Mill Road NW. Open 11:30–1:30 Wednesday through Saturday; 6–9:30 Monday through Saturday. One of the top restaurants in the city and certainly one of the most romantic, Bacchanalia serves lunch and an impeccable four-course, prix fixe dinner. Suave glamour is achieved in an old warehouse space where chef-spouses Clifford Harrison and Anne Quatrano blend cultural traditions as diverse as Californian nouvelle cuisine and continental European dishes. No smoking. Lunch, $22, dinner $65.

&. **Einstein's** (404-876-7925; www .einsteinsatlanta.com), 1077 Juniper Street NE. Open 11–11 Monday through Thursday, 11–midnight Friday, 10–midnight Saturday, 10–11 Sunday; bar open one hour past closing. Einstein's occupies a couple of bungalows just blocks from the arts district. Lunch and dinner choices range from salads and special sandwiches such as the jerk chicken or portobello and Brie melt to salads and hearty fare such as steaks and chops. Brunch runs the gamut from French toast to steak and eggs. In good weather, dine outside on the tree-shaded patio, which has earned the restaurant the Best Outdoor Dining Experience in Atlanta from *Creative Loafing*. Smoking in the bar only. Lunch and dinner $4–17, brunch $7–18.

&. **Midcity Cuisine** (404-888-8700; www.midcitycuisine.com), 1545 Peachtree Street. Open 11:30–2:30 weekdays; 5–11 Monday through Thursday, 5–midnight Friday and Saturday, 5–10 Sunday; 11–3 Sunday for brunch. Chef Shaun Doty, considered one of Atlanta's top chefs, operates this trendy but understated New American brasserie, which serves inspired, seasonally influenced specialties such as antipasto on crisp Sardinian flatbread or pork sausages and mash with Belgian beer sauce. The beautifully laid-out terrace is considered one of the most dramatic in Atlanta. Smoking at lunchtime on the patio only, at dinnertime in the bar and on the patio. Lunch $6–14, $16–18 for dinner; Sunday night all-you-can eat pizza for $10.

&. **Nan Thai Fine Dining** (404-870-9933; www.nanfinedining.com), 1350 Spring Street. Open 11–2:30 weekdays; 5:30–10 Monday through Thursday, 5:30–11 Friday, 5–11 Saturday, 5–10 Sunday. The decor in the soaring dining room follows the Thai zodiac. Cream banquettes, silk pillows in cream and mocha, and neutral carpet serve as a background for soaring red columns—and all of it combines to create a bold yet still understated look. Fancy ingredients such as lobster tail or lamb come in intricate presentations. The curries are especially noteworthy, and a chef's table at the exhibition kitchen provides a glimpse of culinary artistry. Smoking outdoors only. $31–50.

&. **Park 75 Restaurant** (404-253-3840; www.fourseasons.com/atlanta), 75 14th Street NE. Open 6:30–11 for breakfast, 11:30–2 for lunch, 3–4 for tea, and 5:30–10:30 for dinner Monday through Saturday; 7–10 for breakfast, 11–2 for brunch, and 3–4 for tea Sunday; afternoon tea reservations required 24 hours in advance. Located in the luxurious Four Seasons Hotel, the restaurant's ambience is a rich combination of styles and textures. What's more, it is described as "an opulent oasis and the best place in the world for Sunday brunch" by the Zagat restaurant survey. Park 75 is one of only two restaurants in Georgia to receive a *Mobil Travel Guide* four-star rating. The New American cuisine is considered culinary art, from the sea scallops Rockefeller to the rack of spring meadow lamb. Smoking in the lounge only. Reservations suggested for all meals. Breakfast or lunch $15–30, dinner $28–60, brunch $42, afternoon tea $21.

South City Kitchen (404-873-7358; www.southcitykitchen.com), 1144 Crescent Avenue NE. Open 11–3:30 daily; 5–11 Monday through Thursday, 5–midnight Friday and Saturday, 5–10 Sunday. The restaurant is located in a renovated historic home near the Woodruff Arts Center and High Museum of Art. Not a faithful restoration, this remodeling involved gutting and opening up the interior to result in a sleek, steel-and-glass look with an open kitchen and a long, snazzy bar. Billed as "where the low country meets the high-rises," the South City Kitchen serves imaginative, nouvelle Southern cuisine with low country and Southwestern influences. Some specialties include Charleston she-crab soup, buttermilk fried chicken, and grilled Georgia mountain trout. When the weather's warm and breezy, outdoor dining is popular. Smoking in the bar and on the patio only. Wheelchair accessible on the patio and ground floor; restrooms not wheelchair accessible. Lunch $6–15, brunch $8–15, dinner $14–25.

& **Veni Vidi Vici** (404-875-8424; www.buckheadrestaurants.com), 41 14th Street. Open 11:30–11 Monday through Thursday, 11:30–midnight Friday, 5–midnight Saturday, 5–10 Sunday. Reservations recommended. This northern Italian restaurant is the only fine dining establishment we know of that's located in a parking garage. The restaurant, situated on the ground floor with a small outdoor area, is convenient to many of Midtown's soaring skyscrapers as well as to the Robert W. Woodruff Arts Center, making it perfect for pre-performance dining. Sleek and sophisticated inside, Veni Vidi Vici serves entrées such as calves' liver, salmon, lamb, and veal and rotisserie specialties such as suckling pig and roasted young rabbit. Outdoor seating is available in good weather. No smoking. Entrées $13–18; full meal about $48.

In Virginia-Highland

& **Babette's** (404-523-9121; www .babettescafe.com), 573 North Highland Avenue. Open 5:50–10 Tuesday through Saturday, 5–9 Sunday; 10:30–2 Sunday for brunch. Babette's is a combination farmhouse and bistro located between Inman Park and Poncey-Highlands. Chef-owner Marla Adams creates dishes according to the seasons. The cuisine is a little French, Italian, Spanish, and Mediterranean. Smoking in the bar only. Wheelchair accessible from a ramp on the side. Dinner entrées $14.50–23.75; brunch $5.75–13.50.

Sotto Sotto (404-523-6678; www .sottosottorestaurant.com), 313 North Highland Avenue. Open 5:30–11

Monday through Thursday, 5:30– midnight Friday and Saturday. This smashing Italian restaurant attracts a high-profile crowd to dine on a wide variety of antipasti and pasta. Check to see if one of the monthly "Tour of Italy" dinners is scheduled during your visit. Valet and street parking available. Nonsmoking area. Limited wheelchair accessibility. À la carte entrées $14–24; Chef's Choice three-, four-, or five-course dinners $35–55.

EATING OUT

In Buckhead

🍴 🍷 & **Café Intermezzo** (404-355-0411; www.cafeintermezzo.com), 1845 Peachtree Road NE. Open 10:30 AM–3 AM daily. The Viennese-style café has a full menu of small plates, large plates, soups, salads, and sandwiches. But after a night out on the town attending the symphony or a play, it's a great place to stop in for a nightcap or coffee and dessert accompanied by live entertainment. Choose from 100 pastries, tarts, cakes, pies, and cheesecakes, as well as scores of coffee drinks, teas, beers, wines, and other alcoholic beverages. Lunch available until 5 PM; dinner until late night. No smoking. Breakfast, $6–12, lunch $4–13, dinner and weekend brunch $6–15.

🍴 🍷 & **Eclipse di Luna** (404-846-0449; www.eclipsedeluna.com), 764 Miami Circle. Open 11:30–10 Tuesday through Thursday, 11:30–11 Friday and Saturday, 5–9:30 Sunday. Latin American-, Spanish-, and Brazilian-influenced cuisine is presented in small, tapas-sized portions. The artsy setting in an old warehouse creates a high-energy experience, as does the Sunday bottomless glass of sangria for $10. Live entertainment and a wine tasting on the first Tuesday of each month add to the ambience. No smoking. $2.25–5.

🍴 ♿ **Swan Coach House Restaurant, Gift Shop and Gallery** (404-261-0636; 404-261-4735; www.web guide.com/swancoach.html), 3130 Sloan Drive. Open 11–2:30 daily. Just to the rear of the Atlanta History Center and reached by a separate entrance is the grand coach house–garage of the sumptuous Swan House mansion (see **Atlanta History Center** under *To See—Museums*). Magnificently restored and exquisitely decorated, the carriage house is a favorite place for ladies who lunch as well as for couples and families. Dine on brunch items, soups, salads, sandwiches, and desserts. The carriage house also has an upscale gift shop. No smoking. $10–12.

In Candler Park

🔊 🍴 ♿ **Flying Biscuit Café** (404-687-8888; www.flyingbiscuit.com), 1655 McLendon Avenue. Open 7–10 Sunday through Thursday, 7–10:30 Friday and Saturday. Located in a cheerful and eclectically decorated Craftsman bungalow in the historic Candler Park neighborhood, the Flying Biscuit Café is the home of nonstop breakfast, but the eatery also serves lunch and dinner. Breakfast includes everything from eggs to smoked salmon, and dishes are always accompanied by the famous biscuits. Lunch items include salads, sandwiches, burgers, and more. Dinner choices include salmon, chicken, catfish, and pasta. At the bakery next door, diners can purchase biscuits to take out. No smoking. Breakfast $4.95–8.95, lunch $6.95–8.95, dinner $8.95–13.95.

Downtown

🔊 🍴 **Busy Bee Cafe** (404-525-9212; www.thebusybeecafe.com), 810 Martin Luther King Jr. Drive SW. Open 11–7 Sunday through Friday; closed Saturday. For more than 50 years, locals have flocked to this soul-food café for the "bee-licious" fried chicken, beef stew, and even chitlins, giblets, ham hocks, and neck bones. No smoking. Not wheelchair accessible. $7–9.

🔊 🍴 ♿ **Mary Mac's Tea Room** (404-876-1800; www.marymacs.com), 224 Ponce de Leon Avenue NE. Open 11–9 daily. A local favorite for more than 50 years, Mary Mac's is big on Southern hospitality and heaping helpings of comfort food. Diners pig out on fried chicken, chicken and dumplings, country-fried steak and gravy, fried catfish, meatloaf, turnip and other greens, fried green tomatoes, sweet potato soufflé, home-baked breads, banana pudding, bread pudding with wine sauce, and peach cobbler served with the table wine of the South: sweet tea. No smoking. Lunch $2–5.50, dinner $7.50–16.50.

In Little Five Points

🔊 🍴 ♿ **Front Page News** (404-475-7777; www.fpnnews.com), 351 Moreland Avenue NE. Open 11 AM–midnight Monday through Wednesday, 11 AM–1 AM Thursday, 11 AM–2 AM Friday, 10 AM–2 AM Saturday, 10 AM–midnight Sunday. If you're looking for Cajun flavor and drinks galore, this is the place to come. Walls are covered with front-page newspaper clippings, but the ambience is more New Orleans–like. Smoking and nonsmoking sections available. Entrées $7–20.

🍴 ♿ **The Vortex Bar and Grill** (404-688-1828; www.thevortexbarand

grill.com), 438 Moreland Avenue NE. Open 11 AM–midnight Sunday through Wednesday, 11 AM–3 AM Thursday through Saturday. The first hint a visitor has that this might not be a traditional restaurant is the giant skull with bulging eyes that creates the front of the building. Diners actually enter through the mouth of the skull. Once inside, they discover that this Atlanta institution serves high-quality pub food and a wide variety of alcoholic beverages. Smoking and nonsmoking sections. $8–10.

In Midtown

& **Atmosphere** (678-702-1620; www .atmospherebistro.com), 1620 Piedmont Avenue. Open 11:30–2:00 Saturday, 11:30–2:30 Sunday; 6–10 Tuesday through Thursday, 6–10:30 Friday. Reservations recommended on weekends. Located in a cottage near Ansley Mall, the French restaurant does bistro classics such as duck confit, escargot with white wine, rack of lamb, and salmon tartar, but don't decide what to order until you check out the specials. Smoking in the bar and on the patio only. $14–19.

& **Baraonda Café Italiano** (404-879-9962; www.baraondaatlanta.com), 710 Peachtree Street. Open 11–10:30 Monday through Thursday, 11–midnight Friday, 5–midnight Saturday, noon–10 Sunday. The house specialty is thin Euro-style pizzas baked in an authentic wood-brick oven. In addition to pizzas, the eatery serves antipasti, insalate, calzone, pasta, and secondi; substantial entrées include lamb chops, veal scaloppine, and fish of the day. On Monday nights, "Fifteen for $15" offers a selection of 15 wines for $15. A plus to dining here is that the restaurant is within walking distance of the Fox Theatre. Free

parking available at the Georgian Terrace Hotel, 659 Peachtree Street. Smoking in the bar only. Lunch $4–8.50, dinner $8–17.

& **Front Page News** (404-897-3500; www.fpnnews.com), 1104 Crescent Avenue. The presses start rolling at 11 AM for lunch or weekend brunch; the dinner edition goes until 11 PM. With its brick courtyard, 12-foot-tall cast-iron fountains, flickering gaslights, and lush foliage, it's very reminiscent of New Orleans French Quarter eateries. FPN serves newsworthy Cajun- and Creole-influenced food as well as burgers, po'boys, sandwiches, salads, and fish accompanied by microbrews, martinis, New Orleans–style Hurricanes, and other libations. Smoking only in the bar areas and on the patio downstairs. Lunch $6.95–10.95, dinner $10.95–16.95, brunch $6.95–9.95.

& **Joe's on Juniper** (404-875-6634; www.joesatlanta.com), 1049 Juniper Street NE. Open 11 AM–2 AM Monday through Saturday, 11–midnight Sunday; brunch until 3 PM Saturday and Sunday. A renovated historic cottage provides a home for Joe's, which purveys burgers, hot dogs, chili, soup, wings, munchies, salads, sandwiches, and desserts. The restaurant also serves brunch on weekends—here it is known as "blunch"—consisting of eggs Benedict, omelets, French toast, and other goodies. Smoking outside during the day and at the bar in the evening. $6.95–12.95, brunch $5.95–7.95.

& **ONE.midtown kitchen** (404-892-4111; www.onemidtownkitchen .com), 559 Dutch Valley Road. Open 5:30 PM–midnight Monday through Thursday, 5:30–1 AM Friday and Saturday, 5:30–10 Sunday. This hip eatery overlooking Piedmont Park attracts beautiful people, while the innovative and no-hype food focuses on the freshest ingredients and local products. No smoking. Less than $19.

✒ 🍴 ♿ **The Varsity** (404-881-1706; www.thevarsity.com), 61 North Avenue NW. Open 9 AM–11:30 PM Sunday through Thursday, 9 AM–12:30 AM Friday and Saturday. The Varsity started out back in 1928 as a hangout for Georgia Tech students, but grew to become the world's largest drive-in restaurant. The menu is topped with chili dogs, onion rings, fried pies, and the eatery's famous Frosted Orange drink but also includes burgers, BBQ, chicken salad, ham salad, fries, and coleslaw. Diners can enjoy the luxury of curb service or go inside, but know what you want—car hops and counter workers don't brook any lollygagging. After all, they have to keep things moving to dispense 2 miles of franks, 300 gallons of chili, 2,000 pounds of onions, and fried pies to 12,000 to 15,000 customers each day. Be sure to peruse the memorabilia and photos of all the famous people who've eaten here. No smoking. Wheelchair accessible downstairs. Under $5.

🍴 ♿ **Vickery's Crescent Avenue Bar and Grill** (404-881-1106; www .vickerysbarandgrill.com), 1106 Crescent Avenue NE. Open 11–11:30 weekdays (bar open until 1:30 AM), noon–1:30 AM Saturday (bar open until 2:30 AM), 11-11 Sunday (bar open until midnight). Vickery's was opened in 1983 by three guys and their dog as a place to get a stiff drink and a cheeseburger. Today the casual eatery serves a wide variety of appetizers, soups, salads, sandwiches, burgers, and substantial entrées such as salmon, ravioli, tenderloin medal-

lions, pork chops, and seafood. Brunch includes stratas, French toast, pancakes, crepes, and many egg dishes. Smoking in the bar and on the patio only. Wheelchair accessible through front gate. Dinner entrées $12–21, brunch $4.25–12.

In Virginia-Highland

🍴 ♿ **Atkins Park** (404-876-7249; www.atkinspark.com), 794 North Highland Avenue. Open 11 AM–3 AM Monday through Saturday, 11 AM– midnight Sunday. Atlanta's oldest continuously licensed restaurant and bar, Atkins Park has been serving food and drink since 1922. The Creole-influenced menu features gumbo, jambalaya, and po'boys. Although bar grub—including ample appetizers and bulging sandwiches—is served until the wee hours, full dinner service ends at 11 on weeknights and midnight on weekends. Smoking in at the bar and after 11 PM in the dining room. Lunch $8.95–9.95, dinner $10.95–19.95.

🍴 **George's Bar and Restaurant** (404-892-3648), 1041 North Highland Avenue NE. Open 11:30–midnight Monday through Saturday, noon–10 Sunday. Located here since 1961, the down-home neighborhood pub serves burgers, hot dogs, and finger foods such as chicken fingers. The decor features 1960s-era booths, sports memorabilia, and video games. Smoking at the bar only. Not wheelchair accessible. $2.50–7.50.

🍴 ♿ **Manuel's Tavern** (404-525-3447; www.manuelstavern.com), 602 North Highland Avenue. Open 11 AM–2 AM Monday through Saturday, 11 AM–midnight Sunday; brunch until 3 PM Saturday and Sunday. This venerable Atlanta institution founded in 1956 by the late Manuel Maloof is now run by his family. Above-average bar fare includes wings, hot dogs, burgers, and other simple grub. Wide-screen televisions allow diners to watch the Atlanta Braves, other favorite sports teams, and CNN. Manuel's also hosts Atlanta's longest-running improvisational group, Laughing Matters, once a month. Designated nonsmoking areas. $6.50–22.

🦐 **Murphy's** (404-872-0904; www .murphysvh.com), 997 Virginia Avenue. Open 11–10 Monday through Thursday, 11–midnight Friday, 8 AM–midnight Saturday, 8 AM–10 PM Sunday; brunch until 4 PM Saturday and Sunday. Limited reservations accepted; call-ahead seating available for dinner only. Complimentary valet parking offered every evening after 5. A perennial favorite in the epicenter of the Virginia-Highland shopping and nightlife district, Murphy's has a jazzy new design and an ambitious menu. The community bistro is the ideal amalgamation of upscale comfort food, unassuming service, an inviting high-energy ambience, and good prices. The contemporary American cuisine features everything from heirloom tomato and goat cheese bruschetta to burgers with avocado mayonnaise and apple wood–smoked bacon. The recent renovation made room for a sophisticated martini and wine bar and a retail wine shop where weekly wine tastings and seminars are held. No smoking. Limited wheelchair accessibility. Lunch $4.50–15, dinner $4.95–23.95, brunch $4.50–14.

SNACKS

In Buckhead

🥢 🦐 ♿ **Huey's** (404-873-2037; www .hueysrestaurant.com), 1816 Peachtree Road. Open 5:30–10 Monday through Thursday, 5:30–midnight Fri-

OPEN ALL NIGHT
Buckhead never sleeps, so visitors can find a quick bite, an alcoholic libation, coffee, or dessert at any time. These restaurants are always open: **Au Pied de Cochon** at the **InterContinental Buckhead** (404-946-9070), 3315 Peachtree Road (see *Dining Out*); **International House of Pancakes** (404-264-0647), 3122 Peachtree Road NE; **Landmark Diner** (404-816-9090), 3652 Roswell Road NW, a 1950s-style diner; **OK Cafe** (404-233-2888), 1284 West Paces Ferry Road, a campy, folk-artsy place where you can always get breakfast (the jalapeño cheese grits are a favorite; brunch is served weekends until 2 PM); **R. Thomas Deluxe Grill** (404-872-2942; www.rthomasdeluxe-grill.com), 1812 Peachtree Road NW, which serves breakfast, burgers, macrobiotic delights, and vegan and vegetarian cuisine prepared with the most natural and healthful ingredients; **Starbucks** (404-261-8447), 2333 Peachtree Road NE and (404-240-5596), 3330 Piedmont Road NE; **Steak N Shake** (404-262-7051), 3380 Northside Parkway; and three **Waffle House** restaurants: (404-261-4475), 2581 Piedmont Road; (404-231-0023), 3016 Piedmont Road; and (404-816-2378), 3735 Roswell Road.

day and Saturday; brunch 9–3 Saturday and Sunday. Named for Louisiana politician Huey Long, the eatery has a full menu of Cajun and Creole favorites, but it's also a great place to stop in after an evening on the town for beignets and café au lait. Smoking and nonsmoking areas. $8–12.

In Virginia-Highland

🍴 ♿ **Pura Vida** (404-870-9797; www .puravidatapas.com), 656 North Highland Avenue. Open 5:30–10 Sunday through Thursday, 5:30–11:30 Friday and Saturday. Sophisticated tapas include small napoleons of duck and ripe plantains, homemade malanga chips with cremini mushroom dip, Puerto Rican *monfongo*, and saffron flan with vanilla coconut cream. No smoking. Tapas $6 each.

TAKE-OUT

In Buckhead

EatZi's Market and Bakery (404-237-2266), 3221 Peachtree Road. Open 7–10 daily. EatZi's is the place to go for haute provisions such as sushi, exotic produce, prepared meals, imported cheeses, great breads, fine wines, desserts, and fresh flowers. Stop in about an hour before closing to find some great bargains.

COFFEEHOUSES With the current popularity of coffeehouses, there's a Starbucks on practically every corner and numerous other coffeehouses scattered around town.

✳ Entertainment

DANCE **Atlanta Ballet, Atlanta Ballet Centre for Dance Education** (404-873-5811; www.atlantaballet .com), office: 1400 West Peachtree Street. Founded in 1929, the Atlanta Ballet is the oldest continuously running dance company in the nation. The company performs classic works, children's stories, and the annual *Nutcracker* at the Fox Theatre. Call for a schedule of performances and ticket prices.

MUSIC **Atlanta Opera** (404-881-8801; www.atlantaopera.org), office: 728 West Peachtree Street NW. Office open 9–5 weekdays. The group produces four fully staged grand operas annually at the Boisfeuillet Jones Atlanta Civic Center. Call for a schedule of performances and ticket prices.

Atlanta Symphony Orchestra (404-733-5000; 404-733-4900; www.atlanta symphony.org), office: 1280 Peachtree Street NE. At 60 years old, the symphony is relatively young to have achieved such international prominence under the batons of maestros Robert Shaw, Yoel Levi, and Robert Spano. The symphony performs a classical season, a pops series, several family and holiday concerts, and performances by the Atlanta Youth Orchestra, all in the Woodruff Arts Center's Symphony Hall. The symphony also performs an outdoor summer series at Chastain Park Amphitheatre and several other free community concerts around Atlanta. Call for a schedule of performances and ticket prices.

Capitol City Opera Company (404-454-6213; www.ccityopera.com), office: 1266 West Paces Ferry Road, Suite 451. The opera company produces two or three main operas each year, as well as children's programs and weekly "Dinner and Diva" shows at local restaurants. Call for a schedule of performances and ticket prices.

Center Stage (404-885-1365; www .earthlinklive.com), 1374 West Peachtree Street. This venue with stadium-style seating presents the very latest in musical acts. Call for a schedule of performances and ticket prices. Parking available in the lot underneath Vinyl next door for $10 per car and in three nearby lots for $5 per car.

&. **Chastain Park Amphitheatre** (information: 404-733-4900; tickets: 404-733-5000), 4469 Stella Drive NW. Atlanta's favorite outdoor venue is the site of summer concerts with big-name entertainers almost every night of the week. The section right in front of the stage has tables for six; in the rest of the facility folks bring their own TV tables. In either case, concertgoers bring colorful table linens, dinnerware, wine goblets, floral arrangements, candles, and, of course, an elegant picnic dinner. Instead of bringing their own picnic, out-of-town visitors can reserve an elegant repast from Affairs to Remember (404-872-7859) or Proof of the Pudding (404-892-2359; 770-804-9880), and their order will be delivered to the park. In addition, light fare and even flowers and candles can be purchased at the park. Limited smoking. Call for a schedule of events and ticket prices.

Tabernacle (404-659-9022; www .atlantaconcerts.com/tabernacle.html), 152 Luckie Street NW. This historical landmark is a must-see entertainment complex. The sanctuary is the main performance room where acts such as Lenny Kravitz, Smashing Pumpkins, Kid Rock, Lynyrd Skynyrd, Elvis Costello, and Willie Nelson have performed. Call for a schedule of performances and ticket prices (usually $25–45). Tickets available through TicketMaster (404-249-6400) and at all TicketMaster locations. The box office sells tickets only on the night of a performance, which might lead to disappointment in the event of a sold-out show.

NIGHTLIFE Buckhead is the entertainment mecca of the metropolitan Atlanta area. There are 100 bars and restaurants within 2½ blocks of the intersection of Peachtree and East Paces Ferry roads, which makes for easy walking among them. Atlanta law forbids anyone younger than 21 from entering a bar.

&. **Andrews Upstairs** (404-467-1600; www.andrewsupstairs.com), 56 East Andrews Drive NW, Suite 13. Open 8–2:30 Thursday through Saturday, Sunday through Wednesday only if there are special events. The upscale Buckhead music and entertainment venue (formerly the Celebrity Rock Café) features live regional and national music acts, late-night dancing with Atlanta's hottest DJs, and comedy acts. Smoking in designated areas. Tickets vary with the act, but usually about $6 purchased in advance, $8 at the door.

&. **Beluga** (404-869-1090; www .belugamartinibar.com), 3115 Piedmont Road NE. Open 5–3 weekdays, 8–3 Saturday. Buckhead's Beluga has been rated the "Best Piano Bar" by *Atlanta Magazine*. Smoking permitted; cigar friendly. No cover charge; 15 types of martinis $9.50, other drinks $10, beers $3.75–4.75.

&. **Blind Willie's** (404-873-2583), 828 North Highland Avenue. Open 8–1 Sunday through Thursday, 8–2 Friday and Saturday. Named for Thomson, Georgia, native "Blind Willie" McTell, whose "Statesboro Blues" was made popular by the Allman Brothers Band, this world-renowned bar showcases New Orleans– and Chicago-style blues. Cajun and zydeco are sometimes featured, and Cajun-style bar food is served. Parking can cost up to $10, so try to find a place on Greenwood, Drewry, or Briarcliff Place. Smoking permitted. Cover charge $10.

Churchill Grounds (404-876-3030; www.churchillgrounds.com), 660 Peachtree Street NE. Tuesday through Sunday, the doors to the club's Whisper Room open at 9 PM for shows at 9:30 and 11:30. This intimate and sophisticated coffee shop offers much more than just java. In fact, it's considered one of Atlanta's premier jazz clubs. Those with a hunger for more than music can satisfy those cravings with light fare, espresso, cappuccino, and desserts. Smoking allowed only in a very small area in the back of the performance room. Cover charge minimum $10.

Dante's Down the Hatch (404-266-1600; www.dantesdownthehatch.com), 3380 Peachtree Road NE. Open at 4 daily, except 5 Sunday; live music 6–11 Monday, 7–11 Tuesday through Thursday, 6–midnight Friday and Saturday, 7–11 Sunday. Ahoy, mateys! For a truly unique experience, descend into an 18th-century sailing ship anchored in a mythical Mediterranean village surrounded by a moat where live crocodiles lurk. Feast on fondue while listening to some of Atlanta's best live jazz, acoustic guitar, or vocalists. *Atlanta Magazine* has rated Dante's the place for the best live jazz in town. For a special treat, make reservations two nights in advance for the chocolate fondue. Smoking and nonsmoking sections. Wheelchair accessible on the wharf

but not on the ship. Cover charge $7 to sit on the ship; no cover on the wharf.

ESPN Zone (404-682-3776; www.espnzone.com/atlanta), 3030 Peachtree Road. Open 11:30–12:30 Monday through Saturday, 11:30–midnight Sunday. The restaurant and games center in Buckhead features 200 televisions, a screening room, sports simulation arena, and games arcade. No smoking. No cover charge except for special events.

Euclid Avenue Yacht Club (404-688-2582), 1136 Euclid Avenue NE. Open from 3 PM to the wee hours of the morning Monday through Thursday, from noon Friday and Saturday. This Little Five Points neighborhood bar is always packed to the rafters with students, regulars, bikers, and visitors. This is a smoking bar. No cover charge.

Fadó Irish Pub (404-841-0066; www.fadoirishpub.com), 3035 Peachtree Road. Open 11:30–10 Monday through Thursday, 10 AM–3 AM Friday and Saturday, 10:30–10 Sunday. Fadó is the No. 2 seller of Guinness in America, and the eatery's warm, welcoming ambience is a rarity in frenetic Buckhead. Irish pub grub such as corned beef and cabbage, traditional Irish music, international soccer on television, and other fun complete the package. Smoking allowed. No cover charge.

Johnny's Hideaway (404-233-8026; www.johnnyshideaway.com), 3771 Roswell Road. Open from 11 AM until the wee hours of the morning Monday through Saturday, from noon Sunday. The club is definitely popular with the older crowd. Smoking allowed. No cover charge, but there's a two-drink minimum.

& Kenny's Alley at Underground Atlanta (404-523-2311; www.underground-atlanta.com), 50 Upper Alabama Street SW. Occupying a wing at Underground Atlanta, Kenny's Alley features eight clubs that offer high-energy dance music, rock and roll, Latin-influenced music and dance, Las Vegas–style female impersonator shows, reggae, karaoke, and music with an Irish flair. This is the only place in Atlanta where patrons can carry a drink from bar to bar until 4 AM. Valet parking available Thursday through Saturday nights in Coke Plaza in front of the World of Coca-Cola (55 Martin Luther King Jr. Boulevard).

❦ & Limerick Junction (404-874-7147; www.limerickjunction.com), 822 North Highland Avenue. Entertainment 5 PM–1 AM Monday through Wednesday, until 2 AM Thursday through Saturday, until midnight Sunday. Atlanta's oldest Irish pub features traditional Irish music nightly. Guinness and Harp are on tap, and hearty pub food is served. Parking is a big problem, so you might want to take a taxi. Smoking permitted. Cover charge $3 Friday and Saturday only.

& Masquerade (404-577-8178; www.masq.com), 695 North Avenue. Open Wednesday through Saturday nights until 3:30 or 4 AM. The trilevel club (the levels are Heaven, Hell, and Purgatory) is located in an old warehouse in Little Five Points. Entertainment runs to heavy metal and punk bands. Smoking allowed. Wheelchair accessible, but crowding could make it very difficult to navigate. Show charges $8–35. For multiday events, special two- and three-day passes available.

& Star Community Bar (404-681-9018), 437 Moreland Avenue. This Little Five Points site is open from 4 PM Tuesday through Sunday; shows start at 9:30 or 10 weekdays, 10:30 weekends. Acts run the gamut from country to swing to rockabilly to blues. Monday is karaoke night. Smoking allowed. Cover charge usually $3–8.

& Tongue and Groove (404-261-2325; www.tongueandgrooveonline.com), 3055 Peachtree Road in Buckhead. Open 10 PM–3 AM Tuesday, Thursday, Friday, and Saturday; 9–3 Wednesday. Weekend nights feature a DJ playing top 40 hits; Latin music is played on Wednesday nights with free salsa lessons. The high-energy crowd is 21 to 40+. Smoking permitted. Wheelchair accessible on the Peachtree Road side. Cover charge $10 and up.

& Variety Playhouse (404-521-1786; www.variety-playhouse.com), 1099 Euclid Avenue. Located in Little Five Points, Variety Playhouse is a combination theater and nightclub with a mixture of theater seating, tables and chairs, and dancing and standing areas, and it therefore presents a wide variety of entertainment—primarily live concerts. Smoking limited to lobby and smoking deck. Call for a schedule of events and ticket prices. All shows are general admission.

PROFESSIONAL SPORTS ⚓ &

Atlanta Braves (404-249-6400; 404-522-7630; 1-800-326-4000; www.atlanta.braves.mlb.com), 755 Hank Aaron Drive. The major-league Atlanta Braves baseball team plays at **Turner Field** (see *To See—Guided Tours*). For transportation to the stadium, see the **Braves Stadium Shuttle** described in *Getting Around*. There are 178 "skyline" (we translate this as "nosebleed") seats along the far ends of the upper deck. Those adventurous enough to take a chance on same-day tickets might snare one of them for $1. Call for a schedule of games and ticket prices.

♪ & **Atlanta Falcons** (404-249-6400; 1-800-326-4000; www.atlantafalcons .com), One Georgia Dome Drive. The National Football League's Atlanta Falcons play at the **Georgia Dome** (see *To See—Guided Tours*). Call for a schedule of games and ticket prices.

♪ & **Atlanta Hawks** (404-827-3865; www.nba.com/hawks), One Philips Drive. The National Basketball Association's Atlanta Hawks play at Philips Arena. Call for a schedule of games and ticket prices.

♪ & **Atlanta Thrashers** (404-584-PUCK; www.atlantathrashers.com), One Philips Drive. The National Hockey League's Atlanta Thrashers play at Philips Arena. Call for a schedule of games and ticket prices.

♪ & **Georgia Force** (404-222-5770; www.georgiaforce.com), ticket office: One Georgia Dome Drive. The Force plays arena football at Philips Arena. Call for a schedule of games and ticket prices.

SUMMER THEATER Georgia Shakespeare Festival (404-264-0020; www .gashakespeare.org), 4484 Peachtree Road. When driving up Peachtree Road in Buckhead, castle- and battlementlike structures, fluttering flags, and a cheery, circular, yellow and white tentlike building come as a complete surprise. These out-of-place and -time buildings make up Oglethorpe University. Located on the grounds of the university, the flags and tentlike building announce the

Conant Performing Arts Center, home of the Georgia Shakespeare Festival. In midsummer and in October, the Bard's classics, comedies, and opuses come to life along with works by other playwrights. Eat, drink, and be merry by picnicking before the show with catered meals or your own from home. Call for a schedule of performances and ticket prices.

THEATER King Plow Arts Center, Actor's Express Theatre Company, (404-607-7469; www.actorsexpress.com), 887 West Marietta Street NW, Suite J-107. Office open 10–6 weekdays. The troupe produces six main-stage shows each year, often reflecting original works and perspectives particular to Atlanta. Call for a schedule of performances and ticket prices.

& **Agatha's—A Taste of Mystery** (404-875-1610; www.agathas.com), 2935 North Druid Hills Road. Shows at 7:30 Monday through Saturday, 7 Sunday. Participants are asked to arrive 15–30 minutes early. Reservations must be made by phone. Named for—who else?—Agatha Christie, the queen of mystery writers, this campy interactive dinner theater unfolds a mystery during a five-course dinner. Always a farce with humor ranging from lowbrow to literate, the performance is presented by several actors with help from audience members. Shows run for 13 weeks, so you could go back numerous times throughout the year and see different shows. Small smoking area near the bar. $47.50 Monday through Thursday (cocktails extra), $57.50 Friday through Sunday. A $20 per person deposit required; checks preferred to credit cards. Note: Check before you go. Agatha's had to vacate its 18-year home on Peachtree Street, and these quarters are temporary until a new home is complete.

&. **Alliance Theatre Company** (404-733-5000; www.alliancetheatre.org), Woodruff Arts Center, 1280 Peachtree Street. Call for a schedule of performances and ticket prices. The Southeast's premier professional theater and one of the nation's largest regional theater companies presents 10 productions yearly, including classic dramas, comedies, contemporary plays, and regional and world premieres. All are performed in its main theater or its more intimate Hertz Stage, while Theatre for Young Audiences shows are presented in the nearby 14th Street Playhouse.

Ansley Park Playhouse (404-875-1193; www.ansleyparkplayhouse.com), 1545 Peachtree Street. Shows at 8 Thursday through Saturday, 7 Sunday. Atlanta's longest-running production, *Peachtree Battle,* has been playing here for four years of sold-out performances. The topical parody of Atlanta's upper crust is fall-on-the-floor-laughing hysterical to metro residents who catch on to all the "in" jokes, but it's hilarious to out-of-towners as well. $24.50. Advance tickets a must; the production is often sold out six weeks in advance.

&. **Boisfeuillet Jones Atlanta Civic Center** (404-523-6275; www.atlanta civiccenter.com), 395 Piedmont Avenue NE. Named for a prominent Atlanta philanthropist, the civic center hosts many diverse productions and is the performance venue of the **Atlanta Opera** (see *Music*). The stage is the largest in the Southeast and therefore attracts big productions like *Miss Saigon.* Call for a schedule

of events and ticket prices.

♪ &. **Center for Puppetry Arts** (office: 404-873-3089; tickets: 404-873-3391; www.puppet.org), 1404 Spring Street NW. Open 9–5 Tuesday through Saturday, 11–5 Sunday. During the school year, performances at 10 and 11:30 weekdays; 11, 1, and 3 Saturdays. The center (see *To See—Museums*) produces numerous children's and adult shows throughout the year. Call for a schedule of performances. $12.

The Coca-Cola Roxy Theater (404-233-1062; www.atlantamusicguide .com/roxy_tickets.htm), 3110 Roswell Road. This fine old restored building in Buckhead was built as a movie theater in 1927 in the Spanish Baroque style. Today it serves as an intimate venue for national touring musical acts and comedians, as well as regional and local bands and even once-a-month boxing. Call for a schedule of performances and ticket prices.

&. **Ferst Center for the Arts at Georgia Tech** (404-894-9600; www .ferstcenter.org), 349 Ferst Drive NW. Box office open 9–7 weekdays, 10–5 Saturday. This venue features an outstanding selection of concerts, recitals, dance, film, opera, music, and theater from September through May. The center is also the performance venue for **Atlantic Lyric Theatre, Ballethnic Dance Company,** the **Atlanta Gay Men's Chorus,** and numerous one-time events. Call for a schedule of performances and ticket prices. In addition, the facility houses the **Richards and Westbrook Galleries,** which display visual arts by a wide spectrum of artists.

♪ &. **Fox Theatre** (404-881-2013; www.foxtheatre.org), 660 Peachtree Street NE. Originally planned to be the Yaarab Temple Shrine Mosque, the theater was lavishly designed with Moorish, Egyptian, and art deco influences to reflect the then-recent discovery of King Tut's tomb in 1922. The threat of demolition in the 1970s to make room for a parking deck galvanized the local citizenry to form Landmarks, Inc., which saved and restored the theater, now known affectionately as the Fabulous Fox. To date $20 million has been spent on the restoration. Today the magnificent 4,500-seat performance venue, which is designated a National Historic Landmark and a Georgia Museum Building, hosts a wide variety of events, from movies to traveling

THE RESTORED FOX THEATRE IN DOWN-TOWN ATLANTA, AFFECTIONATELY KNOWN AS THE FABULOUS FOX, HOSTS A VARIETY OF EVENTS THROUGHOUT THE YEAR.

Broadway shows to ballet to rock concerts. A tribute to the Fox's movie-palace heritage is the **Summer Film Festival,** a popular series of classic and contemporary films. For a more in-depth tour, the Atlanta Preservation Society offers tours of the theater on Monday and Thursday mornings and twice on Saturday (see *To See— Guided Tours*). Smoking outdoors only. Call for a schedule of performances and ticket prices.

♿ **The New American Shakespeare Tavern** (404-874-5299; www.shakespearetavern.com), 499 Peachtree Street NE. Box office open 1–6 Tuesday through Saturday, 3–6 Sunday. Performances at 7:30 Thursday through Saturday, 6:30 Sunday. Dinner is available from one hour and 15 minutes before the show until five minutes before the show. After dining on British pub food such as Cornish pasty, Cornish gobble, the King's Supper, or shepherd's pie accompanied by Irish ales and premium wines, enjoy the Elizabethan scenery, Renaissance and medieval costumes, and live acoustic music, all of which enhance the boisterous action of one of the Bard's plays. The tavern also performs original works, variety shows, and classics by other playwrights. Smoking outdoors only. Wheelchair accessible from the entrance behind the building. $19.50 Thursday and Sunday, $22.50 Friday, $24.50 Saturday. Ask about discounts and special programs. Dinner prices ($3.75–8.75) are in addition to tickets for the play, so it's possible to purchase tickets to the play only. Seating is on a first-come, first-served basis. Table seating is limited, but all seats can accommodate food and beverages.

Rialto Center for the Performing Arts at Georgia State University (404-651-4727; www.rialtocenter.org), 80 Forsyth Street. Box office open 10–4:30 weekdays. This lovely historic movie theater in the Fairlie-Poplar Historic District has been fully restored and hosts international musical artists as well as theatrical and dance performances. Call for a schedule of events and ticket prices.

Seven Stages Theater (404-522-0911; www.7stages.org), 1105 Euclid Avenue. This avant-garde, cutting-edge theater in Little Five Points presents plays that delve into the social, political, and spiritual values of contemporary issues. Call for a schedule of performances and ticket prices.

Theatrical Outfit (678-528-1500; www.TheatricalOutfit.org), 84 Luckie Street. The longtime Atlanta theatrical organization got a new home in 2004, the intimate 200-seat Balzer Theater located in the old Herren's restaurant space next door to the Rialto. Productions run the gamut from comedy to drama to musicals to one-person shows. Call for a schedule of performances and ticket prices.

✳ Selective Shopping

A shopper's mecca, Buckhead boasts 1,400 upscale retail shops. In addition, two of Atlanta's premier shopping malls are located in the heart of Buckhead. Between the two malls, shoppers can visit 350 trendy stores and numerous restaurants. A shuttle service whisks shoppers from one mall to another.

First there's upscale **Lenox Square** (404-233-6767; www.lenoxsquare .com), 3393 Peachtree Road NE. Open 10–9 Monday through Saturday,

noon–6 Sunday. The largest mall in the Southeast features a Neiman Marcus, Bloomingdale's, Louis Vuitton, Brooks Brothers, Hermes, Versace Jeans Couture, and the Metropolitan Museum of Art Store, among many others. The **Atlanta Convention and Visitors Bureau** (404-222-6688; www.atlanta.net/shopping) offers shopping packages with terrific rates at one of eight Buckhead hotels, complimentary breakfast, parking, and a $25 gift card to use at Lenox Square.

Then there's posh **Phipps Plaza** (404-261-7910; 1-800-810-7700; www .phippsplaza.com), 3500 Peachtree Road NE. Open 10–9 Monday through Saturday, noon–5:30 Sunday. This swanky mall features a Sak's Fifth Avenue, Gianni Versace, Gucci, Giorgio Armani, and Tiffany & Co., among others. The two newest additions to Phipps Plaza are Barneys New York CO-OP and Nordstrom.

Visitors looking for the perfect antiques, works of art, or home accessories need look no further than Buckhead, which has several major interior decorator districts. **Atlanta Decorative Arts Center** (678-904-0663; www.adacdesigncenter.com), 349 and 351 Peachtree Hills Avenue, is primarily wholesale (a business license and a tax ID number are required for entrance), but the facility is open to members of the public who are accompanied by a designer and for occasional sales and seminars. **Miami Circle Market Center** (404-846-0449), 709 Miami Circle, is a collection of 75 antiques shops and galleries. **Buckhead Design Center** (404-876-2543; www.buckheaddesign center.com), 2133 Peachtree Road NE, is a one-stop shopping source for furniture, accessories, and lighting.

Bennett Street (404-352-4430; www.buckhead.org/bennettstreet), 22 Bennett Street NW, boasts more than 50 antiques and arts shops.

BOOKS A Cappella Books (404-681-5128; 1-866-681-5128; www.acappella books.com), 484-C Moreland Avenue NE. Open 11–8 Monday through Thursday, 11–10 Friday and Saturday, noon–7 Sunday. Shop in this Little Five Points store for new, used, and out-of-print books, including Beat literature, progressive and counterculture subjects, and books about music.

Atlanta Book Exchange (404-872-2665), 1000 North Highland Avenue. In this day of large chain bookstores, this independent one is a rarity, and a pleasant one at that. Located in an old house in Virginia-Highland, this no-frills bookstore is packed to the rafters with new books priced 5 percent to 40 percent off, as well as used, out-of-print, and remainder books. Parking in the front and in the back.

C. Dickens (404-231-3825; www .cdickens.com), 56 East Andrews Drive. Open 9–6 Monday through Saturday. Shop at this Buckhead store for fine, rare, and collectible books as well as maps, historical documents, autographs, and manuscripts.

CRAFTS Ten Thousand Villages (404-892-5307; www.tenthousand villages.com), 1056 St. Charles Avenue NE. Open 11–6 weekdays, 10–6 Saturday, noon–6 Sunday. This nonprofit cooperative store works with 70 other stores across the country on a fair-trade model, paying artisans a percentage of the sales of handicrafts from around the world. You'll find everything—saris and wooden animals from Kenya, pottery from Peru, figurines and wooden boxes from Haiti and Bangladesh—at extremely reasonable prices. You'll go home with treasures for yourself or others, and you'll feel good for helping citizens of Third World countries.

FOOD Star Provisions (404-365-0410; www.starprovisions.com), 1198 Howell Mill Road. Open 11–8 Tuesday through Saturday. This Midtown cook's market is owned by the masterminds behind Bacchanalia (see *Where to Eat—Dining Out*) and Floataway Café. You'll find everything here, from restaurant-quality cookware and gadgets to seasonal tableware and linens to gourmet food products such as A-grade foie gras, $100 bottles of vinegar, ahi tuna, and 200 varieties of cheese (most of which are available to taste).

Sweet Auburn Curb Market (404-659-1665; www.terminalmarkets .com/sweetauburn.htm), 209 Edgewood Avenue SE. Open 8–6 Monday through Saturday. Built as an outdoor marketplace in 1918, the market moved indoors in 1924. Today you can buy not only fresh meat, fish, and produce from local and organic farms but also African and Caribbean foods, African clothing, cell phones, flowers, hair-care products, and prescription drugs.

OUTLET STORES Filene's Basement (404-869-4466; www.filenesbasement .com), 3535 Peachtree Road NE. Open 9:30–9:30 Monday through Saturday. Since 1908, Filene's Basement, the oldest and most famous off-price store, has been selling high-end, designer, and couture goods. The annual bridal gown sale is world renowned.

RECORDS AND COMPACT DISCS

Criminal Records (404-215-9511; www.criminal.com), 466 Moreland Avenue. Open 10–10 Monday through Saturday, noon–7 Sunday. This record and CD store in Little Five Points carries a wide variety of merchandise, including alternative music and independent publications.

SPECIAL SHOPS

Junkman's Daughter (404-577-3188), 464 Moreland Avenue. Open 11–7 Monday through Thursday, 11–8 Friday, 11–9 Saturday, noon–7 Sunday. Located in the heart of Little Five Points, this fun, funky alternative shop carries inexpensive club clothing—often leather and often embellished with chains and studs—and other off-the-wall and utterly tacky items.

✳ Special Events

January: **King Week** (404-524-1956; www.kingcenter.org). Call for a schedule of events and prices. The week-long event, sponsored by the **Center for Nonviolent Social Change** (see *To See—Historic Homes and Sites*), produces live performances, religious and inspirational concerts, and educational seminars to honor Nobel Laureate Martin Luther King Jr.

February: **Southeastern Flower Show** (404-888-5638; www.flowershow.org). Open 10–9 Wednesday through Friday, 9–9 Saturday, 9–6 Sunday. The area's premier horticultural event, held at the **Georgia World Congress Center** (see *Guidance*), is a five-day extravaganza featuring 4 acres of landscape and floral exhibitions, garden-related merchandise, and more. During the day, take tea in the elegant Tea Garden, which transforms into a pub at 5. Adults

$15, children 5–15 $6.

March: **St. Patrick's Day Family Festival** (404-523-2311; www.stpatsatlanta.com). The event, which takes place over three days at **Underground Atlanta** (see *To See—Historic Homes and Sites*), features live traditional Irish music and performances by Celtic rock bands, Irish dance contests, children's activities, Irish food and beverages, and unique Irish vendors. The festival ends with the **St. Patrick's Day Parade**. Free.

April: **Atlanta Dogwood Festival** (404-817-6642; www.dogwood.org). Spring in Atlanta is heralded with a three-day art and music festival in Midtown's **Piedmont Park** (see *Green Space—Nature Preserves and Parks*). The fun includes kids' village activities, a rock-climbing wall, and an artist's market. The ever-popular **U.S. Disc Dog Southern Nationals**, hosted by the Greater Atlanta Dog and Disc Club, features demonstrations on Friday afternoon and competitions all day Saturday and Sunday. Free admission; fee for some activities.

Late April: **Inman Park Festival and Tour of Homes** (770-242-4895). The festival consists of the city's largest street market, a juried arts-and-crafts show, a tour of homes, live entertainment, children's activities, a parade, and a wide variety of food and beverages. Free for festival; fee for tour of homes.

May: **Atlanta Jazz Festival** (404-817-6999; www.atlanta.net/visitors/atlanta-jazz-festival.asp). An international roster of artists performs throughout May in numerous venues around the city. The festival culminates with a three-day festival at **Piedmont Park** (see *Green Space—*

Nature Preserves and Parks). The majority of events are free and open to the public except the concert at **Chastain Park**, which costs $48.

National Black Arts Festival (404-730-7315; www.nbaf.org). The 10-day festival celebrates the creative contributions of people of African descent through visual arts, music, theater, and dance in venues all over the city. Call for a schedule of events and ticket prices.

Sweet Auburn SpringFest (404-886-4469; sweetauburn.com/springfest2005). 11–10 Saturday, 2–9 Sunday. Activities include live performances on 10 stages, the Fantastic Fun Zone for kids, Technology Expo, International Craft Market, the Sweet Auburn Film Festival, and more. Free.

December: **Chick-fil-A Bowl and Parade** (404-586-8496; www.peachbowl.com). Prior to the Chick-fil-A Bowl, more than 30 bands; classic cars; giant helium balloons; floats; participating team presidents, bands, cheerleaders, and mascots; and the Chick-fil-A cows parade down Peachtree Street. After the parade, the NCAA football bowl game begins at the **Georgia Dome** (see *To See—Guided Tours*) . Thirty activities connected with the game occur the week prior. The annual event sells out before the teams are even selected, so book early to avoid disappointment.

Children's Health Care of Atlanta Festival of Trees–Children's Christmas Parade (404-785-NOEL for recorded information; www.choa .org). Hours are 10–9 Monday through Saturday, noon–6 Sunday. The festival, Atlanta's premier holiday event, kicks off on the first Saturday

in December with the popular **Children's Christmas Parade.** The parade consists of marching bands, costumed dogs, antique cars, dance groups, holiday-themed floats, giant helium-balloon characters, specialty groups, clowns, and the grand finale: the arrival of Santa and Mrs. Claus (who coincidentally are portrayed by your authors). Santa and Mrs. Claus then proceed to the **Georgia World Congress Center** (see *Guidance*) to officially open the festival, which runs for the next nine days. At the festival, visitors stroll through 54,000 square feet of decorated trees, wreaths, decorator vignettes, gingerbread houses, handmade dollhouses, specialty shops, an array of children's activities and rides, continuous entertainment, and food outlets. Adults $10, seniors and children 2–12 $5.

Festival of Lights (404-223-4412; www.centennialpark.org). For the month of December, **Centennial Olympic Park** (see *Green Space— Nature Preserves and Parks*) is decked out with millions of lights that create lighted scenes. As an extra-special treat, an outdoor ice skating rink provides hours of entertainment for Southerners not used to this activity. Skating is $7 for 90 minutes; rental skates available. Free.

New Year's Eve Peach Drop (404-523-2311; www.underground-atlanta .com). Held at **Underground Atlanta**, (see *To See—Historic Homes and Sites*) the annual midnight drop of the 800-pound peach is preceded by entertainment and activities and followed by a fireworks display and more live performances. Family-oriented activities begin at noon. Free.

MCDONOUGH, HAMPTON, JACKSON, AND LOCUST GROVE

McDonough, now known as "the Geranium City," was incorporated in 1823, two years after Chief William McIntosh of the Creek Indian Nation stood on a large rock at Indian Springs and signed a treaty giving the state of Georgia all rights to the Creek territory between the Ocmulgee and Flint rivers. Henry County was created from these lands and was named for statesman and orator Patrick Henry. Eventually, five counties were carved out of Henry County, earning it the sobriquet "Mother of Counties."

Because this was a highly productive area of Georgia, it was important to the Confederacy. That significance put it high on William Tecumseh Sherman's list to be destroyed by Union troops on the March to the Sea. During Reconstruction, cotton came into importance and prosperity returned.

McDonough grew and thrived until 1843, when it was bypassed by the railroad. In recent years, Pennsylvanian Bob Oglevee was instrumental in getting Oglevee Products to set up a nursery in McDonough to test their hot-weather geraniums. The company offered to plant hundreds of geraniums in the town square, and the town agreed. The City Council then had McDonough recognized as "the Geranium City," and it now hosts a Geranium Festival on the courthouse square, one of metro Atlanta's most popular events. The landscaped square around the 1897 Romanesque-style courthouse boasts ancient oaks and a Confederate monument. Surrounding the square are bustling specialty shops, antiques stores, and boutiques.

McDonough makes a good base of operations for exploring the surrounding area and small towns that are rich in attractions, historical sites, sporting venues, outdoor pursuits, and special events. Easy access to I-75 gives visitors the convenience of going into Atlanta or Macon as well. Venture onto the back roads to see rolling green pastures, quiet leafy woodlands, serene lakes, and quaint towns.

GUIDANCE When planning a trip to the McDonough area, contact the **McDonough Hospitality and Tourism Bureau–McDonough Welcome Center** (770-898-3196; www.tourmcdonough.com), 5 Griffin Street, McDonough 30253. Open 8–5 weekdays, 10–4 Saturday. Stop at the 1920s prototype Standard Oil gas station for local tourism information and admire the black 1920 Model T Ford waiting for a fill-up at the hand-cranked gas pumps. Pick up the brochure

"Historic Sites of McDonough, Georgia" for a walking–driving tour. For more information about the area, including Hampton and Locust Grove, consult the **Henry County Chamber of Commerce, Convention and Visitors Bureau and Welcome Center** (770-957-5786; 1-800-HENRYCO; www.henrycounty .com), 1709 GA 20 West, McDonough 30253. Open 8–5 weekdays, 10–4 Saturday.

To learn more about the Jackson area, including Flovilla and Indian Springs, contact the **Butts County Chamber of Commerce** (770-775-4839; www .jackson-online.com), 206 E. Third Street, Jackson 30233. Open 10–4 weekdays.

GETTING THERE *By air:* The area is served by **Hartsfield-Jackson Atlanta International Airport** (see What's Where in Georgia). Car rentals are available on-site at the airport from **Avis** (404-530-2725), **Budget** (404-530-3000), **Dollar** (1-866-434-2226), **Enterprise** (404-763-5220), **Hertz** (404-530-2925), **National/ Alamo** (404-530-2800), and **Thrifty** (770-996-2350). Off-site car rentals include **Airport Rent a Car of Atlanta** (1-800-905-4997), **EZ Rent a Car** (404-761-4999), and **Payless Car Rental** (404-766-5034).

By bus: **Greyhound Lines** (1-800-231-2222; www.greyhound.com) does not serve any of the towns described in this chapter. The nearest bus station is in Atlanta at 232 Forsyth Street; 404-584-1728. There is another station at the Atlanta airport, 6000 North Terminal Parkway; 404-765-9598. Visitors arriving in Atlanta by bus would need to rent a car to get to the destinations in this chapter and to get around between them, because taxis and mass transit are not a feasible way to travel.

By car: Most of the towns described in this chapter are easily accessed from I-75 south of Atlanta.

COTTON WAS IMPORTANT IN THE EARLY DAYS OF MCDONOUGH AND SURROUNDING AREAS.

By train: **Amtrak** (404-881-3067; 1-800-USA-RAIL; www.amtrak.com) has a station at 1688 Peachtree Street NW in Atlanta. Visitors arriving in Atlanta by train would need to rent a car to get to the destinations in this chapter and to get around between them, because taxis and mass transit are not a feasible way to travel.

GETTING AROUND In addition to car rentals at the airport, car rentals are available from **Enterprise** (678-432-0130), 456 Industrial Boulevard, McDonough. Public transportation is available from **Xpress** (404-463-4782; www.xpressga.com), metro Atlanta's newest public transit service. Fares are $3 one way, $5 round trip. Hours are 5:30 AM–9:30 PM weekdays. Operated in partnership with the Georgia Regional Transportation Authority (GRTA) and 11 counties, the service provides an easy-to-use connection to downtown Atlanta, where passengers can transfer to the MARTA bus/rail system, from Hampton and McDonough.

MEDICAL EMERGENCY Call 911 for life-threatening situations. For other medical attention, go to the **Henry Medical Center** (770-389-2200; www.henry medical.com), 1133 Eagle's Landing Parkway, Stockbridge.

VILLAGES When the railroad bypassed McDonough, **Hampton,** then known as Bear Creek because two surveyors had seen two bears in a tree there, profited from being on the Central of Georgia route. The center of all business activity in the area, the town shipped all the cotton for the surrounding counties. It wasn't unusual to see hundreds of wagons lining the roads, waiting to be unloaded. The town changed its name in 1873 to honor Civil War hero General Wade Hampton of South Carolina. Hampton's historic railroad depot, circa 1881, was constructed with fireproof brick—both an innovation and an extravagance in the 1880s—and is graced with ornate brick detailing in several patterns. Today, Hampton is best known as the home of races at the **Atlanta Motor Speedway**, which draw more visitors than any other sporting event in Georgia. Beautiful historic homes and ancient oaks line the streets. In the spring, dazzling daylilies line the streets, too.

Indian Springs–Flovilla is noted as the site where an infamous Indian treaty was signed. The Indian Springs Hotel, which was built around 1822, even before the community was founded, was owned by Chief William McIntosh. Tours are offered during special events. *Indian Springs State Park* is the oldest state park in the nation.

Jackson, the county seat of Butts County, was incorporated in 1826. The courthouse, which was built in 1898 (Union troops had burned its predecessor in 1864), has Victorian architectural elements, marble floors, and an intact courtroom. The courthouse is open to the public when court is not in session. The most imposing home in Jackson, indeed in most of Georgia, is the Queen Anne–style Carmichael House on Second Street, which was built by a buggy builder in 1897 for the then-astronomical price of $16,000. It remained in the Carmichael family until the 1990s. Although it is a private home, art festivals and other events are often held on the lawns. Jackson's new brick sidewalks, light fixtures, planters, and refurbished storefronts combine to create an inviting atmosphere. Butts County's oldest restaurant, Fresh Air Barbecue, has been run by members of the same family since 1929. Jackson also hosts several annual events: the **Scottish Festival** in April, the **Native American Festival** in September, and **Civil War Days** in November.

Locust Grove was named for a grove of flowering locust trees that could be seen throughout the town. It was a major rail distribution center for cotton, peaches, and other farm products and had three cotton gins and several warehouses. Beginning in 1894, the prosperous town was the home of the Locust Grove Institute, a top-notch college-preparatory school founded by the Locust Grove Baptist Church and Mercer University. It was one of the first schools in Georgia to be accredited by the Association of Schools and Colleges of the Southern States. The Great Depression and the introduction of public schools led to the demise of the school in 1930, but its beautiful main building now houses city government offices. Today, Locust Grove is the home of **Noah's Ark**, a facility for animal rehabilitation, and the **Tanger Outlet Center**.

✳ To See

FOR FAMILIES ♫ ✿ ♿ **Noah's Ark Animal Rehabilitation Center** (770-957-0888; www.noahs-ark.org), 712 LG-Griffin Road, Locust Grove. Office open 9–5 Tuesday through Friday, facility open for tours noon–3 Tuesday through Saturday; closed on major holidays. (Note: All tours are subject to cancellation because of rain, extreme heat or cold, or lack of volunteers.) Noah's Ark, which is located on 250 acres, was created to provide a home for abused, unwanted, and orphaned wild, domestic, and exotic animals and birds. Rehabilitated animals are returned to the wild or their place of origin; animals that can't be released live out their days here in as natural a habitat as possible, as do unwanted exotic animals such as lions, monkeys, and tigers that have no natural habitat in North America. Visitors can walk the nature trails through 40 acres and view the animal habitats. Free; donations accepted.

HISTORIC HOMES AND SITES ♫ ✿ ♿
Heritage Park (770-954-2031; www.co.henry.ga.us), 101 Lake Dow Road, McDonough. Open daylight hours daily. The 129-acre park

NOAH'S ARK FACTS
- The center rehabilitates more than 1,000 animals each year.
- Around 800 to 900 animals are usually in residence at any one time.
- It costs $600 per day to feed all the animals.
- The yearly budget at Noah's Ark is $900,000.
- There are only 27 full-time and part-time employees.
- It takes 300 volunteers to help with animal care and feeding, tours, group projects, and annual events.
- Noah's Ark had to turn away 2,450 animals last year for lack of funds.

straddles two centuries. The **historic village**, which represents what Henry County was like at the turn of the 20th century, was created by moving historic structures from around the county to one location. It includes a 100-year-old corncrib, an 1827 settler's log cabin, an original two-room country schoolhouse, a typical detached cookhouse, the first library building in the county, a 1933 steam locomotive, and Lane's Store, which was built in 1921 and served as a general store for quarry workers as well as a service station and local gathering place. The **Barn Museum** houses county artifacts. A unit in the county's parks and recreation system, the park also features a community garden, the 0.9-mile paved Brian Williams Trail, two playgrounds, a senior center, and a softball complex. Free.

✳ To Do

AUTO RACING ✐ ⬤ **Atlanta Motor Speedway** (770-707-7904; 770-707-7970 for tours; www.atlantamotorspeedway.com; www.gospeedway.com), 1500 Tara Place/US 41 North, Hampton. Office open 8:30–5 weekdays. Call for a schedule of events and ticket prices. Track tours operate daily from the gift shop. The 1.54-mile track is one of the premier motor-sports facilities in America. Its two NASCAR Nextel Cup Series races are the two largest single-day sporting events in Georgia. In fact, the track is the biggest revenue-producing venue in the state. Approximately 160,000 fans converge there to watch their favorite drivers race around the track at heart-stopping speeds. In addition, the track sponsors the NASCAR Craftsman Truck Series and Busch Series racing. Thursday Thunder Legends and Bandolero racing showcase the talents of up-and-coming drivers for 10 weeks during the summer. In use more than 300 days a year, the track also hosts driving schools, concerts, air shows, dog shows, circuses, weddings, and car shows, bringing in more than $455 million annually. The facility also offers tours and behind-the-scenes looks at the entertainment complex. Official track tours include track history, a visit to Petty Garden, a tour of a luxury suite, a peek at the garages and Victory Lane, and two laps in the speedway van. Camping is also available.

BICYCLING See **Dauset Trails Nature Center** under *Green Space—Natures Preserves and Parks.*

BIRDING See **Dauset Trails Nature Center, Newman Wetlands Center, Cubihatcha Outdoor Center, High Falls State Park,** and **Indian Springs State Park** under *Green Space—Nature Preserves and Parks.*

BOATING See **Lake Jackson** under *Green Space—Lakes* and **High Falls State Park** and **Indian Springs State Park** under *Green Space—Nature Preserves and Parks.*

FISHING See **Lake Jackson** under *Green Space—Lakes* and **High Falls State Park** and **Indian Springs State Park** under *Green Space—Nature Preserves and Parks.*

FOR FAMILIES ✐ **Fun Town of Henry County** (770-898-4272), 300 GA 155, McDonough. Open 9–midnight Monday through Thursday, 9–3 AM Friday and Saturday, noon–midnight Sunday. The 8-acre indoor-outdoor family entertainment complex offers two video arcades, billiards, 32 lanes of bowling, a climbing wall, go-carts, laser tag, 18 holes of mini golf, an eight-station batting cage, and a snack bar. Limited wheelchair accessibility on some rides. $2.75–4 per activity.

FRUIT AND BERRY PICKING ✐ ❧ ♿ **H&H Orchards** (678-432-6555; 770-957-4330), 100 Colvin Drive, Locust Grove. Generally open 8–4:30 Monday, Wednesday, Friday, and Saturday in July, but call for schedule to be sure. Pick your own freestone peaches and pay by the bucket.

✐ ❧ ♿ **Little Billie's Strawberry Farm** (770-957-8524; www.littlebillies.com), 2501 GA 20 West, McDonough. The season typically runs from the first week in April through the first week in June. Hours are 9–7 Monday through Saturday, noon–5 Sunday. A veritable sea of strawberries, the farm has 10 acres planted—that's 140,000 plants. The owners say that if they were lined up end to end, the line would be 26 miles long. Visitors can pick their own succulent strawberries fresh from the vine or purchase those already picked. Don't leave without savoring some of their luscious homemade strawberry ice cream made with their very own strawberries. You-pick $1.50 per pound, they-pick $2.25 per pound.

GOLF See Golf Appendix.

HIKING See **Dauset Trails Nature Center, Cubihatcha Outdoor Center,** and **High Falls State Park** under *Green Space—Nature Preserves and Parks.*

HUNTING See Other Activities Appendix.

MINIATURE GOLF See **Fun Town of Henry County** under *To Do—For Families* and **High Falls State Park** and **Indian Springs State Park** under *Green Space—Nature Preserves and Parks.*

SKATEBOARDING See Other Activities Appendix.

SWIMMING See **Lake Jackson** under *Green Space—Lakes* and **High Falls State Park** and **Indian Springs State Park** under *Green Space—Nature Preserves and Parks.*

✳ Green Space

GARDENS ✐ ❧ ♿ **Dauset Trails Nature Center** (770-775-6798; www.dausettrails.com), 360 Mount Vernon Road, Jackson. Open 9–5 Monday through Saturday, noon–5 Sunday. In the Woodland Garden, visitors can see native azaleas, fairy wands, pink lady's slippers, ferns, merry bells, asters, jack-in-the-pulpits, shooting stars, bird's-foot violets, lilies, bloodroot, mayapple, columbine, galax, phlox, trillium, Solomon's seal, and others. Children can get a list at the visitor center for the Pleasure Hunt, a quest to find fun garden ornaments. The Woodland Garden path ends at the Bog Garden, which features two ponds connected by a waterfall, a covered bridge, and a bog filled with irises, lily pads, ferns, turtles, frogs, and the occasional water snake. The Children's Garden features plants that inspire the senses of smell and touch. There is a formal knot garden in the middle. Free; donations accepted.

LAKES �& 🌿 **Lake Jackson** (770-775-4839; www.jackson-lake.com), Jackson Lake Road, Jackson. Open 7 AM–10 PM daily. The 4,700-acre, power-generating lake was created when a dam was built in 1910. Recreation is a secondary benefit. Lake Jackson has several marinas and offers innumerable opportunities for boating, fishing, swimming, and other water sports. One of the best fishing lakes in the state, it yields trophy-size bream, crappie, large-mouth bass, hybrid bass, catfish, and carp. Waterskiing can be enjoyed on the lake and up three major river tributaries. Parking at Lloyd Shoals Park $3.

NATURE PRESERVES AND PARKS �& 🌿 **Cubihatcha Outdoor Center, Towaliga River Preserve** (678-583-3930; www.hcwsa.com/community/cubihatcha .asp), 100 Collins Road, Locust Grove. Loop Trail open 8–5 year-round; River Trail open 8–5 weekdays, April through October. The center is a wetland enhancement and protection corridor created to improve and protect existing wildlife habitats, as well as for public education and enjoyment. Almost 1,000 acres of bottomland, hardwood forest, wetlands, and uplands typical of the Piedmont region provide diverse habitats for mammals, birds, fish, reptiles, amphibians, and insects. The 8-mile River Trail runs along the Towaliga River, while the Loop Trail is 2 miles around. Visitors can take a self-guided tour or arrange in advance for a walk led by a staff naturalist. (Note: The trails may be closed due to inclement weather or management discretion.) Free.

�& 🌿 & **Dauset Trails Nature Center** (770-775-6798; www.dausettrails.com), 360 Mount Vernon Road, Jackson. Open 9–5 Monday through Saturday, noon–5 Sunday; trails open sunrise–10 PM, provided users sign the release form located at the trailhead parking kiosk. (Note: The main entrance gate closes at 5 PM; after that, park at the trailhead outside the fence. Also note that trails are closed when wet.) The nature center offers 1,200 acres of creeks, lakes, ponds, and wildflower fields, while 17 miles of scenic wooded trails attract bikers, hikers, and observers of birds and other wildlife. The trails, marked for beginner, intermediate, and advanced hikers, include rocky terraces, bottomlands, and creeks. Ten miles of trails (separate from the hiking and biking trails) are open for horseback riding (BYOH—bring your own horse). The Wonder Room in the environmental nature education center interprets the area and exhibits live rehabilitated animals such as alligators, turtles, and snakes that are not releasable into the wild. Farm animals—chickens, guinea hens, goats, horses, mules, burros, cows, and pigs—are on view, too. The center also includes several gardens (see *Gardens*). Allow yourself at least two to three hours to see the main exhibits, more if you are hiking or biking. A piece of trivia: "Dauset" was created from the last names of the two people who started the nature center in 1977—Hampton DAUghtry and David SETtle. Free; donations accepted.

✧ ✿ ♿ **High Falls State Park** (478-993-3053; 1-800-864-7275; www.gastate parks.org/info/highfall), 76 High Falls Park Drive, Jackson. Open 7 AM–10 PM. Two hundred years ago, this site was a booming industrial village with a blacksmith shop, cotton gin, gristmill, shoe factory, several stores, and a hotel. In the late 1880s, it became a ghost town when the railroad bypassed it and all the buildings virtually disappeared. All that remains is the foundation of the gristmill. The scenic area and a waterfall on the Towaliga River led to the creation of a state park where visitors now come for many recreational opportunities. The 1,050-acre park features 4½ miles of hiking trails and a 650-acre lake for boating and fishing. Seasonally, visitors can play miniature golf and swim in the park's pool. For boaters, the park offers two ramps along with canoe and fishing-boat rentals. Private boats are allowed, but there is a 10-horsepower limit. Accommodations are available at the campground (see *Lodging—Campgrounds*). Parking $3.

✧ ✿ ♿ **Indian Springs State Park** (770-504-2277; 1-800-864-7275; www .gastateparks.org/info/indspr), 678 Lake Clark Road, Flovilla. Open 7–10 daily. The springs at this park, considered to be one of the oldest state parks in the country, were used by Creek Indians for centuries. The Native Americans believed the spring waters healed the sick and bestowed additional vitality to the well. During the 1800s, the area became a bustling resort town when settlers came to partake of the springs themselves. During the Great Depression, the Civilian Conservation Corps (CCC) built many of the structures within the park, including the springhouse. A museum, which is open seasonally, focuses on the Creek Indians, the resort era, and the CCC. Today the 528-acre park offers water sports on the 105-acre lake, miniature golf, and a short nature trail. Boating facilities include a boat ramp and seasonal pedal-boat rentals. Private boats are permitted, but there is a 10-horsepower limit. The park also offers camping and cottages (see *Lodging— Cottages and Cabins*). Parking $3.

✧ ✿ ♿ **Newman Wetlands Center** (770-603-5606; www.ccwa.us), 2755 Freeman Road, Hampton. Visitor center open 8:30–5 weekdays, September through May; 8:30–5 Tuesday through Saturday, June through August. Trail open 7–7 daily, March through October; 7–5 daily, November through February. A project of the Clayton County Water Authority, the area was

VISITORS TO INDIAN SPRINGS STATE PARK CAN TAKE TO THE WATER IN PEDAL BOATS.

created to demonstrate the importance of preserving wetland environments and to provide public education about natural resource conservation. The 32-acre facility consists of a trail and a visitor/interpretive center. The easy half-mile trail alternates between crushed stone through forested areas and a boardwalk over the swamp. Wheelchairs and strollers can be accommodated on the trail. The visitor center contains a central exhibit and learning lab area, an auditorium where a wetlands video is presented, and rest rooms. During the summer, weekday guided walks are often scheduled. In addition to 130 species of birds, other wildlife such as beaver, river otter, fox, raccoon, muskrat, deer, wild turkey, opossum, and mink have been sighted. Some species stop here during their migrations; others are permanent residents. The Atlanta Audubon Society holds Saturday-morning bird walks here all year. Birding classes and workshops are offered, too. Special programs on topics such as waterfowl, bats, reptiles, and gardening are scheduled annually. The **Wetlands and Watershed Festival** is held on the first Saturday after Labor Day. Free.

See also Parks Appendix.

✳ Lodging
CAMPGROUNDS

In Flovilla
✦ 🐾 🐾 ✿ **Indian Springs State Park** (770-504-2277; 1-800-864-7275; www.gastateparks.org/info/indspr), 678 Lake Clark Road. The park offers 88 tent, trailer, and RV sites as well as a pioneer campground. See also *Gardens— Nature Preserves and Parks.* $18–40.

In Jackson
✦ 🐾 🐾 ✿ **High Falls State Park** (478-993-3053; 1-800-864-7275; www.gastateparks.org/info/highfall), 76 High Falls Park Drive. The park offers 112 tent, trailer, and RV sites as well as a pioneer campground. See also *Gardens—Nature Preserves and Parks.* $18–40.

In McDonough
✦ 🐾 **Atlanta South RV Resort** (770-957-2610; 1-800-778-0668; www.atlantasouthrvresort.com), 281 Mount Olive Road. The campground provides 140 sites with water, sewer, and electric hook-ups as well as camping, cabin, and tent sites. Other amenities include rest rooms, laundry facilities, showers, a dump station, a pool, and a playground. The new clubhouse features a TV viewing area and Internet access. $35.

COTTAGES AND CABINS

In Flovilla
🐾 🐾 ✿ **Indian Springs State Park** (770-504-2277; 1-800-864-7275; www .gastateparks.org/info/indspr), 678 Lake Clark Road. The park features 10 fully equipped cottages. See also *Campgrounds* and *Gardens—Nature Preserves and Parks.* $80–95.

✳ Where to Eat
DINING OUT

In McDonough
✿ **Pilgreen's on Lake Dow** (770-957-4490), 1720 Lake Dow Road. Open 5–9 Monday through Thursday, 5–10 Friday and Saturday. A favorite with locals and well known for steaks and seafood for more than a half century, Pilgreen's offers white-table service with a view of the lake. No smoking. $11–26.

&. **Truman's** (770-320-8686), 32 Jonesboro Street. Open 11–3 Monday through Sunday; 3–9 Monday through Thursday, 3–10 Friday and Saturday. Dine in luxury at a historic home just off the square, where the cuisine is described as "fancy French to down-home." White tablecloths and soft music enhance the romantic atmosphere. Lunch choices include a wide variety of soups, salads, and sandwiches. Dinner entrées range from pasta to filet mignon. You'll also find everything from quesadillas to shrimp po'boys. Don't forget the delicious homemade desserts. No smoking inside; smoking in outdoor seating area. $7–19.

EATING OUT

In McDonough

♪ 🍴 &. **Gritz Family Restaurant** (770-914-0448), 14 Macon Street. Open 7–3 Monday through Saturday. Down-home Southern cooking is served for breakfast and lunch in a casual atmosphere. Start the day with a hearty breakfast of pancakes, omelets, or eggs fixed any way. Breakfast meats include bacon, sausage, ham, steak, chicken, pork, or corned beef hash. Of course, grits and biscuits make an appearance. Lunch entrées such as chicken and dumplings, salmon patties, fried chicken livers, and country-fried steak include two sides and bread. No smoking. $5–10.

&. **PJ's Café** (770-898-5373), 30 Macon Street. Open 11–9 Tuesday through Thursday, 11–10 Friday and Saturday, 11–8 Sunday. Steaks, seafood, and pasta are served in a casual atmosphere. The restaurant features a wine bar, international beers, and outdoor dining. Enjoy the

cozy bar and the beautiful mural in the dining room. No smoking inside; smoking in outdoor seating area. Lunch $4–10, dinner $11–16. Early bird specials 4–6:30 start at $6.95.

✳ Entertainment

DANCE Atlanta Festival Ballet (770-507-2775; www.festivalballet atlanta.com), mailing address: 416 Eagles Landing Parkway, Stockbridge 30281. The only professional dance company on the south side of metro Atlanta, the organization has 18 full-time professional dancers and more than 40 student apprentices in the Festival Ballet School. The company presents two full-length productions each year, including *The Nutcracker* at holiday time and a spring production, as well as a summer repertory program. Although the company is based in nearby Stockbridge (see Southern Suburbs chapter), performances are held at the **Henry County Schools Performing Arts Center** (770-914-7477), 37 Lemon Street, McDonough, as well as the **Clayton County Schools Performing Arts Center.**

MUSIC Henry County Community Chorus (770-389-4393). The 20-member vocal group performs three concerts annually, including a holiday concert in December, a spring performance, and a patriotic concert in the summer. Performances are at the **McDonough Presbyterian Church** or the **Henry County Schools Performing Arts Center** (770-914-7477), 37 Lemon Street, McDonough.

Southern Crescent Symphony Orchestra (770-389-1625), mailing address: 950 Eagles Landing Parkway, Suite 241, Stockbridge 30281. Call for a schedule of events and ticket prices; some concerts are free. The 75-member volunteer community orchestra composed of professional musicians, music educators, amateur musicians, and students presents four to six concerts annually ranging from Christmas sing-alongs to movie music, children's favorites to classical concertos. Although the symphony is based in Stockbridge (see Southern Suburbs chapter), it performs at the **Henry County Schools Performing Arts Center** (770-914-7477), 37 Lemon Street, McDonough, as well as other venues.

THEATER **Henry Players** (770-914-1474; www.henryplayers.com), mailing address: P.O. Box 3083, McDonough 30253. Call for a schedule of performances and ticket prices, which generally run about $10–12. Tickets are also available at several businesses and online. The theatrical company, which consists entirely of volunteers, presents five productions annually and does some charity performances as well. Productions are held at the **Henry County Schools Performing Arts Center** (770-914-7477), 37 Lemon Street, McDonough.

✳ Selective Shopping

Jackson's historic turn-of-the-20th-century downtown features antiques stores, quaint shops, and restaurants. **McDonough**'s historic town square abounds with antiques shops and also features an old-fashioned hardware store and an art design studio. Many of the merchants in McDonough have banded together to offer a booklet of shopping discounts at many of the town's shops, restaurants, and activities. The booklet can be obtained from the **McDonough Hospitality and Tourism Bureau** (see *Guidance*).

FLEA MARKETS **Peachtree Peddlers Flea Market** (770-914-2269; 1-888-661-3532; www.peachtree peddlers.com), 155 Mill Road, McDonough. Open 9–6 Saturday, 10–6 Sunday. The 200,000-square-foot, all-weather flea market features antiques and craft booths as well as booths for just about every item imaginable. Find books, floral arrangements, Georgia produce, gifts, and much, much more. In addition, the facility has a restaurant and hosts craft shows and other special entertainment events. Free.

Sweetie's Flea Market (770-946-4721), 2316 US 19 and US 441, Hampton. Open 8–4:30 Friday through Sunday year-round. Georgia's oldest flea market has a fun country-fair atmosphere and bargains galore. More than 100 dealers sell antiques, collectibles, farm and country items, primitives, and more. There is a snack bar on the premises, too.

OTHER GOODS **Atlanta Motor Speedway Gift Store** (770-707-7970; www.atlantamotorspeedway .com; www.gospeedway.com), 1500 Tara Place/US 41 North, Hampton. Open 9–5 Monday through Saturday, 1–5 Sunday. Shop here for Atlanta Motor Speedway and NASCAR apparel, flags, pins, jewelry, pens, postcards, electronics, and kitchen supplies. The gift shop is in the same building as the ticket office.

Nutmeg's (770-957-6199), 16 Macon Street, on town square, McDonough. Open 10–5:30 Monday, Tuesday, and Thursday through Saturday. The gift shop offers gourmet cookware, tableware, cookbooks, and housewarming gifts. Cooking and tea classes also are offered.

OUTLET STORES Tanger Outlet Center (770-957-5310; 1-800-406-0833; www.tangeroutlet.com), 1000 Tanger Drive, Locust Grove. Open 9–9 Monday through Saturday, noon–6 Sunday; longer hours on Thanksgiving weekend; closed Easter, Thanksgiving, and Christmas. One of the largest outlet centers in the country, this one features more than 60 of the nation's leading brand-name stores with quality merchandise at discount prices. It attracts more than 3.5 million shoppers annually.

✳ Special Events

Spring: **Geranium Festival** (678-432-7112). A more-than-quarter-century tradition on the square in

THE TOWN OF MCDONOUGH WELCOMES FALL WITH A FESTIVAL.

McDonough, the festival features an arts and crafts exhibition and sale, music, other entertainment, and great food. Free.

Summer: **Music on the Square concert series** (Peachtree Music, 770-474-9177). Music on the Square concerts 7–11 on specific dates in May, July, and August at the McDonough town square. Talented bands and soloists perform jazz, rock and roll, classical, and pop music. Concert-goers are invited to bring blankets or chairs, snacks, and beverages to enjoy while listening to music outdoors. Free.

October: **Fall Festival and Chili Cook-Off** (770-898-9868). Held on the McDonough town square, the event features a different kind of chili cooking contest. Instead of being judged according to certain criteria, participants are judged by the public. Participants (applications required) prepare their secret chili recipes ahead of time and bring them to the festival, where they're sold in sample-size cups. The person who sells the most cups wins. Other festival activities include entertainment, arts and crafts, and children's activities. Free admission; nominal fees for some activities.

December: **McDonough Holiday Tour of Homes** (770-957-4150). The tour allows glimpses into six to eight private homes each year to get visitors into the holiday spirit and perhaps give them decorating ideas. Note: The tour is not wheelchair friendly because there are so many steps involved. $8 in advance, $10 on day of tour.

NEWNAN, MORELAND, AND SENOIA

Coweta County was named for the Coweta Indians, a Creek tribe, and its name means "water falls." The county was formed in 1825, when Chief William McIntosh—who was part Scot, part Indian—signed the Treaty of Indian Springs, for which he was killed by his fellow tribesmen.

Coweta County has produced loads of famous folks, from literary giants to entertainers. In addition to authors Erskine Caldwell and Lewis Grizzard (see *To See—Museums*), other celebrities include David Boyd, who illustrates the *You Might Be a Redneck If . . .* books; Margaret Anne Barnes, who wrote *Murder in Coweta County;* country music stars Alan Jackson and Doug Stone; classical music personality Charles Wadsworth, who serves as the musical director of Charleston's Spoleto festival; and football great Drew Hill. Minnie Pearl began her career as a drama coach here as well.

The area should be familiar to moviegoers who have seen *Fried Green Tomatoes, Driving Miss Daisy, Pet Sematary II,* and *The War.* Numerous TV series and productions have been filmed here as well: *I'll Fly Away, Passing Glory, A Christmas Memory,* and *Andersonville,* to name just a few. Riverwood Studios, located on 105 acres in Senoia, is a complete production facility with several sound stages.

Two of the state's designated Scenic Trails travel through this area: the Chattahoochee-Flint Heritage Highway and the Georgia Antiques Trail.

GUIDANCE When planning a trip to the Newnan area, including Grantville, Moreland, Roscoe, Senoia, Sharpsburg, and Turin, contact the **Coweta County Convention and Visitors Bureau and Welcome Center** (770-254-2627; 1-800-826-9382; www.coweta.ga.us), 100 Walt Sanders Memorial Drive, Newnan 30265. Open 9–5 Monday through Saturday, 1–5 Sunday. Pick up a brochure for the Newnan antebellum and Victorian driving tour as well as brochures for Moreland, Senoia, and Grantville tours (see *To See—Scenic Drives*).

Visitors can also consult the **Newnan-Coweta County Chamber of Commerce** (770-253-2270; www.ncchamber.org), 23 Bullsboro Drive, Newnan 30264. Open 9–5 weekdays.

To learn more about Whitesburg, contact the **Carrollton Area Convention** and **Visitors Bureau** (770-214-9746; 1-800-292-0871; www.visitcarrollton.com), 102 North Lakeshore Drive, Carrollton 30117. Open 8:30–5 weekdays.

GETTING THERE *By air:* The nearest airport is **Hartsfield-Jackson Atlanta International Airport** (see What's Where in Georgia). Car rentals are available on-site and off (see What's Where in Georgia).

By bus: The nearest **Greyhound Lines** (1-800-231-2222; www.greyhound.com) bus station is in Atlanta at 232 Forsyth Street; call 404-584-1728. There is another station at the Atlanta airport, 6000 North Terminal Parkway; call 404-765-9598. LaGrange, which is southwest of Newnan, also has a station at 1328 Greenville Street; call 706-882-1897.

By car: The towns described in this chapter are clustered around I-85 south of Atlanta.

By train: The nearest **Amtrak** rail station (404-881-3067; 1-800-USA-RAIL; www.amtrak.com) to this area is in Atlanta at 1688 Peachtree Street NW (see What's Where in Georgia).

MEDICAL EMERGENCY For life-threatening emergencies, call 911. Otherwise, care is available at **Newnan Hospital** (770-253-2330), 80 Jackson Street.

VILLAGES AND NEIGHBORHOODS **Newnan** was founded in 1828 and named for General Daniel Newnan, a War of 1812 veteran and Georgia General Assemblyman, after the area was opened up for settlement in the Land Lottery of 1827. Newnan later became known as the "Hospital City of the Confederacy" because six field hospitals, which served as many as 10,000 wounded soldiers from both the South and North, were located in churches, homes, and other buildings there. A monument erected in 1885 on the east side of the courthouse square honors the Confederate soldiers lost in that war, 63 of whom were laid to rest in Oak Hill Cemetery. The city is renowned for its historic homes built before the Civil War and during the Victorian era, so much so that the motto "the City of Homes" is emblazoned in lights on the old Carnegie Library building in downtown Newnan.

There are numerous historic districts in and around Newnan. The **Newnan Historic District,** a nine-square-block area, was laid out in 1828 in the Washington plan, which includes wide avenues and a public square. This district contains the neo–Greek Revival 1904 courthouse, the first Carnegie-endowed library in Georgia, four religious structures, and the historic black commercial district along Broad Street.

The **Cole Town Historic District,** founded in 1854, is a residential neighborhood with a wide variety of architectural styles.

The **College-Temple Historic District,** laid out in 1828, is an example of a well-planned residential neighborhood where walkways, fences, formal gardens, open lawns, and hedges accent the varied architectural styles. The academy lot was the site of seven schools between 1829 and 1975. The last of those schools now houses the **Male Academy Museum** (see *To See—Museums*).

In contrast to the planned residential neighborhoods, the **Greenville Street–LaGrange Street Historic District** is a patterned development where the principal streets have the oldest and grandest homes, while the infill streets have newer, smaller houses. One of the houses, Buena Vista, served as a Confederate headquarters during the Battle of Brown's Mill in July 1864.

Although it began in 1895, a collection of homes known as the **Platinum Point Historic District** that was built by wealthy Newnan citizens really developed with increased use of automobiles. Built in a parklike atmosphere, the district contains a variety of the revival architecture popular at the turn of the 20th century.

Roscoe–Dunaway Gardens Historic District is actually in Roscoe, a small crossroads community surrounded by farmsteads. The hamlet, which is listed on the National Register of Historic Places, features antebellum homes as well as architectural styles representing the late 19th and early 20th centuries. These farmhouses, large wood-framed barns, and fields depict the prominent role agriculture played and still plays in Coweta County. The only retail establishment left in town is the Roscoe General Store. A mural depicting Roscoe's busier times—when it had eight steam gins, five sawmills, four gristmills, four stores, six churches, and five schools—is painted on the side of the building. **Dunaway Gardens** was recently reopened (see *Green Space—Gardens*).

The town of **Grantville,** which was originally named Calico Corners, was renamed in 1852 for L. P. Grant, president of the Atlantic and LaGrange Railroad. In the late 19th and early 20th centuries, the town flourished with three factories, two banks, a theater, a civic auditorium, and a telephone and telegraph office—all of which earned it the name "Gem of Coweta County." Unfortunately, Grantville declined, and today it is a very small but friendly town.

The **Grantville Historic District** represents a small railroad town that grew up along the tracks. Two historic mills and mill villages remain within the district along with several churches and the passenger and freight depot. One of the most significant homes is Bonnie Castle, an elaborate Romanesque brick home built in 1896 using a variety of styles.

Moreland, originally a railroad stop called Puckett's Station, was once a booming cotton town with a hosiery mill. It was the birthplace of two famous authors: novelist Erskine Caldwell and humorist Lewis Grizzard. Today the small town boasts three museums (see *To See—Museums*), a bike/pedestrian path that winds through town, and a huge Fourth of July weekend celebration (see *Special Events*).

Senoia was developed from a cluster of farms in 1827. When the coming of the railroads brought about the need for an organized community, the town was founded in 1860, then incorporated in 1864. Two railroads intersected in Senoia, and cotton and peaches were shipped from there. It is believed that the town was named for the wife of Chief William McIntosh, Senoya He-ne-ha, who was also his cousin. Much of the original town remains intact as a nationally designated historic district (see *To See—Scenic Drives*). No trip to Senoia would be complete without a visit to the **Buggy Shop Museum** (see *To See—Museums*), a stay at the Culpepper House Bed and Breakfast (see *Lodging—Bed and Break-*

fasts), and shopping at the old-time Hutchinson Hardware. The **Senoia Historic District** contains 150 historic structures representing architectural styles from Greek Revival to Queen Anne. It also includes several antebellum homes that predate the town's development. Most, however, are from the turn of the 20th century.

Old Town Sharpsburg features antiques and craft shops housed in turn-of-the-20th-century buildings.

Whitesburg is known for the **McIntosh Reserve** (see *Green Space—Nature Preserves and Parks*), a recreation area on the site of the plantation of Chief McIntosh, and a superior inn located on the site of a historic mill (see *Lodging—Resorts*).

✳ To See

MUSEUMS ✎ ✤ **Buggy Shop Museum** (770-253-1018), Main Street, Senoia. Open 1–4 on third Saturday and Sunday of each month, April through October, or by appointment. Relive history by viewing buggies, old-time tools and machinery, antique cars, player pianos, Coca-Cola memorabilia, and collectibles from a bygone era. The rustic building that houses the museum was built in 1867. Small admission fee.

✤ ♿ **Coweta County African American Heritage Museum and Research Center** (770-683-7055; www.africanamericanalliance.net), 92 Farmer Street, Newnan. Open 10–4 weekdays. The shotgun house in which the museum is located is an excellent example of historical African American architecture. The museum serves as a repository for artifacts concerning Newnan's African American history and an active research center. A slave cemetery sits under centuries-old giant oak trees on the grounds. An authentic slave cabin is being relocated on the property and will be restored. Free; donations accepted.

✤ ♿ **Erskine Caldwell Birthplace and Museum** (770-251-4438; 770-254-8687; www.coweta.ga.us), East Camp Street on town square, Moreland. Open 1–4 Saturday and Sunday. "The Little Manse" was the birthplace of native son and world-famous author Erskine Caldwell. The small wooden house has been restored to its 1903 appearance and relocated to the town square to serve as a house museum documenting Caldwell's life and accomplishments and to reflect life when the mill dominated the South. The museum features biographical exhibits, personal items, and copies of his books in different languages. Although Caldwell penned 25 novels, he is best remembered for his compelling depictions of the rural South during the Great Depression in *Tobacco Road* and *God's Little Acre*. Adults $2, children $1.

✤ ♿ **Lewis Grizzard Museum** (770-304-1490; 1-800-826-9382; www.cowetaga.com), 2769 US 29 South, Moreland. Open 10–6 daily. Native son Lewis Grizzard, who died from heart disease in 1994 at age 47, was beloved as a Southern humorist,

PRONOUNCE IT CORRECTLY
Senoia looks as if it would be pronounced Seh-NOY-yuh, but locals say Seh-NOY. You'll show that you're a visitor if you mispronounce it.

author, and entertainer. Grizzard put Moreland on the map with his syndicated columns and books such as *Don't Sit Under the Grits Tree with Anyone Else but Me* and *Elvis Is Dead and I Don't Feel So Good Myself* in which he fondly told about his childhood in the small rural town. The museum showcases old typewriters, family photos, mementos, and manuscripts. $1.

✎ ✿ ♿ **Male Academy Museum** (770-251-0207; www.nchistoricalsociety.org), 30 Temple Avenue, Newnan. Open 10–noon and 1–3 Tuesday through Thursday, 2–5 Saturday and Sunday. Once a school for boys, the museum features a Civil War exhibit with an authentic Confederate battle flag, uniforms, soldiers' personal items, artifacts, weaponry, maps, and paintings of the Battle of Brown's Mill. The museum is noted for its extensive collection of 19th- and early 20th-century clothing. $3, younger than 12 free.

✎ ✿ ♿ **Old Mill Museum** (770-254-2627; 1-800-826-9382; www.cowetaga.com), Main Street on town square, Moreland. Open 1–4 Saturday and Sunday by reservation only. The massive brick Moreland Mill on the square was once a hosiery mill. Today it houses town offices, meeting space, and the town museum. Exhibits include artifacts from the building's days as a mill, antique farming equipment, World War II memorabilia, rural Georgia collectibles, and a Smithsonian textile display. Dr. Quigg Young's medical office, which closed years ago, is always open as an exhibit. Outside is a garden planted in memory of longtime resident Lamar Haynes. $2.

SCENIC DRIVES Pick up the brochures for all these tours from the **Coweta County Convention and Visitors Bureau and Welcome Center** (see *Guidance*).

The Chattahoochee-Flint Heritage Highway. runs through Coweta, Troup, Harris, and Meriwether counties from Roscoe to St. Marks. The Creek Indians originally inhabited this land. Today the scenic highway and bike route is filled with historic sites.

Historic Grantville Driving Tour. takes you past lovely homes, among them the Smith-Wilson House and Bonnie Castle. The Renaissance Revival home with its round battlementlike tower is surrounded by an original decorative wrought-iron fence. The original hitching post is still in place as well.

Moreland Driving Tour. takes visitors past the restored history of the town, including the **Old Mill Building** (1894; see *Museums*), the Old Moreland Post Office (1876), Founders Cemetery, and historic homes. Browse for antiques in the old general store.

Newnan Driving Tour. includes five historic districts. Antebellum and Victorian-era houses, which are marked with black metal signs, represent Gothic, Queen Anne, Eastlake, Second Empire, and Colonial Revival styles. Particularly interesting are the Painted Ladies, those Victorian-era houses painted in three or more colors.

Senoia Driving Tour of Homes. points out historic homes, businesses, and churches amid the town's tree-lined streets, 150 historic structures, and a commercial district.

✳ To Do

AUTO RACING ✐ ❧ ♿ **Senoia Speedway** (770-599-6161; www.senoiaspeedway.com), 171 Brown Road, Senoia. Call for a schedule of events. For night races, gates open at 4:30 and races begin at 6:45; for day races, gates open at 12:45 and races begin at 2:45. Events at the speedway include many classes and series: the O'Reilly United Sprint Car Series, the Georgia Asphalt Series, Pro Challenge, Bandoleros, Street Stock, Legends-Pro, Legends-Semi-Pro, Sportsman, and IceMan classes. The demolition derby is another popular event. Adults $10, children younger than 10 $2. For special events, general admission is $15, $20 for positions at the fence, $30 for positions at the pits.

BICYCLING ✐ ❧ **McIntosh Reserve** (770-830-5879; www.carrollcounty.com), 1046 West McIntosh Circle, Whitesburg. Open 8–dusk daily. (Note: The park is gated, and gates close promptly at sundown. Be sure to be out by then if you are not camping there.) Several interconnecting mountain biking trails in the reserve provide 15 miles of riding. Good places to start are the park station and Council Bluff. The trails provide a variety of flat and hilly terrain for beginning and intermediate riders, but there are some sandy, rocky, and eroded areas. And look out: Horses also use the trails and often leave a calling card behind. There is a yearly mountain bike race in August. $2.

CANOEING, KAYAKING, AND RAFTING ✐ ❧ **McIntosh Reserve** (770-830-5879; www.carrollcountyga.com), 1046 West McIntosh Circle, Whitesburg. Open 8–dusk daily. (See the warning above about the gates closing at sundown.) The Chattahoochee River, which forms the southern boundary of the reserve, provides an excellent venue for these paddling sports. $2.

FRIGHTS ✐ ❧ **Horror Hill Haunted Trail and Vertigo Haunted Trail** (770-253-4983; www.horrorhill.com), Newnan. Open evenings at Halloween time. In operation since 1984 and considered to be the largest haunted trail in the Southeast, the route features buildings, cabins, mazes, tunnels, bridges, trapdoors, fog machines, lasers, and strobe lights to create spooky effects. When calling to make a reservation, ask for directions to the first stop on the trail. $12 for Horror Hill Haunted Trail, $20 for both trails.

GOLF See Golf Appendix.

HORSEBACK RIDING See Other Activities Appendix.

SKATING See Other Activities Appendix.

✳ Green Space

GARDENS ✐ ❧ ♿ **Dunaway Gardens** (678-423-4050; www.dunawaygardens.com), 3218 Roscoe Road, Newnan. Open March 15 through November 30, 10–5 Thursday through Saturday, 1–5 Sunday. One of the South's largest natural rock and floral gardens, 25-acre Dunaway Gardens features spring-fed pools, stone waterfalls, and extensive rock paths, walls, and staircases. Dunaway Gardens was created on a former cotton plantation by vaudeville Chautauqua actress Hetty Jane Dunaway and her husband, Wayne Sewell, as part of a larger complex that included a theatrical training center, said to be one of the largest in the 1920s. Many of the company's ballet and theatrical productions were originally previewed at the 1,000-seat amphitheater. Walt and Roy Disney were frequent visitors, and Sarah Ophelia Colley created her Minnie Pearl character here in the 1930s. The gardens remained popular up until the 1950s, when the tearoom was often used for parties and plays were produced in the Patchwork Barn. Dunaway died in 1961 and the gardens were abandoned. Over the years of neglect the historic buildings disappeared, but the walls, walkways, patios, pools, ponds, and waterfalls were salvageable. Jennifer Rae Bingham bought the property in 2000 and spent three years reclaiming the gardens. Today visitors can enjoy the numerous pools, an amphitheater, rockery, many themed gardens, and patios. Little Stone Mountain is a huge outcropping of exposed granite, the base of which underlies the entire garden. It was said to be a favorite campsite of Chief William McIntosh. Adults $10, children $8.

🐾 ♿ **Oak Grove Plantation and Gardens** (770-463-3010; www.oakgrovega .com), 4537 US 29, Newnan. Open periodically for tours. Central to the plantation is the 1830s four-over-four house, which reflects early Plantation Plain and Federal styles. The owners live in the house and it is open only on special occasions, but visitors can admire the exterior architectural details. A restored carriage house offers bed & breakfast accommodations (see *Lodging—Bed and Breakfasts*). Four acres of gardens feature old-fashioned flowers and shrubs as well as herbs and vegetables. There are also other themed areas such as the pool, meditation, secret, formal, patience, shade, rhododendron, sunken, and *sin el agua* (without water) gardens. A historic family cemetery created by former owners that is on the property is attractively planted as well. Oak Grove Plantation Nursery specializes in old-fashioned flowers and shrubs. $5.

NATURE PRESERVES AND PARKS 🐾 ♿ **Coweta County Fairgrounds** (770-254-2685), 275 Pine Road, Newnan. The 65-acre facility hosts the five-day **Coweta County Fair** in September, 4-H events, horse shows, rodeos, dog shows, circuses, and other events. The **Walker Horne Open Air Theater** is a popular site for concerts, stage performances, and weddings. Also within the facility is the **James E. McGuffey Nature Center,** 30 acres of green space with a small pond, wetland environment, forest, and nearly 3 miles of nature trails. The complex also has a hard-surface, wheelchair-accessible trail.

DUNAWAY GARDENS IN NEWNAN IS ONE OF THE SOUTH'S LARGEST GARDENS.

ATLANTA METRO

     McIntosh Reserve (770-830-5879; www.carrollcountyga.com), 1046 West McIntosh Circle, Whitesburg. Open 8–dusk daily. (Note: The reserve is a gated facility and is closed at sundown unless camping arrangements have been made.) The reserve is named for Chief William McIntosh Jr., the son of a Scottish captain in the British Army and a full-blooded Creek Indian woman who belonged to the Wind Clan of the Creek Nation. The park contains part of his plantation, which he called Lochau Talofau, or "Acorn Bluff." McIntosh rose to the rank of chief in the Coweta tribe of the Lower Creeks but was killed May 1, 1825, by his own people, who were angered that he had ceded land to the white settlers.

This area is called a "reserve" because McIntosh reserved some of it for himself. His simple grave is here, as well as a reproduction of his rustic dogtrot-style house. Today, the property—which combines recreational activities, preservation of cultural heritage, education, fish and wildlife management, and conservation of the Chattahoochee River corridor—is used for camping, hiking, fishing, canoeing, rafting, and picnicking. More than 14 miles of trails, enjoyed by hikers, cyclists, and equestrians, wind through the reserve and along the Chattahoochee River, which forms the southern boundary. Model-airplane enthusiasts enjoy the grass airstrip in the lower park near the camping area. Primitive camping can be arranged for weekends only. During the summer, the **Spray and Splash Water Park** is open daily ($1). Annual events include the **Easter Festival, Fall Festival, Native American Pow Wow, Halloween Carnival,** and **Chattahoochee Challenge Car Show.** $2.

CHIEF WILLIAM MCINTOSH

McIntosh, a Lower Creek chief, served America as a distinguished soldier in several battles—including Autossee, Horseshoe Bend, the Creek Indian War, and the Seminole Wars—for which he was awarded the rank of brigadier general in the U.S. Army (the only Indian to ever reach that rank). He fought with Andrew Jackson and even dined with President Thomas Jefferson at the White House. Raised as an Indian, he never knew his Tory father, but since descent was determined through the mother, that was of little importance to the Creeks. He owned a plantation and operated an inn, two taverns, a trading post, and a ferry across the Chattahoochee River. He also owned 72 slaves and had Indians and white men working for him. McIntosh and other Lower Creeks ceded all Creek lands in Georgia west of the Flint River to the U.S. government. He then planned to leave for lands he had been promised in Arkansas. Before he could do that, however, the Upper Creeks killed him, burned the plantation, and destroyed what stock they didn't take, but spared the lives of the women and children.

✳ Lodging
BED & BREAKFASTS

In Newnan
Oak Grove Plantation and Gardens (770-463-3010; 770-841-0789; www.oakgrovega.com), 4537 US 29 North. Located on 20 acres, the plantation is listed on the National Register of Historic Places (see *Green Space—Gardens*). Guest accommodations are offered in the restored tin-roofed carriage house, where two suites boast antique furnishings and private baths with Jacuzzi tubs. The cottage also features a common room stocked with diversions such as games, puzzles, TV, a video and DVD player, and books. There is also a vintage kitchen, which guests are free to use. In addition to enjoying the many different gardens, guests can use the outdoor pool and the playhouse area. Homemade cookies are served in the evening, and the day begins with a hearty breakfast. No smoking. Not wheelchair accessible. $105–155.

In Senoia
Culpepper House (770-599-8182; www.culpepperhouse.com), 35 Broad Street. The house was built in 1871 by Dr. John Addy, a Confederate veteran. The oak trees he planted during that era continue to shade the house and property. The house later belonged to Dr. Wilbur Culpepper and has retained his name. Twelve-foot ceilings and other architectural elements of the period create gracious public rooms and three guest rooms. Guests particularly enjoy the wraparound porch. A generous buffet breakfast is included in the nightly rate. No smoking. Not wheelchair accessible. $95–105.

CAMPGROUNDS

In Whitesburg
♂ 🐾 **McIntosh Reserve** (770-830-5879; www.carrollcounty.com), 1046 West McIntosh Circle. Reservations for primitive camping are restricted to weekends only and can be arranged by calling the office between 9 and 5 weekdays. See also *Green Space—Nature Preserves and Parks.* $10 for county residents, $15 for nonresidents.

RESORTS

In Whitesburg
The Lodges at Historic Banning Mills Country Inn, Executive Retreat and Spa (770-834-9149; 1-866-447-8688; www.HistoricBanningMills.com), 205 Horseshoe Dam Road. The retreat is nestled on 700 wooded acres overlooking the Snake Creek Gorge. Guest accommodations are rooms in the lodge, log cabin suites, and cozy cottages. Many rooms feature a Jacuzzi, gas-log fireplace, refrigerator, microwave, and a deck with a spectacular view. Dining includes a full breakfast, deli box lunch or gourmet picnic basket, and dinner. Amenities at the resort include an Olympic-size swimming pool; tennis, basketball, and sand volleyball courts; an 18-hole putting green; a baseball field; and a horseshoe pit. Hiking along old town trails, Creek Indian paths, old water raceways, and along the Snake River can range from mild to moderately strenuous. Other activities, which are charged separately and range in price from $10 to $70, include fly-fishing, hayrides, skeet shooting, pistol shooting, and kayaking. An on-site spa offers numerous packages and body treatments ranging in price from $30

to $235. No smoking. Not wheelchair accessible. $99–159; ask about special packages.

✳ Where to Eat

DINING OUT

In Newnan

& **Andre's** (770-304-3557), 11 Jefferson Street. Open 5–9:30 Tuesday through Saturday. Serving creative American cuisine, the upscale restaurant features fresh seafood every night. No smoking. $14–26.

& **Brick Yard Restaurant** (770-252-6000), 9 East Court Square. Open from 5 PM Tuesday through Saturday. Newnan's newest fine dining establishment, which is located on the square, serves steaks, seafood, and chef's specials. The restaurant has an extensive wine list and often sponsors wine tastings. Reservations are recommended. No smoking. $18–28.

& **Ten East Washington** (770-502-9100; www.teneastwashington.com), 10 E. Washington Street. Open 5–9 Tuesday through Saturday. Located just off the square, one of Newnan's finest restaurants has earned a reputation for superbly prepared seafood, steaks, and continental cuisine. Chef George Rasovsky concentrates on refinement and fresh products. Live entertainment is offered once a month. No smoking. $14–26.

EATING OUT

In Newnan

✦ ☕ & **Catfish Hollow** (770-502-1223), 2826 GA 154. Open 4:30–9 Tuesday through Thursday, 4:30–10 Friday and Saturday. Naturally, the restaurant serves a multitude of seafood choices, but diners also can choose among steaks, burgers, veggie

plates, and more. No smoking. $8.75–19.

✦ ☕ & **Golden's on the Square** (770-251-4300), 9 E. Gordon Street. Open 11–9 Tuesday through Sunday. Located in a historic downtown building, Golden's has been feeding the citizenry of Newnan for 28 years. Every day, the kitchen staff prepares six to eight made-from-scratch entrées, 12 to 14 freshly steamed vegetables, six to eight salads, and a variety of desserts. All meals are the same price and include a beverage, roll, and butter. No smoking. $6.50.

✦ ☕ & **Gumbeaux—A Cajun Café** (770-304-8144), 385 US 29 North. Open 11–2 Monday through Saturday; 5–9:30 Monday through Thursday, 5–10 Friday and Saturday. This is the best place to go in west Georgia for Cajun dishes such as gumbo and jambalaya. No smoking. $8–12.

✦ ☕ & **Redneck Gourmet Corner Cafe** (770-251-0092; www.redneck gourmet.com), 11 North Court Square. Open 7:30–10:30 AM and 11–3 Monday through Saturday. Breakfast is cooked to order and includes anything you could want, from eggs and breakfast meats to pancakes and French toast. For lunch, diners can enjoy hot and cold sandwiches, salads, soups, daily specials, as well as homemade desserts and cookies. The café, which has been operated by the Smith family for 14 years, is noted for its wide array of hot sauces. Monday's special is BBQ and their "Nearly Famous" Brunswick stew, Thursday features the "Red" Plate Special, and Friday and Saturday are Hot Dawg Days. A new addition is Redneck-without-the-wait take-out. Call 770-683-NECK to place your order. No smoking. Breakfast $5, lunch $4–7.

🐕 🐾 ♿ **Sprayberry's Barbecue**
(770-253-4421; www.sprayberrybbq
.com), 229 Jackson Street, and (770-
253-5080), GA 34 West (exit 47 off I-
85). Open 10:30–9 Monday through
Saturday. Sprayberry's was humorist
Lewis Grizzard's favorite place to eat,
and there's even a dish named after
him. Using a vinegar-based sauce and
slow roasting meat over an oak and
hickory fire, Sprayberry's offers BBQ
chicken and slow-roasted pork,
Brunswick stew, and baby-back ribs.
Grilled fish tacos, meatloaf, and a full
menu are also featured at the original
1926 location in a former gas station
on Jackson Street as well as at the
new location on GA 34 West. Sprayberry's is also renowned for its homemade pies—especially its fried pies.
No smoking. $3.75–14.95.

✳ **Entertainment**
**THEATER Newnan Theatre Com-
pany** (770-683-NCTC; www.newnan
theatre.com), 24 First Avenue, Newnan. The troupe, which has been in
existence since 1975, produces comedies, dramas, musicals, works by
Shakespeare, experimental pieces,
and children's productions. Although
the company has performed in converted warehouses, old cotton mills,
churches, and even open fields, it now
has a home in the former Johnson
Hardware Building. Call for a schedule of performances and ticket prices,
which run about $12 for adults, $10
for seniors and students for the Main-
Stage Series; $2 less for the Artist
Series and the Popcorn Theatre Series.

✳ **Selective Shopping**
ANTIQUES Re-Use the Past (770-
583-3111; www.ReUseThePast.com),
98 Moreland Street, Grantville. Open
noon–5 Wednesday through Monday.
The firm's motto is "If it's old, we
probably have it." Located in an 1895
hosiery mill, the company serves as an
architectural salvage and antiques
store. If you're remodeling a historic
house, this is the place to get antique
heart-pine floorboards, ceiling tin,
doors, Victorian-era stained glass,
bricks, pavers, hinges, doorknobs,
chair rails, and molding, just to name
a few items. If you simply want to add
to your furnishings and decor, the
store carries mirrors, coat hangers,
wall sconces, antique furniture, and
regional pottery.

SPRAYBERRY'S BBQ
The now legendary eatery had its beginning as Houston Sprayberry's gas
station. Sprayberry began selling BBQ sandwiches made on-site with his
special sauce, and soon he was selling so many he closed the pumps and
opened a restaurant. Politicians from U.S. presidents to governors have
campaigned here, and entertainers and athletes stop in as well. Country
music star Alan Jackson waited tables here when he was in high school, so
whenever he's in the area, he stops in for BBQ, Brunswick stew, and lemon
pie. Lewis Grizzard proclaimed Sprayberry's "merely the best barbecue joint
on earth." His choice of meal was a BBQ sandwich, Brunswick stew, and
onion—a combination now known as the Lewis Grizzard Special.

BOOKS **Scott's Book Store** (770-254-9862; www.cityofnewnan.com/businesses/scotts), 28 South Court Square, Newnan. Open 9–6 weekdays, 9–4 Saturday. In addition to a wide selection of books and an extensive children's section, the store carries plush toys, American Girl dolls, and other items. You can purchase tickets here for local events as well.

GIFTS **Collector's Corner** (770-251-6835; www.collectors-corner.net), 8861 GA 54, Sharpsburg. Open 10–6 Monday through Saturday, 1–5 Sunday. This vast shop features antiques, collectibles, gifts, furniture, heritage lace, home and garden accessories, lamps, pictures, mirrors, custom florals, baby and toddler clothing, and much more. Take a break from shopping with a bite in the Jasmine Tea Room and Restaurant. The store has several special events throughout the year.

✳ Special Events

February: **Charles Wadsworth and Friends Concert** (770-253-2270). The native-son pianist and Spoleto musical director performs at Wadsworth Auditorium in Newnan with some of his friends. $30.

April: **Senoia Tour of Homes and Progressive Dinner** (770-251-0207). The Senoia Area Historical Society presents this much-anticipated event, which allows visitors to get a glimpse into several historic homes. $40.

Tour of Homes (770-251-0207). Sponsored by the Newnan-Coweta Historical Society, the tour includes some of Newnan's most beautiful antebellum and Victorian-era homes as well as an art show, antique car show, and trolley tour. $13.

June: **Grantville Day** (770-583-3212). Grantville Day is celebrated with live bands and other entertainment, food, and shopping bargains. Although the festival is called Grantville Day, it is actually held Friday evening, Saturday, and Sunday. Free.

Fourth of July weekend: **Moreland Independence Day Barbecue** (770-251-3428) and **Puckett's Station Arts and Crafts Festival** (770-583-2200; 770-251-3428). For more than half a century, three Moreland-area churches have prepared BBQ pork and stew, which is now served at the Lewis Grizzard Pavilion behind the old Moreland Mill for $6 a plate. Chefs work through the night to cook about 3,000 pounds of meat, and there's already a long line when sales begin at 11 AM. The arts and crafts fair, which is named for Moreland's original name, begins at 9 AM. Activities free except for dinner.

July: **Annual Watermelon Festival** (770-252-9400; 770-254-2627; 1-800-826-9382). Everyone gets free watermelon at this popular Sharpsburg event, and there's also a watermelon seed–spitting contest, antiques dealers, crafts vendors, and old-fashioned games. Free.

August: **Turin Antique Farm Power Show and Tractor Pull** (770-254-2627; 1-800-826-9382). Held the third weekend in August in downtown Turin, the event is sponsored by the West Georgia 2-Cylinder Club. The event begins on Friday with a block party and dance. Saturday morning features 100-plus antique tractors (pre-1965) in a parade at 10 AM. Other events include a slow race, hand-start race, powder puff pull for ladies, and pedal race for kids. Free.

Labor Day weekend: **Powers' Cross-**

roads Country Fair and Art Festival (770-253-2011; www.newnan.com/cowetafestivals/powers). Open 9–5 Saturday through Monday. One of the outstanding events in the nation, the fair at historic Powers Plantation in Newnan features 250 or more juried artists and craftspeople, continuous entertainment, a wide variety of food, a children's play area, and demonstrations of plantation skills. Free parking at remote lots and free shuttle buses are provided. Adults $5, seniors and military $4, children ages 5–12 $2.

December: **Newnan Candlelight Tour of Homes** (770-253-8866). The walking tour features homes, churches, and businesses along with lavish refreshments and evening entertainment. $15.

NORTHERN SUBURBS(NORTHSIDE): TALLAPOOSA TO SOCIAL CIRCLE

Atlanta was once surrounded by small municipalities, some of which predated the city, as well as by seemingly endless rural regions of fields and forests. As the metropolitan area grew—and grew—these towns appeared to be swallowed up. Although it's sometimes hard to distinguish one from another, many still exist as governmental entities and each has its own distinct personality. More than simply bedroom communities for Atlanta, these municipalities offer numerous activities, attractions, lodgings, restaurants, and special events to draw the visitor.

All the towns described in this chapter lie north of I-20, stretching from the Alabama-Georgia state line to Covington, which is east of Atlanta. In fact, the vast majority of these towns lie right along I-20. A few of them are a bit farther north. Marietta and Kennesaw are easily reached from I-75, and Roswell and Alpharetta from GA 400. A traveler interested in visiting some of these towns could start on one side of the city and spend a couple days and nights exploring the area on the east or west side of Atlanta, stay overnight in the city, and then take a few days to explore the area on the other side of the city. Another alternative would be to use Atlanta as a hub and make day trips to the east and west of the city.

The most recognizable natural landmark in the region is Stone Mountain. About 300 million years ago, intense heat and pressure forced molten rock upward. When it cooled, the lava coalesced into compact granite crystals—an unusual mixture of feldspar, mica, and quartz—but it still remained 2 miles beneath the earth's surface. Over the next 200 million years, erosion not only exposed the mass but left 583 acres uncovered at a height of 825 feet above the surface: what we know today as Stone Mountain. Pieces of soapstone bowls and dishes found at the base of the mountain indicate that Native Americans lived around the mountain as long as 5,000 years ago. Long used as a landmark and gathering place by Native Americans and early American settlers, the massive mountain is now the centerpiece of Stone Mountain Park.

In 1909 C. Helen Plane had the idea of memorializing the Confederacy with a carving on the mountain. After several false starts, the carving was finally completed in 1970. It depicts Confederate President Jefferson Davis and Generals Robert E. Lee and Thomas "Stonewall" Jackson astride their steeds. The area of the figures measures 90 by 190 feet and is surrounded by a 3-acre carved surface that is 400 feet above the ground and recessed 42 feet into the mountain. With the carving as a centerpiece, the ever-evolving park has developed.

The second most significant landmark is Kennesaw Mountain. A major Civil War battle occurred here, and the area is now a national battlefield park (see *To See—Historic Homes and Sites*).

GUIDANCE For more information about Alpharetta, contact the **Alpharetta Convention and Visitors Bureau** (678-297-2811; 1-800-294-0923; www .awesomealpharetta.com), 3060 Royal Boulevard S., Suite 145, Alpharetta 30022. Open 8:30–5 Monday through Thursday, 8:30–4:30 Friday. Also consult or stop by the friendly **Alpharetta Welcome Center** (678-297-0102; 1-800-294-0923; www.awesomealpharetta.com), 20 N. Main Street, Alpharetta 30004. Open 9–5 weekdays, 10–4 Saturday.

To learn more about Conyers, contact the **Conyers Convention and Visitors Bureau–Conyers Welcome Center** (770-929-4270; 770-602-2606; 1-800-CONYERS; www.conyersga.com), 1184 Scott Street, Conyers 30012. Open 8–5 weekdays.

For more information about Covington, contact the **Covington–Newton County Convention and Visitors Bureau and Welcome Center** (770-787-3868; 1-800-616-8626; www.newtonchamber.com), 2101 Clark Street, Covington 30014. Open 9–5 weekdays, 10–4 Saturday. Pick up a brochure for the walking/driving tour, which has 46 points of interest.

Those planning a trip to the Decatur–DeKalb County area should contact the **DeKalb Convention and Visitors Bureau** (770-492-5000; 1-800-999-6055; www.dcvb.org), 1957 Lakeside Parkway, Suite 510, Tucker 30084. Open 8:30–5 weekdays.

To find out more about Kennesaw, call the **City of Kennesaw** (770-422-9714; www.kennesaw.ga.us). For information on all of Cobb County, contact the **Cobb County Convention and Visitors Bureau** (678-303-2622; 1-800-451-3480; www.cobbcvb.com), One Galleria Parkway, Atlanta 30339. Open 8:30–5:30 weekdays.

When planning a trip to the Lawrenceville area, contact the **Lawrenceville Tourism and Trade Association** (678-226-2639; www.visitlawrenceville.com), 162 E. Crogan Street, Suite K, Lawrenceville 30046. Open 8–5 weekdays.

For information about Lithonia, contact the **Greater Lithonia–Snapfinger Woods Chamber of Commerce** (770-482-1808), P.O. Box, Lithonia 30074.

When planning a trip to the Marietta area, contact the **Marietta Welcome Center and Visitors Bureau** (770-429-1115; 1-800-835-0445; www.marietta square.com), 4 Depot Street, Marietta 30060. Open 9–5 weekdays, 10–4 Saturday, 1–4 Sunday. Located in the charming 1898 Nashville, Chattanooga, and St. Louis Railway Company passenger train depot, the welcome center features the video *Marietta, My Hometown*, narrated by former Marietta resident Joanne Woodward. The depot was built on the site of the 1840s Western and Atlantic Railroad depot, which was destroyed by Union troops in 1864.

For more information about Monroe, contact the **Walton County Chamber of Commerce** (770-267-6594; www.waltonchamber.org), 323 W. Spring Street, Monroe 30655. Open 9–5 Monday through Thursday, 9–4 Friday.

When planning a trip to the Roswell area, contact the **Historic Roswell Convention and Visitors Bureau–Visitor Center** (770-640-3253; 1-800-776-7935; www.cvb.roswell.ga.us), 617 Atlanta Street, Roswell 30075. Open 9–5 weekdays, 10–4 Saturday, noon–3 Sunday. Stop here to watch a film, examine historic exhibits, and get pamphlets and advice. A brochure for a self-guided walking/driving tour is also available. Guided tours offered by the **Roswell Historical Society** (770-992-1665; www.roswellhs.com) depart from the visitor center at 10 AM Wednesday and 1 PM Saturday. These tours and audio cassette tours cost $5.

To learn more about Social Circle, contact the **Social Circle Visitors Center** (770-464-1866), 294 N. Cherokee Road, Social Circle 30025.

To find out more about **Stone Mountain Park,** US 78 in Stone Mountain, call 770-498-5690 or 1-800-317-2006, or visit the web site at www.stonemountain park.com. The park and its attractions are featured many times throughout this chapter, so we list the contact information, hours, and admission fees only once—here. The park is open 6 AM–midnight daily; the individual attractions generally operate 10–8 daily in summer with shorter hours the remainder of the year. An $8 parking fee per vehicle is required for entrance to the park (bicyclists and pedestrians can enter for free). Other attractions are priced at about $7 each, so you can pay for only what you use. If you intend to visit more than three attractions, it would be wise to purchase a One-Day All Attractions Pass combination ticket: ages 12 and older $20, seniors and military $18, ages 3–11 $17; $13 after 4 PM. Ride the Ducks is an additional add-on to the All Attractions Pass. Because some attractions are open seasonally, there is a Limited Attraction Pass, which costs $18 for those age 12 and older, $15 for ages 3–11; $13 after 2 PM.

For information about Stone Mountain Village, contact the **Stone Mountain Village Visitor's Center** (770-879-4971; www.stonemountainvillage.com), 891 Main Street, Stone Mountain 30083. Open 10–4 Monday through Saturday. **Main Street Stone Mountain Guided Walking Tours** leave from here (see *To See—Guided Tours*).

As you cross the state line from Alabama into Georgia, there is the **Georgia Visitor Information Center—Tallapoosa** (770-574-2621; www.georgiaonmymind .org), I-20 East, Tallapoosa 30176. Open 8:30–5:30 daily.

GETTING THERE *By air:* Visitors to the northern suburbs fly into **Hartsfield-Jackson Atlanta International Airport**. Car rentals are available on- and off-site. Several companies offer shuttle service to various towns. (See What's Where in Georgia.)

By bus: **Greyhound Lines** (404-584-1728; 1-800-231-2222; www.greyhound .com) provides service to downtown Atlanta. There is also a station in Marietta (770-427-3011; 1-800-231-2222; www.greyhound.com), 1250 S. Marietta Parkway SE, Marietta.

By car: North-south I-75 and I-85, which meet in downtown Atlanta, make access from the Northeast and Midwest easy. East-west I-20 traverses downtown as well and connects Birmingham and Augusta. I-285 serves as the circular bypass of the city.

By train: **Amtrak** (404-881-3060; 1-800-872-7245; www.amtrak.com) provides service to the Buckhead section of Atlanta.

GETTING AROUND Visitors to the northern suburbs need a car to get around—their own or a rental. There is some mass transportation. (See What's Where in Georgia.)

MEDICAL EMERGENCY For life-threatening situations, call 911. For immediate care in Conyers and nearby towns, help is available at the **Rockdale Medical Center** (770-918-3000), 1412 Milstead Avenue NE, Conyers. For immediate care in Covington and surrounding towns, go to the **Newton Medical Center** (770-786-7053), 5126 Hospital Drive NE, Covington. In Dallas, assistance is available at **WellStar Paulding Hospital** (770-445-4411; www.wellstar.org), 601 W. Memorial Drive, Dallas. Immediate care is available in the Decatur area at **Decatur Hospital** (404-501-6700; www.drhs.org), 450 N. Candler Street, Decatur; **DeKalb Medical Center** (404-501-7720; www.drhs.org), 2701 N. Decatur Road, Decatur; **Egleston Children's at Emory University** (404-325-9800; www.choa.org), 101 W. Ponce de Leon Avenue, Atlanta; and **Emory University Hospital** (404-327-7565), 555 Asbury Circle NE, Atlanta. For situations needing immediate attention in Marietta or Kennesaw, care is available at **WellStar Kennestone Hospital** (770-793-5000; www.wellstar.org), 677 Church Street, Marietta. For immediate medical care in Roswell or Alpharetta, go to the **North Fulton Medical Center** (770-751-2500; www.northfultonregional.com), 300 Hospital Boulevard, Roswell. For immediate care in Stone Mountain, Lawrenceville, and the surrounding area, help is available at **DeKalb Medical Center** (404-501-8100), 5900 Hillandale Drive, Lithonia.

VILLAGES AND NEIGHBORHOODS Alpharetta, just a few miles to the north of Roswell on US 19, is a fashionable bedroom community, although it is also the home of many international companies. With nearly 200 restaurants featuring practically every cuisine imaginable, Alpharetta has become a premier dining destination in metro Atlanta. Evening entertainment includes live music ranging from rock to jazz, as well as coffeehouses with poetry readings and their own music.

Conyers is the little railroad village that grew and grew. The community has produced country singer Brenda Lee, Academy Award–winning actress Holly Hunter, former federal budget director James Miller, and three Pulitzer Prize winners. Recently revitalized, Conyers's Olde Towne district features numerous historic sites as well as a botanical garden, pavilion, streetscapes, shops, and restaurants. In addition, Conyers is home to the **Georgia International Horse Park** (see *To See—Equestrian Events*), and the **Haralson Mill Covered Bridge** (see *To See—Covered Bridges*), as well as the annual **Conyers Cherry Blossom Festival** (see *Special Events*).

If **Covington** and Newton County look familiar, it may be because the town and surrounding area have been used as the backdrop for so many movies and television shows—morphing from a Civil War village to a 1950s town or a modern-day city—that the town has earned the title "Hollywood of the South." The popular TV series *In the Heat of the Night* was filmed here for seven years in the 1980s, as were several episodes of *The Dukes of Hazzard* and the series *Savannah* and *I'll Fly Away*. Movies shot here run the gamut from *A Man Called Peter* in the 1950s to *Cannonball Run* and *My Cousin Vinny*. Covington's courthouse, so familiar from TV shows and movies, was built in 1884 and is one of only five in the state constructed in the Second Empire style, inspired by French architecture during the reign of Napoleon III. The town, which boasts one of Georgia's largest National Register Historic Districts, has numerous beautifully preserved antebellum and Victorian-era homes that can be seen from the outside on a walking/driving tour.

Decatur, named after naval hero Stephen Decatur, was formed on a rise where two Indian trails intersected, then chartered in 1823. The town predates Atlanta and, in fact, if Decatur hadn't turned down a railroad's proposal to build a major station there, Atlanta might never have existed at all. Although the city limits of Decatur are barely perceptible from neighboring Atlanta, today's Decatur is still imbued with small-town charm, characterized by tree-lined streets, historic attractions, and international culture and cuisine. Delightfully walkable downtown Decatur boasts numerous restaurants, many with outdoor seating, and more than 120 retail shops. On the serious side, the city is the home of the Centers for Disease Control, Emory University, Agnes Scott College, and several significant museums.

Historic Decatur has several historic districts. The tree-lined **Clairmont Historic District,** the northern entryway to Decatur, features architecturally interesting homes from the 1920s. **Historic Sycamore Street,** originally known as Covington Road, was part of a stagecoach route to Augusta. It is the location of some of the grandest houses in town, including the High House, where General William Tecumseh Sherman stopped during the Civil War. The **M.A.K. Local Historic District,** named for McDonough Street, Adams Street, and Kings Highway, was Decatur's first residential subdivision. The neighborhood offers excellent examples of Craftsman-style homes that were popular during the first three decades of the 20th century. **Oakhurst,** one of the oldest sections in Decatur, was actually an independent town known as the City of Oakhurst. Annexed by Decatur in the 1920s, it features many examples of bungalow-style residences. **South Candler Street**—called "the road to the depot" in Caroline McKinney Clarke's *The Story of Decatur 1823–1899*—is home to Agnes Scott College and some of the loveliest Victorian-era homes in the city. Agnes Scott College was established in 1889 as the Decatur Female Academy and in 1907 was the first fully accredited school in Georgia. The campus covers eight blocks and includes many historic residential properties as well as the Bradley Observatory, which is open to the public on the second Friday of each month.

Kennesaw, just north of Marietta, was originally called Big Shanty because it was a construction camp for Irish railroad workers who lived in shanty houses there in the 1830s and 1840s. During the Civil War, Union raiders stole the

General from here and attempted to flee to Chattanooga—an episode known as the Great Locomotive Chase. Their intent was to tear up tracks behind them to disrupt rail service to the Atlanta area, but they failed. At nearby Kennesaw Mountain, Confederate troops held off Union troops for several weeks. After the war, the name of the town was changed to commemorate the battle. Today the town has five historic districts and the **Southern Museum of Civil War and Locomotive History** (see *To See—Museums*). Kennesaw's 1908 railroad depot has been restored and is often the site of fairs and festivals. The town is also a site on the Blue and Gray Trail and the Dixie Highway Trail.

Lawrenceville, the county seat of Gwinnett County, was incorporated in 1821, making it the second-oldest city in the metropolitan Atlanta area. It was named for Captain James Lawrence, commander of the frigate *Chesapeake* during the War of 1812. Although mortally wounded, Captain Lawrence uttered the now-famous battle cry, "Don't give up the ship!" Historic downtown Lawrenceville on US 29 is a mix of restaurants and antiques, craft, and retail shops.

Lilburn, also on US 29, was founded in 1890. A devastating fire and economic hard times in the 1920s almost spelled the end for Lilburn, but the Old Town district was revitalized, and shops and restaurants now occupy the historic buildings.

Lithonia's name was created by a Greek teacher who combined the Greek words *litho*, meaning "rock," with *onia*, meaning "to create." The name is very appropriate because the town sits near massive Stone Mountain, which is created of Lithonia gneiss.

Marietta (pronounced May-retta by locals), founded in 1834, became a summer resort town for south Georgia planters seeking relief from the heat and malaria of the coastal region. The town's location at the foothills of the mountains contributed to its milder, very appealing climate. Fine hotels like the Kennesaw House, which now houses the **Marietta Museum of History** (see *To See—Museums*), welcomed visitors, many of whom stayed for months.

During the Civil War, Andrews's Raiders stayed in Marietta the night before they stole a train pulled by a locomotive called the *General,* thus beginning the famous Great Locomotive Chase. General Sherman ordered most of the buildings around the town square burned during the war, but spared most of the residential areas. It was from Marietta that Sherman had the captured women and children mill workers from Roswell and Lithia Springs charged with treason and shipped to the North to be imprisoned or placed in servitude.

In the 20th century, the Dixie Highway, which passes through Marietta, was a major route for Northerners on their way to and from Florida. Until the construction of the interstate highways, many travelers stayed, ate, or went sightseeing in Marietta or Kennesaw during their trips.

Today Marietta has a population of 61,000 and is the state's ninth-largest city. Because Marietta's residential areas survived the Civil War, the city is blessed with five historic districts. **Northwest Marietta Historic District,** the city's oldest designated historic district, runs from Kennesaw Avenue to Powder Springs Road and includes numerous historic Greek Revival–style homes. **Whit-**

lock **Avenue Historic District,** which borders the Kennesaw Mountain National Battlefield Park, includes several historic homes. **Atlanta/Frazier Street Historic District,** Marietta's most recently designated district, borders the railroad tracks near the Confederate Cemetery and includes several more historic homes. **Washington Avenue Historic District,** on the east side of the city, includes the Marietta National Cemetery and "Lawyer's Row," mid- to late-19th-century houses now adapted for use as attorneys' offices. **Church/Cherokee Historic District** includes two parallel tree-lined streets that head north from the square. This neighborhood includes Victorian-era homes and several historic churches.

Pick up a copy of the "Historic Marietta Walking/Driving Tour" brochure from the **Marietta Welcome Center** (see *Guidance*). It describes 57 historic structures you can walk or drive by, most of which are private homes. The charming turn-of-the-20th-century town square is the prettiest in Georgia. More than 70 antiques and specialty shops, restaurants, theaters, and museums surround the square, and several bed & breakfasts are located nearby. Marietta is also the gateway to the state-designated Blue and Gray Trail and Georgia's Dixie Highway Trail, as well as the northwest Georgia mountains.

THE BIG CHICKEN

When relating Marietta's rich historical background, one can go from the sublime to the ridiculous. Around Marietta, all things point to or away from the much beloved Big Chicken, so directions anywhere in the vicinity generally include references to the giant fowl: "Turn right at the Big Chicken," "Go 4 miles past the Big Chicken"—you get the idea. The 56-foot-tall, red and white sheet-metal chicken with its opening and closing beak and rolling eyes presides over the intersection of US 41/Cobb Parkway and GA 20/Roswell Road east of Marietta proper, where it has been since 1963, when it was erected as the landmark identifying a local fast-food joint. Scores of Northerners saw the big bird on their way to and from Florida when US 41 was the main route. The eatery was bought by Kentucky Fried Chicken in 1980, and as the end of the century approached, company executives began making noises about tearing the chicken down to make this KFC conform to others. But the citizenry grumbled. In 1993 a tornado severely damaged the big fella, and KFC decided once and for all to tear it down, but the company was soon flooded with protests from locals and folks around the world. The company even had to install a special toll-free number to handle the volume of calls that were coming from as far away as Japan. Bowing to the inevitable, executives spent $700,000 to restore the big guy to his former glory. Thank goodness the icon remains at his post. How else would we be able to find our way?

Monroe, named for James Monroe, fifth president of the United States, is called "the City of Governors" because the small town produced four Georgia governors. The fully restored courthouse is the center of Monroe's large historic district.

Roswell was a textile mill town before and during the Civil War. On July 5, 1864, as Union troops advanced, retreating Confederate troops burned the covered bridge at the Chattahoochee River to slow their progress. Not so easily deterred, Union troops found a place to ford the river and entered Roswell anyway. Although Theophile Roche, the French foreman of the mill, tried to claim neutrality by flying the French flag, he fooled no one and on July 7 the mills were burned. Fortunately, the town and homes were spared.

All the mill workers, who were primarily young women and children, were charged with treason by orders from General Sherman. Apparently he feared that these plucky women would somehow find a way to make the things the Confederacy needed, so also by his orders, they were marched west to Marietta (a railhead the Union had already captured) and put on trains for the North. Many were imprisoned for the duration of the war, while others were forced into servitude to Northern families and businesses until they could escape or the war ended. Although many returned to Roswell after the war or at least let their families know where they were, others were never seen or heard from again, giving rise to the legend of the missing Roswell women and children. Several factual and fictional accounts of this story have been written for adults and children, including *Roswell Women* by Frances Patton Statham and *Turn Homeward, Hannalee* by Patricia Beatty.

After the war, the mills were rebuilt and Roswell remained a small but successful textile town until the mid-1970s, when the mills closed for good. The town's proximity to Atlanta, however, guaranteed that rather than dying, as most Southern textile towns had done, Roswell prospered. Now, although Roswell has grown to be the seventh most populous city in Georgia and the home of offices of many national companies, it is primarily a very affluent bedroom community for Atlanta.

Because the town was spared during the Civil War, Roswell's 640-acre historic district, of which 122 acres are listed on the National Register of Historic Places, is filled with period homes, churches, and businesses—many of which serve as museum houses, museums, restaurants, and shops. Among those open to the public as house museums are **Bulloch Hall, Barrington Hall,** and the **Archibald Smith Plantation Home** (see *To See—Historic Homes and Sites*).

Stone Mountain Village, the gateway to Stone Mountain Park, is located just outside the park's West Gate. Established in 1845 and first named New Gibraltar, the village that is now Stone Mountain was a railroad community, center for Georgia's granite industry, and a popular tourist spot from the earliest days. In fact, Stone Mountain Depot was a strategic point for General Sherman's Union troops in their campaign to destroy Atlanta during the Civil War. The Union army destroyed much of the village and 5 miles of rail line, although buildings used as hospitals were spared. The village's historic commercial buildings once housed hotels, banks, and general stores that served the granite workers. Today, these same structures house 50 specialty stores, antiques shops, galleries, and restaurants. Streets surrounding the commercial area are filled with antebellum mansions, Victorian-era cottages, and bungalows. Two of these operate as bed & breakfasts. In all, the National Register of Historic Places Historic District (1830–1940) contains 275 properties and two historic cemeteries.

✳ To See

COVERED BRIDGES ✍ 🐾 **Concord Covered Bridge** (770-431-2858), Concord Road between Hicks Road and S. Cobb Drive, Smyrna. Open daily. Listed on the National Register of Historic Places, the bridge is the centerpiece of the Concord Covered Bridge Historic District, which also contains four historic homes, a railroad trestle bridge, and a gristmill. The bridge, which was built around 1840, was burned during the Civil War but was reconstructed. The only covered bridge still in use on a public highway in metropolitan Atlanta, it is 133 feet long, 16 feet wide, and 13 feet high. Ruff's Mill, which was built in 1850, saw action during the Civil War Battle of Atlanta and operated until the 1930s. The Rock House, a fieldstone structure built in 1910 as a summer residence for a wealthy Atlanta family, is particularly interesting because no two windows are alike. Free.

✍ 🐾 **Haralson Mill Covered Bridge** (770-929-4001; 770-785-5919), Haralson Mill Road off Bethel Road, Conyers. Open daily. Visitors can actually drive through this covered bridge, the first of its kind built in Georgia since the late 1890s. The bridge, which is located at the northeast corner of Randy Poynter Lake at Black Shoals Park, replicates covered bridge design similar to the 1820s Town Lattice Truss design. The bridge, which consists of three 50-foot spans with solid concrete piers and spill-through abutments, was built with Georgia wood products and labor. Surrounding the bridge is the Haralson Mill Historic District, which includes the Haralson Mill House, a general store, the old mill site, and a blacksmith shop. Free.

CULTURAL SITES ✍ 🐾 ♿ **Callanwolde Fine Arts Center** (404-872-5338; www.callanwolde.org), 980 Briarcliff Road NE, Atlanta. Office open 9–5 weekdays; gallery open 10–8 weekdays, 10–3 Saturday; art/gift shop open 11–3:30 Monday through Saturday; conservatory open 10–4 weekdays. Although this is primarily a center for art, literary, music, and dance classes, the home itself is worthy of a visit. The sprawling 27,000-square-foot Gothic-Tudor mansion in the historic Druid Hills neighborhood was built in 1920 for Charles Howard Candler, the oldest son of Coca-Cola Company founder Asa Candler. The designer was Henry Hornbostle, the architect who designed Emory University. One of the most outstanding features is a magnificent 3,742-pipe Aeolian organ, the largest in existence in playable condition in a residence. It's astounding that anyone would ever consider destroying this magnificent house, but it was slated for demolition in 1971 when concerned citizens organized to save it. Now listed on the National Register of Historic Places, the mansion is surrounded by 12 lush acres and several outbuildings. An on-site conservatory is the headquarters of the DeKalb County Federation of Garden Clubs. Many exhibits and performances occur during the year, the most widely anticipated of which is **Christmas**

at **Callanwolde,** when the home is dressed up in holiday finery by local decorators and opened for tours. There are also monthly poetry readings, family storytelling evenings, Friday-night jazz concerts, and Sunday-afternoon classical piano concerts. Free concerts by the Callanwolde Concert Band and performances by the Atlanta Young Singers of Callanwolde are also on the schedule. Free except for special events.

EQUESTRIAN EVENTS ✔ ✿ ♿ **Georgia International Horse Park** (770-860-4190; 1-800-860-4224; www.georgiahorsepark.com), 1996 Centennial Olympic Parkway, Conyers. Office open 8–5 weekdays. Call or consult the web site for a schedule of events and ticket prices. Best known as the scene of the equestrian and mountain biking competitions and the final two events of the modern pentathlon at the 1996 Centennial Olympic Summer Games, today the sprawling 1,400-acre multiuse park hosts events such as rodeos, barrel-racing competitions, dressage shows, fairs, concerts, and festivals almost every day of the year. The park also boasts RV camping, the Hawthorn Suites Golf Resort Hotel, Cherokee Run Golf Club, Big Haynes Creek Nature Center, and trails for mountain biking and horseback riding (see separate entries in *To Do*).

✔ ✿ ♿ **Wills Park Equestrian Center** (678-297-6120; www.alpharetta.ga.us/main.city.parks.parkfacilities.html), 11915 Wills Road, Alpharetta. Outdoor and covered show rings provide the backdrop for an astounding array of English and Western horse shows, dressage events, rodeos, dog shows, dog agility trials, and concerts. Call for a schedule of events and prices.

GUIDED TOURS ✔ ✿ **Ghost Talk–Ghost Walk** (770-649-9922), Roswell. Tours at 8 Friday; reservations required (check the web site for the possibility of Saturday-night tours). The 1½-hour, easy walking tour of Roswell's Historic District includes plenty of chills and thrills concerning the spirits that are said to live behind the walls of the mansions and workers' dwellings in the mill village. Meet at the bandstand in the square at 7:45 and bring a flashlight. Adults $15, children younger than 10 $10.

✿ **Historic Tours** and **Storytelling Tours** (770-640-3253; 1-800-776-7935), 617 Atlanta Street, Roswell. Historic Tours 1 PM Saturday and 10 AM Wednesday; Storytelling Tours third Sunday of each month. Call for exact times. During the Historic Tours, you'll stroll Roswell's historic streets with a guide and hear about the town's early settlers and the turbulent Civil War era. Storytelling Tours are led by guides who weave tales of Roswell's mills and settlers. Historic Tours $2; Storytelling Tours $8.

✿ **Main Street Stone Mountain Village Guided Walking Tours** (770-465-6776 weekdays; 770-879-4971 weekends; www.mainstreetstonemountain.com), 891 Main Street, Stone Mountain Village. Tours of the historic downtown leave from the **Stone Mountain Visitor's Center** red caboose (see *Guidance*) at 11 AM every Saturday between April and mid-November. The one-hour guided tour highlights the development of the village between the 1830s and the 1940s. Adults $5, seniors and students $4.

HISTORIC HOMES AND SITES 🐾 ♿ **Antebellum Brumby Hall and Gardens**
(770-427-2500; 1-888-685-2500; www.brumbyhall.com), 500 Powder Springs
Road, Marietta. House open 9–5 weekdays; gardens open 24/7. The lovely raised
Greek Revival–style house was built by Colonel Anoldus VanderHorst Brumby,
the first superintendent of the Georgia Military Institute, which was located on
adjacent property until it was destroyed during the Civil War. Brumby Hall
served as a Union hospital during the war, and legend has it that General Sherman spared the house because he and Brumby had been friends at West Point.
Make time to wander in the formal boxwood, topiary, rose, annual, perennial,
and knot gardens, which were designed in 1930 by Hubert Bond Owens,
founder of the School of Landscape Architecture at the University of Georgia.
His original 1925 drawings were used to restore the gardens to their former
splendor. Free.

🖊 🐾 ♿ **Archibald Smith Plantation Home** (770-641-3978; www.archibaldsmith
plantation.org), 935 Alpharetta Street, Roswell. Tours hourly 10–3 Monday
through Saturday, 1–3 Sunday. The original 300-acre farm was created by
Archibald Smith, who had migrated to Roswell from coastal Georgia. Built in
1845, the house was lived in for 150 years by three successive generations of the
Smith family until they donated the property to the city. All the furnishings,
therefore, are original, which is very unusual. What is even more interesting,
considering that the remaining 3-acre property is now completely surrounded by
the bustling city of Roswell, is that 10 original outbuildings survive, including
barns, the carriage house, corncrib, greenhouse, kitchen building, slave cabin,
springhouse, and well. Wheelchair accessible on the first floor only. Adults $8,
seniors $7, children 6–12 $6. A combination ticket (adults $18, children $15)
includes admission to Barrington Hall and Bulloch Hall (see below).

🖊 🐾 ♿ **Barrington Hall** (770-640-3855), 535 Barrington Drive, Roswell. Tours
on the hour 1–3 Monday through Saturday, 1–3 Sunday. The house, which only
recently opened to the public, is considered to be one of the finest examples of
Greek Revival Temple architecture in the United States. It was completed in
1842 for Barrington King, son of Roswell founder Roswell King, and lived in by
four generations of the same family: Kings, Bakers, and Simpsons. The house is
furnished with many original pieces. Several original outbuildings survive,
including the smokehouse, icehouse, and kitchen building as well as two wells.
Limited wheelchair accessibility. Adults $8, children 6–12 $6. A combination
ticket (adults $18, children $15) includes admission to the Archibald Smith Plantation House (see above) and Bulloch Hall (see below).

🖊 🐾 ♿ **Bulloch Hall** (706-992-1731; www.bullochhall.org), 180 Bulloch Avenue,
Roswell. Tours 10–3 Monday through Saturday, 1–3 Sunday. The most significant historic site in Roswell, Bulloch Hall, which was built in 1840, was the
home of Major James Stephens Bulloch, one of the town's first settlers and the
grandson of an early Georgia governor, Archibald Bulloch. Major Bulloch's
daughter, Martha "Mittie" Bulloch, married Theodore Roosevelt Sr. in the dining room of Bulloch Hall on December 22, 1853. They went on to become the
parents of President Theodore Roosevelt Jr. and, through their other son, Elliott,
the grandparents of first lady Eleanor Roosevelt. In 1905, President Teddy Roo-

sevelt visited his mother's former home and spoke to Roswell residents from the bandstand in the town square. Bulloch Hall was constructed of heart pine in the Greek temple style with a full pedimented portico and is considered one of the best examples of the style in Georgia. The interior style, typical of the period, was called "four-square"—four principal rooms and a central hall on each floor. The kitchen is in the basement rather than in a separate building (as was more common at the time), and it features a beehive oven. Osage orange trees were planted near the house because of their ability to discourage flies and rodents, and many of them still survive today along with shade and fruit trees. In fact, 142 trees on the property are listed on the Historic Tree Register. Today the lovingly restored home is filled with gracious period pieces, including some original china used by the Bullochs. The dogtrot-style slave quarters, which were reconstructed on the original site, include a period room and an exhibit, "Slave Life in the Piedmont." Bulloch Hall is home to many active guilds—quilting, openhearth cooking, sampler (needlework), gardening, and archaeology—which demonstrate old-time skills at special events. Several special events—the month-long **Christmas at Bulloch Hall,** Civil War encampments, **Osage Orange Festival, Halloween at the Hall,** storytelling programs, and summer camps for children—occur throughout the year. Wheelchair accessible on the main floor only. Adults $8, children 6–12 $6. A combination ticket (adults $18, children $15) includes admission to the Archibald Smith Plantation House and Barrington Hall (see above).

🏛️ ♿ **Historic Complex of the DeKalb Historical Society** (404-373-1088; www.dekalbhistory.org), Adair Park on West Trinity Place, Decatur. Call for hours and guided tour reservations. The complex, which backs to a pleasant, shady park, features three antebellum structures. The oldest is the **Biffle Cabin,** which was built by a Revolutionary War veteran between 1825 and 1840. The log cabin was relocated here from a knoll overlooking Barbashela Creek. The **Thomas-Barber Cabin,** once a stagecoach stop on the Old McDonough Road, was built by Hayden Thomas. The **Benjamin Franklin Swanton House,** a one-story frame home built between 1830 and 1840, is considered Decatur's oldest house (as opposed to a cabin). Legend has it that a Yankee soldier was held captive in an upstairs closet during the Battle of Atlanta. The house serves as a

BULLOCH HALL IS THE MOST SIGNIFICANT HISTORIC SITE IN ROSWELL.

small museum. Also on the property is the **Mary Gay House,** which is named for the author of *Life in Dixie During the War* and used for special events. Even when the houses aren't open, visitors can walk around them and peek in the windows. Free.

✍ ✿ ⚐ **Kennesaw Mountain National Battlefield Park** (770-427-4286; www .nps.gov/kemo), 900 Kennesaw Mountain Drive off Old US 41 and Stilesboro Road, Kennesaw. Open dawn–dusk daily; visitor center open 8:30–5 weekdays, 8:30–6 Saturday and Sunday. Hours extended in the summer. The site of a major Civil War battle on June 27, 1864, which temporarily thwarted the advance of Union troops from Chattanooga to Atlanta, the 2,884-acre park commemorates the Atlanta Campaign. A film at the visitor center describes the battle, and exhibits depict the life of Civil War soldiers. Living-history programs and ranger talks are presented in the summer. The park features 16 miles of hiking trails, monuments, and re-created military positions as well as recreation areas and picnicking facilities. On summer weekends a shuttle bus carries visitors almost to the summit of the mountain. From there they can walk the rest of the way to the top where, on a clear day, they'll be rewarded with the best view of downtown Atlanta. Free.

✿ **McDaniel-Tichenor House** (770-267-5602; www.mcdaniel-tichenor.org), 319 McDaniel Street, Monroe. Open 10–4 Tuesday through Friday. This gracious mansion was the retirement home of Governor Henry Dickerson McDaniel, wounded Civil War veteran, lawyer, businessman, and governor of Georgia during Reconstruction. The house was originally designed in the Victorian Italianate Villa style, but it was extensively renovated in the 1930s in the neoclassical style you see today. Original period features such as original woodwork, doors, and faux marbleized fireplace mantels have been beautifully restored. The eclectically furnished interior features pieces from the late-18th to the mid-20th centuries and includes the governor's carved mahogany bed. One of the interesting things about this house is that it was occupied by several generations of only one family. $3.

✍ ⚐ **Michael C. Carlos Museum of Emory University** (404-727-4282; www .carlos.emory.edu), 571 South Kilgo Street NE, Atlanta. Open 10–5 Tuesday through Saturday, noon–5 Sunday; docent-led tours at 2:30 Thursday and Sunday. Visitors can get wrapped up in the art and architecture of ancient civilizations as they view the large collection at the South's largest archaeological museum. The facility's 16,000 objects offer a glimpse of 9,000 years of art history and include extremely rare ancient Egyptian, Greek, and Roman pieces as well as works on paper from the Middle Ages through the present. Other present-day works come from the Middle East, Near East, Asia, sub-Saharan Africa, and Oceania. From the Western Hemisphere, the collection includes ceramics from Nicaragua and Costa Rica and burial urns from Colombia. $7; audio tours (recommended) can be rented for $3.

✍ ✿ ⚐ **Monastery of the Holy Spirit** (770-438-8705; www.trappist.net), 2625 US 212 SW, Conyers. Open 4 AM–9 PM daily. Abbey Church open daily at 7 AM for morning prayer and Mass, 5:30 PM for evening prayer, 8:15 PM for night prayer. The monastery was begun in 1944 by a group of Cistercian monks. Sitting amid 2,000 acres of woodlands and lakes, the retreat offers peaceful walking paths and picnic areas. Sights to see at the monastery include the beautiful **Abbey Church, Welcome Center, Retreat House, Bonsai Greenhouse,** and **Gift Shop.** In the gift shop you'll find Monk's Fruitcake, Monk's Fudge, Monk's Coffee from a sister monastery in Venezuela, and religious items that include fine art reproductions, statuary, 14-carat and sterling silver jewelry, CDs, cassettes, software, videos, and a wide variety of books. In the greenhouse, bonsai novices and enthusiasts can purchase pottery from among the largest selection of Tokoname pots in the United States. Korean mica pots, books, videos, accessories, tools, wire, and fertilizer are also available. Free.

✏ 🐾 ♿ **Pickett's Mill Battlefield State Historic Site** (770-505-3485; www.gastateparks.org/info/picketts), 4432 Mount Tabor Church Road, Dallas. Open 9–5 Tuesday through Saturday, noon–5 Sunday. On May 27, 1864, a Confederate victory here by 10,000 soldiers under the command of General Patrick Cleburne slowed down the Union advance on Atlanta by a week. Today the battlefield is one of the best preserved in the nation. Located on 760 acres, the historic site has preserved earthworks; an interpretive center with an introductory film and exhibits of artifacts; 4 miles of hiking trails divided into Red, White, and Blue Trails to coincide with troop movements; and picnicking areas. Living-history programs are held on the first and third weekends of each month. Adults $2.50, seniors and children 6–18 $1.25.

🐾 ♿ **The Root House Museum** (770-426-4982), 145 Denmead Street, Marietta. Open 11–4 Tuesday through Saturday. One of the oldest surviving frame houses in Marietta, the 1845 Plantation Plain–style Root House offers a glimpse into the life of a middle-class merchant family. The simple frame house is furnished with period pieces typical of the 1850s. Also on the property is a re-created kitchen house with a working 1850s cookstove as well as flower beds and vegetable plots with plants that were available in Cobb County before 1860. Wheelchair accessible on first floor only. Adults $4, seniors $3, children $2.

✏ 🐾 **Stone Mountain Park Antebellum Plantation**. The plantation, created by moving 19 buildings constructed between 1790 and 1845 to this site, portrays the lifestyle of 19th-century Georgians. In addition to the graceful manor house, other typical plantation outbuildings include a cookhouse, slave cabins, overseer's house, and blacksmith shop. Period gardens and a farmyard with live animals lend an air of authenticity. Several special events occur on the grounds throughout the year. (See *Guidance* for prices and other details.) Limited wheelchair accessibility.

MUSEUMS ✏ 🐾 ♿ **Antique Car and Treasure Museum at Stone Mountain Park**. This nostalgic exhibit showcases 40 vintage cars, including some that are one-of-a-kind, like Buck Rogers's Rocket Car. The short-lived Tucker displayed here was briefly built in Georgia. Other modes of transportation aren't neglected—there are 60 vintage bikes and 15 pedal cars. Music is represented by five band organs, 22 player pianos, and 30 jukeboxes. There are also carousel animals, period clothing, and thousands of other 20th-century artifacts. (See *Guidance* for prices and other details.)

✏ 🐾 ♿ **Bud Jones Taxidermy Wildlife Museum** (770-574-7480; www.bud

jonestaxidermy.com), 359 GA 120 East, Tallapoosa. Open 8–5 weekdays, 9–noon Saturday. Bud Jones's expertise is so well known, he has mounted a full-sized elephant for the Alabama Museum of Natural History in nearby Anniston and has created a full-sized American mastodon and a giant beaver for the South Carolina State Museum in Columbia. At this museum off US 78 near the Atlanta border, visitors will see exotic North American and African animal, fish, bird, and reptile mounts as well as an extensive fossil collection. Free.

✍ 🐾 ♿ **Confederate Hall Historical and Environmental Education Center**. At Confederate Hall, located at the base of Stone Mountain's walk up trail, visitors can learn about the geological and ecological history of the mountain, explore interactive exhibits, and view *The Battle for Georgia—A History of the Civil War in Georgia*, a 25-minute documentary narrated by Hal Holbrook. Exhibits include a life-sized cave with a video about the origin of the mountain. A huge three-dimensional map enhanced by lights and sound effects depicts the Battle of Atlanta and the March to the Sea. Other exhibits include Civil War uniforms and other artifacts. Admission free; $8 park parking fee. (See *Guidance* for details on Stone Mountain Park.)

✍ 🐾 ♿ **Discovering Stone Mountain Museum at Memorial Hall** (770-413-5086; www.stonemountainpark.com), US 78 East, Stone Mountain Park. Open 10–8 daily in summer, shorter hours remainder of year. This museum tells the story behind Stone Mountain and displays true-to-scale elements from the world's largest relief carving. In addition, exhibits tell about local history and the Civil War. (See *Guidance* for prices and other details.)

🐾 ♿ **Marietta/Cobb Museum of Art** (770-528-1444; www.mariettasquare .com/mcma), 30 Atlanta Street, Marietta. Open 11–5 Tuesday through Saturday, 1–5 Sunday. The only all-American art museum in the metro area, this repository featuring 19th- and 20th-century regional art sponsors four annual special exhibits and children's activities. It is housed in an imposing many-columned Classical Revival building that was originally constructed to serve as a federal post office and was later used as a library. Adults $5, seniors and children $3.

✍ 🐾 ♿ **Marietta Fire Museum** (770-794-5460), 112 Haynes Street, Marietta. Open 8–5 weekdays. Housed at the Marietta Fire Station and featuring fire-fighting equipment from the 1800s to the present, the museum is the home of *Aurora*, a horse-drawn Silsby Steamer fire engine in service from 1879 to 1921.

✍ 🐾 ♿ **Marietta *Gone with the Wind* Museum/Scarlett on the Square** (770-794-5576; www.gwtwmarietta.com), 18 Whitlock Avenue, Marietta. Open 10–5 Monday through Saturday. Housed in an 1880s warehouse just off the town square, the museum features a privately owned collection of movie memorabilia, including original costumes, conceptual artwork, scripts, props, photographs, rare press and publicity books, premiere programs, promotional items, and more. Among the treasures are the original Bengaline silk honeymoon gown worn by Vivien Leigh, some of Margaret Mitchell's personal volumes of the novel, contracts, foreign versions of the novel, and foreign film posters. One display is dedicated to the African American members of the cast. Adults $7, seniors and students $6, children younger than 8 free.

PASSPORT TO FUN

The **Marietta Heritage Passport** allows admission to three heritage museums for just $10, a 30 percent savings off the total cost of an adult admission to each site. The passport, which includes the Marietta Museum of History, the Root House Museum, and the Marietta *Gone with the Wind* Museum/Scarlett on the Square, is available for $10 at the Marietta Welcome Center (see *Guidance*). The card is valid for one year from purchase but is not valid for special exhibits or with other discounts.

♂ 🐾 ♿ **Marietta Museum of History** (770-528-0430; www.mariettasquare .com/history_museum.html), 1 Depot Street, Marietta. Open 10–4 Monday through Saturday, 1–4 Sunday. The second floor of the old 1855 Kennesaw House hotel provides a home for the local history museum and its collection of artifacts that tell Marietta's story from the time of the Native Americans to the present. Operating under the name Fletcher House in 1862, the hotel was the base from which Andrews's Raiders launched their bold move to steal the *General*. Other displays include antique quilts and furnishings, mannequins in vintage clothing from various periods, and sewing arts. The Homelife Gallery houses 19th- and 20th-century clothing and accessories, inventions from the turn of the 20th century, a complete 1940s kitchen, and a vignette featuring the bachelor suite of Yankee spy Henry Green Cole. The Civil War Gallery features uniforms, weapons, a battle flag, one of General Sherman's hairpins (a twisted rail), and a military document signed by Abraham Lincoln. The General History Gallery tells the story of Native Americans, the gold rush, local businesses, influential Mariettans, the growth of the Bell Bomber Plant (which became Lockheed Martin), and displays from all of America's wars. Adults $3, seniors and students $2, children $1.

♂ 🐾 ♿ **Southern Museum of Civil War and Locomotive History** (770-427-2117; www.southernmuseum.org), 2829 Cherokee Street, Kennesaw. Open 9:30–5 Monday through Saturday, noon–5 Sunday. This Smithsonian-affiliated museum describes how the locomotive has shaped history. Visitors learn the crucial role railroads played during the Civil War and how a locomotive factory aided in rebuilding the South after the war. On display is one of the most famous locomotives in the South: the *General*, which was hijacked by Union raiders during the Civil War but recaptured by Southerners after an 86-mile chase. The museum also displays a multimillion-dollar collection of Civil War relics as well as the Glover Machine Works collection and traveling Smithsonian exhibits. Adults $7.50, seniors $6.50, children 6–12 $5.50.

♂ 🐾 ♿ **West Georgia Museum of Tallapoosa** (770-574-3125; www.westgeorgia museum.com), 21 W. Lyon Street, Tallapoosa. Open 9–3 Tuesday through Friday, 9–5 Saturday. Extensive displays focus on local history and paleontology. From the prehistoric area visitors see a 30-foot *Tyrannosaurus rex*, seven smaller dinosaurs, a real dinosaur egg from China, and a 300 million-year-old fossilized tree from Alabama. Natural history is traced through mounted animals native to

Haralson County. Native American displays include arrowheads and other artifacts, while early American history is described through a fully stocked general store and a fully furnished log cabin. The evolution of transportation over the past 100 years or so is shown through buggies, wagons, and early automobiles. The Lithia Springs Hotel in Tallapoosa, built between 1890 and 1892, was the largest wooden building east of the Mississippi. Although the hotel no longer exists, numerous items from the hotel, including a registration book with George Vanderbilt's signature, are exhibited here. Each month a special changing display keeps visitors coming back. Adults $2, children $1.

SCENIC DRIVES For a driving tour of Marietta's Civil War sites, the **Cannonball Trail,** pick up a brochure from the **Marietta Welcome Center and Visitors Bureau** (770-429-1115; 1-800-835-0445; www.mariettasquare.com), 4 Depot Street, Marietta.

✧ ❀ ♿ **Kennesaw Mountain National Battlefield Park** (770-427-4286; www.nps.gov/kemo), 900 Kennesaw Mountain Drive off Old US 41 and Stilesboro Road, Kennesaw. The visitor center provides a brochure for a self-guided walking/driving tour of the park. The four sites on the trail are the overlook at the summit of Kennesaw Mountain, where visitors can get a panoramic view of north Georgia, including the Atlanta skyline; Pigeon Hill entrenchments reached by a foot trail; Cheatham Hill, known as the Dead Angle, where fierce fighting occurred during the Civil War; and Kolb's Farm, where an 1836 log house has been restored but is not open to the public.

WINERY TOUR ❀ ♿ **Fox Vineyards Winery,** (770-787-5402), 225 GA 11 South, Social Circle. Open for tours and tastings 10–6 Wednesday through Saturday, 1–6 Sunday. The local award-winning winery grows seven varieties of European *vinifera* and French-American hybrids on its 15-acre vineyard and produces transitional wines such as cabernet sauvignon, chardonnay, merlot, and Riesling as well as some unusual wines with names like Ambrosia, Antebellum Rose, Bonny Blueberry, Muscadew, Scarlet Fox, Scuppedew, Sherrie, and Strawberry Shortcake. Tours, tastings, and wine sales are available.

✳ To Do

BALLOONING **Adventures Aloft Hot-Air Ballooning** (770-963-0149; www.ballooningamerica.com), 2029 Crystal Lake Drive, Lawrenceville. Call for flight schedules and prices. Flights are conducted at dawn and about two hours after sunset, weather permitting. Each trip is custom-designed and includes refreshments and a traditional toast.

BICYCLING ✧ ❀ The **PATH Foundation** (404-875-7284; www.pathfoundation.org), mailing address: P.O. Box 14327, Atlanta 30324, has been instrumental in developing bike paths in the metropolitan Atlanta area. The most ambitious of these trails is the **Silver Comet Trail** (see *Hiking*), which begins in Smyrna and ends 60 miles later at the Alabama line, where it connects with the 33-mile Chief Ladiga Trail. For information on renting regular and three-wheel recumbent bikes and skates or obtaining other related services, visit the **Silver Comet Depot** (770-819-3279; www.silvercometdepot.com), 4342 Floyd Road, Mableton. Open 9–6 Monday through Wednesday and Friday through Sunday, 9–7 Thursday; longer hours in summer. The company also sponsors group walks and rides and provides some shuttle service. The **Stone Mountain Trail,** a portion of the Atlanta-DeKalb Trail System, will extend 18 miles from Georgia Tech (see the Atlanta chapter) to Stone Mountain Park. At this time, 12 miles have been completed from Clarkston to the park. To learn more about the trail system, including places to park, hospitals, rest rooms, water, MARTA access, and other points of interest, purchase the "Atlanta-DeKalb Greenway Trail Guide" from the PATH Foundation for $5.50 plus Georgia tax.

BOAT EXCURSIONS ✈ 🐾 **Ride the Ducks Adventure at Stone Mountain Park.** The amphibious sight-seeing experience makes a 40-minute tour of the park by road and then plunges into Stone Mountain Lake. These unusual vehicles are modeled after the World War II amphibious DUKWS. $9 per person in addition to $8 park parking fee (see *Guidance* for other park details.).

✈ 🐾 ♿ **Riverboat Cruise.** Open 10–8 daily in summer, shorter hours remainder of year. Relax on the first or second deck of the *Scarlett O'Hara* as the replica paddle-wheeler plies the waters of 363-acre Stone Mountain Lake, cruising by natural areas, the beach and water park, the golf course, the campground, the gristmill, the Evergreen Hotel and Conference Center, and the carillon. If the time is right, passengers will hear a concert ringing out from the carillon bell tower, which was donated to the park after being exhibited at the 1964 World's Fair. (See *Guidance* for prices and other details regarding Stone Mountain Park.)

BOATING ✈ 🐾 **Rental Boats at Stone Mountain Park.** The country store at the campground offers rowboats for use on Stone Mountain Lake. No private boats are permitted after 11 AM on weekends and on holidays between May 1 and September 30. Private boats are limited to 10-horsepower motors. Pedal boats can be borrowed at the steamboat landing where the *Scarlett O'Hara* docks (see above); their use is included in the One-Day All Attractions Pass. Boat rental $20 per day. (See *Guidance* for other park details.)

CANOEING, KAYAKING, AND RAFTING On a hot summer day, there's nothing more refreshing than floating down the Chattahoochee River in a raft. This popular activity is known as "Shootin' the Hooch." The water stays about 50 degrees, so if you get too hot all you have to do is splash yourself with water. **Chattahoochee Outfitters** (770-650-1008; www.shootthehooch.com) Rentals and return shuttle service are available seasonally from their Johnson Ferry and Powers Island outposts. Bring your own picnic, because the leisurely trip takes between 2½ and 6 hours, depending on the outpost location and the speed of the river flow. U.S. Coast Guard–approved life jackets are required, and anyone younger than 18 must be accompanied by an adult. Raft rentals begin at $100 for four-person raft; shuttle service $10 per person.

✈ 🐾 **Chattahoochee River Outfitters** (404-274-6912), Chattahoochee River

Park, Azalea Drive, Roswell. Open 10–8 daily. Canoe, kayak, or raft the Chatta-hoochee River as it flows through Roswell. The company provides return shuttle service for rafters who have floated down the river. Canoe and kayak rentals $12 per hour plus $75 deposit; raft rentals $100 for four-person raft, $120 for six-per-son raft, $160 for eight-person raft.

FOR FAMILIES ✍ 🐾 ♿ **Crossroads at Stone Mountain.** Some stores may stay open until the laser show begins at 9:30. Visitors travel back in time to an 1870s Southern village at this park-within-a-park. Here they'll meet fascinating cos-tumed characters and skilled craftspeople who demonstrate such old-time skills as glassblowing, candle making, candy and ice-cream making, blacksmithing, and grinding meal at the gristmill. Crossroads village includes Tall Tales of the South, Georgia's only 4-D theater; the Treehouse Challenge; and the Great Barn, Atlan-ta's largest indoor play experience (see separate entries below). Admission to the Crossroads village is free; $8 park parking fee. Some of the individual attractions have a fee or are included in the One-Day All Attractions Pass. (See *Guidance* for prices and other details.)

✍ 🐾 **The Great Barn at Stone Mountain.** The gigantic barnlike structure fea-tures a series of interactive games geared toward teaching children about harvest time. (See *Guidance* for prices and other details.)

✍ ♿ **Six Flags American Adventures** (770-948-9290; www.sixflags.com/aadventures), 250 Cobb Parkway, Marietta. Open weekends March through May and mid-August through October; daily June through mid-August; closed November through February. Call for exact hours or check the web site. This nostalgic, family-oriented theme park is created to resemble a turn-of-the-20th-century town. Popular activities include the four-story, 40,000-square-foot Foam Factory and the outdoor Fun Forest, which features go-cart rides, bumper cars, laser tag, miniature golf, a mini roller coaster, carousel, kiddie play area, and arcade. Children taller than 36 inches $16, adults and children shorter than 36 inches $6; parking $6. Rates vary by season, and there are numerous specials.

✍ ♿ **Six Flags Over Georgia** (770-948-9290; www.sixflags.com/parks/over georgia), 275 Riverside Parkway, Austell. Open weekends March through Memorial Day and Labor Day through end of October; daily in summer. Hours vary widely, so call ahead or consult the web site. It's always playtime at this fam-ily-oriented theme park, which features 100 rides, including 10 white-knuckle coasters such as the Georgia Scorcher, one of the Southeast's tallest and fastest stand-up coasters; the Georgia Cyclone, the South's only twister coaster; and Acrophobia, a 200-foot rotating tower drop. Other family and not-for-the-faint-of-heart thrill coasters include the massive Goliath roller-coaster, Superman—Ultimate Flight and Batman the Ride. A variety of shows and other entertainment extravaganzas last late into the night on 10 stages. The park's newest additions are Skull Island, the world's largest interactive water-play struc-ture, and Wile E. Coyote Canyon Blaster, a roller coaster. Adults $50, children $30. Parking $10.

✍ ♿ **Six Flags White Water** (770-948-9290; www.whitewaterpark.com; www .sixflags.com/parks/whitewater), 250 Cobb Parkway, Marietta. Open 10–6 weekends in May and week before Memorial Day, then 10–8 daily Memorial Day weekend through Labor Day. The 35-acre site contains all the necessary ingredients for cooling off on hot summer days. Named one of the top 10 water parks in America as well as the Most Scenic Water Park in the country by *USA Today*, the complex offers 50 "splash-tastic" water rides that are fun for the whole family. The 90-foot-tall Cliffhanger provides one of the world's largest free falls, and the Tornado sends thrill-seekers down a 132-foot-long tunnel, throws them into a giant open-ended funnel, and drenches them under a waterfall. The park also features tree-shaded waterfalls, a lazy Little Hooch River, the Atlanta Ocean wave pool, a family raft ride, and the four-story Tree House Island. Five food concessions, a gift shop, and the after-dark "Dive-In Movie" provide even more fun. Adults $35, children shorter than 48 inches $25; parking $8.

♂ ♣ ♿ **Skyride at Stone Mountain Park.** Cable cars whisk visitors from the base of the mountain to the summit and afford a close-up view of the carving. Many visitors choose to take the Skyride to the summit and then walk down. $4 one-way or $7 round-trip per person in addition to $8 park parking fee (See *Guidance*).

♂ ♣ ♿ **Stone Mountain Park.** Call for event schedules and fees, as they vary seasonally. The park, Georgia's most-visited attraction, has something for everyone in the way of outdoor entertainment and recreation. Central to the park is the world's largest exposed mass of granite as well as the world's largest bas-relief sculpture, which depicts Confederate President Jefferson Davis and Generals Robert E. Lee and Stonewall Jackson. Surrounding the 825-foot mountain are 3,300 acres of forests, lakes, and parkland. Attractions include an antebellum plantation (*To See—Historic Homes and Sites*), Confederate Hall Historical and Environmental Center (*To See—Museums*), the 1870s town of Crossroads, a 4-D theater, the Great Barn, Ride the Ducks sight-seeing tour, a riverboat cruise, mountaintop skyride, scenic train ride, and the Lasershow Spectacular—a 40-minute extravaganza of colorful lasers, surround sound, and fantastic fireworks (see separate entries throughout this section). Recreation includes canoeing, boating, golf, hiking, miniature golf, a water slide complex, and tennis (see separate entries in this section). Festivals and other special events occur year-round (see *Special Events*). Accommodations are offered in two hotels and at a campground (see *Lodging*), and numerous restaurants please any palate (see *Where to Eat*). (See *Guidance* for prices and other park details.)

♂ ♣ ♿ **Sun Valley Beach** (770-943-5900; 1-888-811-7390; www.sunvalleybeach.com), 5350 Holloman Road, Powder Springs. Open daily May 15 through Labor Day, weekends in September (hours are too variable to include here, so check the web site). Landlocked metro Atlantans will think they're in paradise at this inland beach. Sun Valley Beach was the forerunner of modern water parks. In operation since 1964, the facility nestled amid 40 acres of pines features the Southeast's largest swimming pool, which is surrounded by white sandy beaches. The complex boasts 11 water slides, a dolphin fountain, showering umbrella, Tarzan ropes, zip line, diving platform, obstacle course, go-cart track, beach volleyball courts, sports fields, tennis courts, horseshoes, ball fields, and picnicking facilities. Adults $16, children 2–11 $14.

✄ 🐾 **Treehouse Challenge at Stone Mountain Park.** The three-story outdoor attraction is actually two dueling tree houses where teams pit the boys against the girls in more than a dozen interactive games. Participants use their hands and wits to master games and try to accumulate the most points. (See *Guidance* for prices and park details.)

✄ 🐾 ⚅ **Yellow River Game Ranch** (770-972-6643; 1-877-972-6643; www .yellowrivergameranch.com), 4525 US 78, Lilburn. Open 9:30–6 daily (last tickets sold at 5). The most acclaimed resident of this 25-acre game preserve is General Beauregard Lee, Georgia's weather prognosticator. The famous groundhog comes out of his Tara-like abode on February 2 and foretells the weather in the South just as Punxsutawney Phil does in the North, though General Lee correctly predicts an early spring much more often than his Northern cousin does. Visitors to the ranch can see 600 animals, including black bears, bobcats, the largest herd of buffalo east of the Mississippi, cougars, coyotes, foxes, goats, mountain lions, pigs, raccoons, sheep and lambs, white-tailed deer, and other animals indigenous to Georgia. The small fry (and even jaded adults) are won over by feeding the deer with specially purchased feed. Spring and summer, when there are babies, are favorite months to visit. Adults $8, children $7.

FRIGHTS ✄ ⚅ **Fright Fest** (770-948-9290; www.sixflags.com/parks/overgeorgia), Six Flags Over Georgia, 275 Riverside Parkway, Austell. Open Friday through Sunday in October. Hours vary widely, so call ahead or consult the web site. Ghouls and goblins transform the entire park into an eerie city filled with haunted houses, scary shows, and other frightfully good fun. Adults $50, children $30; parking $10.

✄ **Tour of Southern Ghosts.** Held after dark until 10 PM on 13 evenings during the Halloween season, the tour consists of tales told by costumed tellers as they guide groups around the lantern-lit grounds of Stone Mountain Park's Antebellum Plantation (see *To See—Historic Homes and Sites*). Stories are a little scary, often humorous, but never so frightening that they're inappropriate for young audiences. Reservations and tickets are strongly recommended to avoid standing in long lines and perhaps being disappointed. Call for the admission fee, which doesn't include the $8 park parking fee.

GOLF **Stone Mountain Golf Club at Stone Mountain Park** (770-465-3278; www.stonemountaingolf.com), Stonewall Jackson Drive, Stone Mountain Park. Open 7 AM–to dusk daily. Managed by Marriott Golf, the club offers 36 championship holes on the Lakemont and Stonemont courses. The Stonemont Course has been named one of the top 25 public courses in the country by *Golf Digest*. A driving range, putting green, practice facilities, pro shop, PGA instruction, clubhouse with locker rooms, and the Commons Restaurant are also available. $28–62.

HIKING ✄ 🐾 **Arabia Mountain Trails** (770-484-3060; www.arabiaalliance.org), 3787 Klondike Road, Lithonia. Open daylight hours daily. The Davidson–Arabia Mountain Nature Preserve features a paved path for walking, biking, and skating, as well as several unpaved marked and unmarked paths varying in length from a half mile to a mile. These paths can be combined for a longer hike of 3.3 miles. The most challenging path is the Bradley Peak Trail, which leads to the top of the 954-foot mountain. Free.

✍ 🐾 🐕 **Chattahoochee River National Recreation Area** (678-538-1200; www .nps.gov/chat). The Sope Creek unit of the 48-mile-long park is located on Paper Mill Road between Terrell Mill Road and Johnson Ferry Road in Marietta. It offers several miles of easy to difficult hiking trails, and mountain biking is allowed on designated stretches of the trails. A moderate hike takes you to the ruins of the Marietta Manufacturing Mill. The Powers Island unit has an easy 1-mile trail, the Johnson Ferry South unit has a 1½–mile trail, and the Johnson Ferry North unit has 2½ miles of easy trails. The Cochran Shoals unit contains easy to difficult trails, including a 3-mile fitness trail and a 3-mile bike loop. See the Atlanta chapter for more information about the recreation area.

✍ 🐕 **Georgia Wildlife Federation** (770-787-7887; www.gwf.org), 11600 Hazel-brand Road, Covington. Open daylight hours daily. The 115-acre grounds of the federation's headquarters offer woodlands, wetlands, meadow habitats, and demonstration wildlife habitat gardens. Visitors enjoy ambling along the Dog-wood Trail as it meanders past the tupelo gum river swamp and along the Alcovy River. The newest addition is the Alcovy Conservation Center, which contains office, classroom, and library space. The center is popular for bird-watching and picnicking. Deer, fox squirrels, otters, and a variety of songbirds are just a few of the year-round residents. Free.

✍ 🐕 **Kennesaw Mountain National Battlefield Park** (770-427-4286; www .nps.gov/kemo), 900 Kennesaw Mountain Drive off Old US 41 and Stilesboro Road, Kennesaw. The park's trails offer short walks and long hikes. Various starting points on the trails create 2-, 5-, 10-, and 16-mile round-trip hikes. All the trails require moderately steep climbing. There is limited water and no shelter or food along the trails.

✍ 🐕 **Nature Trails of Stone Mountain Park.** The park is filled with 10 miles of easy to difficult trails that encourage visitors to enjoy the beauty of the seasons, the natural wonders, and the striking vistas while they get their exercise. The most difficult trail is the steep 1.3-mile **Walk-Up Trail** to the 1,683-feet-above-sea-level summit. Our suggestion is that, unless you're in very good shape, you take the Skyride ($4 one-way) to the top and walk down. If you walk up and ride down, there is no transportation back to the parking lot from which you started. Along the Walk-Up Trail visitors will see the 2-inch-tall red stonecrop, golden ragweed, and the Confederate yellow daisy. Fifteen other genera of rare plants grow on the mountain outcrops and along the trails. The short loop **Nature Trail** is associated with the Nature Garden, where visitors can wander among native plants, flowering shrubs, and mountain streams. The lengthy 7-mile-plus **Cherokee Trail** with two connecting trails wraps all the way around the mountain. The site of the 1996 Centennial Olympic Summer Games archery and cycling events, the area encompasses the **Songbird Habitat and Trail,** a 1-mile trail with a variety of plant life and food for a wide array of birds. Along many of these paths, visitors can see vegetation that is native to Georgia and/or

Stone Mountain Park. Trail use free; $8 park parking fee. (See *Guidance* for park details.)

✍ 🐾 🍃 ♿ **Silver Comet Trail** (770-528-3658; www.pathfoundation.org). The trail connects the Atlanta metropolitan area to the Alabama state line—a 60-mile journey. A former railroad route for the *Silver Comet* passenger train, which ran from Boston to Birmingham between 1947 and 1968, the track has been taken up and paved so that the roadbed provides opportunities for walking, jogging, hiking, cycling, and skating. The trail is also suitable for baby strollers and wheelchairs. Those with their own horse can avail themselves of portions of the trail, and leashed pets are welcome. No motorized vehicles are allowed. The trail, which crosses six trestles and bridges, offers scenic views and access to Heritage Park, a 105-acre nature preserve. A 1.7-mile spur trail goes to the ruins of a woolen mill. Four trailheads offer parking, rest rooms, and water fountains. The trail also can be accessed from several cross streets. It is patrolled by bicycle-mounted Cobb County police officers. For more information about the trail, contact **Cobb County Parks, Recreation and Cultural Affairs** (770-528-8840; www.cobbcounty.org) or the web site at www.trailexpress.com, which provides directions to the trailheads. The trail connects to the Wild Horse Creek Trail (see below) in Powder Springs and to the 33-mile Chief Ladiga Trail at the Georgia-Alabama state line, then continues on to Anniston, Alabama, which creates even more possibilities. See *Bicycling* for information about the shuttle service (reservations required) provided by the **Silver Comet Depot,** a year-round Volksmarch center.

✍ 🐾 🍃 **Vickery Creek Unit, Chattahoochee River National Recreation Area** (678-538-1200; www.nps.gov/chat/hiking.htm), Roswell. The topography of the heavily wooded park includes steep cliffs and rocky outcroppings as well as level terrain. A total of 11½ miles of trails for all abilities crisscross the park along the creek or provide rigorous climbs over ridges. Within the park are the ruins of several mill buildings and an 1860s man-made mill dam that creates a cascading waterfall. Free; $2 if parking off Riverside Drive.

✍ 🐾 🍃 ♿ **Wild Horse Creek Trail** (770-439-2500), Powder Springs. Open daylight hours daily; closed immediately after a rainstorm. This area saw a lot of action as Union troops advanced on Atlanta in 1864. Today, a 10-foot-wide, 1½-mile paved trail is used by cyclists, skaters, runners, and walkers. The trail, which begins at Macedonia Road and ends at Carter Road, is the first in a proposed citywide network of trails. It is appropriate for baby strollers, wheelchairs, and pets on leashes. Motorized vehicles and horses are not permitted. Along the way, users can see the largest red maple tree in the state or view the wetlands from an observation tower. Amenities include a rest area near Powder Springs Road, two emergency call boxes, and parking and rest-room facilities at Wild Horse Creek Park. The bicycle unit of the Powder Springs Police Department provides security. The trail also connects to the Silver Comet Trail (see above).

HORSEBACK RIDING ✍ 🍃 **Georgia International Horse Park** (770-860-4190; 1-800-860-4224; www.georgiahorsepark.com), 1996 Centennial Olympic Parkway, Conyers. Open daylight to dusk daily, but closed occasionally for special events (see *To See—Equestrian Events*), so check the web site. For those who can BYOH (bring your own horse), the park features more than 15 miles of horse trails that offer scenic views of the former Olympic Endurance Course as they wind through wooded areas and open pastureland and past streams. Varied trail lengths and links between trails allow riders to choose their own route and tailor their own ride. A large map of the trails is posted at each check-in shelter, and there are individual take-away maps as well. $5 per-day trail fee collected on the honor system, $35 annual pass.

MINIATURE GOLF ✍ ☙ **Stone Mountain Park Mini Golf.** The course offers 36 holes of entertainment for the whole family. (See *Guidance* for prices and other park details.)

MOUNTAIN BIKING ✍ ☙ **Georgia International Horse Park** (770-860-4190; 1-800-860-4224; www.georgiahorsepark.com), 1996 Centennial Olympic Parkway, Conyers. Open daylight to dusk daily, but closed occasionally for special events (see *To See—Equestrian Events*), so check the web site. The park offers 8 miles of riding and 1,032 feet of elevation change on the first-ever Olympic mountain biking course in the world. A large map of the trails is posted at each check-in shelter, and there are individual take-away maps as well. $5 per-day trail fee collected on the honor system, $35 annual pass.

SKYDIVING **Skydive Monroe** (1-800-SKYDIVE), Monroe Municipal Airport, 528 Tower Street, Monroe. Open 9–sunset Wednesday through Sunday, by appointment only Monday and Tuesday. There are only four skydiving drop zones in Georgia, and this is the closest one to metro Atlanta. Skydive Monroe serves a mix of new jumpers, belly-fliers, and free-fliers. The company belongs to the U.S. Parachute Association and follows that organization's safety standards. Courses are taught by USPA-rated staff. $160 for the course and one jump; $125–245 for further training and jumps.

SPORTS EXPERIENCES **Andretti Speed Lab** (770-992-5688; www.andretti speedlab.com), 11000 Alpharetta Highway, Roswell. Open 3–10 PM Monday through Thursday, 3 PM–1 AM Friday, 11 AM–1 AM Saturday, noon–10 PM Sunday. This indoor complex boasts racing-related entertainment for adventure seekers. Visitors can suit up in authentic racing gear and get behind the wheel of a high-performance, Italian-designed SuperCart. Two indoor courses were patterned after famous European courses. The Game Lab is an interactive arcade with the latest in video and virtual-reality games, including football, basketball, soccer, and racing simulators. The high-energy facility also offers a three-story rock-climbing wall, a ropes course, and 100 satellite-linked televisions as well as Sky-Box Sports Bar and a Fuddrucker's restaurant. Racing is not suitable for preteen children. $7 for a license, $18 for one race, $48 for three races; $9 for three climbs on rock wall; 50¢–$1.50 for arcade games.

TENNIS ✍ ☙ **Stone Mountain International Tennis Center at Stone Mountain Park** (770-413-5288; www.stonemountainpark.com), 5525 Bermuda

Road, Stone Mountain. Open 8:30–9 weekdays, 8–6 weekends. Site of the 1996 Centennial Olympic Summer Games tennis events, the center features 15 lighted Plexi-Cushion courts available for public play; another is reserved for tournaments and concerts. Racquet rentals and instruction are available, and there is a pro shop. $10 per 1½ hours per court; ball machine $15 per hour.

TRAIN EXCURSIONS *✐ 🏵* **Scenic Railroad and Live Show at Stone Mountain Park.** Riding aboard vintage rail cars, passengers enjoy the 5-mile, 30-minute journey around the base of the mountain. Board the train at the Memorial Railroad Depot (where tickets can be purchased) or the Whistle Stop Depot. The train is pulled by the *General II*, a replica of the famous train that was hijacked by Union raiders during the Civil War but chased down and recaptured. On weekends in May and daily in the summer, costumed actors perform a short show when the train passes the replica of a pioneer town. (See *Guidance* for prices and other park details.)

THE *GENERAL II* PULLS A TRAIN THAT CARRIES GUESTS AROUND THE BASE OF STONE MOUNTAIN.

✳ Green Space

GARDENS *✐ 🏵 ♿* **Vines Botanical Gardens and Manor House** (770-466-7532; www.vinesbotanicalgardens.com), 3500 Oak Grove Road, Loganville. Open 10–5 Monday through Saturday. Originally the private estate of Charles "Boe" and Myrna Adams, the 25-acre estate on US 78 between Snellville and Monroe was donated to Gwinnett County for use as a public park. The site is named in honor of Myrna's father, Odie O. Vines, an avid gardener. Beautifully landscaped gardens embrace curving pathways, a picturesque lake, fountains, and imported sculptures. Several niche gardens include Pappy's Garden, the Whimsical Garden, Asian Garden, Southscape Garden, White Garden, and Rose Garden. A light lunch of burgers, quiches, and sandwiches is served 11–2 weekdays. Adults $5, children and seniors $4.

See also **Antebellum Brumby Hall and Gardens** under *To See—Historic Homes and Sites.*

NATURE PRESERVES AND PARKS *✐ 🏵* **Autrey Mill Nature Preserve**

and Heritage Center (770-360-8844; www.autreymill.org), 9770 Autrey Mill
Road, Alpharetta. Grounds open 8–dusk daily; center open 10–4 weekdays, 10–2
Saturday. Located on 46 acres of forest and the site of an old cotton plantation,
Autrey Mill offers scenic creeks, rocky shoals, spring seeps, picturesque cliffs,
mature trees, wildflowers, native plants, wildlife, and 1½ miles of hiking trails.
Circa late 1800s farmhouses from the plantation days remain: The Tenant Farmhouse is filled with tools and furnishings from bygone days; the 1880s Summer-
our House is being restored; and the rustic visitor center displays exhibits. The
park offers special programs and events, including an Easter egg hunt, environmental activities, music programs, summer camp, trail walks, and Young Artist
Days. Free.

❧ ✿ **Big Haynes Creek Nature Center** (770-860-4190; 1-800-860-4224;
www.georgiahorsepark.com), 1996 Centennial Olympic Parkway, Conyers. Within
the **Georgia International Horse Park** (see *To See—Equestrian Events*), 173
acres are designated as a preserve dedicated to the preservation and study of
native plants and wildlife. The preserve features 1.4 miles of riding trails and 2.6
miles of walking trails. A learning center, native plant garden, wildflower meadow, endangered species protection area, outdoor teaching theaters, elevated
boardwalk, canoe trails, picnic areas, and primitive camping areas are planned,
so stay tuned. Free.

✿ ♿ **Black Shoals Park** (770-785-5922; 770-761-1611; www.rockdalecounty.org),
3001 Black Shoals Road, Conyers. Open daily, 7–9 summer, 7–6 winter; boats
must be off the water a half-hour before closing. No gasoline motors of any kind
are permitted. Fishing, boating, and canoeing are the primary activities in this
park surrounding Randy Poynter Lake, a 650-acre reservoir, but hiking and picnicking are popular as well. The Georgia Department of Natural Resources
stocks the lake with largemouth bass, assorted bream, and catfish. The park features a boat ramp, fishing pier, and picnic pavilion. A **Veterans Memorial Park**
(www.walkofheroes.com) is in the works. $5 per person, $5 per boat or canoe.

❧ ✿ ♿ **Chattahoochee Nature Center** (770-992-2055; www.chattnature
center.com), 9135 Willeo Road, Roswell. Open 9–5 Monday through Saturday,
noon–5 Sunday. Visitors can get in touch with nature at this facility, where
boardwalks and nature trails allow access to the 127-acre site and miles of freshwater ponds, river marshes, and wooded uplands that hug the Chattahoochee
River. More than 30 species of wildlife call the nature center home. Among the
popular exhibits is a beaver dam complete with beavers. Raptor aviaries display
birds of prey that have been rehabilitated here and can't be returned to the wild.
The nature center offers tours and hosts educational programs and special
events throughout the year, including seasonal canoe trips on the river. Adults
$3, children 3–12 and seniors $2.

❧ ✿ ♿ **Sweetwater Creek State Conservation Park** (770-732-5871;
www.gastateparks.org/info/sweetwater), Mount Vernon Road, Lithia Springs.
Park open 7–10; visitor center open 8–5; trails close at dark. This is the third
most visited park in the state system and the most visited park without overnight
facilities. More than 2,500 acres of peaceful wilderness and 9 miles of trails are
located just west of Atlanta. A forest trail follows a stream to the ruins of the

TRAILS AT THE CHATTAHOOCHEE NATURE CENTER IN ROSWELL ALLOW GUESTS TO
EXPLORE FLORA AND FAUNA THAT SURROUND THE CHATTAHOOCHEE.

New Manchester Manufacturing Company, a textile mill that was burned during
the Civil War. Its workers (mostly women and children) were charged with treason, marched to Marietta, and put on trains for the North, where they were
either imprisoned or forced into servitude to Northern families and businesses
for the duration of the war. From the mills, the trail climbs rocky bluffs and
affords views of the shoals below. The park's streams and 215-acre George Sparks
Reservoir provide recreation for anglers. (Electric motors only are allowed.) Fishing supplies and snacks are available in the park's bait shop along with canoe and
fishing-boat rentals. The park also features picnicking facilities, a butterfly garden, and periodic interpretive programs such as history walks in February, wildflower walks in April, a Native American festival in June, and New Manchester
Days in September. Children love to feed the ducks in the pond. Maps and park
information can be found at the visitor center. Parking $3, boat ramp fee $2.

See also **Vickery Creek Unit, Chattahoochee River National Recreation
Area,** under *To Do—Hiking.*

RECREATION AREAS ✿ ✸ The **Chattahoochee River National Recreation
Area** (678-538-1200) is a 48-mile stretch of the Chattahoochee River. Along the

way are numerous day-use parks where visitors can enjoy boating (see *To Do—Canoing, Kayaking, and Rafting*), fishing, hiking (see *To Do*), and wildlife observation (see *Nature Preserves and Parks*). The units in the area described by this chapter include Cochran Shoals, Sope Creek, Powers Island, Johnson Ferry North, Johnson Ferry South, and Vickery Creek (see *To Do—Hiking*). Cochran Shoals offers several trails, including one that is wheelchair accessible. Sope Creek has stone ruins from a paper manufacturing company that produced much of the South's paper from 1855 to 1902. Powers Island is named for James Powers, who ferried travelers across the river before there were bridges.

RIVERS ♂ ♣ **Chattahoochee River.** The mighty Chattahoochee, which is the Cherokee word for "River of the Painted Rock," begins as Chattahoochee Spring in the northeast Georgia mountains near the White-Union County line and wends its way to Lake Seminole at the Georgia-Florida border. On the way it creates the border between Georgia and Alabama as well as several lakes. The river and its banks offer opportunities for fishing, hiking, picnicking, canoeing, and rafting. Visitors may see wildflowers, wildlife, and waterfowl. The City of Roswell created a River Parkway, an important link in the Roswell Trail System, along several miles of the river. Dotted along the River Parkway are the **Chattahoochee River Park** on Azalea Drive, **Riverside Park** on Riverside Road, and the **Don White Memorial Park** on Riverside Drive.

✳ Lodging

BED & BREAKFASTS

In Covington
♣ **2119 the Inn** (770-787-0037; www.2119theinn.com), 2119 Emory Street NW. One of Covington's most historic homes, this handsome residence, built in 1905 for the city's first postmaster, John Lamar Callaway Sr., features large, inviting verandas on both floors. The beautifully furnished inn offers three uniquely decorated guest accommodations with sitting areas and private baths. A continental breakfast is served in the sunny solarium. No smoking. Limited wheelchair accessibility. $95; discounts for multiple nights.

In Decatur
♣ 🐾 **Garden House Bed and Breakfast** (404-377-3057; www.home.earthlink.net/~gardenhouse135), 135 Garden Lane. Located just four blocks from downtown Decatur, this B&B offers a second-floor suite in a

home that was built in the 1940s. Guests can choose any type breakfast: continental, full, low-carb, or whatever they'd like. Small dogs accepted. No smoking. Not wheelchair accessible. $85.

🐾 **Sycamore House in Old Decatur** (404-378-0685; www.city-directory.com/sycamorehouse), 624 Sycamore Street. Located in an almost 100-year-old Prairie-style mansion on a tree-lined residential street, this B&B has been lovingly restored and handsomely furnished with an eclectic mixture of antiques and contemporary pieces accented by contemporary artwork. Two upstairs rooms share a bath, while the downstairs suite has a private bath. Guests enjoy a heated pool, hot tub, and waterfall in the garden—an unexpected oasis. Full breakfast is included.

The B&B is located within a five-minute walk of downtown Decatur, Agnes Scott College, and either the Avondale or Decatur rail stations. Pets accepted. No smoking. Not wheelchair accessible. $90–110.

In Marietta
Sixty Polk Street Inn Bed and Breakfast (770-419-1688; 1-800-845-7266; www.sixtypolkstreet.com), 60 Polk Street. Built in 1852, this Victorian-era residence was lived in by one family from 1890 to 1980. Now fully restored, it operates as a bed & breakfast with four guest chambers furnished in styles from Victorian to Empire. No smoking. Not wheelchair accessible. $95–150.

The Stanley House Bed and Breakfast (770-426-1881), 236 Church Street. When visitors see this large, stately Queen Anne Victorian, they find it hard to imagine that the house was built in 1895 as a summer "cottage" by Mrs. Felie Woodrow, an aunt of Woodrow Wilson. Now an ele-gant bed & breakfast, the inn offers four guest rooms. No smoking. Not wheelchair accessible. $125.

The Whitlock Inn Bed and Breakfast (770-428-1495; www.whitlockinn.com), 57 Whitlock Avenue. Built around 1900, this lovely home was the residence of one family for 60 years. It's a perfect example of the "wedding cake" style of architecture so popular at the turn of the 20th century, so it's no surprise that so many weddings are held here. The property has operated since 1994 as an inn with five luxurious, individually decorated guest rooms furnished with period antiques. No smoking. Limited wheelchair accessibility. $100–125.

In Roswell
Ten-Fifty Canton Street Bed and Breakfast (770-998-1050), 1050 Canton Street. Built in the late 1800s, the fully restored white clapboard cottage features rooms filled with antiques. It is within easy walking distance of the historic commercial district's numer-

THE VILLAGE INN BED & BREAKFAST SERVED AS A CONFEDERATE HOSPITAL DURING THE CIVIL WAR.

ous quaint shops and restaurants. A continental breakfast is served. No smoking or pets. Limited wheelchair accessibility. Not appropriate for children. $125–160.

In Stone Mountain Village
Village Inn Bed and Breakfast (770-469-3459; 1-800-214-8385; www.villageinnbb.com), 992 Ridge Avenue. Located in a stately home built in the 1820s as a roadside inn, the structure is the oldest building in Stone Mountain Village. It served as a Confederate hospital during the Civil War and was therefore spared during Sherman's March to the Sea. The inn has six guest rooms, including Scarlett's Room and Rhett's Room, each with two-person whirlpool tubs. Some guest chambers also boast a gas fireplace and/or a veranda. The Ballroom Suite has a sitting area with a daybed and a trundle bed, a refrigerator, a microwave, and a shower and whirlpool therapy tub. Full breakfast is included. Smoking outdoors only. Limited wheelchair accessibility. $129–169.

In Villa Rica
∅ ⴟ **Twin Oaks on MelaCari Bed and Breakfast Cottages** (770-459-4374; www.twinoaksmc.com), 9565 E. Liberty Road. Visitors get the better of two worlds at this upscale 23-acre farm. City slickers who want to get away from it all can enjoy the farm menagerie that includes cats, dogs, Canada geese, mallards, peacocks, a pot-bellied pig, and white mute swans. They can fish in the pond or swim in the pool. But there are no bunkhouse accommodations here. Guest quarters are in swanky, sophisticated, private cottages. Scarlett's Cottage, done in *Gone with the Wind* style, overlooks the goldfish and koi

pond. The Cozy Spot Cottage has a view of the pond and the garden. Swan Cottage boasts a large porch overlooking the ponds and gardens. Guests enjoy a bountiful continental breakfast Sunday through Thursday; on Friday and Saturday, guests take pleasure in a full country breakfast. No smoking. Wheelchair accessible. $109–189.

CAMPGROUNDS

In Conyers
∅ **Georgia International Horse Park** (770-860-4190; 1-800-860-4224; www.georgiahorsepark.com), 1996 Centennial Olympic Parkway. Office open 8–5 weekdays. Reservations required. The full-service park near the stable complex and Walker Arena complex offers 50 sites with full water, electric, and sewer hookups. The park also offers shower facilities. Call for price ranges.

In Stone Mountain Park
∅ ⴟ **Stone Mountain Park Campground** (770-498-5710; 1-800-385-9807; www.stonemountainpark.com), US 78 East. Situated on 363-acre Stone Mountain Lake, the campground features 441 full- and partial-hookup sites as well as primitive sites. Amenities include a campground store (from which you can rent rowboats), laundry facilities, a playground, snack bar, swimming pool, and volleyball court. $23–45.

INNS AND HOTELS

In Atlanta
∅ ⴟ **Renaissance Waverly Hotel** (770-953-4500; 1-888-391-8724; www.renaissancehotels.com), 2450 Galleria Parkway. The Renaissance Waverly is one of the only AAA four-

diamond hostelries in the northwest quadrant of metro Atlanta and one of the most luxurious hotels in the immediate area. The 14-floor hotel features 497 upscale guest rooms, 24 elegant suites, and a concierge level as well as indoor and outdoor pools, a fitness center, and spa services. Restaurants include the Atrium Café and the Waverly Coffee Bar for breakfast and lunch, and the Saddles Sports Bar and the Waverly Grill for dinner. $100–200.

🐾 ♿ **University Inn at Emory** (1-800-654-8591; www.univinn.com), 1767 N. Decatur Road. Guest accommodations are located in several buildings on the Emory University campus. Most rooms are roomy and have a microwave/refrigerator combination. The Guest House features the most economical accommodations, and many of its rooms have a kitchen. Oxford Hall offers long-term housing for those who do not require daily services. For all guests, the inn offers a complimentary continental breakfast and afternoon refreshments daily. Beer and wine are available weekdays. Rooms are equipped with high-speed Internet access or modem connections and voice mail; the inn's business center offers fax, printing, and Internet access. Pet friendly. No smoking. Some rooms are wheelchair accessible. $74–159 in the Guest House, $144–154 in the inn; $210–350 weekly for efficiencies in Oxford Hall (seven-day minimum).

RESORTS

In Conyers
♿ 🐾 ♿ **Hawthorn Suites Golf Resort** (770-761-9155; 1-800-527-1133; www.georgiahorsepark.com), 1659 Centennial Olympic Parkway.

Overlooking the seventh hole of the Cherokee Run Golf Club, the hotel boasts 77 one-, two-, and three-bedroom suites as well as an outdoor heated pool and whirlpool, bar, guest laundry facilities, fitness center, convenience and gift shop, and business center. A hot breakfast is served daily, and there's a manager's reception Monday through Thursday evenings. Pets allowed. Smoking and nonsmoking rooms available. Some rooms are wheelchair accessible. $99-$119.

In Marietta
♿ ♿ **Marietta Conference Center and Resort** (770-427-2500; 1-888-685-2500; www.mariettaresort.com), 500 Powder Springs Road. This magnificent AAA four-diamond hotel, which resembles the world-famous Greenbrier in West Virginia, sits on the site of the old Georgia Military Institute, which was destroyed by Union troops during the Civil War. Choose from 199 elegantly furnished guest rooms or nine parlor suites. Each offers a spectacular view of the Atlanta skyline or the golf course and Kennesaw Mountain. Other amenities include a restaurant, bar, billiard room, outdoor pool, fitness club, golf course, and lighted tennis courts. On the grounds is the historic **Antebellum Brumby Hall and Gardens,** the only surviving building from the school era (see *To See—Historic Homes and Sites*). Smoking and non-smoking rooms available; no smoking in restaurant; smoking allowed in pub. Wheelchair accessible. $99–179.

✳ Where to Eat
DINING OUT

In Alpharetta
♿ **Cabernet** (770-777-5955; www

.cabernetsteakhouse.com), 5575 Windward Parkway. Open 11–2 weekdays; 5–10 Sunday through Thursday, 5–11 Friday and Saturday. The menu features the highest grade of prime aged beef and fresh seafood flown in daily. Chef Richard Holley also has introduced prix fixe dinners on Friday and Saturday; the three-course meal includes an appetizer, entrée, dessert, and a glass of cabernet for $35. Thursdays with a Twist or an Olive feature classic martinis, complimentary hors d'oeuvres, and live jazz 5:30–7:30. Smoking in bar only. Lunch from $9.95, dinner $19.95–38.95.

&. **Killer Creek** (770-649-0064; www .killerrestaurants.com), 1700 Mansell Road. Open 11–2 Monday through Saturday; 5–10 Monday through Thursday, 5–11 Friday and Saturday, 5–9 Sunday; Sunday brunch 11:30–2:30. Voted one of the best steakhouses in Atlanta and a Taste of Alpharetta winner, this upscale restaurant offers premium steaks and fresh seafood. In addition, Killer Creek also features signature cocktails and live entertainment on Wednesday, Friday, and Saturday nights. Smoking in bar only. Lunch under $10, dinner $19.95–39.95.

&. **Rainwater** (770-777-0033; www .rainwaterrestaurant.com), 11655 Haynes Bridge Road. Open 11:30–2 weekdays; 5:30–9 Monday through Thursday, 5:30–10 Friday and Saturday. Rainwater's New American cuisine is heavily influenced by that of northern California and the Pacific Northwest. Lunch offers a variety of salads and sandwiches. Dinner, which is a more formal affair, features such highlights as certified Angus filet, roasted halibut, and Rainwater's signature crabcake. Smoking allowed in one room and on patio. Lunch $10–16, dinner $20–36.

&. **Sage** (770-569-9199; www.sage woodfiretavern.com), 11405 Haynes Bridge Road. Open 11–10 Monday through Thursday, 11–11 Friday, 5–11 Saturday and Sunday; lounge and bar open until 1 AM. Casual ambience paired with city chic serves as a pleasant backdrop for contemporary American cuisine with global influences. Fresh fish, hand-cut steaks, chops, and chicken are prepared over a hickory-oak wood-fire grill. Live music is offered 6–9 Wednesday through Saturday; DJs take over after 9. Thursdays they spin '60s and '70s tunes; Friday the DJ plays techno songs. Smoking in bar only. Lunch under $9.95, dinner $10.95–17.95.

&. **Shiraz** (770-751-7272; www.shiraz -alfredo.com), 11950 Jones Bridge Road. Open 11:30–3 Tuesday through Saturday, 12:30–4:30 Sunday; 5–10 Tuesday through Saturday, 5:30–10 Sunday. This is the most lavish Persian restaurant in the Atlanta metro area. Exotic spreads, chafing dishes of steamed basmati rice, stewed meats and vegetables, and platters stacked high with kebabs are just a few of the choices diners can enjoy. Make a real Persian meal by having the traditional tea service. No smoking. Lunch buffet $9.95, from menu $11–18, dinner $22–28.

&. **Village Tavern** (770-777-6490; www.villagetavern.com), 11555 Rainwater Drive. Open 11–10 Monday through Thursday, 11–11 Friday, 4–11 Saturday, 10–10 Sunday with brunch served 10–3. In this upscale yet casual restaurant, exposed timber beams, warm colors, and a stone fireplace set the stage for traditional and modern fare and an award-winning wine list. Smoking in bar only. $13–27.

& **Vinny's** (770-772-4644; www .knowheretogogh.com), 5355 Windward Parkway. Open 11–midnight Monday through Saturday, 5–10 Sunday. A sibling to the original Van Gogh's in Roswell (see below), Vinny's is also a salute to Vincent Van Gogh. Italian-inspired entrées range from sea bass to lamb to cowboy rib eye, with many other meat and seafood choices filling out the menu. Smoking in bar only. Lunch entrées average $10, dinner entrées $15–29.

In Atlanta

✐ ✦ & **The Dining Room at Fernbank** (404-929-6300; www.fernbank .edu/museum/visitordining.html), 767 Clifton Road NE. Open 11–4 Monday through Saturday, noon–4 Sunday. Located within the Fernbank Museum of Natural History, the eatery serves sandwiches, salads, specialty entrées, light snacks, and refreshing beverages in comfortable surroundings with a spectacular view of Fernbank Forest. No smoking. $2.25–6.

& **Ray's on the River** (770-955-1187; raysrestaurants.com), 6700 Powers Ferry Road. Open 11–2:30 weekdays; 5–10 Monday through Thursday, 5–11 Friday and Saturday, 5–9 Sunday; 9:30–3 Sunday for brunch. Ray's is one of a very few restaurants in metro Atlanta blessed with a location on the banks of the languid Chattahoochee River. Diners vie for window or patio seating to couple a fine meal with a beautiful view. Seafood is prominently featured, and guests also can choose among pork chops, chicken, prime rib, steak, and lobster. The award-winning Sunday brunch features 80 items from peel-and-eat shrimp to mussels marinated in vinaigrette, a carving station, made-to-order omelets, a waffle station, and a vast assortment of desserts. Enjoy live music in the bar 7–10 Thursday and a cookout and music on the patio 5–8 Friday, weather permitting. No smoking (even outside). Lunch $5.75–16, dinner $16.50–37.

In Chamblee

✐ & **57th Fighter Group** (770-457-7227), 3829 Clairmont Road. Open 4–10 Monday through Thursday, 4–11 Friday and Saturday, 10–10 Sunday. World War II nostalgia and splendid views of small planes taking off and landing at DeKalb-Peachtree Airport are the major attractions here. The scene is set with a seemingly bombed-out French farmhouse and WWII planes and vehicles outside, and black-and-white photos of wartime scenes inside. The food includes favorites such as calamari, beer cheese soup, steak, and seafood. DJs spin tunes on the weekends, and there is often live entertainment. No smoking except on patio. $15–35.

In Decatur

& **Floataway Café** (404-892-1414; www.starprovisions.com/float), 1123 Zonolite Road. Open 5–10 Tuesday through Saturday; reservations recommended. Operated by the same team as Midtown's Bacchanalia, the restaurant serves fresh California cuisine reminiscent of Napa Valley and Italian countryside dishes embellished with local produce. Many dishes are cooked in a wood-fire oven or grill. The restaurant, located in a former warehouse along a purely industrial street, is named for the former tenant, the Floataway Door Company. The last time we were there, it was raining so hard we thought we would float away, but we enjoyed a wonderful dinner amid the chic decor. No smoking. $15–23.

ქ **Sage on Sycamore** (404-373-5574; www.thebistros.com), 121 Sycamore Street. Open 11:30–2 Tuesday through Friday; 5:30–9:30 Tuesday through Thursday, 5:30–10:30 Friday and Saturday, 5–9 Sunday; 11:30–2:30 Sunday for brunch. Located behind the historic courthouse on the square, the restaurant serves eclectic American and international cuisine. Many restaurants claim to have an extensive wine list, but Sage delivers with 150 wines, 50 of which are available by the glass. No smoking. Lunch $7.50–15, dinner $21–30, brunch $4.50–12.

ქ **The Supper Club** (404-370-1207; www.supperclubdecatur.com), 308 W. Ponce de Leon Avenue at Ponce Place, Suite H. Open 6–10 Wednesday through Sunday. *Atlanta Magazine* deems this intimate restaurant the Best Place in Atlanta to Seduce a Man. We can assure you that ladies would like to be seduced amid the Supper Club's flickering candlelight and crushed velvet, too. If you're planning on popping the question, there's no better spot than the private, exotic hookah room. The cuisine features seasonal European bistro favorites and is vegetarian friendly. No smoking. $15–28.

In Marietta

✦ ქ **Hamilton's** (770-427-2500; www.mariettaresort.com), 500 Powder Springs Road. Open 6:30–10 AM, 11:30 AM–2 PM, and 6–10 PM daily. Located at the Marietta Conference Center and Resort, the elegant restaurant is fashioned after Southern estates of the 1800s. New South cuisine features seasonally changing menus. No smoking. Breakfast $9, lunch $15, dinner $17–29.

Shillings Top of the Square (770-428-9520), 19 North Park Square. Open 5:30–11 Tuesday through Saturday. The restaurant offers formal dining with crisp table linens and candlelight, while its large windows provide a romantic view of Marietta Square. Dinner choices might include seafood, steaks, chops, chicken, or lamb. Live piano music and a full bar add to the ambience. No smoking. Not wheelchair accessible. $18–23.

ქ **Slovakia Restaurant** (770-792-4443; www.slovakiarestaurant.com), 164 Roswell Street. Open 6–10 PM Tuesday through Saturday, 11:30–2 Sunday for brunch. Aged wood and traditional costumes create an Old World ambience that serves as an elegant backdrop for delicious dishes. Native Slovakians Stefan and Ivana Bencik create traditional dishes such as sauerkraut soup, *tarator* (cold cucumber soup), *halusky* (Slovakian potato spaetzle with cheese and bacon), pierogies, goulash, and entrées using beef, pork, sausage, duck, veal, chicken, and seafood. Specialties include chateaubriand and beef Wellington. Save room for desserts such as strudels or *palacinky* Patrik, Slovakian pancakes with jam, strawberries, whipped cream, chocolate, pecans, and ice cream. On Saturday evenings, the banquet facility portion of the restaurant becomes Murder on the Square, a dinner theater that presents a different play each month. $11.95–24.95, three-course dinner and play $38.

In Roswell

ქ **dick and harry's** (770-641-8757; www.dickandharrys.com), 1570 Holcomb Bridge Road, Suite 810.

Open 11:30–2:30 weekdays; 5:30–10 Monday through Thursday, 5:30–11 Friday and Saturday. Dick and Harry are brothers Richard and Harold Marmulstein. Their contemporary American cuisine at this upscale casual restaurant features fish, seafood, steaks, chops, and award-winning crabcakes. In fact, their menu is so diverse, you can get everything here from special Passover meals to ice cream. Smoking in bar only. $17–30.

Pastis (770-640-3870), 936 Canton Street. Open 11:30–2:30 and 5:30–10 daily. This trendy little restaurant in the heart of the Roswell art gallery district has an award-winning wine list and menu featuring French cuisine. Popular places to dine are by the fireplace or on the balcony overlooking historic Canton Street. Among the accolades heaped on Pastis by various Atlanta publications are Best Steaks, Best French Food, Best Live Music, Best Neighborhood Bar, Best Trendy Hangout, Best Romantic Restaurant, and Best Overall Restaurant. Smoking in bar only. Not wheelchair accessible. $17–30.

& **Salvatore Trattoria** (770-645-9983), 292 S. Atlanta Street. Open 5:30–9 Monday through Saturday; reservations not accepted. Salvatore Mattielo serves Neapolitan-influenced Italian cuisine here. Some specialties include linguine with seafood, veal with tomato and mushrooms, pasta fagioli, calamari with marinara sauce and yellow peppers, penne all'amatriciana, and homemade cannoli. Smoking at bar only. $12–25.

& **Van Gogh's** (770-993-1156; www .knowwheretogogh.com), 70 W. Crossville Road. Open 11:30–11 weekdays; 5–11 Saturday, 5–9 Sunday; Sunday brunch 11:30–2:30. The Zagat Survey considers Van Gogh's to be one of the best restaurants in the entire metropolitan Atlanta area. The contemporary stone and rustic wood structure once housed a California-style restaurant. These days, the formal traditional furnishings and decor are somewhat at odds with the casual structure, but nothing takes away from the fabulous cuisine or the extensive wine list. Van Gogh's wine cellar, which features more than 500 selections representing the world's greatest wine regions, has received *Wine Spectator*'s Award of Excellence several years running—one of only five such awards in the state. Lunch might include such delicacies as a grilled salmon BLT, a grilled bison burger, or a crabcake sandwich. Dinner choices include seared sea scallops, grilled chipotle-marinated pork tenderloin, roast rack of lamb, or confit and crisp-seared breast of duck. Save room for the to-die-for desserts. Smoking in bar only. Lunch entrées average $10, dinner entrées $16–29.

In Social Circle

♪ ⚑ & **Blue Willow Inn** (770-464-2131; 1-800-552-8813; www.blue willowinn.com), 294 N. Cherokee Road/GA 11. Open Tuesday through Sunday for lunch and dinner; reservations recommended. Located in an imposing turn-of-the-20th-century Greek Revival mansion, the elegantly furnished restaurant earned the *Southern Living* Readers' Choice Award as Best Small Town Restaurant from 1996 until the award was retired in 2000. In 2001 and 2002, the restaurant earned the magazine's Best Country Cooking award, and it's also been recognized by *USA Today*, *Gourmet* magazine, and the Food Network. The restaurant serves a traditional, upscale Southern buffet that includes four to five meats, nine to 10 vegetables, soups, salads, biscuits, muffins, corn bread, and desserts, all served with "the Champagne of the South"—sweet tea. No smoking. Wheelchair accessible downstairs only. Lunch $10.95–$13.95, dinner $13.95–21.95, Sunday brunch $15.95.

In Stone Mountain Village

& **The Sycamore Grill** (770-465-6789), 5329 Mimosa Drive. Open 11:30–2:30 Tuesday through Saturday; 5:30–9 Tuesday through Thursday, 5:30–9:30 Saturday. Named for the 150-year-old sycamore tree that shades its verandas, the restaurant is located in a circa 1836 hotel, one of the oldest structures in Stone Mountain Village. A stone stake in the front yard marks the spot from which Andrew Johnson, the first mayor of New Gibraltar (as the town was then called), laid out the town. The two-story, white clapboard house was built in the style of the basic Charleston townhouse. It served as the first post office of Stone Mountain and as a hospital during the Civil War, the reason it was spared during Sherman's March to the Sea. Exquisite dinner entrées include fresh lump blue crabcakes, Georgia mountain trout, quail, Angus filet mignon, pork chops, New Zealand rack of lamb, duck breast, and other delicacies. Luncheon items include soups and salads as well as entrées such as trout, salmon, steak, chicken, and pork chops. Smoking on patio only. Wheelchair accessible downstairs and on patio. Lunch $8–12, dinner $19–32.

EATING OUT

In Conyers

✍ 🍴 & **Seven Gables Restaurant**

(770-922-8824; www.sevengables restaurant.com), 1897 GA 20 SE. Open 5:30–10 daily. This fine dining restaurant, a longtime favorite, is famous for its Dover sole, filet mignon béarnaise, rack of lamb, New York strip Madagascar, Italian sausage, homemade breads and pasta, scrumptious desserts, and fresh dressings, soups, and sauces. The restaurant features a full bar and an extensive wine list. Live entertainment is offered weekends in the bar beginning at 9. No smoking. $12.95–18.95.

In Decatur

🍴 & **The Angel** (404-687-5299), 426 W. Ponce de Leon Avenue. Open 11:30–1 AM Monday through Thursday, 11:30–2 AM Friday and Saturday, 11:30–10 Sunday. The atmosphere is old English pub; the cuisine features traditional British favorites such as bangers and mash, fish-and-chips, and braised cabbage. Beverages include a variety of beers on tap and wine. The child-friendly pub also features outdoor seating. Smoking outside only. $10–20.

🍴 & **Café Alsace** (404-373-5622), 121 E. Ponce de Leon Avenue. Open 11:30–2:30 Tuesday through Friday; 6–10 Tuesday through Saturday; 10–2 Sunday for brunch. This small, cozy, traditional French bistro has only 12 tables, but it's big on flavor. The French cuisine has a German twist with specialties such as spaetzle with Alsatian noodles, as well as a wide array of quiches, seafood, soups, salads, and sandwiches. Outdoor seating. No smoking. $12–20.

🍴 & **Café Lily** (404-371-9119; www .cafelily.com), 308 W. Ponce de Leon Avenue. Open 11:30–2:30 weekdays; 5:30–10 Monday through Thursday, 5:30–11 Friday and Saturday; 10:30–9:30 Sunday. This friendly neighborhood bistro offers a variety of Mediterranean dishes. You could make an entire dinner from appetizers such as Prince Edward Island mussels Posillipo or shrimp beignets. No smoking. $10–18.

In Kennesaw

🍷 **The Trackside Grill** (770-499-0874; www.tracksidegrill.com), 2840 S. Main Street. Open 11–3 weekdays; 5–9 Monday through Thursday, 5–10 Friday and Saturday; 11–3 Sunday for brunch. At lunchtime, choose from soups, salads, sandwiches such as the fried green tomato BLT, and entrées such as seafood, chicken, beef, and meatloaf. Dinner choices include those as well as pork chops, steaks, and pot roast. Brunch choices run the gamut from a fried green tomato Benedict to all kinds of egg dishes to Charleston shrimp and grits to surf and turf. Save room for the maple-bourbon bread pudding with praline ice cream and caramel sauce. Mondays feature wine by the glass or bottle for half price. Every Wednesday is designated for catfish and blues, so wear blue (denim's good) and enjoy BBQ ribs, fried pickles, and catfish. Every Thursday is Pasta Night, which features an array of dishes for $10. The restaurant also offers a special wine dinner on the third Tuesday of each month, when four special courses are paired with four wines for $49.95 per person. Lunch $5–12, dinner $5–19, brunch $8–17.

In Marietta

🍷 🍴 ♿ **Dave and Buster's** (770-951-5554; www.daveandbusters.com), 2215 Dave and Buster's Drive. Open 11:30 AM daily; closes at midnight Sunday through Wednesday, 1 AM Thursday, 2 AM Friday and Saturday. Food, while plentiful and good, takes

second place to the state-of-the-art interactive video games, virtual-reality simulators, pocket billiards, shuffleboard, and entertainment to be found here. Fine dining is offered in the Grand Dining Room; lighter and more casual fare is available at the Viewpoint Bar and the Midway Bar. Children are allowed when accompanied by adults, but their curfew is 10. No smoking in dining areas. $8–20.

In Roswell

🍷 ♿ **Dreamland Barbecue** (678-352-7999; www.dreamlandbbq.com), 10730 Alpharetta Highway. Open 10–10 Monday through Saturday, 11–10 Sunday. The one-of-a-kind Dreamland has been an institution in Tuscaloosa, Alabama, where it was a favorite of local citizens, University of Alabama students, Crimson Tide football players and coaches, and tourists. But it was a bit of a drive if Roswellians got a hankering for Dreamland barbecue, so it was exciting when a sister restaurant opened here. The choices are primarily ribs and sandwiches served with side dishes such as coleslaw and baked beans and a pile of napkins. Smoking at the bar only. $7–18.

🍷 **Greenwood's on Green Street** (770-992-5383), 1087 Green Street. Open 11:30–2:30 Sunday; 5–10 Wednesday through Saturday; 5–9 Sunday. At this casual, down-home Southern eatery, owner Bill Greenwood creates signature dishes such as meatloaf, pork chops, chicken pot pie, and luscious homemade desserts, but even items as fine as duck are featured. No smoking. Limited wheelchair accessibility in one area of restaurant; rest rooms not wheelchair accessible. Credit cards not accepted, but checks are. $10.95–19.50.

✳ Entertainment

Arts at Emory (box office 404-727-5050; www.emory.edu/ARTS), 1641 N. Decatur Road. Box office open 10–6 weekdays. Emory University offers a wide range of arts programs open to the public, including Theater-Emory, Music at Emory, dance performances, and visual arts exhibitions.

DANCE Atlanta Chinese Dance Company (770-449-4953; www.atlantachinesedance.org), 5377 New Peachtree Road, Chamblee. The company was created to promote the development, advancement, and appreciation of Chinese dance and culture and has performed all over the metropolitan Atlanta area. Performances include classic Chinese dance styles, ethnic folk dances, and adaptations of modern dance drama performed in authentic, historically accurate costumes. Audiences delight in the colorful fabrics, platform shoes, tall headdresses, and other adornments. Call for a schedule of events, performance venues, and ticket prices.

MUSIC ✿ ♿ Mable House Barnes Amphitheatre (770-819-7765; www.mablehouseamphitheatre.com), 5239 Floyd Road, Mableton. Box office open 10–4 Monday through Saturday. One of the Atlanta metro area's newest performance venues, the 2,200-seat concert hall is located in a wooded setting on the property of the historic Mable House. The publicly owned outdoor venue provides all kinds of entertainment, including concerts, musical theater, dance, symphonic music, plays, and multi-discipline performances. It offers tables for four, fixed seats, and lawn seating. Call for a schedule of performances and ticket prices.

NIGHTLIFE ♣ ♿ Cowboy's Nightclub and Bar (770-426-5006), 1750 N. Roberts Road, Kennesaw. Open 7 PM–2 AM Thursday and Friday, 6 PM–3 AM Saturday, 9–11 PM Sunday. Cowboy's is a mega country-music venue with a huge dance floor and local and nationally known bands. You'll find everyone here, from boot-scootin' rednecks to city slickers—often decked out in rhinestones and fringe. Free line dancing and couples dancing lessons are given 6–8 Saturday. And, oh yes, just as in *Urban Cowboy*, there's even a mechanical bull. Although it is generally an adult club, on Sunday Cowboy's sponsors family night with free dance lessons and free pizza (while it lasts). No alcohol is served, the club is smoke-free, and all ages are welcome for family night. Smoking is allowed Thursday through Saturday only. $7 Thursday through Saturday (ladies free on Thursday), $10 Sunday.

♣ Eddie's Attic (404-377-4976; www.eddiesattic.com), 515-B N. McDonough Street, Decatur. Bar open 4 PM–12:30 AM Monday through Thursday, 4 PM–2 AM Friday and Saturday; kitchen open 4–10:30 Monday through Thursday, 4–11:30 Friday and Saturday. The covered patio and pool room are for those 21+; on Friday and Saturday there is an all-ages early show 7–8:30, otherwise 21+. The center of Atlanta's singer-songwriter scene, the club features the finest acoustic players every night. The club also has billiards and a popular covered deck. Monday is open mic night, with 20 acts performing two songs each. Tuesday is no-limit Texas Hold 'Em Poker at 7. Friday features a happy hour on the patio with free appetizers 5–7. No smoking in music room; patio and pool room allow smoking. Not wheelchair accessible. Cover charge $6–10 for music room, no cover for use of other facilities; dining $4–7.75.

♣ ♿ **Twain's Billiards and Tap** (404-373-0063), 211 E. Trinity Place, Decatur. Open 11:30 AM–2 AM Monday through Saturday, 11:30 AM–12:30 AM Sunday. Not your pool room of old, Twain's features 20 Brunswick gold-crown tables as well as shuffleboard. Typical bar fare is served. No smoking. Wheelchair accessible. $6.

OUTDOOR DRAMA ✐ ♣ ♿ **Laser-show Spectacular at Stone Mountain Park.** The seasonal laser show begins at 9:30 nightly in the summer, earlier on Saturdays in September and October. The world's largest laser show features a flame cannon and laser canopy, as well as surround sound and special effects choreographed to popular and patriotic music. The event culminates with a spectacular fireworks display. Free with $8 park parking fee (See *Guidance* for park details).

THEATER ✐ ♣ ♿ **ART Station** (770-469-1105; www.artstation.org), 5384 Manor Drive, Stone Mountain Village. Gallery open 10–5 Tuesday through Friday, 1–3 Saturday; also open Mondays during the summer. Call for schedule of theatrical performances. The contemporary, multidisciplinary arts center—housed in a historic trolley barn and power station that was active until 1948—stages six

or seven productions each year. Galleries feature the works of prominent artists, and the center sponsors numerous other events for adults and children. Gallery free; donations appreciated; prices for theatrical events vary.

♿ **Georgia Ensemble Theater** (770-641-1260; www.get.org), 950 Forrest Street, Roswell. The season of professional dramas, comedies, and musicals lasts from February through August. Both season subscriptions and single tickets are available. Call for a schedule and ticket prices.

✐ **Onstage Atlanta and Abracadabra Children's Theatre** (404-378-9901; www.onstageatlanta.com), 2597 N. Decatur Road, Decatur. The company presents dramas, musicals, and comedies and also boasts an interactive, educational theater for children. Call for a schedule of events and ticket prices.

✐ **PushPush Theater/SmallTall Theater** (404-377-6332; www.push pushtheater.com), 121 New Street, Decatur. Not surprisingly, PushPush Theater, which produces films, theatrical productions, and musical performances, pushes the envelope when it comes to exploring new ideas and encouraging artists to take risks that more traditional organizations would not. Twelve major professional productions are presented each year as well as youth programs by the Small-Tall Theater. Call for a schedule of events and ticket prices.

♿ **Roswell Cultural Arts Center** (770-594-6232; 770-641-1260; www.roswellgov.com), 950 Forrest Street, Roswell. Box office open 12:30–6 Tuesday through Saturday. The center hosts theater, dance, musical, and puppet show performances, as well as cultural events such as pageants, celebrations, and exhibits year-round. It is the home of the Georgia Ensemble Theater (see above). Call for a schedule of performances and prices.

🌿 ♿ **Tall Tales of the South 4D Theater at Stone Mountain Park**. Shows every 20 to 30 minutes. All your senses are engaged during the 3-D movie and 4-D special effects revolving around two young children's foray into a swamp. Note: If you or someone in your party doesn't want to get slightly wet or are afraid of snakes, critters, or things that go bump in the night, this attraction may not be for you. (See *Guidance* for prices.)

Theatre Decatur (404-373-5311; www.theatredecatur.com), 430 W. Trinity Place, Decatur. Call for a schedule of events and ticket prices, which range from $14 to $24. For 26 years, the professional, nonequity, nonprofit theater has been producing mysteries, comedies, musicals, and children's programs.

♿ **Theatre in the Square and Alley Theater** (770-422-8369; www.theatre inthesquare.com), 11 Whitlock Avenue, Marietta. This intimate theater, housed in a charming restored cotton warehouse, offers award-winning Broadway-caliber productions year-round, including holiday shows, shows for young people, and a play-reading series featuring works by regional playwrights. The theater has been called "the most charming performing space in the Southeast" by *Southern Living* magazine. A second set of plays is offered in the very intimate Alley Theater. Wheelchair accessible. Call for a schedule of performances and ticket prices.

✳ **Selective Shopping**

BICYCLE SHOPS Bone Shakers Bicycle Shop (770-222-BONE; www .boneshakersbicycle.com), 3279 New MacLand Road, Powder Springs. Open 11–7 weekdays, 11–5 Saturday. Located within riding distance of the Silver Comet Trail, the Wild Horse Creek Trail, and the BMX track at Wild Horse Creek Park (see *To Do—Hiking*), the shop offers sales, repairs, and a limited number of rentals.

FOOD Harry's Farmer's Market (770-664-6300), 1180 Upper Hembree Road, Roswell. Open 9–9 Monday through Saturday, 9–8 Sunday. Residents of the northern suburbs don't have to go to Decatur or south of the airport to shop at a farmer's market. Some visitors have likened Harry's to a culinary theme park or a chef's playground. You can get all kinds of exotic ingredients from around the world here.

Your DeKalb Farmers Market (404-377-6400; www.dekalbfarmers market.com), 3000 E. Ponce de Leon Avenue, Decatur. Open 9–9 daily. Just about every fresh-grown ingredient you can think of is available at the world's largest indoor farmer's market. Without ever leaving the metro area, you have a passport to exotic places and delicious corners of the world. The market boasts a dizzying array of selections from more than 50 countries: cheese, coffee, deli items, fish, fruits, meat, produce, regional snacks, seafood, spices, vegetables, wine, and other foodstuffs. A restaurant and bakery are on-site, and tours are available.

GIFTS Stone Mountain General Store (770-469-9331), 935 Main

Street, Stone Mountain Village. Open 10–6 Monday through Saturday, noon–5 Sunday. Advertising that it carries everything from "wind chimes to washboards," the emporium stocks household and kitchen gadgets, accessories, bird-feeding supplies, sun catchers, garden accessories, pottery, candles, and souvenirs.

OTHER GOODS The Brumby Chair Company (770-425-1875; www .brumbyrocker.com), 37 West Park Square, Marietta. Open 10–5 Monday through Saturday. In 1875, the Brumby family began to make generous oak rocking chairs for Southern verandas. Over time, the popularity of the jumbo rockers led the company to produce other sizes: a double-courting rocker, a smaller lady rocker, a baby rocker, a footstool, and now, in the age of laptop computers, a lap desk rocker. The solid Appalachian red oak rockers come in six stained finishes and two paint colors. No matter what size you choose, the rocker is bound to become a family heirloom. Craftspeople actually assemble the chairs and cane the seats at the store, where visitors also can examine antique Brumby rockers and photographs of famous Georgians with their Brumby rockers. When Jimmy Carter was president, he took them to the White House.

OUTLET MALLS Discover Mills (678-847-5000; 1-866-GAMILLS; www.discovermills.com), 5900 Sugarloaf Parkway, Lawrenceville. Open 10–9 Monday through Saturday, noon–6 Sunday. Among the 200 retailers are Last Call from Neiman Marcus, Off-Fifth (Saks Fifth Avenue), Kenneth Cole New York

Outlet, and Pro Shops Outdoor World. The mall also has several restaurants and offers periodic entertainment such as talent shows, concerts, and other family-oriented events.

SPECIAL STORES Bass Pro Shops Outdoor World (770-847-5500; www .bassproshops.com), 5900 Sugarloaf Parkway, Suite 129, Lawrenceville. Open 9–10 Monday through Saturday, 11–7 Sunday. The outdoor enthusiast will find everything here, from flyfishing and saltwater fishing equipment to hunting needs, camping accessories, apparel, and footwear.

✳ Special Events

March: **Conyers Cherry Blossom Festival** (770-602-2606; www .conyerscherryblossom.com). The festival, which is held at the Georgia International Horse Park in Conyers, features 400 food and art booths. Other activities include croquet and golf tournaments, a queen's pageant, hot dog– and cherry pie–eating contests, and an Easter egg hunt. Admission free; $5 parking fee.

Easter: **Annual Easter Sunrise Service at Stone Mountain Park** (770-498-5690; www.stonemountainpark .com). The park gates and the Skyride open at 4 AM, services begin at approximately 6:15 AM. The park sponsors two simultaneous, nondenominational Easter sunrise services—one on top of the mountain and one on the Memorial Lawn at the base of the mountain. Parking is available at the Skyride or Crossroads lots (and Confederate Hall lot for those walking to the top). Skyride costs $7 per person for those who wish to ride to the top of the mountain and back; otherwise, visitors can attend the Memorial Lawn service at no additional charge, and visitors who hike to the mountaintop service can do so for free.

April: **Foxhall Cup** (www.foxhall cup.com), Foxhall Farms, Douglasville. The vigorous three-day international event is the national championship of eventing for the Fédération Equestre Internationale. The Foxhall Cup, one of only two international three-star-level competitions in the United States, offers a challenging cross-country course with the world's largest water jump complex, a dressage tent, and grand-prix-style show jumping. The overall purse is $50,000. The event also includes an opening gala, children's activities, equitation demonstrations, a wine tasting, a parade of competitors, and a concert. $10 general admission, $5 parking, $40 VIP daily ticket, $125 VIP four-day ticket.

May: **Decatur Arts Festival and Garden Tour** (404-371-9583; 404-371-8262; www.decaturatsalliance .org). This annual festival in its 17th year includes performances by the Decatur Civic Chorus, a literary arts festival, fine art exhibition, film festival, children's arts festival, dance performances, concerts on the square, artists' market, garden tour, and more. Most events are free; tickets for garden tour $15.

May and September: **Concerts on the Square** (404-371-9583; 404-371-8262). Every Saturday night during these months, live bands entertain picnicking concert-goers in Decatur. Free.

May through October: **Roswell Riverside Sounds** (770-594-6187; www.roswellgov.com), Riverside Park, 575 Riverside Road, Roswell. Held at

7:30 PM on first Saturday of each month, May through October. The outdoor concert series features a wide variety of musical genres that might include roots rock, country, rock and roll, jazz, rhythm and blues, soul, swing, or Latin American. Food concessions are available, as are free parking and rest rooms. Free.

June: **Beach Party** (404-371-9583; 404-371-8262). Landlocked Decatur is transformed into a tropical paradise when the city brings in 60 tons of sand and turns the square into a beach complete with wading pools, a lighthouse, flamingos, and palm trees. Activities include a street dance, children's boardwalk games, a special beach movie on a giant inflatable screen, face painting, and more. Some events free; some have a small charge.

Roswell Magnolia Storytelling Festival (770-640-3253; 1-800-776-7935), 180 Bulloch Avenue, Roswell. The general public is invited to the grounds of historic Bulloch Hall to listen to storytellers, musicians, and interpreters from around the Southeast who gather to share stories passed down through generations. The event includes performances, workshops, open-mic programs, a tall-tale contest, and more. Admission for the full two-day festival: adults $25, seniors and children younger than 12 $20; one-day only: adults $15, seniors and children $12; partial day: $10 for everyone no matter what age; Roswell, Mysteries, Legends and Lies $10 for all ages; Roswell Ghost Tour $10 for all ages.

September: **Yellow Daisy Festival** (770-498-5690; www.stonemountain park.com). The festival runs Thursday through Sunday at Stone Mountain

Park; call for exact dates. The festival is considered to be America's top arts and crafts show. More than 450 artists and crafters from 38 states and two foreign countries display and sell their wares. The festival also includes daily live entertainment, children's corner activities, clogging and craft demonstrations, and fabulous food. Festival admission is free with $8 park parking fee.

October: **Folk Tales on the Rails** (770-422-9714). Storytellers portraying pirates, settlers, and Georgia founder James Oglethorpe mesmerize children and adults. The festival, which is held at the Southern Museum of Civil War and Locomotive History in Kennesaw, also includes hayrides and a treasure hunt. Free.

Great Decatur Beer Tasting Festival (404-371-9583; 404-371-8262). Hundreds of local and international beers are available on the square during the city's most popular event. The festival also includes music and food. The $30 entry fee includes a special tasting glass; proceeds benefit community charities. Children and pets not allowed.

Highland Games (770-498-5690; www.stonemountainpark.com). Two days of Scottish fun at Stone Mountain Park include Highland athletic events; Highland dancing; competitions in piping, drumming, and harping; kirking of the tartans; clan challenge events; a parade of the tartans; border collie herding demonstrations; clan and tartan information tents; many colorful Scottish shops; and traditional Scottish food. All events occur rain or shine. Admission charged in addition to $8 park parking fee.

November: **Pow Wow and Indian Festival** (770-498-5690; www.stonemountainpark.com). Visitors to Stone Mountain Park explore a living history tepee village with tepee styles dating back to the late 1800s. Native American demonstrations include fire starting, brain tanning, hide scraping, flint napping, pottery making, and primitive tool technology. The powwow also draws Native American dancers from across the country. Visitors watch high-energy dance and drum competitions while warriors on horseback do battle in the Shield Dance. Admission charged in addition to $8 park parking fee.

Wine Tasting Festival (404-371-9583; 404-371-8262). More than 100 wines from around the world are available for tasting at this event on Decatur's square. The $30 entry fee, which benefits the Decatur Arts Alliance, includes a commemorative wine glass.

November and December: **A Merry Olde Marietta Christmas** (770-429-1115; 1-800-835-0445; www.marietta square.com). Two months of special events include holiday theater performances and the much-anticipated **Marietta Pilgrimage Christmas Home Tour,** which is held on the first full weekend in December. The tour visits six historic private homes and eight public buildings. Shuttle service is provided along the route for the day tour but not the candlelight tour. Pilgrimage hours are 9–6 Saturday, 10–6 Sunday; Saturday candlelight tour runs 7–9:30. $12–25.

Stone Mountain Christmas (770-498-5690; www.stonemountainpark .com). Yes, you can have a white

Christmas in Atlanta. The festival at Stone Mountain Park features "snow" and fireworks, the Christmas story aboard the train, lively holiday shows, millions of lights in the Crossroads village, and more. Adults $13 plus tax, children 3–11 $11 plus tax.

December: **Decatur Holiday Candlelight Tour of Homes** (404-371-9583; 404-371-8262). Tour a variety of Decatur's beautiful homes and other important points of interest decked out in their holiday best. $15 in advance; $20 at the door.

SOUTHERN SUBURBS (SOUTH-SIDE): CARROLLTON TO MORROW)

With the exception of Carrollton, the primary area described in this chapter is called the Southern Crescent because it hugs the south side of Atlanta. To the casual observer, these municipalities seem to blend imperceptibly with each other and with the city of Atlanta, but in reality each is distinct from the others and is imbued with civic pride. This was also *Gone with the Wind* territory. Margaret Mitchell's grandparents lived here, and when young Peggy visited them, she met their neighbors and heard fascinating stories that inspired her to create the characters in her book. Don't come looking for Tara, however, or you'll be disappointed. It never actually existed. However, there are homes from the period that are open for tours.

It's somewhat surprising, considering the proximity to Atlanta, that there are so many parks, nature preserves, and green spaces here, but nature lovers who visit the Southern Crescent will not be disappointed. Farther west, in fact almost to the Georgia-Alabama state line, is Carrollton, the home of the University of West Georgia and John Tanner State Park.

GUIDANCE Before planning a trip to the Carrollton area, contact the **Carrollton Area Convention and Visitors Bureau** (770-214-9746; 1-800-292-0871; www.visitcarrollton.com), 102 N. Lakeshore Drive, Carrollton 30117. Open 8:30–5 weekdays.

To plan a trip to College Park, Fairburn, or Palmetto, contact the **Atlanta Convention and Visitors Bureau** (404-521-6688; 1-800-ATLANTA; www.acvb .com), 233 Peachtree Street NE, Suite 100, Atlanta 30303. Open 8:30–5:30 weekdays. Also consult the web site www.atlanta.net for up-to-date information on hotel and restaurant reservations, directions, guidebooks, maps, and help in creating an itinerary. There is an **Atlanta CVB Visitor Center** at Hartsfield-Jackson Atlanta International Airport, 6000 North Terminal Parkway, Atlanta, which is open 9–9 weekdays, 9–6 Saturday, and 12:30–6 Sunday.

For specific information about Fairburn, contact **Fairburn City Hall** (770-964-2244; www.fairburn.com/copy_of_fairburn_com), 56 Malone Street, Fairburn 30213. Open 8–5 weekdays.

To learn more about Fayetteville and Peachtree City, consult the **Fayette County Chamber of Commerce** (770-461-9983; www.fayettechamber.org), 200 Courthouse Square, Fayetteville 30214.

When planning a trip to the Jonesboro or Morrow area, contact the **Clayton County Convention and Visitors Bureau–Jonesboro Depot Welcome Center** (770-478-4800; 1-800-662-7829; wwwvisitscarlett.com), 104 N. Main Street, Jonesboro 30236. Open 8:30–5:30 weekdays, 10–4 Saturday. Pick up a brochure for the *Gone with the Wind* Historic District Driving Tour here.

To find out more about Morrow, contact the **Morrow Tourist Center** (770-968-1623; www.morrowtourism.com), 6475 Jonesboro Road, Morrow 30260. Open 8:30–5 Tuesday through Saturday.

GETTING THERE *By air:* Visitors to this area fly into **Hartsfield-Jackson Atlanta International Airport** (see What's Where in Georgia). Car rentals are available on- and off-site. There are also numerous shuttle companies, and several hotels have free shuttles to their properties; check ahead when you make your hotel reservation.

By bus: **Greyhound Lines** (404-762-9581; www.greyhound.com), 438 Henry Ford II Avenue, Hapeville, serves most of the municipalities in this chapter. The next nearest station is in downtown Atlanta (see What's Where in Georgia).

By car: The interstate system makes access to these municipalities easy. North-south routes I-75 and I-85 as well as east-west route I-20 meet in downtown Atlanta. The bypass I-285 circles the entire city. After I-75 and I-85 meet, they branch off south of the city, with I-85 continuing to the southwest through Fairburn and Palmetto and I-75 continuing to the southeast through Morrow. Most of the municipalities in this chapter can be reached easily from I-75, I-85, and I-285. Carrollton is south of I-20 on US 27.

By train: The nearest **Amtrak** (404-881-3067; 1-800-USA-RAIL; www.amtrak .com) station is in Atlanta (see What's Where in Georgia).

GETTING AROUND Two companies offer mass transit (see What's Where in Georgia).

MEDICAL EMERGENCIES For life-threatening emergencies, call 911. For other urgent care, there are numerous hospitals in the Southern Crescent: **South Fulton Medical Center** (404-305-3500), 1170 Cleveland Avenue, East Point; **Fayette Community Hospital** (770-719-7070), 1255 GA 54 West, Fayetteville; **Georgia Baptist Urgent Care** (770-461-6666), 105 Yorktown Drive, Fayetteville; **Fairview Day Hospital** (770-473-0404), 102 W. Mimosa Drive, Suite #101, Jonesboro; **Piedmont Clinic** (770-486-5000), 201 Prime Court, Peachtree City; **Southern Regional Medical Center** (770-991-8000), 11 Upper Riverdale Road SW, Riverdale; and **Henry Medical Center** (770-389-2200), 1133 Eagles Landing Parkway, Stockbridge. In Carrollton, help is available at **Tanner Medical Center** (770-836-9666; www.tanner.org), 705 Dixie Street, Carrollton.

VILLAGES In **Carrollton,** the University of West Georgia offers numerous gallery shows, sporting events, and cultural performances. Outdoor enthusiasts enjoy John Tanner State Park, which has a lake with the largest sand swimming beach among Georgia's state parks, as well as boat rentals, hiking trails, miniature golf, a campground, and motel rooms.

College Park was established in 1896 along the tracks of the Atlanta and West Point Railway. The historic city center is well preserved and, along with several residential neighborhoods, 606 acres are recognized as a National Historic Register District, the fourth-largest in the state. Among the 857 designated structures, 29 architectural styles are represented. The east-west streets were named for colleges and universities, the north-south streets for people. Many of the historic buildings along Main Street house specialty shops and restaurants.

Fairburn's slogan is "History Lives Here." The historic downtown is a cluster of antiques shops, boutiques, and restaurants. Visitors should see the Confederate flag monument, the Confederate soldiers monument, the Fairburn cemetery, the grave of the first female sheriff, and the World War I monument. The **Georgia Renaissance Festival** (see *Special Events*) brings a quarter-million visitors to Fairburn each spring.

Fayetteville was established in 1823 and later became the county seat of Fayette County, which had been formed two years earlier. Both the town and the county are named for the Marquis de Lafayette, a French nobleman who aided the colonists during the Revolutionary War. Fayetteville's courthouse, which was built in 1825, is the largest in Georgia. Listed on the National Register of Historic Places, it claims to have the world's longest courthouse bench. Margaret Mitchell did a lot of research for *Gone with the Wind* at the courthouse, and some of her great-grandfather's family members are buried in the Fayetteville City Cemetery. Today Fayetteville has several museums and historic homes open to the public and is the site of several festivals (see *To See—Historic Homes and Sites* and *Museums*).

Jonesboro is the legendary land of *Gone with the Wind*. More than 70 years after the burning of Atlanta, Margaret Mitchell spun a tale about her relatives and local characters in Clayton County. Her book became the best-selling novel of all time and was made into a movie in 1939, introducing Jonesboro and Clayton County to people all over the world. Thousands of visitors from around the globe come searching for Mitchell's mythical Tara. Although they are disappointed not to find it, there are plenty of other attractions connected with the author and her opus.

Morrow began as Morrow Station in 1846, a stop on the railroad line between Jonesboro and Atlanta. Known as the "Whistle Stop," the area gained popularity and was transformed from a farming community to a business and retail center. Today Morrow is the home of Spivey Hall and Clayton College and State University.

Palmetto got its name from South Carolina's Palmetto Rifles troops, which marched through the area on the way to fight in Mexico. Palmetto is the home of an outstanding bed & breakfast, several well-known restaurants, and a nature center.

Peachtree City, the largest city in Fayette County, is a planned community with 90 miles of pedestrian and golf cart paths, three championship golf courses, two lakes, a state-of-the-art tennis center, a full-sized BMX course, and an aquatic center.

GUIDED TOURS ✂ *Gone with the Wind*—**The Tour** (770-477-8864; www.peter bonner.com), 104 N. Main Street, Jonesboro. Peter Bonner's Historical and Hysterical Tours leads the way at 1 PM Monday through Saturday from the 1867 train depot in the center of Jonesboro. Pete, costumed as a common Confederate soldier, is a font of local knowledge. He spins tales about the Battle of Jonesboro and about the local true stories that influenced Margaret Mitchell to write *Gone with the Wind* as he guides visitors around town for 90-minutes $15.

HISTORIC HOMES AND SITES ✂ 🐾 ♿ **Stately Oaks** (770-473-0197; www .historicaljonesboro.org), 100 Carriage Lane, Jonesboro. Open 10–4 weekdays and most Saturdays, but check ahead. The grand, white-columned planter's home was built in 1839. Soldiers camped on the lawns during the Civil War. Tours of the home are conducted by costumed docents who interpret customs and lifestyles of the rural South. Also on the grounds are a log cookhouse, the old-fashioned 1894 Juddy's Country Store, and a one-room schoolhouse. Living-history demonstrations are conducted periodically, and many festivals and special events occur year-round. Adults $8, seniors $6, children $4.

MUSEUMS 🐾 ♿ **Holliday-Dorsey-Fife House** (770-716-5332; www.fayetteville-ga-us.org), 140 W. Lamar Avenue, Fayetteville. Open 10–5 Thursday through Saturday. Located in an 1855 Greek Revival house built by the uncle of infamous outlaw Doc Holliday, the museum features *Gone with the Wind* memorabilia; Civil War relics and documents, particularly from the Fayette Rifle Greys, Company I, 10th Georgia Volunteers; local Fayetteville history artifacts; and genealogical information about the three families who owned the house, which Doc Holliday actually visited. Margaret Mitchell's grandmother stayed in this house when it was used as a dormitory for the Fayetteville Academy. Be sure to stop at the Down South Treasures Museum Shop. Adults $5, seniors $4.

🐾 ♿ **Road to Tara Museum** (770-478-4800; 1-800-662-7829; www .visitscarlett.com), 104 N. Main Street, Jonesboro. Open 8:30–5:30 weekdays, 10–4 Saturday; last ticket sold 45 minutes before closing. Located in the warehouse portion of the historic Jonesboro depot, which also houses the town's welcome center, the museum focuses on Jonesboro's part in the Civil War and the book *Gone with the Wind*. The museum boasts the largest collection of *Gone with the Wind* book and movie memorabilia in the country, including seats from the Lowe's Grand Theater in Atlanta, where the 1939 premiere was held.

TOURS OF STATELY OAKS IN JONESBORO REVEAL WHAT LIFE WAS LIKE IN THE RURAL SOUTH IN THE MID-1800S.

An original mural depicts scenes from the movie. A new exhibit called "Gone with the Girdle" centers on the emancipation of women's clothing. Adults $5, students and seniors $4. A Premier Pass that permits entrance to five Margaret Mitchell/*Gone with the Wind*/Civil War sites in Jonesboro and Atlanta is available here for $34.95.

✳ To Do

FOR FAMILIES ✄ 🐾 ♿ **The Beach at Clayton County International Park** (770-473-5425; www.thebeachccip.com), 2300 GA 138 Southeast, Jonesboro. Park open 8–8 daily year-round; beach open 8–8 daily except Mondays, Memorial Day weekend through Labor Day weekend; open weekends only after school starts, usually in early August. This multiuse park offers a little bit of everything to keep families busy. The **Beach Waterpark** (770-477-3766) is a spring-fed lake with a sandy beach, an adventure kiddie pool, water slides, a water trampoline, and a sun deck. In the same area, the **Nassau Arcade Center** features an indoor playground, snack bar, beach store, and changing facilities. The **Tennis Center** (678-479-5016) offers 17 hard courts, a pro shop with showers, lessons, and league play. There are often drills and round robins, too. **Muscle Beach Fitness** (770-472-8093) is a full gym with strength machines, free weights, cardio equipment, and International Sports Science Association trainers. Classes include body sculpting, cardio, kick boxing, and yoga. A park-within-a-park, the **Hiking and Biking Trails** (770-477-3766) offer paved and naturalized trails accessible 8–8 year-round. Eleven **Volleyball Courts** (770-477-3766) allow beach volleyball play where the world's greatest athletes competed during the 1996 Centennial Olympic Summer Games. Or bring your own gear and drop a line into the **Fishing Lakes** (770-477-3766) for bass, bream, or catfish. A proper fishing license is required. Several concession stands are available. Adults 13–54 $9, seniors and children 3–12 $7. Parking $2. Season beach admission and parking passes available.

✳ Green Space

NATURE PRESERVES AND PARKS ✄ 🐾 ♿ **Cochran Mill Nature Preserve** (770-306-0914; www.cochranmillnaturecenter.org), 6875 Cochran Mill Road, Palmetto. Open 9–3 Monday through Saturday. Fifty heavily wooded acres provide opportunities for hiking, wildlife observation, and environmental education programs. The center has many reptiles, birds, and amphibians. All have been injured and rehabilitated but can't be released back into the wild. Several special events include **Snake Day** in August, the **Wild Trail Trot 5K Run** in September, and the **Halloween Hayride and Family Festival** in October. Adults $1, children 50¢.

✄ 🐾 ♿ **Cochran Mill Park** (404-730-6200), 6875 Cochran Mill Road, Palmetto. The park, located adjacent to the nature preserve (see above), offers hiking, jogging, horse trails (BYOH—bring your own horse), a playground, and primitive camping.

✄ 🐾 ♿ **Flat Creek Nature Center** (770-486-7774), 201 McIntosh Trail, Peachtree City. Open daylight hours daily. The 513-acre center, operated by the Southern Conservation Trust, is adjacent to 3½ miles of paved paths, a 1,200-foot boardwalk, and two viewing platforms extending into the wetlands. The area sustains a wide variety of trees and plants. The educational center offers classes, camps, workshops, and programs throughout the year. Free.

In Carrollton

✐ 🏕 🐾 ♿ **John Tanner State Park** (770-830-2222; 1-800-864-7275; www.gastate parks.org/info/jtanner), 354 Tanner's Beach Road/GA 16. The park features 32 tent, trailer, and RV sites as well as a group lodge and a pioneer campground. $15–20.

✐ 🐾 ♿ **Panola Mountain State Conservation Park** (770-389-7801; www .gastateparks.org/info/panolamt), 2600 GA 155 Southwest, Stockbridge. Open 7–6 daily, September 15 through April 14; 7–9 daily, April 15 through September 14; interpretive center open 9–5 Tuesday through Friday, noon–5 weekends. The 100-acre granite mountain, designated a National Natural Landmark, is located within a 1,026-acre park. The conservation park provides a home for rare plants and animals. Visitors can explore 2 miles of nature trails and a 1-mile fitness trail on their own or join ranger-led nature programs and 3.5-mile guided hikes of the restricted-access mountain Tuesday through Saturday (reservations required). The interpretive center features animal exhibits. Pets and bicycles are not permitted on the trails. Parking $3.

✐ 🐾 ♿ **W. H. Reynolds Memorial Nature Preserve** (770-603-4188; web.co.clayton.ga.us/reynolds/about.htm), 5665 Reynolds Road, Morrow. Visitor center open 8:30–5:30 weekdays, 9–1 first Saturday of each month; park open 8:30–dusk daily. The 146-acre woodland and wetland preserve is dedicated to conservation. The center began with the donation of 130 acres by Judge William "Bill" Huie Reynolds in 1976. Sixteen acres were added to that in 1997. Among the park's attributes are ponds, streams, hardwood forests, piers, pavilions, bridges, a demonstration heritage herb and vegetable garden featuring varieties from the late 1800s, a butterfly and hummingbird garden, and a historic barn with displays of late-19th- and early-20th-century farm implements. The Nature Center houses a collection of native reptiles and amphibians as well as an observation honeybee hive and environmental education exhibits. Visitors can enjoy 4.5 miles of well-defined trails that run in half-mile loops that bring hikers back to their starting point. The Georgia Native Plants Trail is wheelchair accessible and also features Braille trail markers. Free.

✳ Lodging

BED & BREAKFASTS

In Carrollton
Maple Street Inn Bed and Breakfast (770-214-8950; www.bobs mansion.com/maplestreetinn), 338 Maple Street. This stately home with its inviting wraparound porch was built in 1910 by prosperous businessman L. C. Mandeville as a wedding gift to his son John and his bride. This family occupied the home until the late 1950s. Guest rooms are spacious, high-ceilinged retreats with all the modern conveniences. A hearty breakfast is included in the nightly rate. The property also features fine and casual dining (see *Where to Eat*). No smoking. Not wheelchair accessible. $89–109.

In Jonesboro
♿ **The Jonesboro Greenhouse** (770-477-2084; www.jonesborogreen

house.com), 139 College Street. The second story of an elegant house provides luxurious bed & breakfast accommodations. The bedrooms, appropriately named after *Gone with the Wind* characters Scarlett O'Hara, Rhett Butler, Melanie Wilkes, and Ashley Wilkes, are furnished with antiques and props from the movie. Scarlett's and Rhett's rooms can connect to create a suite, as can Ashley's and Melanie's rooms. Some of the bathrooms feature claw-foot tubs. The day begins with a lavish Southern breakfast buffet laden with pastries, drop-biscuits with jellies and preserves, eggs, ham, and sausage. No smoking. One wheelchair-accessible room on first floor. $90–120.

In Palmetto

Serenbe Bed and Breakfast Farm (770-463-2610; www.serenbe .com), 10950 Hutcheson Ferry Road. Guests experience farm life with an elegant twist at this B&B, where accommodations and cuisine are decidedly upscale. Guest rooms are in a restored 1930s horse barn; a lake house; two newly constructed, envi-ronmentally friendly cottages; and a private two-bedroom cottage. More than 100 animals live at Serenbe: chickens, bunnies, goats, pigs, and horses. Yes, you can feed the animals or gather eggs, but you also can enjoy afternoon tea, bedtime snacks, and a full country breakfast. Swim in the pool or soak in the outdoor hot tub, both of which are surrounded by glorious gardens. Play croquet or hike the trails to streams, waterfalls, or a lake, then take some time to laze in the cabana's twin-bed-sized swings. Hayrides and roasting marshmallows around a camp fire are sometime highlights. No smoking. Limited wheelchair accessibility. $140–250.

CAMPGROUNDS

In Carrollton

John Tanner State Park (770-830-2222; 1-800-864-7275; www .gastateparks.org/info/jtanner), 354 Tanner's Beach Road/GA 16. The park features 32 tent, trailer, and RV sites as well as a group lodge and a pioneer campground. $15–20.

✳ Where to Eat

DINING OUT

In Carrollton

Maple Street Mansion (770-834-2657; www.maplestreetmansion.com; www.bobmansion.com), 401 Maple Street. Open 11 AM–1:30 AM Tuesday through Saturday. This gorgeous Queen Anne Victorian-style mansion is immediately identified by its tower, wraparound porch, and porte cochère. It was built between 1889 and 1894 by L. C. Mandeville, a prosperous cotton grower, mill owner, merchant, and banker. Then known as Mandeville House, the mansion used a copper vat

THE MAIN HOUSE AT SERENBE BED AND BREAKFAST FARM IN PALMETTO

on the third floor to provide running water to the floors below and was one of the first homes in town to boast electricity and a telephone. Today the mansion houses a fine dining restaurant as well as a casual eatery in a railroad car on the property, and bed & breakfast accommodations (see *Lodging—Bed and Breakfasts*). Some visitors have experienced manifestations of the ghost of Eugenia Mandeville Watkins. The eclectic cuisine features traditional Southern favorites, salads, sandwiches, and varied choices from lasagna to grilled teriyaki chicken. Dinner choices run the gamut from quesadillas to chili and also feature numerous chicken, beef, pork, and seafood entrées. Save room for the Maple Hill Pie, the restaurant's version of mud pie. Late-night bites are primarily finger foods, and the bar often provides live entertainment. No smoking until 10 PM, then smoking permitted in sports bar. Lunch $5.95–8.95, dinner $10.95–19.95, late-night bar food $1.59–5.99.

In College Park

♪ & **The Feed Store** (404-209-7979), 3841 Main Street. Open 11–2 weekdays; 5–10 Monday through Thursday, 5–11 Friday and Saturday. Look for the mural of a horse on the side of the historic building, which actually was a feed store operated well into the 1980s by the current owner's grandmother. Many rustic architectural elements such as exposed brick have been retained and combined with sleek modern touches for an eclectic look. Antique farm implements grace the walls. The cuisine is described as artful New American. No smoking. Lunch $8–14, dinner $13–26.

& **Kosmos Café** (404-766-3788), 3383 Main Street. Open 11–2:30 and 5–10 Monday through Saturday. *Kosmos* means "beautiful thing" in Greek.

THE MANSION GHOST

Various reports of the sounds of footsteps when no one is there, numerous sightings of the silhouette of a turn-of-the-20th-century woman, mysterious manifestations caught on still film and video, and other unexplained occurrences such as a cupboard opening by itself seem to confirm that Mandeville House/Maple Street Mansion Restaurant does indeed have a ghost. Since it has never harmed anyone, it is believed to be friendly and merely watchful. Why the ghost is believed to be that of Mary Eugenia Mandeville is shrouded in mystery. Eugenia, as she was known, was born in 1878, the oldest child of L. C. Mandeville, who built the house. Numerous stories have taken root over the years that Eugenia committed suicide in the house after the untimely death of her husband. If these stories were true, folks would certainly be justified in believing Eugenia to be the ghost. Those rumors have been completely dispelled, however, by descendants and public records that confirm she died of cancer at age 37 in Atlanta, and that her husband did not predecease her. Perhaps the ghost is someone else, or perhaps Eugenia returned to her happy childhood home. Either way, a ghost story is always fun.

The American cuisine, which is always prepared with the freshest ingredients, shows influences from Europe, Latin America, and Asia. Lunch choices range from soups to salads to sandwiches and include plates such as jerk chicken with collards, coconut rice, and papaya salsa. Dinner entrées feature steaks, pasta, chicken, pork, duck, and seafood dishes. There are a variety of vegetarian dishes for noncarnivores. No smoking while food is being served; after the kitchen closes, smoking is permitted. Lunch $5–10, dinner $12–23.

EATING OUT

In Carrollton

🌺 **The Lazy Donkey** (770-834-6002), 334 Bankhead Highway. Open 11:30–9:30 Tuesday through Thursday, 11:30–10 Friday and Saturday. This understated eatery serves Mexican and Latin cuisine in simple rooms and an outdoor eating area decorated with Mexican art to set the mood. The lunch menu features salads, black bean soup, nachos, quesadillas, enchiladas, chili, fajitas, Cuban sandwiches, and chicken, beef, and fish entrées. Many of the luncheon selections are available for dinner as well, including pork medallions, beef tenderloin, chicken dishes, and pasta. If you're not absolutely stuffed, try the butter pecan ice cream tostada or the sopaipilla, a fried tortilla pastry served with cinnamon and honey. No smoking. Limited wheelchair accessibility. Lunch $3.99–9.99 for dinner $9.29–12.99.

&. **Pearl's Café** (770-830-9795), 301 Adamson Square. Open 11:30–2 daily (Sunday it's brunch); 5–9 Sunday through Thursday, 5–9:30 Friday and Saturday. Located in a restored building on Adamson Square, the restaurant uses local and organic products to create internationally inspired cuisine from burgers to steaks. No smoking. $8–23.

In College Park

🎷 🌺 &. **The Brake Pad** (404-766-1515), 3403 Main Street. Open 11 AM–2 AM daily. An old gas station has been transformed into a funky bar and eatery where you can fuel up with appetizers, burgers, quesadillas, sandwiches, salads, and other pub food. In nice weather, diners enjoy eating and drinking on the patio. The Brake Pad has an extensive selection of beers, and you can get late-night fare until closing. Smoking on patio only. $7–15.

✳ Entertainment

MUSIC 🎷 &. **Frederick Brown Jr. Amphitheater** (770-631-0630; www.amphitheater.org), 201 McIntosh Trail, Peachtree City. Affectionately known as the Fred (as opposed to the Atlanta sports stadium, which is known as the Ted), the amphitheater is an intimate setting in which to enjoy a wide variety of entertainment, including a summer concert series with a variety of top acts. Call for a schedule of events and ticket prices.

🎷 &. **HiFi Buys Amphitheatre** (404-627-9704), 2002 Lakewood Way, East Point. This outdoor performance venue, built in 1989, is designed to offer a state-of-the-art musical experience for artists and patrons alike. Some seats are under a covered area and there's plenty of lawn seating. Nationally renowned acts stop by regularly. Call for a schedule of performances and ticket prices.

🎷 &. **Spivey Hall** (770-960-4200; www.spiveyhall.org), 5900 N. Lee Street, Morrow. Box office open 9–5 weekdays. Located on the campus of

Clayton College and State University, this magnificent performance hall is the scene of the finest in piano, vocal, chamber, choral, classical, jazz, organ, string, and other musical entertainment. The acoustically perfect Spivey Hall is also the home of the magnificent Albert Schweitzer Memorial Pipe Organ, a 4,413-pipe organ built in Italy. The hall's acclaimed concert series receives national attention thanks to frequent appearances on National Public Radio's *Performance Today*. There is also a summer jazz and pops series. Recent developments have included the formation of the Spivey Hall Children's Choir, the Spivey Hall Young Artists, and the Children's Concert Series. Call for a schedule of performances and ticket prices.

♪ ♿ **The Villages Amphitheater** (770-460-0686; www.villagesamphi theater.com), 301 Lafayette, Fayetteville. In the heart of downtown Fayetteville is a state-of-the art venue that provides a setting for a full schedule of local, regional, and national entertainment and concerts. Orchestra tables and tiered table areas are popular choices for enjoying the shows. Call for a schedule of events and ticket prices.

✳ Selective Shopping

BOOKS **Horton's Books and Gifts** (770-832-8021; www.hortonsbooks .com), 410 Adamson Square, Carrollton. Open 9–6 Monday through Wednesday, 9–8 Thursday and Friday, 10–8 Saturday. As certified by the American Booksellers Association, Horton's is the oldest bookstore in Georgia, the third-oldest in the South, and the 10th-oldest in America. Antique cases display new books for sale, and shoppers can find used

books and books on tape in the basement. Sales of books, cards, and gifts are rung up on the store's original 1892 cash register. Shoppers enjoy interacting with Chloe the cat, who lives in the shop and sponsors Chloe's Kids, a book club for children.

FOOD ♪ ♨ ♿ **Atlanta State Farmer's Market** (404-361-7577; 1-800-662-7829), 16 Forest Parkway, Forest Park. Open 24/7 except Christmas Day. The South's largest farmer's market and one of the biggest in the world, the 150-acre site offers a dizzying array of produce; fruit; plants and flowers; homemade items such as pickles, jams, and relishes; and seasonal items such as pumpkins in October and Christmas trees at holiday time. Take a tour of the farmer's market via the **Fresh Express Trolley Tour** ($3 person). The open-sided trolley operates four days a week in good weather. **Georgia Grown Visitors Center and Gifts,** which is located on the grounds of the farmer's market, sells a variety of Georgia foodstuffs and souvenirs. The facility also dispenses travel information for the entire state of Georgia. Events at the market include the **Peachblossom Bluegrass Festival** in April and the **Georgia Grown MarketFest,** an arts and crafts festival, in October.

✳ Special Events

Mid-April through early June: **Renaissance Festival** (770-964-8575). Open 10:30–6 Saturday and Sunday plus Memorial Day, rain or shine. The multiacre kingdom in Fairburn re-creates a 16th-century European country faire in a village of Tudor homes and enchanting cottages. There you can shop like a queen for handcrafted treasures, watch demonstrations of age-old arts, feast like a king on treats like steak on a stake or smoked turkey legs, rollick on dozens of games and rides for all ages in the medieval amusement park, and revel with a cast of costumed characters (costumes are even available for rent if you want to participate). Ten stages present music and comedy acts, rope walking, balancing stunts, magic shows, sword swallowing, and juggling. You also can cheer on your favorite in the joust or the Hack and Slash sword fight. Wheelchair accessible. Adults $15.95, seniors $12.95, children 6–12 $7.50; game and rides $1–5.

Fall: **Battle of Jonesboro Civil War Reenactment** (770-478-4800; 1-800-662-7829). The battle was a decisive event in Union General William Tecumseh Sherman's March to the Sea because the Battle of Jonesboro marked the end of the Atlanta campaign. The reenactment of hostilities, which features 500 Yanks and Rebs,

THE TOWN OF FAIRBURN HOSTS A RENAIS-SANCE FESTIVAL EVERY SPRING.

ATLANTA STATE FARMER'S MARKET FACTS

- 90 tractor-trailer loads of goods are unloaded every day.
- The market has a $3 billion impact on the area each year.
- 3,500 vendors, purchasers, and other visitors visit the market daily.

occurs on a Saturday and Sunday each fall. At the end of the day Saturday, soldiers entrench themselves using shovels and period-replica spoons. On Sunday, Union troops win the battle. Visitors also enjoy glimpses into camp life, tents, weapons, diet, and drilling. Sutler tents are set up next to Jonesboro's historic Stately Oaks to purvey period replicas. Some activities free; others have a small charge.

October: **The Great Georgia Air Show** (770-632-0365; www.thegreat georgiaairshow.com). The annual air show in Peachtree City features performances by professional civilian performers and military demonstration teams. Thirty World War II planes do a flyby, and some are available for rides. There are also arts and crafts, children's activities, rock climbing, food and beverages, and World War II memorabilia for sale. Tickets are available at some Kroger stores and online at www.aircraftspruce.com. In advance: adults $13, children age 6–12 $5; at the gate: adults $18, children $7. Free parking with shuttle service available at Starrs Mill High School.

The Coast

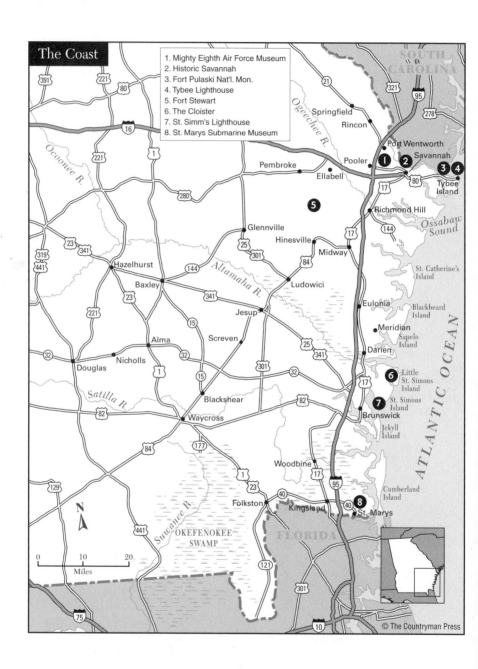

The Coast

1. Mighty Eighth Air Force Museum
2. Historic Savannah
3. Fort Pulaski Nat'l. Mon.
4. Tybee Lighthouse
5. Fort Stewart
6. The Cloister
7. St. Simm's Lighthouse
8. St. Marys Submarine Museum

© The Countryman Press

INTRODUCTION

Pristine barrier islands with dunes and maritime forests, hushed mysterious swamps, unspoiled beaches rimmed with swaying sea oats, untouched tidal marshes, and abundant wildlife characterize the coastal region of the state, as do historic towns and villages, glamorous resorts, and outdoor recreation.

The coast is the cradle of Georgia history. It is here that Spanish monks set up missions in areas inhabited by Guale Indians. This is where General James Oglethorpe established the colony of Georgia—making it the 13th colony—and where several forts were built, stretching along the coast. The coast is where the Spanish were defeated by the British and where some relatively insignificant Revolutionary War battles occurred. The coastal region is also where slaves were imported to work the rice and cotton plantations. During the Civil War, the capture of Savannah was the culmination of Union General William Tecumseh Sherman's March to the Sea in 1864, which hastened the war's end a few months later. The area continues to make history: Just a few years ago, Sea Island played host to the G8 Summit.

Savannah, America's first planned city, is the centerpiece of the region. It was, after all, the colony's first city and first capital. Most of the historic squares laid out by General Oglethorpe still exist, surrounded by magnificently restored Greek Revival and Regency homes, many of which now operate as bed & breakfasts, small inns, restaurants, museums, and shops. Savannah's Historic District is one of the largest in the country. Walking, horse and carriage, trolley, and van tours of the historic district are offered. Savannah is also reputed to be the most haunted city in America, and visitors enjoy a choice of several ghost tours of the Historic District.

Other important colonial towns include Brunswick, Darien, Midway, and St. Marys. Sites with important African American history include Seabrook Village near Midway and Hog Hammock on Sapelo Island, where the Gullah culture survives along with its Geechee language, a Creole form of pidgin English. Although steeped in history, Brunswick and Savannah are active and important ports, as they always have been. Brunswick, which claims to be the Shrimp Capital of the World, is the home of Brunswick Stew.

The barrier islands, each of which has a distinct personality, are accessible by causeway, ferry, or private boat. Cumberland Island, where wild horses gallop on the beach, is designated as a national seashore. Jekyll Island, once the winter retreat of 100 millionaires and their families, is now a resort island, as are Sea Island—the home of the famed resort the Cloister at Sea Island—Tybee, and St. Simons islands. Little St. Simons, although privately owned, welcomes overnight guests. Several other islands are national wildlife refuges.

The region is dotted with nine state parks and historic sites. With so much of the area bordered by or surrounded by water, it's no wonder that water-based activities—boating, canoeing, kayaking, dolphin-watching, fresh- and saltwater fishing, sailing, and scuba diving—are so popular. Naturally, seafood is prominently featured on the menus of numerous restaurants.

Alligators, snakes, wading birds, bobcats, and the cast of the *Pogo* comic strip are the residents of the murky Okefenokee Swamp, which Native Americans called "the land of the trembling earth." One of the last wild places in America, the preserve is a perfect place for canoeing and wildlife observation. Several sites in or near the park depict the difficulties and dangers endured by early settlers.

BRUNSWICK AND THE GOLDEN ISLES

The Spanish pushed north from Florida looking for gold, but they didn't find the precious metal. Instead, they found the coastal barrier-island treasures they called Islas de Oro—the Golden Isles. In fact, if the Spanish hadn't lost a battle to the English on St. Simons Island in 1742, Spanish might be the primary language in Georgia today.

Brunswick and the Golden Isles—as Jekyll, St. Simons, Little St. Simons, and Sea islands are known—are ideal destinations for relaxed getaways. Lush natural beauty, a quiet atmosphere, countless outdoor sports pursuits, and abundant wildlife to observe combine to provide the ideal vacation. Sun-drenched beaches, dolphin tours, turtle walks, 216 holes of golf, fishing, canoeing and kayaking, surfing, windsurfing, scuba diving, boating, bicycling, and numerous other outdoor pursuits attract both the visitor who wants to do little or nothing and the visitor who craves activity. Historic treasures include forts, homes, and a lighthouse, while romance abounds at the beaches and resorts as well as on carriage rides and sunset cruises.

The 486-foot-tall, 7,780-foot-long Sidney Lanier Bridge, US 17, spanning the Brunswick River is Georgia's tallest cable-stayed bridge. Connecting Brunswick on the mainland to St. Simons and Sea islands, it resembles a huge sailing ship and is a beautiful sight to see. Meanwhile, Cumberland Island, which is accessible only by boat, survives in its almost natural state, which makes it attractive to outdoors enthusiasts and travelers interested in ecotourism.

Accommodations of all kinds include bed & breakfasts, intimate inns, condominiums, resort hotels, chain hotels, and campgrounds. Four of *Conde Nast Traveler's* nine Georgia properties on its Gold List of Best Places to Stay are located along the state's coast: the Cloister at Sea Island, Greyfield Inn on Cumberland Island, the Lodge on Little St. Simons Island, and the Lodge at Sea Island. Eateries run the gamut from fine dining establishments specializing in seafood to casual delis where you can get a sandwich. Visitors also have fun exploring several small mainland towns such as St. Marys, the gateway to Cumberland Island, and Folkston, the gateway to the mysterious Okefenokee Swamp.

GUIDANCE When planning a trip to Brunswick and the Golden Isles, contact the **Brunswick and the Golden Isles Convention and Visitors Bureau and Chamber of Commerce** (1-800-933-2627; www.bgicvb.com), 4 Glynn Avenue, Brunswick 31520. Open 8:30–5 weekdays. Once you arrive in the area, stop in at the **Brunswick I-95 Welcome Center** (1-800-933-2627; www.bgicvb.com), 200 I-95, Brunswick 31525, or the **Brunswick US 17 Welcome Center** (1-800-933-2627; www.bgicvb.com), 2000 Glynn Avenue, Brunswick 31520. Both open 9–5 daily. At the US 17 location, visitors can see the original Brunswick stew pot as well as a short video about the area.

For information specific to Jekyll Island, contact the **Jekyll Island Convention and Visitors Bureau** (912-635-4155; 1-877-4-JEKYLL; www.jekyllisland.com), 1 Beachview Drive, Jekyll Island 31527. Open 8–5 weekdays. When in the area, stop by the **Jekyll Island Welcome Center** (912-635-3636), 901 Jekyll Causeway, Jekyll Island 31527. Open 9–5 daily.

Information about Folkston can be obtained from the **Okefenokee Chamber of Commerce, Folkston–Charlton County Development Authority** (912-496-2536; www.folkston.com), 202 W. Main Street, Folkston 31537. Open 8:30–5 weekdays.

For information about Kingsland, Cumberland Island, and the Okefenokee National Wildlife Refuge, consult the **City of Kingsland Welcome Center and Convention and Visitors Bureau** (912-729-5999; 1-800-433-0255; www.visitkingsland.com), 107 S. Lee Street, Kingsland 31548. Open 8–5 weekdays.

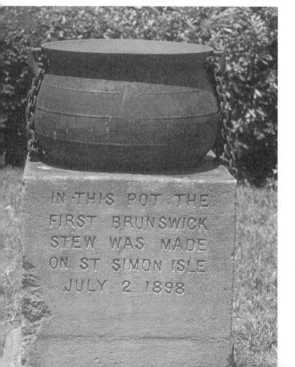

AT THE BRUNSWICK US 17 WELCOME CENTER, VISITORS CAN SEE THE ORIGINAL BRUNSWICK STEW POT.

When in the area, stop by the **Georgia Visitor Information Center-Kingsland** (912-729-3253; www.georgiaonmymind.org), 2424 Haddock Road (exit 1 off I-95), Kingsland 31548. Open 8:30–5:30 daily.

For information about St. Marys, consult the **St. Marys Welcome Center and Tourism Council** (912-882-4000; 1-800-868-8687; www.stmaryswelcome.com), 406 Osborne Street, St. Marys 31558. Open 9–5 Monday through Saturday, 1–4 Sunday. While at the welcome center, pick up a brochure for the **Historic District Braille Trail,** which has Braille markers describing 38 historic sites. For more information about this area, contact the **Camden–Kings Bay Chamber of Commerce** (912-729-5840; 1-800-868-8687; www.camdenchamber.com), 2603 Osborne Road, Suite R, St. Marys 31558. Open 9–5 weekdays.

When visiting St. Simons Island, stop by the **St. Simons Island Visitors Center** (1-800-933-2627), 530-B Beachview Drive. Open 9–5 daily.

GETTING THERE *By air:* **Brunswick Golden Isles Airport** (912-265-2070; ext. 4), 500 Connole Street, Brunswick, offers direct flights to and from Atlanta four times daily aboard Delta jets. Rental cars are available at the Brunswick airport from **Avis** (1-800-831-2847) and **Hertz** (1-800-654-3131). Jekyll Island and St. Simons Island are less than a half-hour from the airport. Otherwise, visitors can use the **Savannah–Hilton Head International Airport** (912-964-0514; 1-877-FLY-2-SAV), 400 Airways Avenue, Savannah, just an hour's drive north, or **Jacksonville International Airport** (904-741-4902), 2400 Yankee Clipper Drive, Jacksonville, Florida, an hour to an hour and a half south. For car rentals at the Savannah airport, see the Savannah chapter. At the Jacksonville airport, car rentals are available from **Alamo** (904-741-4580), **Avis** (904-741-2327), **Budget** (904-741-9910), **Dollar** (904-741-4614), **Enterprise** (904-741-4326), **Hertz** (904-741-2151), and **Thrifty** (904-741-4366).

By bus: **Greyhound Lines** (912-265-2800; 1-800-231-2222; www.greyhound .com) has a terminal at 1101 Gloucester Street in Brunswick.

By car: The two major north-south routes are US 17 and I-95. The major east-west route into Brunswick is US 82 and into St. Marys is GA 40.

By train: The nearest **Amtrak** (1-800-USA-RAIL) stations are in Savannah (see Savannah chapter) and in Jacksonville, Florida, at 3570 Clifford Lane.

GETTING AROUND In addition to car rentals at the airport, in Brunswick, rentals are also available from **Auto Rentals of Brunswick** (912-264-0530), 3576 Darien Highway. **St. Simons Transit Company** (912-638-5678), 105 Marina Drive, operates a fleet of 40 tour boats, yachts, tour buses, and trolleys to provide sight-seeing tours, dolphin tours, dinner cruises, party-boat fishing, shark hunts, and ecotours.

Cumberland Island and Little St. Simons are reached only by ferry, and vehicles are not available for visitors. For ferry service to Cumberland Island, see *Green Space—Nature Preserves and Parks.*

MEDICAL EMERGENCY In life-threatening situations, call 911. For other urgent care, go to **Southeast Georgia Health System** (912-466-7000), 2415 Parkwood Drive in Brunswick. For immediate but less urgent care, go to **Glynn Immediate Care** (912-267-7600), 3400 Parkwood Drive in Brunswick. Open 8–8 weekdays, noon–6 weekends and holidays.

VILLAGES Brunswick, the gateway to the Golden Isles, has an extensive historic district. One of the most special events that takes place there is the annual Blessing of the Fleet on Mother's Day at Mary Ross Waterfront Park. The Portuguese tradition, held yearly, features a parade of brightly decorated shrimp boats passing the park for the blessing.

On **Cumberland Island,** wild horses frolic along vast stretches of pristine beaches. Cumberland, which is the nation's largest wilderness island, is 18 miles long and 3 miles wide with a total of 36,415 acres, of which 16,850 are marsh, mudflats, and tidal creeks. The national seashore island is accessible only by ferry from St. Marys, and the number of visitors per day is limited to 300. The island was owned at one time by Thomas Carnegie, younger brother and business partner of financier Andrew Carnegie. Thomas and his wife, Lucy, built a mansion they called Dungeness in the late 1800s, although Thomas died before it was completed. Lucy finished the home and went on to acquire 90 percent of the island. She built four additional mansions for her children. Dungeness is now only a ruin. Among the other mansions, Plum Orchard is occasionally open for tours and Greyfield is now a luxury inn. The only other accommodations on the island are campgrounds. Cumberland is a living laboratory of Georgia's treasured resources. In addition to a huge expanse of unspoiled beach, the island features marshlands, palmetto stands, tall pines, and moss-draped live-oak forests inhabited by wild horses, deer, bobcats, boars, turkeys, armadillos, sea turtles, and many species of birds.

Jekyll Island has a unique history. It was once described as "the richest, the most exclusive, and the most inaccessible club in the world" (*Munsey's Magazine,* 1904). The Jekyll Island Club was founded in 1886 as the private winter retreat of 100 of America's richest and most elite families—Morgans, Astors, Rockefellers, Pulitzers, and Vanderbilts among them. The ornate Queen Anne–style clubhouse was the center of activity. Some families stayed there; others built grand mansions they called "cottages" because they had no kitchens: Everyone ate at the club. They played golf, tennis, and croquet and hunted for game birds. This idyllic lifestyle lasted for 40 years. When the railroads extended into Florida, the wealthy families moved on to other trendy locations. The island was purchased by the state of Georgia for $675,000, which insures that 35 percent of it will remain in its natural state. The Jekyll Island National Historic Landmark District, the 240-acre riverfront compound used by the millionaires, has been preserved and is one of the largest ongoing restoration projects in the Southeast, if not the country. The Jekyll Island Club has become a luxury hotel (see *Lodgings—Inns and Resorts*), and several of the Victorian-era homes are open for tours (see *To See—Historic Homes and Sites*). Other hotels, inns, bed & breakfasts, restaurants, shops, and sporting options make Jekyll Island an ideal family vacation spot. You don't even have to be a millionaire.

Kingsland was once owned by King George II of England. After the colony of Georgia was granted a charter from King George, another king, John King, acquired enough land to become the largest plantation owner in the area. Today Kingsland is the home of the Naval Submarine Base Kings Bay.

Little St. Simons is a privately owned 10,000-acre barrier island with 7 miles of undeveloped beach. It is reached only by private ferry from Hampton Marina on St. Simons Island. The beach is designated an Important Bird Area; 286 species have been seen there. Hiking, fishing, canoeing, kayaking, and other nature-based activities are popular pursuits. Most guests stay in the island's lodge, but a limited number of daytrips are available, too.

JEKYLL ISLAND FUN FACTS

• General James Oglethorpe, founder of the colony of Georgia, named the island for Sir Joseph Jekyll, Master of the Rolls in Parliament, who had supported the founding of the colony.

• Horton House, now a tabby ruin, was constructed in 1743 and is one of the oldest structures in Georgia.

• The first golf course on the island was constructed in 1898.

• In 1910, leaders in banking finance met on Jekyll Island to discuss ways to address financial panic. This meeting led to the Aldrich Act and the establishment of the Federal Reserve System.

• During the 1910s and 1920s, the Red Bug, an early version of the dune buggy, was the main mode of transportation on the island.

• In 1915, AT&T President Theodore Vail placed the first transcontinental telephone call—from Jekyll Island.

• In 1954, the Jekyll Island Causeway was completed, linking the island to the mainland for the first time. Previous transportation was by ferry.

• Jekyll Island has been recognized as an Important Bird Area by the Audubon Society.

• In 2003, 204 sea turtles laid their eggs on the island's beaches.

THE JEKYLL ISLAND CLUB WAS FOUNDED IN 1886 AS THE PRIVATE WINTER RETREAT OF 100 OF AMERICA'S RICHEST FAMILIES.

Okefenokee Swamp is a dark, brooding, swamp that can be accessed from the sleepy little town of **Folkston.** Known as the Land of the Trembling Earth, the wilderness encompasses 396,000 acres, or 700 square miles, making it the largest swamp in North America. The swamp is home to the American alligator, 234 species of birds, and many other examples of flora and fauna. It has been the site of several movies, including *Swamp Water* (1941) and *Lure of the Wilderness* (1952).

St. Marys, a small coastal village that serves as the gateway to Cumberland Island, is one of Georgia's best-kept secrets. After the Timicuan Indians, Spanish occupation began here in 1566, so St. Marys claims to be the second-oldest town in the United States after St. Augustine, Florida. The charming town boasts 38 National Register of Historic Places sites within walking distance of each other, a waterfront pavilion, and numerous bed & breakfasts located in historic homes and buildings. The Historic Braille Trail, located in downtown St. Marys, features Braille markers at 18 historic sites.

St. Simons is the largest and most populated of Georgia's barrier islands. Its approximately 27,000 acres include 4 miles of beaches, uplands, and marshes. Among its noted visitors was author Eugenia Price, who was so enthralled with the island, she moved there and set *Beloved Invader, Lighthouse, New Moon Rising,* and several other books on the island.

Ritzy **Sea Island** was the vision of early automobile mogul Howard Carl Coffin, who built up the island as a kind of residential-resort club for the wealthy. Management has remained in the family for four generations. The gated enclave offers 5 miles of scenic beach as well as multimillion-dollar private homes and the posh, historic the Cloister at Sea Island resort, which features a hotel and elegant villas in the Spanish-Mediterranean style as well as golf facilities and a top-notch spa (see *Lodging—Inns and Resorts*). Over the years, Sea Island has been visited by five presidents, was the site of Winston Churchill's daughter's wedding, and recently hosted a G8 Summit. George H. W. and Barbara Bush spent their honeymoon at the Cloister. Today the Island is accessible only to overnight guests.

✴ To See

FOR FAMILIES ✐ ❈ **Tidelands Nature Center** (912-635-5032; 912-635-4117; www.tidelands4h.org), 100 South Riverview Drive, Jekyll Island. Open 9–4 Monday through Saturday, 10–2 Sunday. Nature walks at 9 Monday, Wednesday, and Friday, February through September; Monday and Wednesday, October through January. The center, which is operated by the University of Georgia Cooperative Extension Service, provides hands-on marine science exhibits, live animal displays, marsh kayak tours, and nature walks. Visitors observe native species of fish, turtles, crabs, snakes, alligators, and other coastal critters. Among the exhibits are an underwater dock–touch tank display, an alligator tank–freshwater display, a 1,100-gallon sea-turtle tank, and a marsh model. Ninety-minute public nature walks led by experienced guides explore the beach, maritime forest, and/or marsh. Be sure to call ahead, as walks leave from different locations. Three-hour guided kayak tours of Jekyll Creek are available, or visitors may rent a canoe and explore on their own. Admission to nature center: $1: nature walks: adults $5, children 8–17 $3; kayak tours: adults $45, tandem $65, children 7–15 $25.

HISTORIC HOMES AND SITES ✂ ✿ **Fort Frederica National Monument** (912-638-3639; www.nps.gov/fofr), Frederica Road, St. Simons Island. Open 9–5 daily except Christmas Day; movies shown every half-hour. In the 18th century, the land that is now Georgia lay between British South Carolina and Spanish Florida, and was known as debatable land. It was the epicenter of a centuries-old imperial conflict between those two countries. In 1736, just three years after Georgia's first settlement was begun in Savannah, this fort was built by General James Oglethorpe to protect the southern boundary of the new colony of Georgia. After the British repulsed the Spanish attempt to retake St. Simons Island, the garrison was disbanded and the community fell into decline. The remnants of the fortress—built with tabby, an oyster-shell cement—remain, and there are historical tours as well as hiking and nature trails. $3 walk-ins or cyclists, $5 vehicle.

✂ ✿ **Hofwyl-Broadfield Plantation State Historic Site** (912-264-7333; www .gastateparks.org/info/hofwyl), 5556 US 17 North, Brunswick. Open 9–5 Tuesday through Saturday, 2–5:30 Sunday. Last main house tour at 4:15 Tuesday through Saturday, 4:45 Sunday. A visit to Hofwyl-Broadfield Plantation provides a glimpse into life on a former rice plantation converted to a dairy farm when the rice economy failed. Begin at the visitor center by watching a film about the history of the plantation and the families who lived there. You also can see fine silver and a model of a working rice plantation. The pleasant walk from the visitor center to the historic house provides glimpses of salt marsh along the Altamaha River, magnolias, Spanish moss–draped live oaks, and playful goats. The simple 1850s home is filled with family antiques and books. $2.50–5.

✂ ✿ ❬ **Jekyll Island National Historic Landmark District** (912-635-4036), Jekyll Island History Center, 100 Stable Road. Open 9–5 daily; tours leave at 11, 1, and 3. As described in the introduction to this chapter, Jekyll Island was the exclusive elite winter conclave of 100 wealthy families from 1886 through the beginning of World War II. Tour the 240-acre site by tram beginning at the Jekyll Island History Center (see *Museums*), where you can purchase tickets, watch an orientation video, and shop. The tram tour includes admission to two of the island's "cottages." Periodically there are special tours that focus on restoration, folklore, and families. In addition, Mistletoe Cottage showcases the work of nationally renowned Jekyll Island sculptor Rosario Fiore. Exhibit hours are 2–4 weekends. Adults $17.50, children 6–18 $6.50.

MUSEUMS ✂ ✿ ❬ **Cumberland Island National Seashore Museum** (912-882-4336; 1-888-817-3421; www.nps.gov/cuis; www.stmaryswelcome.com), Osborne Street, St. Marys. Open 1–4 daily except Christmas Day. The museum in St. Marys was created to provide a glimpse of the island for the benefit of those who are unable to visit it in person. The museum contains artifacts from the Native Americans, African Americans, and Carnegie family members who inhabited Cumberland Island. Free.

✏ 🍴 ♿ **Jekyll Island History Center** (912-635-4036), 100 Stable Road, Jekyll Island. Open 9–5 daily. Begin a tour of the Jekyll Island National Historic Landmark District at this center, where you can see an orientation film about the island's inhabitants from Native Americans to the present. Tram tours leave from here (see **Jekyll Island National Historic Landmark District** under *Historic Homes and Sites*). Free.

✏ 🍴 ♿ **Maritime Center at the Historic Coast Guard Station** (Coastal Georgia Historical Society: 912-638-4666), 4201 First Street, East Beach, St. Simons Island. Open 10–5 Monday through Saturday, 1:30–5 Sunday. Located in the 1935 Coast Guard Station on East Beach, the museum interprets the region's natural assets and maritime and military history through the letters and field journal entries of Ollie, a fictitious Coast Guardsman, and his dog Scuttle. Seven galleries are filled with hands-on exhibits. Adults $6, children 6–11 $3; family discount and combination tickets, which also include St. Simons Lighthouse (see below), are available.

🍴 **Orange Hall House Museum** (912-673-8118; 912-576-3644 for automated information; www.orangehall.org; www.stmaryswelcome.com), 311 Osborne Street, St. Marys. Open 9–4 Monday through Saturday, 1–4 Sunday. The stately, stereotypical Southern Greek Revival mansion with its massive fluted columns and Doric capitals was built in the early to mid-1800s and is filled with artifacts from the area. During the Civil War it served as a headquarters for Union troops and remained relatively unharmed. Adults $3, children $1.

✏ 🍴 ♿ **St. Marys Submarine Museum** (912-882-2782; www.stmaryssubmuseum .com), 102 St. Marys Street, St. Marys. Open 10–4 Tuesday through Saturday, 1–5 Sunday. Nearby Kingsland is the home of the Naval Submarine Base Kings

THE ORANGE HALL HOUSE MUSEUM IS FILLED WITH ARTIFACTS FROM THE EARLY AND MID-1800S.

Bay. The base is not open for tours, but this submarine museum tells the story of the submarine force in the United States and abroad. The self-guided tour takes one to two hours and includes an operational periscope, a submarine helm station, models of torpedoes, deep-sea fishing suits, uniforms, models of submarines, memorabilia, photos, patrol reports, films, and books. The small, unassuming building can be readily identified by the submarine periscope jutting from the roof. Visitors can peer at the waterfront through the periscope. Adults $4, seniors and active-duty military $3, children 6–18 $2.

✂ 🐾 ♿ **St. Simons Island Lighthouse Museum** (912-638-4666; www.saintsimons lighthouse.org), 101 12th Street, St. Simons Island. Open 10–5 Monday through Saturday, 1:30–5 Sunday (last climb to the top at 4:30). The restored, 104-foot, 1872 lighthouse remains a navigational aid for St. Simons Sound. The tower is open for climbing, and the 1872 keeper's cottage houses a museum with exhibits about this and other lighthouses. Adults $5, children 6–11 $2.50.

NATURAL BEAUTY SPOTS See **Cumberland Island National Seashore** under *Green Space—Nature Preserves and Parks.*

SPECIAL PLACES ✂ 🐾 ♿ **Brunswick Shrimp Docks–Mary Ross Waterfront Park–Liberty Ship Memorial,** Bay and Gloucester streets, Brunswick. Open daily. The park along the docks is a perfect place from which to watch the butterfly-netted shrimp boats come and go. Early morning and late afternoon are the best times. When the boats return, they are usually laden with the day's shrimp catch and the treasures of the sea that may be on the dinner table that evening in one of Brunswick's restaurants. Shop at the **Brunswick Harbor Market,** a farmer's market, at the park. Also in the park is the **Liberty Ship Memorial Plaza,** where visitors can see a scale-model of a Liberty ship similar to those built in Brunswick's shipyards during World War II. The multipurpose park also features an outdoor musical playscape for children and an amphitheater where a wide variety of festivals and events occur throughout the year. In addition, the park is a romantic place to watch a spectacular sunset. Free.

✂ 🐾 ♿ **Folkston Funnel Train Watching Platform** (912-496-2536; www.folkston .com), 103 North First Street, Folkston. Open daily. Train buffs are finding it harder and harder to find places to watch the magnificent behemoths. Folkston is located on CSXT's double-track mainline, known as the CSXT Funnel out of Florida. This covered viewing platform with benches allows train watchers to see up to 70 trains per day, including eight Amtrak trains and intermodal and mixed freight trains. Visitors can activate a scanner to listen to train engineers as they pass through the town. During Folkston's Okefenokee Festival in October, the Orlando Society of Model Railroaders sets up an elaborate train layout. Free.

✳ To Do

BICYCLING On Jekyll Island, visitors can explore more than 20 miles of paved, winding trails that are perfect for cycling, walking, and jogging. Trails pass historic sites, beaches, marshes, and maritime forests. Rentals of 16-, 20-, 24-, and

26-inch bikes are available by the hour, day, or week next to the miniature golf course on North Beachview Drive. Helmets and child seats are also available. Open 9–5 daily. Bike rentals are also available at the Jekyll Island Campground (see *Lodging*) and at many hotels.

On St. Simons, bike paths wind around the airport, through the village, and along the marsh at East Beach as well as the entire length of Frederica Road. Rentals and purchases of equipment are available at a number of locations.

✐ ❀ **Benjy's Bike Shop** (912-638-6766), 130 Retreat Plaza, St. Simons Island. Open 10–6 Monday through Saturday. The full-service bike shop offers rentals of adult and child beach cruisers and mountain bikes, baby seats, training wheels, and tag-alongs as well as repairs, bike accessories, and apparel. $8 per hour, $16 per 24-hour day, $35 per week.

✐ ❀ **Wheel Fun Rentals** (912-634-0606; www.wheelfunrentals.com), main location: 532 Ocean Boulevard, St. Simons Island. Open 9–dusk daily, May through August; call for hours remainder of year. The company, which also has outlets on Jekyll Island, offers much more than simple beach cruisers and moun- tain bikes. Wheel Fun provides pedal-powered fun for all ages and sizes with single and double surreys, deuce coupes, choppers, quad sports, and slingshots in addition to child tag-alongs, child seats, and jogging strollers. Hourly rates: $6 for standard bike to $25 for double surrey; half-day, full-day, and weekly rates available.

See also **Okefenokee Adventures** under *Boat Excursions.*

BIRDING ✐ ❀ **Colonial Coast Birding Trail** (912-882-4000; 1-800-868-8687; downloadable map available at www.georgiawildlife.dnr.state.ga.us/content/birding trailmap.asp). Southeast Georgia is a birder's paradise, offering a wide variety of habitats and species. Along the 18-site trail, which stretches from Savannah south to St. Marys and the Okefenokee Swamp, shorelines, salt marshes, old rice fields, woodlands, tidal rivers, and freshwater wetlands are just a few of the habi- tats to explore. In addition to a plentiful year-round bird population, Jekyll Island is a resting place in the spring and fall for migrating species on the Atlantic Flyway. The trail sponsors the annual Colonial Coast Birding and Nature Festival in October (see *Special Events*). Free.

BOAT EXCURSIONS ✐ **Okefenokee Adventures** (912-496-7156; 1-866- THESWAMP; www.okefenokeeadventures.com), Okefenokee Parkway off GA 121, Folkston. Call for schedules and fees. The visitor-services partner of the Okefenokee National Wildlife Refuge (see *Green Space—Nature Preserves and Parks*) offers guided interpretive tours including multiday excursions. Sunset tours are particularly popular. The outfitter also rents bicycles, canoes, motor- boats, and kayaks. While there, enjoy a light lunch at the Camp Cornelia Café.

✐ **Up the Creek Xpeditions and Outfitters** (912-882-0911; 1-877-UPTHE- CREEK; www.upthecreektrips.com), 111 Osborne Street, St. Marys. Call for schedules and fees. The company offers guided half-day, full-day, and overnight kayak trips, rentals, and instruction.

CANOEING AND KAYAKING The ocean and marshes provide ideal locations for this mode of exploration. Rentals, instruction, and guided excursions are available. For those who have never tried ocean kayaking, these vessels are lightweight, easily maneuverable, and more stable than their freshwater counterparts.

✔ **Southeast Adventure Outfitters** (912-265-5292; www.southeastadventures .com), 1200 Glynn Avenue, Brunswick. Call for a schedule of trips and prices. The company offers year-round guided kayak tours around the offshore islands as well as inland marsh and Altamaha and Satilla river tours.

CARRIAGE RIDES ✔ **Victoria's Carriages and Beach Trail Rides** (912-635-9500), 100 Stable Road, Jekyll Island. Call for hours and fees; reservations required. The company offers narrated carriage tours of the historic district, trail rides on the beach and in maritime forests, hayrides, sunset rides, and couple rides. Moonlit rides depart from the Jekyll Island Club Hotel (see *Lodging*) Monday through Saturday evenings.

DIVING Although Georgia's waters are murky near the shore, they clear to crystal blue offshore. Many artificial reefs have been developed around sunken ships, and a variety of scuba services are available. Gray's Reef is an outstanding diving area.

✔ **Island Dive Center and Tours** (912-638-6590; 1-800-940-3483; www.island divecenter.com), Golden Isles Marina, 101 Marina Drive, St. Simons Island. Call for schedules. The full-service facility offers snorkeling and scuba classes, guided dives, air fills, tours, and equipment rentals, sales, and service. Fees vary by activity.

DOLPHIN WATCHING See **St. Simons Transit Company** under *Getting Around* and **Weadore Sailing** under *Sailing.*

FISHING The Georgia coast boasts access to deep-sea fishing as well as 700,000 acres of salt marsh, tidal creeks, and freshwater rivers. Opportunities for deep-sea, surf, inshore river, and lake fishing abound here. There are also numerous bridges and piers from which to fish. Anglers catch tarpon, whiting, red drum, sea trout, triple tail, spotted sea trout, striped mullet, sheepshank, black drum, and many others. Numerous marinas and experienced guides are available. A Georgia fishing license is required, and there may be limitations on the size and number of some species.

Public fishing is available at the St. Simons Island fishing pier, along the Torras Causeway, and at older bridgeheads. Good shore fishing can be found at Gould's Inlet on East Beach. Crabbing is also a popular activity, using hand lines from low docks or with crab pots and traps from bridges and piers. The Golden Isles Marina adjacent to the Torras Causeway on the Frederica River and the Hampton Point Marina at the north end of the island offer a full range of services, including charters. The St. Simons Boating and Fishing Club is a public facility.

✔ **Coastal Expeditions Charter Fishing and Dolphin Tours** (912-265-0392; www.coastalcharterfishing.com), One Harbor Road, at Jekyll Island Marina. Call for schedules and prices. Fishing, dolphin-watching, and birding tours are offered daily. Specialties include inshore charters for trout and bass, near-shore charters for shark and tarpon, and deep-sea charters.

FRIGHTS ✍ ♿ **St. Simons Ghost Tour** (912-638-2756; www.ghosttoursofstsimons .com), 669 North Golf Villas, St. Simons Island. Thursday through Saturday, March 15 through May; Tuesday through Saturday, June through August; Saturday only, September and October; all tours at 9 PM. The fun and informative 1½-hour lamplight walking tour explores Olde St. Simons. Participants experience frightful tales of folklore, mystery, legends, lovers, and the lost while discovering more about the island and its history. Tours depart from St. Simons Village near the pier.

GOLF Jekyll Island offers 63 holes of golf with three 18-hole courses and a historic nine-hole course, making the island Georgia's largest public golf resort. Jekyll Island hotels offer all-inclusive golf passport packages that allow players to experience these four courses and six others along the coast.

Great Dunes Golf Course (912-635-2170), Shell Road and Beachview Drive, Jekyll Island. Open 8–6 daily; earlier closing in winter. The historic nine-hole course, which was originally built in the late 1800s, lies along the ocean. Today the course still attracts and challenges golfers with its alternating simple and difficult holes. $27 riding, $19 walking; discounts for juniors, replay, and twilight hours.

Jekyll Island Golf Club (912-635-2368), 322 Captain Wylly Road, Jekyll Island. First tee time at 8 AM, last tee time two hours before dark. The club actually includes three 18-hole championship courses from a central clubhouse: **Indian Mounds, Oleander** (which is considered the most difficult), and **Pine Lake.** The facility also includes a putting green, driving range, practice bunker, pro shop, and restaurant. $57 riding, $40 walking; discounts for juniors, replay, and twilight play.

See also Golf Appendix and *Lodging—Inns and Resorts* for more courses in Folkston, Kingsland, and St. Simons Island.

HIKING ✍ **Earth Day Nature Trail** (912-264-7218), Coastal Resources Office, One Conservation Way, off US 17 at Sidney Lanier Bridge, Brunswick. The self-guided trail through salt marshes, tidal ponds, and coastal hammock high ground provides endless opportunities for bird-watching and wildlife observation. Wading birds are abundant, and visitors may catch a glimpse of an eagle or osprey on the nesting platform provided for them. There are observation decks and an observation tower, and binoculars are available for checkout. Free.

HORSEBACK RIDING See Victoria's Carriages and Beach Trail Rides under *Carriage Rides.*

MINIATURE GOLF ✍ 🐾 **Jekyll Island Mini Golf** (912-635-2648), North Beachview Drive at Shell Road, Jekyll Island. Open 9–6 Sunday through Thursday,

9–10 Friday and Saturday, weather permitting. Two lighted, old-time, 18-hole courses are located across from the beach. $5.30 per person per game, $12 three-game pass, $35 10-game pass.

NATURE TOURS ✪ ♿ **Salt Marsh Nature Tours** (912-638-9354; www.marshtours.com), 1000 Hampton River Club Drive, at Hampton River Club Marina, St. Simons Island. Call for schedules. Captain Jeanne and Captain Jim offer one-to-three-hour nature tours of the marshes and tidal creeks between St. Simons Island and Little St. Simons Island aboard *Marsh Hen,* their pontoon boat. They impart historical information as well as pointing out vegetation, birds, and mammals. $30–55.

NATURE WALKS ✪ **Sea Turtle Walks** (912-635-2284; 912-635-4036), 196 Stable Road, Jekyll Island. Call for schedules and prices. Guides conduct walks that teach about sea turtles and their habitats, and participants search for turtle tracks and nesting loggerhead turtle mothers. Tours leave from the historic district's Jekyll Island History Center (see *To See—Historic Homes and Sites*).

See also **Tidelands Nature Center** under *To See—For Families*.

SAILING ✪ **Weadore Sailing** (912-223-4419; www.weadoresailing.com), Jekyll Harbor Marina, One Harbor Road, Jekyll Island. Operates Monday through Saturday, late March through October. The company offers sailing and dolphin tours off the coast. Two- to eight-hour trips aboard the 31-foot *Bombay Clipper* include sunset, dolphin, and moonlight cruises. Lessons and small boat rentals are also available. Two-hour cruises: adults $30, children younger than 12 $20; other cruises $120–500. Reservations required.

SUMMER YOUTH PROGRAMS ✪ **Camp Cloister** at the Cloister at Sea Island (912-638-3611; 1-800-732-4752; www.seaisland.com), 100 First Street, Sea Island. Camp Cloister is available Monday through Saturday year-round. The resort has earned many accolades from readers of *Conde Nast Traveler* and *Travel and Leisure,* including being named the Best Resort for Families in the United States and Canada. The superior Children's Activity Center contains table tennis, air hockey, and other games. Special children's programs are conducted during the summer, spring break, and other holidays. Camp Cloister is available for children ages 3–11; sometimes groups are broken up into ages 3–8 and 9–11. Activities might include turtle walks, dunes discovery, fishing, sand sculpture, contests, tie-dye on the beach, boat rides, and more. Older youth can participate in tennis and golf clinics and round robins. The resort also offers movies, teen bowling, Jeep safaris, and much more. $10–35 per day or activity; participation by reservation only.

✪ **Club Juniors** at Jekyll Island Club Hotel (912-635-2600; 1-800-535-9547), 371 Riverview Drive, Jekyll Island. Available 9–4 Monday through Saturday during summer months. The small fry can enjoy fun-filled days of bicycle safaris, beach fun, crabbing, crafts, tennis, swimming, croquet, miniature golf, board games, contests, hiking and nature walks, treasure hunts, and a visit to Summer

BRUNSWICK AND THE GOLDEN ISLES

Waves Water Park (see *Water Parks*). $10 per half-day, $18 per day for hotel guests; $13 per half-day, $25 per day for others (some activities require additional fee).

TENNIS ♪ **Jekyll Island Tennis Center** (912-635-3154; www.gate.net/~jitc), 400 Captain Wylly Road, Jekyll Island. Open 9–6 daily for open play; evening and night play until 10 PM available by reservation only prior to 6 PM day of play. Recognized as one of the finest municipal facilities in the country, the center offers 13 award-winning, fast-dry clay courts, of which seven are lighted, as well as a pro shop, racquet stringing, and instruction for every level of play. $18 per hour for play; ball machine $18 per hour; racquet and hopper rental $3.

On St. Simons, there are tennis courts at Sea Palms Golf and Tennis Resort, the Island Club, and the King and Prince Beach and Golf Resort (see *Lodging*), as well as public courts at Mallory Park and Epworth Park.

TROLLEY RIDES ♪ **St. Simons Trolley** (912-638-8954; www.stsimonstours.com), Village Pier, St. Simons Island. Tours at 11 and 1 in April, June, and July; one tour at 11 other months. Getting around St. Simons can be fun aboard one of the antique trolleys operated by the St. Simons Transit Company (see *Getting Around*). The 90-minute narrated tours pass all the important sites on the island—the lighthouse, Bloody Marsh, Fort Frederica, and Retreat Plantation, to name just a few—and make a stop at Christ Church. Adults $20, children 4–12 $10; advance tickets and reservations not required.

WATER PARKS ♪ **Summer Waves Water Park** (912-635-2074; www.summer waves.com), 210 South Riverview Drive, Jekyll Island. Open May through Labor Day weekend; call for exact days and hours. The 11-acre, family-oriented water park features more than a million gallons of water used for a lazy river, a wave pool the size of a football field, a kiddie pool, and several exciting water slides with names such as Pirate's Passage, Nature's Revenge, and Thunder and Lightning. There are height restrictions on some rides. Locker rentals and concessions are available, and lifejackets are provided for small children. Those above 4 feet tall $18.95, those under 4 feet tall $14.95, ages 3 and younger free; senior night and other discounts available.

✳ Green Space

BEACHES This coastal area and its barrier islands are rich in beaches: St. Simons offers 10 miles of beaches, Little St. Simons has more than 7 miles of sand, Cumberland Island boasts more than 17 miles of pristine beach, and Jekyll Island offers 10 miles of uncrowded, unspoiled beaches.

NATURE PRESERVES AND PARKS ♪ ✿ 👣 ♿ **Crooked River State Park** (912-882-5256; 1-800-864-7275; www.gastateparks.org/info/crookriv), 6222 Charlie Smith Sr. Highway, St. Marys. Open 7–10 daily. The 500-acre park on the Crooked River features maritime forest and salt marshes. Water sports such as saltwater fishing, boating, and kayaking are the primary activities, but 4 miles of trails attract hikers, and the park offers an Olympic-size swimming pool, playground, and miniature golf course. Accommodations are offered in cottages (some of which are dog-friendly) and campgrounds (see *Lodging*). Parking $3.

 **Cumberland Island National Seashore** (912-882-4335; 1-888-817-3421; www.nps.gov/cuis), landside office: 107 St. Marys Street, St. Marys. Access is by ferry only, and reservations are strongly recommended to avoid disappointment. Two morning departures and two afternoon returns Sunday through Tuesday and an additional return Wednesday through Saturday, March 1 through November 30; two morning departures and two afternoon returns Thursday through Monday, December 1 through February 28. In all cases, the last ferry back to the mainland leaves the island at 5:30. The majority of Cumberland Island, the largest and southernmost of Georgia's barrier islands, is preserved as a national seashore. Secluded white, sandy beaches and a complex ecological system characterize the island. Popular travel guides have rated the island beaches A+ for beaches and sand quality, and the site has been named one of America's top beaches by the Travel Channel. Popular activities include beachcombing and shell gathering, swimming, sunning, walking and hiking (no vehicles allowed), fishing (a license is required and can be purchased in St. Marys; light tackle only can be used, and you must bring your own), camping (see *Lodging—Campgrounds*), and seasonal ranger-led programs. There are also several man-made sites to see on the island. Dungeness Ruins is the remains of a home built in 1884 by Thomas Carnegie. The simple First African Baptist Church served as a church, community hall, and school for the island's early African Americans. It gained worldwide recognition when it served as the site of John F. Kennedy Jr.'s marriage to Carolyn Bissett. Plum Orchard Mansion, which was built by the Carnegie

FAMILIES FLOCK TO THE SUMMER WAVES WATER PARK ON JEKYLL ISLAND.

family in 1898, is sometimes open for ranger-guided tours. The Ice House Museum is open daily. Note: There are no stores on Cumberland Island. St. Marys businesses and the ferry carry sandwiches, snacks, beverages, and souvenirs. Visitors should wear comfortable clothing and shoes and bring food, drinks, suntan lotion, insect repellent, rain gear, and sunglasses. You must carry out what you bring in. No pets or bicycles are permitted on the ferry. For those whose idea of roughing it is room service, luxurious accommodations are available at the privately operated Greyfield Inn (see *Lodging—Inns and Resorts*). Park day-use fee $4, in addition to ferry service: adults $15, seniors $12, children 12 and younger $10.

✐ 🦎 **Okefenokee National Wildlife Refuge, East Entrance–Suwannee Canal Recreation Area** (912-496-7836; 912-496-7156; 1-866-THE-SWAMP), 3324 Okefenokee Parkway, Folkston. Open 7–7:30 daily, March 1 through September 10; 8–6 remainder of year. The Okefenokee NWR is the largest wildlife refuge in the eastern United States as well as being one of the oldest and best-preserved freshwater areas in America. It is a vast bog occupying a saucer-shaped depression that was once an ocean floor. The swamp, which boasts 120 miles of canoe trails, is made up of upland islands, moss-draped cypress forests, scrub-shrub vegetation, prairie wetlands, waterways, and open lakes. In addition to alligators, the swamp is home to other reptiles, amphibians, bobcats, white-tailed deer, black bears, songbirds, birds of prey, wading birds, and migrating waterfowl. Winter is an excellent time to see the endangered Florida sandhill crane, and spring is the time to catch a glimpse of red-cockaded woodpeckers. Human habitation has included Native Americans, early settlers, canal builders, and lumbermen. Visit the preserved Chesser Island Homestead, the hardscrabble home place of the Chesser family for more than 100 years, to see the primitive conditions in which the family eked out an existence. The Swamp's Edge Information Center offers interpretive nature exhibits. Activities at the park include a driving tour, biking, walking and hiking, boating, fishing, hunting, wildlife observation, interpretive programs, and special events. One recommended short jaunt is the 1.5-mile round-trip boardwalk trail to Seagrove Lake and the Owl's Roost observation tower. There are several other half-mile to mile-long hiking trials, and canoe trails range from 12 to 55 miles long. Wilderness canoeing and camping on raised platforms are offered by permit only. Guided boat tours are offered, and canoe, kayak, motorboat, and bike rentals are available. There is also a snack bar and gift shop. (See also the Waycross chapter and the Valdosta chapter in 5, Souther Rivers, for more information about the swamp.) $5.

ALLIGATORS PASS THE TIME AT THE OKE-FENOKEE NATIONAL WILDLIFE REFUGE.

✳ Lodging
BED AND BREAKFASTS

In Brunswick

Brunswick Manor (912-265-6889; www.brunswickmanor.com), 825 Egmont Street. The stately 1886 home, which overlooks an original 1771 park in the Old Town residential district, offers three elegant guest rooms with private baths and plenty of luxurious amenities. Outside, guests are invited to enjoy the wrap-around veranda, the arbored patio, and the hot tub. A delicious breakfast is included. Smoking outdoors only. Not wheelchair accessible. $99–120.

McKinnin House (912-261-9100; 1-866-261-9100; www.mckinnonhouse bandb.com), 1001 Egmont Street. Located in the heart of Old Town Brunswick, the imposing home was built in 1902 for a lumber magnate. Seventeen Corinthian columns support the upstairs and downstairs verandas, where guests often enjoy afternoon refreshments. Family heirlooms and period reproductions characterize the public and guest rooms. Guests enjoy private baths, sweeping verandas, a Southern gourmet breakfast, and afternoon tea. Smoking outdoors only. Not wheelchair accessible. $100–135.

WatersHill Bed and Breakfast (912-264-4262; www.watershill.com), 728 Union Street. The intimate retreat with modern amenities is located in a historic home in Old Town Brunswick. Five elegantly appointed guest rooms feature private baths. Porches, gardens, fountains, and a koi pond entice guests outdoors. No smoking. Not wheelchair accessible. $85–115.

In Folkston

Folkston House (912-496-3445; www.folkstonhouse.com), 802 Kingsland Drive. Folkston House was built at the turn of the 20th century, although it has been modified several times. Seven guest rooms with private baths are decorated in individual styles with period antiques. A full Southern breakfast is included. Children older than 8 are welcome. Smoking outdoors only. Not wheelchair accessible. $85–130.

🍴 ♿ **Inn at Folkston Bed and Breakfast** (912-496-6256; 1-888-509-6246; www.innatfolkston.com), 509 West Main Street. The fully restored 1920s Craftsman-style bungalow features four antique-filled guest rooms, each uniquely decorated with an individual theme. All feature amenities you'd expect to find in an upscale hotel: feather beds, down comforters, robes, hair dryers, and more. Some rooms boast a gas-log fireplace, a private screened porch, and/or a whirlpool tub. The inn also features a large porch, a six-person hot tub, an herb garden, and 2 acres on which to wander. Nightly rates include a full hot breakfast and an evening social hour. Children of all ages welcome. Smoking outdoors only. One room wheelchair accessible. $120–170.

In St. Marys

Emma's Bed and Breakfast (912-882-4199; www.emmasbedandbreak fast.com), 300 West Conyers Street. Located in a lovely, traditional-style home on 4 tranquil acres in downtown St. Marys, Emma's is named for Emma Bealey, who came here as a bride in 1911. The nine individually themed guest rooms and suites in the main house and an additional building have private baths. The grounds feature beautiful gardens. No smoking. Not wheelchair accessible. $119–169; two-night minimum during holidays or special events.

⅄ **Goodbread House Bed and Breakfast** (912-882-7490; www.good breadhouse.com), 209 Osborne Street. Located in a historic house on the main thoroughfare in St. Marys, Goodbread House, with its attractive upstairs and downstairs verandas, features guest rooms whimsically named for famous couples—Rhett and Scarlett, Guinevere and Lancelot, Gabriel and Evangeline, Gable and Lombard, and Lucy and Ricky—each with a private bath. The nightly rate includes a sumptuous breakfast and an afternoon social hour. No smoking. Wheelchair accessible. $124–134.

⌀ ⅄ **Spencer House Inn** (912-882-1872; 1-877-820-1872; www.spencer houseinn.com), 200 Osborne Street. Spencer House has a long history as a hotel. It was built in 1872 by Captain William T. Spencer and was known as the finest hotel in St. Marys and southeast Georgia. The stately pink building with upstairs and downstairs verandas features 14 rooms and suites with private baths. Fine antiques and reproductions furnish public spaces and guest rooms. A full buffet breakfast is served in the cheery breakfast room. No smoking. Wheelchair accessible. $100–185; minimum stay may be required during holidays or special events.

On St. Simons

Beach Bed and Breakfast (912-634-2800; 1-877-634-2800; www .beachbedandbreakfast.com), 907 Beachview Drive. Six large, airy, sunny rooms and suites feature a variety of bedding, but all have private baths. Some boast a fireplace, balcony, or Jacuzzi. The nightly rate includes a full breakfast, beverages, bicycles, beach chairs, and towels. No smoking. Not wheelchair accessible. $240–500.

⌀ ⅄ **Village Inn and Pub** (912-634-6056; 1-888-635-6111; www.village innandpub.com), 500 Mallory Street. A restored 1930s beach cottage serves as the heart of this inn. Designed around the original cottage, the newly constructed inn integrates the architecture of the neighborhood and the facade of the cottage. Accommodations, decorated to celebrate the luxury and tastes of the '30s with modern amenities, range from standard rooms to junior suites and deluxe rooms, most with private balconies. In the evening, enjoy the pub's wild-orchid martini or other libations in an Old English atmosphere. The inn also has a pool and gardens, and therapeutic massages are available by reservation. Continental breakfast, served on the pub's sun porch, is included. No smoking except on balconies or other outdoor locations. Wheelchair accessible. $140–210; peak season March 1 through Labor Day weekend.

CAMPGROUNDS

In Brunswick

⌀ ⅏ ⅄ **Blythe Island Regional Park** (912-261-3805; 1-800-343-7855), 6616 Blythe Island Highway. The 1,100-acre public park offers a full-service campground, excellent freshwater and saltwater fishing, a marina, boat ramp, boat rental, freshwater swimming lake, bait sales, walking and biking trails, two lighted tennis courts, field archery range, tournament horseshoe courts, and laundry facilities. $22 for tent sites, $23 for RV sites with water and electricity, $25 for full hookups.

On Cumberland Island

⌀ ⅏ **Backcountry** and **sea camps** (912-882-4335; 1-888-817-3421; www

.nps.gov/cuis). Two types of camping are offered on Cumberland Island. Developed sea campgrounds offer rest rooms, cold-water showers, and drinking water, and campfires are permitted. Backcountry camps offer only drinking water. Campfires are not permitted, so a camp stove is required. Keep in mind that back-country campsites may be up to 10 miles from the dock; campers must walk both ways while carrying all their equipment. There are no stores, so you must pack in and out everything you need. $2 per person per dayfor backcountry primitive camping, $4 per person per day for sea camp developed camping; $4 day-use fee in addition to camping fee plus the cost of ferry passage to and from the island (see **Cumberland Island National Seashore** under *Green Space—Nature Preserves and Parks*); reservations required.

On Jekyll Island
Jekyll Island Campground
(912-635-3021; 1-866-658-3021; www.jekyllisland.com/where/camping .html), 1197 North Riverview Drive. Eighteen wooded acres on the island's north end provide the site for 199 tent and RV campsites—some with full hookups, others with partial hookups—and some primitive sites. The campground also features a camp store, coin laundry, rest rooms with showers, and bicycle rentals. $18.99 for tent sites; $22 for water and electric sites; $25.99 for back-in, full-service sites; $27.99 for pull-through, full-service sites.

In St. Marys
Crooked River State Park
(912-882-5256; 1-800-864-7275; www .gastateparks.org/info/crookriv), 6222 Charlie Smith Sr. Highway. The park

offers 62 tent, trailer, and RV sites shaded by Spanish moss-draped oaks. A pioneer campground also is available. $20–25.

CONDOS
On St. Simons Island
The Beach Club (912-638-5450), 1440 Ocean Boulevard. The ocean-front condominium complex features 152 fully furnished, two-bedroom, two-bath units with complete kitchens and laundry facilities. Amenities include an oceanside pool, play-ground, hot tubs, an observation deck, and a boardwalk. $170–275.

North Breakers Condominiums (912-638-1244 for information; 912-638-0328 for reservations), 1470 Wood Avenue. The oceanfront condo-minium complex features fully fur-nished, two-bedroom, two-bath units with complete kitchens and laundry facilities. Amenities include an ocean-side pool, a Jacuzzi, and a children's pool. $160–260.

Shipwatch Condominiums (912-638-5450), 1524 Wood Ave-nue. Located near the historic Coast Guard Station on the beach, the facility offers fully furnished two-bedroom, two-bath condomini-ums with complete kitchens and laundry facilities. Amenities include an outdoor pool and a boardwalk. $159–199.

St. Simons Grand Oceanfront Villas (912-638-2407), 1400 Ocean Boulevard. The gated oceanfront condominium community offers 25 elegant, fully furnished units with kitchens and laundry facilities. Ameni-ties include a heated pool, landscaped grounds, and ponds with lighted foun-tains. $300–650.

In Brunswick

✍ 🐾 **Guest Cottages and Suites**
(912-264-6767), 150 Venture Drive.
Fifty well-appointed, fully equipped
cottages offer kitchens with full-size
refrigerators and microwaves. The
main house features 15 individual
rooms and suites. Continental breakfast is included. $50–79.95.

In Folkston

✍ 🐾 **Okefenokee Pastimes Cabins**
(912-496-4472; www.okefenokee.com),
GA 121 South, Folkston. Okefenokee
Adventures (see *To Do— Boat Excursions*) offers three levels of cabins. All
have heat and air conditioning, but
none have phones or televisions.
Deluxe cabins feature a private bath,
equipped kitchenette, and screened
porch. Log cabins are similar but do
not have a bathroom; guests use the
communal bathroom. Linens are provided for the deluxe and log cabins.
Camping cabins are basically a climate-controlled roof over your head.
There are no bathrooms, kitchenettes,
or linens, and you must clean the
cabin when you leave. $95 for deluxe
cabins, $65 for log cabins, $45 for
camping cabins; multinight discounts
available for all.

On Jekyll Island

✍ **Jekyll Realty Vacation Rentals**
(912-635-3301; 1-888-333-5055; www
.jekyll-island.com), Jekyll Shopping
Center. Fully furnished and equipped
one- to-five bedroom homes, apartments, and villas are available by the
week and month or for shorter periods when available.

✍ **Parker-Kaufman, Realtors** (912-
635-2512; 1-888-453-5955; www
.parker-kaufman.com/jekyll), 22
Beachview Drive. More than 100
accommodations are available in one-
to six-bedroom cottages and condos.
Weekly and monthly rates are available as well as shorter stays when
available.

In St. Marys

✍ 🐾 🐕 **Crooked River State Park**
(912-882-5256; 1-800-864-7275; www
.gastateparks.org/info/crookriv), 6222
Charlie Smith Sr. Highway, St. Marys.
Eleven cottages overlook the river at
this state park. Several allow dogs.
$85–110.

INNS AND RESORTS

On Cumberland Island

✍ ♿ **Greyfield Inn** (904-261-6408;
1-866-410-8051; www.greyfieldinn
.com), mailing address: 8 North Second Street, Fernandina Beach, FL
32035. Although the majority of Cumberland Island is national seashore,
some areas remain in private hands.
Greyfield, a historic 1901 mansion
built as a wedding present for Lucy
and Thomas Carnegie's daughter,
Margaret Ricketson, is still in the
hands of descendants of the Carnegie
family. Decorated with family heirlooms and antiques, the inn provides
an elegant, private retreat from the
busy daily world. Eleven guest rooms
and suites feature private, adjacent, or
shared baths. The daily rate includes
accommodations; ferry transportation
to the island; a full Southern breakfast, picnic lunch, and formal candlelit
gourmet dinner; naturalist-led Jeep
tours of the island; complimentary
wine on Sunday; and unlimited use of
bicycles and sports, fishing, and beach
equipment. Children 6 and older welcome. No smoking. Wheelchair accessible. $350–575 midweek off-season,
$395–575 weekends and midweek
high season; two-night minimum stay

required except three-night minimum on holidays.

On Jekyll Island

✿ & **Jekyll Island Club Hotel** (912-635-2600; 1-800-535-9547; www.jekyllclub.com), 371 Riverview Drive. Built in 1887, the main structure was the clubhouse for the private Jekyll Island Club (see *To See—Historic Homes and Sites*). A National Historic Landmark, the hotel offers 157 first-class accommodations in five historic settings: the main hotel in the clubhouse, the 1901 Clubhouse Annex, the 1896 Sans Souci apartments, 1917 Crane Cottage, and 1904 Cherokee Cottage. Guest rooms and suites are nicely appointed with period reproductions. Amenities include fine dining at the **Grand Dining Room** and the **Courtyard at Crane** as well as casual dining at **Café Solterra** (see *Where to Eat*), an outdoor heated pool, a croquet lawn, seasonal children's programs (see *To Do—Summer Youth Programs*), room service, five gift shops, and concierge service. Smoking and nonsmoking rooms available. Wheelchair accessible. $149–399; American Plan or Modified American Plan available at additional cost.

On Little St. Simons Island

✿ & **The Lodge on Little St. Simons** (912-638-7472; 1-888-733-5774; www.littlestsimonsisland.com), depart from 1000 Hampton Point Drive on St. Simons Island. In addition to being named to *Conde Nast Traveler*'s prestigious Gold List of Best Places to Stay in 2006, the resort has been honored by other reports. *Southern Living* has recognized the island resort for having one of the best beaches in the South, and *The Robb Report* has named it one of the World's 10 Great Escapes. Overnight guests are limited

to 30 people, who are housed in 15 guest rooms located in five rustic cottages that were constructed in 1917, 1926, the 1930s, and the 1970s. The Hunting Lodge, the heart of the island, is where guests meet for meals, cocktail hour, games, and socializing. The nightly rate includes three meals, accommodations, horseback riding, guided interpretive programs, boating, biking, bird-watching, fishing, and use of sports equipment. No smoking. Wheelchair accessible. All-inclusive room rates $450 off-season–$675 weekends and holidays; entire cottages $800–2,500; entire island $6,000–8,000.

On Sea Island

✿ & **The Cloister at Sea Island** (912-638-3611; 1-800-732-4752; www.seaisland.com), 100 First Street. The legendary resort began in 1928 with a Spanish-style building on beautifully landscaped grounds. Recently the historic building was replaced with a new one. Ranked "Number One Resort in the U.S." by the readers of *Conde Nast Traveler*, the resort's $200 million improvement plan included the complete rebuilding of the main building, new River House wings, new dining and lounge facilities, and a new spa. Those who are appalled at the idea of demolishing the original hotel should know that the look of the original design remains. The specialty woods, fixtures, stained glass, and mantels from the renowned Spanish Lounge were salvaged so the room could be reconstructed in the new building. Elegantly appointed guest rooms and suites with all the most luxurious amenities are found in the hotel, villas, and cottages. Extras at the resort include 5 miles of private beach, three championship golf courses and a Golf Learning Center, 25 tennis courts, golf and tennis pro shops, a shooting school, five gift shops, five restaurants, three swimming pools, an award-winning spa, a private beach, children's programs, and many special themed events throughout the year. The equestrian program offers ring rides, trail rides, beach rides, lessons, clinics, stable tours, and a petting zoo. Hobie Cat sailboats, sea kayaks, beach funcycles, and boogie boards are available for rent. Three-to nine-bedroom villas are also available. The main dining room is a throwback to a truly elegant era: Jackets for gentlemen and boys older than 12 and slacks and a collared shirt for boys 12 and younger are required for dinner. Note: Travelers must be overnight guests at the Cloister to enjoy the activities or restaurants. Smoking and nonsmoking rooms available. Wheelchair accessible. $230–450.

♪ & **The Lodge at Sea Island** (912-634-4300; 1-866-465-3563; www.sea island.com), 100 Retreat Avenue. Part of the Cloister, the Lodge at Sea Island is geared to golfers. It's one of only 24 properties worldwide to have earned both Mobil five stars and AAA five diamonds, and it's also been named the "Best Golf Resort in the U.S." by the *Robb Report*. The hotel is luxurious in the style of a private manor, with butlers available 24 hours a day to attend to any need or wish. Guests also have use of all the amenities at the Cloister. Smoking and nonsmoking rooms available. Wheelchair accessible. $450–650.

On St. Simons Island

♪ & **King and Prince Beach and Golf Resort** (912-638-3631; 1-800-342-0212; www.kingandprince.com),

201 Arnold Road. Located directly on the beach, the elegant, Mediterranean-style hotel, a member of Historic Hotels of America, offers handsomely decorated guest rooms and suites—many of them oceanfront—as well as oceanfront cabanas. Amenities include an indoor heated pool and hot tub in the atrium lobby, four outdoor pools, two clay tennis courts, a fitness room, and a full-service oceanfront restaurant noted for its Friday-night seafood buffet and Sunday brunch. Seasonal poolside dining also is offered. Golfers can play at the Hampton Club at Hampton Plantation. Only four smoking rooms available; remainder are nonsmoking. Wheelchair accessible. $119–500.

& **Ocean Inn and Suites** (912-634-2122; 1-877-OCEAN-INN), 599 Beachview Drive. The island's newest luxury-suite hotel, located across from the lighthouse, beach, and Neptune Park, boasts a saltwater jetted outdoor pool, a daily complimentary breakfast, and an evening manager's reception with an ice cream social. No smoking. Wheelchair accessible. $219–300.

& **Sea Palms Golf and Tennis Resort** (912-638-3351; 1-800-841-6268; www.seapalms.com), 5445 Frederica Road. Luxurious guest rooms, suites, and one- to four-bedroom villas overlook the Marshes of Glynn. Amenities include 27 holes of championship golf, a private beach club, full-service restaurants, a health and racquet club, three clay tennis courts, three outdoor pools, a children's wading pool, volleyball court, and horseshoe pits. A personal trainer is available, as are bike rentals. The St. Simons Beach Club offers private beach access, a pool, Jacuzzi tub, beach chair rentals, and a snack bar.

Only seven smoking rooms; remainder are nonsmoking. Wheelchair accessible. $159–499 February 1 through Thanksgiving; $119–489 off-season.

OTHER LODGINGS

On St. Simons

🎣 🐾 ♿ **Epworth-by-the-Sea** (912-638-8688; www.epworthbythesea .com), 100 Arthur J. Moore Drive. This Methodist Retreat Center (open to all), an 83-acre retreat located on the banks of the historic Frederica River, features 10 motels from basic 1950s style to upscale new construction, 12 family apartments, and 13 youth buildings—all told accommodating 1,000 people. Exceptional accommodations are offered in the VIP House, which was originally built in 1880 as the office for a sawmill. Meals are served cafeteria-style in several dining rooms. Guests can use the outdoor pool (open seasonally), lighted tennis courts, two fishing piers, four dining rooms, and covered basketball courts. Dolphin tours and a museum are also available. No smoking. Wheelchair accessible. $61–100.

✳ Where to Eat

DINING OUT

On Jekyll Island

♿ **Blackbeard's Seafood Restaurant** (912-635-3522), North Beachview Drive. Open 11–3:30; 5–10 Sunday through Thursday, 5–11 Friday and Saturday. This nautically themed beachfront family restaurant offers authentic island and low-country cuisine, specializing in fresh seafood in addition to a wide variety of appetizers, entrées, nightly specials, and desserts. Dine inside or out on the deck overlooking the beach. No smoking. Wheelchair accessible. $10–22.

♿ **Jekyll Island Club Hotel** (912-635-2600; www.jekyllclub.com), 375 Riverview Drive. Grand Dining Room open 7–11 AM Monday through Saturday (until 10 Sunday), 11:30–2, and 6–10; Sunday brunch 10:45–2 (reservations requested, ext. 1002). Courtyard at Crane open 11–4 daily, 5:30–9 Sunday through Thursday. The elite historic hotel offers several dining options, including the **Grand Dining Room** and the **Courtyard at Crane.** The palatial Grand Dining Room in the main hotel offers lunch with appetizers, soups, salads, sandwiches, and specialties, while dinner features seafood, duck, pork, chicken, quail, and beef dishes. Jackets are requested for gentlemen at the evening meal. The Grand Dining Room's Sunday Brunch features seafood, meats, pâtés, cheeses, breads, omelets, entrées that change weekly, and a dessert buffet. The **Courtyard at Crane** is located adjacent to the hotel in one of the restored "cottages," now used as additional lodging. The cuisine there is Mediterranean influenced with Spanish and Moroccan specialties. Alfresco dining in the courtyard is a popular option. Lunch features salads, seafood, burgers, sandwiches, and chicken. Dinner choices include salads, chicken, steak, veal, lobster, pastas, steaks, and vegetarian entrées. In addition, the hotel offers casual dining at **Café Solterra** and **Vincent's Pub** (see *Eating Out*). No smoking. Wheelchair accessible. Grand Dining Room: $15–25; Sunday brunch $21.95 for adults, $10.95 for children younger than 12. Courtyard at Crane: $15–25.

In St. Marys

& **Borrell Creek Landing** (912-673-6300), 1101 US 40 East. Open 11:30–2:30 and 5–10 weekdays. The restaurant is noted for a variety of entrées, many of which feature steaks and seafood, and a view of the creek. No smoking. Wheelchair accessible. Lunch $6–12, dinner $15–34.

On St. Simons Island

& **Barbara Jean's** (912-634-6500; www.barbara-jeans.com), 214 Mallory Street. Open 11–10 daily in summer; otherwise 11–9 Sunday through Thursday, 11–10 Friday and Saturday. The restaurant features Southern dining specializing in signature crab dishes. In fact, the restaurant's motto is, "If you don't have anything else, try the crab cakes!" These Eastern Shore of Maryland–style crabcakes are prepared different ways and in different sizes. You can have them as appetizers, on sandwiches, or as an entrée. Numerous other kinds of seafood are offered along with meat loaf, pot roast, turkey, pork chops, chicken, steaks, homemade soups, sandwiches, and desserts. No smoking. Wheelchair accessible. $8–20.

& **Chelsea Restaurant** (912-638-2047; www.chelsea-ssi.com), 1226 Ocean Boulevard. Open from 5:30 PM daily; reservations recommended. A warm ambience and delicious food combine to create a memorable evening. Menu choices range from rack of lamb to a variety of fresh seafood, crepes, pasta, steaks, chicken, and prime rib. No smoking. Wheelchair accessible. $9–35; early dinner specials 5:30–6:30 $11.95.

& **George's Mediterranean Café** (912-634-9633), 228 Redfern Village. Open 11–2 and 5–10 daily. George's boasts a cuisine that is primarily Greek with French and Italian influ-

ences. Luncheon choices include a vast array of appetizers, soups, salads, pitas, and pasta. Dinner entrées range from moussaka to filet and lobster tail, and include many chicken, lamb, veal, and seafood choices. No smoking. Wheelchair accessible. Lunch $5.95–17.95, dinner $13.95–22.95.

& **Halyard's** (912-638-9100; www.halyardsrestaurant.com), Shops at Sea Island, Sea Island Road, Suite 19. Open 6–10 Monday through Saturday. Superbly prepared and presented island cuisine ranges from Maine lobster to prime New York strip steak. The restaurant is also renowned for its exceptional service and good wine list. No smoking. Wheelchair accessible. $18–35.

✐ & **The King and Prince Beach and Golf Resort** (912-638-3631, ext. 5321; www.kingandprince.com), 201 Arnold Road. Open 7–10 daily; 11–3 Monday through Saturday; 5–10 daily, Friday seafood buffet 5–9; Sunday brunch 11–2. An island tradition for more than 70 years, the oceanfront hotel's restaurant offers three meals daily as well as special buffets on Friday and Sunday. The Friday-night seafood buffet features more than 30 items, including authentic low-country boil, a vast variety of other seafood, and a "cornucopia of decadent desserts." The gargantuan Sunday-brunch buffet features a seafood table, a complete breakfast buffet, cooked-to-order omelets and Belgian waffles, a carving station with four meats, and desserts galore. No smoking. Wheelchair accessible. Daily breakfast buffet $9.95, lunch $17.95, dinner $27.95; Friday-night seafood buffet $21.95 (children's menu available); Sunday brunch buffet $17.95 for adults, $8.95 for children 7–12.

In Brunswick

✍ 🍴 ♿ **Spanky's Seafood Bar and Grill** (Marshside location 912-267-6100; Mallside location 912-554-0222), Marshside location, 1200 Glynn Avenue; Mallside location, 704 Mall Boulevard. Marshside location open 11–9 Sunday through Thursday, 11–10:30 Friday and Saturday; Mallside location open 10:30–10 Sunday through Thursday, 11–11 Friday and Saturday. Spanky's offers a wide variety of appetizers, stews, salads, chicken dishes, hot dogs, burgers, stackers, steaks, and seafood platters served all day in a casual atmosphere. The Marshside location offers one of the best views in the Golden Isles. Smoking outdoors only. Wheelchair accessible. $5.95–17.95.

In Folkston

✍ ♿ **Okefenokee Restaurant** (912-496-3263), South Second Street. Open 6:30 AM–9 PM Monday through Saturday. Local folks gather here for batter-fried bacon and catfish dinners and other real Southern home cooking. Out-of-towners are always impressed by the large portions and reasonable prices. Breakfast and lunch are served, and there is a buffet dinner featuring steaks, seafood, and freshwater fish. No smoking. Wheelchair accessible. Breakfast $3.50–4.75, lunch $6.99–10, dinner $10–15.

On Jekyll Island

✍ 🍴 ♿ **Café Solterra** (912-635-2500; www.jekyllclub.com), 371 Riverview Drive. Open 8 AM–10 PM daily. For casual dining at the Jekyll Island Club Hotel, the café serves muffins and pastries, deli sandwiches, soups, and pizza. Also at the hotel, Vincent's Pub serves cocktails and light fare from 5:30 until late night. No smoking. Wheelchair accessible. $7–15.

In St. Marys

✍ 🍴 ♿ **Riverside Café** (912-882-3466; www.riversidecafe.com), 106 St. Marys Street. Open 7:30 AM–9 PM Monday through Saturday. Located on the waterfront in the historic district, the restaurant serves three meals daily. Luncheon choices include homemade soups, pita and other sandwiches, and a wide variety of salads. Dinner from the grill includes charbroiled steaks and lamb chops. Smoking outdoors only. Wheelchair accessible. Breakfast $1.95–8.95, lunch $5.95–9.95, dinner $5.95–16.95.

On St. Simons

✍ 🍴 ♿ **The 4th of May Café and Deli** (912-638-5444; www.saintsimons.com/4thofmay), 444 Ocean Boulevard at Mallory Street. Open 7 AM–1 PM daily. Get your day off to a good start with eye-opening omelets, breakfast burritos, griddle goodies, and à la carte items. If you don't want to get up and get dressed to come in, delivery is available. There are different luncheon specials daily as well as seafood, salads, deli sandwiches, fresh-baked breads, home-cooked vegetables, and desserts. There's a children's menu, too. No smoking. Wheelchair accessible. $2.95–6.95 for breakfast, $2.75–12.95 for lunch.

✳ Entertainment

GAMBLING CRUISES **Emerald Princess II Casino Cruises** (912-265-3558; 1-800-842-0115; www.emeraldprincesscasino.com), One GISCO Point Drive, Brunswick. Cruises at 7 PM Monday through Thursday, 11 AM and 7 PM Friday through Sunday. Reservations are preferred, guests must be at least 18 years old. Passengers can enjoy a light meal and gambling. Once the boat reaches international waters, gamblers can choose from blackjack, stud poker, slot machines, and roulette. Free 15-minute lessons are provided prior to the casino opening. $10 (higher on holidays and for special events).

THEATER The Island Players (912-638-3031; www.theislandplayers.com), 1409 Newcastle Street, Brunswick. Call for a schedule of performances and ticket prices. Local thespians present live productions year-round at the theater. Children's theater and camps also are offered.

Ritz Theater (912-262-6934; www .goldenislesarts.org), 1530 Newcastle Street, Brunswick. Call for a schedule of productions and prices. Live productions with local, regional, national, and international artists are performed year-round at this renovated theater in Old Town Brunswick. Art exhibits also are staged. Built in 1898 as the Grand Opera House, the structure also houses shops and offices.

✳ Selective Shopping

ANTIQUES A. Clark Antiques (912-882-1801; www.aclarkantiques.com), 314 Osborne Street, St. Marys. Open "weekdays sometimes, weekends whenever," so call ahead. The Archibald Clark House, which was built in 1801 and is the oldest house in St. Marys, serves as the home of A. Clark Antiques. The house has been lived in by only two families and was the home of the current owner's great-great-great-grandfather. The upscale shop carries Toby mugs, pewter, Blue Willow, Wedgwood, cut glass, transferware, Majolica, and much more.

BOOKS Jekyll Books and Antiques (912-635-2080), 101 Old Plantation Road, Jekyll Island. Open 9:30–5:30 daily. The shop offers new and used books, antiques, collectibles, and gift items, as well as an opportunity to see Furness Cottage, one of the cottages in the Jekyll Island National Historic Landmark District (see *Villages*). It was once used as the infirmary building.

GIFTS Jekyll Island Museum Gift Shop (912-635-4168), 100 Stable Road, Jekyll Island. Open 9–5 daily. The shop, located in the Jekyll Island History Center (see *To See—Museums*), carries quality reproduction historical gifts.

OTHER GOODS Santa's Christmas Shoppe (912-635-3804), 17-A Pier Road, Jekyll Island. Open 9:30–5:30 daily. The year-round emporium offers a wide variety of fine gifts, holiday decorations, and name-brand collectibles such as Christopher Radko, Byers' Choice, Fontanini nativities, and Possible Dreams.

✳ Special Events

August: **Georgia Sea Island Festival** (912-638-8549; www.ssafrican amerheritage.org). Enjoy Gullah and Geechee craft demonstrations, a live performance by the famed Georgia Sea Island Singers, native Georgia cuisine, and more at this event on St. Simons Island. Free.

September: **Catfish Festival** (1-800-433-0225; www.visitkingsland.com/festivals.html). The annual Labor Day weekend festival in Kingsland features crispy, Southern-fried, and Cajun catfish and other foods; country music; entertainment by nationally known artists; a parade; arts and crafts; a children's amusement area; a classic car and tractor exhibition; and other activities. Free; some activities have a small charge.

October: **Brunswick Rockin' Stewbilee** (1-800-933-2627; www.brunswickstewbilee.com). Held in Brunswick's Mary Ross Park, the event is a Brunswick stew cook-off. In addition, the festival features a concert by one or more nationally known groups ($25 in advance, $35 at the gate), Pooch Parade, antique car show, and children's activities. Walking tours of the historic district are also available: $15–20; no tour tickets sold day of festival. Festival free.

Colonial Coast Birding and Nature Festival (912-882-4000; 1-800-868-8687; www.coastalgeorgiabirding.org). Participants see how many species they can spot in a one-day period. During the festival in St. Marys there are exhibitions by vendors and conservation groups, children's activities, arts and crafts, and a raptor show. Festival free; some activities have a small charge.

Okefenokee Festival (www.visitkingsland.com/festivals.html#FEST). The festival, held at the old train depot in Folkston, features a parade, entertainment, food, arts and crafts, and a street dance. Festival free; some activities have a small charge.

DARIEN AND THE COAST

Being sandwiched as it is between Savannah and the Golden Isles, the unsung Georgia coast is full of treasures that are often overlooked by travelers but well worth the effort to seek out and explore. Georgia has 100 miles of coastline on the Atlantic Ocean, but if bays, islands, and river mouths are counted, the state boasts 2,344 miles of coastline. Soldiers, sailors, Native Americans, timber barons, and even pirates once flourished here, as did forts and rice plantations.

The coast, where the serene and natural surroundings promote a slower pace of life, is dotted with small towns (see *Villages*), historic sites, picturesque waterfronts, shopping enclaves, myriad seafood restaurants, and accommodations that vary from campgrounds to bed & breakfasts to chain hotels. Nature lovers find deserted stretches of beach, marsh, or forest where they are the only inhabitants besides the turtles, alligators, or shorebirds. Historians can trace the events of colonial days, the American Revolution, the Civil War and Sherman's March to the Sea, and postwar and turn-of-the-20th-century African American history. The Gullah-Geechee culture, that of descendants of freed plantation slaves, survives on Sapelo Island.

Quaint shrimp boats line the waterfronts, and area restaurants serve freshly caught shrimp, oysters, fish, crab, and other delicacies of the sea prepared from favorite regional recipes. Barbecue and other traditional Southern cuisine also are prominently featured. During the shrimp season, fresh sweet Georgia shrimp can be purchased from local markets.

GUIDANCE For information about Darien and Eulonia, contact the **McIntosh County Chamber of Commerce–Welcome Center** (912-437-6684; www .mcintoshcounty.com), 105 Fort King George Drive, Darien 31305. Open 9–5 Monday through Saturday. The welcome center is located in a park right on the waterfront where shrimp boats dock. Picnic facilities and public fishing docks are available.

To find out more about Hinesville and Midway, consult the **Liberty County Chamber and Development Authority** (912-368-4445; 1-888-384-9814; www.libertycounty.org), 500 East Oglethorpe Highway, Hinesville 31313. Open 9–5 weekdays.

To learn more about Ellabelle and Richmond Hill, contact **Bryan County** (912-653-3819; www.bryancountyga.com), 116 Lanier Street, Pembroke 31321.

For more specific information about Richmond Hill, contact the **Richmond Hill Convention and Visitors Bureau** (912-756-2676; 1-800-807-4848; www.richmondhillcvb.org), 85 Richard R. Davis Drive, Richmond Hill 31324. Open 8:30–5 weekdays. Stop by the **Richmond Hill Local Welcome Center** (912-756-3697; 1-800-807-4848; www.richmondhillcvb.org), GA 144 and Timber Trail Road, Richmond Hill 31324. Open 10–4 Monday through Saturday.

To learn more about Sapelo Island, consult the **Sapelo Island Visitors Center** (912-437-3224; www.sapelonerr.org), One Landing Road, Meridian 31319. Open 7:30–5:30 Tuesday through Friday, 7:30–8:30 Saturday, 7:30–5:30 Sunday.

GETTING THERE *By air:* The closest airports to this region are Brunswick Golden Isles Airport (see Brunswick chapter), Savannah/Hilton Head International Airport (see Savannah chapter), and Jacksonville International Airport in Florida (see Brunswick chapter). All offer rental cars.

By bus: **Greyhound Lines** (912-876-3855), 1112 West Oglethorpe Avenue, Hinesville. Otherwise, the nearest stops are in Savannah or Brunswick (see those chapters).

By car: Travel up and down the Georgia coast is easy. For the quickest route, use I-95; for the most scenic route, use US 17.

By train: **Amtrak** (1-800-USA-RAIL) stops in Jesup (176 Northwest Broad Street), Savannah (see Savannah chapter), and Jacksonville, Florida (see Brunswick chapter).

GETTING AROUND A car is necessary to explore this region—either your own or a rental. Rental cars are available in Savannah, Brunswick, and Jacksonville, Florida, if you arrive in any of those cities by air, bus, or train (see Savannah and Brunswick chapters). Rental cars are available in Darien from **Lilliston Ford** (912-437-6602).

MEDICAL EMERGENCY In life-threatening situations, call 911. For other urgent care in this region, help is available at **Liberty Regional Medical Center** (912-369-9400), 462 Elma G. Miles Parkway, Hinesville. Other nearby hospitals are in Savannah and Brunswick (see those chapters).

VILLAGES The area that became **Darien** began humbly as the home of Guale (pronounced Wally) Indians. The Spaniards briefly had a mission there called Santo Domingo de

GEORGIA HAS 100 MILES OF COASTLINE ON THE ATLANTIC OCEAN.

Talaje. When the English and Scottish Highlanders arrived, they built Fort King George (see *To See—Historic Homes and Sites*) in 1736—just three years after Savannah and the colony of Georgia were founded. In fact, Darien is the second-oldest planned town in Georgia. Darien eventually became a major seaport on the East Coast and the Southeast's foremost exporter of lumber, a title it retained until 1925, when the industry died due to overcutting. Today, commercial fishing and forestry are the area's largest employers.

Noted primarily as the home of Fort Stewart, **Hinesville** has a revitalized downtown with restaurants and specialty shops. Manufacturing companies, which purvey everything from wrapping paper to sportswear, offer outlet prices.

Originally called Ways Station, **Richmond Hill** was in the center of rice plantation country. These plantations, which were heavily dependent on slave labor, were ravaged at the end of the Civil War by Sherman's troops, which destroyed the area's economic livelihood and residents' way of life. The desperate years from 1865 to 1925 were mostly noted for malaria and moonshine. Then Henry Ford and his wife, Clara, decided to build a winter retreat on the site of the former Richmond Plantation. The philanthropist, who eventually owned 85,000 acres, also constructed a sawmill, drained the swamps, and subsidized health care. He started the first kindergarten and built schools, a church, commissary, trade school, community house, and homes for 600 employees. Along with Thomas Edison and Harvey Firestone, he formed the Edison Botanic Society and attempted to transform agricultural products into goods for the auto industry. Ford Farms changed the former rice plantations into truck gardens, which produced iceberg lettuce and 365 varieties of soybeans. The town was renamed Richmond Hill in 1941.

Georgia's fourth-largest barrier island, **Sapelo Island** is rich in human history. Located 5 miles off the mainland, it was inhabited by Paleo-Indians as long as 4,000 years ago. They left several shell middens, including a shell ring 15 feet high and 200 feet in diameter. The ruins of a French plantation known as Chocolate, which was built more than 200 years ago, also remain. In the early 1800s, Thomas Spalding introduced plantations that cultivated Sea Island cotton, corn, and sugar cane. These plantations were dependent on the labor of 400 slaves imported from Charleston and the West Indies, so the island has significant African American history and culture. Freed slaves from the island's plantations found peace in isolated communities such as Hog Hammock—a 434-acre area deeded to African Americans by Spalding—where the Gullah culture is still rich today. Their culture, customs, and songs have been preserved along with the unique Geechee or Gullah language, a Creole form of pidgin English.

Several other white men have added to the island's history. Howard Coffin, the founder of the Hudson Motor Company, bought Sapelo and renovated and enlarged the Spalding home, adding both indoor and outdoor swimming pools and a bowling alley. Beginning in 1934, R. J. Reynolds, tobacco magnate of the Reynolds Tobacco Company, owned the island for more than 30 years and conducted agricultural experimentation. He established the Sapelo Island Research Foundation in 1949 and donated a portion of the island to the University of Georgia to use as a marine research laboratory. In 1969, the northern part of the island was sold to the state and became a wildlife refuge, while the southern part was acquired by the state and the National Oceanic and Atmospheric Administration for the Sapelo Island National Estuarine Research Reserve. Today the island's pine and hardwood forests, salt marsh, and 2 miles of wide beach are protected from development, and the newly restored lighthouse is once again wearing its original red-and-white-striped pattern. Sapelo Island is reached only by ferry from Meridian (see **Sapelo Island Visitor Center** under *To See—Guided Tours*).

✳ To See

FOR FAMILIES ✍ ✿ ♿ **Cay Creek Wetlands Interpretive Center** (912-884-3344), Charlie Butler Road, Midway. Open 8–4 weekdays. The area is an excellent example of tidal, freshwater wetlands, with several different ecosystems amid sites that are either permanently wet or alternate between wet and dry conditions. A variety of trees, birds, mammals, reptiles, amphibians, and insects make their homes here. The center offers only trails at this time, but a boardwalk and an interpretive center are in the planning stages. Free.

GUIDED TOURS ✍ ♿ **Harris Neck Cultural and Eco Tours** (912-437-7821; www.mcintoshseed.org), P.O. Box 2355, Darien. Call for a schedule and tour prices. Heritage and history tours focus on the African American community of Harris Neck (now a wildlife refuge).

✍ ✿ **Nature and Historic Tours** (912-437-6985; www.opengatesbnb.com), 301 Franklin Street, Darien. Tours by appointment only. Nature tours concentrate on the Altamaha River, marshlands, and isolated islands. $30 per hour for up to six people.

✍ ♿ **Sapelo Island Visitor Center–Sapelo Island Reserve and Reynolds Mansion** (mainland visitor center 912-437-3224; park 912-485-2299; www.gastateparks.org/info/sapelo), visitor center, One Landing Road, Meridian. Visitor center open 7:30–5:30 Tuesday through Friday, 8–5:30 Saturday, 1:30–5 Sunday; public tours 8:30–12:30 Wednesday (mansion and island) and 9–1 Saturday (lighthouse and island), September through May; additional tours 8:30–12:30 Friday (lighthouse and island), June through August; extended tours 8:30–3 last Tuesday of the month (lighthouse, mansion, and island), March through October. Transportation to the island is by a 30-minute ferry ride through tidal creeks and marshes for those on guided tours only; reservations required for tours, Reynolds Mansion, and camping. Nature trails are available at the visitor center. The island boasts a beach boardwalk, nature trail, and wildlife observation tower. Popular activities include fishing, bird-watching, beach-combing, hiking, and kayaking. The reserve is a 6,100-acre coastal plain estuary protected on its seaward side by a 16,006-acre Pleistocene barrier island.

The newly restored lighthouse was built in 1820 to serve as a guide for mariners transiting Doboy Sound to and from the port of Darien. It was in service until 1905. After years of neglect, it was restored in 1998 with its original red-and-white-striped day mark and is once again working as an aid to navigation. Visitors can climb to the top for a view of the island and see exhibits in the oil house. For more information about the lighthouse, refer to www.lighthousefriends.com.

Accommodations for individual travelers are offered in private cottages not associated with the state park. Accommodations at the Reynolds Mansion and a pioneer campground are available for groups only. Note: Insect repellent is recommended spring through fall. $10 for guided tour, which includes ferry fee of $1 each way.

✇ ♿ **Spirit of Sapelo Tours** (912-485-2170; www.georgiacoast.com), Sapelo Island. Call for reservations and fees (tour fees are in addition to ferry fee to reach the island). The company, operated by descendants of slaves, offers three-hour tours of the island, including their community of Hog Hammock, aboard handicapped-accessible minibuses. Hog Hammock, 434 acres deeded to them by Thomas Spalding, was named for Sampson Hog, who served as caretaker of the Spalding hogs. Picnic lunches and hayrides can be arranged for an additional fee.

HISTORIC HOMES AND SITES ✇ ❀ **Dorchester Academy National Historic Site** (912-884-2347), US 84, Midway. Open 11–2 Tuesday through Friday, 2–4 Saturday. The academy was founded after the Civil War as a school for freed slaves. By 1917, it was accredited and had eight buildings and 300 students. The academy ceased to function as a school in the 1940s; the remaining Georgian Revival building now serves as a community center and museum. Dr. Martin Luther King Jr. prepared here for the 1963 Birmingham campaign. Special events include a Black Expo and A Day at Old Dorchester. Free.

✇ ❀ ♿ **Fort King George Historic Site** (912-437-4770; www.gastateparks .org/info/ftkinggeorge), One Fort King George Drive, Darien. Open 9–5 Tuesday through Saturday, 2–5:30 Sunday. From 1721 to 1736, this small Altamaha River fort garrisoned by His Majesty's Independent Company was the southernmost outpost of the British Empire in North America. At the palisaded earthen fort, soldiers endured hardships from disease, threats from the Spanish and Native Americans, and the harsh environment. Eventually the fort was abandoned, but then General James Oglethorpe, founder of Georgia, brought Scottish Highlanders to the site in 1736. They called the settlement Darien. The fort and several buildings are reconstructions built using old records and drawings. Remains of three sawmills and tabby (oyster-shell cement) ruins are visible. The interpretive center has a film that traces the history of the area. Numerous special events during the year include living-history demonstrations, battle reenactments, walking tours, Scottish Heritage Days in March, **Winter Muster and Candle Lantern Tour** in November, and **Drums along the Altamaha,** also in November (see *Special Events*). Adults $5, seniors $4.50, children $2.50.

✇ ❀ ♿ **Fort McAllister State Historic Park** (912-727-2339; 1-800-864-7275; www.gastateparks.org/info/ftmcallister; www.fortmcallister.org), 3894 Fort McAllister Road, Richmond Hill. Park open 7–10 daily; museum open 8–5. Noted for the best preserved sand and mud earthwork fortifications surviving from the Confederacy, the 1,725-acre park is located on the south bank of the Great Ogeechee River. The fort was attacked seven times by Union forces but withstood these assaults until it was captured in 1864 by Union General William

Tecumseh Sherman at the end of his infamous March to the Sea. Henry Ford once owned the site and was instrumental in restoring it in the 1930s. The new Civil War museum inside the visitor center is designed to resemble a bombproof and contains Civil War exhibits, artifacts relating to many periods in the fort's history, a video for viewing, and a gift shop. A covered outdoor display is dedicated to the recovered artifacts of the CSS *Nashville*, a blockade runner that was sunk in the Ogeechee River. There is a well-developed and signed nature trail through the Redbird Creek area. To learn more about the park's recreational facilities, see *Green Space—Nature Preserves and Parks*. Accommodations are available at campgrounds and cottages (see *Lodging—Campgrounds* and *Lodging—Cottages and Cabins*). $2.50–4; parking fee $3.

✐ ✿ ᕹ **Fort Morris State Historic Site** (912-884-5999; 1-800-864-7275; www .gastateparks.org/info/ftmorris; www.fortmorris.org), 2559 Fort Morris Road, Midway. Open 9–5 Tuesday through Saturday, 2–5:30 Sunday. The principal attraction at this 70-acre park is the historic fort, but there is also a 1-mile nature trail, part of the Colonial Coast Birding Trail. The importance of the site was apparent from the time of the Continental Congress in 1776. The participants saw the strategic advantage of protecting the growing seaport of Sunbury from the British, so the bluff on the Medway River was fortified and garrisoned by a small group of patriots. When the British first tried to get the fort to surrender, Colonel John McIntosh is reported to have replied, "Come and take it!" Although the British withdrew at that time, they returned 45 days later and captured the fort. Later renamed Fort Defiance, it was used during the War of 1812 and the Civil War. Today earthworks remain, and the visitor center offers a film called *Sunbury Sleeps*. Exhibits chronicle the history of the fort, military and civilian life from the colonial to antebellum periods, and the lost town of Sunbury. A trail leads to the cemetery, which is the only vestige of the once bustling town. Firing of period weapons is often demonstrated. Special events feature reenactments with costumed interpreters, including an **Independence Day Colonial Fair** on July Fourth and **"Come and Take It!"** in November (see *Special Events*). $1.50–2.50.

✐ ✿ **LeConte Woodmanston National Historic Place** (912-884-6500; www .libertytrail.com), off US 17 on Barrington Ferry Road, Midway. Call for hours; closed December through mid-February; special tours by appointment. Once the home of Dr. Louis LeConte, the property was one of the state's first inland-swamp rice plantations and is now a nature preserve. Its once world-famous 18th-century gardens are being re-created with heirloom plants. Visitors can see the cypress forest, stroll the Avenue of Oaks, and walk the interpretive trail through the Bulltown Swamp blackwater ecosystem. Adults $2.

✿ **Midway National Historic District** (912-884-5837), Martin Road, Midway. Cemetery open at all times; museum open 10–4 Tuesday through Saturday, 2–4 Sunday. The 18th-century district contains a church built in 1792, a museum in a raised cottage (see *Museums*), and a cemetery. The simple white-frame New England–style church served as Union General William Tecumseh Sherman's cavalry foraging headquarters during the Civil War. The cavalrymen plundered area plantations and corralled animals in the cemetery. Among the 1,200 graves are those of two Revolutionary War generals (one was Daniel Stewart, the great-grandfather of Theodore Roosevelt) and a state governor. The cemetery, which was laid out in the 1750s, also is reputed to house the ghost of a slave. To this day, the church has no heating system or artificial lights. Special events in the Midway Historic District include a church service on the last Sunday in April and an annual Christmas tea at the museum. (Note: Visitors can obtain a key for the church from the museum or from the service station across the street from the church.) Adults $3, students $1.

✦ ✹ ♿ **Seabrook Village** (912-884-7008), 660 Trade Hill Road, Midway. Open 10–5 Tuesday through Saturday and by appointment. The remnants of this African American village contain eight turn-of-the-20th-century buildings, including a one-room school that operated from 1895 to 1940. Costumed living-history interpreters are on hand only for groups of 15 or more or for special events. During these times, visitors are presented with aspects of old-time village life through interactive activities such as grinding corn or washing using a scrub board. Walking tours $5 for adults.

MUSEUMS ✦ ✹ ♿ **Fort Stewart Military Museum** (912-767-7885; www .stewart.army.mil), Building T904, 2022 Frank Cochran Drive, Hinesville. Open 10–4 Tuesday through Saturday. Group tours are given on request. The museum traces the history of the fort—the largest military post east of the Mississippi River—from its inception in 1940 to the present, as well as presenting the story of the Third Infantry Division (Mechanized), which makes its home there. Changing exhibits feature objects from World War I, World War II, the Korean War, Desert Storm, and current military activities. Note: Due to heightened security, visitors are required to stop at the main gate and provide proof of auto registration, insurance, and a driver's license to receive a visitor's pass. Free.

✹ **Midway Museum** (912-884-5837), US 17, Midway. Open 10–4 Tuesday through Saturday, 2–4 Sunday. The museum, which is located in a typical 18th-century raised plantation cottage, contains documents and exhibits as well as furniture and art typical of early coastal homes from colonial days to the Civil War. The museum's gift shop carries a good selection of books about local history. Adults $3, students $1.

THE HISTORIC MIDWAY CHURCH WAS BUILT IN 1792.

✹ **Richmond Hill Historical Society and Museum** (912-756-3697; 1-800-807-4848; www.richmondhill cvb.org), GA 144 and Timber Trail Road, Richmond Hill. Open 10–4 Monday through Saturday. Housed in the old Ford kindergarten building, the museum's exhibits focus on Henry

Ford's development of the town of Richmond Hill with photographs, displays, and artifacts. Other exhibits depict the plantation era. A one-room schoolhouse and country store of the early 1900s are re-created. Free, but donations accepted.

SCENIC DRIVES ✐ ❦ **The Historic Liberty Trail** (www.libertytrail.com). The driving tour offers history, culture, and ecology. Beginning at exit 76 on I-95, the trail has nine major attractions: the Midway National Historic District, Dorchester Academy National Historic Place, LeConte Woodmanston National Historic Place, Seabrook Village, Fort Morris State Historic Site, Melon Bluff birding trail (see *To Do—Birding*), Cay Creek Wetlands Interpretive Center (see *To See—For Families*), Fort Stewart Museum (see *To See—Museums*), (see *To See—Historic Homes and Sites* for all) and Sunbury Cemetery. A map is available on the web site.

SPECIAL PLACES ✐ ❦ ♿ **Smallest Church in America** (912-832-5922), US 17, Eulonia. Open daily. Services are held the third Sunday of each month at this diminutive church, which is only 10 feet wide by 15 feet long and seats only 12. Little larger than a child's playhouse, albeit with stained-glass windows from England, the church was built in 1949. Mrs. Agnes Harper wanted it to serve as a place of meditation and rest for weary travelers. Free.

WALKS ✐ ❦ **"A Tour Highlighting Historic Sites, Trees, and Bike Path"–Historic Darien Walking Tours** (912-437-6684; www.mcintoshcounty .com), 105 Fort King George Drive, Darien. The free brochure, which is available at the Welcome Center (see *Guidance*), describes a self-guided tour of the scenic waterfront, historic squares, and important landmarks. The brochure also describes the 7-mile pedestrian-biking trail, which stretches to Fort King George Historic Site.

✴ To Do

BALLOONING ✐ **Feather Air Hot-Air Balloons** (912-858-2529; 1-888-277-5819; www.feather-air.com), 4326 Wilma Edwards Road, Ellabelle. Call for schedules, reservations, and prices. The company offers 45-minute to one-hour flights that float over 10 miles of country, field, and swamps.

BICYCLING ✐ ❦ ♿ **Darien Walking and Bike Paths.** A series of paths lined with Spanish moss–laden live oaks connect the downtown waterfront with Fort King George.

BIRDING ✐ ❦ **Devendorf Forested Flyways Birding Trail at Melon Bluff** (1-888-246-8188; www.melonbluff.com), off US 84, Midway. Open 9–4 daily, September 15 through May 15. Melon Bluff consists of 3,000 acres with 25 miles of grassy, forested trails and more than 300 species of birds, including some that are rare or endangered; birding is the prime attraction here. The 2.5-mile interpretive birding trail runs from the nature center through pine uplands, mixed hardwood forest, and swamps to Hidden Lake. Signs highlight various ecological concepts related to birds and forests. Hiking, biking, and accommodations are also offered (see **Melon Bluff Nature and Heritage Reserve** under *Green Space—Nature Preserves and Parks*). Day-use fee $3.

BOAT EXCURSIONS ✍ **Altamaha Coastal Tours** (912-437-6010; www.altamaha .com), 229 Fort King George Drive, Darien. Call for a schedule. Guided canoe and sea kayak tours are offered. Day trips $50, overnight trips $150.

BOATING ✍ **Fort McAllister Marina** (912-727-2632), 3203 Fort McAllister Road, Richmond Hill. Open 7–7 daily. The marina offers fishing charters and tours by the fort. There is a large boat show each year, too.

✍ **Ogeechee Outpost** (912-748-6716; www.ogeecheeoutpost.com), 182 Rose Drive, Ellabelle. Call for schedules, reservations, and prices. The company offers guided overnight trips, instruction, and canoe and kayak rentals.

DOLPHIN-WATCHING See Brunswick chapter for several companies that offer dolphin tours.

FISHING An abundance of rivers and proximity to the ocean have attracted anglers for years. Charter boats, public marinas and boat ramps, fishing piers and docks, bait and tackle shops, and guide services are available. Fishing licenses are required. (See the Fishing Appendix for inshore and offshore fishing charters.)

GOLF See Golf Appendix.

✳ Green Space

BEACHES Those on Blackbeard Island and Sapelo Island are among the most pristine in the state.

NATURE PRESERVES AND PARKS ✍ ❧ **Altamaha Waterfowl Management Area** (912-262-3173), US 17 South, Darien. Open daylight hours daily. Visitors can learn about the role of managed wetlands in the conservation of wildlife through the Ansley-Hodges M.A.R.S.H. Project. Free.

✍ ❧ **Blackbeard Island National Wildlife Refuge** (912-652-4415; www.fws.gov/ blackbeardisland), Alligator Alley, Blackbeard Island. Open sunrise–sunset daily. Blackbeard Island, which is accessible only by boat, serves as a preserve and breeding ground for wildlife and migratory birds. More than 3,000 acres are designated as a national wilderness area. The preserve is popular for bird-watching and wildlife observation, hiking along existing scenic trails and roads, and fishing in the saltwater creeks. Endangered species such as loggerhead sea turtles, American bald eagles, wood storks, and piping plovers are often seen here, along with large concentrations of waterfowl, wading birds, shorebirds, songbirds, raptors, deer, and alligators. Island free; fee for private ferry from Shellman Bluff on mainland.

✑ 🌱 **Butler Island Rice Plantation** (912-437-6684), US 17 South, Butler Island. Open daylight hours daily. Once one of the largest plantations in the South, the property was purchased by Captain Pierce Butler of Philadelphia to grow rice. He married famous British actress Fanny Kemble, who was horrified by the treatment of slaves when she visited the plantation. Her book, *Journal of a Residence on a Georgia Plantation*, is believed to have swayed the British to oppose slavery and the Civil War. The property is open for picnicking, fishing, and bird-watching. Free.

✑ 🌱 ♿ **Cay Creek Wetland Interpretive Center** (912-884-3344; www.liberty trail.com), 189 Charlie Butler Road, Midway. Open 8–4 weekdays. Paths along the marsh wetlands permit visitors to view native plants and various kinds of wildlife in several different ecosystems. Earthen berms are actually the remnants of dikes used when the area was a rice plantation. Plans are under way for a boardwalk and an interpretive center. Free.

✑ 🌱 ♿ **Darien Waterfront Park–Vernon Square** (912-437-6684; www .mcintoshcounty.com), Darien. Open daily. During the 19th century, this area was the commercial, cultural, social, and religious center of Darien. Today, the park is a popular place to come for biking, fishing, and picnicking. Free.

✑ 🌱 ♿ **Fort McAllister State Park** (912-727-2339; 1-800-864-7275; www.ga stateparks.org/info/ftmcallister), 3894 Fort McAllister Road, Richmond Hill. Park open 7 AM–10 PM daily; museum open 8–5. Giant live oaks and surrounding salt marsh create a quiet haven where visitors enjoy outdoor recreation. Boat ramps, a dock, and a fishing pier attract anglers, while hikers and bikers enjoy 4.3 miles of trails. Canoe and kayak rentals are available. $1.50–2.50; rentals additional.

✑ 🌱 ♿ **Harris Neck Wildlife Refuge** (912-832-4608; 912-652-4415), US 17 and Harris Neck Road, Eulonia. Open daylight hours daily; access by personal boat from public boat ramp on Barbour River at termination of GA 131 or through outfitter company tours (see, for example, **Harris Neck Cultural and Eco Tours** under *To See—Guided Tours*). Enjoy nature at this 2,762-acre preserve with salt marshes, grasslands, mixed deciduous forest, and cropland. Many species of birds can be observed, including hundreds of egrets, wood storks, and herons in the summer and ducks in the winter. There are 15 miles of paved roads and trails, a boat ramp and fishing pier, biking trails, and observation decks. Fishing in the tidal creeks is excellent. Free to individual visitors for self-guided tours and use; fees charged for guided tours.

✑ 🌱 ♿ **Melon Bluff Nature and Heritage Reserve** (912-884-5779; 1-888-246-8188; www.melonbluff.com), 2999 Islands Highway, Midway. Open 9–4

THE TREASURE OF BLACKBEARD ISLAND
Blackbeard Island was named for the infamous pirate Edward Teach, alias Blackbeard, who plied the waters off the coast of the Southeast. Rumor has it that some of his ill-gotten gains are buried here, but no trace of his booty has ever been found. Instead, the treasures of the island are pristine beaches and dunes, freshwater and salt marshes, maritime forests, and abundant wildlife.

daily, September 15 through May 15. This 3,000-acre, privately owned preserve is located on land that was once a rice plantation and is now in the heart of the Colonial Coast Birding Trail. Habitats, which range from salt marsh to woodlands and creek swamps, support a wide variety of birds and wildlife. Twenty-five miles of all-season unpaved trails crisscross the property. Biking, birding, hiking, and canoe and kayak expeditions are available. The nature center features exhibits and sponsors educational programs. The gift shop–bookstore also sells snacks and offers equipment rental. (See also **Devendorf Forested Flyways Birding Trail** under *To Do—Birding*.) No smoking, pets, alcohol, or firearms. Day-use fee $3; $15 per horse per day trail riding fee (for prearranged groups of 10 or more); other fees vary by activity.

RIVERS   **Altamaha River** (www.altamahariver.org). Dubbed one of the 75 "Last Great Places" in the world by the Nature Conservancy, the 100-mile river, which winds through cypress swamps and tidal marshes and empties into the sea near Darien, flows freely with no dams. The river's banks are dotted with boat ramps and landings, bait and tackle shops, and marked hiking trails for those who enjoy boating, fishing, water sports, and wildlife observation. The Altamaha River Canoe Trail Map is available on the web site.

Ogeechee River. Part of the 245-mile blackwater river, which begins in the Piedmont region, flows through the lower coastal plain and tidal marsh of this area before emptying into the sea at Ossabaw Sound. Wildlife often sighted includes raccoons, deer, otters, beavers, mink, water snakes, alligators, wading birds, wood storks, southern bald eagles, and occasionally manatees. The river is particularly popular with canoeists and anglers.

✳ Lodging
BED & BREAKFASTS

In Darien
Blue Heron Inn Bed and Breakfast (912-437-4304), One Blue Heron Lane. Located in a contemporary home at the edge of a marsh and tidal creek, the bed & breakfast offers four guest rooms with private baths, three floors of porches and decks from which to admire the scenery, a full breakfast, and afternoon wine and hors d'oeuvres. Blue Heron Inn offers the closest accommodations to Shellman Bluff and the ferry to Sapelo Island. No smoking. Not wheelchair accessible. $85–130.

Open Gates Bed and Breakfast (912-437-6985; www.opengatesbnb .com), 301 Franklin Street. The huge Victorian home overlooking historic Vernon Square was built in 1876 by a local timber baron. Today the home offers five guest rooms—four with private baths—each distinctively decorated. Overnight rates include evening wine and light hors d'oeuvres and a full Southern breakfast. Guests enjoy the elegant common rooms and the outdoor pool. No smoking. Not wheelchair accessible. $90–125.

In Eulonia
McIntosh Manor (912-832-3198; www.sapelomain.com), US 17. The eclectically furnished 1905 house provides a homey, comfortable ambience. Two of the guest rooms share a bath, which makes them desirable for a family or two couples traveling togeth-

er. The B&B's suite has a private bath. A full breakfast is served. No smoking. Limited wheelchair accessibility (one bedroom on first floor but steps to climb to get into house). $79.

In Midway

✒ ♿ **Palmyra Plantation Barn and Palmyra Plantation Cottage at Melon Bluff** (912-884-5779; 1-888-246-8188; www.melonbluff.com), 2999 Islands Parkway. Horses and mules were once housed in the barn along with corn in the corncrib, grain in the feed room, and hay in the second-story loft. Now the barn has been transformed into a comfortable B&B with nine guest rooms and suites decorated with country charm. The nightly rate for rooms in the Palmyra Plantation Barn includes a full breakfast, afternoon hors d'oeuvres, daily guest activities, free movies, and use of the pool, trails, and bikes, as well as admission to the Melon Bluff Nature and Heritage Reserve and discounts for kayaking. The 1840 cottage is ideal for two to six people in the same party. Meal and maid service are not included with stays in the cottage but can be arranged for an additional fee. No smoking; no pets; children 8 and older welcome. One room on first floor is wheelchair accessible. $150–225.

CAMPGROUNDS

In Darien
See Campgrounds Appendix.

In Richmond Hill
✒ 🐾 🐾 ♿ **Fort McAllister State Historic Park** (912-727-2339; 1-800-864-7275; www.gastateparks.org/info/ftmcallister), 3894 Fort McAllister Road. Located amid giant live oaks and alongside a beautiful salt marsh, camping facilities include 65 tent,

trailer, and RV sites with water and electric hookups as well as backcountry primitive campsites and a pioneer campground. Amenities include two comfort stations with toilets, heated showers, and laundry facilities; a playground; and a dock and boat ramp. Campers have access to all the park's amenities. $17–25.

✒ 🐾 ♿ **WaterWay RV Park** (912-756-2296), US 17 at Kingferry Bridge. Located on the banks of the Ogeechee River, the campground offers a boat ramp, a river dock, full hookups, two shower houses, laundry facilities, and a game room. $30.

COTTAGES AND CABINS

In Ellabelle
✒ 🐾 **Ogeechee Outpost Camping** (912-748-6716; www.ogeecheeoutpost.com), 182 Rose Drive. Cabin rentals include use of a boat or canoe. $50.

In Richmond Hill
✒ 🐾 **Fort McAllister State Historic Park** (912-727-2339; 1-800-864-7275; www.gastateparks.org/info/ftmcallister), 3894 Fort McAllister Road. The park offers three traditional cottages and new cottages on stilts with beautiful views of the sunrise and the salt marsh. $100–110.

✳ Where to Eat

DINING OUT In this laid-back area of the coast, few restaurants are so elegant they fit our definition of fine dining and, indeed, locals concur. Rather, there are dozens of popular casual eateries—many specializing in all types of seafood prepared a variety of ways. Using our price definition for fine dining entrées being more than $20, however, these restaurants fit the category.

In Crescent

⏴ ♿ **Pelican Point** (912-832-4295; www.pelicanpointseafood.com), Sapelo Avenue. Open 5–10 weekdays, 4–11 Saturday, noon–10 Sunday. A local favorite for 20 years, the restaurant overlooks the Sapelo River. The family's six shrimp boats are docked next door, guaranteeing the freshest, biggest, and highest-quality catch. The family also raises littleneck clams. Although diners can order from the à la carte menu, many prefer the enormous seafood buffet, which features a variety of seafood as well as prime rib and chicken, a 30-item salad bar, and a dessert station. There's entertainment in the piano bar on Friday and Saturday evenings. Smoking allowed. Wheelchair accessible. $16.95–23.95.

In Darien

⏴ 🍽 ♿ **Skipper's Fish Camp Restaurant and Oyster Bar** (912-437-FISH), 85 Screven Street. Open 11–9 daily. The fish-camp theme and open-air oyster bar set just the right tone for dining on local seafood like Georgia white shrimp and flounder, as well as steaks and slow-smoked barbecue ribs, while enjoying the views of the Darien River. No smoking. Wheelchair accessible. $11–24.95.

In Eulonia

⏴ ♿ **Sapelo Station Crossing** (912-832-3555; www.sapelostation.com), US 17. Open 11–3 Tuesday through Friday, 5:30–9:30 Wednesday through Saturday. Although the restaurant has linen tablecloths and napkins, it is still casual. The menu features steaks, fresh seafood, and Italian-inspired dishes. Lunch items include salads and sandwiches. Live entertainment is often offered on Friday and Saturday evenings (call ahead to see if anyone is playing and if there is a cover

charge). No smoking. Wheelchair accessible. $14–25.

In Hinesville

⏴ ♿ **Elrod's of Hinesville** (912-368-5444), 137 West Hendry Street, Suite #8. Open 11–2 weekdays, 5–10 Monday through Saturday. At this casual eatery, lunch choices include sandwiches, salads, and chicken fingers. Menu items for dinner include mahimahi, strip steak, and T-bone steaks. No smoking in restaurant; smoking allowed in the bar. Wheelchair accessible. Lunch $8.95–10.95, dinner $10–30.

In Midway

⏴ 🍽 ♿ **Shrimp Docks at Sunbury** (912-884-6130; www.shrimpdocks .com), 138 Galley Lane. Open 5–10 Wednesday through Saturday; reservations accepted. The casual eatery overlooking the Medway River, Ossabaw Island, and St. Catherine's Island features po'boy sandwiches and all types of seafood as well as rib eye, New York strip, and filet mignon. No smoking. Wheelchair accessible. $11.95–22.95.

⏴ ♿ **Sunbury Crab Company** (912-884-8640), 541 Brigantine Dunmore Road. Open 5–10 Wednesday through Friday, noon–midnight Saturday and Sunday. Overlooking the Medway River and exuding a Key West atmosphere, the restaurant features specialties like crabcakes, crab stew, burgers, and Cuban sandwiches. No smoking. Wheelchair accessible. Lunch $6.95, dinner $24.95.

In Richmond Hill

⏴ ♿ **Steamers Restaurant and Raw Bar** (912-756-3979), 2518 US 17. Open 5–10 Monday through Thursday, 5–10:30 Friday and Saturday, 5–9 Sunday. Although it doesn't overlook the water, this popular eatery has a fish-camp ambience. In addition to a raw bar to die for, the restaurant offers all kinds of seafood, including local fish caught fresh every day, low-country boil, ribs, and more. No smoking. Wheelchair accessible. $7.95–29.95.

In Shellman Bluff

& **500 Marshview Restaurant** (912-832-4500), 500 Marshview Drive. Open 5–10 Tuesday through Saturday, 10–3 Sunday. Located at the Sapelo Hammock Golf Course near Eulonia, this white-linen restaurant provides a wonderful panoramic view of the 18th hole and the marsh. Among the menu options are local fresh fish, seafood, steaks, and lasagna. No smoking. Wheelchair accessible. $12–18.

EATING OUT

In Darien

✐ 🦐 & **B&J's Family Restaurant and Pizza Place** (912-437-2122), 901 North Street/US 17. Open 8–9 Monday through Saturday, 8–2:30 Sunday. This is where the locals go to eat. The eatery is noted for its breakfast, lunch, and dinner buffets—particularly the Saturday and Sunday buffets. No smoking. Wheelchair accessible. Breakfast $5.95, lunch $7, dinner $18.95–22.95.

In Midway

✐ 🦐 & **Holton's Seafood** (912-884-9151), 13711 US 84. Open 11–9 Sunday through Thursday, 11–10 Friday and Saturday. Don't pass up this unassuming eatery where the specialties are fried shrimp, coleslaw, and French silk pie. The restaurant also serves flounder, shrimp, scallops, oysters, and crab—many of which can be prepared boiled, broiled, or fried. No smoking. Wheelchair accessible. Lunch $5–10, Dinner $9–15.

In Townsend

✐ 🦐 & **Buccaneer Club** (912-832-5171), Buccaneer Club Road. Open 5–9:30 Tuesday through Thursday, 5–10:30 Friday and Saturday. This seafood restaurant is located on the banks of the Sapelo River near Eulonia, where diners can watch the picturesque shrimp boats come and go. The eatery takes its name from an old bar and private club that once stood on this spot. Menu choices range from burgers and steak to shrimp and crab. No smoking. Wheelchair accessible. $16–20.

✳ Entertainment

MUSIC **Hinesville Area Arts Council Series** (Call Pastor Alan Miller at the Hinesville First United Methodist Church, 912-368-2200; 912-368-2124). Call for a schedule of events and prices, which average $7. The council sponsors a series of performances at the Brewton Parker College Auditorium, 2140 East Oglethorpe Highway.

✳ Selective Shopping

For the most part, specialized shopping isn't part of life in these small towns. For out-of-the-ordinary shopping, residents go to Savannah, Brunswick, or the Golden Isles. Darien is an exception, as it has quaint shops and an outlet mall.

Historic Darien Shopping (912-437-6684; www.mcintoshcounty.com), US 17, Darien. Open 9–5 Monday through Saturday. The shops of the historic district contain antique and gift shops as well as a restaurant.

OUTLET MALLS **Georgia Islands Factory Shoppes** (912-437-8360; 888-545-7224; www.horizongroup

.com), One Magnolia Bluff Way, Darien. Open 10–8 Monday through Saturday, 11–6 Sunday. Located at I-95's exit 49, the outlet mall boasts more than 35 stores from Bass to Zales.

✳ Special Events

Spring: **Blessing of the Fleet Festival** (912-437-6684). Activities begin Friday with a parade, fish fry, and art festival in Darien. On Sunday morning, elaborately decorated boats parade by while clerics from several denominations bless them from the bridge as they pass. The weekend may occur in March, April, or May, so call for exact dates. Most activities free.

May: **Henry Ford Days Festival** (912-756-3697; www.forddaysfestival .com). The old-time festival in Richmond Hill features games, food, arts and crafts, concerts, a Civil War reenactment, and the Cruisin' the Hill Open Vehicle Show, Car Corral, and Swap Meet. A trolley takes visitors to the Ford plantation. Festival free; trolley and plantation tour $5, free for children younger than 10.

July: **Independence Day Colonial Fair** (912-884-5999). Held at Fort

DEMONSTRATIONS OF PERIOD WEAPONS ARE PART OF "COME AND TAKE IT!" HELD EACH NOVEMBER IN MIDWAY AT FORT MORRIS STATE HISTORIC SITE.

Morris State Historic Site in Midway, the celebration includes cannon and black-powder demonstrations, colonial games of skill, and reenactors. Free.

October: **Great Ogeechee Seafood Festival** (912-756-3444; 1-800-834-3960; www.goseafoodfestival.com). Held Friday evening through Sunday afternoon the third weekend in October, the Richmond Hill festival features great Southern seafood; arts and crafts; a carnival; a classic car show; and live entertainment from bands and pop singers, dancers, fencers, cheerleaders, and more. The finale features fireworks. $2–5.

November: **"Come and Take It!"** (912-884-5999). Colonial demonstrations, musket and cannon drills, a tactical skirmish, and costumed interpreters discussing soldier and civilian life pay homage to Fort Morris's role in the American Revolution. Held in Midway. $1.50–3.

Drums along the Altamaha (912-437-4770). This event at the Fort King George Historic Site in Darien features a battle reenactment, artillery and musket firings, baking and brewing demonstrations, arts and crafts, coastal maritime history, and Native American skills. Festival activities included with regular admission. (See **Fort King George Historic Site** under *To See—Historic Homes and Sites.*)

Winter Muster and Candle Lantern Tour (912-727-2339). At this event at Fort McAllister State Historic Park in Richmond Hill, you will learn about the last days of the fort before it was captured by Union forces. The battle begins at 4 PM and the tour at 6. Adults $4, seniors $3.50, children $2.50, plus regular $3 parking fee.

SAVANNAH AND TYBEE ISLAND

Savannah, literally Georgia's first city, is also known as the "Queen City of the South." This gracious town was wrenched from raw wilderness in 1733 when English General James Oglethorpe founded the colony of Georgia and its first settlement. A bluff overlooking the Savannah River upriver from the coast was chosen because it created a strategic buffer between South Carolina and the Spanish in northern Florida. Savannah served as the capital of the colony, then of the state, from 1733 to 1782 and prospered as a port city for the exportation of cotton.

One of Oglethorpe's greatest legacies was his city plan, which was laid out on a grid with 24 parklike squares, most of which remain to this day. The squares have burgeoned with now-mature live oak trees draped with gently swaying Spanish moss. Over the years, the city has added monuments and fountains as well as lush landscaping featuring azaleas, oleanders, and magnolias among other Southern favorites. These oases serve as resting and gathering places and are often the scenes of festivals and other events.

Around the squares, gracious neighborhoods of stately homes developed, some areas punctuated by majestic churches and genteel businesses. During the Civil War, Union General William Tecumseh Sherman captured the city at Christmastime in 1864 but refrained from destroying it. By contrast, in the 1950s, some of these structural treasures were being destroyed and disappearing at an alarming rate—being replaced by insignificant buildings in the name of "progress."

Fortunately, Savannah's citizens woke up to what they were losing, and preservationists banded together to save what was left. In 1966 a 2.2-square-mile area was designated as a National Landmark Historic District by the National Trust for Historic Preservation. Today this area remains one of the largest such districts in the country. More than 1,800 structures have been saved and restored, and they now serve as private homes, museum houses, inns, bed & breakfasts, and other businesses that attract scores of visitors.

The compact area and orderly arrangement of streets make Savannah a particularly easy walking city—another plus for tourism. In recent years, the cultlike following created by the fame of John Berendt's book *Midnight in the Garden of Good and Evil* (known locally and frequently referred to in this chapter as "the

Book") and the subsequent movie have brought thousands of new visitors to Savannah. Once there, they share the many charms of the state's fourth-largest city.

Many experts in the paranormal consider Savannah the most haunted city in America. Long-dead abandoned lovers, children who died before their time, Civil War and Revolutionary War soldiers, pirates, sailors, and yellow fever victims allegedly still populate Savannah. Because so many tourist attractions, restaurants, and lodgings are located in historic buildings, visitors are just as likely as not to encounter some of these spirits. Several tour companies offer trolley or walking tours that teach visitors about these restless spirits.

Located just 20 minutes away, off the coast of Savannah, is Tybee Island, where bathing suits, shorts, and flip-flops are de rigueur. With its 3 miles of pristine beach, the family-oriented beach is still lost in the '50s, although it gets posher every year. A low-key attitude, quaint rental cottages—many as old as 100 years—mom-and-pop motels, and casual eateries coupled with a lack of high rises and amusement parks create an appealing destination for a laid-back vacation for all ages. Sunbathing, all kinds of boating and water sports, surf fishing, sand-castle building, crabbing, shelling, and bird-watching are just a few of the delights awaiting visitors to this island paradise.

GUIDANCE There are several excellent sources of information about Savannah and Tybee Island. When planning your trip from home, you can contact the **Savannah Area Convention and Visitors Bureau and Chamber of Commerce** (912-644-6400; 1-877-SAVANNAH; www.savannah-visit.com; www.savannahchamber.com), P.O. Box 1628, Savannah, 31402, for a Savannah Travel Planner and other information. The street address is 101 East Bay Street.

When you arrive in Savannah, there are four visitor information centers with staff and brochures to help you. The **Savannah Visitor Information Center** (912-944-0455), 301 Martin Luther King Jr. Boulevard, Savannah 31401, is open 8:30–5 weekdays, 9–5 Saturday, Sunday, and holidays. There is an introductory movie at this location, and you can leave your car here and join one of the many tours offered by different companies or take advantage of the public transportation available. The **River Street Hospitality Center** (912-651-6662), One River Street, Savannah 31401, is open 10–10 daily.

If you are arriving by air, the **Savannah Airport Visitor Information Center** (912-964-1109), 464 Airways Avenue, Savannah 31401, is open 10–6 daily. On the way into the city on I-95, there is the **Georgia Visitor Information Center at Savannah** (912-963-2546; www.georgiaonmymind.org), I-95, Mile Marker 111, Port Wentworth 31407. Open 8:30–5:30 daily.

The **Tybee Island Visitors Center** (912-786-5444; 1-800-868-BEACH; www.tybeevisit.com; www.tybeeonline.com; www.tybeeisland.com), US 80 at Campbell Avenue, Tybee Island 31328, is open 10–6 daily during the summer, weekends the rest of the year.

The **Pooler Area Chamber of Commerce** (912-748-9121; www.pooler-ga.com), 308 US 80 East, Pooler 31322, is open 9–5 weekdays.

For information about Springfield, contact the **Effingham County Chamber**

of **Commerce** (912-754-3301; 1-866-754-3301; www.effinghamcounty.com), 520
West Third Street, Springfield 31329. It's open 8:30–5 weekdays.

GETTING THERE *By air:* Eight airlines fly into **Savannah/Hilton Head International Airport** (912-964-0514; www.savannahairport.com), 400 Airways Avenue, located off I-95 at exit 104 just 10 miles west of downtown: **AirTran, Continental Express, Delta** and **Delta Connection, Independence Air, Northwest Airlink, United Express,** and **US Airways.** Numerous car rental companies, public transportation, hotel shuttles, and taxis offer transportation from the airport to Savannah and Tybee Island. (See What's Where in Georgia for further details.)

By bus: Savannah is a regular stop on **Greyhound Lines** (912-232-2135; www
.greyhound.com) routes. Buses arrive at the terminal at 610 Oglethorpe Avenue.

By car: Along the coast of the eastern United States, take I-95, getting off at exit 99 onto I-16 East, which ends in downtown Savannah at Montgomery Street. If continuing to Tybee Island, take US 80 from East Liberty Street in downtown Savannah to the island.

By train: **Amtrak** (912-234-2611; 1-800-872-7245; www.amtrak.com), 2611 Seaboard Coastline Drive, uses Savannah as a major stop on its Atlantic coast service between New York and Miami. Daily service to and from Savannah is available aboard the *Silver Star, Silver Palm,* and *Silver Meteor.* Service is coach or, with reservations, first class in superliner sleeping cars.

GETTING AROUND Numerous options make getting around Savannah easy. Because of the parking problems in the historic district, you might want to take advantage of these other alternatives. If you're staying in the historic district, walking is by far the most pleasant choice. Free and convenient, the ✿ **CAT Shuttle** operated by **Chatham Area Transit** (912-233-5767; www.catchacat
.org), 900 East Gwinnett Street, makes 32 stops throughout the historic district, including shops, attractions, and hotels.

Savannah has a plethora of tour company options. At last count, there were 53 offering general tours and/or specializing in subjects as diverse as African American history, "the Book," the Civil War, ghosts, pirates, and pubs. Many tour companies offer guided tours via trolleys and/or buses, some with on-and-off privileges. Among them, just a few include **Gray Line Trolley Tours** (912-234-8687; www.grayline.com), 1115 Louisville Road; **Old Savannah Tours** (912-234-8128; 1-800-517-9007; oldsavannahtours.com); and **Old Town Trolley** (912-233-0083; www.oldtowntrolley.com), 234 Martin Luther King Jr. Boulevard. All depart from the Savannah Visitor Information Center and pick up at some hotels.

What's more romantic than touring the city to the clip-clop of a horse-drawn carriage? Several companies offer day and nighttime tours, among them **Carriage Tours of Savannah** (912-236-6756) and **Historic Savannah Carriage Tours** (912-443-9333; 1-888-837-1011).

Some of the most popular tours are walking tours, and some of these are given after dark. Most tour guides meet participants in a central location rather than at their offices, so we supply only the telephone and web site information here. **Savannah by Foot** (912-238-3843; www.savannahtours.com) and the **Savannah Walks** (912-238-WALKS) are just two of many. (See *Entertainment* for ghost tours.)

If you are staying outside the historic district or want to explore outside it, Chatham Area Transit (see above) also offers for-fee (75 cents per ride or $12 for a weekly pass) bus routes within the city and Chatham County.

Car rentals are available from **Alamo** (912-964-7364), **Avis** (912-964-1781), **Budget** (912-964-4600), **Economy Rent-a-Car** (912-352-7042), **Enterprise Rent-a-Car** (912-920-1093), **Hertz** (912-964-9595), **National** (912-964-1771), and **Thrifty** (912-966-2277).

The easiest and most pleasant way to travel across the river from River Street in the historic district to the Westin Savannah Harbor Golf Resort and Spa and the Savannah International Trade and Convention Center on Hutchinson Island is by way of the water taxis operated by ❧ **Belles Ferry** (912-447-4000; www .savtcc.com) from the City Hall dock. The cost is $3 per person round-trip, and the taxis operate every 10 to 15 minutes between 7 AM and 11 PM daily.

On Tybee Island, trolley tours are available from May through September.

PARKING On-street parking in the Savannah Historic District is practically all metered and can be extremely difficult for sightseers to find. Even many inns and bed & breakfasts have little off-street parking, and guests must park at meters on the street. The good news is that metered parking is free on weekends, and city-owned parking lots are free on Sunday. But don't let your vacation be

CARRIAGE TOURS PROVIDE A UNIQUE WAY TO SEE SAVANNAH.

ruined at other times by getting a ticket or having your car booted or towed. There are several convenient for-fee parking lots and garages, both public and private, within easy walking distances of most tourist sites, accommodations, restaurants, and nightspots.

Tourists may purchase an $8, 48-hour parking pass from the Savannah Visitor Information Center, the Parking Services Division, and various hotels and inns. The pass allows one hour or more of free parking on meters, free parking in the city lots and garages, and extended time in time-limit zones. During the St. Patrick's Day parade, parking on the parade route is prohibited, so be sure to learn the route in advance. Also, be aware of schedules for street cleaning when parking may be prohibited or may be changed from one side of the street to another. If you have questions about parking, Parking Services 912-651-6470 officers can answer them.

On-street parking in the commercial and beach areas on Tybee Island is also metered and can be scarce in the high season, especially on weekends and holidays. Several for-fee parking lots a few blocks from the beach are available. In contrast to the situation with some accommodations in Savannah, most accommodations on Tybee Island have adequate off-street parking.

WHEN TO GO Savannah is a year-round destination, though it's particularly beautiful in the spring when the azaleas are blooming and at Christmas when many of the homes and inns are beautifully decorated and open for tours. A visit during the St. Patrick's celebration requires advance planning. Accommodations for the popular St. Patrick's event often need to be booked a year in advance and usually require a several-night minimum stay and full nonrefundable payment in advance.

As a beach destination, Tybee Island is most sought out during the summer months. September and October are ideal—the air and water temperatures are delightful and the crowds are gone. If swimming is not your primary reason for visiting, Tybee can be enchanting for walking, biking, bird-watching, and shelling in the off-season months. Because Tybee Island is more heavily visited in the summer, some establishments have restricted hours or may even close in the winter, so call ahead.

MEDICAL EMERGENCY Call 911 for immediate assistance. Otherwise, care is available in Savannah at **Memorial Health University Medical Center** (912-350-8000), 4700 Waters Avenue; **St. Joseph's Hospital** (912-819-4100), 11705 Mercy Boulevard; or **Candler Hospital** (912-819-6000), 5353 Reynolds Street. For non-life-threatening situations on Tybee Island, the **Tybee Medical Center** (912-786-8866), Butler Avenue at Tybrisa Street, is open six days a week: 9–5 Monday, Tuesday, Thursday, and Friday; 9–1 Wednesday and Saturday.

✴ To See

FOR FAMILIES ✐ ❀ **Tybee Island Light Station** (912-786-5801; www.tybee lighthouse.org), 30 Meddin Drive, Tybee Island. Open 9–5:30 daily except Tuesdays and St. Patrick's Day, Thanksgiving, Christmas, and New Year's Days. Last

EAT YOUR PICNIC LUNCH WITH A VIEW OF TYBEE PIER

tickets sold at 4:30. This light station is one of this country's most intact, still having most of its historic support buildings—several keepers' cottages, the summer kitchen, garage, and fuel storage building—in addition to the lighthouse. Some kind of light on this spot has been guiding mariners safely into the Savannah River for more than 270 years. The first was built in 1736; Georgia's first public structure, at that time it was the tallest lighthouse in America. A later lighthouse, the first with interior stairs, had to have George Washington's approval. The current 154-foot, 178-step lighthouse was built in 1867 on the base of one from 1773. It wears its 1916 day-mark color scheme and is one of the few surviving American lighthouses to have its original First Order Fresnel lens. The Head Keeper's Cottage has been restored and furnished to reflect an earlier era. The adjacent museum in the summer kitchen displays lighthouse artifacts and local Tybee historical items. Adults $6, children and seniors $5, children 5 and younger free.

✇ ✇ **Tybee Island Marine Science Center** (912-786-5917; www.tybee msc.org), 1510 the Strand at 14th Street, Tybee Island. Open 9–5 Wednesday through Monday, 9–noon Tuesday. This small center interprets marine life with touch tanks, aquariums, and other exhibits. There are monthly Discovery Beach Walks and other programs throughout the year, as well as a summer Sea Camp for children age 3–12. Adults $4, children $3.

✇ **Tybee Turtle Tour** (912-786-5920; www.tybeearts.org). Just in case you don't have the opportunity to see a live sea turtle while you're visiting the island, the Tybee Arts Association is helping save the endangered creature through ecological education in public art. So far 10 huge fiberglass sea trutles have been whimsically decorated by local artist and placed around the island. The goal is to complete 50 turtles. An amusing afternoon can be had searching for and photograhing the turtles such as Bert, Myrtle, Mermaid Rodeo Bareback Rider, Terra Turtle, and Hey-Diddle Turtle. Stop by the Tybee Island Visitor Information Center on US 80 (see *Guidance*) to get a map showing the locations of the turtles.

✇ ✇ ♿ **University of Georgia Marine Science Complex and Aquarium** (912-598-2496; www.uga.edu/aquarium), 30 Ocean Science Circle, Savannah.

Open 9–4 weekdays, noon–5 Saturday. Part of the university's Marine Extension Service, the complex conducts studies on coastal sea life found in the tidal creeks of salt marshes, ocean beaches, and open waters of the continental shelf, including live bottom areas such as Gray's Reef National Marine Sanctuary off Sapelo Island. The 14-tank aquarium exhibit shows 200 live examples that represent 50 species of fish, turtles, and invertebrates, including some of the more spectacular Georgia marine life such as *Octopus vulgaris,* the loggerhead turtle, the shark sucker, and the longnose gar. Among the other permanent and traveling exhibits are archaeological finds such as the fossils of sharks, giant armadillos, whales, mastodons, and woolly mammoths dredged from the Skidaway River. Other exhibits showcase Native American and Gullah cultures as well as the works of local artists. Alongside the Intracoastal Waterway are a nature trail and a picnic area, while the Jay Wolf Nature Trail meanders through the ruins of the old Roebling plantation. Summer camps offer fun and education to children age 6–15. Several special events include the **Coastweeks Celebration** open house in the fall and the annual **Underwater and Coastal Georgia Art and Photography Contest.** Adults $2, children 3–12 $1, children younger than 3 free.

FORTS ✍ 🐾 ♿ **Fort Pulaski National Monument** (912-786-5787; www.nps .gov/fopu), US 80 East, Savannah. Open 9–5:15 daily, September through May; 9–7 daily, June through August. The star-shaped fort, located on Cockspur Island between Savannah and Tybee Island, was once a masterpiece among brick-and-masonry forts. In fact, when Confederate forces occupied it during the early Civil War, they thought it was invincible. Unfortunately, it fell to the Union's rifled artillery in less than 30 hours, and that defeat marked the end of masonry forts. Today the fort is interpreted through a film and exhibits in the visitor center as well as ranger-led programs in the fort. See towering walls, artillery tunnels, the drawbridge, and two moats. Nature trails and picnic grounds round out the offerings. Wheelchair accessible. $3, children younger than 16 free.

✍ 🐾 ♿ **Old Fort Jackson** (912-232-3945; www.chsgeorgia.org/jackson), One Fort Jackson Road, Savannah. Open 9–5 daily. The oldest standing fort in Georgia, Old Fort Jackson perches on a bluff above the Savannah River. Once a Revolutionary War fort, it saw action during both the War of 1812 and the Civil War as well. Cannons, small arms, tools, and machinery are among the interpretive exhibits, along with artifacts from the sunken ironclad CSS *Georgia,* which rests 40 feet below the surface of the Savannah River in front of the fort. Between June 15 and August 15, weapons are demonstrated and cannon fired at 11 AM and 2 PM daily. Among the cannons is the largest black-powder cannon ever fired in America. Battlefield reenactments and special events are ongoing throughout the year, and the fort is also a great place from which to watch the ships sailing up and down the Savannah River. Adults $4, children, seniors, and military $3, children younger than 6 free.

HISTORIC HOMES AND SITES ✍ 🐾 **Andrew Low House** (912-233-6854; www .andrewlowhouse.com), 329 Abercorn Street, Savannah. Open 10–4:30 Monday through Wednesday, Friday, and Saturday, noon–4:30 Sunday. This gracious

Greek Revival– and Italianate-style home was the site where the first Girl Scout troop in America was organized: in 1912 by Juliette Gordon Low, a Savannah native. (For more about the founder, see Juliette Gordon Low National Birthplace, below.) This 1848 structure had been the home of Mrs. Low's father-in-law, Andrew Low, who was a cotton merchant. The young couple inherited the house upon his death. The classical design of the structure also shows West Indian plantation-style influences. The property also contains what is considered to be Savannah's most notable collection of classical furnishings from the period 1800–1850. Purchased by the Colonial Dames in 1928, the Andrew Low House was Savannah's first historic house museum. Adults $8, children 12 and younger and Girl Scouts $4.50.

🏛 ♿ **Bonaventure Cemetery** (912-651-6843), 330 Bonaventure Road, Savannah. Open 8–5 daily. Massive moss-draped oaks stand guard over elegant statuary and headstones dating back more than two centuries in this cemetery on the banks of the Wilmington River. The cemetery is the final resting place of some of Savannah's most famous former residents, such as Pulitzer Prize–winning poet Conrad Aiken and lyricist and Academy Award winner Johnny Mercer, as well as Confederate generals, plantation owners, and lesser-knowns such as a little girl named Gracie whose likeness tops her tomb. The cemetery also figured prominently in *Midnight in the Garden of Good and Evil*. It was here that the narrator sipped martinis and learned about Savannah society. In fact, so many visitors come because of "the Book" that the famous Bird Girl statue had to be removed and now reposes at the Telfair Academy of Arts and Sciences (see *Museums*). Danny Hansford, whose murder is the central theme of the book, is buried in nearby Greenwich Cemetery. Free.

🏛 **Colonial Park Cemetery** (912-651-6610), Abercorn Street and Oglethorpe Avenue, Savannah. Filled with fascinating markers and tombs watched over by ancient magnolias, Colonial Park Cemetery, the oldest graveyard in Savannah, entombed many of Savannah's early colonists from 1750 to 1853. Among those resting here are Archibald Bulloch, the first governor of Georgia, and Button Gwinnett, a Revolutionary War hero and signer of the Declaration of Independence. A point of interest is the hand-carved graffiti on many of the headstones, the work of Union soldiers camped in the cemetery during the Civil War. Look for deaths dated before births and other oddities. Free.

🏛 **Flannery O'Connor Childhood Home** (912-233-6014), 207 East Charlton Street, Lafayette Square, Savannah. Open 1–4 Saturday and Sunday. Get a glimpse into the early life of the famous Georgia novelist and short-story writer at this house, where she lived until she was 13. Built in 1856, the home is furnished as it might have been when the O'Connor family lived there in the 1920s and 1930s. In addition, the center offers special literary programs in the fall and spring. $5.

🏛 **Green-Meldrim House** (912-232-1251), 14 West Macon Street near Madison Square, Savannah. Open 10–3 Tuesday and Thursday through Saturday. Closed Veterans Day week and from mid-December to mid-January. Considered to be one of Georgia's finest examples of neo–Gothic Revival architecture, this circa 1850 house serves as the parish house of St. John's Episcopal Church. During the Civil War occupation by Union troops, the house was the headquarters of General William Tecumseh Sherman. It was in one of the bedrooms that Sherman wrote his famous telegram telling President Lincoln that he was presenting Savannah to him as a Christmas gift. Today the house has been fully restored and appropriately furnished. Adults $5, children and seniors $2.

🌿 **Isaiah Davenport House Museum** (912-236-8097; www.davenportsavga.com), 324 East State Street, Columbia Square, Savannah. Open 10–4 Monday through Saturday, 1–4 Sunday. Built between 1815 and 1820 by master builder Isaiah Davenport, the house is a stellar example of Federal architecture and features outstanding architectural details such as delicate plasterwork, an elliptical cantilevered staircase, and Ionic-Tuscan columns. Furnishings include a fine collection of Davenport china, Chippendale and Sheraton furnishings, and period decorative arts. This house was the first restoration project of the Historic Savannah Foundation. In fact, it was the threatened demolition of this house that served as the catalyst for the preservation movement in Savannah and led to the foundation's formation. Adults $7, children and seniors $3.50.

✍ 🌿 ♿ **Juliette Gordon Low National Birthplace** (912-233-4501; www.girlscouts.org/about/birthplace), 10 East Oglethorpe Avenue, Savannah. Open 10–4 Monday, Tuesday, and Thursday through Saturday, 11–4 Sunday. Closed New Year's Day through January 14; check for hours near major holidays. The home, which was Savannah's first designated National Historic Landmark, is of interest whether you've ever had any association with the Girl Scouts of America or not. This lovely 1820 Regency-style town house was the childhood home of the founder of the girls' organization and has been restored to the period of her residency, 1860 to 1886. In addition to the fine classical interior details, visitors will be interested in many original family pieces. In May, the birthplace sponsors the **Celebrate Girl Scouting** festival, which spills out into Wright Square. Adults $8, children and students $5. Discounts for seniors, Girl Scouts, and families.

🌿 **King-Tisdell Cottage** (912-234-8000; www.kingtisdell.org), 514 East Huntingdon Street, Savannah. Open noon–5 Tuesday through Saturday. A beautifully restored 1896 cottage with unusually intricate gingerbread trim on the porch and dormers, the house is a museum highlighting the contributions of African Americans. Among the exhibits are 19th-century art objects, documents, and furniture. Adults $4, seniors and children $2.

The Mercer Williams House Museum (912-236-6352; 1-877-430-6352; www.mercerhouse.com), 429 Bull Street, Savannah. Open 10:30–3:40 Monday through Saturday, 12:30–4 Sunday. Originally built in the 1860s for General Hugh W. Mercer, the great-grandfather of songster Johnny Mercer, this stately house was purchased in 1969 by antiques dealer and preservationist Jim Williams. During his career, Williams saved more than 50 historic homes in the area. Opulently restored, the Monterey Square home is furnished with 17th-through 19th-century furniture and art. Although you won't hear a word about it on the tour, this house and the late Mr. Williams played pivotal roles in the real-life saga that inspired *Midnight in the Garden of Good and Evil*. Before leaving, be sure to stop in at the Carriage House Shop, 430 Whitaker Street; open 10–4:30 weekdays, 10–5 Saturday, 10:30–4 Sunday. Adults $12.50, students $8.

🌿 **Owens-Thomas House** (912-233-9743; www.telfair.org), 124 Abercorn Street, Savannah. Open noon–5 Monday, 10–5 Tuesday through Saturday, 1–5 Sunday. This mansion, considered to be one of the finest examples of the Regency style in America, was designed by William Jay and built between 1816 and 1819. Many of the furnishings are original to the Thomas family. In the Owens-Thomas Carriage House, the lives and stories of Savannah slaves are told through items in the Acacia Collection. Adults $9, seniors $8, college students $6, children 5–12 $4. A $14 two-site combo ticket also allows admission to the Telfair Academy of Arts and Sciences or the Jepson Center for the Arts; an $18 three-site combo ticket allows admission to all three sites (see *Museums*).

✒ 🌿 ♿ **Wormsloe Historic Site** (912-353-3023; www.gastateparks.org/info/wormsloe), 7601 Skidaway Road, Savannah. Open 9–5 Tuesday through Saturday, 2–5:30 Sunday. Located on the Isle of Hope, Wormsloe was a royal grant to Noble Jones, one of Georgia's first colonists, in 1756. It remained in the same family until 1974, when it was given to the Georgia Heritage Trust. A beautiful oak-lined drive leads visitors to the ruins of the home. The site is interpreted at the visitor center with exhibits of items excavated at Wormsloe and audiovisual programming about the founding of the 13th colony. Make a day of it by wandering along the nature trails to see the tabby (oyster-shell cement) fortification and the Fort Wimberly earthworks. The living-history area is the scene of periodic special programs by costumed staff who demonstrate skills and crafts necessary to early settlers. Call for a schedule of these special events. In February, the Colonial Faire and Muster highlights 18th-century life with military drills, crafts demonstrations, music, and dance. Adults $2.50, children and seniors $1.50.

MUSEUMS 🌿 ♿ **Historic Effingham Society's Old Jail Museum** (912-826-4705; 912-754-6240; www.effinghamcounty.com), 1002 Pine Street, Springfield. Open 2–5 Sunday. Almost three-quarters of a century old, the old jail houses Revolutionary and Native American artifacts. Free.

🌿 ♿ **Massie Heritage Interpretation Center** (912-651-7380; www.massieschool.com), 207 East Gordon Street, Savannah. Open 9–4 weekdays. The center, housed in the only remaining structure of Georgia's oldest chartered school system, is the repository of exhibits explaining Savannah's outstanding architecture. Self-guided tours $3, guided $5, children younger than 4 free.

✒ 🌿 ♿ **Mighty Eighth Air Force Museum** (912-748-8888; www.mightyeighth.org), 175 Bourne Avenue, Pooler. Open 9–5 daily. Exhibits range from World War II to the present. One of the highlights is a simulated B-17 bombing mission where visitors can experience a bomber crew's harrowing flight over Nazi Germany. At another exhibit, visitors can test their skills as a waist gunner. "The Fly Girls of World War II" exhibit is devoted to women in aviation, particularly the unsung heroes of the Women Airforce Service Pilots. Outdoors, the Chapel of the Fallen Eagles occupies a replica of a 15th-century English church. Thirteen stained-glass windows honor World War II airmen. Aircraft on view include an F-4 Phantom, B-47 Stratojet, MiG-17 Fresco, Boeing-Stearman PT-17 Kaydet, and Messerschmitt ME-163 B Komet. The museum is an affiliate of the Smithsonian Institution. Adults $10, seniors $9, children 6–12 $6, children younger than 6 free. Lunch is available in the English-style pub 11–2 Monday through Saturday.

🍴 ♿ **Ralph Mark Gilbert Civil Rights Museum** (912-231-8900; www.savannah civilrightsmuseum.com), 460 Martin Luther King Jr. Boulevard, Savannah. Open 9–5 Monday through Saturday. The museum explores Savannah's African American history and culture with special emphasis on Savannah's struggle against segregation. While you're at the museum, pick up a "Negro Heritage Trail" brochure, which details three separate walking or driving tours pertinent to black history. Adults $4, seniors $3, children $2.

✎ 🍴 **Roundhouse Railroad Museum** (912-651-6823; www.chsgeorgia.org/roundhouse), 601 West Harris Street, Savannah. Open 9–5 daily. This complex, which actually contains 13 original structures, includes the oldest and most complete antebellum locomotive repair shop and roundhouse still in existence in the country. Exhibits include two of the oldest surviving steam engines, as well as other antique locomotives, machinery, and rolling stock. Adults $4, children and seniors $3.50, children younger than 6 free.

🍴 ♿ **Saltzburger Museum and Church** (912-826-5629; www.georgiasaltzburgers .com/information.htm), 2980 Ebenezer Road, Rincon. Open 3–5 Wednesday, Saturday, and Sunday. In 1734, 60 Lutheran religious exiles from the Principality and Archbishopric of Salzburg arrived in Georgia, where they founded the town of Ebenezer on the Savannah River. The museum, which traces the history of this group, is located on the site of the Ebenezer Orphanage, the first in the state. Free.

✎ 🍴 ♿ **Savannah History Museum** (912-238-1779; www.chsgeorgia.org/shm), 303 Martin Luther King Jr. Boulevard, Savannah. Open 8:30–5 weekdays, 9–5 weekends. Numerous exhibits and a film detail more than 260 years of the city's history. The building, which was the passenger station for the Central of Georgia Railway, also houses a prop from the movie *Forrest Gump:* the bench on which the hero sat while waiting for the bus in Chippewa Square. Adults $4, children and seniors $3.50, children younger than 6 free.

✎ 🍴 **Ships of the Sea Maritime Museum** (912-232-1511; www.shipsofthesea.org), 41 Martin Luther King Jr. Boulevard, Savannah. Open 10–5 Tuesday through Sunday. Housed in the elegant William Scarborough House, the museum displays ship models and maritime antiques representing 2,000 years of seagoing history with primary focus on the 18th and 19th centuries. Intricate models represent sail steamers, warships, tugs, supertankers, and more. Among the other exhibits are scrimshaw art and maritime paintings. Scarborough was the principal owner of the *Savannah,* the first steamship to cross the Atlantic. In addition to the outstanding exhibits inside, at the rear of the house there is a lovely garden—the largest in the historic district. Adults $7, children and seniors $5.

✎ 🍴 ♿ **Telfair Academy of Arts and Sciences and Jepson Center for the Arts** (912-790-8800; www.telfair.org), 121 Barnard Street, Savannah. Open noon–5 Monday, 10–5 Tuesday through Saturday, 1–5 Sunday. Docent-led tours at 2 PM daily, additional tours at 1 PM Thursday and Friday, 11 AM Saturday. The South's oldest public art museum, the Telfair Academy of Arts and Sciences is housed in a magnificent mansion designed and built by William Jay in 1818. Opulent period rooms are meticulously restored to their 1819 appearance to serve as an elegant backdrop for the extensive collection of fine and decorative arts, including original family furnishings. A large wing added in 1883 contains superb American and European paintings and sculpture. Aficionados of *Midnight in the Garden of Good and Evil* enjoy seeing the famous Bird Girl statue from the cover of "the Book." Although it once graced Bonaventure Cemetery, it had to be moved for its own protection. The museum has recently opened the state-of-the-art **Jepson Center for the Arts** in a striking modern Moshe Safdie–designed building nearby (207 West York Street). The Jepson displays 20th- and 21st-century art as well as Southern and African American art, photography, works on paper, and outdoor sculpture. The Jepson's children's gallery displays interactive exhibits inspired by works in the museum's collection. The Jepson Center features multilevel interactive galleries, an auditorium, museum store, café, and sculpture gardens. Separate admission to the main museum, the Jepson Center, and the Owens-Thomas House (see *Historic Homes and Sites*) or combination tickets are available. One museum: adults $9, seniors $8, children 5–12 $4. A $14 two-site combo ticket and an $18 three-site combo ticket are available.

SPECIAL PLACES

✂ ✺ **Savannah Riverfront, Riverfront Plaza, and Factor's Walk**, River Street between Martin Luther King Jr. Boulevard and East Broad Street. The Savannah River is the heart of the historic district, and on its south bank is River Street. In past centuries, the street was lined with cotton warehouses and offices of the factors (cotton brokers). The streets were paved with ballast stones, which had been carried in ships to distribute the weight and then discarded. Today River Street is still paved with ballast stones, but the cotton warehouses contain inns, restaurants, nightspots, shops, boutiques, galleries, and artists' studios. **Riverfront Plaza,** a nine-block brick-paved esplanade stretching between City Hall and the Savannah Marriott Riverfront, is dotted with fountains, landscaping, benches, and a children's play area. Always hopping with activity, the plaza is often the scene of festivals, special events, and entertainment. At the far end of the plaza is the **Waving Girl Statue,** which depicts Florence Martus, a young woman whose sailor boyfriend went off to sea and never returned. No one knows whether he died or just changed his mind, but Florence greeted every ship that entered the port of Savannah from 1887 to 1931, anticipating his return. Nearby the **Olympic Cauldron Sculpture** commemorates the sailing events from the 1996 Summer Olympic Games, which were held off the coast of Savannah. First-Saturday festivals are held on Riverfront Plaza each month. **Factor's Walk** is located between River and Bay streets on the bluff above the river. This area was a 19th-century center of commerce for cotton merchants. Offices were on the upper level, warehouses on the lower level. Bridgeways connect the buildings. Riverfront Plaza is wheelchair accessible, as is Factor's Walk. The ballastone paving makes crossing River Street difficult.

AUTO RACING ✿ ♿ **Oglethorpe Speedway Park** (912-964-7223; www.ospracing .net), 200 Jesup Road, Pooler. The park sponsors NASCAR-sanctioned events on weekends. Call for a schedule of events and ticket prices.

BICYCLING One of the most pleasant ways to get around Tybee Island is by bicycle, and the hard-packed beach is even conducive to bike riding. Bring your own or rent one when you get there. **Jaime's Sundance Bicycle Shop** (912-786-9469), 22 Tybrisa Street, Tybee Island, offers rentals, repairs, accessories, child carriers and tagalongs, strollers, and wagons. Guided bike tours by appointment. **Pack Rat** (912-786-4013), 14th Street and Butler Avenue, Tybee Island, offers rentals, sales, and repairs.

BIRDING Numerous locations are excellent for bird-watching, from the beaches to the state park to the national wildlife refuge. ✿ 🐦 **Colonial Coast Birding Trail,** 681 Fort Argyle Road, Savannah. Measuring more than 112 miles along the coast of Georgia, this trail has 18 stops—some with 18th- and 19th-century sites that were once part of plantations. The northern portion of the trail is near Savannah. Free.

BOATING ✿ **Ogeechee River Canoe and Kayak Rentals** (912-964-0202, www .ogeecheecanoe.com), 318 Dublin Road, Pooler. The company offers guided and unguided canoe trips, return shuttle service, and training. Call for schedules and fees.

For public **boat ramps,** see Marinas/Boat Landings Appendix.

CRUISES ✿ 🐦 ♿ **River Street Riverboat Company** (912-232-6404; 1-800-786-6404; www.savannahriverboat.com), 9 East River Street, Savannah. Schedules vary between winter and summer, so call for a timetable of narrated sight-seeing, lunch, brunch, dinner, and moonlight cruises. Make a voyage of discovery aboard the *Savannah River Queen* or the *Georgia Queen,* replicas of old-fashioned paddle-wheelers. In addition to the types of cruises listed above, the company also provides specialty cruises such as gospel, murder-mystery, and Valentine cruises. Wheelchair access on first deck. Basic sight-seeing cruise: adults $16.95, children younger than 12 $14.95, children 3 and younger free. Call for prices of other cruises.

DOLPHIN-WATCHING ✿ **Capt. Mike's Dolphin Tours** (912-786-5858; 1-800-242-0166; www.tybeedolphins.com), Lazaretto Creek Marina, Tybee Island. Mailing address: P.O. Box 787, Tybee Island 31328. Open 9–5 daily. Tours offered at different times depending on season. Reservations recommended. The SS *Dolphin,* a small *African Queen*–like vessel, provides a magical cruise to catch sight of playful bottle-nosed dolphins. Even on a bad day when no dolphins appear, you'll still enjoy the sight-seeing, which passes Old Cockspur Lighthouse, Fort Pulaski, and the north beach of the island. Adults $12, children 12 and younger $5.

✒ **Dolphin Magic** (912-897-4990; 1-800-721-1240), mailing address: P.O. Box 30247, Savannah 31401. Offered seasonally, the dolphin tour aboard Savannah's largest dolphin-watching vessel leaves daily from River Street behind the Hyatt. Not wheelchair accessible. Adults $22, children 3–12 $11, children younger than 3 free.

FISHING An area bounded by the ocean and crisscrossed with rivers is a fisherman's heaven. You can throw a line in almost anywhere, but be aware of fishing laws. Numerous companies offer guided inland fishing trips and deep–sea charters. See Fishing Appendix for a list of piers in the area. See What's Where in Georgia for fishing regulations.

GOLF Mild year-round weather makes for perfect golfing, and the Savannah area boasts 30 golf courses within 30 miles of town. Savannah is also the home of the Senior PGA's Liberty Mutual Legends of Golf tournament.

Henderson Golf Course (912-920-4653; 912-921-5879; www.hendersongolf club.com), One Al Henderson Drive, Savannah. Considered Savannah's best public course, Henderson has 18 holes, a practice facility, and a lighted driving range. Call for hours and prices.

See also Golf Appendix.

KAYAKING The rivers and marshes that abound around Savannah and Tybee Island are perfect for still-water kayaking, while the ocean provides challenges for sea kayakers. Several companies provide kayaks, lessons, and guides.

Alakai Outfitters and Surf Company (912-786-4000; 912-786-4997; www .alakaioutfitters.com), 1213 US 80, Suite A, Tybee Island, rents kayaks, surfboards, and body boards; gives lessons; and provides adventure travel. Guided tour $38; rentals $28 for single-person kayak, $50 for double.

Sea Kayak Georgia (912-786-8732; 1-888-529-2542; www.seakayakgeorgia .com), 1102 US 80, Tybee Island. Open year-round. Sea Kayak Georgia provides experiential education and adventure travel. Basic and advanced kayak instruction and certifications sanctioned by the American Canoe Association and the British Canoe Union are offered. Half-day to multiday trips with camping or overnights at a bed & breakfast take paddlers to places steeped in scenic beauty as well as cultural and natural history. Sea Kayak Georgia also offers kayak and equipment rentals as well as the largest selection of composite sea kayaks for sale in the Southeast. Instruction: from $125 for half-day introductory course to $925 for multiday advanced course. Overnight rates: start at $95 for full day of kayaking, plus accommodations at bed & breakfast next door $70–130 per night. Full overnight trip for two, including all meals and camping gear, $325–350.

MARINAS See Marinas/Boat Landings Appendix.

OUTDOOR ADVENTURES ✒ ✿ ও **Oatland Island Education Center** (912-897-3773; www.oatlandisland.org), 711 Sandtown Road, Oatland Island. Open 9–5 weekdays, 10–5 Saturday; closed Sunday (except for one Super Museum Sunday each year). Among the 175 acres of oaks, pines, and magnolias is a 1.75-mile nature trail that provides opportunities to observe large enclosures with more than 50 indigenous species of wildlife native to the state—shorebirds, bears, alligators, panthers, otters, deer, timber wolves, bison, and diverse raptors among them. Youngsters can see and feed farm animals in the barnyard. The facility is owned by the Savannah–Chatham County School System as an environmental education center, but it is open to the public. $2.

✿ **Old Savannah-Tybee Railroad Historic and Scenic Trail,** US 80 East, Tybee Island. Open daily. At the turn of the 20th century, visitors were transported from Savannah to Tybee Island by train. With the construction of bridges and roadways, the railroad was no longer needed and the tracks fell into disuse and disrepair. Eventually the tracks were taken up and the 6.5-mile roadbed converted to a walking-jogging-bicycling trail. The tree-lined trail provides excellent views of the Savannah River and marshes, along with glimpses of native wildlife—brown pelicans, red-tailed hawks, box turtles, and alligators. Free.

✿ **Wilderness Southeast** (912-897-5108; www.wilderness-southeast.org), 711 Sandtown Road, Savannah. Open year-round. This outdoor school offers overnight wilderness discovery adventures including canoeing, hiking, and sailing. Call for a schedule of events. Price dependent on the activity.

SPAS & **Savannah Day Spa** (912-234-9100; www.savannahdayspa.com), 110 Barnard Street. Open 10–6 Monday through Saturday (extended hours until 9 on Wednesday and Thursday), noon–5 Sunday. The full-service day spa offers facials, body treatments, hydrotherapy, waxing, manicures, and tanning services.

See also the **Mansion on Forsyth Park** under *Lodging—Inns and Hotels* and **Westin Savannah Harbor Golf Resort and Spa** under *Lodging—Resorts.*

SWIMMING With the beaches and other water around Savannah and Tybee Island, there are limitless places to swim. On the occasional rainy day, check out *✿* & **The Chatham County Aquatic Center** (912-652-6793), 7240 Sallie Mood Drive, Savannah. Open 6 AM–8 PM weekdays, 8 AM–6 PM Saturday. A state-of-the-art swimming complex, the 50,000-square-foot facility contains an Olympic-sized pool, therapeutic pool, and Nautilus weight equipment. Programs include water aerobics, swimming lessons, and general recreational swimming. Adults $5, seniors $4, children 3–10 $3.

TENNIS See Other Activities Appendix.

✳ Green Space

BEACHES The beaches of Tybee Island are wide and usually hard-packed. Protected by dunes covered with gently swaying sea oats, these beaches provide endless hours of fun in the sun. Not only can you just lie on the beach and read or vegetate, you can walk or jog, hunt for shells, build sand castles, bury someone in the sand, fly a kite, scoot across the waves on a boogie board, wind surf, fish in the surf, and even ride a bike. The beaches are public, and there are numerous access points.

GARDENS 🐾 ♿ **Bamboo Farm and Coastal Gardens** (912-921-5460), US 17 South and Canebrake Road, Savannah. Open 9–4 weekends, closed weekends and major holidays. Operated by the University of Georgia's College of Agricultural and Environmental Sciences, the 52-acre experimental station contains many plant collections and gardens. The gardens began on this site with three plants more than 100 years ago. Today, the farm boasts the largest collections of bamboo in North America, with more than 140 varieties of both shade- and sun-loving bamboos—some of which are the only specimens in this hemisphere. In the Cottage Garden, old and new varieties of perennials, annuals, and bulbs are tested. The Xeriscape Garden demonstrates water-wise landscaping and is used to teach water conservation practices. Collections of butterfly plants, ornamental grasses, crape myrtles, ferns, ornamental vines, 16 varieties of Southern magnolias, and 600 varieties of daylilies are also exhibited. Of further interest to gardeners are projects demonstrating composting, vegetables, fruits, flowers, shrubs, and turf varieties. A palm collection also has been started. Free. Special events throughout the year include a wild-game supper, spring and fall gardening festivals, and an annual Sunday supper in the strawberry patch.

♿ 🐾 **Chatham County Garden Center and Botanical Gardens** (912-355-3883), 1388 Eisenhower Drive, Savannah. Gardens open 9:30–4:30 daily; garden center open 10–2 weekdays. The Savannah Area Council of Garden Clubs maintains 10 acres of gardens featuring roses, perennials, herbs and vegetables, and seasonal beds. The garden center is housed in a 1840s-era farmhouse. $3 donation encouraged.

NATURE PRESERVES AND PARKS 🐾 ♿ **Bacon Regional Park** (912-652-6780), 6262 Skidaway Road, Savannah. The largest regional park in Chatham County covers 500 acres and boasts a municipal golf course, tennis courts, soccer fields, ball fields, the Chatham County Aquatic Center, a weight-lifting center, and Lake Mayer Community Park. The park-within-a-park has a 35-acre fishing lake, a jogging-walking track with fitness stations, picnic areas, basketball and tennis courts, a remote-control auto racetrack, and an outdoor skating rink designed for in-line hockey. This park also offers a conditioning course for people in wheelchairs.

🐾 ♿ **Daffin Park** (912-651-6610), Victory Drive at Waters Avenue, Savannah. The park offers broad sidewalks; playgrounds; a pond; a fountain; athletic fields for baseball, softball, and soccer; tennis and basketball courts; and an outdoor, Olympic-sized swimming pool. At the eastern end of the park is Grayson Stadium, home of the Sand Gnats (see *Entertainment—Professional Sports*).

♿ **Emmet Park,** along East Bay Street above Factor's Walk and along River Street between Lincoln and Houston streets, Savannah. In addition to ancient live-oak trees, the park contains the Old Harbor Light, which dates to 1852 and warned mariners of British vessels scuttled off the coast in 1779; a fountain commemorating three ships named for Savannah; a Vietnam Memorial; the Oglethorpe Bench, which marks the site of Georgia founding father General James Oglethorpe's landing; and the Celtic Cross, also known as the Irish Monument.

✐ ✿ ♿ **Forsyth Park** (912-351-3852), bounded by Gaston, Whitaker, Drayton, and Hall streets, Savannah. Always open. Forsyth Park, created in 1851 and the largest of Savannah's squares, is 20 acres of green punctuated with wide sidewalks, an ornate fountain, a Confederate monument and other monuments and memorials, and the Fragrant Garden for the Blind. In addition, the park offers many athletic facilities, including two playgrounds, lighted tennis and basketball courts, playing fields, a 1-mile jogging course, and a summer wading fountain. Wheelchair accessible. Free.

✐ ✿ ♿ **Historic Savannah-Ogeechee Barge Canal Museum and Nature Center** (912-748-8068; www.socanalmuseum.com), 681 Fort Argyle Road, Savannah. Open 9–5 daily. Interpretive exhibits and artifacts in the museum teach visitors about the canal. Although it has not been in use for more than 100 years, the canal features four lift locks that are being restored. The 184-acre nature center encompasses river swamp, pine flatland, and sandhill habitats supporting a diversity of migratory birds, reptiles, and other animal life such as the endangered gopher tortoise. Walk alongside the 16.5-mile canal, which links the Savannah and Ogeechee rivers. Adults $2, children and seniors $1, children younger than 5 free. In April, the museum sponsors Swamp Thing, a festival with guided tours and reenactments.

✐ ✿ ♿ **Savannah National Wildlife Refuge** (912-652-4415), access from GA 25 north of Port Wentworth, or SC 170 south of Hardeeville, South Carolina. Open sunrise–sunset. The 26,349-acre refuge, which lies on both the Georgia and South Carolina sides of the Savannah River just upriver from Savannah, is a haven for wildlife. Fish, fowl, and alligators call the refuge home. Its position on the Atlantic Flyway brings in thousands of migratory birds and ducks during the winter, followed by songbirds during the spring and fall. Among the endangered species that call the refuge home are bald eagles, wood storks, manatees, and shortnose sturgeon. The 4-mile Laurel Hill Wildlife Drive off SC 170 is open to vehicular traffic throughout the year. The refuge also offers short hiking trails along which you can see remnants of old plantations with small cemeteries and foundations of slave cabins. The Cistern Trail leads to a huge brick circle where the plantation collected freshwater. Picnicking facilities are available. Call for hunting and fishing times and regulations. Don't forget the bug spray. Free.

✐ ✿ ♿ **Skidaway Island State Park** (912-598-2300; www.gastateparks.org/info/skidaway), 52 Diamond Causeway, Savannah. Open 7 AM–10 PM daily. This 588-acre barrier island has both saltwater and freshwater due to estuaries and marshes that flow through the area. The park borders Skidaway Narrows, a part of the Intracoastal Waterway. In addition to 1- and 3-mile nature and hiking trails that showcase local flora and fauna, the park has earthworks and a lookout tower, a museum and interpretive center, a giant ground sloth exhibit, and a birding station. The park also offers tent and trailer sites, a playground, picnic shelters, fishing, and a Junior Olympic-sized swimming pool. Most facilities handicapped accessible. Free.

THE COAST

✳ Lodging

Most visitors to Savannah prefer to stay in the historic district, which is home to several new and historic award-winning hotels, as well as numerous historic inns and bed & breakfasts where luxury abounds. These hostelries may be positioned along the Savannah River overlooking River Street or located in delightful neighborhoods of 18th- and 19th-century homes, but all are within walking distance of Savannah's primary sights. In addition to the lodgings described here, you might want to check out these web sites: www.romanticinnsofsavannah.com and www.historicinns-savannah.com.

Sun, sand, sea, and salty breezes draw visitors to Tybee Island, where accommodations are found in small hotels and motels, condos, small inns and bed & breakfasts, and rental cottages—some beachfront. Many of the inns and bed & breakfasts offer extras such as afternoon tea or a cocktail hour.

BED & BREAKFASTS

In Savannah

✂ ♿ **Ballastone Inn** (912-236-1484; 1-800-822-4553; www.ballastone.com), 14 East Oglethorpe Avenue. Named one of the most romantic inns in the country by *Brides* magazine and *Glamour,* the four-diamond Ballastone Inn, housed in an 1853 mansion, is truly a diamond among Savannah's many gems. Guest rooms and suites, many of which sport working fireplaces and/or whirlpool tubs, are exquisitely furnished with ornately carved rice poster or canopy beds and other antiques. Among the many amenities are breakfast, midday refreshments, afternoon tea, predinner

hors d'oeuvres, robes, and turndown service. Smoking in courtyard only. Wheelchair accessible. $215–395.

✂ ♿ **Eliza Thompson House** (912-236-3620; 1-800-348-9378; www .elizathompsonhouse.com), 5 West Jones Street. The 1847 town house and carriage house have been lovingly restored to house 25 spacious rooms and suites with all the amenities a modern traveler could want. The beautifully landscaped courtyard exuding Old South formality provides a quiet oasis in which guests can relax. Other niceties include a deluxe continental breakfast, afternoon wine and cheese, and evening desserts. No smoking. One wheelchair-accessible room. Prices from $149.

Foley House (912-232-6622; www .foleyinn.com), 14 West Hull Street, Chippewa Square. Foley House occupies two 1896 Federal-style town houses restored in minute detail. Each of the 18 guest rooms is a handsomely appointed masterpiece. Many guest chambers boast a working fireplace and/or a whirlpool tub. Throughout the day, guests are pampered with a hearty full breakfast, formal afternoon tea, early evening hors d'oeuvres, and late evening cordials. The inn has earned a AAA four-diamond rating. Smoking allowed on porches and balconies only. Not wheelchair accessible. $215–375.

♨ **Forsyth Park Inn** (912-233-6800; www.forsythparkinn.com), 102 West Hall Street. This wonderful old mansion that sits on a lushly landscaped lot across the street from Forsyth Park. Elegantly furnished with period antiques, guest rooms feature fireplaces and all the modern amenities. Guests are indulged with a high level of service as well as evening wine and hors d'oeuvres, plus turndown service with cordials and dessert. Pets welcome in cottage only. No smoking. Not wheelchair accessible. $175–230.

&. **Gaston Gallery Bed and Breakfast** (912-238-3294; 1-800-671-0716; www.gastongallery.com), 211 East Gaston Street. The Gaston Gallery, an elegant Italianate town house, was built in 1876 and has been meticulously restored and furnished with antiques and period reproductions. Among its premier features are its long verandas and second-story galleries, both of which invite sitting in a rocker with a book or a cool drink. A full breakfast and evening hors d'oeuvres are included. No smoking. Some whirlpool tubs and some rooms wheelchair accessible. $100–215.

&. **The Gastonian** (912-232-2869; 1-800-322-6603; www.gastonian.com), 220 East Gaston Street. This AAA four-diamond inn, recognized as one of the most romantic inns in the Southeast, offers 14 luxurious guest rooms as well as three two-room suites—all with a fireplace, some with a whirlpool tub—in two historic 1868 homes and a carriage house. Public and guest rooms are lavishly decorated and furnished in Georgian and Regency styles. Guests enjoy a full Southern breakfast, afternoon tea, evening desserts, and nightly turndown service. Ask about the ghost of Eleanor Richardson, whose portrait hangs over the mantelpiece in the front parlor. No smoking. One room with wheelchair access. $215–415.

&. **Hamilton-Turner Inn** (912-233-1833; 1-888-448-8849), 330 Abercorn Street, Lafayette Square. This AAA four-diamond property is one of the most beautiful and luxurious inns in Savannah. Known around town as the

"Grand Victorian Lady," the residence was built in 1873 and features public rooms and guest chambers furnished with Empire, Eastlake, and Renaissance Revival antiques. Guests enjoy a full Southern breakfast and afternoon tea. Smoking in courtyard only. Some rooms wheelchair accessible. $175–350.

&. **Kehoe House** (912-232-1020; 1-800-820-1020; www.kehoehouse .com), 123 Habersham Street. This magnificent Renaissance Revival mansion was built in 1892 on Columbia Square. Listed on the National Register of Historic Places, Kehoe House has been exquisitely restored and enhanced with antiques and period reproductions. Sumptuous guest rooms feature luxurious beds, and some boast a private or shared porch. An experienced staff pampers guests with a full gourmet breakfast, afternoon tea and hors d'oeuvres, nightly turndown, a concierge, laundry, and limited room service. No smoking. Elevator makes most rooms wheelchair accessible; one bathroom fully adapted for handicapped. $269–469.

Magnolia Place Inn (912-236-7674; 1-800-238-7674; www.magnolia placeinn.com), 503 Whitaker Street. This inn offers superb accommodations in the main house and simpler but more commodious accommodations in three nearby row houses, which are more suitable for families or larger groups. Some guest chambers in the main house boast a fireplace and/or a whirlpool tub, but all have antique furnishings and special accessories from around the world. Indulged guests enjoy a full breakfast, afternoon tea, evening cordials, and nightly turndown service. Oh, and by the way, there's a ghost. Children are welcome in row houses. No smoking. Not wheelchair accessible. $175–275.

✂ & **President's Quarters** (912-233-1600; 1-800-233-1776; www .presidentsquarters.com), 225 East President Street, Oglethorpe Square. Many of the elegant rooms and suites in these twin 1855 Federal-style town houses feature a whirlpool tub, steam shower, and/or a gas-log fireplace. Amenities include a gourmet continental-plus breakfast, afternoon refreshments, plush robes, nightly turndown service, room service, 24-hour concierge, an elevator, courtyard, lap pool, outdoor hot tub, and off-street parking. Children welcome. No smoking. Many rooms wheelchair accessible. $150–235.

MAGNOLIA PLACE INN

Senator's Gate Bed & Breakfast (912-233-6398; www.thesenatorsgate .com), 226 East Hall Street. This B&B offers luxurious accommodations in a magnificently restored Italianate mansion built in 1885 for state Senator R. E. Lester. Located on one of the historic district's best-preserved streets, the property offers four spacious, elegant guest rooms in the main house, as well as accommodations in the carriage house. Luxury is the name of the game here, where there are amenities such as whirlpool tubs and heated towel racks. A delicious gourmet breakfast and tender loving care from gracious hosts guarantee a memorable stay. No smoking. Not wheelchair accessible. $155–300.

17 Hundred 90 Inn (912-236-7122; www.17hundred90.com), 307 East President Street. Built in the year for which it is named, this is Savannah's oldest inn. Among 14 guest rooms handsomely decorated with antiques and Scalamandre fabrics in old Savannah designs, 12 of the rooms feature a fireplace. Room 204 is said to be inhabited by the ghost of the original owner, to which we can attest. The inn also boasts an award-winning restaurant and lounge (see *Where to Eat—Dining Out*) that is one of the locals' favorite places to eat and drink. No smoking. Not wheelchair accessible. $129–169.

On Tybee Island
Lighthouse Inn Bed and Breakfast (912-786-0901; 1-866-786-0901; www.tybeebb.com), 16 Meddin Drive. Cute as a button, this intimate inn is located near the beach, the lighthouse, and the North Beach Grill (see *Eating Out*). Get to know Susie and Stuart, the friendly owners, while

rocking on the shady veranda. No smoking. Not wheelchair accessible. $125–165.

17th Street Inn Bed and Breakfast (912-786-0607; 1-888-909-0607; www.tybeeinn.com), 12 17th Street. Located just a half block from the beach, this small inn offers efficiency apartments with kitchenettes and private porches. Smoking on porches or decks only. Not wheelchair accessible. $120–190.

Tybee Island Inn (912-786-9255; 1-866-892-4667; www.tybeeislandinn.com), 24 Van Horn Street. Once the recreation hall of Fort Screven, the building has been cleverly renovated to accommodate an intimate bed & breakfast located near the beach and lighthouse. No smoking. Not wheelchair accessible. $119–159.

EFFICIENCIES

In Savannah

🦐 ✍ **Sea Cabins** (912-790-8122; www.sea-cabins.com), 430 East River Street. Billed as "Bed and View," these fully equipped apartments, which sleep up to six, have balconies overlooking River Street and the Savannah River. Reservations are accepted nightly or weekly. No smoking. Not wheelchair accessible. $169 for two guests, $249 for six guests.

🦐 ✍ ♿ **Suites on Lafayette** (912-233-7815; www.suitesonlafayette.com), 201 East Charlton Street, Lafayette Square. Centrally located in the historic district, these two- and three-bedroom apartments feature gourmet kitchens, fireplaces in every room, and private porches. No smoking. One four-bedroom suite wheelchair accessible. $149–300.

In Savannah

🐾 ✍ ♿ **East Bay Inn** (912-238-1225; 1-800-500-1225; www.eastbayinn.com), 225 East Bay Street. The location alone, just across from Factor's Walk and River Street, makes this historic hotel—housed in a former cotton warehouse—an attractive place to stay. Charm, romance, elegant decor, and personalized service are important as well. Travelers with a pet, however, choose the East Bay Inn because their four-legged friends are also welcome in specified rooms. Other amenities include a restaurant, deluxe continental breakfast, morning newspaper, evening wine and sherry, and turndown service with a sweet treat. Smoking in first-floor rooms only. Elevator makes inn fully wheelchair accessible. $139–215.

✍ ♿ **Marshall House** (912-644-7896; 1-800-589-6304; www.marshallhouse.com), 123 East Broughton Street. Originally built as a hotel in 1851, the Marshall House declined along with Broughton Street and was closed and decaying for many years. With the renaissance of Broughton Street, however, the hotel was fully restored, reopening in 1999 with a restaurant and lounge. Today the four-star hotel, which was named the Best Hotel in Savannah by *Connect Savannah* magazine in 2004, blends Savannah's past with stylish decor and all the modern amenities and conveniences. Among them: an elevator for wheelchair access, off-street parking—a premium in Savannah—robes, turndown service, complimentary continental breakfast, and health-club privileges. Artifacts discovered during the renovation are displayed throughout the hotel. No smoking. $129–210.

♪ & **Mulberry Inn** (912-238-1200; 1-877-468-1200; www.savannahhotel .com), 601 East Bay Street. Located in an elegantly restored former Coca-Cola Bottling Works, this award-winning, full-service hotel features gracious rooms and suites, a charming courtyard and café, Sgt. Jasper's Tavern, afternoon tea with a live pianist, concierge services, a fitness center, and an outdoor pool and hot tub. Most rooms nonsmoking, but eight rooms reserved for smokers. Four rooms wheelchair accessible. $159–259.

🐾 ♪ **Olde Harbour Inn** (912-234-4100; 1-800-553-6533; www.olde harbourinn.com), 508 East Factor's Walk. Olde Harbour Inn offers one of the city's best views of the Savannah River and River Street. Built in 1892, the building began life as a cotton warehouse and shipping center. After a brief life as a condominium complex, the structure became an all-suites hotel. Now, each guest chamber is either an efficiency or a full apartment with one or more bedrooms—all furnished in period reproductions. Deluxe continental breakfast and afternoon candlelight wine and hors d'oeuvres provide opportunities for guests to mingle. Pets welcome. No smoking. Not wheelchair accessible. $149–250.

♪ & **Planters Inn** (912-232-5678; 1-800-554-1187; www.plantersinn savannah), 29 Abercorn Street, Reynolds Square. An intimate historic hotel built in 1912, Planters Inn blends the warmth and charm of a small inn with the services of a large hotel. High-ceilinged guest rooms feature four-poster beds and lavish bed and window coverings done in reproductions of old Savannah fabrics.

Continental breakfast, afternoon wine, nightly turndown service, and valet parking round out the amenities. No smoking. An elevator makes accommodations wheelchair accessible. $129–279.

♪ & **River Street Inn** (912-234-6400; 1-800-253-4229; www.river streetinn.com), 115 East River Street. Offering riverfront hospitality at its best, the historic River Street Inn, built in 1817 as a cotton warehouse, boasts spacious rooms—many with balconies overlooking the river and River Street. With themes that range from sea captain to English chintz, guest chambers feature all the modern conveniences. The hotel also offers two restaurants and three bars, an elevator, billiard room, concierge service, an hors d'oeuvres reception, and nightly turndown service. Children younger than 16 stay free in the room with parents and using existing bedding. Nonsmoking rooms available. Wheelchair accessible. $132–279.

INNS AND HOTELS

In Savannah

& **Mansion on Forsyth Park** (912-238-5158; www.mansiononforsyth park.com), 700 Drayton Street. This new, chic, and luxurious hostelry offers irresistible accommodations, culinary experiences, and spa services in a restored 1888 historic property around which an addition was built. A successful blend of old and new, the property features dramatic architecture, lavish interiors, and lush gardens. Amenities include the five-star full-service Poseidon Spa, fitness center, 700 Drayton gourmet restaurant, 700 Kitchen cooking school, Grand Bohemian Art Gallery, 24-hour concierge, and business services. No smoking. Some rooms wheelchair accessible. $249–329.

✒ ♿ **Savannah Marriott Riverfront** (912-233-7722; 1-800-228-9290), 100 General McIntosh Boulevard. Overlook the Savannah River from your spacious room. The 337-room, 46-suite hotel also offers a concierge level, indoor and outdoor pools, whirlpool, fitness facility, and two restaurants. The hotel is just a short stroll from River Street and Riverwalk. Nonsmoking rooms available. Wheelchair accessible. $159–189.

RESORTS

In Savannah
✒ ♿ **Westin Savannah Harbor Golf Resort and Spa** (912-201-2000; 1-888-625-5144), One Resort Drive. A AAA four-diamond resort located on Hutchinson Island on the Savannah River across from the historic district, the Westin is Savannah's newest luxury hotel. In addition to more than 400 rooms with Westin's signature beds and baths, the resort hotel features a restaurant and lounge, fitness center, riverside Jacuzzi, cabanas, heated pool, four lighted tennis courts, and a 400-foot water dock. The property also boasts a championship golf course designed by Sam Snead and Robert Cupp, as well as the renowned Greenbrier Spa. Water-taxi service is available to River Street and downtown Savannah. The hotel is adjacent to the Savannah International Trade and Convention Center. No smoking. Wheelchair accessible. $110–400.

On Tybee Island
✒ ♿ **Ocean Plaza Resort** (912-786-7777; 1-800-215-6370; www.ocean plaza.com), 1401 Strand Avenue. Tybee Island's only large hotel, the

Ocean Plaza features rooms and suites, many of them oceanfront. The hotel also features two swimming pools. The hotel's Dolphin Reef Restaurant and Lounge, which is open daily for breakfast, lunch, and dinner, specializes in seafood and steaks. Smoking and nonsmoking rooms available. Wheelchair accessible. $49–190.

CAMPGROUNDS

In Savannah
☙ **Bellaire Woods Campground** (912-748-4000), 805 Fort Argyle Road. Twenty-four shaded acres along the Ogeechee River offer shady, pull-through sites, a bathhouse, convenience store, children's playground, outdoor pool, boat ramp, fishing and boating, laundry facilities, and on-site RV repairs. $30–35.

On Tybee Island
☙ ✒ **River's End Campground and RV Park** (912-786-5518; 1-800-786-1016), 915 Polk Street. Conveniently located within walking distance of the lighthouse, Fort Screven, and the beach, River's End has 130 shady tent and RV sites with full hookups as well as a laundry, dumping site, fuel, picnic tables, bathhouse, a pool, and a camp store. $34–39; cabin rentals $60–100.

COTTAGES

On Tybee Island
✒ **Tybee Cottages** (912-786-6746; 1-877-524-9819; www.tybeecottages .com), P.O. Box 1226. Offers daily and weekly rentals of one- and two-bedroom condos or cottages with up to five bedrooms—many waterfront. $1,100–3,500 per week with accommodations for four to 17.

✳ Where to Eat

Savannah is a virtual cornucopia of award-winning restaurants featuring eclectic cuisines ranging from low country and other Southern traditional favorites to ethnic cuisines such as Asian, Caribbean, English, French, Greek, Irish, Italian, Moroccan, and Southwestern, to name a few. Tybee Island is noted for its plentitude of casual seafood eateries, although it also has several outstanding upscale restaurants. When eating out in Savannah and Tybee Island, it's best to forget the diet and leave the calorie counter at home.

DINING OUT

In Savannah

&. **Chart House Restaurant** (912-234-6686; www.chart-house.com), 202 West Bay Street. Open 5–10 Monday through Saturday, 5–9 Sunday. Although part of a national chain, each Chart House Restaurant is located in a historically significant building that has been lovingly restored. The Savannah location is no different, occupying a converted sugar and cotton warehouse reputed to be the oldest masonry building in Georgia. Proceed from raw-bar selections to appetizers, soups, and salads— including the signature Chart House Salad—then move on to fresh fish and seafood specialties or prime rib, steaks, and chicken. Top off your gastronomic delight with a dessert such as Hot Chocolate Lava Cake. No smoking. Wheelchair ramp on Bay Street side. Entrées $15–25.

Elizabeth on 37th (912-236-5547; www.elizabethon37th.com), 105 East 37th Street. Open 6–10 daily. Located in a lavish Greek Revival–style Southern mansion built in 1900, the restaurant is the creation of chef Elizabeth Terry, winner of the prestigious James Beard Award. Terry's devotion to classic Southern cooking led her to extensively research 18th- and 19th-century Savannah cooking in order to create her contemporary recipes. Although she is no longer involved in the restaurant, Terry's culinary legacy is still evident. Spacious dining rooms exquisitely embellished with beautiful architectural details and a palette of historic Savannah colors and patterns serve as an elegant backdrop for your epicurean delights. Seasonal menus showcase the bounty of local seafood and produce, including herbs from the restaurant's own gardens. Reservations by phone required (e-mail reservations not accepted). No smoking. Not wheelchair accessible. Entrées $24.95–39.95.

&. **Garibaldi** (912-232-7118), 315 West Congress Street. Open 5:30–10:30 Sunday through Thursday, 5:30–midnight Friday and Saturday. Garibaldi serves local seafood specialties such as flounder and tuna, creative chicken and veal entrées, and other European dishes with an Italian flair. Housed in a historic firehouse, the restaurant is filled with colorful Impressionistic murals. The crowd tends to be young and lively. Start with the house favorite, calamari, and finish with a sinful dessert. No smoking. Wheelchair accessible. Entrées $14–35.

&. **Il Pasticcio** (912-231-8888), 2 East Broughton Street. Open 5:30–10 Monday through Thursday, 5:30– midnight Friday and Saturday, 5:30–9:30 Sunday. The name, which means "joyful chaos," is a perfect moniker for this high-voltage Italian restaurant. Located in a former department store, the eatery features an open kitchen and circular wine bar. Original Italian dishes and original artwork blend to create a trend-setting restaurant. Smoking allowed in one section. Wheelchair accessible. Entrées in $20 range.

Olde Pink House (912-232-4286), 23 Abercorn Street. Open 5:30–10 Sunday through Thursday, 5:30–11 Friday and Saturday. Contemporary and colonial Georgian and Caribbean-influenced cuisine is served in one of Savannah's oldest mansions. Signature dishes include crispy scorched flounder, crab-stuffed grouper, and rack of lamb. Smoking in tavern only. Not wheelchair accessible. Entrées $14.95–29.95.

⌀ & **The Pirates' House** (912-233-5757; www.thepirateshouse.com), 20 East Broad Street. Open 6–9 Monday through Thursday, 6–9:30 Friday and Saturday. Originally an inn for seafarers, this 1753 tavern reportedly became a rendezvous for bloodthirsty pirates. In fact, rumors persist that a tunnel extends from the old rum cellar under the Captain's Room to the river and that drunken sailors were carried unconscious through the tunnel to ships waiting in the harbor. What's more, some of the action in Robert Louis Stevenson's *Treasure Island* is supposed to have occurred at the Pirates' House. Old Captain Flint, who originally buried the treasure, is supposed to have died here with cohort Billy Bones at his side. Pages from a rare early edition of the book decorate the walls in some of the 15 dining rooms. Today, the site's treasure is its delicious food—particularly its seafood and Southern specialties—drink, and rousing good times. Also on the premises is **45 South** (912-

233-1881), a five-star restaurant. No smoking. Wheelchair ramp into restaurant, but may be small steps inside. Entrées in $20 range.

& **The River House** (912-234-1900; 1-800-317-1912; www.riverhouse seafood.com), 125 West River Street. Open 11–10 daily, 11 Friday and Saturday. This popular restaurant is located in a converted 1850s cotton warehouse, where you can sit riverside and watch the ships and tugs sail by while savoring genuine Savannah flavors, fresh seafood dishes, and home-baked breads and desserts. Some signature dishes include pecan-encrusted tilapia and low-country grits, yellowfin tuna, or veal chop au poivre, as well as po'boys and pizzettas. No smoking. For wheelchair access, ask staff to open special door. Lunch entrées about $10, dinner entrées $20–30.

17 Hundred 90 Restaurant (912-236-7122; www.17hundred90.com), 307 East President Street. Restaurant open 11:30–2 weekdays, 6–10 nightly. Pub open 11 AM to whenever weekdays, 6 PM to whenever weekends; happy hour with hors d'oeuvres 4:30–7 weekdays. This restaurant delivers a fine dining experience: wonderful entrées and professional service in an elegant setting with original brick floors and fireplaces. Lunch menus feature soups, salads, sandwiches, and entrées such as crabcakes, pasta, catch of the day, and chicken. Dinner entrées feature seafood, veal, rack of lamb, beef, and duck. *Georgia Trend* singled out the restaurant as a favorite spot for "financiers, business people, and professionals." *Gourmet* and *Travelhost* magazines have heaped accolades on it as well. The restaurant's pub has been a local hangout for years—especially with its popular happy hour. Smoking in lounge only. Not wheelchair accessible. Lunch under $10, dinner $20–30.

On Tybee Island

& **Georges' of Tybee** (912-786-9730; www.georgesoftybee.com), 1105 US 80 East. Open 6–10 Tuesday through Sunday. Upscale dining at its best can be found at this trendy restaurant, the brainchild of George Jackson and George Spriggs. Located in a historic building reported to have served as a railroad depot, the restaurant actually exudes the charm and warmth of a private home. The cuisine is described as American fusion, and the presentation and service are exemplary. Begin with Georges' signature soup—crab with sweet corn, leek, and artichoke scented with thyme—then move on to other appetizers, salads, and entrées, among which might be grilled rack of lamb, blackened grouper, iron-seared yellowfin tuna, tomato basil linguinei, fire-grilled pismo rib eye, or barbecue-rubbed beef tenderloin. No smoking. Wheelchair accessible. $8–$32.

& **Sundae Café and Deli** (912-786-7694), US 80 East and Jones Avenue. Open 9–10 daily. Tucked on the other side of the deli and ice cream shop is a fine dining restaurant that serves lunch and dinner. Tablecloths, cloth napkins, and flickering candlelight set the stage for entrées such as black and white sesame–encrusted yellowfin tuna, char-grilled filet mignon, bacon-wrapped and crab-stuffed jumbo shrimp, and other delicacies. No smoking. Wheelchair accessible. Lunch entrées under $10, dinner entrées under $20.

& **Tango** (912-786-8264), 1106 US 80 East. Open 6–10 daily, Sunday brunch 11–3. This trendy eatery serves equatorial cuisine with an emphasis on the Caribbean, but you might find dishes from Vietnam, Indonesia, and Hong Kong as well. Feast on such specialties as conch fritters, mahimahi, and black beans and rice with fried plantains. Eat inside or on the back porch overlooking the marsh. No smoking. Wheelchair accessible. Starters and salads under $10, entrées $16–29.

EATING OUT

In Savannah

& **Crystal Beer Parlor** (912-443-9200; www.crystalbeerparlor.net), 301 West Jones Street. Open 11–10 Monday through Thursday, 11–midnight Friday and Saturday. Locals and visitors frequent the Crystal Beer Parlor for American fare and laid-back entertainment on Friday nights. The old speakeasy-style restaurant began during Prohibition in the 1930s. These days, the Beer Parlor Ramblers house band plays New Orleans–style Dixieland jazz and big-band music on Friday nights. No smoking. Wheelchair accessible. Entrées $6–20.

& **Huey's** (912-234-7385), 115 River Street. Open daily for breakfast, lunch, and dinner. Whether you just want a beignet (a square, holeless doughnut covered in powdered sugar) or a New Orleans–inspired meal of po'boys, red beans and rice, jambalaya, or other Cajun favorites, this fun eatery is the place to go. A table outside or by the window allows diners to people-watch while getting a glimpse of the ships and other boats plying the river. If you eat outside, you can bring your dog. When we asked for a bowl of water for our two cocker spaniels, they were supplied with a porcelain bowl with a lemon wedge on the edge. Smoking in bar area only. Wheelchair accessible. $2.25–$13.95.

☏ ☕ ♿ **The Lady & Sons** (912-233-2600; www.ladyandsons.com), 102 West Congress Street. Open 11–3 and 5 until whenever Monday through Saturday, 11–5 Sunday. Voted the best buffet in Savannah by *Connect Savannah* magazine, this restaurant serves Southern cuisine some call Georgia Coastal and others call Plantation Country. We just call it good. Favorites include Southern fried chicken, collard greens, barbecued pork ribs, low-country boil, and macaroni and cheese, but there's much more comfort food from which to choose. No smoking. Wheelchair accessible. Lunch buffet $12.99, dinner buffet $16.99.

☏ ☕ ♿ **Mrs. Wilkes Dining Room** (912-232-5997; www.mrswilkes.com), 107 Jones Street. Open 11 AM–2 PM weekdays. Although the inimitable Mrs. Wilkes passed on to culinary heaven in 2002 at age 95, family members still operate the famous restaurant where folks come from all over for a bountiful, all-you-can-eat, down-home Southern feast served family-style. Your guaranteed-to-be-interesting table mates may be from anywhere in the world. Neither credit cards nor reservations are accepted. Get in line early if you don't want to be disappointed. No smoking. Wheelchair accessible. $13 flat fee.

On Tybee Island

☏ ♿ **A. J.'s Dockside Restaurant** (912-786-9533), 1315 Chatham Avenue. Open 11–3 and 5–10 Tuesday through Sunday. Don't be discouraged by the unimpressive streetside facade of this delightful eatery—all the action is on the dock

jutting out into the Back River, where you can watch the glorious sunsets (there are a few tables inside and on a covered deck for the occasional rainy day). A wide variety of appetizers, soups, salads, sandwiches, and entrées such as shrimp Creole, jambalaya pasta, rib eye, pork chops, and more satisfy any appetite. Diners may come by car or boat, and there is live entertainment in-season. No smoking inside. Wheelchair accessible (if arriving by boat, ramp from boat dock very steep at low tide). Lunch $7–10, dinner $13–$25.

☏ ☕ ♿ **The Breakfast Club** (912-786-5984), 1500 Butler Avenue. Frequented by locals and consistently voted the best place for breakfast in the Savannah area, this very casual restaurant offers simple, hearty breakfast and lunch fare for the budget-conscious traveler. Primary to the menu are ice-cold, fresh-squeezed orange juice and eggs just about any way you like them—including a variety of omelets with names such as Father Guido Sarducci—accompanied by grits and toast. Hash browns and waffles also figure prominently. Lunch items include burgers, sandwiches, and specials. After such a huge meal, you'll have plenty of energy for a long walk on the beach or a bike ride. No smoking. Wheelchair accessible. $3–7.

☏ ☕ ♿ **The Crab Shack at Chimney Creek** (912-786-9857; www.thecrab shack.com), 40 Estill Hammock Road. Open 11:30–10 Monday through Thursday, 11:30–11 Friday through Sunday. Billed as "Where the Elite Eat in Their Bare Feet," the Crab Shack has been a local tradition since 1983. What began as a fishing camp is now a popular, casual, indoor-outdoor eatery that serves all kinds of seafood. Naturally, crabs of all types top the menu, but you can feast on clams, oysters, shrimp, and low-country boil. The occasional diner who doesn't care for seafood can choose from chicken, ribs, pork, chili, and hot dogs. Picnic tables have a hole in the middle and a trash can underneath so you can dispose of your shells. Paper towels serve as napkins. You get the picture. A gift shop and a pool of tiny alligators offer some distractions for those waiting in line, a given in-season. You also can have your boat put in or taken out of the water here. No smoking inside. Wheelchair accessible. $3.99–$40.

🦐 ♿ **Huc-A-Poos Bites and Booze** (912-786-5900; www.hucapoos.com), US 80 in the Shops at Tybee Oaks. Open 4–midnight weekdays, 11 AM–midnight Saturday and Sunday. Tucked away in a shady grove, Huc-

THE CRAB SHACK

The ramshackle appearance of the building and grounds—the name, after all, is "Shack"—just points out that this is an old fishing camp grown up. Since the 1930s, there has been some kind of fish camp on these 4 acres of high ground overlooking Chimney Creek. In the beginning, locals put their boats in the water here and bought bait and simple "necessaries"—which included cold beer. Then spaces were rented out for a few small camper trailers, and the Chimney Creek Fishing Camp was born.

Jack and Belinda Flanigan, displaced locals who had left the area for the frenetic pace of Atlanta, decided to return to their roots when the fish camp was for sale in 1983. At first they ran the camp and marina while studying for their captain's licenses. Soon Jack was running offshore charters and Belinda was running inshore fishing trips, and both were hearing that their guests wanted a place to gather and cook the crabs, shrimp, and fish they had caught. So a table appeared here and there, and locals, friends, and strangers soon followed.

A business license was obtained in 1987, and the Crab Shack was born. Jack did the cooking and Belinda waited tables. Then folks wanted a libation with their meal. A liquor license came next, and the Flanigans and their friends had an old-fashioned barn raising, but this one was a "bar raising."

Now picnic tables cover several decks and fill screened buildings where folks can still enjoy a meal on a rainy day. Relics from the old days—including the marina and bait-shop building from the '30s, which now houses the Gift Shack, and the rest-room building from the '50s—contribute to the overall dilapidated look. But they don't detract from the picturesque location where you can watch dolphins play or gaze at the stunning sunsets as you dine al fresco amid hundred-year-old live oaks. Come by boat or car, in your shorts or your bathing suit, and you'll be perfectly at home at the Crab Shack.

A-Poos (named after a racehorse) is a casual eatery that specializes in build-your-own pizzas, wraps, nachos, hot dogs, gyros, chili, and a large selection of beers. A full bar and live entertainment make this a fun place to spend a late evening. Smoking allowed. Wheelchair accessible. $12–15.

✒ ✿ ♿ **North Beach Grill** (912-786-9003; www.georgesoftybee.com), 41-A Meddin Drive. Open 11:30–3 and 5–9:30 daily in-season, weekends only off-season. Don't be put off by the shanty appearance; there's good food and good times in store. The cuisine is innovative, Caribbean-inspired fare such as grilled plantains with chutney, conch fritters and fish tacos, or a chunky crabmeat sandwich. The menu also offers the usual burgers, hot dogs, and wings for lunch and jerk pork or chicken, duck, and rib eye for dinner. Top off your meal with a Red Stripe beer, and you'd swear you were in the islands. No smoking inside. Wheelchair accessible. Lunch entrées under $10, dinner entrées under $20.

✒ ✿ **Sunrise** (912-786-7473), 1511 Butler Avenue. Open 6–2 daily. While tourists are lined up to get into the Breakfast Club, locals stroll on over to the less-crowded Sunrise for a hearty breakfast or lunch. All kinds of eggs, omelets, pancakes, waffles, and French toast fill the breakfast menu. Sandwiches, burgers, steaks, chicken, and salads make up the lunch menu. A breakfast buffet is served on weekends and holidays, and a lunch buffet on weekdays. No smoking. Not wheelchair accessible. Most entrées $5 or under.

TEAROOMS

In Savannah
✒ ✿ ♿ **Gryphon Tea Room** (912-525-5880), 337 Bull Street. Open 8:30–9:30 weekdays, 10–9:30 Saturday. Owned by the Savannah College of Art and Design, the Gryphon is located in the meticulously restored former A. A. Solomon's and Company drug store, which has been converted to resemble a Parisian tearoom while retaining many of the architectural features of the old apothecary, such as the Tiffany glass globes featuring the gryphons that lend the tearoom its name. The Gryphon serves breakfast and lunch, but the pièce de résistance is afternoon tea served from 4 to 6. There is also a selection of specialty coffees. No smoking. Wheelchair accessible. High tea $12, lunch $7–11.

✳ Entertainment

HAUNTED TOURS Savannah claims to be the most haunted city in America, and plenty of strange occurrences have been documented there. Whether or not you believe in the supernatural, these tours, which usually gather after dark in a central location, are mesmerizing. One is offered by **Haunting Tours** (912-234-3571; www.hauntingstour.com). Adults $17–21, children 6–14 $6. Another is the **Creepy Crawl: Haunted Pub Tour,** operated by Savannah by Foot Tours (912-238-3843; www.savannah-tours.com/CreepyCrawl.asp). Voted Savannah's Best Tour by *Connect Savannah* magazine, the Creepy Crawl is an enjoyable after-dark walk with spirited tales of ghosts, witchery, and voodoo along with stops (and drinks) at some of Savannah's most interesting pubs. Reservations required. $15 per person, not including gratuities.

♿ **Murder Afloat** (912-232-6404; 1-800-786-6404; www.murderafloat

.com), Thursday nights April through August. Tours depart from a site next to the Hyatt on River Street. Become an amateur sleuth as a puzzling murder mystery unfolds around you during a 1½-hour cruise along the riverfront. Professional actors dramatize an original whodunit at various places on the boat, and guests are encouraged to circulate, question suspects, uncover clues, and compare notes with others. A prize is given for solving the crime. No smoking. Wheelchair accessible on first deck. Adults $24.95, children younger than 12 $17.50.

MOVIES Friends of the Tybee Theater (912-313-4687; www.tybee theater.com), Tybee Island. The group offers movies under the stars on the grounds of the Tybee Lighthouse on the third Saturday of May, June, July, and August. Movies start 30 minutes after sunset. Bring your lawn chairs, blankets, a picnic, and a cooler. The proceeds from the movies, which cost $5, are used as a fund-raiser for the eventual restoration of the historic Tybee Theater. Children younger than 3 free. Pets not allowed. Don't forget bug spray.

MUSIC Jazz has been a tradition in Savannah since Reconstruction-era brass bands were popular in the city. Vaudeville, ragtime, and rhythm and blues followed. Today, contemporary jazz stylings can be heard at various venues, and a plentitude of musical performances can be heard at theaters, houses of worship, and festivals. Music is integral to the **St. Patrick's Day** celebration as well as the **Savannah Music Festival** and **Savannah Jazz Festival** (see *Special Events*). Savannah is also part of the **Georgia**

Music Trail, which includes Atlanta, Athens, and Macon, too. For more information on the trail, consult www .georgia.org/tourism/music_trail/ index.asp.

♪ ₺ *Jukebox Journey* (912-233-7764; www.savannahtheatre.com), Savannah Theatre, 222 Bull Street, Chippewa Square, Savannah. Performances at 8 Wednesday through Saturday, matinees at 3 Saturday and Sunday. The musical scene from the 1940s to the present is depicted in a bright, colorful, fast-moving production filled with popular music, peppy choreography, lavish costumes, and comedy skits, all of which have made *Jukebox Journey* downtown's No. 1 entertainment extravaganza. Wheelchair accessible. $30.

₺ **Savannah Symphony Orchestra** (912-236-9877; 1-800-537-7894), 225 Abercorn Street, Savannah. Box office open 9–5 weekdays. Call for a schedule of events and prices. Savannah's orchestra is one of only two fully professional orchestras in Georgia (Atlanta's is the other). The yearly nine-concert Masterworks series is performed at the Savannah Civic Center's Johnny Mercer Theatre. During the year, the orchestra also performs at Forsyth Park, at the Telfair Academy of Arts and Sciences, in churches, and at other venues.

NIGHTSPOTS As much as there is to do in Savannah during the day, the city really sparkles at night, with a variety of clubs featuring jazz and blues, Latin salsa, bluegrass, swing, oldies, and every genre in between.

Club 1 (912-232-0200; www.clubone -online.com), One Jefferson Street, Savannah. Open 5 PM–3 AM Monday through Saturday, Sunday until 2 AM.

Club 1 has been voted Savannah's top dance club since 1997 by readers of *Connect Savannah* magazine. Activities include Tuesday trivia night, Wednesday talent night, and Thursday Gothic and show night, but the premier event is a not-to-be-missed monthly appearance by the one-and-only Lady Chablis of *Midnight in the Garden of Good and Evil* fame. Smoking permitted. Wheelchair accessible on first floor only. Note: Shows are on the second floor, which is not wheelchair accessible. $6 general admission, $10 for a show, $25 for Lady Chablis.

& **Savannah Smiles Dueling Pianos Saloon** (912-527-6453), 314-B Williamson Street, Savannah. Open 5 PM–3 AM Wednesday through Friday, 5:30 PM–3 AM Saturday, 5:30 PM–2 AM Sunday. Get there early, because this nightspot with continuous dueling piano music is so popular that parking is at a premium and the venue fills up fast. Smoking allowed. Wheelchair accessible. $5 cover charge; food $6–8.

& **Tubby's Tank House** (912-233-0770), 115 East River Street, Savannah. Open 11–10 Monday through Thursday and Sunday, 11–11 Friday and Saturday. Tubby's offers a happy hour and live entertainment (weather permitting) daily on River Street's largest balcony, as well as seafood, sandwiches, and the like. Smoking outside only. Wheelchair accessible. $10–20.

& **Wet Willie's** (912-233-5650; www.wetwillies.com), 101 East River Street, Savannah. Open 11 AM–1 AM Monday through Thursday, 11 AM–2 AM Friday and Saturday, 12:30 PM–1 AM Sunday. Now with several locations nationwide, Wet Willie's started right here on Savannah's River Street in 1989. Famous for its daiquiris and other frozen drinks with names such as Sex on the Beach, Shock Treatment, and Willie's Electric Tea, the establishment also offers live entertainment including disc jockeys, karaoke, dancing, and trivia contests. No smoking. Wheelchair accessible. $2–7.

PROFESSIONAL SPORTS & & **Savannah Sand Gnats** (912-351-9150; www.sandgnats.com), Victory Drive and Bee Road, Savannah (mailing address: P.O. Box 3783, Savannah 31313). The minor-league team, an affiliate of the Washington Nationals, competes in the Class-A South Atlantic League. The team plays about 70 home games at Grayson Stadium in Daffin Park between April and Labor Day. Tickets can be purchased at the gate or by calling ahead.

THEATER & **The Lucas Theatre** (912-525-5040; www.lucastheatre.com), 32 Abercorn Street, Reynolds Square, Savannah. The Lucas Theatre is an icon of a bygone era. Built in 1921 as the first and only movie palace in Savannah, the opulent Italian Renaissance theater contains 1,250 seats. It closed in 1976, and although it was once slated for demolition, the theater was saved and fully restored, including its majestic 40-foot-wide ceiling dome, intricately detailed Adam-style plasterwork, Wedgwood-inspired colors, and gold-leaf accents. It reopened in 2000 and today is a premier performing arts center offering musical theater, classic performances, and concerts by top artists. Call for a schedule of events and prices.

& **Trustees Theater** (box office 912-

525-5050; www.trusteestheater.com), 216 East Broughton Street, Savannah. Formerly the Weis Theater, Trustees was once part of Savannah's thriving post–World War II theater district. It claimed to be fireproof, had one of the largest movie screens in the Southeast, had air-conditioning, and was lavishly decorated in the Art Moderne style. As in other cities, the theater and others nearby failed as movie theaters followed residents to the suburbs, and it closed in 1980. Fortunately, it was bought and restored by the Savannah College of Art and Design and now plays host to the school's productions, student film screenings, national headline acts, concerts, lectures, and the annual Savannah Film and Video Festival. Call for a schedule of events and prices.

✳ Selective Shopping

Quaint ballast-stone streets along Savannah's River Street and Factor's Walk are lined with shops and boutiques purveying everything from pralines to kites to nautical-themed apparel and gifts. Several blocks away, but still within the historic district, City Market—known as the "Art and Soul of Savannah"—is a four-block courtyard alive with art studios, galleries, specialty shops, restaurants, and nightspots. Bull and Broughton streets are the heart of Savannah's antiques district.

Tybee Island has a growing number of upscale galleries and shops, but shopping there is primarily limited to beach clothing, equipment, and souvenirs.

ANTIQUES Clipper Trading Company, Inc. (912-443-9111; 1-800-390-0498; www.clippertrading.com), 506 West Jones Street, Savannah. Open 9:30–5:30 Monday through Saturday. Clipper Trading imports artwork, antique furniture, china, collectibles, crafts, and home accent pieces from Southeast Asia and China.

ART GALLERIES City Market Art Center (912-232-4903), Jefferson and St. Julian streets, City Market, Savannah. Hours vary on weekdays; open most weekends. The center is actually a community of 35 working artists who make and sell their work in studio and gallery lofts.

Gallery by the Sea (912-786-7979), US 80 and Campbell Avenue, Tybee Island. Open 9–5:30 daily. Home to the artists of the Tybee Arts Association, the gallery shows the work of 80 local and regional artists.

The Nautilus Studio Gallery (912-786-4462; www.lindalindeborg.com), 701 US 80 East, Tybee Island. Open afternoons and evenings on weekends March through December or by appointment. This is actually the home of watercolorist Linda Lindeborg. Meet her in her studio, where you can purchase originals and prints.

Ray Ellis Gallery (1-800-752-4865), 205 West Congress Street, Savannah. Open 10–4 Monday through Saturday. The gallery exhibits the watercolors, oils, and bronzes of Ray Ellis exclusively, as well as limited- and open-edition prints and books.

BOOKS The Casual Reader Used Bookstore (912-786-7655), 1213 US 80 East, Tybee Island. Open 10–6 Tuesday through Sunday. Because beach visits and summer reading go hand in hand, visitors devour books and may exhaust the supply they brought from home. You can trade in your finished books at the only bookstore on Tybee, which has a huge selection that more than likely includes your favorite authors. The shop also rents DVDs.

E. Shaver, Bookseller (912-234-7257), 326 Bull Street, Savannah. Open 9–6 Monday through Saturday. With 12 rooms of books, this exceptional bookstore offers an extensive collection of hardbacks and paperbacks, specializing in architecture, decorative arts, and regional history. The shop also carries antique maps.

FLEA MARKETS Keller's Flea Market (912-927-4848; www.ilovefleas .com), 5901 Ogeechee Road, Savannah. Open 8–6 every weekend year-round. The full-service flea market includes 600 stalls where you can find just about anything. Look for the giant cow. The site also includes restaurants and camping facilities for the serious shopper. Wheelchair accessible. No pets allowed. Free parking and admission.

FOOD Savannah is known for its pralines and other sweets. The following stores sell everything your sweet tooth could desire.

River Street Sweets (912-234-4608; www.riverstreetsweets.com), 13 East River Street, Savannah. Open 9–8 daily, Friday and Saturday until 11. This is Savannah's original candy store, and it's where you can find its world-famous pralines as well as gourmet Southern candies and gift baskets.

Savannah Candy Kitchen (912-233-8411; www.savannahcandy.com), 225 East River Street, Savannah. Open 9:30–10 daily. Pecan pralines and fudge are specialties, but the sweetshop also sells cakes, pies, and gift baskets.

Savannah Sweets (912-355-3539; 1-800-423-1314; www.savannahsweets .com), 7804 Abercorn Street, Savannah. Open 10–9 Monday through Saturday, noon–6 Sunday. This shop specializes in pecan candies, glazed pecans, sugar and spice pecans, pralines, caramels, brittles, fudge, and divinity.

GIFTS Nautilus Chic on the Beach (912-659-9371; www.lindalindeborg .com), 1213 US 80 East, Tybee Island. Open 10–5 Wednesday through Saturday, 11–4 Sunday. Merchandise includes prints by artist Linda Lindeborg's (see Nautilus Studio Gallery under *Art Galleries*) and handcrafted decorative arts. Linda herself is here Wednesday through Friday.

Very Jeri (912-786-7718; www.very jeri.com), 1213 US 80 East, Tybee Island. Open 10ish until whenever Tuesday through Saturday, 1ish to whenever Sunday. Guaranteed to put a smile on your face, this shop sells whimsical local art and beachy home accessories in happy colors. Flip-flops are featured on everything from paintings to jewelry to T-shirts to fan pulls. Representations of the Tybee Lighthouse appear on tiles, cookie tins, aprons, cards, plaques, and ornaments. Jeri paints Petraits—3-D papier-mâché-on-canvas pet portraits. You can buy one she has created or have her create a custom work of your pet.

OUTLET MALLS Savannah Festival Factory Stores, (912-925-3089), 11 Gateway Boulevard, Savannah. Open 9–9 Monday through Saturday, 11–6 Sunday. The facility features a restaurant and 30 brand-name outlet stores, including Bon Worth, Dress Barn, Corning Revere, Book Warehouse, Paper Factory, and Bass Outlet.

SPECIAL STORES **"The Book" Gift Shop and Midnight Museum** (912-233-3867; 1-888-833-3867 for orders only; www.midnightinsavannah.com), 127 East Gordon Street, Calhoun Square, Savannah. Open 10:30–5 Monday through Saturday, 12:30–4:30 Sunday. Your one-stop shop for fine Savannah gifts is the city's only official headquarters for *Midnight* information, products, and memorabilia, including autographed books. The shop also offers daily bus and walking tours to sites described in "the Book."

The Christmas Shop (912-234-5243; 1-800-569-0330; www.the-christmas -shop.com), 307 Bull Street, Savannah. Open 9:30–6 Monday through Saturday, noon–3 Sunday. Shop here for the finest in Christmas collectibles, ornaments, and decorations, as well as designer jewelry and handbags, and infant and children's clothing.

Saints and Shamrocks (912-233-8855; www.saints-shamrocks.com), 309 Bull Street, Savannah. The city is so Irish, it's only natural that an Irish-themed store would find its home there. The family-owned Saints and Shamrocks is a tasteful, upscale book, gift, and religious gift shop. No trashy souvenirs cluttering the shelves here.

Savannah Sails and Rails (912-232-7201), 423 East River Street, Savannah. A not-to-be-missed shop, this fascinating emporium features an astounding array of kites, windsocks, flags, LGB trains, toys, and much more. If you're looking for a state, U.S., country, or historic flag, you can probably find it here, or owner Pat Robinson can get it for you. She can

even order a custom-made flag using your graphics or hers. The store is the largest LGB retailer in the Southeast.

✳ Special Events

Known as the "Hostess City of the South," Savannah boasts more than 200 citywide festivals and events each year, so there's bound to be something to appeal to every traveler, no matter what your age group or interests. Among the premier events in the city and on Tybee Island are these:

February: The **Black Heritage Festival** (912-356-2448; www.savstate edu/bhf05/index.htm) includes a variety of cultural activities presented by Savannah State University and the City of Savannah's Department of Cultural Affairs. Free.

The **Savannah Irish Festival** (912-232-3448; www.savannahirish.org) celebrates everything Irish. Free.

March: A Savannah tradition for 180 years, the annual **St. Patrick's Day Parade** (912-233-4804) is the second largest in the nation. In addition to the parade, three days of activities create a nonstop party. Be prepared for green water in the fountains, green fireworks, pets adorned in green costumes, and green food and beverages. Parade and most activities free.

Truly "Southern, Soulful, and Sophisticated," the **Savannah Music Festival** (912-234-3378; www.savannah musicfestival.org) is a two-week musical feast offering one-time-only performances and world premieres showcasing blues, jazz, and other indigenous music from the Deep South; newly composed chamber music; ballet; and internationally renowned musicians in concert. Some events free; other events $5–75.

The annual **Tour of Homes and Gardens** (912-234-8054; www .savannahtourofhomes.org) offers self-guided walking tours of private homes and gardens in the historic district. Walking tour $35, special events and seminars $16–65.

May: **Fine Arts on the River** weekends (912-232-7731), sponsored by the Savannah Art Association, showcase the best in Savannah's visual and performing arts. This major arts festival includes a juried art exhibit, an arts and crafts show, performances by the Savannah Symphony and other groups, food, a wine tasting, and children's activities. Fireworks serve as a grand finale. Free.

The **Sand Arts Festival** (912-525-5225; www.scad.edu), held near the lighthouse on Tybee Island, features competitions using sand and objects such as shells and seaweed to create sand castles, sand sculptures, sand reliefs, and wind sculpture. Free.

August: **Annual Seafood and Music Fest** (912-786-5444) features seafood, live concerts, and other activities on Tybee Island's north beach parking lot. Call for ticket prices.

September: The **Savannah Jazz Festival** (912-232-2222) showcases the best in local and regional jazz artists at venues in City Market and Forsyth Park. Free.

EVERY MARCH, SAVANNAH PUTS ON THE DOG FOR ITS ANNUAL ST. PATRICK'S DAY PARADE.

December: **Christmas in Savannah** (912-234-0295) includes a festival of trees, open houses at shops and artists' studios, tours of homes and inns, a holiday door contest, parade, arts and crafts festival, and live performances. Among the much-anticipated events is the **Christmas Lighted Boat Parade** (1-800-786-6404). Most activities free.

The annual **Tybee Island Christmas Boat Parade** features whimsically decorated boats. Call Frank's Outboard and Jetsports (912-786-4032) or Lazaretto Creek Marina (912-786-5848) for details. Free.

WAYCROSS

Waycross, at the northern end of the 450,000-acre Okefenokee National Wildlife Refuge, offers something for everyone. History buffs will be enthralled by the Okefenokee Heritage Center and the Southern Forest World museums. For the nature-minded, the Okefenokee Swamp offers a glimpse of a one-of-a-kind ecosystem. Catch all the history and cultural exhibits at Obediah's Okefenok and the Okefenokee Swamp Park's pioneer area, where you can see what life was like for the early settlers of this unusual area. Train enthusiasts will be dumb-struck by "Rice Yard," the second-largest computerized rail yard for CSX in the United States. It can be studied in comfort from the patio area at the visitor center in downtown Waycross. While there, be sure to pick up a copy of the "Historic Walking Tour" guide, which will lead visitors on a tour that details the pioneer, Native American, and environmental history of this area.

Waycross owes its development to the Plant System Railroad, which laid tracks in this area in the mid-1800s. As railroad traffic increased, the prosperity of the town grew. Today, the railroad is still the number-one employer in the county. The Waycross Tourism Bureau and Visitor Center, the Waycross-Ware County Chamber of Commerce, and other local businesses are housed in the restored train depot.

Waycross is also home to the Green Frog, a restaurant built in the 1930s by the Dardin brothers, who went on to found the Red Lobster restaurant chain. Other famous natives include Pernell Roberts, Gram Parsons, Ozzie Davis, and Burt Reynolds. Interestingly, alligators outnumber people in this fascinating region. Do not touch, taunt or feed them, especially the babies. The mother is always nearby and they are very fast, even on land.

GUIDANCE When planning a trip to the Waycross area, contact the **Waycross Tourism Bureau and Visitor Center** (912-283-3744; www.okefenokee tourism.org), 315-A Plant Avenue, Waycross, 31501. Open 9–5 weekdays.

To learn more about Alma, consult the **Alma–Bacon County Chamber of Commerce** (912-632-5859; www.abcchamber.org), 1120 West 12th Street, Alma 31510, or stop by the **Alma–Bacon County Welcome Center** (912-632-0019), Bacon County Courthouse, 502 West 12th Street, Alma 31510. Open 8–5 weekdays.

Visitors planning a trip to Baxley should contact the **Baxley-Appling County Board of Tourism** (912-367-7731; www.baxley.org), 305 West Parker Street, Baxley 31513. Open 8–5 weekdays.

For information about Blackshear, contact the **Pierce County Chamber of Commerce** (912-449-7044), 200 Central Avenue, Blackshear 31516. Open 8–3 weekdays. The chamber shares the historic depot with the Pierce County Heritage Museum (see *To See—Museums*).

For information about Douglas, contact the **Douglas–Coffee County Chamber of Commerce and Welcome Center** (912-384-1873; 1-888-426-3334; www.douglas.org), 211 South Gaskin Avenue, Douglas 31533. Open 8–5 weekdays.

To learn more about Glennville, consult the **Glennville Welcome Center** (912-654-1380; www.tattnall.com), 136 South Main Street, Glennville 30427. Open 9–5 weekdays.

To find out more about Hazlehurst, contact the **Hazlehurst–Jeff Davis Board of Tourism/Jeff Davis County Chamber of Commerce** (912-375-4543; www .hazlehurst-jeffdavis.com), 95 East Jarman Street, Hazlehurst 31539. Open 8–5 weekdays. The facility dispenses information about agricultural tours and the local folklife play.

For information about Jesup, contact the **Wayne County Chamber of Commerce** (912-427-2028; 1-888-224-5983; www.waynechamber.com), 124 NW Broad Street, Jesup 31545. Open 9–5 weekdays.

GETTING THERE *By air:* Fly into **Middle Georgia Regional Airport** in Macon (see Macon chapter in 3, Historic South) or **Hartsfield-Jackson Atlanta International Airport** (see What's Where in Georgia).

By bus: **Greyhound Lines** (912-283-7211; 1-800-231-2222; www.greyhound.com) has a terminal at 405 Tebeau Street in Waycross. There is also a Greyhound station in Jesup at 105 Cherry Street; call 912-588-0888 for details.

By car: Waycross is located at the junctions of US 1, 82, and 84 in the southeastern corner of Georgia, situated at the northern edge of the Okefenokee National Park and Wilderness Area. Jesup is located off I-95 about 60 miles south of Savannah and about 60 miles north of Jacksonville, Florida NW.

By train: **Amtrak** (1-800-872-7245; www.amtrak.com), 176 NW Broad Street, has been stopping in Jesup since the 1980s. The station is open 30 minutes prior to arrival, but there is no staff at this station. Contact Amtrak directly or see a local travel agent for tickets.

MEDICAL EMERGENCY For life threatening emergencies, call 911. For other health issues, contact **Bacon County Hospital** (912-632-8961), 302 South Wayne Street, Alma; **Satilla Regional Medical Center** (912-283-3030; www .satilla.org), 410 Darling Avenue, Waycross; **Tattnall Regional Hospital** (912-255-4731), 247 South Main Street, Reidsville; or **Wayne Memorial Hospital** (912-427-6811; www.mhweb.com), 865 South First Street, Jesup.

VILLAGES Alma got its name by combining the first three letters of four of Georgia's past and current capitals: Augusta, Louisville, Milledgeville, and, of course, Atlanta. The people of this agrarian community are truly friendly, perhaps due to the slower pace of life here. When driving the winding country roads, however, you'll see more soybeans, corn, tobacco, cotton, and blueberries than people.

Tiny **Baxley** is the county seat of Appling County. Like Waycross, Baxley, once known as "Station Number Seven," came into being largely due to the railroad. Caroline Miller (Georgia's first Pulitzer Prize winner) was living here when she wrote *Lamb in His Bosom* in the early 1930s, and it was in this community that she learned about the dignity and courage of the state's early settlers. Adventurers will enjoy exploring the undimmed Altamaha River, the second-largest watershed on the eastern seaboard. The Nature Conservancy has dubbed it "Georgia's Natural Treasure, One of America's Last Great Places."

Modern downtown **Hazlehurst** features a historic district with many specialty stores. The city also hosts the state's largest horse auction every Friday.

Jesup's local economy has always been heavily influenced by the proximity of the Altamaha River, the railroads, and the timber industry. It has long marked the intersection of the Atlantic and Gulf Railroad (now CXS) and the Macon and Brunswick Railroad (now Norfolk Southern). To this day, these industries are the number-one employers in the county.

✴ To See

FOR FAMILIES ✐ ✾ **Southern Forest World Museum** (912-285-4056), 1440 North Augusta Avenue, Waycross. Open 9–5 Tuesday through Saturday. Museum visitors can listen to the "talking tree," a model of a loblolly pine tree that tells the story of this species, which dominated the economy of the area for more than a century. Then they can climb the winding stairway built inside a huge pine-tree replica and later get their picture taken inside a huge cypress tree or atop the Agent Lumber Company's No. 3 steam engine. $2.

MUMMIES IN AMERICA?

Well, it seems that one of the most fascinating items on exhibit at the Southern Forest World Museum is a mummified dog called Stuckey. Nature, not Egyptian priests, created this mummy. No one knows how long ago it happened, but the dog apparently chased a small animal into a hollow tree and actually climbed up inside the chimneylike space, where he got stuck and died. Instead of decomposing, the dog was mummified by a combination of updrafts, which prevented the scent from attracting predators, the dry environment, and tannic acid in the tree. He was discovered, almost perfectly preserved, when loggers cut down the tree and were cutting it into pulpwood lengths.

HISTORIC HOMES AND SITES ✦ ✿ & **Obediah's Okefenok** (912-287-0090; www.okefenokeeswamp.com), 5115 Swamp Road, Waycross. Open 10–5 daily. 'Round about 130 years ago, the legendary Obediah Barber was known as the King of the Okefenokee. His homestead, including the original cabin, syrup boiler shelter, smokehouse, potato crib, eight-stall livestock barn, cotton gin, blacksmith's shop, and gristmill, has been preserved as a National Historic Site. Scattered around the site are several small museums containing historic exhibits and artifacts from that time period. The park is also home to more than 70 animals that are native to the Okefenokee area, and they can be seen along the trails and boardwalk. Adults $4.50, seniors $3.50, children 6–17 $3, children 5 and younger free.

MUSEUMS ✦ ✿ & **Appling County Heritage Center** (912-367-8133), 209 Thomas Street, Baxley. Open noon–4:30 Tuesday, Thursday, and Friday. The facility is the repository of the county's historical and genealogical records, as well as an extensive collection of artifacts pertaining to the turpentine industry and exhibits about agriculture, African American history, and war history. Among the displays are 19th- and 20th-century memorabilia, county architectural items, and collections and publications by local historians. Free.

✦ ✿ **Glennville-Tattnall Museum** (912-654-2461), South Hillman Street, Glennville. Open 1–3 Saturday and Sunday; weekdays by appointment. This museum houses a collection of exhibits relating to art, science, and local culture and history. Its goal is to teach "young people to learn from the past, live in the present, and plan for the future." Free, but donations accepted.

✿ & **Hazlehurst Historical Museum** (912-375-2557), 61 East Coffee Street, Hazlehurst. Open 2–5 weekdays. The turn-of-the-20th-century raised cottage that houses the museum is on the Georgia Historic Register and the National Register of Historic Places. Inside are artifacts pertaining to rural Georgia. Donations accepted.

✦ ✿ & **Heritage Station Museum** (912-389-3461; www.cityofdouglas.com), 219 West Ward Street, Douglas. Open 10–4 Tuesday through Saturday. Located in the historic Georgia & Florida Railroad Depot, the museum displays railroad history through original G&F documents, furnishings, and period clothing. In addition, the center exhibits Douglas and Coffee County history. Adults $1.

✿ **Jones Creek Church Museum** (912-545-2437; 912-545-9315; www.wcolweb.com/jonescreek), US 301 North, Ludowici. Open by appointment only. The historic 1856 church features a slave gallery and original cemetery. The "baptism hole" is at Jones Creek. Free.

✦ ✿ **Little Red Caboose** (912-427-3233; 1-888-224-5983), 101 East Cherry Street, Jesup. Open 1–5 weekdays. The caboose is used as a museum to exhibit Wayne County history from General "Mad" Anthony Wayne to the railroad boom. Free.

✦ & **Okefenokee Heritage Center** (912-285-4260; www.okeheritage.org; www.okefenokkeetourism.org), 1460 North Augusta Avenue, Waycross. Open 10–4:30

Tuesday through Sunday. The first thing that catches your eye is the 1912 steam locomotive No. 9 sitting outside of the museum. Visitors are encouraged to climb aboard the locomotive as well as the passenger cars. The old train depot and an 1800s cabin are filled with all the necessities of pioneer life, while the museum houses a large Native American exhibit that includes the requisite arrowheads collection, pottery, a campsite display, and tools. Other exhibits focus on African Americans and pioneers and include walk-through displays of an old Colonial-style home, an early 1900s schoolhouse, and a church. The one-of-a-kind "Sacred Heart Gospel Sing" exhibit is an interactive musical display. Adults $3, children and seniors $2.

🐾 ♿ **Pierce County Heritage Museum and Depot** (912-449-7044), 200 South Central Avenue, Blackshear. Open 8–3 weekdays. The 1902 depot houses a museum that exhibits Civil War and local history artifacts. A genealogical library is also on-site. Free.

✳ To Do

BICYCLING See the **SPAR Bicycle Ride** in **Annual Dogwood Festival** under *Special Events.*

BIRDING The east entrance to the Okefenokee Swamp has 2.5 miles of hiking trails and a 4,000-foot boardwalk. These wilderness walkways attract hundreds of bird-watchers right about sunset.

BOAT EXCURSIONS ⚓ **Altamaha and Ocmulgee River Excursions** (912-375-4543; www.hazlehurst-jeffdavis.com), 95 East Jarman Street, Hazlehurst. Call for schedules and prices. Canoe, kayak, or raft down the scenic rivers by yourself or with experienced guides.

⚓ **Three Rivers Expeditions** (912-379-1371; www.3riverexp.com), 13 Victor Street, Hazlehurst. Call for a schedule and fees. The company offers full-service canoe and kayak rentals, guides, and return shuttle service.

CANOE TRIPS See **Canoe-Canoe Outfitters** in Statesboro chapter in 3, Historic South, for guided tours in the Okefenokee Swamp to visit the cypress forests, scrub-scrub areas, lakes, and wet prairies. For the really adventurous, arrange an overnight trip where you'll camp on raised wooden platforms by night and during the day visit the islands where Native Americans and early settlers lived. This is a one-of-a-kind chance to visit nature in one of its most unusual environments.

FISHING See *Green Space—Lakes*, and *Recreation Areas.*

FOR FAMILIES ⚓ 🐾 ♿ **Okefenokee Swamp Park** (912-283-0583; www.oke swamp.com), GA 177, Waycross. Open 9–5:30 daily. Located on the northern edge of the Okefenokee National Wildlife Refuge, the park acts as one of the gateways into the "Land of Trembling Earth"—the Great Okefenokee Swamp—

FAMILIES CAN SEE CYPRESS TREES GROWING AT THE OKEFENOKEE SWAMP PARK.

via guided boat tour, train excursion, or on foot. Visitors get a glimpse of the original Native American waterways and have a chance to see local wildlife in its natural habitat. They also are invited to visit Pioneer Island, a re-creation of pioneer life in the swamp. Adults $12, children 5–11 $11, children younger than 4 free.

GOLF 🎣 **The Lakes at Laura Walker Golf Course** (912-285-6154; www.golf georgia.org), 550 Laura Walker Road, Waycross. This recently opened, Steve Burns–designed championship golf course uses natural sand for the bunkers. In addition to being a challenging 18-hole course, its proximity to the swamps make it the habitat for local wildlife, including deer, herons, box turtles, quail, red-tailed foxes, and alligators. The course also features a clubhouse, a golf pro, unlimited weekday play, and junior/senior discounts. $30–35.

See also Golf Appendix.

TENNIS See Other Activities Appendix.

TRAIN EXCURSION 🎣 **Okefenokee Railroad Tour** (912-283-0583; www.okeswamp.com). The *Lady Suwanee* operates 9–5 daily except Thanksgiving and Christmas. A 1.5-mile-long train ride takes visitors into the swamp, where they can hear stories about swamp life and see a honeybee farm, turpentine farm, Seminole Indian village, and moonshine still. A stop at Pioneer Island gives visitors a glimpse into the world of this area's early settlers and also features native animals in their own habitat. It also includes a tour of Wildes Cabin Museum and a visit to the country store. Interestingly, the Seminole Indians named this area Okefenokee or "land of the trembling earth" because of the many floating islands in the swamp. Many of them will support the weight of a person, but when you step on them, they shake. The cost of this unique excursion is included in the $12 admission to Okefenokee Swamp Park (See *For Families*).

✳ Green Space

LAKES ✧ ☜ **Lake Lindsay Grace** (912-579-6475), 1167 Griffis Road, Screven (on US 84). Open daily. The lake provides numerous opportunities for all water sports. Free.

NATURE PRESERVES AND PARKS ✧ ☜ ⅙ **General Coffee State Park** (912-384-7082; www.gastateparks.org/info/gencoffee), GA 32, Douglas. Open 7–10 daily. The 1,511-acre park features a lake, a pitcher-plant bog, a swimming pool, and a nature trail and boardwalk. Recreational opportunities include boating and fishing. Farm buildings and live animals impart agricultural history. Camping available (see *Lodging—Campgrounds*). Parking $3, free on Wednesday.

✧ ☜ ⅙ **Laura S. Walker State Park** (912-287-4900; 1-800-864-7275; www .gastateparks.org/info/lwalker), 5653 Laura Walker Road off GA 177, Waycross. Open 7 AM–10 PM daily. One of Georgia's few parks named for a woman, this one honors the Georgia writer, teacher, civic leader, and naturalist who worked

THE LAKES AT LAURA WALKER GOLF COURSE IS WAYCROSS'S NEWEST COURSE.

for the preservation of trees. The park covers 626 acres, including a 120-acre lake known for its great bass fishing as well as for canoeing, boating, and waterskiing. For those who prefer to stay on land, the park includes 2 miles of nature trails that meander through the loblolly pines and show off the natural beauty of the area. Keep an eye out for carnivorous pitcher plants, saw palmettos, and various oaks, as well as wildlife such as the shy gopher tortoise, yellow-shafted flickers, warblers, owls, great blue herons, and even alligators. The park also features a golf course (see *ToDo—Golf*). Other recreational opportunities include a swimming pool, fishing dock, boat ramp, and canoe and fishing-boat rentals. Accommodations are offered at the campground (see *Lodging*). Parking $3.

See also Parks Appendix.

RECREATION AREAS ✧ ☜ ⅙ **Lake Mayers Public Recreation Area** (912-367-8177), 100 Oak Street, Baxley. Open daily. Lake Mayers offers fishing for largemouth bass, bream, crappie, bluegill, shellcracker, and catfish. Facilities include a swimming beach, boat launch, rest rooms, and picnicking facilities. Free.

RIVERS ✦ ❀ **Altamaha River–Altamaha Canoe Trail** (912-367-8133; www.altamahariver.org; www.altamahariverkeeper.org), Baxley. Open daily. The Nature Conservancy has proclaimed the Altamaha River "Georgia's Natural Treasure, One of America's Last Great Places." The river, which borders Appling County, is the second-largest watershed on the eastern seaboard. Completely undammed, it is crossed only five times by roads and twice by rail lines, so its natural beauty is largely undisturbed. It flows 137 miles through 11 counties from its head, where the Oconee and Ocmulgee rivers come together north of Baxley, to its delta on the coast. Surrounded by more than 2 million acres of forest land, the river provides a habitat for more than 130 species of birds, plants, and animals, including many that are rare and endangered, and it is a mecca for canoeing, kayaking, fishing, and bird-watching. A popular biannual event is the Altamaha River Rat Run, a canoe and kayak excursion in the spring and fall. Free.

✳ Lodging
BED & BREAKFASTS

In Hazlehurst
❀ ♿ **Garden Gate Inn** (912-375-5035), 572 Bell Telephone Road. The B&B is located about a half mile outside Hazlehurst in a 100-year old restored home on a 100-acre farm with a stream. The front of the home features a pleasant half-wraparound porch; there's another large porch in back. Inside, the decor contains a mixture of cottage and traditional furnishings. This inn offers three guest rooms, all with private baths. Guests are welcome to enjoy the common room with its television, piano, and card table. The host offers an assortment of board games to while away the evenings, and guests are also invited to wander the grounds. Visiting the animals, which include a donkey, baby rabbits, geese, ducks, and chickens, is always relaxing. No smoking. Wheelchair accessible. (Showers wheelchair accessible, and two rooms offer higher commodes. Special showerheads in each bathroom to prevent scalding or freezing water.) $65 including breakfast and snack.

In Waycross
Pond View Downtown & Inn (912-283-9300; 1-866-582-5149; www.bbonline.com/ga/pondview), 311 Pendleton Street. This B&B has four elegantly decorated guest rooms on the second floor. All the upscale amenities are featured, including private baths. There's a restaurant downstairs. No smoking. Not wheelchair accessible. $81–129.

CAMPGROUNDS

In Douglas
✦ ❀ ❀ ♿ **General Coffee State Park** (912-384-7082; 1-800-864-7275; www.gastateparks.org/info/gencoffee), 46 John Coffee Road, GA 32. This park features 50 tent, trailer, and RV sites. Amenities include a 4-acre lake, a swimming pool, outdoor amphitheater, seven picnic shelters ($30), a group shelter that seats 180 ($135), a 4-mile hiking trail with boardwalks, history and nature programs, fishing,

and canoe and pedal-boat rentals. $16–18; pioneer camping $15 and up.

In Screven

Happy Acres Resort Campgrounds (912-586-6781; 1-877-288-6456; www.happyacresresort.com), 5441 Odum Road South. This campground boasts 130 RV sites that can accommodate any size RV. It is open year-round and features two clubhouses, modem-friendly phone hookups, a swimming pool, fishing, boating, hiking, and a picnic area. It is located next to 250-acre Lake Lindsay Grace (see *Green Space—Lakes*). The camp store sells both hunting and fishing licenses as well as various staples. $20 per night.

In Waycross

Laura S. Walker State Park (912-287-4900; 1-800-864-7275; www.gastateparks.org/info/lwalker), 5653 Laura Walker Road off GA 177. The park offers 44 tent, trailer, and RV sites and two pioneer campgrounds. There is also a group camp that sleeps 142. $17–25; $360 for group camp.

See also Campgrounds Appendix.

COTTAGES AND CABINS

In Douglas

General Coffee State Park (912-384-7082; 1-800-864-7275; www.gastateparks.org/info/gencoffee), 46 John Coffee Road, GA 32. The park offers six fully equipped cottages for rent. See *Green Space—Nature Preserves and Parks* for park amenities and attractions. $60–80.

In Glennville

Adamson's Fish Camp at Beard's Bluff (912-654-3632), US 301 South. Cabins rent for $20 per night, $25 with shower and laundry access. Cookhouses with a stove, sink,

and refrigerator rent for $12–18 and seat six to 12.

✳ Where to Eat

DINING OUT

In Waycross

Andrew's Café and Grill (912-285-1545), 412 Elizabeth Street. Open 5:30–10 Thursday through Saturday. Andrew's is one of Waycross's best dining experiences, a place where guests can get steaks, seafood, salads, pasta, and homemade soups and desserts. No smoking. Wheelchair accessible. $8–24.

Cavagnaro's (912-285-4000), 1810 Francis Street. Open 11–10 Monday through Thursday, 11–11 Friday and Saturday, 11–9 Sunday. An interesting combination of Italian restaurant and sports bar, this eatery serves good Italian entrées plus steaks and seafood. It has a good wine list, too. No smoking. Wheelchair accessible. $7–25.

Pond View Downtown (912-283-9300; 1-866-582-5149; www.bbonline.com/ga/pondview), 311 Pendleton Street. Open 5:30–9 Tuesday through Saturday. Perfect for an intimate and romantic evening of fine dining, the restaurant serves favorites such as crabcakes, beef tenderloin, sautéed grouper, and melt-in-your-mouth desserts. No smoking. Wheelchair accessible. $9–26.

EATING OUT

In Baxley

B & F Restaurant (912-367-4766), 500 West Parker Street. Open 5 AM–9 PM daily. This popular eatery serves homemade breakfasts, sandwiches, and traditional Southern dinners. No smoking. Wheelchair accessible. Around $5.

🔪 🏵 ♿ **Captain Joe's Seafood Restaurant** (912-367-7795), 508 Golden Isles Parkway East. Open 11–9 Monday through Thursday, 11–10 Friday and Saturday, 11–9:30 Sunday. Seafood, steaks, hamburgers, and chicken are served with various sides. No smoking. Wheelchair accessible. $10–18.

🔪 🏵 ♿ **Carter's Fried Chicken** (912-367-4108), 501 North Boulevard. Open 9–9 weekdays, 9–10 Saturday. Besides fried chicken, the restaurant serves fish, shrimp, and cube-steak dinners. No smoking. Wheelchair accessible. $4 per person for a meat and two vegetables.

🔪 🏵 ♿ **Fuji Express Japanese Steakhouse** (912-366-9444), 201 West Parker Street. Open 11–9 Monday through Thursday, 11–10 Friday through Sunday. The restaurant serves steak, chicken, seafood, fried rice, and vegetables. No smoking. Wheelchair accessible. Around $8.

🔪 🏵 ♿ **Sweet Temptations Bakery** (912-367-5700), 603 West Parker Street. Open 6 AM–5:30 PM weekdays, 7 AM–noon Saturday. Popular menu items include soups and sandwiches served on homemade breads. The bakery and café also makes its own chicken and tuna salads. No smoking. Wheelchair accessible. $4.

🔪 🏵 ♿ **Tradition's Restaurant and Tavern** (912-367-5855), 69 Comas Street. Open 11–2 and 5–10 weekdays, 11–10 Saturday. Tradition's specializes in black Angus steak, prime rib, and seafood. No smoking. Wheelchair accessible. $15.

In Jesup

🔪 🏵 ♿ **Doc Holiday's** (912-530-8321), 106 East Pine Street. Open 11–9 Monday through Thursday, 11–midnight Friday, 5–midnight Saturday. Menu favorites include hand-cut and aged Black Angus steaks grilled over an open flame, homemade salad dressings, and fried cheesecake. The restaurant is famous for its homemade baked bread and honey butter. Smoking in tavern only. Wheelchair accessible. $8–19.

🔪 🏵 ♿ **Jones Kitchen** (912-427-4100), 526 West Cherry Street. Open 11 AM–2 PM Monday through Saturday. This restaurant offers good old-fashioned country cooking, including fried chicken, pork chops, and an assortment of vegetables. No smoking. Wheelchair accessible. $3.50.

🔪 🏵 ♿ **Mister J's Steak, Potato & BBQ** (912-530-9228), 123 Sunset Boulevard. Open 10:30–8 Monday through Saturday, 11–2 Sunday. As the name suggests, this restaurant specializes in steaks, stuffed baked potatoes, and barbecue. No smoking. Wheelchair accessible. $5.

🔪 🏵 ♿ **Overpass Steak & Ribs** (912-530-6900), 123 East Pine Street. Open 11–10 Monday through Saturday. The restaurant offers steaks, chicken, pork, seafood, and ribs with your choice of vegetable and a salad. No smoking. Wheelchair accessible. Entrées average $12.

🔪 🏵 ♿ **Sugar 'N Spice Bake Shop** (912-427-9956), 185 NW Broad Street. Open 6 AM–2 PM Tuesday and Wednesday, 6–6 Thursday and Friday, 6–1 Saturday. Homemade chicken and tuna salads, sandwiches, and sweets round out the menu here. No smoking. Wheelchair accessible. Sandwiches average $3.50.

In Screven

🔪 🏵 ♿ **Screven Restaurant** (912-579-6608), 118 East J. L. Tyre Street.

Open 5 AM–2 PM weekdays, 7 AM–2 PM weekends. Menu favorites include meat loaf, fried chicken, and a wide variety of home-style vegetables. No smoking. Wheelchair accessible. $5.50 for a meat and two vegetables.

In Waycross

🛈 🍴 ♿ **Carlo's** (912-283-5393), 501 City Boulevard. Open 11–10 Monday through Thursday and Sunday, 11–11 Friday and Saturday. Enjoy Cajun and Latin cuisine, including crawfish ètouffée, jambalaya, shrimp Creole, po'boys, and more. No smoking. Wheelchair accessible. $5–11.

🛈 🍴 ♿ **Cedar River** (912-338-0074), 2456 Memorial Drive. Open 11–9 Monday through Thursday, 11–10 Friday and Saturday. The popular eatery has been serving seafood, steak, chicken breasts, pastas, and other favorites since 1977. No smoking. Wheelchair accessible. Prices start at $3.99.

🛈 🍴 ♿ **Jerry J's Country Café** (912-287-1303), 1404 Plant Avenue. Open 6 AM–8 PM Monday through Thursday, 6 AM–9 PM Friday and Saturday. This is the place to go for big meals in Waycross. The restaurant serves breakfast, lunch, and dinner. Menu favorites include huge handmade biscuits and all the other breakfast staples as well as meat and vegetable plates like your grandmother used to make. The hardest thing is narrowing down your choices. No smoking. Wheelchair accessible. $6 for meat and two vegetables.

🛈 🍴 ♿ **KD's Café** (912-285-3300), 504 Elizabeth Street. Open 11–2 weekdays, 6–9:30 Friday. This favorite lunch eatery for Waycross residents, located in the downtown historic district, serves soups, salads, sand-

wiches, subs, barbecue, lasagna, chicken, pasta, burgers, Brunswick stew, sweet-potato fries, and a daily lunch special. No smoking. Wheelchair accessible. $4–14.

🛈 🍴 **M. T. Taters** (912-338-0099), 1713 Knight Avenue. Open 11–9 Monday through Saturday. Every kind of stuffed baked potato you can think of is offered, as well as hot dogs, barbecue, and chicken strips. No smoking. Not wheelchair accessible. $2–6.

🛈 🍴 **Three Pigs Bar-B-Q** (912-283-8234), Central Avenue Extension. Open 11–9 Thursday through Saturday. Located inside the Okefenokee Swamp Park, the restaurant serves steak, shrimp, catfish, and sandwiches. No smoking. Wheelchair accessible. $4–24.

COFFEEHOUSES

In Baxley

🍴 ♿ **Common Ground Coffee and Eatery** (912-366-9997), 20 NW Park Avenue. Open 7 AM–4:30 PM Monday through Thursday, 7 AM–9 PM Friday, 8 AM–1 PM Saturday. The coffeehouse offers specialty coffees along with soups and sandwiches. No smoking. Wheelchair accessible. Average price under $5.

In Waycross

🍴 ♿ **Hot Toddy** (912-285-0100), 506 Elizabeth Street. Open 7 AM–10 PM Monday through Saturday, 1–10 Sunday. The coffeehouse specializes in coffees, cappuccinos, espressos, lattes, fruit smoothies, pastries, and special treats. No smoking. Wheelchair accessible. Under $5.

✳ Entertainment

Appling County Arts Council (912-

367-7615). Events take place primarily at the Appling County Elementary Complex in Baxley or the City Auditorium. Call for schedule of performances, information on the particular venue, and ticket prices. This group exists to enhance appreciation for the arts in Appling County and hosts numerous programs each year, including performances by the South Georgia Ballet and the Valdosta Symphony Orchestra, piano concerts, madrigal singers, and art shows.

THEATER Altamaha Community Theatre (912-427-4240) presents a season of adult shows throughout the year and a children's theater production each summer. Performances are usually at the Presbyterian Church, 297 South Brunswick Street, in Baxley. Call for a schedule, ticket prices, and other details.

Martin Centre (912-384-5978; www.cityofdouglas.com), 109 East Ashley Street, Douglas. The historic 1940s art deco–style theater has been restored as a multiuse performance venue where numerous theatrical and musical programs are presented. Call for a schedule of performances and ticket prices.

Wayne County Productions (912-427-2028). This community theater pulls together local talent to host singing, dancing, and theatrical productions, which are performed at the new Wayne County High School on Jacket Drive. Past performances include a Christmas program, hilarious '50s and '60s musical shows, country music concerts, and gospel shows. Best of all, proceeds benefit local charities. Call for a schedule of events and ticket prices.

ANTIQUES Al's Antique Emporium (912-367-0808), 906 East Parker Street, Baxley. Open 10–6 weekdays, 9–5 Saturday. Rare finds include tobacco memorabilia, reproduction pieces, and furnishings from the 1700s to the 1950s.

McCurdy's on Main (912-654-4004; www.mccurdysonmain.com), 208 South Main Street, Glennville. Open 8:30–5:30 weekdays, 8:30–1 Saturday. This spacious establishment has been in business for more than 30 years, specializing in antiques and unique gifts.

The Plunder Place (912-366-9727), GA 15 South, Baxley. Open 1–6 Monday through Saturday. This emporium specializes in antiques and country decor, fresh produce, pottery, and flowers. Check to see when there might be an auction.

GIFTS ✐ ✿ **Old Red Barn Gift Shop and McSimmons Barnyard** (912-375-4641; 912-375-5035), 566 Bell Telephone Road, Hazlehurst. Open 10–6 Tuesday through Friday, 10–2 Saturday. While parents might come to this 50-year-old barn to browse through the gift shop, youngsters enjoy Daisy the cow, Jenny the donkey, and other farmyard friends.

✳ Special Events

Monthly: **Waresboro Mudbog** (912-283-3744; www.waresboromudbog.com). This monthly event, held the third Saturday of each month about 12 miles outside Waycross, features trucks and other vehicles from all over south Georgia and north Florida trying to make a full pull through the mud pit. Very few make it without getting bogged down. The event's motto is, "NASCAR—500 miles in 3 hours, NHRA—¼ mile in 30 seconds, Waresboro Mudbog—200 feet . . . if you're lucky." $10 to participate; free for spectators.

March: **Annual Dogwood Festival** (912-427-2028). Activities include a 1-mile/5K Family Fun Run, SPAR Bike Ride, Wayne County Young Farmers Truck Pull, arts and crafts, and more fun-filled events for the whole family throughout Jesup. This event takes place on the fourth Saturday and Sunday in March. Free.

Peaches to Beaches Yard Sale (912-367-7731). Those die-hard shoppers looking for bargains in Hazlehurst will want to check out some sections of the 172-mile yard sale, held the second Friday and Saturday of March. Free.

April: **Baxley Tree Fest** (912-367-7731). A celebration of the forestry industry and outdoor recreation, this three-day festival's highlights include a street dance, outdoor expo, parade, antique tractor show, sports events, "Treeography" photo contest, motorcycle show, petting zoo, and much more. Free, except $2 for street dance.

Swamp Fest (912-283-3744; www.swampfest.com). The annual Swamp Fest is held the first weekend in April. Activities include a parade, street dance, concert, arts and crafts, great Southern cooking, a beauty pageant, live theater, and children's entertainment. The festival takes place in downtown Waycross, although some events are held at the Waycross fairgrounds. Free.

June: **Shriners' Annual All-Night Gospel Sing** (912-283-3744). For more than 40 years the Shriners have sponsored an event that includes nationally known gospel groups and a talent search that showcases performers from all over the Southeast. This annual event at the Okefenokee Fairgrounds in Waycross usually takes place the last weekend in June, beginning on Friday night and lasting until the wee hours of Saturday morning. $13 in advance; $15 at the door.

October: **Guysie Mule Roundup** (912-632-5859). The two-day event held on a Friday and Saturday on GA 32 between Alma and Nicholls features displays of antique barn implements and old-fashioned tools. Demonstrations show the way farm chores were once accomplished. The roundup also features a rodeo, parade, food, and wagon rides. $4; children 12 and younger free.

November: **Smokin' on the Square/National Barbecue Festival** (912-384-4555; www.cityofdouglas.com). After three years of hosting the Smokin' on the Square barbecue festival downtown, Douglas expanded this event to the National Barbecue Festival Best of the Best in 2004. Representatives from more than 38 states competed to determine the best barbecue in the nation. Call for a list of events and admission process.

December: **Christmas Lights in the Park** (912-283-0583; www.okeswamp.com). Ride the train on a 30- to 40-minute trip through the Okefenokee Swamp Park in Waycross to see this spectacular light show and other decorations. Adults $6, children 3–11 $4 .

Historical South 3

INTRODUCTION

The Historic South area of the state is, indeed, Georgia's heartland. In some ways, the region is the most stereotypically Southern, with lots of small towns and white-columned mansions, but the area is also quite diverse.

The region in the rolling hills of the Piedmont contains several small cities, each of which has a very distinct personality. Among these are Athens, home of the University of Georgia; Augusta, home of the Masters golf tournament, the Augusta Futurity cutting-horse competition, and several important boating events; Macon, home of several major museums and state halls of fame as well as the annual International Cherry Blossom Festival; Milledgeville, Georgia's capital at the time of secession; Statesboro, home of Georgia Southern University; and Warner Robins, home of Robins Air Force Base and the Museum of Aviation.

The region also contains many charming small towns, a national forest, some major rivers, several significant lakes, 15 state parks, historic sites, and some interesting special events. The Historic South is the only area touched by all of Georgia's other tourism regions—Atlanta Metro, the Coast, the Mountains, and Southern Rivers—and it's also bordered on the east by South Carolina.

One would expect such a large area to be far from homogeneous. Thus the region is further subdivided into the state-designated Classic South, represented by Augusta, Washington, Thomson, and several smaller towns; Historic Heartland, represented by Macon, Athens, Barnesville, Conyers, Covington, Eatonton, Fort Valley, Juliette, Milledgeville, Monroe, Monticello, Perry, Social Circle, Warner Robins, Watkinsville, and other small towns; and Magnolia Midlands, represented by Dublin, Eastman, Fitzgerald, Hawkinsville, Statesboro, Vidalia, and a few other towns.

The entire region is famous for its peaches, pecans, and coveted sweet Vidalia onions, but it's also well known for fruitcake produced by two companies in the small town of Claxton.

Golf is synonymous with the Masters golf tournament in Augusta, but the sport is widely available at several state parks and resorts such as those around Lake Oconee. This is also horse country, and different events are held at the

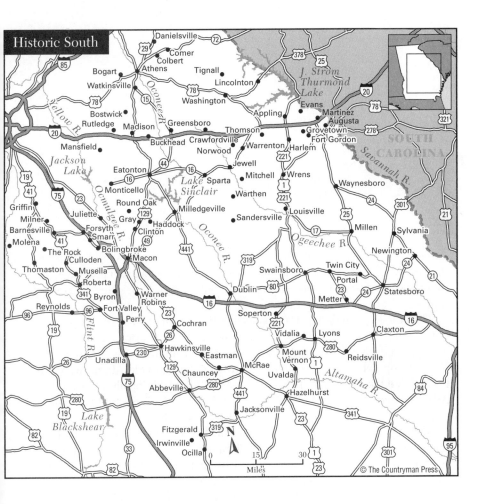

Georgia International Horse Park in Conyers and the Lawrence Bennett Harness Horse Training Facility in Hawkinsville.

The region's multifaceted history is represented by such sites as the Tubman African American Museum in Macon; the Ocmulgee National Monument, also in Macon; the Governor's Mansion in Milledgeville; Callaway Plantation in Washington; Jarrell Plantation in Juliette; and the Boyhood Home of President Woodrow Wilson in Augusta.

Outdoor recreation is not neglected. The lakes and the rivers provide ample opportunities for various types of boating, fishing, and other water sports. The Altamaha River, formed by the confluence of the Ocmulgee, Oconee, and Ohoopee rivers, is the largest river system east of the Mississippi and supports more than 100 species of endangered plants and animals.

ATHENS

I t's not for its name only that Athens—named for its Old World predecessor, the Greek center of higher learning—is known as "the Classic City." Even its tree-lined neighborhoods are showcases of antebellum Greek Revival architecture.

The city was founded in 1806 concurrently with the University of Georgia (UGA), the nation's first state-chartered university. For various reasons, the city was spared during the Civil War, leaving much to admire today. For one thing, Union troops who were directed to destroy rail lines around Athens were ambushed and taken prisoner by Confederate troops. Additionally, after the fall of Atlanta, Union General William Tecumseh Sherman's March to the Sea moved southeast toward Milledgeville and thus bypassed Athens.

Although the city suffered during the Civil War and Reconstruction, it bounced back quickly. Athens's antebellum economy was based on cotton, railroad transportation, and textiles. Its flourishing textile mills created growth unparalleled in the New South.

Today Athens is the fifth-largest city in the state and the largest city in the northeast Georgia Piedmont region, with a population of 102,000. It is dominated by the ever-growing university. As with all college towns, the presence of the university means there is a healthy variety of museums, cultural events, sports venues, restaurants, and nightspots. In fact, Athens has been named one of America's Top 25 Arts Destinations by *AmericanStyle magazine*.

With its bohemian allure and downtown district filled with enough clubs to earn the city the title "Live Music Central" from the *New York Times* and the "#1 Music Mecca/College Music Scene in America" by *Rolling Stone* magazine, Athens is a major site on the **Georgia Music Trail,** which also includes Atlanta, Macon, and Savannah. From a long history of folk music to the advent of bands such as the B-52s and R.E.M. in the early 1980s, to present-day bands such as Widespread Panic and Drive-By Truckers, Athens has long cultivated musicians and other artists. (Just a little piece of trivia: On April 18, 1998, downtown Athens hosted the largest CD release party in history when local band Widespread Panic gave a free concert attended by 100,000 fans.) With blues, classical, country, hip-hop, rock, and every alternative genre playing on a continuous basis, Athens provides one of the most eclectic and affordable music scenes in the world.

GUIDANCE Before your trip, consult the **Athens Convention and Visitors Bureau** (706-357-4430; 1-800-653-0603; www.visitathensga.com), 300 North Thomas Street, Athens 30601, for information. Open 8–5 weekdays.

Once you arrive in Athens, stop by the **Athens Welcome Center** (706-353-1820; www.visitathensga.com/welcome_center.cfm), 280 East Dougherty Street, Athens 30601. Open daily 10–5 in fall and winter, 10–6 in spring and summer. Housed in the historic Federal-style **Church-Waddell-Brumby House,** the center provides maps, brochures, self-guided tours of more than 50 sites, and visitor information. For more information about the house, see *To See—Historic Homes and Sites*. Guided tours given by **Classic City Tours** (706-208-TOUR) depart from the center at 2 PM daily. Before leaving the Welcome Center, pick up the brochures "Athens Music Walking Tour," a 28-stop self-guided tour to some of the most significant spots in the city's rich musical history; a "A Walking Tour of Downtown Athens"; "Georgia's Antebellum Trail," a 100-mile trail of pre–Civil War sites that stretches south to Macon and for which Athens is the northern gateway; and "Heartland of the Confederacy Trail," a Civil War heritage trail.

For more information about the University of Georgia campus, consult the following organizations. The **UGA Visitors Center** (706-542-0842, www.uga.edu/~visctr), Four Towers Building, College Station Road, Athens 30602. Open 8–5 weekdays, 9–5 Saturday, 1–5 Sunday; closed on official university holidays. The visitor center, housed in a former dairy barn called the Four Towers Building because of its four silos, provides assistance and information about the university. Stay awhile to see the displays that focus on university history, campus life, and distinguished alumni. The "Campus Arboretum Walking Tour of Trees" brochure is available at the UGA Visitors Center, too. The **UGA Alumni Association** (706-542-2251; www.alumni.uga.edu.), 298 Hull Street, is housed in the historic 1825 **Wray-Nicholson House,** which is open for tours. Open 8–5 weekdays.

For information about Watkinsville, consult the **Oconee County Visitors Bureau** (706-769-5197; www.oconeecounty.com), US 441, Watkinsville 30677.

GETTING THERE *By air:* Air transportation is into **Athens–Ben Epps Airport** (706-613-3420; www.athensairport.net). Named for Georgia's first aviator, Ben Epps, who began building and flying planes in Athens in 1907, the airport is served by **US Airways Express** (1-800-428-4322). Many visitors may prefer to fly into Atlanta (see What's Where in Georgia). Car rentals are available through **Hertz** (706-543-5984) at the airport.

By bus: **Southeastern Stages/Greyhound Lines** (706-549-2255; www.southeasternstages.com), 220 West Broad Street, provides direct service.

By car: The major highway routes into Athens are GA 15, US 78, and US 129/441; GA Loop 10 goes around the city.

GETTING AROUND The **Athens Transit System** (706-613-3430; www.athenstransit.com/routeinformation.html) provides public transit transportation throughout the Athens area. Downtown, rental cars are available from **Budget**

Rent-A-Car (706-353-0600), 1870 West Broad Street, and **Enterprise Rent-A-Car** (706-543-0771), 2080 Timothy Road.

PARKING Adequate parking (except for UGA football home-game weekends) is available at four for-fee parking decks downtown, and there is also on-street, metered parking. There are new parking decks at the Classic Center and one at College Avenue. At the University of Georgia, there is a free lot for short-term parking adjacent to the visitor center (obtain a pass inside the center). Additional visitor parking is available in for-fee lots and parking decks around the campus. The one at North Campus is very convenient to downtown.

WHEN TO GO In the autumn, if you aren't attending a UGA football home game, we strongly urge you avoid the city, which will be crowded, traffic-choked, and expensive. Graduation weekend is a similar story. In addition, Athens is not totally friendly to the weekend visitor. Many of the major attractions are open only on weekdays, although the situation is gradually being resolved. The Georgia Museum of Art and the State Botanical Garden of Georgia, for example, are open on weekends.

MEDICAL EMERGENCY For life-threatening situations, call 911. Otherwise, medical attention is available at **Athens Regional Medical Center** (706-475-7000; www.armc.org), 1199 Prince Avenue, or at **St. Mary's Hospital** (706-548-7581; www.stmarysathens.org), 1230 Baxter Street.

VILLAGES AND NEIGHBORHOODS Athens is teeming with National Register of Historic Places–designated neighborhoods: **Athens Warehouse,** a commercial area on Foundry Street; **Bloomfield Street,** a residential area of Craftsman bungalows; **Boulevard,** a turn-of-the-20th-century streetcar district; **Buena Vista Heights,** a neighborhood of small cottages; **Cobbham,** an area of imposing Queen Anne Victorian homes; **Old North Campus–UGA,** where the first permanent college buildings were erected in 1806; the **Prince Avenue** corridor, with the best examples of Greek Revival homes; and **Shotgun Row,** a collection of narrow shotgun cottages. Other historic districts include Dearing Street, Downtown Athens, Milledge Avenue, Milledge Circle, Oglethorpe Avenue, Reese Street, Rocksprings, and West Hancock Avenue. All these neighborhoods make excellent walking tours. Get information from the welcome center.

When visiting sleepy little nearby **Watkinsville,** it's hard to believe that the town was once considered for the site of the University of Georgia. It was decided, however, that the existence of the Eagle Tavern made the town "too frivolous an atmosphere for studious young gentlemen." Those who made the decision to locate the school in Athens must be turning over in their graves, because over the years UGA has earned the dubious reputation of being a party school. Today Watkinsville has a plethora of artists' studios and galleries. It is also the home of the Oconee Cultural Arts Foundation, which hosts exhibits in a 1902 schoolhouse.

✳ To See

COVERED BRIDGES ✐ ❀ ♿ Elders Mill Covered Bridge, Elders Mill
Road/GA 15 over Rose Creek, Watkinsville. Always accessible. Free. Not only is
this one of just 16 covered bridges remaining in the state, it is one of the last still
in use on a public road. The bridge was originally constructed in 1897 over Calls
Creek between Athens and Watkinsville, but in 1924 it was relocated to cross
Big Rose Creek. It's truly amazing that the bridge is able to carry traffic without
the support of underlying steel beams.

CULTURAL SITES ✐ ❀ ♿ Lyndon House Arts Center, Ware-Lyndon House
(706-613-3623; www.itown.com/athens/lyndonhouse), 293 Hoyt Street, Athens.
Open noon–9 Tuesday and Thursday, 9–5 Wednesday, Friday, and Saturday.
Guided tours are available with 48-hour advance reservations. Originally located
in a circa-1850 house considered to be one of the most historically significant
homes in the city, the community visual arts center has recently been renovated
and expanded to feature galleries, a children's wing, artists' workshops, a gift
shop, and a perennial garden. The **Visual Arts Guild of Athens** (706-546-7580)
is based at the arts center. Now that its rooms are no longer needed as galleries,

---

WHO LET THE DAWGS OUT?

The **"We Let the Dawgs Out"** public art exhibit (www.weletthedawgsout
.com) can be found at various locations throughout Athens. Always accessible. Even before the internationally known Cow Parade (painted fiberglass
bovines as public art) came to Atlanta temporarily, Athens was the first city
in Georgia to create such public art with an animal theme, turning the entire
area into an outdoor museum. The project was sponsored by the Athens-
Oconee Junior Woman's Club and funded by city, art, and private sectors.
Naturally, the animal of choice was not as mundane as a cow but, rather,
was the Athens icon—the bulldog. That's "dawg" to the uninitiated. More
than three dozen larger-than-life bulldawgs were created, and each is a
unique representation of the vision of a different local artist. Just a few of
these fine whimsical canines include Caesar Dawgustus, Carmen Miran-
dawg, Dawgwood, the Blue Dawg of Happiness, and A-pooch-ecary. You
get the idea. Rather than auctioning off the pooches as other such projects
have done, the bulldawgs are on permanent display around the city. Finding
them makes a pleasant and amusing walking and/or driving tour. Don't forget your camera. More than a dozen dawgs are clustered in the downtown
area and another 10 in the Five Points area; others are scattered farther
afield. To find them, go to the web site above and print a map showing the
locations of all the dawgs, or pick up a map from the Athens Welcome Center. This is one tour that will guarantee a smile. Free.

the completely restored Ware-Lyndon House, one of the few antebellum homes in Athens with Italianate elements, is open as a house museum. Free.

🏛 ♿ **University of Georgia Historic North Campus** lies between Lumpkin, Jackson, Broad, and Baldwin streets. Despite the fact that the bulldog, Uga, may appear to be the most familiar representation of the university, the landmark cast-iron **arch,** through which students and visitors enter the North Campus, is officially featured as the logo of the university. The cast-iron fencing around the area was originally not just for decorative purposes; it kept grazing animals out of the quadrangle. This section of the university, the location of the original campus in the early 1800s, features Greek Revival architecture, handsome gardens, and majestic trees. Among the historically significant buildings is the **UGA Chapel,** home of George Cooke's painting of St. Peter's Cathedral. Measuring 17 by 23½ feet, it was the largest framed oil painting in the world at the time of its completion in 1847.

GUIDED TOURS Guided tours given by ✒ **Classic City Tours** (706-208-TOUR) depart from the Athens Welcome Center at 2 PM daily. If you're lucky, Janet Clark will be your guide. We consider her the most knowledgeable source of information in the city. Tours are $15. Although the three Athens house museums listed in this section are open to the public for tours by individuals, Classic City Tours offers a guided tour of historic interiors of these museums at 4 PM Tuesday and Thursday. The price of $20 per person includes the price of admission to each museum. Classic City Tours also offers specialty tours such as the Haunted History Tour in October.

✒ 🏛 **UGA Visitors Center Tours** (706-542-0842; www.uga.edu/~visctr/). Open 8–5 weekdays, 9–5 Saturday, 1–5 Sunday; closed on official university holidays. The center provides guided walking and van tours (reservations required)— three on weekdays, two on Saturday, one on Sunday. These tours via minibus last one hour and involve walking as well as riding. Free.

HISTORIC HOMES AND SITES 🏛 **Church-Waddell-Brumby House** (706-353-1820; www.visitathensga.com/welcome_center.cfm). Open 10–5 daily in fall and winter, 10–6 in spring and summer. The historic Federal-style house serves as the city's welcome center (see *Guidance*). Built in 1820, the house itself is considered to be the oldest house in Athens. It was built for UGA mathematics professor Alonzo Church and later became the home of university president Moses Waddell. The rescue and restoration of this house in the 1970s sparked the historic preservation movement in Athens. Besides serving as the welcome center, the house is a museum filled with period furniture and decorative arts. Free.

✒ 🏛 ♿ **Double-Barreled Cannon**, Cannon Park on City Hall lawn at College and Hancock streets, Athens. Open daily. Probably the most unusual weapon from the Civil War, this unique cannon was built in 1863 at a local foundry when the uneasy citizenry dreaded an attack by invading Union armies. This one-of-a-kind weapon designed by Athenian house builder John Gilleland was a prototype for a hoped-for superweapon. The theory was that two cannonballs attached by a chain would be fired simultaneously and would mow down everything in their path, including wide swaths of the enemy, before striking their target. Unfortunately, the first firing was spectacularly unsuccessful. An observer noted that the cannonballs "plowed up an acre of ground, tore up a cornfield, mowed down saplings, and the chain broke, the balls going in opposite directions, one of the balls killed a cow in a distant field, while the other knocked down the chimney from a log cabin. The observers scattered as though the entire Yankee army had turned loose in that vicinity." Although no other copy was ever built, the original sits on the Court House lawn, facing north—just in case. The unusual weapon has been featured in *Ripley's Believe It or Not*. Free.

THIS UNIQUE DOUBLE-BARRELED CANNON WAS BUILT IN ATHENS IN 1863 TO PROTECT THE TOWN FROM UNION FORCES.

🐾 ♿ **Taylor-Grady House** (706-549-8688), 634 Prince Avenue, Athens. Open 9–1 and 2–5 weekdays. Guided tours available through Athens Welcome Center. Famed journalist, orator, and editor of the *Atlanta Constitution* Henry Grady, who was credited with reuniting the North and South and establishing the concept of the New South after the Civil War, lived in this gorgeous 1844 Greek Revival residence during his collegiate career. The exterior of the imposing mansion is bordered by 13 columns representing the 13 original states. These soaring columns are connected by delicate ironwork. Operated by the Junior League, the site is filled with graceful period pieces. Adults $3; children younger than 12 free.

✎ 🐾 ♿ **Tree That Owns Itself,** Deering and Finley streets, Athens. If you simply drive by without knowing what you're seeing, you'd think this was just an ordinary tree. You'd be wrong, however. Professor William H. Jackson loved the shade of the great white oak on his property so much that in the 1890s he deeded the tree to itself along with 8 feet of land on all four sides. Unfortunately, the 100-foot tall, 15-foot diameter tree blew down in a 1942 windstorm, but what was considered a tragedy by the fond citizenry had a happy ending. A new tree grew from one of the acorns of the original, and today Jackson Oak Jr. rivals its parent in size.

MUSEUMS ✎ 🐾 ♿ **Butts-Mehre Heritage Hall and Sports Museum** (706-542-9036), Pinecrest Drive and Lumpkin Street, Athens. Open 8–5 weekdays, 2–5 weekends, limited hours on days of home football games. Named for two former coaches, Wallace Butts and Harry Mehre, the museum is housed in a striking building constructed of red granite accentuated with black glass. Inside, the displays showcase more than 100 years of athletic accomplishments of UGA students such as Herschel Walker and Frankie Sinkwich, whose Heisman Trophies are on display. Free.

🪶 🌿 ♿ **Eagle Tavern Museum and Welcome Center** (706-769-5197, www .oconeecounty.com), 26 North Main Street, Watkinsville. Open 10–5 Monday through Saturday. This humble building, one of the oldest structures in Oconee County, began life in 1789 as a fort, built to protect settlers from Indians. It remained a fort until 1801, when it opened as a stagecoach stop and tavern. The structure has been restored to its Federal Plain–style appearance. The "two up, two down" interior is furnished with simple 1700s pieces to replicate a tavern downstairs and stagecoach-stop hostelry upstairs. Among the exhibits are artifacts excavated on the property. Free.

🌿 ♿ **Garden Club of Georgia** (706-227-5369; www.uga.edu/gardenclub/New Home.html), 2450 South Milledge Avenue, Athens. Open 8–noon and 1–5 weekdays. Headquarters of the 16,000 Georgia garden clubs, the organization occupies a neoclassical structure situated on a hill overlooking the Heritage Garden at the **State Botanical Garden of Georgia** (see *Green Space—Gardens*). In addition to administrative offices, the building contains a decorative arts museum and an impressive collection of museum-quality antiques. Tours $2 (call for appointment one day in advance).

🌿 ♿ **Georgia Museum of Art** (706-542-4662; www.uga.edu/gamuseum), 90 Carlton Street, Athens. Open 10–5 Tuesday and Thursday through Saturday, 10–9 Wednesday, 1–5 Sunday; closed Monday and most state and federal holidays. Located in the East Campus Triangle in the Performing and Visual Arts Complex, the museum is the Official State Art Museum. The permanent collection features more than 8,000 works that focus primarily on 19th- and early 20th-century American paintings. Other collections include the Kress Collection of Italian Renaissance paintings; a significant collection of American, European, and Oriental prints from the Renaissance to the present; and a growing collec-

THE BUTTS-MEHRE HERITAGE HALL AND SPORTS MUSEUM FOCUSES ON THE ATHLETIC ACCOMPLISHMENTS OF UNIVERSITY OF GEORGIA STUDENTS.

tion of decorative arts. Obviously all these works can't be displayed at once, so the museum produces 20 culturally and artistically diverse shows each year featuring pieces from the permanent collection and works from traveling museum and private collections. Self-guided; guided tours available by reservation with two weeks' notice. $2 suggested donation. Plan to lunch or have some light refreshments at the museum's **Figgie's Café,** (see *Where to Eat—Eating Out*).

✐ 🐾 **Georgia Museum of Natural History** (706-542-1663; naturalhistory.uga .edu), Natural History Building, East Campus Drive and Cedar Street, UGA campus, Athens. Visitors may park in lot adjacent to building; request a parking permit from museum office. Open for tours at 4 Friday. Fourteen separate collections of objects, artifacts, and specimens relating to the natural history of Georgia and the Southeast are housed at the museum, ranked as ninth in the nation among natural history museums. The Archaeology Laboratory houses more than 3 million artifacts and specimens chronicling 12,000 years of human settlement and includes stone tools, plant and skeletal remains, and pottery. Free.

✐ 🐾 ♿ **ITA Collegiate Tennis Hall of Fame** (706-542-8064), UGA South Campus, Athens. Open 9–noon and 2–5 weekdays. Guided tours by reservation. Using photographs and equipment of legends of the Intercollegiate Tennis Association, the hall of fame honors more than 150 players, coaches, and contributors dating back to 1883, including Arthur Ashe, Jimmy Connors, and Stan Smith. Free.

SELF-GUIDED TOURS ✐ **Heartland of the Confederacy Civil War Trail** (www.visitathensga.com/civilwartrail). The Leader's Trail section of this regional self-guided heritage trail, which stretches from Gainesville to Crawfordville, features 45 historic sites, 24 of which are located within Athens and Clarke County. The local sites include historical monuments, homes belonging to Confederate leaders, and unusual relics. Maps are available at the Athens Welcome Center (see *Guidance*).

SPECIAL PLACES ✐ 🐾 ♿ **UGA Memorial,** western end of Sanford Stadium, UGA campus, 310 Sanford Drive, Athens. Fans of the University of Georgia football teams worship Uga, the English bulldog mascot, named the nation's best mascot by *Sports Illustrated.* For almost 60 years, one after another of these six (so far) "damn good dogs" has presided over regular-season games and post-season bowl games. When Ugas depart for doggie heaven, they are interred at the stadium in a marble vault and memorialized with a plaque presided over by a bronze statue. Fans place flowers and other tributes on the vaults and, just like rubbing a Bud-

SIMPLE ITEMS FROM THE 1700S FURNISH THE EAGLE TAVERN MUSEUM AND WELCOME CENTER.

dha's tummy for good luck, pat the muzzle of the statue for good fortune. Visitors can see the memorial during home games or during campus tours from the UGA Visitors Center (see *Guidance*). Free.

WALKING TOUR ❧ **Athens Music History Walking Tour** (contact the Athens Welcome Center at 706-353-1820; www.visitathensga.com/music.tour.cfm). This 28-stop self-guided tour of Athens's music heritage will tell you everything you ever wanted to know about the local music scene, including the humble spots where many famous bands got their start. At some of the stops, such as **Weaver D's Fine Foods, the Grit, Copper Creek Brewing Company, 40 Watt Club,** or **Georgia Theatre,** you can get a meal or a drink or enjoy live entertainment. Free.

✳ To Do

GOLF See Golf Appendix.

HIKING Check out all the parks listed under *Green Space—Nature Preserves and Parks,* and don't forget the 5 miles of trails within the **State Botanical Garden of Georgia** (see *Green Space—Gardens*).

SKATING See Other Activities Appendix.

SWIMMING See Other Activities Appendix.

TENNIS See Other Activities Appendix.

✳ Green Space

GARDENS ❧ ♿ **Founders Memorial Garden** (706-227-5369; www.sed.edu/facilities/founders), 325 South Lumpkin Street, Athens. Open daily during daylight hours except during events. The first garden club in America was begun by 12 ladies in Athens in 1891. In 1946, this small formal garden on the North University Campus was created to commemorate that event. The garden serves not only as a museum of landscape design but also as a natural laboratory for botany, forestry, and related disciplines. The layout of the 1½-acre garden consists of winding walkways, a formal boxwood garden, two courtyards, a fountain, a perennial garden, and an arboretum. A centerpiece of the garden, the early 1800s house, is used by the School of Environmental Design. Free.

❧ **North Georgia Garden and Specialty Nursery Trail** (contact Athens Convention and Visitors Bureau: 706-357-4430; 1-800-653-0603; www.visitathensga .com). Along the historic US 441 Heritage Corridor between I-85 and I-20 is the most concentrated and diverse group of specialty nurseries and gardens in the Southeast. The array of plants is unequaled.

✐ ❧ ♿ **State Botanical Garden of Georgia** (706-542-1244; www.uga.edu/bot garden), 2450 South Milledge Avenue, Athens. Open year-round. Grounds open 8–8 daily, April through September; 8–6 daily, October through March. Conser-

vatory/visitor center open 9–4:30 Tuesday through Saturday, 11:30–4:30 Sunday.
Guided tours by reservation. Encompassing 313 acres, the complex features dramatic gorges and spring-fed streams in addition to the formal gardens. Five
miles of trails wander along wooded, flower-lined vistas, providing plenty of
opportunities to enjoy native flora and fauna. Most of these trails are wheelchair-
friendly, but not all. Special collections include magnolias, native and adapted
trees and shrubs including shade and ornamental trees, poisonous and medicinal
plants, a bog garden, and herbaceous flower gardens. In the **Dunson Native
Flora Garden,** more than 300 native Southeastern species are showcased. In
addition, a dazzling three-story **tropical conservatory** houses a rain forest of
tropical and semitropical plants and seasonal annuals. Of special interest is the
magnificent collection of orchids.

Clute's Kugel, located in the pavilion overlooking the international garden, is a
perfectly balanced 816-pound black granite sphere that floats and revolves on a
thin sheet of water. It was named for a young boy, Clute Barrow Nelson, who
died from a brain tumor. Also on the
grounds is the lovely **Day Chapel**
and the headquarters of the Garden
Club of Georgia (see *To See—Museums*). Families can rent a **Garden
Adventure Pack,** filled with hands-
on activities for children. Call ahead
to reserve a pack. Admission to gardens free.

NATURE PRESERVES AND PARKS
♂ ✿ ♿ **Lake Herrick Beach and
Pavilion** (706-542-5060), off College
Station Road, Athens. Swimming area
open 11–5 Friday through Sunday. The
small lake is adjacent to UGA's intra-
mural fields and Oconee Forest Park.
The park features a sandy beach for
volleyball, and the lake provides canoeing; canoe rentals are available. A fitness trail with 20 stations wraps
around the lake and some of the athletic fields and connects to the
Oconee Forest Trail. Admission $3;
UGA students, faculty, and staff
members free. Most of the trails are
wheelchair accessible, but not all.

♂ ✿ ♿ **Memorial Park and Bear
Hollow Wildlife Trail** (park 706-
613-3580; zoo 706-613-3616; www
.athensclarkecounty.com/bearhollow),

THE FOUNDERS MEMORIAL GARDEN IN
ATHENS COMMEMORATES THE FOUNDING OF
THE FIRST GARDEN CLUB IN AMERICA.

293 Gran Ellen Drive, Athens. Open 8–sunset weekdays, 9–sunset weekends and holidays. Guided trail tours by reservation. The 72-acre park contains nature trails, a recreation building, a lake for fishing and paddleboating, basketball court, pool, picnic areas, and playground. More than 120 species of native animals including black bears, bobcats, white-tailed deer, river otters, owls, and others may be viewed on the Bear Hollow Wildlife Trail. Memorial Day features living history.

✍ ✇ ☗ ❧ **North Oconee River Greenway and Heritage Trail** (706-613-3615, Ext. 242; www.athensgreenway.com), 205 Old Commerce Road, Athens. Open sunrise–sunset daily. Seven miles of paved and dirt trails enjoyed by hikers, bikers, and joggers connect Sandy Creek Park, Sandy Creek Nature Center, North Oconee River Park, Dudley Park, and the UGA campus. A 4-mile section of the trail system consists of a 10-foot-wide paved, lighted trail. The park also offers boating, canoe launches and landings, fishing, and a picnic area. Leashed dogs are welcome. Free.

✍ ✇ ☗ **Oconee Forest Park** (706-542-1571; www.warnell.forestry.uga.edu/warnell/ofp), UGA Recreational Sports Complex, College Station and East Campus roads, Athens. Open daily during daylight hours. With 60 acres, the 100-year-old forest park features 15-acre Lake Herrick, lakeshore hiking trails, a 1.2-mile mountain biking trail, a picnic area, and the Teaching Tree Trail—actually a network of trails with more than 100 identified native trees and shrubs. Mature oak and hickory trees mingle with tulip poplars and the largest scarlet oak tree in Georgia. There's an off-leash area for dogs and a pond where they can swim. Free.

✍ ✇ ❧ **Sandy Creek Nature Center** (706-613-3615; www.sandycreeknature center.com), 205 Old Commerce Road, Athens. Trails open sunrise–sunset daily; center open 8:30–5:30 Tuesday through Saturday; naturalist-led walks at 10 AM Saturday. In addition to 225 acres of pristine woodland, fields, and marshlands that are home to numerous native species, the center also features 4 miles of trails, interactive exhibits, and environmental education programs. A wide variety of activities range from stargazing to salamander searches. The newest addition to the center is **ENSAT** (Environment, Natural Science, and Appropriate Technology) **Center,** a state-of-the-art learning laboratory that features live animal exhibits and handicapped-accessible trails. The center highlights energy-saving and "green" technology, construction, and architecture. Free.

✍ ✇ ☗ **Sandy Creek Park** (706-613-3631; www.sandycreekpark.com), 400 Bob Holman Road, Athens. Open 7–9 daily in summer; 8–6 daily in winter. Centered on 260-acre **Lake Chapman,** the 782-acre park offers a visitor center, boat rentals, picnicking, fishing, camping, and swimming as well as playgrounds. There are also private dog runs and a group play area for your four-legged friends. The lake is fully stocked with bass, brim, and crappie, though you must have a valid fishing license. You can bring your own boat, but no gas motors are allowed. Sports areas feature tennis courts, a basketball court, and all kinds of ball fields. There's a 4-mile trail to the Sandy Creek Nature Center and a 3-mile trail alongside the lake. Some of the trails are available for horseback riding. Adults $2; younger than 4 and older than 64 free. Primitive camping available for $5 per night.

See also Parks Appendix.

✳ Lodging

BED & BREAKFASTS

In Athens

♿ **Magnolia Terrace Guesthouse**
(706-548-3860), 227 Hill Street. Up-scale accommodations are offered in this bed & breakfast located in the Cobbham Historic District, which is convenient to the university and down-town. The opulent Classic Revival home with its long, wicker-filled veran-da was built in 1903 Meticulously restored in 1994 and opened as a bed & breakfast, it features beveled glass, hardwood floors, high ceilings, decora-tive mantels, and ornamental moldings. Some of the charming guest accommo-dations include a working fireplace and/or a whirlpool tub. The price includes a continental-plus breakfast on weekdays and a full breakfast on weekends. No smoking. Some wheel-chair accessibility. $85-150.

♿ **Nicholson House Historic Inn**
(706-353-2200; www.nicholsoninn
.com), 6295 Jefferson Road. A true getaway even though it's located with-in 5 miles of town, this magnificent Colonial Revival home built in 1820 is surrounded by 34 acres of open meadows, rolling hills, and heavily wooded areas. Lavishly appointed, the inn offers five guest rooms and three suites between the main house and a converted carriage house. Your day gets off to a perfect start with a full hearty breakfast and it ends peaceful-ly with complimentary sherry to guar-antee a good night's rest. Adults over 17 only. No smoking indoors; smoking permitted on veranda and patios. One ground-floor room wheelchair acces-sible. $109–159; extra $35 for a third person in Carriage House suites; spe-cial event surcharges may apply for graduation and football weekends.

In Watkinsville

♿ ♿ **Ashford Manor Bed and Breakfast** (706-769-2633, www
.ambedandbreakfast.com), 5 Harden Hill Road. The 5-acre Ashford Estate overlooks Watkinsville's distinguished Main Street with its antiques shops and art galleries, but it is still seclud-ed by its border of magnolias, red-buds, and pines. What's truly amazing is that the Victorian house, which was built in 1893, was occupied by the same family for 100 years. Six gra-cious guest rooms, a bridal suite, and a two-story penthouse feature private baths. Among the landscaped gardens you can enjoy a gazebo, a pool, and paths leading to woods and a creek. Concerts in the Ashford Manor Con-cert Series on the lawn are held the first and third Mondays from May through October. Dogs accepted. In June, **Grace's Doggie Birthday Party** is a party for dogs and the peo-ple who love them (see *Special Events*). No smoking. Wheelchair accessible. $89–150.

CAMPGROUNDS See Campgrounds Appendix.

INNS AND HOTELS

In Athens

♿ **College Gameday Suites** (706-583-4500; www.gamedaycenters.com/
georgia.html), 250 West Broad Street. This unique college-market property offers 65 UGA-themed suites with one, two, or three bedrooms. The fully furnished suites are within walk-ing distance of restaurants, shopping, and entertainment. The facility offers a fitness center, covered parking, concierge service, high-speed Internet access, and a club room. No smoking. Wheelchair accessible. $99–195.

ᴦ **The Foundry Park Inn and Spa**
(706-549-7020; 1-866-9ATHENS;
www.foundryparkinn.com), 295 East
Dougherty Street. Built on the 4-acre
site of a former foundry, this upscale
boutique property features 119 luxurious rooms and suites. In addition, the
inn offers meeting facilities, a full-
service spa, fine dining at the historic
1829 **Nathan Hoyt House Restaurant** (see *Where to Eat—Dining
Out*), and food and live music at the
**Athens Steam Company Pub. The
Day Spa** (706-425-9700) showcases a
wide variety of treatments. Smoking
rooms available. Wheelchair accessible. $99–130.

✳ Where to Eat
DINING OUT

In Athens
ᴦ **The Basil Press** (706-227-8926),
104 Washington Street. Open
11:30–2:30 and 5:30–10 daily. Popular
with the artsy crowd as well as with
UGA faculty and businesspeople, the
restaurant features continental fusion
cuisine and a nice selection of French
and California wines. No smoking.
Wheelchair accessible. Lunch $6–10,
dinner $11–25.

ᴦ **East-West Bistro** (706-546-9378;
www.hlamarthomas.net), 351 East
Broad Street. Open 11–10 Monday
through Saturday; noon–3 (brunch)
and 3–10 Sunday. Somewhat schizophrenic, this eatery, the brainchild of
chef Lamar Thomas, is actually two
restaurants in one. The "east" part is a
casual, moderately priced downstairs
restaurant that serves Japanese-Amer-
ican fusion cuisine and has a lively bar
scene. The "west" part is the more
upscale, more formal, more expensive
upstairs restaurant, which serves

Northern Italian cuisine, considered
by many to be the best in Athens. No
smoking. Wheelchair accessible.
Lunch under $10, dinner $10–25;
brunch $6–8.

ᴦ **Five and Ten** (706-546-7300;
www.fiveandten.com), 1653 South
Lumpkin Street. Open 5:30–10 Monday through Thursday, 5:30–11 Friday
and Saturday; brunch 10:30–2:30
Sundays. Considered by many to be
the best fine dining venue in Athens,
the trendy Five and Ten is under the
direction of nationally acclaimed chef
Hugh Acheson, who is known for putting fun twists on old standards on the
seasonally changing menu. (Acheson
earned national acclaim as one of
Food and Wine magazine's Top 10
New Chefs in America in 2002.) No
smoking. Wheelchair accessible.
Lunch and brunch $7–12, dinner
$15–25.

ᴦ **Harry Bissett's New Orleans
Cafe** (706-353-7065; www.harry
bissetts.com), 279 East Broad Street.
Open 5:30–10 Monday, Saturday
11:30–3 and 5:30–10 Tuesday through
Thursday, 5:30–11 Friday and Saturday, 11–3:30 (brunch) and 5:30–10
Sunday. Located just across the street
from UGA's arch in a converted historic drugstore with a skylit atrium,
this legendary upscale restaurant specializes in Cajun and Creole cuisine
but also offers steak, veal, quail, and
seafood. Try the weekend brunch. No
smoking. Wheelchair accessible. Lunch
and brunch $6–11, dinner $14–26.

ᴦ **Hoyt House Restaurant** (706-
425-0444; www.foundryparkinn.com),
295 East Dougherty Street. Open
7–11 daily; 6–10 Friday and Saturday,
brunch 11–2 Sunday. The on-site
restaurant of the **Foundry Park Inn
and Spa** (see *Lodging—Inns and*

Hotels), the Hoyt House Restaurant, housed in the 1829 Nathan Hoyt home, is one of the most upscale places to eat in Athens. The contemporary American fusion cuisine menu is both traditional and trendy. For a special romantic evening, choose a three- or four-course dinner with wine pairings from the extensive wine list. No smoking. Wheelchair accessible. Breakfast $8–10, dinner $18–28, brunch $8–12.

EATING OUT

In Athens

✔ 🕏 🕭 **Big City Bread** (706-543-1187; www.bigcitybread.net), 393 North Finley Street. Open 7–6 Monday through Saturday, 7–3 Sunday. A great place for a leisurely breakfast, this laid-back bakery specializes in an array of fresh breads and fabulous pastries. The eatery serves lunch and dinner as well. Smoking on patio only. Wheelchair accessible. $3–11.

🕏 🕭 **Figgie's Cafe** (706-542-6727; www.uga.edu/gamuseum), 90 Carlton Street. Open 10 AM–2 PM weekdays. Although most diners are **Georgia Museum of Art** patrons (see *To See—Museums*), the gourmet sandwich- and rotating soup-based menu is worth the trip. Save room for dessert. No smoking. Wheelchair accessible. $4.50–5.50.

✔ 🕏 **Garden Room Cafe** (706-542-6359; www.uga.edu/botgarden), 2450 South Milledgeville Avenue. Open 11:30–2:30 Tuesday through Friday, 11:30–3 Saturday and Sunday. Located in the conservatory of the **State Botanical Garden of Georgia** (see *Green Space—Gardens*), this casual eatery offers light meals along with a beautiful view of the outdoors. You also can enjoy the monthly art

exhibits. No smoking. Not wheelchair accessible. Any two items $5.95, three items $7.95.

✔ 🕏 🕭 **The Grit** (706-543-6592; www.thegrit.com), 199 Prince Avenue. Open 11–10 weekdays, 10–3 (brunch) and 5–10 Saturday and Sunday. Although you can get grits in this dinerlike eatery, the primary focus is on good, healthful Southern vegetarian cuisine. No smoking. Wheelchair accessible. Under $8.

🕏 🕭 **Last Resort Grill** (706-549-0810; www.lastresortgrill.com), 184 West Clayton Street. Open 11–3 Monday through Saturday; 5–10 Sunday through Thursday, 5–11 Friday and Saturday, brunch 11–3 Sunday. Nouvelle Southern cuisine is served in a building that was once a nightclub where R.E.M. and the B-52s got their start. The ambience is casual and the prices affordable. Specialties such as the cornmeal-battered fried green tomato sandwich topped with Vidalia-bacon dressing, grilled salmon, or north Georgia trout top the menu. No smoking before 11 PM. Wheelchair accessible on lower-level bar and patio only. Brunch and lunch $7, dinner under $15.

✔ 🕏 🕭 **Weaver D's Fine Foods** (706-353-7797), 1016 East Broad Street. Open 11–6 Monday through Saturday. "The fried chicken's on and we're waitin' for ya" is the friendly invitation at this restaurant. This Athens institution looks pretty inauspicious in its white concrete building, but it was made famous by R.E.M.'s "Automatic for the People" album—named for a sign that hangs outside the eatery. The sign refers to good food and quick, efficient service with a smile. Serving up "soul food that rocks," a typical lunch might consist of fried chicken, pork chops, catfish, barbecue, steak and gravy, or meat loaf. No smoking. Wheelchair accessible. $4–9.

✐ ♨ ♿ **Wilson's Soul Food** (706-353-7289), 351 North Hull Street. Open 11–4 daily. The home-cookin' eatery serves comfort foods and homemade desserts, among which a favorite is sweet-potato custard. No smoking. Wheelchair accessible. $6 for meat and two vegetables, $7.50 for meat and three vegetables.

In Danielsville

♨ ♿ **Zeb's Place BBQ** (706-795-2701), 5742 US 29 North. Open 9–9 Tuesday through Saturday. Talk about staying power; Zeb's has been cooking up chopped pork barbecue, shank barbecue, Brunswick stew, and specialty ham since 1946. No smoking. Wheelchair accessible. Around $7.50.

SNACKS

In Athens

♨ ♿ **The Grill** (706-543-4770), 171 College Avenue. Open 24/7. In this downtown diner, you can get burgers, fries, and a milk shake. If you're in the mood for something more substantial, the menu includes hot sandwiches, crinkle-cut fries with feta dressing, the local specialty, and vegetarian offerings. You can get an ample breakfast from midnight to noon. No smoking. Wheelchair accessible. $2.50–8.

✐ ♨ ♿ **The Varsity** (706-548-6325; www.thevarsity.com), 1000 West Broad Street. Open 10–10 Sunday through Thursday, 10–midnight Friday and Saturday. With its original location still in operation in Atlanta after 65 years, the hot dogs, onion rings, greasy fries, and frosted orange drinks are beloved by Georgians. No

smoking. Wheelchair accessible. $1–6.25 (cash only).

COFFEEHOUSES

In Athens

✐ ♨ ♿ **Jittery Joe's Coffee Roasting Company** (706-208-1979), 1210 South Milledge Avenue (with two other locations in the city). Open 6:30 AM–midnight weekdays, 7:30 AM–midnight weekends. Athens's favorite coffee shop's slogan is "Jittery Joe's— Because life is too short to drink grocery store coffee." True to the company philosophy, Jittery Joe's claims to serve the freshest coffee in town, with several varieties of locally roasted coffees served hot, cold, or frozen. In addition, you can get tea, soft drinks, bagels, pastries, and desserts. No smoking. Wheelchair accessible. $1.80–4.

✳ Entertainment

COLLEGE SPORTS University of Georgia (UGA Visitors Center, 706-542-0842; www.uga.edu/visctr). For schedules and tickets to UGA games and sporting events, contact the **UGA Athletic Association** (706-542-1231; www.georgiadogs.com). The university boasts 21 Division 1-A sports teams that have won 10 national championships and 22 Southeastern Conference championships since 1998. Football is played at **Sanford Stadium** (706-542-9036), Sanford Drive; basketball and gymnastics use **Stegeman Coliseum** (706-542-3579), Carlton Street; swim meets and volleyball tournaments occur at the **Ramsey Student Center for Physical Activities** (706-542-3579), Carlton Street.

DANCE Athens Ballet Theatre– Athens School of Ballet (706-353-

2082; www.itown.com/athens/abt),
mailing address: 126 Barrington
Drive, Athens 30605. Call for a
schedule performance times and
prices. Organized in 1973, the Athens
Ballet Theatre produces several full-
length ballets each year with performances at the Morton Theater or the
Classic Center Theatre (see *Theater*).

**MUSIC Athens Symphony Orches-
tra** (706-425-4205; www.athens
synphony.org), mailing address: P.O.
Box 5244, Athens 30604. For ticket
information, contact the box office at
the Classic Center Theatre (706-357-
4444), 300 North Thomas Street.
Since 1979, the community orchestra
has been entertaining Athenians with
winter, spring, pops, and Christmas
concerts. Most performances are held
at the Classic Center Theatre. Free,
but tickets required. They can be
picked up at Classic Center box office
Monday two weeks prior to concert;
maximum four tickets per family.

NIGHTLIFE & 40 Watt Club (706-
549-7871; www.40watt.com), 285
West Washington Street, Athens.
Open 10 PM–2:45 AM daily unless
nationally touring band is performing,
at which time opening is 9 PM. The
world-famous nightclub, named for
the single 40-watt bulb that barely
provided the illumination in the original location on opening night in 1978,
offers live music six nights a week and
a DJ on the seventh night. Although
the club is best known for rock, it also
books some R&B. No smoking.
Wheelchair accessible, including rest
rooms. Cover $5–6. Admission cash
only; bars take credit cards. Some
bands require ticketed admission.
Ticket may be purchased at the club;
online at the club's web site; at **Low**

Yo Yo Stuff Records (706-227-6199),
285 West Washington Street, Athens);
and at **Schoolkids Records** (706-
353-1666); 264 East Clayton Street,
Athens.

Georgia Theatre (706-353-3405;
www.georgiatheatre.com), 215 North
Lumpkin Street, Athens. Call or consult web site for a schedule of events
and prices. One of the city's most
revered venues, this theater helped
launch the careers of numerous musicians. It was built in 1889, but extensive renovations in 1935 resulted in
the current art deco facade. Today it
is used as a nightclub venue for popular bands.

& **Tasty World** (706-543-0797;
www.tastyworld.net), 213 East Broad
Street, Athens. First-floor Music Hall
open 4 PM–2 AM Monday through Saturday, second floor open 10 PM–2 AM.
Voted Best Party Venue by the *Athens
Banner-Herald* two years running.
Downstairs is an intimate atmosphere
for bands playing everything from jazz
to punk to Norwegian death metal to
indie-rock, bluegrass, country, grind-
core, pop, rap, salsa, and hip-hop.
Upstairs there is a salsa night once a
week and a swing night—both with
lessons. The second floor also features
pool tables, video games, a full bar,
and a terrific view of downtown. No
smoking until 11 PM. Wheelchair
accessible. $5 cover charge after 10 PM.

THEATER Classic Center Theatre
(box office 706-357-4444; 1-800-864-
4160; www.classiccenter.com), 300
North Thomas Street, Athens. Box
office open 10–6 Monday through
Saturday (weekdays only in summer).
Call for a schedule of events and
prices. The state-of-the-art, 2,050-seat
theater is the venue for national

Broadway touring companies, a country music series, headline entertainers, the **Athens Symphony Orchestra** (see *Music*), and other productions.

Morton Theater (706-613-3770; www.mortontheatre.com), 195 West Washington Street, Athens. Call for a schedule of events and prices. Free tours by reservation. One of the country's first and oldest surviving vaudeville theaters, the Morton was built in 1910 and owned by African American politician and businessman M. B. Morton. During its heyday, it hosted performers such as Louis Armstrong, Cab Calloway, Duke Ellington, and Bessie Smith. Now listed on the National Register of Historic Places, the theater serves as a community performing arts venue with a wide range of dramatic and musical performances.

University of Georgia Performing Arts Center (box office 706-542-4400; www.uga.edu/pac), 230 River Road, Athens. Call for a schedule of events and prices. The center is home to the **Athens Symphony Orchesta** (see *Music*), Dance Fest, the Showtime Series, Traditions Series, and the Ramsey Hall Concert Series, as well as an outstanding lineup of award-winning local, regional, and national talent. The center has two theaters: the 1,100-seat Hogdson Hall and the 360-seat Ramsey Hall. Last-minute tickets frequently available.

✴ Selective Shopping

ANTIQUES Athens Antique Mall (706-354-0108), 4615 Atlanta Highway, Bogart. Open 10–6 daily. The largest antiques emporium in the Athens area, the mall has 25 dealers who offer European and American antiques.

Athens Five Points District, centered on Milledge Avenue, Milledge Circle, and Lumpkin Street in Athens, is an area of 1920s and 1930s homes now teeming with antiques and other shops such as Appointments at Five, the Cat's Pajamas, the Garden Gate, and Jingles.

ART GALLERIES Chappelle Gallery in the Historic Haygood House (706-310-0985), 25 South Main Street, Watkinsville. Open 10–5:30 Monday through Saturday. The gallery showcases American crafts including drawings, paintings, pottery, blown glass, stained glass, wood, wrought iron, candles, and other works by local, regional, and national artists.

Fire Hall No. 2 (706-353-1801), 489 Prince Avenue, Athens. Call for hours. Located in a triangular 1901 structure, the two-story Victorian firehouse at Hill and Prince avenues anchors one end of the Cobbham Historic District. In its newest incarnation, the old fire hall contains an art gallery and is also the home of the Athens-Clark Heritage Foundation.

Oconee Cultural Arts Foundation (706-769-4565; www.ocaf.com), 34 School Street, Watkinsville. Several nationally recognized artists live and work in Oconee County. The Oconee Cultural Arts Center, located in a 1902 four-room brick schoolhouse, provides exhibition space for contemporary art, folk art, and various crafts, as well as musical and theatrical performances.

CRAFTS Happy Valley Pottery (706-769-5922), 1210 Carson Graves Road, Watkinsville. Open 8–4 Monday through Saturday. Founded in 1970 and named after a Walt Disney production, the facility features on-site pottery-making and glass-blowing demonstrations.

FLEA MARKETS J&J Flea Market (706-613-2410), 11661 Commerce Road, Athens. Open 8–5 daily. An astounding 750 outside tables and 400 inside booths are crammed with bargains in antiques, crafts, collectibles, and everything retro from boiled peanuts to live chickens to tube socks. During the summer months, farmers sell their homegrown produce. Three restaurants including the Flea Bite Café keep hungry shoppers on the property.

RECORDS Wuxtry Records (706-369-9428; www.wuxtryrecords.com), 197 East Clayton Street, Athens. Open 10–7 weekdays, 11–7 Saturday, noon–6 Sunday. A locally owned music shop established in 1975, Wuxtry Records was the first-of-its-kind used-record outlet. Considered part museum and part record shop, it has offered mainstream and obscure albums as well as a vast array of CDs, cassettes, and publications. R.E.M.'s Peter Buck worked here, and in fact, he and fellow band member Michael Stipe met here.

SPECIAL STORES The Junkman's Daughter's Brother (706-543-4454), 458 East Clayton Street, Athens. Open 10:30–7 Monday through Saturday, noon–6 Sunday. A sibling to the trendy Junkman's Daughter in Atlanta's funky Little Five Points neighborhood, the emporium carries cool clothes, leather and studs, costumes, and posters. Wheelchair accessible.

✳ Special Events

March: **Robert Osborne's Classic Film Festival**, held at the Classic Center Theatre, 300 North Thomas Street, Athens (call Classic Center box office at 706-357-4444 or consult web sites at www.grady.uga.edu/osbornefest or www.peabody.grady.uga.edu/osbornefest). Hosted by Robert Osborne, host of Turner Classic Movies and columnist for the *Hollywood Reporter,* the four-day festival glamorizes the days of Old Hollywood with screenings of newly remastered classic movies. Special guests discuss the films. $10 per film, $60 for festival pass.

April or May: **Athens Human Rights Festival** (706-208-8674; www.athenshumanrightsfest.org), College Square downtown. For more than a quarter century, the two-day festival has been an activist tradition that combines politics, music, outdoor fun and a full lineup of local musicians as well as art and entertainment interspersed with speakers and political activists from around the world. Free.

June: **AthFest Music and Arts Festival** (706-548-1973; www.athfest.com), downtown Athens at outside stages and in clubs. The four-day music and arts festival showcases local talent and includes as many as 150 bands, a juried artists' market, a nighttime "Club Crawl," a music seminar, and activities for children at KidsFest. A compilation CD is released each year to showcase new music and groups. Performances at outdoor stages free; all-venue weekend wristbands that include performances in clubs $10–15.

❀ **Grace's Doggie Birthday Party** (706-769-2633; www.gracesbirthday.com). Held on the grounds of the **Ashford Manor Bed and Breakfast** (see *Lodging—Bed & Breakfasts*), 5

Harden Hill Road in Watkinsville, the party for pooches and their human guests features entertainment, a silent auction, and contests. The fun-filled event has been featured in *Southern Living* magazine. $15.

Oct. 31: **Halloween, Athens Style** (www.flagpole.com). Bands and fans alike dress in wild costumes at the city's world-renowned night clubs. It's a fright to behold. Consult the web site for a performance schedule. Included in regular club entrance fees.

November and December: **Christmas in Athens** (706-357-4430; www .christmasinathens.com). A compilation of almost 150 events throughout November and December. One of the premier Christmas in Athens activities is the **Downtown Athens Christmas Parade of Lights** (706-613-3589; 706-613-3580), traditionally held the first Thursday after Thanksgiving. Another popular Christmas in Athens event is the **Annual Singing Christmas Tree** (706-357-4444; www .athenssingingtree.org), a musical, orchestral, and dramatic production by the Prince Avenue Baptist Church, with seven performances traditionally held the third weekend in December at the Classic Center Theatre, 300 North Thomas Street. Some Christmas in Athens events free; individual events $8–14.

AUGUSTA

Augusta is Georgia's second-oldest city (dating from 1736) as well as its second largest, with a population of 193,000. Once Savannah had been settled in 1733, explorers and settlers followed the Savannah River north and developed a remote trading post at what is now Augusta—named for Princess Augusta, the mother of King George III. St. Paul's Church sits on the site of Fort Augusta, the original location of the city.

The area first served as a fur trading outpost. Settlers then attempted unsuccessfully to grow tobacco, so cotton was tried next. In 100 years, Augusta developed into the second-largest inland cotton market in the world. The city served as the state capital from 1783 to 1795 and saw action in the French and Indian, Revolutionary, and Civil wars. Despite the fact that Confederate ammunition was made here, the city was spared.

The Augusta Canal, which was built in 1846 and expanded in 1872 to harness the power of the Savannah River and to attract manufacturing to the South, was constructed by Irish, Italians, Chinese, slaves, and free blacks—all of whose influence can still be seen today. The canal saw 25,000 bales of cotton a year moved along its banks. During this era of "White Gold," it was reported that when cotton bales were stacked ready for shipping, a person could walk from bale to bale for more than a mile without ever putting a foot on the ground. Reaching from the headgates in Columbia County to downtown Augusta, the canal is a nationally designated heritage area. The canal and its associated tow path, where mules used to pull the barges, offers opportunities for hiking, cycling, fishing, and canoeing or kayaking.

Although the Savannah River was the instrument of the city's commercial and industrial success, it hasn't always been a hospitable neighbor. Several great floods left residents getting around the streets by boat. A levee was built to hold back the river, but even it was breached in 1929, when the river crested at more than 45 feet. Unfortunately, the city also suffered a great fire in 1916 that devastated 32 blocks.

Located on the Piedmont Fall Line, Augusta was considered upcountry by coastal residents who fled there in the summer for the cooler temperatures. Augusta's prosperity, coupled with the felicitous weather and the fact that the city was the end of the line for north-south railroads for many years, made

Augusta a playground for the rich and famous. President William Howard Taft, John D. Rockefeller, and Harvey Firestone were only a few of the elite who wintered in Augusta's luxury hotels. Sadly, none of those hotels survives today.

It was during the resort era that the first golf courses were laid out. Golf legend Bobby Jones built his dream course in the 1930s on the site of the Fruitlands Nursery. Today, golf legends play the Augusta National Golf Club each April during the annual Masters golf tournament. Be forewarned, however, that the Augusta National Golf Club, where the Masters is played, is a private club and does not allow visitors on the grounds at any time. Admission to the tournament is by a special badge for which there is a lengthy waiting list.

In addition to golf, Augusta is also known for other sporting events such as the Augusta Futurity, a cutting-horse event, and the Barrel Horse World Championships. Known as "the Watersports Capital of the Southeast," Augusta also hosts several rowing and racing events.

GUIDANCE

When planning a trip to the Augusta area, contact the **Augusta Metropolitan Convention and Visitors Bureau** (706-823-6600; 1-800-726-0243; www .augustaga.org), 1450 Greene Street, Enterprise Mill, Augusta 30901. (Mailing address: P.O. Box 1331, Augusta 30903-1331). Open 8:30–5 weekdays.

The **Augusta Visitor Information Center** (706-724-4067), 560 Reynolds Street, Augusta 30901, is located inside the **Augusta Museum of History** (see *To See—Museums*). Open 10–5 Monday through Saturday, 1–5 Sunday.

There is also a **Georgia State Visitor Center** (706-737-1446) on I-20 westbound just inside the Georgia–South Carolina state line in Martinez. Open 8:30–5:30 daily.

The Savannah Rapids Visitor Center (706-868-3349; www.savannahrapids .com), 3300 Evans-to-Lock Road, Martinez 30907, is located in Columbia County at the headgates of the Augusta Canal. Housed in the historic lockkeeper's home, the center provides brochures and other information (see *Green Spaces— Nature Preserves and Parks*).

Additional sources of information are the **Augusta Canal Authority** (706-823-0440), 20 Eighth Street, Augusta 30901, for information about the canal and its recreational opportunities, and **Historic Augusta** (706-724-0436), 111 10th Street, Augusta 30901, for historic information about the city and tour information.

For Masters golf credentials, housing, hospitality, and transportation services, contact **Ticket Daddy LLC** (706-364-4250; 1-888-642-4200; www.TicketDaddy .com), the Atrium Building, 3633 Wheeler Road, Suite 270, Augusta 30901.

For information about Appling, Evans, Grovetown, Harlem, and Martinez, contact the **Columbia County Chamber of Commerce** (706-651-0018; www .columbiacountychamber.com), 4424 Evans to Locks Road, Evans 30809.

To find out more about **Fort Gordon,** consult the web site at www.gordon .army.mil.

For information about Thomson, contact the **Thomson-McDuffie Tourism**

Convention and Visitors Bureau (706-597-1000; www.thomson-mdduffie
.org), 111 Railroad Street, Thomson 30824. Open 8:30–5 Monday through
Thursday, 8:30–4 Friday.

GETTING THERE *By air:* **Augusta Regional Airport** (706-798-3236; 1-866-860-
9809; www.AugustaRegionalAirport.com) is served by **Atlantic Southeast Airlines** (1-800-221-1212) and **US Airways Express** (1-800-428-4322).

Some visitors will choose to fly in to **Hartsfield-Jackson Atlanta International
Airport** (see What's Where in Georgia) and take a shuttle or rental car to Augusta.

By bus: **Southeastern Stages** (706-722-6411; www.southeasternstages.com),
1128 Greene Street, serves Augusta directly and connects to **Greyhound Lines**
(1-800-229-9424; www.greyhound.com), 1128 Greene Street.

By car: Major highways that serve Augusta are I-20 and I-520 (which circles the
city), US 1, US 25, US 78, and US 278.

GETTING AROUND Car rentals can be obtained from **Alamo** (1-800-327-9633),
Avis (1-800-331-1212), **Budget** (1-800-227-3678), **Economy** (706-737-6006),
Enterprise (1-800-325-8007), **Hertz** (1-800-654-3131), and **National** (1-800-
227-7368). Local bus service with numerous routes is offered by **Augusta Public Transit** (706-821-1719).

WHEN TO GO The **Masters** golf tournament is a ticketed event, and tickets are
almost impossible to obtain (see *Special Events*). If you are not one of the privi-
leged few with tickets, we strongly urge you not to visit Augusta during the first
week in April. Not only are accommodations almost impossible to find, they are
outrageously expensive. Traffic is heavy and restaurants are crowded. With 51
other glorious weeks in which to visit, why subject yourself to the aggravation?

MEDICAL EMERGENCY For life-threatening situations, call 911. Otherwise,
medical help can be sought at these Augusta hospitals: **Doctors Hospital** (706-
651-3232), 3651 Wheeler Road; **Medical College of Georgia Medical Center** (706-721-CARE; 1-800-736-CARE; www.mcghealth.org), 1120 15th Street;
St. Joseph Hospital (706-481-7000), 2260 Wrightsboro Road; or **University
Hospital** (706-722-9011), 1350 Walton Way; or **Children's Medical Center**
(706-721-KIDS; 1-888-721-KIDS; www.mcghealth.org), 1446 Harper Street.

VILLAGES AND NEIGHBORHOODS **Augusta** boasts several historic neighborhoods of tree-lined streets and majestic mansions that are appropriate for walking and/or driving tours. The **Summerville–Gould's Corner** neighborhood,
locally known as "the Hill" because of its lofty location above the city, is a time
warp where Greek Revival mansions vie for attention with Italian Renaissance
Victorians. The **Olde Town Pinch Gut Historic District** also features many
historical styles popular at the turn of the 20th century. The neighborhood
derived its unusual name from the corsets with which ladies cinched themselves
in those days. The **Laney-Walker Historic District** is the heart of what was
the African American business district in the days of segregation.

Nearby **McDuffie County**'s roots go back to 1768 with the settlement of Wrightsborough by Quakers from New Jersey. This was Georgia's only Quaker settlement and marked the southernmost point of Quaker migration in North America. Today sights of white-columned mansions, beautiful lakes, thick forests, and lush rolling countryside epitomize the South. Only a few sites remain to reveal evidence that Wrightsborough ever existed.

Thomson, the area's major town, boasts several attractions to draw visitors. In 1913 Thomson adopted the motto "Camellia City of the South." This appellation may be disputed by other cities, but the area has ideal climatic conditions and a perfect combination of soils to produce an astounding array of these beautiful blooms from late fall to early spring.

Tiny **Harlem** is known as the birthplace of Oliver Hardy, half of the silver-screen comedy team of Laurel and Hardy, and is the home of the annual **Oliver Hardy Festival** (see **Laurel and Hardy Museum** under *To See—Museums*).

✳ To See

Purchase an ✿ **Augusta Gallery Pass** from the visitor information center and other venues. The pass allows entrance to nine attractions and galleries. The cost is $20 and if you visit at least four places, you'll have paid for the pass and can enjoy all the other attractions gratis.

CULTURAL SITES Augusta boasts several interesting monuments. For more information about any of them, consult the Augusta Metropolitan Convention and Visitors Bureau (see *Guidance*).

🐾 ☸ ✿ ♿ **Confederate Monument,** between Seventh and Eighth streets at Broad Street, is unusual in that it honors the common soldier with a Confederate private featured on the top, while Generals Robert E. Lee, Stonewall Jackson, T. R. R. Cobb, and W. H. T. Walker encircle the base.

🐾 ☸ ✿ ♿ **Confederate Powderworks Chimney,** 1717 Gooodrich Street. The only permanent structure ever built by the Confederate States of America was the Confederate Powderworks in Augusta, created to manufacture ammunition. During its brief operation, the Powderworks manufactured 2 million pounds of gunpowder. Although the building is long gone, the chimney remains and is a visible, if silent, reminder of the Confederacy.

🐾 ☸ ✿ ♿ **Haunted Pillar,** Fifth and Broad streets, is a local legend. The pillar was part of the Lower City Market. The story goes that an itinerant evangelist was refused permission to preach at the market, so he put a curse on it. In 1878 a cyclone destroyed the market with the exception of this pillar. Legend has it that several attempts have been made to remove or move the pillar, all to no avail.

🐾 ☸ ✿ ♿ **Signers Monument,** Greene and Monument streets. The obelisk marks the burial spot of two of three Georgia signers of the Declaration of Independence: Lyman Hall and George Walton.

In Thomson, the **Women of the Confederacy Monument,** 111 Railroad Street, is one of the few such monuments in the South. It was created from Italian marble sometime between 1910 and 1920 in Florence, Italy. The base contains the names of Confederate soldiers from Thomson.

FOR FAMILIES 🐾 💧 ♿ **National Science Center's Fort Discovery** (706-821-0200; 1-800-325-5445; www.nscdiscovery.org), 1 Seventh Street, Augusta. Open 10–5 Monday through Saturday, noon–5 Sunday. Science, math, and technology are on display at this playground for children and adults, with its more than 270 hands-on, interactive exhibits. Visitors learn about and experience technologies involved with automation, communications, computers, and electronics. Among the most popular attractions are the StarLab Planetarium, KidScape for budding scientists younger than 7, the Martian Towers climbing structure, and the Paul S. Simon Discovery Theater. Field trips, overnight camp-ins, summer camps, and workshops are other well-liked activities. Adults $8, children and seniors $6.

💧 ♿ **Pine Top Farm Horse Trails** (706-595-3792; www.pinetopfarm.com), 1393 Augusta Road/US 78/278, Thomson. Six times throughout the year, Pine Top Farm Equestrian Center hosts nationally sanctioned horse trials such as the United States Combined Training Association event—a three-phase competition including dressage, cross-country, and show jumping. The facility was a 1996 pre-Olympic training site for five counties, was the site of the 1995 Pan-American selection trials, and hosted the 1999 Georgia Games Equestrian Competition. Call for a schedule and prices.

GUIDED TOURS 💧 🐾 **Saturday Guided Historic Tours** (706-724-4067). Tours depart at 1:30 from outside Augusta Visitor Information Center, Sixth and Reynolds streets. By reservation only. Taking one of these fascinating driving tours is an opportunity to see Augusta in the company of local guides who impart their love of the city's rich history. To tour on your own, request a copy of "Discover Augusta on Foot" from the Augusta Metropolitan Convention and Visitors Bureau (see *Guidance*). Guided tour: adults $10, children younger than 12 $5.

HISTORIC HOMES AND SITES 🐾 **Augusta Cotton Exchange,** Eighth and Reynolds streets at Riverwalk, Augusta. Visitors may examine these exhibits during regular banking hours, 9–4 Monday through Thursday, 9–6 Friday. The Cotton Exchange, an Augusta icon that served for many

NOW A BANK, THE AUGUSTA COTTON EXCHANGE WAS ONCE THE SECOND-LARGEST COTTON MARKET IN THE WORLD.

years as the city's Welcome Center, is now owned and operated as a bank by Georgia Bank and Trust Company. Built in 1886, the Cotton Exchange, which was once the second-largest cotton market in the world, housed the business activities of cotton farmers, brokers, and buyers. The bank has retained all the historic exchange furniture, the chalkboard with cotton prices listed as of the day the exchange closed, scales, cotton hooks, a tester, a model of the evil boll weevil, and other memorabilia. Free.

🏛 ✐ ♿ **The Boyhood Home of President Woodrow Wilson** (706-722-9828; www.wilsonboyhoodhome.org), 419 Seventh Street, Augusta. Open 10–5 Tuesday through Saturday. This is the oldest presidential site in Georgia. From 1860 to 1870, the future 28th president of the United States, Thomas "Tommy" Woodrow Wilson, lived in the manse of the First Presbyterian Church while his father served as the church's pastor. The house has been restored by Historic Augusta and opened to the public. Wilson's sojourn here, which lasted from age 3 to 13, occurred during the Civil War, and the wounded soldiers he saw on the lawns of the church undoubtedly affected his later views about war. The house museum shows 14 rooms, including Tommy's bedroom, each furnished with original and period pieces, as well as the Carriage House–Stable where the future president played with his friends. Look for the place where he signed his name in the house. Wilson visited while he was president and reminisced about how that period had affected his life. Note: Only first floor is wheelchair-accessible. Adults $5, Seniors $4, children through 12th grade $3.

🏛 **Ezekiel Harris House** (706-737-2820; www.augustamuseum.org/eh.htm), 1822 Broad Street, Augusta. Open 10–4:30 Tuesday through Saturday. Built in 1797, the house is a reminder of the days when tobacco, not cotton, was king. It is the second-oldest building in Augusta. Ezekiel Harris established a tobacco inspection station and warehouse and laid out a town he called Harrisburg, which he hoped would rival Augusta. He also offered accommodations in his house. Considered to be the finest 18th-century house in Georgia, it is an outstanding example of early Federal-style architecture. Adults $2, children $1.

🏛 **Historic Wrightsborough** (Thomson-McDuffie Tourism Convention and Visitors Bureau: 706-597-1000), Wrightsborough Road, Thomson. Open on request. This settlement was created by Quakers from North Carolina in 1768. The last of the planned colonial towns, the town of Wrightsborough was surveyed and laid out in 1769 and incorporated in 1799. All that remains is the simple Wrightsboro Methodist Church and Cemetery. Informative signs describe the history of the site. Because historic Wrightsborough is located in a rural area 7 miles southwest of Thomson and is not staffed, it is best to stop in town at the CVB at 111 Railroad Street to get specific directions and to pick up a key. Free.

🏛 **Meadow Garden, George Walton Historic Site** (706-724-4174), 1320 Independence Way (13th Street at Walton Way), Augusta. Open 10–4 weekdays, Saturdays by appointment. The oldest documented house in Augusta, Meadow Garden was built in 1792. It was the home of George Walton, one of Georgia's signers of the Declaration of Independence who, at 35, was the youngest signer. Walton went on to have distinguished careers as a soldier, a legislator, a judge, and eventually the governor of Georgia. The house was saved from demolition by the Georgia State Society of the Daughters of the American Revolution in 1900 and opened as a house museum in 1901. As such it is the oldest house museum in Georgia. The house you will see includes additions made between 1825 and 1840 and is filled with simple colonial-era furnishings. Adults $4, seniors $3.50, college students $3, children $1.

🌿 **Rock House** (Thomson-McDuffie Tourism Convention and Visitors Bureau: 706-597-1000), Rock House Road, Thomson. Open daily. Built in 1785, the Rock House is the oldest stone residence in Georgia and is listed on the National Register of Historic Places. Its substantial design, flanked by chimneys at both ends, is typical of the New Jersey area where many of the area's Quakers originated. Amazingly enough, the simple structure was occupied until the 1930s. It is owned by the Wrightsboro Quaker Foundation. Free.

🌿 ♿ **Sacred Heart Cultural Center** (706-826-4700; www.sacredheartaugusta .org), 1301 Greene Street, Augusta. Open 9–5 weekdays. An architectural masterpiece built between 1897 and 1900, this graceful building was once a Catholic church. Deconsecrated when the congregation moved to the suburbs, the building was in danger of demolition before it was saved and restored to have a new life as the heart of Augusta's cultural community with offices of the ballet, opera, symphony, and other arts organizations. The red-brick, double-spired Romanesque church features no less than 15 brick patterns. Inside, feast your eyes on the stained-glass windows, elaborate altar, and Italian columns among other fine examples of Old World craftsmanship. Many concerts and other special events are held here throughout the year. Guided tour $2; donations accepted for self-guided tours.

🌿 **Ware's Folly, Gertrude Herbert Institute of Art** (706-722-5495; www .ghia.org), 506 Telfair Street, Augusta. Open 10–5 Tuesday through Friday, Saturday by appointment. So exorbitant ($40,000) was the cost of Nicholas Ware's Federal-style home in 1818 that locals called it Ware's Folly. Itself a work of art, the mansion has among its features a double exterior stairway, fluted pilasters, a three-story elliptical staircase, and elegant bay windows. Mrs. Olivia A. Herbert, a New Yorker who wintered in Augusta, bought the mansion and renovated it. In 1937 she gifted it as a permanent home for the Augusta Art Club in memory of her daughter, Gertrude Herbert Dunn. Today the institute offers art classes and workshops and presents several major art exhibitions each year. Free.

🌿 **Watson Homes** (706-595-7777; www.watson-brown.org), 310 Tom Watson Way, Thomson. Open 10–5 weekdays; tours on the hour until 4. Thomson was the home of controversial lawyer, statesman, senator, author, and publisher Thomas E. Watson. He was best known for founding the Georgia People's Party in 1891 and running unsuccessfully as the party's vice presidential candidate, but he is also acknowledged as the father of the rural free mail delivery system. His birthplace and two of his later homes are owned and operated by the Watson-Brown Foundation. The simple **Thomas E. Watson Birthplace** is a cabin built in 1830 and moved here from its original location 3 miles away. The **Thomas E. Watson House** was built in 1865 and acquired by Watson in 1881. Today the house serves as the administrative headquarters of the foundation but is open for tours. Filled with photographs, memorabilia, and period furniture, it is surrounded by 6 acres of gardens. Lastly, in 1900 Watson acquired **Hickory Hill,** which was built around 1864. He added impressive Greek Revival elements, enlarged the house, and added modern conveniences such as electricity and indoor plumbing. After extensive renovation, it has been restored to its 1920 appearance and features original furnishings throughout as well as memorabilia depicting the senator's life and career. Surrounding the house are support structures such as the corncrib, smokehouse, pigeon cote, garage, and even a one-room schoolhouse. There are gardens and orchards, too. Adults $3, seniors $2, children 5–18 $1.

MUSEUMS ⚡ ✎ ♿ **Augusta Canal Interpretive Center** (706-823-0440; www.augustacanal.com), 1450 Greene Street, Augusta. Open 9:30–5:30 Monday through Saturday, 1–5:30 Sunday; closed Monday, December through February. One of the pivotal factors in the development of Augusta was the Augusta Canal. Now designated as the Augusta Canal National Heritage Area—Georgia's only officially designated National Heritage Area—the 8-mile waterway is the only intact industrial canal in the country in continuous use since its construction in the 1840s. The interpretive center is appropriately housed in the renovated 19th-century **Enterprise Mill**, an important landmark itself. Built in 1877, by 1900 it had 33,000 spindles and 928 looms. It employed more than 400 workers, who manufactured more than 10.8 million yards of cloth yearly, the equivalent of 6,200 miles of fabric. The center narrates the story of the canal and the Southern textile industry it made possible. Begin a tour with the movie **The Power of a Canal** and then see the exhibits, which include models, working mill machinery, and more. Many of the exhibits are interactive. A highlight of any visit to the center can be a **Petersburg Boat Guided Tour,** which glides past natural and historic sites. The only Petersburg tour boats in the world, the shallow-draft, 49-passenger boats were modeled on the long wooden vessels powered by six-man African American crews that carried cargo on the river and canal. These boats are the largest electrically powered boats in America. Boat tours are held weather permitting, and shortened hours are in effect in winter. The tow path and nature trails along the canal are also worth exploring. Get a free self-guided tour map of the canal from the **Augusta Canal Authority** offices (see *Guidance*) or the interpretative center. Admission to center: adults $6, seniors $5, children 4–12 $4. One-hour guided boat tour with admission to center: adults $10, seniors $8, children $6. Three-hour sunset boat tour (offered on weekends) and admission to center: adults $17, seniors $15, children $10.

THE AUGUST CANAL INTERPRETIVE CENTER TELLS THE STORY OF THE AUGUSTA CANAL AND THE TEXTILE INDUSTRY IT MADE POSSIBLE.

🐾 ⚲ �& **Augusta Museum of History** (706-722-8454; www.augustamuseum .org), 560 Reynolds Street, Augusta. Open 10–5 Tuesday through Saturday, 1–5 Sunday. Filled with fascinating exhibits, some of them interactive, the museum has 15,000 artifacts that chronicle Augusta's 12,000-year history from its prehistoric physical geography to the Paleo-Indian period to the present, concentrating on the area's transformation from a trading post to an industrial and commercial center. The Confederate collection features uniforms, flags, and weapons. Among other interesting artifacts are Edgefield pottery from nearby South Carolina, Masters golf tournament memorabilia, and one of Godfather of Soul James Brown's costumes. This museum allows visitors to clean cotton in a replica cotton gin, as well as view a Petersburg boat, a restored 1917 steam locomotive, and a reconstructed 1930s gas station. In the Susan L. Still Children's Discovery Gallery, named for the astronaut, youngsters can pack a canoe, sit at the controls of a space shuttle, and dress up and play games of children from throughout Augusta's history. Documentaries are shown continuously in the History Theater. Adults $6, seniors $5, children 6–18 $4.

🐾 �& **Grovetown Museum** (706-868-6338), 106 West Robison Avenue, Grovetown. Open 10–4 Friday, 1–4 Saturday and Sunday. Artifacts and other exhibits describing the local area are housed in a 100-year-old building. One exhibit pertains to local poet Paul H. Paine. Among the military memorabilia on display are uniforms from World War II, Korea, and Vietnam donated by local veterans. Free.

🐾 ⚲ �& **Laurel and Hardy Museum** (706-556-0401; 1-888-288-9108; www .laurelandhardymuseum.org), 250 North Louisville Street, Harlem. Open 9–4 weekdays, 10–4 Saturday, 1–4 Sunday. Visitors can yuck it up as they watch old Laurel and Hardy films and see other memorabilia concerning Oliver Hardy, the more rotund of the duo, who entered the world's stage in Harlem in 1892. Although he attended Georgia Military College in Milledgeville, the Atlanta Conservatory of Music, and even the University of Georgia School of Law, entertainment was in his blood. He left for Hollywood in 1918 and paired up with Englishman Stan Laurel. Together they made more than 100 films and worked on the stage and in radio and television. In addition to the film clips, visitors can see movie posters, photographs, and souvenirs related to Hardy's career. In October, the town keeps his legacy alive by sponsoring the **Oliver Hardy Festival.** The highlight of the festival is the look-alike contest, during which dozens of fussbudget Olivers roam the streets, wringing their hands and declaring, "This is a fine mess you've gotten us into." Crafts, a carnival, entertainment, a parade, more movies, and a street dance keep the town hopping. Free.

🐾 ⚲ �& **Lucy Craft Laney Museum of Black History** (706-724-3576; www .lucycraftlaneymuseum.com), 1116 Phillips Street, Augusta. Open 9–5 Tuesday through Friday, 10–4 Saturday, 2–5 Sunday. Serving an important function in the central Savannah River area, the museum is the only one in the area focusing on African Americans. The museum is housed in the modest house of Lucy Craft Laney, who, although born a slave, graduated from Atlanta University and became a famous educator. Among her many accomplishments were Augusta's first kindergarten for African Americans, the first nurse's training classes for black women, and the Haines Normal and Industrial Institute, which educated thousands of African American students. Artifacts from Laney's life and exhibits about notable Augustans are among several permanent exhibits and collections. While you're visiting the museum, save enough time to stroll through the Period Garden. Adults $3, children $1.

🦟 ♿ **Morris Museum of Art** (706-724-7501; www.themorris.org), One Tenth Street, Augusta. Open 10–5 Tuesday through Saturday, noon–5 Sunday. This site, known as the Museum of Painting in the South, exhibits the work of Southern artists from the antebellum period to the present, with some of the exhibits focusing on Civil War art, the black presence in Southern art, and Southern Impressionism. The museum, located on Riverwalk downtown, has recently been honored by being named an affiliate of the Smithsonian Institution. Adults $3; military, students, and seniors $2; children free when admitted with an adult. Free on Sunday.

🖋 🦟 ♿ **U.S. Army Signal Corps Museum** (706-791-2818), Conrad Hall, Building 29807, Fort Gordon. Open 8–4 Tuesday through Friday, 10–4 Saturday; closed Sunday, Monday, and federal holidays. Exhibits trace the development of the Signal Corps from its beginning in 1860 to the present. The museum has more than 10,000 objects in its collections. Among the interesting exhibits are those focusing on Signal Corps aviation and the World War I "Hello Girls." The Signal Corps winter flight school was located in Augusta from 1911 to 1913. Free.

SPECIAL PLACES 🦟 🖋 ♿ **Riverwalk Augusta,** which hugs the river between Seventh and 10th streets, is a jewel in Augusta's crown. The wonderful park is created along and on top of a flood-protection levee. A paved walkway allows visitors to stroll at their own pace while enjoying the landscaped slopes, inspect markers chronicling important events in Augusta's past, and see Hero's Overlook,

RIVERWALK AUGUSTA ALLOWS VISITORS TO LEARN ABOUT AUGUSTA'S PAST WHILE STROLLING ALONG THE SAVANNAH RIVER.

which is dedicated to members of the armed forces. In addition, visitors see flags that have flown over the region, a children's playground, and **Takarazuka,** a waterfall and miniature Japanese garden display donated by the people of Augusta's sister city. Entrances at Eighth Street and 10th Street have granite markers that show the height and date of Augusta's most devastating floods. Erupting from the antique brickwork that paves the courtyard of the Eighth Street entrance is a dancing fountain that is an irresistible draw to kids of all ages—whether they're dressed for getting wet or not. The position of the **Jessye Norman Amphitheater** on the banks of the river allows spectators to enjoy concerts and other local, regional, and national entertainment from land or water. Riverwalk hosts many festivals and other events throughout the year. Free.

✳ To Do

BICYCLING ✐ 🌳 **Augusta Canal Trail**, along the old tow path, offers the best cycling in the area. Another good spot is the challenging 8-mile **Rock Dam Trail** at **Mistletoe State Park** (see *Green Space—Nature Preserves and Parks*). It's best to bring your own bikes, because rentals are very limited.

✐ **Chain Reaction Cycling** (706-855-2024), 3920 Roberts Road, Martinez, offers comfort and mountain bikes. Rental $20 per day.

See also **Little River Marina and Family Resort** under *Lodging—Cottages*.

BOAT EXCURSIONS See **Augusta Canal Interpretive Center** under *To See—Museums*.

BOATING ✐ ♿ **Augusta Riverwalk Marina** (706-722-1388), One Fifth Street, Augusta. Open 11–5 weekdays, 10–5 Saturday, noon–5 Sunday. The marina offers the only full service for boaters along the Savannah River between Savannah and Augusta. There are 68 slips with full hookups, a store with supplies and refreshments, pontoon boat rentals, and public rest rooms.

✐ ♿ **Little River Marina and Family Resort** (706-541-1358), 4271 Old Lincolnton Road, Appling. Open 9–6 weekdays, 8–8 Saturday and Sunday. The full-service marina on Clarks Hill Lake offers year-round fishing; bicycle rentals; canoe, kayak, and boat rentals; professionally licensed guide services; and a camp store as well as cabins, campsites, and a restaurant (see *Lodging—Cottages*). The facility also has a party boat and offers lake tours.

✐ ♿ **Trade Winds Marina Yacht Club** (706-541-1380), 5577 Marina Parkway, Appling. Open 8:30–5:30 daily Memorial Day to Labor Day, 9–5 off-season. The full-service marina on Clarks Hill Lake offers boat rentals, guide service referrals, picnic shelters, and cabins.

CANOEING AND KAYAKING Canoeing and kayaking are available on both the Savannah River and the canal. Augusta outfitters such as **AWOL (American Outfitters Limited)** (706-738-8500), 2328 Washington Road, and **Broadway Tackle and Canoe Rentals** (706-738-8848), 1730 Broad Street, have drop-off and pickup points on both.

FISHING Freshwater fishing at its best attracts many anglers to this section of the state. A license is required (see fishing regulations in What's Where in Georgia). One of the best bass fishing spots in the country is at **Mistletoe State Park** (see *Green Space—Nature Preserves and Parks*).

FOR FAMILIES ✿ ♂ ⅃ **Funsville** (706-863-3087; www.funsvilleaugusta.org), 4350 Wheeler Road, Martinez. Open Memorial Day to Labor Day, 10–10 weekdays, until 1 AM Saturday, noon–9 Sunday. The Augusta area's largest arcade features the Water Zone, a Venetian carousel, bumper boats, two miniature-golf courses, six amusement rides, two racetracks, and an indoor playground. Free admission; each ride charged separately.

GOLF Jones Creek Golf Club (706-860-4228; www.jonescreekgolfclub.com), 777 Jones Creek Drive, Evans. Open 7:30–6 daily, until 7 PM during daylight-saving time. Considered by many to be the best public course in America and consistently rated as one of *Golf Digest's* premier public courses, Jones Creek, a Rees Jones–designed, 18-hole, 6,900-yard course, is often called "the poor man's Augusta National." It also has a practice facility and driving range and offers instruction. $45 Monday through Thursday, $55 Friday through Sunday, carts included.

HIKING Most hiking trails in these parts are easy walking—the only difference is the length. For a short, easy hike, try the 1.2-mile **Turkey Trot Trail**, the 1.3-mile **Clatt Creek Trail,** or the 1.9-mile **Twin Oaks Trail** in **Mistletoe State Park** (see *Green Space—Nature Preserves and Parks*). For longer hikes, try the 4.1-mile **Cook's Trail** at **Sandy Creek Park** (see *Green Space—Nature Preserves and Parks*) or the 8½-mile **Augusta Canal Trail** that runs between Martinez and downtown (see *To See—Museums*). Keep in mind that these distances are one-way.

HORSEBACK RIDING ♂ ✿ **Hilltop Riding Stable** (706-791-4864), Range Road, Building 509, Fort Gordon. Open riding available 9–3:45 Saturday and Sunday; all other days by reservation. Miniature ponies as well as beginner, intermediate, and advanced horses are available. The stable also offers youth horse camps, family fun days, and riding lessons. One-hour trail ride, unsponsored civilians, $20.

TENNIS See Other Activities Appendix.

TRAP AND SKEET SHOOTING See Other Activities Appendix.

WINERY TOURS ✿ ⅃ **1810 Country Inn and Winery** (706-595-8311; 1-800-515-1810; www.1810countryinnandwinery.com), 254 North Seymour, Thomson. Free tours and tastings 10:30–5 Monday through Saturday. The last time we visited, this was a quaint country inn with accommodations in the main house and a simple cottage. Today the 66-acre complex blends the charm of the classic South and the passion for the age-old tradition of winemaking with 19 acres of grapevines, a boutique winery producing small quantities of several types of wine, a restaurant and tasting room, a gift shop, and several more cottages (see *Lodging* and *Where to Eat*).

GARDENS Augusta's slogan, "Garden City of the South," was chosen in the early 20th century because the city had so many large private gardens. An emphasis on gardens is still evident today.

🏛 🖉 ♿ **Georgia Golf Hall of Fame's Botanical Gardens** (706-724-4443; www.gghf.org), One 11th Street, Augusta. Open 9–5 Tuesday through Saturday, 1–5 Sunday. Because Augusta is world famous as the host of the Masters golf tournament, it was natural that the city would be chosen as the future site of the Georgia Golf Hall of Fame. It will be located on 17 acres near the Savannah River. The first step in creating the complex is the completion of an 8-acre botanical garden. Aquatic, Asian, azalea, bulb, butterfly, children's, coastal, cottage, formal, gold medal, rose, turf and grass, and Xeriscape gardens make up more than a dozen beautifully landscaped and meticulously maintained display gardens. The Rose Garden showcases more than 800 varieties of miniature roses. Punctuating the landscape are ponds, fountains, and waterfalls, as well as life-size bronze sculptures of some of golf's great masters, including Ben Hogan, Bobby Jones, Ray Floyd, Byron Nelson, Jack Nicklaus, and Arnold Palmer. Adults $5.50, students and seniors $4.50, children 4–12 $3.50.

🏛 🖉 ♿ **Monroe Kimbrel Gardens** (706-595-8886; www.watson-brown.org), 310 Tom Watson Way, Thomson. Open 8–5 weekdays, weekends by appointment. Operated as an outdoor classroom by the Watson-Brown Foundation, the gardens cover 4 acres and encompass lawns, ponds, and wetlands. Flora and fauna are Georgia natives found in the Piedmont region. Free.

LAKES 🏛 🖉 **Clarks Hill Lake–Thurmond Lake**. This schizophrenic lake straddles the border of two states and is called Clarks Hill Lake on the Georgia side and Strom Thurmond Lake on the South Carolina side (although Congress passed a bill in 1988 to change its official name to Thurmond). No matter what you call it, with 70,000 surface acres, it is the largest man-made Corps of Engineers lake east of the Mississippi River. The lake also boasts 1,200 miles of shoreline, six state parks, two county parks, and numerous Corps of Engineers and private campgrounds. Boating, swimming, hunting, fishing, and picnicking opportunities abound. Hikers can enjoy 15 miles of the Bartram Trail. Several marinas offer boat rentals and more.

NATURE PRESERVES AND PARKS
🏛 🖉 ♿ **Augusta Common**, mid-900 block of Broad Street, Augusta. The

THIS STATUE OF BYRON NELSON CAN BE FOUND AT THE GEORGIA GOLF HALL OF FAME'S BOTANICAL GARDENS.

city's newest park links Broad Street to the Riverwalk and serves as the scene of many festivals such as Arts in the Heart of Augusta, which is held in September. Free.

🌸 𝒮 ♿ **Mistletoe State Park** (706-541-0321; 1-800-864-7275; www.gastate parks.org/info/mistletoe), 3723 Mistletoe Road, Appling. Open 7 AM–10 PM. Located on the shores of Clarks Hill Lake, the park is known as one of the best bass-fishing spots in the country. The lake itself has no limit on boats, and three boat ramps make access easy. The park was named for Mistletoe Junction, a nearby place where folks gathered mistletoe at the turn of the 20th century. In addition to fishing, the park offers a swimming beach, nature and bike trails, canoe and fishing-boat rentals, cottages, and campsites. The park is the scene of the Fall Family Fest in October. Parking $3.

🌸 𝒮 ♿ **Phinizy Swamp Nature Park** (706-828-2109; www.phinzyswamp.org), Lock-and-Dam Road, Augusta. Open noon–dusk weekdays, dawn–dusk weekends. Although it's located near the city, this park boasts more than 1,100 acres of swampland, which provide a haven for birds and wildlife. Miles of nature trails and boardwalks as well as observation towers allow visitors to view a variety of wildlife, including blue herons, bobcats, red-shouldered hawks, otters, and alligators. Free.

🌸 𝒮 **Savannah Rapids Visitor Center** (706-868-3349; www.savannahrapids .com), 3300 Evans-to-Lock Road, Martinez. Open 10–4 Tuesday through Saturday, 11–3 Sunday. Located in a historic lockkeeper's home, the center offers visitor information, a re-creation of the lockkeeper's bedroom, and other exhibits including a pictorial history of Columbia County and exhibits describing the significance of the Augusta Canal. Other exhibits change quarterly. Bull Sluice identifies the first of the rapids that stretch more than 4 miles downstream and mark the fall line between the Piedmont Plateau and the Coastal Plain as well as the end of navigation up the Savannah River from the ocean. A breathtaking view of the turbulent rapids is just one reason to visit this park, because it also offers opportunities for hiking, canoeing, kayaking, fishing, and bicycling. From here the scenic 8½-mile trail extends to downtown. The park is the scene of the Columbia County Art and Renaissance Festival and the New Horizons Art Festival, both in October. Free.

🌸 𝒮 ♿ **Springfield Village Park** (706-724-1056; 1-800-726-0243; www.historic springfield.com), 1200 block of Reynolds Street, Augusta. Open 11–3 weekdays. Guided tours by reservation. Built by renowned African American sculptor Richard Hunt to honor those who created and worshipped at the adjacent **Springfield Baptist Church** (114 12th Street)—the oldest African American church in the nation still in continuous existence—a 45-foot stainless-steel sculpture called *The Tower of Aspiration* presides over a reflecting pond in the 2½-acre park. The church was founded in 1787 and still stands on its original site. Free.

🌸 𝒮 ♿ **Wildwood Park** (706-541-0586), 6212 Holloway Road, Appling. Open 8 AM–11 PM daily. Located on Clarks Hill Lake, the park offers beaches, boat ramps, a 12-mile horse trail, a nature trail, biking trails, fishing, campsites, picnicking, and volleyball. Day use $3.

RECREATION AREAS See Parks Appendix.

✻ Lodging

BED & BREAKFASTS

In Augusta

🐾 ♿ **The Azalea Inn Bed and Breakfast** (706-724-3454), 312-334 Greene Street. A perfect place for romantic getaways and special occasions, the multibuilding Azalea Inn is also favored by business and convention visitors to Augusta. Located in the heart of Olde Town, the inn is actually three restored Victorian houses. Reflecting a relaxed time and way of life, the inn features 21 elegantly decorated guest suites furnished with tasteful antiques. Some guest chambers might include a kitchenette, sun porch, whirlpool tub, and/or fireplace. Continental breakfast is included in the nightly rate. No smoking. Two rooms wheelchair accessible. $99–109; $139–$380 during Masters week.

🐾 **Queen Anne Inn** (706-723-0045; 1-877-460-0045; www.queenanne augusta.com), 406 Greene Street. Located in an imposing three-story Victorian house in Olde Town, the inn offers seven antique-filled guest accommodations, most with a fireplace. One particularly romantic suite features a heart-shaped two-person whirlpool tub. Amenities include an outdoor Jacuzzi. No smoking. Not wheelchair accessible. $59–99.

In Thomson

🐾 ♿ **1810 Country Inn and Winery** (706-595-3156; 1-800-515-1810), 254 North Seymour Drive. A romantic image of the Old South is evoked on this traditional estate, where accommodations are offered in nine guest chambers in the Georgia Plantation Plain–style main house and in several cottages and the old smokehouse, which offer one to three rooms or suites. Nineteenth-century ambience is smoothly blended with 21st-century convenience to ensure a perfect getaway. Among the many amenities are a full old-fashioned breakfast, an outdoor heated pool and spa, and golf and tennis privileges at a nearby country club. Several rooms boast a fireplace, refrigerator, full kitchen, and/or private porch. No smoking. Main house not wheelchair accessible, but the two cottages are. $70–125; packages that include additional meals, a winery tour, and strawberries and champagne available.

CAMPGROUNDS

In Appling

✎ 🐾 🐾 ♿ **Mistletoe State Park** (706-541-0321; 1-800-864-7275; www.gastateparks.org/info/mistletoe). The park features 92 tent, trailer, and RV sites as well as four walk-in sites (see *Green Space—Nature Preserves and Parks*). $15–17 for tent, trailer, RV sites; $7.50 for primitive walk-in sites.

See also Campgrounds Appendix.

COTTAGES

In Appling

✎ ♿ **Little River Marina and Family Resort** (706-541-1358; www.aces triperguide.com). The resort offers motel room-type cabins ($65), efficiencies with a refrigerator and hot plate ($90), and cottages (one bedroom $100, two bedroom $110). There are no phones or television. See *To Do—Boating*.

✎ 🐾 🐾 ♿ **Mistletoe State Park** (706-541-0321; 1-800-864-7275; www.gastateparks.org/info/mistletoe). The park offers 10 fully equipped lakeside cottages, five of which are log cabins, as well as a camper cabin that sleeps four. $30 for camper cabin, $100 for cottages. See *Green Space— Nature Preserves and Parks.*

INNS AND HOTELS

In Augusta

🌿 ♿ **Partridge Inn** (706-737-8888; 1-800-476-6888; www.partridge inn.com), 2110 Walton Way. This stately inn, the "grand dame" of Augusta hostelries, began as a private residence in 1879. Perched on a hill-side overlooking downtown, the structure grew and grew over the years and eventually became a hotel. Although it was never as big as some of the hotels from the city's golden resort era from 1889 to 1930, it is the only one to survive. Today, beautifully restored and elegantly furnished, the inn offers 156 rooms, suites, and studios. One of the inn's most entrancing features is the wide expanse of verandas and balconies—perfect places to relax in a rocking chair with a cool drink. In addition to luxurious accommodations, the inn boasts a restaurant, lounge, pool, elevator, and exercise facility. The lobby is a mini museum in itself, with old photographs, postcards, newspaper clippings, letters, and other artifacts from the inn's long history. Smoking and nonsmoking rooms available. Wheelchair accessible. $99–149.

🌿 🐾 ♿ **Radisson Riverfront Hotel Augusta** (706-722-8900), Two 10th Street. Although the hotel is fairly new, its construction blends well with the historic warehouses along the Riverwalk. Among its many attributes are river and Riverwalk views. The 234-room hotel features all the modern conveniences, along with a riverside pool, restaurant, and lounge.

Small pets welcome. Smoking and nonsmoking rooms available. Eleven guest rooms and all public areas wheelchair accessible. $139–370.

✳ Where to Eat

DINING OUT

In Augusta

♿ **French Market Grill** (706-737-4865), 425 Highland Avenue, in the Surrey Center. Open 11–10 weekdays, 11–11 weekends. Consistently voted the best restaurant in Augusta, the eatery serves spicy Louisiana cuisine as well as a large variety of wines and beers from around the world. Smoking and nonsmoking sections. Wheelchair accessible. $16–20.

♿ **La Maison on Telfair** (706-722-4805), 404 Telfair Street. Open 6–10 Monday through Saturday. Occupying a beautifully restored home built in 1853 in Olde Town, the restaurant is a perfect place for a romantic dinner. The restaurant serves such specialties as wild game and seafood with French, German, and Swiss influences. Reservations recommended. No smoking. Wheelchair accessible. $16–28.

♿ **Partridge Inn Bar and Grill** (706-737-8888), 2110 Walton Way. Open 6:30–10 daily; 11–10 weekdays, 11–11 weekends; brunch 11–2 Sunday. Dinner specialties include prime rib and red snapper. The bar is a hot place for jazz on Friday and Saturday nights, and the Sunday brunch buffet is both gargantuan and accompanied by a live pianist. Smoking permitted after 9 PM. Wheelchair accessible. Dinner $14–25, Sunday brunch $25.

♿ **T-Bonz** (706-737-8325), 2856 Washington Road. Open 11–10 weekdays, 11–11 weekends. There's no doubt why the restaurant has been named the best place for steaks in Augusta for 14 years by *Metro Spirit* magazine. There's a band on Friday and Saturday nights, but no cover charge. No smoking. Wheelchair accessible. $11–22.

In Thomson
& 1810 Country Inn and Winery (706-595-8323 for reservations; 1-800-515-1810), 254 North Seymour. Open 11:30–2:30 Tuesday through Friday, 5:30–9:30 Wednesday through Saturday, 11:30–2 Sunday brunch. A casually elegant atmosphere showcases a modern American menu featuring such dishes as panfried catfish with Gulf shrimp and cheese grits, roasted free-range chicken breast, or Southern seafood linguine. Naturally, the inn's own wines are offered to accompany your meal. No smoking. Wheelchair accessible. $4–14 for lunch and $15–25 for dinner

EATING OUT

In Augusta
& Boll Weevil Cafe (706-722-7772), 10 Ninth Street. Open 11–10 Sunday through Thursday, 11–11 Friday and Saturday. A great place for a quick lunch or snack, the eatery serves a variety of Southern and Southwestern cuisine as well as wings, soups, salads, sandwiches, pizzas, and a staggering array of desserts. No smoking. Wheelchair accessible. $6–12.

& Fat Man's Cafe (706-733-1740), 1717 Laney Walker Boulevard. Open 11–4 weekdays. Before or after a marathon shopping experience at Fat Man's Forest (see "Something for Everyone" sidebar under *Shopping—Special Stores*), refuel with a meal of comfort food at this down-home restaurant. Local favorites include

squash casserole, turnip greens, candied yams, macaroni and cheese, barbecue, ham, liver, and fried chicken finished off with banana pudding. The restaurant also serves hamburgers, hot dogs, and numerous varieties of sandwiches, soups, and salads. No smoking. Wheelchair accessible. $3–5.

& Mally's Bagels-n-Grits (706-736-0770), 15 Seventh Street. Open 6–3 weekdays, 7–3 Saturday and Sunday. A well-known place to head for breakfast or lunch, Mally's serves such specialties as grits Benedict and sun-dried tomato bagels in the morning. Lunch might consist of homemade soups of the day, hot sandwiches, salads, and wraps. No smoking. Wheelchair accessible. $1–9.

& Sunshine Bakery (706-724-2302), 1209 Broad Street. Open 9:30–5:30 weekdays. Sunshine Bakery's been a favorite for lunch with locals since the 1950s, and for good reason. Sandwiches such as Reubens, Dutch Rhubuns, pastrami, and other choices get folks lining up early to get in, to say nothing of the potato soup and brats. Lunch is served all day, so it's best not to go around noon. Whatever your luncheon choice, wash it down with a lemony Sunshine Tea. Both smoking and nonsmoking areas. Wheelchair accessible. $3.50–6.50.

✳ Entertainment
DANCE Augusta Ballet (706-261-0555), offices at Sacred Heart Cultural Arts Center, 1301 Greene Street, Augusta. Four productions a year are performed at the Imperial Theatre (745 Broad Street) between October and May. Call for a schedule of performances and prices.

Augusta Dance Theatre (706-860-

1852), 639 Furys Ferry Road, Martinez. Box office hours 4–6 Monday, Tuesday, and Thursday; 4:30–5:30 Wednesday; 10:30–12:30 Saturday. Celebrating its 20th season in 2005, the Academy of Ballet produces a variety of performances each year. Call for a schedule of events and prices.

MUSIC **Augusta Choral Society** (706-826-4713), Sacred Heart Cultural Center, 1301 Greene Street, Augusta. The choral society performs major choral works, new compositions, holiday favorites, and lighter classical works—often accompanied by members of the Augusta Symphony. Single tickets: Adults $20, seniors and students $16. Season tickets available.

Augusta Symphony (706-826-4705; www.augustasymphony.org), box office at Sacred Heart Cultural Center, 1301 Greene Street, Suite 200, Augusta; open 9–5 weekdays. The symphony, which celebrated its 50th anniversary in 2005, performs classical, pops, family, world premiere, and chamber concerts at various venues around the city. Tickets generally $10–$40.

NIGHTLIFE ♿ **Fox's Lair** (706-828-5600, www.thefoxslair.com), 349 Telfair Street, Augusta. Open 4–midnight Tuesday through Thursday, 4–2 Friday, 7–2 Saturday. This English-style neighborhood pub, located on the basement level of a B&B, the Old Town Inn, is an old favorite of locals and visitors alike. There is live Irish music Friday and Saturday evenings. Smoking area. Wheelchair accessible. No cover charge.

♿ **Soul Bar** (706-724-8880), 984 Broad Street, Augusta. Open 8 PM–3 AM Monday through Saturday. A mecca for James Brown fans, this soul and funk bar offers live entertainment and dancing. Smoking area. Wheelchair accessible. No cover charge.

PROFESSIONAL SPORTS **Augusta GreenJackets** (706-736-7889; www.greenjackets.net), Lake Olmstead Stadium, 78 Milledge Road, Augusta. The minor-league baseball team is a class-A affiliate of the San Francisco Giants. The season runs early April through September. Call for a schedule and prices.

Augusta Lynx (706-724-4423; www.augusta.lynx.com), office at 712 Telfair Street, Augusta. A member of the very popular and fast-growing East Coast Hockey League, the AA hockey Lynx play in the Augusta-Richmond County Civic Center. The season runs October through early April. Call for a schedule and prices.

THEATER **The Fort Gordon Dinner Theatre** (706-791-4389; box office 706-793-8552), Third Avenue, Building 32100, Fort Gordon. Dinner at 7, followed by show at 8. A six-show season features plays such as *Barefoot in the Park, Caught in the Net, Passing the Buck, Pippin,* and *Wait Until Dark.* Civilians $30, $16 for show only.

The Imperial Theatre (706-722-8293; www.imperialtheatre.com), 745 Broad Street, Augusta. The theater was built in 1917 after a terrible fire that devastated much of downtown Augusta. It hosted vaudeville, silent movies, and then "talkies." Today it hosts live stage performances and is the home of the Augusta Opera and Augusta Ballet. Call for a schedule of events and prices.

✳ Selective Shopping

ANTIQUES Riverwalk Antique Depot (706-724-5648), 505 Reynolds Street, Augusta. Open 10–6 Tuesday through Saturday, 1–6 Sunday. A city block of antiques and collectibles is located in a historic rail depot.

ART GALLERIES Artist's Row (706-774-1006; 706-823-6600; 1-800-726-0243), 700–1200 blocks of Broad Street, Augusta. Centered on the 1100 block, this is really a collection of two dozen art galleries, working studios, specialty boutiques, and one-of-a-kind bistros and cafés housed in restored 19th- and early 20th-century storefronts. Something for everyone includes original works, prints, posters, golf prints, jewelry, and crafts. Demonstrations, artists' chats, and receptions take place monthly during **First Friday** gatherings (see *Special Events*).

Gertrude Herbert Institute of Art (706-722-5495), in Ware's Folly, 509 Telfair Street, Augusta. Open 10–5 Tuesday through Friday, Saturday by appointment. (See *To See—Historic Homes and Sites* for more information about the mansion.) The institute sponsors at least six major exhibitions a year, showcasing the works of students as well as local and regional artists. Each exhibition lasts six to eight weeks. Free.

Sacred Heart Cultural Center (706-826-4700), 1301 Greene Street, Augusta. Open 9–5 weekdays. The gift shop features works by regional artists as well as other quality gifts and books. See *To See—Historic Homes and Sites*. $1.

FLEA MARKETS The Barnyard Flea Market (706-793-8800; 1-866-993-8800), 1625 Doug Barnard Parkway, Augusta. Open Friday through Sunday. The ultimate garage sale features 600 dealers.

✳ Special Events

Monthly: **First Friday** (CVB: 706-823-6600; 1-800-726-0243; www .augustaga.org), Artists' Row on Broad Street between 10th and 11th streets,

---

SPECIAL STORES

SOMETHING FOR EVERYONE

Fat Man's Forest (706-722-1796; www.fatmans.com), 1545 Laney Walker Boulevard, Augusta. Open 10–9 Monday through Saturday, 12:30–8 Sunday. It's been around since 1948 and is consistently rated the number one place for Augusta gifts, but that doesn't give you a clue about what you'll find here. There's no better place to shop for Halloween and Christmas decorations and costumes, but the warren of nooks and crannies is open year-round, purveying decorations for all holidays—especially St. Patrick's Day and Easter. But it doesn't stop there. The emporium includes a costume shop and florist as well as just about everything you could ever conceivably want, such as bumper stickers, candles, candy, flags, incense, pictures, piñatas, plants, posters, pots and pans, pottery, souvenirs, T-shirts, and wicker. Make a day of it, and when you're weak from hunger, go next door to Fat Man's Cafe (see *Where to Eat—Eating Out*).

Augusta. This event features art exhibitions, demonstrations, and an opportunity to meet various artists in an outdoor setting. Free.

January: **Augusta Futurity** (706-724-0851; www.augustafuturity.com), held at Augusta–Richmond County Civic Center, address, Augusta. This is the largest cutting-horse tournament east of the Mississippi and one of the top 10 in the world. The fast-paced event features the country's foremost professional riders and horses competing for hundreds of thousands of dollars in prizes. Totally western in flavor, the event features working broncs, a horse-and-wagon parade, evening shows, and an exposition of western wear and gear. Adults $12, children $2; reserved seats for three final events $13.50–16.50.

April: Practice-round tickets for the **Masters** golf tournament (706-667-6000), Augusta National Golf Club, Augusta, are available through a lottery system. Call for details.

May: **Blind Willie Blues Festival** (706-597-1000; www.blindwillie.com). Held the third week in May in Thomson, the festival honors the pioneer and all-time great country blues 12-string guitarist William Samuel "Blind Willie" McTell, who was born south of Thomson in 1901. McTell was posthumously inducted into the Georgia Music Hall of Fame in 1990 for his more than 120 songs, including "Statesboro Blues," which was made famous by the Allman Brothers Band.

The festival features a variety of local and national talent. $20 in advance, $25 at the gate.

July: **Augusta Southern Nationals Dragboat Races** (1-800-726-0243; www.augustasouthernnationals.org), centered around Augusta Riverwalk Marina (see *To Do—Boating*). This is a weekend of supercharged hydroplane and flat-bottomed boats competing in nine classes. Considered the world's richest drag-boat race, the event carries more than $120,000 in prizes. $15 per day in advance, $18 at the gate; $25 for both days.

November: **Head of the South Rowing Regatta** (706-821-2875), held on the Savannah River opposite the Riverwalk in downtown Augusta. This weekend race showcases some of the South's best rowing teams, including more than one Olympic competitor. Free.

Blessing of the Hounds at the Belle Meade Fox Hunt (Thomson-McDuffie CVB: 706-597-1000). The hunt season begins on the first Saturday in November with Thomson's Blessing of the Hounds, which includes the story of St. Hubert—the patron saint of hunters—and the presentation of St. Hubert medals to the riders. Visitors are then welcome to follow the hunt and to watch the scarlet-coated hunters and the well-trained hounds from the comfort of Tally-Ho wagons pulled by tractors and pickup trucks. Spectators free; $50 to ride a Tally-Ho wagon.

BARNESVILLE

This charming, laid-back area of central Georgia is characterized by small towns, dairy farms, the timber industry, and antiques shops. In the past, Barnesville was the Buggy Capital of the World and Forsyth served as a Civil War hospital town.

Today visitors can enjoy a historic plantation, museums, two covered bridges, numerous bed & breakfasts in grand historic homes, a railroad excursion, and a wide variety of festivals that celebrate everything from buggies to barbecue, forsythias to fried green tomatoes. The Flint River, Lake Juliette, many parks, and wide-open spaces provide endless opportunities for canoeing and kayaking, mountain biking, off-road excursions, hiking, and even skydiving.

GUIDANCE When planning a trip to Barnesville or Milner, contact the **Barnesville–Lamar County Chamber of Commerce** (770-358-5884; www.barnesville.org; www.cityofbarnesville.com), 100 Commerce Place, Barnesville 30204. Open 9–5 weekdays. Get information here for the **Barnesville Walking Tour.**

For more information about Forsyth, Bolingbroke, Culloden, Juliette, and Smarr, contact the **Forsyth–Monroe County Chamber of Commerce** (478-994-9239; 1-888-642-4628; www.forsyth-monroechamber.com), 267 Tift College Drive, Forsyth 31029. Open 8–5 weekdays. Ask about the **Historic Forsyth Walking Tour** and the **Monroe County Driving Tour.** Both tours begin at the courthouse and feature Civil War monuments, landmarks, and antebellum homes. The driving tour also includes the McCowen Cemetery, the towns of Bolingbroke and Culloden, Ham's Store, and Russellville Baptist Church. For more specific information about Juliette, consult the web site at www.juliettega.com.

To learn more about Griffin, consult the **Griffin Regional Welcome Center/ Griffin–Spalding Chamber of Commerce** (770-228-8200; 770-228-2356; www.griffinchamber.com), 143 North Hill Street, Griffin 30223. Open 8–5 weekdays. The welcome center also houses a museum and art exhibits.

For information about Clinton and Gray, contact the **Jones County–Gray Chamber of Commerce** (478-986-1123), 161 West Clinton Street, Gray 31032.

To learn more about Molena, contact **Pike County** (770-567-3406), P.O. Box 377, Zebulon 30295.

To learn more about Thomaston, consult the **Thomaston–Upson County Chamber of Commerce** (706-647-9686; www.thomastonchamber.com), 213 East Gordon Street, Thomaston 30286. Open 8:30–5 Monday through Thursday, 8–4:30 Friday. You can pick up information for a driving or walking tour past Thomaston's historic homes (many of which are private residences) or find the information online at www.thomastonchamber.com/historichomes.asp.

GETTING THERE *By air:* The nearest airport to this region is in Macon (see Macon chapter). Because Atlanta is also close by, it is often easier to fly into **Hartsfield-Jackson Atlanta International Airport** (see What's Where in Georgia).

By bus: The nearest **Greyhound Lines** (1-800-231-2222; www.greyhound.com) station is in Macon (see Macon chapter).

By car: Most of the towns in this chapter lie between I-85 and I-75, south of Atlanta and north of Macon.

By train: The nearest **Amtrak** station is in Atlanta (see What's Where in Georgia).

GETTING AROUND In Barnesville, car rentals are available from **Alamo** (1-888-426-3304) and **Hertz** (1-800-654-3131); in Forsyth, from **Enterprise** (478-992-8640); in Griffin, from **Economy** (770-227-5966) and **Enterprise** (770-233-2830; 1-800-736-8222).

MEDICAL EMERGENCY In a life-threatening emergency, call 911. For other immediate care, assistance is available at **Monroe County Hospital** (478-994-3478), 88 Martin Luther King Jr. Drive, Forsyth; **Spalding Regional Medical Center** (770-228-2721), 601 South Eighth Street, Griffin; and **Upson Regional Medical Center** (706-647-8111), 801 West Gordon Street, Thomaston.

Macon may be the closest city to where you are if you are visiting Bolingbroke, Clinton, or Gray. Care is available there at the **Medical Center of Central Georgia** (478-633-1353), 777 Hemlock Street, Macon (see Macon chapter).

If you are visiting Molena, you are about equidistant to Thomaston, LaGrange, or Newnan. In LaGrange, contact **West Georgia Medical Center** (706-882-1411), 1514 Vernon Road (see LaGrange chapter in 5, Southern Rivers). In Newnan, contact **Newnan Hospital** (770-253-2330), 80 Jackson Street (see Newnan chapter in 1, Atlanta Metro).

VILLAGES AND NEIGHBORHOODS **Barnesville** enjoyed its heyday from before the Civil War until the 1880s. During that time the small town had four buggy factories and produced 16,000 horse-drawn buggies annually along with wagons, carts, and hearses, which earned the town the title "Buggy Capital of the World." Today Barnesville boasts a museum, an art gallery–studio, gift shops, and many restaurants. The town celebrates its history with the annual **Barnesville Buggy Days** (see *Special Events*).

Bolingbroke is a former railroad and farming community that has developed into an antiques lover's paradise, complete with shops and an old-fashioned soda fountain.

Clinton was once one of the fastest-growing centers of trade and culture in this part of Georgia. Today it is a sleepy village known as "the town that time forgot." Part of the small town is designated as the Old Clinton Historic District, which is listed on the National Register of Historic Places to preserve a dozen homes built between 1808 and 1830. A brochure for a self-guided tour is available from the Jones County–Gray Chamber of Commerce, 161 West Clinton Street in nearby Gray. Clinton also offers several yearly and monthly events, including tours of the historic homes sponsored by the Clinton Historical Society, **Old Clinton War Days** (see *Special Events*), and the **Ole Clinton Opry** (see *Entertainment*).

Culloden was named for William Culloden, a well-known Scotsman and trader. A battle took place here 10 days after the Civil War was over because word that Lee had surrendered had not yet reached the area. Today Culloden is the scene of **Culloden Highland Games and Scottish festival** (see *Special Events*).

Forsyth became a hospital center during the Civil War. After the battles of Atlanta, Stone Mountain, and Jonesboro, 20,000 wounded soldiers were sent here. The Monroe County Courthouse, Monroe Female College, Hilliard Institute, Lumpkin Hotel, stores, and private homes were pressed into service, and there were still so many wounded, tents had to be used. After the boll weevil decimated the cotton economy, the county turned to dairy farms and timber. Forsyth's historical mid to late 1800s commercial district is centered by 1896 Courthouse Square, where the **Forsythia Festival** is held each spring (see *Special Events*).

Griffin is called the Iris City because the Flint River Iris Society promotes and grows irises, sponsors an iris show in the spring, and offers an iris sale in the late summer. Another of Griffin's claims to fame is that it was the birthplace of the infamous outlaw Doc Holliday. Today Griffin has several museums and historic sites open to the public. Each May, the city sponsors the **Great Griffin Mayfling.**

Jones County is the site of **Jarrell Plantation Historic Site** and the **Piedmont National Wildlife Refuge,** while **Gray,** the county seat, has a magnificent 1905 courthouse surrounded by a park with a gazebo and fountain. An antiques shop occupies the oldest house in town.

Juliette was a thriving Monroe County community along the railroad tracks and the Ocmulgee River in the early 1900s. Unfortunately, time and changes in the economy left Juliette a virtual ghost town. In 1991, however, its river, railroad line, abandoned mill, and quaint old buildings brought Juliette a new prosperity. The small town's abandoned air was made famous as the site where the film *Fried Green Tomatoes* was filmed. Although the fictional story takes place in Alabama, author Fanny Flagg thought Juliette perfectly represented the town she envisioned. Fans of the movie will want to have lunch and

JULIETTE IS HOME TO THE WHISTLE STOP CAFÉ, MADE FAMOUS IN THE MOVIE *FRIED GREEN TOMATOES.*

some fried green tomatoes at the real **Whistle Stop Café** (see *Where to Eat—Eating Out*) and then shop up and down McCrackin Street for gifts and souvenirs. Rumor has it that the story is Broadway-bound, which should bring even more visitors to Juliette. The **Green Tomato Festival** (see *Special Events*) is held annually.

Thomaston, imbued with small-town charm, has twice been listed in the book *100 Best Small Towns in America*. Thomaston boasts several museums and historic houses, a restored art deco theater, a covered bridge, and quaint antiques and gift shops around the courthouse square. The city also hosts an Emancipation Proclamation Celebration each May, the nation's oldest and longest running such event. It includes speeches, a parade, and a candlelight prayer service. **Sprewell Bluff State Park** is nearby (see *Green Space—Nature Preserves and Parks*).

✳ To See

COVERED BRIDGES ✿ ❡ ⚹ **Auchumpkee Creek Covered Bridge,** on Allen Road off US 19 South, Thomaston. Open daily. Covered bridges are so precious, when one is lost it's a great tragedy. The original 96-foot-long town lattice-design bridge in this location was built in 1892. Unfortunately it was destroyed by the devastating south Georgia floods of 1994 but has since been authentically rebuilt by a nationally renowned covered-bridge craftsman using portions of the original bridge. Many of the original building techniques were used, including the use of a team of draft horses to help pull the structure across the creek. Free.

HISTORIC HOMES AND SITES ❡ ⚹ **Bailey-Tebault House** (770-229-2432; www.gshistoricalsociety.org/bthouse.htm), 633 Meriwether Street, Griffin. Open by appointment. Now serving as the headquarters of the Griffin-Spalding Historical Society, the handsome Greek Revival home was built between 1859 and 1862 by Colonel David J. Bailey, a lawyer, state representative, state senator, and creator of the 30th Georgia Regiment of the Confederate Army. The home probably would have been destroyed during Union General William Tecumseh Sherman's March to the Sea, except for the fact that Mrs. Bailey opened it as a hospital for the wounded from both sides of the conflict. It is reported that Margaret Mitchell modeled the fictional Twelve Oaks on the Bailey-Tebault House (this is not the only home that makes that claim). After Colonel and Mrs. Bailey's deaths, the house was inherited by their daughter, Mrs. S. H. Tebault, who never lived there after her marriage, which means that no one named Tebault ever lived in the house. The home remained in the family until 1971, when it became a funeral home. The Griffin-Spalding Historical Society acquired it in 1987. The elegant home has been restored recently along with three original outbuildings, including the apothecary and two dependencies. The grounds are being restored as well, with the Mary Smalley Garden, a fenced annual garden, maintained by the Griffin Garden Club. Free.

✿ ❡ ⚹ **Jarrell Plantation Historic Site** (478-986-5172; www.gastateparks .org/info/jarrell), 711 Jarrell Plantation Road, Juliette. Open 9–5 Tuesday through Saturday, 2–5:30 Sunday. This is not the grand plantation of the stereotypical Old South but, rather, a self-contained, self-supporting working farm depicting the period from the 1840s to the 1940s. Generations of the Jarrell family lived and worked here from 1847, when John Fitz Jarrell built the first simple heart-pine house and made many of the furnishings. In 1895, his son Dick built another house for his family. In 1974, the buildings and artifacts were willed to the state and constitute one of the largest and most complete collections of original family relics in Georgia. Several rustic homes on the site contain looms, spinning wheels, quilting frames, a cobbler's bench, and a wood-burning stove. A small museum in the visitor center includes exhibits and a film. Many other buildings are scattered around the grounds, including a sawmill, cotton gin, gristmill, sugarcane press, syrup evaporator, carpenter shop, blacksmith shop, shingle mill, smokehouses, wheat houses, and barn. Farm animals and equipment, a garden, and grape arbors lend an air of authenticity. Special events and exhibitions, which feature sheep shearing, spinning, weaving, blacksmithing, and woodstove cooking, occur throughout the year. Wheelchair access is limited. An adjacent Jarrell home retained by family members offers bed & breakfast accommodations (see **Jarrell 1920 House** under *Lodging*). Adults $4, children $2.50.

MUSEUMS ✇ ✤ **Doc Holliday Museum** (770-229-2705), 209 North 13th Street, Griffin. Open by appointment only. America's best-known (or should we say infamous) dentist is memorialized through exhibits of previously unpublished photographs, historical documents, and books that trace the life and times of Doc Holliday. Plans are in the works to move the museum into a building that was actually owned by Doc Holliday. Free.

✤ ✤ **Griffin Museum and Art Gallery** (770-228-8200), 143 North Hill Street, Griffin. Open 8–5 weekdays. The museum, located within the Welcome Center (see *Guidance*), chronicles the history of Griffin and Spalding County and features the work of local artists. Free.

✇ ✤ **Old Jail Museum and Archives** (770-358-0150), 326 Thomaston Street, Barnesville. Open 10–5 Wednesday, 10–2 Saturday, 2–5 Sunday. The museum, which is located in the old Lamar County Jail, chronicles Barnesville's history as the Buggy Capital of the World. In addition to buggies and buggy memorabilia, artifacts include uniforms, dresses, antique toys and dolls, and household items. The Old Crowder Brothers Scale House on the property houses a collection of buggies and carriages, while the archives house materials back to the early 1800s. Suggested donation $1.

♂ ☙ ♿ **Roosevelt Railroad Museum** (404-392-6103; www.rooseveltrailroad .com), 3030 Teamon Road, Griffin. Open 1–7 second weekend of each month (may be closed in winter and does not operate in inclement weather, so call ahead); trains leave every half-hour. The 7-mile tour over the former Southern Railways "M" line begins at the famous Towaliga trestle and goes south to Experiment, passing through the site of Camp Stephens, which was the largest Confederate training camp in Georgia. The museum features three steam loco-motives: ones built in 1892, 1909, and 1921. In addition to regular tours, there is a three-day Halloween Special close to that holiday, and November tours are designated as Fall Leaves Specials. Note: Anyone in need of handicapped acces-sibility should notify the railroad at least one day in advance so arrangements can be made. Tickets for scenic rail tours $6.

> **ROOSEVELT RAILROAD MUSEUM FACTS**
> * President Franklin D. Roosevelt made more than 50 trips over the railroad while traveling between Washington, D.C., and Warm Springs, Georgia.
> * On April 13, 1945, President Roosevelt made his last trip. His funeral train traveled the railroad from Warm Springs to Washington, D.C., and then on to Hyde Park, New York.
> * The 101st Airborne Company E Band of Brothers traveled over the railroad from Atlanta to Fort Benning, Georgia, where its members completed their parachute training.
> * Doc Holliday traveled from Griffin, Georgia, to Dallas, Texas, aboard the Houston and Texas Central.

✳ To Do

BICYCLING See **Gerald L. Lawhorn Canoe Base and Training Center** under *For Families.*

BIRDING See **Piedmont National Wildlife Refuge** and **Sprewell Bluff State Park** under *Green Space—Nature Preserves and Parks.*

CANOEING AND KAYAKING ♂ ♿ **Flint River Outdoor Center** (706-647-2633; www.flintriverfun.com), 4429 Woodland Road, Thomaston. Open 9–9 Monday through Thursday, 9–10 Friday and Saturday, 9–6 Sunday. Half-day, full-day, and two-day canoe trips on the Flint River are offered along with canoe, accessory, and tube rentals and return shuttle service. Guided trips with three class II rapids are available weekdays by reservation with a minimum of 12 participants required. RV and primitive camping are also available. Fees vary by activity.

See also **Flint River** under *Green Space—Rivers* and **Gerald L. Lawhorn Canoe Base and Training Center** under *For Families.*

FISHING See **Flint River** under *Green Space—Rivers* and **Lake Juliette** under *Green Space—Lakes.*

FOR FAMILIES ✒ **Gerald L. Lawhorn Canoe Base and Training Center** (706-646-2255; www.thunderbsa.org), Thunder Scout Reservation, 1166 Dripping Rock Road, Molena. Office open 9–5 weekdays. Much more than a canoeing outpost, this facility offers an 8.2-mile looping trail for beginner to advanced mountain bikers, 1,106 feet of climbing trails, and 15 miles of hiking trails. For organized groups, the facility offers canoeing, rappelling, and ropes courses. Call for schedules of events and prices.

GOLF See Golf appendix.

HIKING See **Gerald L. Lawhorn Canoe Base and Training Center** under *For Families* and **Piedmont National Wildlife Refuge** and **Sprewell Bluff State Park** under *Green Space—Nature Preserves and Parks.*

OFF-ROAD RIDING ✒ **Rocky Creek ATV Trail** (478-885-2266; 478-885-2338), 4637 GA 34 (mailing address: 446 Main Street), Culloden. Open 10:30–5:30 on first full weekend of the month; Sunday Mud Run at 2 PM. Riders of four-wheel and two-wheel ATVs and motorcycles enjoy 19.8 miles of dirt trails, mud, jumps, creeks, and bridges. Camping facilities are available. $20 per day per machine; $30 per machine for two-day weekend pass.

SHOOTING SPORTS ♿ **Meadows National Gun Club** (478-994-9910), 1064 Rumble Road, Smarr. Open 10–6 Wednesday through Sunday. The 400-acre world-class gun club facility, which was the site of the 1998 U.S. Open Sporting Clays Championship, offers a 100-bird sporting clays course with 12 stations and a 25-bird five-stand sporting clays course. $35 per 100 rounds for clays course, $7 per 25 rounds for five-stand course.

SKYDIVING **Skydive Atlanta** (706-647-9701; 1-800-276-DIVE; www.skydive atlanta.com), 2333 Delray Road, Thomaston. Open 8–sunset weekends, by appointment weekdays. Whether you're an expert thrill seeker or a wannabe, Skydive Atlanta has a certified instructor appropriate for your experience level. Call for fees.

SWIMMING See **Lake Juliette** under *Green Space—Lakes.*

TRAIN EXCURSIONS See **Roosevelt Railroad Museum** under *To See—Museums.*

TUBING See **Flint River** under *Green Space—Rivers,* **Flint River Outdoor Center** under *Canoeing and Kayaking,* and **Gerald L. Lawhorn Canoe Base and Training Center** under *For Families.*

WHITE-WATER RAFTING See **Flint River** under *Green Space—Rivers* and **Flint River Outdoor Center** under *Canoeing and Kayaking.*

✳ Green Space

GARDENS ✐ ✿ ♿ **University of Georgia Research and Education Garden** (770-229-6107; www.griffin.uga.edu/garden), Georgia Station, 1109 Experiment Street, Griffin. Open 9–4 weekdays year-round, 1–5 Sunday May through September. Encompassing 65 acres, the garden demonstrates new approaches to environmental gardening, including the latest landscape and turf grass findings. The gardens consist of 17 theme gardens, including a garden for the disabled, a children's garden, rock garden, water garden, butterfly garden, bog garden, Xeriscape (plants that need little water), and gardens devoted to perennials, native plants, herbs, ornamental grasses, heirloom plants and flowers, antique roses, irises and daylilies, turf, and wildflowers. Free.

LAKES ✐ ✿ **Lake Juliette** (478-994-9239; 1-888-642-4628; 1-888-GPC-LAKE; www.southerncompany.com/gapower), US 23/GA 87, Juliette. Open 7–10 daily. Operated in cooperation with the Georgia Department of Natural Resources, this 3,600-acre lake is strictly for fishing, whether along its banks or by boat. Boats with engines greater than 25 horsepower are prohibited, as are waterskiing and Jet Skiing. In the surrounding lands, a public boat ramp, picnicking, primitive campsites, and developed campsites with hookups are available. Access free; fees for some activities.

NATURE PRESERVES AND PARKS

✐ ✿ ♿ **Piedmont National Wildlife Refuge** (478-986-5441; www.piedmont .fws.gov), 718 Juliette Road, Round Oak. Open daylight hours daily; visitor center open 7:30–5 weekdays, 9–5 Saturday. The 35,000-acre refuge, administered by the U.S. Fish and Wildlife Service, offers fishing, 18 miles of hiking trails, and a wildlife drive. Loblolly pines on the ridges, hardwoods along creek bottoms, coves, streams, and beaver ponds all combine to create an ideal habitat for 200 species of migrating birds and waterfowl, as well as beavers, raccoons, opossums, turkeys, and deer. Educational programs, fishing, and hunting are available. Transportation through the preserve is primarily by way of gravel roads and footpaths. Three trails range from 0.9 mile to 2.9 miles. The best time to catch a glimpse of the red-cockaded woodpecker, by the way, is April through July. The Allison Lake Trail is the best place to view wintering waterfowl and wading birds. Free.

✐ ✿ ♿ **Sprewell Bluff State Park** (706-646-6026; www.gastateparks.org/info/ sprewell), 740 Sprewell Bluff Road, Thomaston. Open 7–sunset. This little-known and undeveloped 1,372-acre park on the banks of the Flint River is truly a spot to get away from it all. There's a ramp for those who want to put canoes, kayaks, and rafts into the river, and fishing for bass and catfish is a popular pastime. A 3-mile trail hugs the riverbank and climbs among rocky bluffs from which visitors can get excellent views of the river. Picnicking, horseshoes, and volleyball round out the activities. Parking $3.

RIVERS **Flint River.** One of the major rivers in Georgia, the Flint flows from the Atlanta metropolitan area to the Florida border, providing scenic beauty and many recreational opportunities including canoe and kayak trips, tubing, white-water rafting trips, and fishing (see **Flint River Outdoor Center** under *To Do—Canoeing and Kayaking* and **Gerald L. Lawhorn Canoe Base and Training Center** under *To Do—For Families*).

✳ Lodging
BED & BREAKFASTS

In Barnesville
& **Tarleton Oaks Bed and Breakfast/*Gone with the Wind* Hall of Stars Museum** (770-358-4989; 1-877-LUV-GWTW; www.tarleton-oaks.com), 643 Greenwood Street. Guest rooms are spacious and furnished with period antiques. Each features a private bath, sitting area, fireplace, and cable television, but guests at Tarleton Oaks are in for many special treats. First of all, the owner and proprietor is Fred Crane, who played Brent Tarleton in *Gone with the Wind.* He can regale you with many tales from the making of the film and how it has affected the last 65 years of his life. He'll also happily relate the story of the resident ghost. Secondly, the 1849 Greek Revival house, which served as a Confederate headquarters and hospital during the Civil War, contains the *Gone with the Wind* Hall of Stars Museum, a collection of rare *GWTW* memorabilia, including items worn by cast members and one of author Margaret Mitchell's own copies of the book with her notations written in it. Fred and his wife, Terry, open the museum to guests at 4 PM. At 8 PM, guests are given the opportunity to see a three-hour presentation, "Rare Photography from *Gone with the Wind,*" which includes scenes cut from the movie and behind-the-scenes photos. *GWTW* items are for

THOSE WHO LOVE THE OUTDOORS WILL LOVE SPREWELL BLUFF STATE PARK ALONG THE BANKS OF THE FLINT RIVER.

sale in the gift shop. A gourmet breakfast is served in the Tara Dining Room. It's obvious that Southern hospitality is not gone with the wind at Tarleton Oaks. No smoking. Wheelchair accessible. $150 and up.

In Forsyth
✿ **Uncle Frank's Restaurant and Inn** (478-994-2160), 22 West Main Street. This charming and very affordable inn was formerly known as the Forsyth Square Restaurant and Inn. Located in a fully restored circa 1925 furniture store in downtown Forsyth right across from the courthouse, this establishment has a popular restaurant as well as 10 bed & breakfast rooms and suites upstairs. A full country breakfast at the restaurant is included.

No smoking. Not wheelchair accessible. $49–$89.

In Juliette

Jarrell 1920 House (478-986-3972; 1-888-574-5434, ext. 1920; www.jarrellhouse.com), 715 Jarrell Plantation Road. This circa 1920 home was originally part of the **Jarrell Plantation** (see *To See—Historic Homes and Sites*) and was the third home built on the farm as well as the fanciest, though it is still a simple plantation country house. The floors, walls, and ceilings are rare heart pine—felled, milled, and assembled by the family on-site at the plantation. The bed & breakfast enjoys a quiet, wooded setting just 30 minutes south of Macon. Accommodations are offered in Dick and Mamie's Room, which has an adjoining bath, or in the Guest Room, which has a bath down the hall. Weeknight guests are treated to a full buffet breakfast; weekend guests enjoy a continental breakfast on Saturday and a full breakfast buffet on Sunday, and receive a coupon for a lunch discount at the **Whistle Stop Café** (see *Where to Eat—Eating Out*). Also part of a stay at the bed & breakfast is a free pass to the **Jarrell Plantation Historic Site.** The B&B is only suitable for well-behaved children older than 12. No smoking. Not wheelchair accessible. $95–$175.

In Thomaston

Woodall House Bed and Breakfast (706-647-7044), 324 West Main Street. This large 1910 residence with a wide wraparound veranda sits on an expansive shaded lot. Inside, Victorian-era antiques create an elegant but comfortable ambience with four guest rooms. No smoking. Not wheelchair accessible. $69–$79.

CAMPGROUNDS

In Juliette

Dames Ferry Park (478-994-7945; 1-888-GPC-LAKE; www.georgiapower.com/gpclake), 9546 US 23/GA 87. This all-service campground on the shores of Lake Juliette

THE JARRELL 1920 HOUSE OCCUPIES A QUIET SPOT SOUTH OF MACON.

provides RV and tent sites, a dump station, rest room and shower facilities, a public boat launch, and a beach. $3–$16.

In Thomaston
See **Flint River Outdoor Center** under *To Do—Canoeing and Kayaking.* See also Campgrounds appendix.

✳ Where to Eat
DINING OUT

In Forsyth
✎ ⅙ **Grits Café** (478-994-8325; www .gritscafe.com), 17 West Johnston Street. Open 11–2 Tuesday through Saturday, 5:30–9 Tuesday through Thursday, 5:30–10 Friday and Saturday. The Grits Café offers contemporary Southern cuisine with Cajun, Southwestern, and Asian flair. Located in a restored 125-year-old building, the café provides upscale but casual dining in a comfortable environment. Menu items include dishes with grits and Vidalia onions, barbecue, fried green tomatoes, a wide array of salads, daily specials, wraps, quesadillas, seafood, sandwiches, and blue plate specials. Look for special events such as wine tastings, wine dinners, guest speakers, and theme dinners. No smoking. Wheelchair accessible. Lunch $4.25–13.75, dinner $16.75–23.75.

In Griffin
⅙ **Manhattan's Restaurant** (770-228-5442), 1707 North Expressway. Open 11–10 Monday through Thursday, 11–11 Friday and Saturday, 11–8:30 Sunday. Menu items at the upscale restaurant run the gamut from prime rib, steak, and seafood to pasta and even take-out. Smoking permitted in a completely separate area. Wheelchair accessible. $9.95–24.95.

In Bolingbroke
✎ ❀ ⅙ **Twyla Faye's Tea Room and Soda Fountain** (478-994-0031), 6025 US 41 South. Open 11–3 weekdays, 11–4 Saturday. The old-fashioned soda fountain serves soda fountain treats, blue plate specials, salads, soups, and sandwiches. No smoking. Wheelchair accessible. $3.25–5.95.

In Forsyth
✎ ❀ ⅙ **This Little Piggy Bar-B-Q** (478-994-0618), 866 Indian Springs Drive. Open 11–8 Monday through Saturday. The casual eatery serves pulled pork and chicken barbecue as well as ribs, but no beef. No smoking. Wheelchair accessible. $4.75–$6.75.

In Griffin
✎ ❀ ⅙ **Margo's Italian Restaurant** (770-229-4602), 1136 West Taylor Street. Open 11–9:30 Monday through Thursday, 11–10 Friday, 11–4 Saturday. The restaurant specializes in Italian and Mediterranean cuisine, and its menu features pasta, prime rib, and seafood. No smoking. Wheelchair accessible. Lunch $5.65–6.99, dinner $10–15.

In Juliette
✎ ❀ ⅙ **Whistle Stop Café** (478-992-8886; 1-888-642-4628; www.the whistlestocafe.com), 443 McCracken Street. Open 11–4 Tuesday through Sunday. Just step through the screen door and you'll be transported to the *Fried Green Tomatoes* movie set. Furniture and memorabilia re-create the 1930s and 1940s depicted in the movie. The 1927 general-merchandise store operated until 1972 and then served as a real estate office, timber consulting firm, and antiques shop before being "discovered" and turned into the café. Naturally, green toma-

toes, lightly battered and fried, top the menu choices, but you can find plenty of other Southern favorites such as polk salit, barbecue, burgers, and sandwiches for lunch. An early dinner usually consists of meat and one or two vegetables with a mason jar of sweet tea and bread. Make room for a fruit cobbler or pound cake and fruit for dessert. No smoking. Wheelchair accessible. Lunch $3.50–6.25, dinner $6.50–7.25.

COFFEEHOUSES AND TEAROOMS

In Thomaston
🍵 **A Time Remembered, Southern Style Tearoom** (706-647-9405; www.atimeremembered.net), 505 Stewart Avenue. Open for tea 11–4 Wednesday through Saturday; gift shop open 10–5 Wednesday through Saturday. Reservations required for tea. The charming tearoom is located in the historic Sidney Barron House, which dates from the early 1830s, making it one of the oldest homes in Thomaston. The tearoom offers several different tea services, the most popular of which is full afternoon tea. This event, served on an eclectic mixture of antique china and silver, features three-tiered trays stacked with scones, fruit, finger sandwiches, sweets, Devonshire cream, lemon curd, and a main entrée as well as a selection of teas. Memories of yesteryear include antique hats, luxurious furs, and dainty gloves that visiting ladies may don, as well as special hats for gentlemen. The gift shop offers fine loose-leaf teas, tea ware and accoutrements, and many old-fashioned items. Etiquette classes and seminars on the art of taking tea are offered occasionally. Cream tea $6.95, light afternoon tea $10.95, full afternoon tea $14.95, high tea $26.

❋ **Entertainment**

MUSIC **The Ole Clinton Opry** (call Paul Moncrief at 478-986-6587), 215 Old GA 18, Gray. Held 6–9:30 every Friday. The event, which attracts 200 to 250 people, showcases regional bluegrass, country, and gospel talent. Admission free, but donations accepted.

THEATER **Main Street Players** (770-229-9916; www.mainstreetplayers.org), 115 North Hill Street, Griffin. After six years of planning, the community theater group presented its first play in 2001. The old Woolworth's building has been renovated to serve as the 100-seat, black-box theater, where a full season of plays is presented each year. Call for a schedule of performances. Adults $18, seniors $15, students $10.

Ritz Theater (706-647-2749 or 706-647-7022 for showtimes; 706-647-5372 for tour information), 114 South Church Street, Thomaston. The beautifully restored 1930s art deco–style theater shows first-run and classic movies throughout the year and also hosts live performances. Redesigned for the comfort of today's audiences, the theater's seats feature retractable armrests with cup holders and folding countertop-style tables. A few of the original seats are on display as mementos. The newly renovated VIP balcony for adults age 21 and up serves wine and beer. The facility operates as a café during the day and offers coffee and desserts to movie-goers at night. Call for a schedule. Adults $5, children and seniors $4.

❋ **Selective Shopping**

FLEA MARKETS **Griffin Flea Market** (678-688-2325), 329 East

Solomon Street, Griffin. Open 8–6 Friday through Sunday. Twenty-five dealers sell antiques, baby items, dolls, furniture, kitchen and household items, jewelry, and tools.

GIFTS **S&P Specialties** (478-994-1374), 445 McCrackin Street, Juliette. Open 11–4 daily. Located in the old train depot, the shop purveys jewelry, purses, scarves, gift items, antiques, and home decor.

✳ Special Events

March: **Forsythia Festival** (478-994-9239; 1-888-642-4628; www.forsyth-monroechamber.com). The family-oriented festival on the Courthouse Square in Forsyth features arts and crafts, a children's fair, 5K and fun runs, sporting tournaments, live entertainment, a chili cook-off and yellow dessert contest, foods, a beauty pageant, classic car show, treasure hunt, pancake breakfast, and a presentation of the Forsythia Festival musical—"Songs of America." Free.

April: **Barnesville BBQ and Blues Festival** (770-358-5884; www.barnesville.org). This Florida BBQ Association–sanctioned event, held Friday night and Saturday in Barnesville, features entertainment by live blues bands, a classic car show, and a horseshoe-pitching tournament. $5 in advance, $7 at the gate.

Culloden Highland Games and Scottish Festival (478-885-2595; www.culloddengames.com). Culloden's festival features kilted gentlemen participating in traditional Highland games. Other activities include bagpiping, dancing, drumming, authentic food, whiskey tasting, Scottish wares, and information on clans. $10.

May: **Old Clinton War Days** (478-986-6383). This Clinton Historical Society–sponsored event features a re-enactment of the Federal occupation of Clinton. $5 per day.

September: **Barnesville Buggy Days** (770-358-5884; www.barnesville.org). The celebration of Barnesville's glory days as a preeminent buggy-manufacturing center features 150 artists and craftspeople as well as historic buggies on display outdoors and at the Old Jail Museum; food; 10K, 5K, and 1-mile fun runs; tennis and softball tournaments; and the Buggy Blast Fun Park, a new attraction with a rock-climbing wall, racetrack, pony rides, and a spider jump. A gala parade features buggies, floats, 250 horses, and civic groups. Park at Lamar County High School and ride the free Buggy Days van. The van operates 9–6 Saturday, 1–5 Sunday. Festival free; some activities have a small charge.

October: **Green Tomato Festival** (478-974-0716; www.juliettega.com). This festival in Juliette is filled with arts and crafts vendors, live entertainment, antiques and collectibles, children's pony rides, hayrides, and games. Naturally, fried green tomatoes are featured along with other food. Free.

FORSYTHIA

All seven varieties of forsythia shrubs—known for their bright yellow, star-shaped flowers—are related to the olive family. The flowers appear in the early spring before the leaves. The shrub was named for the Scottish horticulturist William Forsyth (1737–1804).

HAWKINSVILLE, EASTMAN, AND FITZGERALD

L ocated in the heart of Georgia, this area of rural countryside and small towns has some interesting Civil War history, including the capture of fleeing Confederate President Jefferson Davis near Irwinville and the creation of a village settled by former soldiers from the North and South.

Hawkinsville and Pulaski County's love affair with harness racing began in 1894, when the Pulaski County Fair Association held its first official harness races and Northerners realized that Georgia's mild climate and red clay provided an excellent combination for conditioning young horses. Now known as "the Harness Horse Capital," Hawkinsville has been a winter home for American and Canadian harness horses since 1920. Several world champions have been trained on Hawkinsville tracks.

The region is also popular for outdoor recreational pursuits such as ATV riding, canoeing and kayaking, boating, fishing, hunting, and wildlife observation.

The area is home to some unusual festivals, too, including those dedicated to harness racing, wild chickens, gum swamps, pumpkins, bluegrass, and wild hogs.

GUIDANCE Information about Abbeville is available from the **City of Abbeville** (229-467-3201; abbevillegeorgia.gov), 215 South Depot, Abbeville 31001.

For information about Cochran, contact the **Cochran–Bleckley County Chamber of Commerce** (478-934-2965), 318 Second Street, Cochran 31014. Open 8:30–5 weekdays.

To learn more about Chauncey and/or Eastman, call the **Eastman–Dodge County Chamber of Commerce and Local Welcome Center** (478-374-4723; www.eastman-georgia.com), 116 Ninth Avenue, Eastman 31023. Open 8:30–5 weekdays, 9–noon Saturday.

To find out more about Fitzgerald, contact the **Fitzgerald Area Convention and Visitors Bureau** (229-426-5033; 1-800-386-4642; www.fitzgeraldga.org), 115 South Main Street, Fitzgerald 31750. Open 8–5 weekdays. Get information on the town's Architectural Treasures Tour, A Captured President Tour, and A Tale of Two Cities Tour here. Information also can be obtained from the **Fitzgerald–Ben Hill County Chamber of Commerce** (229-426-5035; www.fitzgeraldchamber.org), 126 East Pine Street, Fitzgerald 31750.

Information about Hawkinsville, including the Hawkinsville Historic Driving Tour, can be obtained from the **Hawkinsville–Pulaski County Chamber of Commerce** (478-783-1717; www.hawkinsville.org), 108 North Lumpkin Street, Hawkinsville 31036. Open 9–5 weekdays.

For more information about Irwinville, contact the **town of Irwinville** (229-468-9441; www.irwincounty.georgia.gov), 207 South Irwin Avenue, Irwinville 31774.

To learn more about McRae, contact the **Telfair Chamber of Commerce** (229-868-6365; www.mcraega.net; www.telfairco.com), 120 East Oak Street, McRae 31055.

Find out more about Unadilla by contacting the **city of Unadilla** (478-627-3022; www.unadillageorgia.gov), P.O. Box 307, Unadilla 31091.

GETTING THERE *By air:* This area is served by **Hartsfield-Jackson Atlanta International Airport**. For more information about the airlines and car rentals at the airport, see What's Where in Georgia.

By bus: **Greyhound Lines** (1-800-231-2222; www.greyhound.com) does not provide service to the area described in this chapter. The nearest stations are in Macon (see Macon chapter) or Dublin (see Statesboro chapter). A bus passenger arriving in either of those towns would need to rent a car to get to and around these towns.

By car: Hawkinsville lies between the north-south route I-75 and the east-west route I-16. The primary U.S. highways through the area are 23, 129, and 341.

By train: The nearest **Amtrak** (404-881-3067; 1-800-USA-RAIL; www.amtrak.com) stations are in Atlanta or Columbus (see What's Where in Georgia and the Columbus chapter in 5, Southern Rivers). An arriving rail passenger would then need a rental car.

GETTING AROUND Car rentals are available from **Freedom Rent-A-Car** (478-934-6351) in Cochran and **Shorty's Used Cars** (478-374-0814) in Eastman. The catch-22 is that, with the exception of travelers arriving in Hawkinsville by shuttle from Atlanta, a visitor would need to have a car already to get to these towns.

MEDICAL EMERGENCY Immediate care is available at **Bleckley Memorial Hospital** (478-934-6211), 145 East Peacock Street, Cochran; **Dodge County Hospital** (478-374-4000; 478-374-0494), 901 Griffin Avenue, Eastman; and **Dorminy Medical Center** (229-424-7100), 200 Perry House Road, Fitzgerald. Pulaski County–Hawkinsville does not have 911 service.

VILLAGES **Abbeville** in Wilcox County was settled by French Huguenots and was the home of John C. Calhoun, vice president of the United States from 1825 to 1832. The Civil War's Battle of Breakfast Creek occurred near Abbeville and a Confederate monument stands in front of the courthouse, which was built in 1903. The area, famous for being home to a large number of wild hogs, is called "the Wild Hog Capital of Georgia." A popular event is the **Ocmulgee Wild Hog Festival,** held each May (see *Special Events*).

Chauncey in Dodge County is in prime quail-hunting territory and is also home to a mineral spring that is the heart of a recreational resort.

Cochran, the county seat of Bleckley County, was established in 1869 and named for Arthur E. Cochran, president of the Macon and Brunswick Railroad. Middle Georgia College, which is located here, is the oldest two-year college in the nation. Cochran sponsors several annual festivals, including the Gum Swamp Festival in May and the Great Pumpkin Festival in October.

Dodge County was created in 1870 as the 134th Georgia county and was named for William E. Dodge, a New Yorker who owned vast tracks of timberland in Georgia. He was instrumental in getting Congress to remove taxation from timber, and when he learned that a county was being named in his honor, he built the county's first courthouse in 1908 as a gift.

Eastman, the largest town, is the home of the original Stuckey Candy Plant, renowned for its pecan roll, and is known as "the Candy Capital of Georgia." At one time Stuckey had 320 outlets along U.S. highways and employed 1,000 people. After dwindling to 100 outlets, the company was sold to Standard Candy, which is famous for its Goo Goo Cluster. The plant in Eastman continues to operate. An important festival in Eastman is Dickens of a Christmas in December. Nearby Rhine hosts the Spring Lake Bluegrass Festival–Old Timers Fiddler's Reunion.

Fitzgerald is a Southern town with a Yankee foundation. In the 1890s, P. H. Fitzgerald, an Indianapolis newspaperman and veterans' pension attorney who was a Union drummer boy in his youth, decided that as part of the healing process between North and South, a colony should be created where former soldiers from both sides could live together. He thought the colony should be in the South so aging Union soldiers could escape harsh winters and drought.

More than just an idea, the American Tribune Soldiers Colony, also known as the Old Soldiers Colony Company, actually came into fruition in 1895 on 50,000 acres purchased for that purpose. It was rather ironic that the area chosen was so close to the place where Confederate President Jefferson Davis was captured. Nearly 3,000 former soldiers from both sides came from 38 states to fulfill the dream. These soldiers were able to conquer their painful feelings and forge lifelong friendships. They named the streets for Ulysses S. Grant and William T. Sherman as well as Robert E. Lee and Stonewall Jackson. Other streets are named for both Northern and Southern trees and flowers. In the early years, a harvest celebration was planned that would include both Union and Confederate parades, but on the day of the event all marched together as one.

The experiment seems to have worked. The town continues to prosper and is known as "Where North and South Reunited." Its Evergreen Cemetery is filled with the graves of the town's early Rebel and Yank settlers.

Today Fitzgerald's historic downtown is a 16-block National Historic Register District with venerable buildings, brick streets, sidewalks paved in blue and gray bricks, and landscaped parks. The 1902 railroad depot houses the Blue and Gray Museum (see *To See—Museums*). In April Fitzgerald celebrates the **Georgia Harmony Jubilee** in honor of the town's origins (see *Special Events*).

THE FITZGERALD CHICKENS

One of Fitzgerald's more amusing and endearing present-day idiosyncrasies is the presence of wild Burmese chickens. Visitors see the brilliantly plumed fowl wandering around town, greeting locals and visitors, roosting in trees, and guiding their biddies around. Traffic stops to let them cross the streets. They were originally introduced all over the state by the Department of Natural Resources in the 1960s as an additional game bird to be hunted like pheasant or quail. For whatever reason, the chickens never took hold anywhere in Georgia but here. Soon the chickens realized they could get free handouts by venturing into town. They've multiplied, of course, so at one time removing them was discussed, but the majority of the citizenry has become so attached to them that the idea was quickly dropped. The annual **Fitzgerald Wild Chicken Festival** celebrates these wild residents (see *Special Events*).

Hawkinsville is home to the 86-acre Lawrence Bennett Harness Training Facility, which can be toured, and sponsors the **Hawkinsville Harness Festival and Spring Celebration** (see *Special Events*).

Irwin County, the 45th county created in Georgia, was formed in 1818 and encompassed all of south-central Georgia. Several other counties were created from this area, and today Irwin County contains the upper reaches of the Alapaha, Satilla, and Willachoochee rivers. Irwinville was the county seat during the Civil War, but that honor is now held by Ocilla. Several endangered species still survive in Irwin County: the Florida panther, the peregrine falcon, and the southern bald eagle.

The area between what is now **Irwinville** and Fitzgerald became an important footnote to history on May 9, 1865, when Confederate President Jefferson Davis, his family, and some of his staff were captured here by Union troops. Although the Civil War was officially over and the Confederate cabinet had been dissolved, Davis was headed to Louisiana and Texas, where he hoped to reunite rebel forces and continue the fight. As they were camping in this pine forest, they had no idea that two groups of Union soldiers were in close pursuit. As it happened, neither of the Union detachments knew of the existence of the other and they began firing at each other. Davis and his party were caught between them and captured.

Jacksonville and **Unadilla** are known for outdoor recreational opportunities.

McRae, the county seat of Telfair County, was incorporated in 1874 and named for a pioneering Scottish family. Known as "the Crossroads City," McRae is located at the intersection of US 23/341, 280, 319, and 441. The small town's square contains a Statue of Liberty, a Liberty Bell, and a war memorial. McRae was the home of two former Georgia governors: Eugene Talmadge and Herman Eugene Talmadge. Little Ocmulgee State Park is nearby (see *To Do—Golf, To Do—Miniature Golf, Green Space—Nature Preserves and Parks, Lodging—Camp-*

grounds, Lodging—Cottages, Lodging—Inns and Resorts, and *Where to Eat— Eating Out*).

✴ To See

CULTURAL SITES 🐾 ♿ **Butler Brown Gallery** (478-892-9323; 1-866-481-5980), GA 26 East, Hawkinsville. Open 10–5 Tuesday through Friday, 11–3 Saturday. See the works of world-renowned artist Butler Brown, whose paintings have hung in the White House. Free. Classes are available, too.

See also **Historic Opera House** under *Entertainment—Theater*.

FOR FAMILIES ✐ 🐾 ♿ **Bowens Mill Fish Hatchery** (229-426-5272), 1773 Bowens Mill Highway, Fitzgerald. Open 8–4:30 weekdays. This hatchery raises bluegill, redear sunfish, channel catfish, and largemouth bass. A 45-minute tour is offered, but two days' advance notice is required.

✐ 🐾 **Fallen Star Ranch** (478-374-3111; www.fallenstarranch.com), 796 Reedy Branch Road, Eastman. Open by appointment. The farm breeds, raises, and sells miniature horses. Children weighing less than 50 pounds can ride the horses. The farm is named for Georgiaites, natural glass formed when an asteroid or meteorite collides with the earth. They are the rarest variety of tektites—95 percent of which are found nearby. Free.

✐ 🐾 **Owen and Williams Fish Farm** (478-892-3144; www.owenandwilliams .com), US 280, Hawkinsville. Open 8–5 weekdays, 8–noon Saturday. The bream, catfish, and grass carp that are raised here are used to stock fishing ponds around the state. Free.

HISTORIC HOMES AND SITES 🐾 ♿ **Evergreen Cemetery,** Benjamin Hill Drive East, Fitzgerald. Open 8–5 daily. Brochures are available for a self-guided tour. Among the notable Fitzgerald citizens buried here is Lewis Clute, who is credited with capturing Jefferson Davis. This is also the final resting place for Civil War soldiers William J. Bush, who lived to be the oldest Georgia veteran, and Jerome Moss, who was Union General William Tecumseh Sherman's drummer boy. The cemetery took its name from the Gettysburg cemetery over which the famous battle was fought. Street names within the cemetery take their names from the Gettysburg cemetery as well: Cemetery Ridge Road, Emmitsburg Road, Little Round Top Lane, and Seminary Ridge Road. Other streets include Confederate Lane and Union Road. Free.

✐ 🐾 ♿ **Jefferson Davis Memorial State Historic Site** (229-831-2335; www .gastateparks.org/info/jeffd), 338 Jeff Davis Park Road, Fitzgerald. Open 9–5 Tuesday through Saturday, 2–5:30 Sunday. This 13-acre park marks the spot where Confederate President Jefferson Davis and some of his staff were captured on May 9, 1865, after the official end of the Civil War. At the museum, visitors can watch a video about the event and see Civil War memorabilia, including a preserved piece of the tree where Davis was standing when he was captured. The park also features a small nature trail and picnic facilities. Adults $3, children $1.75. Several special events occur throughout the year, including "1860s

Christmas," when visitors can enjoy candlelit tours, period refreshments, caroling, crafts, decorations, and a visit from Santa.

🎣 🐾 ♿ **Liberty Square,** downtown McRae. Open daily. The grounds of the quaint square are adorned with miniature monuments, including a 1/12th size Statue of Liberty and a replica of the Liberty Bell. The square also contains a memorial to fallen soldiers from the area. Free.

🐾 ♿ **Orphans Cemetery, Williamson Mausoleum,** Orphan Cemetery Road, Eastman. Cemetery open daylight hours daily. This 1887 cemetery is dedicated to a young man who was orphaned and left to raise his five younger brothers. A. G. Williamson commissioned this impressive mausoleum with life-sized figures of himself, his wife, and his nephew, J. G. Williamson. The elder Mr. Williamson sent a photograph of what he wanted to an Italian sculptor in 1887, and the mausoleum was rendered in marble, then sent to Eastman. The cemetery also contains other ornate memorials from the Victorian era. Free.

MUSEUMS 🎣 🐾 ♿ **Blue and Gray Museum** (229-426-5069; www.fitzgerald .ga.org), 116 North Johnston Street, Fitzgerald. Open year-round, 10–4 Tuesday through Saturday, 1–5 Sunday. The museum chronicles the history of Fitzgerald's creation as a haven for soldiers from both sides of the Civil War. Among the exhibits are photos and mementos from the colony's beginnings as well as Union and Confederate battle relics and other artifacts. Among the interesting artifacts are a key from Andersonville Prison, a war drum dated 1861 and used in Fitzgerald parades for more than a century, and a Southern Cross of Honor medal. The Hall of Honor lists the names of Fitzgerald's pioneers, and the film *Marching as One* tells the story of the town's founding. Other exhibits include uniforms, arms, and medals used in all of this country's major conflicts. One section is dedicated to Fitzgerald native son and Congressional Medal of Honor winner General Raymond G. Davis. Adults $3, students $2, children $1.

🎣 🐾 ♿ **Fitzgerald Fire Engine Museum** (229-426-5030), 315 East Pine Street, Fitzgerald. Open 10–4 daily. The Fitzgerald Fire Department began way back in 1895. The current department displays a collection of antique equipment, including horse-drawn apparatus and the first gasoline engine the department acquired, in 1915. Kids can slide down the original brass firefighter's pole and take home a red hat of their own. Visitors also can view sparkling up-to-the-minute engines and equipment next door. Adults $3, children $1. Free.

✳ **To Do**

BOAT EXCURSIONS 🎣 **Ocmulgee Outfitters** (478-231-9381; 478-230-8499; www.ocmulgeeoutfitters.com),

SOUTHERN CROSS OF HONOR
Although the Union created the Congressional Medal of Honor during the Civil War, the Confederacy had nothing similar. After the war, the United Daughters of the Confederacy created the Southern Cross of Honor to award the service of every soldier who had fought for the Confederate States of America. In all, they presented 78,000 medals.

Hawkinsville (call for directions). Open 9–dusk Saturday and Sunday. Guided canoe and kayak trips of the Ocmulgee River, including overnight trips, that are offered should be booked two weeks in advance. Okefenokee Swamp trips should be booked two months in advance. All trips include an experienced guide, all equipment, and meals. The company's specialty is the 12-mile Ocmulgee River Trek from Dykes Landing near Cochran to the Hawkinsville City Landing. The trip takes four to six hours. $40 per canoe or two-person kayak per day; Ocmulgee River Trek $40; call for other fees.

BOATING ✐ ❀ **Telfair County Boat Landing,** Ocmulgee River at the US 341 Bridge, Lumber City (east of Hawkinsville). Open daily. Several boat landings permit easy access to the river for boaters and anglers. Free.

FISHING ✐ ❀ ⬧ **Georgia DNR Dodge County Public Fishing Area** (478-374-6765; www.gofishgeorgia.com), 325 Dodge Lake Road, Eastman. A Georgia fishing license is required. Open 6 AM–8 PM daily. The 104-acre lake is stocked with bluegill, bream, channel catfish, crappie, redear sunfish, and largemouth bass. The facility also features a boat ramp, fish-cleaning station, pier, rest rooms, an interpretive nature trail, and a picnic area. Some facilities wheelchair accessible. Free.

FOR FAMILIES ✐ ❀ ⬧ **Jay Bird Springs** (229-868-2728), 1221 Jay Bird Springs Road, Chauncey. Pool open seasonally; other attractions open year-round, 11–8 Wednesday, Thursday, and Sunday, 11–11 Friday and Saturday. The 40-acre, family-oriented recreational facility features the first public swimming pool in Georgia: a spring-fed 60-by-100-foot swimming pool with a 310-foot water slide. In addition, the resort has a miniature-golf course, a roller-skating rink, a game room, ball fields, picnic grounds, and lodging. $6–9 for pool, $6 for skating.

GOLF **Southern Hills Golf Club** (478-783-0600; www.southernhills golf.com), US 129/GA 247 North, Hawkinsville. Generally open full daylight–two hours before dusk, weather permitting. Call to be sure. The semiprivate, 18-hole course is 6,741 yards, par 72. The rolling terrain features a change in elevation of 131 feet. *Golf Digest* readers voted it one of the top five golfing values in the country and the service as the third best. $27 weekdays, $32.50 weekends.

✐ ❀ **Wallace Adams Golf Course at Little Ocmulgee State Park** (229-868-6651; 1-888-882-8906; www.gastateparks.org/info/liocmulgee; www.golfgeorgia.org), US 441 North, McRae. Open 8–dusk. The state park boasts an 18-hole, 6,625-yard, par-72 course along with clubhouse, pro shop, instruction, and snack bar. The course is characterized by loblolly pines, magnolias, and willows. The older back nine is wider open than the newer front nine. $30 weekdays, $34 weekends and holidays.

HOW DID JAY BIRD SPRINGS GET ITS NAME?

The area was settled in 1900. Folklore says that a black man with an injured leg was led to the springs by a jay bird, and the mineral waters healed his injury.

HORSE RACING ♂ 🐎 ♿ **Lawrence Bennett Harness Training Facility** (478-892-3240), US 129 South, Hawkinsville. Open daylight hours October through May. The South's only training facility for harness racing trains trotters and pacers on half-mile and mile tracks. Visitors are welcome to watch the training or simply visit with the horses. Free. The annual **Hawkinsville Harness Festival and Spring Celebration** (see *Special Events*) is held each April, and rodeos occur once a month.

HUNTING Barksdale Bobwhite Plantation (478-934-6916; www.barksdale plantation.com), Longstreet Road, Cochran. Open October 1 through March 31. In addition to guided hunts for chukar, deer, pheasant, quail, turkey, and wild hog, the 2,700-acre facility offers a skeet range and lodging. Call for reservations and fees.

McCranie Plantation (478-374-7293; www.mccranieplantation.com), 2662 Chauncey Rhine Highway, Eastman. Open October through March by reservation only. Different settings on 3,000 acres range from thin or thick cover to field edges. Clear-cuts provide excellent opportunities for quail hunting. Guides, hunting vehicles, and dogs are provided. $200–350 for quail hunting, $75 for fishing.

MINIATURE GOLF ♂ 🐎 ♿ **Little Ocmulgee State Park and Lodge** (229-868-7474; 1-800-864-7275; www .gastateparks.org/info/liocmulgee), off US 441, McRae. Open sunup–10 PM daily. The mini golf course replicates the state park's **Wallace Adams Golf Course** (see *Golf*). $2.

See also **Jay Bird Springs** under *For Families.*

OFF-ROAD RIDING 🐎 ♿ **Big Creek Trail Rides** (478-783-2968; www.bigcreektrailride.com), GA 230 West, Hawkinsville. Open for two-day rides the second weekend of each month and one-day rides the fourth Saturday of each month. More than 15 miles of trails crisscrossing 500 acres offer everything from rolling pastures and beautiful scenery for the beginning or more relaxed rider to difficult trails and "mud that would trap a bear" for the extreme rider. Dirt bikes, dune buggies, and mud-bogging vehicles are welcome. The facility offers concessions and primitive campsites. Check for occasional rides for horses only. $15 per person per day, $20 per person per weekend; includes primitive camping.

THE LAWRENCE BENNETT HARNESS TRAINING FACILITY WELCOMES VISITORS OCTOBER THROUGH MAY.

✳ Green Space

NATURE PRESERVES AND PARKS 🖉 🐾 ♿ **Grand Plaza Park** (229-426-5033; 1-800-386-4642; www.fitzgeraldga.org). Open daily. Green space located in the heart of downtown celebrates Fitzgerald's heritage. Landscaped with flowers, trees, and other greenery, the park's central attractions include topiaries of Union and Confederate generals shaking hands and a giant Burmese chicken. A fountain, an original hitching post, granite benches, brick arches from Monitor High School, and ironwork columns from the Empire hotel, which once stood on the spot, punctuate the park. Outdoor performances are often held here, and chess aficionados can make use of the park's life-sized chessboard and pieces. Free.

🖉 🐾 **Horse Creek Wildlife Management Area** (229-868-6365; www.telfairco.com), 120 East Oak Street, Jacksonville. Open dawn–dusk daily. The preserve offers fishing, hiking, and hunting. Free; check for hunting fees.

🖉 🐾 🐾 ♿ **Little Ocmulgee State Park and Lodge** (229-868-7474; 1-800-864-7275; www.gastateparks.org/info/liocmulgee), off US 441, McRae. This 1,265-acre park of sand hills and pine forests has a plethora of recreational amenities, including a golf course (see *To Do—Golf*), miniature golf (see *To Do—Miniature Golf*), a 265-acre lake with a swimming beach, a swimming pool, boat ramp, canoe and pedal boat rentals, two lighted tennis courts, and an amphitheater. Fishing, boating, and waterskiing are popular pursuits, and the park has a water-ski ramp. The 2½-mile Oak Ridge Trail meanders through scrub oaks and pine toward a buzzard roost and boardwalk. Wildlife seen along the trail might include the harmless indigo snake or the endangered gopher tortoise. Accommodations include a lodge, campground, and cottages (see *Lodging*). Pets are permitted in the campground and cottages but not the lodge. Parking $3.

🖉 🐾 **Oakbin Pond Preserve** (404-873-6946; www.nature.org/georgia), Oakbin Road off US 41 (parallels I-75), Unadilla. Open 9–5 weekdays. The preserve features a cypress pond, boardwalk, wetlands, and hiking trails through the uplands. The area is of particular interest to birdwatchers during spring and fall migrations. (Note: Some ponds are restricted.) Free.

See also Parks Appendix.

RIVERS Ocmulgee River (229-426-5100). The river provides countless opportunities for boating, tubing, fishing, wildlife observation, and camping. Anglers try their luck fishing for largemouth bass, bream, catfish, and trout. In fact, the world-record 22-pound largemouth bass was caught near Ben Hill County Landing (near Fitzgerald). The area surrounding the river abounds with deer, wild turkey, quail, and other wildlife. Camping is available on the honor system.

✳ Lodging

BED & BREAKFASTS

In Eastman

🐾 ♿ **Dodge Hill Inn** (478-374-2644; www.dodgehillinn.com), 5021 Ninth Avenue. This gracious home was built in 1912 by N. W. Hurst, the town's first school superintendent. During the 1920s, the Cooke family owned the house and Mrs. Cooke planted hundreds of camellias and other flowering bushes, many of which are still flourishing. The inn is furnished with antiques and accessorized with bisque figurines, oil paintings, antique toys, and old glass and china. Guest accommodations are offered in two suites, two guest rooms, and two nearby guest houses. All rooms offer refrigerators, and the guest houses boast a full kitchen. A full breakfast is included in the nightly rate. No smoking. Wheelchair accessible. $79.50–99 for rooms, $89.50–99 for suites, $95–125 for guest houses.

In Fitzgerald
🌸 ♿ **Dorminy-Massee House Bed and Breakfast Inn** (229-423-3123; www.members.tripod.com/~dmhouse), 516 West Central Avenue. The opulent mansion, which is within walking distance of the historic downtown, was built in 1915 by J. J. "Captain Jack" Dorminy, who personally picked the heart pine used in the construction. He lived there until his death in 1952, after which his daughter Eulalie Dorminy Massee inherited the house and lived there until her death in 1995. Today it is owned and operated by her son Marion, her grandson Mark, and their wives. The house features spacious rooms with high ceilings and lavish furnishings and decor. Eight luxurious guest rooms are offered. The landscaped grounds boast a goldfish pond, smokehouse, greenhouse, and gazebo. A continental breakfast is included in the nightly rate. No smoking. Two rooms on first floor wheelchair accessible. $75–85.

In Hawkinsville
🌸 ♿ **Betty Faye's Bed and Breakfast** (478-892-3494; www.bettyfayes.com), 417 Commerce Street. The historic farmhouse is more than 100

years old. In fact, the original part of the house was constructed in 1836 and then added on to over the years. Six guest rooms are offered: two with king-sized beds, three with queens, and one with a double bed. No smoking. Wheelchair accessible. $59–$69.

In McRae
🌸 **The Parker House Inn** (229-868-2326; 1-877-495-7030; www.telfairco.com), 301 Huckabee Street. The inn's six rooms offer basic, economical accommodations. No smoking. Not wheelchair accessible. $50–60.

In Unadilla
🌸 **Sugar Hill Bed and Breakfast** (478-627-3557; www.sugarhill.bizhosting.com), 2540 Sugar Hill Road. This mid-1800s farmhouse is located just 4 miles from I-75, but a world and a century away. Its idyllic country setting offers solitude, peace, and quiet. Family antiques, three fireplaces, two common rooms, a rocker-filled front porch, and a swimming pool entice guests to unwind. Mom and Pop's Room boasts a two-person whirlpool tub, a sitting area, and a gas-log fireplace. Ask about children. No alcohol. No smoking. Not wheelchair accessible. $55–75.

CAMPGROUNDS

In Chauncey
🎣 🌸 ♿ **Jay Bird Springs Resort and Campground** (229-868-2728), 1221 Jay Bird Springs Road. The resort offers a variety of accommodations as well as recreational activities (see *To Do—For Families*). $16 for full hookups, $12 for tent sites, $50–150 for motel rooms and cottages.

In Hawkinsville
🎣 🐾 🌸 ♿ **Lawrence Bennett Har-**

ness Training Facility and Campground (478-892-3240; www.hawkins villega.net), US 129 South. Reservations required. In addition to camping facilities, including wheelchair-accessible RV sites, the campground offers fishing and golf privileges. Pets allowed. $12–15.

In McRae

🗡 🐾 🎗 ⅋ Little Ocmulgee State Park and Lodge (229-868-7474; 1-800-864-7275; www.gastateparks.org/info/liocmulgee), off US 441. The state park offers 55 tent, trailer, and RV sites with cable TV hookups as well as a rustic group pioneer campground. Visitors enjoy all the amenities of a resort state park (see *Green Space—Nature Preserves and Parks*). $17–19.

COTTAGES AND CABINS

In McRae

🗡 🐾 🎗 ⅋ Little Ocmulgee State Park and Lodge (229-868-7474; 1-800-864-7275; www.gastateparks.org/info/liocmulgee), off US 441. The park features 10 fully equipped one- and two-bedroom lakeside cottages. Visitors enjoy all the benefits of a resort state park (see *Green Space—Nature Preserves and Parks*). $70–95.

INNS AND RESORTS

In McRae

🗡 🎗 ⅋ The Lodge at Little Ocmulgee State Park (229-868-7474; 1-800-864-7275; www.gastateparks.org/info/liocmulgee), off US 441. The state park's 60-room, two-junior-suite lodge features a restaurant with a golf-course view. Visitors enjoy all the amenities of a resort state park (see *Green Space—Nature Preserves and Parks*). $60–70.

✳ Where to Eat

DINING OUT

In Hawkinsville

🗡 🎗 ⅋ Steakhouse Restaurant (478-892-3383), US 341 Bypass. Open 11–9 Monday through Saturday, 11–2:30 Sunday. This is where locals go for lunch and dinner and the best steaks in town. No smoking. Wheelchair accessible. $5–20.

EATING OUT

In Fitzgerald

🗡 🎗 Cirillo's Pizza (229-622-0044), 113 South Main Street. Open 9–9 weekdays, 5–9 Saturday. Cirillo's serves the most authentic Italian pizza in town. No smoking. Not wheelchair accessible. $5–$15.

🗡 🎗 ⅋ Floyd's Bar-B-Q (229-423-3013), 121 Benjamin H. Hill Drive West. Open 6 AM–2 PM Monday through Saturday, 6 PM–9 PM Thursday and Friday The old-fashioned hamburger and barbecue house has been a favorite for four generations. Steaks and sandwiches also are served. No smoking. Wheelchair accessible. $3–10.

🗡 🎗 ⅋ Huc-A-Poo's (229-426-7503), 116 South Grant Street. Open 5–10 Wednesday through Saturday (bar open until 2 AM). The casual eatery serves pizza, sandwiches, wraps, and chili. Nothing on the menu is fried. No smoking. Wheelchair accessible. $5–10.

In Hawkinsville

🗡 🎗 ⅋ Tom and Sandy's Horseshoe Restaurant (478-892-3526), 539 Broad Street. Open 6 AM–2 PM Monday through Saturday, 11 AM–3 PM Sunday. Country cooking is the staple here, and the full country breakfast is a great way to start the day. No smoking. Wheelchair accessible. Breakfast $4–7, lunch buffet $5.95.

In McRae

♂ 🐾 ♿ **Fairway Grill** (229-868-7474) at the Lodge at Little Ocmulgee State Park, off US 441. Open 7–10 and 11–2 daily, 5–9 Monday through Saturday. Overlooking the sixth and seventh holes on the Wallace Adams Golf Course, the restaurant offers buffets and à la carte selections. Beer and wine are offered. No smoking. Wheelchair accessible. $8.99 for buffet, $3–5 for sandwiches.

✳ Entertainment

MUSIC Po' Boy Opry (229-426-5060; 1-800-386-4642), 217 East Pine Street, Fitzgerald. Open 6–midnight Saturday. Either bring your own fiddle, guitar, or other instrument to join in with local musicians on stage, or sit back and listen. Gospel and country-western are the specialties, but you might hear blues or oldies, too. Free.

THEATER Grand Theatre (229-426-5090; 1-800-386-4642), 119 South Main Street, Fitzgerald. Box office open 8–5 weekdays. Built in the 1930s in the art deco style, this theater has been restored to serve as a venue for the performing arts. Call for a schedule of events and prices.

Historic Opera House (478-783-1884; www.hawkinsville.org), 100 North Lumpkin Street, Hawkinsville. The restored opera house, which boasts near-perfect acoustics, stages concerts and other live performances. Be sure to admire the hand-painted canvas stage curtain. Call for a schedule of performances and ticket prices. Free tours 10–4 daily by reservation.

✳ Selective Shopping

ANTIQUES Hawkinsville Antique Mall (478-783-3607), 226 North Lumpkin Street, Hawkinsville. Open 10–5 Monday through Saturday, 1–5 Sunday. Multiple dealers sell antiques and collectibles.

Juliet's Antiques (229-424-5040), 214 South Main Street, Fitzgerald. Open 11–6 Monday through Saturday. Browse through this shop—which is owned and operated by the descendant of an original settler—for dishes, folk art, furniture, quilts, and more.

Wendy's Antiques and Interiors (229-423-5593), 110 East Pine Street, Fitzgerald. Open 10:30–noon and 1–5:30 Monday, Tuesday, Thursday, and Friday. Shop here for an eclectic variety of antiques, collectibles, and decorative arts.

ART GALLERIES Colony Art Gallery (229-426-5038), 126 East Pine Street, Fitzgerald. Open 10–4 Monday, Tuesday, Thursday, and Friday, 10–noon Wednesday. Area artists display crafts, folk art, paintings, pottery, and stained glass in an old five-and-ten. The wildlife paintings of local artist Ronald Goodman and the folk-art dogs made by local artist Ray Minshew are displayed here, too.

FOOD Fitzgerald Farmers Market (229-426-5060), South Sherman and East Pine streets, Fitzgerald. Open 8–6 Monday through Saturday. Local growers sell fresh produce year-round.

Gooseneck Farms (478-783-1063; www.gooseneckfarms.com), US 129 South, Hawkinsville. Open 10–6 Monday through Saturday, September through December. A self-proclaimed "Nuthouse," the emporium offers items made with locally produced pecans as well as other gourmet gifts.

GIFTS Jenny K.'s Gift Gallery (229-424-0930), 120 South Grant Street, Fitzgerald. Open 9–6 Monday through Saturday. Among the gifts for every age and interest are items with rooster and chicken motifs in honor of the town's famous residents. The store also specializes in gift baskets.

SPECIAL STORES Fitzgerald Five-Story Plaza (229-426-5033; 1-800-386-4642), 128 South Grant Street, Fitzgerald. Open 9–6 Monday through Saturday. Shoppers can find just about anything in these 40 shops under one roof.

✳ Special Events

March: **Fitzgerald Wild Chicken Festival** (229-423-7660). Fitzgerald's wild Burmese chickens are celebrated with wildlife displays, boats, RVs, and other outdoor equipment. Free.

April: **Georgia Harmony Jubilee** (229-426-5033; 1-800-386-4642). Fitzgerald's weeklong festival celebrates the history, heritage, and har-mony of "the City Where America Reunited." The jubilee includes an arts and crafts marketplace, concert, dance, children's activities, food, music, and more. Very special activities include a presentation of "Our Friends, Our Enemies," the founding story; a parade with flag bearers from all 50 states; and a re-creation of the 1896 Roll Call of the States. Some events free, others $3–10.

Hawkinsville Harness Festival and Spring Celebration (478-783-1717). In addition to harness races, this two-day festival at the Lawrence Bennett Harness Training Facility includes arts and crafts, fireworks, concerts, beauty pageants, a golf tournament, hayrides, a reptile show, clowns, magic, rides, cartoon characters, and food. Adults $5, children $2.

May: **Ocmulgee Wild Hog Festival** (229-467-2144). Abbeville's festival in Lion's Park features food, arts and crafts, live musical entertainment, horse and carriage rides, a Saturday-night dance, and various contests such as hog baying. Of course, wild boars are displayed, too. $2.

RACES ARE JUST ONE PART OF THE HAWKINSVILLE HARNESS FESTIVAL AND SPRING CELE-BRATION, HELD EACH APRIL.

MACON

Known as the "City of White Columns and Cherry Blossoms," Macon is one of the most gracious cities in the South. Blessedly spared during the Civil War, it still showcases its profusion of significant historic structures. Macon boasts 5,500 individual structures in 11 historic districts listed on the National Register of Historic Places, including 70 antebellum and 19 plantation homes. In all, the city has more acreage on the prestigious register than any other city in Georgia.

Something else it has in profusion is cherry trees. Although anytime is a good time to visit, the best time is in the spring, when the city is canopied by the pink blossoms of 285,000 Yoshino cherry trees—more than any other city in the world. Washington, D.C., so well-known for its cherry trees, has a mere 5,000.

Georgians have left their stamp on every genre of music, from ragtime and blues to smooth soul and punk rock. Many of these musicians called Macon home. During the 1950s and 1960s, nightclubs flourished up and down Broadway. R&B radio personalities commanded the airwaves, and the careers of Little Richard, Otis Redding, and James Brown were launched. In the 1970s, the combination of Capricorn Records and the Allman Brothers Band made Macon the home of Southern Rock.

In addition to Macon's musical heritage, the city's central location in the state made it a natural to be the site of the **Georgia Music Hall of Fame** (see *To See—Cultural Sites*) and a site on the **Georgia Music Trail** along with Atlanta, Athens, and Savannah.

Georgians also have made an indelible mark on virtually every sport. Olympic champions, professional superstars, and legendary coaches are native sons and daughters. Once again, Macon was tapped: as the site of the **Georgia Sports Hall of Fame** (see *To See—Museums*).

A plethora of small towns around Macon each have one or more attractions to keep visitors in the region. Byron has an abundance of interesting shops, antiques stores, and restaurants in its historic district. The town also has a small museum in its railroad depot as well as an antique-car mall, an antiques mall, and an outlet mall.

GUIDANCE

Before making a trip to the Macon area, contact the **Macon–Bibb County Convention and Visitors Bureau** (478-743-3401; 1-800-768-3401; www

.maconga.org), 200 Cherry Street, Macon 31201. Open 9–5 Monday through Saturday. Located in the historic 1916 Terminal Station, the CVB's Welcome Center dispenses brochures and advice. Guided tours leave from there, or visitors can pick up a self-guided tour map.

Visitors also can get information from the **Macon I-75 Welcome Center** (478-994-9191), I-75 at Mile Marker 179, Macon 31201. Open 9–5:30 daily.

For information about Byron, contact the **Byron Convention and Visitors Bureau and Welcome Center** (478-956-2409; 1-888-686-3496; www.byronga .com), 100 West Heritage Boulevard, Byron 31008, housed in the former Vinson's Pharmacy, circa 1910. Open 9–4 weekdays. There's also a satellite welcome center at the **Big Peach Antique Mall and Welcome Center** (478-956-6256), 119 Peach Parkway, Byron 31008.

Contact the **Peach County Chamber of Commerce–Welcome Center** (478-825-3733; www.peachcountyga.com), 201 Oakland Heights Parkway, Fort Valley 31030, to learn more about Fort Valley and Peach County.

To learn more about Perry, contact the **Perry Area Convention and Visitors Bureau–Perry Welcome Center** (478-988-8000; www.perryga.com), 101 General Courtney Hodges Boulevard, Perry 31069. Open 8:30–5 weekdays, 9–4 Saturday; Memorial Day through Labor Day, also 1–5 Sunday. Pick up a brochure for the Historic Perry Walking-Driving Tour of more than 50 historic locations in Perry.

For information about Roberta, contact the **Roberta–Crawford County Chamber of Commerce** (478-836-3825; www.robertacrawfordchamber.org), 38 Wright Avenue, Roberta 31078. Open 8:30–noon weekdays.

For information about Warner Robins, contact **Warner Robins Convention and Visitors Bureau–E. L. Greenway Welcome Center** (478-922-5100; 1-888-288-WRGA; www.warner-robins.org), 99 North First Street, Warner Robins 31093, located in the historic train depot. To learn more about visiting the air force base, contact the **Robins Air Force Base Visitors Center** (478-926-4208; events hotline recording 478-926-2137).

GETTING THERE *By air:* **Middle Georgia Regional Airport Macon** (478-788-3760; www.cityofmacon.net/CityDept/aviation.htm), 1000 Terminal Drive, Macon, is serviced by Delta's **Atlantic Southeast Airlines**. Car rentals are available on-site from **Alamo/National** (478-788-5385), **Avis** (478-788-3840), **Budget** (478-784-7130), **Enterprise** (478-784-8633), and **Hertz** (478-788-3600). Because Macon is so close to Atlanta, however, most travelers would rather use **Hartsfield-Jackson Atlanta International Airport** (see What's Where in Georgia). If flying into Atlanta, visitors can rent a car from numerous vendors on-site at the airport and off-site (see What's Where in Georgia).

By bus: **Greyhound Lines** (478-743-2868; www.greyhound.com), provides service to Macon at 65 Spring Street. There is also a Greyhound station in Warner Robins (478-329-1614), 522 North Davis Drive. **Georgia Trailways** (478-743-8489), 448 Pine Street, links Macon with regional destinations.

By car: Access to Macon is extremely easy by either I-75 from the north and south or I-16 from the east—both of which intersect in Macon.

By train: The closest rail service is **Amtrak** (1-800-872-7245; www.amtrak.com) to Atlanta (see What's Where in Georgia). Greyhound, however, does have connecting service to Amtrak from its station (see *By bus,* above).

GETTING AROUND Intracity bus service is offered by **Macon–Bibb County Transit Authority** (478-746-1318; www.mta-mac.com), which operates 20 buses in the city, including the **Macon Intown Trolley Service.** The trolley provides a 25-minute minibus tour of downtown Macon. A real bargain at 25¢, the trolley allows on-and-off privileges.

MEDICAL EMERGENCY For life-threatening emergencies, call 911. For something less serious, care is available in Macon at the **Medical Center of Central Georgia** (478-633-1353), 777 Hemlock Street. In Warner Robins, care is available at **Houston Medical Center** (478-922-4281; www.hhc.org), 1601 Watson Boulevard. In Perry, care is available at **Perry Hospital** (478-987-3600; www .hhc.org), 1120 Morningside Drive.

VILLAGES AND NEIGHBORHOODS Macon has numerous historic neighborhoods. **Ingleside Village,** Ingleside Avenue between Rogers and Corbin avenues, is becoming known as Antiques Alley with its collection of quaint shops (see *Selective Shopping*).

Pleasant Hill Historic District, bounded by College, Neal, Rogers, and Vineville streets, was one of the first African American neighborhoods in the country to be listed on the National Register of Historic Places. It was the childhood home of "Little Richard" Penniman, the "Architect of Rock and Roll."

Fort Valley, the county seat of Peach County, Georgia's youngest county, is known for camellias, peaches, and pecans. In fact, Fort Valley—which would be named Fox Valley if not for a mistake made by the U.S. Postal Service in Washington—is known as "the Peach Capital of Georgia." Peach season is May through August, while pecan season runs October through January. William Tecumseh Sherman and his Union troops bypassed Fort Valley on the March to the Sea, so the historic district features homes from that period. The city's cemetery contains grave markers of both Confederate and Union soldiers.

Perry, named for naval hero Oliver Hazard Perry, is known as the crossroads of Georgia because of its central location, where three major state and federal highways (I-75, US 341, and US 41, which parallels I-75) intersect and the Golden Isles Parkway begins. The small city, three hours from the north Georgia mountains and three hours from the coast, is featured on three state tourism trails: the **Antiques Trail**, the **Peachblossom Trail**, and the **Andersonville Trail**. An agricultural center, Perry is also the site of the **Georgia National Fair** (see *Special Events*) and numerous sporting competitions.

Roberta was the site of the first Indian agency on the Flint River and the burial place of the first Indian agent, Benjamin Hawkins. Roberta is also the home of Georgia's oldest continuously operating peach-packing operation, where several automation processes were first introduced. Botanist William Bartram discovered the oak-leaf hydrangea near the small town, and Roberta's unique position on Georgia's Piedmont fall line encouraged a thriving pottery industry in the 1800s and 100 years of sand mining.

Warner Robins is the home of the Air Logistics Center at Robins Air Force Base, Georgia's largest single employer. The center is Georgia's largest industrial complex and one of only three such centers in the country. Both the town and Air Force base were named for Brigadier General Augustine Warner Robins. A fast-growing aviation museum also calls the town home.

✳ To See

CULTURAL SITES ✐ ✇ ♿ **Georgia Music Hall of Fame** (478-750-8555; 1-888-GAROCKS; www.gamusichall.com), 200 Martin Luther King Jr. Boulevard, Macon. Open 9–5 Monday through Saturday, 1–5 Sunday. Georgia and Macon's rich musical heritage is explored at this state-of-the-art museum, which is the state's official music museum. Permanent collections and regularly changing exhibits of music memorabilia as well as interactive shows cover the lives and careers of more than 450 artists, all of whom were born in Georgia, lived in Georgia, began their careers in Georgia, or contributed to the musical life of Georgia.

Since 1979, more than 80 artists have been inducted into the hall of fame. The lives of Macon artists such as "Little Richard" Penniman, Otis Redding, Lena Horne, and the Allman brothers are highlighted along with many, many others. In Tune Town, the main exhibit hall, vintage rooms devoted to every genre from classical to rhythm and blues to country explore a particular style through instruments, costumes, photographs, videos, audio landscapes, photos, posters, and other artifacts. The Music Factory Children's Wing has many interactive exhibits that introduce youngsters to the world of music.

In the interactive Gretsch Theater, audience members vote to choose videos from various musical genres. The newest exhibit is "the Great Gretsch Sound," a large array of Gretsch guitars and drums, which are manufactured by Fred Gretsch Enterprises in Pooler, Georgia. Among the historic and current instruments are the type used by Chet Atkins, George Harrison, Brian Setzer, and other guitarists and drums such as those used by Charlie Watts of the Rolling Stones. Naturally, the museum store carries a wide variety of CDs and cassette recordings as well as other music-themed clothing and gift items. Adults $8, seniors and students with ID $6, children 4–16 $3.50, children younger than 4 free.

MACON IS HOME TO THE GEORGIA MUSIC HALL OF FAME.

FOR FAMILIES ✐ ✇ ♿ **Georgia National Fairgrounds and Agricenter** (478-987-3247; 1-800-987-

3247; www.gnfa.com), 401 Larry Walker Parkway, Perry. Call for a schedule of events and prices. The premier event at this vast multipurpose facility is October's **Georgia National Fair** (see *Special Events*), which attracts 360,000 visitors, but other events include concerts, horse shows, livestock competitions, rodeos, RV rallies, and sporting events. The parklike setting with a fountain, lakes, gardens, and picnic facilities invites visitors to stop by even when no events are in progress. Admission to complex free.

GUIDED TOURS ♂ **Around Town Tours of Historic Macon** (478-743-3401; 1-800-768-3401; www.maconga.org), 200 Cherry Street, Macon. Open 10–6 Monday through Saturday. This is an easy way to visit Macon's mansions, museums, and other attractions. The Downtown Tour visits three attractions all in the same block. You can tour four more by hopping on the Intown Trolley, which loops around town all day and has on-and-off privileges, so you can tour at your leisure. Depending on tour, adults $15, youth $9; combination tour: adults $29, children $16.50.

HISTORIC HOMES AND SITES ♠ **Anderson House Museum** (478-825-6475), 1005 State University Drive, Fort Valley. Open 10–4 Monday, Wednesday, and Friday. Formerly the home for the president of Fort Valley State University, which began as a black land-grant school and is now a research institution, the residence is now a house museum furnished in the style of the late 1800s. The Biggs Collection is one of the finest accumulations from the turn of the 20th century—so fine, in fact, that it was sought by the Smithsonian. Free.

♠ ᘗ **Cannonball House and Civil War Museum** (478-745-5982; www.cannonballhouse.org), 856 Mulberry Street, Macon. Open 10–5 Monday through Saturday. There's a lot to see here, but the house is named for the 12-pound nonexplosive cannonball that crashed into it during the Civil War in 1864, coming to rest on the hall floor, where you can still see it today. In fact, the house had the dubious distinction of being the only one hit in Macon during the halfhearted attack by Union troops. A stereotypical white-columned Southern Greek Revival, the gracious home built in 1853 is filled with period antiques. Two rooms are furnished as replicas of chambers at Old Wesleyan College, the first woman's college in the country and home of the first national sorority. The adjacent brick kitchen and servants' quarters building is a repository for Civil War artifacts, including several that purportedly belonged to Mrs. Robert E. Lee. Call ahead so that staff can set up ramp over back stairs; no access to second floor. Adults $5, seniors and military $4, students $1, children younger than 6 free.

♠ ᘗ **Hay House** (478-742-8155; www.hayhouse.org), 934 Georgia Avenue, Macon. Open 10–5 Monday through Saturday, 1–5 Sunday (last tour at 4). One of Macon's most magnificent houses, the 18,000-square-foot Hay House is a prime example of the Italian Renaissance Revival style. Known as the "Palace of the South," it was built between 1855 and 1859 by William Butler Johnston, who later became the keeper of the Confederate treasury. The mansion has been featured on the A&E Channel series *America's Castles*. Amazingly, the grand home was occupied by only two families throughout its history before it was acquired by the Georgia Trust for Historic Preservation. Nearly fully restored, the house displays numerous examples of the exquisite workmanship of the period when it was built, such as 12-foot-high, 500-pound front doors; 16- and 30-foot ceilings; carved Carerra marble mantelpieces, ornately embossed cornices, medallions, and moldings; stained glass; marbleized faux finishes; and intricate trompe l'oeil wall and ceiling paintings. At the time of its construction, the Hay House incorporated such then-unheard-of amenities as indoor plumbing, walk-in closets, an elevator, an intercom, and the best ventilation system ever designed for an American home until the invention of air-conditioning. Eighteen rooms are filled with sumptuous 18th- and 19th-century antiques and objets d'art. Adults $8, seniors and military $7, children $4.

✒ 🐾 ♿ **Ocmulgee National Monument** (478-752-8257; www.nps.gov/ocmu), 1207 Emery Highway, Macon. Open 9–5 daily except Christmas and New Year's Day. Seven impressive temple and burial mounds from the Mississippian Period (A.D. 900 to 1100), the tallest of which is 45 feet tall, remain on the 683-acre historic site. A ceremonial earth lodge where tribal political and religious meetings were held has been reconstructed on the original 1,000-year-old floor. The interpretive center features artifacts such as axes, clay pipes, beads, knives, and other weapons from the six distinct Native American groups that occupied the site as well as later traders. A film traces Native American history in the area over 12,000 years. The park also features 5 miles of walking trails (see *To Do—Hiking*), and visitors can stomp their feet to the primitive beat of Native American ceremonial dances each September at the **Ocmulgee Indian Celebration** (see *Special Events*). Free.

EXPLORE NATIVE AMERICAN TRADITIONS AND SITES AT THE OCMULGEE NATIONAL MONUMENT IN MACON.

🐾 ♿ **Sidney Lanier Cottage** (478-743-3851; www.historicmacon.org), 935 High Street, Macon. Open 10–4 Monday through Saturday (last tour at 3:30). Famous Southern poet and musician Sidney Lanier was born in 1842 in this house, the home of his grandparents. Despite his fame as the author of the poems *The Marshes of Glynn* and *Song of the Chattahoochee*, Lanier was also a linguist, mathematician, musician, and lawyer. He served in the Confederate Army and was captured and imprisoned by the Union. It was during his incarceration that he lost his health, which he never regained, and he died at age 31. At the cottage, see his writings, his flute, and even his bride's tiny wedding gown. Local historian Marty Willet often portrays Sidney. Adults $5, seniors and active military $4, children 6–18 $3, children under 6 free.

MUSEUMS ✧ ✦ ✧ **Byron Depot** (478-956-3600; www.byronga.com), 101 East Heritage Boulevard, Byron. Call for hours. The town's 1870 railroad depot reputedly saw more area-grown peaches shipped through it on a daily basis in the 1920s and 1930s than anywhere else in the world. The depot, once abandoned, has been restored to its turn-of-the-20th-century appearance and now serves as a small museum that contains a pictorial history of the town as well as historical memorabilia about trains. The caboose houses model train exhibits. Keys are available at Byron City Hall or the Byron Convention and Visitors Bureauee (see *Guidance*). Free.

✧ ✦ ✧ **Georgia Children's Museum** (478-755-9539; www.georgiachildrens museum.org), 382 Cherry Street and Martin Luther King Jr. Boulevard, Macon. Open 9:30–5 Tuesday through Saturday, noon–5 Sunday. Macon's newest attraction, which opened its first two floors in April 2005 and another in the fall of 2006, completes a collection of museums adjacent to the Union Terminal Welcome Center—joining the **Georgia Music Hall of Fame** (see *Cultural Sites*) and the **Georgia Sports Hall of Fame,** and soon to be joined by the **Tubman African American Museum** (see separate entries below). The historic **Douglass Theatre** (see *Entertainment—Theater*) is nearby, making the area a one-stop entertainment district. Everywhere in the children's museum are colorful murals of children at play and engaged in learning activities, each painted by artist Arrin Freeman. What will be a six-floor museum already features the **Riverside Ford Theatre for Young Audiences**—a black-box theater where professional and amateur performances are held, as well as theatrical arts exhibits. Separate floors are devoted to interactive exhibits. In addition, a café and ice cream shop provide a welcome break. After-school, school break, and summer programs are offered (see *To Do—Day Camps*). Admission $5, but subject to change.

✧ ✦ ✧ **Georgia Sports Hall of Fame** (478-752-1585; www.georgiasportshall offame.com), 301 Cherry Street, Macon. Open 9–5 Monday through Saturday, 1–5 Sunday. Exhibits honor high school, college, amateur, professional, and Olympic teams and individuals as well as legendary coaches. Baseball's Hank Aaron, boxing's Evander Holyfield, golf's Bobby Jones and Nancy Lopez, racing's Bill Elliott, and football's Herschel Walker are just a few athletic superstars to call Georgia home. Their exploits and those of many others are showcased at America's largest sports hall of fame. Displays, audiovisual presentations, and interactive games, where you can exercise your body and your mind, keep visitors busy. Adults $8, children 6–16 $3.50.

✧ ✦ ✧ **Museum of Arts and Sciences** (478-477-3232; www.masmacon.com), 4182 Forsyth Road, Macon. Open 9–8 Monday, 9–5 Tuesday through Saturday, 1–5 Sunday. Daily shows: live animals at 3, planetarium at 4; check about extra shows. This is a place for families—particularly those with young children—to discover the world. The "arts" side permits visitors to examine the beauty of original works of art in changing and permanent exhibits, including the Gunn

Collection of Boehm Porcelains. On the "sciences" side, visitors can journey to outer space in the planetarium; see live tamarind monkeys and parrots in an enclosed animal habitat with a replica of a giant banyan tree; watch and identify birds at the bird-watching window; experience hands-on adventures in the three-story Discovery House, which includes an artist's garret, a humanist's study, a globe room, Poet's Corner, and a scientist's workshop; and hike the nature trails on the 18-acre property to see a turn-of-the-20th-century caboose, a historic cabin, and several outdoor sculptures. The star of the museum is a 40 million-year-old whale-skeleton fossil found in the area, which would indicate that Macon was once close to the sea. The **Mark Smith Planetarium** offers daily galaxy shows in a 40-foot dome. On clear Friday nights, visitors can view the real night sky from the **Observatory**. The museum's recent affiliation with the Smithsonian Institution will enable the facility to get important traveling exhibitions. Adults $7, seniors $6, students 12 and older $5, children 2–11 $4.

✎ 🐾 ♿ **Tubman African American Museum** (478-743-8544; www.tubman museum.com), 340 Walnut Street, Macon. Open 9–5 Monday through Saturday, 2–5 Sunday. Named in honor of Harriett Tubman, mastermind of the Civil War Underground Railroad, the museum is the state's largest museum devoted to African American history and culture. What began as a grassroots effort to recognize the triumphs of blacks has grown to the extent that the museum garners international recognition. The museum devotes 14 exhibition galleries to the journey and accomplishments of African Americans from Africa to modern America and includes the esteemed Noel Collection of African art. Among the most fascinating exhibits are those devoted to inventions of African Americans. In the Inventors Room, you'll learn about the African American creators of the automated traffic signal, barbed harpoon, corn planter, eye dropper, fire extinguisher, gas mask, goggles, horseshoes, ironing board, lawn sprinkler, linoleum, oxygen tanks, postal letter box, a precursor of the riding lawnmower, and the wildly popular Super Soaker. You'll also hear about African Americans who contributed to the invention of the first electric lights and the first open-heart surgery. Art includes paintings, tapestries, carved ivory, masks, and textiles from Africa. Permanent collections are augmented by touring national and international exhibitions. The museum is also home to the Pan African Festival. Adults $5, children $3.

✎ 🐾 ♿ **U.S. Air Force Museum of Aviation–Georgia Aviation Hall of Fame** (478-926-6870; 1-888-807-3359; www.museumofaviation.org), US 129/GA 247 South and Russell Parkway, Warner Robins. Open 9–5 daily. Visitors' spirits will soar at the indoor-outdoor Museum of Aviation, the fastest-growing aviation museum in the Southeast and the country's fourth-largest aviation museum. It's "Just PLANE Fun!" to tour the more than 200,000 square feet of space in four buildings filled with interactive exhibits and historical displays of more than 90 military aircraft. The oldest aircraft is an 1896 glider; outstanding modern aircraft include the F-15A and the SR-71 Blackbird, the fastest plane on earth. Exhibits focus on World War II, Korea, Desert Storm, the Flying Tigers, Tuskegee Airmen, and China-Burma-India Hump pilots. In the "Footsteps of Giants" display, the lives of famous Georgians are examined: President Jimmy

Carter, United Nations Ambassador Andrew Young, Congressman Carl Vinson, and Senators Walter F. George, Herman Tallmadge, and Sam Nunn. Films are shown continuously in the **Robert L. Scott Vistascope Theater**. The Hall of Fame commemorates the careers of distinguished men and women who have made significant contributions to aviation in Georgia, such as Ben Epps Sr., the first man to fly in Georgia; Jacques Ballard, the first African American military aviator; and Robert L. Scott, World War II ace and author of *God Is My Co-Pilot*. In the Heritage Building, "Windows to the Distant Past," a sight-and-sound exhibit, explores the cultures of Native Americans. Have lunch in the Victory Café and watch planes take off at Robins Air Force Base next door. Free.

SPECIAL PLACES ✿ **Rose Hill Cemetery** (478-743-3401; 1-800-768-3401; www.gabba.org/rosehill.htm), 1091 Riverside Drive, Macon. Open daylight hours. A beautiful example of the Victorian park movement, the 65-acre cemetery is one of the oldest memorial parks in the nation, having been founded in 1840, just 17 years after Macon. It is named for its founder, Simri Rose, whose ornate grave is in the cemetery. The burial ground's opulent monuments, mausoleums, and vaults mark the final resting places of many famous Macon residents, including three Georgia governors, two U.S. senators, a congressman, and 31 Macon mayors. The graveyard has Jewish, Catholic, Protestant, and African American sections. The Confederate section contains the remains of more than 600 Civil War soldiers, reinterred here from the places where they fell in battle.

THE GRAVE OF JOHN B. ROSS JUHAN IS ONE OF THE POIGNANT MARKERS AT THE ROSE HILL CEMETERY.

The graves that attract the most interest, however, are those of rock and roll legends Duane Allman and Berry Oakley. Both members of the Allman Brothers Band, they were killed in separate motorcycle accidents in 1971 and 1972 near the same spot. They rest side by side on a tranquil terrace overlooking the Ocmulgee River, where they often came in life to smoke and drink and look for inspiration for their songs. In the past, visitors who came to pay their respects and read the flowery inscriptions on their gravestones often left liquor, cigarettes, and beer in tribute. Today, the grave sites are watched over and protected by Berry's sister, Candace, who is often there to make sure the graves are properly honored. Also in the cemetery are the graves of "Little Martha" and "Elizabeth Reed," both of whom were mentioned in the band's songs.

Also memorialized at the cemetery is Lieutenant Bobby, a dog that President Calvin Coolidge allowed to remain in the military with his master even after the little dog's useful military life was over. Tragically, Lieutenant Bobby met an unexpected demise when he fell down an elevator shaft in a Macon hotel in 1936. He's buried among the human dead with a proper headstone. Six years later, when his master, D. C. Harris Jr. died, he was laid to rest next to his dog.

One of the most poignant memorials is that of John B. Ross, the eight-year-old son of W. A. and Elizabeth Jane Juhan. Little John wanted to be a fireman when he grew up, and he spent so much time at Defiance Company No. 5 that he was made their mascot. His touching gravestone was created to look as though it is draped with his child-sized fireman's cape, hat, and belt.

The steeply terraced cemetery gives beautiful views of the river and the Ocmulgee Heritage Trail on the other side. Guided walking tours are given periodically, but participants should be forewarned about how steep some of the hills are. Cars can drive around most of the cemetery, but the roads are narrow. Free.

✳ To Do

AUTO RACING ✎ **Silver Dollar Raceway** (478-847-4414; www.silverdollarraceway.com), GA 96 West, Reynolds. Open weekends, January through November. The quarter-mile National Hot Rod Association–sanctioned drag strip sponsors turn-and-test events and quarter-mile points series races. Call for a schedule of events and prices.

DAY CAMPS ✎ **Camp Discovery** is sponsored by the **Museum of Arts and Sciences** (478-477-3232; www.masmacon.com), 4182 Forsyth Road, Macon. Hours 9–4 weekdays. Children ages 4–10 experience the entire museum through arts and crafts and hands-on exhibits. Full-day rates for the week: $110 members, $130 nonmembers; half-day rates for the week (9–noon or 1–4); $60 members, $80 nonmembers.

The ✎ **Georgia Children's Museum** (478-755-9539; www.georgiachildresmuseum.org), 382 Cherry Street, Macon, offers a **Summer Camp,** which runs from the end of May through July and meets 7:30–6 weekdays. Children age 6–12 are invited to participate. $80 per week per child plus $45 one-time registration fee; drop-ins $20 per day. The **First Street Arts Center** (478-745-0844) next door, associated with the children's museum, offers a program with the same rates and times. Both include exploration of art, theater, journalism, cooking, creative writing, and magic, to name just a few.

FACTORY TOURS ✎ 🍑 ♿ **Lane Packing Company** (478-825-3592; 1-800-27-PEACH; www.lanepacking.com), 50 Lane Road, Fort Valley. Open 8–8 daily September through mid-May, 9–5 daily mid-May through August. The fourth-generation, family-owned company grows 30 varieties of peaches and 10 kinds of pecans, as well as strawberries and asparagus. During the peach season mid-May through August, the state-of-the-art packing facility is bustling with activity as peaches are harvested, cleaned, sorted, boxed, and shipped. Inside, the self-guided plant tour shows how more than 300,000 peaches per hour are carefully weighed, counted, separated, and packed to prevent bruising. Visitors can get a bird's-eye view of the operation from overhead walkways. A guided tram tour takes visitors through acres and acres of peach and pecan orchards; reservations suggested. You may want to have lunch at the Peachtree Café, but for sure you'll want to enjoy some peach cobbler or peach ice cream. Shop for Southern gifts and Georgia food items in the Just Peachy Gift Shop, or buy some fruit or nuts to take home from the roadside market. Visitors can pick their own strawberries March through May; pecan season is October through January. The company also has a full-service mail order department. Facility wheelchair accessible, but tram difficult for those who can't stand or step up into it. Self-guided tours free; tram tours $5.

FOR FAMILIES ✔ ♿ **DJ's Galaxy Quest** (478-329-8002), 815 Russell Parkway, Warner Robins. Open 11–8 Thursday, 11–10 Friday and Saturday, 1–8 Sunday. Other hours available for private parties. The facility's activities include miniature golf, laser tag, and a roller coaster, to name just a few. Rates are based on each child's age and activity level. Average for three hours of entertainment about $15 per child.

✔ **Starcadia Entertainment Park** (478-475-9880; www.starcadia.net), 150 Starcadia Circle, Macon. Open year-round. Hours vary by season and event, so call ahead or visit the web site for specifics. Six acres filled with Go-Karts, blaster boats, a rock-climbing wall, miniature golf, race cars, a bungee trampoline high jump, billiard tables, and an indoor arcade provide plenty of fun for active families. Entry to park free, individual charges for rides and games; during wristband events, all-inclusive rates $10–20.

FRUIT AND BERRY PICKING ✔ 🍑 **Big 6 Farm** (478-825-7504; www.big6farm .com), 5575 Zenith Mill Road, Fort Valley. Open May through August, 8–6 Monday through Saturday; November through January, 8–5 weekdays. The second-largest peach grower in the county, Big 6 Farm allows visitors to pick their own succulent fruit. Prices vary according to crop conditions.

✔ 🍑 **Taylor Orchards** (478-847-4186; www.taylororchards.com), GA 96, Reynolds. Call for hours. Pick your own strawberries April 1 through May 30, and purchase just-picked peaches mid-May through July 31. Fresh ice cream, too. Prices vary.

See also **Lane Packing Company** under *Factory Tours*.

GOLF See Golf Appendix.

HIKING ✔ 🍃 **Ocmulgee National Monument** (478-752-8257; www.nps.gov/ ocmu), 1207 Emery Highway, Macon. Open 9–5 year-round except Christmas and New Year's Day. Five easy trails, together covering almost 6 miles, crisscross the historic site and offer opportunities to view deer and other four-legged critters, as well as ducks and water birds. The longest path is the Human Cultural Trail. At 4 miles in length, it focuses on the Indian mounds (see *To See—Historic Homes and Sites*). The mile-long River Trail leads naturally enough to the Ocmulgee River. Along the 0.4-mile Wildflower Trail, visitors may see wildlife as well as wildflowers. The 0.3-mile Loop Trail meets the 0.25-mile Opelofa Trail, which circles swampy lowland. Free.

TENNIS See Other Activities Appendix.

WALKING TOURS ♠ **Lights on Macon** is a self-guided walking tour past 33 mansions dramatically lit in a nighttime display of Southern grandeur that bathes each mansion in a warm glow. Get a walking tour brochure from the welcome center so you can follow the route and learn something about the various architectural gems. Free.

✳ Green Space

GARDENS ✍ ♠ ৬ **American Camellia Society–Massee Lane Gardens–Annabelle Lundy Fetterman Educational Museum** (478-967-2358; www .camellias-acs.com), 100 Massee Lane, Fort Valley. Open 10–4:30 Tuesday through Saturday, 1–4:30 Sunday. Guided tours by reservation. Naturally, the stars in this 9-acre garden on the grounds of the headquarters of the American Camellia Society are the 2,000 camellia bushes that bloom from late fall to early spring. Red, white, pink, and variegated blooms are spectacular from October through March. Other flowers, however, are not neglected. Seasonal flora is found in the Kitty Frank Daffodil Garden, the Marvin Jernigan Native Azalea Garden, and the Scheibert Rose Garden. Daylilies, annuals, perennials, and chrysanthemums are featured in their seasons.

In addition, the Brown and Hall Environmental Garden showcases plants indigenous to the Southeast, and the peaceful Abendroth Japanese Garden features a koi pond. The landscaped greenhouse contains camellias, azaleas, and other plants.

This garden began in the 1930s as the private garden of David C. Strother. In addition to planting his flowers and flowering shrubs, he collected millstones from corn-grinding mills in middle Georgia and old wire mile markers, which can still be seen around the garden. He donated the property to the American Camellia Society in 1966. An orientation slide show informs visitors about camellias and the garden.

Within the gardens, the **Stevens-Taylor** and the **Fetterman Museum galleries** contain the world's largest public display of Edward Marshall Boehm porcelain sculptures of birds and flowers. Also on display are porcelains created by Connoisseur, Cybis, and other world-renowned studios.

The newest attraction is the Children's Garden, where the small fry can dig for "fossils," play in the playground, or run to their heart's content while Mom and Dad relax in old-fashioned swings. Special events at the garden include the **Festival of Camellias** throughout February (see *Special Events*) and the Daylily

Extravaganza throughout June. Adults $5, seniors $4, children younger than 12 free.

NATURE PRESERVES AND PARKS ✐ ✿ ♿ **Freedom Park** (478-751-9248), 3301 Roff Avenue, Macon. Open 9 AM–10 PM weekdays, noon–5 Saturday. Twenty-seven acres of recreational facilities include a 7-acre lake stocked with bass, bream, channel catfish, crappie, and other species. It is open to licensed anglers April through October. In addition, the park sports a game room, playground, softball and baseball fields, and a swimming pool. General admission free; swimming pool $1.

✐ ✿ ♿ **Ocmulgee Heritage Trail, Gateway Park** (478-722-9909; www.new townmacon.com/ocmulgee-heritage-trail.htm), New Town Macon, 479 Cherry Street, Macon. This 2-mile, flat, paved path on the banks of the Ocmulgee River is popular with walkers, joggers, and in-line skaters. When complete, the trail will stretch 10 miles from the **Ocmulgee National Monument** (see *To See— Historic Homes and Sites*) to the Old Waterworks Park. At the entrance, visitors will find the **Otis Redding Statue.** The life-sized bronze statue of the legendary singer-songwriter of "Sittin' on the Dock of the Bay" fame sits on a set of pilings overlooking the river, holding a guitar, pen, and paper. It's not difficult to imagine where inspiration for this hit song came from.

RECREATION AREAS ✐ ✿ ♿ **Lake Tobesofkee Recreation Area** (478-474-8770; www.maconga.org), 6600 Mosely Dixon Road, Macon. Open 6–10 daily. Surrounding a 1,750-acre lake with 35 miles of shoreline boasting three white-sand beaches, the recreation area actually contains Arrowhead Park, Sandy Beach Park, and Claystone Park, which among them offer boat ramps, picnicking, playgrounds, and tennis. There is also a full-service marina and a lakeside restaurant. Fishing for several types of bass, bream, catfish, and crappie; boating; camping; and swimming are also popular pastimes. A well-liked annual event is the Arrowhead Arts and Crafts Festival each October. Day use $3, camping $15.

✴ Lodging

BED & BREAKFASTS

In Macon

♿ **1842 Inn** (478-747-1842; 1-800-336-1842; www.1842inn.com), 353 College Avenue. Luxurious AAA four-diamond accommodations are offered in this antebellum Greek Revival mansion and its Victorian-era cottage. Set in one of the city's most beautiful and best preserved historic neighborhoods, the imposing residence boasts a huge veranda with 18 soaring columns. All of the opulent guest rooms feature antiques, artwork, ornate beds, and a writing desk. Some boast a working fireplace and/or a whirlpool tub. Afternoon refreshments and a delicious breakfast are highlights of each day. No smoking. Some rooms wheelchair accessible. $230 plus 10 percent service charge; see web site for special discounts.

In Perry
Swift Street Bed and Breakfast (478-988-9148; 1-877-607-7794; www.bbonline.com/ga/swiftstreet), 1204 Swift Street. At this intimate, two-bedroom B&B, guests are delighted

to find a fireplace in one room and a whirlpool in the other. Smoking allowed on large front porch with comfortable rocking chairs. Not wheelchair accessible. $85–110 includes full breakfast and afternoon snack.

CAMPGROUNDS

In Macon

✍ 🐾 🏕 **Lake Tobesofkee Recreation Area** (478-474-8770; www.co.bibb.ga.us/laketobesofkee), 6600 Moseley Dixon Road. Amenities include boating, fishing, camping, lighted tennis courts, a playground, white-sand beach, covered picnic pavilions, and a softball field. Pets allowed, but must be kept leashed. $15–18 per campsite.

In Perry

✍ 🐾 **Fair Harbor RV Park** (478-988-8844; 1-877-988-8844; www.fairharborrvpark.com), 515 Marshallville Road. Camp around a fishing pond among 100 shady acres located adjacent to the Georgia National Fairgrounds and Agricenter. $24 per campsite, additional $2.50 for high-speed Internet connection.

INNS AND HOTELS

In Macon

✍ 🏕 ♿ **Crowne Plaza Macon** (478-746-1461; 1-800-227-6963; www.crowneplaza.com), 108 First Street. The upscale, high-rise Crowne Plaza offers 200 guest rooms with all the modern conveniences as well as concierge services, a pool, sauna, fitness center, restaurant, café, bar, and lounge. Smoking and nonsmoking rooms available. Wheelchair accessible. Pet friendly. $94–119.

In Perry

✍ 🐾 ♿ **New Perry Hotel** (478-987-1000; 1-800-877-3779; www.newperryhotel.com), 800 Main Street. Although it was built in 1925 and the newest rooms added in 1956, it's called the New Perry Hotel because it's built on the site of the original 1870s hostelry, Cox's Inn, which was built as a stagecoach stop. Before the advent of interstate highways, the hotel was on a major route to Florida, and travelers planned their itinerary to stay or eat a meal here. Guest rooms are offered in the main hotel and a poolside annex. Even today, for lots of folks, it's the dining room that brings them here (see *Where to Eat—Eating Out*). Recently the hotel has been named a National Historic Site. Smoking rooms available; no smoking in public areas or restaurants. Wheelchair accessible. $45–90.

RESORTS

In Perry

♿ **Henderson Village** (478-988-8696; 1-888-615-9722; www.hendersonvillage.com), 125 South Langston Circle. Scattered around 18 shady acres on this AAA four-diamond property are four stately 19th-century homes with sprawling verandas and white columns, as well as six simple tenant cottages—each containing luxurious guest accommodations with antique or reproduction furnishings, a gas-log fireplace, a claw-foot or jetted tub, and beautiful decorative accents. Twenty-four guest suites are offered in all. Naturally, the guest chambers in the homes are more formal than those in the tenant cottages. Delicious haute cuisine is served in the historic Langston House Restaurant (see *Where to Eat—Dining Out*). A lovely formal garden and a swimming pool are among other amenities on the property. Many sporting excursions can be arranged on the **Gamelands at Henderson Village,** an exceptional 3,400-acre hunting preserve of timberlands, pastures, and croplands. In addition to bird and wild game hunting, the facility offers five-stand sporting clays, pond and creek fishing for bass and bream, horseback riding, mule-drawn wagon rides, and hiking. No smoking. Wheelchair accessible. $175–300.

✳ Where to Eat

DINING OUT

In Macon

🦐 ♿ **Bert's** (478-742-9100), 442 Cherry Street. Open 11:30–2 weekdays, 5:30–9 Wednesday through Saturday. Bert's is a charming place to dine in the downtown area. The lunch menu includes a large variety of salads and sandwiches. Dinner features seafood, chicken, veal, beef, and pasta. Save room for the delicious desserts. No smoking. Wheelchair accessible. Lunch $6–8; dinner $7–22.

♿ **Tic Toc Room** (478-744-0123), 408 Martin Luther King Jr. Boulevard. Open 4–10 Tuesday through Thursday, 4–11 Friday and Saturday. The upscale restaurant serves sophisticated Southern cuisine. Menu items include sushi, beef items, seafood, and creative chef's specials. Other enticements include an elaborate wine and martini list. Dress is business casual. Smoking permitted in bar. Wheelchair accessible. About $25.

EATING OUT

In Macon

🦐 🍴 ♿ **Fincher's Barbecue** (478-788-1900), 3947 Houston Avenue. Open 9–9 Monday through Saturday,

11–2 Sunday. The only barbecue to go into space with NASA, Fincher's serves up the flavor of the South and even has curb service. Smoking permitted. Wheelchair accessible. Around $6.50.

🦐 🍴 ♿ **H&H Restaurant** (478-742-9810), 807 Forsyth Street. Open 7–4 Monday through Saturday. Meat–and–three soul-food plates include enough meat, vegetables, bread, and a beverage to appease even the most voracious appetite. Back when the Allman Brothers Band was getting started and the band members didn't have more than a few dollars, they'd come in and place one order, and they'd all share it. When they got famous, they'd fly Mama Louise out to California to cook for them. The casual eatery is complete with a funky jukebox and memorabilia-covered walls. No smoking. Wheelchair accessible. $6–7.

🦐 ♿ **Len Berg's** (478-742-9255), 240 Post Office Alley. Open 11–2:30 weekdays. Southern home-cookin' specialties include salmon croquettes, mac and cheese, fresh vegetables, homemade rolls, fried oysters or catfish, and macaroon pie. Len Berg's

GUESTS CAN RELAX IN THE LUXURIOUS ACCOMMODATIONS FOUND AT THE HENDERSON VILLAGE RESORT IN PERRY.

has been named one of Georgia's top 50 restaurants by *Georgia Trend* magazine. No smoking. Wheelchair accessible. $5–7 (no credit cards).

🐾 🍴 ♿ **Nu-Way Weiners** (478-743-1368; www.nu-wayweiners.com), 430 Cotton Avenue. Open 6 AM–7 PM weekdays, 7 AM–6 PM Saturday. An institution in this location and sporting the same neon sign since 1916, this hot-doggery is one of the two oldest hot dog stands in the country. The restaurant purveys private-label pork and beef wieners, secret-recipe chili, burgers, and sandwiches. The signature dog is dressed with mustard, onions, the aforementioned chili, and barbecue sauce, but if that combination isn't to your liking, you can have it your way. It's obvious why their slogan, "I'd go a long way for a Nu-Way," has stuck for nearly 90 years. Note that the dictionary spells franks "wiener," but Nu-Way spells it "weiner." Who can argue with success? No smoking. Wheelchair accessible. Under $5.

🍴 ♿ **Willow on Fifth Restaurant** (478-745-9007; www.willowonfifth .com), 325 Fifth Street. Open 11–3 and 5–8 daily. Feast on the best of traditional Southern cooking at this sister restaurant to the world-famous Blue Willow Inn in Social Circle. You'll find a bountiful buffet of meats, vegetables, fruits, salads, and desserts. No smoking. Wheelchair accessible. $8.95 includes beverage.

In Perry
♿ **Langston House Restaurant** (478-988-8696; 1-888-615-9722; www .hendersonvillage.com), 125 South Langston Circle. Open 7–10:30 and 11–2:30 daily, 6–9 Sunday through Thursday, 6–10 Friday and Saturday. Located in a 19th-century house in

the historic Henderson Village resort (see *Lodging—Resorts*), the restaurant serves three meals a day except dinner on Sunday. For dinner, guests might be treated to such specialties as barbecued salmon, rack of lamb, or sea bass. Favorites include breakfast sandwiches, fried catfish, and chicken specialties. No smoking. Wheelchair accessible. Breakfast prices vary, lunch about $12, dinner $40.

🐾 🍴 ♿ **The Restaurant at the New Perry Hotel** (478-218-7701; 1-800-877-3779), 800 Main Street. Open 11:30–2 Tuesday through Saturday, 5–9 Tuesday through Thursday, 5–9:30 Friday and Saturday, brunch 11–3 Sunday. Fresh flowers from the hotel's year-round gardens embellish the white-starched tablecloths. The menu is typical Southern comfort food. Visitors can expect dishes such as chopped steak, mackerel, salmon croquettes, or turkey accompanied by a relish tray, salad, soup, and three vegetables. Save room for the pecan pie. No smoking. Wheelchair accessible. Lunch about $10, dinner about $20.

For more casual dining, the hotel also offers the **Tavery.** Open 5–9:30 Monday through Thursday, 5–10 Friday and Saturday, with a happy hour 5–6:30 each of those days. The Tavery has a full bar, an extensive wine list, a bar menu, and patio dining on the terrace. No smoking. Wheelchair accessible.

✳ Entertainment
MUSIC **Grand Opera House** (478-301-5460; www.mercer.edu/thegrand), 639 Mulberry Street, Macon. Open only for performances. Built in 1884 as the Academy of Music, the Grand Opera House boasts one of the largest

stages in the South—it's seven stories high. Over its many-year history, such superstars of the day as Burns and Allen, Houdini, Sarah Bernhardt, Bob Hope, and Will Rogers trod the boards here. Restored to its former opulence, the Grand now serves as the performing arts center for **Mercer University** and hosts performances by the **Macon Symphony Orchestra** (see below), Broadway touring companies, and other arts and cultural events. Call for a schedule of events and prices.

Macon City Auditorium (478-752-8400), 415 First Street, Macon. The auditorium has the world's largest copper dome, and its proscenium displays a mural depicting Macon's leaders through history. The facility hosts bands and other performances. Call for a schedule of events and prices.

Macon Concert Association (478-477-3741; www.maconarts.org), Porter Auditorium, Wesleyan College, 4760 Forsyth Street, Macon. This all-volunteer organization, celebrating its 73rd season in 2006, sponsors four productions each year featuring international artists and ensembles. Programs include dance, classical music, and jazz. $15–20; call for specific performance information.

Macon Symphony Orchestra (478-301-5300; www.maconsymphony .com), offices: 400 Popular Street, Macon. The symphony presents six classical concerts, four pops concerts, and six Macon-Mercer Symphony Youth Orchestra concerts. Most regular subscription series concerts are presented at the Grand Opera House (see above), although sometimes they are performed at the City Auditorium (see above). Before the classical concerts, preconcert lectures led by Mae-

stro Adrian Gnam and featured guest artists are held in conjunction with a four-course dinner at the **Macon City Club** (478-738-9000; 355 First Avenue, fourth floor). $22.50 plus tax and tip; reservations must be made three days prior to concert. The symphony often performs in outlying areas such as Milledgeville, Fort Valley, Eatonton, Griffin, Hawkinsville, Warner Robins, and Henderson Village, so check schedules if you are going to be in those towns. A free outdoor Picnic Pops Concert is held at a downtown location with the youth orchestra. Call for a schedule of performances and ticket prices (usually adults $30, students with ID $15). Purchase tickets by calling box office or online at symphony's web site.

Mercer University (478-301-2700), 1400 Coleman Avenue, Macon. The Music Department presents numerous classical and jazz performances by faculty, students, and visiting artists. Call for performance schedule and prices.

✍ 🐌 **Powersville Opry** (478-953-1406), Powersville Road, Byron. Open 5–9:30 Saturday. Bluegrass, country, and gospel are played to standing-room-only crowds. You never know who might sit in with the musicians at this old store turned concert venue. Admission free, but donations welcome.

PROFESSIONAL SPORTS Macon Blaze (478-803-2700; www.the maconblaze.com), 200 Cherry Street, Macon. Part of the World Basketball Association, the Macon Blaze season runs late April through August. They are the hosts of the annual Black College All-Star game in April. Call for game schedules and ticket prices.

Macon Trax Hockey Club (478-743-6010; www.macontrax.com), offices: 433 Cherry Street, Suite A, Macon. Part of the Atlantic Coast Hockey League, the team plays home games at the Macon Centreplex sports arena from October to May. Call for schedule and prices.

THEATER Douglass Theatre (478-742-2000; www.douglasstheatre.org), 355 Martin Luther King Jr. Boulevard, Macon. Open 10–5 weekdays. A significant African American theater built in 1921, the Douglass hosted such performers as Count Basie, Cab Calloway, Ma Rainey, and Bessie Smith. Otis Redding was discovered here, and Little Richard and Godfather of Soul James Brown performed here as well, but the theater closed in 1972 and slumbered for 20 years before renovations began. Beautifully restored, the state-of-the-art theater now hosts 3-D films, live musical and theatrical performances, and meetings. Call for schedule and prices. Donations accepted for tours.

Macon Little Theater (478-477-3342; 478-471-7529), 4220 Forsyth Road, Macon. Located adjacent to the Museum of Arts and Sciences. Yearly productions include at least one musical and a tribute to Patsy Cline. Funded entirely by membership and private donations. Call for a schedule of productions. Adults $16, seniors $14, students $11.

Perry Players Community Theatre (478-987-5354; www.perryplayers .org), 909 Main Street, Perry. The Perry Players, performing since 1962, put on three or four productions each year and are housed in a renovated horse barn. Entirely self-supporting through private donations. Call for

information about their annual summer youth workshop. Adults $10, students and seniors $6.

Theater Macon (478-477-9485), offices: 434 Cherry Street, Macon. During the regular season, the organization presents seven productions. The Stage Two Season has weekend productions, one-act plays, poetry readings, and cabaret acts. Call for a performance schedule and prices.

Warner Robins Little Theatre (478-929-4579; www.wrlt.org), 502 South Pleasant Hill Road, Warner Robins. This busy little theater hosts five performances per season. Call for schedule of performances. Season pass $50; individual tickets $12.

✳ Selective Shopping

Ingleside Village Shopping and Arts District (478-743-3401; 1-800-768-3401), Ingleside Avenue, Macon. The district is a trendy area filled with art galleries and specialty shops that purvey antiques, books, clothing, gifts, and home accents.

ANTIQUES Big Peach Antique Mall and Welcome Center (478-956-6256), 119 Peach Parkway, Byron. Open 10–7 Monday through Saturday, noon–6 Sunday. Instantly identifiable from I-75 because of its towering peach (not counting the pedestal, the giant peach measures 75 feet from stem to tip and is 28 feet in diameter), this mall offers 230 dealers selling antiques, collectibles, china, and other fine items in 40,000 square feet of retail space. Make time to stop for a picture of the Big Peach and slurp down a peach ice-cream cone.

Generation Gap (478-956-2678), 123 Peachtree Park, Byron. Open 9–5 weekdays. This unique family-owned business focusing on the sale of classic cars, open and enclosed trailers, and antiques has been operating since 1975. The vintage cars at this old-time car mall emporium range in quality from 100-point show cars to those needing work. Most are ready to drive. For those who aren't in the market for a classic car, this is a fantastic opportunity to see many of them in one spot, displayed in a museumlike atmosphere alongside airplanes, trolleys, race cars, bathtub boats, and one-of-a-kind items. A group of antiques dealers sell everything from automobiles to Civil War artifacts, collectibles, glassware, and more.

ART GALLERIES Macon Arts Gallery (478-743-6940; www.macon arts.org), 414 Cherry Street, Macon. Open 9–5 weekdays. Local artists show their one-of-a-kind creations, with new works added frequently.

CLOTHING The Art of Dreams (478-742-5737), 339 Cotton Avenue, Macon. Open 10–5:30 weekdays, 10–4 Saturday. This unique shop purveys elegant and sophisticated ladies' clothing and accessories.

The Barnes House (478-743-1909), 807 Cherry Street, Macon. Open 9:30–5:30 weekdays, 9:30–4:30 Saturday. Serving Macon since 1927, the store offers coats downstairs and gifts upstairs.

Karla's Shoe Boutique (478-741-2066), 603 Cherry Street, Macon. Open 10–5:30 Monday through Saturday, 10–4 Saturday. Owned by Zelma Redding and Karla Redding-Andrews, the widow and daughter of Otis Redding, the store offers the finest in designer footwear and accessories.

FOOD Dickey Farms (478-836-4362; 1-800-732-2442; www.gapeaches .com), 3440 Old US 341, Musella. Open 8–7 weekdays, 8–6 weekends. Purchase peaches and other peachy treats from the oldest operating packing house in Georgia.

Jolly Nut Company (478-825-7733; 1-800-332-1505; www.jollynut.com), 100 Commercial Heights, Fort Valley. Open January through October, 9–5 weekdays; November and December, 9–5:30 Monday through Saturday. Founded in 1924, the historic store sells Georgia gifts and pecans. Don't miss the free samples.

Priester's Pecans Candy Kitchen and Restaurant (478-987-6080; 1-800-277-3226; www.priester.com), 106 Fairview Drive, Perry. Open 8–9 Friday and Saturday. Watch pecan pralines, divinity, fudge, sugared nuts, and other sweets being made, and sample all the homemade candies. If it's mealtime, visitors can enjoy the lunch buffet or weekend seafood dinner buffet.

OUTLET MALLS Peach Festival Outlet Shops at Byron (478-956-1855), 331 GA 49 North, Byron. Open 10–9 Monday through Saturday, noon–6 Sunday. This center provides middle Georgia's only outlet shopping. The center features dozens of brand-name stores such as Corning, Dress Barn, Fieldcrest, Hanes, Hushpuppies, and Samsonite, purveying goods from kitchenware to clothing. The Byron Plantation Southern Deli and Store is also on-site.

✳ Special Events

Early February: **Festival of Camellias** at the American Camellia Society–Massee Lane Gardens (478-967-2358).

The monthlong celebration in Fort Valley includes senior days, deluxe tours, music Saturdays, box lunch days, a fashion show and luncheon, camellia sales, clinics, and workshops. Included with regular admission; free first Saturday in February. See *Green Space—Gardens.*

March: **International Cherry Blossom Festival** (478-751-7429; www .cherryblossom.com). For 10 days, visitors to Macon are treated to more than 400 activities, extravagant displays of springtime beauty, and exciting festivities—all situated under a pink canopy of blossoms. Among the activities are headliner concerts, old-fashioned dances, and daily performances in Central City Park. Festival free; some events have a charge.

Macon, Gardens, Mansions and Moonlight (contact Hay House for tickets, 478-742-8155; www.hay house.org). This event consists of three tours: a Historic Homes Tour, Secret Gardens Tour, and Moonlight Tour of Homes. Attendees who purchase the combination ticket for all three tours also get a bonus tour of the Hay House (see *To See—Historic Homes and Sites*). Other events during the three-day tour weekend (for which tickets are sold separately) are Mint Juleps and Supper with Sidney at the Sidney Lanier Cottage; a Rose Hill Ramble at Rose Hill Cemetery; and the Garden Market Preview Party. $8 for Moonlight Tour of Homes–$44 for combination of tours. Free events include three-day Garden Market plant sale at Central City Park and seminars by noted gardeners.

Peaches to Beaches Antiques and Yard Sale (contact Golden Isles Parkway Association, 912-375-5035; www.goldenislesparkway.org). This 172-mile-long yard sale connects the peach-growing counties of middle Georgia to the Golden Isles of the coast, stopping in 17 communities along the way, including Perry. If you like to haggle, then this March event is the Super Bowl of yard sales for you. Free.

April and May: **Live at Five Happy Hour Concert Series** (478-750-8555; 1-888-GA-ROCKS; www.ga musichall.com). For six Tuesday evenings throughout April and early May, the Tune Town area of the **Georgia Music Hall of Fame** (see *To See—Cultural Sites*) features concerts for all ages. Concerts may be from any genre of music. Beverages are available. Series included in regular admission price.

April and October: **Mossy Creek Barnyard Festival** (478-922-8265; www.mossycreekfestival.com). Held 6 miles east of I-75 near Perry and Warner Robins. Open 10–5:30 Saturday and Sunday. The award-winning weekend fair, named one of the top 20 events in the Southeast and one of the top 100 events in North America, features pioneer demonstrations, continuous music and storytelling, arts and crafts, and hayrides. Adults $5, children $1. Parking free.

May: **Battle of Byron** (478-956-2409; 1-888-686-3496; www.byronga .com). Activities include a barbecue, gospel singing, parade, pet show, sock hop, sports tournaments, and square dancing. Free.

June: **Georgia Peach Festival** (478-825-4002; 1-877-322-4371, www .gapeachfestival.org). Some activities occur in Fort Valley and others in Byron. Georgia's Official Food Festival, the fair's highlight is the world's largest peach cobbler, a juicy 6-by-9-

foot dessert. Other activities include a hat contest, street dance, barbecue cook-off, Glitz and Glamour Ball, Peach Queen Pageant, an art show, and an ice-cream making contest. $1.

September: **Georgia Music Week** (800-768-3401; www.maconga.com). Sponsored by the **Georgia Music Hall of Fame** (see *To See—Cultural Sites*), this musical extravaganza is a celebration of the state's musical heritage, consisting of daily and nightly concerts in a variety of venues and genres in Macon. Premier events include the weeklong Brown Bag Boogie luncheon concert series, the Jammin' in the Street outdoor concert, and themed exhibits and programs in the museum. Brown Bag Boogie luncheon concerts and Jammin' in the Street concert free; call for times and prices of other special events.

Ocmulgee Indian Celebration (478-752-8257; www.nps.gov/ocmu). Held the third weekend in September at the **Ocmulgee National Monument** (see *To See—Historic Homes and Sites*), this festival is a gathering of Creeks, Cherokees, Chickasaws, Choctaws, and Seminoles. They perform ancient ceremonial dances in colorful regalia and tell of Native American legends and lore. Among the food choices are roasted corn, buffalo burgers, and Indian tacos. Music, art, and native crafts round out the activities. Adults $5, children free.

October: **Georgia National Fair** (478-987-3247; 1-800-YUR-FAIR, www.gnfa.com). Open 8 AM–10 PM daily. A 10-day fall exposition, this family-oriented festival includes a circus, games, home and fine arts competitions, horse shows, livestock events, midway rides, youth exhibits, and food. Nights are filled with concerts, entertainment, and fireworks. General admission: adults $6, children 10 and younger free. Rides charged individually.

Wings and Wheels Car Show (478-923-6600; www.museumofaviation .org). Held at the Museum of Aviation, address, in Warner Robins. The annual show features more than 250 show vehicles on display, a "for sale" car corral, and special attractions. Call for exact date. Free.

MADISON TO WASHINGTON

The Piedmont country between Georgia's mountainous region and its coastal plain is the heart of the state's Historic South region. Not only is it centrally located, but it is the most stereotypically Southern area of Georgia. Although Union General William Tecumseh Sherman's infamous March to the Sea came right through the heartland and resulted in immense destruction of plantations and towns, much was spared and survives to this day. In fact, Madison is known as the "town Sherman refused to burn." This entire area of Georgia's historic heartland is a living museum to a less harried time in U.S. history, and it contains shining examples of plantation architecture.

Many of the wonderful historic plantation and in-town properties are featured on much-anticipated annual tours of homes, which sell out early, so don't lollygag when making your reservations. Others are used as elegant bed & breakfasts. Outside of Savannah, this area has one of the largest concentrations of B&Bs in the state, and in a region where expansive front porches are de rigueur, it's no surprise that Southern hospitality is at its best here. Still other historic properties create homes for a variety of museums. The region is an important part of the **Georgia Antique Trail** and the **Antebellum Trail.** After you get off the interstate, scenic byways wind past pastoral fields and through quaint villages inviting visitors to stop by for a spell.

Cotton may have been king at one time, but recreation—and golf in particular—is king now. State parks and resorts offer outstanding opportunities to golfers of all abilities. Several lakes and state parks as well as a national forest provide innumerable choices for water sports and other outdoor recreation including hiking, biking, swimming, bird-watching, boating, fishing, horseback riding, and shooting sports. Lake Oconee claims to have more fish per cubic yard than any other lake in Georgia.

GUIDANCE Before visiting Madison, Buckhead, or Rutledge, contact the **Madison–Morgan County Chamber of Commerce, Convention and Visitors Bureau, Madison Welcome Center** (706-342-4454; 1-800-709-7406; www.madisonga.org), 115 East Jefferson Street, Madison 30650. Open 8:30–5 weekdays, 10–5 Saturday, 1–4 Sunday.

When planning a trip to the Eatonton area, contact the **Eatonton-Putnam**

Chamber of Commerce (706-485-7701; www.eatonton.com), 105 South Washington Avenue, Eatonton 31024. Open 8:30–5 weekdays. Information is available here for the **Alice Walker Driving Tour, Historic Walking Tour of Eatonton,** and the **Antebellum Trail.**

For information about Greensboro, consult the **Greene County Chamber of Commerce** (706-453-7592; 1-866-341-4466; www.greeneccoc.org; www.oconee .com), 111 North Main Street, Greensboro 30642. Open 9–5 weekdays, 10–3 Saturday.

To learn about Lincolnton, consult the **Lincolnton–Lincoln County Chamber of Commerce** (706-359-7970; www.lincolncountyga.org), 112 North Washington Street, Lincolnton 30817. Located in the historic Lamar-Blanchard House, the chamber is open 8:30–5 weekdays.

For more information about Monticello, consult the **Monticello–Jasper County Chamber of Commerce** (706-468-8994; www.monticelloga.org), 123 West Washington Street, Monticello 31064. Open 9–5 weekdays. The office also serves as the **Monticello Crossroads Trailhead and Visitors Center.** At the visitor center, you can see a small exhibit about Trisha Yearwood and get a brochure for the **Monticello Historic District Driving Tour** and a brochure for the **Monticello Crossroads Scenic Byway.**

To learn more about Warrenton, contact the **Warren County Chamber of Commerce** (706-465-9604; www.warrencountyga.org), 552 Main Street, Warrenton 30838. Open 11–5 weekdays.

When planning a trip to the Washington area, contact the **Washington–Wilkes County Chamber of Commerce** (706-678-2013; www.washingtonwilkes.com), 104 East Liberty Street, Washington 30673. Open 9–5 weekdays.

GETTING THERE *By air:* Most visitors to this area who are arriving by air fly into **Hartsfield-Jackson Atlanta International Airport** (see What's Where in Georgia). Visitors also could fly into **Middle Georgia Regional Airport** (478-788-3760; www.cityofmacon.net/CityDept/aviation.htm), 1000 Terminal Drive, Macon, which is serviced by Delta's **Atlantic Southeast Airlines** (1-800-325-1999). Car rentals are available there from **Alamo/National** (478-788-5385), **Avis** (478-788-3840), **Budget** (478-784-7130), **Enterprise** (478-784-8633), and **Hertz** (478-788-3600).

By bus: **Greyhound Lines** (706-549-2255; 1-800-231-2222; www.greyhound .com) operates service to Crawfordville, Greensboro, Madison, and Washington.

By car: This chapter has two completely separate nodes, but all the towns are found just north or south of I-20. The western node contains Buckhead, Eatonton, Greensboro, Madison, Monticello, and Rutledge. The eastern node contains Crawfordville, Lincolnton, Norwood, Warrenton, and Washington. Various routes will take you to the charming towns, so get a good Georgia map.

By train: **Amtrak** (1-800-USA-RAIL) operates service to Atlanta (see What's Where in Georgia) and Augusta (see Augusta chapter).

GETTING AROUND This area has no mass transit or taxi service, and rental cars are available only at the Atlanta or Macon airports.

MEDICAL EMERGENCY For life-threatening emergencies, call 911. For other health-care needs contact **Wills Memorial Hospital** (706-678-2151), 120 Gordon Street, Washington. In Greene County contact **Minnie G. Boswell Memorial Hospital** (706-453-7331), 120 Siloam Road, Greensboro, or **Putnam General Hospital** (706-485-2711), 101 Lake Oconee Parkway, Eatonton. Medical assistance can be found in Madison at **Morgan Memorial Hospital** (706-342-1667), 1077 South Main Street.

VILLAGES Before the Civil War, **Madison** was known as the most cultured and aristocratic town on the stage route from Charleston to New Orleans, but during the Civil War it became known as "the Town Sherman Refused to Burn." Madison was on the direct path of Sherman's March to the Sea from Atlanta to Savannah, and the expectation was that it would be put to the torch as so many other towns were. After 140 years, the question still remains unanswered: Why was Madison spared? According to one story, Senator Joshua Hill was a friend of Sherman's brother and had been an early foe of secession. It is reported that he was able to come to a gentleman's agreement with Sherman that would save the town from being burned. Whether there's any truth to this conjecture or not, this fortuitous fact that Madison and its outstanding architecture—a large portion of which was built between 1830 and 1860—was spared resulted in the town being named a designated historic district by the Department of the Interior in 1974. One of the first such districts in Georgia, it is also one of the largest in the country. A few historic homes are open for tours year-round, and several tours throughout the year allow visitors to get a glimpse into private residences.

Eatonton bills itself as "Close to Everything, Next to Perfect." The town has a rich storytelling and literary history. Two of Eatonton's most famous citizens are Joel Chandler Harris, creator of the Uncle Remus tales, and Alice Walker, author of *The Color Purple, The Temple of My Familiar,* and other books. Harris was born in Eatonton in 1848. His first collection of poems and proverbs was published in 1881 as *Uncle Remus: His Songs and Sayings.*

Greensboro was founded in 1786 and boasts five historic districts and seven historic sites, including Bethesda Baptist Church (organized in 1785), the original campus of Mercer University (1830), Jefferson Hall and Heard-Carpenter House (1830), and the Greensboro Old Gaol (1807). The area is a hub for family activities and events.

Besides being the home of country-music star Trisha Yearwood, the entire city of **Monticello**, including the downtown shopping district, is listed on the National Register of Historic Places.

Washington, which was the site of the Revolutionary War Battle of Kettle Creek, has several history museums and an intact plantation now open for tours.

✳ To See

CULTURAL SITES 🗡 🐾 ♿ **Madison-Morgan Cultural Arts Center** (706-342-4743; www.madisonmorgancultural.org; www.morgan.public.lib.ga.us/madmorg), 434 South Main Street, Madison. Open 10–5 Tuesday through Saturday, 2–5 Sunday. The majestic 1895 Romanesque Revival–style schoolhouse was one of

the first graded schools in the South. The structure currently houses a history
museum, a performing arts center, and several authentically restored and furnished turn-of-the-20th-century classrooms. In addition, the museum is filled with
19th-century decorative arts, historical artifacts, and information about the Piedmont region of Georgia, as well as permanent and traveling art exhibits. A variety
of performances are given in the apse-shaped auditorium (see *Entertainment—
Theater*). Adults $3, seniors $2.50, children $2.

FOR FAMILIES 🗸 🐾 ♿ **Br'er Rabbit Statue,** Courthouse Square, Eatonton.
Open daily. The large, sprightly, brightly dressed statue is a tribute to the star of
the tales author Joel Chandler Harris heard from slaves. When stopping to take a
photo here, imagine what devilment Br'er Rabbit is contemplating to inflict on
Br'er Fox and Br'er Bear. Free.

GUIDED TOURS Confederate Gold, Majestic Mansions, and **An Unreconstructed Rebel** tours (706-678-2013 between 1 and 4 PM). The Madison–Morgan
County Chamber of Commerce sponsors guided tours from 1½ hours to 6½
hours. Call for reservations and locations. $6–25 depending on length and number
of attractions covered.

HISTORIC HOMES AND SITES 🗸 🐾 **Callaway Plantation** (706-678-7060; www
.washingtonwilkes.com/attractions.html), US 78, Washington. Open 10–5 Tuesday through Saturday, 2–5 Sunday. A living-history museum, the facility has
three historic houses and primitive crafts and even allows visitors to pick cotton.
Sightseers can follow the original family from its humble log cabin beginnings all
the way to life in this beautiful Greek Revival manor house. Limited wheelchair
accessibility. Adults $4, children 6–13 $2.
🐾 ♿ **Heritage Hall** (706-342-9627; 1-800-545-8771; www.friendsofheritage
hall.com), 277 South Main Street, Madison. Open 11–4:30 Tuesday through Saturday, 1:30–4:30 Sunday. Built circa 1811, this gracious, many-columned structure is furnished with period pieces. Be sure to look for a unique feature of this
historic home: Many windows have etchings on them. These were done by the
daughters and granddaughters of Dr. Elijah Evans Jones, the home's second
owner. While you are there, ask about the ghost room and the Christmas tour.
Adults $5, students $2, children 12 and younger free.
🗸 🐾 ♿ **Rock Eagle Effigy** (706-484-2800; www.rockeagle4H.org), Rock Eagle
4-H Center, 350 Rock Eagle Road, Eatonton. Open dawn–dusk daily. The rock representation of an eagle is the oldest and most unusual attraction in the state. The
prone bird, which measures 102 feet from head to tail and 120 feet across while
rising 10 feet from the ground, is thought to have been created 2,000 years ago by
Woodland Indians as a ceremonial meeting place. The milky quartz rocks used to
construct the giant bird range from baseball-size stones to boulders and were
brought from as far as 100 miles away in an era when there were no horses or
wheeled vehicles on this continent. For the best view and photo op, climb the observation tower (not wheelchair accessible). Boating and fishing are allowed on the 4-H
center's 110-acre lake, but swimming is not permitted. (**Rock Hawk,** also located in

THE ROCK EAGLE EFFIGY, WHICH RISES 10 FEET FROM THE GROUND IN EATONTON, IS THOUGHT TO HAVE BEEN CREATED 2,000 YEARS AGO BY WOODLAND INDIANS.

Putnam County, is a sister mound of similar construction. This site is located at the entrance to Georgia Power's **Shoal Park** on Lake Oconee.) Free.

🐾 ♿ **Rogers House and Rose Cottage** (706-343-0190; www.madisonga .org/attractions.htm), 179 East Jefferson Street, Madison. Open 10–4:30 Monday through Saturday, 1:30–4:30 Sunday. Located on the same property, the two houses represent two different time periods. The Rogers House, circa 1810, is one of the oldest Piedmont Plain–style homes in the county and is filled with period furnishings. Rose Cottage, circa 1891, was built by Adeline Rose, who was born into slavery. $3 for both houses.

MUSEUMS ♿ **Madison Museum of Fine Art** (706-342-8320; www.madison museum.org), 290 Hancock Street, Madison. Open 1–5 Sunday through Friday, 11–5 Saturday. The permanent collection includes works by Picasso and Batistello, an Italian Old Master. Other exhibits include works by Rembrandt, Renoir, Dali, and Calder, while changing exhibits entice visitors to return again and again.

✍ 🐾 ♿ **Morgan County African American Museum** (706-342-9191), 156 Academy Street, Madison. Open 10–4 Tuesday through Friday, noon–4 Saturday. This museum, dedicated to African American heritage and contributions to Southern culture, is located in the historic 1890s Moore House. Exhibits illustrate the African origins of Morgan County blacks and seek to preserve and promote a greater awareness of contributions African Americans have made to the South. Adults $3, children $2.

✍ 🐾 **Robert Toombs House Historic Site** (706-678-2226; 1-800-864-7275; www.gastateparks.org/info/rtoombs), 216 East Robert Toombs Avenue, Washington. Open 9–5 Tuesday through Saturday, 2–5 Sunday. This stately, white-columned home was the residence of Confederate leader Robert Toombs. A legend in his own time, Toombs was a wealthy planter and lawyer who became a state legislator and U.S. senator, eventually evolving into a fiery secessionist. He served five months as the Confederate secretary of state, but resigned to serve as a brigadier general in the Army of Northern Virginia. After the Civil War, he was one of only a few who refused to sign an oath of allegiance to the Union, calling himself an Unreconstructed Rebel. He helped create the Georgia state constitution in 1877. His home is filled with Toombs family furniture as well as Civil War exhibits. Visitors also should see the dramatic film about Toombs and tour the grounds. $1.75–3.

🐾 **Steffen Thomas Museum** (706-342-7557; www.steffenthomas.org), 4200

Bethany Road, Buckhead. Open 1–4 Tuesday through Saturday. Inside a steel warehouse is a wondrous art museum filled floor to ceiling with Expressionist oil paintings, watercolors, mosaics, and sculptures—all the work of the late Steffen Thomas. Thomas immigrated to Atlanta from Germany in the 1920s and lived there until his death in 1990. He is known for having created the Alabama Memorial at Vicksburg National Military Park in Mississippi and a bronze bust of George Washington Carver, which is displayed at the Tuskegee Institute in Alabama. The works he created for himself are displayed here. The subject matter ranges from women to landscapes, pets to farm animals. Adults $5, seniors and students $3, children free.

🏛 🍴 ⚿ **Uncle Remus Museum** (706-485-6856; www.eatonton.com), 2414 Oak Street/US 441 South, Eatonton. Open 10–5 Monday through Saturday, 2–5 Sunday; closed Tuesdays, September through May. Several authentic slave cabins were combined in Turner Park to create this museum dedicated to Joel Chandler Harris and his critters. Among the displays are shadow-box scenes of the critters, first editions, and other Harris memorabilia. A portrait of Uncle Remus and the little boy as they appeared in the Disney movie *Song of the South* hangs over the fireplace. The surrounding park contains historic outbuildings and old-fashioned farm tools. Adults $1, children 50¢.

🏛 🍴 ⚿ **Washington Historical Museum** (706-678-2105), 308 East Robert Toombs Avenue, Washington. Open 10–5 Tuesday through Saturday, 2–5 Sunday. Visitors learn about the history of Washington and Wilkes County by viewing Native American and Civil War artifacts and other memorabilia. This house museum is decorated with authentic period furnishings, has a replica of a plantation kitchen, and includes displays about prehistoric Indian life, the Battle of Kettle Creek, and Native American pottery. Adults $3, children 5–12 $2, children under 5 free.

SPECIAL PLACES 🏛 🍴 **Scull Shoals Archaeological Site** (706-453-7592; 1-866-341-4466; www.greeneccoc.org), Macedonia Church Road, Greensboro. Open daily. Visitors may see active archaeological digs under way at these pre-Columbian-era Indian mounds on the site of the now-defunct village of Scull Shoals. The extinct 19th-century mill village once included Georgia's first paper mill and a water-powered cotton mill, as well as gristmills, sawmills, a four-story brick textile mill, stores, and homes. Flooding caused the demise of the mills in the 1880s, and the town was abandoned in the 1920s. The 2,200-acre site is now an experimental forest area, a hub for environmental education, and a research center for the study of the history of technology, economics,

THE UNCLE REMUS MUSEUM IN EATONTON IS DEDICATED TO JOEL CHANDLER HARRIS, CREATOR OF THE UNCLE REMUS TALES, AND THE CHARACTERS WHOSE STORIES HE TOLD.

THE TALES OF UNCLE REMUS

Joel Chandler Harris was born into utter poverty in 1848, but through the care of others who recognized his potential, he received an education. The postmaster used to give him discarded papers and magazines to satisfy his hunger for learning. At age 13, Harris was hired as a printer's devil for the *Countryman,* a newspaper published by Joseph Addison Turner on his plantation, Turnwold. It was while working here that Harris began his lifelong friendship with the plantation's African Americans and the animals he later wrote about. Harris always insisted that he was not the author of the tales, but only the compiler. He eventually produced nine books with 183 different stories in which the lowly and enslaved always outwit their masters. These stories have been translated into 27 languages.

medicine, forestry, landscape use, and other subjects. **Scull Shoals Historical Area, Oconee National Forest,** is reached by a gravel road or a 1-mile hiking trail that leads past the ruins of this once-prosperous town. From there, the **Boarding House Trail** leads to the ruins of an old boardinghouse. The **Indian Mounds Trail** traverses the Oconee River flood plain to two prehistoric mounds. Free.

✳ To Do

BICYCLING ✐ ❧ A brochure for a **self-guided bicycling tour** of Eatonton is available from the Eatonton-Putnam Chamber of Commerce (706-485-8565). A local biker has mapped out the community in a very scenic and energetic ride for the entire family. Call for details.

CARRIAGE RIDES ✐ ❧ **Double C Carriage Tours** (706-742-7972; 706-224-4539; www.doubleccarriages.com) operates horse-and-buggy tours of downtown Madison. Call for times. All tours are narrated by professional staff and highlight special points of interest in the historic district. 20-minute rides $10 per person, 40-minute rides $15 per person.

FOR FAMILIES ✐ ❧ **Second Time Around Mini Farm** (706-678-4902; www .secondtimearoundminifarm.com), 146 Hendry Lane, Washington. See animals such as macaws, babydoll sheep, llamas, goats, potbellied pigs, miniature donkeys, and Japanese koi in natural-looking habitats. Paddleboats are also available, as are accommodations in private bungalows (see *Lodging—Bed & Breakfasts*). Not wheelchair accessible. Adults $10, children $8; reservations required.

GOLF ❧ **The Creek at Hard Labor** (706-557-3006; 1-888-353-4592; www.golf georgia.org), 1400 Knox Chapel Road, Rutledge. Open 7–7 daily. One of Georgia's best golf values, the 18-hole course is intersected by Hard Labor Creek, which creates water hazards on five holes. The course features a pro shop, driving range, unlimited weekday play, and junior and senior discounts. $37–42.

Golf Club at Cuscowilla (706-485-0094; www.cuscowilla.com), 126 Cuscowilla Drive, Eatonton. Open 7–7 daily. Four championship courses blend with the rolling meadows and pine forests that dot the shores of Lake Oconee. This highly acclaimed course features a pro shop, practice green, driving range, swimming, and tennis. Guest accommodations are also available (see *Lodging—Inns and Resorts*). Greens fees start at $65.

Harbor Club (1-800-505-4653; www.harborclub.com), One Club Drive, Greensboro. Open 8–7 daily. This 18-hole course offers a challenge to golfers of all skill levels. Many holes border Lake Oconee or one of the facility's natural streams. $69 weekdays, $79 weekends, including cart.

Reynolds Plantation Golf Club (706-485-0235; www.reynoldsplantation.com), 112 Plantation Drive, Eatonton. Open 8–7 daily. This beautiful property boasts five world-class golf courses, with a sixth scheduled to open in early 2007. There are currently 81 uniquely sculpted holes, many of which enjoy breathtaking views of Lake Oconee. The Oconee Course offers 6,702 yards of challenging play as well as a Dave Pelz Scoring Game School, a caddie-concierge program, and customized club fitting. The 6,545-yard Great Waters Course also features a 10,000-square-foot putting green. The 6,698-yard Plantation Course features a practice range with two bunkers and five target greens. Its 19th Hole Grill and Lounge is a great place to have lunch or unwind. The National Course actually consists of three nine-hole courses: the Ridge, the Bluff, and the Cove, which together have more than 100 bunkers. The courses are open only to guests staying at the **Ritz-Carlton Lodge, Reynolds Plantation** (see *Lodging—Inns and Resorts*), or those with a temporary membership, of which there are several types available to travelers (call for details). Greens fees $90 winter–$260 peak weekends.

See also Golf Appendix.

SPAS &. **The Ritz-Carlton Lodge, Reynolds Plantation** (706-467-7185), One Lake Oconee Greensboro Trail. Open 8–8 daily. The spa, which is ranked fourth on *Travel + Leisure*'s list of Top Resort Spas in the United States and Canada, offers an impressive variety of spa treatments. Many are inspired by Southern ingredients such as magnolia, gardenia, primrose, eucalyptus oil, and Oconee mud. Reservations are required two to three weeks in advance. (For more information about this resort, see *Golf*, *Lodging—Inns and Resorts*, and *Where to Eat—Eating Out*.)

WALKING TOURS 🍃 **The Walking Tour of Madison** (1-800-709-7406). Discover the unexpected in historic Madison by taking this self-guided walking tour, which begins at the Madison Welcome Center on the Square. This 1.4-mile tour is a pleasant and healthy way to see some of the finest architecture that the South has to offer. Driving routes are available as well. Free.

WATER SPORTS Waterskiing opportunities abound on nearby **Lake Oconee, Clarks Hill Lake, Lake Jackson** and **Lake Sinclair.** Fishing, swimming, and boating are other popular water sports. See *Green Space—Lakes*.

LAKES ✐ ❧ **Clarks Hill Lake** (706-359-7970; www.lincolncountyga.org), 2959 McCormick Highway/US 378 East, Lincolnton. Open daily. A mecca for watersports enthusiasts, Clarks Hill Lake straddles the Georgia–South Carolina border. It is known as Strom Thurmond Lake on the South Carolina side. The lake, which is the largest reservoir in the Southeast, boasts 1,200 miles of shoreline, of which 400 miles are in Lincoln County. With its 11 Corps of Engineers recreation areas, 13 Corps campgrounds, five commercial marinas, six state parks, and four county parks, it attracts 6 million visitors per year. Free.

✐ ❧ **Lake Jackson** (706-468-8994; www.monticelloga.com), GA 16 and GA 212, Monticello. Open daily. The Alcovy, South, and Yellow rivers meet at Lloyd Shoals Dam, which was built in the early 1900s to create a lake for swimming, fishing, boating, and other water sports. Free.

✐ ❧ **Lake Oconee** (706-453-7592; 1-866-341-4466; www.oconee.com), GA 44 South/Lake Oconee Parkway, Greensboro. Open daily. In 1980 Georgia Power Company built Wallace Dam, creating a 19,000-acre lake to supply hydroelectric power for the region. The resulting Lake Oconee, the second-largest lake in Georgia, supports a world-class resort community with access from numerous places from Eatonton to Greensboro. The 374 miles of shoreline provide ideal locations for marinas, beaches, restaurants, lodging, and golf courses. Water sports include boating, fishing, swimming, and waterskiing. Camping, hiking, bird-watching, and picnicking are other popular activities. Access to lake free; some activities have fees.

✐ ❧ **Lake Sinclair** (706-485-7701; www.eatonton.com), Eatonton. Open daily. Public boat ramps, bird-watching, tailrace fishing, and other water activities are available at this 14,750-acre lake with 417 miles of shoreline. Free.

NATURE PRESERVES AND PARKS ✐ ❧ ♿ **A. H. Stephens State Historic Park** (706-456-2602; 1-800-864-7275; www.gastateparks.org/info/ahsteph), 456 Alexander Street North, Crawfordville. Park open 7–10 daily; museum and Liberty Hall open 9–5 Tuesday through Saturday, 2–5 Sunday. This park combines Civil War history with outdoor recreation. Central to the park is Liberty Hall, the home of A. H. Stephens, who served as the vice president of the Confederate States of America and later as governor of Georgia. The home, which was built after the Civil War in 1875, has been restored to that period and furnished with period pieces and Stephens memorabilia. The adjacent museum contains one of the finest collections of Civil War artifacts in the state. A statue of the "Little Giant" marks his grave site. Surrounding the historic site is a 1,177-acre park with fishing lakes, a junior Olympic-size swimming pool open seasonally, 3 miles of walking trails—one of which is ADA accessible—and 12 miles of horseback riding trails (BYOH—bring your own horse). Private boats with electric motors are permitted, and fishing and pedal boats are available for rent. Lodging is offered at the campground and in cottages (see *Lodging*). Park parking $3; admission to museum and Liberty Hall: Adults $2.50, children $1.50.

✐ ❧ ♿ **Elijah Clark State Park and Museum** (706-359-3458; www.gastate

parks.org/info/elijah), 2959 McCormick Highway, Lincolnton. Park open 7–10
daily; museum open weekends April through November. Located on the western
shores of Clarks Hill Lake, the 447-acre park is named for a frontiersman and
war hero who led pioneers during the Revolutionary War. He and his wife, Hannah, are buried here. A renovated log cabin serves as a museum where furniture,
utensils, and tools from the late 1780s are displayed. Recreational facilities include a swimming beach, playground, miniature golf, shuffleboard courts, four
boat ramps, and 3.75 miles of hiking trails. Accommodations are available in cottages and campsites (see *Lodging*). Parking $3, free on Wednesday.

✍ ♠ ⅏ **Hard Labor Creek State Park** (706-557-3001; 1-800-864-7275; www
.gastateparks.org/info/hardlabor), US 278/Fairplay Road (parallels I-20), Rutledge. Open 7–10 daily; reservations required for equestrian camping. The origin
of this park's name is shrouded in mystery. Two possibilities seem likely. Some
believe the area was named by Native Americans who found it difficult to ford
the creek here. Others believe that the area was named by slaves who tilled the
fields. Regardless of where it got its name, the wooded 5,804-acre park has a
wide range of recreational opportunities. It is well known for its golf course (see
To Do—Golf), but is equally popular for its 24.5 miles of hiking trails and 22
miles of horseback riding trails (BYOH—bring your own horse), as well as lakes,
fishing, and a lakeside beach open for swimming in the summer. Horseback riders will find 30 rental stalls for their equine friends, as well as a riding ring and
12 equestrian campsites. Canoes, fishing boats, and pedal boats are available to
rent. Accommodations are available at campgrounds and in cottages (see *Lodging*). Parking $3, free on Wednesday.

✍ ♠ **Oconee National Forest** (706-485-7110; www.monticelloga.com), office at
1199 Madison Road, Eatonton. Open daily. The forest consists of 16,000 acres of
public lands with two wildlife management areas. Hiking, camping, bird-watching,
and wildlife observation are popular activities. The forest includes the **Sinclair
Recreational Area** on Lake Sinclair as well as two recreational areas with boat
access on Lake Oconee. In addition to numerous hiking trails, five horseback
riding trails meander through the woodlands (BYOH—bring your own horse;
there are no rentals). Camping is permitted forestwide. Stop by the office for the
brochure "A Guide to the Chattahoochee-Oconee National Forests." Free.

✳ Lodging
BED & BREAKFASTS

In Greensboro
♠ **Higdon House Bed and Breakfast** (706-453-2511; www.higdon
houseinn.com), 301 West Green
Street. This elegant Victorian-era
house more than 160 years old is
located on more than 2 acres of landscaped gardens and pecan trees in the
beautiful Lake Oconee District. A full

breakfast and afternoon wine and
cheese on the veranda are included.
Smoking permitted on veranda. Not
wheelchair accessible. $99. Credit
cards not accepted.

♠ ⅏ **Washington Grass Inn** (706-
467-2520; www.washingtongrass.com),
2281 Fuller Road. The gracious
Southern past is in residence at this

beautiful Victorian-era home, which is situated on 13 peaceful acres. The three guest rooms share a common bath. Full breakfast is included; other gourmet meals are available for an additional charge. Smoking permitted in summer kitchen. $85.

In Madison

♣ ᴧ **Brady Inn** (706-342-4400; www .bradyinn.com), 250 North Second Street. Enjoy the charm of the Victorian era in two tastefully and lovingly restored private homes. Besides the full breakfast with complimentary morning newspaper, a selection of homemade goodies and beverages is always available in the dining room. All seven guest rooms boast private baths. No smoking. Two rooms wheelchair accessible, but baths not handicapped equipped. $90–100.

♣ **Burnett Place** (706-342-4034; www.burnettplace.com), 317 Old Post Road. Located in the heart of the historic district, this B&B offers personal service, graceful accommodations, and exceptional breakfasts. There are three elegantly decorated guest rooms, each with a private bath. No smoking. Not wheelchair accessible. $85–95.

♪ ᴧ **Farmhouse Inn** (706-342-7933; www.thefarmhouseinn.com), 1051 Meadow Lane. Rediscover life's simple pleasures at this 100-acre farm. Families enjoy the inn's many farm animals, walking trails, and lake frontage. Canoeing on the Apalachee River is another option. Guest accommodations include five private rooms and two separate cottages. Smoking permitted on terrace outside Red Barn Meeting Room. Wheelchair accessible, but baths not handicapped equipped. $125–375.

Madison Oaks Inn and Garden (706-343-9990; www.madisonoaks inn.com), 766 East Avenue. This 1905 Greek Revival mansion offers accommodations truly befitting of the rich history, architecture, gardens, and antiques of Madison. Each of the four guest rooms features a private bath, superior linens, satellite TV, plush robes, and early morning coffee or tea service. A full gourmet breakfast is included. Smoking permitted outdoors. Not wheelchair accessible. $185–250.

♪ **Southern Cross Ranch** (706-342-8027; www.southcross.com), 1670 Bethany Church Road. Various meal plans and even all-inclusive packages that include horseback riding are offered at this resort. Sixteen theme-decorated guest rooms offer something for everyone. All rooms have private bath, AC, television, VCR, and telephone with data port. After a strenuous horseback ride, cool off in the outdoor pool or relax in the hot tub. Tours of the property also can be arranged for those not staying overnight (tour only: adults $10, children $8); see the web site for additional offerings. English, French, and German are spoken here. Smoking permitted outdoors. Not wheelchair accessible. $80–240.

In Washington

♪ 🐾 ᴧ **Babe's House Bed and Breakfast** (706-678-2083), 415 East Robert Toombs Avenue. This property offers a private two-bedroom guest cottage with its own kitchen, living and dining rooms, screened-in porch, and private bath. The owners are delighted to welcome well-behaved children and pets. No smoking. $100–150.

1894 Inn (706-678-1174; 1-866-466-1894; www.1894inn.com), 202 West

Robert Toombs Avenue. Five guest rooms, all with private baths, offer visitors the opportunity to relax in a warm and friendly setting. Knowledgeable hosts are happy to supply guests with information on the abundant area attractions. Full breakfast. No smoking. Not wheelchair accessible. $105–125.

✂ ☻ ♿ **Holly Ridge Country Inn** (706-285-2594), 2221 Sandtown Road. Two historical houses were joined on this quiet 100-acre property in 1985. After extensive renovation, the property opened in 1987 as a country inn. Guests can choose from eight authentically furnished rooms with private baths. Other amenities include a sun room, parlor, extra-large dining room, and wraparound porch with swings, rockers, and wicker furniture. This exciting property also boasts a pond with an authentic log cabin, an old post office, and a country store, all of which are currently being renovated for use as guest cottages. The breakfast of your choice (from continental to a full Southern meal) is included in the price of your stay. Innkeepers Roger and Vivian Walker welcome well-behaved children and pets. No smoking. $95–125.

♿ **Hunter Finnell House** (706-678-7953; 706-678-1477), 217 Lexington Avenue. Guest accommodations include two bedrooms with double beds, one sitting room, kitchen, dining room, laundry, central heat and air, a large back yard, and a deck. Smoking allowed. $80–140.

✂ ☻ **Second Time Around Mini Farm** (706-678-4902; www.second timearoundminifarm.com), 146 Hendry Lane. Enjoy a private bungalow by the pool at this truly unique facility surrounded by pastures, ponds, and gardens. Wake up to a leisurely breakfast served poolside, then catch your own dinner and cook it in your own outdoor kitchen. Experience the agricultural life at this working farm

THE HOLLY RIDGE COUNTRY INN IN WASHINGTON

(see *To Do—For Families*). Your children and pets are welcome here, too. Smoking permitted outdoors. Not wheelchair accessible. $125.

❧ **Sleighter House** (706-678-3166; www.sleighterhouse.com), 307 North Alexander Avenue. Built in 1827, this house was originally a women's seminary. Today it features four tastefully decorated guest rooms with queen-sized beds. Morning coffee or tea service is included along with a candlelight breakfast. Guests are encouraged to participate in classes on topics such as candle making, cooking, and floral arranging. Bicycles are available and picnic baskets can be ordered. No smoking. Not wheelchair accessible. $85.

The Washington Plantation Bed and Breakfast (706-678-2006; 1-877-405-9956; www.washingtonplantation.com), 15 Lexington Avenue. This lovely old home once ruled over a 3,000-acre plantation. Today, it offers guests a glimpse of the South's gracious past. Five spacious guest rooms with private baths are decorated with both comfort and elegance in mind. All rooms have a television, telephone, and wireless Internet access. Smoking permitted on veranda. Not wheelchair accessible. $125–185.

Wisteria Hall (706-678-7779), 225 East Robert Toombs Avenue. One of the oldest buildings in Washington, this circa 1700 house is furnished with a comfortable mixture of period antiques and modern designs. Guest accommodations are in three rooms with private baths. Full breakfast is included. Smoking permitted on grounds, but not in house. Not wheelchair accessible. $95–125.

CAMPGROUNDS

In Crawfordville

🖉 🐾 ❧ **A. H. Stephens State Historic Park** (706-456-2602; 1-800-864-7275; www.gastateparks.org/info/ahsteph), 456 Alexander Street North. Camping facilities include 25 tent, trailer, and RV sites, as well as a group campground and a pioneer campground. See *Green Space—Nature Preserves and Parks.* $16–20.

In Lincolnton

🖉 🐾 ❧ **Elijah Clark State Park and Museum** (706-359-3458; www.gastateparks.org/info/elijah), 2959 McCormick Highway. The park offers 165 tent, trailer, and RV sites nestled in the forest, as well as a pioneer campground and a country store. See *Green Space—Nature Preserves and Parks.* $18–25.

In Rutledge

🖉 🐾 ❧ **Hard Labor Creek State Park** (706-557-3001; 1-800-864-7275; www.gastateparks.org/info/hardlabor), Fairplay Road. Camping facilities include 51 tent, trailer, and RV sites as well as two group camps and a pioneer campground. Amenities include a swimming beach, bathhouse, two lakes, horse stables and trails, four picnic shelters, and one barbecue pit. $22–30.

COTTAGES AND CABINS For all three parks, see also *Green Space—Nature Preserves and Parks.*

In Crawfordville

🖉 🐾 ❧ **A. H. Stephens State Historic Park** (706-456-2602; 1-800-864-7275; www.gastateparks.org/info/ahsteph), 456 Alexander Street North. The park offers four fully equipped cottages. $60–85.

In Lincolnton

♂ ♟ ♞ **Elijah Clark State Park and Museum** (706-359-3458; www.gastateparks.org/info/elijah), 2959 McCormick Highway. The park has 20 cottages located at the water's edge. $70–100.

In Rutledge

♂ ♟ ♞ **Hard Labor Creek State Park** (706-557-3001; 1-800-864-7275; www.gastateparks.org/info/hardlabor), Fairplay Road. The park offers 20 fully equipped cottages. $85–95.

HOTELS

In Washington

♿ **The Fitzpatrick Hotel** (706-678-5900; www.thefitzpatrickhotel.com), West Public Square. Built in 1898, the venerable hotel sat empty for 50 years, beginning in 1952, but recently has been restored and reopened with 17 guest rooms, a restaurant, and retail space. The current owners have furnished this Queen Anne Victorian property in period reproductions and antiques. All rooms have queen-sized beds and private baths. No smoking. $75–139.

INNS AND RESORTS

In Eatonton

♂ **Cuscowilla Resort on Lake Oconee** (706-485-9616; 1-800-458-5351; www.cuscowilla.com), 126 Cuscowilla Drive. Amenities include a golf course (see *To Do—Golf*), swimming pool, restaurant, two tennis courts, walking trails, and a spa with a certified massage therapist on staff. Call for a list of spa treatments, rates, and hours. Accommodations are in golf cottages or fabulous lakeside villas. No smoking. Not wheelchair accessible. $125–650.

THE RITZ-CARLTON LODGE, REYNOLDS PLANTATION, IN GREENSBORO

In Greensboro

♞ **Granite Shoals Lodge** (706-453-7639), 3991 Walker Church Road. The standard rooms with two double beds and private bath are 50 feet from the water at this fishing lodge. There is a boat ramp, restaurant, and marina on the property. No swimming. Smoking permitted. Not wheelchair accessible. $59.95.

♿ **The Ritz-Carlton Lodge, Reynolds Plantation** (706-467-0600; 1-800-241-3333; www.ritzcarlton.com/resorts/reynolds_plantation), One Lake Oconee Trail. The AAA four-diamond property, ranked seventh on the list of Top Hotels and Resorts in America by *Travel & Leisure,* is a new concept in Ritz-Carlton accommodations. Instead of a typical high-rise urban hotel, the lodge is a 251-room facility that sprawls across a knoll in the manner of the great resorts of the early 20th century. What doesn't change from a traveler's expectations is the legendary Ritz-Carlton level of service. In addition to sumptuous accommodations on the secluded shores of Lake Oconee in central Georgia, the resort offers a golf course (see *To Do—Golf*), an award-winning spa (see *To Do—Spas*), exemplary cuisine (see *Where to Eat—Eating Out*), and activities from fishing to waterskiing to canoeing. Smoking and non-smoking rooms available. $195–5,000.

✳ Where to Eat
DINING OUT

In Eatonton
& **Waterside & Veranda Café** (706-484-2044), 126 Cuscowilla Drive. Open 5:30–10 Wednesday through Sunday. Poolside service offered 11:30–4 Wednesday through Sunday. This restaurant specializes in club cuisine with a Southern flair. Menu favorites include beef tenderloin, Dover sole, stuffed sea bass, and other seafood dishes. Smoking permitted in bar area. Around $20.

In Greensboro
& **The Clubhouse** (1-800-505-4653), One Club Drive. Open 11–3:30 (11–2:30 Sunday for brunch) and 5–9 daily. Both formal and informal dining rooms and a comfortable lounge can be found at this fine-dining restaurant, where specialties include lamb, veal, and beef tenderloin. No smoking. Around $24.

✔ & **Gaby's on the Lake** (706-467-0600), 100 Linger Longer Road. Open 11–3:30 and 5–10 daily; closed during winter. This delightful poolside restaurant also offers splendid views of Lake Oconee, so guests can enjoy casual dining in a beautiful setting. Menu items for lunch include salads and traditional hot and cold sandwiches. Dinner enticements include rosemary-rubbed grilled chicken, blackened redfish, grilled filet of beef, or mussels steamed in white wine. A children's menu is available. No smoking. Lunch $6–14, dinner $18–28.

EATING OUT

In Eatonton
✔ ❦ & **Hugs Restaurant** (706-484-4847), 103 Harmony Crossing NE, Suite 6. Open 11–2 and 5–9 Tuesday through Saturday. The lunch menu features sandwiches, burgers, subs, and chicken fingers. Dinner is a little more formal, with shrimp, chicken Romano, specialty pasta dishes, steak, and seafood. No smoking. Lunch about $7, dinner $12–13 .

In Greensboro
❦ **Granite Shoals Marina** (706-453-7639), 3991 Walker Church Road. The marina's restaurant specializes in fresh shrimp and catfish, grilled steaks, burgers, and homemade sandwiches. Amenities at the marina, which is open year-round, include lodging, gas, groceries, and fishing tackle. Smoking allowed at this adults-only fishing lodge. Not wheelchair accessible. $8–12.

✔ ❦ & **The Lobby Lounge** at the Ritz-Carlton Lodge, Reynolds Plantation (706-467-0600), 100 Linger Longer Road. Open 3–midnight weekdays, 1–1 Friday and Saturday. Enjoy a snifter of cognac and a good cigar as you look over the soothing shores of Lake Oconee from the fabulous veranda. Inside, enjoy light fare by the fireplace. Favorites include fried oysters, shrimp cocktail, crab, hush puppies, soups, and salads. The Lobby Lounge is the perfect place for a cocktail before dinner or a drink before bedtime. On Friday and Saturday nights, enjoy live entertainment 8 PM–12 AM. No smoking. $10–15.

✔ ❦ & **The Plantation Grill at Reynolds Plantation** (706-467-0600), 100 Linger Longer Road. Open 9–9 Tuesday through Saturday, noon–2:30 and 5:30–8:30 Sunday. Menu items range from salads to sandwiches, steaks to seafood. Golfers can dine here between rounds, and there is a Sunday brunch as well. No smoking. $7 and up.

🔖 **The Towne House Restaurant** (706-453-2729), 102 South Main Street. Open 7–2 Monday through Saturday. This cafeteria-style restaurant offers Southern soul food and country favorites such as fried chicken, macaroni and cheese, and a variety of vegetables and desserts. No smoking. A meat and two vegetables runs $4.75.

In Lincolnton

✐ 🔖 ♿ **Goolsby's Store** (706-359-3577), Augusta Highway. Open 11:30–2 Thursday and Friday, 11:30–2 and 5–8 Saturday and Sunday. In addition to laying claim to the "Best Hot Dogs in Town," this restaurant serves good Southern barbecue in a cafeteria setting. Menu favorites include fried chicken breasts, fried pork loin, generously proportioned ribs, grilled chicken, fresh catfish, and their famous fried corn fritters. No smoking. Lunch around $6, dinner $7–10.

✐ 🔖 ♿ **Soap Creek Restaurant** (706-359-3125), off US 378. Open 5–9:30 Thursday through Saturday. Soap Creek specializes in catfish, steaks, and seafood. Thursday all-you-can-eat seafood buffet; Friday and Saturday have all-you-can-eat catfish. No smoking. $7–19.95.

In Madison

✐ 🔖 ♿ **Adrian's Place** (706-342-1600), 342 West Washington Street. Open 11–2:30 weekdays. The menu at this cafeteria-style restaurant changes daily. Try their vegetable plate. No smoking. $6–7.50.

✐ 🔖 ♿ **Amici Italian Café** (706-342-0000), 113 South Main Street. Open 11:30–9:30 Monday through Thursday, 11:30–11 Friday, 11:30–10 Saturday, noon–9 Sunday. Menu favorites include calzones, 25 varieties of pizza, hot and cold subs, wings, and salads. No smoking. About $10–15.

✐ 🔖 ♿ **Hallie Jane's Market and Catering** (706-342-2837), 144 Academy Street. Open 11–3 Monday through Saturday. Specializing in "gourmet to go," this restaurant has a hot and cold bar that features fresh salads, soups, and homemade casseroles, to name just a few. In addition to a fascinatingly eclectic blend of cuisine, Hallie Jane's has another unique feature: Prices are determined by the pound. No smoking. About $4–8 per person.

✐ 🔖 ♿ **Madison Chop House Grill** (706-342-9009), 202 South Main Street. Open 11–9 Sunday through Thursday, 11–10 Friday and Saturday. The specialty here is American cuisine. Menu favorites include pasta, salmon, steaks, and salads. No smoking. About $12.

✐ 🔖 ♿ **Marlow's Café** (706-342-7172), 169 South Main Street. Open 7–2:30 Monday through Saturday, 11–3 Sunday. Most folks come for the country buffet, a bargain including a drink. À la carte items such as hamburgers, french fries, chicken salad, and other homemade favorites are also available. No smoking. $7.95–9.95.

In Tignall

✐ 🔖 ♿ **Kumback Café** (706-285-2831), 112 Independence Street. Open 6 AM–2 PM Tuesday through Saturday, 5–9 Friday and Saturday. You'll find all your favorite breakfast and short-order items on the menu as well as steaks, shrimp, and catfish at dinnertime. Smoking permitted. About $6.

In Warrenton

🍴 ♿ **Miss Jane's** (706-465-3882), 110 West Main Street. Open 4:30 AM–2 PM Monday through Saturday, 6:30 AM–2 PM Sunday. Breakfast favorites fill the morning menu. A changing lunch menu is chock-full of country favorites that delight afternoon patrons. No smoking. About $6.

In Washington

🍴 ♿ **Home Café** (706-678-2231), 1001 North Bypass East. Open 6–10:30, 11–2, and 5–9 Monday through Saturday; 6–2 Sunday. The menu changes daily, but some favorites include roast beef and gravy, fried catfish, country-fried steak, homemade vegetables, and more. No smoking. Breakfast and lunch under $6; dinner $5.95–12.95.

🍷 🍴 ♿ **Miller's Bistro** (706-678-4446), 9 East Public Square. Open 11:30–4:30 Sunday through Tuesday, 11–3 Thursday through Saturday, 6–9 Saturday. Menu items cover every taste, from open-face and club sandwiches at lunch to catfish, half a chicken, Cornish game hens, blackened salmon, and rib-eye steaks for dinner. On Sunday the eatery features a soul-food buffet with all your favorite comfort foods. There is a smoking section. Lunch around $7, dinner $13.

🍷 🍴 ♿ **Washington Jockey Club** (706-678-1672), 5 East Public Square. Open 11–2 and 5–9 daily, until 10:30 Friday and Saturday. The menu covers the bases, from sandwiches and burgers to Gulf Coast seafood, specialty pastas, steak, and entrée salads. Smoking permitted in bar. Lunch around $6–7, dinner a little more .

🍷 🍴 ♿ **Watchmakers Restaurant** (706-678-5901), 16 West Public Square. Open 11:30–2 Tuesday through Saturday, 5:30–9 Friday and Saturday, 11–2 Sunday. Menu salads, a daily blue plate special, chicken items, and fried green tomato sandwiches are favorites with the lunch crowd. At dinnertime feast on salmon, organic chicken breast, scallops, steaks, barbecued quail, and more. No smoking. Lunch $7, dinner $9–21.

COFFEEHOUSES

In Madison

🍴 ♿ **Barista's Coffeehouse and Café** (706-342-9803), 115 West Jefferson Street. Open 7 AM–9 PM weekdays, 9–10 Saturday, 11–4 Sunday. Soups, salads, sandwiches, cakes, pastries, muffins, brownies, scones, cappuccino, and espresso are among the favorite menu items here. No smoking. $6.

✳ Entertainment

THEATER Madison-Morgan Cultural Arts Center (706-342-4743; www.madisonmorgancultural.org), 434 South Main Street, Madison. This intimate 397-seat theater contains original woodwork, ceilings, seats, and chandeliers (circa 1895). Music, lectures, dance, and theater presentations feature such notables as the Alvin Ailey Dance Company, the Atlanta Symphony Orchestra, Nnenna Freelon, the Royal Shakespeare Company, Mischa Dichter, Bobby McFerrin, and the Vienna Boys Choir. (See *To See—Museums* for more about this building's architecture and museum hours.) Call for a schedule of events and ticket prices.

✳ Selective Shopping

ANTIQUES **Attic Treasures** (706-342-7197), 121 South Main Street, Madison. Open 10–5:30 daily. This delightful shop specializes in jewelry, silver, Oriental and African art, glassware, ceramics, sports equipment, military memorabilia (especially Civil War and World War II), musical instruments, and children's books.

Barn Raising Antiques (706-557-2956), 118 Fairplay Street, Rutledge. Open 11–6 Tuesday through Saturday. This quaint shop specializes in gifts, collectibles, antiques, and handcrafted items.

Greensboro Antique Mall (706-453-9100; www.antiquesofthelake.com), 101 South Main Street, Greensboro. Open 10–5:30 Monday through Saturday. Shop here not only for antiques, furniture, jewelry, and collectibles but also for unusual items.

In High Cotton (706-342-7777), 158 West Jefferson Street, Madison. Open 10–5:30 Monday through Saturday, 1–5 Sunday. This charming store carries a little bit of everything. Merchandise includes but is not limited to furniture, mirrors, wrought iron, wicker, lamps, and candles.

J & K Fleas An'Tiques (706-557-9188), 122 Fairplay Street, Rutledge. Open 10–6 Tuesday through Saturday. Despite its name, this is not where you'll find your average flea-market junk. This store specializes in high-end antique furnishings. Patrons come from all over the United States to shop this upscale collection of treasures from the past.

ART GALLERIES **Genuine Georgia, an Artist Marketplace** (706 453-1440), 101 North Main Street, Greensboro. Open 10–7 Monday through Saturday, 1–5 Sunday. This artists' emporium features the work of more than 130 Georgia artisans. Items for sale include heritage crafts, Okefenokee palmetto dolls and fans, pine-needle baskets, folk art and fine art paintings, pottery (both utilitarian and decorative), birdhouses, silks, weavings, a genuine Georgia pantry section with gourmet foods from all over the state, and a book center that features Georgia authors.

Steffen Thomas Museum & Archives (706 342-7557; www.steffen thomas.org), 4200 Bethany Road, Buckhead. Open 1–4 Tuesday through Saturday. Stop by this quirky museum (see *To See—Museums*) to see or to purchase the works of Steffen Thomas.

CRAFTS **Craftsman's Row** (706-557-9020; 1-800-709-7406; www.madison ga.org), US 278/Fairplay Street, Rutledge. Open 10–6 Monday through Saturday, 1–5 Sunday. This two-block area is filled with artisans' shops where craftspeople cane chairs, hook rugs, quilt, carve wood, and create other works of art.

See also **Genuine Georgia, an Artisan Marketplace** under *Art Galleries*.

FLEA MARKETS **Madison Mall and Flea Market** (706-342-0018), 1291 Eatonton Highway, Madison. Open 10–5 Monday through Thursday, 10–6:30 Friday and Saturday. More than 60 vendors participate in this massive enterprise. Treasure hunters will be delighted by the wide variety of merchandise on display.

✳ Special Events

Spring: **Spring Tour of Homes**

(706-342-4743). Visit gracious old homes and gardens along Madison's beautiful tree-lined streets. This walking and driving tour is self-guided. Call for details because dates vary from year to year. $20.

April: **Southland Jubilee** (706-453-7592). The historic business district of Greensboro is the setting for this unique family festival. Activities include three different stages of live music, juried arts and crafts, heritage craft demonstrations, living-history interpreters, children's games, agricultural exhibits, an antique car show, a parade, cow milking, a petting zoo, pony rides, food, and more. Call for exact date. Free.

Washington-Wilkes Tour of Homes (706-678-2013). Held annually in Washington on the first Saturday in April, this event features tours of several private homes, churches, public buildings, museums, and other sites. $3.

May and September: **Cruise-In on the Square Antique Car Show** (706-678-2013). Antique cars and trucks cruise the streets of Washington and are displayed in the square during this event, held on the second Saturday of May and September. Free.

October: **Jack's Creek Farm Festival** (706-343-1855). A trip to this Madison pumpkin farm is the ideal October activity. In addition to finding an endless assortment of pumpkins, children of all ages will be delighted by the petting zoo, hayrides, and a corn maze. Call for dates and details.

Mule Day Southern Heritage Festival (706-678-2013). Held on the second Saturday in October at Callaway Plantation in Washington, this event celebrates plantation life in the Old South with mule contests, primitive demonstrations, food, an arts and crafts show, and lots more fun. Free.

December: **Christmas at Callaway Plantation** (706-678-2013). This event, held on the second Saturday in December, allows visitors to enjoy a plantation Christmas the way the first settlers of Wilkes County experienced it. The entire plantation in Washington is beautifully decorated, and music adds to the atmosphere. Free.

Historic Town and Country Holiday Tour (706-342-4454; 1-800-709-7406). Candlelight tours of six different Madison homes are highlighted during four days in December. Call for exact dates and times. $20–25 for two tours.

MILLEDGEVILLE

This area of Georgia is characterized by rolling hills, red clay, pine trees, and hardwoods. Native Americans lived here 12,000 years ago, as evidenced by earthen mounds, pottery, tools, and weapons that have survived. Several Indian trading trails converged near what is now Milledgeville.

The town, which served as the state capital from 1807 to 1868, is the only city in the country besides Washington, D.C., designed specifically to be a capital. When Union troops occupied Milledgeville, they burned the military arsenal and stabled their horses in St. Stephen's Episcopal Church while pouring molasses down the pipes of the organ. Although various romantic legends claim to know why Union General William Tecumseh Sherman spared the city on his March to the Sea from Atlanta to Savannah, the real, mundane reason was probably that the city had no military significance.

Because Milledgeville survived the Civil War, it is considered to be the only remaining example of a complete Federal-era city in America. As is not surprising in an old town with so much history, Milledgeville is well known for its ghosts, among them Miss Sue and the banshee.

GUIDANCE When planning a trip to Milledgeville, contact the **Milledgeville–Baldwin County Convention and Visitors Bureau and Welcome Center** (478-452-4687; 1-800-653-1804; www.milledgevillecvb.com), 200 West Hancock Street, Milledgeville 31061. After you arrive in town, you can pick up information on Andalusia tours and the Historic Trolley Tour, as well as brochures for self-guided walking-driving tours (see *To Do—Guided Tours* and *To Do—Historic Homes and Sites*). Check out the Convention and Visitors Bureau web site, which offers coupons and special packages.

For information about Louisville and Wrens, contact the **Jefferson County Chamber of Commerce** (478-625-8134, www.jeffersoncounty.org), 302 East Broad Street, Louisville 30434. Open 9–5 weekdays.

To learn more about Sandersville, call the **Washington County Chamber of Commerce** (478-552-3288; www.washingtoncounty-ga.com), 131 West Haynes Street, Sandersville 31082.

For more information about Sparta, contact SHARE, the **Sparta-Hancock**

Alliance for Revitalization and Empowerment (706-444-7462), 325 Broad Street, Sparta 31087.

GETTING THERE *By air:* The **Baldwin County Airport,** 216 Airport Road (off US 441), Milledgeville, has a 5,000-foot airstrip for private aircraft. Otherwise, visitors fly into nearby **Middle Georgia Regional Airport** in Macon (see Macon chapter) on **American Airlines** (1-800-443-7300), **Delta** (1-800-221-1212), **Northwest Airlines** (1-800-225-2525), or **United Airlines** (1-800-241-6522) and then rent a car.

By bus: The nearest **Greyhound Lines** (1-800-231-2222; www.greyhound.com) service is to Macon (see Macon chapter).

By car: The towns described in this chapter are clustered along US 441 and US 1/221 between I-20 and I-16.

By train: The nearest **Amtrak** station is in Atlanta (see What's Where in Georgia).

GETTING AROUND When visiting these small towns, it's imperative to have a car—either your own or a rental. There are few taxis and no public transit. The towns themselves are some distance apart.

MEDICAL EMERGENCY For life-threatening emergencies call 911 or go to **Oconee Regional Hospital** (478-454-3500), 821 North Cobb Street, Milledgeville.

VILLAGES AND NEIGHBORHOODS The charming small towns of **Haddock, Mitchell,** and **Wrens** have their own sight-seeing attractions or recreational activities to offer.

Lake Sinclair, the only large lake in this region, offers almost limitless opportunities for water sports.

Tiny **Louisville** (pronounced Lewisville) was the state capital from 1795 to 1806. Named for France's Louis XVI, the entire town was laid out and its buildings, including the governor's mansion and the capital, constructed before inhabitants moved in.

Sandersville claims to be the kaolin capital of the world. This white alumina-silicate clay, one of Georgia's most important minerals, is used in hundreds of goods, from paper products to ceramics.

While in **Sparta**, admire the Hancock County Courthouse, a masterpiece of Victorian architecture constructed between 1881 and 1883, and Confederate Square, which has a Confederate monument on its grounds.

✳ To See

CULTURAL SITES 🅐 ♿ **Allied Arts Cultural Center–John Marlor House** (478-452-3950; www.milledgevillecvb.com), 201 North Wayne Street, Milledgeville. Open 9–5 weekdays. This beautiful Federal-style house was built in the 1830s by John Marlor as a wedding present for his second wife. Today it houses the Allied Arts Center and the Elizabeth Marlor Bethune Art Gallery, which offers works by local artists and traveling exhibits throughout the year. Free.

🦞 ♿ **Flannery O'Connor Memorial Room** (478-445-4047; www.library.gcsu .edu/~sc/foc.html), Ida Dillard Russell Library at Georgia College and State University, Clark and Montgomery streets, Milledgeville. Open 8–4 weekdays when school is in session. Furnished in the style of the 1870s, the room features pieces from Andalusia Farm (see *Historic Homes and Sites*), the home where Flannery O'Connor wrote most of her fiction. Also on display are her personal library of more than 700 books and other memorabilia, including letters, manuscripts, and paintings by the author. A short film chronicles her life story and early death. Many papers are available only to scholars by reservation. Free.

GUIDED TOURS 🖋 🦞 **Milledgeville Historic Trolley Tour** (478-452-4687; 1-800-653-1804; www.milledgevillecvb.com), 200 West Hancock Street, Milledgeville. Leaves at 10 AM weekdays, 2 PM Saturday, from Convention and Visitors Bureau. The tour makes rotating visits to the Old Governor's Mansion, Old Capitol, St. Stephen's Episcopal Church, Lockerly Hall, or the Stetson-Sanford House. Stops vary daily. Visitors who purchase a trolley tour receive a discount on the Old Governor's Mansion tour (see *Historic Homes and Sites*). Adults $10, children 6–16 $5.

HISTORIC HOMES AND SITES 🦞 **Andalusia Farm** (478-454-4029; www .andalusiafarm.org), US 441 North, Milledgeville. Open 10–4 Monday, Tuesday, and Saturday or by appointment. This dairy farm–home of Flannery O'Connor is where the world-renowned author wrote two of her novels, *The Violent Bear It Away* and *Wise Blood,* as well as a number of the short stories for which she is so famous. Tours of the white, two-story main house from the 1850s include the PBS video *The Displaced Person*; Flannery's bedroom, where she did most of her writing; and the dining room, kitchen, and addition. Visitors are then free to wander around the farm, where they can see various farm buildings, ponds, a creek, and several ecosystems, and perhaps catch a glimpse of some wildlife. Free, but donations accepted.

🖋 🦞 **Lockerly Hall** (478-452-2112; www.lockerlyarboretum.org), 1534 Irwinton Road, Milledgeville. Open 8:30–4:30 weekdays. Built in 1839, the mansion is an outstanding example of plantation architecture. Built around 1839 and lived in by only six families, the house was once known as Rose Hill because such a profusion of wild Cherokee roses grew in the region. Gardens still surround the house today. Lockerly Hall is the centerpiece of **Lockerly Arboretum** (see *Green Space—Nature Preserves and Parks*). $3.

🦞 ♿ **Market House,** center of Broad Street, Louisville. Constructed in the late 1700s at the intersection of two trails, this timber, open-air structure contains a bronze bell that was made in France in 1772 for a New Orleans convent. The bell never made it to New Orleans, however, because it was captured by pirates off the coast of Savannah. When it was put on the auction block, it was purchased and brought to Louisville, the state capital at the time, where it was used as a community warning system in the event of a possible Indian attack. Later the bell rang out to celebrate the independence of the 13 colonies, and even later it announced Georgia's secession from the Union. This open-air market is also the only remaining slave-trade site in the state.

🌹 ♿ **Memory Hill Cemetery,** Franklin and Liberty streets, Milledgeville. Open daily. Land for this cemetery was designated when the town plan was laid out in 1803 as one of four public squares of 20 acres each. It later became known as Cemetery Square. Flannery O'Connor's grave site is here, as are those of U.S. Congressman Carl Vinson and other Georgia statesmen. On the infamous side, notorious stagecoach and train robber Bill Miner is buried here as well. In addition, the cemetery contains some interesting African American graves. In front of each headstone is a metal rod with hooks and chains attached to it. One link means the person was born into slavery, two means he or she was born and lived in slavery, and three means the person was born, lived, and died in slavery. Several Revolutionary and Civil War soldiers are buried here as well. Free.

🌹 ♿ **Old Governor's Mansion** (478-445-4545; www.gcsu.edu/mansion), 120 South Clark Street, Milledgeville. Open 10–4 Tuesday through Saturday, 2–4 Sunday. Guided tours are given on the hour. Built in 1839, the pink stucco-covered mansion was home to 10 Georgia governors through the antebellum, Civil War, and Reconstruction periods until the state capital was moved to Atlanta in 1868. Union General William Tecumseh Sherman used the mansion as his headquarters on November 22, 1864, during his March to the Sea. When the capital was moved to Atlanta, the building was given to Georgia Normal and Industrial College (now Georgia College and State University) as the founding building of that institution. The Old Governor's Mansion is considered to be one of the country's most outstanding examples of High Greek Revival–style residences. An extensive three-year renovation has returned the mansion to its 1850s appearance, complete with its original layout, colors, and lighting. The tour includes the main floor, the bedroom level, and the servants' area. One of the biggest surprises is the rotunda and 40-foot dome, which can't be seen from the street. Make sure to note the intricate gilding in the interior of the dome. Adults $10, seniors $6, students $2, children younger than 6 free.

MUSEUMS 🌹 ♿ **Brown House Museum** (478-552-1965), 268 North Harris Street, Sandersville. Open 2–5 Tuesday and Thursday. Union General William Tecumseh Sherman used this house as his headquarters when he and his army passed through Sandersville on the March to the Sea. Restored to its original condition, the house displays Sandersville and Civil War artifacts. Donations accepted.

THE OLD GOVERNOR'S MANSION IN MILLEDGEVILLE WAS BUILT IN 1839.

🌹 ♿ **Museum and Archives of Georgia Education** (478-445-4391; www.library.gcsu.edu/~sc/magepages), 131 South Clark Street, Milledgeville. Open 1–5 Tuesday through Friday. Corinthian columns and graceful Palladian windows characterize this circa 1900 Classical Revival building, which houses artifacts, memorabilia, and records chronicling the development of education in Georgia. One gallery features rotating exhibits. Free.

✦ ✤ **Ogeechee River Mill** (478-552-2393), Hamburg State Park, 6071 Hamburg State Park Road, Mitchell. Call ahead, as operating hours vary. There has been a mill on this site for the past 170 years, although it has been known by many different names. Today visitors can enjoy a demonstration of how cornmeal was ground by this water-powered gristmill. Be sure to take home a package of their famous hush-puppy mix. Admission free, parking $2.

✦ ✤ ♿ **Old State Capitol Building, Georgia's Antebellum Capital Museum** (478-453-1803; www.oldcapitalmuseum.com), 201 East Greene Street, Milledgeville. Open 10–noon and 1–3 Monday, Wednesday, and Friday. Built around 1807, the Old Capitol Building is considered to be the finest example of the Gothic Revival style in America. It may also be the oldest public building in the country. It served as the seat of government for the state of Georgia from 1807 to 1868. It was here in the legislative chambers that the Secession Convention was held in 1861. During the brief time that Union troops held the town in November 1864, they conducted a mock assembly of the legislature here and "repealed" the Ordinance of Secession. The north and south gates were constructed from bricks recovered from the arsenal destroyed by Sherman's troops. Since 1879, the Georgia Military College has occupied the historic site, and today it serves primarily as a classroom building, but the House Chamber operates as **Georgia's Antebellum Capitol Museum** with exhibits on area history and culture, including period furnishings and memorabilia. Each of the five galleries depicts a different era in the history of the former capital. $2.

✤ ♿ **Sparta–Hancock County Museum** (706-444-7462; www.historicsparta hancock.org), 719 Elm Street, Sparta. Open 9–5 weekdays, weekends by appointment only. The highlight display examines the life of Hancock County author Amanda America Dickson, who wrote *A House Divided*. Other displays feature local arts and crafts, including quilts and wood carvings. Of further interest is an exhibit that chronicles the life of a wealthy plantation owner's daughter who discovers the truth about her biracial heritage. Adults $3, seniors $2, children $1.

✴ To Do

BIRDING Mississippi kites, osprey, waterfowl, great blue herons, snowy and common egrets, pine siskins, Carolina wrens, and a wide variety of woodpeckers, to name just a few, can be found at the **Baldwin Forest Public Fishing Area** (see *Fishing*).

BOATING On Lake Sinclair, boat rentals are available from **Sinclair Marina** (478-452-3620), 170 NE Sinclair Marina Road. Kayaks rentals are available from **Lazy River Kayaks**

THE OLD STATE CAPITOL BUILDING, NOW OCCUPIED BY PART OF GEORGIA MILITARY COLLEGE, IS ALSO HOME TO GEORGIA'S ANTEBELLUM CAPITOL MUSEUM.

(478-453-0248), 38 SE Old River Bridge Road. Other marina facilities are available at **Bass Boat House Shop** (478-452-5112), 140 Bass Road NE; **Crooked Creek Marina** (706-485-7558), 208 Crooked Creek Road; and **Highgrove Harbor** (706-484-9885), 105 Mays Road.

FARM TOURS ✔ ✿ **Olive Forge Herb Farm** (478-932-5737; e-mail oliveforge @alltel.net), 161 Brown's Crossing, Haddock. Open 9–5 Thursday through Saturday, other days by appointment. This unique attraction offers 360 varieties of herbs, including 18 varieties of rosemary. Olive Forge also features a gift shop with culinary items and toiletries made at the farm. Herbal refreshments available. Free.

See also **Andalusia Farm** under *To See—Historic Homes and Sites* and **Gourd Farm** under *Selective Shopping—Other Goods*.

FISHING ✔ ✿ **Baldwin Forest Public Fishing Area** (478-453-7832). From Milledgeville travel south on US 441, go approximately 3 miles south of GA 243 intersection to point where highway crosses Little Black Creek, follow signs to entrance of public fishing area. Facility not staffed. This 2,500-acre park boasts five ponds covering 51 acres of water that provides angling for channel catfish, largemouth bass, and bream. Bird-watching is also excellent. No fees.

See also **Bartram Forest** and **Hamburg State Park** under *Green Space—Nature Preserves and Parks*.

GOLF See Golf Appendix.

✳ Green Space

LAKES ✔ ✿ & **Lake Sinclair** (706-485-8704; 1-888-472-5253; www.southernco .com/gapower/lakes), US 441, Milledgeville. Open daily year-round. Halfway between Atlanta and Augusta, this popular 15,300-acre lake with 417 miles of shoreline spans Oconee, Greene, Morgan, Putnam, Hancock, and Baldwin counties and offers boating, fishing, and other water sports. In addition to several major fishing tournaments, visitors can find accommodations of all sorts as well as several marinas (see *To Do—Boating*), recreation areas, and restaurants. Lake Sinclair also claims to be the cleanest lake in the state. Free.

NATURE PRESERVES AND PARKS ✔ ✿ & **Bartram Forest** (478-445-2119), 2892 US 441 South, Milledgeville. Open 8–4:30 weekdays. In prehistoric times, the area was a shallow sea, as evidenced by the soil found in an erosion ravine. In 1794, the area was inhabited by Native Americans. Today, three looping walking trails with educational stations provide opportunities for bird-watching and plant and wildlife observation. The facility also offers a pavilion, garden, and fishing. Free.

✔ 🐾 ✿ & **Hamburg State Park** (478-552-2393; www.gastateparks.org/info/hamburg), 6071 Hamburg State Park Road, Mitchell. Open 7–10 daily. It's not just outdoor adventures that await visitors to this park. Sure, there's Little Ocmulgee River–fed Hamburg Lake and its associated water sports, as well as a boat ramp, boat rentals, a fishing pier, and nature and hiking trails. But the park also features a working circa 1921 gristmill and a country store where you can buy freshly ground cornmeal from the mill. The park's museum exhibits agricultural tools and appliances used in rural Georgia. The park offers 30 shady tent, trailer, and RV sites along the lake's edge. Pets are permitted at the campground. Parking/day-use fee $3, camping $15–17.

✍ 🐾 **Lockerly Arboretum** (478-452-2112; www.lockerlyarboretum.org), 1534 Irwinton Road, Milledgeville. Open 8:30–4:30 weekdays year-round, Saturday 1–5 October through May and 10–2 June through September. Fifty acres contain many types of native trees, shrubs, herb beds, flower gardens, and vineyards. The floral gardens feature iris, daylily, rhododendron, bulb, and perennial gardens, and there is also a tropical and desert greenhouse. In addition to educational exhibits, the arboretum features trails, a stream, and a tiny museum. Admission to arboretum free. Admission to **Lockerly Hall** (see *To See—Historic Homes and Sites*) $3.

✹ Lodging

BED & BREAKFASTS

In Louisville
🐾 **Old Town Plantation** (888-754-2717), 8910 GA 17 South. This 4,000-acre resort with three guest houses is open year-round. Activities include tennis, swimming, and fishing. Guests are also invited to use the weight room or visit the old gristmill (circa 1825) on the property. No smoking. Not wheelchair accessible. $85.

In Milledgeville
Antebellum Inn (478-453-3993; www.antebelluminn.com), 200 North Columbia Street. The inn is a late-1800s Greek Revival home with all the modern amenities. Verandas, lushly landscaped lawns, and a swimming pool create a restful oasis. No smoking. Not wheelchair accessible. $79–129.

♿ **Guest House** (478-452-3098), 520 West Hancock Street. Comfort and privacy are the top priority at this B&B, which has two lovely suites. In addition to the sleeping area, each suite has a parlor and a private bath. A full breakfast is included. No smoking. Wheelchair accessible. $90–150.

CAMPGOUNDS

In Milledgeville
✍ 🏕 🐾 **Little River Park Campground** (478-452-1605), 3069 North Columbia Street. Get there early, as sites are first-come, first-served. RV campsites offer all the modern amenities. The campground also features a lake with a beach, picnic tables, and grills. $19 per night, $125 per week.

✍ 🐾 **Scenic Mountain RV Park and Campground** (478-453-8683; 1-800-716-3015), 2686 Irwinton Road. This 108-acre facility offers full hookups on spacious lots. Amenities include five stocked ponds, a nature trail, phone, cable, a clubhouse, bathhouse, pool, and spa. $24 per night, $150 per week.

In Mitchell
See **Hamburg State Park** under *Green Space—Nature Preserves and Parks.*

CONDOS

In Milledgeville
✍ **Lake Sinclair Villages** (478-453-2068; 1-800-837-0036; www.lake sinclairvillages.com), 1000 Marigold Road. These lakeside condos are large

enough for several couples or a multi-generational family. Amenities include tennis and basketball courts, an outdoor pool, horseshoes, shuffleboard, grills, and a boat launch. $250–330 for three-day weekend (three-night minimum required); weekly rates also available.

✳ Where to Eat
DINING OUT

In Louisville
✦ ♿ **Emily's on West Broad** (478-625-0102; www.emilysonwestbroad.com), 401 West Broad Street. Open 11–2:30 and 5:30–9 Thursday through Saturday. Mouth-watering gourmet favorites are served for lunch and dinner in a cozy, inviting atmosphere. A self-playing baby grand piano provides soft jazz background music. Don't miss the delectable desserts. A gift shop that specializes in the work of local artists is open 10–5 Wednesday through Saturday. No smoking. Wheelchair accessible. Lunch $6–8; dinner varies.

In Milledgeville
⌕ ✦ ♿ **Chobys Landing Restaurant** (478-453-9744), 3090 US 441 North. Open 4:30–9 Thursday and Sunday, 4:30–10 Friday and Saturday. This casual restaurant on Lake Sinclair delights diners with catfish, chicken, shrimp, scallops, steak, and awesome prime rib. No smoking. Wheelchair accessible. $10–17.

♿ **119 Chops** (478-452-8119), 119 Wayne Street. Open 5 PM–midnight Tuesday through Saturday; bar open until 2 AM. This casual, fine-dining steakhouse offers steak lovers choices up to 32 ounces (allow 45 minutes to cook it to medium). Other fare includes fish, chops, homemade meatloaf, and pasta. No smoking. Wheelchair accessible through back entrance. $7–30.

EATING OUT

In Milledgeville
✦ ♿ **Amici's** (478-452-5003), 101 West Hancock Street. Open 11–10 daily; bar open until 2 AM. Menu selections include salads, sandwiches, and pasta. No smoking until 11 PM. Wheelchair accessible. $6–17.

✦ ♿ **Café South** (478-452-3164), 132 Harwick Street. Open 11–2 daily. Vegetarian selections are available at this Southern buffet. No smoking. Wheelchair accessible. $6.15 per person, $5.50 for seniors.

⌕ ✦ ♿ **Pig in a Pit** (478-414-1744), 1835 North Columbia Road. Open 11–9. Not surprisingly, this barbecue restaurant specializes in on-site pit-cooked beef, pork, chicken, and finger-lickin' ribs as well as Buffalo wings, chicken tenders, sandwiches, and low-carb wraps. All the eatery's delicious side dishes are homemade on-site as well. No smoking. Wheelchair accessible. $3–15.

⌕ ✦ ♿ **Zaxby's** (478-452-1027), 1700 North Columbia Street. Open 10:30–10. This chain eatery specializes in chicken fingers and Buffalo wings. No smoking. Wheelchair accessible. $3–15.

✳ Selective Shopping
ANTIQUES **Black Sheep Antiques** (478-453-7148), 125 South Wayne Street, Milledgeville. Open 10–6 Tuesday through Saturday. Black Sheep specializes in "the stuff your mother and grandmother had that you wish you had never thrown out," including furniture, china, decorative

items, pictures, linens, antique tools, and McCoy items such as vases, planters, and mixing bowls.

Grapevine Antiques (478-451-0556), 117 West Hancock Street, Milledgeville. Open 10–7 Tuesday through Saturday, 1–6 Sunday. Grapevine purveys everything from junk to treasures in 30,000 square feet of space. With everything from 1800s antiques to new items, the emporium advertises that "if you name it—we probably have it."

Jean's Antiques (478-452-1550), 2205 Irwinton Road, Milledgeville. Open 10–5 Tuesday through Saturday. The store has eight rooms spread over two circa 1920 houses. Browse here for blanket chests, love seats, 1800s antiques, coffee tables, chess tables, handcrafted items, pottery, clocks, Coca-Cola memorabilia, McCoy pottery, and Masonic memorabilia.

OTHER GOODS 🖋 🐌 **Gourd Farm** (706-547-6784), 1089 Hoyt Braswell Road, Wrens. Open 8 AM–dark daily. If you want any size gourd to use as a birdhouse or for any decorative purpose, this farm is the place to come. You can also buy homemade syrups and fresh produce.

✳ Special Events

April or May: **Spring Home and Garden Tour** (478-454-3646). Get a glimpse of some of Milledgeville's finest private homes and their beautifully manicured gardens. Call for details. $20 in advance; $25 that day.

June: **Southern Rock Bikefest** (478-453-7057; www.milledgevillethunder rally.com), US 441 South, Milledgeville. This festival features good food, entertainment, amusement, and fun.

Call for specific date. $35 adults, $25 children.

August: **Hamp Brown Bottom Festival** (478-452-5904). Held on the third weekend in August in one of Milledgeville's oldest neighborhoods, once called "the Bourbon Street of Milledgeville." This African American festival comes alive with food and entertainment. A free soul-food dinner on Sunday is followed by a gospel sing. Free.

October: **Haunted Trolley Tours** (478-452-4687). Take a ride on the spooky side and experience the thrills and chills of days gone by. Costumed actors play scary spirits, revealing lurid tales that have made Milledgeville one of the spookiest towns in Georgia. See where the ghosts live and hear stories about the spirits who still lurk in this world. Adults $15 in advance, $20 at the time of tour (don't take a chance on waiting until the last minute; tour may be full), $25 for tour and dinner; children $8 for tour, $10 for tour and dinner.

November: **Sweetwater Festival** (478-414-4014; www.milledgeville mainstreet.com). Named in honor of the spring discovered in 1803, this festival in downtown Milledgeville features live music, a barbecue cook-off, an artists' market, an antique car show, and special children's activities in the Kid's Corner. Adults $5, children $2.

November or December: **Old Governor's Mansion Candlelight Tour** (478-445-4545), 120 South Clark Street, Milledgeville. Take a candlelit tour of the restored mansion completely decorated for the holidays and enjoy entertainment by local choirs. Adults $10 ($7 in advance), seniors $6, students $2.

STATESBORO TO WAYNESBORO TO DUBLIN

With a few exceptions, this tranquil area of central to eastern Georgia is characterized by rural agricultural areas and small towns with populations ranging from 500 to 3,500. Regardless of size, each municipality has something unique to offer.

One of the larger small-towns is Statesboro in Bulloch County, with a population of nearly 23,000. Statesboro, which has been named one of the 100 best small towns in America by author Michael Crompton, is the home of Georgia Southern University. Like most universities, GSU offers many benefits to the general public, from theatrical and musical performances to museums, botanical gardens, and a renowned raptor center. Interestingly, the town, which is believed to have been named in honor of the statehood of Georgia, is the only Statesboro in America.

Bulloch County was named for Archibald Bulloch, who presided over the Provincial Congress on July 4, 1775, and became Georgia's first provincial governor, in 1776. A traveler to early Statesboro (then spelled Statesborough) noted that the residents were hard workers, but also hard drinkers. Supposedly at that time there were only three public buildings: a log courthouse, a log whiskey shop, and a boardinghouse. One hundred years later, the Jaeckel Hotel opened and was renowned for having the finest accommodations in the area. Celebrities such as Henry Ford, William Jennings Bryan, and Cornelius Vanderbilt stayed at the hotel and enjoyed its Southern hospitality. Today, that structure serves as Statesboro City Hall.

Potential visitors to this area of Georgia may be very familiar with some of the products of the region without being aware of the towns or rural areas from which they come. The Vidalia area, for example, known around the world for its sweet onions, is blessed with the perfect climate and soil to produce this wonderful vegetable. The town of Vidalia and the others near it were settled at the turn of the 20th century along the Savannah, Americus & Montgomery Railroad.

Of further interest—and regardless of the fact that some comedians claim that there is only one fruitcake in the world, which just keeps getting passed around—the small town of Claxton has two famous fruitcake-baking companies that together produce more than 7 million pounds of the sweet treat annually.

Tattnall County is one of the largest and most diversified agricultural counties in the state. Besides producing more than half of the world's Vidalia onions, this area—also known as "the Breadbasket of Georgia" and the state's tomato capital—grows produce from blackberries to watermelon and everything in between. Visit **Farm Fresh Tattnall** (see *Selective Shopping—Food*) for the best of what's in-season during your visit.

GUIDANCE If you are planning a trip to the Statesboro area, contact the **Statesboro Convention and Visitors Bureau** (912-489-1869; 1-800-568-3301; www .visit-statesboro.com), 332 South Main Street, Statesboro 30458. Open 8:30–5 weekdays.

To find out more about Claxton, contact the **Claxton–Evans County Chamber of Commerce and Welcome Center** (912-739-1391; www.claxtonevans chamber.com), 4 North Duval Street/US 301 North, Claxton 30417. Open 8–5 weekdays.

For more information about Dublin, consult the **Dublin–Laurens County Chamber of Commerce** (478-272-5546; www.dublin-georgia.com), 1200 Bellevue Avenue, Dublin 31021. Open 8:30–5 weekdays. Pick up a brochure for the Dublin's Walking Tour of Historic Downtown from the chamber. Further information can be obtained from the **Dublin–Laurens County Welcome Center** (478-272-5766; www.dublin-georgia.com), I-16 at US 441, Dublin 31021. Open 8:30–5 Monday through Saturday.

To learn more about Metter, contact the **Metter–Candler County Chamber of Commerce** (912-685-2159; www.metter-candler.com), 1210 South Lewis Street, Metter 30439. Open 9–5 weekdays. This location, which was once the 1928 Metter Commissary, also serves as the **Metter Local Welcome Center** (912-685-6988), which is open 9–5 Monday through Saturday, 1–5 Sunday (seasonally).

For information about Millen and the surrounding area, contact the **Jenkins County Chamber of Commerce** (478-982-5595; www.millenjenkinscounty .org), 548 Cotton Avenue, Millen 30442. Open 9–5 weekdays.

To learn more about Reidsville, consult the **Greater Tattnall Chamber of Commerce and Reidsville Welcome Center** (912-557-6323), 120 Brazell Street, Reidsville 30453. Open 8–5 weekdays.

For more information about Soperton, contact the **Soperton–Treutlen County Chamber of Commerce** (912-529-6868; www.soperton.org), 402 Second Street, Soperton 30457. Open 8–5 weekdays. Stop by the **Million Pines Visitors Welcome Center** (912-529-6263), I-16 at GA 29, Soperton 30457, where the 1845 log cabin serves as a museum and visitor center.

For information about Swainsboro, contact the **Swainsboro–Emanuel County Chamber of Commerce** (478-237-6426; www.emanuelchamber.org), 102 South Main Street, Swainsboro 30401. Open 8:30–5 weekdays.

Information about Sylvania and the surrounding area (as well as the entire state of Georgia) can be picked up at the **Georgia Visitor Information Center– Sylvania** (912-829-3331; www.georgiaonmymind.org), 8463 Burton's Ferry Highway, Sylvania 30467. Open 8:30–5:30 weekdays. This visitor center claims to be the oldest in the country. Information is also available at the **Screven Coun-**

ty Chamber of Commerce (912-564-7878; www.screvencounty.com), 101 South Main Street, Sylvania 30467. Open 9–5 weekdays.

To learn more about Vidalia, contact the **Vidalia Area Convention and Visitors Bureau** (912-538-8687; www.vidaliaarea.com), 100 Vidalia Sweet Onion Drive, Vidalia 30474. Open 8:30–5 weekdays. Get information here about Vidalia farm tours. You also can contact the **Toombs-Montgomery Chamber of Commerce and Development Authority** (912-537-4466; www.toombsmontgomery chamber.com), 2805 East First Street, Vidalia 30474. Open 8:30–5 weekdays.

To learn more about Waynesboro, contact the **Burke County Chamber of Commerce** (706-554-5451; www.burkechamber.com), 241 East Sixth Street, Waynesboro 30830. Open 9–5 weekdays.

GETTING THERE *By air:* The closest airport is 55 miles away in Savannah (see Savannah chapter in 2, The Coast).

By bus: **Greyhound Lines** (1-800-231-2222; www.greyhound.com) stops just west of Claxton at **Carroll's Texaco/Food Mart** (912-739-1944), 6494 US 280 West, Hagen. In Dublin, there is a **Greyhound office** (478-272-2912) at 620 East Jackson Street. The bus service also makes stops in Lyons, Metter, Reidsville, Soperton, Swainsboro, Sylvania, Vidalia, and Waynesboro.

By car: The towns in this chapter are stretched out to the north or south of I-16. North-south highways include US 301, 25, 1, and 221.

By train: **Amtrak** (1-800-USA-RAIL; www.amtrak.com) provides service as far as Augusta and Savannah (see those chapters).

GETTING AROUND Getting around in these small towns requires a car—either your own or a rental. There is no mass transportation and no taxi service.

MEDICAL EMERGENCY In the case of life-threatening emergency, call 911. Otherwise contact **Emanuel Medical Center** (478-289-1100), 117 Kite Road, Swainsboro; **Tattnall Regional Hospital** (912-255-4731), 247 South Main Street, Reidsville; or **Meadows Regional Medical Center** (912-537-3641), 1015 First Street East, Vidalia.

VILLAGES AND NEIGHBORHOODS The **Savannah Avenue Historic District,** located on Savannah Avenue in Statesboro, was the town's first suburb in the early 1900s. Many of the original homes and gardens have been preserved.

Claxton's famed **Rattlesnake Roundup** (see *Special Events*) began in 1968, when a local boy was bitten several times by an eastern diamondback rattler as family members were picking vegetables on their farm. Fortunately, swift and skilled medical attention saved the child's life, but it took a year for him to recover and even after that he had side effects. A group of residents decided to learn more about rattlesnakes, formed the Evans County Wildlife Club, and eventually sponsored the roundup—the purpose of which is to "educate, not eradicate."

The area around **Dublin,** "the Emerald City," is a haven for sportsmen who

enjoy tennis, golf, fishing, and hunting. It is St. Patrick's Day, however, for which
the small town is famous. While Savannah's St. Patrick's Day celebrations are the
second largest in the nation, Dublin's are the second largest in Georgia.

When Colonel Samuel H. Hawkins of Americus was building railroad depots
along the route of the Savannah, Americus & Montgomery Railroad, he named
some of the stations after places he'd visited in Europe. The **Lyons** depot was
named after Lyons, France, and a town soon grew up around the station. Today
Lyons, which possesses the only complete set of weights-and-measures scales in
Georgia, boasts several hidden treasures such as New Deal public art.

Metter, the county seat of Candler County, was established solely as a stop on
the railroad and was incorporated in 1903. Legend has it that a railroad official
named the town for his wife because he "met her" there. Today Metter is the
home of **Guido Gardens,** an evangelistic association (see *Green Space—Gardens*).

Millen is the home of **Magnolia Springs State Park,** which was named for the
crystal-clear spring that puts out 9 million gallons of 64-degree water every day
(see *Green Space—Nature Preserves and Parks*).

Mount Vernon, incorporated in 1872, was named after George Washington's
home in Virginia. Today it is the home of Brewton-Parker College, which has a
historic village on campus.

Soperton, named for Benjamin Franklin Soper, a construction engineer with
the Macon, Dublin & Savannah Railroad, was incorporated in 1902. The only
incorporated municipality in Treutlen County, it is known as "Million Pines City"
but should actually be called "Seven Million Pines City" because James Fowler
planted more than 7 million pine seedlings on 10,000 acres here. Pine by-products
are an important part of the local economy, and the most important annual event
is November's **Million Pines Arts and Crafts Festival** (see *Special Events*).

Swainsboro, named for Colonel Stephen Swain, a member of the state legislature, was incorporated in 1854. The name of the town was changed to Paris
for a brief period but soon was returned to its original name. Today the city of
nearly 7,000 is the home of East Georgia College and Swainsboro Technical
Institute, as well as several outstanding bed & breakfasts and restaurants located
in its historic homes. Nearby is **George L. Smith State Park** (see *Green
Space—Nature Preserves and Parks*).

Sylvania, the "Welcome Station City," was established as the county seat of
Screven County in 1847. In Latin, Sylvania means "place in the woods," which
was and is symbolic for the beautiful surroundings of the city. The Revolutionary
War battle of Brier Creek took place not far from here. Unlike many nearby
towns, whose downtowns reflect the architecture of the late 1800s, Sylvania's
buildings represent the styles of the 1920s and 1930s.

Waynesboro is known as the "Bird Dog Capital of the World" because of the
annual bird-dog field trials (see *Special Events*) held here every year. In fact,
people come from all over the world to enter and observe these competitions to
determine whose bird dog is the best of the best. Waynesboro also offers
antiques shops, old churches, and the **Burke County Museum** (see *To See—
Museums*).

✴ To See

COVERED BRIDGES ✍ ☜ ᕼ **Parrish Mill Bridge** (478-763-2759; www.ga stateparks.org/info/georgels), George L. Smith State Park, 371 George L. Smith State Park Road, Twin City. Open 7–10 daily. George L. Smith State Park is located off GA 23 between Twin City and Metter, and within it lies a most unusual covered bridge. In fact, it is unique in the state of Georgia because the bridge, a gristmill, a sawmill, and a dam are all lodged under one roof. The structure was built in 1880 on beautiful Fifteen Mile Creek. The doors at each end can be opened to allow passage, but you'll have to walk through the bridge because it is closed to vehicular traffic. Free; parking $3.

FOR FAMILIES ✍ ☜ ᕼ **Center for Wildlife Education and Lamar Q. Ball Jr. Raptor Center** (912-681-0831; 1-800-568-3301; welcome.georgiasouthern.edu/ wildlife), Old Register Road, Georgia Southern University, Statesboro. Open 9–5 weekdays, 1–5 Sunday, September through May; closed June through August. Many species of native birds of prey live here among 4 acres of natural woodland habitats. The center also has a large collection of reptiles and amphibians. The hit of a visit is a raptor show presented at 3 PM weekends, and those who aren't turned off by snakes enjoy the reptile show at 2. Children enjoy finding the 50 hidden animals in the Down-to-Earth Encounter and the 17 stations along the Children's Discovery Trail, where they can look for animal tracks, antlers, bird nests, eggshells, feathers, skeletons, snake skins, and turtle shells. They can even climb into a life-sized eagle's nest for a photo opportunity. Free.

✍ ☜ ᕼ **Claxton Bakery** (912-739-3441; 1-800-841-4211; www.claxtonfruitcake .com), 203 West Main Street, Claxton. Open 8–5 Monday through Saturday. Between September and December, millions of pounds of fruitcake are baked and shipped by this world-renowned bakery, but it's not the only fruitcake bakery in Claxton (see next entry). Free.

✍ ☜ ᕼ **Georgia Fruit Cake Company** (912-739-2683; www.georgiafruitcake company.com), 5 South Duval Street, Claxton. Open 7–4:30 weekdays. This fourth-generation, family-owned bakery is famed for its homemade fruit-cakes. Free.

✍ ☜ ᕼ **Vidalia Onion Factory and Gift Shop** (912-526-3466; 1-800-227-6646; www.vidaliaonion.com), 3309 East First Street, Vidalia. Factory tours available by appointment only April through mid-June; gift shop open 9–6 Monday through Saturday, 1–5 Sunday year-round. Stop by and get a behind-the-scenes glimpse into what happens to a Vidalia onion before it gets to the grocery store. The process is fascinating. (See also *Selective Shopping—Food*.) Free.

HISTORIC HOMES AND SITES ✒ ✿ ♿ **Historic Village at Brewton-Parker College** (912-583-2241; 1-800-342-1087), US 280, Mount Vernon. Open daily. No time machine is needed to visit the past in Mount Vernon. The village's Cooper-Conner House is considered to be one of the oldest houses in Montgomery County. It was originally built by slave labor at the fork of the Oconee and Ocmulgee rivers in 1799 for Richard Cooper, a Revolutionary War hero. The house was moved to its current site because it was being torn down by hunters who were using it for firewood. Free.

MUSEUMS ✿ ♿ **Altama Museum of Art and History** (912-537-1911; www .vidaliaga.com), 611 Jackson Street, Vidalia. Hours vary, so call first. Housed in the 1911 Brazell House, the museum's permanent collection includes 18th- and 19th-century American and European prints, 18th- and 19th-century Libby porcelain collections, John James Audubon first-edition hand-colored prints, and 20th-century Southern paintings. The museum also shows the work of visiting artists. Free.

✿ ♿ **Burke County Museum** (706-554-4889; www.home.bellsouth.net/p/PWP -bcmuseum), 536 Liberty Street, Waynesboro. Open 8–4 weekdays; weekends and holidays by appointment. The museum, which is located in the 1858 J. D. Roberts house, features county-related artifacts and memorabilia that will intrigue many a history buff. Over the years the structure served as a doctor's office annex and a military shop. Free.

✿ ♿ **Dublin-Laurens Museum** (478-272-9242), 311 Academy Avenue, Dublin. Open 1–4:30 Tuesday through Friday. The graceful building, which serves as a repository for county memorabilia, was built as a library with a grant from Andrew Carnegie in 1904. Today it serves as the museum and the home of the Laurens County Historical Society. Free.

✒ ✿ ♿ **Georgia Southern University Museum** (912-681-5444; ceps.georgia-southern.edu/museum), Rosenwald Building, Southern Drive, Georgia Southern University, Statesboro. Open 9–5 weekdays, 2–5 Saturday and Sunday. The stars at this natural-history museum are a 26-foot fossil of a mosasaur, the prehistoric *T. rex* of the sea, which is believed to be 78 million years old, and *Georgiacetus vogtlensis*, the oldest whale fossil found in North America. Free.

SPECIAL PLACES ✿ **Meinhardt Vineyards Winery** (912-839-2458), 305 Kennedy Pond Road, Statesboro. Open Thursday through Sunday. Meinhardt Vineyards and Winery, southeast Georgia's first winery, specializes in muscadine wine. What was a 15-year family winemaking hobby became a business in 2004 with the opening of the winery. A relaxing atmosphere and scenic views are extra-added features of a visit to the winery for complimentary tastings and tours. Free.

✴ To Do

BICYCLING ✍ ✿ **Yamassee Bicycle Trail** (contact Vidalia Area Convention and Visitors Bureau, 912-538-8687). This 27-mile trail allows the whole family to pedal past beautiful farm country, historic churches, and huge pine forests. You'll also pass through the Long Pond, Alston, and Uvalda communities, where you can learn a little about their histories and purchase refreshments. Call for a trail map.

See also **George L. Smith State Park** under *Green Space—Nature Preserves and Parks.*

BOATING ✍ **Canoe Canoe Outfitters** (912-526-8222; www.canoecanoe.com), 3008 US 280 East, Lyons. The outfitter company knows the flat rivers of south Georgia as well as the camps and where the fish bite. Canoe Canoe furnishes everything from paddles to gourmet camp cuisine. Trips range from several hours to overnight trips to custom-designed excursions on Pendleton Creek and the Altamaha, Ocmulgee, Ohoopee, and Oconee rivers. Call for prices.

Three Rivers Expeditions ✍ (912-379-1371; 912-363-CANU; www.3riverexp .com), mailing address: Charlie J. Ford, 13 Victor Street, Hazelhurst 31539. The outfitter offers services to the Altamaha, Ohoopee, Oconee, Ocmulgee, and Little Ocmulgee rivers, including rentals, shuttle service, retail sales of boats and gear, and guide service. Call for prices.

See also **George L. Smith State Park, Gordonia-Alatamaha State Park,** and **Magnolia Springs State Park** under *Green Space—Nature Preserves and Parks.*

FARM TOURS ✍ ✿ **Pecan Orchard Plantation,** located 10 minutes from Vidalia, offers an outdoor classroom-type experience that the whole family will find interesting. Pack a picnic and spend the day at this entertaining working farm. Activities include a petting zoo, hayrides, corn maze (seasonal), Easter egg hunt (seasonal), a visit to the pumpkin patch (seasonal), ol' time fishing, and lessons about fruit and agriculture in Mrs. Scott's outdoor classroom. Sometimes they even make old-fashioned cane syrup. Special activities are scheduled during the **Vidalia Onion Festival** (see *Special Events*). Tours must be arranged in advance through the **Vidalia Area Convention and Visitors Bureau** (912-538-8687; e-mail vacvb@bellsouth.net). $5.

FISHING ✍ ✿ **Evans County Public Fishing Area** (912-739-1139; 912-685-6424, www.gofishgeorgia.com), US 280 East, Claxton. Open daily. The three-lake fishing compound features a boat ramp, boardwalk, picnicking facilities, and primitive campsites. A fishing license is required. Free.

See also **George L. Smith State Park, Gordonia-Alatamaha State Park,** and **Magnolia Springs State Park** under *Green Space—Nature Preserves and Parks.*

FRUIT AND BERRY PICKING ✍ ✿ **Clark Farm and Produce** (912-865-3200;

www.clarkfarmandproduce.com), 1699 Clark Farm Road, Portal. Open 9–7
Monday through Saturday, April 1 through October 31; call to verify availability.
At this working farm, visitors can take a tour, pick their own strawberries in season, enjoy strawberry ice cream year-round, or choose a pumpkin and take a
hayride in the autumn. Berries $1.50 per pound.

GOLF See Golf Appendix.

HIKING See **George L. Smith State Park** and **Magnolia Springs State Park**
under *Green Space—Nature Preserves and Parks.*

MINIATURE GOLF See **Gordonia-Alatamaha State Park** under *Green Space—
Nature Preserves and Parks.*

SKYDIVING Skydive Statesboro (912-764-2737), 401 Airport Drive, Statesboro. This facility offers instruction, gear rental and sales, covered parking, and
much more. Call for details and prices.

SWIMMING AND WATER PLAY ✒ ❧ & **Splash in the Boro** (912-764-5637;
www.splashintheboro.com), off GA 24, Statesboro. Water park open May
through Labor Day; therapy and competition pools open year-round. This 5-acre
family water park and aquatics center, located in **Mill Creek Regional Park**,
features three water slides, zero-depth entry pools, water guns, valves that shoot
water unexpectedly all over the pool, a bucket that dumps 600 gallons of water
every three minutes, an 800-foot Lazy River, a four-lane therapy pool, and a 25-
meter competition pool. A bubble dome covers the therapy and competition
pools during colder months for year-round operation of those facilities. Winter
activities include water aerobics, lap swimming, open recreational swimming,
open exercise and therapy swimming, and swimming lessons. $9 adults, $7
youth; summer passes available.
See also Parks Appendix and **Gordonia-Alatamaha State Park** and **Magnolia
Springs State Park** under *Green Space—Nature Preserves and Parks.*

TENNIS See also Other Activities Appendix and **Gordonia-Alatamaha State
Park** under *Green Space—Nature Preserves and Parks.*

✳ Green Space

GARDENS ✒ ❧ & **Georgia Southern University Botanical Garden** (912-681-
1149; welcome.georgiasouthern.edu/garden), 1505 Bland Avenue, Statesboro.
Gardens open 9–dusk daily; garden center cottage open 10–4 Tuesday through
Saturday, 1–4 Sunday. This preserve for native plants, Southern gardens, and
microhabitats of the Coastal Plain features gardens and a turn-of-the-20th-century
cottage now used as the garden center. Free.

✒ ❧ & **Guido Gardens** (912-685-2222; www.GuidoGardens.com), 600 North
Lewis Street, Metter. Open for tours 8–noon and 1–5 weekdays; reservations
suggested. The gardens contain the Chapel in the Pines as well as arbors,

bridges, a gazebo, topiaries, and water attractions. During the Christmas season, the gardens are filled with a million lights and lighted sculptures. Free.

NATURE PRESERVES AND PARKS ♂ 🐾 ♿ **George L. Smith State Park** (478-763-2759; 1-800-864-7275; www.gastateparks.org/info/georgels), 371 George L. Smith State Park Road, Twin City. Open 7–10 daily. Named for a Georgia legislator, this quiet, 1,634-acre park is popular with sports enthusiasts. Anglers and canoeists enjoy the lake, while birdwatchers look for blue herons and white ibis. Hikers stretch their legs on 11 miles of trails while they keep an eagle eye out for the endangered gopher tortoise. Bikers also use the trails. Located right on the water's edge of 412-acre Cypress Lake, the circa 1880 Parrish Mill at the park is a combination gristmill, sawmill, covered bridge, and dam (see **Parrish Mill Bridge** under *To See—Covered Bridges*). Private boats are permitted, but motors are limited to 10 horsepower. Canoes and fishing and pedal-boat rentals are available. Accommodations are offered at tent, trailer, and RV sites as well as at a primitive campground and in four cottages (see *Lodging*). Parking $3.

♂ 🐾 ♿ **Gordonia-Alatamaha State Park** (912-557-7744; 1-800-864-7275; www.gastateparks.org/info/gordonalt), off US 280, Reidsville. Open 7–10 daily. The park's unusual name comes from the rare Gordonia tree (a member of the bay family) and the original spelling of the Altamaha River. The 462-acre park is visited for golf (see Golf Appendix) and water sports. At the small 12-acre lake, visitors can fish or rent fishing and pedal boats seasonally. Private boats are not permitted. Land-loving anglers can fish from the docks, and children like looking for beaver dams from the observation deck. The park also features a swimming pool, tennis courts, miniature golf, and camping (see *Lodgings*). Parking $3; swimming $3; mini golf $2.50; paddleboats $2.50 per hour.

♂ 🐾 ♿ **Magnolia Springs State Park** (478-982-1660; www.gastateparks.org/info/magspr), 1053 Magnolia Springs Drive, Millen. Park open 7–10 daily; aquarium open 9–4 daily. The 1,071-acre park is best known for its crystal-clear springs from which 7 million gallons of water flow each day. Visitors can admire the springs from a boardwalk that spans the water and offers a good place from which to view wildlife such as alligators, turtles, ibis, heron, and other species. A 28-acre lake is popular for boating and fishing. Other recreational amenities include three playgrounds, a swimming pool, 10 miles of hiking and biking trails, a wheelchair-accessible fishing dock, and a boat ramp. There are canoe and fishing boat rentals, and private boats are allowed. During the Civil War, a prison called Camp Lawton occupied the site, and the earthen breastworks that surrounded the prison remain today. One of the most special features of this park is the **Bo Ginn Aquarium and Aquatic Educational Center** (478-982-4168), 1061 Hatchery Road, where 26 freshwater tanks display native fish, reptiles, and turtles. Accommodations are available in cottages and campgrounds (see *Lodgings*). Parking $3; admission to aquarium free.

RIVERS ♂ 🐾 **Canoochee River,** access at US 301 North, US 280 East, and GA 169 North, Claxton. Open daily. Public landings attract anglers (a fishing license is required), boaters, and swimmers to the shores of the river. Free.

✳ Lodging

BED & BREAKFASTS

In Claxton

🐾 **Smith House Inn** (912-739-8095), 610 West Liberty Street. This quaint, circa 1910 B&B offers four comfortably decorated guest rooms with private baths. A full breakfast is included. No smoking. Not wheelchair accessible. $75–$100.

In Dublin

🐾 ♿ **Come Home to the Country B&B** (478-275-8766; www.dublin farm.com), 875 James Currie Road. This country-style B&B is located on a picturesque farm in the scenic and peaceful countryside of middle Georgia. It offers four guest rooms with private baths. The hosts speak English, German, and Italian. Sumptuous breakfast included. No smoking. $60–85.

Page House (478-275-4551; www.pagehousebb.com), 711 Bellevue Avenue. This beautiful and elegant antebellum home features five spacious guest rooms and one honeymoon suite. Full gourmet breakfast included. No smoking. Not wheelchair accessible. $89–119.

In Statesboro

♿ **Beaver House Inn Bed and Breakfast and Restaurant** (912-764-2821; www.beaverhouseinn.com), 121 South Main Street. This antebellum home houses a fine restaurant. There is also a Victorian cottage that serves as a guest house. No smoking. $89–249.

🐾 ♿ **Georgia's Bed and Breakfast** (912-489-6330), 123 South Zetterower Avenue. This historic home has four guest rooms, all with private baths. A full breakfast is included. No smoking. $80.

In Swainsboro

🐾 **Coleman House Bed and Breakfast** (478-237-9100; www.coleman houseinn.com), 323 North Main Street. This magnificent 1904 Painted Lady boasts 10,000 square feet of living space, 98 windows, 11 fireplaces, 500 spindles, 2,000 feet of porches, and a widow's walk. Luxurious guest rooms feature all the modern amenities. The B&B also features a restaurant (see *Where to Eat—Dining Out*). No smoking. Not wheelchair accessible. $55 and up.

🐾 ♿ **Edenfield House Inn** (478-237-3007; www.bbonline.com/ga/eden field), 426 West Church Street. This charming inn offers six guest rooms with private baths. Amenities include individual heat and air-conditioning controls, wireless Internet, hair dryers, coffeepots, a garden, and a wraparound porch with rockers. All accommodations include a full breakfast. No smoking. $65–$120.

In Waynesboro

🐾 **Steadman House Bed and Breakfast** (706-437-1228; 1-877-853-9439; www.steadmanhouse.com), 828 Liberty Street. This stately yellow brick Mediterranean mansion with a red tile roof is surrounded by beautifully tended grounds and gardens.

THE COLEMAN HOUSE BED AND BREAKFAST IN SWAINSBORO

Four guest rooms are individually decorated and furnished with antiques. Full breakfast and snacks included. No smoking except outside. Not wheelchair accessible. $75.

CAMPGROUNDS

In Millen

✍ 🐾 🌺 **Magnolia Springs State Park** (478-982-1660; www.gastateparks .org/info/magspr), 1053 Magnolia Springs Drive. The park features 26 tent, trailer, and RV sites as well as three walk-in sites and two pioneer campgrounds. In addition, there is a group camp lodge that sleeps 94. $13–20; $460 for lodge.

In Reidsville

✍ 🐾 🌺 **Gordonia-Alatamaha State Park** (912-557-7744; 1-800-864-7275; www.gastateparks.org/info/gordonalt), off US 280 West. This park campground offers 26 tent, trailer, and RV sites and features a large playground, basketball hoop, volleyball net, miniature golf, swimming pool, picnic shelters and picnic tables, and a 12-acre lake with fishing and pedal boats. All campsites have water and electric hookups; some have sewage hookups as well. The campground also offers a dump station. At the far end of the park is Brazell's Creek Golf Course (see Golf Appendix). Maps and guides are available free at the park's welcome station. $14–20.

In Twin City

✍ 🐾 🌺 **George L. Smith State Park** (478-763-2759; 1-800-864-7275; www .gastateparks.org/info/georgels), 371 George L. Smith State Park Road. The park provides 25 tent, trailer, and RV sites right at the water's edge as well as a pioneer campground. $19–25.

COTTAGES AND CABINS

In Millen

✍ 🐾 **Magnolia Springs State Park** (478-982-1660; www.gastateparks.org/ info/magspr), 1053 Magnolia Springs Drive. The park offers five fully equipped cottages as well as a group lodge that sleeps 16. $60–105; $95–105 for lodge.

In Twin City

✍ 🐾 🌺 **George L. Smith State Park** (478-763-2759; 1-800-864-7275; www .gastateparks.org/info/georgels), 371 George L. Smith State Park Road. Four fully equipped cottages with gas fireplaces and screened porches are nestled in the woods. $70–85.

✳ Where to Eat

DINING OUT

In Dublin

♿ **Come Home to the Country B&B** (478-275-8766; www.dublin farm.com), 875 James Currie Road. Open at 7 PM every Friday and Saturday; also on special occasions such as Mother's Day and Father's Day. Reservations required, as the restaurant offers only one seating for this authentic fixed-price, five-course Italian meal. No smoking. $25.

In Statesboro

♿ **Blue Moon Café** (912-489-1094), 40 East Main Street. Open 11–3 Monday through Saturday; 5–9:30 Thursday through Saturday. The lunch menu features a wide variety of deli-style sandwiches. Dinner choices include duck, crabcakes, certified Angus steaks, foie gras, grouper, salmon, and salads. No smoking. Lunch about $7; dinner $20.

♿ **French Quarter Café** (912-489-3233), 106 Savannah Avenue. Open 11–10; bar stays open until midnight. This New Orleans–style eatery features ètouffée, seafood, jambalaya, steaks, bourbon chicken, and more. Smoking permitted in balcony area. $8–21.

In Swainsboro

♿ **Coleman House Bed and Breakfast** (478-237-9100; www.coleman houseinn.com), 323 North Main Street. Open 11–2 Sunday through Friday; reservations required for holidays. Located in a gorgeous 1904 Victorian mansion with a wraparound porch and a widow's walk, the restaurant serves a lunch buffet and à la carte choices. No smoking. Buffet $11.

EATING OUT

In Lyons

✎ ♘ ♿ **Chatters Restaurant** (912-526-8040), 674 NW Broad Street. Open 5 AM–9 PM Monday through Saturday, 11–3 Sunday. Don't miss the seafood buffet on Friday and Saturday nights. No smoking. About $10.

In Statesboro

✎ ♘ ♿ **Ocean Galley Seafood** (912-489-4145), 503 Northside Drive East. Open 11–9 Sunday through Thursday, 11–10 Friday and Saturday. Menu favorites include seafood, steaks, hamburgers, chicken fingers, grilled chicken, and specialty salads. No smoking. About $10.

✎ ♘ ♿ **Snooky's Restaurant** (912-764-7190), 409 Fair Road. Open 6 AM–9 PM weekdays, 6–2 Saturday. This home-style restaurant features a buffet with all your favorite country comfort foods. No smoking. About $5.

In Swainsboro

✎ ♘ ♿ **The Old Home Place** (478-237-9600), 686 South Main Street. Open 11–9 Monday through Saturday, 11–2 Sunday. This home-cooking restaurant features steak and seafood in addition to a daily buffet. No smoking. About $8.

In Vidalia

✎ ♘ ♿ **Old Rodeo** (912-537-0071), 1601 First Street. Open 11–9 Tuesday through Sunday. The restaurant specializes in traditional Mexican fare. No smoking. About $9.

COFFEEHOUSES

In Statesboro

♘ ♿ **Daily Grind** (912-489-5070), 124 Savannah Avenue, Suite #1-E. Open 7–10 Monday through Thursday, 7–11 Friday, 8–11 Saturday. Traditional coffeehouse fare is served at a very reasonable price. No smoking. $3–5.

✎ ♘ ♿ **Maui Smoothies and Coffee House** (912-681-7979), 620 Fair Road, Suite #2. Open 6:30 AM–9 PM weekdays, 8–9 Saturday, noon–6 Sunday. In addition to smoothies and coffee, this casual eatery offers sandwiches and salads. No smoking. About $4.

✵ Entertainment

MUSIC Statesboro Georgia Southern Symphony (912-681-5396; www .georgiasouthern.edu/music), mailing address: P.O. Box 2311, Statesboro 30459. The semiprofessional orchestra presents three subscription concerts, two youth shows, one outdoor pops concert, and a holiday program each year. Call for a schedule of performances and ticket prices.

Vidalia Community Chorus (912-537-1911) presents a two- to three-concert season featuring a variety of music including classical, jazz, pop, Broadway, and Christmas favorites. Performances are at the Southeastern Technical College. Call ORCA—the **Ohoopee Regional Council for the Arts** (912-537-8459)—for schedule and tickets. $10.

THEATER **David H. Averitt Center for the Arts** (912-212-2787; www.averittcenterforthearts.org), 33 East Main Street, Statesboro. Box office and galleries open 9–7 weekdays, 11–4 Saturday, 1–4 Sunday. The center, which occupies the historic Old Bank of Statesboro (circa 1911) and the old Georgia Theater (circa 1936), provides a permanent home for the arts in Statesboro and features the Emma Kelly Theater, a main gallery, and a student gallery. $5–21 depending on performance.

Georgia Southern University Theater South (912-486-7999; 1-866-PAC-ARTS; www.georgiasouthern.edu/pac). The university center presents 10 shows yearly with nationally and internationally known artists in music, dance, and theater at the school's Performing Arts Center. Call for a schedule of performances. $30–45.

ORCA—the Ohoopee Regional Council for the Arts (912-537-8459) features world-class performances throughout the year at the Toombs Auditorium at Southeastern Technical College. There are three plays in the Really Awesome Performances for Kids series and three shows in the Performing Arts Series. Call for a schedule. Adults $15–20, children $3–5.

Theatre Dublin (478-277-5060), 314 Academy Avenue, Dublin. The renovated theater serves as an arts center for a variety of performances. Call for a schedule of performances and ticket prices.

✳ **Selective Shopping**

FOOD **Farm Fresh Tattnall** (912-557-6724; www.farmfreshtattnall.com), P.O. Box 30453, Reidsville. This organization is a cooperative of 18 roadside and pick-your-own farms in Tattnall County. Visitors can find

THE LADY OF 6,000 SONGS
Bulloch County native daughter Emma Kelly was renowned for her encyclopedic knowledge of the popular music of the late Johnny Mercer and others and her ability to play it on request. In addition to playing and singing for local church services, civic clubs, graduations, proms, and recitals, she often played in clubs in Savannah. When author John Berendt wrote his famous book, *Midnight in the Garden of Good and Evil,* he dedicated an entire chapter to the talents of Mrs. Kelly, which resulted in her playing a cameo role as herself in the 1997 movie directed by Clint Eastwood. A national concert tour followed, and in 1998 Mrs. Kelly was inducted into the Georgia Music Hall of Fame. She died in January 2001 at the age of 83.

every fresh product from peaches and strawberries to Vidalia onions, sweet potatoes, and turnip greens. Consult the web site to see what's in season during your visit.

Vidalia Onion Factory and Gift Shop (912-526-3466; 1-800-227-6646), 3309 East First Street, Vidalia. Factory open April through mid-June; gift shop open 9–6 Monday through Saturday and 1–5 Sunday year-round. Don't leave the Vidalia area without taking home some onion products—not only the sweet onions themselves, but sauces, dressings, relishes, pickles, and other delicacies made with them. The shop also offers onion ring mix, cookbooks, a microwave onion cooker, souvenirs, collectibles, and Christmas ornaments. The café specializes in fried onion rings.

✴ Special Events

January: **Annual Bird Dog Field Trials** (706-554-5451). These field trials are among the oldest in the country. **Georgia Open Shooting Dog Championship Field Trials,** the **Georgialina Field Trials,** and the **Southeastern Field Trials** attract hundreds of dogs, handlers, horses, judges, field marshals, and spectators from all over the world for a month-long series of shooting dog championship events at Di-Lane Plantation Wildlife Management Area in Waynesboro. Free for spectators.

March: **Claxton Rattlesnake Roundup** (912-739-3820; www.claxtonrattlesnakeroundup.com). This event, held in Claxton on the second weekend in March, features rattlesnakes on exhibit, prizes for hunters, live snake milking for venom, a 100-unit parade, handmade arts and crafts, educational lectures, live music, cloggers, queen's coronation, gospel singing, children's activities, and food. Ages 6 and older $6.

April: **Tales from the Altamaha—A Georgia Folk Life Play** (912-526-6445; www.lyonsga.com). For two weeks, playgoers are transported back to a time when Southern traditions were just being forged. The unforgettable blend of comedy, music, and drama, based on the writings of Colonel T. Ross Sharpe, is performed by a cast of 100 volunteers in the newly renovated Blue Marquee Theater in Lyons. The play describes the lives, loves, losses, scandals, and plain ol' gossip of rural south Georgia. $15.

Vidalia Onion Festival (912-538-8687; www.vidaliaonionfestival.com). This annual something-for-everyone event in Vidalia features an air show (the Blue Angels performed in 2005); arts and crafts; a cooking school; fireworks; street dance; beauty pageant; carnival; a chef's competition using Vidalia onions; several sports competitions; live entertainment; midway rides; a rodeo; an antique car, truck, and motorcycle show; an onion-eating contest; lots of food; and a train ride on the SAM Shortline Railroad. During the festival, **Pecan Orchard Plantation** (see *To Do—Farm Tours*) is open 9–8 Wednesday through Saturday and 1–8 Sunday for special activities, including the Sweet Vidalia Onion Oat Field Maze. A charge for some events. Call for details and prices.

October: **South Georgia Jaycee Fair** (478-237-6426). Held every year during the first week in October in Swainsboro, the fair features commercial and 4-H exhibits, animal competitions, nightly beauty pageants, midway rides, great food, games, and live entertainment. Adults $4, children 6–12 $3.

November: **Million Pines Arts and Crafts Festival** (912-529-6868), at Iva Park, 421 Main Street East, Soperton. The festival features arts and crafts sales and demonstrations of how these skills were used in days gone by, live entertainment, and old-time fair food, including Georgia's famous boiled peanuts and pork rinds. Adults $4, children 6 and younger free; parking and shuttle free.

The Mountains 4

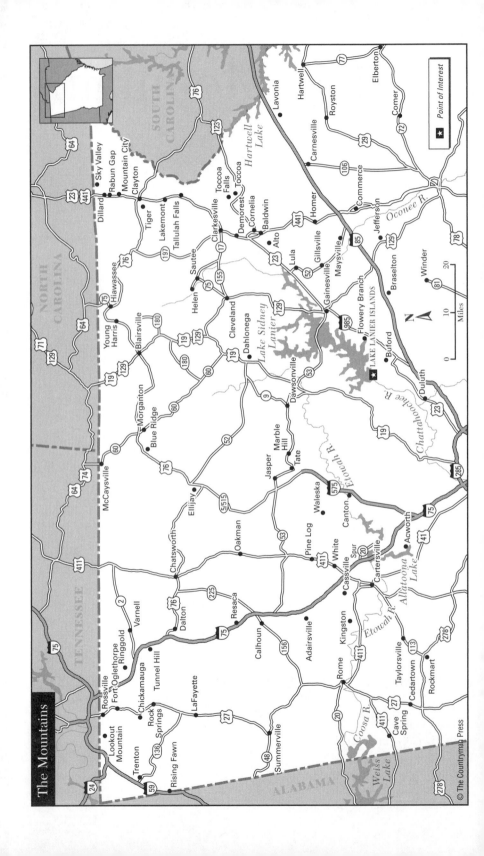

The Mountains

© The Countryman Press

INTRODUCTION

Mountains cover the entire northern part of Georgia from Alabama to South Carolina and bordering Tennessee and North Carolina. Sensational scenery is one of the biggest draws for visitors to the mountainous area of northern Georgia. Crystal-clear blue skies permit visitors to enjoy long-range vistas from rugged mountaintops such as Brasstown Bald, one of the highest points in the East. Throughout the region, steep slopes are covered with brilliant wildflowers in the spring and flamboyantly hued leaves in the fall. The Chattahoochee National Forest encompasses 750,000 acres with 10 wilderness areas, 1,367 miles of trout streams, and 430 miles of hiking trails. The Appalachian Trail begins—or ends, depending how you look at it—in north Georgia.

Water plays a prominent role in north Georgia, whether it plummets over a rocky precipice to create a cascading waterfall, drifts serenely in a glassy-surfaced lake, or careens down a tumultuous white-water river such as the Chattooga or the Ocoee. Lakes Allatoona, Blue Ridge, Burton, Carters, Hartwell, Lanier, Rabun, Tallulah, Tugaloo, and several others provide plentiful opportunities for popular activities such as fishing, boating, swimming, and waterskiing. Although some of these lakes are the most visited in the nation, many of them didn't even exist 100 years ago. Because Georgia didn't experience glacial action during the last Ice Age, the scouring necessary to create lakes left the region with few large, naturally occurring lakes. It was only in the early years of the 20th century that the need for power generation, navigation, and flood control led the U.S. Army Corps of Engineers, Georgia Power, and the Tennessee Valley Authority to create dams and reservoirs—the by-product of which is water-borne recreation.

With all these lakes, rivers, forests, and trails in the area, outdoor recreation is a major reason for tourists to flock to the mountains. In fact, this region is the cradle of tourism in the state. From early times, wealthy families from the coast and southern Georgia escaped to the mountains for the entire summer to avoid the heat of their homes and the diseases rampant in the hotter climes. Railroads later brought middle-class visitors from all over the state for prolonged stays. Nowadays auto travelers can make the trip for as little as a day. The region contains the highest concentration of Georgia's state parks and historic sites: 24 parks, which offer something for almost everyone.

History is not just a footnote in north Georgia. The area is imbued with Native American history. The Cherokee capital of New Echota that flourished near what is present-day Calhoun lasted until America's first gold rush in the hills around Dahlonega. After that event, the Native Americans were forced off their land and sent west along the Trail of Tears. Today's travelers can visit the Etowah Indian Mounds Historic Park and other important Native American sites along the Chieftains Trail. They also can stop by the Dahlonega Gold Museum Historic Site, tour a gold mine, or even pan for gold.

The first European settlers in this area were sturdy, self-sufficient mountaineers who led a hardscrabble life. Learn about them at the Foxfire Museum in Mountain City or the Northeast Georgia History Museum in Gainesville among others. Northwest Georgia was the site of many important Civil War battles and the scene of the famous Great Locomotive Chase in which Union spies stole a locomotive called the *General.* Numerous Civil War sites can be seen along the Blue and Gray Trail, and several battles are re-enacted annually.

Agriculture makes a different and less significant contribution to this area than it does to more southerly parts of the state, but apples play a major role, and the success of growing grapes has led to the creation of several wineries. Different types of farms are open for tours and other activities such as corn mazes and hayrides.

A few of the unusual or unexpected attractions in north Georgia include the Bavarian-style village of Helen, BabyLand General Hospital (the birthplace of the Cabbage Patch Kids), the Booth Western Art Museum, and Rock City Gardens.

CARTERSVILLE AND BLUE RIDGE

Northwest Georgia occupies the southern reach of the Blue Ridge Mountains. The area has more changes in topography than the lower two-thirds of the state and has, therefore, been attracting tourists since the 1800s. Early visitors often came to escape the heat and diseases of the low country and often stayed for months at a time. Before the first tourists, however, the area was inhabited by Native Americans, including Mississippian Mound Builders and Cherokees, and then by white settlers. Many historical attractions include Native American sites and Civil War battlefields and cemeteries. Historical trails include the **Blue and Gray Trail** and the **Chieftains Trail.**

Despite the modern-day existence of interstate highways, small cities, and other signs of "progress," the area remains very much as it was hundreds of years ago. Vast acreage, including the Cohutta Wilderness, is covered by the Chattahoochee National Forest. State parks and U.S. Forest Service recreation areas also keep much of northwest Georgia in its natural state. Lakes Allatoona, Acworth, and Blue Ridge as well as the Toccoa River provide fishing, boating, and other water sports. Other outdoor recreational opportunities range from hiking to mountain biking, horseback riding to white-water rafting.

In addition to natural beauty, northwest Georgia offers a covered bridge; Indian mounds; the world's first Coca-Cola sign; museums dedicated to geology, famous residents, Native Americans, African Americans, and even western art; farm tours concentrating on everything from alpacas to apples; one of Georgia's last drive-in movies; a scenic railroad ride; and an array of festivals and special events. Accommodations range from bed & breakfasts to cabins to campgrounds, while dining options range from casual eateries to fine restaurants.

GUIDANCE When planning a trip to the Cartersville area, including Cassville and White, contact the **Cartersville–Bartow County Convention and Visitors Bureau, Georgia Local Welcome Center** (770-387-1357; 1-800-733-2280; www.notatlanta.org), One Friendship Plaza, Cartersville 30120. Open 8:30–5 weekdays, 11–4 Saturday. Housed in an 1856 railroad depot, the bureau offers information on attractions, driving tours, and history in addition to lodging, restaurants, and shopping. Train watchers enjoy the 45 to 60 trains that pass by each day.

To find out more about Acworth, contact the **Acworth Area Convention and Visitors Bureau** (770-974-8813; www.acworth.org), 4415 Senator Russell Avenue, Acworth 30101. Open 8–5 weekdays. Pick up a brochure for a 30-site walking tour of historic Acworth here.

For information about Canton and Waleska, call the **Cherokee County Chamber of Commerce** (770-345-0400; www.cherokee-chamber.com), 3605 Marietta Highway, Canton 30114. Open 9–5 weekdays.

For information about Blue Ridge and McCaysville, contact the **Fannin County Chamber of Commerce and Local Welcome Center** (706-632-5680; 1-800-899-MTNS; www.blueridgemountains.com), 3990 Appalachian Highway, Blue Ridge 30513. Open 8–5 weekdays, 9–5 Saturday, 1–5 Sunday. The center provides information on back-roads tours and other attractions.

For information about Ellijay and East Ellijay, consult the **Gilmer County Chamber of Commerce and Welcome Center** (706-635-7400; www.gilmer chamber.com), 369 Craig Street, East Ellijay 30539. Open 9–5 weekdays, 10–4 Saturday and Sunday.

To learn more about Jasper and Marble Hill, contact the **Pickens County Chamber of Commerce** (706-692-5600; www.pickenschamber.com), 500 Stegall Drive, Jasper 30143. Open 9–5 weekdays.

GETTING THERE *By air:* The nearest airports to this region are **Hartsfield-Jackson Atlanta International Airport** (see What's Where in Georgia) and **Chattanooga Metropolitan Airport** (423-855-2200), 1001 Airport Road, Chattanooga, Tennessee. Car rentals are available at both airports, and there is some shuttle service.

By bus: The nearest **Greyhound Lines** stations are in Dalton (see Dalton chapter), Atlanta (see What's Where in Georgia), and Chattanooga, Tennessee, at 960 Airport Road (423-892-1277).

By car: I-75, US 441, I-575, and GA 5/515 run north-south through northwest Georgia. GA 53 and US 76 run east-west.

By train: The nearest **Amtrak** stations are in Atlanta (see What's Where in Georgia) and Toccoa (see Clarkesville chapter).

GETTING AROUND In Cartersville, car rentals are available from **Budget** (770-606-0340) and **Enterprise** (770-607-2020).

WHEN TO GO North Georgia is the only area of the state that gets much snow, although even here it is rare. Do plan accordingly in the winter. Due to colder temperatures and the possibility of severe weather, some campgrounds and other establishments close for a few months in the winter, so be sure to check ahead to avoid disappointment.

MEDICAL EMERGENCY In a life-threatening emergency, call 911. For other immediate needs, medical assistance is available at **Cartersville Medical Center** (770-382-1530; www.cartersvillemedical.com), 960 Joe Frank Harris Park-

way, Cartersville; **Fannin Regional Hospital** (706-632-3711; www.fannin
regionalhospital.com), 2855 Old GA 5, Blue Ridge; **North Georgia Medical
Center** (706-276-4741; www.northgeorgiamedicalcenter.com), 1362 South Main
Street, Ellijay; and **Northside Hospital-Cherokee** (770-720-5100; www
.northsidecherokee.com), 201 Hospital Road, Canton.

VILLAGES During the Civil War, Union troops camped in the **Acworth** area,
and homes and churches were used as field headquarters and hospitals. Union
General William Tecumseh Sherman was headquartered in Acworth for several
days. When the Union troops left Acworth, they burned much of the town. The
cotton economy brought prosperity to Acworth by the late 1870s, and new
homes and businesses were built. These are the historic buildings visitors see
today. The small town's **Collins Avenue Historic District** showcases 150 years
of architecture. **Lake Allatoona** and **Lake Acworth** were built in the 1950s,
earning Acworth the nickname "Lake City" and providing numerous recreational
opportunities (see *Green Space—Lakes*).

Blue Ridge in Fannin County is considered the gateway to the Blue Ridge
Mountains. During the early 1900s, the Marietta and North Georgia Railroad
brought large numbers of tourists to Blue Ridge because of its pure mineral
waters, which turned the small town into an elite health resort. Today visitors
come to ride the scenic railroad (see *To Do—Train Excursions*) and to shop for
Appalachian arts and crafts, antiques, mountain furnishings, apples, trout, and
items made from alpaca wool. Art fairs, gallery tours, exhibitions, receptions, festivals, concerts, and plays occur throughout the year.

Cartersville is rich in history, culture, scenic beauty, and recreational opportunities. Evidence of human habitation here goes back as far as 10,000 B.C.
The first historic documentation was written in 1540 by Hernando de Soto,
who visited the area and described the Mound Builder civilization. Creeks and
Cherokees later inhabited the area until driven out and sent along the Trail of
Tears. The Civil War intruded upon Cartersville, though it suffered little damage compared to other nearby towns. After the war, the railroads and natural
resources brought great prosperity to the area. Today one of its greatest assets
is tourism.

Cassville was once the cultural center of north Georgia, with two colleges, four
hotels, and a newspaper. The town even had wooden sidewalks. Georgia's first
Supreme Court decision was delivered at Cassville, in 1856, and many Cherokee
legal battles took place at the Cassville Courthouse. The town was decimated by
the Civil War, however. Residents were given only 20 minutes' notice to flee, and
no images or official records survived. All that remained afterward were three
houses, two churches, and a Confederate cemetery. In the 20th century, Cassville enjoyed being on the route of the Dixie Highway, the nation's first planned
interstate highway. During the 1930s, the Works Progress Administration constructed an Atlanta Campaign Pocket Park there. The old post office, which
operated until the 1990s, houses the Cassville History Museum.

McCaysville is schizophrenic. The town has a blue line painted down the middle of the main street. On one side of the line you are in McCaysville, Georgia;

on the other side, you are in Copperhill, Tennessee. A favorite photo op is to pose with one foot in each state.

✳ To See

COVERED BRIDGES ✍ ⚲ ⚬ **Euharlee Covered Bridge and History Museum** (770-607-2017), 116 Covered Bridge Road, Cartersville. Museum open 1–4:30 most weekdays. One of only 16 covered bridges left in Georgia and part of the state's Covered Bridge Trail, the Euharlee Bridge was built by Washington King in 1886. Although the town of Euharlee was bustling with several mills in the 1840s, it is now virtually a ghost town. Remains of the old town include a well, courthouse, blacksmith shop, gristmill ruins, and commissary. Buildings still in use include a store, Baptist and Presbyterian churches, and a parsonage. The museum, located in an 1850 cowshed next to the bridge, is a good source of information about the town. Pick up the "Historic Euharlee Georgia" brochure here. Free.

HISTORIC HOMES AND SITES ✍ ⚲ ⚬ **Etowah Indian Mound Historic Site** (770-387-3747; www.gastateparks.org/info/etowah), 813 Indian Mounds Road SE, Cartersville. Open 9–5 Tuesday through Saturday, 2–5:30 Sunday. This area on the scenic banks of the Etowah River was home to several thousand Native Americans between 1000 and 1550, a time period known as the Mississippian era. During this time their great achievement was a series of earthen mounds used socially and ceremonially for temples and tombs. The mounds were seen by de Soto on his exploration through the area in 1540, although the civilization was rapidly declining by then. Today the 54-acre site preserves the mounds as well as the area where there was a village surrounded by a defensive ditch. The interpretive center houses artifacts, beads, ornaments, pot shards, and other artifacts found on the site. "Ike" and "Mike," the two largest carved-stone effigies ever discovered at a Mound Builder site, also are on display. Wooden stairs permit

ONE OF THE EARTHEN MOUNDS CREATED BY NATIVE AMERICANS AT THE ETOWAH INDIAN MOUND HISTORIC SITE IN CARTERSVILLE

visitors to climb to the top of the largest mound (63 feet tall and covering 3 acres) for a wonderful panoramic view and a glimpse of the V-shaped, piled-stone traps the natives built to catch fish and mussels. The site is an important stop on the **Georgia Chieftains Trail.** Note: Interpretive center and paths wheelchair accessible; top of mound is not. Adults $3, seniors $2.50, children $2.

✍ ❧ ♿ **Kirby-Quinton Heritage Cabin–Old Pickens County Jail** (706-268-3129; www.marblevalley.org), 141 North Main Street, Jasper. Open 2–5 Saturday and Sunday. The jail-residence was constructed in 1906 with the living quarters for the jailer and his family on the first floor and the cellblocks on the second floor. This arrangement served the county until 1982. Some of the antique furniture includes a rope bed, spinning wheel, and crib. $2.

MUSEUMS ✍ ❧ ♿ **Bartow History Center** (770-382-3818; www.bartowhistory center.org), 13 North Wall Street, Cartersville. Open 10–5 Tuesday through Saturday (Thursday until 8), 1–5 Sunday. The museum, a site on Georgia's **Blue and Gray Trail,** preserves the cultural, industrial, and agricultural heritage of the county. Displays follow the footsteps of the Cherokee, march with Civil War soldiers, and visit a 20th-century dentist's office. Trade, politics, and transportation are examined through artifacts, archival material, and oral histories from pioneer settlements to the early 20th century. Adults $3, seniors $2.50, children $2.

✍ ❧ ♿ **Booth Western Art Museum** (770-607-6361; www.boothmuseum.org), 501 Museum Drive, Cartersville. Open 10–5 Tuesday through Saturday (Thursday until 8), 1–5 Sunday; tours at 1:30 daily; café open 10–3:30 Tuesday through Saturday. This stunning museum, the only one of its kind in the Southeast and the second-largest museum in Georgia, showcases contemporary western art as well as Civil War art, presidential photographs and letters, and other items. The collection consists of 200 paintings and sculptures by more than 100 of the 20th century's best-known western artists—most of whom are still living. All U.S. presidents are represented by a painting or photograph and a typed or signed document in the Presidential Gallery. Another exhibit, "Illustration and Movie Star Art," features western movie posters. An orientation film, *The American West,* is shown continuously. The Sagebrush Ranch children's gallery features a replica of a stagecoach and a horse the small fry can climb on; an artist's studio; a bunkhouse where they can dress up in costumes; "Tall Tales Barn," where they can watch vintage western TV programs; a fully outfitted chuck wagon; and a puzzle corral, branding station, and barrel computer station. The museum's café serves sandwiches, salads, soups, chili, and desserts. Special events at the museum include the **Southeastern Cowboy Symposium** and **Georgia Cowboy Poetry Gathering** held each March and October (see *Special Events*). Wheelchair accessible; limited number of wheelchairs available, and closed caption orientation film offered. Adults $8, seniors and active military $6, children 13–18 $5, 12 and younger free.

✍ ❧ ♿ **Funk Heritage Center** (770-720-5970; www.reinhardt.edu/funk.htm), 7300 Reinhardt College Circle, Waleska. Open 9–4 weekdays, 10–5 Saturday, 1–5 Sunday. Located on the campus of Reinhardt College and designated as the state's official Frontier and Southeastern Indian Interpretive Center, the museum is devoted to Native American history as well as the pioneer experience of early Appalachian settlers. The contemporary building was inspired by Indian designs. Highlights include dioramas, interactive displays, artifacts, contemporary Native American art, and thousands of tools from more than 100 crafts and trades from the 18th and 19th centuries. On the grounds is a re-created 19th-century settlers village. Adults $6, seniors $5.50, children $4.

✒ 🏵 **Lake Allatoona Visitors Center** (770-382-4700), GA Spur 20 at Allatoona Dam, Cartersville. Open 8–6 daily, April through September; 8–4:30 daily, October through March. A multimedia presentation and numerous exhibits tell the stories of Native American history and culture; the U.S. Army Corps of Engineers from its inception in the Revolutionary War; the Civil War, including the Battle of Allatoona Pass; the geology of Bartow County; and the building of Lake Allatoona. A short walk takes visitors to the Allatoona Dam overlook to view the dam and powerhouse. One of the other hiking trails—an easy, 0.7-mile trail that runs along a railroad bed once used by mining trains—leads to the Cooper's Furnace Day Use Area (see *Green Space—Nature Preserves and Parks*). The moderate, 1-mile Laurel Ridge Trail runs along slopes overlooking the Etowah River Valley. The museum is a site on Georgia's **Blue and Gray Trail**. Free.

🏵 ♿ **Noble Hill–Wheeler Memorial Center** (770-383-3392; www.notatlanta .org), 2361 Joe Frank Harris Parkway, Cassville. Open 9–4 Tuesday through Saturday. This black history museum and cultural center is housed in the first school in north Georgia to be built with Rosenwald funds, which were specifically designated to be used for the education of African American children. Wheelchair accessible. Free; donations accepted.

🏵 ♿ **Rose Lawn Museum** (770-387-5162; www.roselawnmuseum.com), 224 West Cherokee Avenue, Cartersville. Open 10–noon and 1–5 Tuesday through Friday, but call first to verify. Samuel Porter Jones, a noted evangelist of the 1800s, lived in this restored 1850 mansion, which now serves as a museum. The facility contains writings and memorabilia related to Jones as well as to Rebecca Latimer Felton, a Bartow County resident who became the first woman to serve in the U.S. Senate. Adults $3, children 12 and younger $2.

ONE OF THE DISPLAYS AT THE WEINMAN MINERAL MUSEUM IN WHITE

✒ 🏵 ♿ **Weinman Mineral Museum** (770-386-0576; www.weinmanmuseum .org), 51 Mineral Museum Drive, White. Open 10–5 Monday through Saturday. The museum, which features an extensive collection of minerals from Georgia and around the world as well as fossil displays and antique mining equipment, is considered to be the finest mineral museum in the Southeast. Gold and gemstones are displayed, and youngsters particularly enjoy the simulated cave tunnel and hands-on exhibits. Outdoor activities include fossil hunting and gold panning. Adults $4, seniors $3.50, children 6–11 $3.

SCENIC DRIVES ✒ 🐾 **Georgia Mountain Parkway Trail.** The 65-mile route stretches from Jasper to Hiawassee. Along the trail are nostalgic towns, beautiful scenery, seasonal festivals, and ample opportunities for outdoor pursuits such as camping, canoeing, fishing, kayaking, and white-water rafting.

✒ 🐾 **Southern Highroads Trail** (706-633-6706; www.southernhighroads.org). This 360-mile scenic route goes through four states. The Georgia section stretches from Blue Ridge to Clayton (see Clarkesville chapter) and provides scenic beauty and Appalachian history and culture. Free.

✳ To Do

BICYCLING ✒ 🐾 **Ridgeway Mountain Bike Trail** (706-334-2248; www.carters .sam.usace.army.mil), US 76/GA 282, Ellijay. Open daily. The 6-mile trail has advanced and intermediate sections to challenge riders of various skill levels. Trail use free; parking $4.

BOATING ✒ 🐾 **Toccoa River Canoe Trail** (706-632-5680; 1-800-899-6867; www.blueridgemountains.com), 3990 Appalachian Highway, Blue Ridge. A 17-mile class II river winds through the Chattahoochee National Forest. Call for maps and suggested take-out points.

See also Marinas/Boat Landings Appendix.

FARM TOURS ✒ 🐾 **Apple Orchard Alley**, GA 52 East, East Ellijay. Open daily during apple season, August through December. Gilmer County is Georgia's apple capital. Eleven of the county's 18 apple orchards are along GA 52. Free.

✒ 🐾 **Pettit Creek Farms** (770-386-8688; www.PettitCreekFarms.com), 337 Cassville Road, Cartersville. Open October through December; call for hours and admission fees. During October, the farm offers the Pumpkin Pickin' Patch where you can choose the perfect pumpkin for your jack-o'-lantern. During the second weekend of October, the **Pumpkinfest** arts and crafts festival is held. See a camel, zebra, Patagonian cavy, emu, ponies, buffalo, and traditional farm animals. Beginning the day after Thanksgiving, you can choose your own Christmas tree, take a hayride tour of the farm, and enjoy a drive-through holiday lights display.

✒ 🐾 ♿ **Sugar Creek Alpaca Farm** (706-258-4494; 1-888-662-8253; www .sugarcreekfarmandinn.com), 1050 Cox Road, Blue Ridge. Guided tours by reservation. Visit this farm to see a growing herd of suri alpacas from Bolivia and adorable babydoll sheep. Alpacas, which are considerably smaller than their camel and llama relatives, are noted for their high-quality, silky fleece, which is prized for making sweaters and shawls. The small babydoll sheep have cute teddy-bear faces and make good pets. Their wool is in the same class as cashmere and is ideal when blended with Angora rabbit or goat wool. Free.

FISHING See **Lake Acworth** and **Lake Blue Ridge** under *Green Space—Lakes.*

FOR FAMILIES ✐ ⚐ ♿ **Cagle's Dairy MAIZE** (770-345-5591; www.caglesdairy
.com/MAIZE2.htm), 362 Stringer Road, Canton. Open 3:30–11 Friday, 10–11
Saturday, 10–6 Sunday, Labor Day through mid-November. The working dairy,
which also offers farm tours year round, creates an intricate corn maze with lots
of twists and turns each autumn. Maze $9, hayride and bonfire $7, $14 for both.

✐ ⚐ ♿ **Swan Center Outreach** (770-893-3525, www.swancenter.org), 75 Swan
Center Drive, Marble Hill. Open 10:30–4:30 Wednesday through Sunday. The
sanctuary for rescued animals offers trail rides, children's horse camps, and a
petting zoo. Lodging is available. Tours free; prices of other activities vary.

FRUIT AND BERRY PICKING ✐ ⚐ ♿ **Hillcrest Orchards** (706-273-3838; www
.hillcrestorchards.net), 9696 GA 52 East, Ellijay. Open 9–6 weekdays, September
1 through November 30. In addition to pick-your-own fruit, the farm sells
apples, cider, sorghum syrup, mountain honey, and apple butter. Activities
include wagon rides, a nature trail, and a petting zoo. $5.

✐ ⚐ ♿ **Mercier Orchards** (706-632-2364; www.mercier-orchards.com), GA 5
North, Blue Ridge. Open 8–6 Monday through Saturday, noon–6 Sunday; pick-
your-own 10–4 weekends in September. Mercier Orchards is one of the largest
apple orchards in the Southeast. For more than 60 years, four generations of one
family have been growing and selling more than 30 varieties of fruit, including
20 varieties of apples as well as blueberries, blackberries, raspberries, and peaches.
In addition, the property features a farmer's market that offers cider, jellies,
jams, pickled okra, smoked trout, sourwood honey, and gift items; a bakery that
produces apple cider doughnuts, apple bread, pies, cakes, apple dumplings, fritters, and fried pies; and deli items.

GOLF See Golf Appendix.

HIKING ✐ ⚐ **Allatoona Pass Trail** (770-606-8862), Old Allatoona Road,
Cartersville. Open dawn–dusk daily. The 190-foot-deep pass was used as a railroad bed of the Western and Atlantic Railroad. A Civil War battle occurred here
on October 5, 1864, and visitors can still see trenches and fortifications constructed by Union troops. Two and a half miles of interpretive signs explain the
battle. Free.

✐ ⚐ **Aska Trails** (706-632-5680; 1-800-899-6867; www.blueridgemountains
.com/aska_trails.html), 3990 Appalachian Highway, Blue Ridge. Open year-
round. The Aska Trails area is a 17-mile hiking and mountain biking trail system
through Chattahoochee National Forest lands near Deep Gap. Trail sections
range from 1 to 5½ miles, vary in difficulty, and run from the shores of Lake
Blue Ridge to 3,200 feet in elevation. Free.

✐ ⚐ **Benton MacKaye Trail** (for information, e-mail contactBMTA@bmta.org)
extends nearly 300 miles through the Appalachian Mountains, part of it in Georgia beginning at Springer Mountain. The trail, which is rated strenuous, passes
through some of the most remote backcountry in Georgia and crosses the

Appalachian Trail several times. There are numerous access points and trailheads—including 16 in Georgia—which create many options for short or long, one-way or round-trip hikes. Permits are required only for backcountry camping. Free.

✎ 🐾 **Riverside Park, Vineyard Mountain Trail,** Allatoona Dam Road, Cartersville. Open 8–9:30 daily. Three difficult trails take hikers along steep slopes overlooking the Etowah River, Allatoona Dam, and Lake Allatoona. Free.

See also **Lake Allatoona Visitors Center** under *To See—Museums* and **Cooper's Furnace Day Use Area** and **Red Top Mountain State Park** under *Green Space—Nature Preserves and Parks.*

HORSEBACK RIDING ✎ **Adventure Trail Rides** (706-258-2276; www.adventure trailrides.com), Blue Ridge. Call or consult the web site for directions. Open for rides 10–noon, 1–3, and 4–6, but call ahead. Guided rides explore easy scenic trails, more advanced terrain, and steep terrain and winding trails suitable only for advanced riders. $30–45 depending on level of difficulty.

✎ **Blanche Manor Riding Stables** (706-455-RIDE; www.blancemanor.com), 181 Deal Hollow Road, Blue Ridge. Rides at 10, noon, and 3 daily. Guided trail rides wind through the north Georgia mountains. Hayrides, dinner rides, and bonfire rides are also available. $28–35 depending on length.

✎ **Double D Trail Rides** (706-632-6975; www.doubledtrailrides.com), 1474 Pack Creek Road, Blue Ridge. Reservations required. Guided trail rides use quarter horses for riders of all skill levels. $35 for 90-minute ride, $45 for three-hour ride, $60 for full-day ride with lunch.

✎ **Mule Top Mountain Outfitters** (706-632-0076; www.muletop.com), 319 Hells Hollow Road, Blue Ridge. Reservations required. Not for the fainthearted, these adventurous rides are on steep trails with slow walking and tight turns. $25 for one-hour ride, $35 for two-hour ride, $45 for three-hour ride, $55 for four-hour ride.

MINIATURE GOLF ✎ 🐾 ♿ **Gilmer Golf and Games** (706-698-4653), 7286 GA 515 North, Ellijay. Open March 1 through December 1; call for hours and prices. In addition to miniature golf, the facility offers batting cages and video game rooms.

TRAIN EXCURSIONS ✎ **Blue Ridge Scenic Railway** (706-632-9833; 1-800-934-1898; www.brscenic.com), 241 Depot Street, Blue Ridge. Call for schedule. The nostalgic train, which winds 26 miles through rolling hills alongside the Toccoa River to McCaysville, has both open and closed cars. Weekends in December, the railway offers the **Blue Ridge Scenic Railway Christmas Express,** which includes visits from Santa and Mrs. Claus and the elves, Christmas stories, and caroling. Adults $32.10, seniors $27.82, children 2–12 $16.05.

WHITE-WATER RAFTING ✎ Call the **Fannin County Welcome Center** (706-632-5680; 1-800-899-6867) for information about experienced guides and outfitters.

❋ Green Space

LAKES ✔ ✿ ♿ **Allatoona Lake and Visitors Center** (678-721-6700; allatoona.sam.usace.army.mil), 1138 GA 20 Spur, Cartersville. Visitor center open 8–4:30 daily. In addition to water sports, the lake and surrounding land offer hiking trails and camping (see *Lodging*). Free.

✔ ✿ ♿ **Lake Acworth** (770-974-3112), City of Acworth Parks and Recreation Department, 4375 Russell Square, Acworth. Open daylight hours daily. The 90-acre urban lake offers fishing, boating (electric motors only), boat ramps, picnicking, swimming in the summer, a playground, and a concession stand. The lake is stocked with channel catfish, largemouth bass, bluegill, redear sunfish, crappie, carp, and bullheads. Free.

✔ ✿ ♿ **Lake Blue Ridge** (www.georgialakeonfo.com/blueridge), located within the Chattahoochee National Forest, Blue Ridge. Formed by a Tennessee Valley Authority dam, the 3,290-acre lake's crystal-clear blue waters contain the head-waters of the Toccoa River, one of the state's most pristine rivers. Boating, camping, hiking, picnicking, and waterskiing are popular pastimes. Trout fishing is particularly popular with anglers, but the lake also contains bass, bream, catfish, crappie, perch, and other species. There is an overlook near the dam as well as a canoe and kayak launch below it. When water is released, the river provides class I and II float trips.

NATURE PRESERVES AND PARKS ✔ ✿ ♿ **Acworth Beach, Cauble Park** (770-917-1234; www.acworth.org), Beach Street, Acworth. Park open 7–11 daily year-round; beach open Memorial Day–Labor Day. Boating, fishing, swimming, and occasional outdoor concerts keep families busy here. Admission free; parking $5 on weekends.

✔ ✿ ♿ **Cooper's Furnace Day Use Area** (678-721-6700), River Road, Cartersville. Open 8–dusk daily, March through October. The site, which is on Georgia's **Blue and Gray Trail** at the base of Allatoona Dam, is the last reminder of the town of Etowah (now under the waters of Lake Allatoona) and Cooper's Iron Works. Mark Anthony Cooper sold the iron manufacturing facilities to the Confederacy in 1863, and it was destroyed by Union forces in 1864. The town and most of the remnants of the iron industry were lost when the man-made lake was created in 1950. A lone cold-blast furnace is the only memorial to the iron empire. Visitors can hike the nature trail to an overlook atop the dam. Wheelchair accessible. Free.

✔ ✿ ♿ ❋ **Red Top Mountain State Park and Lodge** (770-975-0055; 1-800-864-7275; www.gastateparks.org/info/redtop), 50 Lodge Road, Cartersville. Open 7–10 daily. This popular 1,428-acre state park on the shores of 12,000-acre Allatoona Lake features a swimming beach, pool, boating, fishing, hiking, picnicking, tennis, and miniature golf. The mountain, once an important iron mining area, is named for the soil's rich red color. Twelve miles of wooded hiking trails wind through the park. A 0.75-mile paved trail behind the restaurant is suitable for wheelchairs and strollers. A special attraction is the reconstructed 1860s homestead, which is open and staffed on Saturdays and used for heritage events during **Spring Time at the Homestead, Harvest Time at the Homestead,** and the **Mountain Music Series,** which offers bluegrass music and storytelling at 8 Saturdays, May through July. The park also hosts many other special activities, including **Halloween Hayrides; For the Birds**—a program of bird walks, slide presentations, and raptor shows; **Archaeology at the Red Top;** and an **Iron Pour** in which molten iron ore is poured at 2,800 degrees Fahrenheit. Accommodations are offered in a hotel-style lodge, in cottages, or at a campground. The campground offers 92 tent and RV sites as well as a yurt. Sixty-eight sites offer water and electric hookups; the remainder are primitive sites. One site is wheelchair accessible. Campsites $18–22; yurt $35. The park offers 18 fully equipped cabins, two of which are wheelchair accessible. No smoking. $89–119; some holidays have three- or four-night minimum. The park also offers a 33-room lodge, which is home to the Mountain Cove Restaurant. No smoking. Wheelchair accessible. $69–89. State park parking/day-use fee $3.

RIVERS ⚓ 🐟 the **Toccoa River** is a popular destination for tubing, canoeing, kayaking, and trout fishing. It flows into Lake Blue Ridge, then journeys down a wide valley known as the McCaysville Basin. Trout fishermen favor this area of the river. After the river leaves McCaysville, it becomes the Ocoee, a world-class white-water river and the site of the 1996 Summer Olympic Games' white-water events.

✳ Lodging

BED & BREAKFASTS

In Blue Ridge

Blue Ridge Inn (706-632-0222; www.blueridgeinnbandb.com), 477 West First Street. One of the oldest residences in Blue Ridge, the three-story Victorian-era inn features 12-foot ceilings, heart-pine floors, original hand-carved woodwork, claw-foot tubs, eight fireplaces, and a rocking-chair porch. Accommodations are in three rooms and a suite with private en suite baths and three other rooms with private hall baths. Room decor is based on themes such as roses, Marilyn Monroe, sports, garden, cabin, lighthouse, and safari. A full country breakfast is included in the nightly rate. The inn is within easy walking distance of the Blue Ridge Scenic Railway depot, shops, and restaurants. No smoking. Not wheelchair accessible. $89–129.

Sugar Creek Farm and Inn (706-258-4494; 1-888-662-8253; www.sugarcreekfarmandinn.com), 1050 Cox Road. The 11-acre working alpaca and babydoll sheep farm offers accommodations in a house that has been extensively renovated to create a bed & breakfast. Three upstairs rooms feature sitting areas and private baths; the two downstairs rooms share a bath. An extensive menu of gourmet breakfast entrées ensures that guests get their day off to a healthy start. Smoking allowed. Not wheelchair accessible. $70–125; two-night minimum May through October.

THE MOUNTAINS

In Acworth

♂ 🦐 Holiday Harbor Marina, Campsites, and Resort (770-974-2575; www.lakeallatoona.net), 5989 Groovers Landing Road. The campground offers 28 campsites with partial hookups as well as a camp store, restaurant, and boat rentals. Campsites $20. Seven waterfront cabins each offer a kitchen, living room with fireplace, dining room, two bedrooms, one or two bathrooms, a deck, and a courtesy boat dock. Smoking and nonsmoking cabins. Not wheelchair accessible. $115–135 per night, $545 per week.

In Blue Ridge

There are numerous **U.S. Forest Service campgrounds** (706-632-3031; www.fs.fed.us/conf) in this area. Check on reservations and rates for all of them. See also campgrounds appendix.

In Cartersville

The area has numerous **U.S. Corps of Engineers campgrounds** (678-721-6700; 1-877-444-6777; www.alla toona.sam.usace.army.mil/Allatoona/camping). Check on information, reservations, and rates for all of them. See also campgrounds appendix.

See also **Red Top Mountain State Park** under *Green Space—Nature Preserves and Parks.*

COTTAGES AND CABINS

In Acworth

See **Holiday Harbor Marina, Campsites, and Resort** under *Campgrounds.*

In Cartersville

See **Red Top Mountain State Park** under *Green Space—Nature Preserves and Parks.*

INNS AND RESORTS

In Cartersville

See **Red Top Mountain State Park and Lodge** under *Green Space—Nature Preserves and Parks.*

In Ellijay

♂ Whitepath Mountain Resort (706-276-7199; www.whitepath lodge.com), 987 Shenandoah Drive. Enjoy gorgeous mountain views and manicured gardens at this retreat. Accommodations are in two-bedroom villas with fully equipped kitchens, gas fireplaces, and private porches and decks. Swimming in the pool, golf, tennis, horseshoes, and basketball are popular activities. No smoking. Villas not wheelchair accessible, although common room in lodge is. $100–220; two-night minimum on weekends; some three-night minimums at peak times.

OTHER LODGINGS

In Jasper

Rolin' Hills Garden and Gallery (770-893-2096; www.rolinhills.com), 5850 Cove Road. The home, which is located on 10 wooded acres near the beginning of the Appalachian Trail, is furnished with many items handcrafted by owner Tony Lumley and accented with wife Lynn's original paintings. Accommodations are provided in the Rustic Room, which has a queen bed, a large private bath, and a private entrance with a porch. Guests traveling with an extra person can reserve the Garden Room, which has one twin bed and shares a bath. Rolin' Hills Gardens has something we have seen at no other: a disco. Tony was a DJ in a former life, and the couple also taught disco lessons. So Tony has outfitted a room behind the house with a disco ball, light and sound equipment, and his huge music collection of records and CDs. Because accommodations are rented to only one party of one to three people at a time, guests can play music and dance to their hearts' content without bothering anyone. During the day, guests enjoy the gardens filled with more than 500 varieties of daylilies and perennials accented with a koi pond. No pets. No smoking. Limited wheelchair accessibility; back door is at ground level, but bathrooms and doors cannot accommodate wheelchairs. $75–115.

✳ Where to Eat
DINING OUT
In Blue Ridge
♂ ₺ **Victorian House Restaurant** (706-258-2275), 224 West Main Street. Open 11:30–3 Monday, Tuesday, and Thursday through Sunday; 5–9 Thursday through Saturday. The restaurant re-creates the Victorian era with its architecture and the use of 1900-style china, glassware, and decor. The cuisine features both Southern and Italian influences. Luncheon choices include a wide variety of appetizers, soups, salads, sandwiches, quiches, and entrées such as chicken, trout, and pasta. Dinner choices include many of the same items as well as boar, pork, beef, veal, and seafood. Smoking on covered patio only. Wheelchair accessible from rear of restaurant. Lunch $5.99–13.99, dinner $12.99–22.99.

♂ ₷ ₺ **Appalachian Grill** (770-607-5357), 14 East Church Street. Open 11–9 Monday through Thursday, 11–10 Friday and Saturday. On the historic square "under the bridge" (a highway overpass), this casual yet upscale eatery is eclectic in decor and cuisine as well as in its choice of background music. The ambience is warmed by stone and brick walls and aged wood, while music ranges from bluegrass to country to blues to light rock. Dinner entrées include steaks, prime rib, seafood, chicken, and pork. No smoking. Wheelchair accessible, but all seating is in booths, so wheelchair must be set at end of table. Lunch $7–12, dinner $13–21.

D. Morgan's Restaurant and Wine Bar (770-383-3535; www.dmorgans.com), 28 West Main Street. Open 5–10 Tuesday through Saturday; wine bar open 5–midnight. Located in a historic 1800s building in downtown Cartersville, this upscale, white-linen restaurant serves New American cuisine that features seafood, chicken, pork chops, duck cassoulet, beef, veal, and rack of lamb. No smoking. Wheelchair accessible. $16–29.

EATING OUT
In Cartersville
♂ ₷ ₺ **Church Street Tea Garden** (678-721-5025), 119 West Church Street. Open 11–3 Tuesday through Saturday. Enjoy salads, quiche, crêpes, soups, and sandwiches with a choice of 15 varieties of tea. No smoking. Wheelchair accessible. $7–13.

♂ ₷ ₺ **The Four Way,** (no phone) Main and Gilmer streets. Open 6 AM–3 PM Monday through Saturday. For more than 50 years, this restaurant has been serving Southern specialties and ethnic delights such as hamburger with gravy and the world's sloppiest chili dogs. Lines are often out the door because there are only about a dozen stools. Take-out might be a better option. No smoking. Wheelchair accessible. $4–10.

✎ ⚘ **Riverwalk Bakery and Café at Grove Park** (770-607-BAKE), 700 Douthit Ferry Road, Suite 710. Open 7–5 Monday, Tuesday, Thursday, and Friday; 7–3 Wednesday and Saturday. The café serves delectable baked goods, distinctive coffees, specialty sandwiches, and gourmet salads. Lunch is served from 11 to closing. No smoking. Not wheelchair accessible. $4.99–6.25.

✎ ⚘ ♿ **The Village Porch Café** (770-386-3100), 25 North Wall Street. Open 10:30–3 Tuesday through Friday, 7:30–3 Saturday. Choose from more than 20 sandwiches, Italian sodas, and ice cream. No smoking. Wheelchair accessible. $4.50–6.50.

✳ **Entertainment**

The **Blue Ridge Mountain Arts Association** (706-632-2144) sponsors seasonal exhibits and gallery tours as well as **Concerts in the Park** in July and August, the **Arts in the Park Festival** on Memorial Day weekend, and the **Wildlife Festival of the Arts** (see *Special Events*) in September.

MOVIES ✎ ⚘ **Swan Drive-In** (1-888-469-1955; www.swan-drivein.com), 651 Summit Street, Blue Ridge. One of four remaining drive-ins in Georgia, the family-oriented Swan began operation in 1955 and continues to offer first-run movies year-round. Adults $5, children ages 4–11 $2.

THEATER **Blue Ridge Community Theater** (706-632-9223; www.blueridgecommunitytheater.com), Hampton Square, 11 Mountain Street, Suite D, Blue Ridge. Shows are usually Friday and Saturday evenings and Sunday afternoons. The volunteer group presents a full calendar of drama, comedy, and musicals. The Sunny D Children's Theater Workshop offers a summer camp and a Christmas production. Call for a schedule of productions. Tickets average $12.50.

Cobb Playhouse and Studio (770-565-3995; www.cobbplayhouse.com), 4857 North Main Street, Suite 240, Acworth. The theater organization is actually a collection of six theater companies, an arts education program, and an art studio. Call for a schedule of events. $8–16; dinner theater $38.

Grand Theatre of Cartersville (information 770-386-7343; tickets 770-607-3686; www.thegrandtheatre.org), 7 North Wall Street, Cartersville. Built in the 1920s and fully restored, the theater hosts a wide variety of performing arts events throughout the year. Call for a schedule of performances and ticket prices.

Legion Theater and the Pumphouse Players (770-387-2620; www.pumphouseplayers.com), 114-C Main Street, Cartersville. Formed in the 1960s, the troupe of community players performs a variety of genres from musicals to Shakespeare. Call for a schedule of performances and ticket prices.

✳ **Selective Shopping**

Cartersville Historic Downtown

Shopping District (770-387-1357; 1-800-733-2280; www.notatlanta.org), One Friendship Plaza, Cartersville. The area contains more than 46 shops and 15 restaurants.

ANTIQUES You'll be captivated by **Acworth's** Victorian village–style downtown, where you'll find many antiques shops.

Bradford Place Antiques (770-607-6922), 18 South Wall Street, Cartersville. Open 10:30–6 Monday through Saturday. The shop specializes in rare books by local authors. Gordy pottery, decorative antiques, chair caning, and antique restoration are also offered.

High Country Art and Antiques (706-632-6882), 715 East Main Street, Blue Ridge. Open 10–5 Monday and Wednesday through Saturday, noon–5 Sunday. The shop displays 1,000 works by 65 local and regional painters, potters, and sculptors.

CLOTHING Georgia Mountain Fibers (706-632-6767; www.georgia mountainfiber.com), Hampton Square, 11 Mountain Street, Suite A, Blue Ridge. Open noon–6 Tuesday through Friday, noon–8 Saturday; longer hours in summer. The shop sells dyed and natural alpaca yarns as well as yarn produced from llamas, cashmere goats, and yaks. In partnership with **Fleece to Fashion USA** (www.FleeceToFashion.com), the enterprise also offers handwoven and hand- or machine-knit sweaters, shawls, hats, scarves, mittens, socks, and baby layettes and blankets. They can even custom-create something for you.

FOOD See **Hillcrest Orchards** and

Mercier Orchards under *To Do—Fruit and Berry Picking.*

✴ Special Events

March: **Cowboy Poetry Gathering** (770-387-1300; www.boothmuseum .org). Held in conjunction with Cartersville's Booth Western Art Museum, the event features artists' presentations and workshops, art and history programs, a concert at the Grand Theatre, children's activities, a poetry- and song-writing workshop, blacksmithing demonstration, and Dutch-oven cooking contest. (Included with regular admission; see **Booth Western Art Museum** under *To See— Museums.*)

September: **Apple Pickin' Jubilee** at Hillcrest Orchards (706-273-3838), 9696 GA 52 East, Ellijay. General hours 9–6 weekends, last two weekends of September (call ahead to be sure of dates and times). Pick all the apples you can shake a stick at, and visit the petting zoo. Except for the apple picking, these festivities continue throughout the month of October. $5; additional $3 petting zoo.

Wildlife Festival of the Arts (706-632-2144). Held in the Blue Ridge City Park, the event features the works of the finest wildlife artists in the Southeast. Other events include forest service information, fly-fishing demonstrations, food, and entertainment. Free.

October: **Southeastern Cowboy Symposium** (770-387-1300; www .boothmuseum.org), Cartersville. Activities include cowboy poetry and music, a reenactment of the Gunfight at the OK Corral, chuck-

APPLES ARE THE STAR EVERY SEPTEMBER AT HILLCREST ORCHARDS IN ELLIJAY.

wagon cooking demonstrations, Native American programs, children's activities, western fashion shows, artists offering everything from jewelry to bows and arrows to leather goods, a frontier camp, an Indian encampment, concerts, and Cowboy Church on Sunday. Admission the same as museum admission; see **Booth Western Art Museum** under *To See—Museums;* nominal fee charged for children's activities; concerts $5–25.

CLARKESVILLE TO CLAYTON

Located at the southern end of the Blue Ridge Mountains—so named for the blue haze that covers them year-round—this area is widely visited thanks to the Chattahoochee National Forest's hundreds of miles of trails, numerous lakes, mountain streams, and nature preserves. The region is a mecca for outdoor enthusiasts in search of mountain biking, golf, fishing, horseback riding, canoeing, kayaking, white-water rafting, camping, backpacking, and wilderness adventures. An abundance of waterfalls range from dramatic torrents to delicate cascades. Few are visible from the road or parking lots, so hikes—most of which are short—are required to get a glimpse of them. The scenery is spectacular and local residents are friendly.

The area is also rich in quaint villages, historic country inns, country cooking and fine dining, and shopping for antiques, folk art, pottery, fine crafts, and handmade country pine furniture.

This region has a wealth of Native American history because north Georgia was the capital of the Cherokee Nation during the mid-1700s. Visitors enjoy stories, legends, and lore about that era.

GUIDANCE When planning a trip to the Clarkesville area—including Alto, Cornelia, and Demorest—consult the **Habersham County Welcome Center** (706-754-2296; www.seehabersham.com), Mauldin House, 458 Jefferson Street, Clarkesville 30523. Open 10–4 Tuesday through Friday, 10–2 Saturday. Another source of information is the **Habersham County Chamber of Commerce** (706-778-4654; 1-800-835-2559; www.habershamchamber.com), 668 Clarkesville Street, Cornelia 30531. Open 8:30–5 weekdays.

To learn more about Clayton and the surrounding area—including Dillard, Lakemont, Mountain City, Rabun Gap, Sky Valley, Tallulah Falls, and Tiger—contact the **Rabun County Chamber–Rabun Convention and Visitors Bureau and Welcome Center** (706-782-4812; www.gamountains

---

RABUN BALD MOUNTAIN

According to Indian legend, the 4,690-foot mountain is inhabited by fire-breathing demon people. Even in the 21st century, campers and other visitors often report strange sounds in the night.

.com), 232 US 441 North, Clayton 30525. Open 9–5 weekdays; April through October also open 9–3 Saturday.

To find out more about Toccoa, contact the **Toccoa–Stephens County Chamber of Commerce** (706-886-2132; 1-877-6TOCCOA; www.toccoagachamber .com), 901 East Currahee Street, Toccoa 30577. Open 8:30–5 weekdays.

GETTING THERE *By air:* The closest airports to this area are **Athens–Ben Epps Airport** (see Athens chapter in 3, Historic South); **Hartsfield-Jackson Atlanta International Airport** in Atlanta (see What's Where in Georgia); **Greenville-Spartanburg International Airport** (864-877-7426), 2000 GSP Drive, Greer, South Carolina; and **Asheville Regional Airport** (828-684-2226), 708 Airport Road, Fletcher, North Carolina.

Greenville-Spartanburg International Airport is served by **American Eagle, Continental, Delta,** and **Independence Air**. Car rentals are available from **Alamo/National** (1-800-328-4567), **Avis** (1-800-331-1212), **Budget** (1-800-527-0700), **Hertz** (1-800-654-3131), and **Thrifty** (1-800-367-2277). Asheville Regional Airport is served by **Continental, Delta, Northwest,** and **US Airways.** Car rentals are available there from **Avis, Budget, Enterprise** (1-800-261-7331), and **Hertz.**

By bus: The nearest **Greyhound Lines** station is in Gainesville (see Gainesville chapter).

By car: I-85 and I-985 running north-south near the area make access easy. The primary north-south route within the region is US 441.

By train: **Amtrak** (1-800-USA-RAIL; www.amtrak.com), 47 North Alexandria Street, Toccoa. The *Crescent*, which travels from New York City to Atlanta and New Orleans via Washington, D.C., stops in Toccoa.

WHEN TO GO It's not unusual for the mountainous area to get snow or ice in the winter, although it rarely stays on the ground very long, but travelers should be aware of the possibility. Some campgrounds and other establishments close for a few months in the winter, so it's best to call ahead to check.

MEDICAL EMERGENCY In life-threatening situations, call 911. Immediate care is available at the **Habersham County Medical Center** (706-754-2161; hcm-cmed.org), 541 Historic US 441, Demorest; **Rabun County Memorial Hospital** (706-782-4233), South Main Street, Clayton; and **Stephens County Hospital** (706-282-4200), 2003 Falls Road, Toccoa.

VILLAGES Clarkesville, in Habersham County, is a pleasant small town noted for bed & breakfasts and shopping for mountain arts and crafts. **Moccasin Creek State Park** is located nearby (see *Green Space—Nature Preserves and Parks*). A Civil War ironworks in the county produced guns and cannons for the Confederacy, which might have marked it for destruction as Union forces moved south, but it was spared when Confederate troops turned back the Union Cavalry near Currahee Mountain.

Clayton is world-renowned as the home of the Foxfire series, a collection of oral histories gathered by local high school students and published in magazines and books.

Cornelia is a small former railroad town in apple country. In fact, the fruit is so important to the economy, a monument to it has been erected (see **Big Red Apple Monument** under *To See—Historic Homes and Sites*).

Dillard, a gateway to the Smoky Mountains, is known for an all-you-can-eat restaurant (see *Where to Eat—Dining Out*). Several state parks are nearby.

Mountain City is a recreation and retirement haven bordered by the Appalachian National Scenic Trail and the wild and scenic white-water Chattooga River. The town is also the home of the **Foxfire Museum**, which exhibits artifacts relating to Appalachian life (see *To See—Museums*).

Sky Valley had the distinction of having one of the two southernmost ski resorts in the country (the other was in northern Alabama) from 1969 until very recently. Formerly a cattle ranch, the 2,500-acre site is in a stream valley surrounded by mountain ridges that rise to as high as 4,200 feet. Although it rarely snows in Georgia and certainly doesn't snow often enough to create a base for skiing, this elevation produced temperatures that allowed for man-made snow. Unfortunately, a series of warm winters and the inability to make and maintain snow made the ski resort financially unviable. The City of Sky Valley, which embraces the resort, is still a popular golf destination (see *To Do—Golf* and *Lodging—Inns & Resorts*). To reach Sky Valley, visitors must drive into North Carolina and enter from the north.

The town of **Tallulah Falls** lies partially in Rabun County and partially in Habersham County. Three state parks are nearby, as is a portion of the Appalachian Trail.

Tiger, in Rabun County, claims to be "Where Spring Spends the Summer" because the average temperature in August is 79.8 degrees. Annual rainfall of 70 inches yields lush forests, wildflowers, and colorful leaves in October.

Toccoa means "beautiful" in the Cherokee language. Sadly, many lives were lost here in the 1970s when an earthen dam broke. Today a lovely waterfall can be viewed on the grounds of Toccoa Falls College (see *To Do—Waterfalls*).

✳ To See

CULTURAL SITES ✐ ✿ **Georgia Heritage Center for the Arts** (706-754-5989; www.experiencegeorgiaarts.com), 11785 US 441 South, Tallulah Falls. Open 10–5 Monday through Saturday, 1–5 Sunday. The arts center promotes emerging Georgia artists. Free.

HISTORIC HOMES AND SITES ✐ ✿ ♿ **Big Red Apple Monument,** 102 Grant Place, Cornelia. Open daily. Apples have been such an important part of Cornelia's economy since the early 1900s that town fathers erected a monument to the crisp, sweet fruit in 1926. The concrete apple weighs 5,200 pounds and is 7 feet tall and 22 feet around, making it the largest apple monument in the world. Free.

🔲 🏛 ♿ **Mauldin House** (706-754-2296; www.seehabersham.com), 458 Jefferson Street, Clarkesville. Open 10–4 Tuesday through Saturday, 10–2 Saturday. The late 19th-century building houses the Habersham County Welcome Center as well as a room filled with Victorian furniture and another filled with artifacts. The house began as a very small, simple structure and was enlarged in 1904 and 1925 until it achieved its current Victorian cottage style. Adjacent to the house is Mrs. Mauldin's **Millinery Shop** of the same period. The building is considered to be one of the oldest commercial buildings in town. Hats—including an antebellum wedding bonnet and baby bonnets—feathers, lace, gloves, and jewelry of the period are displayed. The hats are rotated in and out seasonally. Also on the grounds is the **Big Holly Cabin,** built around 1819 and later moved to this location. The cabin is furnished with a rope bed, plank table, and simple utilitarian items such as a corn-husk broom. Free.

🔲 🏛 ♿ **Traveler's Rest Historic Site** (706-886-2256; www.gastateparks.org/info/travelers), 8162 Riverdale Road, Toccoa. Open 9–5 Thursday through Saturday, 2–5:30 Sunday. Built in 1833 as the plantation house of Devereaux Jarrett, the "richest man in the Tugaloo Valley," this building was the center of his thriving plantation. It was later enlarged to be used as an inn. The structure features a 90-foot-long porch. Inside are antique furnishings of the period—many of them original to the site and some made by local craftsman Caleb Shaw. $2.50–4.

MUSEUMS 🔲 🏛 ♿ **Foxfire Museum** (706-746-5828; www.foxfire.org), 200 Foxfire Lane, Mountain City. Open 8:30–4:30 Monday through Saturday. Dedicated to the heritage and culture of the Appalachian Mountains, the museum displays many examples of the resilience of the area's early settlers. Visitors can experience Southern Appalachia as documented, photographed, and recorded by the students of Rabun County over the past four decades and shared with the world through *The Foxfire Magazine* and *The Foxfire Book* series. The magazine began in 1966 as an attempt to engage high school English students and increase their interest in learning. In 1972, an anthology of magazine articles was published as the first *Foxfire Book.* Ten more books have been published with total sales of 8.5 million copies. Royalties from the books paid for the land and the acquisition or construction of more than 20 log structures that now comprise the Foxfire Museum. The site includes a gristmill, blacksmith shop, church, and several single- and multiroom cabins. A wagon collection is another treat. Self-guided tours for visitors focus on artifacts displayed in and around the cabins. Adults $5, children 10 and younger free.

🔲 🏛 ♿ **Johnny Mize Athletic Center and Museum** (706-778-3000; www.piedmont.edu), 280 Laurel Avenue, Demorest. Open 6 AM–10 PM daily. The museum, named for the former Piedmont College baseball player and Hall of Famer who played for the Cardinals, Giants, and Yankees, features memorabilia from his career. Free.

🔲 🏛 ♿ **Loudermilk Boarding House Museum** (706-778-2001; www.joni mabe.com), 271 Foreacre Street, Cornelia. Open 10–5 Friday and Saturday. Joni Mabe is so enthralled—dare we say obsessed?—with Elvis Presley, she has amassed 30,000 items associated with the King of Rock and Roll. Her collection, dubbed Joni Mabe's Panoramic Encyclopedia of Everything Elvis, toured the world for 14 years before it finally found a permanent home in 2000 on the third floor of Mabe's great-grandparents' circa 1908 boardinghouse in Cornelia. Mabe professes to have been collecting since Elvis died in 1977. Among all the photos, newspaper and magazine articles, souvenirs, and books about the King are some particularly special pieces. She has a vial that purportedly contains Elvis sweat and a toenail she personally picked up from the carpet of the Jungle Room at Graceland. Even Mabe admits that the authenticity of these artifacts is iffy. Her prize possession, however, is a wart removed from Elvis by his doctor. The gift shop stocks everything Elvis as well as Mabe's own artwork. A highly anticipated annual event at the museum is the **Big E Celebration** honoring the King's death. This is when visitors can see Elvis impersonators and eat his favorite peanut butter and banana sandwiches or Moon Pies. Adults $5, children 6 and younger free.

✍ ᠑ ᠘ **Tallulah Falls Railroad Museum** (Rabun Gap–Nacoochee School, 706-746-7467; 1-800-543-7467; www.rabungap.org; www.railga.com/oddend/rabun gap.html), US 441, Rabun Gap. Open 9–5 Friday through Sunday, April 1 through late October or early November; open daily Memorial Day to Labor Day; or by appointment. Students at the Rabun Gap–Nacoochee School built a replica of the depot that served the former Tallulah Falls Railway, which once ran through Rabun Gap and brought visitors to the cool mountains at the turn of the 20th century. Exhibits include railroad artifacts and a 2-foot-gauge locomotive, passenger car, flatcar, caboose, and tracks built by students. Adults $2, children $1.

✍ ᠑ ᠘ **Tallulah Falls School Museum** (706-754-0400, ext. 3530; www.tallulah falls.org), Old US 441, Tallulah Falls. Open 8:30–4:30 weekdays. Located in Giddings Cottage on the school's campus, the museum traces the history of the Tallulah Falls School through artifacts, photographs, and paintings. Free.

SCENIC DRIVES ✍ ᠑ **Scenic Highway GA 197** (706-947-0030; www.scenic197 .com). From Clarkesville head north on Georgia Scenic Highway 197, part of the Southern Highroads Trail, along which you can shop for antiques, herbs, gifts, and crafts; stop for lunch; fish or wade in a creek; buy boiled peanuts; meander through gardens; have dinner; and spend the night. Then slide down the famous sliding rock on Wildcat Creek, a headwater stream that feeds into Lake Burton.

SPECIAL PLACES ✍ ᠘ **Sky Valley Golf Resort** (706-746-5303; 1-800-437-2416; www.skyvalley.com), 1 Sky Valley Way, Sky Valley. Resort open year-round. The 2,300-acre, four-season resort is popular for golf (see *To Do—Golf*), fishing, and hiking. There is also a restaurant and lounge. Accommodations are available in rental cottages and homes (see *Lodging—Inns & Resorts*). Overnight visitors enjoy the swimming pool, tennis courts, and fitness center. Prices vary by activity.

WINERIES ᠑ ᠘ **Persimmon Creek Vineyards** (706-212-7380; www .persimmoncreekwine.com), 81 Vineyard Lane, Clayton. Open 11–6 Saturdays, April through October; November through March by appointment. Reputedly once the home of active moonshine stills, the property near Lake Burton and Lake Rabun is now a 101-acre vineyard. The winery is best known for its Riesling, merlot, cabernet franc, and Seyval blanc. Wine dinners and tastings are scheduled periodically. Winery free; charges for special events.

🐾 ♿ **Tiger Mountain Vineyards** (706-782-4777; 706-782-9256), 2592 Old US 441, Tiger. Open 1–5 Tuesday through Friday, 11–6 Saturday during summer; weekends only remainder of the year. The 2,000-foot elevation, mineral-rich soil, and well-drained slopes combine to produce award-winning wines, including cabernet franc, malbec, and cabernet sauvignon. Since 1999, the vineyard's six red and one white have won many national and international awards. Vineyard parties are scheduled in fall and spring. Winery free; charges for some special events.

✳ To Do

BICYCLING 🚲 🐾 The **U.S. Forest Service** (770-297-3000; www.fs.fed.us) maintains several dirt or gravel roads that are suitable for recreational use. Riding varies from easy to strenuous. Free.

BOATING Numerous lakes (see *Green Space—Lakes*) provide endless opportunities for motorboating. These same lakes and some rivers (see *Green Space—Rivers*) also provide opportunities for canoeing, kayaking, and even white-water rafting.

FISHING 🚲 🐾 ♿ **Andy's Trout Farm** (706-746-2550; www.andystroutfarm.com), Betty's Creek Road, Dillard. Open 10–5 Monday through Saturday, 1–5 Sunday, April through November. Catch rainbow trout on the 350-acre farm, which has a lake and well-stocked ponds. No license is required and there is no limit to your catch (you must keep what you catch, not release them). Trout can be shipped at an additional fee. Tour the hatchery or hike a nature trail that winds through the forest, across streams, and past a waterfall. Gold and gem panning is also avail-

THE AREA'S LAKES ARE PERFECT FOR CANOEING OR KAYAKING.

able at $5 per bucket. Kids can enjoy a ride on Andy's Recycled Kiddie Train, and all ages enjoy pedal boats on the lake. Appalachian entertainment is offered around the campfire. Andy's also offers RV campsites (see *Lodging—Campgrounds*) and cabins (see *Lodging—Cottages and Cabins*). Fishing costs $3.50 per pound for what you catch; 50¢ pole rental; $2.25 for bait and worms; cleaning 50¢ per fish.

🎣 🦌 ♿ **Lake Burton Trout Hatchery** (706-947-3112), 3695 GA 197 North, Clarkesville. Open 8–4:30 daily. Of course the primary reason to come here is to fish for brown and rainbow trout, but there's also a well-stocked children's catfish pond, boating, waterskiing, picnicking, and wildlife viewing areas. Free.

River North Fly Fishing (404-403-2808; www.rivernorthflyfishing.com), 1850 Hardman Road, Clarkesville. Call for hours and fees. Professional guides accompany anglers to some of north Georgia's best fast-water, deep-hole fly-fishing.

GOLF **Kingwood Golf Club and Resort** (706-212-4100; 1-866-KINGWOOD; www.kingwoodresort.com), 401 Country Club Road, Clayton. Open daylight hours in summer; 12:30 or 1–dusk in winter (some holes may not be playable in winter if ground is frozen). Dramatic changes in elevation make this 18-hole, 6,016-yard, par-71 course very challenging. Three tees for each hole accommodate any level of player. $40.20 weekdays, $51.40 weekends, $18.70 cart rental.

Sky Valley Golf Resort (706-746-5303; 1-800-437-2416; www.skyvalley.com), 696 Sky Valley Way, Sky Valley. Open 8:30–5 in summer; in winter, course opens as conditions permit after greens thaw. This 18-hole, 6,450-yard championship golf course is located in a mountain valley at the Georgia–North Carolina line. Playing the course not only challenges your skills but provides views of mountains, streams, waterfalls, and vegetation. The club has a driving range, a pro shop, and instruction. $55 before 1 PM, $45 after 1 PM; higher rates during holiday periods; afternoon rates not valid during holiday periods.

See also Golf Appendix.

HIKING Nearby hiking trails include Currahee Mountain, Broad River, Panther Creek, Yonah Dam, Minnehaha, Bartram, and Coleman River. See also the Chattahoochee National Forest, Moccasin Creek State Park, and Tallulah Gorge State Park under *Green Space—Nature Preserves and Parks.*

HORSEBACK RIDING 🐎 **Dillard House Stables** (706-746-2038; 706-782-5630 after hours; www.dillardhousestables.com), Old Dillard Road, Dillard. Open daily by reservation; rides go out 9–4:30. The stable offers many different kinds of rides: 30-minute and one-hour farm rides, one-hour river rides, 1½–hour trail rides, children's ring rides, and all-day Chattooga wilderness rides. Lessons are also available. $20–150; average $30.

🐎 **Sunburst Stables** (706-947-7433; 1-800-806-1953; www.sunburststables .com), 3181 GA 255, Clarkesville. Open 10–4 daily. Take a group trail ride or enjoy a private lesson in the Chattahoochee National Forest. The company also offers overnight rides of up to four days, summer camps, camping facilities, and several cabins—one with a hot tub to soak your weary bones after a day of riding

($109 per night). $25–65 for regular trail rides depending on length; $75 for half-day restaurant ride with stop for breakfast or lunch.

OFF-ROAD RIDING ✐ ✿ **Locust Stake ATV Area** (U.S. Forest Service, 770-297-3000; www.fs.fed.us/conf/rec/orv_info.htm), Locust Stake Road, Toccoa. The forest service offers several off-road riding experiences. Locust Stake, located near the north fork of the Broad River west of Toccoa, provides 17 miles of trails for two-, three-, and four-wheel vehicles. Designated trails range from easy to extremely difficult. Users must stay on signed trails to prevent damage to the area.

SPAS ♿ **Spa at Kingwood Golf Club and Resort** (706-212-4100; 1-866-KINGWOOD; www.kingwoodresort.com), 401 Country Club Road, Clayton. Open 7–9 daily, March 1 through November 30; 7–7 remainder of the year. The spa offers massages, reflexology, Vichy showers, mud wraps, facials, therapeutic treatments, manicures, and pedicures. Call for prices.

WATERFALLS Several web sites provide information about Georgia's waterfalls: www.n-georgia.com/waterfal.htm; www.ngeorgia.com/naturally/waterfalls.html; and www.georgiatrails.com/waterfalls.html. Note: The rocks are deceptively slippery around these falls. Exercise caution, and don't get too close to the edge.

✐ ✿ **Becky Branch Falls** (706-782-3320), Warwoman Road, Clayton. Open daylight hours daily. This small, 20-foot cascade just five minutes from downtown is easily accessible by taking a short walk up a trail to a bridge at the base of the falls. Free.

✐ ✿ **Dick's Creek Falls** (706-782-3320), off Sandy Ford Road, Clayton. Open daylight hours daily. A viewing area at the top of the falls permits a view of the 60-foot drop over a granite mound into the Chattooga River. Free.

✐ ✿ **Holcomb Creek Falls and Ammons Creek Falls** (706-782-3320), Hale Ridge Road, Clayton. Open daylight hours daily. Holcomb Creek Falls drops and flows over shoals for 150 feet, and Ammons Creek Falls has an observation deck. Other waterfalls in the Clayton area include **Angel-Panther Falls, Martin Creek Falls,** and **Mud Creek Falls.** Free.

✐ ✿ **Minnehaha Falls** (706-782-3320), off Bear Gap Road, Tallulah Falls. Open daylight hours daily. The waterfall is 100 feet high, and the 0.4-mile Minnehaha Trail leads to the base of the falls. Free.

✐ ✿ **Panther Creek Falls** (706-782-3320), Warwoman Road, Clarkesville. Open daylight hours daily. The 5.5-mile hike to the falls means that it is seen only by those willing to make the 11-mile roundtrip trek through hemlock and white pine forests and along steep, rocky bluffs. The trail is noted for its variety of wildflowers and ferns. Trout fishermen enjoy the stream. Free.

✐ ✿ ♿ **Toccoa Falls** (706-886-6831; 1-800-868-3257; www.tfc.edu/consider/falls.htm), GA 17 Alt., Toccoa Falls. Open 8:30–6 weekdays, 8:30–5 Saturday, noon–5 Sunday. Located on the grounds of Toccoa Falls College, the 186-foot waterfall is 26 feet taller than Niagara Falls. A short, level path leads to the base of the falls. Visitors can enjoy the landscaped grounds as well as the gift shop and the Gate Cottage Restaurant, which offers a Sunday buffet. A monument is dedicated to those who lost their lives when an earthen dam broke in the 1970s. Adults $1, seniors and children 50¢.

WHITE-WATER RAFTING *Nantahala Outdoor Center* (864-638-5980; 1-800-232-7238; www.noc.com), off US 76 East, Clayton. Open 8–5 daily. The center offers exciting guided white-water rafting trips on the Chattooga and Oconee rivers, as well as kayaking instruction, a range of paddling classes, adventure tours, and equipment rentals. The adventure extends beyond the river with mountain biking, hiking, lake kayaking, and more. Prices vary by activity.

Southeastern Expeditions—Chattooga River Rafting (404-329-0433; 1-800-868-7238; www.southeasternexpeditions.com), 7350 US 76 East, Clayton. The season runs March through October. The adventure company offers white-water rafting, canoe and kayak instruction, and overnight trips. Fees vary by activity.

Wildwater Rafting (864-647-9587; 1-800-451-9972; www.wildwaterrafting .com), off US 76, Clayton. Open daily; hours vary seasonally. The company offers rafting trips on the Oconee, Chattooga, Pigeon, and Nantahala rivers, depending on the season. Kayak clinics also are available. Fees vary by activity.

✳ Green Space

LAKES *Georgia Power Company* (706-782-4014; 1-888-GPCLAKE; www .georgiapower.com/gpclake or www.southernco.com/gapower/lakes/ng_lakes) operates several lakes in this area for power generation and recreation. These lakes provide opportunities for swimming, boating, fishing, hiking, and picnicking. Some also have camping facilities. Most are open daylight hours daily and most activities are free.

Lake Burton (706-782-4014; 1-888-GPCLAKE), 4 Seed Lake Road, Lakemont. The most popular lake in the area.

Lake Tugaloo, off US 441 North, Tallulah Falls. Boats are restricted to less than 25 horsepower.

LAKE BURTON

✈ ❦ ♿ **Tallulah Falls Lake,** off US 441 South, Tallulah Falls. The small lake, which covers 63 acres, has a mere 3.6 miles of shoreline, part of which is in **Tallulah Gorge State Park.**

NATURE PRESERVES AND PARKS ✈ ❦ ♞ ♿ Black Rock Mountain State

Park (706-746-2141; 1-800-864-7275; www.gastateparks.org/info/blackrock), Black Rock Mountain Parkway, Mountain City. Open 7–10 daily. With an altitude of 3,640 feet, this is the highest state park in Georgia. The 1,738-acre site, named for its sheer, dark-colored biotite gneiss cliffs, is located on the Eastern Continental Divide. Scenic overlooks provide spectacular 80-mile vistas of the southern Appalachian Mountains and four states: Georgia, Tennessee, and North and South Carolina. The park also offers a summit visitor center and fishing for bass, bream, catfish, perch, and trout on a 17-acre lake. A new fishing pier is wheelchair accessible. Eleven miles of hiking trails pass lush forests, cascading streams, small waterfalls, and wildflowers. Accommodations are available in cottages and at campgrounds (see *Lodging*). Parking $3.

✈ ❦ **Chattahoochee National Forest** (770-297-3000; www.fs.fed.us/conf) spans 18 north Georgia counties and covers nearly 750,000 acres with more than 450 miles of trails, 1,600 miles of road, and 2,200 miles of rivers and streams— all of which provide endless opportunities for outdoor pursuits. The pristine, undeveloped forest is laced with wildlife management tracts, recreation areas, and scenic regions. Recreational activities include off-road riding, mountain biking, horseback riding, hiking, fishing, hunting, and camping. Access to forest free; some activities have fees.

✈ ❦ ♞ ♿ **Moccasin Creek State Park** (706-947-3194; 1-800-864-7275; www .gastateparks.org/info/moccasin), 3655 GA 197 North, Clarkesville. Open 7–10 daily. Moccasin Creek is located on the shores of 2,800-acre Lake Burton. Although the park is located in the north Georgia mountains, the terrain is relatively flat, which makes it ideal for children's bicycles and wheelchairs. The park offers a boat ramp, seasonal canoe rentals, a wheelchair-accessible fishing pier,

---

TALLULAH GORGE

Tallulah Gorge is one of the most spectacular chasms east of the Mississippi. Considered to be one of the Seven Wonders of Georgia, it is reputed to be the oldest gorge in the United States. It was carved over millions of years by the Tallulah River, which flows through Lakes Burton, Seed, and Rabun to join the Tugaloo River, eating its way through quartzite rock along the way. The 2-mile-long, 1,100-foot-deep chasm is second in depth only to the Grand Canyon. When the water is flowing freely (it is regulated by Georgia Power), three falls, the highest of which is 700 feet, plummet into the canyon. The company releases more water on the first two weekends in April and the first three weekends in November, at which time the river is suitable for advanced white-water kayaking.

and RV camping. Hiking trails and a Department of Natural Resources trout-rearing station are located nearby. Parking $3.

♂ 🐾 ♿ **Tallulah Gorge State Park** (706-754-7970; 1-800-864-7274; www .gastateparks.org/info/tallulah), 338 Jane Hurt Yarn Drive, Tallulah Falls. Park open 8–dark daily; interpretive center open 8–5 daily. Visitors can hike several rim trails to overlooks to get a clear view of the gorge and falls, sheer cliffs, and rock formations. The more intrepid hikers can obtain a free permit (limit 100 hikers per day) to hike down in the gorge, and the brave can venture out onto the new suspension bridge that sways 80 feet above the bottom. Exhibits in the Jane Hurt Yarn Interpretive Center focus on the resort era, the rugged terrain, and the fragile ecosystem. An award-winning film takes visitors on a spectacular excursion through the gorge. The 2,689-acre park also contains a 63-acre fishing lake with a swimming beach, more than 20 miles of hiking and biking trails, a 1.7-mile paved "Rails to Trails" path, tennis courts, picnicking, and camping facilities (see *Lodging*). Parking $4.

RECREATION AREAS The **U.S. Forest Service** (706-782-3320; www.fs.fed.us/ conf) operates several recreation areas. Unless otherwise indicated, the recreation areas listed here are open daylight hours daily.

♂ 🐾 ♿ **Rabun Beach Recreation Area,** Lake Rabun Road South/County Road 10, Clayton. Open 7–10 daily (until 11 on weekends), mid-April to end of November. In addition to swimming, boating, and fishing, visitors enjoy hiking and picnicking. Campsites also available by reservation. Day use free.

RIVERS ♂ **Chattooga Wild and Scenic River** (760-782-3320; www.nps.gov/ rivers/wsr-chattooga.html), US 76 East, Clayton. Open daily. Daredevils can enjoy a heart-pounding, wet-and-wild ride on class II to class V white-water rapids on this river, which extends 56.9 miles through the Chattahoochee National Forest. Of that mileage, 39.8 miles are designated wild, 2.5 miles scenic, and 14.6 miles recreational. From spring through fall, outfitters offer half-day, full-day, and overnight raft trips on Sections III and IV, which boast 30 rapids. River access free; fees for activities vary.

✳ Lodging
BED & BREAKFASTS

In Alto
♿ **The Lodge on Apple Pie Ridge** (706-776-6012; 1-888-339-1374; www .lodgeonapplepieridge.com), 2154 Apple Pie Ridge Road. Skilled artisans took two years to transform old pine logs, local stone, and reclaimed wood into this handsome lodge on a wooded hillside. All rooms boast a private bath and a private balcony or covered patio. For a particularly romantic stay, choose the Royal Gala or the Braeburn room, both of which have jetted tubs for two. Outdoors, guests enjoy the mountain views and landscaped grounds, fields of wild-flowers, herb gardens, grape arbors, and blueberry groves. An arrival snack, evening dessert, turndown service with chocolates, and a full breakfast are included. No smoking.

One room wheelchair accessible. $139–159; multiple-night stays may be required during holiday periods.

In Clarkesville

🐾 **Burns-Sutton Inn** (706-754-5565; www.bbonline.com/ga/burns-sutton), 855 Washington Street. This 1901 Victorian house features stained-glass windows, delicate cutwork, and hand-carved fireplace mantels. Six handsomely decorated guest rooms have private baths, some of which feature a claw-foot tub or whirlpool tub. Two rooms boast a gas fireplace. Guests also enjoy the wraparound porches and the acre of landscaped grounds. A full breakfast is served. Well-behaved children welcome. No pets. Smoking

THE INTERIOR OF GLEN ELLA SPRINGS INN IN CLARKESVILLE

outdoors only. Not wheelchair accessible. $75–125.

🐾 ♿ **Glen Ella Springs Inn** (706-754-7295; 1-877-456-7527; www .glenella.com), 1789 Bear Gap Road. Travel down a gravel road and leave the hustle and bustle of daily life behind. This historic inn, which was built as a private home in 1875 and expanded to an inn in 1890, is a member of the prestigious Select Registry, Distinguished Inns of North America. Imbued with casual elegance, Glen Ella offers comfortable, handsomely appointed, rustic guest rooms and suites furnished with king- or queen-sized beds, antiques, and locally hand-crafted items. Each has a private bath, but TV is blessedly absent. Suites boast a whirlpool tub and a gas-log fireplace. All rooms open onto common porches well supplied with rocking chairs. The inn sits on 17 acres with formal gardens, meadows, woods, and an outdoor pool. In addition, the inn is well-known for fine dining (see *Where to Eat—Dining Out*) and a high level of personal service. A full breakfast is included. Alcoholic beverages are not served, but guests and diners are welcome to bring their own. No smoking. Some rooms wheelchair accessible. $165–265; two-night minimums required on weekends during high season; frequent guest discounts and last-minute specials available.

In Clayton

♿ **Beechwood Inn** (706-782-5485; 1-866-782-2485; www.beechwood inn.ws), 220 Beechwood Drive. Recently inducted into the Select Registry, Distinguished Inns of North America, Beechwood Inn joins four others as the only five such honored inns in north Georgia. The 1922 inn offers rustic elegance on a mountain-side overlooking Clayton and Black Rock Mountain across the valley. Guest rooms filled with antiques and locally crafted primitive pieces offer queen-sized beds with luxury linens and private baths. Most rooms boast a working fireplace and/or private balcony. Guests enjoy relaxing on the porches or wandering in the lushly landscaped 100-year-old herb and wildflower gardens. A gourmet breakfast begins each day, and afternoon wine tastings also are offered. The inn is known for its wine and food events, many of which include a four-course gourmet dinner. No smoking. One room on first floor wheelchair accessible. $139–159.

In Dillard

White Hall Inn (706-746-5511; 1-888-883-7708; www.whitehallinn .com), 205 Carolina Street. The stately house has an interesting history. It was created from three existing mill houses in Athens in 1848. It was moved in 1890 to a different place on the property, where it served as a school. In 1906, the house was disassembled, and each piece was numbered and transported to Mountain City by train. The pieces were then hauled to this location by ox-drawn carts and reassembled over a period of three years. Each guest room is named for a flower and furnished simply to recall times past. Each has a private bath, some with claw-foot tubs, one with a shower for two. Accommodations are also offered in two cottages called the Loft and the Tool Shed, which are furnished more rustically than the rooms in the main house. Guests enjoy sitting in rocking chairs or swings on the huge white-columned front porch, where they can get a panoramic view of fields,

mountains, and the town below. A full gourmet breakfast is served Monday through Saturday; a continental breakfast is served Sunday. No children younger than 14. No pets. No smoking indoors. Not wheelchair accessible. $159.

In Lakemont

✐ ✿ **Lake Rabun Hotel, Restaurant, Bar, and Marina** (706-782-4946; www.lakerabunhotel.com), 35 Andrea Drive. The rustic 1922 hotel sitting across the road from Lake Rabun is surrounded by the Chattahoochee National Forest. The local historic landmark remains almost exactly as it was built, complete with wood-paneled walls and exposed beams. Rooms are simply decorated with rustic furniture, and most of them share baths. Televisions are located in the great room and in the bar, and plenty of board games keep guests entertained. The restaurant serves country cooking (see *Where to Eat—Eating Out*). The marina is 4 miles from the hotel and has a dock and a bar that serves drinks and simple fare. No smoking. Very limited wheelchair accessibility; bathrooms cannot accommodate wheelchairs. $89 for one night, $79 per night for multiple nights.

In Rabun Gap

*✐ 🐾 �& * **Sylvan Falls Mill Bed and Breakfast** (706-746-7138; www .sylvanfallsmill.com), 156 Taylor's Chapel Road. The mill was built in 1840 at the base of a 100-foot waterfall that powers it. The B&B's simple rooms—like those you might have found at your grandmother's house—feature private baths, and the Fireplace Room has a gas-burning fireplace. In addition to enjoying the waterfall, guests can wander through

flower and herb gardens. A full breakfast is served. Before guests leave, they often stock up on freshly ground yellow or white grits, yellow or white cornmeal, and whole wheat or rye flour. Pets welcome. No smoking. One room wheelchair accessible. $115; two-night minimum on holidays and during leaf season.

✐ **York House Bed and Breakfast** (706-746-2068; 1-800-231-9675; www .gamountains.com/yorkhouse), 416 York House Road. The inn, tucked in a scenic valley and surrounded by hemlocks and pre–Civil War Norwegian spruces, has been offering hospitality since 1896. Listed on the National Register of Historic Places, it is the oldest inn in Georgia to be in continuous operation. Each of the 13 guest rooms is furnished with its own individual style. Rooms feature private baths and entrances onto a rocking-chair porch. No pets. No smoking inside. Limited wheelchair accessibility; there are ramps, but doorways aren't wide enough for wheelchairs, and bathrooms not fully equipped. $89–119.

In Toccoa

Simmons-Bond Inn Bed and Breakfast (706-282-5183; 1-877-658-0746; www.simmons-bond.com), 130 West Tugaloo Street. The inn occupies a beautiful 1903 Queen Anne–Greek Revival home. Graciously furnished rooms feature private baths and modern conveniences. A large gourmet breakfast is served. No smoking. Not wheelchair accessible. $59–109.

CAMPGROUNDS

In Clarkesville

✐ ☙ ✤ **Moccasin Creek State Park** (706-947-3194; 1-800-864-7275; www .gastateparks.org/info/mocassin), 3655

GA 197 North. The park boasts 54 tent, trailer, and RV sites. $14–24.

In Clayton

The **U.S. Forest Service** (706-782-3320; www.fs.fed.us/conf) operates several campgrounds in the Chattahoochee National Forest. Check for information, rates, and reservations. These campgrounds are **Rabun Beach Campground,** Lake Rabun Road South; **Sandy Bottom Campground,** Forest Road 70; **Tallulah River Campground,** Forest Road 70; **Tate Branch Campground,** Forest Road 70; and **Wills Knob Campground,** Wills Knob Road.

In Dillard

✐ ✤ **Andy's Trout Farm, Cabins, and Campground** (706-746-2550; www.andystroutfarm.com), Betty's Creek Road. Open March through November. Andy's offers 12 sites with water, 30-amp electric, and sewer hookups. There is no bathhouse. To learn more about fishing and other activities at Andy's, see *To Do— Fishing.* $12; seventh night free if staying a week.

In Lakemont

✐ ✤ **Seed Lake Campground** (706-782-4014; 1;888-GPC-LAKE; www .georgiapower.com/gpclake), Crow Creek Road. Open seasonally. The Georgia Power campground offers sites for tents, trailers, and RVs; water and electric hookups; showers and rest rooms; laundry facilities; and a dump station. There is a beach area, too. Tent sites $14, RV sites $16; reservations required 10 days in advance; two-night minimum.

In Mountain City

✐ ☙ ✤ & **Black Rock Mountain State Park** (706-746-2141; 1-800-864-7275; www.gastateparks.org/info/

blackrock), Black Rock Mountain Parkway. The park offers 48 tent, trailer, and RV sites with cable TV hookups; 12 walk-in sites; four back-country campsites; and the highest pioneer campground in the state. $3–75.

In Tallulah Falls

✒ 🏕 🐾 ♿ **Tallulah Gorge State Park** (706-754-7970; 1-800-864-7274; www .gastateparks.org/info/tallulah), 338 Jane Hurt Yarn Drive. The park offers 50 tent, trailer, and RV sites as well as a pioneer campground and a back-country Adirondack shelter. $20–25.

COTTAGES AND CABINS

In Clarkesville

✒ **Burton Woods Cabins and Lodging** (706-947-3926; 706-219-9027), 220 Brookwoods Lane. One- to four-bedroom cottages that accommodate four to 12 people are staggered up the mountainside near Lake Burton. All cabins feature fireplaces and fully equipped kitchens. The two- to four-bedroom cabins have dishwashers and a washer and dryer. For a family reunion or group of friends, accommodations are offered in a lodge with seven bedrooms, five bathrooms, and two kitchens. There's also a recreation building on the property, lawn games, and pontoon boat rentals. Ask about pets. No smoking. Not wheelchair accessible. $60–175.

In Demorest

✒ ♿ **Twin Rivers Resort** (706-754-2010; 1-866-754-2010; www.twin riverscabins.com), 210 Twin Rivers Resort Drive. The resort consists of a lodge and a complex of 10 secluded luxury cabins located on a 325-acre reserve between the Chattahoochee and Soque rivers with 2 miles of river frontage. The resort prefers no alco-

hol, but if visitors bring it, it must be kept indoors. No pets. No smoking. Lodge rooms and one cabin wheelchair accessible. $115–250 depending on size of cabin.

In Dillard

✒ 🐾 ♿ **Andy's Trout Farm, Cabins, and Campground** (706-746-2550; www.andystroutfarm.com), Betty's Creek Road. The cabins on Betty's Creek are surrounded by rhododendrons and hemlocks. Each has a kitchen with basic supplies, a living-dining room, a bathroom, and a porch. Ages 10 and older welcome. One-bedroom cabin $60, two-bedroom cabin $80; additional guests $5; seventh night free if staying a week.

✒ **Chalet Village** (706-746-5348; 1-800-541-0671; www.dillardhouse .com), 768 Franklin Street. Twenty-five A-frame chalets, each of which accommodates two to 10 people, offer fully equipped kitchens and several bedrooms and baths. Some have a Jacuzzi and/or a fireplace. No smoking. Not wheelchair accessible. $89–179.

In Mountain City

✒ 🏕 🐾 ♿ **Black Rock Mountain State Park** (706-746-2141; 1-800-864-7275; www.gastateparks.org/info/ blackrock), Black Rock Mountain Parkway. The park has 10 fully equipped cottages. $75–115.

INNS AND RESORTS

In Clayton

✒ ♿ **Kingwood Golf Club and Resort** (706-212-4100; 1-866-KING-WOOD; www.kingwoodresort.com), 401 Country Club Road. Accommodations are offered in lodge rooms as well as fully equipped two- and three-bedroom condominiums and rental homes. The resort features an 18-hole

CLARKESVILLE TO CLAYTON

golf course; tennis courts; indoor and outdoor swimming pools; a fitness center with a Jacuzzi, steam room, and wet and dry saunas; and a spa. Dining is offered in the main dining room, the Back Porch, and the Fireside Lounge (see *Where to Eat— Dining Out*). Guests enjoy a complimentary breakfast, and the inn also offers a Friday-night reception with live music and complimentary wine, beer, and hors d'oeuvres. No smoking. Wheelchair accessible. Lodge rooms $140–160, condominiums $250–300, rental homes $399; condos and rental homes have two-night minimum stay.

In Dillard

♂ & **Dillard House** (706-746-5348; 1-800-541-0671; www.dillardhouse .com), 768 Franklin Street. An outstanding place for a family escape, the 100-year-old working farm offers a petting zoo, tennis, swimming, horseback riding, a waterfall ride, an outdoor hot tub, two stocked trout ponds, volleyball, and horseshoes. Accommodations are offered in the Old Inn (the original Dillard House), as well as in chalets, motels, and cottages, some of which are at other sites. The chalets, which are at a 90-acre location 2 miles away, include small A-frames and chalets big enough to accommodate a large family reunion. Each chalet features a living room with a fireplace and a fully equipped kitchen, and some have a Jacuzzi tub. The Chalet Village has a swimming pool, outdoor hot tub, tennis courts, a trout pond, and hiking trails. Cottages, most of which have a fully equipped kitchen, sleep two to eight people. Motel-style accommodations include some Jacuzzi and fireplace suites and some with a refrigerator

and microwave. No smoking. Wheelchair accessible. $79–199.

In Sky Valley

♂ **Sky Valley Golf Resort** (706-746-5962; www.skyvalleyvacationrentals .com), 3608 GA 246 North. A wide variety of comfortable lodgings at the resort range from one-bedroom chalets to condos to upscale rental homes with up to five bedrooms on the golf course. Some have fireplaces and/or hot tubs. No smoking. Not wheelchair accessible. $165–300 nightly; $950–1,500 weekly.

✴ Where to Eat

DINING OUT

In Clarkesville

& **Glen Ella Springs Inn** (706-754-7295; 1-877-456-7527; www.glenella .com), 1789 Bear Gap Road. Open 6–9 daily. The restaurant at this rustic inn (see *Lodging—Bed and Breakfasts*) has won numerous accolades from *Georgia Trend Magazine* and *Southern Living*, among others. Exceptional cuisine features regional recipes and local ingredients to create a distinctive American Continental flavor with a touch of the South. All the desserts are homemade. Alcohol is not served, but guests may bring their own. No smoking. Wheelchair accessible. $20–27.

In Clayton

♂ **Julia's Surf and Turf** (706-782-2052), US 441. Open 4–9 Tuesday through Saturday. A varied menu that includes steaks and seafood awaits guests in search of fine dining in a casual atmosphere. No smoking. Limited wheelchair accessibility; bathroom doors not fully accessible. $14–28.

♂ & **Kingwood Golf Club and Resort** (706-212-4100; 1-866-KING-

WOOD; www.kingwoodresort.com), 401 Country Club Road. Open 7:30–10 and 11–2 daily; 6–9 Sunday through Thursday, 6–10 Friday and Saturday (somewhat shorter hours in winter). The **Dining Room,** which overlooks the ninth-hole green, serves three meals daily. The varied cuisine features seasonal menus and nightly specials. On holidays, the Dining Room features grand buffets and entertainment. The all-season **Back Porch** offers beautiful mountain views and casual dining for three meals daily. The **Fireside Lounge** features a fireplace, a 96-inch projection television, cocktails, and light fare. Denim is prohibited in the Dining Room; guests who wish to wear denim can eat on the Back Porch. No smoking. Wheelchair accessible. Breakfast $8.95, lunch $3.95–12, dinner $12–25.

In Dillard

✍ 🍴 ♿ **Dillard House** (706-746-5348; 1-800-541-0671; www.dillardhouse .com), 768 Franklin Street. Open 7–10 and 11:30–8 daily. Check the diet at the door when dining at this nationally renowned, down-home, all-you-can-eat restaurant. There are no menus. Instead, generous portions of farm-fresh, mountain-grown home cooking like Grandma used to fix are served family-style. Expect country ham, country-fried steak, fried chicken, pork chops, a dozen vegetables and sides, and yummy desserts. You won't leave the table hungry. No smoking. Wheelchair accessible. Lunch $18–19, dinner $20–21, $19.95 all day Sunday.

EATING OUT

In Dillard

✍ 🍴 ♿ **The Cupboard Café** (706-746-5700), US 441. Open 7–9 Monday through Saturday. The restaurant serves a wide assortment of country favorites, including steak, barbecue, fried chicken, meat loaf, vegetables, corn bread, pastas, and homemade desserts. The café also has a gift shop (see *Selective Shopping*). No smoking. Wheelchair accessible. Breakfast $3.95–7.99, lunch $5–10, dinner $5.99–15.99.

In Lakemont

✍ **Lake Rabun Hotel, Restaurant, Bar, and Marina** (706-782-4946; www.lakerabunhotel.com), 35 Andrea Drive. Open from 11:30 Friday and Saturday; 5:30–9:30 Wednesday, Thursday, and Sunday; 5:30–10 Friday and Saturday. The restaurant serves country cooking that includes fresh vegetables, casseroles, barbecue, meats, and fish. Dinner entrées run the gamut from vegetable plates to a 9-ounce filet mignon. Save room for their pies, cakes, and cobblers. No smoking. Not wheelchair accessible. Lunch $3.95–9.95, dinner $10.95–26.95.

✳ Entertainment

MOVIES ✍ 🍴 ♿ **Tiger Drive-In** (706-782-1611; www.tigerdrivein .com), 2956 Old US 441, Tiger. Gates open at 5:30 Friday and Saturday, movie begins at 7; on some Sundays gates open at 5, movie begins at 6:30. One of only a few nostalgic drive-ins still operating in Georgia, the Tiger Drive-In offers two-for-one showings of first-run movies on the weekends. Adults $6, children 4–11 $3.

MUSIC Northeast Georgia Community Concert Association (706-297-7121). Call for a schedule of guest artists. The series offers national and international entertainment from early fall to late spring. Adults $15, children $10 in advance; $20 at the door.

Toccoa Symphony Orchestra and Chorus (706-886-7959). Celebrating its 30th season, the symphony presents concerts in December, March, and May at the Georgia Baptist Assembly's Garrison Auditorium. Adjuncts of the symphony are the Toccoa Brass Ensemble, a string quartet, and the chorus, which perform throughout the year. Adults $7 in advance, $10 at the door; children $3 in advance, $5 at the door.

THEATER **Toccoa Stephens County Community Theater** (706-282-9799; www.tscct.org). Call for a schedule of performances. The group offers musical and nonmusical productions throughout the year at various venues, but primarily at the Schaefer Center for the Performing Arts in downtown Toccoa. The group also uses the Java Station coffeehouse for dinner–theater productions. Adults $10–15, children ages 8–12 $8–10; discounts for seniors.

✳ Selective Shopping

ANTIQUES ✿ **Old Clarkesville Mill** (706-839-1583; www.oldclarkes villemill.com), 583 Grant Street, Clarkesville. Art and antique mall open 10–6 Monday through Saturday, 1–5 Sunday; shops open 10–6 Tuesday through Saturday; bowling center open 10–10 Monday through Thursday, 10–midnight Friday and Saturday, 1–9 Sunday. The 6½-acre Old Clarkesville Mill is the perfect destination for shopping and family fun, offering everything from art classes to bowling lessons. There are shops filled with art, antiques, discount books, clothing, pottery, furniture, and home decor, as well as a bowling center, billiards, and a video arcade.

Whistlestop Cornerstone Antique Market (706-282-1386), 202 North Sage Street, Toccoa. Open 10–5:30 Monday through Saturday, 1–5 Sunday. Shop here for antiques, collectibles, crafts, furniture, silver, glass, porcelain, and American pottery dating back to the early 1800s.

ART GALLERIES **Burton Gallery and Emporium** (706-947-1351; 1-877-947-1351; www.burtongallery .net), 295 Cherokee Ridge Drive, Clarkesville. Open 10–6 Wednesday through Monday spring through fall; winter hours 10–5 Friday, Saturday, and Monday, noon–5 Sunday. The eclectic gallery carries everything from fine art to folk art as well as high-quality handcrafted items representing the works of 350 artists. Children enjoy the koi pond and waterfall.

Tallulah Gallery (706-754-6020; www.tallulahgallery.com), 580 Scenic Loop 15, Tallulah Falls. Open 10–5 daily, April through December and winter weekends. The gallery offers fine Southern art, including folk art, original paintings, pottery, raku, sculpture, fiber art, jewelry, and photography. Books and furniture can be found here, too. All proceeds go to the scholarship fund of Tallulah Falls School.

CRAFTS **Mark of the Potter** (706-947-3440; www.markofthepotter.com), 9982 GA 197 North, Clarkesville. Open 10–6 daily in summer, 10–5 daily in winter. Located inside Grandpa Watts' Grist Mill on the picturesque Soque River, the shop purveys quality, handcrafted, contemporary artworks in wood, metal, pottery, and handblown glass. The mill has been restored and a deck added so visitors can get a better view of the falls and the huge native trout.

FOOD **Appletree Farms** (706-776-8381; www.appletreefarms.com), 4005 US 23/GA 365 South, Alto. Open 9:30–5:30 Monday through Saturday, 11–3 Sunday; tasting room open 9:30–5:30 Monday through Saturday, 12:30–3 Sunday. The working farm features a country store that sells fresh organic produce. In addition, the emporium features a restaurant; a gift shop that carries a wide array of garden accessories, home decor, artwork, folk and contemporary pottery, toys, games, and Christmas items; live entertainment on Saturday nights; and the Habersham Winery Tasting Room.

Hillside Orchard Farms (706-782-0858; 1-866-782-4995; www.hillside orchard.com), 28 Sorghum Mill Drive, Lakemont. Open 9–6 daily. The roadside country store is filled with seasonal produce, jams, jellies, and other goodies in a jar. You also can purchase gift baskets and fall decorations. The newest attraction is panning for gems at the indoor gem mine. Special events include a corn maze in the fall (it's haunted in October), bluegrass music on Saturday afternoons, and **Old Time Farm Day** on the last Saturday in October.

Jaemor Farm Market (770-869-3999; www.jamsjellies.com), 5340 Cornelia Highway, Alto. Open 7–6 Monday through Saturday, January through March; 7–7 Monday through Saturday, 1–6 Sunday, April through August; 7–6 Monday through Saturday, 1–6 Sunday, September through December. Jaemor Farms grows fruits and vegetables on 100 acres. The peach and apple orchards produce 30 varieties of peaches and 15 varieties of apples. The market specializes in fresh seasonal fruits and vegetables as well as jams, jellies, canned goods, pickles, relishes, barbecue sauce, cider, salad dressing, salsas, marinades, hot sauces, apple and peach products, Vidalia onion products, and more. Their homemade fried pies are famous in these parts. In addition, the market features handmade farmhouse furniture and pottery for the yard.

FURNITURE **Amish Red Barn** (706-754-8235), 6345 GA 17, Clarkesville. Open 10–6 Friday and Saturday, 10–5 Sunday. The store offers Amish furniture, artwork, quilts, and crafts from Pennsylvania and Ohio.

GIFTS **Cupboard Café Gift Shop** (706-746-5700), US 441, Dillard. Open 7–9 Monday through Saturday. The shop carries candles; wooden toys; homemade fudge, jams, jellies, and preserves; greeting cards; plush toys; recorded dulcimer music; wind chimes; and Christmas collectibles.

SPECIAL STORES **Barker's Mill** (706-746-6921; www.barkersmill.net firms.com), Betty's Creek Road, Rabun Gap. Open noon–4 first Saturday of each month. The historic mill has been providing milling services since the 1880s. The current mill, which was built in 1944 on the site of an older mill, still produces and sells whole-wheat flour from hard winter wheat, buckwheat flour from Pennsylvania-grown buckwheat, and grits and meal from locally grown hybrid yellow and nonhybrid white corn. Speckled grits and cornmeal are produced from white "keener" corn. A 12-foot overshot wheel powers the mill and the two 16-inch flint/granite stones that do the grinding. If you bring your own grain to be ground, the miller charges one-quarter of what he grinds. The store also carries wool yarn.

✳ Special Events

May: **Community Celebration Picnic** (706-746-5828). The picnic, held at the Foxfire Museum on Black Rock Mountain, Mountain City, honors the folks who have shared their time, stories, and skills with hundreds of Foxfire students to keep Appalachian heritage alive. The picnic includes a covered-dish dinner, live music, and exhibits by crafters and artists. Shuttle service runs from parking areas on US 441. Admission fee: Bring a covered dish.

October: **Fall Festival** (706-746-5828). Sponsored by the Foxfire Museum and held in the Dillard City Hall, the fun-filled day features exhibits, demonstrations of old-time skills, children's events, traditional music, raffles, and food. $4–5.

December: **Toccoa Christmasfest** (706-886-2132). Held the first weekend in December, the holiday extravaganza features a luncheon concert, living Christmas tree, live Nativity scene, toy train, festival of trees, art show, food, crafts, parade, tour of homes, performances by the Toccoa Symphony Orchestra and Chorus, carriage rides, and the arrival of Santa. Free.

DAHLONEGA TO HELEN

Although everyone has heard of the 1849 California gold rush, Dahlonega was actually the site of the nation's first gold rush 20 years earlier in what was then the Cherokee Nation in north Georgia. The rush caused the towns of Auraria and Dahlonega to grow and prosper, and a U.S. Mint was established in Dahlonega, where more than $6 million in gold was coined between 1838 and 1861. Even the domes of North Georgia College and State University in Dahlonega and the Georgia Capitol in Atlanta are covered with gold leaf mined in Dahlonega.

Although active mining stopped more than 150 years ago, it's believed that enough gold remains in the ground to pave the square around the Dahlonega courthouse 1 foot deep. These days, however, panning for gold is purely a pastime for tourists.

Dahlonega also serves as the gateway to the northeast Georgia mountains area, which contains many charming small towns with numerous attractions (see *Villages*) but which may be better known as an outdoor lover's paradise. Rivers, a national forest, recreation areas, wildlife management areas, and numerous state parks provide innumerable opportunities for trout fishing, horseback riding, tubing, white-water rafting, mountain biking, and hiking. The region has more waterfalls and wineries than any other area of the state as well as a large selection of bed & breakfasts.

GUIDANCE When planning a trip to the Dahlonega area, contact the **Dahlonega-Lumpkin County Chamber of Commerce and Visitors Center** (706-864-3711; 1-800-231-5543; www.dahlonega.org), 13 South Park Street, Dahlonega 30533. Open 9–5:30 daily. Pick up a brochure for "Dahlonega's Mountain Magic Self-Guided Auto Tour," which takes you through the Chattahoochee National Forest.

For more information about Dawsonville, consult the **Dawson County Chamber of Commerce** (706-265-6278; 1-877-302-9271; www.dawson.org), 54 GA 53 West, Dawsonville 30534, which is housed in the old jail. Open 8–5 weekdays.

To learn more about Cleveland, call the **White County Chamber of Commerce** (706-865-5356; www.whitecountychamber.org), 122 North Main Street, Cleveland 30528, also located in an old jail. Open 8–4:30 weekdays.

For information about Helen, contact the **Alpine Helen–White County Convention Center and Visitors Bureau** (706-878-2181; 1-800-858-8027; www .helenga.org), 726 Brucken Strasse, Helen 30545. Open 9–5 Monday through Saturday, 10–4 Sunday. Also, contact the **Greater Helen Area Chamber of Commerce** (706-878-1619; www.helenchamber.com), 1074 Edelweiss Strasse, Helen 30545. Open 10–5 weekdays.

GETTING THERE *By air:* Most visitors who plan to arrive by air for a visit to the north Georgia mountains will fly into **Hartsfield-Jackson Atlanta International Airport** (see What's Where in Georgia). It would then be necessary to rent a car to reach and tour the area covered in this chapter. Car rentals are available on-site at the airport; off-site car rentals are also available. For a complete of airlines and car rental companies, see What's Where in Georgia.

By bus: The closest stop on **Greyhound Line**'s (1-800-231-2222; www.grey hound.com) Georgia route is in Gainesville (see Gainesville chapter). It would then be necessary to rent a car to reach and tour the destinations in this chapter.

By car: Access to this area is easy from Atlanta from I-85, I-985, and US 19/GA 400.

By train: The nearest **Amtrak** (1-800-USA-RAIL; www.amtrak.com) station is in Gainesville (see Gainesville chapter).

GETTING AROUND US 129 is another north-south route. GA 53 is the major east-west route.

WHEN TO GO During the winter, temperatures can be somewhat unpredictable. For example, in the course of a week, it's not unusual to experience a fairly warm sunny day, a miserably dreary rainy day, or a snowy winter wonderland. Be forewarned: The narrow country lanes can be severely clogged during the fall leaf season.

MEDICAL EMERGENCY For life-threatening emergencies, call 911. For other health-care needs, contact **Chestatee Regional Hospital** (706-864-6136), 227 Mountain Drive, Dahlonega.

VILLAGES Dawsonville is considered to be the birthplace of auto racing in Georgia and is also the home of NASCAR legend and hometown hero "Awesome Bill from Dawsonville" Bill Elliott.

Helen, a replica of a Bavarian village nestled in the midst of the north Georgia mountains, is a curiosity. It's the place to go in north Georgia to shop 'til you drop. There are dozens of stores selling a wide assortment of merchandise—homemade quilts, candles, Christmas decorations, apparel, Georgia foods and nuts, antiques, bath and body products, gourd crafts, wines, pottery, silver jewelry, *Gone with the Wind* memorabilia, and so on. The list is endless. Start at one end of Main Street and see if you have the stamina to shop all the way down and all the way back. Don't forget to stop for snacks in the numerous eateries along the way.

The Sautee and Nacoochee valleys have been established as an official his-

HELEN REBORN

The tiny hamlet of Helen was once a logging town. When the industry moved on, the village began to die. Residents refused to let that happen, however, and set about to find a way to revive the economy. What they came up with was quite innovative. Bavarian facades were put on the buildings, vendors of Bavarian-type merchandise were recruited to fill the empty stores, and German restaurants attracted diners from miles around. The concept has been so wildly successful that Helen is booming. The result may be a little hokey, with a theme-park or Disneyesque ambience, but everyone should visit Helen at least once.

BAVARIAN ARCHITECTURE IN HELEN

toric district and named one of "the 100 Best Small Arts Towns in America" in a recent book.

✳ To See

COVERED BRIDGES 🌊 🐾 **Stovall Mill Covered Bridge** (www.georgiahistory .com/stovall.htm), GA 255, Sautee. Open daily. A pull-over observation area allows a good view of the state's shortest clear-span covered bridge. Built in 1895 in the Kingpost design, it is only 33 feet long and one span wide. Free.

FOR FAMILIES 🌊 🐾 **BabyLand General Hospital** (706-865-2171; www .cabbagepatchkids.com), 73 West Underwood Street, Cleveland. Open 9–5 Monday through Saturday, 10–5 Sunday. Fun is born at this museum–attraction–retail store located in a turn-of-the-20th-century medical clinic dedicated to the Cabbage Patch Kids, the brainchildren of native son Xavier Roberts that now number 100 million worldwide. Those who visit the clinic can watch Kids being "born" from Mother Cabbages in the Cabbage Patch and placed in incubators. When the Kids are ready to be placed for adoption, LPNs (Licensed Patch Nurses) are available for consultations. Vignettes throughout the clinic show Kids in every aspect of play. Dolls and outfits are for sale. (See *Selective Shopping.*) Free.

✑ 🐾 ♿ **Black Forest Bear Park and Reptile Exhibit** (706-878-7043; www .blackforestbearpark.com), 8160 South Main Street, Helen. Open 10–7 week-days, 10–8 Saturday, 10–6 Sunday. The park has a collection of live bears used to educate people about different species and their habitats. The reptile exhibit features many large snakes, including all the poisonous snakes found in North America. Bear exhibit $4, reptile exhibit $1.

✑ 🐾 ♿ **Charlemagne's Kingdom** (706-878-2200; www.georgiamodelrailroad .com), 8808 North Main Street, Helen. Open 10–6 daily; shorter hours in winter. A small-scale version of Germany from the North Sea to the Alps has been cre-ated, with HO-scale railroads running on 400 feet of track through the 20-by-50-foot layout. Accurate topography, 300 buildings in alpine architecture, seaports, bridges, autobahns, towns, villages, lakes, rivers, and 800 figures along with sound effects lend authenticity. Marvel at the 4-foot-tall carved glockenspiel fig-ures in colorful traditional dress as they dance to German music three times a day. Adults $5, children $2.50.

✑ ♿ **Kangaroo Conservation Center** (706-265-6100; www.kangaroocenter.com), 222 Bailey-Waters Road, Dawsonville. Tours at 10:30 and 1:30 Tuesday through Saturday. The facility is not open at other times, though it is open on the occa-sional Monday, so it can't hurt to call and check. Visitors must be a minimum of 8 years old or in second grade for admittance. Bounce on over to this unusual 87-acre wildlife conservation and exotic animal breeding facility. Amazingly enough, this center, one of only three American Zoo and Aquarium Association-accredited zoological facilities in Georgia, boasts the largest collection of kangaroos outside Australia. More than 200 red, western grey, and eastern grey kangaroos are on view to visitors through an educational and adventure-filled 1½-hour guided bus tour. Also on view are the only blue-winged kookaburras on exhibit in North America. The **Billabong Encounter** is a free-flight aviary and greenhouse exhibiting Australian plants and fauna such as parrots and small mammals, including tiny kangaroos. Visitors also can see Bennett's wallabies, burros, spring-haas, dik-diks, cranes, and ducks. The tiny brush-tailed bettong (an endangered species) and the agile wallaby are seen only rarely in North America. The **Aussie Walkabout** is a quarter-mile scenic hiking trail. Adults $27.50, children $22.50.

GUIDED TOURS ♿ **Smithgall Woods–Dukes Creek Conservation Area and Lodge** (706-878-3087; 1-800-318-5248; www.smithgallwoods.com; www.gastate parks.org/info/smithgall), 61 Tsalaki Trail, Helen. Open 7–6 daily. Van tours offered daily at 12:30; call for fees. Once a private 5,555-acre estate, this beautiful property offers catch-and-release trout fishing on Georgia's premier trout stream, Dukes Creek (reservations required; see *To Do—Fishing*), as well as biking, hiking, pic-nicking, and wildlife observation. Four miles of trails and 18 miles of roads allow hikers and cyclists to explore far afield. An elegant lodge and several cottages provide upscale accommodations for overnight guests (see *Lodging—Resorts*).

✒ ❦ **Nora Mill Granary** (706-878-1280; 1-800-
927-2375; www.noramill.com), 7107 South Main Street/GA75, Helen. Open 9–5
weekdays, 9–6 Saturday, 10–5 Sunday; closed Christmas Day. Nora Mill, an
authentic working gristmill, was constructed in 1876 on the banks of the Chattahoochee River. The Fain family still grinds grain using the original French burr
stones and sells grits and meal as well as jams and home-baked pies. Free.

❦ **Sautee-Nacoochee Indian Mounds** (706-878-2181; 1-800-858-8027; www
.helenga.org), GA 75 and GA 17, Helen. Although this mound, believed to have
been built by Native Americans between 10,000 and 2500 B.C., is located on the private property of the Hardman-Nichols Estate, it is clearly visible from both highways
and you can pull off the highway to photograph it. The mound is reputed to be the
final resting place of two tragic lovers from warring Cherokee and Chickasaw tribes.
The Victorian gazebo, which sits atop the mound, was a much more recent addition.

MUSEUMS ✒ ❦ ♿ **Alpine Antique Auto and Buggy Museum** (706-878-0072;
www.alpinemusem.com), 115 Escowee Drive, Helen. Open 10–9 daily. More than
100 antique automobiles from the early 1990s to the late 1970s are displayed,
including an 1840 hearse and a Civil War ambulance. Buggies and pieces of farm
equipment are exhibited, too. Adults $8, children $5, seniors 80 and older free.

✒ ❦ ♿ **Dahlonega Gold Museum Historic Site** (706-864-2257; www.gastate
parks.org/info/dahlonega), One Public Square, Dahlonega. Open 9–5 Monday
through Saturday, 10–5 Sunday. Literally located in the center of the historic
town square, the structure in which the museum is housed was the original
Lumpkin County Courthouse. Built in 1836 on the site of a log cabin, the courthouse is the oldest public building in north Georgia. The museum tells the story
of the local gold rush and mining in Georgia through a film and exhibits that
include mining tools and equipment as well as gold nuggets (one weighing more
than 5 ounces) and gold coins—all very well protected, of course. Adults $4, sen-
iors $2.50, children 6–18 $3.

❦ ♿ **Folk Pottery Museum of Northeast Georgia** (706-878-3300; www
.folkpotterymuseum.com), 283 GA 255, Sautee-Nacoochee. Open 10–5 weekdays, noon–5 Saturday and Sunday. Located at the Sautee-Nacoochee Art Center (see *Entertainment—Theater*), this museum contains an extensive collection
of more than 150 rare pieces of folk pottery dating from the 1840s to the present. It is the only such collection in the Southeast. Activities at the museum
include audiovisual presentations, programs, demonstrations by local potters,
seminars, and special tours. Adults $4, children and seniors $2.

✒ ❦ **Old Sautee Store** (706-878-2281; 1-888-463-9853; www.sauteestore.com),
GA 17 at GA 255, Sautee. Open 10–5:30 Monday through Saturday, noon–5:30
Sunday. Established in 1872, the original store served the community with general
merchandise and was even the post office for the entire valley until the 1940s. The
original front portion of the store is reminiscent of an old-time country store, complete with old fixtures and merchandise from yesteryear in museumlike displays,
but now visitors also can shop for special gifts and enjoy coffee and a bagel. Free.

❦ **Scarlett's Secret** (706-878-1028; www.scarlettsecret.com), 1902 GA 17,

Sautee. Open 10:30–4 weekdays, 10:30–5 Saturday, 1–4 Sunday. Appropriately located in a plantation-style home furnished in *Gone with the Wind* style, the museum contains *GWTW* and Civil War memorabilia. Scarlett's Secret also offers a tearoom and a gift shop that sells vintage and new *GWTW* merchandise. Adults $2.50, children younger than 12 free.

NATURAL BEAUTY SPOTS ✒ 🍃 **Neel's Gap Lookout Point and Mountain Crossings at Walasi-Yi Information Center** (706-745-6095), US 19, Dahlonega. The Appalachian Trail passes directly through this rustic center, which was built during the New Deal in 1937. Outside, the overlook offers stunning views. You can buy hiking gear, maps, guidebooks, and picnic supplies as well as homemade crafts.

SCENIC DRIVES ✒ 🍃 **Russell-Brasstown Scenic Byway** (www.dot.state.ga.us/ DOT/planprog/planning/projects/scenic_byways/index.shtml; click on "Georgia Scenic Byways"). This 41-mile scenic loop that stretches between Helen and Hiawassee reveals some of the most dramatic scenery in the state. It was awarded National Scenic Byway designation on June 15, 2000. Included in the route is Brasstown Bald (Georgia's highest mountain), the Bavarian-themed town of Helen, several wildlife management areas, the headwaters of the Chattahoochee River, and a section of the Appalachian Trail. Along the way several state parks offer an array of recreational opportunities such as hiking, camping, and fishing. One of the highlights is **Anna Ruby Falls** (see *To Do—Waterfalls*).

✒ 🍃 **Sautee-Nacoochee Valleys–Scenic 197–Southern Highroads Trail** (706-878-2181; www.southernhighroads.org). The Sautee-Nacoochee Valleys Association and the Scenic 197 Business Association have joined with the Southern Highroads Trail Association to create a special gateway loop route.

✳ To Do

BALLOONING **David Bristol Hot-Air Balloon Rides** (706-878-1449; www .goballooning.net), Helen. Soar high above the north Georgia mountains for a bird's-eye view of the region. Call for schedules, prices, and reservations.

BICYCLING ✒ 🍃 **Woody's Mountain Bikes** (706-878-3715; www.helenga.org/ woodys), 457 GA 356, Helen. Open March through November, 10–6 Wenesday through Monday. Woody, a former Florida state mountain bike champion, operates a full-service mountain bicycle shop that provides sales, repairs, bike rentals, and escorted tours suitable for all skill levels over some of the 60 bike trails in the north Georgia mountains. Rentals include a bicycle, helmet, and, in some cases, return shuttle service. May through October, intermediate bikers are welcome to join regular Thursday-night rides leaving at 6 PM sharp. Beginning in mid-April and lasting through early fall, training rides are held at 7:30 AM every Saturday. The $45 Gap Ride is the most popular for families. Reservations recommended. Call for prices.

BOAT EXCURSIONS ✒ **Appalachian Outfitters River Trips** (706-864-7117; 1-

800-426-7117; www.canoegeorgia.com), 2084 South Chestatee/GA 60 South, Dahlonega. Open daily June through August; Thursday through Sunday in April, May, and September. Reservations are strongly suggested. Thrills and chills are guaranteed on half-hour to overnight guided canoe, kayak, and tube trips on the Chestatee and Etowah rivers. Call for prices.

🛶 **Wildwood Outfitters** (706-865-4451; 1-800-553-2715; www.wildwood outfitters.com), 7272 South Main Street, Helen. Outpost open 10–6 daily March through September; retail shop open daily year-round. Guided and unguided canoe, kayak, and raft trips (class I and II) are available, as well as rock-climbing instruction and camping. Equipment is also available for sale. Call for prices.

CARRIAGE RIDES 🛶 🐾 **Horne's Buggy Rides** (706-878-3658; www.helenga.org/ hornesbuggyrides), 165 Dandy Lane, Helen. Open daily. The company offers rides through the picturesque, Bavarian-style streets of Helen. Adults $5, children $3. See also *Horseback Riding*.

FARM TOURS 🛶 🐾 ♿ **Bradley's Pumpkin Patch and Christmas Trees** (706-265-1447; www.bradleyspumpkinpatch.com), 55 Lawrence Drive, Dawsonville. Open 10–8 Thursday through Sunday in autumn. Visitors can pick their own pumpkins to take home to create jack-o'-lanterns. They also can pick out fresh apples, gourds, and Indian corn or even a Christmas tree in season. The gift shop carries honey, apple cider, and other goodies. Free.

🛶 🐾 ♿ **Burt's Farm** (706-265-3701; 1-800-600-BURT; www.burtsfarm.com), 4801 GA 53 East, Dawsonville. Open 9–6 daily, September 1 through November 15. In the autumn, Burt's is a sea of colorful pumpkins, gourds, and Indian corn. Visitors also can watch corn being processed for popcorn, take a tractor-pulled hayride on weekends, and see talking pumpkin heads. The gift shop carries honey, cider, popcorn, and an array of autumn decorations. Farm visit free; call for hayride prices.

🛶 🐾 **Joe's Rows Corn Maze** (706-878-JOES), 1497 Lynch Mountain Road, Sautee. Who would have thought that getting lost could be so much fun? Open from mid-August, as soon as corn is about yea high, until end of October; 5–10 Wednesday through Friday, noon–11 Saturday, 1–10 Sunday. Other attractions include a potato cannon, a pumpkin patch, a petting zoo, and a haunted maze that begins in late October, just in time for Halloween. Adults $10, children 4–9 $8.

🛶 🐾 **Uncle Shuck's Corn Maze and Pumpkin Patch** (770-772-6223; 1-888-OSHUCKS; www.uncleshucks.com), GA 53 East, Dawsonville. Call for hours and prices. The challenging, intricate maze with 3 miles of trails and fun for all ages is created from a cornfield each autumn. In addition, the farm sells pumpkins, gourds, and Indian corn. On weekends prior to Halloween, ghosts, goblins, and witches take over the maze dusk–10 PM.

FISHING **Smithgall Woods–Dukes Creek Conservation Area** (706-878-3087; 1-800-318-5248; www.gastateparks.org/info/smithgall), 61 Tsalaki Trail, Helen. North Georgia's premier trout stream, Dukes Creek, runs through this property and offers superb fishing opportunities. Catch-and-release trout fishing and shuttle service are offered on certain days of the week. Reservations required, so always check ahead. Call for schedules and prices.

Unicoi Outfitters (706-878-3083; www.unicoioutfitters.com), 7280 South Main Street/GA 75, Helen. A must-stop place for fly-fisherman or wannabes, the company offers fly-fishing and tying classes, as well as guided fly-fishing excursions. The fly shop, of course, stocks fly-fishing equipment. Call for hours and fees.

FOR FAMILIES ♂ ✿ ♿ **Alpine Amusement Park** (706-878-2306; www.helenga .org/alpineamusementpark), 419 Edelweiss Strasse, Helen. Open 1–11 daily in summer; during fall and spring 1–1 Saturday, 1–8 Sunday. While not a giant theme park, the family entertainment center features Go-Karts, a Tilt-A-Whirl, the largest bumper boat pool in Georgia, and a 40-foot Ferris wheel, as well as miniature golf and arcade games. Each ride $2; Go-Karts, bumper boats, and miniature golf, each $6.

♂ ✿ ♿ **Chestatee Wildlife Preserve** (678-859-6820; www.chestateewildlife preserve.org), 469 Old Dahlonega Highway, Dahlonega. Open 10–4 daily. The area promotes preservation of exotic and domestic wildlife through education. Located on 20 acres, the preserve is the home of 100 animals including tigers, lions, cougars, camels, and others. Adults $10, children younger than 12 $5.

♂ ✿ ♿ **Nacoochee Village** (www.nacoocheevillage.com). Phone numbers and addresses listed with individual entries. Located just a half-mile south of Helen, the village boasts a variety of activities for the entire family, including **Nora Mill Granary,** a historic gristmill (see *To See—Historic Homes and Sites*); antiques shops (see *Selective Shopping—Antiques*); the **Nacoochee Grill** (see *Where to Eat—Dining Out*); a candle shop and a paint-your-own pottery studio (see *Selective Shopping—Crafts*); a day spa (see *Spas*); and cabin rentals (see *Lodging— Cottages and Cabins*). Free.

♂ ✿ ♿ **Thunder Road U.S.A.–Georgia Racing Hall of Fame** (706-216-7223; www.thunderroadusa.com), 415 GA 53 East, Dawsonville. Open 10–6 weekends. This exciting attraction features the largest remote-controlled car track in North America as well as full-sized race car simulators. Racing cars and Bill Elliott memorabilia also are sure to enthrall, while the Georgia Racing Hall of Fame recognizes the contributions of motor sports in the state. The hall of fame features items such as the first NASCAR trophy ever awarded, historic racing vehicles, and videos of memorable moments in racing history played in a replica of a drive-in theater. Adults $8.50, seniors $7.50, children 6–12 $6.50; simulator extra.

GEM AND GOLD PANNING ♂ ✿ ♿ **Dukes Creek Mine** (706-878-2625), GA 75, Helen. Open 10:30–dark daily. Pan for gold and screen for gems or fossils. With so many choices, everyone from your future geologist to your future princess will be hooked. Individual buckets $8–9; family buckets $40.

♂ ✿ ♿ **Gold 'n Gem Grubbin' Mine** (706-865-5454; www.goldngem.com), 75 Gold Nugget Lane, Cleveland. Open 9–6 daily in summer, 9–5 remainder of the year. Visitors can try their luck panning for gold and gemstones. Between spring and fall you can tour the mine, too. Fishing and camping are also available. Call for prices.

GOLF ♨ **Innsbruck Golf Club** (706-878-2100; 1-800-642-2709; www.inns bruckgolfclub.com), 664 Bahn Innsbruck, Helen. Voted one of the best golf courses in the country by *Golf Digest,* Innsbruck was designed to challenge both the avid golfer and the enthusiastic novice. Amenities include a swimming pool, tennis court, and clubhouse. Summer rates $39 weekdays, $49 weekends; winter rates $29 weekdays, $39 weekends; senior discounts.

See also Golf Appendix.

HIKING ✐ ♨ **Appalachian Trail** (706-265-6278; 706-265-8888; www .appalachiantrail.org). Always accessible. The southern terminus of the 2,174-mile footpath is at Springer Mountain. Access to the 78-mile Georgia section of the trail, the most hiked trail in Georgia, is via an 8-mile approach trail from Amicalola Falls State Park and from seven other spots between there and Bly Gap at the North Carolina border. The easiest access is at the Walasi-Yi Center, where the trail crosses US 19 north of Dahlonega. Free.

HORSEBACK RIDING ✐ **Appalachian Adventures at Spring Mountain** (706-344-2451), 697 Guy Waters Road, Dahlonega. Call for hours. These proprietors know the land in this area well. They should—their predecessors have been here since the 1800s, when one of their ancestors married into the Cherokee tribe. In addition to horseback riding adventures, they'll be happy to arrange mountain biking, hayrides, cookouts, trout and striper fishing, spring turkey hunts, canoeing and kayaking, and pontoon rentals for their clients. Prices vary by activity.

✐ **Chattahoochee Back Country Treks** (706-482-8302; 706-864-8329), 1420 Chester Road, Dahlonega. Call for hours. This family-run stable offers professional instruction and guidance for all levels of horsemanship. Although beginners may wish to stick to the day-trips, more advanced equestrians will enjoy several days and nights of backcountry exploration and camping. Prices vary by activity.

✐ **Chattahoochee Stables** (706-878-7000; www.helenga.org/chattahoochee stables), GA 17, Helen. Open 10–6 daily year-round. Reservations suggested but not required. All ages can ride and there are no weight limits. Have a *City Slicker* experience on one of these one-hour, 3½-mile guided trail rides on a 143-acre ranch in the Sautee-Nacoochee Valley. Riders enjoy lush scenery and perhaps see some wildlife. $20–30.

✐ **Cross Creek Stables** (706-878-1600; 706-878-3327; www.nacoocheevillage .com), 7017 South Main Street, Helen. Rides go out every day except Wednesday, weather permitting. Hours vary; call for times and prices. These rides meander past scenic rivers and along mountain trails. Horses are available for all levels of experience, and ponies are available for the younger set.

✐ **Gold City Corral and Carriage Company** (706-867-9395; www.goldcity corral.com), 49 Forrest Hills Road, Dahlonega. Open daily. First rides leave at 10 AM, and rides operate every two hours until 6. Call for reservations. The company offers guided one- and two-hour rides down forest trails and scenic mountain back roads. Half-day trail rides with lunch included are also offered, as are chuck-wagon dinner rides and carriage rides. For the more experienced rider, try an overnight camping trip. One- and two-hour trail rides $25 per person per hour; half-day ride $100. Call for prices for dinner, carriage, and overnight rides.

🖉 **Sunny Farms North** (706-867-9167), 1332 Longbranch Road, Dahlonega. Riders see pastures and mountain trails on these one- or two-hour trail rides. Call for times and fees.

MINE TOURS 🖉 ♿ **Consolidated Gold Mine** (706-864-8473; www.consolidated goldmine.com), 185 Consolidated Gold Mine Road, Dahlonega. Open 10–5 daily in summer, 10–4 daily in winter. Although the mine closed 100 years ago, it was the largest gold mine east of the Mississippi when it was operating. Guides take you 250 feet below ground on a tour of a massive underground network of tunnels while explaining the techniques used by early miners. Once back on the surface, you can learn how to pan for gold or gemstones. (Mine tour not wheelchair accessible.) Adults $11, children age 4–14 $7, including tour and gold panning.

🖉 ♿ **Crisson Gold Mine** (706-864-6363; www.crissongoldmine.com), 2736 Morrison Moore Parkway East, Dahlonega. Open daily: 10–6 weekends and during the summer, 10–5 remainder of the year. This mine, which began operation in 1847, opened as a gold-panning destination in 1970 and is operated by the fourth generation of a mining family. Georgia's only stamp mill, its 120-year-old machine was used to crush rock so the gold could be removed. Visitors see other working mine machinery and can pan for gold or gemstones. Indoor panning is offered in the winter. Call for prices.

A GOLD-PANNING DEMONSTRATION AT CONSOLIDATED GOLD MINE

MINIATURE GOLF 🖉 ♿ **Alpine Miniature Golf** (706-878-3328), 7914 South Main Street, Helen. Open in summer 10–10 Sunday through Thursday, 10–11 Friday and Saturday; in winter, weekends only. This quaint course was designed to resemble a tiny Bavarian village. Children of all ages will be charmed by its miniature chalets and lodges. Adults $6.75, children younger than 12 $4.75.

See also **Alpine Amusement Park** under *To Do—For Families.*

SPAS ♿ **Forrest Hills Mountain Hideaway Resort** (706-534-3244; 1-800-654-6313; www.ForrestHillsResort.com), 135 Forrest Hills Road, Dahlonega. The menu of spa services offered here is comprehensive and unique. The facility offers everything from paraffin facials to reflexology to stone massage to full-body massage. Couples also can enjoy private couples massage training. $45–200 depending on services. See also *Lodging—Cottages and Cabins.*

&. **Mandela Wellness Spa and Retreat** (706-878-0036), 47 Wingo Drive, Sautee-Nacoochee. Open 9:30–5:30 Monday through Saturday. Reservations suggested. This day spa offers European facials and body treatments, therapeutic massage, herbal and mineral aromatherapy baths, yoga, t'ai chi, meditation classes, holistic counseling, and weight-loss and smoking-cessation programs. Call for prices.

See also **Mountain Laurel Creek Inn and Spa** and **Pura Vida USA** under *Lodging—Bed & Breakfasts.*

TUBING ♂ ♣ **Cool River Tubing** (706-878-2665; 1-800-896-4595; www.cool rivertubing.com), 590 Edelweiss Drive, Helen. Open 9–6 daily, Memorial Day through Labor Day. Enjoy scenic one- or two-hour floats down the Chattahoochee River or try the water slide. $5.

♂ ♣ **Helen Tubing** (706-878-1082; www.helentubing.com), 9917 GA 75 North, Helen. Open daily, Memorial Day through Labor Day. Float down the Hooch on 1½- or 3-hour trips or enjoy the water park's slides, tubes, and lazy river. The facility also has a game room and gift shop. Tubing $3; water park: adults $25, anyone under 48 inches tall $15, children 5 and under free.

THE TOP OF SPECTACULAR AMICALOLA FALLS

WATERFALLS ♂ ♣ &. **Amicalola Falls and Amicalola Falls State Park and Lodge** (park: 706-265-4703; lodge: 706-265-8888; reservations: 1-800-864-7275; www.gastateparks.org/info/amicalola; www.amicalolafalls.com), 240 Amicalola Falls State Park Road, Dawsonville. Open 7 AM–10 PM daily. The star of this 829-acre park is, of course, the spectacular waterfall. In fact, *Amicalola* is the Cherokee word for "tumbling waters." With a drop of 729 feet, Amicalola is one of the highest waterfalls in the Southeast and is included in the Seven Wonders of Georgia. Visitors can drive almost to the base of the falls to admire it without any strenuous exercise, but there is one trail that leads about halfway up from the bottom and another trail that leads partway down from the top.

Exercise caution, because the rocky paths can be slippery due to spray from the falls. The popular park has numerous other attractions as well (see *Green Space—Nature Preserves and Parks,* and *Lodging—Campgrounds, Cottages and Cabins* and *Inns & Hotels*). Parking $3.

✒ ❀ ♿ **Anna Ruby Falls** (706-754-6221; www.fs.fed.us/conf/press/arf-hours .htm), GA 356, Helen. Open 9–8 daily in summer, 9–7 daily in spring and fall, 9–6 daily in winter. Anna Ruby Falls is actually two falls: Curtis Creek and York Creek flow parallel to each other, then drop as side-by-side cascades. Curtis Falls plummets 150 feet; York Falls plunges 50 feet. In addition to the double falls, the area on Tray Mountain features hiking, picnicking, a visitor center, and a craft shop. The Lion's Eye interpretive trail, a half mile round trip, is accessible to people with visual and physical disabilities. Adults $1, children younger than 6 free.

✒ ❀ **DeSoto Falls and DeSoto Falls Recreation Area** (706-745-6928; www.fs.fed.us/conf/desotocp.htm), US 19/129 North, Dahlonega. Open 7 AM– 10 PM daily. Explorer Hernando de Soto scouted in this area in the 1500s, and a plate of armor reputedly was found near here in the 1880s; hence the name DeSoto was chosen for the falls. Because the elevation changes from 2,000 feet to 3,400 feet within a very small area, the streams that flow through the area plummet from the higher level to the lower in three separate falls. Two can be reached by easy hiking trails; the third requires a strenuous trek. In addition to viewing the falls, visitors can enjoy camping, fishing, hiking, picnicking, and wildlife viewing at the recreation area. Free.

✒ ❀ ♿ **Dukes Creek Falls and Recreation Area** (706-754-6221; www.fs.fed.us/conf/dukescreek.htm), GA 348, Helen. Open 8 AM–10 PM daily. Dukes Creek Falls plummet 400 feet into a scenic gorge, which can be reached by a steep half-mile trail. The path has a series of switchbacks, however, so it's not too strenuous. Despite its name, the falls are actually on Davis Creek at its confluence with Dukes Creek. An observation deck at the foot of the falls allows a beautiful view. The upper portion of the trail from the parking lot to an observation deck that permits a glimpse of the falls from above is wheelchair accessible. Free.

✒ ❀ **Raven Cliffs Falls** (706-754-6221; www.fs.fed.us/conf), Russell-Brasstown Scenic Byway, Helen. Open daylight hours daily. Considered to be the most unusual waterfall in the area, Raven Cliffs Falls results from water flowing through a split in the face of a solid rock outcropping. $3.

WHITE-WATER RAFTING See **Appalachian Outfitters River Trips** and **Wildwood Outfitters** under *Boat Excursions.*

WILDERNESS SCHOOL ✒ **Medicine Bow** (706-864-5928; www.medicinebow .net), 104 Medicine Bow, Dahlonega. Call for a schedule of classes and fees. Classes for all ages in ancient skills and Native American lore teach students about man's unique relationship with the forest. There are parent-child weeknds and summer camp, too.

WINERY TOURS 🍷 ♿ **Dahlonega Tasting Room** (706-864-8275), 16 North Park Street, Dahlonega. Call for hours and fees. This establishment features reserve wines and a tasting facility, along with a shop that sells wine accessories, home decor, and gift items, and also has a wedding registry.

🍷 **Frogtown Cellars** (706-865-0687; www.frogtownwine.com), 3300 Damascus Church Road, Dahlonega. Tasting room open noon–6 Saturday, noon–5 Sunday. Tours and tastings available; group tours for 10 or more by appointment. This 28-acre vineyard produces 15 varieties of wine made with 100 percent Frogtown grapes. Many visitors prefer to skip the tour and get right to the wine. The facility also serves lunch (see *Where to Eat—Eating Out*). Tours and tastings $7 for eight whites and rosés, $10 for seven reds; groups $10 per person for five wines.

🍷 **Habersham Winery** (706-878-9463; www.habershamwinery.com), 7025 South Main Street/GA 75, Helen. Open 10–6 Monday through Saturday, 12:30–6 Sunday. One of Georgia's oldest and largest wineries, Habersham operates an outlet in Nacoochee Village just south of Helen, where visitors can sample wines and view the tank room, oak barrel room, and bottling line. A large gift shop features wine-related merchandise and gourmet food products.

🍷 ♿ 🐾 **Three Sisters Vineyards and Winery** (706-865-9463; www.three sistersvineyard.com), 439 Vineyard Way, Dahlonega. Tasting room open 11–6 Thursday through Saturday, 1–6 Sunday, other weekdays by appointment. Offerings include complimentary wine tastings and a $10 Vintner's Tasting, where up to six wines are sampled. The 184-acre vineyard boasts a rustic, laid-back, casual atmosphere. Children are welcome and pets are permitted on the property, though not in the winery. Wheelchair accessible. Free.

🍷 **Wolf Mountain Vineyards and Winery** (706-867-9862; www.wolfmountain vineyards.com), 180 Wolf Mountain Trail, Dahlonega. Open noon–5 Thursday through Sunday, March through mid-December; tastings Thursday and Friday for $5; Educational Winemaker; tours and Tastings available on the hour, noon–5 Saturday and Sunday, for $10; tours and tastings for groups of 10 or more at other times by appointment. This boutique winery produces wines from 100 percent Georgia-grown grapes handpicked at the 1,800-foot elevation north of Dahlonega. Enjoy the beautiful views, winery tour, a delicious lunch or sumptuous brunch buffet in the Vineyard Café (see *Where to Eat—Eating Out*), and delicious wines. Tours free.

✳ Green Space

NATURE PRESERVES AND PARKS 🌿 🍷 ♿ **Amicalola Falls State Park and Lodge** (park: 706-265-4703; lodge: 706-265-8888; 1-800-864-7275; www .gastateparks.org/info/amicalola; www.amicalolafalls.com), 240 Amicalola Falls State Park Road, Dawsonville. Open 7 AM–10 PM daily. In addition to Amicalola Falls (see *To Do—Waterfalls*), there are other hiking trails, including an 8-mile access trail to the southern end of the Appalachian Trail and access to the 20-room **Len Foote Hike Inn** (see *Lodging—Other Lodging*), which can only be reached on foot. The popular park also features an interpretive center, weekend programs, a 57-room lodge with a restaurant, 14 cottages, and camping (see *Lodging—Inns & Hotels*). Parking $3.

✒ 🐾 **Chattahoochee National Forest** (770-297-3000; www.fs.fed.us/
conf) spans 18 north Georgia counties and covers nearly 750,000 acres with
more than 450 miles of trails, more than 1,600 miles of "road," and 2,200 miles
of rivers and streams—all of which provide endless opportunities for outdoor
pursuits. The pristine, undeveloped forest is laced with wildlife management
tracts, recreation areas, and scenic regions. Recreational activities include off-
road riding, mountain biking, horseback riding, hiking, fishing, hunting, and
camping. Access free; some activities have fees.

✒ 🐾 ♿ **Unicoi State Park and Lodge** (programs: 706-878-3983; lodge: 706-
878-2201 or 1-800-864-7275; www.gastateparks.org/info/unicoi), 1788 GA 356,
Helen. Open 7 AM–10 PM daily. Beautiful mountain scenery and a 53-acre lake
bring families to this 1,050-acre park for outdoor pursuits. The park has biking
and hiking trails, a swimming beach, seasonal canoe and pedal-boat rentals,
handicapped-accessible fishing docks, a ropes course, four lighted tennis courts,
a softball and volleyball area, and various ranger programs that focus on natural,
cultural, historical, and recreational resources. Hikers and cyclists enjoy 12 miles
of scenic mountain hiking trails and 8 miles of biking trails. Especially popular
are those leading to **Anna Ruby Falls** (see *To Do—Waterfalls*) and the town of
Helen. Overnight guests can stay in the lodge (see *Lodging—Inns & Hotels*),
which has a restaurant, in the cottages, or at the campground. Craft lovers
shouldn't miss the gift shop, which carries handmade quilts, pottery, and other
local mountain crafts. Parking $3.

See also Parks Appendix.

RECREATION AREAS See Parks Appendix.

✳ Lodging
BED & BREAKFASTS

In Cleveland
Caffrey Springs Inn (706-348-6034;
www.helenga.org/caffreysprings),
1111 Satterfield Road. This contemporary home, which sits on 27 wooded acres, features floor-to-ceiling
windows with spectacular mountain
views. Accommodations run from a
standard room with a double bed to a
full suite with all the amenities,
including a Jacuzzi. A full breakfast is
included. No smoking. Not wheelchair accessible. $70–110.

✒ 🐾 ♿ **Lodge at Windy Acres** (706-
865-6635; 1-800-435-5032; www
.n-georgia.com/TheLodge.htm), 16
Windy Acres Road. This comfortable

retreat, located halfway between
Helen and Cleveland, was built in
1988 specifically to be a B&B. There
are five queen rooms with private
baths and a porch or deck access.
Other amenities include a library and
game room, laundry facilities, a fireplace in the common area, and
kitchen privileges. A full breakfast is
included. Smoking outdoors only.
Wheelchair accessible, but bathrooms
not handicapped equipped. $69–85.

In Dahlonega
✒ 🐾 ♿ **Cedar House Inn and Yurts**
(706-867-9446; www.georgia
mountaininn.com), 6463 US 19

North. This eco-friendly B&B offers two types of accommodations. The charming white-pine-paneled rooms have queen beds, private baths, and private entrances. Guests are also free to enjoy the common living and dining rooms, as well as the patios and other outdoor spaces. The facility also offers unique yurts (a domed canvas structure on a wooden base) in the woods. No smoking. Rooms in main house wheelchair accessible. $95 from October 1 through November 15; $90 rest of the year.

Historic Worley House Bed and Breakfast (706-864-7002; 1-800-348-8094; www.bbonline.com/ga/worley), 168 West Main Street. Once a stagecoach stop, this 1845 home just off the square in Dahlonega now operates as an upscale B&B. In mint condition and furnished with graceful antiques, it features cozy, romantic rooms, some with fireplaces, all with private baths. Full country breakfast included. Smoking outdoors only. Not wheelchair accessible. $109–149; all-inclusive packages available.

Lily Creek Lodge (706-864-6848; 1-888-844-2694; www.lilycreeklodge .com), 2608 Auraria Road. Experience a European-style getaway at this cozy and romantic lodge nestled in the woods. This three-diamond facility offers 13 guest rooms furnished with European antiques and art from around the world. Amenities include a secluded swimming pool, a comfortable and relaxing tree house, and the lodge's great room, the perfect place for guests to meet new friends. No smoking. Not wheelchair accessible. $99–175.

Mountain Laurel Creek Inn and Spa (706-867-8134; www.mountain laurelcreek.com), 202 Talmer Grizzle Road. Dahlonega's newest B&B, this special mountain getaway has three deluxe guest suites, all with two-person whirlpools, separate showers, private balconies, and sitting areas with a fireplace. Great mountain views and sumptuous breakfasts are just some of the inn's other highlights. If that's not enough, visit the **Oasis Spa** and enjoy a massage or skin treatment. No smoking. Not wheelchair accessible. $120–140.

&. **Mountain Top Lodge at Dahlonega** (706-864-5257; 1-800-526-9754; www.mountaintoplodge .net), 447 Mountain Top Lodge Road. Relax in the beautiful 5-acre setting and enjoy the scenery from this private mountaintop location. Some of the nine guest rooms in this facility boast Jacuzzis and fireplaces. Another unique amenity is a back porch with a sweeping view of the north Georgia mountains and valley below. A crow's nest with a telescope further enhances viewing opportunities. Full gourmet breakfast included. No smoking. Wheelchair accessible. $135–210.

Royal Guard Inn (706-864-1713; 1-877-659-0739; www.royalguardinn .com), 65 South Park Street. Afternoon tea and evening wine and cheese are among the highlights at this historic home nestled in the shelter of an enormous magnolia tree just off the square in downtown Dahlonega. Each guest room features a queen-sized bed and a private bath. Televisions and phones are not provided in order that guests may truly absorb the tranquility of this mountain setting. No smoking. Not wheelchair accessible. $100–125.

In Helen
&. **Black Forest B&B and Luxury Cabins** (706-878-3995; www.black

forest-bb.com), 8902 North Main Street. This charming and quaint facility offers several lodging solutions, from charming individual rooms to private cabins. Best of all, the B & B is located within easy walking distance of all the area's best attractions. No smoking. Wheelchair accessible. $150–250.

♿ **Lucille's Mountain Top Inn** (706-878-5055; 1-866-245-4777; www .lucillesmountaintopinn.com), 964 Rabun Road. Experience mountain luxury at this deluxe facility. Rates include rooms with private baths (some with Jacuzzis and see-through fireplaces), mountain or valley views, robes, and towel warmers. Children younger than 14 not permitted. No smoking. Wheelchair accessible. $135–210.

In Sautee
♿ **Bernie's Nacoochee Valley Guest House** (706-878-3830; www .letsgotobernies.com), 2220 GA 17. Besides cozy, intimate rooms, guests are treated to a full breakfast and use of the pleasant library, fireplaces, decks, and gardens. No smoking. Limited wheelchair accessibility from patio porch. $99–125.

Sautee Inn (706-878-8287; www .sauteeinn.com), 2178 GA 17. Open April through October. This historic 1892 home features a wraparound porch with views of the Smoky Mountains, terraced gardens, and cozy and comfortable guest rooms with full-, queen-, or king-sized beds. Baths are shared. The antiques throughout the inn are available for purchase, and a country breakfast is included with each stay. Children and pets not permitted. No smoking. Not wheelchair accessible. $95–135.

✂ ⎈ ♿ **Stovall House Bed and Breakfast** (706-878-3355; www .stovallhouse.com), 1526 GA 255 North. This intimate 1837 farmhouse is located on 26 acres. The five guest rooms have mountain views in all directions. Each is furnished with antiques and has its own bath. A continental breakfast is included. For other dining options, try the warm and friendly restaurant (see *Where to Eat—Dining Out*); reservations recommended. Children welcome, but no pets. Restricted smoking. Wheelchair accessible. $60–92.

CAMPGROUNDS

In Cleveland
✂ ⎈ **Gold 'n Gem Grubbin' Mine** (706-865-5454; www.goldngem.com), 75 Gold Nugget Road. After you've panned for gold and gems, found your treasure, and had it mounted (see *To Do—Gem and Gold Mining*), camp in this beautiful tent and RV campground. Tent sites are primitive, but RV sites have full hookups. Campground amenities include a clean log-cabin bathhouse, an 18-hole miniature-golf course, and a stocked fishing pond. There is also a studio apartment adjacent to the bathhouse that sleeps two (call for price and availability). Tent sites $18, $20 on river; RV sites with full hookups $28.

✂ ⎈ **Leisure Acres Campground** (706-865-6466; www.leisureacrescamp ground.com), 3840 Westmoreland Road. Open year-round. This campground offers both full-hookup pull-through RV sites and tent sites. Amenities include a swimming pool, playground, coin-operated laundry, modern bathrooms with hot showers, a game room, pavilion, fishing pond, and cool mountain stream. $24.

In Dawsonville

✈ 🐾 🍃 **Amicalola Falls State Park** (706-265-8888; 1-800-864-7275; www.gastateparks.org/info/amicalola), 240 Amicalola Falls State Park Road. The campground features 24 tent, trailer, and RV sites. $17–19.

In Helen

✈ 🐾 🍃 **Unicoi State Park** (programs: 706-878-3983; lodge: 706-878-2201 or 1-800-864-7275; www.gastateparks .org/info/unicoi), 1788 GA 356. The park offers 82 tent, trailer, and RV sites as well as 33 walk-in sites. $20–24.

In Sautee

✈ 🍃 **Sleepy Hollow Campground** (706-878-2618), 307 Sleepy Hollow Road. This 90-acre campground is surrounded by a national forest and has a 10-acre fishing lake, firewood for sale, hiking, creekside camping, hot showers, a picnic pavilion, and a playground. Tent sites $18, $20 with water and electric; full RV hookup with water, sewage, and electric $22.

COTTAGES AND CABINS

In Dahlonega

🐾 ✈ ♿ **Bend of the River Cabins and Chalets** (706-219-2040), 319 Horseshoe Lane. Located between Dahlonega and Helen, the cabins, chalets, and private homes are available year-round and can accommodate from one to 14 guests. Some of the units are even wheelchair accessible. Others are pet friendly. Priced for every budget; call for details.

In Dawsonville

✈ 🐾 🍃 **Amicalola Falls State Park and Lodge** (706-265-8888; 1-800-864-7275; www.gastateparks.org/info/amicalola), 418 Amicalola Falls Lodge Road. The park features 14

fully equipped cottages. No smoking. Wheelchair accessible. $79–159.

🍃 **Amicalola View** (706-265-8154), 200 Sign Broad Gap Road. This lovely two-bedroom log cabin has a full kitchen, dining room, covered front porch, and private deck. Located next to the state park; the view of the falls is spectacular here. Smoking outdoors only. Not wheelchair accessible. $100; two-night minimum.

In Helen

Georgia Mountain Madness Cabins (706-878-2201; 1-888-534-6452; www.gamountainmadness.com), 190 Mountain Madness Drive. The adults-only timber-framed cabins are tucked away on 60 acres to ensure maximum privacy. In fact, each cabin is located on 1 acre that has been left as natural as possible. Furthermore, the property borders a portion of the 700,000-acre Chattahoochee National Forest. Cabins feature a private hot tub, basic cable and VCR, an open-faced woodstove, and a deck. No smoking. Not wheelchair accessible. $70–150.

✈ ♿ **Nacoochee Cabins** (706-878-2300), 7275 South Main Street. These secluded mountain cabins come in two sizes. The quaint lodgings are comfortably decorated and include Jacuzzi tubs, full kitchens, and back porches with rocking chairs. No smoking. Wheelchair accessible. $99–109.

✈ **Tanglewood Resort Cabins** (706-878-3286), GA 356. The rustic log cabins range in size from one to six bedrooms, all nestled on 75 wooded acres near Unicoi State Park and not far from Helen. No smoking. Wheelchair accessible. $85–535.

✈ 🐾 🍃 ♿ **Unicoi State Park** (programs: 706-878-3983; lodge: 706-878-2201 or 1-800-864-7275; www.gastate

parks.org/info/unicoi; cabins: www .helenga.org/cabins), 1788 GA 356. The park features 30 cottages. No smoking. Wheelchair accessible. $90–139.

See also **Black Forest B & B and Luxury Cabins** and **Cedar House Inn and Yurts** under *Bed & Breakfasts,* **Edelweiss German Country Inn and Restaurant** under *Inns and Hotels,* and listings under *Resorts,* many of which also have cabins.

INNS AND HOTELS

In Dahlonega

🎗 **Smith House** (706-867-7000; 1-800-852-9577; www.smithhouse.com), 84 South Chestatee Street. Located in a house that was built as a family home in 1899, the Smith House has served as an inn and restaurant (see *Eating Out*) since the 1920s. Some of the simple rooms are located in the historic house, while others are in an addition of more recent construction. The inn also features a swimming pool, and guests can pan for gold. The inn is within easy walking distance of the historic Dahlonega town square, attractions, theaters, and restaurants. No smoking. Not wheelchair accessible. $79–250.

In Dawsonville

🎗 🏞 ♿ **Amicalola Falls State Park and Lodge** (706-265-8888; 1-800-864-7275; www.gastateparks.org/info/ amicalola), 418 Amicalola Falls Lodge Road. The 57-room, four-story lodge features guest rooms and suites with private porches and breathtaking views through huge windows, as well as a restaurant that serves a buffet for breakfast, lunch, and dinner. No smoking. Wheelchair accessible. $69–139.

In Helen

🎗 🏞 ♿ **Unicoi State Park and Lodge** (706-878-2201; 1-800-864-

7275; www.gastateparks.org/info/ unicoi), 1788 GA 356. The modern 100-room lodge features an all-buffet restaurant, conference center, and craft shop. No smoking. Wheelchair accessible. $69–129.

In Sautee

🎗 **Edelweiss German Country Inn and Restaurant** (706-865-7371), 747 Duncan Ridge Road. In addition to eight comfortable rooms and private cabins, this inn has a recreation and relaxation area complete with picnic tables, grills, a gazebo, and a nature trail. The restaurant features Old World German cooking as well as many American favorites (see *Where to Eat—Eating Out*). There is also a fully stocked deli and gourmet food shop. Smoking outdoors only. One cabin wheelchair accessible. $85–119; $105–139 during Oktoberfest.

RESORTS

In Cleveland

♿ **Cannon Falls Lodge** (706-348-7919; www.cannonfallslodge.com), Cleveland. Call for hours and fees for fishing; reservations required. In order to protect guests' privacy, the lodge does not publish its address. Once you have a guaranteed reservation, however, you will be provided with the address and directions. This secluded facility offers guests the opportunity to escape the hustle and bustle of everyday life and experience nature in a pristine environment. Anglers from all over the nation are attracted to the beautiful and secluded fly-fishing experience offered here. Cabins $185.

In Dahlonega

♿ **Forrest Hills Mountain Hideaway Resort** (706-534-3244; 1-800-

654-6313; www.forresthillsresort.com), 135 Forrest Hills Road. Located on 140 acres adjacent to the Chattahoochee National Forest, this resort provides private cabins with an accent on romance. Whether styled as rustic, contemporary, or Victorian, each cabin is in a private wooded area and features a whirlpool tub for two, fireplace, and private deck. Accommodations are also offered in bilevel luxury suites and group lodges ranging in size from four to 16 bedrooms. Resort amenities consist of four dining rooms to cater to individual needs (including candlelit dinners in the Secret Garden dining room for couples only), massages, a day spa (see *To Do—Spas*), an outdoor pool, tennis courts, and riding stables. Excursions offered at Forrest Hills by Gold City Corral include guided trail rides, carriage rides, horseback riding, horse-drawn wagon rides, and half-day adventures. The property also boasts a wedding pavilion and a wedding chapel. No smoking. Wheelchair accessible. $99–159; weekend packages available.

&. **Pura Vida USA** (706-865-7678; www.puravidausa.com), 400 Blueberry Hill. Of fairly recent construction, this 1920s-style farmhouse is the perfect setting for returning to the intrinsic rhythms of nature. View 80 pristine hillside acres from the large wraparound porch. Settle in to one of 12 guest rooms or, for more privacy, try one of the "Bear Den" cabins set amid lush woodlands. Enjoy international spa services (see *To Do—Spas*) and a restaurant that specializes in healthy gourmet cooking. No smoking. One room wheelchair accessible. $100–160.

In Helen
&. **Innsbruck Resort and Golf Club** (706-878-2400; www.innsbruck resort.com), 664 Bahn Innsbruck. This all-suite hostelry, which resembles a Bavarian castle, offers accommodations ranging from one-bedroom suites to four-bedroom homes with modern comforts such as a fireplace or a whirlpool tub. Recreational facilities include an 18-hole golf course, tennis courts, pool, hot tub, and bar and grill. Smoking permitted. Wheelchair accessible. $75–249.

&. **The Lodge at Smithgall Woods** (706-878-3087; 1-800-318-5248; www.gastateparks.org/info/smithgall), 61 Tsalaki Trail. In addition to elegant accommodations in the rustic lodge, the property also has five intimate cottages. Because the retreat provides exceptional privacy, it is ideal for romantic getaways. Rates include accommodations, meals, and activities. No smoking. Some units are wheelchair accessible. $189 and up.

In Sautee
&. **Helen Black Bear Resort** (706-865-0093; 1-877-734-2467; www.helenblackbearresort.com), 210 Dawn Way. The resort provides a serene base from which guests can explore the area. The 11-suite lodge is furnished with antiques; 13 luxury log cabins contain full kitchens, fireplaces, hot tubs, and decks. Each suite or cabin features a theme. The resort also features a log wedding chapel and the Black Bear Dinner Theatre (see *Entertainment—Theater*). Come for Sunday brunch in the lodge's Sautee Grill. No smoking. Two cabins wheelchair accessible. $149 and up.

OTHER LODGING

In Dahlonega
Hiker Hostel (770-312-7342), 7693 US 19 North. This

unique facility is located just north of Dahlonega near the Appalachian Trail. The staff will cheerfully supply shuttle service for people who are hiking during the day or even overnight. For those coming off the Appalachian or other trails, they will even provide transportation to local restaurants. No smoking. Not wheelchair accessible. $15 for shared bunk room, $34 for private room.

In Dawsonville

✄ 🐾 **Len Foote Hike Inn** (706-867-6203; 1-800-581-8032; www.hike-inn.com), 240 Amicalola Falls Lodge Road. This special 20-room eco-lodge retreat just for hikers, located at **Amicalola Falls State Park** (see *Green Space—Nature Preserves & Parks*), is reached by a 5-mile trail through the Blue Ridge Mountains. A bathhouse with hot showers is centrally located. A hearty breakfast and dinner are included, and trail lunches can be ordered for an additional fee. No smoking. Not wheelchair accessible. $97 for single occupancy, $70 per person for double; discounts available for children younger than 12.

✳ Where to Eat

DINING OUT

In Dahlonega

♿ **Corkscrew Café** (706-867-8551), 51 West Main Street. Open 11:30–9 Tuesday through Thursday, 11:30–10 Friday and Saturday, noon–9 Sunday (brunch noon–3). Lunch favorites include quiche, paninis, seafood, and a variety of sandwiches. Dinner entrées include filet mignon, lamb, pork, duck, beef tips, local fish, and seafood. The restaurant, located next to the Holly Theater, is the perfect place to eat before the show. No

smoking. Wheelchair accessible. Lunch $9–10; dinner $16–30.

The McGuire House (706-864-6829), 135 North Chestatee Street. Open 4–9 Monday through Thursday, 4–10 Friday and Saturday. The restaurant specializes in steak and seafood. No smoking. Not wheelchair accessible. $16–21.

♿ **The Oar House** (706-864-9938), 3072 East GA 52. Open 11–9 Monday through Thursday, 11–10 Friday and Saturday. This contemporary bistro offers casual fine dining. Menu items include seafood, lamb, beef, and pasta. No smoking in eating area. Wheelchair accessible. $16–24.

♿ **Vineyard Café at Wolf Mountain Vineyards** (706-867-9862), 180 Wolf Mountain Road. Open March through mid-December, noon–3 Friday and Saturday; 12:30–3 Sunday (brunch). Experience gourmet dining in a casual setting with beautiful mountain views. While dining, accompany your meal with the handcrafted wines (see *To Do—Winery Tours*). Live entertainment is offered in April, July, September, and October. No smoking. Wheelchair accessible. Lunch $6.25–10.50, brunch $25.

✄ 🐾 ♿ **Wylie's Restaurant** (706-867-6324), 19 North Chestatee Street. Open 8–9 Monday through Thursday, 8–10 Friday and Saturday, noon–8 Sunday; **Down Under Pub** open 5–midnight. This upscale eatery located in an old house on the historic town square serves delicious soups, salads, and sandwiches for lunch and steaks and seafood for dinner. Wylie's is known for fun, food, music, and trivia. No smoking in restaurant. Wheelchair accessible. $11.

In Helen

🍴 ♿ **Nacoochee Grill** (706-878-8020), 7277 South Main Street. Open 11:30–9 Monday through Thursday, 11:30–10 Friday and Saturday, 11–3:30 and 4:30–9 Sunday. A renovated 1900s farmhouse is the location of this ultrasuccessful "live-fire" grill. Hand-carved Angus steaks, fresh Gulf seafood, ribs, and chops are cooked to perfection over apple wood, oak, and hickory. No smoking. Wheelchair accessible from side entrance. Less than $16.

In Sautee

🍴 ♿ **Stovall House** (706-878-3355; www.stovallhouse.com), 1526 GA 255 North. Open 5:30–8:30 Thursday through Saturday, 11–2 Sunday for brunch. This renowned farmhouse restaurant features regional and continental gourmet meals in a relaxed and casual atmosphere. Favorite menu items include citrus trout, lamb chops, chicken, pasta, or pork scaloppine. No smoking. Wheelchair accessible. $18–20.

EATING OUT

In Cleveland

🍴 ♿ **Turner's Corner Café** (706-865-6150), 10 Turner's Corner Road. Open 11–9 Thursday through Sunday. Featuring riverside dining since 1928, the restaurant is most acclaimed for fresh mountain trout, barbecue ribs, desserts, daily specials, soups, and sandwiches. No smoking. Wheelchair accessible. Less than $11.

In Dahlonega

🍴 **Back Porch Oyster Bar** (678-898-8773), 93 North Public Square. Open 5:30–midnight Thursday through Saturday. The focus at this second-floor restaurant as the name

suggests, is on fresh seafood. Live entertainment is offered, too. No smoking. Not wheelchair accessible. Less than $12.

🍴 ♿ **Caruso's Italian Restaurant,** home of **Dahlonega Brewing Company** (706-864-4664), 19-B East Main Street. Open 11–midnight daily, but kitchen closes at 9. Menu favorites include an array of pasta dishes and pizzas. The restaurant is also the home of the northernmost brewpub in Georgia. Several of the beers produced are on tap. No smoking. Wheelchair accessible. Less than $11.

🍴 ♿ **Frogtown Cellars** (706-865-0867), 300 Damascus Church Road. Open noon–4 Saturday, noon–3 Sunday. Panini sandwiches (served with a side salad), soups, and pastas are favorites at this unique restaurant connected with the winery (see *To Do—Winery Tours*). No smoking. Wheelchair accessible. $9–12.

🍴 **Jack's Café** (706-864-9169), 44 Public Square. Open 11–5 weekdays, 8:30–5 Saturday and Sunday. Jack's features a variety of sandwiches and soups. No smoking. Not wheelchair accessible. $4–6.

🍴 ♿ **Rick's Restaurant** (706-864-9422), 47 South Park Street. Open 11:30–9 Sunday through Thursday, 11:30–10 Friday and Saturday. For a beautiful and casual dining experience, try this historic house just off the town square. Menu favorites include everything from a grilled-cheese sandwich to elegant eggplant Napoleon. Other selections include pasta, salads, sandwiches, fish, chicken, and steak. No smoking. Wheelchair accessible. $5–17.

🍴 ♿ **Smith House** (706-867-7000; 1-800-852-9577; www.smithhouse

.com), 84 South Chestatee Street. Open 11–3 and 4–7 Tuesday through Sunday. The menu, served family-style, includes heaping helpings of fried chicken, honey-cured ham, and a dozen or so vegetables and side dishes, all culminating in traditional Southern desserts like peach cobbler. No smoking. Wheelchair accessible. $11–16.

In Dawsonville

✒ ✿ ♿ **Dawsonville Pool Room** (706-265-2792; www.dawsonville poolroom.com), 78 East First Street. Open 10–10 Sunday through Thursday, 10–11 Friday and Saturday. Part hamburger joint, part pool room, part museum, this popular eatery displays a collection of racing memorabilia from the career of native son "Awesome Bill from Dawsonville" Bill Elliott. No smoking. Wheelchair accessible. About $5; pool $1 per game.

✿ ♿ **Tea with the Queen** (706-265-2800; www.teawiththequeen.com), 408 GA 9 North. Open 11–3 Tuesday through Saturday. Tea lovers and the ladies who lunch will find everything they love at this charming boutique restaurant. Choose your favorite tea and add scones, finger sandwiches, fresh fruits, and delectable sweets to this elegant repast. For the heartier appetite, the restaurant offers soups, salads, sandwiches, and quiche. Shoppers will be charmed by an assortment of merchandise, including a nice selection of accessories for members of the Red Hat Society. No smoking. Wheelchair accessible. $7–17.

In Helen

✒ ✿ ♿ **Café International** (706-878-3102), Main Street/GA 75. Open 11–9 Monday through Saturday, 11–8 Sunday; November through March, open only for lunch. In addition to Reubens, for which the eatery is noted, other menu items include salads, sandwiches, lemon-pepper trout, veal and chicken parmigianas, and German specialties such as knackwurst, schnitzels, and strudels. Sit out on the covered deck overlooking the river, where you can enjoy gentle breezes and watch folks wading in the stream or floating by on inner tubes. Smoking permitted on deck. Wheelchair accessible. Lunch about $7, more for dinner.

✒ ✿ ♿ **Hofer's Bakery and Café** (706-878-8200), 8758 North Main Street. Open 8–5 daily. This authentic Bavarian bakery and café offers an amazing collection of cakes, pies, pastries, and European breads. In addition, the restaurant also serves a relaxed breakfast and lunch in the dining area until 3 daily. Menu favorites include schnitzel, bratwursts, spaetzle, Reubens, and po'boys. On holidays and during Oktoberfest, a dinner menu is added as well. No smoking. Wheelchair accessible. $7–15.

✒ ✿ ♿ **Old Bavaria Inn Restaurant** (706-878-3729), 8619 South Main Street. Open 11–8 Sunday through Thursday, 11–9 Friday and Saturday. The restaurant serves authentic German and American cuisine, specializing in favorites such as schnitzels, sauerbraten, sausages, Reubens, German potato pancakes, beer-battered mushrooms, smoked salmon, spaetzle, fresh local trout, and homemade apple strudel. No smoking. Wheelchair accessible. Around $9.

✒ ✿ ♿ **Safari Steakhouse & Grill, Inc.** (706-878-2083), 8717 North Main Street. Open 11–9 daily. One wonders why there's an African safari-themed restaurant in Bavarian Helen, but ours is not to reason why—obviously it's working. The menu includes great sandwiches, burgers, and appetizers, as well as delicious steak, seafood, and chicken dinners. Children enjoy choosing from the Pigmy Meals and virgin cocktails. Smoking and nonsmoking areas. Wheelchair accessible. $8–24.

In Sautee

◊ ♦ 占 **Edelweiss German Inn and Restaurant** (706-865-7371; www.edelweissgermaninn.com), 351 Duncan Bridge Road. Open 11–3:30 and 5–9 daily (until 8 Sunday). Treat yourself to a taste of Old Bavaria and experience hearty German fare such as bratwursts, schnitzels, sauerbraten, and rouladen, as well as steaks and barbecued ribs. No smoking. Wheelchair accessible. $10.

COFFEEHOUSES

In Dahlonega

◊ ♦ 占 **Crimson Moon** (706-864-3982), 24 North Park Street. Open noon–6 Sunday, noon–midnight Wednesday through Saturday. In addition to all your coffee favorites, menu selections include sandwiches, desserts, baked potatoes, soups, quiche, and salads. Live entertainment is offered every weekend. No smoking. Wheelchair accessible. Around $6.

In Helen

◊ ♦ 占 **Doodle's Coffee and Cream** (706-878-8245), 7275 South Main Street. Hours vary according to season, so be sure to call for the best time to visit. Step back in time to the simple pleasures of yesteryear and sample delicious old-fashioned ice cream, traditionally brewed specialty coffee drinks made from locally roasted beans, and dessert favorites such as

muffins, pastries, cakes, and cookies. No smoking. Wheelchair accessible. Around $2.50.

✳ Entertainment

THEATER ◊ ♦ 占 **Black Bear Dinner Theatre** (706-865-0074; www.blackbeardinnertheatre.com), 210 Dawn Way, Sautee. Shows run Thursday through Saturday evenings, with dinner at 7 and performance at 8; Sunday matinees feature the meal at 1 and show at 2. Call for a schedule of performances. A new component of the Black Bear Resort, the state-of-the-art theater facility mounts a new live stage production every month, each one featuring a buffet menu themed to the production. Productions have ranged from the intimate *I Do! I Do!* to a fully staged presentation of *Man of La Mancha.* Adults $40, students and seniors $37, children $25.

◊ ♦ **Buisson Art Center** (706-867-0050), 199 Choice Street, Dahlonega. Open 10–11 daily. A consortium that promotes the arts in north Georgia, the center includes a children's theater, a dinner theater, a music hall, and an art gallery. Past performances have included such favorites as *Charlotte's Web.* Call for a schedule of events. Tickets: adults $10, children and students $6.

◊ **Historic Holly Theatre** (706-864-3759; www.hollytheater.com), 69 West Main Street, Dahlonega. Box office hours 11–7 weekdays, 9–5 Saturday. A small restored movie theater, the Holly offers movies, theatrical performances, dinner theater, children's theater, and other special performances. Past shows have included such favorites as *Willy Wonka and the Chocolate Factory.* Call for a schedule of performances and prices.

☞ **Remember When Theatre** (706-878-SHOW; www.rememberwhen theatre.com), 115 Escowee Drive, Helen. Performances at 8 Saturday; doors open at 6:30. Take a stroll down memory lane with shows such as *Mark Pitt's Tribute to Elvis*, a variety show that pays homage to "the King." The theater also has a piano bar on Friday and Saturday evenings and an indoor Go-Kart ride. Call for a schedule of performances and prices.

☞ ⊕ ♿ **Sautee-Nacoochee Art Center** (706-878-3300; www.snca.org), 283 GA 255 North, Sautee. This thriving community arts center contains not only a theater in the old cafeteria but also an on-site regional history museum and an art gallery. Housed in an old 1928 schoolhouse situated on 8 acres, the center offers community theater productions, concerts, playwright readings, lectures, environmental workshops, summer youth camps, and visual and performing-arts classes. The history museum features Native American artifacts, pioneer tools, gold-mining relics, old photographs, and school memorabilia. Monthly community folk dances are held in the old gymnasium. The newest addition is a wing showcasing the best of north Georgia folk potters (see *To See—Museums*). The only known surviving slave cabin in northeast Georgia has been relocated to the campus as well. Museum and gallery free. Call for a schedule of performances and ticket prices.

✳ Selective Shopping

ANTIQUES Forever Treasures Antiques (706-878-1010), 8749 North Main Street, Helen. Open 10–5 daily. This dramatic shop specializes in estate pieces, porcelains, and cut crystal. There is always a fascinating, eclectic array of merchandise.

Nacoochee Village Antiques (706-878-4069), 7091 South Main Street, Helen. Open 10–6 daily. Discover treasures and bargains at Helen's largest antiques gallery. The emporium specializes in antique furniture, kitchen and dining ware, books, and paintings. Don't miss the attic Christmas store.

CRAFTS The Chattahoochee Candle Company (706-878-7668), 7086 Main Street South, Nacoochee Village. Open 10–5 daily. Helen's newest home–fragrance candle shop specializes in candles of all shapes and sizes, including customized candles for all occasions. Many are made with mountain ingredients.

Country Store at Skylake (706-878-2292; www.helenga.org/countrystore), 69 Skylake, Sautee. Open 9:30–5 Monday through Saturday, noon–5 Sunday. This emporium sells arts and crafts, gifts, and accent pieces. Visitors also enjoy its café and old-fashioned soda fountain.

♿ **The Glassblowing Shop** (706-864-9022; 1-888-868-6995; www .glassblowingshop.com), 10 South Chestatee Street, Dahlonega. Open 10–6 daily. Call for specific demonstration times. Enjoy these clear and brightly colored works of art. Favorites include frogs, hummingbirds, feeders, and garden orbs, but there is tons more to choose from. Wheelchair accessible.

The Gourd Place (706-865-4048; www.gourdplace.com), 2319 Duncan Bridge Road, Sautee. Open 10–5 Monday through Saturday, 1–5 Sunday; closed January through March except by appointment. The retail shop sells interesting items made from gourds, while the museum features more than 200 gourds from 23 countries.

The Willows (706-878-1344), 7275 South Main Street, Nacoochee Village. Open 10–6 Monday through Saturday, noon–6 Sunday. This unique shop allows budding artists to paint their own pottery. Most days visitors can observe the resident potters at their wheels.

OUTLET MALLS **North Georgia Premium Outlets** (706-216-3609; www.premiumoutlets.com/northgeorgia), 800 US 19/GA 400 South, Dawsonville. Open 10–9 Monday through Saturday, noon–6 Sunday. The upscale center features 140 designer apparel and brand-name stores such as Off 5th (a Saks Fifth Avenue outlet), Banana Republic, Coach, Escada, Hugo Bass, Liz Claiborne, Gap, Polo Ralph Lauren, Timberland, Tommy Hilfiger, and many more. Services include a large food pavilion, stroller rentals, wheelchairs, and a children's play area.

SPECIAL STORES **BabyLand General Hospital** (706-865-2171; www.cabbagepatchkids.com), 73 West Underwood Street, Cleveland. Open 9–5 Monday through Saturday, 10–5 Sunday. After visiting the museum (see *To See—For Families*), proceed to the gift shop, where visitors can "adopt" a Cabbage Patch Kid, then outfit and accessorize it for every possible occasion.

✳ Special Events

March or April: **Easter Eggstravaganza** (706-865-5356). Held in Cleveland the Friday and Saturday of Easter weekend, the event features a parade, breakfast with the Easter Bunny, a 30,000+ egg hunt for children, a treasure hunt for adults, and an arts and crafts fair. Free except for $7 breakfast.

April: **Bear on the Square** (678-787-0530). This annual music festival takes place in historic downtown Dahlonega. Events include concerts, workshops, jam sessions, a children's play and teddy-bear picnic, storytelling, mountain dancing, a pie contest, and a country auction featuring folk art and gifts. Outdoor events free; concert prices free–$10.

May: **Mountain Flower Arts Festival** (706-867-6829). This juried event draws artists from all over the country and attracts thousands of people to the picturesque mountain village of Dahlonega. Free.

June: **Georgia Wine Country Festival** (706-865-WINE). Held the first Saturday and Sunday in June in Dahlonega, this two-day event highlights Georgia's many wine resources.

BABYLAND GENERAL HOSPITAL, BIRTHPLACE OF THE CABBAGE PATCH KIDS

Activities include live music, gourmet food, folk art, farm exhibits and live demonstrations, hot-air balloon rides, a petting zoo and children's area, a silent auction, and wagon rides. Adults $20; designated drivers $10; children free.

Mountain Top Rodeo (706-864-6444). Selected as one of the Southeast Tourism Society's Top 20 Events of 2004, this Professional Rodeo Cowboys Association rodeo features world-class competition in Dahlonega's beautiful mountain setting. Adults $10 in advance, $12 at the gate; children $5.

June, July, and August: **Bavarian Nights of Summer** (706-878-1619), held at Festhalle beer garden, 1074 Edelweiss Strasse, Helen. This event takes place 7–11 every Saturday evening from mid-June until mid-August. Authentic Bavarian musicians oompah the night away. You'll being doing the polka before you know it. $5.

July: **Family Day Independence Day Celebration** (706-864-3365). This Dahlonega event, a perennial winner of the Southeast Tourism Society's Top July Events designation, is the largest celebration of its kind in north Georgia. Events include patriotic speeches, a flag-raising ceremony, clogging, music, arts and crafts demonstrations, gold panning, food, and fireworks. Free.

September: **Autumnfest** (706-505-3485). This event takes place the third weekend in September every year around the historic town square in Dahlonega. The area is festively decorated with natural materials, and events are focused toward reminiscing about days gone by. Highlights include food, a pie contest, cakewalk, bluegrass jam session, gospel music, scarecrow auction, farmer's market, demonstrations of bygone skills, wagon rides with story tours, and 1862 dancing in period attire. Proceeds benefit Habitat for Humanity. Free.

Mid-September through early November: **Oktoberfest** (706-878-1908; www.helenchamber.com). What started more than 70 years ago as a small-town festival has grown into one of the most talked-about events in the state. Although the name suggests October only, this festival actually goes on for two entire months. Favorite activities include browsing Helen's many unique shops, a visit (or two) to a beer garden, and at night a trip to the famous Festhalle, where entertainment includes German bands, dancing, food, beer, and much more. Book your reservations early, as lodging during this event sells out fast. Free; admission charges for some events.

October: **1828 Gold Rush** (706-864-3711; 706-864-7247). This tradition in its 51st year takes place on the third weekend in October in Dahlonega. Celebrate the 1828 discovery of "gold in them thar hills." History is re-created with buck dancing, greased-pig chasing, a beard contest, fashion show, gold-panning contest, king and queen coronation, wrist-wrestling contest, hog-calling contest, pioneer parade, and more than 300 arts and crafts exhibitors. Free.

DALTON AND NORTHWEST GEORGIA

Nestled in the foothills of the Appalachian Mountains, this area of extreme northwest Georgia features serene, fertile valleys and plateaus. Wind and water have sculpted the limestone and sandstone for millions of years, creating awe-inspiring cliffs, dramatic waterfalls, incredible rock formations, and panoramic valleys with hundreds of varieties of ferns, flowers, plants, shrubs, and trees. In addition to scenic beauty, the area offers an abundance of recreational opportunities, from cave exploration to hang gliding.

The area is also rich in Native American and Civil War history, and many sites are on the **Blue and Gray Trail,** which traces battles and events from Chattanooga to Atlanta. Whitfield County has 32 historical markers, more than any other Georgia county. For more information, consult the web site at www.ngeorgia.com/travel/bgtrail.html. Several sites are on the **Georgia Civil War Heritage Trails,** which interpret the events that took place in the state. For more information, consult the web site at www.gcwht.org or call 1-800-331-3258.

Visitors to this area enjoy carpet factories and sales showrooms, an outlet mall, the famous Rock City Gardens, museums, a winery, state parks, wilderness areas, lakes, and even ghost tours. Among the many quaint towns to explore, Dalton is the primary city.

GUIDANCE To learn about northwest Georgia, stop at the **Georgia Visitor Information Center–Ringgold** (706-937-4211; www.georgiaonmymind.org), 2726 I-75 South, Ringgold 30736. Open 8:30–5:30 daily; rest rooms open 7 AM–11 PM.

For information about Chatsworth, contact the **Chatsworth Local Welcome Center, Chatsworth–Murray County Chamber of Commerce and Welcome Center** (706-695-6060; 1-800-969-9490; www.murraycountychamber.com), 126 North Third Street, Chatsworth 30705. Open 8:30–5:30 Monday through Thursday, 8:30–5 Friday.

To learn more about Dalton, Tunnel Hill, and Varnell, contact the **Dalton-Whitfield Convention and Visitors Bureau** (706-270-9960; 1-800-331-3258; www.daltoncvb.com), 2211 Dug Gap Battle Road, Dalton 30720. Open 8:30–5 weekdays. When you arrive in the area, visit the **Dalton Welcome Center**

(706-272-7676; 1-800-824-7469; www.nwgtcc.com), located inside the Northwest Georgia Trade and Convention Center at the same address as the CVB. Open 8:30–5 daily.

For information about Fort Oglethorpe and Ringgold, contact the **Catoosa County Chamber of Commerce** (706-965-5201; 1-877-965-5201; www.gate waytogeorgia.com), 264 Catoosa Circle, Ringgold 30736. Open 8:30–5 weekdays.

To learn more about Chickamauga, LaFayette, Lookout Mountain, and Rossville, contact the **Walker County Chamber of Commerce** (706-375-7702; www.walkercochamber.com), 10052 North US 27, Rock Spring 30739.

For information about Rising Fawn and Trenton, contact the **Dade County Chamber of Commerce** (706-657-4488, www.dadechamber.com), 111 Railway Lane, Trenton 30752.

GETTING THERE *By air:* The nearest airports to this region are **Hartsfield-Jackson Atlanta International Airport** (see What's Where in Georgia) and **Chattanooga Metropolitan Airport** (423-855-2202; www.chattairport.com), 1001 Airport Road, Chattanooga, Tennessee. The Chattanooga airport is served by **American Eagle, ASA/ComAir, Northwest Airlink,** and **US Airways.** Car rentals are available at the Chattanooga airport from **Avis** (423-855-2232), **Budget** (423-855-2224), **Enterprise** (423-894-0707), **Hertz** (423-855-8131), and **National** (423-855-2229).

By bus: Service to this area is provided by **Greyhound Lines** (706-278-3139; 1-800-231-2222; www.greyhound.com), 448 North Thornton Avenue, Dalton.

By car: Northwest Georgia is bisected by the north-south route I-75, so access to the area is easy. Get off the interstate and explore via the scenic routes US 27 and US 411 and east-west US 76. I-59 and I-24 connect this corner of Georgia to Alabama and Tennessee.

By train: The nearest **Amtrak** (1-800-USA-RAIL; www.amtrak.com) station is in Atlanta (see What's Where in Georgia).

GETTING AROUND In Dalton, rental cars can be obtained from **Enterprise Rent-A-Car** (706-226-7770), 1507 East Walnut Avenue. In Chatsworth, car rentals are available from **Enterprise** (706-517-1544).

WHEN TO GO The mountainous areas of Georgia occasionally get snow that sticks to the ground for a couple days and impedes transportation. A few campgrounds and other establishments close for several months in the winter, so be sure to call ahead to avoid disappointment.

MEDICAL EMERGENCY In life-threatening emergencies, call 911. For other immediate care, help is available in Dalton at **Hamilton Health Care System** (706-272-6100; www.hamiltonhealth.com), 1200 Memorial Drive; in Fort Oglethorpe at **Hutcheson Medical Center** (706-858-2000; www.hutcheson.org), 100 Gross Crescent Circle; and in Chatsworth at **Murray Medical Center** (706-695-4564), 707 Old Ellijay Road.

Dalton, located 90 miles north of Atlanta and 25 miles south of Chattanooga, boasts more than 100 carpet outlets, earning the title "Carpet Capital of the World." The town also offers Cherokee and Civil War history as well as discount shopping. After Native Americans were ousted from the region in 1838, the Western and Atlantic Railroad began laying track, and settlers came. Before the city was incorporated, it was known as Cross Plains. In 1852 the City of Dalton was laid out in a 1-mile radius from a survey post where the Dalton Depot now stands.

During the Civil War, Confederate hospitals and manufacturing facilities in Dalton were important for supporting the South's efforts. In May 1864, after the Union victory at Chattanooga, the war turned south toward Atlanta, and several important battles occurred nearby.

Dalton once had the nickname "Peacock Alley" because of the wide array of chenille bedspreads hung out for sale along the highway. This significant cottage industry—a truly American business—began in the early 1900s when a farm girl named Catherine Evans Whitener used the colonial art of tufting to make a bedspread she sold for $2.50. Soon all the ladies in the area were making them. By the 1950s, advances in technology transformed the bedspread industry into carpet making—now a multimillion-dollar industry.

Today historic downtown Dalton features a theater, shopping, and restaurants. Downtown Dalton is a great place for train viewing, too. The CSX and Norfolk-Southern lines travel side by side, and more than 35 trains pass through each day. Stop at the **Dalton Welcome Center** in the **Northwest Georgia Trade and Convention Center** (706-272-7676; 1-800-824-7469; www.nwgtcc.com) to pick up a brochure for the **Chieftans Trail** (www.chieftainstrail.com), a 150-mile path that dates back to 1000 B.C. Nine sites open to the public are included on the trail.

Chickamauga, once known as Crawfish Springs, was the site of one of the bloodiest battles of the Civil War. The Battle of Chickamauga, fought nearby on September 19 and 20, 1863, was one of the early battles in the Union's push toward Atlanta from Chattanooga and was a rare victory for the Confederacy, although it resulted in 34,000 casualties total. The small town near the site of one of the first National Battlefield Parks in the nation has several historic sites and an elegant bed & breakfast.

Durham Iron and Coal Company later built long lines of beehive ovens to turn coal into coke for iron and steel foundries in Chattanooga, a practice that continued until the coal ran out during the Depression. A

THE U.S. CARPET INDUSTRY
• The United States supplies 45 percent of the world's carpet.
• 80 percent of the U.S. carpet market is supplied by mills within a 65-mile radius of Dalton, Georgia.
• 90 percent of the carpet produced is tufted, a process that grew out of the chenille bedspread industry.
• The Georgia manufacturer with the largest number of employees is a carpet manufacturer.

Chickamauga park created around the ovens has wetlands demonstration ponds, a bird sanctuary, and a nature trail. The park is the site of the **Arts and Crafts Festival** held each September in conjunction with **War Between the States Day.** At that event, reenactors erect a camp and living-history demonstration area around the springs. Nearby, the **Holland-Watson Veterans Memorial Park,** which displays a Huey helicopter, honors Chickamauga veterans of all American wars.

Fort Oglethorpe was established in 1902 and served as the home of the sixth, seventh, 10th, 11th, and 12th Cavalries. During World War I, the parade ground served as a detention camp for enemy aliens and prisoners of war. During the 1920s and 1930s, the fort became one of the most elite posts in the country, complete with polo matches and fox hunts. In fact, the Sunday-afternoon polo matches were so famous throughout northwest Georgia and southeast Tennessee, the parade ground became known as the Polo Field. Equally renowned were the fort's horse shows, drill team, mounted band, and mounted guard performances.

During World War II, the post became an induction center and once again served as an internment center for enemy aliens and POWs. In 1943, it became a training center for the Women's Third Army Corps. At the end of the war, the post became a center for processing returning GIs until it was closed in 1947. Across from the fort grounds is the Georgia unit of the **Chickamauga and Chattanooga National Military Park.**

THE BATTLE OF TUNNEL HILL REENACTMENT TAKES PLACE ON THIS RURAL PROPERTY NEAR THE TOWN AND TUNNEL.

Lookout Mountain was formed millions of years ago. Native Americans inhabited it, and two missionaries arrived in 1823 to minister to them. They described the area as a citadel of rocks arranged in streets and lanes (hence Rock City). The slopes of the mountain saw much action during the Civil War. A Union officer and a Confederate nurse both contended that seven states could be seen from the summit. Beginning in the 1890s, Lookout Mountain became a major attraction, with grand hotels and three railroads to the top. Generations of Americans and foreign visitors were familiar with "See Rock City" signs painted on barn roofs.

Tunnel Hill came into being when a 1,477-foot tunnel was built through Chetoogeta Mountain to connect the

ROCK CITY BARNS

When Garnet and Frieda Carter opened Rock City Gardens to the public in 1932, Garnet realized that the attraction was so far off the beaten path he needed to get people's attention in a big way. He hired a sign painter named Chuck Byers to travel the nation's highways and offer to paint farmer's barns for free if they would agree to let him paint "See Rock City" in huge letters on the roof. At one time there were 900 of these barns, and they could be seen as far north as Michigan and as far west as Texas. Sadly, only a few of these treasured national landmarks remain.

port of Augusta to the Tennessee River Valley. Construction began in 1848, and the first Western and Atlantic train passed through in 1850. The new town of Atlanta became one of the railroad's major hubs. The tunnel was the site of several historical events during the Civil War. Afterward, heavier rail traffic and larger train cars often caused trains to become stuck in the tunnel, so a larger parallel tunnel was built in 1928. The abandoned tunnel was neglected for 70 years but was restored and reopened to the public in 2000 in time for its 150th birthday. Today the tunnel and several historic attractions and festivals bring tourists to Tunnel Hill.

SPECTACULAR VIEWS AWAIT VISITORS TO ROCK CITY GARDENS AT LOOKOUT MOUNTAIN.

✳ To See

FOR FAMILIES ✐ 🐾 ♿ **Rock City Gardens** (706-820-2531; 1-800-854-0675; www.seerockcity.com), 1400 Patton Road, Lookout Mountain. Open year-round from 8:30 AM, closes at different times depending on season. Gigantic and often bizarre rock formations created over millions of years by changing temperatures, wind, and water create the basis for this 14-acre park. During the 1920s, Garnet and Frieda Carter created their own private garden here, eventually opening it to the public in 1932. Today 4,100 feet of paths wind through rock formations where visitors can get spectacular views and enjoy 400 different species of native wildflowers, plants, shrubs, and trees. The brave-hearted will want to test their courage on the 180-foot Swing-

Along Bridge. The more faint-of-heart will enjoy Fat Man's Squeeze, Fairyland Caverns, Mother Goose Village, the 90-foot waterfall, and the view of seven states from Lover's Leap. Rock City sponsors many special events throughout the year: **Birds of Prey Take Flight** (Memorial Day weekend through Labor Day weekend), **Rock City Fairytale Festival** (end of June), **Spring Blooms at Rock City** (late March through May), **Summer Blooms at Rock City** (late June through September), the **Enchanted Maize** (see *To Do—For Families*), **Rock City's Beautiful Fall Colors** (October and November), and **Enchanted Garden of Lights and Winter Wonderland** (mid-November through December; see *Special Events*). Partially handicapped accessible. Pets allowed on a leash. Adults $12.95, children 3–12 $6.95; admission for Enchanted Garden of Lights: adults $13.95, children $7.95; both day and night: adults $5 additional, children $4 additional.

GUIDED TOURS 🐾 **Carpet Mill Tours** (706-281-1289; 1-800-331-3258). Weekdays, subject to availability. Carpet mill tours lasting about 1½ hours can be arranged through the Dalton Convention and Visitors Bureau. No one under 16 allowed in the mill. Free.

HISTORIC HOMES AND SITES ✎ 🐾 ♿ **Chickamauga and Chattanooga National Military Park** (706-866-9241; www.nps.gov/chch), 3370 Lafayette Road, Fort Oglethorpe. Visitor center open 8–4:45 daily; park open daylight hours. The scene of a bloody battle that resulted in a rare Confederate victory, the Chickamauga battlefield in Georgia is part of the country's oldest and largest military park. Preserved by veterans from the North and South, the 8,000-acre park—which also includes several sites in Chattanooga, Tennessee—was the first of its kind in the country and endures as a symbol of unity. Nearly a million visitors tour the battlefield annually, making it the most visited military park in the country. Begin at the Chickamauga visitor center to see an audiovisual presentation describing the battle, view the Fuller Gun Collection and other exhibits, and pick up a brochure for a self-guided tour. The Georgia area of the park features driving roads, hiking paths, horse trails (BYOH—bring your own horse), monuments, cannons, and historical markers. The best place from which to get a bird's-eye view of the battlefield is from the top of the 85-foot Wilder Tower, a memorial to Colonel John T. Wilder, who commanded the Lightning Brigade. In addition to the Georgia attractions in the park described here, there are several attractions in Tennessee, including the Cravens House and Point Park. Partially handicapped accessible. Admission to visitor center and Chickamauga battlefield free; admission to Point Park unit in Chattanooga $3.

✎ 🐾 **Chief John Ross House** (706-866-5171), 212 Andrew Street at East Lake Avenue, Rossville. Open 10–2 daily, June through September. The original part of this two-story log home was begun in 1797 by Scotsman John McDonald. His union with a Cherokee woman produced a long line of descendants. John Ross, McDonald's grandson, moved into the house as a boy to live with his grandparents. Eventually he became a successful businessman, a ferry operator, and a chief of the Cherokee Nation. The house served as a post office, schoolhouse, country store, and council room while Ross lived there. Ross was forced off the land at the time of the Trail of Tears. Free; donations accepted.

✒ ☃ ♿ **Chief Vann House Historic Site** (706-695-2598; www.gastateparks.org/info/chiefvann), 82 GA 225 North, Chatsworth. Open 9–5 Tuesday through Saturday, 2–5:30 Sunday; last tour 45 minutes prior to closing. Called the "Showplace of the Cherokee Nation," this beautiful two-story Federal-style residence was the home of Cherokee Chief James Vann, a political leader and wealthy plantation owner. Constructed in 1804, this was the first brick home within the Cherokee Nation and the only mansion built by an early Native American. The interior features a "floating" or cantilevered staircase, hand carvings of the Cherokee rose, and period furniture. Vann brought Moravian missionaries to the Cherokee Nation to build schools and teach the children, and they established the Springplace Moravian Mission School. His son, Joseph, inherited the home and became a Cherokee statesman and businessman. "Rich Joe," as he was known, was forced off the property when the Cherokee were removed from Georgia and sent along the Trail of Tears. Also located on the grounds are a small log cabin and the **Robert E. Chambers Interpretive Center,** which has several exhibits and a short video interpreting Native American life and the clash of cultures with settlers. The most special event of the year is the **Moravian Christmas at the Chief Vann House,** held the second weekend in December. Located just 300 yards from the house is the **Springplace Mission Cemetery,** where such notables as Chief Charles R. Hicks, Margaret "Peggy" Vann Crutchfield (James Vann's widow), and missionary Anna Rosina Gambold are buried. Visitor center and first floor of house wheelchair accessible. Adults $4, seniors $2.50, children 6–18 $2.

✒ ☃ ♿ **Dalton Depot** (706-226-3160), 110 Depot Street, Dalton. Built in 1847 and used by the railroad until 1978, the facility is one of only a few surviving antebellum depots. During the Civil War, it served as a Confederate Army ordnance depot. During the Great Locomotive Chase in 1862 (see Northern Suburbs chapter in 1, Atlanta Metro), it was here that 17-year-old Southerner Edward Henderson was dropped off to telegraph a message to Chattanooga to stop the stolen *General.* Today the depot houses a restaurant and lounge (see *Where to Eat—Eating Out*). The original survey post around which Dalton was laid out is still embedded in the wooden floor of the depot.

THE CHIEF VANN HOUSE HISTORIC SITE IN CHATSWORTH

✑ 🐾 **Dug Gap Battle Park** (706-278-0217; 1-800-331-3258), West Dug Gap Battle Road, Dalton. Open daylight hours daily. Although outnumbered 10–to–1, on May 8, 1864, Confederate soldiers successfully repelled a Union attack by using a stone wall and constructing 1,200-foot breastwork entrenchments that are still evident. Visitors also can take the Dug Gap Mountain hiking trail to the summit and enjoy scenic views of Dalton and the surrounding area. Free.

✑ 🐾 **Emery Center** (706-277-7633), 110 West Emery Street, Dalton. Open 1–4 Thursday through Saturday. Guided tours by appointment. Formerly the Emery Street School, the institution was constructed in 1886 to educate African American children. Until the end of segregation, the school included kindergarten through 12th grade. Eventually threatened with demolition, it was rescued by concerned citizens for use as a museum and multicultural center. It houses the Cornelia M. Easley Media Center, Enduring Echoes Memory and Honor Room, Children's Learning Center, and Military Room. "In Freedom's Footsteps" traces African American life from Africa to the civil rights movement. Free.

Gordon-Lee Mansion (706-375-4728; 1-800-487-4728; www.gordon-lee mansion.com), 217 Cove Road, Chickamauga. The historic home was built between 1840 and 1847 with bricks made on the grounds. It is the last surviving structure used during the Battle of Chickamauga. Union General William S. Rosecrans used the home for his headquarters during the battle, and the home's graceful library served as a grisly operating room. It was reported that there was so much blood on the floors that they had to be covered with mats. The mansion, which now operates as a luxurious bed & breakfast (see *Lodging—Bed & Breakfasts*), is not open for tours except in December, when candlelight tours are offered.

✑ 🐾 ♿ **Lee and Gordon's Mills** (706-375-6801), 71 Red Belt Road, Chickamauga. Park open 10–5 Tuesday through Saturday during winter, longer in summer; mill open only during special events. Located on the east bank of Chickamauga Creek, the original mill, which was built by James Gordon, was constructed in 1836. During the 1863 Civil War Battle of Chickamauga, the mill served as the headquarters of the Confederate Army of Tennessee under the command of General Braxton Bragg. On the second day of the battle, Bragg withdrew to

GENERAL HOOD'S LEG

Confederate General John Bell Hood had been seriously wounded at Gettysburg, resulting in the loss of use of one of his arms. Then he was so grievously wounded in the leg at Chickamauga that it had to be amputated. Amputated limbs were normally discarded, but the doctors were so certain that Hood would die, they sent his leg along with him when he was moved to the Clisby Austin House in nearby Tunnel Hill so it could be buried with him. As he so often did, however, Hood rallied and went on to fight in many more battles. Therefore, his leg was buried in the family cemetery at the Clisby Austin House.

LaFayette, and Union troops occupied the mill. The original mill burned in 1867 and was replaced by one built by James Lee. That mill has been restored to operating condition, and cornmeal ground there can be purchased during special events. Free.

✎ ⚘ **Prater's Mill** (706-694-6455; www.pratersmill.org), 500 Prater's Mill Road/GA 2, Varnell. Park open daylight hours daily; mill building open only during festivals. The historic gristmill was built by slaves in 1855, but the Civil War intruded on the area not long after that. The grounds were used by 600 Union soldiers under Colonel Eli Long in February 1864 and then by 2,500 Confederate soldiers under General Joseph Wheeler two months later. Today the site offers fishing on Cohulla Creek, hiking on a nature trail, and popular spring and fall country fairs (see *Special Events*).

✎ ⚘ ♿ **Tunnel Hill Heritage Center–Western and Atlantic Railroad Tunnel** (706-673-3300; 1-800-331-3258; www.tunnelhillheritagecenter.com), 215 Clisby Austin Road, Dalton. Open 10–6 Monday through Saturday in summer, 9–5 in winter. The 1,477-foot tunnel built by the Western and Atlantic Railroad through Chetoogeta Mountain is the oldest tunnel south of the Mason-Dixon Line and was the first link between the Atlantic and the Ohio Valley. Completed in 1850, it was the engineering marvel of its time. It also was the site of several skirmishes during the Civil War and figured in the Great Locomotive Chase. Near the tunnel is the historic 1850 **Clisby Austin House**, which was built to be a summer getaway in the cool mountains but was used as a hospital during the Battle of Chickamauga. Confederate General John Bell Hood was sent there to recuperate. General Sherman used the house as a headquarters during the Battle of Dalton on May 7, 1864, as he planned the final legs of the Atlanta Campaign.

Located in another building, the heritage center houses historical displays about the Tunnel Hill area, local families, the Clisby Austin House, Foster Cemetery, the Great Locomotive Chase, and Peacock Alley. Exhibits about Civil War and railroad history and Native American artifacts also are displayed. The CSX Railroad tracks adjacent to the heritage center are perfect for train viewing and photography because they are part of a busy rail corridor between Dalton and Chattanooga. The **Battle of Tunnel Hill Reenactment** takes place here each September (see *Special Events*), and April's **Celtic and Heritage Festival** highlights Scottish and Cherokee influences on the area. Adults $2.50, children 12 and younger $1.50.

MUSEUMS ✎ ⚘ ♿ **Crown Gardens and Archives, Whitfield-Murray Historical Society** (706-278-0217), 715 Chattanooga Avenue, Dalton. Gardens and archives open 9–5 Tuesday through Thursday, 9–noon Friday, by appointment Saturday; museum–Hamilton House open by appointment. The museum is located in the circa 1840 **Hamilton House,** the oldest house in Dalton. It was used by Confederate General Joseph H. Lewis as headquarters for the Kentucky Orphan Brigade. In 1876 the house was sold to Crown Cotton Mills and was used as the superintendent's headquarters for many years. Today it serves as a museum with exhibits about Dalton's textile industry, chenille tufting, Native American history, the Civil War, and Georgia poet Robert Loveman. Among the special attractions are the Ellis Owen Pharmaceutical Collection and the Black Heritage Room, which showcases the contributions of many influential African Americans in the region. Also at the site are beautiful gardens and the archives of the historical society, which are housed in the 1855 Crown Cotton Mill office. Free; donations accepted.

✆ ✎ ⅙ **Walker County Regional Heritage and Train Museum** (706-375-4488), 200 Gordon Street, Chickamauga. Open 10–4 Monday through Saturday. The first railroad with a stop at Chickamauga (then Crawfish Springs) made two daily round trips between Chattanooga, Tennessee, and Cedartown (see Rome chapter). Trains pulled by steam locomotives still make excursions from Chattanooga during the summer with stops at the Chickamauga Depot. The stone depot built by Central of Georgia Railroad has been restored and now houses exhibits of Native American artifacts and displays about the Civil War, World War I, and antique guns and furniture. Guests also can see a complete working display of Lionel O-gauge model trains that date back to the 1940s. Free.

SCENIC DRIVES Backroads and Battlefields (1-800-331-3258; www.nw georgiabackroads.com). Stop at the Dalton Visitors Center (2211 Dug Gap Battle Road) to pick up a brochure for this historic and scenic tour of northwest Georgia.

Cohutta-Chattahoochee Scenic Byway (1-800-331-3258; www.nwgeorgia backroads.com). Stop at the Dalton Visitors Center (2211 Dug Gap Battle Road), to learn about this 54-mile corridor, which highlights the scenic, cultural, and historic rural back roads from Dalton east to the top of Fort Mountain, including Chatsworth, historic Prater's Mill, and Fort Mountain State Park.

✳ To Do

FISHING See *Green Space—Lakes* and Fishing Appendix.

FOR FAMILIES Enchanted Maize by Rock City (706-820-2531; 1-800-854-0675; www.seerockcity.com). Open noon–8 or 10 Thursday through Sunday, September and October. The twists and turns of the intricately designed 10-acre cornfield maze at Blowing Springs Farm at the base of Lookout Mountain also includes the **Spooky Acres Halloween Maze** on weekends in October, hayrides, a playground, a kiddie hay maze, hay pyramid, pumpkin patch, refreshments, and more. Adults $8, children 4–12 $6; during Spooky Acres, adults $9, children $7.

✆ ✎ ⅙ **Lake Winnepesaukah** (706-866-5681; 1-877-525-3946; www.lakewin-nie.com), 1730 Lakeview Drive, Rossville. Open: Thursday through Sunday, April through September; hours vary (longest hours are 10–10), so call ahead. Affectionately known as Lake Winnie, this family-oriented amusement park has been open since 1925. In addition to popular rides such as the Cannonball Coasters, Matterhorn, Genie, Tilt-A-Whirl, and an antique carousel, the park offers 30 other thrill, family, and kiddie rides as well as an arcade, miniature golf, paddleboats, a gift shop, and a picnic area. $3; rides priced individually (tickets 80¢ each; rides take two to five tickets), full-day unlimited ride pass $19.

FRIGHTS ✐ ✿ **Dalton Ghost Tours** (www.daltonghosttours.com). Open Friday and Saturday throughout October; tours at 7 and 9. Departs from the wooden deck across from the **historic Wink Theatre** on West Crawford Street (see *Entertainment—Theater*). Connie Scott and her ghost troupe enact eerie tales, chilling lore, and ghostly legends by candlelight. Many of the tales relate to the Wink Theatre. Adults $10, children $5.

GOLF See Golf Appendix.

HANG GLIDING ✐ ✿ **Lookout Mountain Flight Park and Training Center** (706-398-3541; 1-800-688-5637; www.hanglide.com), 7201 Scenic Highway, Rising Fawn. Office and pro shop open 9–6 Thursday through Monday; training center open at 7:45 daily; tandem flights at 9 and 6 during summer and fall, 9 and 4 during spring and winter; discovery tandem flights 9 AM–30 minutes before dark. Enjoy a special view of Lookout Mountain while quietly soaring 2,000 feet over the area. Lessons are available as well as tandem flights with instructors, but if you don't want to participate, spectators are welcome, too. The 44-acre mountain retreat also offers camping and lodging. Fees vary by activity; tandem flight $139.

HIKING ✐ ✿ **Disney Trail.** Named for Confederate soldier George Disney, whose grave site lies at the end of the trail, this steep path that ascends Rocky Face Mountain is the most challenging short trail in the state.

✐ ✿ **Pinhoti Trail, National Forest Service** (706-766-3800; www.georgia pinhoti.org), accessible across from Dug Gap Battle Park (see *To See—Historic Homes and Sites*) and several other points. Consult the web site for a complete trail guide. Open daylight hours daily. *Pinhoti* is the Cherokee word for "turkey," so the trail is blazed with representations of turkey feet. When complete, the multiuse trail will be the state's longest. Plans call for it to be 245 miles long, connecting the Appalachian Trail in northeast Georgia to the Talladega National Forest in Alabama. Free.

See also *Green Space—Nature Preserves & Parks*.

HORSEBACK RIDING ✐ **Fort Mountain Stables** (706-517-4906; www .n-georgia.com/horseback.htm), 181 Mountain Park Road, Chatsworth. Office open 9–5 weekdays. Horseback riding adventures are offered on 37 miles of scenic trails at Fort Mountain State Park (see *Green Space—Nature Preserves & Parks*). Call for fees.

MINIATURE GOLF ✐ ✿ **Dalton Falls Miniature Golf** (706-272-3574; www .daltonfallsgolf.com), 2817 Airport Road, Dalton. Open April through Labor Day, 4–9 Monday through Thursday, 4–10 Friday, 11–10 Saturday, 2–9 Sunday; shorter hours off-season. The facility features an 18-hole course, an arcade room, and a concession stand. Adults $5.60, children $4.60; check for many specials.

MOUNTAIN BIKING See **Fort Mountain State Park** under *Green Space— Nature Preserves & Parks*.

WINERY TOURS 🐾 ⅃ **Georgia Winery Taste Center** (706-937-2177; www
.georgiawines.com), Battlefield Parkway, Ringgold. Open 10–6 Monday through
Saturday. The 52-acre site has been producing wines since 1983. Reds, whites,
rosés, and blushes are produced primarily from muscadine grapes. The gift shop
offers wines, gourmet foods, gifts with a wine or grape theme, and winemaking
supplies. Free.

✳ Green Space

LAKES ⌀ 🐾 ⅃ **Carters Lake** (706-334-2248; 706-276-4891; www.carterslake
.com; carters.sam.usace.army.mil). Located at the southern end of the Blue
Ridge Mountains, this is one of the most scenic lakes in the Southeast as well as
one of the best recreational reservoirs. Impounding the Coosawattee River, the
3,220-acre lake and its surrounding area boast eight public-use parks. The area is
perfect for boating (launching ramps and rentals available), camping, fishing,
hiking, hunting, mountain biking, and picnicking. Camping and cottages are
available (see *Lodging—Inns & Resorts*).

CLOUDLAND CANYON STATE PARK IN RIS-
ING FAWN

⌀ 🐾 **Lookout Lake** (706-395-1970),
GA 136 East, Rising Fawn. Open daylight hours daily in-season; closed in
winter. The small lake is popular for
fishing for bass, catfish, and bluegills.
The lake also offers 12 developed and
some undeveloped campsites. Admission to fish: adults $3, children $2.

NATURE PRESERVES AND PARKS ⌀
🐾 ⅃ 🐾 **Cloudland Canyon State
Park** (706-657-4050; 1-800-864-7275;
www.gastateparks.org/info/cloudland),
122 Cloudland Canyon Park Road,
Rising Fawn. Open 7–10 daily. Spectacular scenery is one of the main reasons visitors come to Cloudland
Canyon State Park at the western
edge of Lookout Mountain. The 3,485-
acre park encompasses a deep gorge
cut by Sitton Gulch Creek, which
results in elevation ranging from 800
to 1,980 feet. Beautiful vistas can be
seen from the picnic area parking lot
as well as from along the rim trail.
Hardy travelers can hike down into
the canyon to view two waterfalls not
visible from the summit. (Just remember: while it's easy going down, it's all
uphill on the way back.) Hikers like

the 4.8-mile West Rim Trail and the 2-mile Backcountry Trail. The park also features tennis courts and a disc-golf course. The park features 73 tent, trailer, and RV sites, 30 walk-in sites, 11 backcountry campsites, and a pioneer campground ($4–40). The park also offers 16 fully equipped cottages ($85–115). Day use $3.

✂ 🐾 ♿ ⛺ **Fort Mountain State Park**
(706-695-2621; 1-800-864-7275; www.gastateparks.org/info/fortmt), 181 Fort Mountain Park Road, Chatsworth. Open 7–10 daily. Named for the ruins of an ancient 855-foot-long rock wall that tops the 2,800-foot-high mountain, the park offers numerous recreational activities. The wall may have been built by Native Americans as a fortification against other tribes, but the most widely held theory is that it was built for ceremonial purposes. Believed to have been constructed around A.D. 500, the wall is situated so that the sun rises and sets perfectly over each end. A hike to the wall takes about 15 minutes. The 3,550-acre park—located in the Chattahoochee National Forest near the Cohutta Wilderness—boasts 14 miles of hiking, 30 miles of mountain biking trails, 37 miles of horseback riding trails, a 17-acre lake with a sandy beach, swimming, pedal-boat rentals, miniature golf, and horseback riding (see *To Do—Horseback Riding*). The park offers 70 tent, trailer, and RV sites as well as four walk-in sites and primitive campsites ($5–20). Fifteen fully equipped two- and three-bedroom cottages ($80–120) also are available. Day use $3; fee for use of mountain biking trails.

✂ 🐾 **Spring Creek Wetlands Preserve** (706-278-1313; 1-800-331-3258; www.dutil.com/springcreek.html), Boyles Mill Road, Dalton. Open 9–6 weekends; reservations required for weekday visits. Well-marked trails provide opportunities for visitors to see a wide variety of flora and fauna in this 200-acre water and wildlife habitat. The preserve supports a secondary trout stream and is the breeding ground for several endangered species. Visitors see frogs, toads, salamanders, wood ducks, reptiles, turtles, snails, great blue herons, and green-backed herons. Free.

✳ Lodging
BED & BREAKFASTS

In Chatsworth
Hearthstone Lodge Bed and Breakfast (706-695-0920; 1-800-695-0905; www.thehearthstonelodge.com), 2755 US 76/GA 282. The beautiful cedar-log home features three guest suites named for apples. Each room offers a private bath, queen-sized bed, sitting area, and entertainment center. The B&B also features five fireplaces, decks and porches, a hot tub, steam room, pool table, and darts. A gourmet breakfast, afternoon refreshments, evening desserts, and bedtime sweets are provided. A short hike takes visitors through forest to creeks and waterfalls. Ages 21 and older only. No smoking. Not wheelchair accessible. $149–209; two-night minimum.

Overlook Inn Bed and Breakfast
(706-517-8810; 1-866-517-8810; www
.theoverlookinn.com), 864 Wilderness
View. Located atop Fort Mountain in
the Cohutta Wilderness with spectacular views of the Blue Ridge Mountains, this rustic inn features
tree-trunk support beams, a stone
fireplace, hardwood floors, and an
antler chandelier. The five surprisingly elegant guest rooms are uniquely
decorated in natural hues. Although
there are blessedly no telephones or
televisions, amenities include private
entrances and porches, in-room or
porch hot tubs, and fireplaces. A
three-course Southern gourmet
breakfast, afternoon wine and cheese,
and candlelight desserts are pleasant
extras. A woodland trail is accessible
from the inn, and Coyote Redd's
mountain-crafts gift shop is on the
property. The inn also operates
Wilderness View Cabin Rentals in
a 100-acre private preserve. Each features a full kitchen, fireplace, and outdoor hot tub. No children. No pets.
Smoking (outdoors only). Limited
wheelchair accessibility. $159–249;
two-night minimum; three-night minimum during fall leaf season and
some holidays.

In Chickamauga
Gordon-Lee Mansion (706-375-
4728; 1-800-487-4728; www.gordon
-leemansion.com), 217 Cove Road.
This white-columned plantation
home, exquisitely furnished in the
manner of the aristocracy of the Civil
War period, is listed on the National
Register of Historic Places and is a
site on the Civil War and Blue and
Gray trails; it now operates as a luxury
bed & breakfast. All rooms have private baths, some with claw-foot tubs,
and the Gold Room boasts a gas fire-

place. An elegant but informal full
breakfast is served in the dining room.
For even more privacy or for a family
or friends traveling together, book the
circa 1900 Log House, which offers
two bedrooms, two bathrooms, a living
room with a gas fireplace, and a
kitchen. (Note: Breakfast is not
included with stays in the Log House.)
Not available in December because of
candlelight tours (see *To See—Historic
Homes and Sites*); closed in January.
Smoking outdoors only. Not wheelchair accessible. $75–125; two-night
minimum on weekends and for Log
House.

In Fort Oglethorpe
**Captain's Quarters Bed and
Breakfast Inn** (706-858-0624; 1-800-
710-6816; www.cqinn.com), 13 Barnhardt Circle. When Fort Oglethorpe
was an active military facility and
home of the sixth, seventh, 10th, 11th,
and 12th Cavalries, the grand turn-of-
the-20th century duplex houses on
Barnhardt Circle provided residences
for the officers. When the fort closed
in 1945, the area became the town of
Fort Oglethorpe and the buildings
were sold at public auction. Captain's
Quarters began operating as a bed &
breakfast in 1988 in half of a former
officer's house. Later, the second half
was incorporated into the B&B.
Accommodations are offered in nine
handsomely decorated rooms and
suites, most with private baths. The
full gourmet breakfast, served with
china, crystal, and silver, is a fine dining experience. No smoking. Not
wheelchair accessible. Rooms
$99–142, suites $153–199.

In Lookout Mountain
✈ & **Chanticleer Inn** (706-820-
2002; 1-866-424-2684; www.stayat
chanticleer.com), 1300 Mockingbird

Lane. A member of Select Registry, Distinguished Inns of North America, this hostelry is located on 5 landscaped acres in the historic Fairyland neighborhood atop Lookout Mountain. The inn, built in the late 1920s, has a mountain-stone exterior similar to that of nearby Rock City Gardens (see *To See—For Families*). Seventeen rooms and five cottages were completely renovated in 2002 using a country theme with English antiques. Each boasts a private bath, cable TV, and feather-top beds. Some rooms have private patios, gas or electric fireplaces, whirlpool tubs, and stocked refrigerators. The inn's swimming pool is open seasonally. A Southern breakfast buffet is served each morning, and afternoon refreshments are also included. No smoking. Wheelchair accessible. $100–200; several special packages available.

Garden Walk Bed and Breakfast Inn (706-820-4127; 1-800-617-0502; www.gardenwalkinn.com), 1206 Lula Lake Road. A series of cottages are nostalgically, romantically, or whimsically decorated in themes. Rooms are available with queen-, king-, or twin-sized beds. Each offers a private bath, refrigerette, coffeemaker, and cable TV. Some feature a fireplace and/or Jacuzzi. Other amenities include an outdoor pool and hot tub along with beautifully landscaped gardens. A full hot breakfast is provided. Adults and youth 16 and older only. Smoking outside or in smoker's lounge only. Limited wheelchair accessibility (one cabin has no steps, but its bathroom will not accommodate a wheelchair). $89–175.

CAMPGROUNDS

In Chatsworth
See **Fort Mountain State Park**

under *Green Space—Nature Preserves and Parks*.

In Rising Fawn
See **Lookout Mountain Flight Park** under *To Do—Hang Gliding*, **Lookout Lake** under *Green Space—Lakes*, and **Cloudland Canyon State Park** under *Green Space—Nature Preserves and Parks*.

In Trenton
✔ 🐾 **Lookout Mountain KOA** (706-657-6815; 1-800-562-1239; www.look outmountainkoa.com), 930 Mountain Shadows Drive. The 37-acre forested site offers beautiful mountain views. Activities and amenities include hiking, a lookout point, and a large pool. Tent sites $18–22, RV sites $26–40, cabins $38–59, Kottage Lodge $95–120.

See also Campgrounds Appendix.

COTTAGES AND CABINS

In Chatsworth
✔ 🐾 **Wilderness View Cabin Rentals** (706-517-8810; www.wilder nessviewcabins.com), 864 Wilderness View. See **Overlook Inn** under *Bed and Breakfasts*.

See also **Fort Mountain State Park** under *Green Space—Nature Preserves and Parks*.

In **Lookout Mountain** see **Chanticleer Inn** under *Bed & Breakfasts*.

In Rising Fawn
See **Cloudland Canyon State Park** under *Green Space—Nature Preserves and Parks*.

INNS AND RESORTS

In Chatsworth
✔ ♿ **Carters Lake Marina and Resort** (706-276-4891; www.carters lake.com), 575 Marina Road. Accom-

modations, which range from basic rooms to cabins to houseboats, fit every budget. Luxury cabins with spectacular views of the lake feature two bedrooms, a sleeping loft, bathroom, gas-log fireplace, fully equipped kitchen, covered porch, deck, and barbecue grill. Family log cabins feature two bedrooms, one bath, a sofa bed, and a fully equipped kitchen. Basic rooms feature one bed and one bath. All basic rooms have a coffeemaker; some also have a refrigerator and microwave. Houseboats feature sleeping for eight, as well as a full kitchen, one bathroom, front and back decks, and an upper deck. They can be rented for three, four, or seven nights. Guests are welcome to bring one personal boat and use the resort's docks at no extra charge; additional boats or Jet Skis are $10 per night. Pontoon boats are available to rent, and a snack bar operates during the summer. For boat customers, service, repairs, fuel, and supplies are available. No smoking. Wheelchair accessible. Lakeside rooms $39.95–49.95, family cabins $95–140; luxury cabins $140–175 for two people; each additional person $15; pontoon boats $155–225; houseboats $850–1,400.

✍ ♿ **Cohutta Lodge and Restaurant** (706-695-9601; www.cohutta lodge.com), 500 Cochise Trail. Located high atop Fort Mountain, the recently renovated rustic lodge provides accommodations, a restaurant (see *Where to Eat—Eating Out*), an enclosed swimming pool, riding stables, hiking trails, mountain biking, and sweeping views of the mountain and valley from the lodge or motel-style annex. No smoking. Wheelchair accessible. $79–159; specials and weekend packages available.

In Chickamauga

✍ ❦ **Hidden Hollow Resort** (706-539-2372; www.hiddenhollowresort .com), 463 Hidden Hollow Lane. The small, secluded resort provides a perfect getaway from modern-day life's hectic pace. The 135 wooded acres lie at the foot and along the side of Lookout Mountain. Guests take long walks, play lawn games, relax on the porches, sit around the fireplace, or participate in sing-alongs or marshmallow roasts. There is a small lake and a creek on the property, too. Accommodations are provided in a quaint country inn or in cozy log cabins, most with fireplaces and all with a kitchen or kitchenette. There is only one central phone and rooms do not have televisions (although you can bring your own). Paddleboats and canoes are available. No smoking. Limited wheelchair accessibility (one cabin has no steps). $40–98.

✳ Where to Eat

DINING OUT

In Rising Fawn

♿ **The Canyon Grill** (706-398-9510; www.cangrill.com), 28 Scenic Highway. Open 5–9 Wednesday through Sunday; call ahead for priority seating. Located at the southern end of Lookout Mountain, the popular restaurant's signature dish is Slash and Burn Catfish, which is crispy fried catfish accompanied by black bean sauce. Other entrées include fish and seafood, duck, pork, pastas, and lamb—many of which are cooked on the eatery's Tuff Grill, which they invented and now sell. The restaurant does not have a liquor license, but diners can BYOB. No smoking. Wheelchair accessible. $14–29.

In Chatsworth

Cohutta Lodge and Restaurant (706-695-9601; www.cohuttalodge.com), 500 Cochise Trail. Open 8–10:30, 11:30–3, and 5–9. The restaurant features several specials: fried chicken buffet on Wednesday, barbecue on Thursday, seafood on Friday, prime rib on Saturday, and brunch on Sunday. No smoking. Wheelchair accessible. Breakfast $8.95, lunch $12.95 ($13.95 on Sunday), dinner $15.95–16.95.

In Chickamauga

🖋 🍽 ♿ **Crystal Spring Smokehouse** (706-375-9269), 501 West Ninth Street. Open 7–8 Tuesday through Friday, 7–3 Saturday. This restaurant specializes in smoked barbecue plates and sandwiches. No smoking. Wheelchair accessible. Breakfast $2.50–6, lunch $4–6, dinner $6–10.

🖋 🍽 ♿ **Greg's Restaurant** (706-375-4788), 207 Lafayette Road. Open 6:30 AM–8 PM Monday through Saturday. A local favorite, the casual eatery offers home cooking as well as live entertainment on Tuesday and Thursday evenings. No smoking. Wheelchair accessible. Breakfast $4.95–6, lunch $5.25–7, dinner $5.25–7.99.

🖋 🍽 ♿ **Scarlett's Tea Room** (706-375-1889), 105 Gordon Street. Open 11–2 Tuesday through Friday, 10–2 Sunday. This restaurant and general store offers Southern-style soups, salads, sandwiches, and desserts. No smoking. Wheelchair accessible. $5.95–6.95.

In Dalton

🖋 🍽 ♿ **Dalton Depot Restaurant and Trackside Cafe** (706-226-3160), 110 Depot Street. Open 11–11 Monday through Saturday. The historic depot (see *To See—Historic Homes and Sites*) is occupied by two restaurants. For a quieter, more personal dining experience in the atmosphere of a bygone era, try the Dalton Depot Restaurant. For a faster pace in a more contemporary setting, the Trackside Cafe has big-screen televisions, video games, interactive trivia games, pool tables and tournaments, live music, and karaoke. Both eateries feature house specialties such as double-cut pork chops, baby-back ribs, chicken or veal parmesan, and shrimp and grits. Their menus also contain a full array of appetizers, seafood, steaks, and lighter fare. Murals and railroad relics are reminders of the building's history. No smoking. Wheelchair accessible. $5.95–19.95.

✳ Entertainment

THEATER Dalton Little Theater (706-226-6618), 210 North Pentz Street, Dalton. With its first production in 1869, the group claims to be the oldest community theater in Georgia. It produces a wide range of shows throughout the year. Call for a schedule of performances and ticket prices.

♿ **Historic Wink Theatre** (706-226-WINK; www.winktheatre.com), 115 West Crawford Street, Dalton. The opulent 1941 theater, designed to be a small-town version of the extravagant Fox Theatre in Atlanta, is the only example of art moderne architecture in north Georgia. The theater had a long career as a movie house until it closed in the 1970s. Now fully restored, it offers a variety of concerts, theatrical productions, classic movies, and other entertainment that keep it filled almost every weekend. Call for a schedule of performances and prices.

✳ Selective Shopping

ANTIQUES Gateway Antiques and Collectibles Mall (706-858-9685; www.gatewayantiques.com), 4103 Cloud Springs Road, Ringgold. Open 9–6 daily. More than 300 dealers purvey everything imaginable in the way of antiques and collectibles.

Le Frou Frou (706-375-7701), 110 Gordon Street, Chickamauga. Open 11–5 weekdays, 11–4 Saturday. The shop carries a blend of vintage and classic antiques as well as the Rachel Ashwell Shabby Chic line of bedding, accessories, and baby items.

BOOKS The Book Nook and Cubby Hole Café (706-226-8886), 229 North Hamilton Street, Dalton. Bookstore open 10–6 Tuesday through Thursday, 10–10 Friday and Saturday; café open 11–2:30 weekdays. Peruse the used hardbacks, paperbacks, and books on tape, then enjoy soups, salads, coffees, and desserts. $3–10.

CARPETS Carpets of Dalton (706-277-3132; 1-800-262-3132; www.carpetsofdalton.com), 3010 Old Dug Gap Road, Dalton. Open 8–7 weekdays, 8–6 Saturday, 1–6 Sunday. The emporium not only is a complete floor covering store but also houses the American Home Showplace, where shoppers can buy quality furniture; Buy the Room, where shoppers can buy furniture at discount prices; and World of Outdoor Living, a place to buy outdoor furniture and accessories.

Myers Carpet Company (706-277-4053; 1-800-297-1972), 3096 North

Dug Gap Road, Dalton. Open 8:30–5:30 weekdays, 10–5:30 Saturday. The company, Dalton's oldest floor-covering retailer, is the largest independent wool carpet dealer in the Southeast. It also produces custom-designed area rugs.

FOOD The Basket Case (706-375-4404), 108 Gordon Street, Chickamauga. Open 10–6 Tuesday through Saturday. The combination gift, cake, and coffee shop offers custom-made baskets, gourmet coffees, and freshly made specialty cakes.

OTHER GOODS The Galleries on Gordon (706-375-9849), 111 Gordon Street, Chickamauga. Open 10–5:30 Tuesday through Friday, 10–4 Saturday. Eighteen shops in one building purvey everything from antiques and art to home and garden decor, pottery, stationery, handbags, gourmet foods, and baby gifts.

OUTLET STORES Dalton Outlet Center (706-277-2688; 1-800-409-7029), 1001 Market Street, Dalton. Open 9–9 Monday through Saturday, noon–6 Sunday. The outlet center features more than 36 designer and specialty shops offering a wide variety of merchandise.

SPECIAL SHOPS Mountain City Mercantile (706-375-3800), 16 Euclid Avenue, Chickamauga. Open 10–6 Thursday through Saturday. Whether you want to purchase authentic Civil War reproductions or just browse, this 19th-century clothier and sutler serves the reenactment and living-history community with quality merchandise that meets historical requirements. The offerings include Confederate and Union uniforms, footwear, accessories, cookware, haversack stuffers, and other items. The shop also offers cowboy merchandise from the period 1830–1899 as well as Victorian-era ladies' clothing and accessories.

✳ Special Events

Mother's Day and Columbus Day weekends: **Prater's Mill Country Fair** (706-694-6455), 500 Prater's Mill Road, Varnell. The old-fashioned country-fair-type festival features quality artists and craftspeople, music, food, and other amusements. The mill, which was built by slaves in 1855 (see *To See—Historic Homes and Sites*), grinds corn during the fair. Adults $5, children under 12 free.

September: **Battle of Tunnel Hill Civil War Reenactment** (706-270-9960; 1-800-331-3258). An exciting battle with 1,000 reenactors, cannon fire, and thundering horses showcases life during the Civil War. Visitors can walk through Union and Confederate camps, shop at sutlers' tents, see the tunnel, and enjoy food and entertainment. Held on the grounds of the historic Clisby Austin House in Tunnel Hill (see *To See—Historic Homes and Sites*). $5 per car.

War Between the States Day and Arts and Crafts Festival (706-375-4728; 1-800-487-4728). This festival in Chickamauga features living-history programs with reenactors demonstrating camp life, artillery firing, period cooking, and life for area farm families affected by the battle. Free.

October: **North Georgia Agricultural Fair** (706-278-1217; www.ngaagfair.com). This popular 10-day agricultural and cultural event in Dalton features livestock, agricultural exhibits, a petting zoo, pony rides, a pageant, wrestling, midway rides and games, food, and live entertainment. Adults $5, children 4–12 $2; special discounts available.

Mid-November through December: **Enchanted Garden of Lights at Rock City Gardens** (706-820-2531; 1-800-854-0675; www.seerockcity.com), 1400 Patton Road, Lookout Mountain. This dazzling lights extravaganza features 25 holiday scenes that transform the garden (see *To See—For Families*) into a fantasyland. "Music Under the Moon" is a concert series held nightly during the holiday period. Adults $13.95, children $7.95; if added to daily admission, adults $5, children $4.

GAINESVILLE AND LAKE LANIER

As the county slogan proclaims, "From shorelines to finish lines to fabulous finds," Gainesville–Hall County offers some of the finest recreation in the South, from water sports to motor sports to major-league football.

Gainesville, once known as Mule Camp Springs, boasts a beautiful art deco–inspired downtown, unlike those of so many Georgia towns with historic town centers from the late 19th century. Although Gainesville's significance as a business and trading center goes back 200 years, a 1936 tornado demolished the downtown and killed many residents. President Franklin D. Roosevelt's New Deal programs made construction of a new downtown possible, thus reflecting the art deco style of the time. A monument to the president is in Roosevelt Square.

In recent years the city has earned the titles "Queen City of the Mountains," "Poultry Capital," and "Hospitality Capital of the World." The revitalized downtown features boutiques, cafés, antiques and collectible shops, and shops featuring the works of local artisans. In May and October, locals and visitors can enjoy Blue Sky Concerts during the noon hour. Bring a lunch or pick one up at a nearby eatery and settle back on one of the square's Victorian benches to enjoy the concert.

Lake Sidney Lanier, named after the beloved Georgia poet, is a 38,000-acre U.S. Army Corps of Engineers lake with 540 miles of shoreline, 60 recreational areas, and seven commercial marinas. The lake, which was formed by the damming of the Chattahoochee River, is a major source of power in Georgia as well as a recreational playground. One of the lake's most popular attractions is Lake Lanier Islands, a resort area with hotels, a water park, golf, horseback riding, and other recreational activities.

GUIDANCE For general information about all the areas covered in this chapter, stop by the **Northeast Georgia Welcome Center** (770-965-9272; www .greaterhallchamber.com), 4700 Lanier Parkway, Flowery Branch 30542. Open 9–5 daily. For other information about the entire area, contact the **Northeast Georgia Mountains Travel Association** (404-231-1820; www.georgia mountains.org).

To find out more about Braselton, Buford, or Duluth, contact the **Gwinnett**

Convention and Visitors Bureau (770-623-3600; 1-888-GWINNETT; www
.gcvb.org), 6500 Sugarloaf Parkway, Suite 200, Duluth 30097.

To learn more about Gainesville, contact the **Gainesville–Hall County Convention and Visitors Bureau** (770-536-5209; 1-888-536-0005; www.gainesville
hallcvb.org), 117 Jesse Jewell Parkway, Gainesville 30503. Open 9–5 weekdays.
Visitors also can stop by the **Greater Hall Chamber and Gainesville Welcome Center** (770-532-6206; www.greaterhallchamber.com), 230 East Butler
Parkway, Gainesville 30501. Open 8:30–5 weekdays.

To find out more about Commerce, call the **Jackson County Area Chamber
of Commerce** (706-335-1897; www.jacksoncountyga.com). Open 8–5 weekdays.

For information about Flowery Branch, contact the **City of Flowery Branch** (770-
967-6371; www.flowerybranchga.org), 5517 Main Street, Flowery Branch 30542.

To learn more about Homer, consult the **Banks County Convention and Visitors Bureau** (706-677-5265; www.bankscountyga.org), 943 Spring Road, Homer
30547. Open 9–5 weekdays. You also could contact the **Banks County Chamber of Commerce** (706-677-2108; 1-800-638-5004; www.bankscountyga.org),
106 Yonah Homer Road, Homer 30547. Open 9–4 weekdays. The chamber is
housed in the Banks County historic courthouse.

For information about Winder, contact the **Barrow County Chamber of
Commerce** (770-867-9444; www.barrowchamber.com), 6 Porter Street, Winder
30680. Open 8:30–5 weekdays.

GETTING THERE *By air:* The nearest full-service airport is **Hartsfield-Jackson
Atlanta International Airport** (1-800-897-1910; www.atlanta-airport.com; see
What's Where in Georgia). Car rentals are available on-site and off-site. Several
shuttle companies offer service to outlying locations.

By bus: In this area, **Greyhound Lines** (770-532-2641; www.greyhound.com)
stops only in Gainesville (1780 Martin Luther King Jr. Boulevard).

By car: The cities and towns described in this chapter are easily accessible from
either I-85 or I-985, which run north-south, as do US 23, US 129, and US 441.
GA 53 runs east-west.

By train: **Amtrak's** (1-800-USA-RAIL; www.amtrak.com) daily *Crescent* makes
one of its three Georgia stops in Gainesville (116 Industrial Boulevard).

MEDICAL EMERGENCY In life-threatening situations, call 911. For other immediate needs in and around Commerce, care is available at **BJC Medical Center**
(706-335-1000), 70 Medical Center Drive. In Duluth, care is available at **Joan
Glancey Memorial Hospital** (770-497-4800), 3215 McClure Bridge Road. In
and around Gainesville and Lake Lanier, help is available at **Northeast Georgia
Medical Center** (770-535-3553), 743 Spring Street NE, Gainesville. In Winder,
help is available at **Columbia Barrow Medical Center** (770-867-3400), 316
North Broad Street. In the eastern portion of this area, the nearest hospitals may
be in Athens: **Athens Regional Medical Center** (706-475-7000; www.armc.org),
1199 Prince Avenue, or **St. Mary's Hospital** (706-548-7581; www.stmarysathens
.org), 1230 Baxter Street.

VILLAGES AND NEIGHBORHOODS In Gainesville, visit the **Green Street Historic District.** Walk or drive along this half-mile, tree-lined historic street to enjoy turn-of-the-20th-century Queen Anne and neoclassical residences and businesses. A walking-tour brochure is available from the Gainesville–Hall County Convention and Visitors Bureau (117 Jesse Jewell Parkway).

Historic Downtown Gainesville's revitalized commercial district, centered around the Downtown Square, features an art center, art galleries, museums, restaurants, and specialty shops.

Braselton was first settled by the Braselton family in 1876. An early Braselton family home now serves as the town hall. Braselton got national attention some years ago when native daughter Kim Basinger bought the entire town with plans to transform it into a major tourist attraction. Although those plans fizzled and Basinger later sold the town, it still has some major attractions—**Mayfield Dairy** and the **Chateau Elan Winery and Resort** (see *To Do—Winery Tours*) being the primary ones.

Buford, named for Algernon Sidney Buford, president of the Atlanta and Richmond Air-Line Railroad, was a stop on the railroad line from Atlanta to Charlotte, North Carolina. From the very beginning, Buford was a bustling business and education center. For many years it was the largest city in Gwinnett County. In fact, a news article in 1902 referred to Buford as the New York of Gwinnett. Leather tanning and the production of shoes, saddles, harnesses, horse collars, and other leather products earned Buford the title "the Leather City." Today the downtown features antiques and collectible shops, restaurants, and the **Buford Artists Colony** (see *To See—Cultural Sites*).

Commerce was the inspiration for Olive Ann Burns's novel *Cold Sassy Tree,* which was filmed as a TNT movie and is currently an opera. Today, Commerce's claim to fame is that it is home to several outlet malls that house more than 125 stores.

Duluth, in Gwinnett County, was originally called Howell Crossing or Howell's Cross Roads. The settlement evolved into a major railroad artery when a railway was built from Howell Crossing to Duluth, Minnesota. At that time, it was decided to rename the Georgia town Duluth as well. It was incorporated in 1876, and Duluth is now the second-largest city in the county. Duluth is the home of an outstanding railroad museum and a regional theater.

Flowery Branch, a spot in Hall County, was established in 1874 along the Georgia Air Line Railroad route from Atlanta to Charlotte, North Carolina. The railroad was the primary artery for people, mail, and goods. Farmers from all over northeast Georgia brought their cotton to Flowery Branch to be ginned, sold, and shipped. Later businesses included furniture, leather goods, and buggies. Sadly, the last scheduled train stop in Flowery Branch was in 1957. From then until the late 1960s, a passenger could flag the train to stop, but now no trains stop in Flowery Branch. The town boasts lake activities, a museum, and the Falcons football team's training facility.

Homer, the county seat of Banks County, was named for Homer Jackson, an early settler, and incorporated in 1859. The Banks County courthouse, built between 1860 and 1863, is one of the four oldest in Georgia. Today it serves as 505 the Banks County Welcome Center and houses the local chamber of commerce offices. Another historic site is the Banks County Jail, which still has its cells, window bars, and hanging trapdoor and houses the county museum.

Jefferson, named for Thomas Jefferson, went through several name changes—first Jeffersonville, then Jeffersonton, before finally settling on the easier name. The small town was the site of the first use of ether for surgical anesthesia. A museum The event and the doctor are commemorated in the **Crawford W. Long Museum** (see *To See—Museums*).

Winder, the county seat of Barrow County, was originally called the Jug, so named because a piece of land had been cleared in the shape of a jug. Later it was called Jug Tavern. When it was incorporated in 1893, the name was changed again to Winder in honor of notable railroad builder and manager John H. Winder. Today Winder boasts a history museum, a racing facility, and a state park.

✳ To See

CULTURAL SITES 🏛 ⚑ **Brenau University Permanent Art Collection** (770-534-6263; www.brenau.edu), One Centennial Circle, Gainesville. Presidents and Sellars Galleries open 10–4 weekdays (until 6 Thursday), 2–5 Sunday; Castelli Gallery open 1–3 weekdays; guided tours of galleries by appointment. The college owns more than 1,000 pieces of original art donated by artists from all over the country in response to an ad placed in *Art in America* magazine. Paintings and other artwork can be found within the buildings, while outdoor sculptures are scattered across the campus. The Presidents Gallery is outside the balcony of Pearce Auditorium; the Sellars Gallery is in the Simmons Visual Arts Center; the Castelli Gallery is in the John S. Burd Center for the Performing Arts. The galleries also sponsor regional, national, and international art exhibits. Free.

🏛 ⚑ **Historic Buford–Tannery Row Artist Colony** (770-904-0572; www.TanneryRowArtistColony.com), 554 West Main Street, Building C, Buford. Hours vary; see below. Historic Buford stretches along Main Street from South Lee Street to Hill Street. The revitalized area boasts antiques shops, art galleries, and monthly arts events. The Tannery Row Artist Colony–Tannery Row Cultural Arts Center has a 13-acre facility in the former Bona Allen Shoe and Horse Collar Factory. Today, 17 artists—including glassblowers, jewelers, painters, photographers, sculptors, and woodcarvers—open their studios 11–9 Saturday to allow the public to view works in progress. Each month there is a festive opening reception 6–9 on the third Saturday for a show of an outstanding artist's work; studios are

FIRST FEMALE MAYOR IN GEORGIA

Alice H. Strickland (1861–1947) promised to clean up the city of Duluth and rid it of "demon rum." She allowed her home to be used as a hospital where children could have their tonsils removed and led conservation movements to protect forestlands. Her donation of an acre of land for a community forest was the first in the area.

open that evening as well. Each month's show can be viewed 1–5 Tuesday through Sunday in the Tannery Row Gallery.

♣ ♿ **Quinlan Visual Arts Center** (770-536-2575; www.quinlanartscenter.org), 514 Green Street NE, Gainesville. Open 9–5 weekdays, 10–4 Saturday, 1–4 Sunday. Located in the Green Street Historic District, this regional arts organization, housed in an imposing Italian Renaissance building, sponsors classes, workshops, and world-class exhibitions. The center owns more than 100 pieces in its permanent collection but also shows the work of emerging, midcareer, and master artists as well as traveling exhibits in its two galleries. Free.

♣ ♿ **Smithgall Arts Center** (770-534-2787; www.theartscouncil.net), 331 Spring Street SW, Gainesville. Open 8:30–5 weekdays. Call for a schedule of events. The arts center is housed in a restored 1914 passenger train depot located next to the downtown square. The depot itself is unusual in that it is the only two-story depot in northeast Georgia. Activities include art exhibitions, the Pearce Series of guest performers, evenings of jazz and theater, outdoor summer concerts, and more (see the **Arts Council** under *Entertainment*. Free.

FOR FAMILIES ✒ ♣ ♿ **Elachee Nature Science Center** (770-535-1976; www.elachee.org), 2125 Elachee Drive, Gainesville. Museum open 10–5 Monday through Saturday; trails open 8–dusk daily (except in extreme weather). The natural history museum and nature complex located in the 1,200-acre Chicopee Woods Nature Preserve features exhibits, live animals, a native plant garden, and 12 miles of hiking trails. The preserve is among the largest land trusts in north Georgia and one of the biggest within city limits east of the Mississippi River. The newest exhibit, "Waters of Time: the Chicopee Woods Story," features two authentic fossilized mosasaur skeletons. Highlights include a Dino Dig box with real fossils to find, a 1-ton petrified log to climb on, a fossil collection to make rubbings from, and goop with which to create forest animal tracks. Astronomy Hall acquaints visitors with the solar system, while a live animal room features fish, reptiles, and amphibians. Red-tailed hawks live in the aviary. Outside are native plant and rain demonstration gardens, a wheelchair-accessible path, a 1-mile loop trail along a gently flowing creek, and longer trails throughout pine forests, hardwood ridges, streams, and wetlands in the preserve. The nature center sponsors many special activities, including **First Quarter Moon Fridays, First Saturday Hikes, Elachee's Spring Bird Festival, Elachee's Annual Snake Day,** and **Elachee's NightFall Halloween Festival.** Museum admission: adults $3, children 2–12 $2; trails free; admission charged for most special events and festivals.

✒ ♣ **Interactive Neighborhood for Kids (INK)** (770-536-1900; www.inkfun.org), 203 Green Street, Gainesville. Open 10–5 Monday through Saturday. The children's museum contains hands-on interactive activities, including a dentist's office, Inkie's Market, Soda Pop's (a '50s diner), a bank, INK Clinic, a train depot, WINK radio station, and more. Guests up to 4 years old can enjoy Preschool Paradise, an area based on *Jack and the Beanstalk*. Not wheelchair accessible. Adults and children 2 and older $6.

✒ ♣ ♿ **Mayfield Dairy Farms** (706-654-9180; 1-888-298-0396; www.mayfielddairy.com), 1160 Broadway Avenue, Braselton. Visitor center open 9–5 weekdays, 9–2 Saturday; call for plant tour times. Begin at the visitor center to see a short film, then tour the milk-processing facility and finish up with an ice cream treat. Free.

HISTORIC HOMES AND SITES 🖉 ⚘ ⚓ **Banks County Historic Courthouse** (706-677-2108; 1-800-638-5004; www.bankscountyga.org), 106 Yonah Homer Road, Homer. Open 9–4 weekdays. One of the four oldest courthouses in Georgia, this one houses the chamber of commerce and the local **Historical Society Museum,** which features art, World War II memorabilia, collector items, and historical records. Free.

🖉 ⚘ ⚓ **Engine 209 Park,** Jesse Jewel Parkway, Gainesville. Open daily. Railroad buffs can examine two historic steam locomotives, the *Gainesville* and the *Midland 209,* as well a coal car and a caboose. The park also features gardens and benches. Free.

🖉 ⚘ ⚓ **Shields-Ethridge Heritage Farm** (706-367-2949; www.shieldsethridge farm.org), 2355 Ethridge Road, Jefferson. Open by appointment only except for special events. This outdoor historical agricultural museum allows visitors to see a blacksmith shop, cotton gin, gristmill, fully stocked commissary, 1900 schoolhouse, mule barn, and a wheat house—some still in use—as well as historic farm equipment. The farm was established by James Shields in 1799 and lived in by generations of the same family for 200 years. Many special events occur at the farm, including the annual **Mule Day,** which includes demonstrations of traditional farm equipment by the Georgia Old Time Plow Club. $5.

MUSEUMS 🖉 ⚘ ⚓ **Barrow County Museum** (770-307-1183), 74 West Athens Street, Winder. Open 1–4 weekdays, Saturday only for special events. The museum is housed in the old Barrow County Jail, which was built in 1915. Listed on the National Register of Historic Places, the building features the original "hanging tower" and three original jail cells. Hundreds of artifacts have been donated by local citizens and placed into exhibits relating to native son Senator Richard B. Russell, county history, and nearby Fort Yargo, which was created as a defense against hostile Indians. Free.

🖉 ⚘ ⚓ **Bete Todd Wages and Princess Lucie Shirazi Vintage Clothing Collections** (770-534-6244; 1-800-252-5119; www.brenau.edu), 406 Academy Street, Gainesville. Open 1–5 Saturday and Sunday. Apparel collections from the early 1880s to the 1960s are displayed in a Victorian-era cottage. Over her lifetime, Wages collected and repaired vintage clothing, eventually amassing 5,000 items. Special emphasis is given to clothing of the Victorian and Edwardian eras. Princess Lucie Jadot Shirazi was born in Belgium in 1908. She married Prince Ali Ahirazi Parvaz, the son of the Shah of Iran, in 1942 and became the sister-in-law of Rita Hayworth. Items of custom and couture apparel from her estate are on display, as are pieces of antique furniture. Free.

🖉 ⚘ ⚓ **Crawford W. Long Museum** (706-367-5307; www.crawfordlong.org), 28 College Street, Jefferson. Open 10–4 Tuesday through Saturday. Known as "the Birthplace of Anesthesia," the museum honors the doctor who performed the first painless surgery, on March 30, 1842, using ether for surgical anesthesia.

In the days when many doctors were self-trained or learned through an apprenticeship, Dr. Long was highly educated. He noticed that friends who were using ether for recreational purposes felt no pain from injuries sustained during their "frolics." He deduced ether could be used for painless surgery, and he was correct. The Medical Museum houses Long's personal artifacts, documents highlighting his life and work in pharmacology, and early anesthesia equipment. The antebellum Pendergrass Store Building houses a re-created 1840s doctor's office and apothecary shop, a replica of a 19th-century general store, and performance space for storytelling, live musical performances, and demonstrations. Outside, the Knot Garden features culinary and medicinal herbs. The Mulberry Tree museum shop carries works by local artisans, books, apparel, keepsakes, children's items, old-fashioned toys, herbal products, and regional souvenirs. The museum offers several history camps during the summer. Free; $1 donation requested.

✐ ❧ **Flowery Branch Historic Train Depot Museum and Historic Caboose** (770-967-6371; www.flowerybranchga.org), Railroad Avenue and Main Street, Flowery Branch. Open 10–1 Saturday. The 100-plus-year-old depot is typical of the Craftsman style. The museum houses exhibits, pictures, and documents relating to the city's history. The 1914 caboose is open to visitors as well, and a simulated railroad track walkway lies along the Railroad Avenue side of the building. Free.

✐ ❧ **Lanier Museum of Natural History** (770-932-4460; www.co.gwinnett.ga .us), 2601 Buford Dam Road, Buford. Open noon–5 Tuesday through Saturday. Among the museum's exhibits are live animals, replicated habitats, rocks, and fossils. Programs focus on gardening, animals, fossils, and environmental studies. $1.

✐ ❧ ♿ **Northeast Georgia History Center** (770-297-5900; www.negahc.org), 322 Academy Street, Gainesville. Open 10–4 Tuesday through Saturday, 1–4 Sunday. In addition to a display chronicling the history of the area, the museum includes a gallery dedicated to Ed Dodd, who created the *Mark Trail* environmental preservation comic strip; exhibits on black history, industrial history, and folk pottery; arts and crafts by north Georgians; the Northeast Georgia Sports Hall of Fame; an exhibit about Confederate General James Longstreet; and a separate railroad museum. Also on the grounds is **Chief White Path's Cabin,**

CHIEF WHITE PATH

Born in 1761, his Cherokee name, Nunna-tsune-ga, translates to "I dwell on the peaceful (or white) path." In 1814, White Path and a small band of Cherokee joined Andrew Jackson to fight the Creeks at the Battle of Horseshoe Bend in Alabama, where they were instrumental in ensuring victory by stealing the Creeks' canoes and cutting off their escape. Unfortunately, the Cherokee were repaid with Andrew Jackson's removal policies. In 1838, when White Path was 77, he helped organize the removal to the West that was later known as the Trail of Tears. White Path didn't make it to Oklahoma but died in Hopkinsville, Kentucky, where he is buried.

circa 1780, a typical Cherokee home. The cabin—originally a one-room dwelling with a loft—was built by White Path's parents in what is now Ellijay (see Cartersville chapter). When land and property were taken away from the Cherokee in 1832, the cabin was acquired by a settler family who added a dog-trot central hallway and another downstairs room, as well as continuing the loft into a full second story. The cabin was relocated here in 1995 with the help of Counte Cooley, a descendant of Chief White Path. Artifacts and authentic period furnishings in the cabin permit visitors to get a glimpse into what life was like for Native Americans and early white settlers in northeast Georgia. The site also features vegetable and herb gardens typical of a Cherokee home. Before leaving the museum, visitors can get information for a self-guided **Longstreet Tour.** General Longstreet, who was considered Robert E. Lee's right-hand man, retired to Gainesville after the war and ran a hotel for 20 years. He is buried in Gainesville at Alta Vista Cemetery. Adults $5, seniors $4, children $3.

🐾 ♿ **Southeastern Railway Museum** (770-476-2013; www.southeasternrailway museum.org), 3595 Peachtree Road, Duluth. Open April through December, 10–5 Thursday through Saturday, noon–5 Sunday of last full weekend of the month, except Christmas and New Year's days; January through March, 10–4 Saturday only. The 30-acre museum site, which is operated by volunteers of the Atlanta Chapter of the National Railway Historical Society and designated as Georgia's Official Transportation History Museum, is dedicated to preserving, restoring, and operating historically significant railway equipment. The chapter owns and displays 90 pieces of rolling stock, including wooden freight cars, vintage steam locomotives, Pullman cars, and maintenance-of-way equipment. Among the vintage cars are a 1910 steam locomotive; the 1911 private car

ONE OF THE TRAINS ON DISPLAY AT THE SOUTHEASTERN RAILWAY MUSEUM

Superb, which was used by President Warren G. Harding in 1923; and the *Washington Club,* a 1930 first-class lounge car. Also on display are a 1940s railway post office, a rare World War II troop kitchen, and a 1922 Pullman coach. The restored locomotive No. 97 pulls the caboose train on the third

> **NO FORKS ALLOWED**
> There is a city ordinance on the books in Gainesville forbidding the use of utensils when eating fried chicken.

Saturday of each month. At other times vintage diesels do the work. The museum sponsors several special events throughout the year, including **Romance on the Rails,** a Valentine's Day dinner; **Caboose Day** in March; and **Railfair** in September. Wheelchair accessibility to the building but not the rail cars. Adults $7, seniors $5 children 2–12 $4.

SPECIAL PLACES 🐾 🐔 ♿ **Poultry Park,** West Academy Street and Jesse Jewell Parkway, Gainesville. The statue of the rooster is a tribute to the poultry industry, which has earned Gainesville the title "Poultry Capital of the World."

✳ To Do

AUTO RACING 🐾 ♿ **Atlanta Dragway** (706-335-2301; 770-682-3782; www.atlantadragway.com), 500 East Ridgeway Road, Commerce. The National Hot Rod Association Power Aid drag-racing facility is the home of the Southern Nationals each May. Call for a schedule of events and ticket prices.

🐾 ♿ **Lanier National Speedway** (770-967-8600; www.lanierspeedway.com), One Raceway Drive, Braselton. Races every Saturday evening, March through October. Georgia's only NASCAR asphalt short track features stock-car races. The speedway hosts 2,500 spectators and 100 competitors every week, with racers coming from all over the Southeast to compete for NASCAR points. Major events include the Southern All Star Stock Car Racing Series, USCS Outlaw Thunder Sprint Cars, ASA Racing Series, and NASCAR All Pro 200. The track offers spectators grandstand seating, track-side parking, and VIP suites. Call for a schedule of events and ticket prices.

🐾 ♿ **Peach State Speedway** (706-387-7490; www.peachstspeedway.com), 388 Lyle Field Road, Jefferson. Among the events held here are the Hooters Pro Cup and Georgia Asphalt Series. Call for a schedule of events and ticket prices.

🐾 ♿ **Road Atlanta** (770-967-6143; 1-800-849-RACE; www.roadatlanta.com), 5300 Winder Highway, Braselton. The area's premier road-racing facility, Road Atlanta features one of the most challenging and exciting racetracks in the country. The 2.54-mile, 12-turn Grand Prix road course, which is home to the American LeMans Series and Panoz Motorsports, hosts internationally acclaimed events such as the Suzuki American Motorcycle Association Superbikes Showdown, Sports Car Club of America Trans Am Southern Dash, and Petit LeMans. Other attractions include professional and amateur auto and motorcycle races, Panoz Racing School, Audi Driving Experience, Audi Teen Driving Experience, Kevin Schwartz Suzuki School, and testing for professional and amateur racing teams. Limited camping is available in the infield for all races; reservations are required. Prebooked hot laps are available to the public. Call for a schedule of events and ticket prices. Parking free for most events; fee for infield parking.

BICYCLING ✔ **The Bike Center at Chateau Elan Winery and Resort** (678-425-6095; www.chateauelanatlanta.com/amenities/bike-trails.html), 100 Rue Charlemagne, Braselton. Open 9–5 Sunday through Thursday, 9–6 Friday and Saturday. Seven miles of trails meander through the 3,500-acre property through wooded areas, quiet nature paths, around the equestrian center, past the vine-yards, along the championship golf courses, and through the exclusive residential area. Bikes, many of them Mountain Comfort models, can be rented at the Bike Depot at the **Stan Smith Tennis Center** (see *Tennis*). Some spa packages include complimentary use of bicycles. Bike rental $20 for two hours for inn guests; nonresidents with their own bikes pay $10 trail maintenance fee.

BIRDING See **Chattahoochee-Oconee National Forest** and **Fort Yargo State Park** under *Green Space—Nature Preserves and Parks.*

BOATING ✔ ♿ **Aqualand Marina** (770-967-6811; www.flagshipmarinas.com/marinas/aqualand/default.htm), 6800 Lights Ferry Road, Flowery Branch. Open 8:30–5:30 daily. The full-service marina offers a fuel dock, pump-out facilities, boat docks, shower and bath facilities, and a fully stocked store. The Windsong Sailing Academy is based here, and visitors can enjoy a meal at the Dockside Grill. Jet Ski and boat rentals are available. Call for rates.

✔ ♿ **Gainesville Marina** (770-536-2171; www.gainesvillemarina.com), 2145 Dawsonville Highway, Gainesville. Open 8–5 weekdays, 9–5 weekends (until 6 Memorial Day through Labor Day). The full-service marina sells new and used boats, provides wet and dry storage and Jet Ski storage, supplies parts and gas, and has a pump-out station, bathhouse, and Skogie's Restaurant.

✔ ♿ **Harbor Landing Marina** (770-932-7255; www.lakelanierislands.com/harbor), 7000 Holiday Road, Lake Lanier Islands. With more than 90 rental boats, Harbor Landing offers the largest fleet on the lake. Choose from ski or pontoon boats or a houseboat (see *Lodging—Other Lodgings*). Call for rates, as they vary widely by type of boat and length of rental; cheapest two-hour rental $109.

✔ ♿ **Holiday Marina on Lake Lanier** (770-945-7201; www.westrec.com/lake lanier.html), 6900 Holiday Road, Buford. Open 8–5 daily. The full-service marina offers boat and Jet Ski rentals and also offers bathhouses and laundry facilities. The surrounding property features rental cabins and restaurants. Call for rates.

FISHING Lake Lanier is noted for its black, spotted, and largemouth bass. The striped bass, which is normally found in salt water, is stocked by the Georgia Department of Natural Resources and has adapted well.

✔ **Harold Nash Lake Lanier Striper and Bass Fishing Guide Service** (770-967-6582; www.lanierfishingguide.com), 5931 Nacoochee Trail, Flowery Branch. The guide service specializes in trophy angling for giant stripers and bass. Call for schedules and fees.

FAMILIES CAN RENT BOATS AT LAKE LANIER ISLANDS AND VARIOUS MARINAS ON THE LAKE.

✐ **Larry's Lanier Guide Services** (770-842-0976; 770-844-0976, www.lanierguide.com), 8850 Bay Drive, Gainesville. Services are offered to novice anglers and pros. Call for a schedule and fees.

FLYING ✐ Lanier Flight Center (678-989-2395; www.lanierflightcenter.com), 1115 Aviation Way, Gainesville. Sight-seeing tours by air over Lake Lanier and the north Georgia mountains are available, as are flying lessons. Call for hours and fees.

FOR FAMILIES ✐ ✤ ♿ Atlanta Falcons Headquarters and Training Facility (770-965-3115; 1-800-241-3489; www.atlantafalcons.com), 4400 Falcons Parkway, Flowery Branch. Call for hours. Fans can watch practices, participate in interactive games, get autographs from players, and tour the Mobile Museum. Housed in two trailer rigs, the facility's interactive museum chronicles the team's history with videos, photos, replica lockers, and more. Special activities for children include Junior Falcons Training Camp; punt, pass, and kick competitions; and appearances by the team's mascot, Freddie Falcon. Fans can purchase team memorabilia and collectibles at the store. Free; off-site parking $5.

✐ ✤ ♿ **Lake Lanier Islands** (770-932-7200; 1-800-840-5253; www.lakelanierislands.com), 7000 Holiday Road, Lake Lanier Islands. This 1,100-acre area on the southernmost shores of Lake Sidney Lanier is a not only a year-round vacation destination but also the most heavily visited water recreation area in the country. Facilities include two luxury hotels, lake house rentals, and lakeside camping as well as two par-72 golf courses, tennis, horseback riding, boat rentals, and a beach and water park (see next entry). Entrance fee $7 per car.

✐ ♿ **Lake Lanier Islands Beach and Waterpark** (770-932-7200; 1-800-840-LAKE; www.lakelanierislands.com/water), 6950 Holiday Road, Buford. Open weekends in May; 10–6 Sunday through Friday, 10–7 Saturday daily late May through early August; weekends only through late September. Located right on the lake, this exciting water park has 12 thrilling water attractions, including Wild Waves, the state's largest wave pool. The small fry enjoy Kiddie Lagoon and Wiggle Waves. The park also boasts a mile-long sandy white beach, beach volleyball, and concessions. Sometimes there are concerts by popular groups. Adults $26.99, children $16.99.

GOLF Chateau Elan Golf Courses (678-425-6050; 1-800-233-9463; www .chateauelanatlanta.com/golf), 6060 Golf Club Drive, Braselton. Open 7:30–dusk. So passionate about golf is Chateau Elan Resort that it has four golf courses: two public 18-hole courses—both of which are rated as among the top four courses in Georgia by the ESPN Zagat Survey; a nine-hole, par-3 executive walking course; and a private course. The public **Chateau Course** is 7,030 yards, par 71, with contoured fairways, three lakes, and two streams. Water comes into play on 10 holes. The public **Woodlands Course** is considered to be the most picturesque of the resort's courses. The 6,735-yard, par-72 course has numerous elevations, lakes, and tree-lined holes. The executive walking course behind the inn is the perfect venue for the golfer without a lot of time, for beginners, or for children. Holes vary in length from less than 100 yards to more than 200 yards. Amenities within the golf complex include clubhouses with restaurants and pro shops at the Chateau and Woodlands courses. Accommodations are available in two- or three-bedroom golf villas in addition to the inn or the spa (see *Lodging*). The practice facility, which has one of the highest ratings in the state, is the home of the **Golf Academy at Chateau Elan.** The program includes comprehensive practice facilities, highly skilled instructors, and video and computer analysis. There is a driving range, short game area, and putting green. $65 Monday through Thursday, $85 Friday through Sunday.

Emerald Pointe Golf Club (770-945-8789; www.lakelanierislands.com/golf), 7000 Holiday Road, Lake Lanier Islands. Open 7:10–5:30 daily. This award-winning, 18-hole, par-72 course boasts 18 holes with dazzling water views of Lake Lanier. The course features instruction, a pro shop, and the Golf Club Grille. $67 Monday through Thursday, $78 Friday through Sunday.

PineIsle Golf Course (1-800-840-5253; www.lakelanierislands.com), 9000 Holiday Road, Lake Lanier Islands. Open 8–dusk weekdays, 7:30–dusk weekends. The 18-hole, 6,596-yard, par-72 resort course designed by Gary Player has numerous holes with lake views. The facility features rentals, lessons, a driving range, putting green, pro shop, and a clubhouse with a restaurant. $49 weekdays, $64 weekends; tee times and lessons should be booked in advance.

See also Golf Appendix.

HORSEBACK RIDING ✔ **Lake Lanier Islands Equestrian Center** (770-932-7233; www.lakelanierislands.com/horse), 7000 Holiday Road, Lake Lanier Islands. Open 10–6 daily; reservations recommended. Saddle up on one of the island's gentle horses for a scenic guided trail ride through the woods and along the lakeshore. Pony rides are available for children 6 and younger. Individual and group western or English lessons are also available. $35 for 45-minute scenic trail ride, $15 for 30-minute pony ride, $25 for half-hour lesson, $40 for hour lesson.

MINIATURE GOLF ✔ 🍴 ♿ **Fort Yargo State Park and Will-A-Way Recreation Area** (770-867-3489; 1-800-864-7275; www.gastateparks.org/info/ftyargo), GA 81, Winder. Open 7 AM–10 PM. See *Green Space—Nature Preserves & Parks.*

✔ 🍴 ♿ **The Oaks Miniature Golf** (770-534-4386; www.oaksminiaturegolf.com), 3709 Whiting Road, Gainesville. Open 11–10 daily. The Oaks is the only mini golf course in the world that immerses visitors in the native environment—the oak-hickory forest of the Georgia Piedmont. The course is also the only one ever to win a design award from the American Society of Landscape Architects for environmental responsibility. There are no windmills or elephants, only a subtle nature theme with native Georgia plants. Until 5 PM: adults $6.25, children $5.25; after 5 PM: $5.

SAILING **Lanier Sailing Academy** (770-945-8810; 1-800-684-9463; www.laniersail.com), 6920 Holiday Road, Buford. Open 9–6 daily. One of the top American Sailing Association schools, the academy offers sailing classes from practical sailing to offshore passage and also provides the largest sailboat rental fleet on Lake Lanier. Call for prices.

SPAS **Great Restorations Day Spa** (770-945-8787, Ext. 6902; www.lakelanierislands.com/accommodations/spa.asp), 7000 Holiday Road, Lake Lanier Islands. Open 10:30–5 daily. Located at the **Emerald Pointe Resort** (see *Lodging—Inns & Resorts*), the spa offers numerous ways to relax and fortify the mind, body, and spirit, including six types of massage and a wide array of body treatments, facials, manicures, pedicures, and hair services. $40–265.

The Healing Arts Spa on Green Street (678-450-1570; www.spaongreenstreet.com), 635 Green Street, Gainesville. Open 10–7 Monday through Saturday (last appointment at 5:30). Located in the beautiful and historic Dunlap House, a Colonial Revival home that until recently was an upscale bed & breakfast, the spa does bioenergetic assessment, acupuncture, massage, body treatments, and skin care. $30–150.

The Spa at Chateau Elan Winery and Resort (1-800-233-WINE; www.chateauelanatlanta.com/spa), 100 Rue Charlemagne, Braselton. Open 9–5 weekdays; weekend appointments as early as 7 AM. Indulgences at the serene and romantic spa are guaranteed to make you feel renewed. Located beside a sparkling lake surrounded by trees, manicured green lawns, and flowering shrubs, the spa is contained within a French country–style spa inn, which also offers unique accommodations (see *Lodging*) and healthful gourmet dining for breakfast, lunch, and dinner at the sunny Fleur-de-lis restaurant. Spa treatments are available à la carte or may be purchased as an overnight package with accommodations at the inn. All-day or overnight spa packages include use of the steam room, sauna, whirlpool, indoor resistance pool, and fitness area, plus classes, a spa lunch, afternoon tea, and a tour of the winery; some overnight packages include other meals as well. The fitness room, which is open 24/7, features a variety of health and fitness equipment. The spa also offers the **LOTUSEA Wellness Program,** which includes a personal health assessment, comprehensive lab testing, classes, and spa amenities. Spa services $42–235; wellness program $200–300.

SPORTING EVENTS ♿ **Chicopee Woods Agricultural Center** (770-531-6855; www.hallcounty.org/parks), 1855 Calvary Church Road, Gainesville. Office open 8–5 weekdays. All kinds of events occur here, including equestrian competitions, rodeos, animal expositions, mountain bike races, archery competitions, and festivals. Call for a schedule of events and ticket prices.

Clarks Bridge Park Olympic Center (770-287-7888; www.lckc.org), 3105 Clarks Bridge Road, Gainesville. Call for a schedule of events and ticket prices. Once the site of the 1996 Centennial Olympic Summer Games' rowing, sprint canoe, and kayak events and the Lanier Canoe 2003 World Championships, the facility has a state-of-the-art finish tower and a unique race course that shelters paddlers from wind and provides clean water year-round. The center provides a permanent facility for two sports and still sponsors national and international canoe, kayak, and rowing events throughout the year. Canoe and kayak rentals are available and there is also a beach and boat ramp.

✇ ও **The Equestrian Center at Chateau Elan** (770-307-3786; www.chateaue-lanatlanta.com/amenities/equestrian.html), 100 Rue Charlemagne, Braselton. With a covered and lighted arena, four large and lighted all-weather rings, two smaller warm-up areas, 196 permanent stalls, and room for 200 temporary stalls, the center is the site of many equestrian and canine shows throughout the year. Concerts, arts and crafts shows, and car shows also are held here. Call for a schedule of events and ticket prices.

See also **Lake Lanier Islands** under *To Do—For Families.*

TENNIS Stan Smith Tennis Center at Chateau Elan Winery and Resort (678-425-60965; www.chateauelanatlanta.com/amenities/tennis/html), 100 Rue Charlemagne, Braselton. Open spring through fall, 9–6 Friday and Saturday, 9–5 Sunday and Tuesday through Thursday; call for winter hours. The center, designed by tennis legend Stan Smith, boasts three clay courts and four hard courts, all lighted for night play. Tennis packages include accommodations at the inn, breakfast in the Versailles Room, a one-hour tennis lesson, two hours of court time, a half-hour use of the ball machine, and use of the spa facilities (fitness room, whirlpool, and resistance pool); spa services are extra. Court use for guests $14; half-hour private lesson $23; packages $215–$315.

WALKING TOURS ✇ ✆ ও **Solar System Tour: Gainesville Scale-Model Walking Tour of Our Solar System** (contact North Georgia Astronomers: scalemodel@northgeorgiaastronomers.org). The 1.8-mile tour takes visitors from the sun, on the square, down to Pluto, on Lake Lanier. Ask for a brochure.

WINERY TOURS Chateau Elan Winery and Resort (678-425-0900; 1-800-233-WINE; www.chateauelanatlanta.com), 100 Rue Charlemagne, Braselton. Open 10–9 daily. Housed in a replica of a 16th-century-style French chateau that rises out of a northeast Georgia field filled with grapevines, this full-production winery is the largest producer of premium wines in Georgia. Approximately 75 acres are planted with *vinifera* French and French-American hybrid grapes from which 22 wines are produced. Wine tours of the operation are offered and culminate with a tasting of several varieties. The winery building also houses two restaurants, an art gallery, and a shop. Free.

Naturally, after touring the winery and tasting some of its vintages, visitors may wish to take some home. **The Wine Market** (ext. 6354), located just adjacent to the tasting room, sells Chateau Elan wines and a wide variety of wine-related gifts as well as Irish crystal, quality golf shirts with the Chateau logo, custom-made gift baskets, and other unique gift items. The **Art Gallery** located in the Chateau Elan Winery, showcases artists working in a wide variety of media; open 10–9 daily. **Le Clos** (see *Where to Eat—Dining Out*) is the winery's fine dining restaurant. The informal, bistro-style **Café Elan** (ext. 6317) has the cozy ambience of a provincial European restaurant where chefs create Mediterranean dishes. Open 11–4 and 5–10 daily; reservations recommended.

✳ Green Space

BEACHES See **Lake Lanier Islands Beach** and Waterpark under *To Do—For Families.*

LAKES **Lake Lanier** is a water-lover's paradise. The huge lake is 26 miles long, covers 38,000 acres, has 540 miles of shoreline, and touches five counties. It offers many water sports and other outdoor recreation. (See *To Do—Boating, Fishing, Flying, For Families, Golf, Horseback Riding, Sailing, Lodging, Campgrounds, Cottages and Villas, Inns and Resorts,* and *Other Lodgings.*)

NATURE PRESERVES AND PARKS 🐾
🦌 **Chattahoochee-Oconee National Forest** (770-297-3000; www.fs.fed.us/conf), 1755 Cleveland Highway, Gainesville. Office open 8–4:30 weekdays; park open daylight hours daily. The vast forest offers opportunities for bird-watching and wildlife observation, camping, fishing, hiking, horseback riding (BYOH—bring your own horse), photography, and riding off-road vehicles. Call or check the web site for specifics, including fees.

🐾 🦌 ♿ **Elachee Nature Preserve** (770-535-1976; www.hallcounty.org/parks), 2125 Elachee Drive, Gainesville. Open 8–dusk daily. *Elachee* is the Cherokee word for "new green earth." The 1,200-acre nature preserve features **Elachee Nature Science Center** (see *To See—For Families*), botanical gardens, nature trails, special programs, and tours. Use of the trails free; admission fee for museum.

THE CHATEAU ELAN WINERY AND RESORT

🖉 🏵 ♿ **Fort Yargo State Park and Will-A-Way Recreation Area** (770-867-3489; 1-800-864-7275; www.gastateparks.org/info/ftyargo), GA 81, Winder. Open 7 AM–10 PM daily. Named for a 1792 log fort built by early settlers as protection against Creek and Cherokee Indians, the 1,814-acre park offers camping and cottages (see *Lodging*), the 260-acre Marbury Creek Reservoir with a swimming beach and boat rentals, 8 miles of hiking and biking trails along the lakeshore, picnicking, and mini golf (see *To Do—Miniature Golf*). Other recreational amenities include boat ramps; seasonal canoe, fishing, and pedal-boat rentals; and tennis courts. The Will-A-Way Recreation Area was specifically designed for challenged populations, so most facilities in the park are wheelchair accessible. Parking $3.

🖉 🏵 ♿ **Hurricane Shoals Park** (706-652-2370), 416 Hurricane Shoals Road, Maysville. Open daylight hours daily. The wooded park is named for the shoals that are popular for swimming and wading. Alongside the stream is an old gristmill, and a heritage village is being developed around it. Other features include a playground and an amphitheater. The **Art in the Park** arts festival is held here in September. Free.

✴ Lodging

BED & BREAKFASTS

In Commerce
🏵 **Harber House Inn** (706-335-9388; 1-877-226-9886; www.harberhouseinn.com), 2280 North Broad Street. Located on 2 acres of rolling hills and walnut, oak, and pecan trees, the graceful 19th-century home features a wraparound porch and fluted Greek Revival columns. The house is named for the Harber family, who lived here for 50 years. Inside, the home is distinguished by 12-foot ceilings, hardwood floors, and floated-glass bow windows. Four individually decorated, antique-filled guest rooms have either one or two double beds. There are two bathrooms, so you may have to share. A hearty full breakfast is included. Special event weekends at nearby University of Georgia, Atlanta Dragway, Atlanta Motor Speedway, Road Atlanta, or Lanier Raceway require reservations and payment 14 days in advance. No smoking. Not wheelchair accessible. $70–$85; checks or cash only.

In Flowery Branch
🖉 🏵 ♿ **Whitworth Inn** (770-967-2386; www.whitworthinn.com), 6593 McEver Road. With its columns and verandas on both floors, the inn looks like a gracious Southern mansion of old, but it was actually built to serve as a bed & breakfast. Ten rooms with private baths are individually decorated to create distinct personalities. Some feature four-poster beds; one has two double beds. A full breakfast is included. No smoking. One room wheelchair accessible. $59–$69.

CAMPGROUNDS

In Buford
🖉 🏵 **Shoal Creek Campground-COE** (770-945-9541; 1-877-444-6777; www.reserveusa.com), 6300 Shadburn Ferry Road. Open April through early October. The U.S. Army Corps of Engineers campground features more than 100 sites with water and electric hookups on Lake Lanier. Amenities

include hot showers, laundry facilities, a boat ramp, playground, dump station, and swimming area. $16–22; reservations must be made two days in advance; two-night minimum on weekends, three-night minimum on holidays.

In Gainesville

🪝 🐾 ♿ **River Forks Park** (770-531-3952; www.hallcounty.org/parks), 3500 Keith Bridge Road. Open March 1 through December 31. The park offers 63 campsites with water and electric hookups, a bathhouse with showers, rest rooms, and a pump-out station, as well as all the facilities of the park. Campsites $20, seniors $15.

At Lake Lanier Islands

🪝 🐾 **Lake Lanier Islands Campground** (1-800-840-LAKE; www.lakelanierislands.com/accommodations/campground.asp), 7000 Holiday Road. The campground offers 300 year-round sites, a fishing pier, pavilion, and camp store. $21–39.

In Winder

🪝 🐾 🐾 ♿ **Fort Yargo State Park and Will-A-Way Recreation Area** (770-867-3489; 1-800-864-7275; www.gastateparks.org/info/ftyargo), GA 81. The park offers 40 tent, trailer, and RV sites; seven walk-in sites; a pioneer campground ($30); and a group camp that sleeps 250. $8–21.

COTTAGES AND CABINS

In Braselton

🪝 ♿ **The Golf Villas at Chateau Elan Winery and Resort** (1-800-233-WINE; www.chateauelanatlanta.com/golf/villas.html), 100 Rue Charlemagne. The villas are located on the 15th fairway of the Chateau Course and within walking distance of the pro shop and Clubhouse Grille (see *To*

Do—Golf). Each villa has two or three bedrooms and baths, a large open plan, a fully equipped kitchen, and a living room with a fireplace. Golf packages include accommodations, breakfast, and one round of golf on the Chateau or Woodlands course. $224–299.

At Lake Lanier Islands

🪝 **The Lake Houses on Lanier** (770-932-7275; 1-800-768-LAKE; www.lakelanierislands.com/accommodations/lakehouses.asp), 7000 Holiday Road. The waterfront New England–style cottages are nestled among towering pines. Each cottage offers two bedrooms and baths, a great room with a fireplace, high-speed Internet access, a washer and dryer, and modern kitchen. Outside on the deck guests will find a gas grill and a heated spa. $259 off-season, $339 in-season.

In Winder

🪝 🐾 🐾 ♿ **Fort Yargo State Park and Will-A-Way Recreation Area** (770-867-3489; 1-800-864-7275; www.gastateparks.org/info/ftyargo), GA 81. The park features three fully equipped cottages. $70–80.

INNS AND RESORTS

In Braselton

🪝 ♿ **The Inn at Chateau Elan Winery and Resort** (678-425-0900; 1-800-233-WINE; www.chateauelanatlanta.com), 100 Rue Charlemagne. The four-star, four-diamond property is truly a resort in every sense of the word, with multitudinous offerings in addition to exquisite guest accommodations. The property, located on the site of a winery, is the flagship of Chateau Elan Hotels and Resorts, a group of luxury properties in the United States and overseas. The

French country chateau–style inn features 277 deluxe guest rooms, including 20 suites, a presidential suite, and 17 wheelchair-accessible rooms. Each guest accommodation boasts all the modern amenities along with a luxurious bath with an oversized tub and separate shower. The inn also features the **Versailles** restaurant, which serves breakfast and lunch buffets and à la carte dinners daily; **L'Auberge** lounge with large-screen televisions, championship-size pool tables, light foods, and live entertainment on Friday and Saturday evenings; a swimming pool; and a conference center. The centerpiece of the resort is the winery (see *To Do—Winery Tours*). The resort also boasts accommodations at the spa (see next entry) and in golf villas (see *Cottages and Cabins*); several golf courses and a golf academy (see *To Do—Golf*); a spa (see *To Do—Spas*); several other restaurants and an Irish pub (see *Where to Eat— Eating Out*); a beauty salon; a fitness room; walking/biking trails and bike rentals (see *To Do—Bicycling*); a tennis center (see *Tennis*); and an equestrian center (see *To Do—Sporting Events*). $209–259.

& **Spa Suites at Chateau Elan Winery and Resort** (678-425-0900; 1-800-233-WINE; www.chateauelan atlanta.com/spa/spa-suites.html), 100 Rue Charlemagne. Located in a separate building from the main inn, the 14 luxurious spa suites exude style and comfort. Each is unique and has a separate mood, among them country French, Victorian wicker, high-tech, Zimbabwe, Oriental, Greek, Gatsby, art deco, fox hunt, Bacchus, and celebration, which has a bright-red pedestal bathtub. $199–274 without Jacuzzi; $224–299 with Jacuzzi.

At Lake Lanier Islands

✋ & **Emerald Pointe Resort** (770-945-8787; www.lakelanierislands.com/ accommodations/emerald.asp), 7000 Holiday Road. The centerpiece of Lake Lanier Islands is the resort hotel, which features 216 guest rooms and suites—many with lake views, high-speed Internet access, and spa services (see **Great Restorations Day Spa** under *To Do—Spas*). The resort has two restaurants: **Windows Restaurant,** open for a breakfast buffet daily as well as special events such as monthly wine-tasting dinners and a summertime seafood buffet; and **Bullfrog's Bar and Grille,** a publike eatery serving lunch and dinner daily. Diners can eat inside or poolside. The resort also offers a championship 18-hole golf course (see *To Do—Golf*), horseback riding (see *To Do—Horseback Riding*), a summertime beach and water park (see *To Do—For Families*), a fleet of rental boats (see *To Do— Boating*), tennis courts, a swimming pool, fitness center, gift shop, business center, and jogging trails. Girlfriends who travel together will enjoy the Girls' Getaway Package, which includes accommodations, massage, and breakfast. $139 in-season, $119 off-season.

OTHER LODGINGS

At Lake Lanier Islands

✋ & **Harbor Landings Houseboats** (1-800-840-LAKE; www.lakelanier islands.com/accommodations/house boats.asp), 7000 Holiday Road. Get away from it all with one of these luxurious, climate-controlled houseboats, which sleep 10 and include a full kitchen, bathrooms, a gas grill, water-slide from the upper deck, and a heated spa. Boats can be rented for three, four, or seven days. $1,899 for three-day weekend rental in-season (Memorial Day to Labor Day), $1,299 off-season; $1,799 for four-day weekday rental in-season, $1,099 off-season; $2,399 for week in-season, $1,699 off-season.

✳ Where to Eat

DINING OUT

In Braselton

& **Le Clos at Chateau Elan Winery and Resort** (678-425-0900, ext. 6317; 1-800-233-WINE; www.chateau elanatlanta.com/dining/leclos-.html), 100 Rue Charlemagne. Open 6–9 Thursday through Sunday; reservations and semiformal attire required. The intimate fine dining room resembles a Mediterranean courtyard. In this setting, seasonal French classic cuisine with American influence is served. Plan to make an evening of it, because the five-course prix-fixe dinner typically takes up to 2½ hours to complete. The staff will recommend two, three, or five wine pairings to accompany the meal for an additional charge, or diners may purchase wine by the bottle. The wine tastings (see *To Do—Winery Tours*) feature Chateau Elan's Georgia Founders Reserve wines. No smoking. Wheelchair accessible. Prix fixe $65, plus wine pairings. $14.50–35.

In Buford

✐ & **Sunday Brunch at Bona Allen Mansion** (770-271-7637; www .turner-events.com), 395 East Main Street. Brunch served nine times yearly; call for schedule. Reservations required. The lavish buffet features a delicious array of regional dishes. Ham, chicken, eggs, and crab are often accompanied by sides such as three-cheese grits, French toast soufflé, salads, fruits, breads, and desserts. The menu changes monthly to take advantage of seasonal delicacies. The grand Italianate-style mansion was

HOUSEBOATS ARE A UNIQUE WAY TO STAY AT LAKE LANIER ISLANDS.

built in 1911 by a local magnate who employed two-thirds of the town's population. Enjoy the 12-foot ceilings, original carved wood paneling, intricate moldings, stained-glass windows, seven fireplaces, and original Italian mural. After dining, stroll through the 6 acres of gardens and manicured lawns punctuated by ancient magnolias, dogwoods, and mighty oaks. The terraced garden provides a flamboyant array of color from spring through fall. Daylilies, gladiolas, roses, spireas, verbena, butterfly bushes, and azaleas are just a few of the blooming plants. Adults $18.50, children 3–10 $11.

In Gainesville

&. **The Bistro at the Boiler Room** (678-450-0115; www.boilerroom.org), 212 Spring Street SW. Open 5–10 Tuesday through Saturday. The full-service restaurant attached to the Boiler Room nightclub offers seafood, hand-cut steaks, chicken, specialty pasta dishes, and signature handmade ice cream desserts. Entertainment nightly in the nightclub (see *Entertainment—Nightlife*). No smoking. Wheelchair accessible. $7–24.

&. **Hudson Steam House** (770-287-1777; www.hudsonsteamhouse.com), 200 Washington Street SW. Open 11–10 Monday through Wednesday, 11–11 Thursday through Saturday. Seafood leads the menu, which includes oysters, shellfish, fish-and-chips, peel-and-eat shrimp, ahi tuna, crabcakes, salmon, and crab legs, but a diner also can get jambalaya, steaks, and surf and turf. No smoking. Wheelchair accessible. $12.95–26.95.

&. **Luna's Restaurant and Piano Lounge** (770-531-0848; www.lunas.com), 200 Main Street. Open 11–2 and 5–10 weekdays, 4–11 Saturday. Located on the ground level of the

Hunt Tower, Luna's offers American-continental fine dining. An intimate romantic ambience is created by wall murals, crisp white table linens, candlelight, and soothing music. Luncheon items include salads, sandwiches, and pastas. Dinner items include steaks, seafood, lamb, chicken, and pork selections. Thursday through Saturday nights, the lounge, with its grand piano and fireplace, offers music, drinks, and cigars. No smoking. Wheelchair accessible. Lunch $7.95–12.95, dinner $12.95–22.95.

&. **Rudolph's Restaurant** (770-534-2226; www.rudolphsdining.com), 700 Green Street. Open 11:30–2 Tuesday through Friday; 5:30–9 Monday through Thursday, 5:30–10 Friday and Saturday; 11:30–2 Sunday for brunch. Continental fine dining is available at elegant and sophisticated Rudolph's, which is housed in the historic 1915 Dixon-Rudolph House. Lunch choices include soups, salads, sandwiches, and entrées such as fish and steak. Dinner choices include steak, fish, lamb, pork, and chicken. The Attic Piano Lounge is open 5:30–10 Friday and Saturday nights for drinks and live entertainment. No smoking. Wheelchair accessible. Lunch and brunch $4.25–16, dinner $14–23.

&. **Tea Tyme Restaurant** (678-450-5770; www.tea-tymedine.com), 110 Main Street. Open 11:30–2:30 and 5:30 until close Tuesday through Saturday. Tea Tyme offers fine dining on the square with cuisine described as New World with the flavors of Europe. Lunch choices include soups, salads, burgers, blue plate specials, calve's liver, and other daily specials. Dinner choices include seafood, chicken, pork, duck, schnitzels, steak, and prime rib. Live music is often offered on weekends, and co-owner Harold Link's art is on display. No smoking. Wheelchair accessible. Lunch $6.99–9.95, dinner $17.99–25.99.

In Jefferson

&. **The Carriage House** (706-367-1989), 1235 Athens Street. Open 11–2:30 weekdays; 5–9 Tuesday through Thursday, 5–10 Friday and Saturday. Operated under the banner of Chateau Elan Winery and Resort, the upscale restaurant is located in a magnificently restored 1886 Victorian-era cottage in what will be the Jefferson Equestrian Estates residential and resort community. The original 1885 plans were for it to be a very large home, but limited funds resulted in a quaint, two-story cottage. Today it is sheltered by mature oaks, locusts, cherries, pines, and poplars. American regional cuisine is served in the Cameo Room, named for an antique alabaster cameo mounted on a wooden plaque near the door, as well as several other intimate dining rooms. No smoking. Wheelchair accessible. Lunch $4.50–9.50, dinner $14.75–29.

EATING OUT

In Braselton

&. **Paddy's Irish Pub at Chateau Elan Winery and Resort** (678-425-0900, ext. 6074; www.chateauelan atlanta.com/dining/paddys-.html), 100 Rue Charlemagne. Open 2–midnight weekdays, noon–1 AM Saturday, 12:30–midnight Sunday. All the fixtures and furnishings at Paddy's are completely authentic, created in Ireland, shipped to the resort, and then reassembled. The pub serves traditional Irish food and beverages and provides Irish music and song on Fri-

day and Saturday evenings beginning at 8:30. Wednesday is open mic night. No smoking. Wheelchair accessible. $9.95–22.95.

In Duluth

&. **Park Café** (678-473-0071; www .parkcafe-duluth.com), 3579 West Lawrenceville Street. Open 11–3 Monday through Saturday; 5–9 Wednesday and Thursday, 5–10 Friday and Saturday; 10–3 Sunday for brunch. Reservations suggested but not required. In this quaint, relaxing restaurant, diners can enjoy casual American dining with a Southern flair. Located in a 106-year-old house overlooking the town green, the eatery serves lunch, dinner, and brunch. There are chef specials almost every evening, special menus to accommodate theater-goers on their way to a production at the **Aurora Theater,** and wine tastings at 6:30 every Wednesday. Dinner entrées include seafood, steaks, salads, and Southern favorites. Some diners prefer the patio, which is enclosed and heated in winter. The café's market sells wine, cheese, gourmet food items, and gift baskets. No smoking. Wheelchair accessible. Brunch $6.25–6.95, lunch $6.50–10.95, dinner $8.95–25.95.

At Lake Lanier Islands
See **Windows** and **Bullfrog's Bar and Grille** at **Emerald Pointe Resort** under Lodging—Inns and Resorts.

SNACKS

In Duluth
&. **The Soda Shop** (678-417-6600; www.TheSodaShopDeli.com), 3122 Hill Street. Open 10:30–9 Monday through Saturday, noon–8 Sunday. This old-fashioned deli on the town

green serves hot and cold sandwiches, soups, and salads, as well as hand-dipped ice cream, milk shakes, sundaes, and sodas. Pizza is available after 4 PM. No smoking. Wheelchair accessible. $4.99–6.99.

✳ Entertainment

The Arts Council (770-534-2787; www.theartscouncil.net), 331 Spring Street SW, Gainesville. The council represents various art forms and sponsors the Pearce Series, Evenings of Intimate Jazz, the outdoor Summer MusicFest, Theatre at the Depot, and numerous other events (see **Smithgall Arts Center** under *Cultural Sites*).

🖉 ♿ **Georgia Mountains Center** (770-534-8420; www.georgiamoun tainscenter.com), 301 Main Street SW, Gainesville. Box office open 8–5 weekdays. Call for a schedule of performances and ticket prices. The event and concert venue presents theatrical performances, musical groups, and other events.

♿ **John S. Burd Center for the Performing Arts** at Brenau University (429 Academy Street), Gainesville. The **Hosch Theater** is the venue for musical concerts, dance and theatrical productions, and other performing arts. The center also houses the **Banks Recital Hall** and an art gallery.

DANCE Gainesville Ballet Company (770-532-4241; www.gainesville ballet.org), mailing address: P.O. Box 1663, Gainesville 30501. Call for a schedule of performances and ticket prices. The company, made up of students and professionals, has been performing classics such as *The Nutcracker* and *Alice in Wonderland* for more than 30 years.

MUSIC The Gainesville Chorale (770-945-2307). The group performs sacred and secular music, including Broadway favorites. Call for a schedule of performances. Average prices: adults $15, seniors $12, children $5.

Lanier Singers (770-534-6234). Call for a schedule of performances and ticket prices. The group, made up of professional and nonprofessional singers, performs a cappella music in Gainesville.

NIGHTLIFE ♿ The Boiler Room (678-450-0115; www.boilerroom.org), 212 Spring Street SW, Gainesville. Open 10 PM–2 AM. Nightly entertainment at the upscale nightclub on the historic downtown square includes national recording artists, local upcoming bands, karaoke, trivia, and DJs. Smoking allowed. Wheelchair accessible. $5 cover charge Friday and Saturday.

THEATER Aurora Theatre (770-476-7926; www.auroratheatre.com), 3087-B Main Street NW, Duluth. For 10 years, the theater company has been presenting a master season of six shows, including musicals, comedies, dramas, and holiday shows. In addition, there are special event productions; a Cabaret Series that includes Halloween, New Year's Eve, and Valentine's performances; and a Children's Playhouse. Teatro del Sol presents Spanish-language productions. Call for a schedule of performances. $22–25.

Gainesville Theatre Alliance (770-718-3624; www.gainesvilletheatre alliance.org), mailing address: P.O. Box 1358, Gainesville 30503. Call for a schedule of performances and ticket prices. The Gainesville Theatre

Alliance (GTA), a collaboration by Gainesville College, Brenau University, and the community through the Theatre Wings organization, is a training ground for theater professionals and educators. GTA is the first college- and community-based theater in the state to be funded by the Georgia Council for the Arts, and it is consistently rated among the top 10 theaters in the state. GTA has performance spaces at Brenau University's **Hosch Theatre,** Pearce Auditorium, and Little Theatre and Gainesville College's Ed Cabell Theatre. GTA produces three drama, comedy, musical, or classic productions annually in November, February, and April. The Discovery Series, often the thesis projects of graduating seniors, can be edgy and more off the beaten path than main-stage productions.

Georgia Mountains Center (770-297-5457; www.georgiamountain center.com), 300 Green Street SE, Gainesville. Call for a schedule of events and ticket prices. Located on the historic square in Gainesville, the multipurpose facility features a performing arts theater and a 2,500-seat arena.

WonderQuest: GTA Theatre for Young Audiences (770-718-3721), mailing address: P.O. Box 2267, Gainesville 30503. This troupe presents literature-based dramas and comedies. Many performances are for schools, but each production has an evening and a Saturday matinee performance open to the public. Call for a schedule of events and ticket prices.

✳ Selective Shopping

Several areas are particularly noted for shopping. The **Flowery Branch Main Street Square** features unique shops and restaurants. **Gainesville's Main Street Marketplace,** built in 1886, is an open-air market with an array of distinctive shops and restaurants. Many people died here during a 1936 tornado, and legend has it that many of their spirits still inhabit the space, but modern-day visitors are more interested in the shops. **Banks Crossing** is one of the most popular outlet centers in the South.

CRAFTS **Raven's Nest Artisans Marketplace** (678-497-1012; www .ravensnestherbals.com), 3109 South Main Street, Duluth. Open 10–6 Tuesday through Friday, 10–5 Saturday. Shop here for handcrafted potpourri, teas, herbs, spices, fragrance oils, herbal bath products, stained glass, jewelry, photography, antiques, folk art, crocheted and knitted items, woodwork, and more. Classes and live musical entertainment are often scheduled.

FLEA MARKETS **Pendergrass Flea Market** (706-693-4466), 5641 US 129 North, Jefferson. Open 9–6 weekends. At the 130,000-square-foot flea market, 350 dealers sell just about anything you can think of, including but not limited to antiques, collectibles, furniture, produce, and even livestock. Stay all day; there's a food court. Free admission and parking.

HOME AND GARDEN **Grassroots Girls** (678-908-2366; www.grassroots girls.com), 3579 West Lawrenceville Street, Duluth. Open 10–5 Tuesday through Saturday; Mondays by appointment. Located in the historic Knox House across from City Hall on the town green, this specialty garden shop offers garden and home accents and furnishings, live plants, and landscape design services.

The Pottery (706-335-3120; 1-800-223-0667), 100 Pottery Road, Commerce. Open 8–8 Monday through Saturday, 11–6 Sunday. This gigantic warehouse emporium sells everything you need for home and garden and also has a huge nursery.

OUTLET STORES **Commerce Factory Stores** (706-335-6352), 199 Pottery Factory Drive, Commerce. Open 9–7 weekdays, 9–9 Saturday, noon–6 Sunday. A pip-squeak compared to its much larger cousin, Tanger Outlets, this center has 20 stores, including Lenox and Dress Barn.

Tanger Outlets of Commerce (706-335-3354; 1-800-405-9828; www .tangeroutlet.com), Tanger I: 111 Tanger Drive; Tanger II: 800 Steven B. Tanger Boulevard, Commerce. Open 9–9 Monday through Saturday, noon–6 Sunday. Located for easy access at US 441 and I-85, the centers offer 125 manufacturer and designer stores ranging from A (Adidas) to Z (Zales). For the serious shopper, several hotels and restaurants are nearby.

POTTERY 🍴 ♿ **Crocker Pottery–Georgia Folk Pottery Center** (770-869-3160), 6345 West Country Line Road, Lula. Open 9–5 weekdays. Michael Crocker, a nationally acclaimed north Georgian folk potter, has work on display at the Smithsonian. He is known for face jugs and jugs encircled by representations of north Georgia snakes. Other folk potters also have their work for sale here.

Hewell's Pottery (770-869-3469; www.hewellspottery.com), 4030 Joe Chandler Road, Gillsville. Open 7:30–5 Monday through Thursday, 7:30–4 Friday and Saturday. Genera-

tions of the Hewell family have been making pottery since 1860—everything from flower pots to glazed collector pieces. Three generations are currently working there. Hewell's is the largest producer of unglazed horticultural ware in the East and Midwest, and it's all created by hand in a 10-wheel shop. The shopping area is open year-round to sell folk pottery fired in a wood-burning groundhog kiln, garden pottery, nostalgic signs, home accessories, and gift items.

Turpin Pottery (706-677-1528), 2500 US 441, Homer. Open 8–4 Monday through Thursday, Friday through Sunday by appointment. Steve Turpin has been creating pottery for more than 30 years, and his pieces are highly sought after. Also for sale are pieces made by Steve's daughter, Abby. She started with face jugs but has moved on to include small chickens and snake jugs.

✳ Special Events

June: **City Lights Festival** (706-335-3164). Held the third weekend in June, this event could be called "Nashville Comes to Commerce." Native son and country music legend "Whispering" Bill Anderson brings stars from Nashville—performers such as Charley Pride, Jimmy Dean, Jan Howard, Mel Tillis, and Vince Gill—to perform at the City Lights Concert. In addition, the festival features eight events over three days, including a golf tournament, Dinner with the Stars, Stars 'N' Cars, Bark in the Park, live music, arts, crafts, and food. Some activities free; others have a small fee.

North Georgia Folk Potters Festival (call Steve Turpin, 706-677-1528). This is an opportunity to purchase directly from a wide variety of potters gathered in one spot in Homer. Older collectible pieces are offered for sale as well. Free.

July through August: **Chateau Elan Summer Concert Series** (678-425-0900; www.chateauelanatlanta.com). Popular local, regional, and national entertainers and bands perform on Saturday nights at these outdoor concerts in Braselton. Tickets include free dance lessons before each show. $30.

August: **Chateau Elan Vineyard Fest** (1-800-233-WINE; www .chateauelanatlanta.com). Activities include the tasting of 80 wines, wine seminars, a food pavilion, a tour of the winery in Braselton, and live entertainment. This event is often sold out far in advance. $42.

September: **Duluth Fall Festival** (770-476-0240; www.duluthfallfestival .com). The weekend festival in Duluth kicks off with a parade, and then the action moves to the Festival Center and Amphitheater, where there are 250 arts and crafts and food vendors, continuous entertainment, a children's area, an auction, and more. Free.

November: **It's a Wonderful House** (www.itsawonderfulhouse.org). Houses open 10–6 (last admittance at 4). This much-anticipated event permits viewing of some of Chateau Elan's private homes bedecked in holiday splendor. Parking is at the winery in Braselton. In addition, there is a gift shop and café. Proceeds benefit the Gwinnett Children's Shelter. $25.

Mid-November through December 30: **Magical Nights of Lights** (770-932-7200; www.lakelanierislands.com). Village open 5–10 nightly. The annual extravaganza at Lake Lanier Islands claims to be the largest animated light display in the world. More than 1 million lights create gigantic animated characters and scenes along a 6½-mile drive. Visitors can tune their car radios to a special station to listen to holiday favorites while making the drive. At the end there is a holiday village, where there's shopping, refreshments, an opportunity to visit with Santa, and a bonfire for roasting marshmallows. $25 per car, $35 per van.

HARTWELL AND ELBERTON

T his area of northeast Georgia is defined by significant lakes and the granite industry. It also has one of the largest concentrations of state parks in Georgia, making it a magnet for outdoor recreation enthusiasts. Here, the waters from the Broad and Savannah rivers are impounded in the largest man-made lake east of the Mississippi. The lake, which straddles the Georgia–South Carolina border, has a split personality. In Georgia it's called Clarks Hill Lake; in South Carolina, Strom Thurmond Lake. Whatever you call it, this lake offers innumerable opportunities for water sports and other outdoor pursuits.

The area is also rich in historic sites, Native American lore, bed & breakfasts, casual eateries, antiques and other shopping, and a variety of special events.

GUIDANCE When planning a trip to Elberton, consult the **Elbert County Chamber and Welcome Center** (706-283-5651; www.elbertga.com), 104 Heard Street, Elberton 30635. Open 8–5 weekdays.

To learn more about Hartwell, contact the **Hart County Chamber of Commerce** (706-376-8590; www.hart-chamber.org), 31 East Howell Street, Hartwell 30643. Open 8:30–5 weekdays.

To find out more about Lavonia, consult the **Lavonia Chamber of Commerce** (706-356-8202; www.lavonia-ga.com), 129 East Main Street, Lavonia 30553. Open 9–noon and 1–5 weekdays. Or stop by the **Georgia Visitor Information Center–Lavonia** (706-356-4019; www.georgiaonmymind.org), 938 County 84, Lavonia 30553. Open 8:30–5:30 daily. In addition to obtaining brochures and other information here, travelers can enjoy the use of picnic tables and grills. There is also a pet walking area.

GETTING THERE *By air:* Most visitors fly into **Hartsfield-Jackson Atlanta International Airport** (see What's Where in Georgia)). Visitors also could fly into **Athens–Ben Epps Airport** in nearby Athens (See Athens chapter in 3, Historic South) or **Greenville-Spartanburg International Airport** in South Carolina. That airport is served by **American, Continental, Delta, Independence, Northwest, United,** and **US Airways** (see What's Where in Georgia).

By bus: **Greyhound Lines** (706-549-2255; 1-800-231-2222; www.greyhound

.com) offers service to nearby Athens (see Athens chapter in 3, Historic South), but then a visitor would have to rent a car to get to and around this area.

By car: The towns described in this chapter are located near the Georgia–South Carolina border and are easily accessed via I-85 from Atlanta to the southwest or from Greenville-Spartanburg, South Carolina, and other points from the northeast. US 29 also runs north-south; GA 72 runs east-west.

By train: **Amtrak** (1-800-USA-RAIL) operates service to Atlanta (see What's Where in Georgia) and Augusta (see Augusta chapter in 3, Historic South), but then a visitor would need a car to get to and around this area.

MEDICAL EMERGENCY For life threatening emergencies, call 911. For immediate care in Elberton, go to **Elbert Memorial Hospital** (706-283-3151), Four Medical Drive, or **Spring Valley Health Care** (706-283-3880), 651 Rhodes Drive. If you need medical attention in Hartwell, contact **Hart County Hospital** (706-856-6100), 138 West Gibson Street.

VILLAGES AND NEIGHBORHOODS **Hart County** and its county seat, **Hartwell,** were named for Nancy Morgan Hart, a Revolutionary War hero. But even before settlers had moved in, the Cherokee met here to trade with tribes from more southerly regions. Their meeting place was known to them as the Center of the World. After the Revolutionary War, veterans settled here; their gravestones can be found in local cemeteries.

The **Hartwell Historic District** has several commercial buildings and residences of historic and architectural interest. Hartwell also is revitalizing its downtown, which is the site of many festivals throughout the year. New, trendy shops and exciting restaurants are popping up near the art center and the historic post office. **Historic Depot Street**, named for the old train station, offers gift shops, antiques stores, art galleries, a candle factory, Bluegrass Music Hall, and the **Hart County Community Theater** (see *Entertainment*).

This hard-rock town of **Elberton,** the top producer of granite in America, calls itself "the Granite Capital of the World" because of the amount of granite extracted from nearby quarries. Most of the stone is produced for gravestones, but some is used for building material and some for sculpture. When in town, be sure to drive by the Elbert County Courthouse, a granite and marble landmark on the square in downtown. Also located on the town square is the Bicentennial Memorial and Fountain, which was donated by the granite industry in 1976. It lists significant periods of local history on 13 panels symbolic of the 13 original colonies. A sculptured American eagle sits atop the central shaft. Before leaving the area, don't miss the **Elberton Granite Museum** (see *To See—Museums*) and the mysterious **Georgia Guidestones** (see *To See—Special Places*).

Tiny **Royston** is best known as the birthplace of baseball great Ty Cobb, and a museum there is dedicated to his career.

The other small towns in this chapter—**Carnesville, Comer,** and **Lavonia**—offer one or more attractions as well as restaurants, lodgings, or special events to keep you in the area.

COVERED BRIDGES ⚔ 🐚 **Cromer's Mill Covered Bridge** (706-384-4659; www
.franklin-county.com), GA 106 East at Nails Creek (access via Baker Road), Carnesville. One of Georgia's precious few remaining covered bridges, this one was
built in 1907, so it is nearing its centennial birthday. The bridge, constructed in
the town lattice design, is one lane wide and 132 feet long.

At **Watson Mill Bridge State Park** (see *Green Space—Nature Preserves and
Parks*), you'll find Georgia's longest covered bridge.

NANCY MORGAN HART—WAR WOMAN

Myth and truth often intermingle, but by any account Nancy was a firebrand
and an exceptional woman. She is reputed to have been a flaming redhead
and more than 6 feet tall.

Around 1760, Nancy married Benjamin Hart, who was related to Thomas
Hart Benton and the wife of Henry Clay. They had eight children and settled
in the Broad River area of northeast Georgia, where they owned 400 acres
on the banks of a creek that the Indians named Wahatchee ("War Woman")
Creek in her honor. There, Nancy grew a medicinal garden and doctored her
family and neighbors. She was reputedly such a crack shot, one side of her
cabin was allegedly covered with antlers from deer she had killed.

During the Revolutionary War, Nancy kept her farm going while her
husband hid from the Tories. She also contributed to the war effort, by dis-
guising herself to gain information. But the story that cemented her legendary reputation concerned a group of Tories who had shot and killed her
neighbor, patriot Colonel John Dooley. These redcoats allegedly came to her
cabin and forced her to cook dinner for them. According to the story, she
regaled them with stories and plied them with drink as she cooked. When
they began to nod off, she sent her daughter, Sukey, to alert neighbors that
she needed help. Meanwhile, she began gathering up their rifles and slip-
ping them out through chinks in the wall.

As the story goes, the soldiers eventually became aware of what she
was doing, so she was forced to hold them at gunpoint. When they tried to
disarm her, she reportedly killed one and wounded another. When her husband and neighbors arrived, they wanted to shoot the rest of the Tories for
killing Dooley, but Nancy said shooting was too good for them, so they were
hanged while she sang "Yankee Doodle." Although some historians didn't
believe the account, six bodies were found in one grave on that very spot in
the early 1900s.

Nancy has a highway, a town, and a county named for her (in fact, this
is the only county in Georgia named for a woman).

HISTORIC HOMES AND SITES ✒ 🐾 **Nancy Hart Cabin** (contact the Elbert County Chamber: 706-283-5651; www.elbertga.com), River Road, Elberton. Open 9–5 Monday through Saturday. Nancy Hart, after whom the county was named, was a skilled doctor and a staunch patriot as well as reputedly being a crack shot. She is most famous, however, for being a spy for the colonials during the Revolutionary War and is credited with capturing several British Tories. The cabin is a replica of the original and is surrounded by 5 acres of park. Free.

MUSEUMS ✒ 🐾 ♿ **Elberton Granite Museum and Exhibit** (706-283-2551; www.egaonline.com), One Granite Plaza, Elberton. Open 2–5 Monday through Saturday. Three stories of self-guided exhibits include antique granite-working tools and historical exhibits, artifacts, educational displays, and materials relating to the past and current granite industry in Elberton. One of the most fascinating items in the museum is the statue called *Dutchy*. The first granite statue created in Elberton, it was meant to be a Civil War memorial. Unfortunately, *Dutchy* was unpopular with local citizens, who thought he looked like a cross between a Pennsylvania Dutchman (hence his name) and a hippopotamus. They also felt that his uniform looked suspiciously Northern. As a result, the statue was pulled down and buried facedown—a sign of military disgrace. After 82 years, *Dutchy* was dug up and run through a car wash to remove the Georgia red clay, and he now resides in the museum. While at the museum, watch the film about the **Georgia Guidestones** (see *Special Places*). The film explains how the monument came to be built, why the site was chosen, a little about the mysterious benefactors without identifying them, and what the various sayings mean. Free.

GEORGIA GUIDESTONES, CALLED AMERICA'S STONEHENGE, WAS ERECTED MYSTERIOUSLY IN A FIELD IN 1980.

✒ 🐾 ♿ **Ty Cobb Museum** (706-245-1825; www.tycobbmuseum.org), 461 Cook Street, Royston. Open 9–4 weekdays, 10–4 Saturday. Native son and baseball great Tyrus Raymond "Ty" Cobb, known as "the Georgia Peach," was born in Royston in 1886. Many years after his death, Cobb is still considered by many to be the best player in baseball history. He set or equaled more records than any other player, and in 1936 he was the first player to be inducted into the Baseball Hall of Fame. His life and career are memorialized at this museum, which features personal belongings, memorabilia, rare films, and photographs. The museum also provides information about baseball history during Cobb's era and his impact on the game. In the Cobb Theater, which boasts a beautiful mural and stadium seating, a video features interviews with players and analysts. Adults $3, seniors and children $2.

SPECIAL PLACES ✍ 🐾 **Georgia Guidestones,** GA 77 North, Elberton. Open daily. This mysterious granite monument consists of three 19-foot-high blue granite stones—reputedly the largest granite blocks ever quarried—connected by a capstone. Called America's Stonehenge, the 119-ton monolith was erected in a field near Elberton in 1980. Only a few people know the identity of the group of sponsors who provided the specifications for the monument, and they're not talking. The stones are engraved with a 10-part philosophical message in 12 languages providing counsel for the preservation of mankind—a total of 4,000 letters sandblasted into the surface. The guidestones also serve as an astrological observatory with a sundial: a diagonal hole aligned to Polaris, the North Star, and a slit that marks the sunrise and sunset at the winter and summer solstices. Before coming to see the guidestones, watch the explanatory film at the **Elberton Granite Museum** (see *Museums*). Free.

☀ To Do

BALLOONING For ballooning information in northeast Georgia, call 1-877-BALLOON.

BICYCLING Several state parks have biking trails. See *Green Space—Lakes* and *Nature Preserves and Parks*.

BOATING See Marinas/Boat Landings Appendix.

GOLF ✍ 🐾 **Arrowhead Pointe at Richard B. Russell State Park** (706-283-6000; 1-877-405-4653; www .gastateparks.org/info/richbruss; www .golfgeorgia.org), 2790 Olympic Rowing Drive, Elberton. Open 8–7 daily. The park's 18-hole, 6,800-yard golf course is called Arrowhead Pointe after the Native American sites that were discovered nearby. Located on a peninsula, the course offers stunning water views, with 10 of the 18 holes skirting the lake. There are no visible houses from any vantage point on the course, which is consistent with the state-park golf-course theme of "no crowds, no houses, no noise." (See

TAKING IN THE GEORGIA SCENERY FROM HOT-AIR BALLOONS

Green Space—Nature Preserves & Parks.) Greens fees $37 weekdays, $42 weekends.

🏌 **Highland Walk Golf Course at Victoria Bryant State Park** (706-245-6770; 1-800-864-7275; www.gastateparks.org/info/vicbryant; www.golfgeorgia.com), 1415 Bryant Park Road, Royston. Open 7–dusk daily. The park's 18-hole course features a clubhouse, pro shop, unlimited weekday play, and junior and senior discounts. (See *Green Space—Nature Preserves and Parks*) $30–36.

See also Golf Appendix.

HORSEBACK RIDING See **Watson Mill Bridge State Park** under *Green Space—Nature Preserves and Parks.*

MINIATURE GOLF See **Tugaloo State Park** under *Green Space—Nature Preserves and Parks.*

SWIMMING See *Green Space—Lakes.*

✳ Green Space

LAKES ✒ 🏌 **Clarks Hill Lake** (706-359-7970; www.lincolncountyga.org), 2959 McCormick Highway/US 378 East, Lincolnton (see Madison chapter in 3, Historic South). Open daily. A mecca for water sports enthusiasts, Clarks Hill Lake straddles the Georgia–South Carolina border. (It's known as Strom Thurmond Lake on the South Carolina side.) This lake, which is the largest reservoir in the Southeast, boasts 1,200 miles of shoreline, of which 400 are in Lincoln County. Its 6 million annual visitors enjoy 11 Corps of Engineers recreation areas and 13 corps campgrounds, five commercial marinas, six state parks, and four county parks. Free.

✒ 🏌 **Lake Hartwell** (706-856-0300; 1-888-893-0678; www.sas.usace.army.mil/lakes/hartwell), US 29 North, Hartwell. Visitor center open 8–4:30 daily. The 55,590-acre lake provides many opportunities for water sports and outdoor recreation.

✒ 🏌 **Lake Richard B. Russell** (706-213-3400; 1-800-944-7207; www.sas.usace.army.mil/lakes/Russell), 4144 Russell Dam Road, Elberton. With 540 miles of shoreline and 26,650 surface acres of water surrounded by an additional 26,500 acres of land, the lake provides multitudinous opportunities for outdoor recreation and water sports. There is a visitor center at the dam and a fishing pier below it.

NATURE PRESERVES AND PARKS ✒ 🏌 ⚓ **Bobby Brown State Park** (706-213-2046; 1-800-864-7275; www.gastateparks.org/info/bobbybrown), 2509 Bobby Brown, Elberton. Open 7–10 daily. The land on which this pretty park sits has an interesting history. In the 1790s an old town called Petersburg, which was surrounded by plantations, was located here, where the Broad and Savannah rivers meet. When the water is low, visitors can still see some of the town's old foundations. The 665-acre park, named in honor of U.S. Navy Lieutenant Robert T. Brown, who lost his life in World War II, uses its location on the shores of

70,000-acre Clarks Hill Lake to offer visitors boating, fishing, and waterskiing.
Park facilities include 2 miles of hiking trails, a swimming pool that's open sea-
sonally, a boat ramp and dock, and seasonal canoe and fishing-boat rentals.
Campsites are offered for those with their own equipment, and the park also
offers yurt (a domed canvas tent with a wooden floor) rentals (see *Lodging—
Campgrounds*). Parking $3.

✒ 🦐 ♿ **Hart State Park** (706-376-8756; 1-800-864-7275; www.gastateparks
.org/info/hart), 330 Hart Road, Hartwell. Open 7–10 daily. Boating, fishing,
swimming, and waterskiing are the primary reasons to visit this park on 55,590-
acre Lake Hartwell (see *Lakes*). A swimming beach, two boat ramps, and docks
offer easy access to all water sports. An angler's heaven, the lake yields largemouth bass, hybrid bass, striper, black crappie, bream, rainbow trout, and
walleyed pike. Canoes, Jon boats, and pontoon boats are rented seasonally. A 1½-
mile multiuse trail attracts hikers and cyclists. Lakeshore accommodations are
offered at campsites and cottages (see *Lodging—Campgrounds* and *Cottages
and Cabins*). Parking $3.

✒ 🦐 ♿ **Richard B. Russell State Park** (706-213-2045; 1-800-864-7275; www
.gastateparks.org/info/richbruss), 2650 Russell Road, Elberton. Open 7–10 daily.
Paleo-Indians lived in the area more than 10,000 years ago at a site now called
Rucker's Bottom, which was completely covered over when 26,500-acre Lake
Richard B. Russell was filled in 1980 (see *Lakes*). Perched on the shores of the
lake, this park offers some of Georgia's best fishing and boating. Facilities for
water sports include a swimming beach, rowing area, boat ramps, and canoe and
pedal boat rentals. Other outdoor pursuits include 6 miles of nature trails, disc golf,
beach volleyball, and a new 18-hole golf course (see *To Do—Golf*). A campground
and cottages provide overnight accommodations (see *Lodging—Campgrounds* and
Cottages and Cabins). Parking $3.

✒ 🦐 ♿ **Tugaloo State Park** (706-356-4362; 1-800-864-7275; www.gastate
parks.org/info/tugaloo), 1763 Tugaloo Road, Lavonia. Open 7–10 daily. The park
is named for the Native American word for the river that flowed freely before
the Hartwell Dam was built to impound Lake Hartwell (see *Lakes*). The park's
location on the lake makes it a popular destination for devotees of water sports.
Fishing is excellent year-round, particularly for largemouth bass. During the
summer, boating, sailing, swimming, and waterskiing are favored pursuits, as are
tennis, volleyball, horseshoes, and miniature golf. Hikers can enjoy the wooded
Crow Tree and Muscadine nature trails. Accommodations are offered at campsites
and in cottages, some of which are dog-friendly (see *Lodging—Campgrounds* and
Cottages and Cabins). Parking $3.

✒ 🦐 ♿ **Victoria Bryant State Park** (706-245-6270; 1-800-864-7275; www.ga
stateparks.org/info/vicbryant), 1105 Bryant Park Road, Royston. Open 7–dark
daily. Visitors come to this park to enjoy the rolling hills of Georgia's upper Piedmont region, hike the 8 miles of trails along the beautiful stream or around the
perimeter, get a glimpse of wildlife, cycle, swim in the park's pool (seasonally), and
play golf (see *To Do—Golf*). Campers can overnight at the park (see *Lodging—
Campgrounds*). Fishing ponds are open only to campers and disabled visitors.
Parking $3.

✄ 🐾 ♿ **Watson Mill Bridge State Park** (706-783-5349; 1-800-864-7275; www .gastateparks.org/info/watson), 650 Watson Mill Road, Comer. Open 7–10 daily. The centerpiece of the 1,018-acre park is Georgia's longest covered bridge still in its original position. The 229-foot bridge was built in 1885 to span the South Fork River and is one of only 16 of the state's original 200 covered bridges still in existence. The scenic park, a mecca for outdoor enthusiasts, offers 5 miles of biking trails and 7 miles of hiking trails; camping in developed and primitive campsites (see *Lodging—Campgrounds*); 12 miles of equestrian trails (BYOH—bring your own horse); fishing for bass, bream, and catfish in the 5-acre millpond; picnicking; and seasonal canoe and pedal-boat rentals. In summertime visitors like to romp in the cool river shoals below the bridge. Accommodations are available in a bunkhouse (see *Lodging—Cottages and Cabins*). There are even accommodations for the horses (reservations required). Admission free; parking $3.

See also Parks Appendix.

✳ Lodging

BED & BREAKFASTS

In Elberton
🐾 **Rainbow Manor Bed and Breakfast** (706-213-0314; www .rainbowmanor.com), 217 Heard Street. Stay in this beautiful antebellum home (circa 1882), which has been lovingly restored and decorated with antiques. Of the five guest rooms, one has a private bath. A full country breakfast is included. No smoking. Not wheelchair accessible. $75–$85.

In Hartwell
Shuler Manor Bed and Breakfast (706-377-3550; 1-866-377-3550; www .shulermanor.com), 714 Early Drive. This lakeside retreat, located on a 2-acre peninsula on Lake Hartwell (see *Green Space—Lakes*), offers a 180-degree view of open water. The newly constructed, Federal-style home offers two large great rooms with fireplaces, a game parlor with billiards and karaoke, and lakeside porches and decks. Other amenities and activities include a large dock with a swim ladder, beach area, outdoor fire pit and hot tub, and murder mystery weekends. Accommodations are also offered in a separate

cottage with a full kitchen. Smoking outdoors only. Limited wheelchair accessibility. $75–400.

♿ **The Skelton House** (706-376-7969; 1-877-556-3790; www.the skeltonhouse.com), 97 Benson Street. This is a B&B where history and traditional elegance embrace contemporary comfort and grace. This lovely inn is on the Select Registry, Distinguished Inns of North America. Seven guest rooms have queen-sized beds, cable televisions with HBO, ceiling fans, private baths, telephones with data ports, and individual thermostats. Full breakfast included. Smoking on porches only. One room wheelchair accessible. $100–135; discounts available for multinight stays.

In Lavonia
♿ **RenStone Bed and Breakfast and Spa** (706-356-1198; 1-866-862-4517; www.renstone.com), 560 Chandler Place Drive. From beautifully appointed rooms to a full range of professional spa services, RenStone is the place to go and be pampered. It is

located in a quiet deep-water cove on Lake Hartwell (see *Green Space— Lakes*), and to ensure maximum privacy, only one party is entertained at a time. The guest suite has a full kitchen, satellite television, a VCR, whirlpool, washer and dryer, a large bath with his-and-hers vanities, and its own lakeside entrance. Continental breakfast included. Smoking on porches and decks only. Wheelchair accessible. $75–$165.

🦐 ♿ **Southern Oaks Bed and Breakfast** (706-356-8382; 1-888-850-8178; www.southernoaksbedand breakfast.com), 30 Baker Street. Built in 1918, this majestic Southern mansion offers an array of delights for overnight guests. Two adjacent buildings were added in 1990 to ensure availability of all the modern amenities. Full Southern breakfast included. Smoking and nonsmoking rooms. Wheelchair accessible. $59.

CAMPGROUNDS *In Comer*

🌊 🐾 🦐 ♿ **Watson Mill Bridge State Park** (706-783-5349; 1-800-864-7275; www.gastateparks.org/info/watson), 650 Watson Mill Road. The park features 21 tent, trailer, and RV sites as well as 11 equestrian campsites and horse stalls ($5 each). $13–19.

In Elberton
🌊 🐾 🦐 ♿ **Bobby Brown State Park** (706-213-2046; 1-800-864-7275; www.gastateparks.org/info/bobby-brown), 2509 Bobby Brown. The park features 61 tent, trailer, and RV sites as well as a pioneer campground for those who have their own equipment. In addition, for those who would like a camping experience but do not have their own equipment, the park offers unusual accommodations in yurts, which are domed tents made of can-

vas over a wooden floor. Campsites $15–25, yurts $45.

🌊 🦐 **Richard B. Russell State Park** (706-213-2045; 1-800-864-7275; www.gastateparks.org/info/richbruss), 2650 Russell Road. The campground, which is near the shoreline of Lake Richard B. Russell, offers 28 tent, trailer, and RV sites with cable TV hookups. $18–21.

In Hartwell
🌊 🐾 🦐 ♿ **Hart State Park** (706-376-8756; 1-800-864-7275; www.gastate parks.org/info/hart), 330 Hart Road. The park offers 78 tent, trailer, and RV sites and 16 walk-in sites. $11–19.

In Lavonia
🌊 🐾 🦐 ♿ **Tugaloo State Park** (706-356-4362; 1-800-864-7275; www.gas tateparks.org/info/tugaloo), 1763 Tugaloo Road. Most of the park's 108 tent, trailer, and RV sites are situated on a wooded peninsula with spectacular views of Lake Hartwell in every direction. There are also five primitive campsites. $8–21.

In Royston
🌊 🐾 🦐 ♿ **Victoria Bryant State Park** (706-245-6270; 1-800-864-7275; www.gastateparks.org/info/vicbryant), 1105 Bryant Park Road. The park features 35 tent, trailer, and RV sites, as well as eight platform tent sites and a pioneer campground. $18–30.

See also Campgrounds Appendix.

COTTAGES AND CABINS

In Comer
🌊 🐾 🦐 ♿ **Watson Mill Bridge State Park** (706-783-5349; 1-800-864-7275; www.gastateparks.org/info/watson), 650 Watson Mill Road. The park features a bunkhouse that sleeps eight. $45 per person.

In Elberton

🔌 🏕 🐾 ♿ **Richard B. Russell State Park** (706-213-2045; 1-800-864-7275; www.gastateparks.org/info/richbruss), 2650 Russell Road. The park features 17 cottages on the shores of Lake Richard B. Russell. $71–91.

In Hartwell

🔌 🐾 ♿ **Hart State Park** (706-376-8756; 1-800-864-7275; www.gastate parks.org/info/hart), 330 Hart Road. The park features five lakeside cottages. $80–100.

In Lavonia

🔌 🏕 🐾 ♿ **Tugaloo State Park** (706-356-4362; 1-800-864-7275; www.ga stateparks.org/info/tugaloo), 1763 Tugaloo Road. All of the park's 20 cottages are located on a wooded peninsula where they have excellent views of Hartwell Lake. Dogs welcome in select cottages. $70–90.

✳ Where to Eat

DINING OUT

In Hartwell

♿ **Waterfall Grille** (706-856-GOLF), Cateechee Golf Club, 140 Cateechee Trail. Open 11:30–2 Tuesday through Saturday; 5:30–9 weekdays, 5:30–10 Saturday and Sunday; 11:30–3 Sunday for brunch. The menu features delicious Southern regional cuisine. Favorites include Georgia white shrimp, prime rib, cold-water lobster tails, sandwiches, chef's specials, unique and creative salads, appetizers, and desserts. Smoking in bar only. Wheelchair accessible. $8–33.

EATING OUT

In Comer

🔌 🐾 ♿ **Three Oak Fish Lodge**

(706-795-3134), David's Home Church Road. Open 5–9 Friday and Saturday. This family restaurant is most sought after for its fish, steaks, and seafood. Credit cards not accepted. No smoking. Wheelchair accessible. $8–12.

In Elberton

🔌 🐾 ♿ **Bank's Bar-Be-Cue** (706-283-8741), 108 Hartwell Highway. Open 5:30 AM–8 PM daily. Menu items include barbecue, fish, chicken, pork chops, and more. The Friday buffet is a popular favorite. No smoking. Wheelchair accessible. $5.50–9.50; buffet $7.49.

🔌 🐾 ♿ **Clara Belle's on College** (706-283-0640), 92 College Avenue. Open 11–2:30 Tuesday through Friday; 5–9 Tuesday through Saturday; 11–5 Sunday. Whether you order soup, salad, a sandwich, or a full surf-and-turf platter, this restaurant has something for every price range. No smoking. Wheelchair accessible. $4–$25.

🔌 🐾 ♿ **Clifford's Restaurant at Beaverdam Marina** (706-213-0079; 706-213-6462; www.Beaverdam Marina.com/Cliffords_Menu.html), 1155 Marina Drive. Open 11–9 Thursday through Saturday. This fun, casual family restaurant specializes in seafood, steaks, and chicken. Nightly specials include prime rib on Friday, chef's specials such as Cajun catfish on Saturday, and snow crab legs on Sunday. No smoking. Wheelchair accessible. $6–15.

🔌 🐾 ♿ **Gardens Restaurant** (706-213-8157), 235 Elbert Street. Open 11–2 and 5–9 daily. Try the lunch buffet (drink extra) or join them for steaks, seafood, and chicken for dinner. No smoking. Wheelchair accessible. $7–8; buffet $5.65.

◢ ◐ ⓑ **Granite City Restaurant** (706-283-6928), 225 College Avenue. Open 5 AM–2 PM daily. This is the place to go for value and all your hometown favorites. Choices change each day. No smoking. Wheelchair accessible. A meat-and-two-vegetable plate costs $5.

◢ ◐ **Time Square** (706-283-1235), 103 Heard Street. Open 11–2. This restaurant serves a wide variety of lunch favorites, including sandwiches, chicken fingers, and salads. No smoking. Not wheelchair accessible. Around $5.

In Hartwell

◢ ◐ ⓑ **Andrew's Coffeehouse and Steakhouse** (706-377-3677), 126 West Franklin Street. Open 7:30–3 and 5:30–9:30 Tuesday through Saturday. Favorites include steak and lobster, seafood, and pasta. No smoking. Wheelchair accessible. Lunch around $7; dinner $13–23.

◢ ◐ ⓑ **Bantam Chef** (706-376-4062), 107 North Forest Avenue. Open 11–10 daily. Favorites include hot dogs, deli and other sandwiches, wings, barbecue, shrimp, and catfish. Smoking permitted outside. Wheelchair accessible. Most items $5.

◢ ◐ ⓑ **Downtown Café and Pizzeria** (706-377-3055), 63 Depot Street. Open 10–9 daily. In addition to great pizza, menu items include authentic pasta dishes as well as seafood. No smoking. Wheelchair accessible. Average $8.

◢ ◐ ⓑ **Jim's Grill** (706-376-9287), 50 South Forest Avenue. Open 6 AM–2 PM daily. The menu can be characterized as old-time soul food. Great value. Favorites include meat loaf, fried chicken, liver and onions, chicken fried steak, turnip greens, and

more. No smoking. Wheelchair accessible. Meat, two vegetables, bread, and drink $4.

In Lavonia

◢ ◐ **Brass Lantern Café and Bakery** (706-356-2877), 211 West Main Street. Open 11–2:30 daily. Enjoy homemade soups and salads, sandwiches, and daily meat specials served with two vegetables. No smoking. Not wheelchair accessible. Around $5.

◢ ◐ ⓑ **Downtown Café and Pizzeria** (706-356-2535), 203 West Main Street. Open 11–9 daily, until 10 on Saturday. Fare includes pizza, a full range of Italian pasta dishes, stromboli, chicken fingers, and salads. No smoking. Wheelchair accessible. About $7.

◢ ◐ ⓑ **Gumlog Bar-B-Que and Fish Lodge** (706-356-4061), GA 328. Open 11–9:45 Friday and Saturday, 11–7:45 Sunday. Besides various barbecue and fish dishes, popular menu items include steaks, burgers, and sandwiches. No smoking. Wheelchair accessible. Most dishes $6.

◢ ◐ ⓑ **La Cabana Mexican Restaurant** (706-356-0747), 934 Ross Place. Open 11–10 daily. This restaurant serves traditional Mexican cuisine along with several American choices. Combo platters are among the most popular items. No smoking. Not wheelchair accessible. Average $6.

TAKE-OUT

In Lavonia

◢ ◐ ⓑ **Finley's Café** (706-356-8281), 12800 Jones Street. Open 10:30–6:30 Monday through Saturday. Menu items include hot dogs, hamburgers, wings, Polish sausages, and much more. Although this is primarily a take-out restaurant, there are two outdoor tables. Smoking outdoors only. Not wheelchair accessible. Very inexpensive.

✳ Entertainment

MUSIC ✍ ♪ **Bluegrass Express** (706-376-3551), 57 Depot Street, Hartwell. Open 7–11 pm Saturday. Visitors can enjoy bluegrass music in a former cotton warehouse every Saturday night. Besides the regular house band, a different guest band is invited to perform each week. Children are free at this family-oriented, alcohol-free facility. A concession stand offers refreshments. $6.

✍ ♪ **Clem's Shoal Creek Music Park** (706-356-1092), 3191 Providence Church Road, Lavonia. This family-oriented, alcohol-free venue offers live bluegrass, country, and gospel entertainment, including a spring and fall bluegrass festival. Call for a schedule of performances and ticket prices.

THEATER **Elberton Theater Foundation** (706-283-1049), 100 South Oliver Street, Elberton. This volunteer theater stages five events per season, plus two children's performances. Additional income is earned by renting the theater out to churches, schools, and various bands. Call for a schedule of events. $5–12, up to $25 when celebrity performs; discounts available for students and seniors.

Hart County Community Theater (706-376-5599), 83 Depot Street, Hartwell. Box office open 10–2 Tuesday through Friday. The group produces plays quarterly. Call for a schedule of performances and ticket prices.

✳ Selective Shopping

ANTIQUES **Restoration House** (706-377-3704) 50 North Forest Avenue, Hartwell. Open Monday and Tuesday by appointment only, 9–5 Wednesday through Saturday, 1:30–5 Sunday. This facility specializes in quality antiques, lamps, Victorian heart quilts, and heritage lace.

ART GALLERIES **Bendzunas Glass Studio and Glass Gallery** (706-783-5869; www.bendzunasglass.com), 89 West South Street, Comer. No regular hours, but visitors encouraged to come by anytime until 10 PM. World-renowned glass artists Paul and Barbara Bendzunas create their imaginative works here, where two generations work side by side in glass and iron.

Blue Bell Gallery (706-783-4665), 89 East North Avenue, Comer. Open 1–6:30 weekdays, all day Saturday and Sunday. The clay studio and gallery represents more than 30 local artists and offers tours and workshops as well as art, dance, and yoga classes. The gallery is located in a circa 1900 sewing plant that once made jeans and overalls. (Restoration is ongoing, so if no one is there, owner Tracy Ingram says they've probably just popped out to Home Depot to pick up something and will be right back.)

Hart Regional Arts Council (706-377-2040), 338 East Howell Street, Hartwell. Open 3–5:30 or 6 Monday through Thursday, noon–5:30 or 6 Friday and Saturday. The nonprofit organization displays and sells a wide variety of works created by local artists and craftspeople.

FLEA MARKETS Franklin County Flea Market (706-245-1126), 1344 Sandycross Road, Royston. Open from sunrise to sunset on Saturday and Sunday. The facility rents space to anyone with something to sell, so you'll see a wide variety of junk-to-treasure merchandise and something different every time you come. Free parking.

Lavonia Antique Market (706-356-1488), 157 West Main Street, Lavonia. Open 10–5:30 Monday through Saturday, 1–5:30 Sunday. This unique facility offers shoppers 12,000 square feet of treasure-hunting space. Get there early and choose from furniture, buttons, glassware, jewelry, linens, and dolls, just to name a few.

✳ Special Events

March: **Antique Boat Show** (706-376-8590). Lake Hartwell provides the backdrop for exhibitors from across the United States to display their classic 1920–1960 wooden boats. Spectators free; parking $1.

Spring Fever Regatta on Lake Hartwell (www.twinhulls.com). The largest catamaran regatta in the United States is advertised as "The World's Finest Regatta by a Dam Site." Call for details. Free for spectators.

April: **Annual Granite Festival** (706-283-5651), Elbert County Fairgrounds, 350 North Oliver Street, Elberton. This fun-filled day for the whole family includes visits to a quarry and skilled craftspeople etching images onto granite. Events include children's activities, food, music, dancing, and arts and crafts. Free.

May and September: **Annual Bluegrass Festival** (706-356-1092), Clem's Shoal Creek Music Park, Hartwell. This family-oriented, alcohol-free venue (see *Entertainment—Music*) offers live bluegrass, country, and gospel entertainment. Call for a schedule of performances and ticket prices.

June: **Bendzunas Glass and Blue Bell Gallery Annual Spring Studio Tours and Open House Exhibitions** (706-783-5869; 706-783-4665; www .bendzunasglass.com). Held the first weekend in June and again in November and December in historic downtown Comer, the tour features glass-blowing, iron-forging, and pot-throwing demonstrations by local artisans. Exhibitions at both galleries feature works from more than 30 local artists and a Friday-evening reception. Free.

August: **Confederate Reenactment** (706-376-8756). This event takes place at Hart State Park, where visitors see weaponry, drilling, and marching while learning about equipment and uniforms from the Civil War. Included in regular $3 parking fee.

September: **ARTS in hARTwell Festival of Heritage and Fine Arts** (706-376-0188). This event on Hartwell Square includes an assortment of activities, including a juried fine arts show, live heritage music, craft demonstrations, storytelling, and children's activities. Free.

October: ✥ ♪ **Loch Hartwell Highland Games and Scottish Festival** (706-376-6761). This festival in Hartwell is filled with Scottish athletic events, massed bagpipe bands on parade, northeast Georgia's Strongest Man competition, shops, food, artisans, Scottish clan tents and genealogists, historical and interactive events, and Scottish entertainment. $10 for one-day pass, $15 for two days; children 12–17 admitted on two-for-one basis for $5 per day.

HIAWASSEE, BLAIRSVILLE, AND YOUNG HARRIS

Most visitors to Hiawassee, Blairsville, and Young Harris come for water sports on Lake Chatuge and Lake Nottely or for hiking and other outdoor pursuits in the Chattahoochee National Forest. Georgia's highest point, Brasstown Bald, is in this area, and the Benton MacKaye and Appalachian trails begin their northward trek along the ridges of the Blue Ridge and Cohutta mountains. The Benton MacKaye Trail follows the western ridge for 250 miles to Virginia, and the Appalachian Trail follows the eastern ridge 2,000 miles to Maine. In August, folks come from near and far for the **Georgia Mountain Fair** (see *Special Events*).

GUIDANCE For more information about Blairsville, contact the **Blairsville–Union County Chamber of Commerce** (706-745-5789; 1-877-745-5789; www.blairsvillechamber.com), 385 Welcome Center Lane, Blairsville 30512. Open May through October, 8:30–4:30 weekdays, 9–1 Saturday.

To learn more about Hiawassee and Young Harris, consult the **Towns County Chamber of Commerce and Local Welcome Center–Towns County Tourism Association** (706-896-4966; 1-800-984-1543; www.mountaintopga.com), 1411 Fuller Circle, Young Harris 30582. Open 9–5 weekdays; April through December, also 9–4 Saturday.

GETTING THERE *By air:* Most air travelers arrive at **Hartsfield-Jackson Atlanta International Airport** (see What's Where in Georgia). Another option is **Chattanooga Metropolitan Airport** (423-855-2200; www.chattairport.com), 1001 Airport Road, Suite 14, Chattanooga, Tennessee. The Chattanooga airport offers flights on five major airlines: **American/American Eagle** (1-800-433-7300), **Delta/ASA** (1-800-282-3424), **Delta/Comair** (1-800-354-9822), **Northwest/Northwest Express** (1-800-428-4322), and **US Air Express** (1-800-428-4322).

By bus: The closest bus service is provided by **Greyhound Lines** (706-278-3139; 1-800-231-2222; www.greyhound.com) to Gainesville (see Gainesville chapter).

By car: Blairsville, Young Harris, and Hiawassee are strung out along US 76 from west to east along the north-central edge of Georgia. There are no interstates in this part of the state except for the extension of I-575 out of Atlanta that becomes GA 5. GA 400 is a multilane limited-access highway out of Atlanta that becomes US 19.

By train: The closest **Amtrak** train service is in Gainesville (see Gainesville chapter).

WHEN TO GO Brasstown Bald, the highest point in the southern United States, has weather comparable to Vermont's. Even down in the valleys, the temperature seldom breaks into the 80s and can easily drop below freezing late into the spring and early in the fall. There can be snow or ice storms in winter. This weather, which is unusual for Georgia, dictates that most visitors prefer visiting from late spring through late fall. Many, however, enjoy visiting around the Christmas season.

MEDICAL EMERGENCY For life-threatening emergencies, call 911. Otherwise, contact **Chatuge Regional Hospital** (706-896-2222), 110 East Main Street, Hiawassee, or **Union General Hospital** (706-745-2111; www.uniongeneral hospital.com), 214 Hospital Street, Blairsville.

VILLAGES **Blairsville** is not only the county seat but the only incorporated town in Union County (which, by the way, was not named for the Federal side during the Civil War, but for the Union Party, which was formed 28 years before that war). Brasstown Bald, the highest point in the state, is nearby (see *To See—Natural Beauty Spots*). The surrounding area is popular for outdoor pursuits, including those offered at **Vogel State Park** (see *Green Space—Nature Preserves & Parks*) and on the Appalachian Trail.

Hiawassee is a Cherokee word meaning "meadow." Although this beautiful town is in the mountains of north Georgia, it is surrounded by many open areas. The town and the Hiawassee River attracted tourists from the 1800s to the 1930s, when wealthy families from the lowlands of Georgia and neighboring states summered in the mountains to escape the heat and disease prevalent in their home areas. Fortunately, the mountains, lakes, and recreational activities have since become affordable for everyone. Another attraction is the **Fred Hamilton Rhododendron Garden** (see *Green Space—Gardens*), which features 2,000 rhododendrons, azaleas, and wildflowers.

Colleges often are named after the towns they are located in, but in the case of **Young Harris**, the town was named for the college. Young Harris College, named for Judge Young Loftin Gerdine Harris, existed before the town came into being. Its planetarium is open to the public. One of the state's fine resorts, **Brasstown Valley Resort** (see *Lodging—Inns & Resorts*), is nearby, as is **Crane Creek Vineyards** (see *To Do—Winery Tours*).

✳ To See

MUSEUMS ✐ ⬢ ㄠ **Misty Mountain Train Museum** (706-745-9819; www .mistymountaininn.com), 4381 Misty Mountain Lane off Town Creek School Road,

Blairsville. Open for tours at 2 Wednesday, Friday, and Saturday, May through December. Located at **Misty Mountain Inn and Cottages** (see *Lodging—Bed & Breakfasts*), the 4,000-square-foot model train layout, which has 14 O-gauge Lionel trains operating on nearly a mile of track with 12 bridges and 15 tunnels, is the largest privately owned O-gauge train collection in the nation. The backdrop represents Georgia and Tennessee. $3 donation requested; proceeds given to charity.

☙ ✿ **Union County Historical Society Museum** (706-745-5493), Old Union County Courthouse on the Square, Blairsville. Open 10–4 Wednesday through Saturday, June through October. The museum contains county memorabilia from Civil War artifacts to 19th-century farm equipment. Adults $2, children $1.

NATURAL BEAUTY SPOTS ☙ ✿ ♿ **Brasstown Bald** (706-745-6928; visitor information center 706-896-2556; www.fs.fed.us/conf), GA 180 Spur, Blairsville. Open daily Memorial Day through October, weekends only March through May and November. At 4,784 feet above sea level, Brasstown Bald is Georgia's highest mountain and one of the highest in the Southeast. From the summit, visitors can see a 360-degree view of four states: Georgia, North Carolina, South Carolina, and Tennessee. Cars can drive most of the way up the mountain. Access to the summit from there is by way of a steep half-mile paved trail or by shuttle in season. Tourists are rewarded at the top with a visitor information center that offers exhibits of flora and fauna not usually found this far south; in fact, they're more typical of Maine. Below the peak to the north and east is the only "cloud forest" in Georgia, an area that's usually dripping wet from the moisture in the clouds that hang low over it. The environmentally sensitive slope features lichen-covered yellow birch and spectacular wildflower displays. The park also features picnicking and four hiking trails ranging from 0.5 to 6 miles. Because of the elevation, the weather can be quite cool, and the area gets snow and ice in the winter. Check the web site at ngeorgia.com/travel/brasstown.html for a weather cam's look at conditions before you go. Parking $3; shuttle $2 round-trip per person.

PLANETARIUMS ☙ ✿ ♿ **Rollins Planetarium** (706-379-4312; 1-800-241-3754; www.yhc.edu/external/planet), One College Street, Young Harris. Open Friday evenings at 8 (June and July shows at 8:30); closed in March. Located on the campus of Young Harris College, this planetarium is one of the largest in the state. It has a 40-foot dome, and guests can relax in reclining seats. Special shows include "Cosmic Concerts" and a Christmas show. The college also has an observatory on state property near Brasstown Valley Resort. Free.

SCENIC DRIVES **Georgia Mountain Parkway** (www.georgiahighcountry.org/gmp). The parkway, which runs 65 miles from Hiawassee to Jasper, is full of stops along the way in nostalgic towns and recreation areas for sight-seeing, shopping, festivals, and outdoor pursuits.

Russell-Brasstown Scenic Byway (www.byways.org/browse/byways/13739). The 41-mile loop trail anchored by Blairsville and Helen runs through the Chattahoochee National Forest and provides some of the most spectacular scenery and views in the state.

BOAT EXCURSIONS Romantic Lake Cruises (828-389-2255; www.romantic lakecruises.net), Dock D, Fieldstone Marina, 3499 US 76 West, Hiawassee. Open daily, April 15 through leaf season in early to mid-November. Cruises on the Lake Chatuge Love Boat include a variety of offerings from a bare-bones one-hour cruise to a sumptuous dinner cruise with live music and complimentary drinks. $50–150.

BOATING ✔ ❧ **Boundary Waters Resort and Marina** (706-896-2530; 1-800-323-3562; www.boundarywatersresort.com), 528 Sunnyside Road, Hiawassee. Open 8:30–5 daily. Located on Lake Chatuge, the full-service marina rents pontoon boats, canoes, kayaks, and paddleboats. Boat rental prices vary.

✔ ❧ **Fieldstone Marina** (706-896-2112), 3499 US 76 West, Hiawassee. Open 9–5 Monday through Thursday, 8–8 Friday through Sunday in summer; 8–5 Monday and Wednesday through Sunday in winter. The full-service marina rents pontoon boats, fishing boats, sailboats, wind riders, Jet Skis, kayaks, and aqua cycles. Rental prices vary.

See also **Lake Chatuge** and **Lake Nottely** under *Green Space—Lakes.*

FISHING ✔ 🐾 ❧ **Hickorynut Cove Trout Farm** (706-896-5341; www.hickory nutcove.com), 2800 Hickorynut Cove, Hiawassee. Open 8–6 daily. Hickorynut Cove has 107 acres surrounded on three sides by wilderness. The farm produces 40,000 pounds of trout annually, and its 5-acre stocked private lake is a great spot for fishing and paddleboating. Staff will clean, bag, and ice your fish for you for 10 percent of the cost of the fish you caught. Bait, tackle, nets, and other equipment can be furnished. Other activities include hiking and feeding the swans and geese. A fully equipped cottage that sleeps up to four is available to rent ($85 per night for two people) and there are bed & breakfast accommodations as well (see **B & B at Swan Lake** under *Lodging—Bed & Breakfasts*). No smoking or pets in cottage. The fishing area is wheelchair accessible; the cottage is not. Admission free; fish caught priced by pound.

✔ ❧ **Upper Hi Fly Fishing Outfitters** (706-896-9075; www.upper-hi-fly.com), 3375 US 76 West, Hiawassee. Open 9–5 Monday through Saturday, 9–2 Sunday; reservations required. Expert guides know the best places and the best techniques for successful fly-fishing. The store carries fishing tackle, clothing, accessories, gifts, and fine art. Call for prices.

FOR FAMILIES ✔ 🐾 ❧ **Brasstown Valley Family Summer Adventure Package** (706-379-9900; 1-800-201-3205; www.brasstownvalley.com), 6321 US 76, Young Harris. Three sessions daily. Children's activities for age 5–12—hayrides, golf challenges, wildlife hikes, and arts and crafts—make an already cool summer destination even better and give parents an opportunity to indulge in their own pursuits. $25 for 10 AM–2 PM session; $35 for 10 AM–4 PM session; $12 for 2–4 PM session; 10 AM sessions include lunch.

✔ 🐾 ❧ **Southern Tree Plantation** (706-745-0601; www.southerntreeplantation.com), 2531 Owltown Road, Blairsville. Open 10–5 Friday and Saturday. Families can choose their own pumpkins in October or their own Christmas tree during the holiday season at this 60-acre farm. The fun doesn't stop there, however, nor is it restricted to October through December. Other family-oriented activities throughout the year include a barnyard playground and maze, horseshoes, volleyball, hayrides, pony rides, fishing, marshmallow roasting around a roaring fire, and train rides aboard the *Southern Tree Express*, a miniature train. The petting zoo allows children to get up-close and personal with lovable farm critters such as Buckwheat the potbellied pig, Bo and Peep the sheep, or Poncho the donkey. Wildlife is represented by Donner the deer. Local crafts also are sold here, and on selected weekends in the fall the farm sponsors a hoedown with bluegrass music and an all-you-can-eat buffet. Southern Tree Plantation is the largest Christmas tree farm in north Georgia, growing more than 25,000 trees at any one time. $8, children 2 and younger free.

GOLF **Brasstown Valley Resort** (706-379-4613; 1-800-201-3205; www.brass townvalley.com), 6321 US 76, Young Harris. Open daylight hours daily. North Georgia's premier mountain golf resort, Brasstown Valley offers an abundance of outdoor activities beyond the award-winning Scottish links–style course designed by Denis Griffiths. The championship par-72 course is consistently ranked by *Golf Digest* as one of the best places to play golf in Georgia and is a member of the prestigious Leading Golf Courses of America. The environmentally sensitive course design uses the natural landscape to create a challenging, well-bunkered course with water on 10 holes. The course also features PGA professional instruction, a driving range, and a pro shop. During the summer season, golfers can get back into the swing of things by attending the **Brasstown Valley Resort's K.I.S.S. Golf School,** which is tailored to women and couples. Led by LPGA pro Lori McCabe and professional instructors, the school features instruction for both novices and experienced players. $65 for 18 holes and cart Monday through Thursday, seniors $39; $80 Friday through Sunday.

Also see Golf Appendix.

HIKING **For the appalachian Trail** (www.appalachiantrail.org), see the Dahlonega chapter.

For the Benton MacKaye Trail (www.bmta.org), see the Cartersville chapter.

HORSEBACK RIDING ✆ **A Step Above Stables** (706-745-9051; www.astep abovestables.net), 3839 South Mauney Road, Blairsville. Open 9–sunset daily; reservations required. The facility offers guided rides along wooded trails and to a Lake Nottely overlook. Ask about the Sunset Ride. Children welcome; day and overnight camps offered in June and July. $25 for one hour, $35 for 1½ hours, $50 for two hours.

✆ **Brasstown Valley Resort** (706-379-4613; 1-800-201-3205; www.brasstown valley.com), 6321 US 76, Young Harris. Rides go out at 10 AM and 1 PM daily; reservations required. This family-oriented resort has added stables. $45 for one hour, $77 for two hours.

🏇 **Trackrock Stables** (706-745-5252; 1-800-826-0073; www.trackrock.com), 4890 Trackrock Camp Road, Blairsville. Open year-round; one-hour rides leave at 11 AM, 1, 2:30 and 4 PM; two-hour rides leave at 10:30 AM and 12:30 PM. Reservations suggested but not required. Guided one-hour trail rides meander through Trackrock Campground, mountain meadows, and along tree-shaded paths beside gurgling streams. They have horses for riders of all skill levels as well as some particularly trained for younger children. Nonriders in your group can enjoy hayrides or spend time fishing, swimming, or hiking. $25 per hour.

LLAMA TREKKING 🏇 **Crystal River Ranch Llama Treks** (706-896-5005; www .crystalriver-ranch.com), 3499 US 76 East, Hiawassee. Open daily; arrive no later than 9:30 AM; treks begin at 10. Reservations required 72 hours in advance; minimum of four people. Take a three- to four-hour hike through the Chattahoochee National Forest accompanied by llamas to carry the supplies for a buffet lunch. The ranch breeds llamas and usually has 40 to 50 on hand. $45.

OUTDOOR ADVENTURES 🏇 **Mountain Adventures at the Fieldstone Resort** (706-896-2262; 1-888-834-4409), 3499 US 76, Hiawassee. Personnel at the resort (see *Lodging*) can plan activities such as canoeing and kayaking, fly-fishing, golf, horseback riding, white-water rafting, and even wine and cheese cruises. Hours and fees vary by activity.

WATERFALLS *Note:* The rocks are deceptively slippery around these falls. Exercise caution.

🏇 🍃 **Helton Creek Falls** (706-745-5789; 1-877-745-5789; www.visitnorth eastgeorgia.com/waterfalls.htm), US 129 South, Blairsville. Open daylight hours daily. The 0.3-mile Helton Creek Falls Trail follows the creek to two waterfalls. The trail accesses the lower falls at both the bottom and top and ends at the bottom of the upper falls. The total vertical drop is more than 100 feet. Free.

🏇 🍃 **High Shoals Falls and High Shoals Scenic Area** (706-745-6928; www.fs.fed.is/conf), Forest Service Road 283 off GA 75, Hiawassee. Open daylight hours daily. An observation deck provides views of five falls. Free.

WINERY TOURS 🍃 ♿ **Crane Creek Vineyards** (706-379-1236; www.crane creekvineyards.com), 916 Crane Creek Road, Young Harris. Open noon–5 Tuesday through Saturday, January through March; 1–6 daily, April through December. The vineyard produces a full spectrum of tradition-

ALL SKILL LEVELS CAN TAKE TO THE TRAILS AT TRACKROCK STABLES IN BLAIRSVILLE.

al wines. Numerous wine dinners are scheduled throughout the year, as well as the **Spring Art and Wine Fest** and the **Fall Harvest Festival.** The Vintner's Tasting in the 1800s farmhouse on Saturday includes a tasting of all of the vineyard's wines and a souvenir glass. Accommodations are available in the single-occupancy Bryson Homestead Guest House. The winery and store are wheelchair accessible, but not tasting room. Tour free; standard tasting $3; Vintner's Tasting $10.

✳ Green Space

GARDENS

✐ ❧ ♿ **Fred Hamilton Rhododendron Garden** (706-896-4191; www.georgia -mountain-fair.com), 1311 Music Hall Drive, Hiawassee. Open daily. In the spring and early summer, more than 3,000 rhododendrons and azaleas bloom alongside wildflowers. Free.

LAKES ✐ ❧ **Lake Chatuge.** The 7,500-acre TVA reservoir, which is shared by Towns County, Georgia, and Clay County, North Carolina, offers numerous water sports and activities.

✐ ❧ **Lake Nottely,** US 19 and US 129 North, Blairsville. Open daylight hours daily. The picturesque 4,180-acre lake with 106 miles of shoreline offers all sorts of water sports, boating, camping, fishing, picnicking, and swimming.

NATURE PRESERVES AND PARKS ✐ ❧ ♿ **Cooper's Creek Wildlife Management Area** (770-535-5700; www.dnr.state.ga.us/dnr/wild), GA 60 at GA 180, Blairsville. Open daylight hours daily. Outdoor fans enjoy the area for bird-watching, camping, fishing, horseback riding (BYOH—bring your own horse), hunting, and picnicking. Free.

✐ ❧ **Sosebee Cove Scenic Area** (706-745-0601; www.fs.fed.us/conf), GA 180, Blairsville. Open daylight hours daily. The area is a large, north-facing cove with many high-elevation flora and fauna. Of particular note are the huge buckeye and tulip trees. The area has a loop trail from which visitors can view the natural beauty of the area and bird-watch. Free.

✐ ❧ ♿ **Swallow Creek Wildlife Management Area** (770-535-5700; www .georgiawildlife.com), off GA 75, Hiawassee. Open daily. This vast 19,000-acre preserve offers opportunities for bird-watching, camping, fishing, hiking, hunting, and picnicking. If you plan to hunt or fish, make sure you have the necessary license and tags. Free.

✐ ❧ ♿ **Vogel State Park** (706-745-2628; 1-800-864-7275; www.gastateparks .org/info/vogel), 7485 Vogel State Park Road, Blairsville. Open 7 AM–10 PM daily. One of the oldest preserves in the state park system, Vogel State Park is located at the foot of Blood Mountain in the Chattahoochee National Forest. The 233-acre park is particularly popular in the autumn, when the area is a sea of brilliant colors. A small 20-acre lake with a beach allows for swimming and fishing, while 17 miles of trails attract hikers and backpackers. In addition, the park features a Civilian Conservation Corps museum, a general store, seasonal miniature golf, and pedal-boat rentals. Accommodations are offered in campsites and cottages (see *Lodging*). Parking $3.

✷ Lodging

BED & BREAKFASTS

In Blairsville

♿ **Davis-Reid Sampson Inn B&B** (706-835-2469; 770-921-8187), 147 Rogers Street. Open only on weekends between June 1 and October 1; reservations required. This 1865 National Registry home is decorated with Victorian-era antiques. No smoking. One wheelchair-accessible room on first floor. $150.

♿ **Highland Falls Bed and Breakfast Inn** (706-835-1926; 1-866-295-7373; www.georgiavacations.com/highlandfallsbb), 4434 Highland Forge East. This three-bedroom B&B has a spectacular mountain view private Jacuzzis and serves a wonderful three- to four-course full breakfast, snacks, and complimentary beverages. No smoking. One room on first floor wheelchair accessible. $129.

Misty Mountain Inn and Cottages (706-745-4786; 1-888-MISTYMN; www.mistymountaininn.com), 4376 Misty Mountain Lane. This comfortable Victorian-era farmhouse is decorated with period antiques. Smoking permitted. No wheelchair access. $70–$85.

In Hiawassee

♿ **Bed and Breakfast at Swan Lake** (706-896-1582; 1-800-896-5341; www.hickorynutcove.com), 2500 Hickorynut Cove. The B&B, which is located on the grounds of the **Hickorynut Cove Trout Farm** (see *To Do—Fishing*) was built in 1991 and describes itself as contemporary rustic. Accommodations are offered in the Hummingbird Hideaway or the Pink Lady's Slipper Suite, both with private baths and a covered patio and porch swing overlooking Swan Lake and Eagle Mountain. Breakfast, included in the nightly rate, is served on the covered veranda, weather permitting. Smoking outside only. Wheelchair accessible. $85.

Guest House at Crane Creek Vineyards (706-379-1236; www.cranecreekvineyards.com), 916 Crane Creek Road. This working winery (see *To Do—Winery Tours*) also offers a 100-year-old restored single-family homestead for guests. If you visit during the late summer or early fall, you can participate in the grape harvest if you so desire. Smoking permitted outside only. Not wheelchair accessible. $100.

Hidden Valley Bed and Breakfast (706-896-4988; 1-866-850-6274; www.hiddenvalleybandbranch.com), 441 Mull Road. This property is located about 2½ miles out of town, tucked back into a little valley that makes you feel as though you were hundreds of miles from the rest of the world. In the evenings, fresh-baked Viennese apple strudel is served. To work off any extra pounds you might have put on, try the spa area with Finnish sauna and Jacuzzi. Swedish massage is also available for an additional fee. No smoking. Not wheelchair accessible. $75.

♿ **Mountain Memories Bed and Breakfast** (706-896-8439; 1-800-335-8439; www.mountainmemoriesbandb.com), 385 Chancey Road. Although this property is technically in town, it doesn't seem like it because it sits on top of a hill that affords guests a panoramic view of both the mountains and Lake Chatuge. Designed for romance, guest accommodations feature a two-person Jacuzzi and private entrance. In addition to the extensive full breakfast (so large the owners say you can skip lunch), an elegant candlelight dessert buffet and coffee are served in the evening. Picnic baskets for two can be provided for an additional fee. Pets permitted with some restrictions; call to inquire. Not equipped for children younger than 12. Smoking permitted outside only. Wheelchair accessible. $129–139; two-night minimum required on holidays and some weekends.

In Young Harris
🌷 🌿 **Creekside Hideaway B&B/ Guesthouse** (706-379-1509; 1-888-882-7335; www.creeksidehideaway .com), 8970 Sharons Way. The property offers B&B rooms, a guest house, and a very rustic log cabin in the woods. The owners allow pets so long as the guest gives notification prior to arrival and signs a Pet Code of Conduct. Smoking outside only. Wheelchair access very limited. $55–89.

CAMPGROUNDS

In Blairsville
🌿 🌷 **Trackrock Campground and Cabins** (706-745-2420; www.track rock.com), 4887 Trackrock Campground Road. This year-round facility offers 95 tree-shaded campsites on 300 acres. Amenities include bathhouses, a recreation building, laundry facilities, and sales of ice, firewood, and liquified petroleum gas. One- and two-bedroom lakeside and rustic wooded cabins are offered as well. These cabins feature a stone fireplace, covered porch, and fully equipped kitchen. Activities include fishing, swimming, horseback riding (separate fee; see *To Do— Horseback Riding*), and hayrides. No smoking in cabins. Cabins not wheelchair accessible. Tents and pop-ups $20; full hookups $22; cabins $99 and up; call for rates for more than two people. Two-night minimum required; three-night minimum on holidays.

🌿 🌿 🌷 **Vogel State Park** (706-745-2628; 1-800-864-7275; www.gastate parks.org/info/vogel), 7485 Vogel State Park Road. This park offers 103 tent, trailer, and RV sites as well as 18 walk-in sites, backcountry sites, and a pioneer campground. $12–40.

CONDOS

In Hiawassee
🌿 ♿ **Fieldstone Resort Condominiums** (706-896-2262; 1-888-834-4409), 3499 US 76 West. Located on the grounds of the resort, the two-, three-, and four-bedroom condos are individually decorated. Many of the resort amenities are available to condo guests. No pets, No smoking. Wheelchair accessible. $279–429 May to October; call for off-season rates.

COTTAGES AND CABINS

In Blairsville
🌿 🌿 🌷 **Vogel State Park** (706-745-2628; 1-800-864-7275; www.gastate parks.org/info/vogel), 7485 Vogel State Park Road. The park features 35 fully equipped cottages, many of them lakeside. $65–125.

See also **Trackrock Campground and Cabins** under *Campgrounds*

INNS AND RESORTS

In Hiawassee
🌿 **Boundary Waters Resort** (706-896-2530; 1-800-323-3562; www .boundarywatersresort.com), 528 Sunnyside Road. Lakeside suites that sleep two to six are offered along with the fully equipped three-bedroom Mallard Point Lake House. Guests receive complimentary dockage for their boats and use of canoes, kayaks, and paddleboats. No pets. No smoking. Limited wheelchair accessibility. Suites $70–150; cabin $135–150; weekly rates available.

♂ ৬ **The Fieldstone Inn Resort**
(706-896-2262; 1-888-834-4409), 3499
US 76 West. Cradled along the shores
of Lake Chatuge, the getaway features
66 upscale rooms with private balconies, complimentary breakfast, the
four-star Old Hiawassee Grill, Yacht
Club Tavern and Grill, swimming
pool, tennis courts, and exercise room.
Fun World at the Fieldstone features
slick-track Go-Karts, rock climbing,
batting cages, miniature golf, laser tag,
a foam factory, more than 100 arcade
games, and Enrico's Pizzeria. Cinemas
Four is a four-theater complex that
features stadium seating and surround
sound. Fieldstone's full-service outfitter, Mountain Adventures, offers boating, Jet Skis, canoeing, kayaking,
sailing, fly-fishing, hiking, and white-
water rafting (see *To Do—Outdoor
Adventures*). Two nonsmoking rooms.
Wheelchair accessible. $109–189.

In Young Harris
♂ ✹ ৬ **Brasstown Valley Resort**
(706-379-9900; 1-800-201-3205; www
.brasstownvalley.com), 6321 US 76.
This luxurious resort offers accommodations in a 134-room lodge and eight
four-bedroom cottages. Renowned for
its high-country cuisine, the restaurant serves authentic north Georgia
dishes paired with wines from local
vintners. Other dining options include
a casual eatery and a cocktail lounge.
Activities on the 503-acre resort
include an 18-hole golf course (see *To
Do—Golf*), four lighted tennis courts,
a swimming pool, state-of-the-art fitness center and spa, stables, 9.2 miles
of interpretive hiking and horseback
riding trails (see *To Do—Horseback
Riding*), Brasstown Creek trout fishing, seasonal children's programs (see
To Do—For Families), and more. Pet-
friendly cottages and some nonsmok-

ing rooms available. Wheelchair
accessible. $169–$179.

OTHER LODGINGS

In Hiawassee
♨ ৬ **Enota Mountain Retreat** (706-
896-9966; www.enota.com), 1000 GA
180. Enota Mountain combines cabin,
RV and tent sites, and a B&B. The
nonprofit spiritual retreat and animal
rescue facility provides accommodations for visitors in order to help
finance its conservation work. No
smoking. One cabin wheelchair accessible. Tent sites $20–26; RV camping
$30–33; cabins $85 for two people to
$165 for eight.

✳ Where to Eat
DINING OUT

In Hiawassee
♂ ৬ **Old Hiawassee Inn at the
Fieldstone Resort** (706-896-2262;
1-888-834-4409), 3499 US 76 West.
Open 7–10 AM and 4–10 PM daily.
This very upscale dining establish-

ROCKING CHAIRS AT THE BRASSTOWN
VALLEY RESORT

ment offers a full country breakfast and serves steaks, freshwater fish, lobster, and pastas for dinner. No smoking. Wheelchair accessible. Breakfast $3.99–7.99, dinner $12.99–30.

In Young Harris

✐ ♿ **Brasstown Valley Resort** (706-379-4613; 1-800-201-3205; www.brass townvalley.com), 6321 US 76. Open 7 AM–10 PM daily. The resort's dinner buffets are particularly popular. Friday night features seafood, and Saturday spotlights prime rib. The à la carte menu is always available. No smoking. Wheelchair accessible. Breakfast and lunch $10.95, dinner $24–26.

EATING OUT

In Hiawassee

✐ ♠ ♿ **Yacht Club Tavern at the Fieldstone Resort** (706-896-2262; 1-888-834-4409), 3499 US 76 West. Open for lunch and dinner daily. This "boater's casual" eatery serves burgers, meat and two sides, soup of the day, and freshly baked desserts. No smoking. Wheelchair accessible. $5.99–12.99.

In Young Harris

✐ ♠ ♿ **Brasstown Valley Resort** (706-379-4613; 1-800-201-3205; www .brasstownvalley.com), 6321 US 76. Open 4–10 daily. **McDivot's Sports Pub** serves burgers, salads, and snacks. No smoking. Wheelchair accessible. Under $10.

✳ Entertainment

MUSIC Anderson Music Hall (706-896-4191; www.georgia-mountain -fair.com), Georgia Mountain Fairgrounds, 1131 Music Hall Road off US 76, Hiawassee. The music hall is the site of many concerts throughout

the year, including the **Country Music Superstar Concerts** and the **Georgia Mountain Bluegrass Festival** (see *Special Events*). Call for schedule and prices.

Hiawassee Opry (706-896-2107), Bell Creek Road, Hiawassee. Old and new country music is performed every Saturday night, April through October. Visiting musicians are invited to participate. Cloggers and a gospel quartet also perform. Free.

✳ Selective Shopping

ANTIQUES Blueberry Hill Collections (706-835-2211), 2987 Town Creek School Road, Blairsville. Open 9–5 weekdays, June 1 through December 31. The emporium purveys all types of antiques and collectibles.

Hiawassee Antique Mall (706-896-0587), 460 North Main Street, Hiawassee. Open 10–5 Monday through Saturday, noon–5 Sunday. Sixty dealers sell a large selection of antiques with an emphasis on mountain country items.

FOOD Puett's Roadside Market (706-379-1304), Young Harris Highway, Young Harris. Open 9–5 daily. Shop here for fresh produce.

SPECIAL STORES Mountain Crossings at Walasi-Yi Center (706-745-6095; www.mountaincrossings.com), 9710 Gainesville Highway/US 19 North, Blairsville. Open daily except Christmas Day; check web site for specific hours. This is the only spot where the 2,172-mile Appalachian Trail actually passes through a building. Built by the Civilian Conservation Corps in 1937, the stone building houses a store where hikers can stock up on supplies and where local art and pottery are sold. The center also offers hostel facilities ($15 per night).

❈ Special Events

May: **Georgia Mountain Bluegrass Festival** (706-896-4191; www .georgia-mountain-fair.com). Held in the Anderson Music Hall at the Georgia Mountain Fair in Hiawassee, the festival features performances by numerous artists and groups. $25 for one-day pass, $40 for two-day pass.

Rhododendron Festival (706-896-4191; www.georgia-mountain-fair .com). Also held at the Georgia Mountain Fair, the festival celebrates the beautiful rhododendron gardens, which bloom from early April to late May. The festival also features craft vendors and food, plus plants for sale. $3.

May through October: **Country Music Superstar Concerts** (706-896-4191; www.georgia-mountain -fair.com). Seven concerts are presented May through October at the Georgia Mountain Fair in Hiawassee (call for exact dates and featured artists). $35–$45 per concert.

August: **Georgia Mountain Fair** (706-896-4191; www.georgia-mountain-fair.com), US 76, Hiawassee. Fair hours: 10–9 Monday through Thursday, 10–10 Friday, 9–10 Saturday, 9–6 Sunday. Towns County's oldest tourist

MOUNTAIN CROSSINGS AT WALASI-YI CENTER IS THE ONLY PLACE WHERE THE APPALACHIAN TRAIL PASSES THROUGH A BUILDING.

attraction, the monthlong celebration features demonstrations of old-time skills, food, arts and crafts, exhibitions, midway rides, and entertainment. $7–$10 for five-day pass, children younger than 10 free; parking $2.

October: **Georgia Mountain Fall Festival** (706-896-4191; www .georgia-mountain-fair.com). Similar to the Georgia Mountain Fair in the summer, the fall festival is also the official **State Fiddlers Convention,** with performances by numerous artists and groups included in the admission price. $7, children younger than 10 free; parking $2.

MOUNTAIN MIDNIGHT COON DOG HOWL

Celebrate New Year's Eve at a unique event where you can come in bibbed overalls or a tux, jeans or a sequined ball gown, and sit on hay bales at tables covered with white linen cloths. Held at the Hiawassee River Trout Lodge (706-896-4966; 1-800-984-1543), the shabby-chic celebration includes an ugly coon dog contest, coon dog howling contest, hog calling contest, favors, entertainment, and champagne for toasting at midnight. Food and beverages available for purchase. $15.

ROME AND CALHOUN

L ocated in the heart of northwest Georgia, this area is rich with history. Long the home of Native Americans, it served as the last capital of the Cherokee Nation, the largest of the five civilized tribes of the Southeast, before the Indians were removed and sent along the Trail of Tears. The Civil War played a significant part in the region's history, and the Battle of Resaca was one of the bloodiest battles in the Atlanta Campaign. For history buffs, numerous museums and historic homes tell the stories of the Native Americans, white settlers, and military campaigns.

Three large rivers flow through the area—the Conasauga, the Oostanaula, and the Coosawattee—as well as numerous smaller rivers and streams. The Chattahoochee National Forest provides splendid views of nature's beauty and a gorgeous setting for outdoor activities, as do several state parks, city and county parks, lakes, and recreation areas.

GUIDANCE When planning a trip to the Rome area, including Cave Spring, contact the **Greater Rome Convention and Visitors Center Bureau and Welcome Center** (706-295-5576; 1-800-444-1834; www.romegeorgia.org), 402 Civic Center Drive, Rome 30161. Open 9–5 weekdays, 9–3 Saturday. The center is located in the old train station, and the Last Stop Gift Shop is in the caboose adjacent to the station.

To learn more about Adairsville, contact the **Adairsville Welcome Center** (770-773-1775; www.notatlanta.org), Open 8–4 weekdays, 10–3 Saturday, 1–3 Sunday.

For more information about Adairsville and Resaca, contact the **Cartersville–Bartow County Convention and Visitors Bureau** (770-387-1357; 1-800-733-2280; www.notatlanta.org), One Friendship Plaza, Cartersville 30120. Open 8:30–5 weekdays, 11–4 Saturday.

For information about Calhoun or Resaca, contact the **Calhoun–Gordon County Convention and Visitors Bureau, Calhoun Local Welcome Center, Gordon County Chamber of Commerce** (706-625-3200; 1-800-887-3811; www.gordonchamber.org), 350 South Wall Street, Calhoun 30701. Open 8:30–5 weekdays, 10–4 Saturday.

To learn more about Cedartown or Rockmart, consult the **Polk County Chamber** **of Commerce** (770-749-1652; www.polk.ofgeorgia.org), 512 Main Street, Cedartown 30125. Open 8:30–5 weekdays, 10–3 Saturday. The chamber has another office at 604 Goodyear Street, Rockmart 30153, which is open 8:30–5 weekdays.

To find out more about the Summerville area, call the **Chattooga County Chamber of Commerce** (706-857-4033; www.chattooga-chamber.org), 44 GA 48, Summerville, GA 30747. Open 9–5 Monday, Tuesday, Thursday, and Friday.

GETTING THERE *By air:* The nearest airports are **Hartsfield-Jackson Atlanta International Airport** in Atlanta and **Chattanooga Metropolitan Airport** in nearby Tennessee (see What's Where in Georgia). Car rentals available at both.

By bus: **Greyhound Lines** (706-291-4775; www.greyhound.com) provides service to Rome (868 Spider Web Drive).

By car: North-south Interstates 75 in Georgia and 59 in Alabama provide easy access to this area, but why not get off the interstates and use the more scenic US 27? East-west routes include US 278 and 411 and GA 20.

By train: The nearest **Amtrak** (1-800-USA-RAIL) station is in Atlanta (see What's Where in Georgia).

GETTING AROUND **Rome Transit** (706-236-4523) offers mass transit service on five routes within the city limits. Service includes paratransit services for the disabled. One-way ticket price: adults $1, seniors and students 50¢. In Rome, car rentals are available from: **Budget** (706-290-0244), **Enterprise** (706-290-1093), **Florida Rent-A-Car** (706-232-9912), **Nugent Auto Rental** (706-232-4400), and **Rent-A-Wreck** (706-232-8391). In Calhoun, car rentals are available from **Enterprise** (706-602-1841) and **Nugent Auto Rental** (706-625-3765).

PARKING Downtown parking on Broad Street in Rome is free and allowed in two-hour increments. Visitors may receive passes for longer parking by contacting the **Greater Rome Convention and Visitors Bureau** (1-800-444-1834). Parking passes are issued on a case-by-case basis and are not allowed for special-event parking.

WHEN TO GO The mountainous areas in the northern part of the state experience longer periods of colder temperatures as well as occasional snow or ice. Some campgrounds and other establishments close for a few months in the winter, so call ahead if traveling in the winter to avoid disappointment.

MEDICAL EMERGENCY For life-threatening situations, call 911. Otherwise, in the Rome area, urgent care is available at **Redmond Regional Medical Center** (706-291-0291; www.redmondregional.com), 501 Redmond Road, Rome, and **Floyd Medical Center** (706-234-8706; www.floyd.org), 304 Turner McCall Boulevard, Rome. Elsewhere in this region, immediate care is available in Calhoun at **Gordon Hospital** (706-629-2895; www.gordonhospital.com), 1035 Red Bud Road, and in Cedartown at **Polk Medical Center** (770-748-2500; www.polk medicalcenter.com), 424 North Main Street.

THE MOUNTAINS

VILLAGES AND NEIGHBORHOODS Rome, the only city in the region described in this chapter, has a population of 91,000 and 800 acres of parkland. Rome boasts Shorter College, one of the finest music schools in the Southeast; Berry College, which has the largest campus in the world; Floyd College; and Coosa Valley Technical College. The official symbol for Rome is its clock tower, which sits atop one of the city's seven hills and is actually a cleverly disguised water tower.

Rome's **Between the Rivers Historic District** is aptly named in that it encompasses the old downtown area of Rome where the town was first founded in 1834. Defined by the Etowah, Oostanaula, and Coosa rivers, this area contains most of Rome's oldest (mostly turn-of-the-20th-century, Victorian-style) homes, churches, and commercial buildings. Broad Street, the second-widest in Georgia, offers many trendy shops and restaurants. Get a walking tour brochure from the visitor center.

Adairsville is noted for the part it played in the Great Locomotive Chase during the Civil War (see Northern Suburbs chapter in 1, Atlanta Metro). In this century, it is also known for the world-class **Barnsley Gardens Resort,** which offers superior accommodations, dining, and sporting options (see listings throughout this chapter). Once a private, 10,000-acre estate called Woodlands, the property has seen its share of tragedies. Julia, wife of original owner Geoffrey Barnsley, died during construction. The Civil War ruined Barnsley's fortunes, and soldiers from both sides ravaged the estate. Later, a 1906 tornado tore the roof off the villa and forced the family into the kitchen annex. The estate was rescued in 1988 by Prince Hubertus Fugger and Princess Alexandra of a small principality in southern Germany. They restored the gardens and stabilized the ruins, then added cottages, dining establishments, a spa, a golf course, and other amenities.

THE CIVIL WAR AND A TORNADO CREATED THE BARNSLEY RUINS IN ADAIRSVILLE.

Adairsville was the first town in Georgia to be listed in its entirety on the National Register of Historic Places. Antebellum and Victorian homes and churches fill the 170-acre historic district. Today it attracts tourists, history buffs, and antiques lovers. Adairsville also hosts the three-day **Great Locomotive Chase Festival** the first weekend in October (see *Special Events*).

Calhoun's past is largely influenced by the Cherokee Indians who lived here. The area eventually became the capital of the Cherokee Nation and was the birthplace of the Cherokee alphabet, written language, and newspaper, the *Cherokee Phoenix* (see **New Echota Cherokee Capital Historic Site** under *Historic Homes and Sites*).

Cave Spring, a classic small Southern town south of Rome, was named for the pure spring found in a limestone cave located in what is now known as **Rolater Park** (see *Green Space—Nature Preserves and Parks*). The town's natural wonders were known to several cultures of Native Americans, and legend has it that tribal meetings and games occurred at the site. The park site also was the campus of the Cave Spring Manual Labor School, later renamed Hearn Academy. One of the historic school buildings now operates as the **Hearn Inn** (see *Lodging—Bed & Breakfasts*), and the old Baptist church is used for weddings, meetings, and special events. Including the school buildings, the picturesque village has 90 structures on the National Register of Historic Places. Homes exhibit Gothic, Queen Anne, and Plantation styles. The 1867 Presbyterian church has been restored and is open to the public as an art gallery on weekends. Still central to the village is the 29-acre park where the spring flows into a pond and then into a 1½–acre swimming pool shaped like the state of Georgia. Cave Spring is widely known for the quality and quantity of its antiques shops, and several antiques, gift, and home decor shops and popular eateries surround the park. A renowned arts and crafts festival also is held each June in the park (see *Special Events*).

Cedartown's claim to fame is that it was the hometown of Sterling Holloway, whose raspy voice portrayed Winnie-the-Pooh. He began performing here in early childhood by putting on neighborhood variety shows. A marker at College Street and Sterling Holloway Place memorializes the native son. Today Cedartown has a history museum and is the home of a skydiving company.

Kingston claims to have more historical markers per capita than any other town in Georgia. Kingston grew during the heyday of the railroads because there was a major rail facility downtown. During the Great Locomotive Chase in April 1862, Andrews's Raiders lost a precious hour in the rail yard until freight trains cleared the tracks. Rescuers missed them by only four minutes but took a locomotive from there to continue the chase. Union General William Tecumseh Sherman headquartered here, consolidating his position early in the Atlanta campaign. While in Kingston during the Civil War, General Sherman made plans for and awaited approval from General Ulysses Grant for his March to the Sea. He destroyed the town when he left. The last contingent of Confederate troops west of the Mississippi was pardoned in Kingston in May 1865. That same year, ladies of the town observed Confederate Memorial Day by decorating the graves of 250 unknown soldiers in the town cemetery on the last Sunday in April. That ceremony became known as Decoration Day and eventually evolved into the Memorial Day we celebrate today, although a separate Confederate Memorial Day is still observed. After the Civil War, Kingston became known for its ministers, whose renown spread on the reports of rail passengers who visited local churches while waiting for their trains. Today Kingston is well known as the home of the Atlanta Steeplechase.

THE LOVE OF HIS LIFE

Geoffrey Barnsley set out to build an estate worthy of his wife, Julia. In 1842 he began construction of a grand 24-room Italianate villa with modern conveniences such as hot and cold running water. He surrounded the villa with formal gardens designed in the style of Andrew Jackson Downing, the architect who designed the grounds of the U.S. Capitol and the White House. Unfortunately, Julia died before the home and gardens were completed. Brokenhearted, Barnsley abandoned construction until Julia allegedly appeared to him in the formal gardens one night and told him she wanted the house finished. You'll find a likeness of Julia on the fountain in the knot garden.

Rockmart's name derived from "Rock Market" because of the abundance of slate, limestone, iron shale, and clay found in the area. A portion of the Silver Comet Trail (see *To See—Special Places*), which will eventually stretch from Atlanta to Anniston, Alabama, runs through the city's park.

✳ To See

CULTURAL SITES ✐ ✍ ♿ **Capitoline Wolf** (607-295-5576; 1-800-444-1834; www.romegeorgia.org), 601 Broad Street, Rome. Open daily. This 1,500-pound statue of a suckling wolf in front of City Hall was a gift from the government of Rome, Italy, to the people of Rome, Georgia, in 1929. The statue is an exact replica of the *Capitoline Wolf* suckling the twins Romulus and Remus (orphaned offspring of Mars, the god of war, and Rhea Silvia, the daughter of King Numitor), an Etruscan statue that stands in the Palazzo dei Conservatori on the Capitoline Hill in Rome. Some folks found the statue so shocking that when important events were scheduled the twins were diapered and the wolf draped. In 1933 one of the twins was stolen and a replacement had to be created. Because of anti-Italy sentiment during World War II and threats to dynamite the statue, it was put into storage until 1952. Free.

THE 1,500-POUND *CAPITOLINE WOLF* STATUE IS IN FRONT OF ROME'S CITY HALL.

GUIDED TOURS ✐ ✍ The **Greater Rome Convention and Visitors Center** (706-295-5576; 1-800-444-1834; www.romegeorgia.org), 402 Civic Center Drive, Rome. At 1 PM every Saturday. Guided tours of historic Rome depart from the visitor center on Jackson Hill. For those who want to tour on their own, the visitor center (open 9–5 weekdays, 9–3 Saturday) offers tapes for self-guided walking tours of Rome's downtown Victorian district as well as brochures marking significant structures. Guided tours: adults $10, children 3–12 $5.

HISTORIC HOMES AND SITES ⚲ ⚲ **Berry College Campus** (706-291-1883; 1-800-220-5504; www.berry.edu/oakhill), 24 Veterans Memorial Highway, Rome. In the early 20th century, Martha Berry began teaching poor children in her playhouse. Eventually her efforts created a college. She called on Henry Ford and other philanthropists for help, and many of the beautiful buildings on campus were constructed with financial contributions from Ford. Today, with 26,000 acres, Berry has the largest campus in the world. Among its interesting sites are Oak Hill and Martha Berry Museum (see *Museums*) and the Old Mill, where corn is sometimes ground with the second-largest working overshot waterwheel in the world. Free.

✍ ⚲ **Clocktower Museum,** Tower Hill in downtown Rome. Museum open April through November, 10–4 Saturday, 1–5 Sunday, or by appointment. The city's water tower was constructed in 1871 and encased in a red brick decagon-shaped structure, which cleverly and completely disguises the steel water tower. A 3-foot space between the exterior walls and the water tower allows for an internal staircase, and a 41-foot superstructure atop the tower contains a clock with four faces and a bell. Visitors can see murals and artifacts from Rome's history and the restored original clockworks. The works of local artist Chuck Schmult also are displayed. You can take the 107 stairs to an observation tower for a panoramic view of historic Rome. Free.

✍ ⚲ ⚲ **New Echota Cherokee Capital Historic Site** (706-624-1321; www .gastateparks.org/info/echota), 1211 Chatsworth Highway NE/GA 225, Calhoun. Open 9–5 Tuesday through Saturday, 2–5:30 Sunday. Contrary to popular opinion, all Native Americans did not live in teepees or grass huts. Many lived just as the white settlers did. In 1825 the Cherokee national legislature established a capital called New Echota at the headwaters of the Oostanaula River, marking one of the earliest experiments in national self-government by an Indian tribe. The Cherokee built log cabins, frame homes, outbuildings, and public structures. They published a bilingual newspaper at an on-site print shop—the first Indian language newspaper in the country. Unfortunately, when gold was discovered in north Georgia, the white men decided to take the land of the Native Americans. A treaty was signed that relinquished all Cherokee land east of the Mississippi River. The infamous Trail of Tears began here with Native Americans assembled for removal to the west in 1838. Today the site contains original and reconstructed buildings, including the council house, courthouse, print shop, missionary Samuel Worcester's home and tavern, an 1805 store, and farm outbuildings such as barns, corncribs, and smokehouses. The modern visitor center provides space for an introductory movie, interpretive exhibits, and a gift shop where visitors can purchase authentic Native American arts, crafts, and music. The site also features a 1-mile nature trail and Coosawattee River fishing. A popular annual event is a **Christmas Candlelight Tour,** held the first Saturday evening in December. At this event, visitors can experience an 1820s Christmas with music, singing, and refreshments by candlelight. $2.50–4.

✏ 🦐 ♿ **Oakleigh** (706-629-1515), 335 South Wall Street, Calhoun. Open 10–4 Monday through Thursday or by appointment. General Sherman used this stately home as his headquarters when his Union troops were advancing from Chattanooga to Atlanta. Today the 1850 house serves as the headquarters of the Gordon County Historical Society. In addition to admiring the home and its antique furniture, female visitors are fascinated by the fantastic collection of nearly 2,000 dolls from the 1930s to the early Barbies, all of which were collected by one woman. The historical society also has many genealogy resources. Free.

✏ 🦐 ♿ **Rome Visitors Center** (706-295-5576; 1-800-444-1834; www.rome georgia.com), 402 Civic Center Drive, Rome. Open 9–5 weekdays, 10–3 Saturday. Not just a dispenser of information, the visitor center is an attraction in and of itself. Located on one of Rome's seven hills, the welcome center is housed in a 1901 train depot. Also on the property is the Boswell Cabin, typical of how pioneer families lived between 1830 and 1850, and several pieces of antique machinery. The Noble Machine Shop lathe, which was built in 1847, was used to make steamboat engines, furnaces, locomotives, and Confederate cannons. The Corliss steam engine served Rome's Southern Cooperative Foundry from 1902 to 1971. The foundry produced so many stoves, heaters, ranges, and grates that Rome became known as the Stove Center of the South. The age of the cotton gin at the center is unknown, but it was the oldest gin in use in 1963.

MUSEUMS ✏ 🦐 ♿ **Chieftains Museum–Major Ridge Home** (706-291-9494; www.chieftainsmuseum.org), 505 Riverside Parkway, Rome. Open 9–3 Tuesday through Friday, 10–4 Saturday. Located on the banks of the Oostanaula River, the original home of Major Ridge, an early 19th-century leader of the Cherokee Nation, was recently given the National Park Service National Trail of Tears designation. Ridge, who tried to conform to white men's culture while preserving his own, served as a mediator during many disputes. He fought with Andrew Jackson at the Battle of Horseshoe Bend in 1814, which is where he earned the rank of major. Ridge and his family were ferryboat operators, storekeepers, tavern owners, and slaveholders. The core house was built in 1794 and enlarged and remodeled many times until it attained its current white clapboard plantation house appearance. Exhibits focus on the Ridge family, artifacts found on the property, the Cherokee, the clash of cultures with white settlers, and the Trail of Tears. Displays include Native American artifacts, photographs, furniture, and artwork. Adults $3, seniors $2, children $1.50.

✏ 🦐 **Eubanks Museum and Gallery** (706-291-2121; 1-800-868-6980), 315 Shorter Avenue, Rome. Open 8:30–5 weekdays. This museum on the campus of Shorter College contains the collection of J. Robert Eubanks, a life trustee and benefactor of the college. Natural-history exhibits display family artifacts from safaris to Africa and India. Other exhibits include antique telephones, early American hardware, and Native American pottery, tools, and hunting items. Free.

🦐 ♿ **Kingston Woman's History Museums** (770-336-5540; 770-387-1357; www.notatlanta.org), 13 East Main Street, Kingston. Open 1–4 Saturday and Sunday or by appointment. Although it started as a women's museum concentrating on candlelit tours, today the Kingston Woman's History Club displays artifacts, scrapbooks, and photographs in two museums. The Civil War Museum portrays the town's role in the Civil War and the Kingston Memorial Day observances, which are the oldest in the nation. The Martha Mulinix Annex displays memorabilia relating to life in Kingston after the Civil War, housing displays of old farm equipment and exhibits related to Kingston schools, stores, and churches. Free; donations accepted.

✍ ❦ ♿ **Oak Hill, Martha Berry Museum** (706-291-1883; 1-800-220-5504; www.berry.edu/oakhill), 24 Veterans Memorial Highway, Rome. Open 10–5 Monday through Saturday. A magnificent example of Colonial Revival architecture, Oak Hill was the home of Martha Berry, founder of the Martha Berry School, which is now Berry College (see *Historic Homes and Sites*). The house, which was built in 1847, remains as it was lived in from 1860 to 1942. The museum chronicles Martha Berry's life and work as related to her founding the school for less fortunate children. The museum also contains an extensive art collection amassed by Miss Berry's sister, Eugenia, wife of Prince Enrico of Italy. The collection includes Italian and American artists and spans 1,000 years. The crowning glory of the estate is the gardens, which were designed between 1927 and 1933. In keeping with early 20th-century landscaping trends, the gardens also display classical statuary and fountains. Trails include the Fernery Nature Trail and Martha Berry's Walkway of Life. Just a small piece of trivia: Oak Hill appeared as the Carmichael mansion in the film *Sweet Home Alabama*. Also on the estate is the Carriage House, which features vintage vehicles; the original log cabin, also known as the "Birthplace of Berry," where Berry began teaching mountain children; and Aunt Martha's Cottage, the recently restored home of Berry's beloved cook and house servant, "Aunt Martha" Freeman. Special events include the **Berry College Ford Festival** and **Candles and Carols.** Adults $5, children 6–12 $3.

❦ **Polk County Historical Society Museum** (770-749-0073; www.polkhist .home.mindspring.com), 611 South Main Street, Cedartown. Open 2–4 Wednesday and 2–5 the fourth Sunday of each month. Once a children's library, the building now houses a local museum where exhibits chronicle the history of the county. Displays include town and farm memorabilia from the 19th through the early 20th century. Free.

❦ ♿ **Roland Hayes Museum** (706-629-2599; www.cgarts.org), 212 South Wall Street, Calhoun. Open 10–9 Monday, 10–4 Tuesday through Thursday, 10–2 Friday and Saturday. Housed within the **Harris Arts Center** (see *Entertainment*), the museum honors Roland Hayes (1887–1977), a native of Calhoun, the son of a slave, and one of the first African Americans to have a concert and operatic career. He performed at Carnegie Hall and all over Europe. The museum displays memorabilia related to Hayes's career. Visitors can listen to his music and see a film about his life. Free.

✍ ❦ ♿ **Rome Area History Museum** (706-235-8051; www.romehistory museum.com), 305 Broad Street, Rome. Open 10–5 Tuesday through Saturday. Exhibits cover subjects such as Native American history, explorer Hernando de Soto's visit to the area, early settlers, and wars from the Civil War to the present. Learn about quilting, weaving, the importance of steamboats and cotton, and the devastation caused when Union troops burned the city to the ground. These stories are told through documents, maps, blueprints, photographs, personal letters, business records, and much more. Adults $3, seniors $2, children 6–12 $1.50.

NATURAL BEAUTY SPOTS ♂ ♞ **Marshall Forest** (706-291-2121; www.nature .org/georgia), Horseleg Creek Road, Rome. Open by appointment. This is one of the last stands of virgin old-growth pine-hardwood forest in the Ridge and Valley Province, a geographical corridor that extends from Pennsylvania to Alabama. It is Georgia's first National Natural Landmark—designated by the U.S. Department of the Interior in 1966—and the only virgin forest in America within city limits. More than 300 species of plants as well as nonthreatened animals, amphibians, snakes, dozens of bird species, and other living organisms inhabit the forest. The 250-acre forest also abounds with self-guided hiking trails that crisscross the area, including a Braille Trail with plant identification tags and 20 stations with plaques written in Braille and English. Free.

SPECIAL PLACES ♂ ♞ ♿ **Silver Comet Trail and Riverwalk** (770-684-8760; 1-800-226-2517), Rockmart. Open daily. This paved rails-to-trails route stretching from Atlanta to the Georgia-Alabama state line is popular with walkers, joggers, skaters, and cyclists. It is accessible from downtown Rockmart. The trail is named for the Seaboard Airline Railroad's silver passenger train, which traveled through here on a route between New York and Birmingham from May 1947 to April 1969. Free.

✳ To Do

BICYCLING ♂ **Barnsley Gardens Resort** (Outpost Sporting Center, 770-773-2457; resort 1-877-773-2447; www.barnsleyresort.com), 597 Barnsley Gardens Road, Adairsville. Reservations required. Rentals include a helmet, water bottle, and trail map. Minimum age 6; adults must accompany riders age 6–11. $12 per hour, $24 for two hours, $30 for four hours, $40 for full day; trail use fee $10 for riders with their own bikes.

BOATING ♂ ♞ **Barnsley Gardens Resort** (Outpost Sporting Center, 770-773-2457; resort 1-877-773-2447; www.barnsleyresort.com), 597 Barnsley Gardens Road, Adairsville. Reservations required. Canoes, kayaks, and johnboats are available on a first-come, first-served basis for use on the resort's 10-acre lake. Boaters must be at least 11 years old unless accompanied by an adult. Complimentary for overnight guests; included in admission price for day visitors.

Rome has 50 miles of canoe trails on the **Oostanaula River.** The gradient drops only 1 foot along the entire length—guaranteeing smooth water and a leisurely paddle. Put-in points are along GA 225.

FARM TOURS ♂ ♞ ♿ **Paradise Pastures Farm and Petting Zoo** (770-382-4119; www.ParadisePastures.com), 650 Taylorsville-Macedonia Road, Taylorsville. Open 10–6 daily, June 1 through September 30; in October 9–9 weekdays, 9–9 Saturday (maze and bonfire available until 10), 1–6 Sunday. The farm offers pet and animal shows in the petting zoo. See llamas, donkeys, miniature donkeys, miniature horses, silky chickens, pigs, goats, pygmy goats, and other animals. The farm has a country store and in October offers hayrides, a corn maze, pumpkin painting, and Saturday-night bonfires. $7.

🌾🐾♿ **Pumpkin Patch Farm** (770-773-2617), 230 Old Dixie Highway, Adairsville. Open 10–5:30 weekends in October. Activities include a petting zoo, hay maze, hayrides, pumpkin and autumn crafts, scarecrow making, and more. Admission free; activity prices vary.

FISHING 🐾 **Barnsley Gardens Resort** (Outpost Sporting Center, 770-773-2457; resort 877-773-2447; www.barnsleyresort.com), 597 Barnsley Gardens Road, Adairsville. Reservations required. Anglers enjoy fly- and spin-fishing on Lower Pond or the 10-acre lake. Instruction is offered, and guides can take anglers on daylong fishing excursions to local rivers such as the Noontoola, a private trophy-trout stream. Minimum age of 14 unless accompanied by an adult. $90–150 for instruction and equipment; if fishing on your own, $25 for fishing permit, $15 for equipment, $4 for lures; $375 for guided fishing trips.

GOLF **Barnsley Gardens Resort** (pro shop 706-773-2555; resort 877-773-2447; www.barnsleyresort.com), 597 Barnsley Gardens Road, Adairsville. Pro shop open 8–6; course opening depends on weather (in winter, frost must be off the course before it can open, then play is until dark), so call for hours. The resort's course, called "the General" for the famous train hijacked during the Great Locomotive Chase, is a Jim Fazio–designed championship course ranked 13th in the state by *Golf Digest*. The 18-hole, 7,350-yard, par-72 course covering 378 acres features an outstanding collection of par-3 holes. The course winds through hardwood forest, tall reeds, cattails, and thick brush past a creek and pond, with abrupt changes in elevation. $100 Monday through Thursday, $115 Friday through Sunday and holidays; afternoon, senior, and junior discounts available.

See also Golf Appendix.

HORSEBACK RIDING 🐾 **Barnsley Gardens Resort** (Outpost Sporting Center, 770-773-2457; resort 877-773-2447; www.barnsleyresort.com), 597 Barnsley Gardens Road, Adairsville. Reservations required. Guests can enjoy a guided western horseback ride. One-hour trail rides, two-hour scenic wilderness rides, and children's rides are offered. Picnic meals can be added to any ride at an additional cost. $80 per hour, $125 for two hours.

🐾 **Zion Farms** (706-235-8002; www.zionfarms.com), 2679 Big Texas Valley Road, Rome. Reservations required. Guided horseback rides of one to three hours are available on this 340-acre estate where riders can enjoy flat green pastures for an easy ride or mountain trails for a more challenging adventure. Riding camps also are offered. Accommodations are available in guest cottages and a bunkhouse (see *Lodging—Inns and Hotels*). $40 for one-hour ride, $60 for two hours, $100 for three-hour picnic ride (minimum of two riders), $100 for fall afternoon hors d'oeuvres ride.

SHOOTING SPORTS **Barnsley Gardens Resort** (Outpost Sporting Center, 770-773-2457; resort 877-773-2447; www.barnsleyresort.com), 597 Barnsley Gardens Road, Adairsville. By appointment 9–4:30 Monday through Saturday; reservations required. The resort offers sporting clays, lessons, and clinics overseen by the prestigious British School of Shooting. $50–125 with Barnsley equipment; $22–67.50 with your own equipment; $50 per hour for lessons.

SKYDIVING **Adventure Skydiving Center** (770-684-3483; 1-800-490-3483; www.ascskydiving.com), 493 Airport Road, Cedartown. Open 9–sunset weekdays. The largest skydiving center in the Southeast offers tandem skydiving with qualified instructors. Participants receive a video or photo of their accomplishment. Call for prices.

Georgia Skydiving Center (706-971-9029; www.georgiaskydivingcenter.com), 304 Russell Field Road NE, Rome. Open 7:30–sunset Wednesday through Sunday. The company offers a full range of skydiving opportunities for the more adventurous among us. The site offers breathtaking panoramas for those who are too faint of heart to try skydiving. Call for prices.

SPAS **Barnsley Gardens Resort** (spa 770-773-7480; resort 877-773-2447; www.barnsleyresort.com), 597 Barnsley Gardens Road, Adairsville. Spa treatments available 9–7 Monday through Saturday, 9–5 Sunday; fitness center and swimming pool open 6 AM–10 PM daily; coed whirlpool open 6 AM–midnight daily. At the Spa at Barnsley Gardens, guests can be pampered with a wide array of massages, skin treatments, body wraps, and aromatherapy. They also can use the large coed whirlpool; ladies' and gentlemen's saunas, steam rooms, and whirlpools; fitness center; and the Grecian-style swimming pool. Must be 18 years old to use spa facilities. Spa rates vary by treatment; packages $275–615.

TENNIS ✍ ❦ **Rome–Floyd County Tennis Center** (706-290-0072), 301 West Third Street SW, Rome. Open 9 AM–11 PM daily. The design of the award-winning center has earned an "Outstanding Tennis Facility Design" award from the U.S. Tennis Association, and *Tennis Magazine* calls Rome one of the top tennis cities in America. The 16-court lighted facility offers instruction and league play and hosts state and regional tournaments. $2 per hour before 5; $2.50 per hour after 5.

❋ Green Space

GARDENS ✍ ❦ ♿ **Barnsley Gardens Resort** (770-773-7480; www.barnsleyresort.com), 597 Barnsley Gardens Road, Adairsville. Open sunrise–sunset daily. The gardens were rescued in 1988 and have been restored to the showcase of the South they once were. Enjoy guided or self-guided tours of the gardens, the manor house ruins, and the small museum. Adults $10, seniors $8, children $5.

LAKES  **Carters Lake** (706-334-2248; www.carters.sam.usace.army.mil), 1850 Carters Dam, Oakman. Open daily. The 3,200-acre U.S. Army Corps of Engineers lake and surrounding 6,000 acres of public land offer opportunities for boating, developed and primitive camping, fishing, hunting, and picnicking. Marinas and cabin and boat rentals are available. Free access to lake; some activities have fees.

NATURE PRESERVES AND PARKS  **Chattahoochee National Forest** (770-297-3000; www.fs.fed.us/conf). Open daylight hours daily except for campers. The pristine, undeveloped forest boasts 750,000 acres, 10 wilderness areas, 2,200 miles of rivers and streams (of which 1,367 miles are trout streams), and 430 miles of hiking trails—many of these located in northwest Georgia. (See also the Cartersville, Clarksville, Dahlonega, Dalton, and Hiawassee chapters.) All of them provide endless opportunities for outdoor pursuits in wildlife management tracts, recreation areas, and scenic regions. Recreational activities include off-road riding, mountain biking, horseback riding, hiking, fishing, hunting, and camping. Free.

James H. Floyd State Park (706-857-0826; 1-800-864-7275; www.ga stateparks.org/info/sloppy), 280 Sloppy Floyd Lake Road off US 27, Summerville. Open 7–10 daily. Isolated from the hustle and bustle of city life, this tranquil 561-acre park is surrounded by rural countryside and the Chattahoochee National Forest (see above). Fishing is offered on two stocked lakes,

THE BEAUTIFUL BARNSLEY GARDENS RESORT IN ADAIRSVILLE

and hikers can use the 3 miles of lake loop trails or access the Pinhoti Trail. Two boat ramps are available (electric motors only are allowed). There are two fishing piers, one of which is wheelchair accessible. Children enjoy the playgrounds, feeding the fish from the boardwalk, and renting pedal boats. There is a **Children's Fishing Rodeo** the first Saturday in June and a **Senior Citizen Fishing Rodeo** the second Saturday in June. The park also offers camping and cottages (see *Lodging*). Parking $3.

✔ 🦌 ♿ **Lock and Dam Regional Park** (706-234-5001; www.rfpra.com), 181 Lock and Dam Road, Rome. Park open 24/7; store open 7–7 Monday through Saturday, 7–5. Sunday. The 73-acre regional park was created around the Mayo Lock and Dam, which was completed and opened for navigation in 1913. Enjoy the best in river fishing as well as canoeing on the Coosa River from the park, which also includes picnic shelters, an exhibition center, horseshoe pits, canoe rentals, and rest rooms. The Coosa River Trading Post sells bait and supplies, while the Coosa River Nature Center has live reptile exhibits and natural history displays. Summer camps are offered at the nature center, and 25 fully equipped RV campsites are available. Parking $2.

✔ 🦌 ♿ **Rolater Park, Cave Spring** (706-777-3962), US 411/GA 53, Cave Spring. Park open daylight hours daily; cave open 10–6 daily in summer. The 300,000-year-old cave, where the spring originates, has impressive stalagmites and the legendary "Devil's Stool" formation. The spring pumps 3 to 4 million gallons of water a day, and the award-winning springwater is noted for its purity and taste. Although it can be purchased commercially, many visitors bring jugs to fill and take home. Park free; cave $1.

✔ 🦌 ♿ **Salacoa Creek Park** (706-629-3490), GA 156, Calhoun. Open 7–8 daily. The 343-acre county park features a 126-acre lake and offers a quality swimming beach, a boat ramp, picnic areas, and fishing. Bass, bream, catfish, and crappie are stocked in the lake. Private boats are permitted on the lake (motorboats are limited to 10 mph) and canoeing is popular. The waters are open for legal fishing when the park is open. Anglers age 16 and older must have a valid state or nonresident fishing license. No night fishing is allowed except during special events. In addition, the park offers nature trails and tent and RV campsites. Free.

RECREATION AREAS ✔ 🦌 ♿ **Rocky Mountain Recreation and Fishing Area** (706-802-5087; www.gofishinggeorgia.com), 4054 Big Texas Valley Road NW, Rome. Open daily; fishing permitted sunrise–sunset. Enjoy nature at its finest as well as outdoor pursuits such as fishing, hunting, picnicking, hiking, camping, and swimming. The 5,000-acre area offers two recreation lakes. Largemouth bass and sunfish are the most common fish caught, but the lakes are also filled with channel catfish, black crappie, and hybrid white-striped bass. Whitetail deer, turkey, and waterfowl are present for wildlife observation. There are two boat ramps. Fishing boats only are allowed and must run at idle speed regardless of boat or motor size. Anglers age 14–65 must have a valid fishing license unless disabled. RV campsites and walk-in sites are available. $3 per car; primitive campsites $7; RV sites $14–28.

✳ Lodging

BED & BREAKFASTS

In Cave Spring

♂ ✿ **Hearn Inn** (706-777-8865), 13 Cedartown Street SW. The 1839 building, once the dormitory for the Cave Spring Manual Labor School or Hearn Academy, now houses a bed and breakfast. Located in Rolater Park, where it has easy access to downtown, the simply furnished inn offers seven rooms, one with a private bath. Other rooms share baths, making them suitable for a family or friends traveling together. A continental breakfast is included in the nightly rate. A communal hot tub is a hit with guests. No smoking. Limited wheelchair accessibility. $65.

✿ **Tumlin House Bed and Breakfast** (706-777-0066; 1-800-939-3880), 38 Alabama Street. The sprawling 1842 home offers four beautifully decorated guest rooms—two with private baths and two with a shared bath. In addition, the B&B boasts a 1,400-square-foot wraparound porch, a screened porch, and a swimming pool. A full gourmet breakfast and afternoon refreshments are included in your stay. Dinner is served on Saturday nights by reservation at an additional cost. The B&B is within easy walking distance of **Rolater Park** (see *Green Space— Nature Preserves and Parks*), antiques shops, and restaurants. No pets. Children 12 and older welcome. Smoking outdoors only. Not wheelchair accessible. $65–85.

In Rome

♿ **Claremont House Bed and Breakfast** (706-291-0900; 1-800-254-4797; www.theclaremonthouse.net), 906 East Second Avenue. One of the most striking Victorian-era mansions

in Rome, the Claremont House (circa 1882) offers elegant guest rooms furnished in Victorian opulence. Spacious guest accommodations feature 14-foot ceilings, heart-pine floors, elaborately carved woodwork, a fireplace, a private bath, gorgeous furnishings, and luxury linens. Included in the nightly rates are a gourmet candlelit breakfast and afternoon refreshments on Friday and Saturday. No smoking. Some rooms wheelchair accessible. $90–150.

Coral River Bed and Breakfast (706-235-9883; www.coralriver.com), 2 Coral Avenue. Located in a newly renovated 1890s home in the Oakdene Historic District, the bed & breakfast offers handsomely appointed guest rooms with king- or queen-sized beds and private baths—some with claw-foot tubs or a Jacuzzi. Amenities include triple-sheeted beds, 300-count sheets, bathrobes and slippers, upgraded bathroom amenities, evening turndown service, a sumptuous Southern breakfast, and afternoon snacks or homemade after-dinner treats. No smoking. Not wheelchair accessible. $99–125; numerous packages available.

In Summerville

✿ **Dillard's Bed and Breakfast** (706-822-9948; www.dillardsbandb .com), 625 East Washington Street. A more-than-100-year-old farmhouse provides three beautifully appointed guest rooms, each with a private bath, television, VCR, and small refrigerator. Two rooms feature a sitting area and a claw-foot tub. A screened porch overlooks the stone patio. No smoking. Not wheelchair accessible. $85.

CAMPGROUNDS AND COTTAGES

In Calhoun

See **Salacoa Creek Park** under

Green Space—Nature Preserves and Parks.

In Rome

See **Lock and Dam Regional Park** under Green Space—Nature Preserves and Parks and Rocky Mountain Recreation and Fishing Area under Green Space—Recreation Areas.

In Summerville

✍ 🌟 ♨ ♿ **James H. Floyd State Park** (706-857-0826; 1-800-864-7275; www.gastateparks.org/info/sloppy), 280 Sloppy Floyd Lake Road off US 27. The park offers four fully equipped cottages as well as 25 tent, trailer, and RV sites and a pioneer campground. Guests can use all the park's facilities. Campsites $20–23; cottages $95–105.

See also **Lock and Dam Regional Park** and **Salacoa Creek Park** in Green Space—Nature Preserves and Parks and **Rocky Mountain Recreation and Fishing Area** in Green Space—Recreation Areas.

INNS AND HOTELS

In Rome

✍ **Zion Farms** (706-235-8002; www.zionfarms.com), 2679 Big Texas Valley Road. The European-style, 340-acre family estate hidden among the pines offers luxurious accommodations in a series of cottages, some with multiple bedrooms, a Jacuzzi tub, and/or a kitchen. Guests enjoy gardens, pastures, ponds, winding mountain trails, secluded picnic areas, a palatial stable, an equestrian gift shop, show arenas, a cross-country course, and more. Activities include horseback riding (additional fee; see To Do—Horseback Riding), fishing, hiking, mountain biking, and estate

tours. A full gourmet country breakfast is included. Boxed picnic lunches and dinners can be provided for an additional fee. Smoking outdoors only. Not wheelchair accessible. Rooms $75; cottages $125–200 per couple, $35 per additional adult, $15 per additional child younger than 10; specials available for two-night weekend stays, weekdays, multiple weekdays, Valentine's weekend.

RESORTS

In Adairsville

✍ 🌟 ♿ **Barnsley Gardens Resort** (770-773-7480; 1-877-773-2447; www.barnsleyresort.com), 597 Barnsley Gardens Road. Thirty-three cottages containing 70 suites feature English-cottage architecture. The cottages sport 12-foot ceilings, heart-pine floors, private porches, and period-inspired private baths with ball-and-claw iron soaking tubs and a separate shower. Each suite is appointed with antiques and fine period reproductions, a king-sized bed, a wood-burning fireplace, and the latest electronics. Many also offer a sofa bed. In addition to superior lodging, fine and casual dining, and a spa, the resort features a golf course, sporting clays, horseback riding, fly-fishing, and bicycle and boat rentals (see separate entries throughout chapter). Kids' Night Out (6–9 every Friday) provides dinner, entertainment, and activities for children age 4–12 ($50 per child; reservations required 24 hours in advance). Pets welcome for additional fee. Vast majority of suites nonsmoking. Four cottages wheelchair accessible. $215–800; many packages and specials available.

✳ Where to Eat

DINING OUT

In Adairsville

♂ ♿ **Barnsley Gardens Resort**
(770-773-2522; 1-877-773-2447; www
.barnsleyresort.com), 597 Barnsley
Gardens Road. Woodlands Grill open
7 AM–10 PM daily; the Rice House
open 5:30–10 PM Friday and Saturday.
World-class dining options abound at
the **Rice House Restaurant** and the
Woodlands Grill. The Rice House,
Barnsley's formal dining restaurant,
serves classic Southern cuisine. Located in an 1854 farmhouse that was the
home of Fleming Rice, the house's
exterior is still marred by bullet holes
from a Civil War battle. Dining
options include the formal dining
room with its original stone fireplace
or the glass-enclosed dining porch
overlooking the gardens and ruins.
Reservations recommended. The
Woodlands Grill, a steakhouse that
serves prime meats and fish, is a little
more casual and has both indoor and
outdoor seating from which guests
enjoy a panoramic view of the golf
course. The restaurant also has an
English pub with a fireplace and billiards table. An international wine and
cheese tasting is offered 5–7 PM Friday. No smoking. Wheelchair accessible. $45 at Woodlands Grill; $50–70
at Rice House.

In Cave Spring

Tumlin House Bed and Breakfast
(706-777-0066; 1-800-939-3880), 38
Alabama Street. Open Saturday 7 PM.
Reservations required. A six-course
gourmet dinner is served at a single
seating. Guests may bring their own
wine. No smoking. Not wheelchair
accessible. $35.

In Rome

♿ **LaScala** (706-238-9000), 413
Broad Street. Open 5:30–10 Monday
through Saturday. This upscale restaurant offers Italian cuisine, traditional
dishes, and candlelight dining as well
as a cozy lounge. Menu choices
include seafood, pastas, gourmet salads, and desserts, and the restaurant
also has a fully stocked bar and an
extensive wine list. No smoking.
Wheelchair accessible. $12.95–25.50.

♿ **Waterfront** (706-378-8700), 112
West Second Avenue. Open 11:30–9
Monday through Thursday, 11:30–10
Friday and Saturday. In warm weather, alfresco dining on the deck is the
favorite choice at this fashionable
restaurant. Otherwise, eat indoors in
the dining room or bar area. The
American/continental menu features
seafood, steaks, and chicken. The sinfully delicious desserts are legendary.
No smoking. Wheelchair accessible.
Lunch $6.95, dinner $14.95–20.95.

EATING OUT

In Adairsville

♂ 🐾 ♿ **Barnsley Gardens Resort**
(770-773-7480; 1-877-773-2447; www
.barnsleyresort.com), 597 Barnsley
Gardens Road. Open seasonally, 4–9
Friday, noon–9 Saturday, noon–6 Sunday; may be closed in inclement
weather. The authentic Bavarian-style
outdoor **Beer Garden** serves imported German beers, including the
house specialty, Munich's Spaten, as
well as cuisine that ranges from
sausages and pretzels to ribs and panini. An open-fire pit warms diners at
night and provides a place to roast
marshmallows. Smoking allowed since
this is outdoors. Wheelchair accessible. $8–14.

✐ 🍴 ♿ **Maggie Mae's Tea Room at the 1902 Stock Exchange** (770-773-1902; www.georgiahighcountry.org/1902stockexchange.html), 124 Public Square. Open 11–2 Tuesday through Saturday. Tearoom fare includes imported teas and coffees, chicken salad, three kinds of quiches, a daily hot special, and a choice of scrumptious desserts such as hummingbird cake, turtle cheesecake, or pie. When the weather is pleasant, eat in the charming brick courtyard. No smoking. Wheelchair accessible. $4.95–6.95.

In Rome

✐ 🍴 ♿ **Country Gentleman** (706-295-0205), 26 Chateau Drive. Open 11–2 and 5–10 weekdays; 5–10 Saturday. A favorite with locals for nearly 30 years, the casual eatery serves grilled seafood, Italian dishes, and steaks. No smoking. Wheelchair accessible. $12–16.

✐ 🍴 ♿ **Harvest Moon Café** (706-292-0099), 234 Broad Street. Open 11–2:30 Monday and Tuesday, 11–10 Wednesday through Saturday, 10:30–2 Sunday. The café is known for specialty sandwiches on home-baked breads, homemade soups, burgers, salads, and delicious desserts at lunchtime. The dinner menu features an extensive array of appetizers, rib-eye steaks, shrimp, pork chops, and pastas. There is also an on-site wine market. No smoking. Wheelchair accessible. Lunch $4–12, dinner $10–22.

✐ 🍴 ♿ **Jefferson's** (706-378-0222), 304 Broad Street. Open 11–10 Monday through Thursday, 11–11 Friday and Saturday, 11:30–10 Sunday. This casual eatery and nightspot serves up hot dogs, nachos, oysters, and seafood, as well as mild, medium hot, or turbo wings. Beer is the most popular beverage and there are many choices, bottled or on tap. No smoking. Wheelchair accessible. $10–15.

✐ 🍴 ♿ **Partridge Café** (706-291-4048), 300 Broad Street. Open 11–6 Sunday through Friday. For more than 60 years, this diner has been offering family-style meat-and-three or à la carte meals featuring regional recipes. No smoking. Wheelchair accessible. $2.60–7.75.

✳ Entertainment

Harris Arts Center (706-629-2599; www.cgarts.org), 212 South Wall Street, Calhoun. Open 10–9 Monday, 10–4 Tuesday through Thursday, 10–2 Friday and Saturday. The center, which occupies the restored 1930-era Rooker Hotel, contains an art gallery, the **Roland Hayes Museum** (see *To See—Museums*), and the Milton Ratner Performing Arts Theater, where the Calhoun Little Theater produces plays and where the Calhoun Community Adult Chorus and Calhoun Community Youth Chorus perform. The art gallery hosts a fine arts show and numerous exhibitions throughout the year. Free to tour building, museum, and art gallery; event prices vary.

Rome Area Council for the Arts (706-295-2787; www.romearts.org), 248 Broad Street, Rome. Gallery open 9–5 weekdays. The council is an umbrella organization for numerous visual, performing, and literary arts organizations in Rome and Floyd County. Performances are presented in various venues. The art gallery sponsors shows that change monthly. Free.

MUSIC Cedartown Civic Auditorium (770-748-4168; 1-877-263-9372; www.ccauditorium.com), 205 East Avenue, Cedartown. Call for a schedule of performances and ticket prices. Performances of all kinds—bluegrass, Broadway, classical, and other genres—are held throughout the year here.

Rome Symphony Orchestra (706-291-7967; www.romesymphony.org), office: P.O. Box 533, Rome 30162. One of the oldest orchestras in the South, the symphony was created in 1921. The orchestra presents a series of four classics concerts and another of three pops concerts at the Rome City Auditorium in addition to outdoor performances during Pops in the Park and the First Friday series. Call for a schedule of performances. In advance: adults $15, seniors $10, students $3; at the door: $20, $15, and $6; season discounts available.

PROFESSIONAL SPORTS 🏊 🎾 ♿

Rome Braves (706-378-5144; 1-800-326-4000; www.romebraves.com), office 755 Braves Boulevard, Rome. Call or visit the web site for a schedule of games. Between April and September, the 2003 South Atlantic League baseball champions play 70 home games at State Mutual Stadium on Veterans Memorial Highway. The **Three Rivers Club** at the stadium is open 11–2 weekdays for lunch. Tickets $4–10.

🏊 🎾 ♿ **Rome Gladiators** (706-853-9265; 1-800-868-6980; www.rome gladiators.decise-direct.com), 315 Shorter Avenue, Rome. Call or visit the web site for a schedule of events and ticket prices. Between March and June, the World Basketball Association team plays home games in the Winthrop-King Centre at Shorter College.

🏊 🎾 ♿ **Rome Renegades** (706-378-7363 for information; 706-291-5281 for tickets; www.romerenegades.com),

office 318 Broad Street, Rome. Box office open 8:30–4:30 weekdays. Call or visit the web site for a schedule of games. Between February and June, the team plays indoor-arena football with home games at the Forum in downtown Rome. $5–20.

THEATER **Public Square Opera House at the 1902 Stock Exchange** (770-773-1902; www .georgiahighcountry.org/1902stock exchange.html), 124 Public Square, Adairsville. Call for a schedule of productions and prices. The facility offers dinner-theater productions highlighting historical themes such as *A Circuit Rider's Wife* by local author Corra Harris, which inspired the film *I'd Climb the Highest Mountain*; Mark Twain's *The Diaries of Adam and Eve*; and Louisa May Alcott's *Little Women*. Special performances are often geared to holidays such as Valentine's Day, Mother's Day, and Christmas. The 1902 Stock Exchange also houses **Maggie Mae's Tea Room** (see *Where to Eat—Eating Out*) as well as numerous shops purveying antiques and collectibles (see *Selective Shopping*).

Rome Little Theatre (706-295-7171; www.romelittletheatre.com), 530 Broad Street, Rome. Call for a schedule of performances. The organization offers quality entertainment for the whole family at the historic 1929 DeSoto Theater in downtown Rome. Each season usually includes a children's show, Christmas show, comedy, drama, and musical. Generally adults $10, students $8.

Theatrical productions also are staged at Shorter and Berry Colleges (see *To See—Historic Homes and Sites* and **Oak Hill** under *To See—Museums*).

ANTIQUES Cave Spring is an antiques mecca with stores like **Blue Willow Antiques and Collectibles** (706-331-1284), 16 Alabama Street; **BW's Emporium, Fudge and Coffee** (706-777-8544), 22 Alabama Street; **Cave Spring Antiques** (706-777-8502), 9 Alabama Street; **Christa's, Etc.** (706-777-3586), 10 Alabama Street; and **Country Roads Antique Mall** (706-777-8397), 19 Rome Road, which houses 30 dealers.

1902 Stock Exchange (770-773-1902; www.georgiahighcountry.org/1902stockexchange.html), 124 Public Square, Adairsville. Open 10–5 Tuesday through Saturday, 1–3 Sunday. Individual gallery shops sell Victorian and Civil War collectibles, fine linens and lace, baby gifts, china, crystal, silver, antique wedding dresses, military weapons, antique furniture, Coke collectibles, Christmas decorations, antique toys, paintings, and prints. The **Corra Harris Bookstore,** named for the novelist from nearby Pine Log and author of *A Circuit Rider's Wife*, carries out-of-print books and works by Georgia authors. The complex also houses **Maggie Mae's Tea Room** (see *Where to Eat— Eating Out*) and the **Public Square Opera House** (see *Entertainment— Theater*).

Kingston Military Antiques (770-336-9354), 17 East Railroad Street, Kingston. Open by appointment only. The store specializes in military antiques, primarily from the Civil War.

FURNITURE **The Country Craftsman** (706-777-8343), 53 Rome Road, Cave Spring. Open 9–5 weekdays, 9–1 Saturday. Shop here for hand-crafted one-of-kind furniture created in all woods, styles, and finishes. Repairs, refinishing, and replacements are also available.

OUTLET STORES **Prime Outlets of Calhoun** (706-602-1305; 1-877-GO-OUTLETS; www.primeoutlets.com), 455 Belwood Road, Calhoun. Open 10–9 Monday through Saturday, noon–6 Sunday. More than 40 designers, manufacturers, and other retailers from Big Dog Sportswear to Wilson's Leather offer discount prices.

✳ Special Events

April: **Atlanta Steeplechase** (404-237-7436; 404-237-2818). Georgia's biggest single horse-racing event, the steeplechase is part of the Triple Crown Circuit and is the region's premier spring social event. The series of races is held at 435-acre Kingston Downs along the Etowah River. Other activities include terrier and pig races; pony rides; a petting zoo; hayrides; an air show and sky dive; hat, tailgating, and tent-party-decor contests; and a parade of hounds. $25 per person plus $20 vehicle pass, packages available for $240–400, which include four to six tickets, parking pass, and a pre-race cocktail party.

May: **Battle of Resaca Reenactment** (706-625-3200; 1-800-887-3811; www.georgiadivision.org/bor_reenactment.html). The reenactment, held the third weekend in May each year, occurs on 650 acres of Chitwood Farm, the battle's original site. In addition to battles both days, spectators see reconstructed breastworks and a redoubt, demonstrations of spinning and other skills, a re-created hospital, civilian and refugee camps, entertainment from a regimental band, and sutlers' and vendors' wares.

There is a memorial service at the Resaca Cemetery on Saturday and a church service on Sunday. Adults $5, children $2; portion of proceeds goes to battlefield preservation.

Silver Hill Rodeo (706-232-7787). Friday and Saturday nights of Memorial Day weekend. Held at Silver Hill Arena in Rome, the event features bronc and bull riding, barrel racing, and calf and cow roping. Gates open at 7 PM for pre-events such as wagon rides for children; main events begin at 8:30. Adults $10, children $5.

June: **Cave Spring Fine Arts and Crafts Festival** (706-777- 3382). Held the second weekend in June at **Rolater Park** (see *Green Space— Nature Preserves & Parks*), the homespun fair features juried artists and an antique car show. $5.

October: **Chiaha Harvest Fair** (706-235-4542). Call for dates. Held on the banks of the Oostanaula River in Rome's Ridge Ferry Park, the festival includes 100 artists, demonstrating craftspeople, continuous live entertainment, Southern cooking, children's art activities, riverboat rides, a wagon train, and historic tours. Admission free; fees for some activities.

Great Locomotive Chase Festival (770-773-3451, ext. 26). Held the first weekend in the Public Square in Adairsville, the festival features arts and crafts, parades, pageants, fireworks, and street dancing. $3.

Heritage Holidays (706-346-6623). The two-week festival in Rome features special events, theatrical productions, concerts, stage shows, live outdoor music, and holiday fairs. Call for dates and prices.

Late October: **Spirits of Barnsley** at Barnsley Gardens Resort (770-773-7480; www.barnsleyresort.com). Tours depart from the Beer Garden at 7:30 and 8 PM. Lamplighters take visitors on after-dark tours and spin spine-tingling tales of former residents. Adults $20, children 6–12 $10.

Southern Rivers 5

INTRODUCTION
PEACHES, PECANS, PEANUTS, PLANTATIONS, AND PRESIDENTS

Located in the southwestern corner of the state, the Southern Rivers region, which is further subdivided into the Plantation Trace and Presidential Pathways, is one of the most tranquil areas of Georgia and the least touristy. The absence of large cities also blessedly means the absence of heavy traffic, so travelers can cruise down miles and miles of almost deserted country roads at their own pace. Just remember to watch for the occasional slow-moving tractor or cotton-picking machinery. This is truly an area where you can get off the beaten track to find one-of-a-kind attractions.

People stereotypically believe that plantations were literally gone with the wind after the Civil War, and so they are quite amazed to learn that not only do vast plantations still exist, but that the region between Thomasville and Tallahassee, Florida, has the largest concentration of working plantations in the country—thus the area being designated as the Plantation Trace.

Two presidents called southwestern Georgia home. Franklin D. Roosevelt came to Warm Springs for polio treatment and ended up building a small house nearby, which came to be known as the Little White House. He died there in 1945 and the house is now a state historic site. Jimmy Carter grew up in Plains and returned there after his presidency, and several sites in and around town are designated as national historic sites. The presidential connection resulted in part of the region being dubbed Presidential Pathways.

Seemingly endless rural areas are filled with farms and orchards that produce peaches, pecans, and peanuts. Purchase the region's bounty in-season and take home numerous products made from them. Visitors also can learn about the importance of agriculture to the area at such sites as the Georgia Agrirama in Tifton, the Old South Farm Museum in Woodland, and Westville in Lumpkin.

One of the most important gardens in the Southeast, Callaway Gardens, is located in this region. Callaway Gardens is also a resort with a variety of lodging options, restaurants, and recreational activities. Flowers are also the main attraction at Ferrell Gardens in LaGrange and in Thomasville, which is known as the Rose City.

Abundant rivers such as the Chattahoochee, Flint, and Ochlocknee; lakes such as Blackshear, George T. Bagby, Seminole, Walter F. George, and West Point;

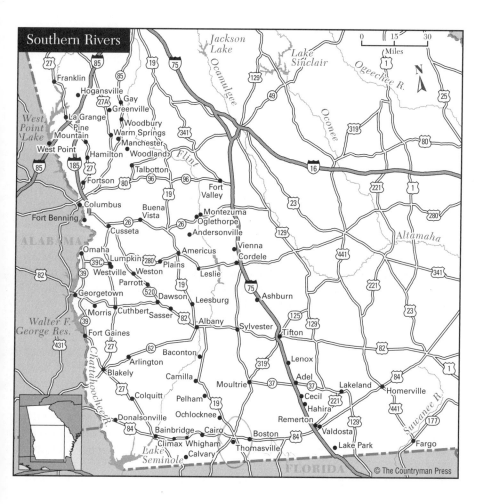

several state parks; and thousands of acres of undeveloped and protected forest lands and preserves provide innumerable opportunities for outdoor recreation.

Only a few small cities dot this area: Albany, Americus, Bainbridge, Columbus, LaGrange, Pine Mountain, Thomasville, Tifton, and Valdosta. Each offers numerous historical attractions and museums as well as a wide range of cultural activities and distinctive accommodations, restaurants, and shopping.

The remainder of the region is made up of dozens of distinctive small towns, each with a special attraction such as the Kolomoki Mounds State Historic Park in Blakely or the Georgia Rural Telephone Museum in Leslie. Eleven state parks and historic sites can be found in this area.

History is always on display in this area. Various aspects of the Civil War can be examined at the Andersonville National Historic Site and National Prisoner of War Museum near Andersonville and the Port Columbus National Civil War Naval Museum in Columbus.

ALBANY

The first residents of what became the Albany area were the Creek Indians, who called it Thronateeska, which meant "the place where flint is picked up." It's no surprise, then, that the Flint River flows through Albany.

The town was founded in 1836 and grew to incorporate several prosperous plantations. There were no battles fought in the area during the Civil War to interrupt production at these plantations, so they were able to supply critical food and cotton for the Confederacy. Albany became a rail center at the turn of the 20th century. Union Station, the convergence point for seven railroads, saw as many as 55 trains a day.

Like most Southern cities, Albany experienced upheaval during the civil rights movement of the 1960s and was the site of marches and protests. But the success of black voter registration led to a runoff election for a city commission seat in 1962. The following spring, all segregation statutes were removed from the books.

Albany, the eighth-biggest city in the state, with a population of 76,000, is currently experiencing an exciting renaissance with significant downtown renewal. The city suffered two devastating floods in the 1990s. In July 1994, Hurricane Hugo dumped 17 inches of rain on the area in a short time and the water rose as much as 8 feet, exceeding the levels of a 500-year flood. A flood of the proportions of a 100-year flood occurred in 1998. Reconstruction from both disasters has given Albany a new lease on life and provided a vibrant backdrop for the city's symphony orchestra, theater, a ballet company, and an excellent art museum.

One of the Seven Wonders of Georgia is found just outside Albany. Radium Springs, the largest natural spring in Georgia, produces 70,000 gallons per minute. The water, which eventually flows into the Flint River, maintains a temperature of 68 degrees year-round.

The plantations of yesteryear are now hunting preserves, and Albany, which is known as the Quail Hunting Capital of the World, annually hosts the Quail Unlimited Celebrity Hunt and the United Kennel Club Coon Dog Hunt. The Flint River and Lake Chehaw provide innumerable opportunities for water sports.

The surrounding small towns and countryside are noted for peanut production, hunting, tennis, and antiques shopping.

GUIDANCE When planning a trip to the Albany area, contact the **Albany Convention and Visitors Bureau and Welcome Center** (229-434-8700; 1-800-475-8700; www.albanyga.com), 225 West Broad Avenue, Albany 31701. Open 8:30–5 weekdays.

For information about Dawson and Parrott, contact the **Dawson–Terrell County Chamber of Commerce** (229-995-2011), 211 West Lee Street, Dawson 39842. Open 9–5 weekdays.

To learn more about Leesburg, contact the **Lee County Chamber of Commerce** (229-759-2422; 1-866-304-9237), 100-B Starksville Avenue, Leesburg 31763. Open 8:30–5 Monday through Thursday, 8:30–4:30 Friday.

For more information about Sasser and Sylvester, contact the **Worth County–Sylvester Chamber of Commerce** (229-776-7718), 301 East Franklin Street, Sylvester 31791. Open 8:30–5 weekdays.

GETTING THERE *By air:* Visitors to Albany can fly into **Southeast Georgia Regional Airport** (229-430-5175; www.ifly.com/southwest-georgia-regional-airport) 3905 Newton Road, Albany, which is served by **Atlantic Southeast Airlines** with four flights from Atlanta daily. Car rentals are available on site from **Avis, Budget, Enterprise, Hertz,** and **Thrifty.** Visitors might also choose to fly into **Hartsfield-Jackson Atlanta International Airport** and rent a car or take a shuttle from there to Albany (see What's Where in Georgia).

Columbus Metropolitan Airport (706-324-2449; www.flycolumbusga.com), 3250 West Britt David Road, Columbus, is served by **ASA/Delta Connection, Northwest,** and **US Air Express.** Passengers arriving at Columbus Metropolitan Airport can rent cars from **Avis** (706-322-2539), **Budget** (706-327-5501), **Enterprise** (706-322-0536), **Hertz** (706-324-2725), and **National** (706-322-4586).

Middle Georgia Regional Airport Macon (478-788-3760; www.airport/kmcn .com), 1000 Terminal Drive, Macon, is serviced by Delta's **Atlantic Southeast Airlines**. Car rentals are available in Macon from **Alamo/National** (478-788-5385), **Avis** (478-788-3840), **Budget** (478-784-7130), **Enterprise** (478-784-8633), and **Hertz** (478-788-3600).

Tallahassee Regional Airport (850-891-7802; www.ci.tallahassee.fl.us/citytlh/ aviation), 3300 Capital Circle SW, Suite 1, Tallahassee, Florida, is served by **Continental Express, Delta Air Lines, Delta Connection/Atlantic Southeast Airlines, Delta Connection/Chautauqua Air Lines, Delta Connection/ Comair, Northwest Airlink,** and **US Airways Express.** On-site car rentals are offered by **Alamo** (1-800-462-5266), **Avis** (1-800-331-1212), **Dollar** (850-575-4255), **Enterprise** (850-575-0603; 1-866-799-7959), **Hertz** (1-800-654-3131), and **National** (1-800-227-7368). Off-site car rentals are also available at several locations around town from **Budget** (1-800-527-7000), **Enterprise** (1-866-799-7959), and **U-Sav** (850-575-7368).

Dothan Regional Airport (334-983-8100), 800 Airport Drive, Dothan, Alabama, is serviced by **Atlantic Southeast Airlines.** Car rentals are available from **Avis** (1-800-331-1212), **Hertz** (1-800-654-3131), and **National** (1-800-227-7368).

By bus: **Greyhound Lines** (1-800-231-2222; www.greyhound.com), 300 West Oglethorpe Boulevard, Albany, offers bus service to Albany.

By car: US 19 and US 82 intersect in Albany. The easiest route to take there is US 82 west from I-75. The smaller towns described here are located along east-west US 82 or north-south US 19.

By train: Rail travel to the Albany area is not convenient. The closest **Amtrak** station (1-800-USA-RAIL; www.amtrak.com) is in Atlanta (see What's Where in Georgia).

GETTING AROUND In Albany, rental cars are available from **Economy Rent-A-Car** (229-883-7141), 524 West Oglethorpe; **Enterprise Rent-A-Car** (229-889-8020), 407 Sands Drive; and **Thrifty Car Rental** (229-434-7368), 712 West Oglethorpe.

MEDICAL EMERGENCY For life-threatening emergency, call 911. For other urgent care in Albany, assistance is available at **Phoebe Putney Memorial Hospital** (912-883-1800), 417 Third Avenue. For assistance in Sylvester, go to **Worth County Hospital** (912-776-6961), 807 South Isabella Street.

VILLAGES Pretty **Dawson**'s downtown historic district is a veritable showcase for architectural styles. The annual tour of homes sponsored by the Dawson Restoration Society features a glimpse inside many antebellum and Victorian-era treasures.

Leesburg is unusual in Georgia in that the town is in Lee County—Georgia towns and counties rarely coincide. The town is noted for an unusual Indian monument and a motor speedway.

Historic **Parrott** was incorporated in 1889 as a cotton-farming community. After a long decline, it was virtually a ghost town. In fact, the hamlet was used for several western movies, including *The Long Riders*. In recent years, however, the downtown has been revitalized and its restored buildings are enjoying new life as antiques shops, boutiques, art galleries, craft shops, and an old-fashioned soda fountain.

Sasser was the site of the Battle of Echouanotchaway Swamp in 1836—a part of the Creek Indian uprisings. Today it has a popular flea market (see *Selective Shopping*) and antiques mall.

STUMPING BOYS

In 1868 a simple lane that was the precursor to the present-day Broad Street in Camilla was created by cutting down virgin pines, leaving their stumps behind. The town's first mayor, T. J. Butler, inaugurated a "stumping contest" in which he contributed dimes to the boys who uprooted the most stumps to clear the lane. He gave dimes from his own pocket because the town treasury had no money in it.

> **GEORGIA PEANUTS**
> • The peanut is Georgia's official state crop, producing $390 million in revenue yearly.
> • Georgia is the nation's largest producer of peanuts, producing nearly 42 percent of the U.S. crop.
> • More than 70 Georgia counties produce 1.5 billion pounds of peanuts annually.
> • Georgia has between 5,000 and 15,000 peanut farms, and 37,000 people work on the farms, in shelling plants, in factories that roast peanuts or make candy or peanut butter from them, or in peanut-related agribusiness.
> • Favorite ways to eat peanuts in Georgia are boiling them in salt water while still in the shells or dropping shelled peanuts in your Coca-Cola.

Sylvester was incorporated in 1898 as the county seat of Worth County. The Sylvester post office is home to a New Deal mural called *Cantaloupe Industry*, painted by Chester J. Tingler in 1939. Worth County, known as "the Peanut Capital of the World," is the home of Universal Blanchers, Birdsong Peanuts, and ConAgra Products (Peter Pan peanut butter). The town and county sponsor the annual **Georgia Peanut Festival** each October, which attracts 10,000 visitors (see *Special Events*).

✳ To See

CULTURAL SITES ⚘ ✿ **Chehaw Indian Monument** (229-759-2422), New York Road, Leesburg. An 8-foot-tall granite monument was erected in 1912 by the Daughters of the American Revolution in honor of Chehaw Indians killed at Chehaw Village.

FOR FAMILIES ⚘ ✿ ♿ **Flint RiverQuarium** (229-639-2650; 1-877-GOFLINT; www.flintriverquarium.com), 101 Pine Avenue, Albany. Open September through May 14, noon–5 weekdays, 10–6 Saturday, 1–6 Sunday; May 15 through August 31, 10–6 Monday through Saturday, 1–6 Sunday. Descend to the depths of an underwater spring without even getting wet at this new aquarium. The facility tells the story of the Apalachicola, Chattahoochee, and Flint River basins and the mysterious blue-hole springs that help create the Flint River, which begins as a tiny trickle south of Atlanta and flows 350 miles to the Gulf of Mexico. The facility also showcases southwest Georgia's unique underwater inhabitants. An open-air, 175,000-gallon freshwater tank is filled with scores of fish, turtles, and alligators native to the area. Also displayed are reptiles, amphibians, and regional plants. The World of Water gives visitors an insider's view of rivers around the world. The Adventure Center, located in an adjacent building, features the three-story-tall, four-story-wide Imagination Theater where IMAX adventure films and special 3-D films are shown. RiverQuarium admission: adults $8.50, seniors $7.50, children 4–12 $6. Imagination Theater admission:

adults $8, seniors $7, children $6. Combination: adults $14, seniors $12.50, children $10.

🛶 🐾 ♿ **Parks at Chehaw** (229-430-5275; www.parksatchehaw.org), 105 Chehaw Road, Albany. Open 9–5 daily. This 800-acre park has a little something for everyone—the Wiregrass Express miniature train ride; water sports at **Lake Chehaw** (see *Green Space—Lakes*); a **BMX Bike Park** (229-894-5822); a Play Park, one of the state's largest play parks for children; a Wild Animal Park; nature trails along Muckalee Creek; picnicking; and camping. An exciting annual event is the **Chehaw Native American Cultural Festival** (see *Special Events*). The centerpiece of the complex is the **Chehaw Wild Animal Park** (229-430-5275), a 100-acre park-within-a-park that is southwest Georgia's only American Zoo Association–accredited wild animal park. It has recently undergone extensive renovations, and its trails and elevated walkways allow visitors to see native Georgia wildlife as well as more exotic fauna such as buffalo, rhinos, elks, llamas, ostriches, lemurs, and zebras roaming in natural habitats. Ben's Barnyard and Children's Farm provides opportunities to get up-close and personal with gentler animals. Wildlife programs given by the park's naturalists occur in the amphitheater at 2 and 3 Saturday and 2:30 and 3:30 Sunday. The alligator feeding at the Muckalee Swampland Station is a big hit on Wednesday and Sunday, but it isn't held in winter. The park was originally designed by Albany native Jim Fowler of *Animal Kingdom*. Admission to park: adults $2, seniors and children 3–17 $1. Admission to both park and zoo: adults $6, seniors and children 3–17 $4. Special events may require additional charge; annual family membership $35.

See also Other Activities Appendix.

HISTORIC HOMES AND SITES 🐾 ♿ **The Albany Civil Rights Movement Museum at Old Mount Zion Church** (229-432-1698; www.members.surf-south.com/~mtzion), 326 Whitney Avenue, Albany. Open 10–4 Wednesday through Saturday, 2–5 Sunday. Located in the historic Freedom District, the Mount Zion Missionary Baptist Church was the site of many mass meetings during the Albany Movement in the early 1960s. Dr. Martin Luther King Jr. and many other civil rights leaders spoke there. Now a museum, the old church, which is set up to reflect its appearance during that period, celebrates the courage of ordinary people who struggled for equality during extraordinary times. The Freedom Singers, a group organized during the civil rights movement, perform at 1 PM on second Saturday of each month. Adults $4, seniors and students $3, children 4–17 $2.

BALD EAGLES AT THE PARKS AT CHEHAW'S WILD ANIMAL PARK

MUSEUMS 🛶 🐾 ♿ **Albany Museum of Art** (229-439-8400; www.albany museum.com), 311 Meadowlark Drive, Albany. Open 10–5 Tuesday through Saturday. Southwest Georgia's only nationally accredited art museum, the Albany Museum of Art offers six galleries. The museum's permanent collection features 19th- and 20th-century American and European art, but it is its sub-Saharan African art that shines. The stunning collection, the largest in the Southeast, features masks, musical instruments, religious and ceremonial devices, sculpture, pottery, baskets, jewelry, gold weights, and textiles. The interactive children's wing is called AMAzing Space. "Full Blown Fridays" combine live musical entertainment 5:30–8:30 on third Friday of each month. Adults $4; children, seniors, college students, members of military $2. Free admission during Thursday Family Arts Night (5–9) and Sunday Afternoon in the Galleries. (Note: The museum is planning to move to bigger and better space in the very near future, so call ahead to make sure of the current address.)

THE ALBANY CIVIL RIGHTS MOVEMENT MUSEUM AT OLD MOUNT ZION CHURCH

✎ 🐾 ♿ **Thronateeska Heritage Center** (229-432-6955; www.heritagecenter.org), Heritage Plaza, 100 West Roosevelt Avenue, Albany. Open noon–4 Thursday through Saturday. Planetarium shows at 2:45 Thursday and Friday; 12:30, 1:30, and 2:30 Saturday; Tuesday evenings June through December. Model railroad exhibit open noon–4 Saturday. Actually a complex of historic buildings and three attractions in one, the center consists of the old railroad depot and an adjacent railway express office, as well as some restored vintage railcars. The History Museum, which occupies the historic 1912 Union Depot, uses changing exhibits of artifacts to trace the history of Albany and southwest Georgia, including the riverboat days and the great floods of 1925 and 1994. In the adjacent Railway Express building, it's always a starry night as the Wetherbee Planetarium presents information about the solar system, stars, and galaxies. Programs change monthly. Also housed in that building is the Science Discovery Center, where visitors can participate in hands-on activities relating to light, electricity, magnetism, sound, weather, and other scientific topics. A model train exhibit, reopened after an absence of several years and operated by the Flint River Model Railroad Club, occupies an old baggage car. Adults $4.25, seniors and children 4–12 $3.25.

✳ To Do

AUTO RACING See Other Activities Appendix.

THE THRONATEESKA HERITAGE CENTER CONSISTS OF AN OLD RAILROAD DEPOT, RAILWAY EXPRESS OFFICE, AND RAILCARS

CANOEING AND KAYAKING ✔ **Flint River Outdoor Center** (706-647-1633; www.flintriverfun.com), 4429 Woodland Drive, Thomaston. The outfitter rents canoes, float tubes, rafts, equipment, and accessories and also provides guided raft trips and shuttle service. In addition, the company has a lodge, RV sites, and primitive camping (see the Barnesville chapter in 3, Historic South). Guided tours over class II rapids are by reservation only for a minimum of 12 people. Call for prices.

✔ **Flint River Outpost** (229-787-3004; www.flintriveroutpost.com), 11151 Old GA 3, Baconton. Open 8–5:30 Tuesday through Sunday. The outfitter provides canoe and kayak rentals, return shuttle service for Flint River trips, and primitive campsites. Prices vary by activity.

FARM TOURS **The Farmyard** (229-883-3308), 3810 Gillionville Road, Albany. Open 9–6 Monday through Saturday. In addition to pumpkin and gourd painting, visitors can pick their own sunflowers or go fishing. Free admission; products for sale.

Mark's Melon Patch (229-698-4750), 8580 Albany Highway, Sasser. Open 8–7 daily. Be sure to bring a flashlight to experience the haunted maze. Other attractions include carved pumpkins, hayrides, and a bouncy house. Choose your own pumpkin or pick sunflowers. The effect of the maze and the jack-o'-lanterns is most dramatic at night and it's less crowded then, too. Many school groups visit during the day. Free admission; products for sale.

FISHING See Fishing Appendix.

FOR FAMILIES ✔ **All-American Fun Park** (229-436-8362), 2608 North Slappey Boulevard, Albany. Open 10–10 Monday through Thursday, 10–midnight Friday, 9–midnight Saturday, 1–midnight Sunday. The family-oriented fun center features 36 holes of miniature golf, the largest game room in the Southeast, bumper boats, Go-Karts, batting cages, laser tag, and a rock-climbing wall. $5 for one activity, $13.50 for three, $35 for 10. Several specials are offered during the season; call for details.

✔ ✿ ♿ **Turtle Grove Play Park** (contact Albany Tomorrow, 229-430-3910), along Front Street, Albany. A magnet for the small fry, the fun park is filled with giant representations of turtles painted with various scenes as well as six interest areas: a Dino Dig, Tot Lot, Critters Area, Big-Kids Area, a mosaic area, and a music area. The park is located next to the Flint RiverQuarium and is also a popular spot from which to watch the Fourth of July fireworks. Free.

FRUIT AND BERRY PICKING See Other Activities Appendix.

GOLF See Golf Appendix.

HIKING See Parks Appendix.

HUNTING See Other Activities Appendix.

SKATING See Other Activities Appendix.

SWIMMING See Other Activities Appendix.

TENNIS See Other Activities Appendix.

TUBING See **Flint River Outdoor Center** and **Flint River Outpost** under *Canoeing and Kayaking.*

WHITE-WATER RAFTING See **Flint River Outdoor Center** and **Flint River Outpost** under *Canoeing and Kayaking.*

✳ Green Space

LAKES ✐ 🦅 **Lake Chehaw** (229-430-5277; www.parksatchehaw.org). On the 1,400-acre lake in Albany, opportunities abound for canoeing, boating, fishing, waterskiing, and picnicking. A canoe trail winds through the lake. See also **Parks at Chehaw** in see *To See—For Families*. Adults $2, children $1.

NATURE PRESERVES AND PARKS ✐ 🦅 ♿ **Veterans Riverfront Park** (229-434-8799; 1-800-475-8700; www.albanyga.com; www.albanytomorrow.com), Oglethorpe Boulevard, Albany. Open dawn–dusk daily. This pleasant park is an appealing place to walk, jog, cycle, or relax with a book. An amphitheater and various monuments honor veterans and victims of several wars. The **Flood of 1994 Memorial** honors those who died and the many volunteers who contributed time and labor to rebuild the city after the catastrophic inundation. The downtown park also features gardens, a fountain that's animated with music and lights, the **Turtle Grove Play Park** (see *To Do—For Families*), the **Greenways Trail System,** and the **Riverwalk.** The park features an interactive water fountain, which is particularly popular on hot summer days, so wear your bathing suit. Free. Also see Parks Appendix.

RIVERS ✐ 🦅 The **Flint River** is central to much of the area's outdoor activities, including boating, fishing, tubing, and other water sports. (See **Flint River Outdoor Center** and **Flint River Outpost** under *To Do—Canoeing and Kayaking.*) The river flows from Atlanta 212 miles south to Lake Blackshear, but because of its meandering nature it actually covers 350 miles. The Flint is one of only 40 rivers in the country that flows more than 200 miles unimpeded by a dam. It also offers the only class II to class IV rapids in south Georgia. Access free; fees for some activities.

✳ Lodging

BED & BREAKFASTS

In Parrott

✎ ✿ **214 Huckaby** (229-623-5545; www.bedandbreakfast.com/georgia/ 214-huckaby-a-bed-and-breakfast-guesthouse.html), 214 Huckaby. Visitors can rent the entire 1917 bungalow on the edge of the town of Parrott. Described as contemporary casual with an emphasis on comfort, the house features a master bedroom plus two additional bedrooms, so it can sleep six. Guests enjoy the huge front and back porches in good weather. As a one-time artist's residence, 214 Huckaby is filled with original art. Fixings are provided for a serve-yourself breakfast, and guests can use the kitchen to prepare other meals. No smoking. Limited wheelchair accessibility. $100–150 for entire house.

CAMPGROUNDS

In Albany

✎ ✿ **Parks at Chehaw** (229-430-5295; www.parksatchehaw.org), 105 Chehaw Park Road. RV sites offer full hookups; tent sites have water hookups. The campground also features a bathhouse, laundry facilities, vending machines, and a dump station. Tent sites $10; RV sites $15, $12 for seniors.

Also see Campgrounds Appendix.

INNS AND HOTELS

In Albany

✎ ✿ **Merry Acres of Albany, Georgia** (229-439-2386; www.merryacres .com), 1504 Dawson Road. Merry Acres is an institution in Albany. The gracious manor house, which serves as the registration and office center, was built in 1934 as a country home, and Albany has since grown up around it. The company retained 10 acres around the house and has built a lodging, dining, shopping, and conference complex connected by gardens and pathways. Lodging is offered in the **Quality Inn Merry Acres** (229-435-7721; 1-888-462-7721) and **Comfort Suites Merry Acres** (229-888-3939; 1-888-726-3939), the only all-suite hotel in Albany. Recreational amenities include a secluded swimming pool and a state-of-the-art fitness center. There's also the **Merry Acres Restaurant** (see *Eating Out*) and **Merry Acres Galleria**, a collection of specialty shops. 75 percent of guest rooms nonsmoking. Wheelchair accessible, including some fully adapted bathrooms. $65–172.

✳ Where to Eat

DINING OUT

In Albany

✎ ✿ ♿ **The Rocket** (229-420-6747; www.albanyrocket.com), 2724 Dawson Road. Open 11–10 Tuesday through Saturday. Fine dining occurs in a retro 1950s atmosphere. Dramatic black and red pair with chrome furniture and crisp white table linens to create a fun-filled atmosphere. Dinner entrées such as Man in the Moon Rib Eye, Filet to the Moon, Aquarius Salmon, and Lunar Eclipse Chicken are finely prepared and presented. Be sure to save room for sinfully delicious desserts with names such as Chocolate Milky Way, Peaches in Space, and Chocolate Exploration. Live entertainment is offered Wednesday through Saturday. No smoking. Wheelchair accessible. Lunch $5.95–10.95, dinner $12.95–18.95.

& **The Sunset Grill** (229-878-6738), 2601 Dawson Road. Open 11–9:30 weekdays, 11–10 Saturday, 11–8 Sunday. The menu includes American and Caribbean dishes, chops, steaks, and pastas. Smoking in bar only. Wheelchair accessible. Lunch $4–8, dinner $12–24.

EATING OUT
In Albany

♂ ♨ & **Merry Acres Restaurant** (229-439-2261; www.merryacres.com), 1504 Dawson Road. Open 11–3 daily. The restaurant serves soups and sandwiches as well as a buffet with two to three meats and a choice of vegetables. No smoking. Wheelchair accessible. $5–7.

In Parrott

♨ & **Chinaberry Café, Antiques and Gifts** (229-623-2233), 118 East Main Street. Open 11–2 Tuesday through Saturday, 6–8 Friday and Saturday. The café serves everything from seafood to rib eye and T-bone steaks. At $9.50, the all-you-can-eat buffet is very popular. No smoking. Wheelchair accessible. $7.50–15.50.

✳ Entertainment

ARTS Albany Area Arts Council (229-439-ARTS; www.albanyarts council.org), 215 North Jackson Street, Albany. Open 9–5 weekdays. Housed in a beautiful historic 1906 Carnegie library, the council presents exhibits showcasing regional artwork as well as seminars, workshops, festivals, tours, and children's programs. Free.

Albany Darton College (229-430-6858; 229-430-6750), 2400 Gillianville Road, Albany. Call for a schedule of events and ticket prices. The college's theater program presents three major

productions a year. Various music ensembles also perform throughout the year, and there are numerous art exhibits.

Albany Municipal Auditorium (229-430-5205), 200 Pine Avenue, Albany. Call for a schedule of performances and ticket prices. The historic auditorium hosts many of Albany's performing arts companies.

Albany State University Department of Fine Arts (229-430-4849), 504 College Drive, Albany. Call for a schedule of events and ticket prices. The university offers numerous performances and exhibitions of student and faculty work. Under the umbrella of the Department of Fine Arts are the ASU Theater Ensemble, the popular Marching Rams Show Band, the Jazz Band, the Concert Band, and the ASU Concert Chorale.

DANCE Albany Ballet Theater (229-430-5205), 200 Pine Avenue, Albany. Call for a schedule of performances and ticket prices. Annual performances held in the **Albany Municipal Auditorium** (see above) include classical and modern ballets as well as jazz.

MUSIC Albany Chorale (229-439-2787), mailing address: P.O. Box 70942, Albany 30708. Call for a schedule of performances and ticket prices. Performing for more than 70 years, the chorale presents everything from Bach to rock, including classical, jazz, madrigal, and American folk music. The chorale also has a Chamber Ensemble that performs with the Albany Symphony Orchestra at Christmas and other times. The season, which runs from late August to June, features three major concerts, a dinner show, and outreach programs.

Albany Concert Association (229-439-2787), mailing address: P.O. Box 1607, Albany 31702. Call for a schedule of performances and ticket prices. Admission is by membership or single ticket. Founded in 1935, the organization sponsors quality entertainment by professional artists. The four- or five-concert series features dance; musical theater; solo instrumentalists; vocal, string, or bass ensembles; and other genres.

Albany Symphony Orchestra (229-430-6799; www.albanysymphony.org), mailing address: P.O. Box 70065, Albany 30707. Call for a schedule of performances and ticket prices. One of southwest Georgia's professional orchestras, the Albany Symphony is under the direction of a full-time resident conductor and performs at **Albany Darton College** and the **Albany Municipal Auditorium.** The orchestra, which is often heard on Peach State Public Radio, performs American music, orchestral repertory, new music, and lesser-known classics. Regional soloists and national and international artists perform with the orchestra. The season includes five subscription concerts, children's concerts, a holiday pops program, and "Pops in the Park at Chehaw."

PROFESSIONAL SPORTS ♂ & **South Georgia Wildcats Arena Football** (229-435-2849; 1-877-945-3849). Call for a schedule of games and ticket prices. Arena football is a hot, fast-paced, action-packed, fan-friendly sport that's sweeping the nation. Albany's Wildcats play eight home games at the James H. Gray Civic Center. Around $10–30.

THEATER Theatre Albany (box office 229-439-7141; www.theatrealbany.com), 514 Pine Avenue, Albany. Box office open noon–4 Tuesday through Friday, noon–2 on certain Saturdays (check the web site), one hour prior to evening and matinee performances. Times and prices vary by production. Formed in 1932, Theatre Albany is the oldest cultural organization in Albany as well as one of its most respected. Productions take place in the John A. Davis House, one of Albany's elegant restored antebellum landmarks. The five-production main-stage season features an eclectic mix of drama, comedy, and musicals. In addition, the theatrical organization offers productions in its intimate Studio Theater, as well as children's theater, reader's theater, and workshops.

✳ Selective Shopping

ANTIQUES Maridean's Marketplace (229-623-4123; www.parrottga.com/Marideans.html), 110 East Main Street, Parrott. Open 10–5 Tuesday through Saturday. The emporium sells European and American antiques, porcelains, and other merchandise.

Mollie Jane's Antique Mall (229-623-5561; www.parrottga.com/molly.html), 125 Main Street, Parrott. Open 11–4 Tuesday through Thursday, 10–5 Friday, 10–6 Saturday, noon–4 Sunday. The market sells antiques and other merchandise.

FLEA MARKETS Sasser Flea Market and Antique Mall (229-698-4578), 8109 Albany Highway, Sasser. Open 10–6 weekdays, 8–6 Saturday and Sunday. Regional vendors gather here to sell a variety of goods. Auctions are held at 7 PM every Tuesday.

FOOD **Mark's Melon Patch** (229-698-4750), 8580 Albany Highway/US 82, Sasser. Open 8–7 daily. Shop here for cantaloupes and watermelons, but also for gourds, Vidalia onions, butter beans, and other fresh produce. Hayrides and a maze are offered at Halloween (see *To Do—Farm Tours*).

SPECIAL STORES **Sound Play** (229-623-5545; www.soundplay.com), 108 Railroad Street, Parrott. Open 10–6 daily. Guided tours are available. Unusual outdoor musical instruments made from recycled materials are fashioned into fanciful shapes.

✳ Special Events

May: **Chehaw Native American Cultural Festival** (229-430-5275; www.parksatchehaw.org). A major cultural event in the entire Southeast, the three-day festival in Albany features traditional Native American crafts, dances, skills demonstrations, and storytelling. Adults $7, children younger than 11 free.

July: **Local Palooza** at the Parks at Chehaw (229-430-5275; www.parks atchehaw.org). The popular Albany event features 12 bands. Adults $7, children younger than 11 free.

October: **Boo at the Zoo** at the Parks at Chehaw (229-430-5275; www .parksatchehaw.org). Have a hauntingly ghoulish time with games, prizes, food, and costume contests at this Halloween event in Albany. Adults $7, children younger than 11 free.

Georgia Peanut Festival (229-776-7718). Held in Sylvester on the fourth Saturday in October. This annual event, which has been celebrated since 1963, features arts and crafts, the Peanut Parade, a barbecue, cuisine utilizing peanuts, a 5K run, bike tour, the Goober Gala dance, Miss Georgia Peanut pageant, and other activities. Free.

AMERICUS

This area of southwest Georgia, while still relatively undiscovered by most travelers, is rich in history, culture, scenic beauty, state parks, and outdoor recreational activities.

The area in and around the sleepy town of Plains is designated as the Jimmy Carter National Historic Site (see *To See—Historic Homes and Sites*). The former president and Nobel Prize winner grew up here and still makes Plains his home, and you may even see him when you're in town. You also can attend Maranantha Baptist Church, where he often teaches Sunday-school classes. President and Mrs. Carter are always on hand for the annual Plains Peanut Festival (see *Special Events*), held each September. The Carters award prizes, watch the parade, and sign their books. The festival's softball game pits President Carter and his Secret Service contingent against Plains High School alumni.

Georgia may be known as the peach state, but peanuts and pecans are major parts of the economy in southwest Georgia. In fact, the area is known as "the Pecan Capital of the World" and is renowned for the nut itself as well as for pies, cakes, cookies, candies, and other treats made from pecans. Several pecan companies have stores where you can sample and purchase pecan products (see *Selective Shopping—Food*). Watermelon is king in Cordele, known as "the Watermelon Capital of the World." This area is also home of the largest barbecue cook-off in the state (see *Special Events*).

The Civil War intruded here as it did almost everywhere in Georgia, but rather than being the site of many battles, this area was home to the notorious prison camp at Andersonville. The prison camp, national cemetery, and National Prisoner of War Museum attract many visitors every year, as does the small village of Andersonville (see *To See—Historic Homes and Sites*).

Some surprises in this region include an 1850s living-history village at Westville, a deep canyon known as Georgia's Little Grand Canyon, and a telephone museum with an outstanding collection. Numerous festivals celebrate or memorialize the watermelon, dogwood, peanuts, and a flood (see *Special Events*).

GUIDANCE For information about Americus, contact the **Americus Welcome Center** (229-928-6059; 1-888-278-6837; www.therealgeorgia.com), 123 West Lamar Street, Americus 31709. Open 9–5 weekdays, 10–4 weekends. Pick up a brochure for the Americus Driving Tour here.

To learn more about Andersonville, contact the **Andersonville Welcome Center** (229-924-2558; www.andersonvillega.freeservers.com), 114 Church Street, Andersonville 31711. Open 9–5 daily. Information about the town, the prison, and the cemetery are available here.

For information on Cordele, contact the **Cordele-Crisp Chamber of Commerce** (229-273-1668; 1-866-426-3566; www.cordele-crisp-chamber.com), 302 East 16th Avenue, Cordele 31015. Open 8:30–5 weekdays.

Find out more about Leslie by contacting the **Town of Leslie** (229-874-5835), 108 Commerce Street, Leslie 31764.

To learn more about Lumpkin, contact the **City of Lumpkin** (229-838-4333; www.lumpkinga.com), Martin Luther King Drive, Lumpkin 31815.

For more information about Montezuma, contact the **Macon County Chamber of Commerce and Welcome Center** (478-472-2391; www.maconcounty ga.com), 109 North Dooly Street, Montezuma 31063. Open 8–5 weekdays. You also can contact the **City of Montezuma** (478-474-8144; www.montezuma-ga.org).

For more information about Omaha, contact the **Four-County Chamber of Commerce** (912-732-2683), 318 Court Street, Cuthbert 31740.

To learn more about Plains, contact the **Plains Visitor Information Center** (229-824-7477), 1763 US 280 East, Plains 31780. Open 8:30–5:30 daily.

For information about Vienna, contact the **Dooly County Chamber of Commerce** (229-268-8275), 117 East Union Street, Vienna 31092. Open 8:30–5 weekdays. Also consult the web site www.cityofvienna.org.

GETTING THERE *By air:* The two closest airports to Americus and the towns described in this chapter are in Columbus and Macon (see those chapters; Macon is in 3, Historic South).

By bus: The closest **Greyhound Lines** stations are also in Columbus and Macon (see those chapters).

By car: The towns and attractions described in this chapter are accessible from I-75 southwest of Atlanta. East-West US 280 and GA 26 connect to I-75 as well as US 19, US 27, and GA 520.

By train: The closest **Amtrak** (1-800-AMTRAK; www.amtrak.com) station is in Atlanta (see What's Where in Georgia).

MEDICAL EMERGENCY In life-threatening situations, call 911. For other urgent care, assistance is available at **Sumter Regional Hospital** (229-924-6011), 100 Wheatley Drive, Americus; **Crisp County Hospital** (229-276-3100), 902 Seventh Street, Cordele; and **Flint River Community Hospital** (478-472-3100), 509 Sumter Street, Montezuma.

VILLAGES Americus, established in 1832, is the county seat of Sumter County. The name Americus is the masculine version of America, which was named for Amerigo Vespucci. Americus is the only city in the nation that uses that name. Some wags claim, however, that the town got its name from "A-Merry-Cuss," a person with a high-spirited zest for life. Four years before his solo flight across the Atlantic in 1927, Charles Lindbergh bought his first plane in Americus. He came to Souther Field, a U.S. Army aviation training camp, to obtain a single-engine World War I–surplus "Jenny." Although he had flown with other barnstormers, when Lindbergh took the plane on a test flight, it was his first solo. The momentous occasion is marked by a plaque at the Americus airport. Famous people from Americus include Dan Reeves, the head coach of the Atlanta Falcons, and Chan Gailey, the coach of the Dallas Cowboys. Today Americus is the international headquarters for Habitat for Humanity, the nonprofit organization dedicated to eliminating substandard housing around the world. Habitat is one of the top 10 homebuilders in the nation.

Andersonville, tiny as it is, became infamous during the Civil War. In 1864, with the war going badly for the Confederacy, it was decided to move Union prisoners of war from near Richmond to an area out of reach of Federal troops. Andersonville was chosen, and Camp Sumter was established as a prison. The unfortunate soldiers are remembered in many ways in a national park, a national cemetery, and several museums.

The area around what is now **Cordele** served as the temporary capital of Georgia during the waning days of the Civil War, when Governor Joseph E. Brown used his rural farmhouse here to escape the Union March to the Sea. Cordele, the county seat, was founded in 1888 at a junction of the Savannah, Americus and Montgomery Railroads. It was named for Cordelia Hawkins, the daughter of the president of the railroad. Today Cordele is so well known nationwide for its big, luscious watermelons it has earned the title "Watermelon Capital of the World."

Leslie, which got its name from a Victorian lady named Leslie Bailey, has hardly changed since her time except for the addition of modern conveniences. Well-kept historic homes line dogwood-framed streets. The town contains a telephone museum (see *To See—Museums*) and is well known for its **Antique Dogwood Festival** (see *Special Events*).

Lumpkin, a charming small town, offers historical sites and outdoor recreation at two state parks nearby.

CORDELE IS KNOWN AS THE "WATERMELON CAPITAL OF THE WORLD."

Montezuma is in Mennonite farm country, where you can pick your own fruit or buy it fresh, and where folk arts and crafts are readily available. Montezuma, which was named for the Aztec warrior by local soldiers returning from the Mexican War, was a railroad and steamboat town on the Flint River. The bustling economic center had hotels, livery stables, cottonseed processing plants, and agricultural industries. Now it is the home of Southern Frozen Foods for the McKenzie Brand of frozen fruits and vegetables, which are sold all over the country. Today, instead of providing an avenue for steamboat transportation, the Flint River supplies the area with natural resources and recreational opportunities. The river, however, has occasionally caused terrible devastation. Major floods hit the area in 1902, 1929, 1948, and 1994, when 20 inches of rain fell in 24 hours, causing the Flint to crest at 35 feet. Montezuma calls itself "the Town That Refused to Drown" and has restored its historic downtown buildings and created new parks and streetscapes.

Plains (population 716) revolves around farming, church, and school. The small rural town produced James Earl "Jimmy" Carter, naval officer, peanut farmer, governor of Georgia, president of the United States, and Nobel Peace Prize winner, who still lives there and often can be seen around town.

What better icon should greet visitors to Plains than the **Smiling Peanut** on GA 45 (south of US 280)? This giant grinning goober, spokesman for this region of Georgia, isn't just any peanut. The 13-foot-tall goober has a very recognizable toothy smile—that of the 39th president. It was constructed by Democratic friends Loretta Townsend, Doyle Kifer, and James Kiley of Evansville, Indiana. Recognizable worldwide, the happy peanut has even appeared on *Jeopardy*. The must-stop photo op is located at the edge of town about a half-mile from Carter's campaign headquarters, which was in the old Seaboard Railroad depot. While in town, visit the **Jimmy Carter National Historic Site** (see *To See—Historic Homes and Sites*).

Vienna (when visiting here, make sure to pronounce the name correctly—it's not pronounced vee-EN-na, but VI-enna) is home to the oldest and largest barbecue cook-off in the state, the **Big Pig Jig** (see *Special Events*).

✳ To See

FOR FAMILIES ✏ ◈ ⚹ **Habitat for Humanity Global Village and Discovery Center and International Headquarters** (229-924-6935; 1-800-HABITAT; www.habitat.org/gvdc), headquarters at 322 West Lamar Street, Americus; Global Village at 721 West Church Street, Americus. Tours 10–3 Tuesday through Saturday. Watch an orientation film at headquarters, then drive a couple blocks to tour the Global Village and Discovery Center. This 6-acre attraction features different types of Habitat residences built in 15 countries. Visitors begin in the Living in Poverty Area, where conditions mirror those experienced by millions of people worldwide—in fact, one in five people live in poverty. In the Village Area, the examples of Habitat houses show how simple local materials can be used to provide adequate housing and an increased standard of living. In the Experience Area, you can actually make bricks and tiles. The Marketplace contains a photo gallery, exhibits, a theater with short films about Habitat, an exploration center, and a store. Adults $6, seniors and students $5, children younger than 6 free.

HISTORIC HOMES AND SITES ✏ ◈ ⚹ **Andersonville Civil War Village** (229-924-2558; www.andersonvillega.freeservers.com), 114 Church Street, Andersonville. The entire center of the tiny town is a restored Civil War–era village where visitors can see the **Drummer Boy Civil War Museum** (see *Museums*) and the

CIVIL WAR HISTORY COMES TO LIFE AT THE ANDERSONVILLE NATIONAL HISTORIC SITE.

controversial **Wirz Monument** (see below). The remainder of the commercial establishments are occupied by shops and restaurants. During the Civil War, Andersonville was where Federal prisoners arrived by rail before being marched to nearby Camp Sumter–Andersonville Civil War Prison. The village became a supply center for the prison. Visitors can explore an old-time farm complete with a log cabin and barn as well as live animals, a sugarcane mill, and a syrup kettle. Andersonville's log-and-fieldstone church, **Pennington St. James,** is open daily. Built in 1927, it was designed by Cramm and Ferguson, the architectural firm that designed St. John the Divine in New York City.

✂ ✆ ♿ **Andersonville National Historic Site** (229-924-0343; www.nps.gov/ande), 496 Cemetery Road, Andersonville. Park grounds, historic prison site, and cemetery open 8–5 daily (until 6 the Sunday before Memorial Day); museum open 8:30–5 daily except Thanksgiving, Christmas, and New Year's Day. A brochure and audiotape are available for a self-guided tour. During the Civil War, Camp Sumter was a notorious Confederate prison where more than 40,000 Union troops were incarcerated in a space that was created to hold 10,000. About 13,000 men died from disease, malnutrition, poor sanitation, overcrowding, and exposure—the highest percentage of deaths at any prison camp, North or South.

After the war, famed nurse Clara Barton came to Andersonville to find out the fate of many missing Union soldiers. She and her helpers located and marked the graves of most of the dead, but 500 remain unknown. The 500-acre site preserves the **Andersonville National Cemetery** and the location of the stockade. On Memorial Day, the cemetery is a sea of small, fluttering American flags placed on every grave.

MIRACLE AT THE ANDERSONVILLE PRISON CAMP

The small granite **Providence Spring House** at the Andersonville National Historic Site marks the site of a miracle at the prison camp. The only source of drinking water within the stockade was a small spring, which was constantly polluted by human waste and by men washing in the water. The prisoners prayed for rain so they could collect clean water and get some relief from the summer heat. During a downpour that cleaned out the creek, lightning struck the ground and a spring began to flow from that spot. Not only did it provide a balm for the POWs, it is still flowing to this day. The springhouse was built over it in 1901 by the Women's Relief Corps.

The historic site is also the home of the **National Prisoner of War Museum,** which traces America's wars from the Revolution to the present and honors more than 800,000 Americans who have been captured during wartime. This is the only unit in the national park system that serves as a memorial to prisoners of war. Begin with the 27-minute film *Echoes of Captivity,* then see touching exhibits that trace the lives of POWs from capture to release or escape. Interactive displays and short video clips heighten the experience. Then walk or drive around the cemetery and prison site. An audio driving tour is available to rent for $1. Interpretive programs are presented at the national park at 11 and 2 daily. During periodic living-history presentations at the site, reenactors describe the inhumane conditions POWs endured. With so much suffering and death here, it's not surprising that ghost stories persist. Sometimes visitors claim to feel hands reaching out to them, while others experience hovering shadows. Others feel cold spots by the Providence Spring and Stockade Creek. Some claim to have seen the ghost of a one-legged Confederate soldier on crutches in the cemetery. (See also *To Do—Hiking* to learn about the **Andersonville Prison Historical Hike.**) Free.

✔ ☏ ♿ **Jimmy Carter National Historic Site** (229-824-4104; www.nps.gov/jica), 300 North Bond Street, Plains. Visitor center open 9–5 daily except Thanksgiving, Christmas, and New Year's Day; depot open 9–4:30; boyhood farm open 10–4. Begin at **Plains High School,** the official State School of Georgia and the visitor center. President Carter, his wife, Rosalynn, and their three sons were all educated here. A film and exhibits of photographs, documents, and other memorabilia in the former classrooms chronicle the life of the former president from tiny Plains to Washington, D.C., and beyond. The visitor center also keeps a schedule of times President Carter teaches Sunday school at Maranantha Baptist Church, which visitors are welcome to attend. Then visit the old **Plains Depot,** Main and M. L. Hudson streets, which was Carter's 1976 campaign headquarters and is the oldest structure in town.

The highlight of a visit to the historic site is the **Carter Boyhood Home,** located in nearby Archery. The 360-acre farm is restored to its 1930s pre-electricity appearance and features the house, barn, blacksmith shop, and pump house. In several rooms, visitors can hear recorded reminiscences of the former president. You can get to the farm by car or aboard the SAM Shortline Railroad (see *To Do—Train Excursions*). Free.

✔ ☏ ♿ **Westville** (229-838-6310; 1-888-733-1850; www.westville.org), One Martin Luther King Drive, Lumpkin. Open 10–5 Tuesday through Saturday. Westville never

YOUNG JIMMY CARTER'S BEDROOM AT THE JIMMY CARTER NATIONAL HISTORIC SITE IN PLAINS

actually existed as a town and no one ever lived here, but by moving more than 30 antebellum homes, stores, workshops, churches, a courthouse, a school, and other buildings from various places in Georgia, a preindustrial town representing the 1850s has been created. Homes run the gamut from log cabins to elegant Greek Revival town houses. Nearly every artifact has been donated. Costumed living-history reenactors demonstrate old-time skills such as quilting, potting, blacksmithing, woodworking, and open-hearth cooking. Gardens are planted as they would have been in the 1850s. There are monthly special events to keep visitors coming back, too. Some of the bigger events are the **Spring Festival, Independence Day Celebration, Harvest Festival,** and **Yuletide Season** (see *Special Events*). Adults $10, seniors and military $8, children 18 and younger $4.

✄ ⚅ **Windsor Hotel** (229-924-1555; 1-888-297-9567; www.windsor-americus.com), 125 West Lamar Street, Americus. Whether you stay at the Windsor or not, you should stop in to admire it and perhaps have a meal in the **Grand Dining Room** (see *Where to Eat—Dining Out*); pamper yourself with some spa services (see *To Do—Spas*); or visit the gift, clothing, art, and antiques shop. A whimsical confection of various architectural styles, the massive hotel, which occupies an entire city block, was fashioned after the finest hotels in 19th-century Europe and built in 1892 to attract winter visitors from the North. It is Italianate in style but also features a Flemish-style stepped roof, a Romanesque tower, and a Moorish atrium. Some famous former guests include heavyweight boxing champion John L. Sullivan, Congressman William Jennings Bryan, American labor leader Eugene V. Debs, and soon-to-be President Franklin D. Roosevelt. It's even rumored that Al Capone and John Dillinger spent the night in what is now the Bridal Suite while their armed bodyguards were posted at the foot of the stairs. The depressions of 1893 and the 1930s seriously impacted tourism and the hotel, and it began a long decline. The hotel finally closed in the 1970s and sat empty for almost 20 years. It was donated to the city by the family of the last owner, and city government had to make a major decision: tear it down for a parking lot or restore it. Fortunately, they chose the latter. The Windsor was beautifully restored and reopened in 1991, and it is one of only five Georgia hotels listed in the National Trust for Historic Preservation's Historic Hotels of America. Many of its original architectural features and fixtures survive.

⚘ ⚅ **Wirz Monument,** downtown square, Andersonville. Because Swiss-born Henry Wirz was the commandant of the infamous Andersonville Confederate Prison, he was held responsible for the terrible conditions there and the resulting deaths of so many Union soldiers. After the South fell, he was tried, convicted, and hanged by the U.S. government for these crimes—the only man on either side convicted and executed. He was still a hero to the South, however, and Southerners claimed that he was just following orders, that conditions were beyond his control, and that Confederate prisoners fared just as badly in Northern prisons, so the United Daughters of the Confederacy erected this granite obelisk as a monument to him.

MUSEUMS ✄ ⚘ **Bedingfield Inn Museum** (229-838-6419), 100 Cotton Street, on the square, Lumpkin. Open 10–5 Tuesday through Saturday, 1–5 Sunday;

guided tours at 10, 1, and 3. The circa 1836 Greek Revival–style building, a former stagecoach inn that also serves as the visitor center for Stewart County, has been restored and furnished to represent the period 1836–1850. The inn and original period furnishings show visitors what overnight stops were like in the early days. If travelers could pay a high price, they would get a private room, but more often several strangers would sleep in the same bed or on the floor. Also located on the property is a dependency kitchen building and an 1845 dogtrot house. Before leaving the museum, pick up a brochure for the **Stagecoach Trail Tour,** a driving tour past 23 pre-1850 homes. Adults $3, children $1.

✒ ☙ ⛫ **Drummer Boy Civil War Museum** (229-924-2558; www.andersonville georgia.com), 117 Church Street, Andersonville. Open 10–5 Thursday through Saturday, 1–5 Sunday. The idea for the museum was based on two drummer boys—one a Yank, one a Reb. Exhibits feature 15 mannequins wearing authentic Civil War uniforms, including a colorful red and blue New York Fire Zouave uniform and, of course, Union and Confederate drummer boy uniforms complete with original drums. Other exhibits display weapons, documents, and photographs taken by famed Civil War photographer Matthew Brady. Flags on exhibit include a 35-star U.S. flag and the last national flag of the Confederacy. An extensive collection of artifacts belonged to General Thomas T. Eckert, president of Western Union and chief of the U.S. Military Telegraph Department under President Lincoln. One of the interesting pieces on display is the bonnet of Mary Surratt, which was removed from her head and given to Eckert just before her hanging with others convicted in the conspiracy to assassinate Lincoln. A large diorama depicts the Andersonville Confederate Prison and the village of Andersonville as they were in 1864. Adults $2, children $1.

✒ ☙ ⛫ **Georgia Rural Telephone Museum** (229-874-4786; www.sowega .net/~museum), 135 Bailey Avenue, Leslie. Open 9–3 weekdays; tours on the hour. It's astonishing that in a town of less than 500 there is one of the world's largest telephone museums. Housed in a circa 1920s cotton warehouse, the astounding personal collection of Tommy C. Smith, owner of Citizens Telephone Company, contains more than 2,000 artifacts. Visitors can trace the evolution of communications in this country from the smoke signals in a re-created Creek Indian village to the modern cell phone. Showcased are some of the oldest, rarest, and largest examples of telecommunications from 1876 to the present. One of the prize artifacts is Alexander Graham Bell's 1876 liquid transmitter, the first transmitter through which a voice was relayed. A re-creation of Bell's workshop includes many of the telephones envisioned by the inventor. Among other exhibits are wooden voice boxes; early pay telephone booths; rare 1882 50-line switchboards; turn-of-the-20th-century headsets; a model of TelStar, the first communications satellite; antique clocks; a late 1800s pipe organ; and antique service vehicles. Several vignettes portray early telephone workers at their jobs. Free.

✒ ☙ ⛫ **Georgia State Cotton Museum** (229-268-2045), 1321 East Union Street, Vienna. Open 9–5 weekdays. Farm tools, cotton bolls, periodicals, a cotton bale, and other agricultural implements tell the story of cotton in this rustic museum. A small patch of cotton is growing outside. Before leaving, be sure to pick up a brochure for the **Driving Tour of Vienna,** which guides visitors past

60 historic buildings, the imposing 1892 Romanesque-style courthouse, and the **Walter F. George Law Museum** (see below). Free.

✏ ✿ ♿ **Georgia Veterans State Park** (229-276-2371; 1-800-864-7275; www .gastateparks.org/info/georgiavet), 2456 US 280 West, Cordele. Open 7–10 daily. Developed to honor U.S. veterans, the 1,308-acre state park features a museum with uniforms, medals, weapons, and other memorabilia from the Revolutionary War through the Gulf War. Outdoors, visitors can get up-close looks at several vintage military airplanes, tanks, and other vehicles. (For information about the park's recreational facilities and lodging, see *To Do—Golf, Green Space—Nature Preserves and Parks,* and *Lodging—Campgrounds.*) Parking $3.

✿ **Walter F. George Law Museum** (229-268-3663; www.historicvienna.com), 106 North Fourth Street, Vienna. Open 9–4 weekdays by appointment. George opened his first law practice in Vienna. From there he went on to several judge-ships, including the Georgia Supreme Court, then served as a U.S. senator from 1922 to 1956, after which he served as President Dwight D. Eisenhower's special ambassador to NATO. He died back home in Vienna in 1957 and is buried here. **Lake Walter F. George** (see *Green Space—Nature Preserves & Parks*) and the School of Law at Mercer University are named for this famous Georgian. Here in his first law office, visitors can see original furniture, photographs, campaign items, and documents relating to the senator's career and private life. Free.

NATURAL BEAUTY SPOTS ✏ ✿ ♿ **Providence Canyon State Conservation Park** (229-838-6202; 1-800-864-7275; www.gastateparks.org/info/providence),

AN UNUSUAL ROCK FORMATION AT PROVI-DENCE CANYON STATE CONSERVATION PARK

GA 39-C, Lumpkin. Open 7–6 daily, September 15 through April 14; 7–9 daily, April 15 through September 14. Known as Georgia's "Little Grand Canyon," this gorge, which is 150 feet deep at its greatest depth, presents a vision of breathtaking pink, orange, red, and purple hues and undulating patterns. Formations resembling aboveground stalagmites punctuate the chasm. What's totally amazing is that the canyon isn't millions of years old but was caused by erosion due to poor farming practices in the 1800s. Visitors can view the ravines from the rim trail or make the 3-mile trek into the canyon. Backpackers can over-night along the 7 miles of backcountry trails. The interpretive center at the 1,109-acre park has exhibits about the formation of the canyon. The rare orange plumleaf azalea grows only in a small 50-mile radius area that stretches from the canyon to Callaway Gardens (see Pine Mountain chapter), and the park is often dotted with colorful wildflowers. In fact, the park is noted for having the largest concentration of wildflowers in Georgia. Special events include **Wildflower Day, Kudzu Takeover Day,** and **Photography Day.** Parking $3.

SCENIC DRIVES **Andersonville Trail** (229-924-2558). The looping trail stretches 75 miles from Byron (see the Macon chapter in 3, Historic South) to Cordele. Visitors enjoy quaint towns, historic homes, museums, cotton and canola fields, peach and pecan orchards, and two national historic sites. Highlights of the trail include Massee Lane Gardens, national headquarters of the American Camellia Society (see Macon chapter); **Habitat for Humanity Global Village and Discovery Center and International Headquarters** (see *To See—For Families*); **Georgia Veterans State Park** (see *To See—Museums*); and the **Museum of Aviation/Georgia Aviation Hall of Fame** (see Macon chapter). Along the way there are numerous opportunities for antiquing and other shopping, camping, fishing, and hunting. Stop at roadside stands for watermelons, peaches, peanuts, and pecans.

✳ To Do

AUTO RACING **Watermelon Capital Speedway** (229-271-9301; www.water meloncapitalspeedway.com), 385 Farmers Market Road, Cordele. The 3/8-mile, medium-banked, high-speed asphalt track is the scene of Bandolero, Legends, Mini Stock, Enduro, Pure Stock, Superstreet, and Pro Late Model races. Call for a schedule of events and ticket prices.

BICYCLING The area is relatively flat and therefore ideal for cycling as long as you bring your own. Particularly pleasant places to ride are the paved roads in **Providence Canyon State Conservation Park** (see *To See—Natural Beauty Spots*), **Georgia Veterans State Park,** and **Florence Marina State Park** (see *Green Space—Nature Preserves & Parks*).

BIRDING See **Providence Canyon State Conservation Park** under *To See— Natural Beauty Spots* and **Georgia Veterans State Park** under *Green Space— Nature Preserves and Parks.*

BOATING 𝄞 **Turkey Creek Outfitters** (229-271-1997; www.turkeycreekoutfitters .com), 991 US 280 West, Cordele. Open 7:30–6 weekdays, 7:30–noon Saturday (Saturday activities continue in the afternoon, but reservations must be made by noon). Serving the Flint River and Lake Blackshear, the company rents a variety of boats as well as Jet Skis and water sports equipment. Guided pontoon cruises and fishing trips are also available, as is guided deer, quail, and turkey hunting. Call for rental fees, as they vary widely depending on type of boat and length of rental.

See also **Flint River** under *Green Space—Rivers;* **Florence Marina State Park** and **Georgia Veterans State Park** under *Green Space—Nature Preserves and Parks;* and **Lake Blackshear** and **Lake Walter F. George** under *Green Space—Lakes.*

598

SOUTHERN RIVERS

FISHING See **Flint River** under *Green Space—Rivers*; **Florence Marina State Park** and **Georgia Veterans State Park** under *Green Space—Nature Preserves and Parks*; and **Lake Blackshear** and **Lake Walter F. George** under *Green Space—Lakes.*

FRUIT AND BERRY PICKING ✔ 🐾 ♿ **Kauffman's Strawberry and Farm Market** (478-472-8833; www.kauffmansstrawberries.com), 1305 Mennonite Church Road, Montezuma. Open 8–7 Monday through Saturday; April 1 through June 15 for strawberries, May 15 through July 31 for peaches. Pick your own strawberries and peaches in season. When you've worked up an appetite or a sweat, cool off with ice cream or lemonade. Take home cakes, pies, tarts, and produce. Fees vary.

GOLF 🐾 **Georgia Veterans Memorial Golf Course** (golf course 229-276-2377; tee times 1-800-434-0982) at **Georgia Veterans State Park** (229-276-2371; 1-800-864-7275; www.gastateparks.org/info/georgiavet), 2459-H US 280 West, Cordele. Open 8–dusk. This 18-hole, 7,059-yard, par-72, four-star championship course was designed by Dennis Griffith. The course's clubhouse features light snacks and drinks as well as a full-service pro shop (229-276-2377). Instruction can include video recording and analysis. $33–37.

HIKING ✔ 🐾 **Andersonville Prison Historical Hike.** The 3-mile walking history lesson explores the **Andersonville National Historic Site** (see *To See—Historic Homes and Sites*) and the town of Andersonville. The route is directed by a questionnaire available at the information desk at the National Prisoner of War Museum, goes through the prison site and into the town of Andersonville, and ends up at the Andersonville National Cemetery.

See also **Georgia Veterans State Park** under *Green Space—Nature Preserves and Parks* and **Providence Canyon State Conservation Park** under *To See— Natural Beauty Spots.*

MINIATURE GOLF ✔ 🐾 See **Florence Marina State Park** under *Green Space— Nature Preserves and Parks.*

SPAS **The Windsor Spa** (229-924-9772), 125 West Lamar Street, Americus. Services include basic Swedish massage, hot lava-stone massage, facials, body wraps, pedisage, manisage, manicures, pedicures, and paraffin dips. $35–165.

SWIMMING See **Florence Marina State Park** and **Georgia Veterans State Park** under *Green Space—Nature Preserves and Parks.*

TENNIS See **Florence Marina State Park** under *Green Space—Nature Preserves and Parks.*

TRAIN EXCURSIONS ✔ **SAM Shortline–Southwest Georgia Excursion Train** (229-276-2715; 1-800-864-7275; 1-877-GA-RAILS; www.samshortline.com), P.O. Box 845, Cordele. Generally operates Friday, Saturday, and Monday, but call or check web site for times and prices. Restored vintage 1949 rail cars provide a nostalgic way to see this area of southwest Georgia along a 42-mile route through pecan country. Called the SAM Shortline because the route was once part of the Savannah, Americus, and Montgomery line, the railroad now operates the Peanut Express, the Americus Adventurer, and the Archery Express between Cordele and Archery with intermediate stops at Georgia Veterans State Park, Leslie, Americus, and Plains. Special runs to additional cities are offered throughout the year. Passengers can get off at any of the stops, do some sightseeing, have a meal, or even stay overnight and then resume their ride.

✳ Green Space

LAKES ✍ 🐾 ♿ **Lake Blackshear** was created in 1930 by damming the Flint River to provide power to Crisp County. The 8,600-acre lake provides water and shore recreation including boating and fishing for bass, crappie, catfish, and bream.

✍ 🐾 ♿ **Lake Walter F. George** on the Chattahoochee River contains 45,000 acres of water surface and innumerable opportunities for water sports and other outdoor recreation. The lake actually has two names. It is called Lake Walter F. George on the Georgia side but is known as Lake Eufaula on the Alabama side.

NATURE PRESERVES AND PARKS ✍ 🐾 ♿ **Florence Marina State Park** (229-838-6870; www.gastateparks.org/info/flormarin), GA 39-C, Omaha. Open 7–10 daily. The 173-acre park is located at the northern end of 45,000-acre Lake Walter F. George on the Georgia side (the lake is known as Lake Eufaula on the Alabama side). Recreational amenities at the park include a natural deep-water marina with 66 slips, a boat ramp and dock, boat rentals, a lighted fishing pier, swimming pool, tennis courts, two playgrounds, a 0.75-mile nature trail, and miniature golf. Other amenities include picnic shelters ($25), laundry and bath facilities, wheelchair-accessible areas, and phones. The park's **Kirbo Interpretive Center** teaches visitors about Native Americans, local history, and nature. Displays include artifacts from prehistoric Paleo-Indians to the present. Accommodations are available (see *Lodging*). Parking $3.

✍ 🐾 ♿ **Georgia Veterans State Park** (229-276-2371; 1-800-864-7275; www.gastateparks.org/info/georgiavet), 2456-H US 280 West, Cordele. Open 7–10 daily. The park is located on the shores of 8,600-acre Lake Blackshear. Water sports include swimming at the beach, fishing, waterskiing, and boating. Private boats are permitted on the lake, and rentals are available at the park's marina. The 1,308-acre park offers even more. It boasts the **Lake Blackshear Resort and Golf Club** (see *To Do—Golf* and *Lodging*) as well as camping, a 1-mile nature trail, a fitness course, a radio-controlled model airplane flying field, a hummingbird-wildflower meadow, and an indoor-outdoor military museum (see *To See—Museums.*) In addition, the **SAM Shortline/Southwest Georgia Excursion Train** stops at the park, giving visitors an opportunity to travel to Plains and back (see *To Do—Train Excursions*). Special events throughout the year include the **Georgia Veterans Memorial Triathlon** in August, the **Fall School Day Fair** in September, and **Tribute to Veterans** in November. Parking $3.

RIVERS The **Flint River** makes a transition north of this area from the Piedmont region to the Coastal Plain. Unlike areas of shoals and rapids where whitewater rafting is possible, this section of the river is characterized by deeply cut, sandy banks and broad, forested floodplains. The river here is deep, wide, and slow. When rainfall is heavy upstream, the river overflows, sometimes with devastating results. Periodic flooding has resulted in a vast floodplain known as the Great Swamp. It actually consists of two swamps—north of GA 96 (which runs east from Columbus to Fort Valley) is the Magnolia Swamp, south of the highway is Beechwood Swamp. During floods they cover thousands of acres. The stream channel is continuously migrating and creating new sandbars, which make good places to camp or fish for flathead and channel catfish. Bends in the river often cause oxbow lakes, which are fishermen's closely guarded secrets. Boating can be impeded by tree snags, but these same snags provide homes for turtles, water snakes, bluegill, and bass. North of Montezuma is an escarped area referred to as the Montezuma Bluffs, where weathering has resulted in a 150-foot escarpment overlooking the Beechwood Swamp and the river. Not only can visitors see fossilized limestone that was part of a marine ecosystem 50 million years ago, but the steep, moist slopes contain one of the state's largest concentrations of the rare and endangered relic trillium. The area remains relatively pristine because access is only by boat.

✳ Lodging

BED & BREAKFASTS

In Americus
& **Americus Garden Inn Bed and Breakfast** (229-931-0122; 1-888-758-4749; www.americusgardeninn.com), 504 Rees Park. This 1848 mansion surrounded by 1.3 acres has a wraparound porch and gingerbread accents. The inn offers eight guest accommodations: two rooms on the first floor, five on the second, and the Executive Suite in the Olde Schoolhouse. Some rooms boast a Jacuzzi. Outdoors, enjoy the garden, gazebo, koi pond, and waterfall. A full gourmet breakfast is included. Smoking outdoors only. Wheelchair accessible. $99–119; on special event weekends, two-night minimum required.

🐾 **1906 Pathway Inn** (229-928-2078; 1-800-889-1466; www.1906 Pathwayinn.com), 501 South Lee Street. The stunning neoclassical home provides the most elegant accommodations in town. Public rooms and guest rooms are beautifully and luxuriously decorated with antiques. The guest rooms are named for famous people connected with the region: Carter, Rosalynn, Lindbergh, Roosevelt, Presidential, and Bell. Make time to enjoy the superb architectural elements, the pleasant veranda, and the gardens. A full gourmet breakfast is included in the nightly rate. Small pets allowed with prior approval and additional fee. Smoking outdoors only. Not wheelchair accessible. $90–125.

In Andersonville
🐾 ✤ & **A Place Away Cottage** (229-924-1044; 229-924-2558), 110 North Oglethorpe Street. This tin-roofed house, a former sharecropper's cottage, exudes rustic country charm. It's really a duplex, offering two rooms with a shared kitchen, which makes it

perfect for a family. One room has two double beds; the other has a queen and a double. No smoking. Wheelchair accessible. $50.

In Montezuma

☀ **Traveler's Rest Bed and Breakfast** (478-472-0085; 478-951-1214; www.travelersrestbb.com), 318 North Dooly Street. Romantic accommodations await in this 1899 home. The luxurious guest accommodations are decorated to reflect Victorian, Civil War, and garden themes. A sumptuous breakfast is served in the Tea Room. Other meals are available for an additional fee. Pets welcome with prior approval. Smoking outdoors only. Not wheelchair accessible. $69–109.

☀ **White House Farm** (478-472-7942; www.whitehousefarmbnb.com), 1679 Mennonite Church Road. The Yoders' home is located on a 250-acre dairy farm. Their two-story home was built in the 1950s with help from members of the Mennonite community—similar to an old-fashioned barn raising. Guest accommodations include cannonball and four-poster beds and soft floral fabrics. A full breakfast gets your day off to a good start. The Yoder family also bakes typical Mennonite favorites. No smoking. Not wheelchair accessible. $70–90.

In Plains

✐ & **Plains Historic Inn and Antique Mall** (229-824-4517; www.plainsgeorgia.com/Plains_Inn.htm), 106 Main Street. In this historic commercial establishment, the ground floor is devoted to an antiques mall, but charming bed & breakfast accommodations can be found upstairs. "Every room is a history lesson," the web site claims. In fact, each guest room is dedicated to a decade in Pres-

ident Jimmy Carter's life, from 1920 to 1980, and the decor of each reflects the style of that era. Guests have access to a large common room and a balcony overlooking the historic square. Complimentary continental breakfast is included. No smoking. Wheelchair accessible. $85–140.

CAMPGROUNDS

In Cordele

✐ ☀ ❀ **Georgia Veterans State Park** (229-276-2371; 1-800-864-7275; www.gastateparks.org/info/georgiavet), 2456-H US 280 West. The park offers 77 tent, trailer, and RV sites with hookups and a pioneer campground. $17–22.

In Lumpkin

✐ ☀ ❀ **Providence Canyon State Conservation Park** (229-838-6202; 1-800-864-7275; www.gastateparks.org/info/providence), GA 39-C. The park has six backcountry campsites as well as a pioneer campground. $4–30.

In Omaha

✐ ☀ ❀ **Florence Marina State Park** (229-838-6870; www.gastateparks.org/info/flormarin), GA 39-C. The park offers 43 tent, trailer, and RV sites with cable TV hookups and all the amenities of the park. $18–20.

See also Campgrounds Appendix.

COTTAGES AND CABINS

In Cordele

✐ ☀ & **Lake Blackshear Resort and Golf Club** (1-800-459-1230; www.lakeblackshearretreat.org/accomm.cfm) at **Georgia Veterans State Park** (229-276-2371; 1-800-864-7275; www.gastateparks.org/info/georgiavet), 2459-H US 280 West. The resort has 10 private, fully equipped cottages, each with two bedrooms, one bath, complete kitchen, living room with a fireplace, and a large screened porch. Guests also enjoy all the other amenities of the park. No smoking. Pets allowed for an additional fee. Some wheelchair accessibility. $99–102 weekdays, $169–179 weekends.

In Omaha

✑ 🎣 🐾 **Florence Marina State Park** (229-838-6670; www.gastateparks .org/info/flormarin), GA 39-C. The park has six fully equipped cottages and eight efficiency units. $50–90.

INNS AND HOTELS

In Americus

✑ ♿ **Windsor Hotel** (229-924-1555; 1-888-297-9567; www.windsor-americus .com), 125 West Lamar Street. (See *To See—Historic Homes and Sites* for a complete description of the structure.) Choose from 53 period-style guest rooms and suites, each different and each with all the modern amenities. There are several two-room executive suites, too. The one on the third floor is named for Jessica Tandy and its connecting room for Hume Cronin. The famous couple stayed at the hotel during the making of the Hallmark Hall of Fame film *To Dance with the White Dog*. In addition there are two suites: the James Earl Carter Presidential Suite and the bridal suite, which has its own private stairway. The **Grand Dining Room** is open for three meals a day and brunch on Sunday (see *Where to Eat—Dining Out*). Cocktails and musical entertainment can be enjoyed in Floyd's Pub and its adjacent veranda. Floyd's is open Monday through Saturday and offers wireless Internet service, a happy hour on weekdays, and Trivia Night on Wednesday. The Windsor also offers

spa services (see *To Do—Spas*). Each November the three-tiered atrium and lobby are transformed into a medieval castle as a backdrop for the songs of madrigal singers. Continental breakfast is included in the nightly rate. Smoking and nonsmoking rooms. Wheelchair accessible. $101–199; numerous special packages available.

RESORTS

In Cordele

✑ ♿ **Lake Blackshear Resort and Golf Club** (229-276-1004; 1-800-459-1230; www.lakeblackshearretreat.org) at **Georgia Veterans State Park** (229-276-2371; 1-800-864-7275; www.gastateparks.org/info/georgiavet), 2459-H US 280 West. The resort offers 14 rooms in the contemporary lodge as well as in 64 villas, each of which has a private screened porch or balcony overlooking the lake. These rooms contain a small refrigerator. Accommodations also are offered in 10 cottages (see *Cottages*). The lodge features **Cordelia's** restaurant (see *Where to Eat—Dining Out*) and 88's Lakeside Bar. Guests have access to all the amenities of the park and Lake Blackshear, including an 18-hole golf course (see *To Do—Golf*), beach and swimming area, fitness center, indoor-outdoor pool with whirlpool, lake activities, nature trail, gift shop, and business center. Smoking and nonsmoking rooms available. Some rooms and villas wheelchair accessible. $159 for rooms, $169 for villas.

✳ Where to Eat

DINING OUT

In Americus

✑ 🐾 ♿ **Grand Dining Room at the Windsor Hotel** (229-924-1555; www .windsor-americus.com), 125 West

Lamar Street. Open 11–2 weekdays, 6–9 Monday through Saturday, 11:30–2 Sunday. Dinner reservations recommended. Savor a sophisticated dining experience in the epitome of Victorian elegance. A buffet is served for lunch and brunch. Dinner choices include regional and national favorites made with beef, seafood, veal, chicken, lamb, and pork. No smoking. Wheelchair accessible. Lunch $8 for buffet or $6–9 à la carte, dinner $14.95–23.95; brunch $9.95.

In Cordele

🎣 🦐 ♿ **Cordelia's** (229-276-1004; 1-800-459-1230; www.lakeblackshear retreat.com) at the Lake Blackshear Resort and Golf Club, 2459-H US 280 West. Open 7–10:30, 11:30–2, and 6–10 daily; 10:30–2 for Sunday brunch; prix-fixe dinner available 6–7:30 Sunday through Thursday. The city of Cordele was named for Cordelia Hawkins in 1888 and she was also the inspiration for this upscale restaurant. The cuisine is a blend of Southern, American, and European, with the dinner menu being primarily classic Italian. Get the day off to a good start with traditional breakfast choices ranging from egg dishes to pancakes, French toast, and Belgian waffles. If you can tear yourself away from outdoor activities, lunches include soups, salads, sandwiches, and specials such as crabcakes, chicken pot pie, jambalaya, meat loaf, pastas, and seafood. À la carte dinner choices include classic Italian fare parmigiana, spaghetti, gnocchi, linguine, or lasagna but also steaks, chicken, veal, pork, lamb, duck, and seafood. In addition to an à la carte menu for dinner, there is also a prix fixe dinner, which includes salad or soup, an entrée, and dessert. A gargantuan Sunday brunch is served.

Diners enjoy lake views while savoring their meal, and some folks even come by boat. Adjacent to the restaurant, 88's Lakeside Bar, named because the state of Georgia was officially created in 1788 and the city was founded in 1888, serves cocktails and light fare in a casual, eclectic setting overlooking the lake. No smoking. Wheelchair accessible. Breakfast $3.50–7.95, lunch $5.95–8.95, dinner $9.95–35.95 à la carte or $16.95 prix fixe, brunch $15.95 for adults, $7.95 for children.

🎣 🦐 ♿ **Daphne Lodge** (229-273-2596), US 280 West. Open 5:30–9 weekdays, 5:30–10 weekends. Located in a red barn nestled among the pines near Georgia Veterans State Park, Daphne Lodge is a great casual place to go for catfish, seafood, and steaks. Lots of small dining rooms are decorated with country charm. No smoking. Wheelchair accessible. $10.95–27.

🦐 ♿ **The Old Inn** (229-273-1229), 2536 US 280 West. Open 5:30–9 weekdays, 5:30–10 weekends. If you're looking for casual fun dining, go to the

FLOYD'S PUB

The quaint watering hole on the second floor of the Windsor Hotel overlooking downtown Americus was named for Floyd Lowery, an employee who worked at the hotel for 40 years. During the restoration, workers found an old safe and were eager to open it and see what was inside. Instead of money, jewels, or stock certificates, it contained one of Floyd's worn-out uniforms. The pub was named in honor of Floyd, but what's ironic about the choice is that Floyd was a complete teetotaler who had never taken a drink.

Old Inn for steaks, catfish, and seafood. The eatery has an excellent wine and beer list, too. No smoking. Wheelchair accessible. $10.95–26.50.

EATING OUT

In Americus

🍴 ♿ **Dingus Magee's** (229-924-6333), 120 North Lee Street. Kitchen open 11–10 Monday through Wednesday, 11–midnight Thursday through Saturday; bar open until midnight Monday through Saturday. Dingus Magee's is a fun-loving place where folks like to get together. The menu includes appetizers, steaks, ribs, seafood, burgers, and chicken fingers. The restaurant is downstairs, while there is a nightclub upstairs with a $10 cover charge. No smoking downstairs until 10 PM, when only those older than 21 are admitted. Smoking allowed in nightclub only. Restaurant wheelchair accessible; nightclub is not. $7.95–20.

🍴 ♿ **Monroe's Hot Dogs and Billiards** (229-924-4106), 318-A West Lamar Street. Open 9:30–10 Monday through Saturday. Monroe's bills their famous hot dogs as "the best dog ever bitten by a man." Drop in to try one out for yourself, and stay to enjoy the billiards and game room. Smoking allowed. Wheelchair accessible. Hot dogs 85¢–$1.05; pool $1.25 per person for 30 minutes.

✂ 🍴 ♿ **The Varsity** (229-924-2461), 716 Felder Street. Open 11–2 and 5–9 Monday through Thursday, 11–9 Friday and Saturday. Home cookin' is what they sell; eat in or take out. Catfish, shrimp, and steak are on the menu. Breakfast items are served anytime except Friday night. No smoking. Wheelchair accessible. $6.50–9.95.

In Andersonville

✂ 🍴 ♿ **Andersonville Restaurant** (229-928-8480), Church Street. Open 11–2 weekdays, 6–9 Friday. Great country cooking includes fish, steaks, and daily specials. No smoking. Wheelchair accessible. Lunch about $5, dinner $10.

In Montezuma

✂ 🍴 ♿ **Yoder's Deitsch Haus Restaurant, Bakery, and Gift Shop** (478-472-2024), 5252 GA 26 East. Open 11:30–2 and 5–8:30 Tuesday, Thursday, Friday, and Saturday; 11:30–2 only on Wednesday. Menu items at the nationally renowned restaurant include roast beef, chicken, fish, chops, casseroles, Southern-style vegetables, and homemade desserts. Pies are a specialty. No smoking. Restaurant wheelchair accessible, rest rooms are not. $7–9.

In Plains

✂ 🍴 ♿ **Mom's Kitchen** (229-824-5458), 203 Church Street. Open 6–3 Tuesday through Thursday, 6–8 Friday and Saturday, 11–3 Sunday. Southern specialties such as corn fritters, sweet-potato pie, and collard greens are served buffet style. No smoking. Wheelchair accessible. Buffet $5.19, sides $1 each.

✳ Entertainment

THEATER ✂ ♿ **Rylander Theatre** (229-931-0001; www.rylander.org), 310 West Lamar Street, Americus. Box office open 11–4 weekdays. Call for a schedule of performances and ticket prices. Americus businessman Walter Rylander constructed this premier performance theater and movie palace in 1921. At that time it was called "the Finest Playhouse South of Atlanta." The theater's interior is a visual feast, featuring ornate plasterwork, beautiful stencil patterns, and painted murals. Despite having closed in 1951 and sitting empty for many years, its architectural details are intact. The beautifully restored theater is now a venue for live performances, organ concerts on the 1928 Moller pipe organ, classic movies, and other special events. Guided tours available.

Sumter Players (229-924-2645; 229-931-0001; www.sumterplayer.org). Box office open 11–4 weekdays; 11–8 Thursday through Saturday on days of performances; 1–2:30 Sunday on days of performances. Call for a schedule of performances. The all-volunteer theater troupe has been entertaining the community for more than 40 years. In addition to a full season of adult productions, the organization also sponsors the Fran Gore Children's Theater, which produces an annual play by and for children. Adults $15; seniors, students, and Habitat volunteers $10; children's theater performances free.

❋ Selective Shopping

ANTIQUES Plains Historic Inn and Antiques Mall (229-824-4517; www.plainsgeorgia.com), 106 Main Street, Plains. Open 10–6 Monday through Saturday, 1–5 Sunday. Twenty-five booths offer a wide variety of antiques and other merchandise. Bed & breakfast accommodations are offered upstairs (see *Lodging*).

CLOTHING The Tog Shop (229-924-8806; 1-800-943-3006; www.togshop.com), 1 Lester Square, Americus. Open 8–5:30 weekdays, 9–5 Saturday. Primarily a mail-order business, the Tog Shop now carries all types of apparel, footwear, and accessories. The Americus headquarters houses the executive offices, fulfillment operation of the mail-order catalog, the manufacturing facility, and a retail store where visitors can peruse the merchandise.

CRAFTS

& **Yoder's Deitsch Haus Restaurant, Bakery, and Gift Shop** (478-472-2024), 5252 GA 26 East, Montezuma. Open 11:30–2 and 5–8:30 Tuesday, Thursday, Friday, and Saturday; 11:30–2 only on Wednesday. Shop here for quality crafts and traditional Pennsylvania Dutch and Southern foods. The business also offers a restaurant (see *Where to Eat—Eating Out*) and a bakery.

FOOD Ellis Brothers Pecans (229-268-9041; 1-800-635-0616; www.werenuts.com), 1315 Tippetsville Road, Vienna. Open 8–7 daily. Purchase pecans and peanuts as well as other nuts; cakes, pies, and candies; cookbooks; gift tins, baskets and boxes; cracking tools; relishes, jams, and jellies; and peaches in-season. Visitors can watch the pecan- and peanut-packing process in-season by appointment.

THE WRAPARONG

What started in the 1940s with a simple terry-cloth saronglike after-bath wrap called the Wraparong grew into a multimillion-dollar business that's still going strong after more than 50 years. Designed by Americus native Gertrude Davenport, who was working as a designer in New York, the Wraparong is in the Costume Institute collection at the Metropolitan Museum of Art as an important example of American loungewear. Davenport returned to Americus to open The Tog Shop factory to meet the demand. She is given credit for the terry-cloth vogue and for being ahead of the market in easy-care fabrics.

Merritt Pecan Company (229-828-6610; 1-800-762-9152; www.merritt-pecan.com), GA 520, Weston. Open 7–8:30 daily. The company, in business since 1980, produces a massive amount of pecans and pecan products, mostly for its mail-order business. The company grows and harvests the pecans on its own farms and processes them in its own plant to sell in shell, as halves and pieces, and as ingredients in fine candies and pies. The store carries a variety of pecan products, peach and may-haw jellies, syrups, regional souvenirs, and cookbooks.

State Farmer's Market (229-276-2335), 1901 US 41 North, Cordele. Open 7 AM–11 PM in summer, otherwise 8–4. The market offers a vast array of fresh seasonal produce and is a major shipping point for watermelons, one of the county's largest cash crops. You also can find fried peanuts, homemade jellies, and seasonal items such as pumpkins and gourds in the fall, Christmas trees during the holidays, and spring flowers and shrubs. Besides all that, you can find arts and crafts, yard art, and cookbooks.

Yoder's Country Market (478-472-2070), 7402 GA 26 East, Montezuma. Open 9–7 weekdays, 9–8 Saturday. Shop here for cheeses, jams, and spices.

✳ Special Events

March: **Andersonville Revisited Living-History Weekend** (229-924-0343). Living history begins with the arrival of the prisoners, and various scenarios continue throughout the weekend. Lantern tours of the prison site are offered Saturday evening. Reservations required for lantern tours cannot be made until February 1. Free.

April: **Antique Dogwood Festival** (229-874-5835). The festival, held in Leslie, features antiques dealers from all over Georgia with a variety of merchandise. $5.

Spring Festival (229-838-6310; 1-888-733-1850). See plowing, planting, and garden preparation using mules. Participate in crafts and games and listen to musicians playing traditional instruments. Included in regular admission to Westville (see *To See— Historic Homes and Sites*).

May and October: **Andersonville Historic Fair** (229-924-2558; www.andersonvillega.freeservers.com). The festival features old-time craftspeople—as well as entertainment. A flea market offers bargains. Adults $4, children $1.50.

July: **Independence Day Celebration** (229-838-6310; 1-888-733-1850). The event in Westville includes a barbecue, musical entertainment, and mid-19th-century games. Visitors also can enjoy watching an 1860s baseball game with rules, equipment, and uniforms of the period. Included in regular admission.

Watermelon Days Festival (229-273-1668; www.cordele-crisp-chamber.com/festival.html). The Cordele festival celebrated its 50th birthday in 2005. For the first two weeks in July, a multitude of events take place at various locations: a pageant, 5K and fun run, car race, entertainment, arts and crafts, parade, photo contest, 4-H dog show, fishing rodeo, horseshoe tournament, waterskiing show, puppet show, Mr. Melon contest, gospel sing, and, of course, watermelon-decorating, seed-spitting, and watermelon-eating contests. A special event is Fireworks on the Flint seen from aboard the SAM Shortline train (see *To Do—Train Excursions*). Festival free; small charge for some activities.

September: **Plains Peanut Festival** (229-824-5373; www.plainsgeorgia .com). The festival celebrates peanut production with a 1-mile fun run and a 5K road race. Former President Jimmy Carter awards the prizes for these events. Then there's a downtown parade with VIPs, beauty queens, bands, and floats. President and Mrs. Carter view the parade from the balcony of the Plains Historic Inn (see *Lodging—Bed & Breakfasts*). The festival continues at Maxine Reese Park on Main Street with arts and crafts, food, and continuous entertainment. The annual folk play If *These Sidewalks Could Talk . . . Comin' Home,* performed on Friday and Saturday evenings, is an amusing look at life in a small town. After the Saturday performance, festival-goers enjoy music under the stars at the Plains welcome center (see *Guidance*). The conclusion of the weekend sees President Carter and the Secret Service battling Plains High School alumni in an annual softball game. Festival free; small charge for some activities.

Late September or early October: **Big Pig Jig** (229-268-8278; 229-268-8275; www.bigpigjig.com), Big Pig Jig Boulevard, Vienna. This is the oldest and largest of Georgia's barbecue cooking championships. In addition to the contest, there's something for everyone at this event: crafts, collectibles, a midway with games, golf tournament, specialty food vendors, hog-calling contests, and barbecue tastings. Evening concerts, a parade, a pageant, children's activities, and the 5K Hog Jog round out the fun. $5 on Saturday during the day; $8 evenings when there is entertainment.

October: **Montezuma's Beaver Creek Festival** (478-472-2391; www .maconcoutyga.org). The annual event, which began after a devastating flood in July 1994, celebrates the accomplishments that continue to be made in reviving the town of Montezuma. The festival features arts and crafts, live entertainment, and the Great Beaver Creek Duck Race. Free.

November: **Harvest Festival** (229-838-6310; 1-888-733-1850). Traditional activities at this Westville event include music, crafts, and skills demonstrations. Included in regular admission.

December: **Yuletide Season** (229-838-6310; 1-888-733-1850). Continuing throughout the Saturdays of the month, activities in Westville include a decorating workshop, a hunt for the yule log, and the Christmas-tree lighting. After Christmas, Westville ends the holiday and ushers in the New Year with the traditional burning of the greens ceremony. Included in regular admission.

BARBECUE IS KING AT THE BIG PIG JIG, HELD EVERY FALL IN VIENNA.

BAINBRIDGE AND SOUTHWEST GEORGIA

This area of extreme southwest Georgia is, in fact, much closer to Alabama and the Florida panhandle than it is to most of Georgia, and it's probably more familiar to travelers from those states than it is to citizens of Georgia. There are no large towns but several large lakes, several state parks, the Chattahoochee and Flint rivers, and lots of opportunities for outdoor recreation.

The area is characterized by small towns and red-clay fields of peanuts, corn, and cotton. Visitors are rewarded with sights such as a covered bridge, murals painted on downtown buildings, a monument to the peanut, a variety of museums, a winery, and the official Georgia folk-life play, *Swamp Gravy*. Some of the state's most unusual festivals—among them those celebrating mules, swine, and even rattlesnakes—draw lots of guests to the region.

GUIDANCE If you are planning a trip to Bainbridge and Climax, contact the **Bainbridge–Decatur County Chamber of Commerce** (229-246-4774; 1-800-243-4774; www.bainbridgegachamber.com), 100 Boat Basin Circle, Bainbridge 39817. Open 8–5 weekdays. When you are in the area, stop by the office, which is located in the **McKenzie-Reynolds House,** a 1921 neo–Classical Revival home. For more information about the entire area of southwest Georgia, call or stop in at the **Southwest Georgia Visitor Information Center** (229-243-8555; www.bainbridgega.com), 101 Airport Road, Bainbridge, GA 39817. Open 8–5 Monday through Saturday. The visitor center provides information on statewide as well as local attractions.

Visitors planning a trip to the Blakely area, including Arlington, should consult the **Blakely–Early County Chamber of Commerce** (229-723-3677; www.blakelyearlychamber.com), 52 Court Square, Blakely 39823. Open 8:30–5 weekdays.

For more information about Colquitt, contact the **Colquitt–Miller County Chamber of Commerce** (229-758-2400; www.colquitt-georgia.com), 302 East College Street, Colquitt 39837. Open 9–5 weekdays.

For information about Cuthbert and Randolph County, contact the **Southwest Georgia Chamber of Commerce** (229-732-2683), 201 North Lumpkin Street, Cuthbert 39840. Open 9–5 weekdays.

To learn more about Donalsonville, contact the **Donalsonville–Seminole** **County Chamber of Commerce** (229-524-2588; www.donalsonvillega.com), 104 Joseph Avenue, Donalsonville 31806. Open 9–5 weekdays. In addition to general information, the **Southern Rivers Birding Trail** (see *To Do—Birding*) guide and map are available here.

To learn more about Fort Gaines, contact the **Clay County Visitors Bureau** **and Information Center** (229-768-2248; www.fortgaines.com), Clay County Library, 208 Hancock Street, Fort Gaines 39851. Open 9–5 weekdays. Both the library and **George T. Bagby State Park and Lodge** (see *Green Space— Nature Preserves & Parks*) provide audio guides and brochures for the **Fort Gaines Walking Tour** (see *To See—Walking Tours*) of the area.

To learn more about Calvary and Whigham as well as Fort Gaines and Cuthbert, contact the **Four-County Chamber of Commerce** (912-732-2683), 318 Court Street, Cuthbert 31740.

GETTING THERE *By air:* Getting to this area by air requires flying into a nearby airport and renting a car. The closest airport to Cuthbert and Fort Gaines is **Columbus Metropolitan Airport** (see Columbus chapter). The closest airport to Blakely, Arlington, and Colquitt is in Dothan, Alabama. **Dothan Regional Airport** (334-983-8100; www.flydothan.com), 800 Airport Drive, is served by **Atlantic Southeast Airlines**. Car rentals are available from **Avis** (1-800-654-3131), **Hertz** (1-800-654-3131), and **National** (1-800-227-7368).

The closest airports to Donalsonville, Bainbridge, Calvary, Whigham, and Climax are in Dothan (see above), or Tallahassee, Florida. **Tallahassee Regional Airport** (850-891-7802; www.ci.tallahassee.fl.us/citytlh/aviation), 3300 Capital Circle SW, Suite 1, Tallahassee, Florida, is served by **Continental Express, Delta Air Lines, Delta Connection/Atlantic Southeast Airlines, Delta Connection/Chautauqua Air Lines, Delta Connection/Comair, Northwest Airlink,** and **US Airways Express**. On-site car rentals are offered by **Alamo** (1-800-462-5266), **Avis** (1-800-331-1212), **Dollar** (850-575-4255), **Enterprise** (850-575-0603), **Hertz** (1-800-654-3131), and **National** (1-800-227-7368). Off-site car rentals are available from **Budget** (1-800-527-7000) and **Thrifty** (850-576-7368).

By bus: The **Greyhound Lines** (229-248-8774) station in Bainbridge (2331 Dothan Highway) is the only one in the area covered by this chapter. The nearest station to Cuthbert and Fort Gaines is in Columbus (see Columbus chapter). The nearest stations to Blakely, Arlington, and Colquitt include the one in Bainbridge, one in Albany (see Albany chapter), or one at 285 South Foster Street in Dothan, Alabama. The nearest station to Donalsonville, Calvary, Whigham, and Climax is the one in Bainbridge. The other options are in Thomasville (see Thomasville chapter), Dothan (see above), or 112 West Tennessee Street in Tallahassee, Florida.

By car: The two major towns are Bainbridge, at US 84 and US 27, and Blakely, at US 27 and GA 62. Cuthbert is at US 27 and US 82.

By train:

MEDICAL EMERGENCY In life-threatening situations, call 911. For other immediate care needs, assistance is available at **Memorial Hospital** (229-246-3500), 1500 East Shotwell Street, Bainbridge, or **Early Memorial Hospital** (229-723-6061), 301 Columbia Street, Blakely.

VILLAGES Bainbridge, located near Lake Seminole, is the county seat of Decatur County. The town was incorporated in 1829 and is named for Commodore William Bainbridge, commander of the USS *Constitution,* "Old Ironsides." Historic downtown Bainbridge surrounds Willis Park and contains an intact group of architecturally significant commercial buildings that date from 1860 to 1920. Numerous outdoor recreational activities are available in the area, including **Seminole State Park** (see *Green Space—Nature Preserves and Parks*).

The city of **Climax** is noted for its annual **Swine Time Festival** (see *Special Events*).

Fort Gaines, established in 1814 around a fort on the Chattahoochee River, is one of the oldest towns in Georgia. The fort was established to protect settlers during the Creek Indian Wars. Fort Gaines's position on the Chattahoochee River led to the town becoming a shipping point for cotton planters on both the Georgia and Alabama sides of the river. Fort Gaines remained a key market until railroads replaced river freight. The tiny town and the surrounding area have numerous attractions, including a museum, two lakes, and several state parks. The area around Fort Gaines is also the last refuge of the *Trillium reliquum,* an endangered plant species, and is the home of the largest magnolia tree in Georgia. Wildlife is plentiful. In fact, Clay County is reputed to have three times more deer than people.

AN INDIAN STATUE IN FORT GAINES

Arlington is noted for several Indian mounds and **Kolomoki Mounds Historic Park** (see *To See—Historic Homes and Sites*).

Blakely is known as "the Peanut Capital of the World" because so many peanut products are made here. A peanut monument on Courthouse Square salutes the industry. Blakely is also known for the Indian mounds nearby, a covered bridge, a 140 plus-

THE SUTHRIE HOUSE IN FORT GAINES

year-old Confederate flagpole, a restored 1930s theater, and several festivals, including **Holidays on the Square.**

With a population of less than 2,000 people, **Colquitt** belies its size in the number of things going on there. Located in the southwest corner of Georgia, Colquitt is 50 miles east of Dothan, Alabama, southwest of Albany, and north of Tallahassee, Florida. The town is known as "the Mayhaw Capital of the World." Mayhaws are a tart fruit from the rose family that grow in swampy areas; boats and nets are often required to harvest them. Colquitt is also the home of a 23-foot carved face of an Indian brave and *Swamp Gravy,* the official Georgia folklife play. Many events occur throughout the year here, including the **National Mayhaw Festival** (see *Special Events*).

Cuthbert's square is graced with the lovely **Tarrer Inn,** which offers luxurious accommodations and also boasts a restaurant (see *Lodging—Bed & Breakfasts* and *Where to Eat—Dining Out*).

Donalsonville's primary attractions are **Lake Seminole** (see *Green Space— Lakes*) and **Seminole State Park** (see *Green Space—Nature Preserves & Parks*).

Whigham hosts the annual **Rattlesnake Roundup,** and **Calvary** hosts the annual **Mule Day** (see *Special Events*).

✳ To See

COVERED BRIDGES 🎣 🦪 ♿ **Coheelee Creek Covered Bridge** (229-273-3741; www.blakelyearlychamber.com), GA 62 and Old River Road, Blakely. Open daily. Built in 1891, the 96-foot-long, two-span bridge, which crosses narrow, rambling Coheelee Creek in Fannie Askew Williams Park, is one of only 16 covered bridges left in Georgia. The bridge has an even more significant designation: It is the southernmost historic, authentic covered bridge in the United States. Free.

CULTURAL SITES ✐ ⍟ ♿ **Donalsonville Murals** (229-524-2588; www.donalson villega.com), 105 South Tennille and South Wiley street, Donalsonville. Local artist Earl Burke painted two murals on local businesses depicting Donalsonville history. Among them are *The Old Depot* on Lions Hall and *Farming of Yesterday* on the north end of Seminole Auto Parts.

✐ ⍟ ♿ **Millennium Murals** (229-758-2400; 229-758-5450; www.colquitt-georgia .com), Town Square and throughout town, Colquitt. Nine murals (so far) painted by artists from all over the United States constitute the project, which was started in 1999. The murals help promote the importance of storytelling and oral histories. *We've Got a Story to Tell* depicts the three dominant cultures of the South—Native American, African American, and European. This mural features not only life-sized figures but native plants, crops, and even insects. When the 10th mural is completed, the project will be eligible to belong to the International Mural Society, which promotes public art.

✐ ⍟ ♿ **Tribute to the American Indian** (229-758-2400; www.colquitt-georgia .com), 166 South First Street/US 27, Colquitt. Hungarian-born sculptor Peter Toth has devoted his life to carving memorial monuments, which he calls "Whispering Giants," in each state in honor of the spirit of the Native Americans who inhabited our land before European settlers arrived. His Georgia contribution is a 23-foot red-oak head of an Indian brave. Toth said he chose Colquitt for the site of Georgia's tribute statue because of the spirit of hospitality, friendship, and cooperation he received when he first visited 20 years ago.

A LOG HOME AT FRONTIER VILLAGE IN FORT GAINES

FOR FAMILIES ✍ 🍴 ♿ **Peanut Monument** (229-273-3741; www.blakelyearly chamber.com), North Main Street, on the square, Blakely. Open daily. Early County produces more peanuts than any other county in America. Although the county has more acres planted in cotton, peanuts produce millions more dollars in income. This monument pays tribute to the crop on which the city and county's economy is based.

HISTORIC HOMES AND SITES ✍ 🍴 ♿ **Frontier Village** (229-768-2248; www .fortgaines.com), Bluff Street, Fort Gaines. Open daily. Its strategic position on a bluff overlooking the Chattahoochee River was the reason for situating a frontier fort here in 1814. It served as an Indian fort in 1836. Bluff Park, where the village is located, has existed since the turn of the 20th century. Many structures have been relocated here to form the village: the 1928 Woman's Club House, a 1928 Boy Scout cabin, an 1820s tollhouse, a gristmill and smokehouse, several log cabins and simple settler houses, and the watchtower of a Confederate fort. Visitors to the park also can see a Civil War cannon, which has rested in the same spot since the war, and the Otis Micco statue. Micco was a Native American overwhelmed by American forces in the early days of the town. The artist, Phillip Andrews, retired in Fort Gaines. Free.

✍ 🍴 ♿ **Kolomoki Mounds Historic Park** (229-724-2150; 1-800-864-7275; www .gastateparks.org/info/kolomoki), US 27, Blakely. Park open 7–10 daily; museum open 8–5 daily except major holidays. Kolomoki is both an important archaeological site and a recreational area. Central to this 1,293-acre park are seven Native American earthen mounds built between A.D. 250 and 950 by Swift Creek and Weeden Island Indians. Although the site, which was one of the most populous settlements north of Mexico, is believed to have been inhabited from 1000 B.C., the highest level of development was between A.D. 350 and 600. The seven mounds include the state's oldest temple mound as well as two burial mounds and four ceremonial mounds. An interpretive museum, partially situated inside an excavated mound, explains the significance of the mounds and displays artifacts discovered on the site. In addition to the archaeologically significant sites in the park, the 1,293-acre preserve also provides 50- and 80-acre lakes, a swimming pool (additional fee charged), boating, fishing, picnicking, miniature golf, and 5 miles of hiking trails. There is a boat ramp and fishing pier, and pedal boats, fishing boats, and canoes can be rented seasonally. Private boats are permitted with a 10-horsepower limit. The park features 43 tent, trailer, and RV campsites ($17–20) as well as three pioneer campgrounds ($20 and up) and a group camp that sleeps 135 ($350–475). Special events include an astronomy program in October, **Kolomoki Festival** in October, and **Christmas at Kolomoki** in December. State park parking/day-use fee $3; museum admission $1.75–3.

✍ 🍴 ♿ **Outpost Replica** (229-768-2248; www.fortgaines.com), Commerce Street, Fort Gaines. Open daily. The replica re-creates in miniature the old fort and village that was used to protect early settlers from Creek and Seminole Indian attacks between 1814 and 1830. This village consists of original log houses from around the city that have been moved to the site. Free.

MUSEUMS 🖾 ♿ **Coleman Opera House and Museum** (229-768-2248; www
.fortgaines.com), Commerce Street, Fort Gaines. Open by appointment only.
The opera house was built in 1880 as an entertainment palace. During the summer, actors and singers from New York came to the theater to fine-tune their
shows before opening in New York. The theater finally closed in 1936 but now
contains Fort Gaines artifacts and memorabilia collected by local historian James
Edgar Coleman. Free.

🖋 🖾 ♿ **Cotton Hall–Storytelling Museum–Museum of Southern Culture**
(229-758-6686; www.swampgravy.com), 116 East Main Street, Colquitt. Open
only during performances, which are given frequently throughout the year. Cotton Hall was built in the 1930s as part of the New Deal, but it was used as a cotton warehouse for only four years before the boll weevil decimated the cotton
industry. Now it has a new life. The community-based folklife museum has
10,000 exhibits relating to Southern culture, rural Southerners, storytelling, and
folklife. Familiar and frequented places around town are re-created: the doctor's
office, barber–beauty shop, railroad depot, post office, newspaper, dry goods
store, picture show, and farm. The characters who operated these businesses
invite visitors to explore the museum through the stories of their ancestors. Visitors also can use the storytelling room to share their own life stories. Free.

🖋 🖾 **Sutton's Corner 1844 Frontier Country Museum** (229-768-2312; www
.suttonscorner.com), 115 Washington Street, Fort Gaines. Open by appointment
only. The store was originally located on the edge of a plantation, but it was
relocated to the site of the Globe Tavern and Inn stagecoach stop in Fort
Gaines. More than 4,000 artifacts, which depict life as it was on the frontier,
make this museum among the top five heritage museums in the United States. It
took more than 10 years for one man—now in his 80s—to accumulate and create the displays. Examine petticoat counters, wooden cash registers, an antique
post office, a gristmill, and many documents. Free.

SCENIC DRIVES 🖾 **Bainbridge Heritage Tour** (229-246-4774; 1-800-243-
4774), brochures can be picked up from several locations: the Bainbridge–
Decatur County Chamber of Commerce (see *Guidance*); **Main Street–Tourism
Office** (229-248-2000; www.bainbridgecity.com), 107 South Broad Street; or the
Southwest Georgia Visitor Information Center (see *Guidance*). Several magnifi-
cent mansions from the turn-of-the-20th century are described.

WALKING TOURS 🖾 **Fort Gaines Walking Tour** (Clay County Visitors Bureau
and Information Center, 229-768-2248; www.fortgaines.com), Clay County
Library, 208 Hancock Street, Fort Gaines. The tour includes 34 historic sites.
Brochures can be picked up at the library or at George T. Bagby State Park and
Lodge off GA 39 in Fort Gaines.

✳ To Do

AIRBOAT RIDES 🖋 **Dixie Twister** (229-246-2553; 229-254-0887). Call ahead to
make arrangements. Departing from **Wingate's Marina** (139 Wingate Road),
Bainbridge, the airboat rides provide an exciting way to see wildlife, including

alligators. The airboat seats three in addition to the driver, so it's not for large families. Morning and late afternoon are the best times for rides. $25.

BIRDING ✍ 🐦 ♿ **Southern Rivers Birding Trail** (478-994-1438). More than 263 species of birds, 20 of them rare and endangered, inhabit the area. This 30-site Georgia Department of Natural Resources trail winds its way from the rolling hills of the Georgia Piedmont to the Coastal Plain and eventually to the Okefenokee Swamp. Many of the prime observation sites are located along the Chattahoochee and Flint rivers. Maps and bird lists are available at local visitor centers or by calling the number above.

BOATING Numerous opportunities are available for sailing, motorboating, water-skiing, canoeing, kayaking, and the use of personal watercraft on **Lake Walter F. George** (see *Green Space—Lakes*) and **Lake George W. Andrews.** Boaters are urged to be cautious of commercial barge traffic, possible underwater hazards, and low-hanging power lines.

See also **Kolomoki Mounds Historic Park** under *To See—Historic Homes and Sites.*

FISHING See **Lake Walter F. George** and **Lake Seminole** under *Green Space—Lakes* as well as the **Chattahoochee River** and the **Flint River** under *Green Space—Rivers.* Although Georgia and Alabama have a reciprocal agreement honoring each other's fishing licenses, the two states differ in daily limits and size restrictions for some species, so check ahead. Bank fishing is excellent at public fishing docks, by bridges, and at the mouths of creeks. The Georgia Department of Natural Resources maintains a series of fish attractors for better fishing. Cedar trees have been placed in the lakes to create new fish concentration areas, and these are marked with buoys.

See also **Kolomoki Mounds Historic Park** under *To See—Historic Homes and Sites.*

GOLF 🐦 **Meadow Links Golf Course at George T. Bagby State Park and Lodge** (pro shop 229-768-3714 or 1-877-591-5574; 1-800-434-0982 for tee times; www.golfgeorgia.com), GA 39, Fort Gaines. Open 8–dusk except Christmas Day; tee times can be scheduled by reservation, which is particularly recommended on weekends and holidays. The state park features Meadow Links, an 18-hole, 7,007-yard, par-72, Willard Byrd–designed golf course that challenges any golfer. This newest state park course was named the sixth-best new affordable public course in America when it opened in 1998. Amenities include a pro shop, snack bar, and instruction. Golf packages are available combined with accommodations in the park's lodge or cottages (see *Green Space—Nature Preserves & Parks*). $30–35; junior and senior discounts.

HIKING The Georgia side of the **Walter F. George Lock and Dam** is used for walking and hiking and also as an exercise area. See also **George T. Bagby State Park and Lodge** under *Green Space—Nature Preserves and Parks* and

Cotton Hill Park Campground under *Lodging—Campgrounds.*

See also **Kolomoki Mounds Historic Park** under *To See—Historic Homes and Sites.*

MINIATURE GOLF See **Seminole State Park** under *Green Space—Nature Preserves and Parks.* See also **Kolomoki Mounds Historic Park** under *To See—Historic Homes and Sites.*

WINERY TOURS 🐾 ♿ **Still Pond Vineyard and Winery** (229-792-6382; 1-800-475-1193; www.stillpond.com), 1575 Still Pond Road, Arlington. Open 11–6 Monday through Saturday. Still Pond is the largest winery in the state as well as the only winery in south Georgia. At Still Pond, you'll find acres and acres of muscadine (also known as scuppernong or swamp grapes) vines. Visitors can tour the vineyards and winery and then enjoy complimentary tastings of the five Still Pond premium wines from the comfort of a custom-made rocking chair. Tastings of other Georgia wines are available for a small fee. In addition to producing its own wines, Still Pond Winery also supplies muscadine juice to other wineries and retailers. The gift shop sells Still Pond wines, wine-related gifts, and cheeses. Several special events occur throughout the year, including spring, summer, and fall wine festivals and a Christmas open house. Free.

> **THE LEGEND OF STILL POND**
> Although we pictured this isolated pond at the Vineyard and winery as being tranquil and serene, therefore "still," that's not how the pond got its name. During the Civil War, the landowner had a still on the banks of the pond, where he turned out peach brandy for exhausted Confederate soldiers to give them some comfort, relaxation, and escape.

✳ Green Space

BEACHES There are man-made beaches at several state parks and day-use areas on **Lake Walter F. George, Lake George W. Andrews,** and **Lake Seminole** as well as at **Cheney Griffin Park** in Bainbridge.

LAKES ⚓ 🐾 ♿ **Lake Seminole** (229-662-2001), Donalsonville. When completed in 1957, Jim Woodruff Lock and Dam created the 37,500-acre lake at the confluence of the Chattahoochee and Flint rivers. The lake was named for the last Native American tribe that was pushed out of Georgia into central Florida. Interpretive displays can be found at the Lake Seminole Visitor Center at the Resource Management Office in nearby Chattahoochee, Florida. The lake's 500 miles of shoreline extend 30 miles up the Chattahoochee and 35 miles up the Flint. The lock and dam improve navigation, generate electricity, and provide recreation. Before construction, the Chattahoochee was only 3 feet deep. Today, a channel 9 feet deep and 100 feet wide allows commercial river traffic to reach Columbus on the Chattahoochee and Bainbridge on the Flint. The area's moderate climate and sandy, acid soils produce a diversity of distinctive Coastal Plain flora, which in turn supports a vast abundance of mammalian, reptilian, amphib-

ian, bird, and fish species. In fact, Lake Seminole is one of the most highly re-
garded fishing lakes in North America for largemouth bass, striped and hybrid
bass, bream, crappie, and catfish. In addition to fishing, the lake is popular for
swimming, boating, and waterskiing. Numerous boat ramps make access to the
lake easy. Fishing supplies, licenses, and other supplies are readily available at
marinas and bait and tackle shops. Boat rentals are also available at marinas. You
can cruise all the way from Columbus, Georgia, to Panama City Beach, Florida,
by going through the locks (call the superintendent for schedules). Shore-based
activities include hiking, hunting, camping, bird-watching, and nature photography.

✒ 🐾 � **Lake Walter F. George, U.S. Army Corps of Engineers Visitors
Center** (229-768-2516; 1-866-772-9542; walterfgeorge.sam.usace.army.mil), off
GA 39, Fort Gaines. Lake open daily dawn–dusk; visitor center open 8–4:30
weekdays year-round, plus 9:30–6 Saturday and Sunday in summer. The 48,000-
acre lake occupies 85 miles of the Chattahoochee River separating Georgia and
Alabama (on the Alabama side, it's called Lake Eufaula). The lake boasts 640
miles of shoreline, 13 Corps of Engineers day-use parks, and four campgrounds.
The day-use parks on the Georgia side of the lake are Pataula Creek, Cool
Branch, East Bank, and River Bluff. Some of the day-use parks offer beaches,
picnic tables, horseshoe pits, and volleyball areas. Most of them have rest rooms.
Fishing is a major attraction, with the principal species being largemouth bass,
white bass, crappie, channel catfish, and bream. Fishing is good from boats,
banks, and piers at the mouth of tributary creeks and along several bridges. The
two states have reciprocal acceptance of state-issued fishing licenses. The lake
also offers boating, camping, swimming, and waterskiing. Access to lake free;
day-use parks with beaches $4, day-use areas with boat launching ramps $3.

NATURE PRESERVES AND PARKS ✒ 🐾 ⅙ **Earl May Boat Basin and Cheney
Griffin Park** (229-248-2000), Boat Basin Circle, Bainbridge. Open daily. This
500-acre park on the banks of the Flint River features a visitor center, swimming
area in a spring-fed lake, boat-launching ramps, fishing pier, 3.4 miles of hiking
and nature trails, a boardwalk along the river, camping, a petting zoo, playground, historic steam locomotive, lighted tennis courts, and a performance
amphitheater where monthly concerts are held from May to October. Free.

✒ 🐾 ⅙ 🌳 **George T. Bagby State Park and Lodge** (229-768-2571; 1-800-
864-7275; www.gastateparks.org/info/georgetb), off GA 39, Fort Gaines. Open
7–10 daily. Located on 48,000-acre **Lake Walter F. George** (see *Lakes*), the
700-acre resort park offers endless water sports. Water enthusiasts are drawn to
its swimming beach, pool, full-service marina, docks and boat ramps, and canoe,
fishing boat, and pontoon boat rentals. Other recreational amenities include an
award-winning golf course with a pro shop (see *To Do—Golf*), tennis courts, 3
miles of hiking trails through hardwoods and pines, beach volleyball, and picnicking. Bird-watching and wildlife observation are popular activities, too.
Accommodations are available in a lodge, in cottages, and in campsites (see
Lodging), and a restaurant is also on-site (see *Where to Eat—Eating Out*). Pets
are permitted in the campground and selected cottages, but not the lodge. Special events throughout the year include a summer nature photography contest,

Labor Day celebration and luau, Halloween celebration, and holiday open house. State park parking/day-use fee $3.

✿ ᰔ �& **Mayhaw Wildlife Management Area** (229-430-4254), north of Colquitt; call for directions. Open 24/7. The 4,700-acre preserve is perfect for bird-watching, hiking, camping, and hunting, and there is also a firing range. Mostly dirt roads take visitors through hardwood bottoms, cypress-gum wetlands, and young and mature pines. Bird-watchers enjoy the ibis and wood storks that congregate here during the summer. Free; fees for hunting.

✿ ᰔ & 🐾 **Seminole State Park** (229-861-3137; 1-800-864-7275; www.gastate parks.org/info/seminole), GA 253, Donalsonville. Open 7–10 daily. Lake Seminole, with 37,500 surface acres, is rated the fifth-best bass-fishing lake in the nation (see *Lakes*). Naturally it is immensely popular for fishing but also for all other water sports, including boating, swimming, and waterskiing, as well as for bird-watching. Although the lake is shallow, natural lime sinkholes create areas of cool, clear water that attract a variety of fish. The 604-acre park features a swimming beach, picnic area, nature trail, and miniature golf. Georgia's state reptile, the endangered gopher tortoise, resides along the 2.2-mile nature trail, which interprets the wire-grass habitat. Canoe and boat rentals are available. Accommodations are available in campsites and cottages (see *Lodging*). The park is located near a wildlife management area, which attracts duck and deer hunters—many of whom stay at the park. Parking $3.

See also **Kolomoki Mounds Historic Park** under *To See—Historic Homes and Sites.*

RIVERS *✿ ᰔ* **Chattahoochee River** (229-524-2588; www.donalsonvillega.com), Neals Landing/GA 91, Donalsonville. Open dawn–dusk daily. The Chattahoochee River begins as a mere trickle in north Georgia, wends its way through metro Atlanta where it is designated as the Chattahoochee River National Recreation Area, then creates the border between Georgia and Alabama before emptying into Lake Seminole at the Georgia-Florida border. The river has rapids in its upper reaches, but the river in this region flows placidly through the Coastal Plain. Although the Chattahoochee is navigable up to Columbus and was once a major transportation artery, today its main uses are for power generation, drinking water, and recreation, and it remains one of the most important ecological and economic assets to the region. Public boat ramps and day-use areas afford opportunities for fishing, boating, waterskiing, bird-watching, picnicking, and hiking. Free.

✿ ᰔ **Flint River,** which begins in metro Atlanta and flows all the way to the Florida border into Lake Seminole, has three distinct sections. The Lower Flint River Basin in the Bainbridge area flows through Coastal Plain and Dougherty Plain. Many natural springs create blue holes, where swimmers cool off on hot summer days because the water temperature is 68 degrees year-round. These cool temperatures are critical to the survival of the Gulf strain of striped bass. Meanwhile, shoals in the river provide habitats for several rare and threatened fish and freshwater shellfish. When the river reaches Bainbridge, it is discharging 3 million to 11 million gallons of water daily, which is essential to the ecosys-

tems of Lake Seminole, the Apalachicola River, Apalachicola Bay, and the Gulf of Mexico. The river provides innumerable opportunities for swimming, fishing, camping, waterskiing, boating, bird-watching, wildlife observation, and plant identification.

❊ Lodging
BED & BREAKFASTS
In Bainbridge
❦ **The Commodore Bed and Breakfast** (229-248-0081; www.bed andbreakfast.com/georgia/the -commodore-b-b.html), 320 Washington Street. The magnificent white-columned antebellum home is the epitome of a Southern mansion. Built in 1840, the virgin longleaf-pine structure is supported by 40-foot-high cypress columns. Guest rooms and public spaces are filled with antiques, fine furniture, and collectibles. The second-floor sitting area features an art gallery. All four accommodations feature a sitting area; two have private baths, two share. Beautifully landscaped grounds boast fountains, a gazebo, and a swimming pool. All this within walking distance of the downtown square and the Flint River. A full breakfast is included. Crate-trained pets permitted. Smoking outdoors only. Not wheelchair accessible. $85–115.

In Colquitt
♪ ⅙ **Tarrer Inn** (229-758-2888; 1-888-282-7737; www.tarrerinn.com), 155 South Cuthbert Street. The inn, built in 1905 and restored in 1994, is listed on the National Register of Historic Places and is the recipient of the prestigious Georgia Trust for Historic Preservation award. Its 12 elegant accommodations are furnished with fine period antiques and boast hand-painted fireplaces and luxurious baths. From embroidered bed linens

to computer data ports, the inn provides a combination of elegance and convenience. A full Southern breakfast is included. For other meals, authentic Southern cuisine is featured at sumptuous lunch and dinner buffets in the dining rooms (see *Where to Eat—Dining Out*). Outstanding personal service proves the truth of Southern hospitality. No smoking. Wheelchair accessible. $99–125.

In Fort Gaines
❦ ⅙ **Sutlive House Bed and Breakfast** (229-768-3546), 204 South Washington Street. Two suites, each with a bedroom, sitting room, and private bath with a Jacuzzi tub, are offered in the 1820 Plantation-style home. No smoking. Wheelchair accessible. $95.

CAMPGROUNDS
In Bainbridge
♪ ❦ **Wingate's Marina** (229-246-0658; www.wingateslodge.com), 139 Wingate Road. Wingate's offers a variety of lodging options, a restaurant (see *Where to Eat—Eating Out*), and a full-service marina with two in-and-out ramps. The campground features a dump station, 30- to 50-amp hookups, a bathhouse, picnic tables, and fire rings. Wingate's also offers a variety of brick cottages, two-bedroom log cabins, motel rooms, and mobile homes. Campsites $20 with full hookups, rooms and cottages $50, cabins $75.

In Blakely

See **Kolomoki Mounds Historic Park** under *To See—Historic Homes and Sites.*

In Donalsonville

See **Seminole State Park** under *Green Space—Nature Preserves and Parks.*

In Fort Gaines

🐾 🦌 ♿ **Cotton Hill Park Campground** (229-768-3061; www.reserve usa.com), GA 39 North. The Corps of Engineers campground, which is open year-round, offers 104 campsites, all with water hookups, 94 with electrical hookups as well. Many of the sites are lakefront. Amenities include a fish-cleaning station, coin laundry, three bathhouses with showers, a boat ramp and courtesy dock, playgrounds, a dump station, and wheelchair-accessible rest rooms and fishing. The campground also features a hiking trail with interpretive markers for nature lovers. Tent sites $16, other sites $18; reservations must be made at least four days in advance; two-night minimum on weekends, three-night minimum on holiday weekends.

George T. Bagby State Park and Lodge (229-768-2571; 1-800-864-7275; www.gastateparks.org/info/ georgetb), off GA 39, Fort Gaines. The park offers five tent, trailer, and RV sites as well as a pioneer campground. $17–21.

In Bainbridge

See **Wingate's Marina** under *Campgrounds.*

In Donalsonville

🐾 🦌 ♿ 🐕 **Seminole State Park**

(229-861-3137; 1-800-864-7275; www .gastateparks.org/info/seminole), 7870 State Park Drive/GA 253. Seminole State Park offers 14 fully equipped cottages; many of which are located at the water's edge and have excellent lake views. Dogs are allowed in campgrounds and selected cottages. $85–100.

In Fort Gaines

George T. Bagby State Park and Lodge (229-768-2571; 1-800-864-7275; www.gastateparks.org/info/ georgetb), off GA 39, Fort Gaines. Guests can stay in one of five two-bedroom cottages, each with digital satellite TV, fireplace, a kitchen with stove and refrigerator, living and dining areas, and all utensils and linens. $80–125.

In Fort Gaines

George T. Bagby State Park and Lodge (229-768-2571; 1-800-864-7275; www.gastateparks.org/info/ georgetb), off GA 39, Fort Gaines. The park's lodge features 60 rooms, including two junior suites, as well as a restaurant. Many of the traditional hotel rooms offer a view of the lake. Each accommodation has modern conveniences such as digital satellite TV and telephones with data ports and voice mail. In addition, there is a group lodge that sleeps 14. No smoking. Wheelchair accessible. Rooms $60–75; group lodge $95–150.

✳ **Where to Eat**

In Colquitt

♿ **Tarrer Inn** (229-758-2888; 1-888-282-7737; www.tarrerinn.com), 155 South Cuthbert Street. Open 11:30–2

Wednesday through Friday and Sunday, 6–9 Thursday and Friday, Saturday evenings during *Swamp Gravy* performances (see *Entertainment—Theater*). Several dining rooms ensure intimate dining. Rich in the tradition of Southern cooking, the restaurant serves buffet-style meals with regional dishes such as fried chicken, glazed pork roast, and catfish, along with a vast array of vegetables, salads, breads, and desserts like peach cobbler, pecan pie, strawberry trifle, and banana pudding. Thursday evenings feature a family-style buffet, and Friday evenings feature a seafood buffet, (except during *Swamp Gravy* performances). No smoking. Wheelchair accessible. $8.50–14.79.

EATING OUT

In Bainbridge

✒ 🍴 ♿ **Boyd's Pit Bar-B-Que and Grill** (229-246-0797), 721 East Calhoun Street. Open 11–3 Monday and Tuesday, 11–7 Wednesday, 11–9 Thursday through Saturday. The specialty here is rubbed and hickory-smoked ribs cooked "Southern, smoky, and slow." Diners can get a half slab, whole slab, basket, or plate of ribs. Check for the night of the all-you-can-eat ribs special. If ribs aren't your thing, there are a wide variety of sandwiches, salads, plates, and burgers, as well as a Kids Korner menu. The eatery advertises its fried tenderloin sandwich as the largest sandwich on a bun. No smoking. Wheelchair accessible. $4.50–8.25.

✒ 🍴 ♿ **The Marketplace Restaurant** (229-246-8550; 1-800-768-8550), 1401 Tallahassee Highway. Open 6–11 and 11–2 daily, 5–9 Monday through Saturday. Located in the Charter House Inn, the restaurant serves three meals every day except Sunday. For breakfast diners can choose from the buffet or the menu. The lunch buffet features a 35-item salad bar, soup of the day, three Southern entrées, vegetables and starches, cobblers, and sweet tea. Dinner features a soup and salad bar and such entrées as prime rib, Angus rib eye, seafood pasta, and smoked pork chops. No smoking. Wheelchair accessible. Buffet $5.95, lunch $5–7 à la carte, dinner $9–18.

🍴 ♿ **Po Boys BBQ at Wingate's Marina** (229-246-0658; www.wingateslodge.com), 139 Wingate Road. Open 6 AM–9 PM. This casual eatery offers eggs, biscuits and gravy, fresh fruit, barbecued ribs, pulled pork, and chicken. No smoking. Wheelchair accessible. Breakfast $2.95–6.95, lunch or dinner $5.95–12.95.

In Fort Gaines

🍴 ♿ **Pilot House Grille at George T. Bagby State Park and Lodge**. (229-768-2571; 1-800-864-7275; www.gastateparks.org/info/georgtb), off GA 39. Open 7–10 and 11:30–3 daily, 5–9 Monday through Saturday. The lakeside restaurant offers sumptuous buffets as well as an à la carte menu. No smoking. Wheelchair accessible. Breakfast $3.25–7, lunch $4.50–7, dinner $7–15.

WHAT IS SWAMP GRAVY?
Indigenous to the area, the stew-like dish is made by pouring fish drippings left in the grease after frying fish over tomatoes, potatoes, onions, and whatever else is at hand. It can be a side dish or even the whole meal if there isn't enough fish for everyone.

SOUTHERN RIVERS

In Cuthbert

🦐 ♿ **Julianna's Antiques, Gifts, and Tea Parlor** (229-732-5523), 104 South Peachtree Street. Open 10–5 Tuesday through Saturday. Reservations required for tea. Located in the original Bank of Randolph, which was built in the 1800s, the Victorian-style tearoom serves English tea with a Southern twist, in the parlor or in the Savannah-style garden. Afternoon Tea features tea sandwiches and sweets; High Tea also features an entrée. The ambience, service, and food are flawless. Even if you don't have tea, peruse the gift shop for wonderful finds including irresistible gifts for the tea lover as well as gift items, antiques, and collectibles. No smoking. Wheelchair accessible. $14.95–18.95.

✳ Entertainment

MUSIC 🎵 🦐 ♿ **River Music Concert Series** (229-248-2010), Performing Arts amphitheater at **Earl May Boat Basin and Cheney Griffin Park** (see *Green Space—Nature Preserves & Parks*), Boat Basin Circle, Bainbridge. Call for a schedule of events. The monthly concerts occur from June through September and feature a variety of musical genres, from gospel to barbershop to Army band selections to '50s music. The July concert also includes fireworks. Bring a blanket or lawn chair and a picnic. Most concerts free.

THEATER **Bainbridge Little Theater** (229-246-8345; www.bainbridge littletheater.com), 220 Troupe Street, Bainbridge (mailing address: P.O. Box 1245, Bainbridge 39818). Call for a schedule of performances. Entertaining Bainbridge residents and those from the surrounding area for more than 30 years, this award-winning theater presents four productions each year, including dramas, comedies, and musicals. Plays: adults $12, students $7; musicals: adults $15, students $10.

Cotton Hall Theater, *Swamp Gravy* (229-758-6686; www.swamp gravy.com), 166 East Main Street, Colquitt. The play is performed weekends in March and October and during the annual Mayhaw Festival in April (see *Events*). Call for a schedule of performances and ticket prices. The Museum of Southern Culture is open only during performances. The restored 70-year-old cotton warehouse is the home of the **Museum of Southern Culture** (see *To See—Historic Homes and Sites*) and the performance venue of Georgia's official folk-life play, *Swamp Gravy*, which depicts the ordinary, comic, and tragic life and culture of rural southwest Georgia families and communities through original and traditional song and dance.

The play, which has a cast of more than 100, was first performed in 1992. With a new play created each year, however, it's still attracting scores of playgoers. All the plays are based on real-life stories obtained from taped interviews and adapted for the stage by a local playwright. *Swamp Gravy* attracted national attention through a Cultural Olympiad appearance at the 1996 Centennial Olympic Summer Games and another at the Kennedy Center. Cotton Hall, which features four stages, arena-style seating, and a state-of-the-art lighting system, hosts other performances throughout the year, such as a *Cotton Hall Christmas*. Tickets about $22.

♿ **Olive Theater** (229-524-1139; 229-524-8259), 203 South Woolfork Avenue, Donalsonville. Call for a schedule of performances and ticket prices. Once a 1930s-era movie palace, the theater has been restored and upgraded to a state-of-the-art performance venue for the productions of the Seminole County Arts Council.

✷ **Selective Shopping**

Market on the Square (229-758-8480), 164 North First Street, Colquitt. Open 10–5:30 weekdays, 10–2 Saturday; special hours during holidays and productions of *Swamp Gravy*. Market on the Square is a mini-mall with 20 shops featuring antiques, arts and crafts, jewelry, gifts, home accents, Christmas items, children's clothing, and food items such as mayhaw jelly and peanut products.

T&W Auction Company (229-248-0640), 3017 Thomasville Highway US 84 East, Bainbridge. Auctions at 6 PM on second and last Saturday of each month; previews 9–4 weekdays. The company specializes in antique auctions and also does estate and business liquidation auctions. Shoppers may find flow blue, various china, pottery, oil paintings, collectibles such as Hummels, art glass, advertising items, jewelry, old coins, Persian rugs, tools, and much more. Although much of the excitement is the auction itself, you don't have to present because left bids and phone bids are accepted.

✷ **Special Events**

January: **Rattlesnake Roundup** (229-762-3774). This event, a popular attraction for 40 years, is held on the last Saturday in January at the Rattlesnake Grounds in Whigham. In addition to snake-handling demonstrations, the festival features arts and crafts, concessions, entertainment, and children's rides. Free.

April: **National Mayhaw Festival** (229-758-2400; www.colquitt-georgia .com). Held the third weekend in April at the Spring Creek Recreational Park in Colquitt, the festival celebrates the mayhaw, small red berries often used in jams and jellies. The event includes a parade, arts and crafts, entertainment, children's activities, Civil War reenactments, a tennis tournament, and food. *Swamp Gravy* is performed Friday and Saturday nights and Sunday afternoon. Festival free; some events have a charge; *Swamp Gravy* performances $22.

July: **Tama Intertribal Pow-Wow** (229-762-3165). Held over the July Fourth weekend in Whigham's Tama Tribal Town, the event is sponsored by the Lower Muscogee Creek Tribe. The festival includes Native American crafts and exhibits as well as dancing, drumming, and storytelling. Bluegrass and gospel are also featured. $5.

November: **Christmas at the Fort** (229-732-6092; 229-881-5797). The annual arts and crafts fair, held at Fort Gaines's **Frontier Village** (see *To See—Historic Homes and Sites*), features arts and crafts vendors, Christmas items, food, continuous entertainment, and demonstrations of old-time skills. The Fort Gaines Methodist Church sells chili and desserts. Shuttle buses take fairgoers to the fort from the nearby senior center. Festival free; some events have a charge.

Mule Day (229-377-MULE). Held in Calvary the first Saturday in November, the festival, which attracts 75,000 visitors, features a parade of mule-drawn wagons; mule judging; a mule show; contests in skills such as plowing; demonstrations of cane grinding, meal grinding, and syrup making; all-day entertainment; arts and crafts booths; a flea market; a slingshot turkey shoot; and food. The Mule Museum takes visitors back to the days of shade tobacco farms. Events prior to Mule Day include a golf tournament, trail ride, chicken dinner, and auction. Festival free; some events have a charge.

Swine Time Festival (229-246-3300). Held the Saturday of Thanksgiving weekend in Climax, the festival features a parade, food, arts and crafts, a homemade quilt auction, entertainment, and demonstrations of old-time skills. Contests include the best-dressed pig, hog and turkey calling, pig racing, a greased pig chase, corn shucking, chitterlings eating, syrup making, and baby crawling. Antique engines and vehicles are displayed. There is a historic log cabin to visit and there are camper sites available at a very reasonable price. Festival free; some activities have a small charge.

Late November through mid-December: **Cotton Hall Christmas** (229-758-5450; www.swampgravy.com). Performances Thursday through Sunday in Colquitt. The folks who bring you *Swamp Gravy* put a Depression-era south Georgia twist on the familiar Dickens story, with the town's stingy cotton gin owner as Old Man Scrooge. Productions include rousing original music along with traditional carols. $20.

COLUMBUS

Although Columbus is far inland from the Gulf of Mexico, the Chattahoochee River is navigable to Columbus, making it a real river city. Therefore, in the 1800s it was a shipbuilding center and, in fact, the Confederate ironclad CSS *Jackson* was built there. Unfortunately, before it could be put into service, it was destroyed by Union troops, with only its below-water hull surviving. It rested on the bottom of the Chattahoochee until it was recovered in the 1960s. Today it is the centerpiece of the Port Columbus Civil War Naval Museum (see *To See— Historic Homes and Sites*).

Throughout the years, three things have played major roles in Columbus's history: cotton, clay, and Coca-Cola.

Columbus also has a rich African American heritage. In addition to Mother of the Blues "Ma" Rainey, Columbus was the home of Eugene Bullard, the world's first black combat aviator, and Horace King, a former slave who became a master bridge builder.

Novelist Carson McCullers, author of *The Heart is a Lonely Hunter* and *The Member of the Wedding*, was also a Columbus native. Visitors can walk or drive by her house at 1519 Stark Avenue, now privately owned, and read the historical marker.

SOFT DRINK CAPITAL

One of Columbus's claims to fame is that it was the birthplace of the world-famous soft drink Coca-Cola. A local pharmacist, Dr. John Stith Pemberton, concocted the original formula for French Wine of Coca, a forerunner of Coca-Cola, in his apothecary shop in 1850 and later dispensed it at a soda fountain. It wasn't until after the Civil War, when he moved to Atlanta, that he perfected the formula and sold it to Asa Candler for a mere $1,750. When Candler sold it in 1917, he made $25 million. What Coca-Cola is worth today is beyond comprehension. Most folks are amazed to learn that not only Coca-Cola but Royal Crown Cola and Nehi were concocted by Columbus citizens as well.

Today bustling Columbus is the state's third-largest city, with a population of 186,000. Among the oddities in Columbus is the Scramble Dog, a strange concoction served at the Dinglewood Pharmacy (see *Where to Eat—Eating Out*). The city also claims to have the highest concentration of barbecue restaurants anywhere.

Nearby is Fort Benning, the world's largest infantry training center and home of the National Infantry Museum (see *To See—Museums*). Tiny Buena Vista is the home of Pasaquan, the colorful compound of an audacious artist (see *To See—Historic Homes and Sites*).

GUIDANCE For information about Columbus and the greater Columbus area including Buena Vista in Marion County, Cusseta in Chattahoochee County, and Fortson in Muscogee County, contact the **Columbus Convention and Visitors Bureau** (706-322-1613; 1-800-999-1613; www.visitcolumbusga.com), 900 Front Avenue, Columbus 31901. Open 8:30–5:30 weekdays, 10–4 Saturday. Stop by to see a video orientation to the city and pick up brochures.

There's also a **Georgia Visitor Information Center** (706-649-7455), 1751 Williams Road, Columbus 31904.

To learn more about Buena Vista, contact the **Buena Vista–Marion County Chamber of Commerce** (229-649-2842; 1-800-647-2842), 107 East Sixth Street, Buena Vista 31803. Open 10–3 weekdays.

See **National Infantry Museum** under *To See—Museums* for more information about Fort Benning.

GETTING THERE *By air:* **Columbus Metropolitan Airport** (706-324-2449; www.flycolumbusga.com) is served by **ASA/Delta Connection, Northwest,** and **US Airways Express**. Passengers can rent cars from **Avis** (706-322-2539), **Budget** (706-327-5501), **Enterprise** (706-322-0536), **Hertz** (706-324-2725), and **National** (706-322-4586). Several hotels provide shuttle service.

By bus: **Greyhound Lines** (1-800-231-2222; www.greyhound.com), 818 Veterans Parkway, provides bus service to and from Columbus.

By car: Columbus is on the Georgia-Alabama line. From the north it is reached by I-85, then I-185. From the south it is reached by US 280. The major east-west route is US 80, plus GA 26 and GA 96.

By train: There is no **Amtrak** service to Columbus. Train riders have to transfer by bus or car from Atlanta, which is three hours to the north.

MEDICAL EMERGENCY For a medical emergency, call 911. For other immediate care needs in Columbus, go to **Columbus Regional Healthcare** (706-571-1000), 710 Center Street; **Doctor's Hospital** (706-571-4262), 616 19th Street; or **Doctor's Hospital HCA** (706-576-4560), 537 18th Street.

NEIGHBORHOODS Columbus has several designated historic neighborhoods: **Uptown**, which includes the Springer Opera House; **High Uptown**, which includes opulent residences such as the **Rankin House** (see *To See—Historic Homes and Sites*), known for its ornamental ironwork; and the **Historic District,**

which encompasses **Heritage Corner** (see *To See—Historic Homes and Sites*), the Chattahoochee promenade, and the **Port Columbus Civil War Naval Museum** (see *To See—Museums*).

✳ To See

HISTORIC HOMES AND SITES ⚲ ❦ **Heritage Corner Tour** (706-323-7979; www.historiccolumbus.com), 708 Broadway, Columbus. Tours at 2 daily. Tour five adjacent houses ranging from a primitive cabin circa 1800 to an elegant mansion circa 1870. One of the houses is the Greek Revival–style **John Stith Pemberton House** (11 Seventh Street), which features family heirlooms and a portrait of the inventor of Coca-Cola. To the rear of the house in the former separate kitchen building is a replica of Pemberton's apothecary shop, which displays marble-topped soda fountain counters and Coca-Cola memorabilia. The **Walker-Peters-Langdon House** (716 Broadway), is a Federal-style cottage built in 1828, the year Columbus was founded, making it the oldest house in the city. One family owned it from 1836 to 1966. The 1870 Italianate **Victorian Townhouse** was the home of Albert Lamar and Sterling Price Gilbert. Also on the grounds are two other homes that were moved there: an 1800s **log cabin** and the 1840 double-pen or dogtrot-style **Woodruff Farm House**, which serves as the headquarters of **Riverfest Weekend** (see *Special Events*) and Heritage Corner Tours. Across the street is **Heritage Park**, a quiet retreat with fountains, statues, and educational plaques. Tour: adults $5, students $1.

⚲ ❦ **Pasaquan** (Pasaquan Preservation Society, 912-649-9444; www.pasaquan.com), Eddie Martin Road off County 78, Buena Vista. Open one Saturday a month May through November or by appointment (but it's worth the effort). This bizarre 4-acre fantasy compound created by artist Eddie Owens Martin (1908–1988), son of a local sharecropper, is one of the most unusual sights anyone will ever see and one of the premier outsider-art sites in the country. Martin, who freely admitted to dabbling in drugs, mystic religions, and the occult, dubbed himself St. EOM (his initials), the Wizard of Pasaquan. Martin claimed that God spoke to him and told him to create Pasaquan, which he translated to mean "bringing the past and future together." Drawing from African, Asian, and Native American mythology, he created flamboyantly painted outdoor sculptures, pagodas, temples, totem poles, and walls. If these figures were envisioned when Martin was in a drug-induced state, it must have been a happy place considering the many representations of smiling humans and grinning snakes. Inside the main house, floors, walls, ceilings, and furniture are also

THE QUIRKY COMPOUND KNOWN AS PASAQUAN OVERFLOWS WITH COLORFUL ART.

painted within an inch of their lives. Upon his death, Martin willed the compound to the Marion County Historical Society, which struggles to preserve it. Admission free, (but the society would be ever so grateful for a $5 donation).

🐾 **Rankin House** (706-322-0756), 1440 Second Avenue, Columbus. Open 9–5 weekdays. Located in the High Uptown Historic District and serving as the headquarters of the Historic Columbus Foundation, the grand 1860s mansion features exquisite iron grillwork, a flying balcony, and lovely Victorian-era antiques. Free.

MUSEUMS 🐾 🐾 ♿ **Columbus Museum** (706-649-0713; www.columbusmuseum .com), 1251 Wynnton Road, Columbus. Open 10–5 Tuesday through Saturday (until 9 on Thursday), 1–5 Sunday. The second-largest museum in the state, the Columbus Museum contains collections of Native American, American Impressionist, and contemporary mixed-media art as well as American furniture and many changing exhibits. The Chattahoochee Legacy is a regional history gallery where a film and life-sized period settings tell the story of the Chattahoochee River Valley. Here visitors see dwellings, an old schoolroom, exhibitions on Rood Creek Indians, and old photos. Hands-on activities in the children's discovery gallery encourage curiosity and imagination. Enjoy fabulous food in a beautiful setting at the museum's **Place for Taste Café,** open 11–2 Tuesday through Friday.

The museum has a satellite facility, the ♿ **Columbus Museum Uptown** (706-221-7580), 1004 Broadway. Open noon–8 Tuesday through Saturday. It is both an exhibition space and a studio program. At this facility, the intimate Dr. Sidney Yarbrough III Gallery features changing exhibits of the latest works from American contemporary artists working in a wide range of media. The Tom Morgan and Mary Lindsay studios offer classes, workshops, and camps. Admission to both museums free.

🐾 🐾 ♿ **National Infantry Museum** (706-545-2958; www.benningmwr.com/ museum.cfm), Building 396, Baltzell Avenue, Fort Benning. Open 10–4:30 weekdays, 12:30–4:30 weekends. Fort Benning is the world's largest infantry training center, so it's no surprise that a museum connected with the foot soldier would be located here or that it houses one of the most complete collections of military memorabilia from U.S. infantrymen. The evolution of the dogface is chronicled from the 1607 wilderness of Virginia to the French and Indian War to the 1991 Persian Gulf War. This museum has an example of every gun ever used by the U.S. Army, and other artifacts from each of America's military engagements are displayed, including uniforms, footwear, mess equipment, helmets, vehicles, military band instruments, captured enemy paraphernalia, military documents signed by each of America's presidents, silver presentation pieces, and much more. Some of the more interesting artifacts include a document signed by John Hancock, a bust of Adolph Hitler, a gas mask for a horse, and a prisoner of war uniform. The collection is so immense it cannot all be exhibited at the same time, so displays change often, giving even frequent visitors something new to see. Films are shown daily in the auditorium. The museum's Quartermaster's Sale Shop sells military-related bears, books, toys, and many other items. Other sites to see at Fort Benning include the **POW Monument,** the **War Dog**

Memorial, and the **Ranger Memorial.** Special events include the **Airborne in Action Show** and the **Mass Parachute Jump.** Free.

✐ 🐾 ♿ **Port Columbus Civil War Naval Museum** (706-327-9798; www.port columbus.org), 1002 Victory Drive, Columbus. Open 9–5 daily. This museum, dedicated to the naval battles of the Civil War, was created to display the remains of two Confederate Navy ships. The museum's star attraction is what remains of the CSS *Jackson,* the largest surviving scratch-made ironclad ship in the world. Since so little of it is left, a steel ghost skeleton was constructed over the hull to give an idea of the ship's size. The hull can be viewed from above and below. The museum's hundreds of exhibits also feature remnants of the CSS *Chattahoochee,* a warship built in Columbus and scuttled by Union troops; a partial replica of the USS *Hartford,* Union Admiral David Farragut's flagship; a full-size sectional reconstruction of the USS *Monitor;* as well as the country's only full-size ironclad Civil War combat simulator. Both Confederate and Union weapons and uniforms are shown, as well as rare Confederate naval flags. To fully understand the story, begin with the audiovisual presentations about the Union attack. Adults $4.50, seniors and active military $3.50, students $3.

NATURAL BEAUTY SPOTS A **waterfall** in downtown Columbus marks the northernmost navigable point on the Chattahoochee River. It can be seen from the **RiverWalk** (see *Special Places*).

SCENIC DRIVES Purchase an area map and enjoy the 68-mile drive from **Columbus to Providence Canyon.** There are good secondary roads that meander south of Columbus, through the forested part of Fort Benning Military Reservation, through various small towns, past the scenic Chattahoochee River and the Walter F. George Lake and Dam, continuing through Florence Marina State Park to beautiful Providence Canyon State Park. Other points of interest along the way include American Indian mounds and Westville Historic Village (c. 1800s). For more information about these sites, see the Americus chapter.

SELF-GUIDED TOURS **Black Heritage Trail Tour.** Pick up a brochure for this driving tour from the **Columbus Convention and Visitors Bureau** (see *Guidance*). Twenty-four sites on this drive-by tour include historic black churches, cemeteries, the Liberty Theater, and the last home of Gertrude "Ma" Rainey. Born to minstrel-show parents in Columbus in 1886, Gertrude Pridgett began performing early. She married Will Rainey, but it didn't last long. She took on the name "Ma" and went on to a career as one of the first female recording stars, earning the titles "Queen of the Blues" and "Mother of the Blues." Someday the house may be a museum, but for now visitors can only drive by her home at 805 Fifth Avenue. Visitors also can drive by the home of Eugene Ballard, the first African American combat pilot.

SPECIAL PLACES ✐ 🐾 ♿ **Columbus RiverWalk,** located along the scenic bluffs and banks of the Chattahoochee River. The 15-mile linear park is a favorite spot for walking, cycling, skating, and fishing. The brick-paved promenade is punctuated with decorative ironwork, gazebos, fountains, historical markers, sculptures, and benches. Free.

✳ To Do

BICYCLING See *Outdoor Adventures.*

BIRDING See **Columbus RiverWalk** under *To Se—Special Places* and **Lake Walter F. George** under *Green Space—Lakes.*

BOATING See **Lake Walter F. George** under *Green Space—Lakes.*

BREWERY TOURS Cannon Brewpub (706-653-2337), 1041 Broadway, Columbus. Tours of this brewery and pub, opened in February 1999, are available by appointment. Call for details.

FISHING 🎣 🦌 ♿ **Cooper Creek Park** (706-563-4546), 4816 Milgen Road, Columbus. Open 10 AM–11 PM Monday through Thursday, 8–8 Friday and Sunday, 8–6 Saturday. BYOT—bring your own tackle.

FOR FAMILIES 🎣 🦌 ♿ **Coca-Cola Space Science Center** (706-649-1470; www.ccssc.org), 701 Front Avenue, Columbus. Open 10–4 Monday through Thursday, 10–8 Friday, 10:30–8 Saturday, closed Sunday. Science center open only to groups of at least 20, but observatory and theater open to all. Hands-on is the byword at this space and astronomy facility, one of 31 Challenger centers in America, where visitors can experience landing on the moon or probing a comet's tail. See a full-sized replica of the nose cone of a NASA space shuttle orbiter, the first Coca-Cola drink dispenser taken into space, a space suit, and an interactive view of 88 constellations. The Mead Observatory is open once a month for astronomical viewing. At the state-of-the-art Omnisphere Planetarium Theater, spectacular laser concerts, star shows, and children's shows take place. Museum admission free; a charge for laser and star shows. Call for a schedule of shows and prices. 🎣 🦌 ♿ **Hollywood Connection** (706-571-3456), 1683 Whittlesey Road, Columbus. Open 11:30–9 Sunday through Thursday, 11:30–midnight Friday and Saturday. There's something for everyone in the family

THE COLUMBUS RIVERWALK ALONG THE CHATTAHOOCHEE RIVER

here. In addition to megaplex movie theaters with stadium seating, the complex offers Caddyshack miniature golf, Fun Zone amusements and rides, Mind Games arcade, Krazy Kars bumper cars, Ultrazone Laser Tag Arena, Xanadu Skate Center, and a teen club. Animal House is a two-story soft play area for younger kids. Lieutenant's, a '50s-style restaurant, is open for lunch daily. Prices vary by activity.

HORSEBACK RIDING ✿ **Snyder Farms Stables** (706-324-4806), 936 McCrary Road, Fortson. Snyder Farms offers one-hour guided trail rides through 100 acres of wooded countryside. Western riding lessons and camps are also offered. Rides are open to age 6 and older. Call for rates and hours.

MINIATURE GOLF See **Hollywood Connection** under *For Families.*

OUTDOOR ADVENTURES ✿ **Chattahoochee Riverwalk Outfitters** (706-660-2999), 1000 Bay Avenue, Columbus. Open 8–8 daily. The company rents bikes, canoes, kayaks, and skates—everything needed for outdoor fun. Call for rates.

SWIMMING See **Lake Walter F. George** under *Green Space—Lakes.*

TENNIS ✿ ✿ **Cooper Creek Tennis Center** (706-317-4186), 4816 Milgen Road, Columbus. Open 8 AM–10 PM Monday through Thursday, 8–8 Friday and Sunday, 8–6 Saturday. This is the South's largest clay-court tennis facility, with a total of 30 lighted courts. $2.50 an hour for Muscogee County residents, $3.50 an hour during peak hours for nonresidents.

WATERFALLS See *To See—Natural Beauty Spots.*

✳ Green Space

LAKES ✿ ✿ ✿ **Lake Walter F. George** (south of Columbus on GA 39) boasts 45,000 acres and includes many opportunities for deep-water fishing. Bird-watchers will want to stay alert as herons, egrets, and the occasional bald eagle inhabit these shores. Families enjoy the **Kirbo Interpretive Center** at **Florence Marina State Park** (see Americus chapter). Parking is $3.

NATURE PRESERVES AND PARKS ✿ ✿ ✿ **Oxbow Meadows Environmental Learning Center** (706-687-4090; www.oxbo.colstate.edu), 3535 South Lumpkin Road, Columbus. Open 10–5 Tuesday through Saturday, noon–5 Sunday. More than 1,600 acres provide homes for native wildlife such as alligators, birds, butterflies, dragonflies, hawks, opossums, owls, and turtles. The center provides opportunities for outdoor education, wildlife observation, and recreation. Two walking trails wind between ponds to allow visitors to see the flora and fauna. The hands-on nature discovery center interprets the natural history of the area with mounted specimens of birds, mammals, and reptiles, along with a small live-animal collection of amphibians, fish, insects, and reptiles. Free.

✳ Lodging

BED & BREAKFASTS

In Buena Vista

🏵 **Sign of the Dove Bed and Breakfast** (229-649-3663; 1-888-690-3663; www.sign-of-the-dove.com), 108 North Church Street. This 1905 historic home is on the National Register of Historic Places. Neoclassical architecture blends Greek and Roman influences with Southern details like the large wraparound porch. Besides the sleeping area, each guest room features a sitting area and a private bath with a claw-foot tub. A restaurant also is on-site. No pets. $75 includes breakfast; $125 and up includes breakfast and a four-course dinner.

In Columbus

♿ **The Gates House Bed & Breakfast** (706-324-6464; 1-800-891-3187; www.gateshouse.com), 737 and 802 Broadway. Painstaking restoration is combined with modern convenience at two properties, West and East, located across the street from each other. Complimentary bicycles and helmets, use of a health club, and movies in the home theater are available to all guests. No smoking. Limited number of wheelchair-accessible rooms. $105–265.

♿ **Rothschild-Pound House Inn and Cottages–Cafe 222** (706-322-4075; 1-800-585-4075; www.thepoundhouseinn.com), 201 Seventh Street. A gorgeous Second Empire Italianate "painted lady" filled with antiques, the mansion offers elegant AAA four-diamond bed & breakfast accommodations—some with fireplaces. In addition to starting the day with a full gourmet mbreakfast, cocktails and hors d'oeuvres are served in the afternoon. In addition to those in the main house, accommodations are offered in fourcottages. No smoking. Wheelchair accessible. $125–265; $225–365 for cottages.

ROTHSCHILD-POUND HOUSE INN IN COLUMBUS

CAMPGROUNDS

In Buena Vista
🚶 ♞ **Country Vista Campground**
(229-649-2267), 1634 GA 41 South.
Amenities include laundry facilities
and separate men's and women's bathhouses. Full hookups with water,
sewer, and electric are available. Tent
sites $14; hookups $18 per day.

In Columbus
🚶 ♞ **Lake Pines Campground and
RV Park** (706-561-9675; www.lake
pines.net), 6404 Garrett Road. Amenities include a bathhouse, laundry, and
swimming pool. Full hookups with
water, sewer, and electric are available. Tent sites $18 per day, $120 per
week; hookups $22 per day, $130–145
per week.

INNS AND HOTELS

In Columbus
🚶 ♿ **Wyndham Hotel** (706-324-
1800), 800 Front Avenue. A section of
the riverfront hotel uses the historic
125-year-old Empire Mills. Coca-Cola
memorabilia lines the walls of Pemberton's Cafe, named for the founder
of the soft drink, while a sporting motif
sets a relaxing backdrop in Hunter's
Lounge. Smoking rooms available.
Wheelchair accessible. $155–195.

✳ Where to Eat
DINING OUT

In Columbus
♿ **Bludau's Goetchius House
Restaurant** (706-324-4863;
www.goetchiushouse.com), 405
Broadway. Open 5–10 Monday
through Thursday, 5–11 Friday and
Saturday. An 1839 New Orleans–style
mansion sets an elegant backdrop for
magnificent continental cuisine.

Fancy wrought iron and floor-to-ceiling windows invoke the Deep South.
The menu might include she-crab
soup, chateaubriand, frog legs,
seafood, and veal. Smoking permitted.
Wheelchair accessible. $7–40.

♿ **Buckhead Grill** (706-571-9995),
5010 Armour Road. Open 5–10 weekdays, 5–11 Saturday. Menu highlights
include Angus beef, fish, pasta, and
ribs, as well as a full array of burgers,
salads, and sandwiches. No smoking.
Wheelchair accessible. $10–25.

EATING OUT

In Columbus
🚶 ♞ ♿ **Country's Barbecue** (706-
563-7604), 3137 Mercury Drive.
There are other locations: **Country's
on Broadway** (706-596-8910), 1329
Broadway, and **Country's North**
(706-660-1415), 6298 Veterans Parkway. All three open 11–10 Sunday
through Thursday, 11–11 Friday and
Saturday. Slow-cooked barbecue
pork, ribs, beef, or chicken cooked
over hickory and oak are the specialties, but the menu includes other
country-cooking favorites. Tuesday
features all-you-can-eat barbecue. No
smoking. Wheelchair accessible.
Around $5.

🚶 ♞ ♿ **Dinglewood Pharmacy**
(706-322-0616), 1939 Wynnton Road.
Open 11–6:30 weekdays, 11–4:30 Saturday. Since the 1940s, the Scramble
Dog has been served at the lunch
counter and booths of this 1918-era
pharmacy. Two hot dogs and a bun
are split open, then piled with cheese,
chili, dill pickles, and mustard, then
topped with oyster crackers. Why a
visitor would want to order anything
else, we can't possibly imagine, but
hamburgers, chicken sandwiches, and
deli sandwiches are also on the menu.

No smoking. Wheelchair accessible through back entrance. Scramble Dog $4.25.

🍽 ⟁ **Minnie's Uptown** (706-322-2766), 104 Eighth Street. Open 10:45–2:30 weekdays. This eatery in the historic district offers award-winning Southern cooking. No smoking. Wheelchair accessible. About $5.50.

✎ 🍽 ⟁ **Miriam's Café and Gallery** (706-327-0707), 1330 13th Street. Open 11–3 Monday through Saturday. Miriam's, an upscale deli with European flair, serves lunch only. There are creative specials every day and exciting menu choices. No smoking. Wheelchair accessible. About $7.

✎ 🍽 ⟁ **The Rankin Quarter** (706-322-8151), 21 East 10th Street. Open 11–3:30 Sunday through Friday. Menu features deli sandwiches, burgers, salads, and grilled items. No smoking. Restaurant wheelchair accessible, but rest rooms are not. Around $6

✎ 🍽 ⟁ **Tavern on the Square** (706-324-2238), 14 11th Street. Open 11–3 daily; 5–8:30 Monday through Wednesday, 5–9:30 Thursday through Saturday. Hearty sandwiches, pasta, seafood, soups, salads, and combos are served in a pub atmosphere. No smoking. Wheelchair accessible. Lunch from $6; dinner $10–20.

✳ Entertainment

MUSIC **Columbus Symphony Orchestra** (706-323-5059; www .csoga.org), 935 First Avenue, Columbus. Founded in 1855, the CSO was the third symphony in America. It performs concerts October through May at the RiverCenter for the Performing Arts (see below). There is also a children's series of concerts.

Call for a schedule of performances and ticket prices.

RiverCenter for the Performing Arts (706-653-7993; 1-888-332-5200; event hotline 706-256-3600; www .rivercenter.org), 900 Broadway, Columbus. Box office open noon–5 weekdays. This enormous showplace, the centerpiece of a new arts and entertainment district, contains multiple recital halls and a theater. The facility is the home of the nationally touring Broadway Series, Columbus Symphony Orchestra (see above), Columbus State University Schwob School of Music, and other local music and dance companies. Call for schedules of events and prices.

NIGHTLIFE ⟁ **Oxygen** (706-596-8397), 1040 Broadway, Columbus. Open 9 PM–3 AM Wednesday through Saturday. Located in the historic district, Oxygen is a high-energy, Top 40 nightclub. Dress is upscale. No smoking. Wheelchair accessible. Cover charge $10; ladies admitted free until 11.

PROFESSIONAL SPORTS ✎ **Columbus Cottonmouths Hockey** (706-571-0086; www.cottonmouths.com), 400 Fourth Street, Columbus. The season runs late October to mid-March. Competing for a decade, the Cottonmouths, a Southern Professional Hockey League team, play at the Columbus Civic Center. During the 2004–2005 season, the Cottonmouths won the SPHL President's Cup Championship. $10–16.

THEATER **Human Experience Theater** (706-323-3689), 1047 Broadway, Columbus. Season runs September through May. Box office open 10–2

Tuesday and Thursday, 2–6 Wednesday, Friday, and Saturday. Unique to this theater is its "bring-your-own-dinner" concept. Call for a schedule and prices.

Liberty Theater Cultural Center (706-653-7566), 813 Eighth Avenue, Columbus. Office open 10–5 weekdays. This historic, 300-seat theater, which opened in 1924, once drew performers such as Cab Calloway, Lena Horne, and Ma Rainey. Now restored, the theater once again hosts performances of dramas and musicals. Call for tours, schedule, and prices.

✅ **Springer Opera House** (706-327-3688; 1-888-332-5200; www.springer operahouse.org), 103 10th Street, Columbus. Tours at 3:30 Monday and Wednesday. A jewel in Columbus's crown, the magnificent plush-and-gilt theater was built in 1871 and saw performances by Irving Berlin, Edwin Booth, John Philip Sousa, Will Rogers, Oscar Wilde, and many other luminaries from the late 1800s through the Great Depression. Like many theaters of the day, it was converted to a movie house and began a long decline. Designated as the State Theater of Georgia, the Springer Opera House has been restored to its 1901 Edwardian splendor. The theater's main-stage season September through May hosts Broadway musicals, comedies, and dramas. In addition, there is an alternative Studio II Series and a colorful Children's Series. Museum areas on the first and second floors display artifacts and furnishings such as 19th-century theater seats, vintage photographs, portraits, programs, posters, and other memorabilia. Call for a schedule of events and ticket prices. Tours free.

✳ Selective Shopping

ART GALLERIES Galleria Riverside (706-653-1950), 11 Ninth Street, Columbus. Open 10–5:30 weekdays, 10–4 Saturday. In addition to artwork, the gallery offers antiques, hand-crafted furniture, and gifts.

Joseph House Gallery Cooperative (706-321-8948), 828 Broadway, Columbus. Open 11–5 Tuesday through Friday, 1–5 Saturday. The historic structure houses the work of 65 regional artists and more than 1,000 original paintings, drawings, pottery, photography, woodwork, and china.

FOOD Columbus Farmers Market (706-649-7448), 318 10th Avenue, Columbus. Open 6 AM–9:30 PM daily. This is the place to go for fresh flowers, fruits, and vegetables.

✳ Special Events

April: **Riverfest Weekend–Salisbury Fair** (706-324-7417). Held the last full weekend in April along the Columbus RiverWalk, this event consists of several parts. The **Salisbury Fair** features artists at work, arts and crafts, a 5K road race, fireworks, and a food court. The **Folklife Village** consists of a folk-art show, crafters, youth art show, fine art exhibition, children's activities, and Native American demonstrations. The **Greater Columbus Pig Jig Barbecue Cook-Off** is a Memphis in May–sanctioned barbecue cook-off. Entertainment features local, regional, and national talent performing jazz, blues, country, and rock on three stages. Other activities include a carnival, collectibles, and even pig racing.

October: **Help the Hooch** and the postcleanup **Watershed Festival.** For more information, contact **Keep Columbus Beautiful** (706-653-4008; www.helpthehooch.org). During the 2004 cleanup, more than 12,000 volunteers turned out to help. Attendance at the Watershed Festival afterward, a reward for all the hard work, was also record-breaking.

LAGRANGE

This area calls itself "Georgia's West Coast" because of its location on the Chattahoochee River and West Point Lake at the Georgia-Alabama border. Together the river and lake provide an immense area of water and endless recreational opportunities.

Historically, the Creek Indians, who occupied west Georgia before the Indian Springs Treaty of 1825, used a warpath that ran through what is now downtown LaGrange. All but a few of the Creeks were gone by 1827, when the area was opened for settlement. The area is primarily rural, with most of the population living in LaGrange and a few small towns.

Visitors primarily come to LaGrange to see its two art museums and two magnificent historic homes. While there, many decide to take the walking tour or watch some drag racing. Outdoor recreation enthusiasts can find a million things to do at West Point Lake, the West Point Wildlife Management Area, and other parks. Campers are particularly pleased with the wide selection of campgrounds.

Visitors to LaGrange's downtown park won't find the statue of a founding father of the state or city, nor a monument to Confederate soldiers, nor a memorial to some politician. Instead they'll see a statue honoring the Marquis de Lafayette, the French hero of the Revolutionary War. In fact, the town itself is named after Lafayette's estate in France. It seems that when Lafayette was traveling through this then undeveloped area in 1825, he remarked that the surroundings reminded him of his home, which he called LaGrange. In 1828, when a seat for Troup County was created, the name LaGrange was chosen for the town. In 1976 city fathers named the downtown park Lafayette Square and commissioned a fountain centered with a bronze statue of Lafayette.

The nearby towns of Franklin, Hogansville, and West Point offer one or more sight-seeing attractions, bed & breakfasts, campgrounds, restaurants, and interesting shops.

GUIDANCE For visitors planning a trip to LaGrange, contact the **LaGrange–Troup County Chamber of Commerce** (706-884-8671; www.lagrange chamber.com), 111 Bull Street, LaGrange 30240. Open 9–5 weekdays. The Chamber of Commerce has brochures on the Chattahoochee Trace, the

> **"HERE YOU GO, LAFAYETTE"**
>
> When Lafayette was in Newnan, he reportedly told Colonel Julius C. Alford about a French custom of tossing a coin into a well to wish for good luck. When Alford left for the Creek Indian War of 1836, he tossed a coin into one of Newnan's two wells and said, "Here you go, Lafayette." All the men who were going off to war did the same, as did their sweethearts, and a custom was born.
>
> Eventually, townsfolk began throwing two coins into the well to double their wish. According to tradition, the first coin is tossed over one's shoulder, standing back-to-back with the statue; the second is tossed while facing the statue.
>
> After the courthouse burned in 1936 and a fountain was placed in the square, people transferred the two-coin custom to the fountain. In 1976, when the statue of Lafayette was placed in the fountain, the phrase "Here you go, Lafayette" took on added meaning.

Chattahoochee-Flint Heritage Highway, the Historic Courthouse Corridor Travel Guide, and the Presidential Pathways Travel Guide.

While in the area, stop at the **Georgia Visitor Information Center** (706-645-3353), I-85 North at the Georgia–Alabama line. Open 8:30–5:30 daily.

For information about Franklin, contact the **Heard County Chamber of Commerce** (706-675-0560; 1-888-331-0560; www.heardgeorgia.org), 121 South Court Square, Franklin 30217. Open 9–5 weekdays.

GETTING THERE *By air:* The nearest commercial airport to LaGrange is **Columbus Metropolitan Airport** (706-324-2449; www.flycolumbusga.com), 3250 West Britt David Road (see Columbus chapter). Five rental firms offer cars at the Columbus airport. Most visitors choose to fly into Atlanta's **Hartsfield-Jackson Atlanta International Airport** (see What's Where in Georgia). Car rentals are available on-site and off-site.

By bus: **Greyhound Lines** (706-882-1897; 1-800-231-2222; www.greyhound.com) has a terminal (1328 Greenville Street) in LaGrange.

By car: LaGrange is 65 miles southwest of Atlanta on I-85. US 27 is the other north-south route.

By train: The closest **Amtrak** (1-800-USA-Rail; www.amtrak.com) station is in Atlanta (see What's Where in Georgia).

GETTING AROUND Rental cars can be obtained in LaGrange from **Advantage Rent-a-Car** (706-812-8797), 1237 Lafayette Parkway, and **Enterprise Rent-a-Car** (706-883-8800), 1504 Lafayette Parkway.

MEDICAL EMERGENCY For life-threatening emergencies, call 911. Otherwise, contact **West Georgia Medical Center** (706-882-1411), 1514 Vernon Road, LaGrange.

✳ To See

CULTURAL SITES ✿ ᕃ **Lamar Dodd Art Center** (706-880-8211; www.lagrange .edu), 302 Forrest Avenue, LaGrange. Open 8:30–4:30 weekdays, September through June. Located in a modern edifice on the campus of LaGrange College, the center houses a permanent collection of the works of 20th-century painter and native son Lamar Dodd. The art center also hosts rotating exhibits of the works of numerous other contemporary painters and graduating seniors. Some interesting Indian artifacts are also part of the permanent display. Free.

FOR FAMILIES See **West Point Lake** under *Green Space—Lakes*, **Hoofer's Gospel Barn** under *Entertainment—Music*, **WaterWiz** under *To Do—Swimming*, and **Highland Marina and Resort** under *Lodging—Inns and Resorts*.

HISTORIC HOMES AND SITES ✿ **Bellevue Historical Home** (706-884-1832), 204 Ben Hill Street, LaGrange. Open 10–noon and 2–5 Tuesday through Saturday. This opulent antebellum home, the former residence of U.S. Senator Benjamin Harvey Hill, is considered one of the finest examples of Greek Revival architecture in Georgia. Designed and built over two years in the early 1850s, the exterior features Ionic columns supporting wide porticos. The structure's outstanding architectural features include unique woodwork such as massive carved cornices over the doors and windows. The interior is further embellished with black Italian marble mantels and ornate plaster ceiling medallions. In the 1930s, the Fuller E. Callaway Foundation purchased the house and later presented it to the LaGrange Womans Club. The house was restored in 1974 and 1975. Bellevue is furnished with period pieces to reflect the 1850s as well as with family mementos such as portraits of Senator Hill and his wife, Caroline Holt Hill, and framed rubbings from Hill family tombstones. In fact, the rosewood piano in the formal parlor has been there since the home's earliest days. Adults $4, students $2.

✧ ✿ ᕃ **Fort Tyler** (334-642-1503; www.forttyler.com), Sixth Avenue and West 10th Street, West Point. Open daylight hours daily. A paved path leads to a small earthen fort built in 1863 and named in honor of General R. C. Tyler, quartermaster of the Confederate army. It was the last Confederate fort to fall at the end of the Civil War. Three cannon replicas are located at the fort, and interpretive signs describe the site. Free.

✿ ᕃ **Hills and Dales** (706-882-3242; www.hillsanddalesestate.org), 1916 Hills and Dales Drive, LaGrange. Open 10–6 Tuesday through Saturday, 1–5 Sunday, March through September; 10–5 Tuesday through Saturday, October through February; closed July 4, Thanksgiving, Christmas Eve, Christmas and New Year's Days. The centerpiece of this 35-acre estate, which opened for tours in the fall of 2004, is the opulent 1916 Italian-style villa. Designed by Neel Reid, one of the founders of the Georgia School of Classicism, the historic estate was the

home of textile magnate Fuller E. Callaway Sr. and his wife, Ida Cason Callaway. Upon their deaths, it passed to their son, Fuller E. Callaway Jr., and his wife, Alice Hand Callaway. After the younger Callaway and his wife passed away, the estate was given to the Fuller E. Callaway Foundation to be opened for the enjoyment and enrichment of the public. The mansion tour includes the majestic rooms and family furnishings on the first floor.

Of equal interest at the same site are the **Ferrell Gardens**, which date to 1841 and are named for Sarah Ferrell, whose family lived on the property in a much smaller house before the Callaways bought the estate and built the mansion. Sarah opened the grounds to the public after church on Sundays, and the Callaways continued the tradition. These gardens feature extensive boxwood plantings in Italian Renaissance and Baroque designs, as well as fountains, descending terraces, a greenhouse, and many religious elements introduced by Sarah. The site also includes an herb garden, a sunken garden, and many planted walks, terraces, and lanes. The Callaways acquired outdoor statuary on their world travels, and many of these pieces continue to grace the gardens as well.

THE ITALIAN-STYLE VILLA IS THE CENTERPIECE OF HILLS AND DALES ESTATE.

Begin at the opulent new **visitor center,** a classically inspired building that blends beautifully with the existing Neel Reid architecture. There you can see educational exhibits and watch a film about Sarah Ferrell and two generations of the Callaway family. Then take a tram up the steep hill to the house for the guided tour and finish by strolling through the gardens on your own. Plan on at least two hours to experience everything. Children younger than 6 are not admitted to the house. House and garden admission: adults $10, students $6. Admission to gardens only: adults $6, students $3.

MUSEUMS 🐾 ♿ **Chattahoochee Valley Art Museum** (706-882-3267; www.cvam-online.org), 112 Lafayette Parkway, LaGrange. Open 9–5 Tuesday through Friday, 11–5 Saturday. Focusing on contemporary art and encompassing more than 500 pieces, the museum annually features 10 to 13 exhibitions showcasing the works of well-known and emerging Southeastern artists. Workshops and gallery talks spotlight artists whose work is currently on display. Every other year, the museum hosts the paintings, prints, and drawings portion of the LaGrange National Biennial, which brings the most current trends in contemporary art to LaGrange. Located just off Lafayette Square in historic downtown LaGrange, the 1892 building itself is interesting because it served as the Troup County Jail until 1946. The building was completely renovated in 1978 to create contemporary galleries, allowing paintings to hang where criminals were once hanged. $1 suggested donation.

⚓ 🦪 **Heard County Historical Center and Museum** (706-675-6507; www
.heardgeorgia.org), 161 Shady Street, Franklin. Open 8:30–noon and 1–5 Tues-
day and Thursday. Located in the county's "Old Jail," the beautiful Romanesque
Revival structure served as the county jail and sheriff's office from 1912 to 1964.
Visitors can still see the cells and gallows, along with other exhibits relating to
county history. Movie buffs delight in learning about local legends such as Miss
Mayhaley Lancaster, a pivotal character from the best-selling novel and movie
Murder in Coweta County. Free.

✳ To Do

AUTO RACING ⚓ 🦪 ♿ **LaGrange–Troup County Speedway** (706-884-6600;
www.troupcountydrag.com), 123 Heard Road, LaGrange. Gates open at 11.
Generally there are exciting races on weekends, among them the Shootout of the
South, Mammoth $8,000 Bracket Weekend, Pro Mod Roundup, Classic Gassers,
and Southern Slingshots–Front Engine Dragsters. Concessions available. Adults
$10, children age 10 and younger free.

BALLOONING For information on hot-air ballooning, visit the web site at www
.hotairballooning.stego.biz.

BICYCLING Contact the LaGrange-Troup County Chamber of Commerce (see
Guidance) to request the bicycling brochure titled, "Backroads Bicycling on
Georgia's Chattahoochee–Flint Heritage Way."

BIRDING According to www.georgiabirding.com, visitors to this area can hope to
spot Carolina chickadees, the tufted titmouse, both the northern cardinal and
the northern mockingbird, great-crested flycatchers, eastern bluebirds, northern
flickers, red-winged blackbirds, wood thrushes, blue jays, indigo buntings, loggerhead shrikes, and Carolina wrens. On West Point Lake, look for little blue
herons, great blue herons, belted kingfishers, ospreys, and various egrets.
See **West Point Wildlife Management Area** under *Green Space—Nature
Preserves and Parks.*

BOATING See Marinas/Boat Landings Appendix.

FISHING Fishing is the most popular activity on **West Point Lake.** A dozen
creeks and 40 square miles of lake provide prime fishing spots for several species
of monster-size bass, bream, channel catfish, and crappie. Bank and pier fishing
is excellent, and all piers are wheelchair accessible. Interestingly, West Point
Lake has more annual fishing tournaments than any other lake in Georgia.

GOLF See Golf Appendix.

SWIMMING ⚓ 🦪 ♿ **WaterWiz** (706-884-0899), 305 Old Roanoke Road, La-
Grange. The popular water park boasts 275- and 300-foot water slides in addition to a 30-by-60-foot swimming pool. The complex also features a batting cage
where future big-leaguers can swing at six balls for 25¢. The batting area stays lit

until 10 PM. $8.95 for children taller than 4 feet tall, $5.95 for children shorter than 4 feet tall, $4.95 for spectators, chaperones, and seniors.

See also Other Activities Appendix.

TENNIS See Other Activities Appendix.

WALKING TOURS 🕯 **Historic Downtown LaGrange Walking Tour** (706-884-1828; 706-884-8671; www.trouparchives.org). Pick up a free brochure in LaGrange from the Troup County Historical Society and Archives, 136 Main Street, or the LaGrange-Troup County Chamber of Commerce (see *Guidance*).

✳ Green Space

BEACHES See **West Point Lake** under *Lakes* and **Highland Marina and Resort** under *Lodging—Resorts*.

LAKES ✍ 🕯 ♿ **West Point Lake** (706-645-2937; 1-877-444-6777; www.west pt.sam.usace.army.mil), 500 Resource Management Drive, West Point. Most facilities open 8–4:30 weekdays, October through March; 8–5 daily, April through September. The U.S. Army Corps of Engineers lake extends 35 miles along the Chattahoochee River. The 26,000-acre reservoir has 500 miles of shoreline and is surrounded by forests. Although the lake's purpose is to control flooding, generate electricity, and maintain depths downstream that permit navigation by tugboats, barges, and other riverboats, it is a mecca for recreation even in the winter, with day-use parks, campgrounds, marinas, beach areas, boat launching areas, and fishing piers surrounding the lake. If water sports are your main interest, there are hundreds of coves and two secluded slalom courses for waterskiing enthusiasts. Without all the heavy traffic of other lakes, West Point is also perfect for tubing, kneeboarding, swimming, and cruising. There is also a white sand beach and a play area for children. For fishermen, this resort is heaven, famous for monster-size largemouth bass, hybrid bass, spotted bass, white bass, stripers, and crappie. It also offers more fishing tournaments than any other lake in the state. Two privately owned marinas provide fuel, repairs, rentals, supplies, and other necessities. Because of West Point Lake's many recreation possibilities and its proximity to three major metropolitan areas, the lake is identified by the Corps of Engineers as a Recreational Demonstration Project, and therefore additional recreational facilities not commonly found at other lakes are provided here. Some of the day-use areas have tennis courts, ball fields, basketball courts, and fishing piers with fish attractors placed under them for the disabled. The **Visitor Center at the Project Management Office** has displays concerning the management of the lake and its lands.

NATURE PRESERVES AND PARKS ✍ 🕯 ♿ **Pyne Road Park** (706-884-1414; www .ohwy.com/ga/p/pynerdpk.htm), GA 109 at West Point Lake, LaGrange. Open 7–10 daily, March through October. Facilities include a beach, boat ramp, ball field, picnic sites, and hiking trails as well as primitive and developed camping areas. Admission free; picnic pavilion rentals $50; primitive tent sites $10, RV hookups $15.

West Point Wildlife Management Area (706-884-3915; 478-825-6354). Nearly 10,000 acres provide habitat for ospreys, bald eagles, deer, bobcats, and dozens of species of songbirds. The area also offers excellent hunting for deer, turkey, doves, quail, wood ducks, and other waterfowl. Hunters need a Georgia Wildlife Management Area stamp to hunt seasonally and participate in special quota hunts.

✴ Lodging

BED & BREAKFASTS

In LaGrange

🕯 **Thyme Away Bed and Breakfast** (706-885-9625), 508 Greenville Street. This attractive Greek Revival B&B (circa 1840) boasts five deluxe guest rooms. Each individually decorated room features a private bath with whirlpool tub, TV, VCR, refrigerator, and wireless Internet access. Be sure to enjoy the beautiful gardens surrounding the house, too. Full breakfast is included. No smoking. Not wheelchair accessible. $75 single, $85 double.

CAMPGROUNDS

In Franklin

🎣 🕯 **Brush Creek Park** (706-675-2267; 706-645-3778), 1328 Brush Creek Park Road. This county-maintained recreation area on West Point Lake offers both primitive and RV campsites, bathhouses, picnic pavilions, a baseball field, basketball court, playground, and direct boat access. Of further interest, this campground is located on the site of the old Indian community of Chatta-hoochee. It is from this early settlement that the Chattahoochee River got its name. $12–16.

In LaGrange

🎣 🕯 **Highland Marina and Resort** (706-882-3437; www.highlandmarina .com), 1000 Seminole Road. If camping is your thing, the marina has many RV sites (sorry, no tent camping). Get

there early because reservations are not accepted and sites rent on a first-come, first-served basis. $25 per night, $150 per week.

🎣 🕯 **Three Creeks Campground** (706-885-7655; www.cityoflagrange .com), 305 Old Roanoke Road. With both pop-up and RV sites, a swimming pool, horseshoes, a bathhouse, laundry facilities, playground, catfish lake, waterslide, and batting cage, this campground has it all. If that's not enough, it's located only a quarter-mile from the closest boat launch at West Point Lake. $18–22.

See also **Pyne Road Park** under *Green Space—Nature Preserves and Parks.*

COTTAGES AND CABINS See **Highland Marina and Resort** under *Resorts.*

RESORTS

In LaGrange

🎣 **Highland Marina and Resort** (706-882-3437), 100 Seminole Road. Georgia's most affordable and beautiful marina is actually a complete resort that sits on 200 acres of peace and quiet. During your stay, enjoy a seemingly endless list of activities or just take time to relax and refresh. Fishermen can angle for largemouth, hybrid, spotted, and white bass as well as stripers and crappie. The resort also has a store that sells fishing tackle, bait, food, and beer and has on-the-water gas pumps to fill up your boat. A restaurant is open for lunch Tuesday through Saturday and for Saturday and Sunday breakfast March through November. The most expensive entrée is $6. In addition to campsites, the resort offers 33 fully equipped, one- to three-bedroom waterfront cabins with full kitchens, central heat and air, cable television, and decks with grills. For complete privacy, rent a private dock for your cabin as well. $69–159 per night, $414–955 per week.

✴ Where to Eat

DINING OUT

In LaGrange

✿ ♿ **Banzai Japanese Steakhouse** (706-882-0750), 1510 Lafayette Parkway. Open 4:30–10 Monday through Thursday, 4:30–11 Friday and Saturday. Enjoy Japanese-style cuisine from grilled chicken to a steak-and-seafood combination platter. Entrées are served with rice and a vegetable. No smoking. Wheelchair accessible. $7–24.

♿ **Basil Leaf** (706-812-1198), 109 Main Street. Open 11–2 Tuesday through Friday, 5:30–9:30 Tuesday through Saturday. This upscale, international restaurant offers Italian-influenced cuisine. Guests enjoy seafood, steaks, chicken, and chef's specials. No smoking. Wheelchair accessible. Lunch $7–10, dinner $15–20.

🍴 ♿ **Spring House Inn** (706-812-1546), One Youngs Mill Road. Open 11–1:30 weekdays, for 5:30–9:30 Monday through Saturday. Lunch specials include delicious Southern favorites. Dinner entrées range from steak to seafood. No smoking. Wheel-

chair accessible. Lunch about $6, dinner $18.

EATING OUT

In Hogansville

✿ 🍴 ♿ **Roger's Bar-B-Q Hogansville** (706-637-4100), 1863 East Main Street. Open 11–9 Monday through Thursday, 11–11 Friday and Saturday. The menu at this 60-year-old barbecue restaurant includes ribs, chicken, steak, stew, and catfish as well as salads, vegetables, and homemade lunches. All the barbecue items are pit cooked on-site. No smoking. Wheelchair accessible. Average $8.

In LaGrange

✿ 🍴 ♿ **Charlie Joseph's** (706-884-5416), 128 Bull Street. Open 9–5:30 Monday through Saturday (Wednesday they close at 2). The menu includes hot dogs, hamburgers, sandwiches, and stews. No smoking. Wheelchair accessible. $2–5.

✿ 🍴 ♿ **Cisco's Café** (706-883-6100), 1600 Vernon Road. Open 11–2 and 5–10 Monday through Thursday, 11–2 and 3–10:30 Friday and Saturday. Cisco's serves traditional Mexican food. Smoking permitted only on patio. Wheelchair accessible. $5–7.

✿ 🍴 ♿ **Hog Heaven** (706-882-7227), 2240 West Point Road. Proclaimed the "Best Barbecue in Troup County" two years in a row by the *LaGrange Daily News*, this restaurant definitely lives up to its name. Menu favorites include baby-back ribs, steaks, burgers, salads, and smoked pork, chicken, and turkey. Fresh-cooked pork skins can be delivered to your table still crackling. There's also a free bucket of peanuts on every table (just throw the shells on the floor). No smoking. Wheelchair accessible. $3–19.

♂ ♨ ❖ **Jim Bob's** (706-882-9917), 108 Corporate Plaza Drive. Open 10–9 Monday through Saturday. Chicken fingers, wings, and catfish fillets are among the specialties of this restaurant. No smoking. Wheelchair accessible. Average $7.

♨ ❖ **Tulla's Bayou Bar and Grill** (706-812-8554), 109 Main Street. Open 11–2 and 5:30–9:30 daily. A lunch buffet features an extensive selection of favorites, or diners can order à la carte. For dinner, the eatery's selection of seafood items is extensive. Nightly specials, steaks, and salads are also available. No smoking. Wheelchair accessible. Lunch buffet $8.99 including beverage, other lunch favorites $6.99–8.99; dinner $7.99–19.99.

♨ ❖ **Venucci** (706-884-9393), 129 Main Street. Open 11–2 and 5:30–9:30 Monday through Saturday. Meals are served family-style at this traditional Italian restaurant. The eatery caters to a business crowd at lunch, and therefore the lunch menu is much more extensive (and also expensive) than the more limited dinner menu. No smoking. Wheelchair accessible. Lunch $7–23, dinner $7–9.

In West Point
♂ ♨ ❖ **Heart of the South Tea Room** (706-643-0544), 1111 Second Avenue. Open 11–3 Sunday through Friday. Menu favorites include salads, sandwiches, muffalettas, po'boys, veggie plates, daily specials, and the tearoom's unique corn-bread salad. No smoking. Wheelchair accessible. Around $7.

TAKE-OUT

In LaGrange
♂ ♨ ❖ **Big Chic** (706-882-5615), 503

Vernon Street. Open 11–8 Tuesday through Saturday, 11–7 Sunday. This take-out-only restaurant has a variety of favorites, including chicken dishes, seafood items, and great desserts. No smoking. Wheelchair accessible. $3–6.

COFFEEHOUSES

In LaGrange
♂ ♨ ❖ **Higher Groundz Family Coffee House** (706-883-6498), 380-A South Davis Road. Open 7–7 Monday through Thursday, 7 AM–11 PM Friday and Saturday. Homemade pasta, chicken, and potato salads; wraps, soups, and sandwiches; specialty coffees, smoothies, and desserts tempt the palate at this family eatery. No smoking. Wheelchair accessible. Average $7.

✳ Entertainment

DANCE **LaGrange Ballet** (706-882-9439; www.lagrangeballet.com), 210 Bull Street, LaGrange. The LaGrange Ballet presents professional-quality dance performances for the southwestern Georgia region. Call for a schedule of events and costs.

MUSIC **Hoofer's Gospel Barn** (706-885-9300; 1-800-844-6737; www.hoofers.com), 3472 Hogansville Road, LaGrange. Top acts in gospel and bluegrass provide plenty of family entertainment. Besides Southern gospel and bluegrass at their finest, Hoofer's also has a restaurant that serves catfish, steak, and seafood in a family atmosphere. Call for a schedule of performances and prices, as both vary dramatically.

LaGrange Symphony (706-882-0662), 301 Church Street, LaGrange. The orchestra enriches the community through music, cultural experience, educational programs, and performance opportunities. Call for performance schedule and ticket prices.

THEATER **Lafayette Society for the Performing Arts** (706-882-9909), 210 Bull Street, LaGrange. This community theater delivers a wide variety of high-quality presentations. Call for a schedule of events and ticket prices.

✴ Selective Shopping

ART GALLERIES **Artists in Residence** (706-885-9900), 300 South Greenwood Street, LaGrange. Open 10–6 weekdays (although office closes 1–2 for lunch. This facility houses a retail store, artists' studios, and a teaching section for arts and pottery.

Gallery on the Square (706-883-6680), 9 East Lafayette Square, LaGrange. Open 10–5 Tuesday through Saturday. Expect to find an art gallery, antiques store, and a framing gallery, just to name a few of the attractions.

FLEA MARKETS **House of Stuff** (706-675-2222), 12740 GA 34 East, Franklin. Open 10–5 Wednesday through Sunday. This pleasant flea market has 40 booths where shoppers can find all kinds of treasures. Of further interest, there is a public auction at 6:30 PM every Friday and Saturday. Free parking.

✴ Special Events

Early May: **An Affair on the Square** (706-882-3267), 112 Lafayette Parkway, LaGrange. Held on the square on the second weekend in May, this fine arts fair, sponsored by the **Chattahoochee Valley Art Museum** (see *To See—Museums*), has lots of food and entertainment for the whole family. Free.

Early July: **Fourth of July festivities** (706-883-1670), 1220 Lafayette Parkway, LaGrange. This Independence Day celebration includes a children's parade, festivities all afternoon at **Pyne Road Park** on West Point Lake (see *Green Space—Nature Preserves & Parks*), and a fireworks display over the lake that night. Free.

October: **Hogansville Hummingbird Festival** (706-637-9497). This charming annual festival is held the third week in October in downtown Hogansville. In addition to a food court and various entertainment, there are sales and demonstrations of unique arts and crafts as well as special children's activities. Free.

PINE MOUNTAIN, CALLAWAY GARDENS, AND WARM SPRINGS

This region is the home of one of the best-known resorts in the Southeast: Callaway Gardens. The vast 14,000-acre garden, resort, and preserve complex was the brainchild of Cason Jewell Callaway and his wife, Virginia Hand Callaway. He longed for a place where man and nature could commingle to the advantage of both. The resort features various types of accommodations and eateries as well as numerous activities and pursuits. Whether you desire a quiet place for leisurely strolls and observation of nature or prefer an action-packed sports experience and other adventures, you can find what you want at Callaway Gardens.

The area described in this chapter is included in the region known as Presidential Pathways because of its association with Franklin D. Roosevelt and Jimmy Carter. (For more information about the part of the Presidential Pathways region that relates to Jimmy Carter, see the Americus chapter.) FDR came to Warm Springs to try the curative waters for relief from his polio. After several visits, he built the only house he ever bought on his own. That home, which became known as the Little White House, draws many visitors annually (see *To See—Historic Homes and Sites*).

THE WARM SPRINGS

Long before Franklin D. Roosevelt founded the Roosevelt Warms Springs Institute for Rehabilitation in 1927, Native Americans had recognized the powers of the springs. Following battle or other injuries, they came to the springs to seek healing. After white settlers discovered the springs, a spa was created there. Water emerging at 900 gallons per minute and maintaining a temperature of 88 degrees year-round made the springs a popular stagecoach stop. Statesmen John C. Calhoun and Henry Clay are known to have visited the springs.

At the turn of the 20th century, well-to-do families began erecting summer homes nearby. A hotel was built as well as a swimming pool so that people could get better access to the warm, buoyant waters. FDR came to the pools and built his own home nearby. Today his institute treats all kinds of disabilities, and the springs are still part of the therapy.

Many other outdoor activities such as fishing, hiking, and horseback riding attract visitors year-round, as do a wild animal park, a covered bridge, an aquarium, museums, and shopping.

GUIDANCE To learn more about Pine Mountain, contact the **Pine Mountain Tourism Association and Welcome Center** (706-663-4000; 1-800-441-3502; www.pinemountain.org), 101 East Broad Street, Pine Mountain 31822. Open 9–5 weekdays, 10–4 Saturday.

For information about Warm Springs, contact the **Warm Springs Area Tourism Association–FDR Warm Springs Welcome Center** (706-655-3322; 1-800-337-1927; www.warmspringsga.ws), One Broad Street, Warm Springs 31830. Open 10–5 Monday through Saturday, 1–4 Sunday.

GETTING THERE *By air:* Pine Mountain is located 60 miles south of **Hartsfield-Jackson Atlanta International Airport** (see What's Where in Georgia). Another option is to fly into **Columbus Metropolitan Airport** (see Columbus chapter).

By bus: **Greyhound Lines** does not stop in any of the towns described in this chapter. The nearest stations are in LaGrange, Columbus, and Fort Benning (see LaGrange and Columbus chapters).

By car: The towns described in this chapter lie between I-75, I-85, and I-185. The primary north-south routes through the area are US 27 Alt. and GA 85.

By train: There is no train service to this area. The closest **Amtrak** station is in Atlanta (see What's Where in Georgia).

GETTING AROUND There are no taxis, buses, or shuttles in the area, so visitors to this area must have a car, either their own or a rental.

MEDICAL EMERGENCY The closest medical facility to Pine Mountain is 17 miles away in LaGrange: **West Georgia Medical Center** (706-882-1411), 1514 Vernon Road.

VILLAGES Callaway Gardens is a world unto itself, with gardens, accommodations, restaurants, shops, and recreational activities. The resort is mentioned many times in this chapter. In order to avoid repetition, the contact information is listed only once here: Callaway Gardens (706-663-2281; 1-800-225-5292; www.callawayonline.com), GA 18 and GA 354, Pine Mountain. See *Green Space— Gardens* for hours and admission fees).

Manchester seems to be in a time warp that left the sleepy village in the Pine Mountain foothills in the 1930s. The town's annual **Railroad Days** is a popular October event (see *Special Events*).

Pine Mountain is the nearest town to Callaway Gardens. Founded in 1882 as the railroad town of Chipley, it's now known as "the Gateway to Callaway," but Pine Mountain has attractions of its own, including a bed & breakfast, a museum, restaurants, and interesting shops.

Warm Springs is deeply rooted in the historical era of four-term President

Franklin D. Roosevelt. Downtown's Warm Springs Village has been restored and now features a bed & breakfast, several restaurants, and numerous shops.

✵ To See

COVERED BRIDGES ✅ 🏵 **Red Oak Covered Bridge,** GA 85 Alt./Covered Bridge Road, Woodbury. Open daylight hours daily. This is the last existing covered bridge built by Horace King, the famous freed slave who became a master bridge builder. Free.

EQUESTRIAN EVENTS See **Steeplechase at Callaway** under *Special Events.*

FOR FAMILIES ✅ ♿ **Butts Mill Farm** (706-663-7400; www.buttsmillfarm.com), 2280 Butts Mill Road, Pine Mountain. Open 10–5 weekdays and Sunday, 10–6 Saturday; last ticket sold one hour prior to closing. Spend a fun day at this operational farm, complete with a gristmill and a covered bridge. Other features include a black bear exhibit, Country Carny Area, fishing, Go-Kart track, hayrides, miniature golf course, petting farm, pony and horseback rides, Super Down Hill Slide, train rides, and a water slide. Adults $11.95, children 3–9 $9.95; some activities such as horseback riding and Go-Karts have an additional fee.

✅ ♿ **Cecil B. Day Butterfly Center** at **Callaway Gardens** (see *Green Space— Gardens*), named for the founder of the Days Inn motel chain and given in his honor by his widow, is a butterfly-filled rain forest in west-central Georgia. In fact, upward of 1,000 butterflies of 50 lepidopteran species call the glass-enclosed space home. One of the oldest and largest butterfly conservatories in North America, it was the first to incorporate butterflies with horticulture and the first in the world to showcase butterflies from Africa. These "flying flowers" nibble on bananas and oranges and, if you're quiet, light on you for colorful photo ops. A video called *On Wings of Wonder* plays continuously.

✅ 🏵 ♿ **Old South Farm Museum and Agricultural Learning Center** (706-674-2894; 1-888-635-0193), Pleasant Valley Road and GA 41, Woodland. Open 9–5 Monday through Saturday. This interactive farm museum features live animals and examples of authentic farm machinery such as balers, combines, cultivators, and hay presses. There is a canning plant, a moonshine still, and a peach-packing shed. The Old South Drive-Through section features Southern farm scenes such as a blacksmith shop, cotton gin, dairy farm, gristmill, poultry house, sawmill, and syrup mill. Adults $3, children 3–12 $1.

✅ ♿ **Virginia Hand Callaway Discovery Center** at **Callaway Gardens** (see *Green Space—Gardens*), situated at the end of Mountain Creek Lake, features informational films, permanent and traveling exhibits, and educational programs. The **"Birds of Prey Show,"** presented at the Discovery Center either outdoors or in, depending on the weather, features free-flying raptors such as the bald eagle. In addition, the Callaway Gardens resort (see *To Do* and *Lodging—Cottages and Cabins*) features 13 man-made lakes for boating, fishing, and swimming, Robin Lake Beach, several swimming pools, a 10-mile biking trail, hiking trails, a fitness trail, boat and bike rentals, a fly-casting center, 36 holes of golf, tennis, lodging, and restaurants. Among the many special events are the Summer Family Adventures, Harvest Festival, Steeplechase at Callaway, and Fantasy in Lights.

⚓ ⚒ **Wild Animal Safari** (706-663-8744; 1-800-367-2751; www.animalsafari .com), 1300 Oak Grove Road, Pine Mountain. Open at 10 daily; closing hours vary by season: 5:30 from day after Labor Day to end of February, 6:30 in March and April, 7:30 May through Labor Day; closed Christmas. This park contains 500 acres, which provide habitats for 200 animal species from six continents. Take a guided Zebra Bus tour in season or drive your own car along the 3½-mile road through the park. Many of the kinder, gentler animals are wandering freely and may come right up to your car to be petted or fed (special food is sold at the park entrance). Some of the more unusual animals are ligers, zedonks, zonies, yakatusi, and guar. An aviary, monkey house, and the Snake Pit (a serpentarium open seasonally) offer views of other exotic species. At Old McDonald's Farm and the Petting Zoo, visitors can cuddle up with more docile critters, bottle-feed a calf, or milk a cow. The park also features the Georgia Wildlife Museum, Baby Land USA, the Barrel of Fun Arcade, Serengeti Gift Shop, and the Giraffe Grill. Don't forget your camera. Adults $13.95, seniors and students 10–16 $12.95, children 3–9 $11.95.

HISTORIC HOMES AND SITES ⚓ ⚒ ⚒ **Little White House Historic Site** (706-655-5870; www.gastateparks.org/info/littlewhite or www.fdr-littlewhitehouse.org), 401 Little White House Road, Warm Springs. Open 9–4:45 daily, last tour at 4. Because Franklin D. Roosevelt inherited his mother's magnificent home at Hyde Park, New York, and then lived in the White House, this small cottage is the only one he ever built on his own. In fact, he personally drew the original plans. After being stricken with polio in 1921, Roosevelt came in 1924 to swim in the waters of what is now known as the Roosevelt–Warm Springs Institute for Rehabilitation, hoping for a cure. Although the cure didn't happen, the waters gave him some relief and, while running for president in 1932, he built a simple vacation cottage on the side of Pine Mountain that later became known as the Little White House. It was during his many trips here that he talked to the county residents and learned of their difficulties. These conversations led to the inspiration for New Deal programs like the Rural Electrification Administration, the Civilian Conservation Corps, and the Tennessee Valley Authority. FDR suffered a stroke here on April 12, 1945, while sitting for a portrait being painted by Elizabeth Shoumatoff, and he died a few hours later.

The house and furnishings have been preserved almost as he left them that day. In fact, the leash of FDR's little Scottie, Fala, is still hanging in the closet. Visitors also can see the guest house and servants' quarters. A new $5 million museum on the property features a film narrated by Walter Cronkite, while "Fireside Chats" play on the radio in a typical 1930s kitchen. Exhibits contain memorabilia about FDR's life and presidency, including his struggle with polio, his role in the country's recovery from the Great Depression, and his leadership in World War II. Two of the most popular exhibits are the unfinished portrait and the president's 1938 Ford convertible, which had been adapted with hand controls. A stagecoach that was owned by FDR and used in local parades is also on display.

More than 100,000 visitors come to the Little White House each year. A commemorative ceremony is held each year on April 12, the date of FDR's death. Adults $7, children and seniors $6; parking free.

NATURAL BEAUTY SPOTS ✔ 🐾 ⅄ **Dowdell's Knob**, at **Franklin D. Roosevelt State Park** (706-663-4858; 1-800-864-7275; www.gastateparks.org/info/fdr), 2970 GA 190, Pine Mountain. Open 7 AM–10 PM daily. A rocky spur of the Pine Mountain ridge, Dowdell's Knob sits at 1,395 feet above sea level, where it offers a panoramic view of Pine Mountain Valley. It was one of President Franklin D. Roosevelt's favorite spots. When Roosevelt drove up here in his 1938 Ford convertible, sometimes alone, sometimes with friends for a picnic, the route was a barely cleared dirt track. Of course, when a president of the United States has a picnic, it may not be the casual affair we mere mortals are accustomed to. It's reported that tables and chairs, linen tablecloths and napkins, china, and silver were part of the setup. Roosevelt made his last trip to Dowdell's Knob on April 10, 1945, just two days before his death. It is reported that he had Secret Service agents drive him there, walk back down the road, and not return until he honked the car's horn. He sat alone in his car for two hours. We can only imagine what he was contemplating. Today the road to Dowdell's Knob is paved, and picnic tables and grills have been added so that visitors can eat and enjoy the view as FDR did. A historical marker titled "This Was His Georgia" tells about FDR's fondness for the spot. Sometimes when FDR came here, aides simply took the seat out of his car for him to sit on. A fund has been established to create a life-sized bronze statue of FDR sitting on a car seat, which will enable visitors to sit beside him for a unique photo op. The memorial also will feature an interpretive panel detailing some of FDR's important programs. Parking $2.

SCENIC DRIVES Chattahoochee Flint River Heritage Highway Tour (US 27) from Roscoe to St. Marks (northwest of Greenville). Part of the 150-mile scenic highway is included in this chapter. The area, once occupied by the Creek Indians, features historic sites, unique architecture, and beautiful vistas.

SPECIAL PLACES ✔ ⅄ **Ida Cason Callaway Memorial Chapel** at **Callaway Gardens** (see *Green Space—Gardens*) is a memorial to Cason Callaway's mother. Situated at the end of a lake, the Gothic-style stone chapel is surrounded by forests and streams. Six striking stained glass windows depict local forests and the changing seasons. The Moller pipe organ fills the chapel and woodlands with heavenly music. A peaceful place for contemplation, the chapel is also very popular for weddings.

✳ To Do

BICYCLING Callaway Gardens (see *Green Space—Gardens*) offers a 10-mile paved **Discovery Bicycle Trail** with gently rolling terrain, which is an invigorating way to see the property. The trail is situated so that it provides access to all the major gardens. Bring your own bike or rent one at the Callaway Discovery Center.

FISHING Callaway Gardens (see *Green Space—Gardens*) offers a variety of opportunities. **Mountain Creek Lake** offers some of the finest fishing in the region, and both spin-fishing and fly-fishing enthusiasts extol the resort. Guides can lead fly-fishing excursions to private lakes. Two-day fishing schools and private lessons also are offered.

GOLF Callaway Gardens Golf. Open 8–5 daily. Opportunities for golfers are almost limitless at this Pine Mountain resort, where superbly designed and meticulously maintained courses feature woodland borders and lakeland settings. The original course, which has been recently renovated, is the 18-hole, par-70 **Lake View** course, designed by world-famous golf architects Dick Wilson and J. B. McGovern. Beautiful landscaping with azaleas, dogwoods, and seasonal flowers belies the challenges of the nine water holes. Recent innovations include new bunkers, TifEagle greens, and new cart paths. The **Mountain View** course, also designed by Wilson, is a 7,057-yard, par-72 championship course, which served for 10 years as the home of the PGA Tour's Buick Challenge. The course is ranked among the nation's top courses by *Golf Digest* and *Golf* magazines. $65–75 for Lake View course, $90–95 for Mountain View course.

HIKING Callaway Gardens (see *Green Space—Gardens*). features **nature trails** varying in length from a half mile to 1.6 miles. These trails showcase plants and wildlife and provide changing scenery throughout the year. Some of the trails are dedicated to azaleas, wildflowers, holly, and rhododendrons. Other trails include the **Mountain Creek Lake Trail, Laurel Springs Trail,** and the **Whippoorwill Lake Trail.**

✦ ☙ **Pine Mountain Trail** (www.pinemountaintrail.org) in **Franklin D. Roosevelt State Park** (see *Green Space—Nature Preserves & Parks*). Get a trail map from the state park office (706-663-4858). Twenty-three miles of blazed trail run from the Callaway Country Store on US 27 in Pine Mountain to the WJSP-TV tower on GA 85 in Warm Springs. The trail, which runs along the ridge, sometimes provides views of the valley, while at other times it winds through forests and past streams, waterfalls, and rocky outcroppings. Various trailheads make it possible to hike small portions of the trail. The 4.3-mile **Dowdell's Knob Loop,** near the center of the trail, is popular for its stunning views and historical backdrop (see *To See— Natural Beauty Spots*). Many claim that the **Wolfden Loop** is the most beautiful trail in the Southeast. The 6½-mile trail passes beaver dams, goes over Hogback Mountain, and continues along the **Mountain Creek Nature Trail.** There are very few steep grades along the entire Pine

GOLFERS HAVE TWO COURSES TO CHOOSE FROM AT CALLAWAY GARDENS.

Mountain Trail, so hiking is not difficult. Those who want to hike the complete length of the trail can camp out at nine different sites.

HORSEBACK RIDING ⚘ **Roosevelt Riding Stables** (706-628-7463; 1-877-696-4613; www.RooseveltStables.com), 1063 Group Camp Road, Pine Mountain. Open daily; call for hours. Saddle up for a horseback-riding adventure on 25 miles of trails that wind through the mountains and valleys of **FDR State Park** (see *Green Space—Nature Preserves & Parks*). Trail rides of various lengths last from one to four hours and accommodate riders of all skill levels. Some rides are coupled with lunch or dinner or overnight excursions. Lessons and wagon rides are also available, and moonlight rides and overnight excursions are offered October through May. $30 per hour; ask about rates for overnight rides.

SHOOTING SPORTS Callaway Gun Club at **Callaway Gardens** (see *Green Space—Gardens*). Open 1–7 Wednesday through Friday and Sunday, 9–7 Saturday. The gun club offers skeet, trap, five-stand, and sporting clays. Professionals can teach novices or help sharpen the skills of the more experienced. $9 if you have your own gun and ammo; call for other rates.

SUMMER YOUTH PROGRAMS ⚘ ♿ **Callaway Summer Family Adventure Program** at **Callaway Gardens** (see *Green Space—Gardens*). What person hasn't wanted to run off and join the circus at one time or another in their life? From early June to early August, kids age 3–12 can fly high at weeklong sessions of this glorified summer camp. Members of the Florida State University Flying High Circus not only provide entertainment in regular circus performances but also serve as camp counselors. There's a wide range of structured activities for 3- to 6-year-olds at the child care center. When children reach the age of 7, they can join the circus, where they'll learn simple magic tricks and circus acts such as juggling, tightrope walking, tumbling, and even flying on a trapeze. Youngsters who have attended year after year progress in the difficulty of acts they can perform. While the kids are busy, Mom and Dad can enjoy the resort's many sports options and amenities. The program also includes parent-child time for campfires, games, movies, scavenger hunts, sports, stage shows, theme dinners, and more. Families are normally housed in the resort's cottages, which have full kitchens (see *Lodging*). Rates for packages including accommodations vary widely, so call for details.

TRAP AND SKEET SHOOTING IS AVAILABLE AT CALLAWAY GARDENS.

SWIMMING ✈ ♿ **Robin Lake Beach** at **Callaway Gardens** (see *Green Space—Gardens*) is the longest inland white-sand beach in the country. In addition to sunning and swimming, other activities around the beach include paddleboats, shuffleboard, miniature golf, and table tennis.

TENNIS ✈ **Mountain Creek Tennis Center** at **Callaway Gardens** (see *Green Space—Gardens*) is consistently recognized as one of the Top 50 Tennis Resorts in America by *Tennis* magazine. Ten outdoor lighted tennis courts and two indoor racquetball courts combine to form an excellent venue. Private and group lessons available. Call for rates.

✳ Green Space

BEACHES See **Robin Lake Beach** under *To Do—Swimming*.

GARDENS

All the following gardens are within Callaway Gardens.
✈ ♿ **Callaway Brothers Azalea Bowl** at **Callaway Gardens** (see below), the world's largest azalea garden, is named for Ely Reeves Callaway and his brother, Fuller Earle Callaway, the father of the garden's founder, Cason Callaway. More than 3,400 hybrid azaleas erupt in pink, red, and white each spring. The rare orange plumleaf azalea, which blooms in profusion at Callaway Gardens, is found only within a 50-mile radius in west Georgia. Additionally, 2,000 trees, shrubs, and seasonal flowers provide an array of color and blooms throughout the year. Bubbling streams, walking paths, an arched bridge, and a reflection pool make this an excellent place to relax.

MR. CASON'S VEGETABLE GARDEN AT CALLAWAY GARDENS

✈ ♿ **Callaway Gardens.** Open 9–5 daily. The 14,000-acre resort features several gardens and natural areas, and within them are even more specialized gardens. Adults $13.91, children 5–12 $6.96. Prices for activities vary.

✈ ♿ **John A. Sibley Horticultural Center** at **Callaway Gardens** (see above), which has recently received a $3.5 million face-lift, contains everything from exotic to native plants, unique Mediterranean plantings, and seasonal displays such as chrysanthemums in the autumn and poinsettias during the holidays. The indoor-outdoor center at Callaway sports a powerful 22-foot waterfall where 350 gallons of water per minute plummet into a pool. The lawns are also planted with seasonal plants. Winding paths and swings invite visitors to linger.

✔ **Lady Bird Johnson Wildflower Trail** (near Callaway's Pioneer Log Cabin) at **Callaway Gardens** (see above) displays plants native to Georgia as well as rare, threatened, and endangered species. Meadow, bog, Coastal Plain, Piedmont forest, and southern Appalachian forest habitats are represented. Along the trail are a gazebo, a waterfall, and a picturesque bridge overlooking Mountain Creek Lake.

✔ �& **Mr. Cason's Vegetable Garden** at **Callaway Gardens** (see above) is a 7.5-acre demonstration garden originally planted by founder Cason Callaway (see above) to demonstrate proper growing techniques. Today flowers, vegetables, fruits, and herbs grow in the garden where Southern segments of the long-running PBS television series *The Victory Garden* are filmed.

✔ �& **Overlook Garden and Azalea Trail** at **Callaway Gardens** (see above) contains an impressive collection of more than 700 varieties of azaleas.

NATURE PRESERVES AND PARKS ✔ 🐾 �& **Franklin D. Roosevelt State Park** (706-663-4858; 1-800-864-7275; www.gastateparks.org/info/fdr), 2970 GA 190, Pine Mountain. Open 7 AM–10 PM daily. Stretching from Pine Mountain to Warm Springs and encompassing more than 9,000 acres, Georgia's largest state park is named for the four-term president who loved the area so much. In fact, his favorite picnic spot, at **Dowdell's Knob** above Kings Gap (see *To See—Natural Beauty Spots*), is within the park. The 23-mile **Pine Mountain Trail** winds through forests of hardwoods and pines, but there are 14 miles of other trails (see *To Do—Hiking*). Two lakes provide opportunities for water sports. Many of the park's buildings and the Liberty Bell–shaped swimming pool were constructed during the Great Depression by the Civilian Conservation Corps. Activities available in the park include backpacking, boating, camping (see *Lodging— Campgrounds*), fishing, horseback riding (see *To Do—Horseback Riding*), and picnicking. Parking $3.

✳ Lodging

BED & BREAKFASTS

In Greenville

�& **Georgian Inn Bed and Breakfast** (706-672-1600; www.georgian place.com), 566 South Talbotton Street/US 27 Alt. Five sumptuous, lavishly decorated rooms with all the modern conveniences are offered in this stately, white-columned historic house. Outdoors, guests can enjoy the summer house; perennial, herb, hummingbird, and butterfly gardens; and typical Southern flowering shrubs such as gardenias, azaleas, camellias,

sasanquas, and others. An abundant Southern country breakfast is offered each morning. No smoking. One downstairs room wheelchair accessible. $220 for two nights.

Grand Wisteria Plantation Bed and Breakfast (706-672-0072; www .grandwisteria.com), 15380 Roosevelt Highway/US 27 Alt. The grand 1832 antebellum plantation manor house offers five beautifully decorated guest rooms with private baths and king- or queen-sized beds. A three-course gourmet breakfast is included in the

MAGNOLIA HALL BED AND BREAKFAST IN HAMILTON

nightly rate, and afternoon refreshments are served. With advance notice, lunch can be served for an additional $30 per couple, a picnic basket can be prepared for $25 per couple, or a four-course gourmet dinner can be served for $60 per couple. Children older than 12 welcome. No smoking. Not wheelchair accessible. $110–155.

In Hamilton

⚿ **Magnolia Hall Bed and Breakfast** (706-628-4566; 1-877-813-4394; www.magnoliahallbb.com), 127 Barnes Mill Road. The gracious antiques-filled Victorian home provides five lovely accommodations. A porch swing and rockers attract guests to the wraparound porch. An elegant breakfast is served in the formal dining room, and a snack basket greets visitors in their rooms. Nightly turndown service is accompanied by chocolates and sherry. No pets. No smoking in house or on porches. One downstairs room wheelchair accessible. $105–125.

In Pine Mountain

⚯ ❀ ⚿ **Chipley Murrah House Bed and Breakfast** (706-663-9801; 1-888-782-0797; www.chipleymurrah.com), 207 West Harris Street. Truly a "wedding cake" type of "painted lady," this gorgeous Queen Anne Victorian home was built in 1895. Today the antiques-filled home offers spacious rooms with private baths (one is in the hall), king- or queen-sized beds, and Southern hospitality. Two- and three-bedroom cottages recently have been constructed on the property. All guests enjoy the wraparound porch, swimming pool, and putting green. A hearty breakfast is served to guests in the main house; breakfast is not included for those staying in the cottages. Children younger than 12 in cottages only. No pets. No smoking. One room on first floor of main house, and cottages, wheelchair accessible, but bathrooms not fully equipped. Rooms $95–140, cottages $140–205; two-night minimum on weekends in main house; closed in January.

In Warm Springs

⚯ ⚿ **Hotel Warm Springs Bed and Breakfast Inn** (706-655-2114; 1-800-366-7616; www.hotelwarmspringsbb .org), 47 Broad Street. It's appropriate that the town's historic 1907-era hotel is once again serving up hospitality, this time as a bed & breakfast. When President Franklin D. Roosevelt was in residence at his nearby Little White House, national and international dignitaries as well as journalists and Secret Service agents stayed at the hotel. Restored to its 1941 appearance, the venerable old hotel offers accommodations in spacious, high-ceilinged rooms filled with antiques and Roosevelt memorabilia. Unexpectedly, the Honeymoon Suite features an oversized, red, heart-shaped hot tub. The nightly rate includes a late-afternoon social hour and a full Southern breakfast with cheese grits. No smoking. Wheelchair accessible. Rooms $75–110, suites $135–195.

CAMPGROUNDS

In Pine Mountain

♂ ❄ ✿ ♿ **Franklin D. Roosevelt State Park** (706-663-4858; www.ga stateparks.org/info/fdr), 2970 GA 190. The park offers 140 tent, trailer, and RV sites as well as a bathhouse. Some sites overlook the lake; others are nestled in the woods. (See *Green Space—Nature Preserves and Parks* for more information about the park.) $15–17.

♂ ✿ **Pine Mountain Campground** (706-663-4329; www.camppine mountain.com), 8804 Hamilton Road. In addition to tent sites and paved pull-through sites with full hookups, the campground offers a swimming pool, playground, miniature golf, horseshoes, volleyball, banana bike rentals, rest rooms, convenience store, laundry facilities, and an activity building for groups of eight or more. The facility also offers two cabins for rent. Tent sites $20, 30-amp hookups $25, 50-amp hookups $27; cabins $70–85.

In Pine Mountain

♂ ♿ **Callaway Gardens.** The resort features spacious one- or two-bedroom cottages at the **Southern Pine Cottages** and luxurious one- to four-bedroom homes at the **Mountain Creek Villas.** All feature a fully equipped kitchen, a living-dining area with a fireplace, a deck, and a screened-in porch. The cottage area has its own swimming pool, laundry, and the Flower Mill restaurant. The villas feature a bathroom for every bedroom and a washer and dryer. The nightly rate includes admission to the gardens, use of the fitness center, and admission to Robin Lake Beach in-season (see *To Do—Swimming*). No smoking. Wheelchair accessible. Cabins $189–329, villas $229–599.

♂ ❄ ♿ **Franklin D. Roosevelt State Park** (706-663-4858; www.ga stateparks.org/info/fdr), 2970 GA 190. The park has 22 historic stone cottages built by the Civilian Conservation Corps. Each is equipped with a fireplace and grill as well as linens and kitchen utensils. Some of the cottages sit on the mountaintop and have fabulous views; others hug the lakeshore. No smoking. Two cottages wheelchair accessible. Pets are allowed in selected cottages. (See *Green Space—Nature Preserves and Parks* for more information about the park.) $60–130.

❄ ♿ **Homestead Log Cabins** (706-663-4951; 1-866-652-2246; www .homesteadcabins.com), Hines Gap Road. Secluded in the mountains in four different locations, but close to attractions, these log cabins, which sleep from two to 16, vary from very rustic to sleek contemporary. Some offer a fireplace, Jacuzzi, and a full kitchen. Many are pet friendly. No smoking. Wheelchair accessible, but bathrooms not totally equipped. $100–450.

☀ ♿ **Mountain Top Inn and Resort** (706-663-4719; 1-800-533-6376; www.hide-away.com), GA 190 and Hines Gap Road. At this unique resort, accommodations are available in log cabins with world-theme guest rooms, fireplaces, and double Jacuzzis. The resort also has hiking trails, tennis, and a pool with a waterfall. For the hopelessly romantic, the resort has a charming **log wedding chapel** (800-ITAKETHEE), so couples can have their wedding and honeymoon on-site. Ask about pets. No smoking. Some wheelchair accessibility. $125 Monday through Thursday, $145 Friday through Sunday.

🎣 ♿ **Pine Mountain Club Chalets Family Resort** (706-663-2211; 1-800-535-7622; www.pinemountain clubchalets.com), 14475 GA 18. Quaint one-, two-, and three-bedroom alpine chalets surround a fishing lake or are nestled in the woods. Each chalet features a fully equipped kitchen, living and dining room, and a private deck. Linens are provided. The resort also features a fishing lake, tennis courts, a swimming pool, a nine-hole miniature golf course, basketball and shuffleboard courts, and a playground. No pets. Smoking and nonsmoking cabins. Wheelchair-accessible cabins available. One-bedroom chalet $99, two-bedroom chalet $135, three-bedroom chalet $165; holidays require three-night minimum.

INNS AND RESORTS

In Pine Mountain
🎣 ♿ **Callaway Gardens** offers motel-room accommodations in the

Mountain Creek Inn, which also features restaurants, a cocktail lounge, and a swimming pool. The nightly rate includes admission to the gardens, use of the fitness center, and admission to Robin Lake Beach (see *To Do—Swimming*) in-season. No smoking. Wheelchair accessible. $134–154.

✳ Where to Eat

DINING OUT

In Pine Mountain
🎣 ♿ There are several options for fine dining at **Callaway Gardens,** including the **Gardens Restaurant** (open 5–9 nightly; $17–33) within the gardens, which has a lovely porch overlooking Mountain Creek Lake and the Lake View Golf Course; the **Piedmont Dining Room** (open 7–2 and 5–9 daily; $15–33) at the Southern Pine Conference Center, which features buffets and an à la carte menu; and the **Plantation Room** (open 6:30–10:30, 11:30–2, and 5–9 daily; $16.50–24.95) in the Mountain Creek Inn, which is famous for its Friday-night seafood buffet.

♿ **Cricket's Restaurant** (706-663-8136; www.cricketsrestaurant.com), GA 18. Open 5–9 nightly. Located in a quaint chalet in a wooded setting, the restaurant offers steak, seafood, and New Orleans cuisine. No smoking. Wheelchair accessible. $10–27.

EATING OUT

In Pine Mountain
🎣 🍴 ♿ There are several options for inexpensive meals at **Callaway Gardens,** including the **Discovery Café** (open 7:30–5:30 daily; $3–7) and **Mountain Creek Café** (open 7:30–5:30 daily; $3.50–6.50), both in

the Callaway Discovery Center and featuring salads and sandwiches; and the **Country Kitchen** (open 6:30–9 daily; $6.95–10.95) in the Callaway Country Store, which serves down-home cooking, including blue plate specials and pit-cooked barbecue.

🍴 ♿ **Rose Cottage** (706-663-7877), 111 East Broad Street. Open 11–3 Sunday through Friday, 11–4 Saturday. This café–tearoom–antiques shop serves gourmet sandwiches, soups, salads, quiche, desserts, English teas, and fine wines. In addition, diners can purchase English antiques and gifts, gourmet foods, and baby's and children's gifts. No smoking. Wheelchair accessible. $5–10.

In Warm Springs

🍸 🍴 ♿ **Bulloch House** (706-655-9068), US 27A/US 41. Open 11–2:30 daily, 5–8:30 Friday and Saturday. "Country with class" is the motto at this popular all-you-can-eat restaurant located in a charming circa 1892 Victorian-style cottage. No smoking. Wheelchair accessible. Lunch $7.95, dinner $9.95.

🍴 ♿ **Victorian Tea Room** (706-655-3508; www.VictorianTeaRoom.biz), 70 Broad Street. Open 11–2:30 daily. The eatery serves Southern cuisine, including hot and cold buffets, daily specials, and fresh baked goods. No smoking. Wheelchair accessible. $6.95.

SNACKS

In Pine Mountain

🍸 🍴 ♿ There are several options for snacks and light meals at **Callaway Gardens,** including **Champions** ($3–7.50) in the Mountain View golf course clubhouse, which offers salads, sandwiches, and bar service; the **Coffee House** ($2.50–6.50) at the Mountain Creek Inn patio, which offers coffee, tea, juice, pastries, fruit, and snacks; **Ironwood Lounge** ($2–10.50) at the Southern Pine Conference Center, which offers cocktails, appetizers, and billiards; and the **Vineyard Green** ($3.50–9.50) in the Mountain Creek Inn, which offers a light menu and cocktails.

🍸 🍴 ♿ **Purple Cow Café** (706-663-8080; www.purplecowcafe.com), 161 North Main Street. Open at 10 AM daily; closing hours vary by season. This is the place to come for ice cream and specialty drinks. The casual eatery offers 24 flavors of Blue Bell ice cream, malts, shakes, smoothies, specialty coffees, espresso, latte, cappuccino, hot chocolate, steamers, and hot teas. For those who desire something more substantial, the café offers deli sandwiches, desserts, and bakery items. Inside the Purple Cow is the **Georgia Winery Tasting Room** (see *Selective Shopping—Other Goods*). No smoking. Restaurant wheelchair accessible, but restrooms not. $2–4.50.

✳ Selective Shopping

Callaway Gardens has numerous shopping outlets. The **Callaway Gardens Country Store** stocks Callaway specialty food items such as their famous muscadine sauce and jelly, as well as home decor, apparel, and more. The **Inn Store** carries souvenirs and home decor. Gift shops in the **Callaway Discovery Center, Day Butterfly Center,** and **Sibley Horticultural Center** purvey nature and garden items. The **Pro Shops** at the golf and tennis facilities make sure visitors are properly outfitted for their respective sports, while **Kingfisher Outfitters** has all the equipment anglers need for fishing. All these items also can be purchased online at www.callawayonline.com.

Warm Springs Village (706-655-3322; 1-800-337-1927; www.warm springsga.ws), 69 Broad Street, Warm Springs. Historic buildings grouped around the Bullochville and Magnolia courtyards contain a variety of specialty shops that purvey everything from furniture and accessories to antiques, fine collectibles, and crafts.

ANTIQUES **Antiques and Crafts Unlimited Mall** (706-655-2468; www .acum.org), 7679 Roosevelt Highway, Warm Springs. Open 10–6 daily. In addition to antiques, this emporium of 114 shops offers art, collectibles, crafts, furniture, glassware, pottery, and more. The **Visions Art Gallery** (www.visionsartgallery.net) features the work of regional artist Arthur Riggs.

Pine Mountain Antique Mall (706-663-8165; 1-800-613-9072; www.pine mountainantiquemall.com), 230 Main Street, Pine Mountain. Open 10–6 daily. Thousands of antiques range from the ordinary to the sublime and include books, coins, dolls, jewelry, period glass, primitives, sterling silver, and wind chimes.

ART GALLERIES **Anne Tutt Gallery and Alexander Kalinen Studio** (706-663-8032; 1-888-282-0021; www .annetuttgallery.com), GA 27 at County 354, Pine Mountain. Open 10–6 Monday through Saturday (2–6 Sunday in December). In addition to Anne's works and those of her husband, Alexander, the gallery shows etched glass, jewelry, pottery, sculpture, and Asian antiques.

OTHER GOODS **Country Gardens** (706-663-7779), 155 Main Street, Pine Mountain. Open 10–6 daily. In addition to everything you could want for your garden, the emporium offers antiques and accessories for the home.

Georgia Winery Tasting Room (706-663-8080), 161 North Main Street, Pine Mountain. Open 10–6 Monday through Saturday. Located inside the **Purple Cow Café** (see *Where to Eat—Snacks*), the tasting room offers the opportunity to sample and buy some of Georgia's fine wines. In addition, a large assortment of wine gifts and accessories are available for purchase.

✳ Special Events

May: **Masters Water-Ski and Wakeboard Tournament** (706-663-2281; 1-800-225-5292; www.callawayonline .com). Held Memorial Day weekend on Callaway Gardens' Robin Lake, the extravaganza has been going strong for almost 50 years. Pavilion seating is available. General admission only; included in Callaway Gardens admission.

Piedmont Lake Garden Railroad Spring Display (706-663-8304), Pine Mountain. Model trains depict the 1890–1900 era on a 60-by-70-foot layout. At the children's area, the kiddies can control 14 different trains themselves. See the Garfield train, Thomas the Tank Engine, Mickey and Goofy handcar, cable cars and more. Free.

May and October: **Cotton Pickin' Fair** (706-538-6814; www.cpfair.com). A peach-packing shed, cotton gin, and an 1891 farmhouse in Gay are some of the attractions. Skilled artisans present their wares and there are also antiques, great Southern food, and live entertainment presented on six stages. Adults $5, children age 4–12 $2.

Summer: **FSU "Flying High" Circus** (706-663-2281; 1-800-225-5292;

www.callawayonline.com). Shows at
8 PM Monday and Friday, 2:30 PM
Tuesday and Thursday, 2:30 and 8 PM
Saturday and Sunday. The popular
event features Florida State University students and children participating
in Callaway Gardens' Summer Family
Program. Included with garden admission; general admission seating only.

September: **Sky High Hot Air Balloon Festival** (706-663-2281; 1-800-
225-5292; www.callawayonline.com).
The premier activity at this festive
event at Callaway Gardens is the balloon glow on Friday night. There are
tethered morning and afternoon
flights throughout the weekend, entertainment, family activities, a barbecue,
classic car show, rock-climbing wall,
sand-castle construction, exhibits, and
Frisbee dog demonstrations. Balloon
rides: adults $10, children $5; rock
climbing wall $5; face painting $2;
some fees for other activities.

October: **Ossahatchee Indian Festival and Pow-Wow** (706-628-7653;
www.ossahatchee.org). The festival in
Hamilton features Native American
dance competitions, primitive skills
demonstrations, and authentic arts,
crafts, and food. Free.

Railroad Days (706-846-5341). The
Saturday railroadiana show at the
Manchester Mill features model layout displays, personal collections, and
vendor sales. A few blocks away, the
Manchester railroad yard features a
covered platform where you can
watch the passing trains. Adults and
children older than 12 $2.

November: **Fala Day** (706-655-5870;
www.fdr-littlewhitehouse.org). The
annual tribute to FDR's little Scottie
is presented in the lower parking lot
of the Little White House Historic
Site in Warm Springs by the Scottie
Club of Greater Atlanta and the
Order of Tartan Dancers. Free admission to festival; those who want to
participate in parade and/or tour
house and museum need to pay
regular admission to Little White
House Historic Site (see *To See—Historic Homes and Sites*).

Steeplechase at Callaway (706-324-
6252). Held at Callaway Gardens, the

STEEPLECHASE AT CALLAWAY

event is the third and final leg of the "Sport of Kings" Challenge in the United States. One of the premier social events in all of southwest Georgia, the steeplechase provides numerous horse races, a decorated buggy parade, junior pony races, Jack Russell terrier races, and lots of food. $20 per person, additional $20 per car for infield parking.

November-December: **Fantasy in Lights** (706-663-2281; 1-800-225-5292; www.callawayonline.com), GA 18 and GA 354, Pine Mountain. Open evenings from Friday before Thanksgiving through late December at Callaway Gardens. A true winter wonderland, this 5-mile drive-through extravaganza of Christmas scenes—illuminated with 8 million white and colored lights—is the largest in the Southeast. At the end of the ride, there are refreshments and a Christmas shop. Admission on weekends: adults $16.05, children $8.03; admission on weeknights: adults $13.91, children $6.96. Tickets must be purchased in advance.

THOMASVILLE

Take time to smell the roses in Thomasville, a city in the Red Hills region of southwest Georgia. The land, with its extremely fertile soil, is home to tall stands of longleaf pines, graceful live oaks, and a profusion of azaleas, dogwood, wisteria, and roses (more about them later).

The town was established in the 1820s with the introduction of cotton plantations. Still prosperous to this day, the region between Thomasville and Tallahassee boasts more working plantations than anywhere in the country—71 plantations encompass more than 300,000 acres. They are private and hidden away behind gates, but one offers accommodations and another is open for tours.

Although most of the South suffered during and after the Civil War, Thomasville prospered. Not only was it far removed from Union forces, but it benefited from its timber industry and an agricultural economy not entirely dependent on cotton. Later, the extension of northern railroads into the area brought commerce, visitors, and new residents.

One of the first cities in Georgia to recognize the importance of historic preservation, Thomasville formed Thomasville Landmarks in 1964. Concentrating on residential restoration, the program has documented seven historic districts in the city. Even though the gargantuan turn-of-the-20th-century hotels of

WINTER RESORT ERA

Thomasville's pleasant climate, lack of mosquito-laden marshes, abundance of wild game, and easy access by railroad caused Northerners to flock to the area in the late 1880s, creating the Winter Resort Era and turning cotton plantations into quail-hunting estates. The Northerners even believed that the area's pine-scented air had beneficial qualities for pulmonary ailments. Large resort hotels sprang up and attracted presidents, potentates, tycoons, and entertainers. Many of these visitors decided to stay at least part of the year and built grand homes they modestly called "cottages." Eventually the railroads pushed into Florida and the fickle idle rich moved on to trendier locales, but Thomasville still retains the charm of that area with many surviving homes.

the Winter Resort Era are "gone with the wind," many of the mansions built during that period survive as private homes and businesses, so the town retains much of the charm of that bygone age. Thomasville was recently named one of the Top Five Main Street Cities in America, and its Main Street Program has restored more than 100 buildings so far.

Thomasville claims to have more roses than people (population 20,000), and if you're riding around the fragrant, colorful streets in the late spring and early summertime, you can easily believe it. The city plants and maintains more than 7,000 rosebushes—each of which blossoms with hundreds of flowers—and many residents nurture their own impressive rose gardens.

The small towns in this region boast one or more attractions, outdoor recreation, lodgings, restaurants, and special events.

GUIDANCE To learn more about Thomasville and Ochlocknee, contact the **Thomasville–Thomas County Visitors Center** (229-227-7099; 1-866-577-3600; www.thomasvillega.com), 401 South Broad Street, Thomasville 31792. Open 9–5 weekdays, 10–3 Saturday. This is the place to pick up brochures for the **Historic Walking and Driving Tour** and the **Thomasville Black History Heritage Trail Tour Guide** (see *To Do—Walking Tours*).

For information about Cairo, contact the **Cairo–Grady County Chamber of Commerce** (229-377-3663; www.cairogachamber.com), 961 North Broad Street, Cairo 39828. Open 8:30–5 weekdays.

To learn about Camilla, contact the **Camilla Chamber of Commerce** (229-336-5255; www.camillageorgia.com), 212 East Broad Street, Camilla 31730. Open 8:30–5 weekdays.

To learn more about Pelham, contact the **Pelham Convention and Visitors Bureau** (229-294-4924), 131-B McLaughlin Street, Pelham 31779. For more information about Pelham as well as Camilla, contact **Mitchell County** (229-336-2000; www.mitchellcountyga.net), P.O. Box 187, Camilla 31730.

GETTING THERE *By air:* The nearest airport is **Tallahassee Regional Airport** (850-891-7802; www.ci.tallahassee.fl.us/citytlh/aviation), which is 35 miles south of Thomasville. The airport is served by **Continental Express, Delta Air Lines, Delta Connection/Atlantic Southeast Airlines, Delta Connection/ Chautauqua Air Lines, Delta Connection/Comair, Northwest Airlink,** and **US Airways Express** (1-800-428-4322). On-site car rentals are offered by **Alamo** (1-800-462-5266), **Avis** (1-800-331-1212), **Dollar** (850-575-4255), **Enterprise** (850-575-0603), **Hertz** (1-800-654-3131), and **National** (1-800-227-7368). Off-site car rentals are available from **Budget** (1-800-527-7000) and **Thrifty** (850-576-7368).

By bus: **Greyhound Lines** (229-226-4422; 1-800-231-2222; www.greyhound .com), 1136 West Jackson Street, serves Thomasville.

By car: Thomasville is at the intersection of US 84/221, US 319, and US 19/GA 300.

By train:

GETTING AROUND If arriving by air into the Tallahassee Regional Airport, see the car rental companies listed above with the airport. Car rentals in Thomasville

MEDICAL EMERGENCY For life-threatening situations, call 911. Medical care in Thomasville is available at **John D. Archbold Memorial Hospital** (229-228-2000; www.archbold.org), 915 Gordon Avenue, and **Archbold Urgent Care Center** (229-228-4136), Pine Tree Boulevard and Remington Avenue. Open 8–8 weekdays, 9–4 Saturday, noon–4 Sunday. Care is available in Camilla at **Mitchell County Hospital** (912-336-5284), 90 East Stephens Street.

NEIGHBORHOODS AND VILLAGES Thomasville boasts several historic districts with a wide range of turn-of-the-20th-century homes and buildings and a vast array of architectural styles. The **Dawson Street Historic District** stretches from Jackson to Wacott streets. The **Downtown Historic District** extends from Walcott and Dawson streets to Broad Street. The **Stevens Street Historic District,** which includes West Calhoun, Oak, Monroe, Stevens, Pine, West Clay, West Washington, Jefferson, Webster, Walcott, Jerger, and Forsyth streets, was a neighborhood for affluent African Americans. Some other historic districts include the **Paradise Park Historic District** and the **Tockwotton–Love Street Historic District.** Numerous historic buildings line **Hansell Street.**

Camilla is the county seat of Mitchell County. The county was named for General Henry Mitchell, a Revolutionary War hero and state senator, and Camilla was named after his 19-year-old daughter. The town is the center of one of the most efficient irrigated agricultural production systems in the world. Crops such as peanuts, pecans, pine trees, cotton, and vegetables are grown nearby and processed in Camilla. Many beautiful landmarks such as antebellum homes, the historic courthouse, and the *Spirit of Camilla* historic steam locomotive line Broad Street. Camilla is also noted for good hunting and boasts several hunting plantations.

An unfortunate event occurred here in 1868, when a group of freedmen who had been expelled from the state legislature began a march to town for a protest rally. They were fired on by whites; nine were killed and 25 to 30 wounded. The event has been known as the Battle of Camilla, the Camilla Massacre, and the Camilla Riot.

Today, Camilla has been named one of the Top Tennis Towns in America by *Racquet Magazine.* For the past 20 years, the town has sponsored the Lite Southeastern Professional Invitational Tournament, which attracts more than two dozen tennis stars. Another much-anticipated yearly event is the **Gnat Days Festival** in May.

Nearby **Cairo** is the home of an astounding collection of antique autos and hosts some interesting and popular festivals along with Camilla and the small towns of **Ochlocknee** and **Pelham.**

✳ To See

CULTURAL SITES 𝄞 🍴 ♿ **Thomasville Cultural Center** (229-226-0588;

www.tccarts.org), 600 East Washington Street, Thomasville. Galleries open 9–5 weekdays, 1–5 Saturday and Sunday. The center hosts art exhibits as well as performances and conducts visual and performing arts classes. In the Orientation Room, artifacts, memorabilia, and photographs offer an in-depth look at the cultural history of the city and county. Multiple galleries on several levels of the center feature the works of local, regional, and national artists on a rotating basis. There is also an impressive permanent gallery, and a period classroom is filled with children's artwork. The three-story building is interesting in itself. It was originally constructed in 1915 for the Eastside Elementary School, the city's first public school built with tax revenue. Free.

FOR FAMILIES ✍ 🕷 ♿ **Cairo Antique Automobile Museum** (229-377-3911; www.mrchick.com), 1125 US 84 East, Cairo. Open 10–4 first Saturday of each month. With an astounding collection of vehicles, this museum showcases antique cars, bicycles, and motorcycles as well as other memorabilia, all collected by one person. Cars from every decade in the 1900s are represented, as are thousands of Matchbox cars. Adults $4, children younger than 6 free.

HISTORIC HOMES AND SITES 🕷 **Hardy Bryan House** (229-226-6016), 312 North Broad Street, Thomasville. Open 2–4 Friday. Considered to be the oldest two-story house in Thomasville, the simple house with upstairs and downstairs porches was built in two stages, in 1833 and 1837. Today, fully restored, it serves as headquarters for Landmarks, Inc., and is open one afternoon a week for tours. $2.

✍ 🕷 **Lapham-Patterson House Historic Site** (229-225-4004; www.gastat parks.org/info/lapham), 626 North Dawson Street, Thomasville. Open 9–5 Tuesday through Saturday, 2–5:30 Sunday. Guided tours start on the hour and last about 45 minutes; last tour at 4. This whimsical Queen Anne house is a testimonial to ingenuity, engineering, and craftsmanship. Some of its interesting architectural features are its fish-scale shingles in several different patterns, Oriental-style molding on the porch, longleaf pine inlaid floors, a double-flue chimney with a walk-through staircase, and a cantilevered balcony, but two things are especially interesting: None of the rooms are square or rectangular, and all 19 rooms have an outside exit. C. W. Lapham, an affluent Chicago shoe manufacturer, had suffered lung damage in the infamous 1871 Chicago fire. When he built this house as a winter "cottage" in 1885, he made sure he could get out easily no matter where he was in his home.

THE LAPHAM-PATTERSON HOUSE HISTORIC SITE OVERFLOWS WITH UNIQUE ARCHITECTURAL FEATURES, AS SEEN FROM THIS VIEW FROM THE REAR.

In addition to satisfying his safety concerns, he made sure the house featured all the modern conveniences of the time: a gas-lighting system, hot and cold running water, and built-in closets. All this was created for the then astronomical price of $4,500. Adults $4, seniors $3.50, children 6–18 $2.

🎈 ♿ **Old Magnolia Cemetery, Lieutenant Henry O. Flipper's Grave,** 700 North Madison Street, Thomasville. Of all the notable African American citizens buried in this graveyard, one is of particular interest. Lieutenant Henry Ossian Flipper, a Thomasville native, was born into slavery in 1856. He went on, however, to become the first African American graduate of the U.S. Military Academy at West Point and subsequently had a career with the U.S. Cavalry's Buffalo soldiers, where he achieved many firsts for African American soldiers: cavalry officer, surveyor, cartographer, civil and mining engineer, translator, editor, author, and special agent for the Justice Department. Unfortunately, Flipper was erroneously accused of embezzling government funds. Although he was found not guilty, his clumsy attempt to replace the money to make the problem go away resulted in a dishonorable discharge from the Army. Through the prodigious efforts of family members, the Army finally granted him a posthumous honorable discharge in 1976, and President Clinton granted him a pardon in 1999, 59 years after his death. To honor his memory, the city of Thomasville named the park across the street from the cemetery Henry O. Flipper Park, and a bust of Flipper resides in the Thomas County Library's Flipper Room.

✒ 🎈 ♿ **Pebble Hill Plantation** (229-226-2344; www.pebblehill.com), 1251 US 319, Thomasville. Open 10–5 Tuesday through Saturday, 1–5 Sunday (final tour at 4); closed in September. Pebble Hill is currently the only one of the Thomasville area's many plantations that is open for tours. With more than 3,000 acres, the plantation is a prime example of the opulent late-19th and early 20th-century shooting plantations developed by wealthy Northerners. Although the plantation had existed as a working farm since 1820 when it had been established by Thomas Jefferson Johnson, the founder of Thomas County, when it was acquired by Cleveland entrepreneur Howard Melville Hanna in 1896, it became a place of leisure pursuits. The original house was destroyed by fire in the 1930s with the exception of the loggia. The current 40-room mansion was designed by Abram Garfield, son of the nation's 20th president. Hanna's granddaughter and last of the Hanna heirs, Elisabeth Ireland Poe, known as "Miss Pansy," filled the house with antique furnishings, period wall murals, decorative arts, silver, an astounding collection of sporting art and wildlife scenes, and an extensive collection of Audubon prints, Native American artifacts, shells, sporting trophies, and other personal mementos. On her death in 1978, Miss Pansy left the estate to be used as a museum. Outside, visitors can tour the stables, kennels, dog hospital, log-cabin schoolhouse, infirmary, fire engine house, garage filled with vintage carriages and autos, swimming pool, graveyards (both human and canine), and a child-size Noah's Ark that serves as a playhouse–jungle gym. Plan on several hours here. Children younger than 6 not permitted in main house, but there are plenty of other things for them to see outdoors. Admission to property: adults $3, children younger than 12 $1.50; mansion tour: adults $7, children 6–12 $3.50.

MUSEUMS  **Grady County Museum and History Center** (229-377-9728), One North Broad Street, Cairo. Open 8–4 Monday and Wednesday, 8–noon Friday. The Grady County Historical Society operates this museum, where visitors can see antiques, collectibles, memorabilia, and photographs that depict the rich heritage of the county. Among the displays are household and agricultural items, but the focal point of the museum is a historic mural on permanent loan from the post office. Free.

Thomas County Museum of History (229-226-7664; www.rose.net/ ~history), 725 North Dawson Street, Thomasville. Open 10–noon and 2–5 Monday through Saturday; last morning tour starts at 11:30, final afternoon tour at 3:30; closed last two weeks in August. Step into this 1923 Jeffersonian Revival house and discover the stories of early Thomasville residents. The story of the Winter Resort Era and its wealthy visitors is told through photographs and artifacts from the hotels and plantations, but African American, Civil War, antebellum, World War II, and pioneer Thomasville history are not neglected. A particularly interesting exhibit details the lives of African American families who lived and worked on plantations. Also located on the grounds are several historic buildings either original to the property or moved from other locations. The circa 1860 **Rufus Smith House** is a pioneer log cabin, while the circa 1877 **Emily Joyner House** is a modest Victorian cottage. Something most visitors have never seen anywhere else is the self-contained **Ewart Bowling Alley,** a turn-of-the-20th-century bowling alley built of heart pine. It is the oldest in Georgia and perhaps the oldest in the South. The newest addition to the complex is the circa 1892 **Metcalf Courthouse,** a simple country courthouse. Adults $5, children 6–18 $1.

SPECIAL PLACES **The Big Oak,** East Monroe and North Crawford streets, Thomasville. The pride and joy of Thomasville is this mighty live oak,

THE BIG OAK IN THOMASVILLE IS MORE THAN 320 YEARS OLD.

which was about 320 years old in 2005. Think about it: That means this oak predates the founding of this nation by many years. The venerable tree is more than
66 feet tall and is 24 feet in circumference, making it the largest live oak east of
the Mississippi. The sprawling branches are often covered with resurrection
fern. Non-Southerners may not be familiar with resurrection fern, which is
found in abundance on this and other trees. It may look as if it's dried up and
dead, but any moisture—even morning dew—brings it miraculously back to life.
In order to protect the Big Oak, there are restrictions about what can be driven
under it. For example, don't try to drive an RV under it. Free.

✳ To Do

BIRDING ✿ ✎ **Birdsong Nature Center** (229-377-4408; 1-800-953-BIRD;
www.freenet.tlh.fl.us/birdsong), 2106 Meridian Road, Thomasville. Open 9–5
Wednesday, Friday, and Saturday; 1–5 Sunday. This pristine sanctuary for birds
and wildlife, located on what was originally Birdsong Plantation, boasts 565 acres
of fields, pine and hardwood forests, ponds, swamps, and wildflower meadows.
The most unusual feature of the center is the Bird Window. Within the historic
house, which now serves as the visitor center, a large picture window allows visitors to observe birds up-close. Providing food for the birds in the intimate
enclosed garden outside the window has attracted more than 160 species. Visitors can easily see 25 different species in one sitting. At the Listening Place, a
screened pavilion overlooking Big Bay Swamp, visitors can hear a symphony of
bird calls and the songs of frogs, alligators, and other wildlife. The Butterfly Garden is vibrant with multicolored butterflies from April through November, while
the best time to see purple martins is from January to July. Ten miles of nature
trails include the Bluebird Trail, along which 40 nest boxes are placed in ideal
bluebird habitat. More than 100 bluebird fledglings are born here each year during the nesting season from mid-March to August. Adults $5, children 4–12 $2.50.

FARM TOURS ✿ ✎ ⬥ **Sweet Grass Dairy** (229-227-0752; www.sweetgrassdairy
.com), 19635 US 19 North, Thomasville. Open three Market Days annually—
one each in the spring, summer, and fall; call or consult web site for exact dates.
The 140-acre working dairy farm produces goat and Jersey cow cheese. The best
time of year to come is in the spring, when there are many lambs, kids, and
piglets. Tours include the milking parlor (the goats are milked at 8:30 AM, so plan
accordingly); the cheese-making area, where visitors can taste several types of
cheese; and time spent in the fields with the animals. Free.

FRUIT AND BERRY PICKING ✎ ✿ **Griffin Farms** (229-226-1008), 9113 GA 188,
Ochlocknee. Open for blueberry picking 7–7 daily, July through mid-August.
Call for availability before you go. The organic farm uses no chemicals. $6 per
gallon to pick your own, $10 per gallon prepicked.

✎ ✿ **Titus Schrock** (229-336-2711), 3312 Lake Pleasant Church Road, Camilla.
The farm offers pick-your-own strawberries during the season March 1 through
July 1. Call for details.

✎ ✿ **Van Strawberry Farm** (229-787-5133), 7 miles north of Camilla on US 19.

Strawberries can be picked here from March to early July. Price varies according to crop conditions. Call for specifics.

GOLF See Golf Appendix.

HORSEBACK RIDING *𝄐* **Horse Around Stables** (229-226-8573), 1002 McKinnon Road, Boston. Trail rides and lessons are offered. Call for prices.

HUNTING AND TRAPSHOOTING **Hickory Nut Hill Hunting Preserve** (229-377-2123; www.hickorynuthill.com), 302 Brookins Drive, Cairo. Open Monday through Saturday and Sunday by appointment. Located between Thomasville and Cairo, the preserve offers trapshooting and half-day and full-day dove, duck, and quail hunting in season. Call for hours and prices.

Myrtlewood Hunting Plantation (229-228-6232; www.myrtlewoodplantation .com), Lower Cairo Road, Thomasville. Office open 8–5 weekdays. Myrtlewood offers a five-stand compact shooting clays course, fishing lakes, and hunting for quail and white-tailed deer. Private lodges are available for overnight accommodations. Prices vary depending on activity.

Rio Piedra Plantation (229-336-1677; 1-800-538-8559; www.riopiedraplantation .com), 5749 Turkey Road, Camilla. Open October through March. Rio Piedra, one of only 25 Orvis-endorsed wing-shooting lodges in the world, invites hunters to experience "the gentleman's sport of quail hunting as it was in the antebellum Old South." Full-day shoots can be arranged with or without lodging and meals, but shoots do include a hunting license, a guide, dogs, and Jeeps. The plantation provides gun rentals and an Orvis pro shop. Sporting clays are also available. For those who stay overnight, accommodations are provided in a contemporary two-story lodge and in nearby cottages. Smoking is allowed only outside. There is a wheelchair-accessible bedroom and bathroom. A full day (dawn until dark) of hunting plus lodging, three meals a day, cocktails, hors d'oeuvres, guide, dogs, 12-bird privilege, and a Jeep costs $695 per person double occupancy.

WALKING TOURS ❧ **Historic Walking and Driving Tour** (www.thomasville ga.com/scenic_tour.htm) Available for purchase for $1.59 from the Thomasville–Thomas County Visitors Center, 401 South Broad Street, the self-guided 4½-mile tour includes more than 70 homes and buildings. Every historic building downtown contains a marker listing the year of construction and the original business that occupied the space, though many of the residences are private homes not open to the public. You can get a sample of what you'll see on the tour by consulting the web site.

❧ **Thomasville Black History Heritage Trail Tour** (www.thomasvillega.com/ black_history.htm). Free booklets available at the visitor center and the Thomas County Historical Society, 725 North Dawson Street, have pictures and an easy-to-follow map. The self-guided tour points out 68 significant African American historical sites, including the grave site of Lieutenant Henry Ossian Flipper (see **Old Magnolia Cemetery** under *Historic Homes and Sites*), a post office named in Flipper's honor, the only remaining African American one-room country

school, the historic Stevens Street Historic District, and the Douglas High   **671**
School Memorial Monument.

THOMASVILLE

✳ Green Space

GARDENS ♨ ⬥ ♿ **Thomasville Rose Garden,** Smith Avenue and Covington Drive near Cherokee Lake, Thomasville. Open daylight hours daily. Although quite small, this colorful garden showcases more than 250 species and more than 500 prize rosebushes. Free.

NATURE PRESERVES AND PARKS ♨ ⬥ ♿ **Paradise Park,** bounded by Broad, Hansell, and Metcalf streets, was originally nicknamed Yankee Paradise because the Northerners who stayed at the resort hotels used the park. John Philip Sousa's band entertained in the bandstand. Today the 26-acre park remains in its natural state for all to enjoy.

RIVERS ⬥ ♨ The **Ochlocknee River** in Cairo has several boat landings and many opportunities for canoeing and fishing.

✳ Lodging

BED & BREAKFASTS

In Camilla

♨ **Eagle Eyrie and the Smoke-house Antiques** (229-336-8811), 135 East Broad Street. This circa 1900 house boasts 22 rooms, four of which are reserved for guests at this charming B&B. A wraparound porch with swings and rockers graces the entrance, and guests are invited to shop for antiques in the converted smokehouse. A full breakfast is included in the nightly rate. Smoking not permitted indoors. Not wheelchair accessible. $85.

In Thomasville

Dawson Street Inn (229-226-7515; www.dawsonstinn.com), 324 North Dawson Street. This typically Southern bed & breakfast, located in the circa 1856 Ephraim Ponder House, was once a dormitory for Young's Female College. The house features a long veranda, high ceilings, grand staircases, and ornate fireplaces. Outside the house are a formal Charleston-style garden and a pool. Other special touches include turn-down service with chocolates, gourmet breakfast, and afternoon refreshments. Together the interior and exterior amenities set the scene for a comfortable stay. No smoking. Not wheelchair accessible. $145–155.

1854 Wright House Bed and Breakfast (229-225-9922; www.1854wrighthouse.com), 415 Fletcher Street. Two spacious guest rooms are available in this antebellum home set amid trees and gardens. Amenities include a multicourse breakfast, bedtime treats, fresh flowers, and personal service. Smoking allowed only on porch. Not wheelchair accessible. $95–125; credit cards accepted.

1884 Paxton House Inn (229-226-5197; www.1884paxtonhouseinn.com), 445 Remington Avenue. Located in an opulent Victorian Gothic mansion recognized for its outstanding renovation by the Georgia Trust for Historic Preservation, this AAA four-diamond B&B offers luxurious accommodations in the historic main house and several recently constructed cottages. The house was originally built by Colonel J. W. Paxton of Wheeling, West Virginia, as a vacation residence during the Winter Resort Era. Owner Susie Sherrod has many fascinating collections from her world travels—Lalique, Waterford, Hummels, and Russian dolls among them. She's just as fascinating herself. Among the surprises are a communal indoor lap pool and a hot tub in one of the cottages. The pool is available for use by all guests 9–9; earlier or later than that, it is available only to guests in that cottage. A gourmet breakfast is served in the Garden Room of the main house with fine china, silver, and crystal. An afternoon tea and lemonade social is available by reservation only 1–3 Monday, Thursday, and Friday for $15 per person. No smoking. Not wheelchair accessible. $165–350.

🍴 ♿ **Evans House Bed and Breakfast** (229-226-1343), 725 East Hansell Street. A cheerful yellow Victorian-neoclassical house built in 1898, the Evans House sports an inviting, wide, wicker-filled veranda. It was once known as the Honeymoon Cottage because so many honeymooners stayed there. Eight individually decorated rooms are created for comfort and relaxation. Among the amenities are a full gourmet breakfast and fresh flowers. Visitors are encouraged to borrow a bicycle and explore the park across the street or the beautiful neighborhood. No smoking. One room wheelchair accessible. Rooms $75–90; suite $85–145.

Magnolia Leaf (229-226-4499), 501 East Washington Street. The Greek Revival bed & breakfast is located amid 3 acres of manicured lawns. Filled with antiques and collectibles, it caters to business travelers. Each of the two suites has two bedrooms and can accommodate four people. A full breakfast is served. No smoking Not wheelchair accessible. $191–391.

🍴 ♿ **Mitchell-Young-Anderson House** (229-226-3463), 319 Oak Street. Built in 1833, the house has had a checkered past as a brothel and a rooming house, but since 1910 it has been in the possession of Emma and Sam Young and their descendants. Before the end of segregation in public accommodations, the Youngs rented rooms to traveling black entertainers. Operated today as a B&B by their great-granddaughter, the home is filled with century-old furniture and art treasures. Smoking only on veranda. Wheelchair accessible. $75.

🍴 **Our Cottage on the Park Bed and Breakfast** (229-227-6327), 801 South Hansell Street. Just across the street from Paradise Park, the quaint Victorian cottage that houses the bed & breakfast offers two suites with period decor. Guests enjoy a complete Southern breakfast. Smoking permitted only on porches. Not wheelchair accessible. $70–80.

Serendipity Cottage (229-226-8111; 1-800-383-7377; www.serendipity cottage.com), 339 East Jefferson Street. Not a mansion, but an ample, comfortable, upper-middle-class home from the turn of the 20th century, the B&B offers gracious public rooms and accommodations in individually decorated guest chambers. Smoking only on porch. Not wheelchair accessible. $115 weeknights, $125 weekend.

♞ Southwoods Bobwhite Bed and Breakfast (229-226-0170), 8025 US 19 South. Although it's only 2½ miles from the city, this bed & breakfast offers visitors all the serenity of the country. There are miles of walking trails through piney woods. German, French, and Spanish are spoken. Smoking outside only. Not wheelchair accessible. $85.

CAMPGROUNDS

In Ochlocknee

♞ **Sugar Mill Plantation RV Park** (229-227-1451), 4857 McMillan Road. In addition to level, shady RV sites, the facility offers cabins, three clubhouses, exercise room, shuffleboard, horseshoes, a basketball court, fish ponds (no license required), fishing pier, hiking trails, rest rooms and showers, laundry, lending library, and even a woodworking shop. $19 per night, $114 per week, $150 per month.

See also Campgrounds Appendix.

In Thomasville

♿ **Melhana, the Grand Plantation** (229-226-2290; 1-888-920-3030; www.melhana.com), 301 Showboat Lane. This AAA four-diamond property is the kind of place almost everyone has dreamed of staying. Pull off the highway and travel down the tree-lined driveway until you come to the magnificent 1820 pink plantation house surrounded by 30 historic cottages, barns, and other buildings—most of which have been converted, along with the main house, to offer accommodations in 38 luxurious rooms and suites. Each exquisite guest chamber has a unique personality with period antiques or reproductions and every possible amenity. Some are further enhanced with a fireplace and/or a whirlpool tub. Hibernia Cottage, the dreamy honeymoon suite, is contained in the old creamery. A lovely indoor heated swimming pool, clay tennis courts, a croquet lawn, and a fitness center round out the resort

LUXURY LIVES AT MELHANA, THE GRAND PLANTATION.

facilities. Continental breakfast is included, or choose the hot plantation breakfast for $12. Fine dining is available Friday and Saturday evenings and Sunday for brunch in the **Chapin Dining Room** (see *Where to Eat— Dining Out*). Also on the property is the Showboat theater, which hosted the first showing of *Gone with the Wind*. Why was a private showing of *GWTW* given here before it was released to the public? The story goes that when Jock Whitney, who had contributed heavily to finance the film, was asked for more money to promote it, he wanted to see what he might be paying for. The studio sent an advance copy and Whitney asked his friend, Mel Hanna Jr., to show the film in his private theater. Although Whitney's opinion is not recorded, his funds were forthcoming and the rest, as they say, is history. No smoking. Some rooms wheelchair accessible. $105–400.

✳ Where to Eat
DINING OUT

In Thomasville
♿ **Chapin Dining Room at Melhana, the Grand Plantation** (229-226-2290; 1-888-920-3030; www.melhana.com), 301 Showboat Lane. Open 5–9 Friday and Saturday, 11:30–2 Sunday for brunch. Reservations required. As befits the gracious estate of which this restaurant is a part, you'll find soft colors, crisp linens, sparkling china and crystal, candlelight, and attentive white-glove service. À la carte choices are available Friday and Saturday evenings, while Sunday's brunch is a buffet. Fresh seafood is brought in from the nearby Gulf Coast, and herbs are picked from the estate's own kitchen garden. In addition to seafood, en-

trées may include Black Angus tenderloin, pork, or lamb. Desserts are to die for, and the wine list is impressive. No smoking. Wheelchair accessible. Dinner $27–35; brunch $22.50, children $11.25.

♿ **Liam's Restaurant** (229-226-9944), 109 East Jackson Street. Open 11–2 Tuesday through Saturday, 5:30–10 Thursday through Saturday. A *Georgia Trend* Silver Spoon Award Winner, the restaurant features eclectic seasonal fare with a rotating menu. In addition to the food, diners enjoy the warm atmosphere, open kitchen, artwork by local artists, Sweet Grass Dairy cheeses, and garden dining when the weather permits. No smoking. Wheelchair accessible. Lunch $7–11, dinner $17–32.

EATING OUT

In Thomasville
🍴 🐾 ♿ **George and Louie's Fresh Seafood Restaurant** (229-226-1218), 216 Remington Avenue. Open 10–9 Monday through Saturday. Located in what was once a 1950s burger joint, this eatery serves up catfish, oyster, scallop, shrimp, and snapper plates accompanied by fries or grits, hush puppies, and salad. Deviled crab, chicken or seafood kebabs, sandwiches, salads, and burgers are also on the menu, but they're really famous for their fried green tomatoes, Greek salads and Greek wines. If you're in a big hurry, call in your order and pick it up at the drive-through window. No smoking. Wheelchair accessible. $9–17.

🐾 ♿ 🍴 **Market Diner** (229-225-1777), 502 Smith Avenue. Open 10:30–9 Monday through Thursday, 10:30–10 Friday and Saturday, 10:30–7:30 Sunday. A bustling place, this restaurant is located in the State Farmer's Market (see *Selective Shopping—Food*). Plain and simple, the eatery's staple is its buffet, but its specialty is chicken gizzards. You also can order seafood platters, quail, a variety of vegetables, and homemade desserts. There's an all-you-can-eat seafood buffet on Friday and Saturday nights. No smoking. Wheelchair accessible. Lunch $6–7 , dinner $9–11.

🍴 ♿ ✿ **Souper Salad Cafe** (229-227-6777; www.toscoga.com), 209 South Broad Street. Open 11–4 weekdays, 11–5 Saturday, noon–4 Sunday. This is the place to eat when shopping for antiques at Toscoga Marketplace Antiques (see *Selective Shopping*). The simple menu features five daily choices of soups, sandwiches, and salads. Smoking outside only. Wheelchair accessible. $2.75–6.95.

SNACKS AND TAKE-OUT

In Thomasville

🍴 ♿ ✿ **The Billiard Academy** (229-226-9981), 121 South Broad Street. Open 8–9 weekdays, 8–6 Saturday. Is it the hot dogs or the billiards or both that bring folks here from far and near? The franks, slathered in a special chili sauce, can be purchased at the sidewalk window or enjoyed at the lunch counter inside. Between 200 and 300 dogs are sold on any normal day, but during festivals and special events the number may soar to 1,000. Billiards are enjoyed in the back room. No smoking. Wheelchair accessible. $1.25 per frank.

🍴 ♿ ✿ **The Scoop Ice Cream and Deli** (229-551-0012), 118-A South Broad Street. Open 9:30–5:30 Monday through Saturday. When in the mood for dessert, stop at the Scoop for fresh ice cream, milk shakes, and sundaes. The eatery also serves salads, sandwiches, and soups. Primarily meant to be a take-out place, there is one table inside and several outside. No smoking. Wheelchair accessible. $1.59–$6.

✳ **Entertainment**

🎭 **Thomasville Cultural Center** (229-226-0588; www.tccarts.org), 600 East Washington Street, Thomasville. Galleries open 9–5 weekdays, 1–5 Saturday and Sunday. Theatrical and musical productions are staged in the newly renovated auditorium. In collaboration with the Thomasville Entertainment Foundation, a nine-month-long season brings national performers to the stage. Classic films are shown during the Summer Music Series, and annual events include the **Plantation Wildlife Arts Festival** (see *Special Events*). Admission to galleries free. Times and prices vary for productions; call for a schedule of events and ticket prices.

MUSIC **Thomasville Entertainment Foundation** (229-226-7404; www .tccarts.org/tef/htm). Performances held at Thomasville Cultural Arts Center auditorium, 600 East Jackson Street, Thomasville. Founded in 1937, the foundation is one of America's oldest all-volunteer concert series presenters. Patrons are treated to internationally renowned dancers, instrumentalists, pianists, and singers in six concerts between October and April. $70 for three-concert classical series; $70 for three-concert pops series; $130 for all six; individual tickets: adults $30, students $15.

THEATER 🎭 **Thomasville On Stage & Company** (229-226-0863), 117

South Broad Street, Thomasville. Performances Friday and Saturday nights and Sunday afternoons. A local theater group, the company stages three shows a year, one of which is usually a musical. Call for a schedule of performances. Adults $12, students $10.

✳ Selective Shopping

ANTIQUES Toscoga Marketplace Antiques (229-227-6777; www.toscoga .com), 209 South Broad Street, Thomasville. Open 10–6 Monday through Saturday, noon–5 Sunday. Ninety dealers offer antiques, collectibles, and gifts. If you work up an appetite, eat at the establishment's **Souper Salad Cafe** (see *Where to Eat—Eating Out*).

Walcott Cottage (229-226-1033), 219 East Washington Street, Thomasville. Open 10–5 Monday through Saturday. Located in the heart of the historic district, the shop features 18th- and 19th-century furniture and accessories, as well as quality needlework kits.

ART GALLERIES Meridian Gallery (229-227-0307), 126 South Broad Street, Thomasville. Open 10–6 weekdays, 10–5 Saturday. The gallery specializes in original works, custom prints, and custom framing.

BOOKS The Bookshelf (229-228-7767), 108 East Jackson Street, Thomasville. Open 9–5:30 weekdays, 10–5:30 Saturday. Those who appreciate the ever-decreasing independent bookstores will want to stop here for a wide selection of new and used books, audio books, cards, and gifts. The store will help you locate out-of-print books, too.

FOOD State Farmer's Market (229-225-4072), 502 Smith Avenue, Thomasville. Open 8–6 Monday through Saturday; auctions held 2–6 Monday through Saturday, May through November. Second in size only to Atlanta's farmer's market in the Southeast, the Thomasville market sells the best and freshest regional produce, everything from mayhaw berries to the world-famous sweet Vidalia onions. Among the homemade jams, jellies, relishes, and pickles is mayhaw jelly, created from berries that grow on trees in swamps. **Market Diner,** the on-site restaurant, is open 10–9:30 daily (see *Where to Eat— Eating Out*). Local cookbooks, white oak baskets, and souvenirs are also available.

GIFTS White's Cottage (229-226-0313), 116 South Broad Street, Thomasville. Open 10–5 Monday through Saturday. The upscale gift shop features gifts for all occasions as well as the only selection of fine loose teas within 100 miles.

✳ Special Events

April: **Thomasville Rose Show, Parade, and Festival** (229-227-3310). Visitors have a blooming good time at this festival, which celebrates the 7,000 rosebushes planted throughout the city. Among the activities are special rose displays; historic home, garden, and museum tours; street dances; arts and crafts shows; walking and running races; a golf classic; Jump for the Roses horse show; the Pebble Hill Plantation Ball; a juried rose show; lectures; nursery vendor displays; and, of course, the parade. During the festival, the Lapham-Patterson House is the

"House of a Hundred Roses," with hundreds of roses on display. Free; some activities have a small fee.

Late April or early May and October: **Picker's Paradise Park Festival** (229-226-6435), 2217 Maddox Road, Ochlocknee. The twice-yearly blue-grass festival is held on a scenic 10-acre lake. Music starts informally on Thursday night but officially starts at 7 on Friday. People are usually playing informally all day in "picking circles." Home-cooked food is also an integral part of the festival. Free Thursday; $10 per day Friday and Saturday.

Early October: **Pelham Wildlife Festival** (229-294-4924). Held on the first Saturday of October, the biggest wildlife event in southwest Georgia features wildlife education shows, arts and crafts, and all-day entertainment. Free.

Fall Sampler at Pebble Hill Plantation (229-226-2344; www.pebble hill.com). Held the first Sunday of October near Thomasville (see *To See—Historic Homes and Sites*). Family fun activities include wagon rides, pony rides, and a petting zoo, as well as demonstrations of horse jumping, dog retrieving, horseshoeing, fall flower arranging, fly-fishing, and kite flying. Adults $5; children younger than 12 $3 (children can get a coloring sheet online and bring it to get in free).

Mid-October: **Thomasville Fly-In** (229-226-4753; www.thomasvillefly in.com). Held the second weekend of the month at Thomasville Municipal Airport. The fastest-growing area of the fly-in is the Vendors and Fly Market. The Aircraft Engine Museum is another draw, and peanut boiling is a long-standing Saturday-morning tradi-

tion. The Rose City Soaring Club offers sailplane and glider rides, and many folks get their first plane ride at the fly-in. Children's activities include a parade and the Candy Drop—50 pounds of candy dropped from a helicopter. Free for spectators; small charge for some activities.

Mid-November: **Plantation Wildlife Arts Festival** (229-226-0588; www .tccarts.org/pwaf.htm). Held in Thomasville 10–5 Saturday and Sunday preceding Thanksgiving. The **Thomasville Cultural Center** (see *To See—Cultural Sites*) presents a juried wildlife arts show featuring painting, sculpture, and photography by renowned artists. Prices for items for sale range from $10 to $50,000. An annual highlight is a visit from *Wild Kingdom* host Jim Fowler, who entertains visitors with furred and feathered wildlife. Other activities include children's activities, demonstrations, lectures, and wildlife and sporting films. Adults $10, children 5–11 $3.

Early December: **Victorian Christmas** (229-227-7020; www.downtown thomasville.com/victorian.html). The 1890s are recreated in Thomasville during two evenings with jingle-bell horse-drawn carriage rides, citizens in period costumes, stores and restaurants decorated for the holidays, and food and holiday delicacies. Most anticipated, however, are the street performances by actors, storytellers, carolers, choirs, dancers, bands, mimes, jugglers, and an organ grinder. Other activities include a Victorian Museum, a live Nativity, and a visit from St. Nicholas. In addition, during Victorian Christmas there is an open house at the **Lapham-Patterson House** (see *To See—Historic Homes* *and Sites*), a holiday show from the Thomasville Music and Drama Troupe, Pebble Hill Plantation's Candlelight Tour (see below), and the Thomas County Museum of History's Candlelight Tour of Homes. Some events free; others, fees vary by activity. Call for details.

Mid-December: **Pebble Hill Plantation's Christmas Candlelight Tour** (229-226-2344; www.pebblehill.com).

Held on Friday and Saturday of second weekend in December near Thomasville (see *To See—Historic Homes and Sites*). Reservations required—must be made *way* in advance. Guests tour the downstairs of the main house, decked out in all its holiday finery, and enjoy a champagne reception, carriage rides, presentations of seasonal music, and a Christmas reading. $45.

TIFTON AND MOULTRIE

In the heart of rural south Georgia, prime agricultural land with scenic, sprawling farmsteads is the norm. The region, however, is a growing leisure destination. The only big towns are Tifton and Moultrie, but there are numerous hamlets with enough attractions and activities to draw visitors. Travelers find plentiful outdoor recreational activities, art museums and galleries, outdoor murals and other public art, historic and quirky museums, gardens, state parks, wildlife refuges, cultural events, unusual festivals, antiques and outlet shopping, and bed & breakfasts in historic homes.

In Georgia, towns and counties with the same name are not usually paired up (Clayton is not in Clayton County, Lumpkin is not in Lumpkin County, and so on), so Tifton and Tift County are unusual in that they were both named for the same family—although not for the same person. Tift County was named for Nelson Tift, and the town of Tifton was named for his nephew, Henry Tift.

GUIDANCE When planning a trip to the Tifton area, contact the **Tifton–Tift County Tourism Association** (229-386-0216; www.tiftontourism.com), 115 West Second Street, Tifton 31793. Another source of information is the **Tifton–Tift County Chamber of Commerce** (229-382-6200; www.tiftonchamber.org), 100 North Central Avenue, Tifton 31794. Open 8:30–4 weekdays.

To learn more about Adel, Cecil, and Lenox, consult the **Adel–Cook County Chamber of Commerce** (229-896-2281; www.adel-cookchamber.org), 100 South Hutchinson Avenue, Adel 31620. Open 8–6 weekdays. While in the area, stop in at the **Georgia–Florida Welcome Center** (229-896-9742), 1203 West Fourth Street, Adel 31620. Open 8–6 daily.

For information about Ashburn, contact the **Ashburn–Turner County Chamber of Commerce** (229-567-9696; 1-800-471-9696; www.turnerchamber.com), 238 East College Avenue, Ashburn 31714. Open 8:30–noon and 1–5 weekdays. Pick up a brochure for the Ashburn Walking-Driving Tour from the chamber.

To learn more about Lakeland, consult the **Lakeland–Lanier County Chamber of Commerce** (229-482-9755), 112 Main Street, Lakeland 31635. Open 9–5 Monday through Thursday.

If planning travel to the Moultrie area, contact the **Moultrie–Colquitt County**

Chamber of Commerce (229-985-2131; 1-888-40-VISIT; www.moultriechamber.com), 116 First Avenue SE, Moultrie 31768. Open 8–5 weekdays.

GETTING THERE *By air:* Tifton is located within one hour's drive of the Valdosta and Albany airports (see Valdosta and Albany chapters).

By bus: Bus service is provided by **Greyhound Lines** (229-382-1868; 1-800-231-2222), 4431 Union Road, Tifton.

By car: Tifton is conveniently located at I-75, US 319, US 82, and US 41.

By train: The nearest **Amtrak** (1-800-USA-RAIL) stations are in Atlanta (see What's Where in Georgia) and Madison, Florida.

OLD MEETS NEW AT THE GEORGIA AGRI-RAMA IN TIFTON.

GETTING AROUND In Tifton, car rentals are available from **Enterprise** (229-382-6614; 1-800-736-8222), 1401 Tift Avenue, or **Thrifty** (229-387-7368; 1-800-847-4389), 1802 US 82 West.

MEDICAL EMERGENCY In life-threatening situations, call 911. For other urgent care, help is available at **Colquitt Regional Medical Center** (229-935-3420; 1-888-262-2762; www.colquittregional.com), 3131 South Main Street, Moultrie, or **Tift Regional Medical Center** (229-382-7120; 1-800-648-1935; www.tiftregional.com), 901 East 18th Street, Tifton. There are some areas, such as around the Paradise Public Fishing Area, where there is no 911 service, so ask an attendant on duty for the local emergency number.

VILLAGES Tifton, the largest municipality in this area, was founded in 1890 by sawmill supervisor Henry Harding Tift. Today 70 percent of the downtown buildings are on the National Register of Historic Places. Because Tifton, listed in the book *100 Best Small Towns in America* by Michael Crampton, participates in the nationwide Main Street improvement program, downtown buildings have been spruced up to house trendy shops, boutiques, and restaurants. The city offers museums, art galleries, shopping, historic sites, and outdoor recreational activities.

Moultrie, the county seat of Colquitt County, was incorporated in 1859 and named for General William Moultrie, a Revolutionary War hero. The city's opulent 1902 courthouse has been voted the prettiest in the state. Moultrie, which rivals Tifton in population, boasts a rejuvenated downtown with more than 50

WHAT'S IN A NAME?

Unusually named **Adel,** originally called Puddleville, has interesting stories about the origin of its name. One story is that the founders of the city and Cook County wanted just a piece of city life for their small town, so they took the middle four letters from the thriving city of PhilADELphia as the name of the town. An alternative legend is that the first postmaster, Joel "Uncle Jack" Parrish, wanted to change the town's name from Puddleville, and when he saw the name "Philadelphia" on a crocus sack, he struck out the first four and the last four letters to create the town's name.

Lenox has a similar story. In the late 1800s, there was a lumber mill town called Mogul. In the early 1900s, the story goes, two farmers were sitting around at the train station watching workers as they loaded an old ox. One farmer reportedly said to the other, "That sure is a lean ox." By dropping the letter *A* from *lean*, the town became Lenox, which today sponsors the annual **Lean-Ox Festival.**

specialty shops and restaurants. Called "the Antique Capital of South Georgia," it boasts 36 downtown antiques dealers. Moultrie is also the home of the **Sunbelt Agricultural Exposition**, the largest farm show in the country (see *Special Events*), and hosts several other festivals. Moultrie is in the midst of prime quail hunting plantations, too.

✷ To See

CULTURAL SITES ❧ ⅛ **Atlantic Coastline Artists Station** (229-382-5589), 119 Love Avenue, Tifton. Open 2–4 Wednesday or by appointment. The town's restored railroad freight depot houses a permanent collection and changing exhibitions. Outside, *Our Town Tifton* is a 30-foot bas-relief folk-art wall that was created by combining the whimsical minisculptures made by hundreds of area residents. Free.

❧ ⅛ **Citizen's Art Collection** (229-382-6231), 130 East First Street, Tifton. Open 8:30–5 weekdays. Several dozen works of art depicting Tifton and south Georgia as seen through the eyes of local and regional artists are displayed at the historic Myon Hotel, which now serves as Tifton City Hall. Free.

❧ ⅛ **Landscape Murals.** Always accessible. Outdoor murals of regional scenes, lakes, and flowers adorn a building at Main and Second streets and another at Commerce Way and Third Street, both in Tifton. Free.

❧ ⅛ **Milltown Murals** (229-482-9755), at Main, Center, and Murrell streets as well as Valdosta Highway, Lakeland. Always accessible. Twenty-three life-size murals painted on downtown buildings depict the citizens, landscape, and important events of Milltown, which was Lakeland's name until 1925. The murals depict life in the 1920s. Maps to help visitors locate all the murals can be obtained from the **Lakeland–Lanier County Chamber of Commerce** (see *Guidance*).

LITTLE ELEPHANT Anyone who has ever wanted to run off and join the circus will smile at this touching little gravestone in the old Pleasant Grove Primitive Baptist Church cemetery on GA 37 in Moultrie. As a boy at the turn of the 20th century, William F. Duggan wanted to do just that. When he grew up, his dream came true and then some—he bought a circus. Duggan died in 1950 and, as a tribute to his father's dream, his son commissioned a gravestone that is topped with the likeness of a baby elephant.

EQUESTRIAN EVENTS ✈ ♿ **Rafter H. Rodeo Arena** (229-985-2652; 229-985-2131), 1331 US 319, Moultrie. The state-of-the-art facility hosts amateur and professional rodeo competitions such as the Georgia Junior Competition and the Sunbelt Southern PRCA Rodeo. A western-wear store is on the property (see *Selective Shopping—Clothing*). Call for a rodeo schedule and ticket prices.

FOR FAMILIES 🏠 ♿ **Ellen Payne Odom Genealogy Library** (229-985-6540), 204 Fifth Street SE, Moultrie. Open 8:30–5:30 Monday through Saturday. The library is a treasure trove of information about the eastern seaboard and migration routes to the West and contains material on 100 Scottish clans and family associations. Genealogical research assistance is available. Free.

VISITORS TO THE GEORGIA AGRIRAMA LIVING HISTORY MUSEUM WILL LEARN ABOUT THE WIRE-GRASS REGION DURING THE PERIOD 1870 TO 1910.

HISTORIC HOMES AND SITES ✈ 🏠 ♿ **Fulwood Garden Center** (229-386-8347), 802 West 12th Street, Tifton. Open for self-guided tours 9–noon weekdays; guided tours by reservation. A beautiful home from the early 1900s has been restored by the Tifton Garden Club and surrounded by a garden filled with native and exotic plants. Free.

✈ ♿ 🏠 **Georgia Agrirama Living History Museum** (229-386-3344; 1-800-767-1875; www.agrirama.com), 1392 Whiddon Mill Road, Tifton. Open 9–5 Tuesday through Saturday. By moving 35 historical homes and commercial buildings from various locations in south Georgia, a town and surrounding farmsteads have been assembled to depict the wire-grass region during the period 1870 to 1910. Costumed docents describe life

in a simpler time and demonstrate old-time skills. In addition to several historic
homes and two farmsteads, the town contains an apothecary, church, cotton gin,
country store, feed and seed store, water-powered gristmill, Masonic lodge,
newspaper office and print shop, railroad depot, sawmill, one-room school, and
turpentine still. A steam locomotive pulls a train of open-air wooden cars around
the site. Visitors can buy small, interesting, old-timey gifts at the country store.
Cotton ginning, cane grinding, and turpentine stilling are demonstrated at various times throughout the year. The Wiregrass Opry performs some Saturday
nights. Among the special events that occur throughout the year are the **Spring
Folk Life and Bluegrass Festival** (see *Special Events*) **Clogging Hoedown,
Historical Halloween Carnival,** and the **1890s Victorian Christmas Celebration.** Adults $7, seniors $6, children 5–16 $4.

✔ ♣ ♿ **Old Colquitt County Jail** (229-985-2131; 1-888-40-VISIT; www
.moultriechamber.com), 116 First Avenue SE, Moultrie. Open 8–5 weekdays.
Now the location of the chamber of commerce, the 1915 building served as a
jail, and the original gallows are still in place. The structure is notable for its Oriental brick, terrazzo floors, and Georgia granite. Free.

MUSEUMS ✔ ♣ ♿ **Crime and Punishment Museum and Last Meal Café**
(229-567-9696; 1-800-471-9696; www.jailmuseum.com), 241 East College Street,
Ashburn. Open 10–5 Tuesday through Saturday. Built in 1906, the Turner County
Jail was nicknamed "Castle Turner" by inmates because of its Romanesque style.
Among things to see here are the original cells, death cell, hanging hook, and
trapdoor where two men were hung for murder. The facility also features the
Last Meal Café (see *Where to Eat—Eating Out*). Adults $6, seniors $4, children 6–17 $2.

✔ ♣ ♿ **Museum of Colquitt County History** (229-890-1626; www.colquitt
musem.org), 500 Fourth Avenue SE, Moultrie. Open for self-guided tours 10–5
Friday and Saturday, 2–5 Sunday, or by appointment; guided tours by reservation. Changing exhibits chronicle the diverse history of the area. Displays range
from Native American history to more recent events such as wars in which
Colquitt County citizens have participated. Artifacts date back to pre-Columbian
times. Free; donations appreciated.

♣ ♿ **Tifton Museum of Arts and Heritage** (229-382-3600), 255 Love Avenue,
Tifton. Open based on exhibit schedule, so call for hours; tours by reservation.
The museum is housed in a restored 1901 Romanesque church, which was
Tifton's first brick church. The building retains its exquisite stained-glass windows and other significant architectural elements such as heart-pine floors,
vaulted ceilings and buttresses, a bell tower, and fanlight doorways. The museum
features quarterly traveling exhibits of paintings, works in wood, porcelain, and
other media. Free; donations appreciated.

SPECIAL PLACES Magnolia Tree Park (229-386-0216), Magnolia Industrial
Park Drive, Tifton. Accessible 24/7. More than 400 years old and 61 feet tall
with a crown spread of 105 feet, the second-largest magnolia in the country is
the star of this park. If this is the second largest, we'd love to see the largest. The

best time to see the tree is in the late spring or early summer, when it is covered with thousands of waxy white blooms. Free.

✳ To Do

AUTO RACING ♂ ᵹ **South Georgia Motorsports Park** (229-896-7000; www .sgmpracing.com), 2521 US 41 North, Cecil. Located near Valdosta, the facility features a full weekly schedule of "dragway" and speedway racing, including monster truck shows, swap meets, and motorcycle days. Tiered seats accommodate 6,000. The 4,100-foot dragway is on one side of the stands; a half-mile oval track for stock car racing is on the other side. Call for a schedule of events and ticket prices.

BICYCLING ♂ ✿ ᵹ **The Bike Trail** (229-985-1056; www.moultriega.com/comm/ lifestyle.htm). Open daily. This Rails-to-Trails project beside South Main Street in downtown Moultrie offers easily accessible opportunities for biking, walking, jogging, and in-line skating. Free.

BIRDING See **Reed Bingham State Park** under *Green Space—Nature Preserves and Parks.* The best locations are near the bridge and dam and along the nature trails at dusk. Buzzard viewing is best in the morning and late afternoon.

FISHING ♂ ✿ ᵹ **Paradise Public Fishing Area** (229-533-4792), Brookfield-Nashville Road off US 82 East, Tifton. Open sunrise–sunset daily. Seventy-one lakes and ponds totaling 550 acres of water provide plenty of fishing opportunities, but you must have a valid fishing license. In addition, there are 568 acres of forest and 123 acres of open fields. The entire Georgia Department of Natural Resources–operated area is excellent for wildlife observation. Many areas can be seen from a vehicle or a small boat, except for some longleaf pine–wire-grass areas, which can be reached only on foot. A variety of wading birds and waterfowl, bald eagles, hawks, many mammals, nine-banded armadillos, snakes, and the endangered gopher tortoise can be seen. (Note: When venturing off roads and trails, snake leggings are recommended.) The facility offers rest rooms, a boat ramp, fishing pier, dock, and primitive camping. Some of the facilities are handicapped accessible. Several tournaments occur throughout the year, some specifically for children. Free.

GOLF See Golf Appendix.

HIKING ♂ ✿ **Robert Simpson Nature Trail** (229-482-9755), North Temple Street, Lakeland. Open dawn–dusk daily. The trail on a 75-acre tract alongside Lake Irma meanders through pristine forested areas where visitors can see abundant plant life, natural bogs, and native wildlife. The exceptional scenery attracts both seasoned and novice hikers. Fishing opportunities are excellent as well. Free.

HUNTING **Live Oak Plantation** (229-896-2112; 1-800-682-4868; www.huntliveoak.com), 675 Plantation Road, Adel. Open daily October 1 through March 31. A sportsman's paradise, the facility offers not only quail and pheasant hunting but also golf and fishing. Bobwhite quail abound on the 3,000-acre private reserve. Professional hunting guides and champion bird dogs lead the way to the action. A handsomely decorated rustic lodge provides accommodations and meals. Prices vary.

MINIATURE GOLF See **Reed Bingham State Park** under *Green Space— Nature Preserves and Parks.*

WALKING TOURS 🐾 **Walking Tour of Moultrie** (www.moultriega.com/h/tour .htm). Go to the web site and print out the walking tour information, which leads visitors past the courthouse, war memorials, and other downtown historic buildings constructed in the Beaux Arts, neoclassical, Colonial Revival, Craftsman–Mediterranean Revival, and art deco styles. In addition, brochures for walking and driving tours of the county are available at the **Moultrie–Colquitt County Chamber of Commerce** (see *Guidance*).

✷ Green Space

NATURE PRESERVES AND PARKS ✍ 🐾 **Banks Lake National Wildlife Refuge** (229-482-9755), US 221, Lakeland. Open dawn–dusk daily. The refuge provides opportunities for wildlife observation, and its boat ramps are popular with boaters who launch from there. Free.

✍ 🐾 ♿ **Bert Harsh Park** (229-985-2131; 1-888-40-VISIT; www.moultrie chamber.com), Fifth Street SE, Moultrie. Open daylight hours daily. This is the first historic grove of trees to be planted in a USA Certified Tree City. Trees in the park were planted and named in honor of Moultrie people and famous Americans, most of them Southern: for example, the Jimmy Carter slash pine, the Juliette Gordon Lowe magnolia, or the Robert E. Lee sweet gum. Free.

✍ 🐾 ♿ **Coastal Plain Research Arboretum** (229-386-3811), South Entomology Drive, Tifton. Open daylight hours daily for self-guided tours; guided tours by reservation. Thirty-eight acres of forest and wetlands provide opportunities for plant identification and wildlife observation. The arboretum is planted with 280 different species of trees, shrubs, and herbaceous plants native to the Coastal Plain of Georgia. Free.

✍ 🐾 ♿ **Reed Bingham State Park** (229-896-3551; 1-800-864-7275; www.ga stateparks.org/info/reedbing), 542 Reed Bingham Road, Adel. Open 7 AM–10 PM daily. Central to the 1,613-acre park is a 375-acre lake, which has become a major boating, fishing, and waterskiing mecca in south Georgia. Fishing for bass, catfish, and crappie is excellent. Recreational amenities include a swimming beach, three boat ramps, a wheelchair-accessible fishing dock, a playground, miniature golf, and 4 miles of hiking trails. Boat rentals are available, too. The park's Coastal Plain Nature Trail and Gopher Tortoise Nature Trail wind through a cypress swamp, sand hills, a pitcher plant bog, and other habitats where visitors may see waterfowl, the endangered gopher tortoise, harmless indigo snakes, and other wildlife; however, the most famous residents are thousands of black vultures and turkey vultures that arrive in November and stay through April. Accommodations are offered at campgrounds (see *Lodging*). Parking $3. See also Parks Appendix.

RIVERS ✍ ♠ ♿ **Alapaha River** (229-482-9755), US 221 and GA 37, Lakeland. Open dawn–dusk daily. The river offers numerous opportunities for fishing, canoeing, bird-watching, and wildlife observation, not to mention simple relaxation. Free.

✳ Lodging
BED & BREAKFASTS

In Moultrie

Barber-Tucker House (229-890-0714; www.moultriebandb.com), 704 Third Street. The epitome of an opulent Southern home, this white-columned mansion built in 1905 is one of the oldest and most beautiful homes in Moultrie. The Barber family lived there for 50 years, and then the Tucker family lived there for 40. Now a luxurious B&B, the Barber-Tucker house continues the tradition of gracious hospitality with extravagant accommodations located in the main house and the carriage house. No smoking. Limited wheelchair accessibility (one room in cottage wheelchair accessible, but dining room in main house is up some steps; breakfast served on patio in good weather or in cottage to accommodate guests in wheelchair). $125–165; two-night minimum.

Pecan Hill Inn Bed and Breakfast (229-985-7869), 2458 Sylvester Highway. The stately 110-year-old Queen Anne Victorian home, also known as the Coleman House, sits on 5 acres with 22 pecan trees. The home has an interesting past, including use as a boardinghouse for teachers and home of the Georgia State Patrol. It is listed on both the Georgia and National Registers of Historic Places. Also on the property is a livestock and cattle barn listed on the National Register and a carriage house. Four well-appointed guest rooms with private baths, fireplaces, and bay windows are offered. A bountiful gourmet breakfast is served. No smoking. Not wheelchair accessible. $115–150.

In Tifton

♠ **Hummingbird's Perch Bed and Breakfast** (229-382-5431), 305 Adams Road, Tifton. Four guest accommodations with private or semiprivate baths are offered in the modern, traditionally styled home, which sits on 7 acres with a fishing pond. A full breakfast is included. No smoking. Not wheelchair accessible. $80.

Mockingbird Ridge (229-382-8454; www.mockingbirdridge.com), 4935 GA 125 North. Many lodgings claim to offer guests a home away from home, but this bed & breakfast really delivers. Accommodations are offered in a private brick home with a bedroom and bath, living room, fully stocked kitchen, front porch, swimming pool, and gardens on 10 acres with a fishing pond. Smoking outdoors only. Not wheelchair accessible. $99 Sunday through Thursday, $125 Friday and Saturday.

CAMPGROUNDS

In Adel

✍ 🐾 🍴 ♿ **Reed Bingham State Park** (229-896-3551; 1-800-864-7275; www.gastateparks.org/info/reedbing), 542 Reed Bingham Road. The park offers 46 tent, trailer, and RV sites as well as a pioneer campground. $15–21.

In Tifton

✍ 🍴 **Amy's South Georgia RV Park** (229-386-8441; reservations 1-800-813-3274; www.amysrvpark.com), 4632 Union Road. The park's 55 pull-through sites offer 30- or 50-amp hookups. Amenities include a swimming pool, playground, and catch-and-release fishing pond. Accommodations also are offered in one cozy cabin. $22.22.

✳ Where to Eat

DINING OUT

In Tifton

✍ 🍴 ♿ **Charles Seafood** (229-382-9696), 711 Carpenter Road North. Open 11–2 Monday through Saturday; 5–9 Monday, 5–10 Tuesday through Saturday. Although the restaurant is casual, it offers the most upscale dining in town. No smoking. Wheelchair accessible. Lunch $5–7, dinner $5–10.

EATING OUT

In Ashburn

✍ 🍴 ♿ **Last Meal Café** (229-567-9696; 1-800-471-9696; www.jailmuseum.com), 241 East College Street. Open 11 AM–1 PM Tuesday through Saturday. There is a long-standing tradition of allowing death-row inmates to request a lavish last meal. The café, located at the **Crime and Punishment Museum** (see *To See—Museums*), serves desserts to die

for (just be glad you don't have to) as well as other favorite Southern dishes. No smoking. Wheelchair accessible. $6.

In Tifton

✍ 🍴 ♿ **Bubba's Ribs & Q** (229-386-2888), 1629 Tift Avenue North. Open 10–1 Monday, 10:30–8:30 Tuesday through Saturday. Barbecue ribs as well as barbecue pork, beef, and chicken sandwiches lead the menu at this casual eatery, but diners also can choose among steaks and other items. No smoking. Wheelchair accessible. $3.65–8.75.

✍ 🍴 ♿ **Giggles Café** (229-382-7997), 3323 US 82 West Open 10–2 Monday through Saturday. This casual eatery serves an array of homemade soups, salads, sandwiches, wraps, and desserts. No smoking. Wheelchair accessible. $2–6.25.

✍ 🍴 ♿ **La Cabana Mexican Restaurant** (229-382-1011), 211 Main Street South. Open 11–10 Monday through Saturday, 11–9 Sunday. This casual eatery serves authentic Mexican cuisine. No smoking. Wheelchair accessible. $5–7.

✳ Entertainment

ARTS Colquitt County Arts Center (229-985-1922), 401 Seventh Avenue SW, Moultrie. Open 9–5 Monday through Thursday, 9–3 Friday. The 1929 Moultrie High School was restored to create this entertainment center. Throughout the year the center stages art exhibits, theatrical performances, and other arts programs. Free admission to building; call for a schedule of events and ticket prices.

MUSIC Arts and Entertainment Series, First Tuesday Series, Stafford Steinway Series (AE and

Steinway Series 229-291-4820; First Tuesday Series 229-391-4943; www.abac.edu/arts). In collaboration with several arts groups, the Tifton–Tift County Arts Council presents an annual series of dance, music, and stage plays performed by artists from all over the world. Performances are held at the Chapel of All Faiths, Howard Auditorium on the campus of Abraham Baldwin Agricultural College, the Tift County High School Performing Arts Center, and other venues. Call for a schedule of events. $5–15.

THEATER Tift Theater for the Performing Arts (229-386-5150; 229-391-3903), 318 Main Street, Tifton. The art deco–style theater in the heart of downtown Tifton was built in 1937 with a Carrara glass facade embellished with neon lights. Fully restored, the theater now hosts local and traveling musical and theatrical performances, pageants, and big-screen movies. Call for a schedule of events and ticket prices.

✳ Selective Shopping

ANTIQUES Moultrie's Antiques Trail (229-890-5455; 1-888-40-VISIT; www.moultriega.com), downtown Moultrie. Open Monday through Saturday; hours vary. Moultrie bills itself as "the Antique Capital of South Georgia" and boats more than 36 antiques dealers purveying middle- to upper-end merchandise.

CLOTHING Hancock's Western Wear (229-985-2652; 229-985-2131), 1331 US 319 North, Moultrie. Open 9–6 weekdays, 9–5 Saturday. Located at the Rafter H. Rodeo Arena (see *To See— Equestrian Events*), the store purveys western boots, jeans, hats, and shirts.

FOOD Calhoun Produce (229-273-1887; www.calhounproduce.com), 5075 Hawpond Road, Ashburn. Open 8–6 daily, March through December. Shoppers can choose from fresh fruits, vegetables, and gift baskets. Take a break from shopping for a treat of ice cream or lemonade.

State Farmer's Market (229-985-2131; 1-888-40-VISIT; www.moultriechamber.com), First Avenue SE, Moultrie. Open 7–6 Monday through Saturday year-round. Locals and visitors can purchase fresh seasonal produce directly from local farmers. It's also a popular place to purchase a Christmas tree in December.

Sumner Pecan Groves (229-546-4322; 1-800-647-0811; www.sumnerpecans.com), 416 North Broad Street, Lenox. Open daily, November through February. V. B. Godwin

THE 1937 TIFT THEATER FOR PERFORMING ARTS HAS BEEN COMPLETELY RESTORED.

THE LOVE AFFAIR FINE ARTS FESTIVAL FEATURES PLENTY OF HANDS-ON ACTIVITIES FOR PARTICIPANTS.

began planting this pecan orchard in 1916, and it's still going strong. Free.

OUTLET STORES King Frog Factory Outlet (229-896-4848), 1203 West Fourth Street, Adel. Open 9–6 Monday through Saturday, 11–5 Sunday. The Green Frog is a landmark travelers rely on to locate the factory-direct outlet stores representing 100 brand names in clothing, shoes, and accessories.

✳ Special Events

March: **Arts in Black Festival** (Abraham Baldwin Arts Connection, 229-391-4820). In Tifton, African and African American heritage is showcased, including music, poetry, storytelling, dance, drums, foods, and crafts. Free.

Fire Ant Festival (229-386-0216). Held on the fourth Saturday of March in Ashburn, this hilarious tribute to south Georgia's nemesis features a car

and bike show, pet parade, art show, strawberry cook-off, beauty pageant, photography contest, and entertainment. Free.

March and November: **Calico Arts and Crafts Shows** (229-985-1968). Artists at more than 300 booths at this Moultrie event show and sell handmade arts and crafts. Adults $5; younger than 12 free.

April: **Spring Folk Life and Bluegrass Festival** (229-386-3848; 1-800-767-1875). The fiddlers' jamboree at the **Georgia Agrirama Living History Museum** (see *To See—Museums*) in Tifton features bluegrass, country, and gospel music; arts and crafts; 1800s games; and demonstrations of old-time skills and activities. The turpentine still operates during this festival, too. Included with museum admission; fees for some activities.

May: **Love Affair Fine Arts Festival** (Abraham Baldwin Arts Connection,

229-391-4820; www.abac.edu/arts/ LoveAffair). The renowned three-day cultural arts extravaganza, which is presented in Fulwood Park and other historic downtown Tifton venues, features quality visual and performing arts. Other events include hands-on activities for children, heritage crafts demonstrations, and strolling performers. The "Concert and Picnic under the Stars" held on Saturday night features a nationally known musical group. Festival admission free; concert tickets: general-admission lawn and bleacher seats $10, table $300.

August: **Southern Wildlife and Outdoor Expo** (229-985-2131; 1-888-40-VISIT). This three-day weekend event in Moultrie celebrates the beauty of the region and the diversity of outdoor activities. Visitors will see and experience the Outfitters Marketplace, outdoor equipment, a petting zoo, skeet and trapshooting, archery, fly-fishing and hunting-dog demonstrations, a rock-climbing wall, exhibits about wildlife conservation, live animal exhibits and shows, the Georgia Conservancy Kids Nature Niche, and juried wildlife fine arts. Multiday pass: adults $6, children 6–11 $4.

October: **Sunbelt Agricultural Exposition** (229-386-0216). Like an old-fashioned county fair on steroids, this Moultrie festival, the largest agricultural expo in North America, features livestock exhibits, stock-dog sheep and cattle trials, alpaca and equine demonstrations, an antique tractor parade, hot-air balloon flights, entertainment, and hunting and fishing demonstrations. Visitors see the wares of more than 1,000 exhibitors. Adults $6; children under 6 free.

December: **Hometown Holiday Celebration** (www.tiftonhometownholidays.com; or contact Tifton–Tift County Tourism Association, 229-386-0216; www.tifttourism.com). A parade, musical performances, live nativity scene, breakfast with Santa, the Candy Cane Express to Fulwood Park's Wonderland Tour of Lights, a tree lighting, arts and crafts, a tour of homes, and the Hall of Trees and Gingerbread Houses at the Museum of Art and Heritage set the mood for the holiday season in Tifton. Some events free; concert $15; tour of homes $10; breakfast with Santa: adults $3, children $2.

VALDOSTA AND THE OKEFENOKEE SWAMP

Valdosta, which is only 18 miles north of the Georgia–Florida border, is named after an estate owned by former Georgia Governor George Troup. The name is believed to have been derived from "Val de Aosta," a district in the Alpine Mountains of Italy. The English translation is "Vale of Beauty." The city certainly lives up to its name with an abundance of flowering azaleas—which have earned Valdosta the nickname "the Azalea City"—as well as gardens blooming throughout the spring and summer.

Valdosta is also known as "Winnersville" because it is the home of the winningest high school football team in the nation. The city, the 10th largest in Georgia, is recognized as the business, cultural, leisure, medical, and retail hub for an 11-county area of south Georgia and north Florida. Another claim to fame is that Valdosta was the boyhood home of notorious outlaw John Henry (Doc) Holliday. His home still exists, but it is a private residence.

Valdosta State University is an integral part of cultural life in Valdosta, presenting theatrical and musical productions and opening its art gallery to the public.

The small towns in this chapter offer attractions, outdoor recreation, special lodgings and restaurants, and fairs and festivals.

THE AZALEA CITY

R. J. Drexel came to Valdosta as its parks superintendent in 1925. He planted azaleas along city streets, in the cemetery, on church grounds, and around government buildings, and each spring he would give five azalea plants to citizens who wanted them. Later the Garden Club sold azaleas for 10 cents each to raise money for the purchase and renovation of the Crescent, a historic home that serves as its headquarters (see *To See—Historic Homes and Sites*). Drexel Park, at Brookwood Drive and Patterson Street, is named in R. J. Drexel's honor, and the Azalea Trail is a scenic driving route through the most beautiful azalea areas (see *To See—Scenic Drives*). One of the biggest events in the community is the Valdosta–Lowndes County Azalea Festival (see Special Events).

GUIDANCE If you are planning a trip to the Valdosta-Remerton area, contact the **Valdosta–Lowndes County Conference Center and Tourism Authority** (229-245-0513; 1-800-569-TOUR; www.valdostatourism.com), 1 Meeting Place, Valdosta 31601. Open 8–5 weekdays. While there, get a brochure for the **Valdosta Historic Driving Tour** (see *To See—Scenic Drives*). When you arrive in the area, visit the **Georgia Visitor Information Center–Valdosta** (229-559-5828), 5584 Mill Store Road, Lake Park 31636. Open 8:30–5 daily.

For information about Fargo and Homerville, contact the **Clinch County Chamber of Commerce** (912-487-2360), 23 West Plant Avenue, Homerville 31634.

To learn more about Hahira, contact **Hahira Better Hometown** (229-794-2567; 229-794-2330; www.hahira.ga.us), 102 South Church Street, Hahira 31632. Open 8–1 weekdays.

To find out about Lake Park, consult the **Lake Park Chamber of Commerce** (229-559-5302), 5208 Jewell Sutch Road, Lake Park 31636. Open 9–5 weekdays.

GETTING THERE *By air:* **Valdosta Regional Airport** (229-333-1833), 1750 Airport Road, Valdosta, is served by **Atlantic Southeast Airline**. Car rentals are available on-site from **Avis** (229-242-4242) and **Hertz** (229-242-7070).

The nearest large commercial airport served by several airlines is **Tallahassee Regional Airport** (850-891-7802; www.ci.tallahassee.fl.us/citytlh/aviation), 3300 Capital Circle SW, Suite 1, Tallahassee, Florida. The airport is served by **Continental Express, Delta Air Lines, Delta Connection/Atlantic Southeast Airlines, Delta Connection/Chautauqua Air Lines, Delta Connection/Comair, Northwest Airlink,** and **US Airways Express**. On-site car rentals are offered by **Alamo** (1-800-462-5266), **Avis** (1-800-331-1212), **Dollar** (850-575-4255), **Enterprise** (850-575-0603), **Hertz** (1-800-654-3131), and **National** (1-800-227-7368). Off-site car rentals are available from **Budget** (1-800-527-7000) and **Thrifty** (850-576-7368).

By bus: Service is provided by **Greyhound Lines** (229-242-8575; 1-800-231-2222; www.greyhound.com), 200 North Oak Street, Valdosta.

By car: These cities and towns are easily accessible from I-75. Other north-south routes are US 129 and US 441; east-west access is via US 84.

By train: The nearest **Amtrak** (1-800-USA-RAIL; www.amtrak.com) station is 27 miles away at 1000 South Range Street in Madison, Florida, which is on the *Sunset Limited* coast-to-coast route with three trains per week.

GETTING AROUND In addition to the car rental companies at the airport (see *Getting There—By Air*), car rentals are also available in Valdosta from **Buggy Works Rent-A-Car** (229-247-5556), 4154 North Valdosta Road; **Enterprise** (229-241-8560), 803 North Ashley Street; and **Thrifty** (229-241-7368), 2704 Bemiss Road.

MEDICAL EMERGENCY In Valdosta, **South Georgia Medical Center** (229-333-1000; www.sgmc.org), 2501 North Patterson Street, offers emergency and urgent-care services and many other medical services. Care is also available at **Smith Northview Hospital** (229-671-2000), 4280 North Valdosta Road.

NEIGHBORHOODS AND VILLAGES Valdosta has several National Register Historic Districts: Brookwood North Historic District, Valdosta Commercial Historic District, East End Historic District, Fairview Historic District, and midtown's North Patterson Street Historic District. Of particular interest is the **Fairview Historic District,** which concentrates on River, Varnedoe, and Wells streets and Central Place downtown. The village of Fairview predates the incorporation of the city of Valdosta. The neighborhood underwent three primary periods of development: 1840–1860; the late 1890s Victorian era, when opulent homes were built; and the 1910–1920s period of Prairie and Craftsman influence.

The small town of **Fargo** east of Valdosta in Clinch County is the western entrance to Okefenokee Swamp through **Stephen C. Foster State Park.** Be sure to visit Billy's Island, one of the best boating and hiking spots in the park.

Hahira, just 11 miles north of Valdosta, is the gateway to the city from the north. This small town hosts several popular annual events, including a **River Run Equestrian Ride** the weekend before Thanksgiving and the **Honey Bee Festival** in October (see *Special Events*).

Lake Park is located 14 miles south of Valdosta. The area is characterized by pine trees and crystal-clear lakes as far as the eye can see. Lake Park is replete with natural beauty, rich history, and year-round shopping and recreation.

The **Okefenokee Swamp**, one of the most intriguing areas in Georgia (or in the country, for that matter), features moss-laden cypress trees reflecting off black swamp waters. Visitors to the **Okefenokee National Wildlife Refuge** can view alligators, turtles, raccoons, black bears, deer, and other creatures from elevated boardwalks, on guided boat trips, or by renting motorboats or canoes.

Remerton was named for Remer Young Lane, president of Valdosta's first bank. The village was established in 1899 to meet the needs of workers at the Strickland Cotton Mills. The mill owned the houses in Remerton and would rent their rooms for 25 cents each. A two-street stretch of preserved houses at Baytree Place and Plum Street now teems with antiques and specialty shops and restaurants. Although the former mill village is now surrounded by the city of Valdosta, it still has its own government and law enforcement.

✳ To See

CULTURAL SITES ✐ 🐾 ♿ **Annette Howell Turner Center for the Arts** (229-247-2787; www.turner-center.org or www.lvac.org), 527 North Patterson Street, Valdosta. Open 10–6 Tuesday through Thursday, 10–4 Friday and Saturday, 1–4 Sunday. Operated by the Lowndes-Valdosta Arts Commission, the center has art galleries and is the home of the Little Actor's Theater, where children put on several productions each

ALL SORTS OF GREENERY GROWS IN THE OKEFENOKEE SWAMP.

year. In addition to four rotating galleries that feature new exhibits each month, the permanent gallery has a collection of East African art. The center also sponsors a spring festival and summer art camps. Free; donations accepted.

HISTORIC HOME AND SITES ✿ ⚹ **Barber-Pittman House** (229-247-8100; www.valdostachamber.com), 416 North Ashley Street, Valdosta. Open 9–5 weekdays. This imposing, white-columned neoclassical home, considered to be one of the most outstanding examples of architectural design in the Southeast, was built in 1915 for E. R. Barber, an inventor and the first bottler of Coca-Cola outside Atlanta. When the house was threatened with demolition, Ola Barber Pittman, the original builder's daughter, bequeathed it to the citizens of Valdosta with a provision that it not be sold. Mrs. Pittman died in 1977, the mansion was restored by local architects and the Valdosta Junior Women's Club in 1979, and it now serves as the home of the **Valdosta–Lowndes County Chamber of Commerce** (see *Guidance*). Visitors are welcome to see the beautiful interior architectural features as well as the original light fixtures, admire the original family furnishings, and stroll the formal gardens. Free.

✿ **The Crescent** (229-244-6747), 904 North Patterson Street, Valdosta. Open 2–5 weekdays or by appointment. Neoclassical in design, the Crescent, built in 1898 by U.S. Senator William Stanley West, acquired its name from the distinctive semicircular portico supported by 13 Doric columns representing the 13 original colonies. The Crescent is Valdosta's most recognized landmark. Rescued from demolition in 1951, it is now the home of the Garden Club of Valdosta and is the scene of many weddings and other special events. At the 23-room mansion, the grand staircase, ballroom, original pieces, and period antiques give a glimpse into turn-of-the-20th-century sophistication. The grounds boast beautiful test gardens, an octagonal schoolhouse, and a quaint chapel. Free, donations accepted.

MUSEUMS ✿ ⚹ **Lowndes County Historical Society and Museum** (229-247-4780; www.valdostamuseum.org), 305 West Central Avenue, Valdosta. Open 10–5 weekdays, 10–2 Saturday. Housed in a historic Carnegie library built in 1913, the museum's exhibits display an extensive collection of artifacts from early Lowndes County families, including historical photographs, documents, costumes, and more. Special displays tell about the local hospital, Moody Air Force Base, and prominent local families. There is also an extensive genealogical library available for research. Free.

SCENIC DRIVES **The Azalea Trail,** available from the Valdosta–Lowndes County Conference Center and Tourism Authority (229-245-0513; 1-800-569-TOUR; www.valdostatourism.com), 1 Meeting Place, Valdosta. The map leads visitors past the most cultivated azalea areas in the city.

Valdosta Historic Driving Tour, available from the Valdosta–Lowndes County Convention and Visitors Bureau (229-245-0513; 1-800-569-TOUR, www.valdostatourism.com), 1 Meeting Place, Valdosta. The tour leads visitors past 56 historic sites, including the early 1900s courthouse, stately homes, churches, and a cemetery.

✳ To Do

BICYCLING Relatively flat terrain and wide-open spaces mean that there are many opportunities for bike riding. The nine-county area is developing a comprehensive bicycle and pedestrian plan to make the region more biker-friendly. As state roads are resurfaced, a 6-foot-wide bike lane is being added, and 4-foot-wide lanes are being added within the city.

BIRDING Opportunities abound for bird-watching. Particularly favorable watching can be found at **Stephen C. Foster State Park, Grand Bay Wildlife Management Area,** and the **Okefenokee National Wildlife Refuge** (see *Green Space—Nature Preserves and Parks*).

BOATING See **Stephen C. Foster State Park, Grand Bay Wildlife Management Area,** and the **Okefenokee National Wildlife Refuge** under *Green Space—Nature Preserves and Parks.*

FISHING See **Stephen C. Foster State Park, Grand Bay Wildlife Management Area,** and the **Okefenokee National Wildlife Refuge** under *Green Space—Nature Preserves and Parks.*

FOR FAMILIES ✐ ᕒ **Wild Adventures Theme Park** (229-219-7080; 1-800-808-0872; www.wildadventures.net), 3766 Old Clyattsville Road, Valdosta. Open year-round; hours vary by season—generally open daily March through Labor Day, Friday through Monday rest of the year, but call ahead to be sure. Splash Island Water Park open during regular park hours March through September, weekends in October. Although this is a family-owned regional park, its 56 rides, including nine roller coasters and five water rides in the new Splash Island

A ROLLER COASTER AT WILD ADVENTURES THEME PARK IN VALDOSTA

Water Park, vie with national theme parks. Splash Island features the five-story Rain Fortress, an interactive wet play area with 21 platforms and various slides. The Safari Train Ride permits views of many of the 500 wild animals scattered in natural habitats throughout the park. Adventure Quest, for which there is an additional fee, is a park-within-a-park with an 18-hole adventure golf course, climbing wall, game arcade, and Go-Kart raceway. Up to a dozen entertainment shows each day may include acrobats, musical revues, and western melodramas. National headliners—from Christian to country, pop to R&B—take the stage at the All-Star Amphitheater. General seating is included in park admission, and visitors are encouraged to bring their own lawn chairs so they can watch the concerts in comfort. Reserved seating under the pavilion is an additional $10–20 depending on the show. Shows such as "Wild Adventures on Ice" are presented at the skating rink. The Lone Star Bar-B-Que restaurant, snack concessions, and several gift shops are on-site. Adults $38.95, seniors and children 3–9 $31.95; second-day free pass for regular-priced tickets. Reduced-price twilight pass after 5 PM on nights when park is open until 10. The Passport, a season pass, permits unlimited admission to the park and to Cypress Gardens in Florida. Parking $7, RV $9.

FRIGHTS ✐ 🐾 ♿ **Wild Adventures Phobia** (229-219-7080; 1-800-808-0872; www.wildadventures.net), 3766 Old Clyattsville Road, Valdosta. At 6:30 PM Thursday through Sunday, September 30 through Halloween Night. The theme park puts a new face on fear with haunted houses, fearsome forests, a terrifying train ride, and other ghastly delights. If you're brave enough, you'll experience the Dominion of the Dead haunted house inhabited by the Grim Reaper, vampires, and the living dead. The other haunted house, Hotel Doom, features 3-D visions of sinister clowns and crazed circus animals. The Terror Train takes you on a frightful journey to the unknown. Throughout the park, menacing characters and ghastly sights and sounds keep you on edge. Even the entertainment takes a dark turn. Boo House features friendlier Halloween fun for the small fry. Shops and restaurants hand out treats, too. Price included in park admission (see **Wild Adventures Theme Park** under *For Families*).

GOLF See Golf Appendix.

HIKING See **Stephen C. Foster State Park, Grand Bay Wildlife Management** Area, and the **Okefenokee National Wildlife Refuge** under *Green Space— Nature Preserves and Parks*.

HORSEBACK RIDING CAMPS ✐ **KB Horse Camp** (229-794-3598), 5548 Bent Creek Circle, Hahira. Three sessions of summer camps, Saturday through Friday; camp also offered during spring break. Call for a schedule of camps. Campers learn to care for a horse, horsemanship skills, barrel racing, and pole bending. Other activities include roping, trail rides, a campfire, and visits to a western store and a horse auction. The week culminates with a rodeo. In addition, the facility offers private and group lessons throughout the year. $400 for day camp, $550 for overnight camp.

WALKING TOURS The Camellia Trail (229-333-5800), Georgia Avenue. Open daily. Take a leisurely stroll along the 3,000-foot trail on the campus of Valdosta State University, which was begun in 1944. During the fall through spring camellia season, more than 430 varieties of camellias are showcased within a longleaf pine grove. A memorial gateway honors the collection's founder, Jewell Whitehead, who was known as "the Camellia Lady." Free.

RENTAL CANOES AT STEPHEN C. FOSTER STATE PARK

✳ Green Space

NATURE PRESERVES AND PARKS ✍ 🏵 **Grand Bay Wildlife Management Area** (229-245-8160), Bemiss Road, Valdosta. Open Saturday and Sunday year-round. The site is composed of 1,350 acres within a 13,000-acre wetlands system, the second-largest natural blackwater cypress-blackgum wetland in the Coastal Plain of Georgia after the Okefenokee Swamp. The preserve is open year-round for fishing, canoeing, hiking, bird and wildlife observation, camping, and deer and small-game hunting. Most access and activities free.

✍ 🏵 ♿ **Okefenokee National Wildlife Refuge** (912-496-7836; www.fws.gov/okefenokee), Folkston (see the Waycross chapter in 2, The Coast). The 680-square-mile wetland wilderness provides crucial habitat for wildlife. For humans, the refuge offers boating, canoeing and kayaking, fishing, camping, wildlife observation, bicycling, hiking, and guided tours. (For much more information about the swamp, see the Waycross chapter in 2, The Coast.) In this area, access to the swamp is through **Stephen C. Foster State Park.**

✍ 🏵 ♿ 🐾 **Stephen C. Foster State Park** (912-637-5274; 1-800-864-7275; www.gastateparks.org/info/scfoster), 17515 GA 177, Fargo. Open 7–7 in fall and winter, 6:30–8:30 in spring and summer. (Because the park is located within the Okefenokee National Wildlife Refuge, the gates are locked at closing.) One of the primary entrances to the primordial Okefenokee Swamp,this remote 80-acre park is named for songwriter Stephen Foster. There is a 1.5-mile Trembling Earth Nature Trail as well as 25 miles of day-use waterways. Canoe and fishing boat rentals are available and private boats are permitted, though there is a 10-horsepower limit. There is a boat ramp for launching, too. Fishing is popular, but don't trail your catch behind the boat; you'll attract alligators. Accommodations are available in cottages and at the campgrounds (see *Lodging*). Stop at the park's new **Suwannee River Interpretive Center** on US 441 to watch a short film about the swamp and to see exhibits and live animals. The building itself has won an award for its environmentally responsible construction. State park parking/day-use fee $3; guided boat tours $6–8.

✳ Lodging

BED & BREAKFASTS

In Valdosta
Fairview Inn Bed and Breakfast
(229-244-6456; www.fairviewinn.info),
416 River Street. Located in the historic Fairview neighborhood, one of Valdosta's oldest, the commodious inn takes visitors back to the opulence of the late 1800s. Five uniquely decorated guest rooms feature modern amenities such as cable television, BOSE CD radios, high-speed Internet access, and hair dryers. A full breakfast is served 7–9 AM. Guests can choose to enjoy their repast in the Old World dining room or the cozy kitchen. The inn is within walking distance of the **Lowndes County Historical Society Museum** (see *To See—Museums*), the historic courthouse, and downtown shops. Smoking outside only. Not wheelchair accessible. $85–125.

CAMPGROUNDS

In Fargo
Stephen C. Foster State Park (912-637-5274; 1-800-864-7275; www.ga stateparks.org/info/scfoster), 17515 GA 177, Fargo. The park offers 66 tent, trailer, and RV sites as well as a pioneer campground. $17–22; $40 for pioneer campground.

See also Campgrounds Appendix.

COTTAGES AND CABINS

In Fargo
Stephen C. Foster State Park (912-637-5274; 1-800-864-7275; www.ga stateparks.org/info/scfoster), 17515 GA 177, Fargo. The park features nine fully equipped cottages. $70–90.

✳ Where to Eat

DINING OUT

In Valdosta
&. **The Bistro Restaurant and Piano Bar** (229-253-1253), 130 North Ashley Street. Open 5–10 Monday through Saturday. The Bistro features fine dining. Its French/American-inspired cuisine includes Angus beef, seafood, chicken, lamb, sashimi tuna, and pasta. No smoking. Wheelchair accessible. $14.95–24.95.

&. **Charlie Tripper's Fine Food and Fruits of the Vine** (229-247-0366; www.charlie-trippers.com), 4479 North Valdosta Road. Open 6–10 Tuesday through Saturday; bar opens at 5. In this four-star, casual-but-fashionable restaurant, intimate dining is assured in small rooms with white table linens and low lighting. The eclectic decor features exposed brick accented with artwork and memorabilia. Entrées include Angus beef, fillets, rib eye, New Zealand lamb, pork, and seafood. Vegetarian plates can be requested. Save room for decadent desserts such as bananas Foster, bread pudding, crème brûlée, cobblers, and tarts. No smoking. Wheelchair accessible. $16.95–25.95.

🍴 &. **Gulio's Greek-Italian Restaurant** (229-333-0929), 105 East Ann Street. Open at 5 PM Tuesday through Saturday. A beautiful setting in a turn-of-the-20th-century home sets the scene for European-inspired cuisine specializing in seafood and char-broiled steaks. Gulio's is not too formal, however. You're just as likely to see jeans as tuxedos. No smoking. Wheelchair accessible. $9–17.

&. **Hannah's Restaurant and Piano Bar** (229-219-0185), 1403 North St. Augustine Road. Open at 5 PM Tuesday through Saturday. Located in the Best Western King of the Road, this fine-dining restaurant offers Angus steaks, seafood, chicken, pasta, nightly specials, and homemade desserts. No smoking. Wheelchair accessible. $11–25.

& **Lulu's Restaurant** (229-242-4000), 132 North Patterson Street. Open 11–2 Tuesday through Friday, 5:30–9 Tuesday through Saturday. Upscale American fine dining features entrées such as curried shrimp, tuna steak, and stuffed pork loin. No smoking. Wheelchair accessible. Lunch $7.95–15.95, dinner $11.95–25.95.

& **The Ravine Grille and Dinner House Restaurant** (229-219-2325), 3374 US 84 West. Open 11–5 Monday through Saturday; 5–10 Monday through Thursday, 5–11 Friday and Saturday; happy hour 4–7 Monday through Saturday. Located at the Kinderlou Forest Golf Club, the restaurant offers fine dining in a casual atmosphere. Fillet, grouper, flounder, combos, oysters, salads, and pasta are featured. Both indoor and outdoor dining afford beautiful views of the course. No smoking. Wheelchair accessible. Lunch $8–14, dinner $18–25.

EATING OUT

In Lake Park

& & **Bayou Bill's South Cajun Grill** (229-559-5820), 234 Lakes Boulevard. Open 4 PM–2 AM Monday through Saturday. The eatery specializes in crawfish, raw oysters, sandwiches, steaks, daily drink specials, and nightly entertainment. Smoking allowed. Wheelchair accessible. Entrée $4.95–14.95; cover charge $5–10 when there are live bands.

In Valdosta

& & **CJ's Pub and Pool** (229-333-0903), 1201 Baytree Road. Open 11 AM–3 AM daily. It's always a party here with Gandy pool tables, 20 televisions, and a famous horseshoe bar. Steaks, pizza, seafood, burgers, sandwiches, soups, and salads are served for lunch, dinner, and late-night snacks. Smoking allowed. Wheelchair accessible. Lunch $5.95–12.95, dinner $10.95–25.

& & & **Covington's** (229-242-2261; www.covingtonscatering.com), 310 North Patterson Street. Open 11–2 Monday through Saturday. Covington's serves soups such as creamy crab as well as appetizers, salads, sandwiches, pasta, lasagna, quesadillas, fish, quiche, and desserts. No smoking. Wheelchair accessible. Breakfast $2–3.75, lunch $5.50–7.95.

& & & **Two Friends Café and Market** (229-242-3282; www.twofriendscafe.com), 3338-B Country Club Road. Open 8 AM–2 PM Tuesday through Friday, 11 AM–3 PM Saturday; market open 10 AM–6 PM Tuesday through Friday, 10 AM–4 PM Saturday. The café offers light breakfast items such as a sweet-potato biscuit with baked ham, homemade granola, muffins, and fruit. Lunch includes the specialty hot baked chicken salad as well as soups, salads, sandwiches, appetizers, and desserts. Take-out items include breads, desserts, casseroles, salads, pastas, quiches, lasagna, jambalaya, pot pie, meat loaf, and appetizers. No smoking. Wheelchair accessible. Breakfast $2–3.75, lunch $6.95–8.95.

✷ Entertainment

MUSIC **Valdosta Symphony Orchestra** (229-333-5804; www.valdosta.edu/music). Four concerts presented annually November to May. The group consists of Valdosta State University faculty as well as students and professional musicians from the community. Guest artists are often featured, and a youth orchestra also performs. Concerts are held in the Fine Arts Building on the Valdosta State University campus. Call for a schedule of performances and ticket prices.

NIGHTLIFE & **Bayou Bill's North Cajun Grill** (229-241-8825), 1811 Jerry Jones Drive, Valdosta. Open 4 PM–2 AM Monday through Saturday. Although a sibling to **Bayou Bill's South** in Lake Park (see *Where to Eat—Eating Out*), this casual eatery serves mainly wings, appetizers, and raw oysters. Bayou Bill's North is known for daily drink specials and nightly entertainment. Smoking allowed. Wheelchair accessible. Cover charge $5 when there is live entertainment.

& **Bungalow's Bar & Grill** (229-253-1760), 1919 Baytree Place, Valdosta. Open 4 PM–3 AM Tuesday through Thursday, noon–3 AM Friday, noon–midnight Saturday, 11–midnight Sunday. Housed in a converted mill worker's home, the facility offers live bands, a big-screen television, pool tables, and darts. Smoking allowed. Wheelchair accessible. Cover charge depends on the group playing.

Loozie Anna's (229-219-7700), 1915 Baytree Road, Valdosta. Open 4 PM–3 AM Monday through Saturday, 4 PM–midnight Sunday. The facility offers blues, Cajun food, a big-screen television, and an outside deck. Smoking allowed. Not wheelchair accessible. Weekend cover $3.

& **Maria's Lounge** (229-247-5302), 1828 East Park Avenue, Valdosta.

Open 7 PM–3 AM Friday and Saturday. The facility offers classic rock and modern country bands, Latin music on Saturday nights, and casino-type games. Smoking allowed. Wheelchair accessible. Cover charge $5.

& **Mikki's** (229-242-3248), 402 Northside Drive, Valdosta. Open 4 PM–2 AM weeknights, 3 PM–2 AM Saturday, 4 PM–midnight Sunday. In addition to live bands, Mikki's offers a big-screen television, pool tables, and darts. Smoking allowed. Wheelchair accessible. Cover charge $5.

THEATER **The Dosta Playhouse** (229-247-8243), 122 North Ashley Street, Valdosta. The art moderne structure, built in 1941, reflects the era just after the Great Depression. Free of much ornamentation, the theater still features glass bricks, porthole windows, and curved corners created to celebrate cruise ships and the automobile. The theater is home to **Theatre Guild-Valdosta,** which presents four main shows and two children's productions each year. Call for a schedule of performances and ticket prices.

Peach State Summer Theater (229-259-7770). The nine-week summer season features three musicals in rotating repertory. Call for a schedule. Performances take place at the Sawyer Theater in the Valdosta State University Fine Arts Building. The professional summer-stock theater company is composed of 60 actors-singers and backup personnel. Previous visitors to Georgia may have experienced the works of this group in its former incarnation as the Jekyll Island Musical Theatre Festival. Tickets $10–20.

Valdosta State University Theatre (229-333-5973; www.valdosta.edu/

comarts/thaseason.html). The theater arts program at the university presents a seven-production season. Call for a schedule of performances. Plays with a small number of actors are presented in the intimate Lab Theatre; larger-scale works are presented in the Sawyer Theatre. Adults $8, seniors $7, children $6; VSU students free.

✳ Selective Shopping
Remerton Village (Plum Street and Baytree Place) in Valdosta features quaint restored mill houses now occupied by specialty shops that offer antiques, collectibles, crafts, a pottery, a coffeehouse, and several restaurants.

ANTIQUES Just off Main (229-794-1118), 103 North Lowndes Street, Hahira. Open 10–5 Tuesday through Saturday. Located in a restored home in the heart of Hahira, the shop sells antiques, furniture, lamps, accessories for the home, and vintage collectibles.

BOOKS Hildegard's (229-247-6802), 101 East Central Avenue, Valdosta. Open 8 AM–11 PM (kitchen open 8. AM–9 PM). The nonprofit bookstore/café features a coffee and tea lounge, deli, wireless Internet access, an art gallery, and performance space.

CLOTHING Country Cobbler (229-242-1430), 1737 Gornto Road, Valdosta. Open 10–9 Monday through Saturday, 1–6 Sunday. Every shoe lover's dream, this store carries a fine and large selection of women's and men's shoes from Steve Madden to Brighton at affordable prices.

FOOD South Georgia Pecan Gift Shop (229-244-0686; 1-800-627-6630), 403 East Hill Avenue, Valdos-

ta. Open 9–5 weekdays. The shop offers a wide variety of fresh nuts, syrups, gift baskets, and much more.

OUTLET STORES Lake Park Outlets (229-559-6822; 1-888-SHOP-333; www.lakeparkoutlets.com), 5327 Mill Store Road, Lake Park. Open 9–8 Monday through Saturday, 10–6 Sunday. Whether you're interested in fashion, gifts, or home accessories, choose from more than 48 famous designer names and national brands at this outlet center. Nestled within the larger factory center, **Farm House Plaza** features 14 shops selling china, books, diamonds and gold, carpets, and linens. The facility also offers an antiques and crafters mall with 125 dealers and a country restaurant.

✳ Special Events
March: **Valdosta–Lowndes County Azalea Festival** (229-247-2787; www.azaleafestival.com). Held in Valdosta's Drexel Park, the event features a parade, sporting events, circus, arts and crafts, musical entertainment, home tours, food, children's activities, and more. An international village displays costumes and exhibits while offering food and entertainment. There are also events in the weeks preceding the festival, including the Azalea Asian Cultural Experience Festival and an international extravaganza with bands, a parade of nations, entertainment, fireworks, and food. Parking is allowed in all Valdosta State University lots. Most events free; small participation fees for children's activities; $15–30 entry fee for race, ride, and fun walk/run.

October: **Hahira Honey Bee Festival** (229-794-3097; 229-794-2813;

www.hahira.ga.us). Sponsored by the Hahira Honey Bee Committee, the weeklong festival features live bee demonstrations, arts and crafts, gospel singing and other live entertainment, a 5K run, beauty pageant, dog show, climbing wall, and parade. Free parking at Pick-In Park on GA 122 West and free shuttle service by trolley. Free.

November: **Lowndes County–South Georgia Fair** (229-242-9316; www .valdostatourism.com). Held at the Lowndes County Civic Center in Valdosta, the fair features livestock shows, exhibits, booths, and carnival rides. Free.

Mid-November through December 30: **Wild Adventures Christmas Wonderland** (229-219-7080; www.wildadventures.net). For this, one of the South's largest holiday celebrations, the Wild Adventures Theme Park in Valdosta (see *To Do—For Families*) is transformed into a magical land filled with millions of dazzling lights, holiday displays, sounds of the season, a living nativity, and holiday shows. The Wonderland Express is a merry train ride and, of course, no visit would be complete without a visit with St. Nicholas. Included in regular park admission.

December 31 through February 28: **Snow Days at Wild Adventures** (229-219-7080; www.wildadventures .net). The festivities at Wild Adventures Theme Park in Valdosta (see *To Do—For Families*) begin with a New Year's Eve celebration, an alcohol-free event that features live concerts, laser shows, and amusement rides. Then, through the miracles of modern technology, south Georgians can enjoy ice skating, a toboggan run, snowman building, marshmallow roasts, and hot chocolate for the next two months. Included in regular park admission.

Appendix

AUTHORS' NOTE

Space limitations prohibited us from including all of Georgia's wonderful activities, attractions, campgrounds, fishing and hunting opportunities, golf courses, marinas and boat landings, and parks, which range from small city parks to vast wildlife refuges. Following are names, contact information, and a brief description of many more things to see and do in Georgia.

ATTRACTIONS TO SEE

1 Atlanta Metro

CULTURAL SITES

In Senoia

Pascova Wedding Chapel (770-599-0144), Pylant Street. Charming chapel has bell tower, original heart-pine floors, hand-carved pine pews, stained glass.

GARDENS

In Sharpsburg

Grandmother's Garden and Pathways of Gold Park (770-254-2627; www.coweta.ga.us), Main Street. Small park with flowers, fragrances, wildlife.

2 The Coast

CULTURAL SITES

On Jekyll Island

Jekyll Island Art Gallery, Goodyear Cottage (912-635-3920), 321 Riverview Drive. Changing exhibits in Goodyear Cottage, one of the magnificent homes in Jekyll Island National Historic Landmark District.

On St. Simons

Glynn Art Association (912-638-8770; www.glynnart.org), 319 Mallory Street. Exhibitions of work by local and regional artists.

Mildred Huie Museum at Mediterranean House (912-638-3057; 1-800-336-9469; www.landmarkscenes.com), 1819 Frederica Road. Memorabilia and works by Mildred Nix Huie—legendary Impressionist artist, sculptor, historian, and writer on St. Simons—displayed in 1929 historic home.

HISTORIC HOMES AND SITES

In St. Marys

McIntosh Sugar Mill Ruins (912-882-4000; 1-800-868-8687; www.stmaryswelcome.com), Charlie Smith Sr. Highway/Spur GA 40. Ruins of 1825 McIntosh Sugar Works mill.

Oak Grove Cemetery (912-882-4000; 1-800-868-8687; www.stmaryswelcome.com), Bartlett and Weed streets. Resting place of soldiers from America's wars, 1801 to present.

On St. Simons

Avenue of Oaks, Frederica Road at Retreat Plantation. Double rows of oak trees from mid-1800s mark entrance to Sea Island Golf Club.

Bloody Marsh Battle Site (912-638-3639; www.nps.gov/fofr), Demere Road. British victory over Spanish at this site in 1742.

Christ Church, Frederica (912-638-8683; www.christchurchfrederica.org), 6329 Frederica Road. Built in 1884 by Anson Phelps Dodge Jr.

Faith Chapel (912-635-4036), 181 Old Plantation Road. Chapel built in 1904 has one of only four signed Louis Comfort Tiffany stained-glass windows.

Gascoigne Bluff, Gascoigne Bluff Road. Area overlooking Frederica River was Native American campground, 16th-century Franciscan monastery, then naval base during colonial times.

MUSEUMS

On Cumberland Island

Ice House Museum (Mainland Visitor Information Center, 877-860-6787). Artifacts and photos dealing with island's history from Native Americans to Carnegie era.

In Folkston

Okefenokee Education and Research Center (912-496-7116), 500 Kingsland Drive. Okefenokee region's natural, cultural, and historical heritage.

Train Museum (912-496-2536; www.folkston.com), Folkston Railroad Depot, 202 West Main Street. Old railroad memorabilia.

On St. Simons

Arthur J. Moore Museum and Library (912-638-8688; www.epworthbythe sea.org), 100 Arthur J. Moore Drive. Located on grounds of Methodist retreat Epworth-by-the-Sea, museum displays items related to Wesley brothers in Georgia, Battle of Bloody Marsh, and colonial and plantation days.

3 Historical South

CULTURAL SITES

In Athens

Lamar Dodd School of Art Gallery (706-542-1511; www.art.uga.edu), Jackson Street. Revolving shows of student, faculty, and professional work.

Studio 2 (706-542-1511; www.visart.uga.edu), 257 West Broad Street. Revolving shows of work by faculty, students, and outside professionals.

Tate Student Center Gallery, Room 309 (706-542-6396; www.uga.edu/union), 153 Tate Student Center, University of Georgia campus. Rotating exhibits of student, local, and international artwork.

In Barnesville

Historic Carnegie Library and Cara Studios Art Gallery (770-358-3132;

www.carastudios.com), One Carnegie Way at Library and Greenwood Streets. Art exhibits, performances, gardens, outdoor sculpture.

In Lyons
New Deal Public Art (call City Hall, 912-526-6318), Lyons Post Office, US 1 North. Terra-cotta relief titled *Wild Duck and Deer* created by Albino Manca in 1942.

In Greensboro
Iron Horse, visible from GA 15. Two-ton public outdoor art.

GARDENS

In Athens
Horticulture Trial Garden (706-542-2471; www.ugatrial.hort.uga.edu), 1111 Plant Science Building, Department of Horticulture, University of Georgia. Ornamentals in seasonally rotating garden.

University of Georgia Arboretum (706-542-0842; www.uga.edu/hort/arboretum/ugacampusarboretum.htm), UGA campus. Diverse collection of trees, shrubs, plants. Brochure "Campus Arboretum Walking Tour of Trees" available at UGA Visitors Center.

University of Georgia Campus (UGA Visitors Center; 706-542-0842). Founders Memorial Garden, President's Club Garden on North Campus, Horticulture Trial Garden on South Campus.

HISTORIC HOMES AND SITES

In Augusta
Magnolia Cemetery (706-821-1746), 702 Third Street. Seven Civil War generals and 900 Confederate soldiers buried here.

In Griffin
Old Soldiers Confederate Cemetery, East Taylor Street. Two Union soldiers buried among 67 Confederate soldiers from 11 states.

In Jewell
Rock Mill Plantation (706-465-3285), Mayfield-Jewell Road. Federal-style historical residence; open by appointment only.

In Lincolnton
Lincoln County Historical Park (706-359-7970; www.lincolncountyga.org), 147 Lumber Street. Historic buildings brought from other locations to create park.

In Louisville
Revolutionary Cemetery, GA 24 West. Final resting place of many Revolutionary War soldiers.

In Macon
Neel Reid Federated Garden Clubs Center (478-742-0921; www.fgcmacon.org), 730 College Street. Four-story English Tudor home furnished with period pieces.

In Soperton
Troup's Tomb, GA 46. Elaborate granite memorial located on plantation of former Georgia Governor George M. Troup.

In Warrenton
Walk the Halls of History (706-465-2171; www.warrencountyga.org), Warren County Courthouse, 521 Main Street. Original artworks depicting local history and heritage.

In Washington
Kettle Creek Revolutionary War Battlefield (706-678-2013; www.washington wilkes.com/attractions.html), Warhill Road. A few gravestones mark where patriots defeated British troops in 1779, breaking British stranglehold on Georgia.

MUSEUMS

In Greensboro
Greene County Historical Society Museum (706-453-7592; 1-866-341-4466), 201 East Greene Street. Railroad memorabilia, Creek Indian artifacts, Rock Jail, L. L. Wyatt Museum (old sheriff's quarters).

In Lyons
Lyons Depot (call City Hall, 912-526-6318), US 280 at Victory Drive. Photographs of Lyons history.

In Milledgeville
Central State Hospital Museum (478-445-1757; www.centralstatehospital.org), Swint Avenue. Story of mental health treatment in this country, 160-year history of this hospital.

In Monticello
Dow's Pulpit Monument, GA 11 and GA 83, Monticello. Rock resembles a pulpit; it's reported that Georgia's famous walking evangelist, the Reverend Lorenzo Dow, preached here.

In Perry
Sam Nunn Exhibit (478-988-6200), 1100 Main Street. Memorabilia trace former U.S. senator's life from childhood in Perry to Washington, D.C.

In Sparta
Glen Mary Plantation (contact Sparta-Hancock Alliance for Revitalization and Empowerment, 706-444-7462), site at 183 Linton Road, Sparta. Grounds of Greek Revival raised cottage, mule barn, private cemetery.

In Thomaston
African-American Museum (706-647-9686), 460 Cedar Row. Authentic shotgun house contains furniture, artifacts.

Pettigrew-White-Stamps House (706-647-1488), 800 South Church Street. Built in 1833, this classically designed home is second-oldest house in Thomaston.

COVERED BRIDGES

In Homer

Blind Suzie (or Lula) Covered Bridge, Antioch Church Road. At only 34 feet in length, this is smallest covered bridge in Georgia and one of smallest in the country.

CULTURAL SITES

In Gainesville/Oakwood

Roy C. Moore Art Gallery (770-718-3707), Gainesville College, 3820 Mundy Mill Road, Oakwood. Touring exhibits and works of college's art majors.

In Hartwell

The Arts Center (706-377-2040), 338 East Howell Street. Regional and national fine arts and crafts.

FOR FAMILIES

In Dahlonega

George Coleman Planetarium (706-864-1471, ext. 1511; www.ngcsu.edu/Academic/Sciences/Planetarium/planetarium.htm), North Georgia College and State University, Sunset Drive.

HISTORIC HOMES AND SITES

In Cartersville

Allatoona Pass Battlefield (770-606-8862; www.allatoonapassbattlefield.org), Old Allatoona Road. Forts, trench works, interpretive trail markers.

In Cassville

Cassville Confederate Cemetery (770-387-1357; 1-800-733-2280; www.not atlanta.org), Cass-White Road. Grave sites of 300 Confederate soldiers.

In Dalton

Atlanta Campaign Pocket Park (706-270-9960; 1-800-331-3258; www.dalton-cvb.com), US 41 North off I-75 at exit 336. Historical markers, relief map show troop movements from Chattanooga to Atlanta.

Confederate Cemetery and Memorial Wall (706-270-9960; 1-800-331-3258; www.daltoncvb.com), West Hill Cemetery between Culyer and Emery streets. Final resting place of 421 Confederate and four unknown Union soldiers.

Joseph E. Johnston Statue (706-270-9960), Hamilton and Crawford streets. Only outdoor statue of Confederate General Joseph E. Johnston.

In Gainesville

Alta Vista Cemetery and Longstreet Gravesite (770-536-5209), 521 Jones Street at Jesse Jewel Parkway. Grave sites of two Georgia governors and Civil War Confederate General James Longstreet.

In Hartwell
Center of the World Monument, US 29 South. Site of Cherokee assembly ground.

Old Dan Tucker's Gravesite (contact Elbert Chamber: 706-283-5651; www.elbertga.com), Heardmont Road, Elberton. Methodist minister whose empathy and kindness toward slaves inspired the song.

In Resaca
Confederate Cemetery–Battle of Resaca (706-625-3200; 1-800-887-3811; www.georgiadivision.org; www.resacabattlefield.org), US 41 North and Confederate Road. Resting place of 450 Confederate soldiers. Battle reenacted each May.

In Ringgold
Old Stone Church Museum (706-935-5232), US 41 and GA 2. 1850 church houses Catoosa County Historical Museum, objects from county life.

In Rockmart
The Roundhouse (770-684-8426), 438 Jones Avenue. Oldest roundhouse in America as well as first cement house in Georgia.

In Rome
Myrtle Hill Cemetery (706-295-5576; 1-800-444-1834; www.romegeorgia.org), Myrtle Street. Final resting place of America's Known Soldier (World War I soldier Charles Graves); President Woodrow Wilson's wife, Ellen Axson Wilson; 377 Civil War soldiers.

In Winder
Russell Family Cemetery, GA 53. Home of late Senator Richard B. Russell and the family cemetery.

MUSEUMS

In Dalton
Georgia Athletic Coaches Association Hall of Fame (706-272-7676; 1-800-824-7469; www.nwgtcc.com), 2211 Dug Gap Battle Road. Likeness and biography of each Georgia high school coach who has been inducted.

In Hartwell
Hart County Historical Museum (706-376-6330), 31 East Howell Street. Located in Teasley-Holland House, museum is good source of county historical information.

NATURAL BEAUTY SPOTS

In Jasper
Burnt Mountain Overlook, Burnt Mountain Road. Breathtaking view of southern end of Appalachian Mountains.

WATERFALLS

In Dahlonega
Dick's Creek Falls (706-505-3485; 1-800-231-5543), call for directions.

Located in Chattahoochee National Forest at confluence of Waters and Dicks creeks.

In Helen

Horse Trough Falls (706-754-6221; www.fs.fed.us/conf), GA 75 and Forest Service Road 44. Short, level trail leads to beautiful falls.

In LaFayette/Villanow

Keown Falls near LaFayette and Villanow. Falls located in Keown Falls Scenic Area. Falls, wildlife, hiking.

5 Southern Rivers

CULTURAL SITES

In Bainbridge

Firehouse Center and Gallery (229-243-1010), 119 West Water Street. Only Mission-style public building in southwest Georgia; 1914 structure is home of Bainbridge–Decatur County Council for the Arts and Decatur County Historical Society.

FOR FAMILIES

In Warm Springs

Warm Springs Regional Fisheries Center and Aquarium (706-655-3382; www.warmsprings.fws.gov), 5308 Spring Street. Aquarium, boardwalk, environmental education unit, fish health and technology centers, national fish hatchery.

HISTORIC HOMES AND SITES

In Blakely

Confederate Flagpole (229-273-3741; www.blakelyearlychamber.com), North Main Street, on the square. Last known wooden Confederate flagpole, from 1861.

In Colquitt

Veterans Memorial Courtyard (229-758-6686), adjacent to Cotton Hall on East Main Street. Tribute to more than 1,900 Miller County veterans who served from Revolutionary to Gulf Wars.

In Valdosta

Sunset Cemetery, North Oak Street. Repository of mausoleums and memorials in landscaped park.

In Warm Springs

Roosevelt–Warm Springs Institute for Rehabilitation/Therapeutic Pools and Springs Complex (706-655-5000; www.rooseveltrehab.org), 6135 Roosevelt Highway. FDR established the institute in 1927. Complex has state-of-the-art rehab facilities as well as historic structures.

MUSEUMS

In Lumpkin/Richland

Richland Rail Museum (229-887-3323), 200 Broad Street. Late-1800s depot houses train-related memorabilia.

OTHER ACTIVITIES TO DO

1 Atlanta Metro

HORSEBACK RIDING

In Newnan
Blue Moon Equestrian Center (770-252-3300; www.bluemoonstables.net), 493 Boone Road. Riding, Raven's Ridge Riding Academy, arts and crafts, snack, lecture, horse movie day.

SKATING

In Jackson
Skate Park (770-775-8228; www.buttscountyrecreation.com/skatepark.html), 576 Ernest Biles Drive. Designed for skateboarders; two quarter-pipe ramps, two wedges, two platform wedges, two grind rails.

In Newnan
Skate Palace (770-254-1999; www.cityofnewnan.com/businesses/skatepalace/skatepalace.html), 195 Walt Sanders Memorial Drive. For standard, speed, and in-line skate enthusiasts. The center also offers Lazer Tag, a Bounce House, and the Dungeon Teen Dance Club.

SPAS

In McDonough
Scarlett's Retreat and Day Spa (678-432-7474; www.scarlettsretreat.com), 22 Jonesboro Road. Selected as *The Atlanta Journal-Constitution* Editor's Pick as "the Best Place to Get the Cares of the World Rubbed Away."

TENNIS

In McDonough
City parks with courts: **Richard Craig Park,** 125 Cedar Street; **Warren Holder Park,** 301 Club Drive; **Sandy Ridge Park,** 1200 Keys Ferry Road.

2 The Coast

BOAT EXCURSIONS

In Folkston
Okefenokee Pastimes (912-496-4472; www.okefenokee.com), GA 121 South. Ecotourism outfitter offers half-day, full-day, and night motor- and paddleboat tours.

In St. Marys
Electric Dream Tours (912-729-4448; www.electricdreamtours.com), 100-B St. Marys Street. Eco-, harbor, and sunset cruises.

In St. Marys

St. Marys Aquatic Center (912-673-8118; www.cia-st-marys.ga.us/aquatic.html), 301 Herb Bauer Drive. Small family water park.

GUIDED TOURS

In St. Marys

Historic St. Marys Tram Tours (912-882-4000; 1-800-868-8687; www.stmarys welcome.com), 406 Osborne Street. For groups—important sights in and around St. Marys.

On St. Simons

Marsh Tours (912-638-9354; www.marshtours.com), 310 Magnolia Avenue. Birding, dolphin watching, historical, and marsh ecosystem tours.

TENNIS

In Savannah

Bacon Park (912-351-3850), 6262 Skidaway Road; **Daffin Park** (912-351-3851), 1001 East Victory Drive; **Forsyth Park** (912-351-3852), Drayton and Gaston streets; **Lake Mayer** (912-652-6780), Montgomery Crossroads and Sallie Mood Drive; **Louis Scott Stell Park** (912-925-8694), Bush Road; **Port Wentworth** (912-966-7428), Warren Drive; **Southbridge Racquet Club** (912-651-5466), 80 Wedgefield Crossing; **Tybee Island Memorial Park** (912-786-4698), Butler Avenue, Tybee Island; and **Wilmington Island Community Park** (912-652-6780), Lang Street and Walthour Road, Wilmington Island.

3 Historical South

AUTO RACING

In Newington

Screven Motor Speedway–Savannah River Dragway (912-857-4884), 6118 Savannah Highway. Races are run in several classes.

ENTERTAINMENT/DANCE

In Athens

University of Georgia Departmental Productions, Department of Dance (706-542-4415; www.franklin.uga.edu/dance), Dance Building, Sanford Drive behind Marine Science Building. Classics to contemporary and original works.

ENTERTAINMENT/MUSIC

In Athens

University of Georgia Departmental Productions, School of Music (706-542-3737; www.uga.edu/~music/events.html), Music Building, 250 River Road. Classics to contemporary and original works.

In Athens
The Annex (760-613-7771), 164 East Clayton Street. Top-40 tunes.

Insomnia (706-316-1000), 131 East Broad Street. DJ; Saturday night devoted to hip-hop.

Last Call (706-353-8869), 420 East Clayton Street.

346 Club (706-227-2124), 346 East Broad Street.

ENTERTAINMENT/THEATER

In Athens
Athens Creative Theatre (706-613-3628; www.athenscreativetheatre.com), 293 Gran Ellen Drive. Well-known shows, works by local artists.

Canopy Studio (706-549-8501; www.canopystudio.com), 160 Tracy Street. Exhibits, performances, classes.

Town and Gown Players (706-208-TOWN; www.townandgownplayers.org; www.nega.net/tandg), Athens Community Theatre, 115 Grady Avenue. Classics, original works.

University of Georgia Departmental Productions, Department of Drama (706-542-2838; www.drama.uga.edu), Fine Arts Building, Baldwin and Lumpkin streets. Classics to contemporary and original works.

EQUESTRIAN EVENTS

In Madison
Four Seasons Farm (706-342-7577), 1356 Plantation Road. Showing of jumpers and show hunters.

FOR FAMILIES

In the Rock
The Rock Ranch (706-647-6374; www.therockranch.com), 5020 Barnesville Highway. Easter egg hunt, fall corn maze.

FRUIT AND BERRY PICKING

In Baxley
Mathews Farms (912-367-4616), 479 Dunn's Lake Road.

In Glennville
Roger Dasher Farms (912-654-4931), GA 144 East.

In Watkinsville
Washington Farms (706-769-0627; www.washingtonfarms.com), 5691 Hog Mountain Road. Pumpkins, strawberries, blackberries, hayrides, petting farm, corn maze.

In Lincolnton
Graves Mountain (706-359-7970). Rare minerals at old mining operation.

HIKING

In Vidalia
Meadows Regional Medical Center Walking Trail, 1703 Meadows Lane. Wooded walking course with trail markers and additional exercises.

OUTDOOR ADVENTURES

In Athens
Georgia Outdoor Recreation Program (706-542-5460). Classes in scuba diving, kayaking, backpacking, fly-fishing, rafting, horseback riding.

Granite Arches Climbing Services (706-552-1619; www.granitearches.com), 265 Oak Grove Road. Rock-climbing lessons, lead and rescue climbing, guide services.

SHOOTING SPORTS

In Augusta
Pinetucky Trap and Skeet Club (706-592-4230), Camp Josey Road/US 1. Pistol and rifle shooting; trap, skeet, and sporting clays.

Shooter's Pistol and Rifle Range (706-860-7778), 1025 Patriot's Way. Indoor range.

In Eatonton
Lake Oconee Sporting Club (706-485-4557; www.oconeeshootingclub.com), 631 Sparta Highway. Skeet and trap fields, sporting clays.

SKATING

In Athens
Skate-A-Round USA (706-546-5951; www.skatearoundusa.com/athensga.htm), 3030 Cherokee Road. Family-oriented rink.

Skatersxtreme Skate Park (706-353-9700; www.skateboardparks.com/georgia/skatersxtreme/athens), 30 Commerce Boulevard. Park for very athletic, serious, adventurous in-line skaters, skateboarders, cyclists.

SPAS

In Douglas
Reflections Day Spa (912-389-1811), 1202 North Madison Avenue. Complete hair and nail care, facials, massages, makeup, glycolic peels, microdermabrasion.

In Milledgeville
Salon 200 (478-454-2155), 2600 North Columbia Street.

Serenity Wellness Spa and Salon (478-453-8158), 107 Sportsman Club Road NE. Hairstyling, manicures, pedicures, facials, massage, pilates.

APPENDIX

In Milledgeville
Dry Creek Farm (478-451-5070), 134 Pettigrew Road NW. Horse care, riding.

SWIMMING

In Athens
Public pools: **Bishop Park** (706-613-3589), 705 Sunset Drive; **East Athens Community Center** (706-613-3593), 400 McKinley Avenue; **Lay Park** (706-613-3596), 297 Hoyt Street; **Memorial Park** (706-613-3580), 293 Gran Ellen Drive; **Rocksprings Park** (706-613-3602), 105 Columbus Avenue.

In Eatonton
County of Putnam Swimming Pool (706-485-0428), 402 West Marion Street.

In Greensboro
Green County Parks and Recreation (706-486-2251), 2741 Old Union Road.

In Lincolnton
Lincolnton Recreation Pool (706-359-2236), Betty G. Ross Park, 800 Madison Street.

TENNIS

In Alma
Alma Recreational Park. Tennis, softball-baseball fields, picnic area, children's play area, nature trail.

In Athens
Athens–Clarke County Parks (706-613-3800) facilities: **Bishop Lake** (706-613-3589), 705 Sunset Drive; **East Athens Community Center** (706-613-3593), 400 McKinley Drive; **Sandy Creek Park** (706-613-3631), 400 Holman Road; **Satterfield Park** (706-613-3589), Cherokee Road.

In Augusta
Newman Tennis Center (706-821-1600), 3103 Wrightsboro Road, has outdoor composition courts and two practice walls.

Also: **Dyess Park** (706-821-2877), 902 Ninth Street; **Hillside Park** (706-796-5025), 2101 Telfair Street; **May Park** (706-724-0504), 622 Fourth Street; **Warren Road Community Center** (706-860-0986), 300 Warren Road; **West Vineland Park** (706-796-5025), 241 West Vineland Road.

In Baxley
Max Deen Memorial Park (912-367-8190; www.baxley.org), 400 Walnut Street.

In Claxton
Evans County Recreation Department (912-739-1434), One Recreation Department Road. Courts located about 1 mile east of Claxton on US 280.

In Macon

John Drew Smith Tennis Center (478-474-5075), 3280 North Ingle Place. 24 lighted courts.

Tatnall Square Tennis Center (478-751-9196), 1155 College Street. 12 lighted courts.

In Warner Robins

Warner Robins Parks and Recreation Department (478-929-1916) facilities: **Fountain Park,** 614 Kimberly Road; **Perkins Park,** 105 Mulberry Street; **Tanner Park,** 200 Carl Vinson Parkway; and **Ted Wright Park,** 2841 Moody Drive.

In Portal

Portal Park (912-489-9062; www.bullochrec.com), 27225 US 80 West/120 Ballfield Lane.

In Statesboro

Memorial Park (912-489-9062; www.bullochrec.com), One Max Lockwood Drive.

In Statesboro/Brooklet

Brooklet Park (912-489-9062; www.bullochrec.com), Cromley Road.

In Sylvania

Sylvania–Screven County Recreation Department (912-564-2388), 320 Millen Road.

4 The Mountains

AUTO RACING

In Blue Ridge

Sugar Creek Raceway (706-632-9083), 2252 Sugar Creek Road. Dirt-track car racing on ⅓-mile clay oval.

In Chatsworth

North Georgia Mini Speedway (706-602-0307; 706-629-5123; www.northgamini speedway.com), 6481 GA 225. Go-Kart racing on ⅕-mile clay oval.

In Rome

Rome International Speedway (706-235-2541; www.dixiespeedway.com), Chulio Road. World's fastest ½-mile dirt track. Regular stock car races, some national events, including the South's biggest short-track stock car race.

FRUIT AND BERRY PICKING

In Royston

Bea's Better Berries (706-245-0954), 2756 Freeman Road.

SHOOTING SPORTS

In Dawsonville

Etowah Valley Game Preserve (706-265-6543; www.etowahvalleygame.com),

120 Leon Jones Road. Sporting clays, five-stand, and trap shooting; pheasant, chukar, and quail hunting.

SUMMER YOUTH PROGRAMS

In Dahlonega
Kindermusik (706-867-0050; www.quigleybooks.com/kindermusik.html), sponsored by **Buisson Art Center,** 199 Choice Street. Wonder of music explored through activities geared to each child's pace.

SWIMMING

In Dawsonville
Chestatee Golf Club (706-216-7336; 1-800-520-8675; www.chestateegolf.net), 777 Dogwood Way. Junior Olympic-sized pool.

TENNIS

In Dawsonville
Chestatee Golf Club (706-216-7336; 1-800-520-8675; www.chestateegolf.net), 777 Dogwood Way. Seven lighted courts.

In Duluth
City of Duluth Parks and Recreation lighted courts: **Bunten Road Park** (770-814-6981), Bunten Road; **W. P. Jones Park** (770-623-2781), Pleasant Hill Road.

In Flowery Branch
Alberta Banks Park, 5575 Jim Crow Road.

In Gainesville
Hall County Parks and Leisure Services (770-531-3952) parks: **Laurel Park,** 3100 Old Cleveland Highway; **Central Park,** 1200 Candler Road.

In Helen
Innsbruck Golf Club (706-878-2100; 1-800-642-2709; www.innsbruckgolf club.com), 664 Bahn Innsbruck. One court for those staying at Innsbruck Resort.
Unicoi State Park (706-878-2201; 1-800-864-7275; www.gastateparks.org/info/ unicoi), 1788 GA 356. Four lighted courts.

In Lula
Rafe Banks Park, 5831 Athens Street.

5 Southern Rivers
AUTO RACING

In Albany
US 19 Dragway (229-431-0077; www.us19dragway.com), 1304 Williamsburg Road. Home to National Hotrod Association–sanctioned events.

Albany Motor Speedway (229-431-0190), 140 Darian Drive. Stock car races on ¼-mile asphalt oval track.

ENTERTAINMENT/MUSIC, THEATER, VISUAL ARTS

In Americus
Georgia Southwest State University (1-800-338-0062), 800 Wheatley Street. Musical theater; instrumental and vocal performances; art gallery; glassblowing facility.

ENTERTAINMENT/NIGHTLIFE

In Americus
Pat's Place (229-924-0033), 1526 South Lee Street. Pub with game room, live music, poetry, pub grub.

In LaGrange
Troup County Parks and Recreation's (706-884-5857; 706-637-9295) **Moonlight Ballroom Dance Club,** Recreation Center, 1220 Lafayette Parkway. Lessons, monthly dances.

EQUESTRIAN EVENTS

In Hamilton
Poplar Place Farm Equestrian Center (706-582-3742; www.poplarplacefarm.com), 8191 US 27. Numerous equestrian events: horse trials, dressage shows, schooling shows, clinics.

In Pine Mountain
Pine Mountain Horse Shows (706-845-9519; 706-663-7787; www.pinemountainhorseshows.com), 649 Butts Mill Road. Schooling shows in dressage, cross-country events.

FOR FAMILIES

In Dawson
Steve Cocke Fish Hatchery (229-995-4486; www.gofishgeorgia.com), 109 Hatchery Access Road. Gulf Coast striped bass.

In Valdosta
Jungle Jym's Family Fun Center (229-247-1271), 3124 North Oak Street Extension. Indoor skating, family activities, batting cages.

FRUIT AND BERRY PICKING

In Leesburg
Calhoun Produce (229-438-9983), 999 Lovers Lane.

In Valdosta
Valdosta Paintball (229-630-5628; www.valdostapaintball.com), 2953 Touchton Road. Six fields, gun, tank, mask, balls.

SKATING

In Albany
Stardust II Skate Center (229-435-0111), 2881 Ledo Road. Skating, special sessions, arcade games.

SWIMMING

In Albany
City of Albany Recreation Department (229-430-5222): **Carver Sports Complex** (229-430-5241), 1023 South McKinley; **Turner Landing Park** (229-430-5245), 1922 Schilling Avenue.

TENNIS

In Albany
City of Albany Recreation Department (229-430-5222) courts: **Carver Sports Complex** (229-430-5241), 1023 South McKinley (open by reservation); **Robert Cross Park,** 3000 South Martin Luther King Jr. Drive; **Tift Park** (229-430-5222), Fifth and Seventh avenues at Jefferson Street and Palmyra Road.

In LaGrange
LaGrange College (706-882-2911; www.lagrange.edu), 601 Broad Street. Outsiders can purchase a pass to Aqua/Sports Complex, which contains tennis courts, indoor pool, outdoor pool, fitness center.

Troup County Parks and Recreation (706-883-1670; www.troupcountyga.org) courts: **Earl Cook Recreation Area, Hardley Creek Park, Ringer Park, Rocky Point Recreation Area, R. Schaefer Day Use Area, Yellowjacket Park.**

In Valdosta
Valdosta Recreation, Parks and Community Affairs Department (229-259-3507) courts: **McKey Park,** 112 Burton Avenue; lighted courts **Scott Park,** 1101 Old Statenville Road.

BOAT LANDINGS AND MARINAS

2 The Coast

In Brunswick
Brunswick Landing Marina (912-262-9264), 2429 Newcastle Street. Fuel, bait, supplies, floating docks, wet and dry storage, laundry facilities, bathhouse.

Brunswick Marina (912-262-9264), 1701 Newcastle Street. Hoist lift, fuel, bait, ice.

Troupe Creek Marina (912-264-3862), 375 Yacht Road. Boat storage, boat services, fishing tackle, food and drinks, fuel, bait, supplies.

Two-Way Marina (912-265-0410), 250 Charlie Gibbs Way (US 17 at Altamaha River). Boat lift, full-time mechanic, fishing charters for onshore and deep-sea fishing, restaurant, gas, supplies, bait.

On Jekyll Island

Jekyll Harbor Resort Marina (912-635-3137; www.jekyllharbor.com), One Harbor Road. Boat slips; floating docks; dry storage; dolphin, fishing, and sailing tours; SeaJay's Restaurant. Those docked at marina can use pool, hot tub, laundry facilities.

Jekyll Island Fishing Pier (contact Jekyll Island Welcome Center, 912-635-3636), North Riverview Drive. Great place for fishing and crabbing.

Jekyll Wharf Marina (912-635-3152), One Pier Road. Docks, hook-ups, fuel, supplies, ice, bike and kayak rentals, rest rooms, bait, charters, water taxi and shuttle services, dolphin tours. Latitude 31 restaurant, Dockside Raw Bar.

Savannah/Tybee Island

Boat landings: **Bell's Landing,** Apache Road off Abercorn on Forest River; **Islands Expressway,** Frank W. Spencer Park on Wilmington River; **Kings River,** US 17 on Ogeechee River; **Lazaretto Creek,** US 80, Tybee Island; **Montgomery,** Whitfield Avenue on Vernon River; **Port Wentworth,** US 17 North (old bridge) and Savannah River; **Salt Creek,** US 17 at Silk Hope; **Skidaway Narrows,** Diamond Causeway near Skidaway Island; **Thunderbolt,** Savannah Marina on Wilmington River.

Bull River Marina (912-897-7300), 8005 Old Tybee Road. Deep-water dockage, boat rentals, ecotours, dolphin cruises, fishing charters.

In St. Marys

Lang's Marina East (912-882-4452), 100 St. Marys Street. Floating dock, fuel, provisions, shower facilities.

4 The Mountains

In Elberton

Beaverdam Marina (706-213-6462), 1155 Marina Drive. Covered boat slips; courtesy dock; pump-out services; gasoline; pontoon boat rentals; fishing guide services; boat ramp; trailer parking; boat repairs; ice, beverages, snacks; Clifford's Restaurant.

In Hartwell

Hartwell Marina (706-376-5441; www.hartwellmarina.com), 149 Hartwell Marina Road. Gas dock, courtesy parking, pump-out station, boat repair services.

5 Southern Rivers

Boat ramps: **Cool Branch Park, Pataula Creek Park, River Bend Park, River Bluff Park,** and **Rood Creek Park** on Georgia side of Lake Walter F. George; **East Bank Park** and **Coheelee Creek Park** on Georgia side of George W. Andrews Lake.

In Albany

City of Albany Recreation Department (229-430-5222) boat landings (and fishing): **Cleve Cox Landing and Park,** Philem Road and Lakeshore Drive; **Cromartie Beach Landing and Park,** Cromartie Beach Road at Maple Street; **Radium Boat Landing and Park,** Radium Springs Road at Marine Corps Ditch; **Turner Landing Park,** Turner Field Road.

In Bainbridge

Wingate's Marina (229-246-0658), 139 Wingate Road. Restaurant, lodging, fishing licenses, tackle, gas, fishing guide services.

In Georgetown

River Bluff Park at Lake Walter F. George (229-768-2516; www.sam.usace .army.mil/op/rec/wfg), off US 82. Boat ramp, fishing pier.

In LaGrange

Highland Marina (706-882-3437; www.highlandmarina.com), 1000 Seminole Road. Bass- and pontoon-boat rentals.

Mitchell Marine (706-884-2594), 370 Davis Road. Retail boat sales and boat-related accessories.

FISHING

2 The Coast

In Brunswick

B&D Marine (912-264-1819), 1200 Glynn Avenue. Deep-sea, offshore, and inshore fishing as well as diving, trolling, sailing, sunset cruises.

Happy Hooker Charters (912-265-3298; 912-270-7997, www.goldenislescharterfishing.com), 408 Howard Drive. Backwater, inshore, and offshore fishing near Jekyll and St. Simons islands.

Hobo Charter Fishing (912-264-5735), 211 Choctaw Road. Inshore and near-shore excursions.

In Darien

Captain Phillip's Boat Charters and Tours (912-437-5708), 1310 Wayne Street.

David Edwards Charters (912-437-6908).

Free Spooling Charters (912-437-8200).

Liquid Asset Offshore Fishing (866-282-0524; www.liquidassetfishing.com).

Savannah/Tybee Island

Fishing piers: **Back River Pier,** Chatham Avenue, Tybee Island; **Frank O. Downing Pier,** Diamond Causeway near Skidaway Island; **Islands Expressway Pier,** Frank W. Spencer Park on Wilmington River; **Lazaretto Creek Pier,** US 80 East, Tybee Island; **Salt Creek Bridge,** US 17 at Silk Hope; **Thunderbolt,** Wilmington River; **Tybee Island Pier–Pavilion,** Tybrisa Street and the Strand.

On St. Simons
St. Simons Island Fishing Pier (912-265-0620), Mallory Street. Located at southern tip of island.

In Woodbine
Fish Masters Charters (912-729-5214; 912-258-6844), 141 Mallard Pointe Drive. Fishing and dive charters.

3 Historical South

In Mansfield
Marben Public Fishing Area (770-784-3121), 543 Elliot Trail. 25 lakes.

4 The Mountains

In Clarksville
Brigadoon Lodge (706-754-1558; 1-888-4BRIGADOON; www.brigadoon-lodge.com), 8137 GA 197 North. Facility on Soque River is favorite of fishermen.

In Ringgold/Cohutta
Cohutta Fisheries Center (706-694-8830), 5350 Red Clay Road NW. Open 8–4:30 weekdays. Ten tanks display warm-water species; bank fishing for channel catfish and trout in-season.

5 Southern Rivers

In Albany
Ken Gardens Park (229-430-5267), 1509-1511 Ken Garden Road.
Sherwood Park, Whispering Pines at Barnesdale Way.

In Camilla
Covey Rise Plantation (229-294-3143; www.coveyrise.com), 9217 GA 65. Guided fly-fishing expeditions on Flint River.

In Talbotton
Big Lazer Public Fishing Area (706-665-8079; www.georgiawildlife.com), Bunkham Road. 195-acre lake with abundant fishing and boat ramp.

In Thomasville
Myrtlewood Hunting Plantation (229-228-6232; www.myrtlewoodplantation.com), Lower Cairo Road. Several stocked fishing lakes.

GOLF

1 Atlanta Metro

In Lithonia
Mystery Valley Golf Course (770-469-6913; www.mysteryvalley.com), 6094 Shadowrock Drive.

In McDonough

The CottonFields Golf Club (770-914-1442; www.cottonfieldsgolf.com), 400 Industrial Boulevard. 18-hole course, practice greens, pro shop, snack bar.

Georgia National Golf Club (770-914-9994; www.georgianational.com), 1715 Lake Dow Road. 18-hole course, pro shop, putting green, chipping green, practice bunker, grill.

In Newnan

Orchard Hills Golf Club (770-251-5683; www.orchardhills.com), 600 GA 16 East. 27-hole championship course, driving range, putting green, pro shop, full-service restaurant.

Pine Ridge National Golf and Country Club (770-683-4727; www.pineridgenational.com), 300 Arbor Springs Parkway. 18-hole semiprivate course, full-service restaurant.

SummerGrove Golf Club (770-251-1800; www.summergrovegolf.com), 335 SummerGrove Parkway. Public 18-hole championship course, three-hole par 3 course, driving range, putting green, chipping green, practice bunker, clubhouse, pro shop, restaurant.

In Tucker

Heritage Golf Club (770-493-4653; www.heritagegolfclub.com), 4445 Britt Road.

2 The Coast

In Black Creek

Black Creek Golf Club (912-858-4653), Bill Fitch Road.

In Blackshear

Lakeview Golf Club (912-449-4411), 510 Golf Club Road. 18-hole course, putting green, driving range, pro shop.

In Brunswick

Coastal Pines Golf Course (912-261-0503), 1 Coastal Pines Circle. Public 18-hole course, practice facility, pro shop, snack bar.

In Folkston

Folkston Golf Club (912-496-7155; www.golfgeorgia.org), 202 Country Club Road. Public 18-hole course, driving range.

In Hinesville

Cherokee Rose Country Club Golf (912-496-7155; www.golfgeorgia.org), 225 Cherokee Trail.

In Kingsland

Laurel Island Links (912-729-7277; www.visitkingsland.com), 233 Marsh Harbour Parkway. Public 18-hole, Davis Love III-designed course, driving range, putting green, practice bunker, pro shop, Meridian Grill.

In Richmond Hill

Waterford Landing Golf Course (912-727-4848; www.richmondhillcvb.com), 731 Waterford Landing Way.

In Rincon

Lost Plantation Golf Club (912-826-2092; www.lostplantationgolf.com), One Clubhouse Drive.

In St. Marys

Osprey Cove Golf Course (912-882-5575; www.ospreycove.com), 123 Osprey Drive. 18-hole championship course, pro shop.

On St. Simons

Hampton Club (912-634-0255; www.hamptonclub.com), 100 Tabbystone. 18-hole course on site of Hampton Plantation with pro shop, instruction, snack bar, driving range, putting green, dining room.

Sea Palms Golf and Tennis Resort (912-638-9041; www.seapalms.com), 5445 Frederica Road. 27 holes of golf, tennis center.

Savannah

Bacon Park Golf Course (912-354-2625; www.baconparkgolf.com), One Shorty Cooper Drive. 27-hole course, driving range, putting greens.

The Club at Savannah Harbor (912-201-2007; 912-201-2260; www.theclubat savannahharbor.net), Two Resort Drive. 18 holes.

Crosswinds Golf Club (912-966-1909; 912-966-0674; www.crosswindsgolfclub .com), 232 James B. Blackburn Drive. 18 championship holes, executive par-three course.

The Lost Plantation (912-826-2092; 1-888-243-5678; www.lostplantationgolf.com), One Clubhouse Drive. 18 holes.

Mary Caulder Golf Course (912-238-7100), West Lathrop Avenue. Semiprivate nine-hole course, putting green.

Southbridge Golf Club (912-651-5455), 415 Southbridge Boulevard. Semiprivate, 18-hole, Rees Jones-designed course, practice facilities, driving range, putting and chipping greens, pro shop, lessons.

On Sea Island

Sea Island Golf Club (912-638-5118; 1-800-732-4752; www.seaisland.com), 100 Hudson Place. Play on three courses is restricted to guests of The Cloister and The Lodge at Sea Island.

In Shellman Bluff

Sapelo Hammock Golf Course (912-832-4653; www.sapelohammockgolfclub), 500 Marshview Drive.

3 Historical South

In Alma

Blueberry Plantation Golf Course (912-632-2772), 315 Ironwood Circle. Semiprivate 18-hole course, putting green, clubhouse, pool.

In Athens

Green Hills Country Club (706-548-6032), 4080 Barnett Shoals Road. 18-hole semiprivate course.

University Golf Course (706-369-5739; 1-800-9DOGTEE; www.golfcourse.uga.edu), 2600 Riverbend Road. Demanding 18-hole, Robert Trent Jones-designed course, driving range, pro shop.

In Augusta
Augusta Golf Course (706-796-5058), 2023 Highland Avenue.

Forest Hills Golf Club (706-733-0001), 1500 Comfort Road.

Goshen Plantation Golf Course (706-793-1035; www.goshenplantation.com), 1601 Goshen Clubhouse Drive.

In Baxley
Appling Country Club (912-367-3582), 4628 Hatch Parkway South. Nine holes, putting green, driving range, swimming pool.

In Bonaire
Waterford Golf Club (478-328-7533), 620 Highway 96. Semiprivate 18-hole course.

In Claxton
Evans Heights Golf Center (912-739-3003), US 301 South. 18 holes, practice green, driving range.

In Colbert
Sunrise Golf Club (706-788-2720; www.sunrisegolfclub.com), 5225 Colbert-Danielsville Road. 18 holes, driving range, clubhouse, snack bar.

In Douglas
Beaver Kreek Golf Club (912-384-8230), 485 Beaver Kreek Road. Challenging course, putting green, driving range, pro shop.

Douglas Community Golf Course (912-384-7353), SGC Tiger Road. 18 holes.

Hinson Hills Golf Course (912-384-8984), 3179 GA 32 East. 18 holes, driving range, putting green, chipping area, pro shop.

In Dublin
Riverview Park Golf Course (478-275-4064), 100 Riverview Drive. 18-hole course, practice green, driving range.

In Forsyth
Forsyth Golf Club (478-994-5328), 400 Country Club Drive. 18 holes.

In Fort Valley
Pine Needles Country Club (478-825-3816), 111 Country Club Road. Nine-hole course.

In Harlem
Three Oaks Golf Club (706-556-1400; www.threeoaksgolfclub.com), 1300 Three Oaks Drive. 18 holes.

In Hazlehurst
Twisted Pines Golf Club (912-375-6697), 270 Uvalda Highway. Nine holes, putting green, driving range, pro shop.

In Jackson
Hickory Hill Golf Course (770-775-2433), 209 Biles Road. Semiprivate 27-hole course, putting green, grill.

In Jesup
Pine Forest Country Club (912-427-6505), GA 301 South. Private, but they'll allow you to play if you're from out of town and call first; putting green, driving range, pro shop.

In Lincolnton
Rocky Branch Golf Club and Country Club (706-359-4303), 4711 Double Branches Road. 18 holes, pro shop, driving range, practice green.

In Macon
Bowden Golf Course (478-742-1610), 3111 Millerfield Road. 18-hole municipal course, driving range, pro shop, snack bar.

Oak Haven Golf Club (478-474-8080), 7359 Thomaston Road. 18-hole semiprivate course.

Oakview Golf and Country Club (478-784-8700; www.oakviewgolf.com), 128 Oakview Club Drive. Semiprivate 18-hole course, driving range, putting green, pro shop, junior Olympic-sized swimming pool.

In Metter
Willow Lake Country Club (912-685-2724), Willow Lake Drive. Semiprivate course, practice green, special teaching area.

In Milledgeville
Little Fishing Creek Golf Course (478-445-0796), 65 GA 22 West. 18-hole public course, pro shop, driving range, practice greens.

In Monticello
Hunter Pope Country Club (706-468-6222), 14617 GA 127. 18 holes, pro shop, driving range, practice green.

In Perry
Houston Lake Country Club (478-218-5253; www.houstonlake.com), 2323 GA 127. 18-hole, par-72 course ranked among the top 50 courses in Georgia, pro shop, practice range, PGA professional instruction.

In Reidsville
Brazell's Creek Golf Course at Gordonia-Alatamaha State Park (912-557-7745; 1-800-434-0982; www.gastateparks.org/info/gordonalt; www.golfgeorgia.org), 355 Golf Course Road. Nine-hole course, pro shop, driving range, practice bunker, putting green, unlimited weekday play, junior/senior discounts.

In Statesboro
Eagle Creek Golf Club (912-839-3933), 7436 GA 46. 18-hole course, practice green, driving range.

Southern Links (912-839-3191), 1031 Golf Club Road. 18-hole course, practice green, driving range.

In Swainsboro
Swainsboro Golf & Country Club (478-237-6116), 557 McCleod Bridge Road. 18-hole course, practice green, driving range.

In Sylvania
Briar Creek Country Club (912-863-4161), 301 North Country Club Road. Nine-hole course, practice green, driving range.

In Vidalia
Rocky Creek Golf Club (912-538-1110), 1916 Foxfire Drive. 18-hole public course, driving range.

In Warner Robins
International City Golf Club (478-322-0276), 100 Sandy Run Lane. 18 holes, practice facility, pro shop, instruction, snack bar.

In Warrenton
The Boulders Golf Course (706-465-2577), 546 Quaker Road. Semiprivate course, pro shop, practice green. No driving range.

In Waynesboro
Waynesboro Country Club (706-554-2262), 336 Herndon Road. 18 holes, practice green, driving range.

In Wrens
Brushy Creek Golf Club (706-547-2816; www.brushycreekgolf.com), 2896 GA 102. Hilly, semiprivate 18-hole course, pro shop.

4 The Mountains

In Acworth
Bentwater Golf Club (770-529-9554; www.bentwater-atlanta.com/golfclub), 100 Golf Links Drive.

Cobblestone Golf Course (770-917-5151; www.cobblestonegolf.com), 4200 Nance Road.

In Adairsville
Indian Ridge Golf Course (706-292-9324), 4333 Adairsville Road Northeast.

In Calhoun
Calhoun Elks Golf Club (706-629-4091), 143 Craigtown Road.

Fields Ferry Golf Course (706-625-5666), 581 Fields Ferry Drive.

In Canton
Bridge Mill Athletic Club (770-345-5500; www.bridgemillgc.com), 1190 Bridge Mill Avenue.

Woodmont Golf Club (770-345-9260; www.woodmontongolfclub.com), 3105 Gaddis Road.

In Cartersville
Green Valley Greens Golf Club (770-382-8510), 157 Rudy York Road Northwest.

Royal Oaks Golf Club (770-382-3999; www.royaloaksgolf.com), 256 Summit Ridge Drive.

In Cedartown
Meadow Lakes Golf Course (770-748-4942), 383 Adams Road.

In Chatsworth
Indian Trace Golf Course (706-695-7353), 730 Mitchell Bridge Road

Spring Lakes Golf Club (706-695-9300), 1591 Spring Place.

In Clarkesville
Apple Mountain Golf Club (706-754-2255; www.applemountaingolfgao.com), 901 Rockford Creek Road.

Orchard Golf and Country Club (706-754-3156; 1-800-754-8543; www.the orchardsclub.com), 1057 Orchard Drive.

In Clayton
Kingwood Resort Golf Club (706-212-4100; 1-866-KINGWOOD; www.kingwood resort.com), 401 Country Club Road.

Rabun County Golf Club (706-782-5500), 1322 Old US 441 South.

In Commerce
Deer Trail Country Club (706-335-3987), 224 Country Club Lane. Nine-hole course, driving range, golf pro.

Sandy Creek Golf Course (706-335-8100; www.eaglegreens.com), 3100 Ila Road. 18-hole championship course, pro shop, golf pro, self-service snack bar.

In Dalton
Nob North Golf Course (706-694-8505), 298 Nob North Drive. A PGA-approved, 18-hole course designed by Gary Player with driving range and practice greens.

In Ellijay
Whitepath Golf Course (706-276-3080), 1156 Shenandoah.

In Flowery Branch
Royal Lakes Golf and Country Club (770-535-8800), 4700 Royal Lakes Drive. Semiprivate 18-hole course, driving range, golf pro.

In Gainesville
Chattahoochee Golf Course (770-532-0066; www.chattahoocheegolfcourse.com), 301 Tommy Aaron Drive. Robert Trent Jones-designed 18-hole course, two putting greens, driving range, practice bunker, chipping green, pro shop, short-order grill.

Chicopee Woods Golf Course (770-534-7322; www.chicopeewoodsgolfcourse .com), 2515 Atlanta Highway. 27 holes divided into three nine-hole courses: **The Village, The Mill,** and **The School,** driving range, chipping green, practice bunker, putting green, full-service grill, pro shop.

In Hartwell
Cateechee Golf Club (706-856-4653; www.cateechee.com), 140 Cateechee

Trail. One of only a few courses worldwide to achieve the coveted and prestigious Audubon International Signature Status. Magnificent course, pro shop, clubhouse, restaurant, lounge, and putting, chipping, and driving practice facilities.

Hartwell Golf Club (706-376-8161; www.hartwellgolf.com), 755 Golf Course Road. 18-hole course, chipping and putting practice areas, driving range, pro shop.

In Homer

Hammer's Glen Golf Course (706-677-3333; www.hammersglen.com), 148 Hammer's Glen Drive. 18-hole, semiprivate course, pro shop, grill, driving range, putting green, chipping green, practice bunker.

In Lafayette

Lafayette Golf Course (706-638-0220), 638 South Main Street.

In Ringgold

Windstone Golf Club (423-894-1231), 9230 Windstone Drive.

In Rockmart

Goodyear Golf Course (770-684-2500), 984 Goodyear Avenue.

In Rome

Horseleg Plantation Country Club Golf Course (706-290-1982), 127 Winding Road Southwest.

Stonebridge Golf Club (706-236-5046; 1-800-336-5046; www.romestonebridge .com), 585 Stonebridge Drive.

In Toccoa

The Pines (706-886-1915), Black Mountain Road.

In Trenton

Air Castle Golf Club (706-657-3616; www.aircastle.com), 2060 Back Valley Road.

Big Sandy Golf Course (706-657-6738), 545 Michaels Road.

In Tunnel Hill

Tunnel Hill Golf Course (706-673-4131), 3449 Chattanooga Road.

In Waleska

Lake Arrowhead Country Club (770-479-5500), 598 Country Club Lane.

In Winder

The Chimneys Golf Course (770-307-4900; www.eaglegreens.com), 338 Monroe Highway. 18 holes, pro shop, snack bar.

Pine Hills Golf Course (770-867-3150), 661 Hog Mountain Road. 18-hole public course, driving range.

In Woodstock

Eagle Watch Golf Club (770-591-1000; www.eaglewatchgolf.com), 3055 Eagle Watch Drive.

Golf Club at Bradshaw Farm (770-592-2222; www.americangolf.com), 3030 Bradshaw Club Drive.

5 Southern Rivers

In Albany
Flint River Municipal Golf Course of Albany (229-430-5267), 2000
McAdams Drive. 18-hole public course, putting green, practice bunker, lounge,
dining room.

River Pointe Golf Course (229-883-4885; www.riverpointegolfcourse.com),
801 River Pointe Drive. 18-hole semiprivate course.

In Americus
Brickyard Plantation Golf Club and RV Park (229-874-1234; www.brickyard
golfclub.com), 1619 US 280 East. Three nine-hole courses: **The Ditches, The
Waters,** and **The Mounds,** pro shop, snack bar.

Wolf Creek Golf Club (229-928-4040), 407 Wolf Creek Drive. 18-hole semiprivate course, driving range.

In Ashburn
Wanee Lake Country Club (229-567-2727), 3821 GA 122 West.

In Bainbridge
Industrial Park Golf Club (229-246-8545), 183 Davis Avenue. Nine-hole public
course, driving range, instruction, pro shop.

In Buena Vista
Cedar Creek Golf and Country Club (229-649-3381), off GA 137. Tough
nine-hole course. Closed Monday.

In Colquitt
Crooked Oak Golf Club (229-758-9200; www.clydesdalemeadows.com), 100
Clubhouse Drive. 18-hole, Arthur Davis-designed, public links-style course, pro
shop, putting green, driving range, clubhouse.

In Columbus
Bull Creek Golf Course (706-561-1614; www.columbusga.org/bullcreek), 7333
Lynch Road. 36 holes on two championship courses.

Godwin Creek Golf Course (706-324-0583), 403 42nd Street. Tough, nine-
hole course.

Oxbow Creek Golf Course (706-689-9977), 3491 South Lumpkin Road. Nine-
hole course.

In Cusseta
Red Oak Golf Club (706-989-3312; www.golfgeorgia.org), 158 Gordy Mill
Pond Road. 18 holes.

In Forsyth
Forsyth Golf Club (478-994-5328), 400 Country Club Drive. 18-hole course,
clubhouse, pro shop.

In Fort Benning

Follow Me Golf Course (706-687-1940), Baltzell Avenue, Building 390. Two 18-hole golf courses, two putting greens, practice green, driving range, pro shop, full-service clubhouse.

In Gray

Lake Jonesco Golf Course (478-986-3206; www.lakejonesco.com), 834 GA 22 East. 18-hole public course, pro shop.

In Griffin

City of Griffin Municipal Golf Course (770-229-6615; www.cityofgriffin.com), City Park, 601-C Camp Northern Road. 18-hole course in the heart of the city, 12-station driving range, pitching and putting green.

Morgan Dairy Golf Club (770-358-2221), 525 Morgan Dairy Road. Public 18-hole course, driving range, chipping and putting greens, snack bar.

In LaGrange

American Legion Golf Course (706-884-4379), Hamilton Road. Nine holes, pro shop, practice green.

The Fields Golf Course (706-845-7425; www.fieldsgolf.com), 257 South Smith Road. Scottish links-style course, 18 championship holes, practice green, driving range, pro shop, croquet court.

In Lake Park

Francis Lake Golf Club (229-559-7961), 5366 Golf Drive. Semiprivate, 18-hole course, swimming pool, tennis courts, pro shop, snack bar.

In Midland

Woodland Hills Golf Club (706-563-5511; www.woodlandhills.net), 599 Day Lake Drive. Par-72 course.

In Tifton

Country Oaks Municipal Golf Course (229-225-4333), 6481 GA 122/Pavo Road. Par-72 course, putting green, driving range, pro shop, snack bar, instruction.

Forest Lakes Golf Course (229-382-7626), 260 Sutton Drive. Public nine-hole course, driving range, putting green.

Tifton Family Golf and Pine Island Golf Club (229-387-7600), 336 Brighton Road. Nine-hole public course, lighted driving range, putting green, pro shop.

In Valdosta

The Golf Place (229-244-7610), 2953 Touchton Road. Lighted driving range.

Kinderlou Forest Golf Club (229-219-2300; www.kinderlou.com), 3374 US 84 West. Davis Love III-designed course, pro shop, restaurant.

Moody Quiet Pines Golf Course (229-257-3297), 15501 Prewitte Street. Nine-hole public course.

Stone Creek Golf Club (229-247-2527; www.gagolf.com/golf.html), 4300 Coleman Road. 18-hole public course, restaurant, pro shop.

Pebblebrook Golf Course (706-846-3809; www.golfatpebblebrook.com), 1116 Pebblebrook Road. Nine Arthur Davis-designed holes, pitching and putting greens, driving range.

In Warm Springs
Roosevelt Memorial Golf Course (706-655-5230), US 27-A/GA 41.

▌HUNTING

South Georgia is famous for quail, deer, dove, turkey, and wild hog hunting. Several of the area's plantations offer guided hunts. Listed below are several of these as well as other places that offer hunting. Also consult the Parks Appendix for waterfowl management areas, wildlife management areas, and other parks and preserves throughout the state that permit hunting.

1 Atlanta Metro

In McDonough
Dogwood Plantation Hunting Preserve (770-957-7005; 770-616-7714), 1409 US 23/GA 42 South. Quail- and pheasant-hunting preserve with an on-site clubhouse, lodging, meals, sporting clays.

4 The Mountains

In Homer
Allen's Fly-Away Shooting Resort (706-677-2019; 1-866-217-0397), 182 Lake Tehama Trail.

5 Southern Rivers

In Arlington
Quail Country Lodge and Conference Center (229-725-4645; www.quail-country.com), 1134 Quail Country Road. Guided hunting, lodging, meals.

In Camilla
Covey Rise Plantation (229-294-3143; www.coveyrise.com), 9217 GA 65. Quail hunting as well as guided fly-fishing expeditions on Flint River.

In Colquitt
Pine Hill Plantation (229-758-2464; www.pinehillplantation.com), 349 Kimbrell Road. Quail hunting on horseback or by customized mule-drawn wagons; Lodging, meals.

In Morris
Clay Hill Hunting (229-768-2820; www.clayhillhunting.com), 728 Days Avenue. Hunting for deer, dove, quail, turkey, and wild hog; lodging, meals.

In Thomasville
Myrtlewood Hunting Plantation (229-228-6232; www.myrtlewoodplantation

.com), Lower Cairo Road. Primarily focused on hunting; also has several stocked fishing lakes.

PARKS

1 Atlanta Metro

In McDonough

Alexander Park (770-954-2031; www.co.henry.ga.us), GA 42. Baseball fields, playground, walking-jogging track, summer concert series.

Red Hawk Nature Preserve Park (770-954-2031; www.co.henry.ga.us), 143 Henry Parkway. Remote-control airplane–helicopter strip, Henry County Model Aerodome, home of Conley Flyers RC Club.

Richard Craig Park (770-954-2031; www.co.henry.ga.us), 125 Zack Hinton Parkway. Ball fields, tennis courts, playground, walking track, community building; hosts **Roberto Clemente World Series of Baseball.**

Windy Hill Park (770-954-2031; www.co.henry.ga.us), 125 South Cedar. Ball fields, fairground–exhibit area, obstacle course, paved walking-jogging track, playground.

2 The Coast

In Baxley

Randall Tuten Environmental Park (912-367-8630; www.baxley.org), US 15 South. Streams, wetlands, ponds, dock, nature trail.

Max Deen Memorial Park (912-367-8190; www.baxley.org), 400 Walnut Street. Pool, tennis, ball fields, picnicking.

Moody Forest Natural Area (912-366-9549; www.baxley.org.nature.org), East River Road. One of America's last remaining old-growth forests; hiking, wildlife observation.

In Glennville

Big Hammock Wildlife Management Area (229-426-5267; www.gohuntgeorgia.com), GA 144. Contains Phillips Natural Area, 800-acre forest that is U.S. Natural Landmark and example of rare ecosystem.

In Jesup

Rayonier Wildlife Management Area (912-262-3173; www.gohuntgeorgia.com), GA 32. Hunting and fishing.

In Ludowici

Griffin Ridge Wildlife Management Area (912-262-3173; www.gohuntgeorgia.com), US 301. Hunting and fishing.

On St. Simons

Neptune Park (912-265-0620; 1-800-933-2627), Beachview Drive. Playground, mini golf, picnic facilities, bandstand, fishing pier, library, theater.

Bullard Creek Wildlife Management Area (912-375-4543; www.hazlehurst-jeffdavis.com), US 221 North. Hunting, fishing, birding, primitive camping.

In Woodbine

Satilla Waterfront Park (912-729-5600), 310 Bedell Avenue. Nature walk, boating, fishing.

3 Historic South

In Appling

Lake Springs Recreation Area (706-541-0150; 1-800-533-3478), 3900 Lake Springs Road. Hiking, biking, fishing, picnicking.

West Dam Recreation Area (706-541-0031), Scons Ferry Road. Fishing, picnicking, water activities.

In Athens

Bishop Park (706-613-3589), 705 Sunset Drive. Tennis courts, playground, athletic fields, swimming pool, trail.

Dudley Park (706-613-3624), 100 Dudley Park Road. Fishing, hiking trails, ball fields, picnicking.

Lake Herrick Beach and Pavilion (706-542-5060), off College Station Road. Canoeing (rentals available), swimming, fitness trail, athletic fields.

Memorial Park and Bear Hollow Wildlife Trail (park 706-613-3580; zoo 706-613-3616; www.athensclarkecounty.com/bearhollow), 293 Gran Ellen Drive. Nature trails, fishing, paddleboating, pool, picnicking, playground.

In Eatonton

Lawrence Shoals Recreation Area (706-485-5494; www.georgiapower.com/gpclakes), 125 Wallace Dam Road NE. Boating, swimming, picnicking, camping.

In Forsyth

Rum Creek Wildlife Management Area (478-994-1438; www.georgiawildlife.com), GA 18. Nature trail, hunting trips, fishing, bird-watching, camping.

In Griffin

Griffin City Park (770-229-6603; www.cityofgriffin.com), Camp Northern Road and Ninth Street. Ball fields, playgrounds, tennis, trails.

In Lincolnton

Amity Recreation Area (1-800-533-3478; www.usace.army.mil), 5870 Thomson Highway. Beach, playground, picnicking.

Bussey Point Recreation Area (1-800-533-3478; www.usace.army.mil), Double Branches Road. Located on Clarks Hill Lake. Hiking, biking, horseback riding, bird-watching, picnicking, primitive camping.

Cherokee Recreation Day Use Area (1-800-533-3478; www.usace.army.mil), 5926 Augusta Highway. Located on Clarks Hill Lake. Water sports.

In Madison

Bowl Springs Park (706-342-4454; 1-800-709-7406; www.madisonga.org), 156 Academy Street. Trails, wildlife observation.

In Statesboro

Statesboro–Bulloch County Parks and Recreation Department (912-764-5637; www.bullochrec.com) operates several city pools.

In Thomson

Big Hart Recreation Area (706-595-8613; 1-800-533-3478), US 78. Picnicking, boat ramp, beaches, playground.

In Watkinsville

Herman C. Michael Park (706-769-3965; www.oconeecounty.com), GA 53 and Elder Road. Ball fields, tennis, fishing, nature trails.

4 The Mountains

In Calhoun

John's Mountain Wildlife Management Area (706-695-6736), Pocket Road. Pocket and Hidden Creek campgrounds, overlook, creek, hiking trails.

In Chatsworth

Lake Conasauga Recreation Area–Lake Conasauga Songbird Management Area (706-695-6736; www.fs.fed.us/conf), 3941 US 76. Trails, campground, fishing, swimming, boating, picnicking, bird-watching, hiking.

Cohutta Wilderness Area (706-695-6736; www.fs.fed.us/conf), 3941 US 76. Recommended for seasoned backpackers and fisherman only; 90 miles of rough-terrain trails.

In Clarkesville

Lake Burton Wildlife Management Area (770-535-5700; www.gawildlife.com), GA 197 North. Backpacking, bird-watching, camping, fishing, hiking, hunting, picnicking.

Panther Creek Falls and Panther Creek Recreation Area, Old US 441 North, Clarkesville. Trail to three waterfalls.

In Clayton

Ellicott Rock Wilderness Area (706-782-3320; www.fs.fed.us/conf), Forest Road 646. Wilderness hiking.

Sandy Bottom Recreation Area, Forest Road 70. Fishing, picnicking, camping.

Southern Nantahala Wilderness Area (706-782-3320; www.fs.fed.us/conf), Forest Road 70. Hiking, ecotourism, wildlife observation.

Tallulah River Recreation Area, Forest Road 70. Trout fishing, hiking in Coleman River Scenic Area.

Tate Branch Recreation Area (706-782-3320; www.fs.fed.us/conf), Forest Road 70. Trout fishing, magnificent scenery.

Warwoman Dell Wildlife Management Area (770-535-5700; www.georgia wildlife.com), Warwoman Dell Road. Bird-watching, camping, fishing, hiking, hunting, picnicking, horse trails.

Willis Knob Recreation Area, Willis Knob Road. Fishing, hiking, horse trails.

In Cleveland

Chestatee Wildlife Management Area (770-535-5700; www.georgiawildlife .com), off US 19. Bird-watching, camping, fishing, hiking, hunting, picnicking.

In Cornelia

Lake Russell Wildlife Management Area (770-535-5700; www.georgiaw-ildlife.com), off GA 123 adjacent to Lake Russell Recreation Area. Hiking, mountain biking, trails.

In Cornelia/Mount Airy

Lake Russell Recreation Area, 304 Lake Russell Road. Boating (no outboard motors), camping, fishing, picnicking, swimming.

In Dahlonega

Blue Ridge Wildlife Management Area (770-535-5700; www.georgia wildlife.com), Lower Blue Ridge WMA is at GA 52 West, Upper Blue Ridge WMA is at GA 60 North. Bird-watching, camping, fishing, hiking, hunting, picnicking, horseback riding trails.

Cooper Creek Scenic Area (706-745-6928; www.fs.fed.us/conf), Forest Road 4 off GA 60. Trout fishing in Cooper Creek and tributaries, camping, hiking.

Dockery Lake Recreation Area (706-745-6928; www.fs.fed.us/conf), Forest Road 654 off GA 60. Picnicking, camping, fishing, hiking.

In Dalton

Dalton Area Parks and Recreation (706-278-5404; recreation.citydalton.net; www.whitfieldcountyga.com/recreation). City's parks feature ball fields, playgrounds, tennis courts.

In Dawsonville

Dawson Forest Wildlife Management Area (770-535-5700; www.georgiaw-ildlife.com), GA 53 West. Bird-watching, camping, canoeing, fishing, hiking, hunting, horse trails, perhaps some wildlife sightings.

In Duluth

City of Duluth Parks and Recreation operates two parks with paved trails and nature trails: **Bunten Road Park** (770-814-6981), Bunten Road; **W. P. Jones Park** (770-623-2781), Pleasant Hill Road.

In Elberton

Broad River Wildlife Management Area (770-918-6400; www.georgiaw-ildlife.com), off GA 79 West. Excellent canoeing.

Elbert County Wildlife Management Area (706-595-4222; www.georgiaw-ildlife.com), off GA 72. Bird-watching, fishing, hunting, picnicking, boat ramp, canoe access.

In Gainesville

Laurel Park (770-535-8280; www.hallcounty.org/parks), 3100 Old Cleveland Highway. Ball fields, playground, tennis, boat ramp, walking trail, Sprayground (children's water playground).

River Forks Park (770-531-3952; www.hallcounty.org/parks.asp), 3500 Keith Bridge Road. Boating, camping, fishing, hiking, swimming beach, boat ramp, sand volleyball, horseshoes, picnicking.

In Hartwell

Hart County Wildlife Management Area (770-535-5700; www.georgia wildlife.com), GA 77 Alternate East. Bird-watching, hunting, picnicking, primitive camping, wildlife observation.

In Helen

Andrews Cove Recreation Area (706-754-6221; www.fs.fed.us/conf), GA 75 North. Camping, old logging trail that leads to Appalachian Trail.

Pete's Park, in center of Helen, has walking and jogging trails, picnicking, beginning of Helen-Unicoi Volksmarch Trail.

Tray Mountain Wilderness Area (706-754-6221; www.fs.fed.us/conf), Forest Road 698 and Appalachian Trail. Primitive wilderness area, plentiful outdoor recreation opportunities.

Upper Chattahoochee River Recreation Area (706-754-6221; www.fs.fed.us/ conf), Forest Road 44. Camping, hiking, picnicking.

In Homer

Wilson Shoals Wildlife Management Area (770-535-5700; www.georgia wildlife.com), off GA 365 on Yonah Road. Bird-watching, wildlife observation, hiking, hunting, photography, primitive camping, shooting.

In LaFayette

Pocket Recreation Area (706-695-6736; www.fs.fed.us/conf). Hiking, camping, picnicking.

In Ringgold

Elsie A. Holmes Nature Park (706-935-5263), 88 Ben Holmes Road. Fishing, hiking.

In Toccoa

Henderson Falls Park (706-886-2132; www.toccoagachamber.com), Henderson Falls Road. Waterfall, nature trail, tennis.

5 Southern Rivers

In Albany

City of Albany Recreation Department (229-430-5222) parks with short trails: **C. W. Heath Park,** East Second Avenue and 1000 Jordan; **Grove Park,** 2603 Rosebriar Avenue at Webster Avenue; **Hillsman Park,** Third Avenue at North Van Buren Street; **Martin Luther King Jr. Park,** South Martin Luther King Jr. Drive; **Riverfront Park** (229-344-PARK), North Front Street between

Pine Avenue and West Broad; **Tift Park** (229-430-5222), Fifth and Seventh
avenues at Jefferson Street and Palmyra Road.

Historic Tift Park (229-430-5222; www.albanyga.com), 1300 North Monroe
Street. Gardens, hiking trails, picnicking, playgrounds, tennis, horseshoes.

In Colquitt
Spring Creek Recreational Park (229-758-6213), 148 West Street. Trail,
boardwalk, bird-watching, ball fields, tennis, picnicking, playground, physical fitness course, fishing, Christmas lights display.

In Georgetown
River Bluff Park at Lake Walter F. George (229-768-2516; www.sam.usace
.army.mil/op/rec/wfg), off GA 82. Boat ramp, fishing pier, water sports.

In Hamilton
Blanton Creek Park (706-643-7737; 1-888-GPC-LAKE; www.georgiapower.com/
gpclake), Lick Skillet Road. Boat ramp, fishing, nature trails, camping.

In Leesburg
Leesburg Central Park, Academy and Fourth streets, has walking trail; **Pirate's
Cove Nature Park,** Pirates Cove Road, has swamp trail and walking path.

In Tifton
Friendly City Park and E. B. Hamilton Complex (229-382-3262), 3199 E.
B. Hamilton Drive. Ball fields, picnicking, playground, pond.

In Valdosta
Langdale Park (229-259-3507; www.valdostacity.com), US 41 North. Nature
trails, bird-watching, picnicking, boat ramp.

McKey Park (229-259-3507; www.valdostacity.com), 112 Burton Avenue. Tennis
center, shuffleboard, handball, picnicking, horseshoes, playgrounds.

Ralph K. Harrington Park (229-333-1887), 509 South Fry Street. Pool, baby pool.

CAMPGROUNDS

2 The Coast

In Baxley
Deen's Campground (912-367-2949), 998 Deen Landing Road.

In Brunswick
Altamaha Regional Park (912-264-2342), 1605 Altamaha Park Road.

Golden Isles Vacation Park (912-261-1025), 7445 Blythe Island Highway.

In Darien
Darien Inland Harbor RV Park (912-437-6172), GA 251 East.

Tall Pines Campground (912-437-3966), GA 251 and I-95.

In Folkston
Traders Hill Park (912-496-3412; 912-496-7037), GA 121 South.

In Glennville
Adamson's Fish Camp at Beard's Bluff (912-654-3632), US 301 South.

In Jesup
Jaycee Landing and Campground (912-588-9222), 230 Jaycee Landing.

In Kingsland
Country Oaks Campground and RV Park (912-729-6212), 768 Carlton Cemetery Road (I-95 at exit 1).

KOA I-95 Kingsland (912-729-3232; 1-800-KOA-3232; www.koa.com), 2970 Scrubby Bluff Road.

In Midway
Martin's Glebe Plantation Campground (912-884-5218), 529 Glebe Road.

In Richmond Hill
KOA Campground (912-756-3396; 1-800-562-8741), US 17 South.

In Woodbine
King George RV Resort (912-729-4110), 1242 Still Road West.

3 Historic South

In Athens
Sandy Creek Park (706-613-3631; www.sandycreekpark.com), 400 Bob Holman Road.

Little River Marina and Family Resort (706-541-1358), 4271 Old Lincolnton Road.

In Cochran
Hillside Bluegrass Park and RV Park (478-934-6694; www.hillsidebluegrass.com), Eastman Highway (US 23/GA 87).

The Woods RV Park (478-230-7115), Mac Thompson Road.

In Dublin
Interstate RV Center (478-956-5511; 1-888-817-0906; www.interstaterv center.com), 305 Chapman Road.

Pinetucky Campground (478-272-6745), 1007 Campground Road.

Robins Travel Park (478-956-2323), 4756 Houser Mill Road.

In Eatonton
Oconee Springs Park (706-485-8423; www.eatonton.com), 109 South Spring Road.

In Fitzgerald
Ellis T. Paulk Park (229-426-5050), Perry House Road.

In Forsyth
KOA Kampgrounds (478-994-2019; 1-800-KOA-8614; www.koa.com/where/GA/10101.htm), 441 South Frontage Road (exit 186 off I-75).

L&D RV Campground (478-994-5401), 1655 GA 18.

In Fort Valley
Ponderosa Campgrounds (478-825-8030), GA 96 and I-75 at exit 142.

In Greensboro
Old Salem Park (706-467-2850; 1-888-472-5254; www.georgiapower.com/gpclake), 1530 Old Salem Road.

In Madison
Country Boy's RV Park (706-342-1799; 1-866-227-8542), 2750 Eatonton Road.

In Metter
Brookwood RV Resort Park at Parrish Lake (912-685-2594; www.bkwdrvbr.com), Route 5, Box 3107.

In Mount Vernon
Brewton–Parker College Campground (912-583-3210), GA 280.
Wiregrass Trail RV Campground (912-557-4185), 268 Catfish Lane.

In Statesboro
Parkwood Motel and RV Campground (912-681-3105; 1-866-727-5967; www.parkwoodrv.com), 12188 US 301 South.

In Sylvania
Pinevale Campground (912-863-4347), 1667 Statesboro Highway.

In Thomaston
Flint River Outdoor Center (706-647-2633; www.flintriverfun.com), 4429 Woodland Road.

In Thomson
Big Hart Recreation Area (706-595-8613; 1-800-533-3478), Russell Landing and Washington roads.
Raysville Campground (706-595-6759; 1-800-533-3478; www.sas.usace.army.mil), 6584 Lincolnton Highway.

In Tignall
Broad River Campground (706-359-2053; 1-800-533-3478; www.reserveusa.com), 8181 Elberton Highway.
Hester's Ferry Campground (706-359-2746; 1-800-533-3478), 1864 Graball Road.

In Vidalia
Vidalia's RV Campground (912-537-6757; 912-537-9499), GA 130 (Loop Road).

In Watkinsville/Bishop
Pine Lake (706-769-5486), 5540 High Shoals Road.

4 The Mountains

In Adairsville
Harvest Moon RV Park (770-773-7320), 1001 Poplar Springs Road.

Leisure Time RV Park (770-877-5063), 881 Poplar Springs Road.

In Blue Ridge
Toccoa Valley Campground (706-838-5208), 11481 Aska Road.

In Calhoun
KOA Campgrounds (706-629-7511; 1-800-KOA-7512; www.koa.com/where/ga/10126.htm), 2523 Red Bud Road NE.

Salacoa Creek Park (706-629-3490), GA 156.

In Cartersville
Allatoona Lake Campground (678-721-6700; 1-877-444-6777), 1138 GA 20 Spur.

Allatoona Landing Marina Resort (770-974-6089; 1-800-346-7305; www.allatoonalandingmarina.com), 24 Allatoona Landing Road.

Clark Creek Campground, North and South (678-721-6700; 1-877-444-6777; allatoona.sam.usace.army.mil), Glade Road.

Gatewood Park (770-387-5163), 244 Bartow Beach Road.

KOA Cartersville (770-382-7330; 1-800-KOA-2841; www.koa.com/where/ga/10120.htm), 800 Cassville White Road.

McKaskey Creek Campground (678-721-6700; 1-877-444-6777; www.allatoona.sam.usace.army.mil), McKaskey Creek Road.

McKinney Campground (678-721-6700; 1-877-444-6777; www.allatoona.sam.usace.army.mil), King's Camp Road.

Old Highway 41 No. 3 Campground (678-721-6700; 1-877-444-6777; www.allatoona.sam.usace.army.mil), Lake Acworth Road.

Upper Stamp Creek Campground (678-721-6700; 1-877-444-6777; www.allatoona.sam.usace.army.mil), Wilderness Camp Road.

In Cedartown
Hightower Falls (770-748-8588; www.hightowerfalls.com), 771 Hightower Falls Road.

In Chatsworth
Lake Conasauga (706-695-6736; www.fs.fed.us/conf), 3941 US 76.

In Dahlonega
Dockery Lake Recreation Area (706-745-6928; www.fs.fed.us/conf/dkrylkcp.htm), Forest Road 654.

In Ellijay
Plum Nelly Campground (404-317-2458; www.gilmerchamber.com), 15828 GA 515 South.

In Hartwell
Milltown Campground–COE, Paynes Creek Campground–COE, and **Wadsadler Campground–COE** (706-856-0300; 1-888-893-0678; www.sas.usace.army.mil/lakes/hartwell/camping.htm), New Prospect Road.

In Maysville
Bell Acres Resort (706-677-2931; www.bellacres.com), 155 Bell Acres Road. (Note: clothing optional.)

In McCaysville
Rolling Thunder River Company and Campground (706-496-5752; www.rollingthunderriverco.com), 20 Hughes Street.

In Oakman
Doll Mountain Campgrounds, Harris Branch Campgrounds, Ridgeway Campground, and **Woodring Branch Campground** (706-276-4413; 1-877-444-6777; carters.sam.usace.army.mil), GA 382.

In Ringgold
Chattanooga South KOA Campground (706-937-4166; 1-800-KOA-4167; www.koacampgrounds.com), 199 KOA Boulevard.

In Rome
Lock and Dam Regional Park (706-234-5001; www.rfpra.com), 181 Lock and Dam Road.

In Rossville
Best Holiday Trav-L-Park (706-891-9766; 1-800-693-2877; www.chattacamp.com), 1623 Mack Smith Road.

In Sautee
Cherokee Campground (706-878-2267), 45 Bethel Road.

In Toccoa
Toccoa RV Park and Campground (706-886-2654), 2136 Oak Valley Road.

5 Southern Rivers

In Albany
Albany RV Resort (229-431-2229), 1218 Liberty Expressway.

Creekside RV Park and Campground (229-886-0504; www.creeksidervcampsite.com), 1437 Hancock Road.

In Americus
Brickyard Plantation RV Park (229-874-1234; www.brickyardgolfclub.com), 1619 US 280 East.

In Andersonville
Andersonville RV Park (229-924-2558; www.andersonvillega.freeservers.com), 114 Church Street.

In Bainbridge
The Place to Be RV Park (229-246-5802; www.theplace2brv.com), 801 West Shotwell Street.

In Buena Vista
Country Vista Campground (229-649-2267), 1634 GA 41 South.

In Columbus
Lake Pines Campground and RV Park (706-561-9675; www.lakepines.net), 6404 Garrett Road.

In Cordele
Cordele KOA (229-273-5454; 1-800-562-0275; www.koa.com), 373 Rockhouse Road East.

Cordele RV Camping (229-271-3111), 191 Floyd Road.

In Franklin
Overnite RV Park (770-854-8695), 100 West Ferry Road. Monthly rates available.

In LaGrange
Holiday Campground (706-884-6818), 954 Abbots Ford Road.

Hoofer's (706-885-9300; 1-800-844-6737; www.hoofers.com), 3472 Hogansville Road.

Ringer Campground (706-645-2937; www.westpt.sam.usace.army.mil), US 27.

Satellite Campground (706-882-5439; www.westpt.sam.usace.army.mil), 1000 County 288.

Whitehall Ridge Campground (706-884-8972; www.westpt.sam.usace.army .mil), 565 Abbots Ford Road.

In Lake Park
Eagles Roost (229-559-5192), 5464 Mill Store Road.

Suncoast RV Campground (229-559-9738), 5230 Jewel Futch Road.

In Moultrie
Boggy Pond Plantation (229-985-5395), 1084 Lanier Road.

In Oglethorpe
Whitewater Creek Park (478-472-8171; www.montezuma-ga.org/chamber/ whitewater.htm), GA 128 North and Whitewater Road.

In Thomasville
City of Roses RV Park (229-228-7275), 277 Old Boston Road (US 319 South and US 84).

In Tifton
Pines Campground (229-382-3500), 18 Casseta Road.

In Valdosta
River Park RV Park (229-244-8397), 1407 St. Augustine Road.

In Vienna
Dixie RV Park (229-268-5712), 866 Campers Haven Road.

In West Point
R. Shaefer Heard Campground (706-645-2404; www.westpt.samusace.army .mil), 101 North Shaefer Road, West Point.

INDEX